D1600565

PRONOUNCING GAELIC-ENGLISH DICTIONARY

COMPILED BY

Neil MacAlpine

GAIRM PUBLICATIONS
29 Waterloo Street
Glasgow
1979

MacAlpine's Gaelic-English Dictionary was first published in 1832, and new editions have frequently been published since then. Now issued in a new and enlarged format.

SBN 901771 22 8

Printed in Scotland by
ROBERT MACLEHOSE AND CO LTD
Printers to the University of Glasgow

KEY.

A has six sounds in the Key.

ā long, like *a* in fame, came, tame.

ȧ, ä, ā², is the short sound of the last, as *a* in fate, rate, gate, final.

â is the sound of *a* in far, fâr, star, stâr.

ă is the short soft sound of the last; as, in farm, fărm.

a is the short and shut sound of *a*, as in can.

à is the nasal sound. The only sounds that approach this, in English, is *a* in palm, calm, psalm. It occurs uniformly before m, mh, and n—sometimes before th; as, in màthair, *mother*; àth, *a ford*; nathair, *a serpent*; math, *good, and its derivatives*; athar, *sky, firmament*;—in some words *n* is introduced for *r* in order to give it the nasal sound; as in cànran, mànran, mànrach, màrran, kàrr-an, màrr-ach; also mànr, màrr, *to obstruct*;—*ai* placed before *mh*, &c. has the same sound, or one nearly allied to *ai* in sprain, strain, brains, as the Scotch pronounce these words:—marked in the key sprèn, strèn, brèns.

á is the short nasal sound; é before *n*, &c. the short one of *ai* or áé.

ȧ in participles thus, tyȧ sounds like short u or aŏ shorter a little, chyaŏ.

āo has nothing like it in English; a pretty correct idea may be formed of it by pronouncing the *u*, in the surname Burns, long; also *u* in gun, without touching the -rns in the first instance, and the -n in the latter. Bāo—gāo—the French *eu* is somewhat like it.

aŏ is the short sound of the last.

E has two sounds, long and short.

ē long, like ee in teem, seem; feed, hired

e, ë, ē², is the short of the above.

è long, as e in there, pronounced long thèr—the η of the Greeks, as the Scotch and Foreigners pronounce it.

é is the short sound of the last.

Before *v*, representing *mh* and *n*, it has a nasal sound—see a nasal changed into ai—also representing ea or eu; as Neumh or Nèamh, nèv, *Heaven*, neamh, név, *venom*.

I has one sound long and short; as, *y* in my, thy; mī, thī, short; as i in sight, might, sĭt, mĭt.

O has four sounds, long and short.

ō, as o in more, mōr, tone, tōn, pole, pōl.

ȯ, ö, ō², short sound of the above.

ô sounds like o in lord, lôrd, cord, kôrd.

ŏ is the short of the last; o shorter.

ò is the long nasal sound, occurring uniformly before mh, and sometimes before n; in many instances the nasal sound of *o* occurs otherwise placed; as, in mòd, *a court of justice*, being a contraction of momhad; also mò, contraction of momha, *greater*; also moit, *fastidiousness*; mothar, *a horrifying voice*; glothar, gag; mògharr bland. The true orthography is momhar, glomhar, &c.

ó is the short nasal sound of o. Even before n, o sounds like o in pole, sole, &c. sometimes; as, tonn, tō²nn, *a wave*; *n* is introduced sometimes to give the nasal sounds merely; thus ònrachd, sònraich, òrr-achg, sòrr-èch; the same as ànrath, àrr-a*h* in a nasal.

U has a great number of sounds.

ū sounds as u in pure, cure, tune.

ů, ü, is the short sound of the last.

û sounds as oo in moor, cool, tool.

ŭ is the short sound of the last.

ù is the same as the French u nearly.

ú is the French short sound.

u the same as the u in under, *or* un- a prefix

Ӽ is a contraction to save room, and represents the primitive sound aŏ-gh', being a kind of a syllable and a half. See -gh'.

-Gh', an idea of this original sound. It is a kind of an ineffectual effort to disjoint your jaws without touching the palate or teeth with your tongue, and at the same time making a strong respiration. It is nearly akin to the Greek χ. It is not possible, without oral instruction, to convey an adequate idea of -gh'.

v², this representing mh, shews that the v is only slightly sounded, the object of mh being chiefly to give the nasal twang to the preceding vowel.

ll², lly', shews that the ll is liquified, as in filial, fē-lyal; for ll and nn initial, see *l* and *n* in the Grammar.

id, de.—This is represented by ėj. It is said that it does not express the true sound. If not, Walker, and Fulton and Knight, must be wrong in pronouncing age, āj;

tedious, tēj-us, and tē-jus, tē-dyus. This sound, when not final, is often exhibited thus, deug, dyăg.

ėn, ėnn, is often not marked at all, the last *n* being always liquified, ēnny'; sometimes marked ėn', ėny', and nn' and nny'.

ty'.—This sound is found in Chris*t*ianity, Kris-tyė-, *or* chė-an-ė-tė. The *t* is thus liquified often by putting j before it, thus, sagairt, sag-arjt, *a priest*; and sometimes by marking it *t'*.

ĕu shews also the short sound of *a*, as in beag, bĕug; ea is the short form of eu, which is always long; eu, ea, ei, are styled always diphthongs: With the exception of the very peculiar sound ao, I do not think there is such in the language, eu long, and its short sounds ea and ei, having both the vowels sounded. Thus, feum, fă-um, the um being pronounced so quick, that they almost form one syllable. They form a syllable and a half, as is seen in ui and oi in buil, toil, bŭ'l, tŏ'l, *i. e.* bŭ-ul, tŏ-ul, being two syllables thrown almost into one.

The orthography of the Gaelic, shews more acuteness and ingenuity in its structure, than any other language the author knows any thing of. It is said, that mh and bh should give way to v;—no such thing!! Bh represents the simple form of v, and mh of v, following the nasal sound; and, besides, bh is only an occasional or accidental form: thus, bò, *a cow*; a bho, uv-v*hō*, *the cow*.

ABBREVIATIONS IN THIS WORK.

A. after *v.* thus, *v. a.*, verb active.
a.. adj. adjective.
Adv. adverb.
Arab. Arabic.
Ar. Arg. peculiar to Argyleshire.
Armst. Arm. Dr. Armstrong's excellent Gaelic Dictionary.
Art. m. article masculine; *art. f.* article feminine, or *a. m.* and *a. f.* or *art. fem.*
a. as. f. aspirated form or *a. f.*
Belg. for Belgic Language.
B. for Bible, also *Bi.—B. B.* Bedel's Bible.
Brit. British.
Buch. Buchanan's Hymns.
Campbell or Campb. Campbell's Poems.
Comp. comparative degree.
Chald. Chaldee.
Coll. collective noun.
Cond. St. Columbus's Conundrums.
Contr. contracted or contraction.
Corr. corrup. corrupted or corruption of.
D. Dan. Danish Language.
D. Buch. D. B. Dugald Buchannan.
Deg. degrees of comparison.
Def. def. v. defective verb.
Dem. pro. pron. demonstrative pronoun.
D. M'L. Dr. M'Leod's Glossary and Dict.
Fut. for future tense.
F. Fr. French.
G. MS. Gaelic Manuscript.
Gen. genitive.
Gill. Gillies's Gaelic Poems.
G. P. or *Prov.* Gaelic Proverbs.
Gr. Greek; *Gt.* Grant's Poems.
Har. for Harris.
Heb. Hebr. Hebrew.
H. S. High. Sc. Highland Society's Dictionary.
I. i. e. id est. that is.
ib. the same.
Imp. Impersonal.
Inten. Intensative.
Inter. or *Int.* interjection.
Interr. interrogative.
Ir. for pure Irish.—*Irish* for Irish Dialect.
Isd. Islands.
Is. Island of Islay, Argyleshire.
Isl. Icelandic.
It. Italian.
K. Ki. Kk. Rev. Mr. Kirk.
K. M. Kenneth Mackenzie.
Lat. L. Latin.
Leg. Popular Legends.
Lw. Lew. Isle of Lewis.
Lit. literally.
Lld. Lluyd. author of a huge manuscript.
Loch. Lochab. for Lochaber.
M. for Island of Mull.
m. masculine gender.
Md. Alexander Macdonald the Poet; also *Macd. Macdon.*
Macaul. Macaulay's History of St. Kilda.
Macf. Macfar. The Rev. Mr. Macfarlane's New Testament, Psalms, or Gaelic Vocabulary.
M'D. Macdougall's Poems, also *Macd.*
Mland. mainland of Argyle; also *Mld.*
Mt. Macint. Mackintyre's Songs.
Mart. Martin's Description of the Highlands.
Mas. masculine gender.
MacC. MacCruiminn, a poet.
M'G. MacG. MacGregor's Poems.
Ml. M'L. Mr. Maclauchlan's translation of Homer, the best Gaelic translation in existence.
Mn. Martin's Highlands.
MS. MSS. manuscript, manuscripts.
Mur. Dr. Murray, late Professor of Oriental Languages, Edinburgh.
N. North, North Highlands; also N. H.
n. f. noun feminine.
n. m. noun masculine.
nom. for nominative case.
Obs. obsolete.
Oss. Ossian's Poems.
P. page; also past tense; participle
P. E. part. expl. particle expletive.
pt. part. for participle.
Past. past tense.
Pers. Persic.
Perf part. perfect participle.
Psh. Perthsh. Perthshire; also P. S.
Per. pro. pron. personal pronoun.
Pl. plural number.
Pref. prefix.
Pre. prep. pro. preposition and pronoun.
Pr. Prov. Gaelic Proverbs; also G. P.
Ps. Psalms of David.
Provin. Provincial word.
R. D. Robb Donn.
R. M'D., R. D., Ranald Macdonald.
S. Rev. Dr. Smith.
R. Rss. Rev. Dr. Ross's Psalms.
Sc. Scot. Scotch, Scottish.
Sh. Shaw, Rev. Dr. Shaw's Vocabulary.

Sg. popular Songs.
Sg. sing. singular number.
Sk. Skye.
Sm. Rev. Dr. Smith.
Sp. Span. Spanish.
St. Stew. Stewart's Songs; also St. Kilda.
Su. Suths. Sutherlandshire; also Suthl.
Syr. Syriac.
Trad. Tradition.
Tt. Teut. Teutonic, *or* Old German, *or* Gaelic.
T. Tt. Turn. Peter Turner's compilation.
V. v. verb active; *n. v.* neuter verb
v. n. verb active and neuter.
Val. Vallancey.
v. irreg. verb irregular.
Voc. Vocabulary.
W. and *W. H.* West Highlands.
Wl. Wel. for Welsh.
West, West H., West Highlands.

BRIATHRADAIR

GAIDHLIG AGUS BEURLA.

A, a, the first letter of the alphabet, called by the Irish *an fhalm*, the elm tree.

A', the gen. and dat. mas. and the nom. and dat. fem. of the article, the; used before three of the labials, b, m, p, and the two palatals, c, g, when aspirated; as, *a'* choin, of the dog; *a'* mhàthair, *the mother; a* phàisde, *of the child*; *a'* ghruagach, *the damsel:* the fourth labial, f, takes an; as, *an* fhir, *of the man; an* fhaobruinn, *of the large ankle; an* fhradhairc, *of the eye-sight*; *an* fheantagach, *the nettle*; *an* fhiolair, *the eagle.*

The aspiration of the f, in these and similar instances, is the cause of many corruptions: hence, àile instead of fàile, *smell*; radharc instead of fradharc, *eye-sight*; àradh in place of fàradh, *a ladder*; aile nan tàirnean, instead of fail nan tàirnean, *the print of the nails*, &c.; but Dr. N. M'Leod has very properly restored fradharc, and many other words, to their correct orthography, paying no regard to the corrupt manner in which they were written formerly. In some places of Argyle, faile, the gen. is used in place of the nom. fail: 2. *a'*, the sign of the present participle (for ag); used before consonants; as, *a'* fàs, *growing*; *a'* dùnadh, *shutting*; *a'* dol, *going:* 3. a', contraction for ann; as, a'd' cheann, *in thy head.*

A, à, *pos. pro.* his, her, hers, its: *a* mhac, *his son*; *a* nighean, *his daughter*; *a* mac, *her son*; *a* nighean, *her daughter*; ellipsed before fh, and a vowel in the mas.; as, 'fhalt, *his hair*; 'aghaidh, *his countenance*: in the feminine an h is interposed between the pronoun and noun; as, *a* h-each, *her horse*; *a* h-eun, *her bird.* When a consonant comes after the fh, the pronoun is retained in the mas.; as, a fhluiche, *his*, or *its wetness*; pronounced, ul-lŭĕch-à: 2. *a*, sign of the infinitive; as, *a* bhualadh, *to strike*; *a* cheangal an duine, *to bind the man*; 3. *a*, é, *prep.* out, out of; *a* tigh na daorsa, *out of the house of bondage*; *a* baile, *out of town, from home*: 4. *a*, sign of the vocative; as, éirich, *a* laoich, *rise hero:* 5. *a*, relative *pro.* who, which, that, and what; as, a' bhean *a* bha, *the woman who was*; an cù *a* bha, *the dog that was.*

Ab, Ăb, *n. m.* an abbot; an ni ni an dara *h-aba* subhach, ni e dubhach an *t-aba* eile, *what makes the one abbot glad, makes the other abbot sad*: abair tri uairean Mac an *Aba*, gun do chab a dhùnadh, *repeat thrice the surname, MacNabb without shutting your gab. Cond.*

Abab, ab-ab′, *int.* fie! pshaw shame *n. m.* filth, dirt.

Ababach, ab-ab′-ach, *a.* filthy, dirty.

Ababachd, ab-ab′-ăchg, *n.f.* filthiness, dirt.

Ababardaich, ab′-ab′-ardd-èch, *n.f.* a disgusting repetition of *abab.*

Abachd, ab′-achg, contraction of abuidheachd, ripeness; pertness.

Abaid, ăb′-ăj, *n. f.* an abbey; a' triall thun na *h-abaid, strolling to the abbey. St.*

Abaideachd, ăb′-ăj-achg, *n.f.* abbacy.

Abaideal, ab′-èj-all, *n.f.* the colic. *Lw.*

Abaidealach, ab′-èj-all-ach, *a.* griping.

Abaidealachd, ab′-èj-al-achg, *n.f.* griping.

Abair, ab′-èr, *v.* say, affirm, express; na *h-abair* ach beag, is *abair* gu maith, *say but little, and say that little well.*

Abairt, ab′-art^2, *n.f.* babbling, recrimination, scolding. *Is.* Politeness, an idiom, *Sh. Ir.*

Abalt, âb′-allt, *a.* expert, proficient, masterly, very able. *Isd.*

Abaltachd, âb′-allt-ăchg, *n.f.* proficiency dexterity, uncommon skill; strength.

Abaltaiche, âb′-allt-èch-â, *n. m.* a proficient, an adept, duine sgileil.

Abardair, ăb′-ar-ddar^2, *n. m.* a dictionary *Sh.*

Abarrach, ab′-arr-ach, *a.* indelicate, as a female; *n. f* a bold masculine female.

Abarrachd, ăb′-arr-achg, *n. f.* indelicacy, as a female, immodesty; impudence, turbulence.

Abartach, ăb′-ărt-ach, *a.* talkative.

Abartachd, ab′-art-ăchg, *n. f.* loquacity, unbecoming boldness, as a female.

Abartair, ab′-art-ar′, *n. m.* a babbler.

Abh, âv, *n. m.* a hose net, a hand net.

Abh, ăvf, *n. f.* the yelp of a terrier; obs. water; hence, abhuinn; *abh*, water, and *inne*, a channel,—a river in Germany.

Abhachd, and **Abhachdas**, âv′-ăchg, and -us, sport, diversion; nar n-aobhar spors' is *abhachdais, a cause of sport and diversion,—Ps.*; ri àbhachd, ann an teaghlach a' Mhoireir, *at our diversion in his Lordship's family.* 2.

Abhachdach, âv′-achg ach, *a.* joyful, merry; gach creutair a' togail an cinn gu h-àbhachdach, *all creatures lifting their heads joyfully.* 10.

Abhadh-ciuil, âv′-Ă-kūll, *n. f.* a musical instrument. *B.* inneal ciuil.

Abhag, ăvf′-ag, *n. f.* a terrier.

Abhagail, ăvf′-ag-al, *a.* terrier-like; *n. m.* yelping; snapping, carping; *a.* carping.

Abhagais, av′-ag-as, *n. f.* a surmise, an evil report—*T.* surmise is *babhd.*

Abhall, av′-all, *n. f.* an orchard; a chraobh a b' àirde 'san *abhall* thu, *the highest tree in the orchard thou wert. St.* Sometimes *abhallghart.*

A bhan, a-vàn′, *ad.* downwards, *b.*

Abharr, ăv′-urr, *n. f.* a silly jest, joke.

Abharrach, ăv′-urr-ach, *a.* given to silly jokes, or jesting. *Is.*

Abharsair, âv′-ar-sar′, *n. m.* Satan.

Abhcaid, ăv′-achg-ăj, *n. f.* silly gibe. *Lw. abhcaideachd,* ludicrous gibing; pleasantry.

Abhlan, ăv′-llan, *n. m.* a wafer; *B. abhlan* coisrigte, *a consecrated wafer,* (cèirean).

Abhras, ăv′-rus, *n. m.* wool, cotton, lint, or any other materials for cloth manufacture.

Abhrasach, av′-rus-ach, *a.* well supplied with materials for cloth manufacture.

Abhrasaiche, ăv′-rus-èch-à, *n. m.* a cloth manufacturer.

Abhsadh, ăv′-sĂ, *n. m.* a tug at a rope. *Sk.*

Abhuinn, av′-ènn, *n. f.* a river, from *abh*, water, obs. and *inne*, a channel; far an taine an *abhuinn* 's ann is mo a fuaim, *where the river is most shallow, it makes the greatest noise.*—Said to a vain-glorious fellow. *See* amhainn.

Abhuist, àv′-èsht, *n. f.* a habit, a practice, a custom; mar a b' *àbhuist* duit, *as you were accustomed to be.*

Ablach, ab′-llach, *n. c.* any thing mangled, a contemptible person.

Ablaich, ab′-llèch, *v* mangle, spoil.

Abrach, contraction of abarrach, and corr of cabrach, belonging to Lochaber.

Abran, ab′-run, *n. m.* an oar-slip; clamhdan, cnot. *I. S.*

Abraon, ab′-rāon, *n. m.* April. *Sh.*

Abstol, abs′-tull, *n. m.* an apostle.

Abstolachd, abs′-tull-ăchg, *n. f.* apostleship.

Abuchadh, ab′-uch-Ă, and, ap′-uch-Ă, *n. m. pt.* state of ripening; maturing, mellow ing, ripening.

Abuich, ab′- *or* ap′-èch, *v.* ripen, mellow maturate; *a.* ripe, mellow.

Abuidh, ab′-è, *a.* ripe, mature; pert; duine *abuidh, a pert meddling person.*

Abuidheachd, ab′-è-ăchg, *n. f.* ripeness, maturity; pertness. This word is writ ten *abuicheachd.*

Aca, achg′-à, *comp. pro.* of them, with them, in their possession; their; as, an tigh *aca, their house*; am fearann *aca, their land* aca siod, *in the possession of those*; agus biodh uachdranachd *aca, and let them have dominion, B.;* theid *aca* air, *they can master it*; mòran *aca* 'g ràdh, *many of them say. S.*

Acaid, achg′-ăj, *n. f.* a stitch; a transient lancinating pain; is trom an *acaid* a tha 'm lot, *intense is the pain that is in my wound, O.;* a stitch.

Acaideach, achg′-aj-ach, *a.* painful, groaning.

Acain, ăchg′-an′, *n. f.* a moan, a sigh; gun och na acain, without alas, or a moan.

Acair, achg′-ur′, *n. f.* an anchor; an acre. —North, a rick of corn; *acairpholl,* a harbour. *Sh.*

Acanaich, ăchg′-an-èch, *f. n.* grief, *D.* sobbing, plaintive moaning.

Acaran, achg′-ar-an, *n. m.* lumber. *N.*

Acarra, achg′-urr-a, *a.* moderate in price lenient, indulgent; settled.

Acarrachd, achg′-urr-achg, abatement moderation, indulgence.

Acarsaid, achg′-urr-sàj. *f. n.* a harbour an anchorage; a haven; roads.

Acastair, achg′-as-tar², an axle-tree. *S.*

Acfhuinn, achg′-ènn, or -fhènn, *n. f.* apparatus, implements, utensils; salve; tools; *acfhuinn* an t-saoir, *the carpenter's tools*; *acfhuinn* air son na coise, *a salve for the foot* (sore foot), 11; *acfhuinn* gunna, *the lock of a gun* (gleus); *acfhuinn* thogalach, *the apparatus for distilling*; harness; tackling: *acfhuinn* an eich, *the horse's harness; acfhuinn* na slaite, *the tackling of the fishing-rod.*

Acfhuinneach, achg′-fènn-ach, &c. *a.* well equipped, well furnished with apparatus.

Ach, ăch, *int.* oh! alas!

Ach, ach, *conj.* but, except, save; *ach* mise, *but me*; *ach* esan, *but him*; tir

Lewis, a field, a meadow); *ach* cha'n 'eil breitheanas ann, *but there is no judgment*; *ach* beag, *almost, nearly*.

ACHADH, ach'-ă, *n. m.* a corn field newly cut, or ready for reaping; bha sinn a' ceangal sguab 'san *achadh, we were binding sheaves in the field*. *B.*

ACHAIN, ach'-an', *n. f.* a supplication.

ACHANACH, ach'-an-ach, *a.* supplicatory. *R.*

ACHANAICH, ăch'-an-ėch, *n. f.* an earnest entreaty, supplication, a solemn appeal or prayer; *v. n.* entreat, beseech earnestly; ach tha mi 'g *achanaich* ort, *but I solemnly entreat of you*.

ACHD, ăchg, *n. m.* an act, a law, a statute; *achd* parlamaid, *an act of parliament*; an objection; 's mòr na *h-achdana* th' agad, *you have many objections*; air na h-uil' *achd, at all events*; *v.* enact.

A CHEUD, à chyădd, *or* a chĕăd, *a.* the first; *a' cheud* bhean, *the first woman*.

ACHLAID, ach'-llăj, *n. f.* chase, faoghaid.

ACHLAIS, ach'-lush, *n. f.* the arm-pit, hollow, or bosom; raimh ga'n sniomh ann an *achlais* nan àrd thonn, *oars twisting in the bosom of lofty waves*.

ACHLASAN, ach'-las-an, *n. m.* any thing carried under the arm; *achlasan* challum chille, see, seud challum chille, St. John's wort.

ACHMHASAN, ach'-vas-an, *n. m.* a reproof, a reprimand, a reprehension, rebuke.

ACHMHASANACH, ach'-'vas-an-ach, *a.* reprehensive; prone to rebuke; reproachful.

ACHMHASANAICH, ach'-'vas-an-ėch, *v.* reprove, rebuke, chide, reprimand, reprehend.

ACHMHASANAICHE, ach'-'vas-an-ėch-ă, *n.m.* reprover, a rebuker, a reprimander.

ACHRANNACH, ăch'-rànn-ăch. *a.* intricate; *achrannaich*, entangle, entwine, (amaili). *Sh.*

ACRACH, achg'-rrach, *a.* hungry; in *Irish*, ocrach.

ACRAICH, achg'-rėch, *v.* drop anchor, moor, come to anchor.

ACRAS, achg'-rrus, *n. m.* hunger; appetite.

ACRASACH, achg'-rras-ach, *a.* hungry-looking, bespeaking poverty

AD, *pro. 2. per.* thy, thine; ann *ad* chiobhlaibh, *or ad* ghialaibh, *in thy jaws*.

AD, add, *n. f.* a hat. *See Ata.*

ADAG, add'-ag, *n. f.* a shock of corn; the fish haddock; (*Sc.* stook).

ADAGAICH, add'-ag-ėch, *v.* gather into shocks, make shocks; ag *adagachadh, making shocks*; *stooking*.

ADH, â'-gh', *n. m.* prosperity, success; sonas is *àdh* ort, *may happiness and success attend you*; Is fearr *àdh* na ealain, *good luck is better than a trade, than dexterity.*

ADHAN, á'-un, *n. m.* a bye-word, a proverb; mu'n d' thuirt, an *t-adhan*, as the proverb says.

ADH-géir, (àine,) liver of fish. *Sk.*

ADHAL, ă'-ul, *n. m.* flesh hook. *Sh.*

ADHALTRACH, aŏ'-alt-rach, *a.* adulterous.

ADHALTRANNACH, aŏ'-ult-runn-ach, *n. m.* an adulterer; *a.* adulterous, guilty o. adultery.

ADHALTRANNAS, aŏ'-alt-runn-us, *n. m.* adultery.

ADHAMH, âv, *n. m.* Adam, the happy man

ADHARC, aŏ'-urk, *or* -archg, *n. f.* a horn.

ADHARCACH, aŏ'-ark-ach, *a.* horned.

ADHARCAN, aŏ'-ark-an, *n. m.* pee-wee, or lap-wing. *See* sagharcan.

ADHART, aŏ'-artt, *n. m.* the head of a bed, (1.) a bolster; front; *H.* progress.

ADHARTAN, aŏ'-artt-an, *n. m.* a pillow.

ADHLACADH, à'-llachg-ă, *p.* burying; *n. m* burial, interment. *B.*

ADHLAIC, â'-llėchg. *v.* bury, inter.

ADHMHOL, â'-voll, *v.* magnify. *B.*

ADHMHOR, âgh'-ur, vur, *a.* prosperous, lucky, happy.

ADHMHORACHD, â-gh' -vur-achg, agh-urachg, *n. m.* prosperity, luck, joyfulness.

AFRAIGHE, ă'-fri-ė, *n. m* preparation for battle.

AG, agg, *n. m.* doubt, hesitation.

AG, ug, sign of the present participle; as, *ag* ràdh, *saying*; *ag* iarruidh, *seeking*; *ag* òl, *drinking*.

AG, agg, for aig, joined to pronouns, and signifying possession; *agad, in your possession*; an tigh *agad, thy house*; a' bhean *agad, thy wife*; an tigh *agaibh, your house*; *againn, in our possession*

AGADH, âg'-ă, an ox. *North.*

AGAIL, ăg'-ăl, *a.* doubtful, sceptical.

AGALACHD, ăg'-al-achg, *n. m.* doubtfulness.

AGAIR, ag'-ur', *v. n.* accuse; tha 'choimhseas 'ga *agairt, his conscience accuses him*; crave; tha e 'g *agairt* orm, *he craves me*; prosecute: tha e 'g *agairt he prosecutes*.

AGAIRT, ag'-art[2], *n. m.* prosecution; accusation; *p.* pursuing, craving; prosecuting; blaming.

AGALLAMH, ag'-al-uv, *n. m.* conference. *St.*

AGAM, ag'-um, *pre.* and *pro.* in my possession; an tigh *agamsa, my house*.

AGARRACH, ag'-urr-ach, *n. m.* pretender.

AGARTACH, ag'-artt-ach, *a.* litigious, vindictive, revengeful.

AGARTACHD, ăg'-ărt-ăchg, *n. f.* litigation litigiousness.

AGARTAS, ăg'-ărt-us, *n. m.* a suit at law, a plea, a suit.

AGH, aŏ'-gh', *n. f.* a heifer, a fawn.

AGHAIB, aŏ'-ėbb, *n. f.* an attempt, an essay, trial; *from* aghaidh and ob, an objection, (differs from oidhirp)

Aghaibeach, aŏ′-ėbb-ach, *a.* persevering, industrious, indefatigable.

Aghaibeachd, aŏ′-ėbb-achg, *n. f.* industry, perseverance, indefatigability.

Aghaidh, aŏgh′-ė, and aŏ′-ė, *n. f.* face, countenance, visage; reproach; thug e 'n *aghaidh* air, *he reproached him*; an *aghaidh* a chéile, *against each other, contrary, opposed, at war*; am *aghaidh, against me*; theirig air *t'aghaidh, go forward*; cuir na *'aghaidh, oppose, thwart him*; cuir na *h-aghaidh, oppose her*; *aghaidh ri aghaidh, face to face.*

Aghann, aŏ′-unn, *n. m.* frying-pan; 2. a goblet, a pan of any kind. *H. S.*

Aghastar, aŏ′-star, *n. m.* a horse halter. *P.*

Agus, ă′-ghus, and ag′-gus, *conj.* and.

Aha, â′-hâ! *inter.* aha!

Aibheis, ev′-ėsh, *n. f.* a place full of fairies; a sea or ocean; a great quantity; the air, *or* atmosphere; an *aibheis* uile làn bhòchdan, *the whole atmosphere full of goblins. Rd.*

Aibheiseach, év′-êsh-ach, *a.* enormous, incredible, vast.

Aibheiseachd, ev′esh-achg, *n. f.* enormity, incredibility, exaggeration.

Aibheiseachadh, év′-êsh-ach-Ă, *p.* exaggerating from envious motives; *n. m.* exaggeration.

Aibheisich, ev′-ėsh-ėch, *v.* exaggerate from envious motives.

Aibhist, īv′-ėsht, *n. f.* an old ruin, 12.

Aibhistear, īv′-ėsht-ar², *n. m.* the devil.

Aibhistearachd, īv′-ėsht-ar-achg, *n. f.* demonism, the conduct of a devil.

Aibhlitir, īv′-llėt-ur², *n. f.* the alphabet, an A, B, C. *Ir.*

Aibhse, ev′-ėsh, *n. f.* a spectre, bòchdan.

Aibideal, ī′-bėj-al, *n. f.* the alphabet.

Aibidealach, ī′-bėj-al-ach, *a.* alphabetical.

Aic', Aice, Aice-se, echg, echg′-â, echg′. â-shâ, *pr.* and *pro. fem.* in her possession, with her, in her; her, *or* hers; an tigh *aice-se, her house*; tha e *aice-se, she has it in her possession.*

Aicheadh, aĕch′-Ă, *n. m.* denial, refusal; se 'n *t-àicheadh* maith dara poing is fhearr 'san lagh, *a strenuous denial is the best point in law.*

Aicheamhail, ăĕch′-uv-al, *n. f.* vengeance, reprisals; na bheireadh *aicheamhail* duibh, *that would make reprisals. M.*

Aicheidh, ăĕch′-ī, *v.* deny, refuse, disavow, renounce; *dh' àicheidh* e 'chreidimh, *he renounced or denied his religion.*

Aideachadh, ăj′-ach-Ă, *n. m.* confession, acknowledgment, avowal; *p.* acknowledging, confessing, avowing; ag *aideachadh* a chionta, *confessing his sin.*

Aideachail, ăj-ach-al, *a.* affirmatory penitent, confessing.

Aidh, âė, *n. m.* and *n. f.* a guest, a stranger, 2.

Aidheachd, ăė′-achg, hospitality.

Aidhmhillteach, aï′-vhēl²-tyach, *n. m.* a beast that steals from the pasture to feed on the growing corn.—*Sk.* a spendthrift.

Aidich, ăj′-ėch, *v.* confess, acknowledge, avow; dh' *aidich* e, *he confessed.*

Aidichte, ăj′-ėch-tyâ, *pt.* confessed, acknowledged, owned, admitted, allowed.

Aidmheil, ăj′-val, *n. f.* confession, profession, persuasion, religious belief; dé 'n *aidmheil* a tha e leantuinn, *what religious belief,* or *persuasion does he follow,* or *profess? v.* believe, profess, confess, admit.

Aidmheileach, aj′-vull-ach, *a.* acquiescent, forthcoming; bithidh mise *aidmheileach* dhuitse, *I will be responsible to you, or acquiescent.*

Aidmheileachd, aj′-vall-achg, *n. f.* acquiescence, responsibility; acknowledgment.

Aidmheiliche, aj′-vâll-ėch-â, *n. m.* a professor, one that follows some creed.

Aifrionn, 'eff-runn, *n. m.* a chapel, (Rach,) mass. *Irish.*

Aig, egg, *pres.* at, near, near to, close by, in possession; *aig* baile, *at home; aig* na dorsaibh, *at the doors;* on account of, for, *aig* meud aigheir, *on account of his excessive joy; in possession;* bh' *aig* duine àraid dithist mhac, *a certain man had two sons;* tha dithist aige, *he has two*; cha'n 'eil mìr aige, *he has not a particle.*

Aigeal, ăĕg′-al, *n. m.* the bottom of the sea, the deep; thuit m' aigne 'san *aigeal, my mind sunk into the bottom, into the abyss. Sk.*

Aigealach, ăĕg′-al-ach, *n. m.* a sounder. 1.

Aigean, ăĕg′-an′, *n. m.* the sea; an abyss; na shuidhe air an *aigein* dhorcha thiugh, *sitting on the dark misty deep;* grunnd an aigein, *the bottom of the abyss. Si.*

Aigeannach, ăĕg′-ann-ach, *n. f.* a self-willed boisterous female; *a.* self-willed, stubborn, mulish, uncontrollable.

Aigeannachd, ăĕg′-ann-achd, *n. f.* stubbornness, a turbulent disposition. *Is.*

Aigeanta, ăĕg′-ann-ta, *a.* self-willed.

Aigeantach, ăĕg′-annt-ach, *n. f.* a turbulent female; *a.* stubborn, mulish.

Aigeantachd. *See* Aigeannachd.

Aighear, ăĕ′- or ī-ghur′, *n. m.* joy; exultation, gladness, mirth, happiness.

Aighearach, ăĕ′-ghurr′-ach, *a.* exulting, joyous, gay, happy; odd, òlach *aighearach, an odd fellow.*

Aighearachd, ăĕ′-ghur′-achg, *n. f.* gladness merriment, mirthfulness; oddness

AIGILEAN, ăĕg′-ĕll-an′, *n.f.* a tagor horn. *H*

AIGNE, ăĕg′-nyà, *pl. n.* and AIGNEAN, the affections, disposition.

AIGNEACH, ăĕg′-nyach, *a.* lively, brisk.

AILBHINN, al′-vyēnn, *n. f.* flint.—*Bible;* a projecting rock, *Is.* a projection; precipice; an deòir a' sileadh mar bhainne na h-*ailbhinn, their tears dropping as water from a projecting rock.* 17. *H;* na shuidhe air *ailbhinn* oillteil, *sitting on a horrific precipice.*

AILEAN, ăĕl′-an′, *n. m.* a green, a plain.

AILEAR, ael′-ar′, a porch, sgath-thigh. *B.*

AILGHEAS, ăĕl′-ghus, fastidiousness, pride; imperiousness; ailgheas dhaoine, *the pride of men. S.*

AILGHEASACH, ăĕl′-ghus-ach, *a.* fastidious; proud, haughty; imperious, arrogant.

AILGHEASACHD, ăĕl′-ghus-achg, *n.f.* fastidiousness, haughtiness; arrogance.

AILIS, ăl′-ēsh, *n. f.* reproach. *D.*

AILL, àĕll, *n. f.* will, desire, pleasure; dé's *àill* leibh, *what is your will? sir, madam;* an ni a b' àill leam, *the thing that I would wish, or desire;* ma 's àill leibh so, *if you wish or desire this;* an *àill* leat, *do you wish?* dean àille do'n éiginn, *let willingness be of necessity.* 3. *A.*

AILL-BHILL, âĕll′-vhēll, *n. m.* bridle-bit. *Sh.*

AILLE, âĕll′-à, *n. f.* beauty, sublimity, glory, dignity; *aille* thalmhaidh air cha bhi, *no earthly beauty shall be found in him.—Par.;* the deg. of comp. of àluinn, *handsome;* ni's *àille, more, or most beautiful, more handsome.*

AILLEACHD, âĕll′-achg, *n. f.* beautifulness, handsomeness, sublimity.

AILLEAD, âĕll′-ud, *n. m.* degree of beauty.

AILLEAGAN, âĕll′-a-gan, *n. m.* a jewel.

AILLEALACHD, ăĕll′-all-achg, *n. f.* modesty.

AILLEANN, ăĕll′-unn, *n. f.* the herb elecampane—a young beau; a minion. *Ir.*

AILLEANTA, ăĕll′-annt-a, *a.* delicate.

AILLEANTACHD, ăĕll′-ant-achg, *n. f.* delicacy, bashfulness; is i *ailleantachd* maise nam ban, *delicacy is the ornament of women. Ar.*

AILLEORT, ăĕll′-ŏrt, *a.* high-rocked. *H. R.*

AILLIONAIR, ăĕll′-an-ar, *n. m.* a caterer. *Ir.*

AILLSE, ăĕll′-shá, *n. m.* a fairy.

AILLSEAG, ăĕll′-shag, *n. f.* a catterpillar.

AILPEAN, Alp′-an′, *n. m.* a man's name.

AILPEANACH, Alp′-an′-ach, *n. m.* a MacAlpine; cnoic is ùillt is Ailpeanaich; ach cuin a thàinig Artaraich, *hills, streams and M'Alpines are contemporaries, but when did the M'Arthurs come.*

AIMBEART, em′-byart′, *n. f.* poverty, *b.*

AIMBEAIRTEACH, ém′-byart′-ach, *a.* poor.

AIMHEAL, éff′-al, or évv′-al, *n. m.* mortification, pique, great vexation; fogh, *aimheal* is fo sgios, *piqued and fatigued.*

AIMHEALACH, évf′-al-ach, *a.* galling, vexing to the utmost; mortifying.

AIMHEALACHD, évf′-al-achg, *n. f.* the greatest mortificatian, *or* vexation.

AIMHEALAICH, évf′-al-ēch, *v.* gall, pique, mortify; vex; air 'aimhealachadh, *galled, vexed.*

AIMHINN, èv′-enn, *n. f.* an oven, a stove: In Irish, *amhann.*

AIMHINNICH, èv′-ēnn-ēch, *v.* stew, seethe.

AIMHLEAS, év′-llās, *n. m.* destruction, ruination, ruin; b'e sin car *t-aimhleis, that would be your ruination;* ag iarraidh m'-aimhleis, *bent on my destruction;* 12 *perverseness; harm, mischief;* a' labhairt *aimhleis, uttering perverseness. B. A.*

AIMHLEASACH, év′-llăss-ach, *a.* destructive, hurtful, ruinous, injurious.

AIMHLEASCAHD, év′-llăs-achg, *n. f.* ruinousness, destructiveness; mischievousness.

AIMHLEATHAN, év′-llan′, strait, narrow.

AIMHLEATHANACHD, ev′-llan2-achg, narrowness, straitness, tightness.

AIMHREIT, év′-rāt′ *or* év-rraj, *n. f.* entanglement, disorder, confusion, disagreement.

AIMHREITEACH, ev′-rat2-ach, *a.* confused, entangled; contentious; duine *aimhreiteach, a contentious person.*

AIMHREITEACHD, év′-rat′- *or* -răj-achg, *n. f.* degree of confusion, *or* disorder; quarrelsomeness.

AIMHREITICH, év′-răt2 *or* -răj-ēch, *v.* entangle, disorder, entwine as thread, put in confusion.

AIMHRIAR, év′-rēăr, *n. f.* mismanagement. *N.*

AIMHRIOCHD, év′-rrúchg, *n. f.* disguise. 10.

AIMLISG, em′-lēshg, *n. f.* confusion, quarrel. *B.*

AIMLISGEACH, em′-llēshg-ach, *a.* quarrelsome.

AIMRID, ém′-rrēj, *a.* barren, as women. *Bible.*

AIMRIDEACH, em′-rrēj-ach, *a.* a barrren woman.

AIMRIDEACHD, ém′-rēj-ăchg, *n. f.* barrenness.

AIMSIR, ém′-shēr, (aim-sior) time; season; weather; a réir na h-aimsir a bhios ann, *according to the weather we may have.*

AIMSIREIL, em′-shēr-al, *a.* temporal; oir tha na nithe a chithear *aimsireil, for the things that are seen are temporal. B.*

AIN, én′, same as *aimh* prefixed to words, and answering to *un,* in, &c. in English.

AINBHEACH, én′-uv-ach, *n.m.* a debt, an obligation; fogh *ainbheach* dhuitse, *under obligations to you;* from *ain* and *fiach,* the *f* being changed into *bh.*—See Professor Murray's *Vs.*

AINBHIOS, én-uv-èss, *n. m.* ignorance; an *ainbhios* duit, *unknown to thee, (ain* and *fios.)*

AINBHIOSACH, en′-uv-èss-ach, *a.* ignorant of; unknown to.

AINBHEIL, én′-val, *n. f.* impertinence. *D.*

AINBHFHIACH, én′-uv-ëăch′, *n. m.* a debt.

AINCHEARD, an- *or* én-chyard, *n. f.* a witticism, a jest.

AINCHEARDACH, an′-chyard-ach, *a.* jocose, sportive, witty, merry.

AINCHEIST, an′-chyäsht, *n. f.* dilemma.

AINCHIS, én′-chèsh, *n. f.* fury, rage. *N.*

AINDEOIN, en′-nyan′, compulsion, reluctance; defiance; a dh' *aindeòin* cò theireadh e, *in defiance of all that would oppose it. M. L's. Motto;* a dheòin na dh' *aindeòin, with, or without one's consent.*

AINDEOINEACH, an′-dyôn′-ach, *a.* reluctant.

AINDEOINEACHD, an′-dyôn′-achg, *n. f.* reluctancy; obstinacy; unwillingness.

AINDEISEAL, an′-dyāsh-al, *a.* unprepared.

AINDREANN, an′-drènn, *n. m.* fretfulness.

AINEAMH, én′-uv, *n. f.* a flaw, blemish, defect, (gaoid.) *Bible;* ceilidh seirc aineimh, *charity conceals faults or blemishes.*

AINE, à′-nyà, *n. f.* the liver of fish; àinean nam piocach, the liver of coal-fish.

AINEARTAICH, en′ art-èch, *n. f.* yawning.

AINEAS, én′-as, *n. f.* passion, fury. 10.

AINEASACH, en′-as-ach, *a.* furious, passionate.

AINEOL, én′-ëŏl, *n. m.* unacquaintance; ann an tìr m' *aineoil, in the country where I am unacquainted;* a' dol air '*aineol, going where not known; a stranger;* cha'n fhaic *aineol,* o'n lear na o'n fhasach, *a stranger from sea, or wilderness, will not behold;* is trom geum bò air a h-*aineol, deep is the low of a cow on strange pasture. H.*

AINEOLACH, en″-ëŏl-ach, *a.* ignorant, illiterate, unintelligent, rude.

AINEOLAS, en″-ëŏl-as, *n. m.* ignorance; is trom an t-ealach an *t-aineolas, ignorance is a heavy burden; boorishness.*

AINFHEOIL, én′-ëôll, *n. f.* proud flesh.

AINGEAL, éng′-al, or én′-nyal, *n. m.* an angel.

AINGEALACH, éng′-al-ach, *a.* angelic.

AINGEALAG, éng′-al-ag, *n. f.* angelica. *M.*

AINGEALTA, éng′-alt-a, *a.* perverse, wicked.

AINGEALTACHD, éng′-alt-achg, *n. f.* perversenesss, wickedness.

AINGIDH, eng′-è, *a.* perverse, wicked.

AINGIDHEACHD, éng′-è-achg, *n. f.* perverseness, wickedness, sin, viciousness.

AINGLIDH, eng-lè, *a.* angelic.

AINICH, àn-èch, *n. f.* panting. *Skye.*

AINID, én′-èj, *a.* vexing.

AINLEAG, én′-lyag, *n. f.* a swallow, *Md.;* *ainleag* mhara, *a sea-martin.*

AINM, én′-um, *n. m.* a name; an *t-ainm* gun an tairbhe, *the name without the benefit;* character; is fhasa deadh *ainm* a chall, na chosnadh, *it is easier to lose a good character, than to gain one.*

AINMEACHADH, en′-um-ach-Ă, *n. m.* and *p.* naming, appointing, denominating.

AINMEACHAS, én′-um-ach-us, *n. m.* a bare name; a nominal thing.

AINMEALACHD, én′-um-all-ăchg, *n. m.* celebrity, fame, reputation; notoriety.

AINMEANNACH, én′-um-ann-ach, *n. m.* a nominative, a denominator. *D.*

AINMEIL, én′-um-al, *a.* namely, celebrated, renowned; dh' fhàs iad sin nan daoine, *ainmeil, those became men of renown. B.*

AINMHIDH, én′-vhè, *n. c.* a brute of the horse species; a beast.

AINMHIDHEACHD, én′-vhè-achg, *n. m.* brutality.

AINMICH, én′-um-èch, *v.* name; mention, fix upon; denominate; ainmichte, *named,* &c.

AINMIG, én′-um-èg, *a.* rare, scarce, seldom; is *ainmig* a thig e, *he seldom comes.*

AINNEAMH. *See* Annamh.

AINNEAMHAG, én′-nuv-ag, *n. f.* a phœnix, 10.

AINNEAL, én′-nyal, *n. m.* a common fire.

AINNEART, én′-nyert, *n. m.* force, violence.

AINNEARTACH, én′-nyert-ach, *a.* oppressive.

AINNEARTACHD, en′-nyert-achg, *n. f.* force, violence, oppression.

AINNIR, én′nyèr, *n. f.* a virgin, (ainfhir.)

AINNIS, en′nyèsh, *a.* poor, needy. *Ps.*

AINNISEACHD, én′-nyèsh-achg, *n. f.* poverty.

AINNIUIGH, én′-nyū, *n. m.* a sigh. *North.*

AINSGEAN, én′-sken, *n. f.* fury, rage.

AINSRIANTA, an-srĕănt′-a, *a.* unbridled, debauched, obstinate. *Sh.*

AINTEAS, ann′-tyäs, *n. m.* inflammation, great heat, zeal. *Bible.*

AINTEASACH, ann′-tyäs-ach, *a.* inflammatory, hot, violent.

AINTEIST, ann′-tyäsht, *n. m.* bad report.

AINTEISTEANAS, ann′-tyäsht-an-us, *n. m.* a bad character, false testimony. *A.*

AINTEISTEIL, ann′-tyāsht-al, *a.* discreditable.

AINTETH, ann′-tyä, *a.* very hot. *L.*

AIR, ăr′, *pre.* upon, on, of, concerning; iomradh *air* do ghliocas, *the fame of thy wisdom, B.;* *air* beinn, *on a mountain;* *air* sgàth, *for the sake of;* *air* ainm, *by name;* *air* bheagan, *possessing little;* *air* an aobhar sin, *for that reason, therefore;* *air* mo shonsa dheth, *for my part, as far as I am concerned*; air éigin, *with much ado; air* a h-aon, *for one*; *air* seachran, *astray*; *air* falbh, *away, from home*; *air* uairibh, *sometimes*; including in itself the same meaning as if joined to the *pro.* e; as, tha eagal *air, he is afraid*; tha acras *air, he is hungry*; tha mòran aige *air, he owes him much*; *air* chor, *so that*; *air* chor eigin, *somehow or other*; duine *air* chor eigin, *some person or other*; *air* mheud is gu'm bheil e, *let it be ever so great*; cha d'fhuair mi ni *air, I got nothing for it*; dé tha cur *air, what is the matter with him? what ails him?*

AIR, ăr', *v.* plough; iadsan a dh'aireas eu-ceart, *they that plough iniquity. Job.*

AIRBHINNEACH, ăr''-vhēnn-ach, *a.* noble.

AIRC, ăĕrk, *n. f.* strait, predicament, poverty; saoi na *airc, a hero in distress. O. A.*; 's mairg a shìneadh lamh na *h-airce* do chridhe na circe, *woe to him who stretches poverty's hand to the hen's heart,—to the illiberal.*

AIRC, âĕrk, *n. f.* an ark, a chest; stad an *àirc, the ark rested. B.*

AIRCEIL, ăĕrk'-al, poor, needy.

AIRCEAS, ăĕrk'-us, *n. f.* poverty.

AIRCLEACH, ăĕrk'-lyach, *n. f.* a cripple; an dall air muin an *aircleich, the blind on the back of the cripple.*

AIRD, ârj, *n. f.* preparation, condition, state; dé'n *àird* a dh'fhàg thu air, *in what condition did you leave him*, or *it?* cuir *àird* air, *prepare*;—quarter of the earth, compass, &c.; O gach *àird, from every quarter*; an *àird* a deas, *the south*; an *àird* an iar, *the west*; an *àird* a tuath, *the north*; an *àird* an ear, *the east*; an *àird* an iar dheas, *the south west*; an *àird* an iar thuath, *the north west*; an *àird* an ear dheas, *the south east*; an *àird* an ear thuath, *the north east*;—a plan or expedient; gu'n deanadh e *àird* air a chur am charaibh, *that he would devise a plan* or *expedient, to put me in possession of it*, 10; an *àird, aloft, upwards.*

AIRDE, ârj'-â, height, stature, highness; dé 'n *àird'* a tha e, *what is his stature*, or *tallness? àirde* nam beann, *the height of the mountains; deg.* more, *or* most high.

AIRDEACHD, ârj'-ăchg, *n. f.* highness.

AIRDEAD, ârj'-ud, *n. f.* degree of height.

AIRDEANNA, ârj'-un-â, *pl.* a constellation.

AIRDEIL, ârj'-al, *a.* ingenious.

AIRE, ăr''-â, *n. f.* attention, heed, notice; thoir an *aire, attend, pay attention, observe*; *more properly*, thoir an fhaire, *be upon the watch.*

AIREACH, âr''-ăch, *n. m.* a dairyman.

AIREACHAIL, ăr''-ach-al, *a.* attentive. *C.*

AIREACHAS, âr''-ach-us, *n. f.* the business of dairyman, summer pasture for black cattle.

AIREAMH, âr2'-uv, *n. m.* number; *v.* count, number, compute; cò dh'airmheas duslach Iacoib, *who can count the dust of Jacob. B.*

AIREAMHACH, âr2'-uv-ach, *a.* numeral, relating to numbers; *n. f.* numerator, an accountant. *Ar.*

AIREAMHACHD, âr2'-uv-achg, *n. f.* numeration, computation: counting, numbering.

AIREAN, aŏr' -an', *n. f.* a ploughman.

AIREANACH, aŏr''-an'-ach, *a.* agricultural

AIREANACHD, aŏr2'-an'-ăchg, *n. f.* agriculture.

AIRFID, ăr'-fĕj, *n. f.* harmony.

AIRFIDEACH, àr'-fĕj-ach, *a.* harmonious, ceòlmhor; *n. m.* a musician.

AIRFIDEACHD, ăr'-fĕj-achg, *n. f.* harmoniousness, melodiousness.

AIRGHEAN, ăr2'-ghen, *n. f.* a symptom.

AIRGIOD, ăr''-gyud', *n. m.* money, silver; se gaol an *airgid* freamh gach uile, *the love of money is the root of all evil*; *airgiod* beo, *quicksilver, mercury*; *airgiod* caguilt, *hearth money*; *airgiod* cinn, *reward money, poll money*; *airgiod* ullamh, *ready money*; *airgiod* caorrach, *slate diamond*; *airgiod* ruadh, *copper money.*

AIRGIODACH, ăr''-gyud-ach, *a.* rich, silvery.

AIRIDH, ăr''-ė, *a.* worthy, deserving, meritorious; cha'n airidh mi, *I am not worthy*; *n. f.* desert, merit; is maith an *airidh* e, *he richly deserves it*; is olc an *airidh, it is a pity.*

AIRIDH, âr''-ė, *n. f.* shealing; hill pasture in summer for black cattle; bothan *airidh, a mountain booth*, or *hut.*

AIRILLEACH, ăr''-il-ach, *n. m.* a sleepy person. *N.*

AIRLEIG, ăĕr''-lyėg, *n. f.* strait; tha mi 'n *airleig, I am in a strait.*

AIRLEIGEACH, ăĕr'-lyėg-ăch, *a.* urgent.

AIRLIS, ĕăr'-lėsh, *n. f.* earnest-penny, pledge.

AIRM, aŏr''-um, *pl.* of arm; arms, weapons; *airm* theine, *fire arms*; *airm* thilgidh, *missive weapons*; gun *airm, without weapons.*

AIRNE, âr''-nyâ, *n. f.* a sloe, a damascene, *in the Bible*, a kidney, reins, (dubhain.)

AIRNEACH, âr''-nyach, *a.* full of sloes, kidneyed; *n. f.* murrainn in cattle. *See* Earrach.

AIRNEIS, ĕăr'-nyash, *n. f.* household furniture, moveables; household stuff. *B.*

AIR-NEO, ăr2-nyŏ', *ad.* else, otherwise; *air-neo* an t-shleagh mu'm bheil do lamh, *otherwise the spear your hand grasps. S.*

AIRSID, ăr'-shėj, *n. f.* unanimity. *Old.*

Airsideach, ar'-shẹj-ach, *a.* unanimous.

Airsneal, ărsh-, *or* ărs'-nyal, *n. m.* drowsiness; languor, depression of spirits; sadness; heaviness.

Airsnealach, ărsh'-nyal-ach, *a.* heavy, sad, drowsy, depressed, melancholy.

Airsnealachd, ărsh'-nyal-achg, *n.f.* drowsiness, sadness, melancholy sadness.

Air son, ăr'-son', *pre.* for, on account of, for the sake of; *air son* nam firean, *for the sake of the righteous; air* mo shonsa, *for me.*

Airtneal, ărty''-nyal. *See* Airsneal.

Ais, ăsh, *n. m.* back; this word is never used but in composition: air *t-ais, back, stand back; backwards;* thàinig e air *'ais, he returned, he came back;* thàinig i air a *h-ais, she returned.*

Aischeimich, ash'-chām-ẹch, *v.* retire, withdraw, back, go backwards. *H. S.*

Aisde, ẹshj'-â, *pr. pre.* out of her, *or* it.

Aiseag, ăsh'-ug, *n. m.* ferry; passage; thar an *aiseig, cross the ferry;* fhuair e an *t-aiseag* a nasgaidh, *he got his passage gratis,* or *free.*

Aiseal, ăsh'-ul, *n. f.* an axle-tree; fun, jollity, *Arm.*; tarrunn *aisil, linch-pin.*

Aiseirigh, ăsh'-ār'-ẹ, *n. f.* resurrection, rising again, *aiseirigh* nam marbh, *the resurrection of the dead. Bible.*

Aisig, ăsh'-ẹg, *v.* ferry over, restore, transfer; aisigidh e, *he will restore, B.*; *aisig* dhomh gàirdeachas do shlàinnte, *restore unto me the joy of thy salvation*; aisigte, *ferried; restored.*

Aisinn, ăsh'-ẹnn, *n. f.* a rib, a dream.

Aisinnleachd, ash-ēnn'-lyachg, *n. f.* a wicked contrivance, a wicked stratagem.

Aisinnleachdach, ăsh-ēnn'-lyăchg-ach, *a.* crafty, plotting, mischievous.

Aisir, ash'-ẹr, *a.* defile, a path.

Aislear, ash'-lyar', *n. m.* spring-tide.

Aisling, ash'-lyẹng, *n. f.* a dream. *B.*

Aislingiche, ăsh'-lyẹng-ẹch-â, *a.* dreamer.

Aislinn, ash'-lyẹnn, *n. f.* a dream, a vision—a second generation, *lit. Islay.*

Aislinneach, ash'-lyen'-ach, *a.* visionary.

Aislinniche, ash'-lyẹn-ẹch-â, *n. c.* dreamer.

Aisneach, ăsh'-nyach, *a.* ribbed.

Ait, ăty', *a.* glad, happy, joyful; odd, funny; òlach *ait, an odd,* or *funny fellow.*

Aite, âty'-â, *n. m.* a place, a situation; *àite* comhnuidh, *a dwelling-place; àite* suidhe, *a seat.*

Aiteach, âty'-ăch, *n. m.* agriculture, farming, cultivation of the land; ri *àiteach, cultivating, farming; an inhabitant;* tha *àitich* innse-torrain fo gheilt, *the inhabitants of Inistore are in terror, S. H.*; a habitation; air neul am bheil an *àiteach* fuar, *on a cloud, is their cold habitation. Oss. H.*

Aiteachadh, âty''-ach-ă, *p.* cultivating, improving; ag *àiteachadh* an fhearainn, *improving,* or *cultivating the land.*

Aiteachas, âty''-ach-us, *n. m.* a colony; colonising; ri *àiteachas, improving waste land.*

Aiteal, ăty''-ăll, *n. m.* a glimpse; fhuair mi *aiteal* dheth, *I got a glimpse of him*; a sprinkling; *aiteal* mine, *a sprinkling of meal*; a slight breeze; *aiteal* an earraich; *the fanning breeze of spring, Oss.*; a tinge; *aiteal* an òir, *the tinge of gold,* 10.; juniper; craobh *aiteil, a juniper tree, B.*; *In. Is.* craobh iubhair; dearcan *aiteil,* na dearcan iubhair, *juniper berries.*

Aitealach, aty''-all-ach, *a.* in glimpses; relating to juniper; in slight breezes.

Aiteam, ăty''-um, *n. f.* a tribe, a people. In the islands, a wicked set of people.

Aiteamh, aty''-uv, *n. m.* a thaw; *v.* thaw tha e 'g *aiteamh, it is thawing.*

Aiteann, ăty''-unn, *n. m.* juniper. *Arm.*

Aitear, â'-tyur², *n. m.* a husbandman.

Aitearachd, â'-tyur²-achg, *n. f.* agriculture.

Aiteas, ăty''-us, *n. m.* joy; gladness; fun, oddness; *t'aiteas, your oddness; aiteas* an sùil Ghorm-àlluinn, *gladness in the eye of Gormallin, O. A.*; a chuireas *aiteas* orm, *that will make me glad, Sm.*; *aiteas* air na sleibhte uaine, *joy on the green mountains, O. A.*

Aith, àẹch, *n. f.* a kiln; *aith* aoil, *a lime kiln. Is.*

Aitheamh, áĕ'-uv, *a.* fathom; fichead *aitheamh, twenty fathoms.*

Aitheamhaich, áĕ'-uv-ẹch, *v.* fathom.

Aitheornach, ă'-ĕŏrn-ach, *n. m.* land where barley was the last crop.

Aithghearr, ă'-ghyàrr, *a.* soon, brief; short; short-tempered; tha e *aithghearr, he is short-tempered;* sgaoil sinn cho *aithghearr, we dispersed so soon,* 3; *n. f.* short time, *or* way; ann an *aithghearr, in a short time*; so an *aithghearr, this is the short way,* or *road;* short method, *or* abridgement.

Aithinn, ăĕ'-ẹn', *n. m.* fire-brand (leus). *B.*

Aithis, ăĕ'-ẹsh, *n. f.* a reproach, check, *B.*; a fit means to do evil. *Islay.*

Aithlis, ăl'-ẹsh, *v.* imitate, mimic, *n. f.* mimicry; reproach, disgrace. *M. L.*

Aithliseach, al'-ẹsh-ach, *a.* imitative.

Aithn, àny', *n. f.* a circle; *àithn* an latha, *broad day-light.* See *faithne.*

Aithn, àny', *v.* command, order, bid, enjoin: dh' *àithn* an tighearn, *the Lord commanded, enjoined,* &c

Aithne, à′-nyà, *n. f.* commandment, injunction, charge; m' àitheanta, *my commandments. B.*

Aithne, á′-nyà, or én′ nyà, *n. f.* knowledge, acquaintance; an *aithne* dhuit, *do you know?* 's *aithne* dhuit, *you know, thou knowest. Ps.*; cha'n *aithne* dhomh, *I know not.*

Aithneach, én′-nyăch, *a.* discerning, considerate, attentive; tha i glè *aithneach, she is considerate enough; n. m.* woodrush, or wild leeks; acquaintance, or a guest; leis nach dragh aithnichean, *by whom acquaintances, or guests, were not counted a trouble. Mt.*

Aithneachadh, én′-ach-Ă, *n. m.* a slight degree; what is discernible: cuir *aithneachadh* an taobh so e, *put it a slight degree this way; p.* knowing, recognising, discerning: a dh' *aithneachadh* gliocais, *to know wisdom.*

Aithneachd, én′-ăchg, *n. f.* discernment, knowledge; humanity.

Aithnich, én′-êch, *v.* know, recognise, discern, perceive; dh' *aithnich* mi, *I knew or recognised*; aithnichte, *known, recognised; plain, obvious.*

Aithreach, ăěr′-ăch, *a.* giving cause to regret; cha'n *aithreach* leam, *I have no cause to regret, I do not regret it;* b' *aithreach* leis an tighearn, *it repented the Lord. B.*

Aithreachas, ăěr-ach-us, *n. m.* repentance, regret, penitence: is amaideach a bhi cuir a mach airgid a cheannach *aithreachais, it is foolish to expend money on the purchasing of repentance.*

Aithris, ăěr′-ésh, *n. f.* imitation, mimicry; report, rehearsal; *v.* imitate; mimic; ag *aithris* ormsa, *imitating or mimicing me;* rehearse, report, affirm; agus dh' *aithris* e na nithe sin uile nan éisdeachd, *and he affirmed, or told all those things in their hearing. B.*

Aithriseach, ăěr′-ésh-ach, *a.* imitative; traditionary, widely celebrated. *D.*

Aitich, âty″-êch, *v.* cultivate, till, improve; ag *àiteachadh* an fhearainn, *cultivating the land;* dwell, inhabit; gach neach a dh' *àitich* colunn riamh, *every one that ever dwelt in a body, D. B.;* drop anchor, moor; dh' *àitich* an long, *the ship anchored.* Oss.; àitichte, *cultivated, improved; inhabited.*

Aitidh, âty″-ê, *a.* damp, moist, wet.

Aitidheachd, âty′-ê-ăchg, *n. f.* moistness, dampness; moisture.

Aitreabh, ăty″-ruv, *n. f.* premises, steading; tigh is *aitreabh, mansion-house and premises;* théid a'n *aitreabh* sìos, *their buildings shall decay. B.*

Aitreabhach, ăty″-ruv-ach, *a.* domestic, belonging to premises; *n. m.* an inhabitant. *B. B.*

Aitreabhail, ăty″-ruv-al, *a.* domestic. *T.*

Al, âll′, *n. m.* brood, offspring, young; generation; a solar dhearc da cuid *àil, gathering berries for her young, O; àl* stiallach, *speckled offspring, B;* an *t-àl* a tha ri teachd, *the generation to come. Sm.*

Alach, âll′-ach, *n. m.* brood; covey; litter; tribe; generation; trà thig an sealgair gun fhios air *àl, when the hunter comes unexpectedly on a covey;* a' mhuc 's a cuid *àil, the sow and her litter; bank of oars, set of nails.*

Alag, al′-ag, *n. f.* hiccup, hard task.

Alaich, âll′-êch, *v. n.* fall to, commence, attack; breed; dh' *àlaich* iad air, *they fell to; they attacked him;* is luath a dh' *àlaich* iad, *soon have they multiplied. H.*

Albainn, al′-ub-ènn, (*g.* alba) Scotland feadh na h-alba, *throughout Scotland.*

Albannach, ăl′-ub-ann-ăch, *n. m.* a Scot, a Scotchman; *a.* Scotch, Scottish.

A lathair, ul-lâ′-ur′, *ad.* present, alive, in existence; tha e *làthair, he is present, he is alive;* thoir a *làthair* a chéile iad, *bring them face to face;* ma bhitheas mi *làthair, if I live.*

A leas, ul -lless′, *ad.* cha ruigear *a leas, there is no need;* cha ruig thu *leas, you* need not.

Alla, all′-à, *a.* wild, fierce. *O.*

Alladh, all′-à, *n. f.* defamation, libel; used in the Bible either as good or bad fame, but never so in Argyle.

Allaban, all′-ă-ban, *n. m.* wandering; more properly *eallaban.*

Allail, ăll′-all, *a.* defamatory, detracting; in *H. S.* excellent, famous.

Allabhuadhach, all′-a-vŭă-ach, *a.* victorious, but in disgrace.

Allamharach, ăll′-văr-ach, *n. m.* a foreigner; a straggler; *a.* foreign, strange.

Allamharachd, ăll′-var-ăchg, *n. m.* straggling, loitering, wandering; savageness.

Allsadh, ăll′-sĂ, *n. m.* a jerk, a sudden inclination of the body.

Allsaich, ăll′-sêch, *v.* jerk; suspend; lean to one side.

Allsporag, all′-spŏr-ag, *n. f.* the throttle of a cow, or any brute.

Allsmuain, ăll′-smŭăin, *n. f.* great buoy.

Allt, âllt, *n. m.* a river with precipitous banks; a river, a brook; *a.* wild.

Alltachd, âllt′-ăchg, *n. f.* savageness. *S.*

Alltan, âllt′-an, *n. m.* a rill, a brook.

A los, ul′-lòs, *adv.* about, intending; *a los* dol dachaidh, *intending,* or *about going home; a los* falbh, *with the intention of going.*

Alp, alp, *v.* dovetail. *See* Ealp.

Alt, ăllt, *n. m.* a joint; as an *alt, out of joint*; a method; ni sinn *alt* eile air, *we will use another method*; air na h-uile *alt, at all events; v.* dovetail, indent.

Altachadh, alt′-ach-Ă, *n. m.* grace before meat; *altachadh* beatha, *welcoming, saluting;* dh' *altaich* iad beath a chéile, *they saluted each other, B.*; 's ann do'n làimh ghlain bu chòir *altachadh, it is the clean hand that should salute—one rogue should not accuse a brother;* the articulation of the joints.

Altaich, allt′-êch, *v.* salute, join.

Altair, âlt′-ar2, *n. m.* an altar.

Altcheangal, ălt′-chéng-al, *n. m.* articulation, inosculation, ceangal nan alt.

Altrum, ălt′-rum, *n. m.* fostering, nursing, rearing; *v.* nurse, foster, rear; cajole.

Altshligeach, alt′-hlég-ach, *a.* crustacious, crusty; like shells.

Aluinn, âll′-ènn, *a.* handsome, very beautiful, elegant, superb.

Aluinneachd, âll′-èn-ăchg, handsomeness, beauty, elegance, superbness.

Am, um, *per. pro.* their, used before words beginning with *b, m, f,* and *p*; as, *am* fearg, *their wrath; am* màthair, *their mother; am* bainne, *their milk; am* pàisd, *their child.*

Am, um, *art. mas. sing.* used before *b, m, f,* and *p,* when not aspirated; as, *am* baile, *the town*; *am* math-ghamhuinn, *the bear*; *am* fear, *the man; am* pòsadh, *the marriage:* used before two feminine nouns; *am* boireannach, am mart, *the woman, the cow.* 2.

Am, um, contraction of ann am; as, *am* thigh, *in my house*; *am* meadhon, *am* mearachd, *in the middle, in the* or, *a mistake*; 2. *interr. par.* used before *b, m, f,* and *p*; as, *am* buail thu, *wilt thou strike? am* falbh thu, *wilt thou go? am* meas thu, *wilt thou esteem?* 3. am, um, for mo, my; as, ann *am* thigh, *in my house;* am, part. expl. see *an* part. expl.

Am, ăm, *n. m.* time, season; opportunity; fit time; se so an *t-àm, this is the time;* am fear a ni 'obair na *h-àm* bithidh e na leth thamh, *he that executes his task in due time shall be half at rest*; gabh *àm* air sin, *watch an opportunity to do that*; *àm* sam bith, *any time*; tha 'n *t-àm* ann, *it is time, it is full time*; *àm* iomchuidh, *fit*, or *proper time*, or *season.*

A mach, um′-măch, *ad.* out, out of; thig *a mach, come out*; *a mach* air a chéile, *at variance; int.* mach! mach! *out! out! go about your business, sir,* (or *madam, if you please.)*

Amach, ăm′-ach, *n. f.* a vulture. *Sh.*

Amadan, ăm-ad-an, *n. m.* a foolish man cha tuig an *t-amadan, the foolish man understands not. B.*

Amadanach, ăm′-a-dan-ach, *a.* foolish, silly-looking; aodann *amadanach, a silly expression of countenance.*

Amadanachd, ăm′-ad-an-achg, *n. f.* silliness; foolishness; the conduct of a fool.

Amadan-mointich, ăm′-ăd-an-môn-tyèch, *a.* dotterel; leth-amadan.

Amaid, âm′-êj, *n. f.* a foolish woman.

Amaideach, ăm′-êj-ach, *a.* like a foolish woman; foolish, silly.

Amaideachd, am′-èj-achg, *n. f.* foolishness, folly, silliness.

Amail, âm′-al, *a.* seasonable, timely.

Amaill, ăm′-èll, *v.* entangle; *dh'amaill* thu an lìon, *you have entangled the net*; obstruct, thwart, hinder.

Amais, am′-êsh, *v. n.* hit; *amais* so, *hit this*; meet, *dh'amais* sinn, *we met;* find, light upon; an *d'amais* thu air, *did you find it*; *amaisidh* na daoine is cha 'n *amais* na cnoic, *men meet, but the hills do not—be not a churl;* is sona an duine a dh' *amaiseas* air gliocas, *happy is the man that finds (that lights upon) wisdom.*

Amalachd, âm′-al-ăchg, *n. f.* seasonableness, timeousness, due time.

Amall, am′-all, *n. m.* a muzzle-bar; cuibh, cuibh-mhor, *one for four horses;* gearr-chuibh, *for two horses. Is.*

Amar, am′-urr, *n. m* the bed of a river; *amar* na h-aimhne, *the bed of the river; amar* caol, *a narrow channel, O.*; a trough, a mill-dam. *N.*

Amas, am′-us, *n. m.* power of hitting, aim; chaill thu *t'amas, you have lost your power of hitting; you have lost your aim*, or *mark.*

Amarlaid, am′-ar-laj, *n. f.* a blustering female, a careless woman.

Amarlaideach, ăm′-ar-laj-ach, *a.* careless; blustering.

A measg, um′-mèsg, *pre.* among.

Amh, áv, *a.* raw, unsodden, unboiled, unroasted.

Amhach, ăvf′-ach, *n. f.* the neck of a brute; a term of contempt for a person's neck.

Amhaidh, ăvf′-è, *a.* sour; as weather, lowering; gloomy.

Amhaidheachd, ăv′-è-ăchg, rawness, gloominess, sulkiness.

A mhain, uv-vhàn′, *ad.* alone, only; cha'n e *a mhàin, not only.*

Amhain, ăvf′-an′, *n. m. a.* entanglement by the neck; lying on the back without power of moving, as a horse.

Amhairc, év′- *or* áv′-èrchg, *v.* look, see, behold, observe, regard, attend; am fea nach *amhairc* roimh, amhaircidh e na lhéigh, *he that will not look before him* *must look behind him—look before you leap.*

AMHARC, ăv′-ark, *n. m.* look, appearance; is bochd an *t-amharc* th' air, *he has a miserable appearance;* view, sight; 'san *amharc, in view, in sight*; a' dol as an *amharc, getting out of sight*; the vizzy of a gun; inspection.

AMHARCACH, áv′-ărk-ach, *a.* considerate, attentive, humane; bha sin *amharcach* uaith, *that was very considerate of him.*

AMHARCAICHE, ăv′-ărk-èch-à, *n. m.* a spectator.

AMHARUS, av′-ur-us, suspicion, doubt; is mòr m' *amharus, I very much suspect*; tha gun *amharus, yes, most undoubtedly, most unquestionably; decidedly so.*

AMHARUSACH, ăv′-ur-us-ach, *a.* suspicious, doubtful; distrustful, ambiguous.

AMHARUSACHD, av′-ur-us-achg, *n. f.* distrustfulness, suspiciousness, ambiguousness.

AMHGHAR, àv′-ghar, *n. m.* affliction, tribulation, anguish, dismay, distress.

AMHGHARACH, àv′-ghar-ach, *a.* afflicted.

AMHLAIR, àv′-llar², a silly inoffensive man.

AMHLAIREACHD, àv′-llar-achg, *n. f.* fooling away one's time; trifling conduct.

AMHLUADH, áv′-lǍ′, *n. m.* confusion, dismay.

AMHLAISG, áv′-llèshg, *n. f.* bad beer.

AMHNARACH, áv-nnàr′-ach, *a.* shameless.

AMHUIL, áv′-ul, *ad.* as, like as, even as; *amhuil* mar Nimord an sealgair cumhachdach, *just as,* or *even as Nimrod the mighty hunter. B.;* is *amhuil* sin a bhios na peacaich, *just so,* or *even so, shall the sinners be. Sm.* Written sometimes *amhluidh; n. f.* attention, regard; na biodh *amhuil* agad da, *never mind him,* or *it;* pay no attention to him, *or* it; air an *amhuil* cheudna, *in like manner.*

AMHUILT, àv′-ult², *n. f.* a hellish trick *or* stratagem; deceit.

AMHUILTEACH, àv′-ult²-ach, *a.* full of bad tricks, deceitful, wicked; full of stratagems.

AMHUILTEACHD, àv′-ult²-achg, *n. f.* extreme deceit, deceitfulness; degree of deceit.

AMHUILTEAR, àv′-ult'-ar', *n. m.* a stratagist, a cunning fellow.

AMHUILTEARACHD, àv′-ult'-ar'-achg, *n. f.* a trick; extreme deceitfulness.

AMLADH, am′-llǍ, *n. m.* impediment, obstruction, entanglement; *p.* entwining, entangling, retarding.

AMLAG, am′-lag, *n. f.* a curl, a ringlet.

AMLAGACH, am′-lag-ăch, *a.* curled, in ringlets.

AMLAGAICH, am′-lag-èch, curl, make into ringlets.

AMRAIDH, am·rrè, *n. m.* cupboard. *Sc.*

AM MAIREACH, um′-màr²-ach, *ad.* to-morrow; *am* muigh, um-mŭè, *out, outside.*

AN, un, *art. mas. sing.* used before all letters, except *b, f, m,* and *p,* which take *am*; as, *an* cù, *the dog*; *an* guth, *the voice*—pronounced ung kû, ung gŭ. It takes t- before vowels; as *an* t-each, *an* t-eun, *the horse, the bird;* takes t- in the gen. and dat. of nouns beginning with *sl, sn, sr*; as, *an* t-sluaigh, *an* t-snàimh, *of the multitude, of the swimming.* The article is often used without being trans lated into English: 1. when the noun is followed by so, siod, sin; as, *an* cù so, *this dog*; am bealach so, *this breach,* or *gate-way*; 2. before a noun preceded by an adjective; as, is mòr *an* duine e, is maith *an* duine e, *he is a great man, he is a good man*; 3. before names of places; as, ann *an* Albainn, anns an Fhraing, *in Scotland, in France.*

AN, un, *poss. pro.* their; as, *an* cuid, *their property*; used before all letters, except *b, f, m, p,* which take am; as, *am* baile, *their town*; *am* fearann; *their land*; *am* màthair, *their mother.*

AN, un, *rel. pro.* as, leis *an* d'fhàg mi e, *with whom I left it*; leis *an* d'fhalbh e, *with whom he went*—contracted before prepositions 'n; as, o'n d'thàinig e, *of whom he is descended.*

AN, un, *int. pro.* as, *an* tu so, *is this you?* used before all letters, except *b, f, m, p,* which take am; as, *am* fac thu, *saw you,* &c.

AN, un, an *expletive particle,* placed before all verbs, excepting those beginning with *b, f, m, p,* which take am, as, gus *an* abair iad, *till they have said.*

ANABAISTEACH, an′-a-basht²-ach, *n. c.* an anabaptist, *a.* relating to an anabaptist.

ANABARR, an′-a-barr, *n. m.* excess, superfluity; sometimes written *anabharr.*

ANABARRACH, an′-a-barr-ach, *a.* exceeding, excessive, desperate, indispensible *anabarrach* feumail, *indispensibly* or *very necessary; anabarrach* aingidh, *desperately wicked*—used as an adverb.

ANABAS, an′-a-bass, *n. m.* dregs. *Bible.*

ANABASACH, an′-a-bass-ach, *a.* muddy.

ANABEACHDAIL, an′-a-bechg′-al, *a.* inattentive,—haughty: 2. not recollecting, not punctual.

ANABHIORACH, an′-a-vèr-ach, *n. m.* centipede, whitloe, meall-coinein.

ANABHUIL, an′-a-vhûll, misapplication.

ANABLACH, an-ab-lach, *n. m.* coarse flesh. 3.

ANABLAS, an′-a-blas, *n. m.* insipidity, a bad or bitter taste, tastelessness, 10.

ANABLASDA, ăn-ă-blas′-dda, *a.* insipid, tasteless, of a bad taste.

ANABLASDACHD, an-a-blas′-ddachg, tastelessness, insipidity, insipidness.

ANABRAIS, an′-a-brash, *n. m.* lust, 10.

ANABUICH, an-ăb′-êch, *a.* unripe. *Bible.*

ANABUIDH, an′-a-bê, *or* êch, unripe.

ANABUIDHEACHD, an′-a-bê-achg, *n. f.* unripenses, immaturity, abortiveness. *Is.*

ANABUIRT, ăn′-a-bŭrt², *n. m.* frenzy, 20.

ANACAIL, ăn′-achg-êl², *v.* manage, 1. defend.

ANACAINNT, an-a-kăént′², *n. f.* abusive language, reproaches, ribaldry. *B.*

ANACAINNTEACH, ăn-a-kăént′-ach, *a.* abusive in language, reproachful.

ANACAIR, an′-achg-ur², *n. f.* sickness, disease.

ANACAITH, an-a-kăĕ′, *v.* squander, waste, be profuse *or* prodigal.

ANACAITHEADH, an-a-kae′-Ă, *n. m.* extravagance, prodigality, waste, profusion, squandering.

ANACAITHTEACH, an-a-kăĕ′-tyach, *a.* prodigal.

ANACEART, an-a-kyărt′, *a.* unjust, partial.

ANACEARTAS, an-a-kyart′-us, *n. m.* injustice, unfairness.

ANACHAOINN, an-a-chāon′², *v.* deplore.

ANACLEACHD, an-ă-klechg′, *v.* discontinue the practice of.

ANACLEACHDAINN, an-a-klechg′-ĕn², *n. f.* want of practice, want of custom.

ANACNEASDA, an-a-krésd′-â, *a.* inhuman, cruel, barbarous, horrid.

ANACNEASDACHD, an-a-krésdd′-achg, *n. f.* barbarity, inhumanity, cruelty.

ANACOTHROM, an′-a-kŏr-um, *n. m.* violence, oppression, unfairness.

ANACOTHROMACH, an-a-kŏr′-um-ach, *a.* uneven; unjust.

ANACRACH, an′-achg-rach, *a.* sick; unwell.

ANACREIDEACH, ăn′-a-kraĕj-ăch, *n. m.* an unbeliever, infidel; *a.* unbelieving, irreligious.

ANACRIOSD, an′-a-krêsdd, *n. m.* antichrist.

ANACRIOSDACHD, an′-a-krêsdd-achg, *n. f.* paganism, heathenism, infidelity.

ANACRIOSDAIL, an-a-krēsdd′-al, *a.* unchristian, inhuman, cruel, barbarous.

ANACRIOSDUIDH, an′-a-krêsdd-ê, *n. m.* infidel, a pagan, a heathen.

ANACUIBHEAS, an-a-kwēss′, *n. m.* immensity, vastness, enormity; a thing incredible.

ANACUIBHEASACH, an-a-kwēss′-ach, *a.* enormous, desperate; *anacuibheasach* aingidh, *desperately wicked*; used as an adverb.

ANACUIBHEASEACHD, an-a-kwēss′-achg, *n. m.* enormousness, immoderateness, terribleness.

ANACUIMSE, an-a-kuêm′-shâ, *n. f.* vastness, immensity, immoderateness, terribleness.

ANACUIMSEACH, an′-a-kûêm-shăch, *a.* vast, exaggerated, exorbitant, enormous.

ANACUIMSEACHD, an′-a-kûêm-shachg, *n. f.* exaggeration, immenseness, vastness.

ANACUIMSICH, an′-a-kûêm-shêch, *v.* exaggerate, make exorbitant.

ANACUIMHNE, an-a-kûêv″-nâ, *n. f.* forgetfulness, negligence, want of memory.

ANACUIMHNEACH, an-a-kûêv″-năch, *a.* forgetful, negligent, inattentive.

ANACUIMHNICH, an′-a-kûêv′-nyêch, *v.* forget, disremember, neglect.

ANACURAM, an-a-kûr′-am, *n. m.* negligence, carelessness, inattention.

ANACURAMACH, an-a-kû′-rum-ach, *a.* inattentive, regardless, negligent.

ANAGEALTACH, ăn-ă-gyălt′-ăch, *a.* fearless.

ANAGHLEUSTA, an-a-ghlāst′-â, *a.* spiritless.

ANAGHNATH, an-a-ghrà, *n. m.* an ill habit, bad practice, *or* custom.

ANAGNATHACH, an′-a-ghrà-ăch, *a.* bad, irregular, unusual. *H.*

ANAGHNEITHEIL, an′-a-ghrè-al, *a.* pernicious, destructive, mischievous.

ANAGHRADH, an′-a-ghrâ-gh′, *n. m.* doating, love. *H.*

ANAGHRADHACH, an-a-ghrâ-gh″-ăch, *a.* loving excessively.

ANAGHRINN, an-a-ghrēnn′, *a.* unkind, inelegant.

ANAGOIREASACH, an-a-gaor″-as-ach, *a.* very needful, requisite; inconvenient, incommodious.

ANAINN, an′-ênn, *n. f.* the eaves, *or* top of a wall.

ANAIL, an′-ul, *n. f.* breath, breeze, rest; *anail* na beatha, *the breath of life. B.; anail* na gaoithe, *the breath of the wind*; the breeze. *O.*; *anail* nan speur, *the breath of the skies, i. e.* the breeze. *O.;* leig *t′-anail, rest,* take your rest; leigibh ur *n-anail, rest yourselves. Bible*; is blàth *anail* na màthar, *affectionate is the breath of a mother.* 12.—*Gen.* Analach.

ANAIMSIR, ăn′-ém-shêr′, *n. f.* unseasonable storm, bad weather, tempest.

ANAIMSIREIL, an-ém′-shêr-al, *a.* unseasonable, stormy, tempestuous.

ANALAICH, an′-al-êch, *n. v.* breathe.

AN-AM, ăn-ăm′, *n. m.* unseasonable time.

ANAM, ăn′-um, *n. m.* soul, spirit, breath.

Anamadach, an′-ăm-ăd-ăch, *a.* lively.

Anamadaich, an-am′-ad-ėch, *n. f.* convulsions.

Anameasarra, ăn-ă-mės′-ăr-a, *a.* intemperate, immoderate, lewd.

Anameasarrachd, ăn-a-mēs′-ăr-ăchg, *n. f.* intemperance, immoderateness.

Anameidhidh, an′-a-mēy′-ė, *a.* premature, abortive.

Anameidheachd, an-a-mėy′-ė-ăchg, prematurity, abortiveness.

Anameinn, ăn′-ă-mėn′, perverseness. *B.*

Amameinneach, ăn-ă-mėn′-ăch, *a.* perverse. *B.*

Anamharus, an-áv′-ăr-us, *n. m.* extreme distrust.

Anamhrusach, an-áv′-rus-ach, *a.* very distrustful, extremely jealous, very suspicious.

Anamoch, an′-am-ach, *a.* late, unseasonable; *n. m.* the evening; 'san *anamoch, in the evening. O. B.*

Anamiann, an′-a-mĕănn, *n. m.* sensuality.

Anamiannach, án′-a-mĕăn-ăch, *a.* lustful.

Anaoibhinn, ăn′-aŏėv-ėn′, *a.* joyless; woeful.

Anaoibhneas, an′-aŏėv-nyus, woe, sorrow.

Anart, â′-nărt, *n. m.* pride. *High. S.*

Anart, ăn′-ărtt′, *n. m.* linen.

Anasta, an′-ast-a, *a.* boisterous, stormy.

Anastachd, an′-ast-achg, *n. f.* toil in bad weather; bad usage; boisterousness.

Andana, ann-dàn′-ă, *a.* presumptuous.

Andanadas and **-achd**, ann-dàn′-ăchg, and -das, *n. f.* presumption.

An de, un-dyā, *or* jā, *ad.* yesterday.

An deigh, un-dyā-y″, *ad.* afterwards, (an deis, un jāsh) *un deigh* so, *afterwards, hereafter, after-hand.*

An deigh laimhe, un′-dyā-y′-láév-ă, *ad.* behind hand, in the back ground; afterwards.

Andiadhachd, ann-dyĕă′-ăchg, *n. f.* ungodliness; for *andiadhaidheachd.*

Andiadhaidh, ann-dyėa′-ė, *a.* ungodly, unholy, wicked, perverse.

Andiadhaidheachd, ann-dyĕă′-ė-ăchg, *n. f.* ungodliness, unholiness, wickedness.

An diugh, un′-dyŭ-gh′, *ad.* to-day.

Andlighe, ănn-ddlė′-ă, *n. m.* unjustness, undutifulness.

Andligheach, ănn-ddlė′-ach, *a.* unjust, not due.

Andochas, ănn-dôch′-us, *n. m.* despondency, distrust, despair.

Andochasach, ănn-dôch′-us-ach, *a.* despondent, mistrustful, distrustful, despairing.

Andoigh, ann′-dôė, *n. f.* bad condition.

Andolas, ann-dôl′-us, *n. m.* sadness, discomfort, distress, unhappiness.

An drasd, un′-drâssd, *ad.* now; at this time.

Anduchasach, ann-dûch-us-ach, *a.* not hereditary.

Anduine, ann′-dun′-ă, *n. c.* a decrepid person, *Is.*; a wicked man, *Irish.*

Aneagal, an′-ā-gal, *n. m.* fearlessness.

Aneagalach, an′-ā-gal-ăch, *a.* fearless.

Anealamh, ăn-ĕal′-uv, *a.* inexpert.

Anealanta, ăn-ĕăl′-ant-a, *a.* unskilful.

An-eanar, un-ĕăn′-ur, *ad. two days hence; an-ònar*, un-ōn′-ur, *three days hence;* an-aonar, un-ùn′-ur, *four days hence, Is.*; *an-eararais*, un′-ĕăr-ăsh, *three days hence. N.*

Anearb, ăn-erb′, *v. n.* distrust, despair; mistrust, doubt, suspect.

Anearbsa, an-erb′-sá, *n. f.* despair, distrust.

Anearbsach, an-erb′-sach, *a.* distrustful, despairing, despondent.

Anearbsachd, an-erb′-sachg, *n. f.* distrustfulness, suspiciousness.

Aneibheinn, an′-ā-vhėn′, *a.* woeful, sad, depressed in spirits.

Aneibhneas, an-āv′-nyus, *n. m.* discomfort, unhappiness, grief, misery.

Aneifeachd, ăn-ăf′-ăchg, *n. m.* inefficacy.

Aneifeachdach, ăn-āf′ăchg-ăch, *a.* ineffectual, inefficient, inefficacious, weak.

Aneireachdail, an-ăr″-achd-al, *a.* indecent, unseemly, unbecoming.

Aneireachdas, an-ăr2′-achg-us, *n. m.* indecency.

Anfhainneachd, an′-an′-ăchg, *n. f.* weakness, feebleness, infirmity, debility.

Anfhann, an′-ann, *a.* weak, feeble, infirm, debilitated, enfeebled.

Anfhannaich, an′-an′-ėch, *v.* weaken, enfeeble, debilitate.

Anfharsuinn, an′-ărs-ėn′, *a.* narrow, strait, tight, circumscribed.

Anfhaighidinn, an-ī′-ėj-ėnn, *n. m.* impatience.

Anfhiachail, an′-ĕăch-al, *a.* unworthy.

Anfhiosrach, an′-ės-rach, *a.* ignorant.

Anfhuras, an-ŭr′-us, *n. m.* impatience.

Anfhurasach, an-ŭr′-as-ach, *a.* impatient, discontented, fretful.

Anglonn, an′-a-glŏnn, *a.* brave, powerful; *n. m.* adversity, distress. *Stewart.*

Aniochd, an-eúchg′, *n. f.* cruelty, oppression,

Aniochdaire, an-eúchg′-ur′-ă, *n. m.* a tyrant.

Aniochdmhoireachd, an-eúchg′-vur-ăchg, *n. f.* unmercifulness, cruelty, oppression, tyranny.

Aniochdmhor, an-ėúch′-vur, *a.* merciless, cruel, oppressive, tyrannical.

Anios, un-ėsh′, *ad.* now, this time.

Aniul, an′-ėūll, *n. m.* want of guidance.

Ann, ănn, *pre.* in existence; an lunn a bh

ann, the race that was, or *existed*; *ann* o shean, *in existence of old, O.*; a th' *ann, that exists, that is*; am bheil thu *ann, are you there? are you in existence?* 2. in, within; *ann* an tigh, *in a house*; *ann* am baile, *in a town*; *ann* am bheachdsa, *in my opinion*: 3. stands for ann e, *in him*; cha 'n 'eil coire sam bith *ann, there is no fault in him*; 4. denoting emphasis; is *ann* a thachair e gu maith dha, *it has (truly) happened well to him*; contracted often *a'*; as, *a'* d' chridhe, for *ann* ad chridhe, *in thy*, or *your heart*; *annam, annad, annaibh, in me, in thee, in you.*

We follow Dr. N. M'Leod, and Dr. Armstrong, in spelling *maith*,—the Irish spell it *maith*, and pronounce it măĕch.

Annamh, ann′-uv, *a.* rare, scarce; is *annamh* a leithid, *his match is seldom met with*; gnothuch *annamh, a rare thing*; *ad.* seldom; is *annamh* a thig thu, *you seldom come.*

Annamhachd, ann′-uv-ăchg, *n. f.* rareness, fewness; rareness of occurrence; scarceness.

Annas, ănn′-ăs, *n. m.* a rarity, a novelty, dainty.

Annasach, ănn′-ăs-ăch, *a.* novel, dainty, new, uncommon.

Annasachd, ann′-as-ăchg, *n. f.* rareness, novelty, scarceness, fewness, uncommonness.

Annlamh, ann′-lav, *n.f.* perplexity. *Rd. M.*

Annlann, ann′-lann, *n. m.* condiment; whatever is eaten with bread &c. commonly called kitchen. *No. West*, ainnlean, *pro.* énn′-lyun.

An nochd, un-nnŏchg′, *ad.* to-night, this night; cha d' thig e *'n nochd, he will not come to-night.*

Anns, ann′-s', *pre.* in, used always before the *art.* the; *anns* a' bhaile, *in the town*; *anns* na mìosaibh, *in the months*: often contracted 's, 'san, 'sa; as, 'sa bhaile, *in the town*; *'san* arm, *in the army.*

Annsa, ann′-sà, *n. m.* great attachment, *or* affection; a thug rùn agus *annsa, that bestowed great love and affection, O.*; also, the *comp.* and *super.* of toigh, *beloved*; is toigh leam thusa ach 's *annsa* leam esan, *I love you, but he is more dear to me*; cò is *annsa* leat, *whom do you like above all others?* b' *annsa* thusa na dearrsa grèine, *more acceptable wert thou than sunbeams. O.*

Annsachd, ănns′-săchg, the greatest attachment; best beloved object; is tu m' *annsachd, thou art my best beloved.* 17.

Annsaoghalta, ann-sāŏ′-ălt-à, *a.* covetous, greedy.

Annsaoghaltachd, ann′-sāo-alt-achg, worldliness, greed.

Annspiorad, an′-spĕr-ad', *n. m.* the devil.

Anntlachd, ann′-ttlăchg, nuisance, disgust, displeasure; indecency.

Anntlachdmhoireachd, ănn-tlăchg′-vur'-ăchg, *n. f.* disgust, disagreeableness, nuisance.

Anntlachdmhor, ănn-tlachg′-vur, *a.* disagreeable, disgusting; unpleasant.

Anrach, àn′-rach, *c.* a wanderer; a weather-beaten person; tha dorus Fhinn do'n *anrach* fial, *Fingal's door is open (liberal) to the wanderer*, or *weather-beaten stranger*; is i do ghnùis do'n *anrach* a' ghrian, *your countenance to the weather-beaten stranger*, or *wanderer, is the sun, A. O.*; *a.* wandering, toiling in vain, disordered, stormy; d' fhalt *anrach, thy streaming*, or *disordered hair. O. Arm.*

Anradh, àn′-rā, disorder, distress, disaster; mac Morna 'se 'm meadhon *anraidh, the son of Morna in the midst of distress.*

An rair, un′-rrīr', *ad.* last night. *Is.*

Anriaghailt, ann′-rēā-ălt', *n. f.* disorder, confusion, uproar, tumult, riot.

Anriaghailteach, ann′-rēā-alt'-ach, *a.* disorderly, confused, riotous, tumultuous.

An roir, an′-rāor', *ad.* last night. *Pr.*

Ansheasgair, an′-hāsg-ur', restless.

Ansheasgaireachd, ann-hāsg′-ar'-achg, *n. f.* restlessness, *Is.*; rudeness, violence, *H.*

Anshocair, an-hochg′-ar', *a.* not properly fixed, unsettled, uneasy; *n. f.* sickness, restlessness; uair *anshocair, unsettled weather.*

Anshogh, an′-hô, *n. m.* discomfort, misery.

Anshoghail, an′-hô-al, *a.* miserable, adverse.

Anstrogh, ann′-strô, *n. m.* prodigality, waste.

Anstroghail, ann′-strô-al, *a.* prodigal, wasteful; very wasteful.

Anstruidh, ann-strūĕ′, *v.* waste, spend, squander.

Anstruidhear, ann-strūĕ′-ar2, *n. m.* a prodigal, a spendthrift, a squanderer.

Anstruidheas, ann-strūĕ′-as, *n. m* prodigality, squandering.

Anstruidheasach, ănn-strūĕ′-as-ach, *a.* wasteful, prodigal, profuse.

Anstruidheasachd, ănn-strūĕ′-as-achg, *n. m.* prodigality, wastefulness, extravagance.

Antighearn, ann-tyē′-urnn, *a.* a tyrant, an oppressor, a despot, (cuingire).

Antighearnail, ann-tyē′-arn-al, *a.* oppressive, tyrannical, cruel.

Antighearnas, ann-tyē′-arn-us, *n. m.* oppression, tyranny, cruelty.

Antiorralachd, ann′-tyērr-all-achd, discomfort, badness of climate, want of snugness.

Antiorrail, ann′-tyērr-al, *a.* uncomfortable.

Antogair, ann-ttogg′-èrr, *v.* lust after.

Antogradh, ann-tog′-rȦ, *n. m.* lust, concupiscence; a criminal propensity, anamiann; a keen desire; ioma gnè antoilibh, *many sorts of lusts*; concupiscence. *B.*

Antoil, ann-tōll′, *n. m.* self-will; lust.

Antoilich, ann′-tōll-èch, *v.* lust after. *L.*

Antrath, ann′-trâ, *a.* unseasonable; *n. m.* an unseasonable time. *H.*

Antrocair, ann-trôchg′-èrr′, *n. f.* cruelty.

Antrocaireach, ănn-trôchg′-ar-ăch, *a.* cruel, merciless, unmerciful.

Antrocaireachd, ănn-trôchg′-arr-achd, *n. f.* cruelty, unmercifulness.

Antrom, ann-trōm′, *a.* grievous to be borne. *M.*

Antromachadh, ann-trōm′-ach-Ȧ, *n. m.* aggravation, aggrieving, aggravating.

Antromaich, ann-trôm′-èch, *v.* aggravate, oppress, overload; ag *antromachadh* do chionta, *aggravating your guilt.*

Antruacanta, ann-trŭăchg′-annt-a, *a.* merciless.

Antruacantachd, ann-trŭăchg′-annt-ăchg, *n. f.* want of feeling, *or* compassion.

Antruas, ann-trŭăs′, *n. m.* want of pity.

Antruime, ann-trŭĕm′-à, *n. f.* oppression, tyranny.

Anuabhar, an′ ŭă-vur, *n. m.* excessive pride; luchd an *anuabhair*, *the excessively proud.*

Anuaibhreach, an′-ŭăĕv-rach, *a.* excessively proud—gentle, kind. *H. S.*

Anuaill, ann′-ŭăĕl, *n. f.* excessive pride; air mhòr *anuaile* is air bheag céille, *excessively proud and senseless, Sg.*; humility. *D.*

Anuailse, an-ŭăĕl′-shà, *n. f.* meanness, baseness.

Anuair, an′-ŭăĕr, *n. f.* an unseasonable storm; bad weather in summer.

A nuair, un′-nŭăr, *ad.* when; written often ’nuair.

Anuallach, an′-ŭăll-ach, *a.* indifferent; not haughty, *D.*; *n. f.* an oppressive burden, *Ar.*

A nuas, à-nŭăs′, *ad.* down, downwards, from above; thig *a nuas, come down.*

Anuasail, an′-ŭăs-al, *a.* low, mean.

An uiridh, un′-ŭĕr-ė, un′ŭĕr-èch, *ad.* last year.

A nunn, un′-nŭnn, *ad.* over, across; *a nunn ’s a null, hither and thither.*

Ao, āo, an inseparable preposition, answering to *un, in, dis,* &c. in English.

Aobhach, ′āo-vach. *See* Aoibheach and Aoibheil.

Aobhar, āo′ vur, *n. m.* cause, reason, materials; *aobhar* bròin, cause of grief; cha’n ’eil *aobhar* gearain ann, *there is no reason to complain*; air an *aobhar* sin, *therefore, for that reason*; *aobhar* còta, *materials for making a coat*; *aobhair* bhròg, *materials for making shoes*; gun *aobhar, without reason,* or *cause*; is mòr m’ *aobhar, great is my reason.*

Aobharach, āo′-vur-ach, *a.* causing, giving rise to.

Aobharrach, āo′-vurr-ach, *c.* a young person, *or* beast, of good or bad promise; is maith an *t-aobharrach* an gamhainn sin, *that stirk promises well*; is tu an *t-aobharrach* ciatach, *you are a youth that promises well indeed.*

Aobrunn. *See* Foab and Foabrunn.

Aocoltach, āo′-kòlt-ach, *a.* unlike, dissimilar, unlikely, not like.

Aocoltachd, āo′-kŏlt-achg, *n. m.* dissimilarity, improbability, unlikelihood.

Aocosalachd, āo′-koss-ăll-ăchg, *n. m.* unlikelihood, improbability; *aocosalachd* a ghnothuich sin, *the improbability of that thing.*

Aocosail, āo′-kos-al, *a.* improbable, unlikely, dissimilar.

Aodach, āo′-ddach, *n. m.* cloth, clothes; *aodach* ’sa bheairt, *cloth in the loom*; cuir ort *t’aodach, put on your clothes*; *aodach* leapa, *bed clothes, bedding*; *aodaich, cloth.* See Eid.

Aodann, āo′-ddunn, *n. m.* face, visage, countenance; a cron a bhios san *oadann*, cha ’n fheudar, a chleith, *the blemish in the face, cannot be hid*; impudence; nach ann aige tha ’n *t-aodann*, *what impudence the fellow has.*

Aodannach, āo′-dunn-ăch, *n. m.* the front of a bridle. *Sh.*

Aodhair, aŏ′-gh-ar′, *n. m.* a herdsman.

Aodocha, āo′-dôch-a, *a.* less probable, less likely.

Aodochas, āo-dôch′-us, *n. m,* despair, despondency, distrust.

Aodochasach, āo-dôch′-us-ach, *a.* hopeless, despairing, despondent, distrustful.

Aodochasachd, āo-dôch′-us-achg, *n. f.* hopelessness.

Aog, āogg, *n. m.* death, a skeleton; is tu an *t-aog* duainidh, *you are a miserable looking skeleton*; a’ dol *aog, getting useless, getting vapid as liquor.*

Aogail, āog′-al, *a.* death-looking.

Aogasg, āo′-gusg, *n. m.* appearance, likeness.

Aogachadh, āogg′-ach-X, *n. m.* and *part.* getting lean, withering, fading, dying by inches. *Md.*

Aognaich, āog′-nyêch, *v.* fade, wither.

Aoibh, āoėv, *n. f.* a cheerful countenance.

Aoibhealachd, āoėv -al-achg, *n. f.* cheerfulness, politeness.

Aoibheil, āoėv′-al, *a.* cheerful, in good humour.

Aoibhinn, āoėv′-ėnn, *a.* pleasant; òigridh *aoibhinn, pleasant,* or *joyous youth. Oss.*

Aoibhneach, āoėv′-nyach, *a.* glad, happy, joyous.

Aoibhneas, āoėv′-nyas, *n. m.* gladness; *aoibhneas* a shlighe, *the gladness,* or *joy of his way. B.*

Aoidh, āoė, *n. m.* a guest; aidh. *W.*

Aoidheachd, āoė′-achg, hospitality; aidheachd. *B.*

Aoidion, āoj-dyēnn, *n. m.* a leak; and sometimes pronounced āoj′-dyan.

Aoidionach, āoj-dyan-ach, *a.* leaky.

Aoidionachd, āoj′-dyăn-achg, *n. f.* leakiness.

Aoil, āoėl, *v.* lime, plaster; manure, with lime.

Aoin, ùėn, *v.* unite, join; air aonadh ris, *united to him.*

Aoine, ùėn′-ă, *n. f.* a fast, *Ir.*; di *h-aoine,* Friday; *aoine* na ceusta, *Good Friday.*

Aoineadh, ùėn′-X, *n. m.* a steep promontory. *Md.*

Aoir, āor′, *v.* satirise, lampoon; *n. f.* a satire, a lampoon; ribaldry; sheet or bolt rope of a sail; fear gealtach 'san *aoir, a timorous person holding the sheet. N. Md.*

Aoireachd, āor′′-ăchg, *n. f.* calumniation, a libel.

Aoirneagan, āor′-nyă-gan′, *n. m.* wallowing, weltering.

Aoirneagain, āor′ nyă-gan′, *v.* wallow, welter; 'ga *aoirneagan* 'na fhuil, *weltering in his blood.*

Aois, āosh, *n. f.* age; old age, antiquity; cia *aois* thu, *what is your age?* 's mairg a dh'iarradh an *aoise, woe to him that wishes extreme old age*; air son '*aoise, for its antiquity*; iarguinn na *h-aoise, the evil effects of old age*; agus bha Noah còig ceud bliadhna a dh' *aois, and Noah was five hundred years of age*; ann an làn *aois, in full age*; 'nuair a thig thu gu *h-aois, when you come to years, a set of people*; *aois*-ciuil, *musician,* obs.

Aol, āoll, *n. m.* lime; ath *aoil, a lime-kiln*; *aol* shuirn, *Ir.*; *aol* gun bhàthadh, *quick-lime, unslackened lime.*

Aolach, āoll′-ach, *n. m.* human excrement, dung.

Aoladair, āoll-a-dăr′, *n. m.* a plasterer, a lime-burner.

Aoladaireachd, āoll′-ad-ăr²-ăchg, plastering, burning lime.

Aolais, āoll′-ash, *n. f.* indolence, *Sk.*, an leisg.

Aolaisdeach, āoll′-ăshj-ach, *a.* lazy, sluggish.

Aolar, āoll′-ur, *a.* abounding in lime.

Aolman, āoll′-man, *n. m.* ointment; olla.

Aom, āom, *v.* incline, bend; bulge; be seduced by; dh' *aom* i leis, *she was seduced by him*; *aomaibh* bhur cluas, *incline your ear, B.*; th' am balla '*g aomadh, the wall bulges*; dh' *aom* e a thriall, *he bent his way, Os.*; *aomaidh* an aitreabh, *their buildings shall decay,* or *bulge. B.*

Aomach, āom′-ach, *a.* inclining, tending, bending.

Aomachd, āom′-achg, *n. f.* inclination *or* tendency; aptness to bulge or belly out.

Aomadh, āom′-X, *n. m.* inclination, or the act or state of inclining, bending, bulging, &c.; tendency.

Aomta, āom′-tyȧ, inclined, bent, bulged.

Aon, ùn, *a.* one; alone, same, only, single; *aon* bhean, *one woman*; *aon* eile, *another one,* another; *aon* sam bith, *any one;* gun *h-aon* eile, *he or she alone;* mar mise *aon* làth, *as I am some day or other*; *aon* seach *aon, without distinction*; m' *aon* chearc, *my only hen*; is *aon* ni e, *it is all the same*; 's esan, an *t-aon* duine air son sin, *he is the best man in the world for that*; 's e fein a tha 'na *aon* duine, *it is he, himself that rules the roast*—that is cook, mate and stewart; tri làithean bha e 'na *aon, three days he was all alone, O.*; gach *aon, every one*; a lion *aon* is *aon, one by one*; mar *aon, united, hand in hand*; gun *aon* duine, *without a single individual*; ann an *aon* tigh ruinne, *in the same house with us;* 'san *aon* luing, *in the same ship, Sg.;* do dh' *aon* seach a chéile, *to the one no more than to the other*; *n. m.* and *f.* an individual, a person; *aon* a thàinig a stigh, *an individual that came in*; *a person that came in.*

Aonach, ùn′-ach, *n. m.* a green plain near the shore on a stony bottom; on a sandy bottom, machair, *a green beach:* a siubhail nan *aonach* ciar, *travelling the dusky plains, Os.;* a meeting; *aonach* na samhna, *the meeting of Martinmas. C.*

Aonachadh, ùn′-ach-X, *pt.* uniting; *f. m.* union—galloping. *Mf.*

Aonachd, ùn′-ăchg, *n. f.* union, unity, concord; *aonachd* an spioraid, *the unity of the spirit;* comhnuidh a ghabhail cuideachd ann an *aonachd, to dwell together in unity. B.*

Aonadh, ùn′-ă, contraction of Aonachadh; air an *aonadh, united. B.*

Aonadharcach, ùn-aŏ′-ark-ach, *n. m.* a unicorn. *B.*

Aonairt, *see* Aoirneagan.

Aonaich, ù′-nyèch, *v.* unite, join into one, add; *aonaich* mo chridhe, *unite my heart. B.*

Aonaichte, ùn′-echt-a, *pt.* united, joined.

Aonar, ùn′-urr, *a.* alone, solitary, singular; duine 'na *aonar, a man all alone,* or *a singular man*; 'na *aonar* 'sa mhonadh, *solitary in the hill*; cha 'n 'eil thu ad *aonar* mar sin, *you are not singular in that respect.*

Aonarach, ùn′-urr-ach, *a.* solitary, lonely; forsaken.

Aonarachd, ùn′-ur-ăchg, *n. f.* solitude, solitariness.

Aonaran, ù′-nur-ăn, *n. m.* a hermit, a recluse, a person left alone, or forsaken; *aonaran* liath nan creag, *the hoary hermit of the rocks. O.*

Aonaranach, ùn′-ur-an-àch, *a.* like a hermit, solitary, lonely forsaken, in solitude, biodh an oidhche sin *aonaranach, let that night be solitary. B.*

Aonaranachd, ùn′-ar-an-ăchg, *n. f.* solitude, solitariness, loneliness.

Aonbharail, ùn′-var-ăĕl, *n. f.* unanimity.

Aonbheachd, ùn′-vyechg, *n. f.* unanimity.

Aonbhith, ùn′-vè, *n. f.* co-essentiality.

Aonbhitheach, ùn′-vé-ach, *a.* co-essential; co-substantial, of the same nature.

Aonchaithreach, ùn′-chăĕr-ach, *n. m.* a fellow-citizen; luchd *aonchaithreach, fellow citizens. Lu. b.*

Aonchasach, ùn′-chas-ach, having a single stalk *or* stem, as an herb.

Aonchridheach, ùn′-chrè-ăch, having like sentiments, unanimous.

Aondathach, ùn′-dă-ăch, *a.* of one colour.

Aon deug, ùn′-dyāg, *a.* eleven.

Aonfhillte, ùn′-ēll2-tyà, simple, sincere, foolish; a deanamh an duine *aonfhillte* glic, *making the simple wise. B. Ir.*

Aonfhillteachd, ùn′-ēll2-tyachg, sincerity; le *aonfhillteachd, with simplicity.*

Aonghin, ùn′-ghènn, *n. m.* an only child; mar *aonghin* mic, *like an only begotten son.*

Aonghneitheach, ùn′-ghrè-ăch, *a.* of one nature, of one kind; homogeneous.

Aonghneithachd, ùn′-ghrè-ăchg, *n. f.* homogeneousness.

Aonghradh, ùn′-ghrâ, *n. m.* the best beloved object; m' *aonghradh, my best beloved.*

Aonghuthach, ùn′-ghŭ-ach, *a.* having one voice or vote; consonous.

Aoninntinn, ùn′-ēnn-tyēnn, *n. f.* one mind, one accord; unanimity.

Aoninntinneach, ùn′-ēnn-tyēnn-ăch, *a.* unanimous, of one mind, *or* intention.

Aon-mhaide, ùn′-vèj-â, *n. m.* a simultaneous pull in rowing.

Aonmharsanta, ùn-var′-san′-ta, *n. m.* a monopoliser.

Aonmharsantachd, ùn′-vhàr-sant-achd, *n. f.* monopoly; exclusive sale of any thing.

Aonsgeulach, ùn′-skéul-ach, *a.* unanimous.

Aonsgoch, ùn′-skŏch, *n. f.* swallow-wort. *Sk.*

Aont, ùntt, *n. m.* assent, admission, acquiescence; tha' mi a toirt *aont* do n' a tha thu 'g ràdh, *I agree with,* or *I yield assent to what you say. H. S.*

Aonta, ùn′-tta, *n. f.* a lease, licence.

Aontachadh, ùn′-ttăch-ă, *p.* acceding, admitting, consenting; tha mi 'g *aontachadh, I accede, I admit,* or *allow;* ag *aontachadh* leis an lagh, *consenting to the law. B.*

Aontachd, ùn′-ttachg, *n. f.* acquiescence, agreement; admission.

Aontaich, ùnt′-èch, *n. v.* agree, yield, consent, admit; dh' *aontaich* i leis, *she yielded*; tha mi 'g *aontachadh* gu'm bheil, *I admit that it is;* thug i air *aontachadh, she constrained him to yield, B.;* na *aontaich* thusa leo, *consent* or *acquiesce thou not*; *aontachaidh* sinn leibh, *we will consent unto you, B. H.*; ma dh' *aontaicheas* tu aon uair, *once you consent* or *acquiesce.*

Aorabh, āor′-uv, *n. m.* constitution, mental *or* bodily; tha galar 'na *aorabh, there is a disease in his constitution.*

Aosda, āosd′-â, *a.* somewhat aged, old aged, ancient, antiquated; an déigh dhomh fàs *aosda, after I have become old. B.*; a bhàird *aosda* na linn a thréig, *ye ancient bards of bye-gone ages, A. O.*

Aor, āor, *n. v.* adore, worship; *aoram* dhuit, *I shall worship thee. Ps.*

Aoradh, āor′-ă, *n. m.* worship, adoration; *p.* adoring; ag *aoradh* dha, *worshipping him.*

Aosdachd, āosd′-achg, *n. f.* agedness, &c.

Aosdana, āos-dàn′-a, *n. m.* a poet, a rehearser of ancient poetry. *O. A.*

Aosmhoireachd, āos′-vur′-achg, *n. f.* agedness; great age, properties of old age.

Aosmhor, āos′-vur, *a.* old; aged.

Aotrom, āo′-trum, *a.* light; giddy; creutair *aotrom, a giddy creature.*

Aotromachadh, āo′-trum-ach-Ă, *n.m.* and *p.* ease, respite, as of a fever; alleviation, abatement, as of rain; tha 'n t-uisge 'g *aotromachadh, the rain abates;* fhuair e *aotromachadh* o'n fhiabhrus, *he got a slight respite,* or *crisis,* or *ease from the fever.*

Aotromaich, āo′-trum-èch, *v. n.* abate, as rain; alleviate, as disease; lighten, ease.

Aotroman, ăŏ′-trum-an, *n. m.* a bladder.

Ap, app, *n. f.* an ape.

Aparr, app′-urr, *a.* expert, (àbalt.) *No.*

Aparran, app′-urr-an, *n. m.* an apron.

Ar, for ur, *pro. ar* fearann, *our land;* takes n- before a vowel; *ar* n-each, *our horse; ar* n-athair, *our father.*

Ar, ar, *n. m.* ploughing; bha na daimh ag âr, *the oxen were ploughing, B.*; *ar* meadhonach, *second ploughing. Is.*

Ar, âr, *n. m.* slaughter; na fuilinn *àr* nan crioduidh, *permit not the slaughter of the Christians*; *artreud, arsèap, a retreat*; *battle*; dàn an *àir, the song of the battle-field;* 'san *àr, in the battle-field* hence, airsid, *unanimity,* from *àr, war*; and sìd, *peace, calm,* or *good humour.*

Ar, ar, *n. m.* a kidney, (dubhan,) geir nan *àr* no nan dubhan, *the fat of the kidneys.*

Arabhaig, ar′-a-vêg, *n. f.* strife. *Sk.*

Arach, âr′-ach, *n. m.* tie, stall-tie for a cow, a collar; remedy, help; cha 'n eil *àrach* air, *there is no remedy, there is no help for it*; cha robh *àrach* agamsa air, *I could not help it. North;* cha 'n' eil cothrom air; *battle-field*; 'na laidhe, 'san *àraich, stretched on the battle-field*; nach seachnadh le 'dheoin an *àrach, who would not willingly shun the battle-field. Sm.*

Arachas, âr′-ach-us, *n. m.* insurance.

Aradair, an agriculturist. *See* Airean.

Araich, âr′-èch, *v.* rear, maintain, support, nourish; is mairg a dh' *araich* thu, *woe to the person that maintained you.*

Araichd, ăr′-èchg, *n. f.* treasure, *or* wealth in clothing; a lady *or* gentleman's clothes given to servants, a present, a perquisite.

Araichdeil, ăr′-èchg-al, *a.* precious; gnothuch *araichdeil, a precious,* or *important affair.*

Araid, âr′-ėj, *a.* certain, particular, peculiar, special; duine *àraid, a certain person*; gu *h-àraid,* especially, particularly; gnothuch *àraid, an important* or *certain affair.*

Araideach, ăr′-ăj-ach, *a.* joyous, glad. *H.*

Araideachd, âr′-ėj-ăchg, *n. f.* importance, singularity, particularity, peculiarity.

Araidh, âr″-ė, for àraid.

Ar-amach, ăr-am-ăch′, *n. m.* rebellion, insurrection, mutiny, treason, conspiracy; rinn iad *ar-amach, they rebelled. B.* 12.

Aran, ăr′-an, *n. m.* bread; *aran* làthail, *daily bread*; livelihood; a tha cumail t' *arain* ruit, *who gives you your livelihood:* 2. cha bhi thu gun *aran, you shall not want a livelihood*; *aran* coirce, *oaten bread; aran* eòrna, *barley bread; aran* cruinneachd, *wheaten bread*; *aran* milis, *ginger bread; aran* peasearach, *pease bread; aran* seagaill, *rye bread; aran* taisbeanta, *shew bread.*

Aranaid, ăr′-ăn-ăj, *n. f.* bread basket.

Aranach, ăr′-ăn-ăch, *n. f.* bridle-rein.

Araon, ă-rāon′, *ad.* both together; bheir an Tighearn solus d' an sùilibh *araon, the the Lord will enlighten both their eyes. araon* thusa agus esan, *both of you.*

Arbhar, arv″-ur, *n. m.* sheaf-corn, standing corn. *B.*

Arbharach, ar′-var-ach, *a.* fertile in corn.

Arbharrachd, ăr′-varr-achg, *n. f.* forming into line, embattling.

Arbhartaich, ar′-văr t-éch, *v.* dispossess, disinherit, forfeit, confiscate; am fearann *arbhartaichte, the confiscated* or *forfeited estates*; *arbharaichte, forfeited.*

Arc, ârk, *n. f.* the cork-tree.

Arcan, ârk′-an, *n. m.* cork; a cork *or* stopple.

Arcuinn, ârk′-ènn, *n. m.* an udder. *Sk.*

Ard, ârd′, *a.* high, lofty; supreme; tall; 's esan is *àirde, he is the tallest,*or *the taller*; beinn *àrd, a lofty hill*; answers to *arch* as a prefix in English; *àrdeaspuig, an archbishop;* before an adjective as a prefix, supplies the place of an adverb; *àrd-shona, supremely blessed*; *àrdèibhneach, ecstactic, exulting in the highest degree*—the English or any other people never separate their prefixes by hyphens.

Ardachadh, ârd′-ach-Ă, *n. m.* and *p.* augmentation, increase; *àrdachadh* tuarasdail, *augmentation* or *increase of salary*; promotion, elevation, exaltation; *àrdachadh* nan amadan, *the promotion of fools, B.;* exalting, promoting, raising; extolling, praising; a' neach dh' *àrdaicheas* e fein, islichear e, *he that exalteth himself shall be abased.*

Ardaich, ârd″-ech, *v.* exalt, extol, raise, promote; elevate; increase; *àrdaich* a thuarasdail, *increase his salary.*

Ardaigneach, ârd″-ăĕg-nyach, *a.* nettlesome.

Ardaingeal, ârd′-ĕn′-nyal, *or* -ĕng′-al, *n. f.* an archangel, a supreme angel.

Ardamas, ârd'-am'-us, *n. m.* high aim, ambition.

Ardan, ârd''-an, *n. m.* an eminence, *or* rising ground; na shuidhe air *àrdan*, *sitting on an eminence*; pride, haughtiness, arrogance, wrath; an *ardan* faoin bha 'anam mòr, *in unavailing wrath was his great soul, O.*; dh' at *àrdan* na chridhe, *wrath swelled in his breast*; gach aon *àrdan*, *every knoll* or *rising ground, A.*; uabhar is *àrdan*, *pride and arrogance. B. id.*

Ardanach, ârd''-an-ach, *a.* high-minded, haughty, arrogant, prone to take offence; spiorad *àrdanach*, *a haughty spirit.*

Ardanachd, ârd''-an-ăchg, *n. f.* haughtiness, proudness, arrogancy, pride.

Ardathair, ârd'-ă'-hyur, *n. m.* a patriarch. 1.

Ardbhaile, ârd''-vhăl-à, *n. m.* a metropolis, a city; esan a ghlacas *àrdbhaile, he that takes a city. B.*

Ardbhandhuichd, ârd'-vănn-dyūchg, *n. f.* an archduchess.

Ardbhreitheamh, ârd-vhră'-uv, *n. m.* a supreme judge; a chief justice.

Ardbhrigheamh, ârd-vhrē'-uv, *n. m.* a supreme justice, *or* judge; lord of session.

Ardcheannabhard, ârd-chyann'-vhărd, a commander-in-chief, a supreme ruler or governor. *Is.*

Ardcheannard, ârd-chyann'-ărd, *n. m.* a chief, a supreme head. *H. S.*

Ardcheannas, ârd-chyann'-as, *n. m.* superiority, *C.*; dominion, pre-eminence, command.

Ardchlachair, ard'-chlăch'-ăr', *n. m.* an architect, a master mason.

Ardchlachaireachd, ârd'-chlăch'-ăr'-ăchg, *n. m.* architecture, business of a master mason.

Ardchomas, ârd'-chôm-us, *n. m.* discretionary power, despotic power, despotism.

Ardchomhairle, ârd''-chŏv'-url'-à, *n. m.* supreme counsel, parliament, a synod.

Ardchomhairliche, ârd''-chŏv'-url'-ėch, *n. m.* a chief counsellor, a consul.

Ardchuan, ârd''-chŭăn, *n. m.* the high sea.

Ardchumhachd, ârd'-chûv'-achg, *n. f.* supreme power *or* authority.

Ardchumhachdach, ârd''-chûv'-achg-ach, *a.* high in dignity and authority.

Arddhruidh, ârd''-ghrŭė, *n. m.* an archdruid.

Arddorus, ârd'-dŏr-us, *n. f.* a lintel.

Ardeaspuig, ârd''-ăs-pėg, *n. m.* archbishop.

Ardeaspuigeachd, ârd''-ăsp-ėg-achg, *n. f.* archbishopric, office of a bishop.

Ardfheamanach, ard''-em-ăn-ăch, *n. m.* a high steward. *H. S.*

Ardfheill, ârd'-āėll', *n. f.* a festival.

Ardfhiosachd, ârd'-ēss'-ăchg, *n. f.* vaticination, prophesying, predicting.

Ardfhaitheas, ard'-hlăĕ'-us, *n. m.* supreme dominion.

Ardflhath, ârd-hlă', *n. m.* a monarch.

Ardfhuain, ârd''-ŭăėm, *n. f.* bombulation.

Ardghleadhraich, ârd''-ghlāo-rrėch, *n. f.* bombulation, loud noise.

Ardghlonn, ârd''-ghlŏnn, a feat. *H. S.*

Ardghniomh, ârd'-ghrēv, *n. m.* a feat, exploit, achievement; treubhas.

Ardghuthach, ard-ghŭ'-ăch, *n. m.* clamorous, shouting loudly.

Ardhith, âr'-yhē, *n. f.* war; havoc.

Ardiarla, ârd'-ēărl'-à, *n. m.* first earl.

Ardinbh, ârd'-ēn'-uv, *n. f.* eminence, excellence, high rank. *H.*

Ardinbheach, ârd''-ēn'-uv-ach, *a.* eminent, excellent, in high rank *or* office.

Ardiolach, ârd''-ēŭl-ăch, *n. f.* loud shout, *H. S.*; acclamation.

Ardmharaiche, ârd-vhăr'-ėch-à, *n. m.* an admiral; priomh *ardmharaiche, lord high admiral. H. S.*

Armdhaighstireachd, ârd'-vhī'-styėr-achg *n. f.* supreme command *or* authority.

Ardmhaor, ârd' vāor', *n. m.* a herald: *ardmhaor* righ, *a pursuivant. H. S.*

Ardmhillidh, ârd'-vhēll'-ė, *n. m.* a heroic chief. *H.*

Ardmholl, ârd''-vhŏll, *v.* magnify, highly praise.

Ardmhoirear, ârd-voyr''-ar', *n. m.* an admiral, a lord president.

Ardrach, ârd''-rrach, *n. f.* an eight-oared galley, a boat.

Ardsgoil, ârd'-skol', *n. f.* classical education, philosophy; a high-school.

Ardsgoilear, ârd''-skol-ar', *n. m.* a philosopher, an excellent scholar—a student.

Ardsgoilearachd, ârd'-skol'-ar'-ăchg, *n. f.* philosophy, choice education.

Ardshagart, ârd''-hăg-urt', *n. m.* a high priest.

Ardshagartachd, ârd-hag'ărt'-ăchg, *n. f.* an high priesthood.

Ardsheanadh, ârd-hen'-nă, *n. m.* a general assembly; parliament. *H.*

Ardsheanair, ârd'-hen'-ăr', *n. m.* a member of a general assembly; a member of any supreme council.

Ardshona, ard'-hon'-a, *a.* supremely happy.

Ardshonas, ârd'-hon'-us, *n. m.* supreme bliss.

Ardthriath, ârd'-hryĕăch', *n. m.* supreme, sovereign, a supreme ruler *or* lord, chief *or* hero.

Arduachdran, ârd'-ŭăchg'-ran, *n. m.* a chief ruler *or* sovereign.

Arduachranachd, ârd-ŭăchg'-ran-ăchg, *n. f.* supreme rule *or* authority.

Ardughdarras, ârd'-û'-ddăr-us, *n. m.* full authority, discretionary power.

Arfuntaich, ăr'-funt-ėch, *v.* disinherit, dispossess, forfeit.

Argarrach, ăr'-gărr-ach, *n. m.* claimant.

Argumaid, ărg'-um-ăj, *n. f.* an argument, a motive, a reason; lionainn mo bheul le *h-argamaidibh, I would fill my mouth with arguments. B.*

Argumaideach, ărg'-um-ăj-ăch, *a.* argumentative, fond of arguments, prone to argue.

Argumaidich, ărg'-um-ăj-ėch, *v.* argue, reason, debate; foil.

A rithist, à'-rrė-ėsht, } *ad.* again, a second
A ris, a'-rēsh, } time.

Ar leam, hăr'-lyam; I should think—more correctly, *their leam.*

Arlogh, ăr'-laŏ, *n. m.* harvest-home, *I.* féisd an arloigh. *Arm.*

Arm, ărm, *n. m.* a weapon; the army; sgian, *arm* a bu mhiann leis, *knife, a weapon he was fond of, A.*; tha e 'san *arm, he is in the army*; chaidh e do'n *arm, he joined the army*; *v.* oil *or* grease, wool, ag *armadh* na h-olla, *anointing or greasing the wool.*

Armach, ărm'-ach, *a.* mailed, covered with armour; gach gaisgeach *armach, every mailed hero, Sm. Ar.*; a warrior; labhair an dubh *armach, the dark warrior spoke. Sg.*

Armachd, ărm'-achg, *n. f.* armour; arms; nigh iad an *armachd, they washed their armour*; *armachd* an t-soluis, *the armour of light. Bible.*

Armadh, ărm'-Ă, *n. m.* oil *or* grease for anointing wool; *p.* anointing or greasing wool.

Armaich, ărm'-ėch, *v.* clothe with armour; gird on arms; *armaichibh* sibh féin, *arm yourselves, B.*; *armaichte, armed, clothed with armour.*

Armailt, ărm'-ăėlt', *n. m.* an army; ann an *armailt, in an army. Bible.*

Armailteach, arm'-ăėlt-ăch, *a.* belonging to an army; having great armies.

Armchaismeachd, ărm-chăsh'-măchg, *n. f.* *an alarm of battle.*

Armchleasach, ărm-chlās'-ach, *a.* expert in military exercise.

Armchliseach, arm'-chlėsh-ach, *a.* expert in battle.

Arm-coise, ărm-kòsh'-ă, *n. m.* infantry.

Arm-oilean, arm-ul'-an', *n. m.* military discipline; drilling.

Armta, ărm'-tyả, *p.* oiled, greased as wool.

Armthaisg, arm'-hăėshg, *n. m.* an armoury; a military magazine, *arm thigh.*

Armun, ărm'-munn, *n. m.* a hero, a warrior; air slios an *armuinn, on the warrior's side. O. S.*

Aros, âr'-us, *n. m.* habitation, house; an loisgear *aros* nam Fiann, *shall the habitation of the Fingalians be burnt?*

Arosach, ar'-us-ach, *a.* habitable.

Arpag, arp'-ag, *n. f.* a harpy.

Arpag, ârp'-ag, a triangular cake. *Is.*

Arrabhalach, ărr'-ă-văll-ăch, *n. m.* a traitor; a treacherous fellow; a person that conceals himself in a house to bear away tidings.

Arrachd, ărr'-achg, *n. m.* spectre, *Md.*

Arraid, àrr'-ăj, *n. f.* toiling in vain.

Arraideach, àrr'-ăj-ach, *a.* toiling and wandering to no purpose.

Arraideachd, àrr'-ăj-ăchg, *n. f.* toil, fatigue; wandering to no purpose.

Arral, ărr'-all, *n. m.* fastidiousness; moit, moinig, *foolish pride.*

Arralach, ărr'-ăl-ăch, *a.* fastidious. *Md.* moiteil, moinigeil.

Arronnach, ărr'-òn-ăch, *a.* fit, decent.

Arusg, ar'-usg, indecency. *No.*

Arsa, ăr'-sa, corruption of Orsa; *orsa* mise, *said I*; *orsa* esan, *said he. See* Latin.

Arsachd, âr'-săchg, *n. f.* antiquity. *Irish.*

Arsaidh, ăr'-sė, *a.* old, decrepid.

Arsaidheachd, ărs'-ė-ăchg, antiquity.

Arsadair, âr'-sa-dar', *n. m.* antiquarian.

Arseap, ăr'shèp, *n. f.* retreat.

Artan, art'-an, *n. f.* a pebble; spiothag, *Ir.*

Artarach, ărtt'-ar-ach, *n. f.* a ship's boat; *M. S.*

Artreud, ăr'-ttrădd, *n. m.* retreat, often transposed, *ratreud.*

Arttheine, ărt-hă'-nyả, *n. f.* a flint. *Ir.*

Aruinn, âr'ènn, *n. f.* kidney; a forest.

As, ess, *pr.* out, of, from; *as* a mhachair, *out of the field*; tha 'n solus air dol *as, the light is going out, is extinguishing*; cuir *as* da, *kill him*; chaidh e *as, he escaped* leig *as, let go*; *a* is used for *as* before consonants; *a* tigh na daorsa, *out of the house of bondage*; cha d'thug mi ni sam bith *as, I took nothing out of it*; dubh *as, blot out*; *as* a chéile, *loosened, disjoined, asunder.*

As, ăs, *n. f.* an ass.

Asad, es-ud', out of thee; *asaibh, out of you.*

Asaibh, **Asaibhse**, es'-uv, es'-uv-shả, *pr.* and *pre.* out of you.

Asaid, ăs-ăj, *n. f.* childbirth; delivery; *v.* deliver, be delivered; dh' *asaideadh*, air mac i, *she was delivered of a son.*

Asaig, (acfhuinn,) apparatus.

Asainn, Asainne, es′-ènn, and -nya, out of us.

Asair, ăs′-ur, *n. m.* an herb, and a shoemaker. *Ir.*

Asal; ăs′-ul, *n. f.* an ass.

Asam, Asamsa, ess′-um-sȧ, out of me.

Asbhuan, Fasbhuan, stubble.

Ascain, ăs′-kăn′, ascend. *Irish.*

Ascall, ăs′-kall, *n. m.* loss, damage. *N.*

Ascaoin, as′-kāoèn, *a.* harsh, inclement, *v.* curse, excommunicate.

Ascairt, as′-kăërt, *n. m.* tow, barrach, *m.*

Asgaill, Asgailt, ăsk′-èll -ăèlt, arm-pit; retreat, the embrace.

A sios, a-shēs′, *ad.* down, downwards.

Aslachadh, as′llach-X, *n. m.* supplication, entreaty; *p.* entreating, supplicating.

Aslaich, as′-llèch, *v.* entreat, supplicate.

Aslonnach, as′-lonn-ach, *a.* prone to tell. *Ir.*

Asp, ăsp, *n. f.* an asp, nathair.

Astail, ăst′-ull, *n. m.* a contemptible fellow. *Is.*; a dwelling; a building. *Md.*

Astairich, ăst′-ur-èch, *v.* go, get under way, as a ship or boat.

Astar, ăst′-ur, *n. m.* a journey; distance; *astar* mòr, *a great distance*; *astar* thri làithean, *three days' journey*; *astar* math air falbh, *a considerable distance off*; fad air *astar*, *far away*; *away*, as a ship; a' dol fogh *astar*, *going under way*; a gearradh a *h-astair*, cutting her way.

Astaraiche, ast′-ur-èch-ȧ, *n. m.* traveller.

As ur, es′-ûr, *ad.* anew, afresh.

At, at′, *n. m.* a swelling, *v.* swell.

Ata, at′-a, *n. f.* a hat.

Ataich, at″-èch, *v.* entreat, request. *Md.*

Ataig, at″ėg, *n. m.* a stake, a palisade. *Md.*

Atamach, at″-ăm-ach, *a.* fondling, indulgent, caressing, lenient, partial.

Atamachd, at″-ăm-ăchg, *n. f.* fondling, an unreasonable person; lenity, indulgence, partiality; gun *atamachd* do dhuine seach duine, ***without partiality to any one.***

Atamaich, at″-dăm-èch, *v.* fondle an unreasonable person, caress, fondle, indulge.

Atcuisle, ăt′-kŭsh′-la, *n. m.* aneurism, a disease of the arteries.

Ath, à, *n. m.* a ford; *àth* na sùl, *the corner of the eye, M. L.*; aig *àthaibh* Arnoin, *at the fords of Arnon*; is fhearr tilleadh am meadhon an *àth*, na bâthadh uile, *it is better to turn in the middle of the ford than to drown yourself*, (completely.)

Ath, â, *n. f.* a kiln; air son mo chuidse do'n ghràn gabhadh an *àth* (àith) teine, *for my part of the grain, I will let the kiln take fire.*

Ath, ă, *a.* next, the next; an *ath* uair, *the next time*; 'san *ath* dhorus, *in the next door*; 'san *ath* mhìosa, *in the next month*: *v.* blush, flinch; na seoid nach *athadh an* cruadail, *the heroes that would not flinch in time of danger*; a prefix, signifying a second time.

Athach, ă′-ăch, *n. m.* a giant, famhair; *a.* bashful, blushing; duine *athach*, *a person easily abashed.*

Athailt, ă′-ălty′, *n. m.* a scar, mark; fail, sliochd.

Athadh, ă′-X, *n. m.* and *p.* a daunt, blush: duine gun nàire gun *athadh*, *a man without shame or confusion of face.*

Athair, ă′-hyur′, *n. m.* a father, an ancestor, *athair* mhort, *parricide, murdering one's father.*

Athairainmach, ă-hyur′-én′-um-ach, *a.* patronymical, *H. S.*

Athair ceile, ăr′-kāl′-ȧ, *n. m.* father-in-law.

Athairealachd, ă′-ur′-al-ăchg, *n. f.* fatherliness, affectionateness, humanity, kindness.

Athaireil, ă′-ur′-al, *a.* fatherly, paternal.

Athairich, ă′-ur′-èch, *v.* father, adopt.

Athairlus, ă′-ur′-lûs, *n. f.* ground ivy.

Athairmhort, ă′-ur-vhŏrt, *n. m.* parricide.

Athairmhortach, ă′-ur′-vhort-ăch, *a.* parricidial.

Athairmortair, ă-ur′-vhŏrt′-ar′, *n. m.* one that kills his father, parricide.

Athairthalmhain. *See* Cairthalmhainn, yarrow, milfoil.

Athais, ă′-èsh, *n. f.* leisure, ease, rest opportunity; air t' *athais*, *do at leisure*, *stop*; a cheud *athais* a bhios orm, *the first leisure I get, the first opportunity.*

Athaiseach, ă′-èsh-ach, *a.* slow, tardy, dilatory, leisurely.

Athaiseachd, ă′-èsh-ăchg, *n. f.* slowness, tardiness, dilatoriness, sluggishness, laziness.

Athaisich, ă′-èsh-èch, *v.* get calmer; abate, as rain; get ease.

Athar, ă′-ur, *n. m.* the evil effects or consequence of any thing; bithidh tu an *athar* sin ri d' bheò, *you shall feel the evil effects of that during your life-time*; *athar* 'na griobhaich,* (grēv-ăch), *the dregs* or *evil effects of the measles*; *athar* òil, *the dregs of a debauch*, or *drink*; *athar* na deilginnich,† *effects* or *dregs of the herpes* or *shingles.*

---

* In Skye, griobhlach, (grúl′-ach); in Invern. griobhrach, (grúr-ăch); in Kintyre, griobhach is pronounced grēff-ach, in many other parts of Argyle gruffy and gru′-ach, —all derived from griobh.

† In Skye, piocas; *Lw.* boiceannach; in

Athar, a'-'hur, *n. m.* the air, atmosphere, the firmament; agus rinn Dia an *t-athar, and God made the firmament*; tha 'n *t-athar* dorcha, *the atmosphere is dark* or *hazy.*

Atharail, á'-hur-al, *a.* atmospheric, etherial, relating to the air.

Athar amharc, ă-hur-áv'-urk, *n.m.* Aëroscopy, the observation of the air.

Athar eolas, á-ur-ĕôl'-us, *n. m.* Aëromancy, the art of divining by the air.

Athar iul, á'-'hur-ĕūl, Aĕrology.

Atharla, ă'-ur-la, *n. f.* a heifer, a quey. *P.*

Athar mheidh, á-hur-vhē'-yh', *n. f.* a barometer.

Atharrach, ă'-ur-ach, *a.* droll. *H.*

Atharrach, ă'-ur-ach, *n. m.* alternative, change, alteration; another; cha 'n 'eil *atharrach* agad r' a dheanadh, *you have no alternative*; cha 'n 'eil math 'na *atharrach, there is no good in a change;* cha d' thàinig *atharrach* riamh, *another never came*; cha 'n e maith an *atharraich* th' air 'aire, *it is not the interest of another he has in view.*

Atharrachadh, ă'-urr-ăch, *n. m.* change, removal, alteration; *atharrachadh* giùlain, *an opposite line of conduct*; 's mòr an *t-atharrachadh* a thàinig air, *there is a great change on him*; *p.* changing, moving.

Atharraich, ă'-urr-ėch, *v.* change, alter, translate, move, make an alteration; *dh'atharraich* iad an aodach, *they changed their garments* or *clothes*; a shaor is a dh' *atharraich* sinn, *that delivered and translated us, B. A.*; *atharraichte, changed, translated.*

Atharrachail, ă'-ărr-ăch-ăl, *a.* changeable, changing, unsteady, given to change.

Atharthomhas, ă-urr-hov''-us, *n. m.* Aërometry; tomhas an athair.

Athbhach, ă'-vach, *n. m.* strength. *Arm.*

Athbheachd, ă'-vhechg, *n. m.* retrospect, a second thought, an after-thought, reconsideration, consideration.

Athbheachdaich, ă-vhechg'-ėch, *v.* look steadfastly, a second time; reconsider.

Athbheothaich, ă-vhyŏ'-ėch, *v.* revive, refresh, re-animate, quicken; rekindle; *athbheothaich* an gealbhan, *rekindle the fire.*

Athbheothachadh, ă-vhyŏ'-ăch-Ă, *n. m.* reviving, rekindling; reanimation; *p.* refreshing, reanimating, rekindling.

Bute, Cow. and L. Side, breac-bhoiceannach; in many other places, peigidh; Lochaber, breac-otrach.

Athbheothachail, ă-vhyŏ'-ăch-al, *a.* refreshing, causing to revive.

Athbhliochd, ă'-vhlyúchg, *n. m.* second month after calving; dhaireadh as a *h-athbhliochd* a' bhò, *the cow was lined the second month after calving.*

Athbhreith, ă'-vrā, regeneration; gus am bi thu air t' *athbhreith, till you are regenerated* or *born again.*

Athbhriathar, ă'-vrĕ-ăr, *n. m.* a repetition, tautology, saying the same thing twice.

Athbhriathach, a-vrĕăr'-ach, *a.* tautological, repeating the same thing. *H.*

Athbhreathrachas, ă'-vrĕăr-ăch-us, *n. m.* tautology, repetition.

Athbriathraiche, ă-vrĕăr'-ėch-ă, *n. m.* a tautologist, one saying the same thing twice.

Athbhrosnachadh, ă-vrŏs'-năch-Ă, *n. m.* rallying *or* re-inspiring with courage, *H.*

Athbhrosnaich, ă-vros'-nnėch, *v.* re-inspire, re-encourage, resume courage.

Athbhuail, ă-vhŭăl', *v.* re-strike, strike again, re-thrash; com' nach d' *athbhuail* thu do shleagh, *why did you not strike again your shield? Oss. Ar.*

Athbhualadh, ă-vhŭăl'-Ă, *n. m.* repercussion; *p.* striking *or* thrashing a second time.

Athbhuannaich, ă-vŭăn'-nėch, *v.* regain, recover, gain a second time.

Aithbhuidhinn, ă-vŭ-hēnn', *v.* regain, recover, retrieve, repossess, gain a second time; *n. m.* a second gaining *or* retrieving.

Athchagainn, ă-chăg'-enn, *v.* chew, *or* ruminate a second time. *H.*

Athchagnadh, ă-chăg'-nĂ, *n. m.* rumination, chewing again, chewing the cud again.

Athchairich, ă-chăr'-ėch, *v.* re-mend.

Athchaithte, ă-chăĕ'-tyă, *p.* greatly worn out.

Athchas, ă-chăs', *v.* retwist, retwine.

Athcheannaich, ă-chyann'-ėch, *v.* repurchase, redeem; ag *athcheannach* na h-aimsir, *redeeming the time. Bible.*

Athcheangal, ă'-chyĕ-al, *or* chéng-al, *n. m.* rebinding, renewal of an agreement.

Athcheangail, a-ché'-ėl, *or* cheng-ėl, *v.* rebind, bind again, renew an agreement.

Athcheannsaich, ă-chyănn'-ssėch, *v.* reconquer, subdue a second time; retrieve.

Athcheasnaich, ă'-chyās-nnėch, *v.* re-examine, examine *or* interrogate again.

Athcheasnachadh, a-chyās'-năch-Ă, re-examination; *p.* re-examining.

Athcheumaich, ă-chyām'-ėch, *v.* retrace, repace, pace a second time. *H*

Athcheumnachadh, ă′-chyām-năch-Ă, *n. m.* retracing; recapitulating.

Athchlaon, ă-chlāon′, *v.* relapse into error, deviate a second time.

Athchlaonadh, ă-chlāon′-Ă, *n. m.* relapsing into error, a second deviation.

Athchog, a-chŏg′, *v.* rebel. *Ml.*

Athchoisich, ă-chŏsh′-ėch, *v.* travel again, retrace, repass.

Athchomain, a-chòm′-an′, *n. f.* a second obligation; recompense, retaliation, requital. *D. D.*

Athchomhairle, ă-chŏv″-url′-à, *n. f.* a second thought, a second advice.

Athchomhairlich, ă-chov′-url-ėch, *v.* re-advise, re-admonish

Athchomhairlichte, ă-chŏv″-url′-ėch-tyà, re-advised, re-admonished.

Athchostus, ă-chŏst′-us, *n. m.* after-cost.

Athchronaich, ă-chrŏn′-ėch, *v.* rebuke a second time.

Athchruinnich, ă-chrūėn′-nyėch, *v.* regather, re-assemble, re-unite, rally as an army.

Athchruinnichte, ă-chrūėn′-nyėcht-tyà, *p.* re-assembled, gathered again, rallied.

Athchruth, ă-chrū′, *n. f.* change of form *or* appearance, transformation.

Athchruthachadh, ă-chrū′-ăch-Ă, *n. m.* regeneration, transformation; *p.* recreating, regenerating, transforming.

Athchruthaich, ă-chru′-ėch, *v.* recreate, transform, regenerate.

Athchuimhne, ă-chūėv″-nyà, *n. f.* recollection, remembrance.

Athchuimhnich, ă-chūėv′-nyėch, *v.* recollect, remember, put in mind a second time.

Athchuimirich, ă-chūėm′-ėr′-ėch, *v.* pare a second time, pare minutely.

Athchum, ă′-chŭm, *v.* shape a second time; keep a second time. *D.*

Athchumadh, ă-chum′-Ă, *n. f.* transformation; *p.* transform, reshape. *B.*

Athchunn, ă-chunn′, *v.* reshape, shape anew; fransform. *Islay.*

Athdhealbh, a′-yhyăl-uv, *v.* transform.

Athdhealbhadh, ă-yhyăl′-uv-Ă, *n. m.* transformation, changing the shape. *H.*

Athdheanadach, ă-yhėn′-ad-ăch, *a.* itinerant, circumlocutory. *H.*

Athdhioghail, ă′-yhŭ-ėl, *v.* retaliate, revenge, recompense evil for evil.

Athdhioghladh, ă-yhù′-lĂ, *n. m.* retaliation, retribution, evil for evil; *p.* revenge a second time.

Athdhioghaltach, ă-yhùll′-tach, *a.* revengeful, vindictive; retributive.

Athdhiol, ă-yhēul′, *v.* repay.

Athdhioladh, ă-yhēul′-Ă, *n. m.* requital

Athdhuin, ă-yhûn′, *v.* reshut.

Athdhruid, ă′-yhrūj, *v.* reshut.

Athdhublachadh, ă-yhûb′-lăch-Ă, *n. m* redoubling, reduplication.

Athdhublaich, à-ghûb′-lėch, *v.* redouble.

Athfhas, ă′-âs, *n. m.* aftergrowth.

Athfhuaraich, ă-ūăr′-ėch, *v.* recool.

Athfhuasgladh, a′-ūăsg-lĂ, *n. m.* releasing *or* untying a second time; ransom.

Athghamhnach, ă-ghăv′-năch, *n. f.* a cow two years without a calf. *H. S.*

Athghin, ă′-ghėn, *v.* regenerate, produce a second time.

Athghineumhinn, ă-ghėn′-uv-ėn, *n. f.* regeneration, reproduction. *H.*

Athghlac, a-ghlăchg′, *v.* retake, apprehend a second time.

Athghlan, ă′-ghlăn, *v.* recleanse, polish, purify; *athghlanta*, recleansed.

Athghoirrid, a′-ghaŏrr-ėj, *n. f.* a short road, way, *or* method; *a.* short-tempered; tha e *athghaoirrid, he is short-tempered.*

Athiarr, ă′-ēărr, *v.* seek *or* search a second time.

Athiarrtas, a′-ēărr-tas, *n. m.* a repetition in prayer; a second searching *or* seeking. *B.*

Athlathachadh, ă′-lă-ăch-Ă, *n. m* procrastinating; procrastination; *athlathaich*, procrastinate. *H. S.*

Athleagh, ă′-lyaă, *v.* remelt.

Athleasachadh, ă′-llās²-ach-Ă, *n. m.* and *p.* reformation, amendment, *B.*; second dunging.

Athleasaich, a-llās′²-ėch, *v.* remend, reform, ameliorate, correct, re-dung.

Athloisg, a′-lóėshg, *v.* re-burn.

Athlorgaich, ă-llŏrg′-ėch, *v.* retrace.

Athmhalairt, ă-vhăl′-ărt′, re-exchange; *n. f.* a second exchange *or* bargain.

Athneartachadh, a-nnert′-ăch-Ă, *n. m.* re-strengthening, recruiting strength, reinforcing.

Athneartaich, ă-nnĕrt′-ėch, *v.* re strengthen, recruit, get new strength.

Athnuadhachadh, ă-nūă′-ăch-Ă, *n. m.* renovation, renewal; tre *athnuadhadh* bhur n-inntinn, *by the renewing of your minds.*

Athnuadhaich, ă′-nnūă-ėch, *v.* renew; air chor a's gu'n *athnuadhaichear* t-òige, *so that thy youth is renewed. B. H.*

Aththill, ă′-hyēll, *v.* return. *B.*

Athreitich, ă′-rrā-tyėch, *v.* disentangle.

Athroinn, ă′-rraŏėn, *v.* subdivide.

Athsgriobh, ă-skrēv′, *v.* transcribe, copy; a dh' *athsgriobh* daoine Heseciah righ Iùda, *which the men of Hesekiah king of Judah copied.*

Athsgriobhadair, ă-skrēv′-ă-dar′, *n. m.* a transcriber, one that copies.

Athsgriobhadh, ă′-skrēv-Ă *n. m.* a transcript, a copy; *p.* transcribing.

Athshealbhachadh, a-hyăl'-văch-Ă, *n. m.* re-inheriting, re-possessing.

Athshealbhaich, a-hyăl'-vèch, *v.* re-inherit, re-possess.

Athsheall, a-hyăll', *v.* look again.

Athshealladh, ă-hyăll'-Ă, *n. m.* the second sight, retrospect.

Athsmaoineachadh, a-smāon''-ăch-Ă, reflection, meditation.

Athsmaoinich, a-smāon'-èch, *v.* think again, meditate,—written *athsmaointich* also.

Athstiuir, a-stūèr', reconduct, steer again.

Aththeoidh, a-hyōè', *v.* warm, *or* simmer again.

Aththill, a-hyēll', *v.* return, come back.

Aththog, ă'-hòg, *v.* rebuild, lift again.

Aththoisich, a'-hôsh-èch, *v.* recommence.

Aththreoraich, ă'-hryôr-èch, *v.* reconduct.

Aththuislich, ă'-hūèsh-lyèch, *v.* relapse.

Aththuit, ă-hût'', *r.* fall again, relapse.

Athurachadh, ă-ûr'-ach-Ă, *n. m.* refreshment; *p.* reviving, refreshing, renovating.

Athuraich, ă-ûr'-èch, *v.* refresh, revive; *athùraichte, refreshed, revived, renovated.*

Atmhoireachd, ăt'-vur'-ăchg, *n. f.*; *atmhoireachd* Iordain, *the swelling of Jordan.*

Atmhor, at''-vur, *a.* swelled, turgid.

Atuinn, a'-ttènn, *n. m.* a palasado, a rafter; a wicket; cachladh cabharnach, clisneach, cliseach, cliaibhneach, *I. S. Sk. P. R.* The letters here refer to the places where *cliseach, cabarnach,* &c. are used.

B

B, the second letter of the Gaelic alphabet, *beath* or *beith*, the birch-tree; it has two sounds; one like *b* in English, as, *baile, a town, beò, alive*; the other aspirated, as, *bhuail*, vvhūăl mi, *I struck. Bh* often forms a syllable of itself; as, *marbh*, mar-uv; garbh, găr-uv, but pronounced quick. The article *an* is changed uniformly in the *nom.* into *am*, before this letter; as, *am baile*, and not, *an baile.*

B', for bu; used before an initial vowel, or *f* aspirated; as, *b'* fhearr leam, *I would prefer*; *b'* uamhasach an latha, *terrible was the day*; *b'* eòlach mise air, *I was well acquainted with him*; *well did I know him.*

Ba! ba! bâ bâ, *int.* a lullaby; *bà! bà!* mo leanabh, *sleep, sleep, my child.*

Ba, bă, *n. f. pl.* cows, kine.

Ba, bâ, *a.* foolish, simple. *Lw.*

Bab, băb, *n. m.* a child's excrement; hence *abab*; some parts of Perthshire, *biob* dean do *bhab.*

Babag, băg'-ăg, *n. f.* a filthy female; confounded sometimes with *pabag*, a tassel.

Babach, băb'-ăch, *a.* filthy, abominable.

Babachd, băb'-ăchg, *n. f.* filthiness, abomination.

Babban, babb'-an, *n. m.* a bobin. (Scotch.

Babhd, băv'-ud, *n. m.* a surmise, a rumour.

Babhdach, băv'-ud-ăch, *a.* spreading a surmise *or* rumour.

Babhdaire, bav'-ud-ăr', *a.* a surmiser. *Is.*

Babhdaireachd, băv'-ud-ăr'-ăchg, *n. f.* spreading rumours.

Babhaid, bav'-ĕj, *n. f.* a tassel. *Ar.*

Babhaideach, băv'-aj-ach, *a.* tufted,

Babhsgannta, bav'-ask-annt-ă, *a.* boastful blustering, but easily frightened.

Babhsganntachd, băv'-ăsk-ănnt-ăchg, *n. f.* cowardice; fright from false alarm.

Babhunn, bâ'vunn, *n. m.* bulwark, rampart; brisidh iad a *bàbhuinn, they shall break her bulwarks, Bible*; thugaibh fainear a *bàbhainn* bhreagh, *mark ye her beautiful bulwarks*; *a fold. Ps.*

Babhunnach, bâv'-unn-ach, *a.* well fenced with bulwarks, secure.

Bac, băchg, *v.* hinder, restrain, obstruct; forbid; na *bac* e, *do not hinder him.*

Bac, băchg, *n. m.* the fulcrum of an oar, *H.*; a sand bank, (Coll;) the notch of a spindle; *bac* an righe, *the bend of the arm*; *bac* na h-easgaid, *the hough*; *bac* mòna, *a peat-pit*; *bac* na h-achlais, *the arm-pit*; *bac* a chruachainn, the haunch.

Bacach, băchg'-ăch, *a.* lame, cripple.

Bacadh, bachg'-Ă, *p.* hindering, restraining.

Bacag, băchg'-ăg, *n. f.* a trip; cuir cas *bhacaig* air, *trip him.*

Bacaiche, băchg'-èch-à, *n. f.* lameness.

Bacaichead, băchg'-èch-ud, *n. f.* degree of lameness, lameness.

Bacail, băchg'-al, *n. f.* a stop, hindrance, obstacle, interruption; *p.* stopping.

Bacan, băchg'-an, *n. f.* a tether-stake, a hinge, *Arm.*; an smeòrach air *bacan, the mavis on a stake. Sg. Ar.*

Bacbhord, bachg'-vhord, *n. m.* windward.

Bach, băch, *n. m.* drunkenness, *Md.*; *bach*-thinneas, *sickness occasioned by drinking. Md.*

Bachall, băch'-ăll, *n. f.* an old shoe, a slipper—a staff, a crosier. *Arm.*

Bachlach, bach'-lach, *a.* curled, in ringlets.

Bachlag, băch'-lăg, *n. f.* a shoot *or* blade, as that of lint, turnip, &c.

Bachoid, băch′-áj, *n. f.* the boss of a shield.

Baclamh, bachg′-llàv, *m. n.* hand-cuff.

Bacrach, bachg′-rach, *n. m.* the name of a Druid that foretold the birth of our Savour. *Armstrong.*

Bad, băd, *n. m.* a tuft, a bunch, a cluster; a grove, clump, thicket; a flock; *bad* chaorach, *a flock of sheep*; *bad* coille, *a clump of trees*; gabhaidh sibh *bad, you shall take a cluster, Bible*; a ragged garment; *North*, a plain, a spot; *v.* cut a tuft here and there; prune.

Bag, băg, *a.* a bag, (teutonic,) a big belly.

Bagaid, băg′-ăj, *n. f.* a corpulent female, *Is.*; in the *Bible*, a cluster; *bagaidean* searbh, *sour clusters.*

Bagaideach, bag′-aj, *a.* corpulent; clustered, full of clusters.

Bagailt, băg′-ăělt, *n. f.* a cluster.

Bagair, bag′-ur′, *v. n.* threaten, denounce evil, terrify, appear like; tha e *bagairt* an uisge, *it appears like rain.*

Bagaire, băg′-ur′-à, *n. m.* a corpulent man.

Bagairt, bag′-ărt′, *n. m.* a threat; *p.* threatening, denouncing; cha d' théid plàst air *bagairt, no plaster is applied to a threat. M. In.*

Bagannta, bag′-annt-a, *a.* corpulent, *b.*

Banganntachd, băg′-annt-achg, *n. f.* corpulency.

Bagarrach, băg′-urr-ăch, *a.* prone to threaten, threatening, denouncing evil.

Bagarrachd, bág′-urr-ăchg, *n. f.* a habit of threatening, denouncing evil.

Bagh, bâ, *n. m.* a bay. *D.*

Bagradh, băg′-rĂ, *n. m.* a threat; *p.* threatening, denouncing evil.

Baibeil, bī′-bal, *a.* terrible, enormous.

Baibh, bīv, *n. m.* a terrible sight; an incredible thing; a fairy, a goblin.

Baibhealachd, bīv′-ăl-ăchg, *n. f.* enormousness, terribleness; exaggeration.

Baibheil, bī′-val, and baŏĕ′-val, *a.* incredible, enormous, terrible, exaggerated; prìs *bhaibheil, an exorbitant price.*

Baideal, băj′-ăll, *n. m.* a pillar of cloud, a cloud, *Is.*; *baideal* neòil, *a pillar of cloud, Ps.*; *a tower*; mo *bhaideal* ard, *my high tower. Sm. A.*

Baidealach, băj′-all-ach, *a* like a pillar, a tower; full of pillars of clouds.

Baidh, bī, *n. f.* a wave. *Irish.*

Baidreach, băj′-rach, *a.* ragged; *n. f.* a ragged garment; *n. c.* a ragged person.

Baidse, bâj′-shà, *n. m.* a musician's fee at a country wedding. *N. Highlands.*

Baidse, bèj′-shà, *n. f.* a voyage; an enormous load or cargo. *W. H.*

Baidsire, bèj′-shèr-à, *n. m.* a voyager, an adventurer.

Baidsireachd, bèj-shèr-achg, *n. f.* adventuring, cruising, sea-faring life.

Baigear, beg′-ar′, *c. n.* a beggar, a mendecant, a pauper,—Teutonic. The Teutonic and Gaelic are the same. *Murray.*

Baigeareachd, beg′-ar′-achg, *n. f.* begging, beggary. pauperism; indigence; begging; pleading.

Baigh, bâė *or* bī-yh′, *n. f.* attachment, fondness, partiality, affection; dh'f heòraich i le *bàigh, she inquired affectionately*; is mòr a *bhaigh* ris, *great is his partiality for him. O. A.*

Baighach, bī′-ăch, *a.* kind; *n. m.* a fa vourite.

Baighealachd, bī′-all-achg, *n. f.* favour, partiality, kindness; benignity, fondness.

Baigheil, bī′-yhal, *a.* favourable; bha thusa *baigheil, thou hast been favourable, B.*; in Islay more frequently *sbaigheil.*

Bail, bă′l, *n. f.* economy; the allowance in a mill to the poor. *Arm.*

Bailbhe, bul′-uv-à, *n. f.* dumbness, muteness; deg. more or most mute *o.* dumb.

Bailbheag, bal′-uv-ag, *n. f.* poppy. *N.*

Bailc, băělk, *n. f.* seasonable rain; genial showers, *Is.*; a shower that comes suddenly.

Bailceach, băělk′-ăch, *a.* in seasonable showers—a strong robust man. *Irish.*

Baile, bă′-llà, *n. m.* a town; a village; *baile* mòr, *a city*; *baile* bhòid, *Rothsay, the town of Bute*, lit.; *baile-margaidh, a market-town*; *baile-puirt, a sea-port town;* home; am bheil t' athair aig *baile, is your father at home?* chaidh e o'n (bho 'n *or* as) *bhaile, he went from home*; am *baile* ad thall, *yonder town*; *the town* or *village opposite*; fear a *bhaile, the gentleman* or *proprietor of the farm* or *village*; a farm; tha *baile* aige, *he has a whole farm*; *pl.* bailte *and* bailtean; leig thusa *bailtean* treuna, *thou hast thrown down mighty cities.*

Baileach, bă′-l-ach, economical, *Arm.*; also used for buileach; "glanaidh e gu ro *bhaileach," he will purge thoroughly. See* Matthew. Dr. Smith, the king of Gaelic scholars, uses this word properly. Na tréig mi gu *buileach, do not forsake me utterly*; also, cha bhuain thu gu *buileach, thou shalt not wholly reap. B.*

Bailgeann, bal′-ĕg-unn, *a.* pie-bald, spotted, white-bellied; sometimes *bailgfhionn.*

Bailisdeir, bal′-ėshj-ar′, *n. m.* a babbler.

Bailidh, bâ′-llyė, *n. m.* a magistrate. *Fr. S.*

Bailidheachd, bâ′-llyė-achg, *n.f.* magistracy.

Bailteachas, băĕl′-tyach-us, *n.f.* planting towns; colonizing. *M. L.*

Bainbh, bán′-uv, *n.f.* a young pig; tha mhuc a teannadh ri *bainbhidheachd, the sow is about pigging. Armstrong.*

Baine, bà-nyå, *n. f.* paleness, whiteness; deg. more *or* most pale *or* white.

Baineasg, ban″-ăsk, *n.f.* a ferret, (Peireid,) *Ir.*

Bainidh, bàn″-ė, and -ėch, *n.f.* fury, rage; tha e air *bànaidh, he is raging, he is quite furious. See* lair bhàn.

Bainisg, ban″-ėshg, *n. f.* a little old woman. *Arm.*

Bainne, ban″-nyå, *n. m.* milk; a drop; gach *bainne, every drop*; cha 'n 'eil *bainne* agam, *I have not a drop*; crodh *bainne, milk cattle*; bò *bhainne, a milk cow*; *bainne* milis, *sweet milk*; *bainne* nùis, *biestings*; *bainne* binndichte, *curdled milk*; *bainne* lom, *skimmed milk*; *bainne* goirt na blàthach, *butter milk*; agus ghabh e ìm agus *bainne, and he took butter and milk. B.*

Bainneach, bán″-nyach, *a.* milky, lacteal.

Bainneachas, bán″-nyăch-us, *n. m.* milkiness. *H.*

Bainnear, bán′-nyur′, *a.* milky; *n.f.* fold for milking sheep, &c. *Lw.*

Bainneardaich, ban″-ărt′-ėch, *n. m.* lazy, drops of rain falling now and then.

Bainnse, bén″-shå, *gen.* of banais.

Bainnseachas, bén″-shăch-us, *n.f.* feasting at weddings; banquetting.

Bainsich, bén″-shėch, *v.* waste. *B. G.*

Baintighearna, benj′-tyurn-å, *n.f.* a proprietor's lady; a lady.

Baintighearnas, bénj″-tyurn-us, *n. m.* the rule or sway of a lady; petticoat government. *M. L.*

Baintighearnachd, bén″-tyurn-achg, *n.f.* ladyship.

Baintreach, benj′-ryach, *n. c.* a widow, a widower; is *baintreach* e, *he is a widower*; is *baintreach* i, *she is a widow*; pronounced in various places ban-trach, and bénj′-ryach, and written often *bantrach*, (bandihireach-dibhireach, *a forsaken person.*)

Bair, băĕr′, *n.f.* gaol; ràinig iad a *bhàir, they reached the gaol*; game at shinty; bhuidhinn iad *bàir, they won a game*; strife. *M. L.*

Bairceinn, băr″-kėnn, *n. m.* side timbers for a house, *A.*; taobhain, *W. H.*

Baird, bârj, *n. m.* poets.—*North,* parks, fences.

Bairich, bâr″-ėch, *n.f.* lowing of cattle.

Bairig. băr″-ėg, *v.* bestow *N.*

Bairlinn, bâr″-lyėnn, *n. f.* summons of removal; an enormous wave.

Bairlinnich, *v.* serve with summons of removal.

Bairneach, bâr″-nyach, *n.f.* a limpet.

Bairneachd, bâr″-nyăchg, *n.f.* judgment. *Ir.*

Baist, *v.* băsht, *v.* baptize; *baiste, baptized.*

Baisteach, băshj′-ach, *n. c.* a baptist; *a.* baptismal, relating to baptism.

Baisteadh, basht′-Ă, *n. m.* baptism; *p.* baptizing; 'ga *bhaisteadh, baptizing him.*

Baite, bâ′-tyå, *p.* drowned; quenched, extinguished; (fig.) overwhelmed; tha m' anam *baite,* gu cràiteach ann am chom, *my soul is overwhelmed grievously within me. Ps. H.*

Baith, băĕch, *n.f.* a lure, a decoy.

Balach, băll′-ach, *n. m.* a fellow, a boor, a young man; a boy.

Balachail, bal′-ach-al, *a.* clownish.

Balachan, bal′-ăch-ăn, *n. m.* a boy, a little boy.

Balachanas, băll′-ăch-an-us, *n. m.* boyhood.

Balbh, băl′-uv, *a.* dumb, mute, quiet, still, bha mi *balbh* tosdach, *I was mute and silent, Ps.*; caoin mar *bhalbh* dhrùchd mhaduinn shèimh, *mild as the still dew of placid morning. O.*

Balbhachd, băl′-uv-ăchg, *n. f.* dumbness.

Balbhan, băl′-uv-ăn, *n. c.* a dumb person.

Balbhanachd, băl′-uv ăn-ăchg, *n.f.* interpretation, *or* communication of ideas by signs, dumb show; ri *balbhanachd, communicating ideas by signs.*

Balc, bălk, *n. m.* balk, land-mark. *L.*

Balcach, bălk′-ach, *a.* splay-footed. *H.*

Balcanta, balk′-ănt-å, *a.* stout; firm.

Balgair, băl′-ug-ur′, *a.* fox, *H.*; sionnach.

Ball, ball, *n. m.* a member; ann ad leabhar sgriobhadh sios mo *bhuill* uile, *in thy book all my members were written, Ps.*; a spot: *ball* dubh, *a black spot*; any part of dress; tha 'n deadh *bhall* aodaich agad an sin, *you have an excellent part of dress there*; a rope; *ball* cainib, *a hempen rope*; *ball* acrach, *a cable*; *ball* dòrbhain, *a mole on the skin*; *ball* bùird, *a butt*; *ball* fanaid, *ball* spòrs, *a laughing-stock*; *ball* seirc, *a beauty spot*; *ball* sinnsireachd, *any old article of family furniture, an heir-loom*; *ball* coise, *a foot-ball*; *ball* speil, *a hand-ball*; *ball* chrith, *tremor, tremor of the limbs*; *ball*-dhearg, *bay-coloured, H.*; *ball* tamailt, *an object of disgrace* or *reproach*; *ball*-sgiath, *a bossy shield*; Fionnghal nam *ball* sgiath, *Fingal of the bossy shield, Oss. A.*; b*all*-sampull, *an example. B.*

BALLA, ball'-a, *n. m.* a wall, a fence.

BALLACH, băll'-ach, *n. m.* spotted, speckled; laogh *ballach, a spotted* or *speckled calf.*

BALLAIRE, báll'-ur' à, *n. m.* a cormorant. *N.*

BALLAN, băll'-an, *n. m.* a teat; *ballan* na boine, *the cow's teat*; a tub a vessel; *ballan* binndeachaidh, *a cheese vat* (fiodhan), *H.*; *ballan* stiallach, *a sort of pillory used of old in the Highlands*; air *ballan* stiallach 'g ad sparradh, *fastening thee to the pillory. Arm.*

BALLART. ball'-ărt, *n. m.* noise, fuss about one's family.

BALLARTACH, ball'-ărt-ăch, *a.* boastful.

BALT, băllt, *n. m.* the welt of a shoe; border, belt; *pl.* built, baltan.

BALTACH, bălt'-ach, *a.* bordered, belted.

BAN, ban, the *gen. plu.* of bean, a woman; b' iongantach do ghràdh dhomhsa, a' toirt barrachd air gràdh nam *ban, thy love to me was wonderful, surpassing the love of women. B.*

BAN, bànn, *a.* pale, wan, white, fair-haired; ni 's *bàine, fairer,* &c.; *n. m.* left hand side of a furrow, in ploughing.

BAN, a prefix in compounds; băn before *f* aspirated, ban and bana in other instances; as, *banfhàidh, a prophetess*; *banacharaid, a female friend.*

BANABA, bănn-ab'-ă, *n. f.* an abbess.

BANABHARAN, bann-a-vhar'-un, *n. f.* a baroness.

BANABHARD, bănn'-a-vhârd, *n. f.* a poetess.

BANACHADH, bàn'-ăch-Ă, *n. m.* and *p.* whitening, growing pale *or* wan.

BANACHARAID, băn'-a-chăr-ėj, *n. f.* a female friend, a female relation.

BANACHEARD, ban'-a-chyărd', *n. f.* a gipsy, a tinker's wife.

BANACHEILEADAIR, ban'-a-chyăl²-a-dăr', *n. f.* an executrix, a female guardian.

BANACHIOBAIR, ban'-a-chēbb-ar', *n. f.* a shepherdess.

BANACHOIGREACH, băn-ă-chŏėg-ryăch, *n. f.* a female stranger.

BANACHOMPANACH, băn'-a-chŏmp-an-ach, *n. f.* a female companion.

BANACHOMPANAS, băn'-a-chomp-an-us, *n. m.* female companionship.

BANACHRUITEAR, băn'-a-chrŭt'-tyăr', *n. f.* a female harper, a female minstrel.

BANACHUISLEANAICHE, băn-a-chŭsh'-lyan'-ech-à, *n. f.* a female performer on a wind instrument.

BANACHURADAIR, ban-a-chûr'-a-dar', *n. f.* an executrix, a female guardian.

BANADHALTRANNACH, bann-aŏ'-allt-runn-ăch, *n. f.* an adulteress.

BANAG, bàn'-ăg, *n. f.* a grilse, gealag.

BANAGHAISGE, ban-a-ghăsg'-à. *n. f.* surprising feats *or* exploits of a female.

BANAGHAISGEACH, ban'-a-ghăshg-ăch, *n. f.* a heroine, an amazon, female warrior.

BANAGHOISTIDH, ban'-a-ghŏsht-ė, *n. f.* a god-mother

BANAGHRUDAIR, ban'-a-ghrû-'dur', *n. f.* the landlady of an inn; a female brewer, a hostess; cagar na *banaghrùdair, the ale-wife's whisper soon turns loud. A.*

BANAIBHISTEAR, bann-īv'-ėsht-ăr,' *n. f.* a she-devil, a fury, a virago.

BANAICH, bàn'-ėch, *v.* to whiten, grow pale

BANAIL, băn'-al, *a.* modest, feminine, becoming a female, comely.

BANAIS, băn'-ėsh, *n. f.* a wedding; fear na *bainnse, the bridegroom*; bean na *bainnse; gen.* bainnse.

BANALACHD, băn'-ăl-ăchg, *n. f.* modesty, behaviour becoming a female.

BANALTRACHD, ban'-ăllt-rrăchg, *n. f.* nursing, fostering, cajoling, the business of a nurse; mach air *bhanaltrachd, out a nursing.*

BANALTRADH, băn'-allt-traŏ, *n. f.* a nurse.

BANALTRAICH, băn'-ăllt-rrėch, *v.* nurse.

BANALTRUIM, băn'-ălt-rūėm, *v.* nurse.

BANALTRUM, băn'-allt-rum, *n. f.* a nurse.

BANALTRUMAS, băn'-ălt-rum-us, *n. f.* nursing; cajoling.

BANAMHAIGHSTIR, ban'-a-vhăĕsh-tyur', *n. f.* a mistress; a schoolmistress.

BANAMHAIGHSTIREAS, ban-à-vhăĕ'-tyur'-us, the rule or sway of a mistress.

BANMHARCAICHE, băn-ă-vhărk'-ėch-à, *n. f.* a female rider.

BANAMHARCAS, băn-ă-vhărk'-us, *n. f.* a marchioness.

BANAMHARSONTA, bann'-a-vhăr-sunt-à, *n. f.* a female merchant.

BANAMHOIREAR, ban'-a-vhoyr-ăr', *n. f.* a noblewoman, the wife of a lord; *ban* must be prefixed almost in every case, when speaking of a female's country; *ban-albannach, ban-sassunnach, ban-fhrangach, ban-duidseach, a Scotswoman, an Englishwoman, a Frenchwoman, a Dutchwoman.*

BANAMHORTAIR, bann-a-vhŏrt'-ar', *n. f.* a female that commits murder.

BANAPHRIONNSA, bănn-a-ffrùnn'-sà, *n. f.* a princess, a king's daughter

BANARACH, ban'-ăr-ăch, *n. f.* a dairy-maid

BANARACHAS, băn'-ăr-ăch-us, *n. f.* the office of a dairy-maid *or* milk-maid.

BANASTIGHE, băn-us-tăĕ'-ė, *n. m.* housewifery, female occupation.

BANBH, băn'-uv, *n. m.* land unploughed for a year, an ancient name for Ireland.

BANC, bănk, *n. m.* a balk, a bank. *Bib.*

BANCHRUTHACH, bàn'-chrû-ach, *a.* pale, wan, pale-complexioned. *H.*

BANDAIDH, bănd''-ė, *a.* modest, delicate, feminine.

BANDIA, ban'-jēă, *or* dyēă, *n. f.* a goddess; ach mar an ceudna gu cuirear teampull na *ban-dè* mòire Diana an neophrìs, *but also that the temple of the great goddess Diana should be despised. Acts* xix. 27.

Bandiabhol, bann-jēā-, *or* -dyēa-'val, *n. f.* a fury, a fiend of a female; a devil.

Bandiuichd, bănn'-jūchg *or* -dyūchg, *n. f.* a dutchess, a duke's wife.

Bandruidh, bănn-'drūė', *n. f.* a sorceress.

Banfhaidh, bănn'-âė, *n. f.* a prophetess; agus ghlac Miriam, a *bhanfhàidh*, piuthar Aaroin tiompan 'na làimh, *and Miriam, the prophetess, Aaron's sister, took a timbrel in her hand.*

Banfhigheach, a female weaver, pronounced benk-ăch. *H. S.*

Banfhiosaiche, bann-ĕss'-ėch-å, *n. f.* a fortune-teller, a gipsy.

Banfhlath, bănn'-hlă, *n. f.* a chief's lady.

Banfhuasglach, băn-ŭăsg'-lach, *a.* menstrual; *banfhuasgladh, menstrual courses. H. S.*

Banfhuaighliche, ban'-ŭăėl-ėch-å, *n. f.* a sempstress, a milliner, a mantua-maker. *Is.*

Banfhuineadair, ban-ŭn''-a-dăr', *n. f.* a female baker, a woman that bakes bread. *Bible.*

Bang, băng, *n. f.* a drum; a' toirt fauim air *banga, making a drum beat masterly.*

Bangaid, băng'-ăj, *n. f.* a feast at the christening of a child; a feast.

Baniarla, bann'-ĕărl-å, *n. f.* a countess.

Banifrionnach, bănn-ēf'-rrunn-ăch, *n. f.* a she-devil; a fury; a furious female, a virago.

Banlaoch, bann-lāoch', *n. f.* a heroine, an amazon, a virago.

Banleigh, bann'-llāĕ-yh', *n. f.* a female skilled in medicine.

Banleoghunn, bann'-lyô-ghunn, *n. f.* a lioness.

Banleomhan, bann'-lyôv-unn, *n. f.* a lioness.

Banlighiche, bann-llē'-ėch-å, *n. f.* a female skilled in medicine.

Bann, bănn, *n. m. a hinge*; *bann* an doruis, *the hinge of the door*; *a security*; théid mise am *bannaibh* dhuit, *I can assure you, I will be bound*; a chain, a tie, a bond, a cord; na *boinn* a b'àill leo iadhadh oirnn, *the cords with which they would wish to surround us*; *a key-stone*; cuir *boinn* anns a' *bhalla, put key-stones in the wall*; *v.* bind, tie, make firm with key-stones; balla air a dheadh *bhannadh, a wall well secured with key-stones*; *bannlàmh, a hand-cuff, a manacle*; *bann* duirn, *a wrist-band*; *plu. boinn.*

Bannag, bănn'-ăg, *n. f.* Christmas-eve, *or* the night before the 25th December; a present *or* treat given at Christmas.

Bannal, bănn'-ăll, a gang, a band, a troop; a covey; *bannal* uchd ruadh, *the red-breasted covey. M. A.*

Bannalach, bann'-all-ach, *a.* in companies, in troops, in gangs, in crowds.

Bannaomh, bann'-nùv, *n. f.* a female saint, a nun.

Bann ceirde, bann'-kùrj-a, *n. m.* a deed of indenture. *H.*

Bannceangal, bănn-che'-al, *or* cheng'-al, *n. m.* a bond, a cautionary bond, *H.*

Banndalach, bănnd'-al-ach, *a.* foppish.

Bann duirn, bann'-dŭr-ėn', *n. m.* wrist band.

Bannlamh, bănn'-llàv, *n. m.* a cubit, a hand-cuff, glas làmh.

Bannshaor, bănn'-hāor, *v.* free, license.

Banntach, bănn'-ttăch, *n. f.* a hinge, a bond *or* obligation.

Banntair bănn'-tar', a drawer of bonds.

Bann seilbhe, bănn'-shyăl-uv, *n. m.* a deed of infeftment; *bann* taisbeanaidh, *a bail-bond.*

Banoidhre, bann-āoėr'-å, *n. f.* an heiress; *banoidhreachd, an estate going to heirs female. H.*

Banoglach, băn'-ŏg-llach, *n. f*, a servant maid, a hand-maiden; searbhant.

Banridire, bann'rúj-ur'-á, *n. f.* a baroness, the wife of a knight.

Banrigh, bănn-rē, a queen.

Banrighinn, bann'-rė-ghėnn, bàr'-ėnn, *n. f.* a queen.

Bansealgair, bann-shyăl'-gar', *n. f.* a huntress.

Bansolairiche, bann-sol'-ar-ėch-å, *n. f.* a cateress.

Banstiuart, bann'-styû-art, *n. f.* a housekeeper, a stewardess.

Bantrach, bann'-trach, *n. f.* a widow, a widower. *Prov.*

Bantrail, bann'-trâil', *n. f.* a bond maid, a female slave, mean woman.

Bantuathnach, bann'-tuă-nach, *n. f.* a farmer's wife; a woman holding a farm.

Baobach, bú'-bach, *n. f.* panic; a terrible fright; *a.* panic-struck, terribly afraid; *n. f.* a female easily frightened.

Baobaire, búb'-ur-å, *n. m.* a panic-struck man, a man easily frightened.

Baobh, *or* **Baoibh**, bāoėv, and bāov, *n. f.* a wicked mischievous female, a fury, a virago; càineam is aoiream a *bhaoibh*, a rinn an t-òran, *let me satirise and lampoon the furious woman that made the song.*

Baobhachd, bāov'-ăchg, *n. f.* the conduct of a foolish woman.

Baodhaisteachadh, baŏ'-ăsht-ach-ă, *n. m.* drenching and fatigue in bad weather.

Baodhaistich, baŏ'-ăsht-ėch, *v.* drench, give a miserable appearance; spoil one's clothes in bad weather. *Isds.*

Baogaid, bāog′-ăj, *n. f* a whim, caprice.

Baogaideach, bāog′-ăj-ach, whimsical, capricious, odd, fanciful; *n. f.* a fanciful whimsical female.

Baogaideachd, bāog′-ăj-ăchg, *n. f.* whimsicality, fancifulness, oddity; capriciousness.

Baogh, bāo′-gh′, *n. f.* a she-spirit.

Baoghal, băo′-all, *n. m.* danger, peril.

Baoghalach, băo′-ăl-ăch, *a.* dangerous, furious; destruction, dangerous, perilous, *b. Sh.*

Baois, bāosh, *n. f.* lust, lewdness, *b.*

Baoiseach, bāosh′-ach, lewd, lustful.

Baoit, baŏėt, *n. f.* a foolish, giddy female.

Baol, bāol, *n. m.* approximation, nearness in doing any thing; *v.* approach *or* come near doing any thing; cha *bhaol* e air, *it will not come near it.*

Baoth, bāoh, *a.* foolish, silly; *baoth* bheus, *immorality, folly*; *boath* chreidheamh, *snperstition*; *boath* shùgradh, *foolish and profane jesting*; *boath* smaointinn, *a foolish thought.*

Bara, băr′-à, *n. m.* a barrow; *bara* roth, *a wheel barrow*; *bara* laimhe, *a hand barrow*; a tumble, *or* inclination; chuir e *bara* dheth féin, *he tumbled himself.*

Barail, băr′-ăl, *n. m.* opinion, belief, conjecture, supposition; tha mi 'm *barail, I suppose*; ma 's math mo *bharailsa, if I judge aright*; a réir mo *bharail, to the best of my belief* or *judgment*; dé do *bharail, what do you think? what is your opinion?* thoir dhomh do *bharail, give me your opinion; tell me your sentiments about this matter; pl.* baralaichean.

Baraisd, băr′-ăshg, *n. f.* the herb *borage.*

Baralach, băr′-ăl-ăch, *a.* hypothetical, conjectural; *gen.* of barail.

Baralachadh, bar′-al-ach-ă, *p.* guessing, supposing, conjecturing.

Baralaich, bar′-al-ėch, *v.* guess, suppose, conjecture.

Baran, băr′-un, *n. m.* a baron, a baronet.

Baranachd, bar′-un-ăchg, *n. f.* a barony.

Barant, bar′-unt′, *n. m.* a surety, *or* reliance; is tu bu *bharant* dòchais dhomh, *thou wast the surety of my hope* or *confidence. Ps.*

Barantach, bar′-ant′-ach, *a.* confident, assured.

Barantaich, bar′-ant-ėch, *v.* warrant.

Barantail, bar′-ant-al, *a.* warrantable.

Barantas, băr′-unt′-us, *n. m.* warrant, commission, power, authority; *barantas* glacaidh, *a warrant to secure* or *apprehend.* Spanish, *barrunto* Basque, *barruntea.*

Barbair, bărb′-ar′, *n. m.* a barber. Lat. *barba*; French, *barbier*; Pers. *berber.*

Barc, bărk, *n. f.* a boat, a skiff; chunnacas *barc, a boat was seen, Ossian*; *v.* rush, as water; muir mhòr a *barcadh* ma 'm cheann, *a huge wave rushing on my head. H.*

Bard, bârrd′, *n. m.* a poet, bard, a rhymer; sheinn am *bard, the bard sung*; *North,* a dyke or fence; (*Suth. sh.*) a park, an inclosure.

Bardachd, bârrd″-ăchg, *n. f.* ribaldry, poetry, satire; lampooning.

Bardail, bârrd″-al, *a.* satirical, poetical.

Bardalachd, bârrd′-al-ăchg, *n. f.* satire, ribaldry; unseemly language.

Bardainn, bârd′-ėnn, *n. f.* summons of removal, (bairlinn.) *Per. shire.*

Bargain, bărg′-ăn′, *n. f.* a bargain, a good pennyworth; *C. Br. bargen,* French, Ital, &c. &c.

Bargainich, bărg′-an′-ėch, *v.* bargain, buy

Barais, băr′-ăsh, *n. m.* the ancient Gaelic name of Paris. *Arm.*

Barlag, bâr′-llag, *n. f.* a rag, a tatter.

Barlagach, bâr″-llag-ăch, *a.* ragged, tattered, full of rags *or* tatters.

Barluadh, bâr′-lŭă, *n. m.* a term in pipe music.

Barp, bărp, *n. f.* a conical heap of stones supposed to be memorials of the dead. *Skye.*

Barr, bârr, *n. m.* crop; tha 'n deadh *bhàrr* aca, *they have an excellent crop*; point, top, tip, end, extremity; *bàrr* na snàthaid, *the point, tip,* or *extremity of the needle*; an sin chuir aingeal an tighearn a mach *bàrr* a bhata, *then the angel of the Lord put forth the end of the staff*; excellence; thug sin *bàrr* air na chualadh mi riamh, *that exceeds* or *excels every thing I ever heard*; a *bhàrr* air sin, *besides, moreover*; *v.* cut off the surface, crop, top; a' *barradh* na mòna, *paring the peat moss*; a' *barradh* a' bhuntata, *cropping the potatoes*; a' *barradh* nan craobh, *pruning the trees*; *in Lw.* cream; *bàrr* a bhrisgin, *silver weed, wild tansy.*

Barrabhall, bărr′-ă-văll, *n. m.* bartizan, battlement; embrazure, obairdhion.

Barrabhard, barr′-a-vhărd, *n. m.* a chief poet; a poet laureate, a graduate in poetry.

Barrabhord, barr′-a-vhŏrd, *n. m.* the deck of a vessel.

Barrabhuidh, bărr′-a-vŭė, *a.* yellow-topped, white-haired, fair-haired.

Barracaideach, barr′-ăchg-ăj-ach, adj. saucy.

Barrach, bărr′-ach, *n, m.* second tow; first tow, *bunnach*; third, *sgath*, (Scotch, *brairds*;) *a.* heaped; excessive. *H.*

Barrachaol, barr'-a-chaŏl, *n. m.* a pyramid; *a.* pyramidal, conical, tapering.

Barrachd, bărr'-ăchg, *n. m.* more, surplus; *barrachd* ortsa, *more than you have*; ma bhios *barrachd* agad, *if you have any surplus* or *excess.*

Barrachdail, bărr'-ăchd-al, *a.* surpassing.

Barradhriopair, bărr'-a-ghrep-ur', *n. m.* a butler. *Irish.*

Barradh, bărr'-Ă, *n. m.* surface, cropping.

Barrail, bârr'-al, *a.* excellent. *M.*

Barraichte, bărr'-ech-tyă, *p.* surpassing.

Barrall, bărr'-ăll, *n. m.* a shoe-tie. *Is.*

Barran, bărr'-ăn, *n. m.* any kind of coping on a fence; thorns, flags, &c.

Barrfhionn, barr'-unn, *a.* fair haired; written *barrunn.*

Barrghniomh, barr'-a-ghrev, *n. m.* a work of supererogation, a transcendent exploit.

Barrghniomhach, bărr-ghrev-ăch, *a.* superfluous.

Barr-ial, bărr-ēăl', *n. m.* shoe tie. *B.*

Barrmais, bărr-măsh', *n. m.* a cornice.

Barrmaisich, barr-măsh'-ech, *v.* ornament.

Bas, băss, *n. f.* the palm of the hand; buailibh bhur *basaibh* uile shluaigh, *clap your hands all ye people, B*; a spoke, a hollow. *H.*

Bas, bâs, death; 's e righ nan uamhas am *bàs, death is the king of terrors*; cha 'n eagal *bàs* ach ruaig, *death is no terror but defeat, O.*; faigh *bàs, die, starve*; gheibh gach ni *bàs, every thing shall die.*

Basaich, bâs'-ech, *v.* die as a brute, starve; a ni sin a *bhàsaicheas* leis féin, *that which dies of itself.*

Basail, bâs'-al, *a.* mortal, deadly.

Basalachd, bâs'-ăl-ăchd, *n. f.* mortality.

Basardaich, băss'-ard'-ech, *n. m.* clapping of hands of joy, acclamation, rejoicing.

Basbaire, băs'-bur,-a, *n. m.* a fencer. *Ir.*

Bascaid, băsk'-ăj, *n. f.* a basket; *Wel.* basgad.

Basdal, băsd'-al, *n. f.* noise, glitter, merriment.

Basdalach, băsd'-al-ach, *a.* cheering, gay; 'nuair thig an gloine *basdalach, when the cheering glass comes round. Mt.*

Basdard, băsd''-ărd', *n. c.* basdard, *Teutonic.*

Basgair, basg'-ăr', *n. f.* mournful, mournful clapping of hands.

Basmhor, bâs'-vur, *a.* mortal, deadly, fatal, subject *or* liable to death.

Basmhorachd, bâs'-vur-àchg, *n. f.* mortality, deadliness; fatality; air an aobhar sin na rìoghachadh am peacadh ann bhur corp *basmhor, therefore let not sin reign in your mortal body.*

Basraich, băs'-rrèch, *n. f.* mournful clapping of hands; is i a' *basraich* a' taomadh a h-osnaich air ceò, *she wailing pouring her groanings on the mist.*

Bata, băt''-â, *n. m.* a staff. *Teut. Fren.*

Bata, bá'-ta, *n. f.* a boat; read always with a *mas. art.* in the *nom.*; am *bàta* and not, a' bhata; stiuireadair a *bhàta, the steersman* or *helmsman of the boat.*

Batail, bát'-ăelt', *n. m.* a battle. *French.*

Batail, bat'-ălt', *n. f.* battle.

Batair, băt'-ur', *n. f.* a cudgeller.

Bath, bâ, *v.* drown, quench, extinguish, *bhàthadh* e, *he was drowned*; *bhàth* i an gealbhan, *she extinguished the fire, (by pouring water on it;) bhàth* e phathadh, *he quenched his thirst.*

Bathadh, bâ'-Ă, *n. m.* a drowning, quenching, slaking, smothering, extinguishing.

Bathach, bâ'-ăch, *n. f.* cow-house, byre.

Bathais, bă'-èsh, *n. f.* forehead, front, impudence; nach ann aige a bha *bhathais, what impudence the fellow had.*

Bathar, bă'-hur, *n. m.* merchandise, goods, wares; *bathar* òir agus airgid agus chlach luachmhor, *the merchandise of gold, and silver, and precious stones. Rev.*

Batharbhord, bă'-hur-vhŏrd, *n. m.* a counter.

Batharnach, bă'-ur-nach, *n. m.* a warehouse, a shop, a store-house.

B'e for bu e; as, *b'e* sin iarrtas do chridhe, *that was the desire of thine heart.*

Beach, bech, *n. m.* a bee; chuartaich iad mi mar *bheachaibh, they surrounded me as bees. B.*

Beachach, bech-ăch, *a.* waspish, abounding with bees.

Beachaid, bèch'-ăj, *n. f.* a bee-hive. *Is.*

Beachan, bech'-un, *n. m.* a wasp; *beachan* each, *a horse-fly.*

Beachd, bechg, opinion, perception, idea, keen observation, judgment; distinct recollection; as a *bheachd, out of his senses* or *judgment*; ma 's math *mo bheachdsa, if I have distinct conception* or *recollection*; mòr na *bheachd, having high ideas,* or *haughty*; tha mi 'san aon *bheachd, I am of the same opinion, I am still of the same opinion*; aim or mark; geur shaighde laoich is ro-chinntiche *beachd, the arrows of the hero of surest aim*; am bheil *beachd* agad far (*or* fail) an d'fhàg thu e, *have you a distinct recollection* or *perception of the place where you left it*; gabh *beachd* air, *pay particular attention, mark well*; cha robh mi cho dorcha gun *bheachd, I was not so ignorant and void of perception, O*; air réir mo *bheachdsa, in my opinion,* or *to the best of my opinion* or *recollection*; cum sin ann do *bheachd, keep that steadily in view*; 's e sin a bha 'm *bheachdsa* 'san am, *that is what I had in view at the time.*—" Translating the Gaelic word for word is what spoils it." *Murray.*

Beachdachadh, bechd'-ăch-Ă, *n. m. p.* meditation, contemplation; *p.* attentively and most minutely observing, paying the greatest attention, meditating, contemplating.

Beachdaich, bechg'-êch, *v.* attend, look steadfastly, perceive, observe; cha *bheachdaich* sùil a h-àite, *an eye cannot perceive or discern her place, S.*; review, criticise.

Beachdaid, bechg'-ăj, *n. f.* an observatory, a watch-tower.

Beachdail, bechg'-al, *a.* keenly observant, attentive; sure in aim; nach *beachdail* an t-sùil a th' aige, *how keenly observant his eye is.*

Beachdair, bechg'-urr, *n. m.* a keen observer, a reviewer *or* critic.

Beachdaireachd, bech'-ar'-achg, *n. f.* criticising; reviewing.

Beachdaidh, bechg'-ê, sure, certain, positive; tha thu *beachdaidh* gu'm bi, *you are quite certain it shall be so*; gu *beachdaidh, most assuredly, most decidedly so.*

Beachdalachd, bechg'-ăl-ăchg, *n. f.* keenness and sureness of perception, great punctuality in observing, sureness of aim.

Beadach, bĕud²'-ăch, *a.* impertinent, pert, petulent, pettish.

Beadachd, bĕud²'-ăchg, *n. m.* impertinence, pertness, petulance, for *beadaidheachd.*

Beadag, bĕud²'-ag, *n. f.* a petulant female.

Beadagan, bĕud'-ă-gan, *n. m.* petulant man.

Beadaidh, bĕud'-ag, *a.* impertinent, petulant, impertinent, pert, capricious, fastidious.

Beadair, bĕud'-ur, *v.* fondle, caress, indulge; cajole, coax.

Beadarrach, bĕud'-urr-ăch, *a.* fondled, caressed, spoiled as a child; fond of; pampered.

Beadradh, bĕud'-rĂ, *n. m.* and *p.* fondling, toying, caressing; flirting; a' *beadradh* r'a leannan, *flirting with his sweetheart.*

Beag, bĕug, *a.* little; short; diminutive; disagreeable: trifling; rud *beag, a little thing*; gnothuch *beag, a trifling business* or *affair;* duine *beag, a diminutive person;* ùine *bheag, a short time*; is *beag* orm thu, *you are disagreeable to me, I hate you;* is *beag* orm coimhthional luchd an uile, *I abominate* or *hate the congregation of evil doers*; iadsan air am *beag* sibh, *they who hate you*; is *beag* so, *this is a (trifling) light thing, Bible;* is *beag* an dolaidh, *it is no great harm, he* or *she richly deserves it*; *n. m.* little, nothing, any, the least, the young, cha d'fhuair thu a' *bheag, thou hast found nothing, B.*; am bheil a' *bheag* do mhaith air, *is it worth any thing*; am *beag* is am mòr, *both great and small*; cha 'n fhaigh a' *bheag* bàs, *nothing shall die*; a' *bheag* a dh' aon ni is leatsa, *any (the least), the least particle of what is thine, B. A.*; is *beag, almost;* is *beag* 's nach do mharbh e mi, *he almost killed me*; rud chi na *big*, 'se ni na *big*; is rud chluinneas iad 's e chanas iad, *what the young see, the young do; and what they hear they repeat—as the old cock crows the young cock learns*; *v.* lessen, destroy.

Beagaich, bĕug'-êch, *v.* lessen; a réir teircid nam bliadhnachan *beagachaidh* tu a luach, *according to the fewness of years thou shalt diminish the price thereof,* (lughdachaidh tu a luach.) *Bible.*

Beagan, bĕug'-an, *n. m.* a little, a few; cha 'n 'eil bacadh air an Tighearn saoradh le mòran na le beagan, *for there is no restraint with the Lord, to save by many or by few*; a lìon *beagan* is *beagan, by degrees, by little and little*; ni sinn e a lìon *beagan* is *beagan, we will do it by degrees; beagan* eile, *a little more*; *beagan* cadail, *a little sleep*; air *bheagan* tuaireim, *possessing little sense*; fan *beagan* ni's fhaide, *stay a little longer*; *beagan* uisge, *a little water*; air *bheagan* maith, *worth little, of no great value, of no great interest.*

Beageagalach, bĕug-ā'-gal-ach, *a.* fearless, bold, intrepid, undaunted.

Beagnarach, beug'-nár-ăch, *a.* shameless, impudent, impertinent.

Beagnarachd, bĕug'-nár-ăchg, *n. f.* shamelessness, impudence.

Beairt, byăĕrt, *n. f.* a loom; eige 'sa *bheairt, a web in the loom;* harness; da steud fo *bheairt, two steeds in harness, Maclachline, Ar.*; *beairt* thuairneir a lathe; *a trace*; *beairtean, ship's rigging. M. L.*

Beairteas, byaêrt''-tyus, *n. m.* wealth, riches, abundance, opulence.

Beairteach, byaêrt'-tyach, *a.* rich, wealthy.

Beairtich, byarrt'-êch, *v.* rig, trim, equip.

Bealach, byăll''-ach, *n. m.* a gap, a breach in a wall *or* fence; a gate-way, a gate; gorge of a mountain; tog am *bealach, build the breach* or *gap.*

Bealaidh, byăl'-ê, broom. *See* Mealaich: bad *mealaich, a tuft of broom.*

Bealamas, byal'-am-us, *n. m.* the refuses of a feast, the crumbs that fall from the table, from the mouth, (lit.) beul-amas.

Bealtuinn, byăll'-tènn, *n. f.* May-day.

Bean, ben, touch, handle. *P.*

Bean, ben'n, a woman, a female; *gen.* mnà and mnatha; *bean* ghlùin, *a midwife; bean* shiùbhlaidh, *a woman in child-bed; bean-tighe, a housewife, a landlady*; *bean* òsd, *the landlady of an inn*; *bean* baile, *the lady* or *proprietress of a village*; *bean* chinnidh, *a kinswoman*; *bean* chìche, *a wet nurse*; *bean* choimhideachd, *a bride maid, a maid of honour*; *bean* nigheadaireachd, *a laundry maid, a washer-woman*; *bean* uasail, *a lady, a gentlewoman*; *bean* bhrathar athar, *a paternal uncle's wife*; *bean* brathar màthar, *a maternal uncle's wife*; *bean* brathar, *a sister-in-law*; *bean* bhochd, *a female mendicant, pauper* or *beggar*; *bean* mic, *a daughter-in-law*; *bean* shìth, *a female fairy.*

Beann, byann, *n. f.* a corner, a skirt; bràigh lìn, air a ceithir *beannaibh, a sheet by the four corners, Acts*; attention, regard; na d' thoir *beann* air dé their e, *pay no attention to what he says*; a horn, *I.*; *gen. pl.* of beinn, a hill.

Beannach, byann'-ăch, *a.* cornered, horned.

Beannachadh, byann-ach-X, *n. m.* a blessing, benediction, grace; iarr *beannachadh, say grace*; *p.* blessing.

Beannachd, byann'-ăchg, *n. m.* a benediction, a blessing; *beannachd* Dhia leat, *may the blessing of God attend you*; tha mo *bheannachdsa* agad, *you have my benediction*; compliments, respects; thoir mo *bheannachd, bring my compliments* or *respects*; farewell; *beannachd* leat, *farewell, adieu*; fàg *beannachd* aige, *leave him farewell, bid him adieu*; *beannachd* do t'anam is buaidh, *a blessing to thy soul and victory, O.*; *beannachd* a sheud is shiubhail leis, *may he fare as he deserves*; *beannachd* bàird, *the poet's congratulation.*

Beannachdail, byănn'-ăchg-ăl, *a.* valedictory, also beannachdach.

Beannachdan, byann'-ăchg-an, *n. m.* an insect that strikes your finger when holding it.

Beannaich, byann'-èch, *v.* bless, salute, hail, invoke a blessing; *beannaich* an Tighearn O m'anam, *bless the Lord, O my soul. B.*

Beannaichte, byann'-èch-tyă, *n. f.* happy, holy, blessed; is *beannaichte* an duine sin nach gluais ann an comhairle nan aingidh, *blessed is the man who walketh not in the counsel of the ungodly. Ps.*

Beanntach, byannt'-ach, *a.* mountainous, hilly; pinnacled, rocky.

Beanntachd, byannt'-achg, *n. f.* a mountainousness, hilliness, steepness.

Beanntaire, byannt'-ăr'-ă, *n. f.* mountaineer, a Highlander.

Beanntainn, byannt'-ènn, *n. m.* an herb.

Beantag, byant'-ag, *n. f.* a fan, fasgnag.

Beantainn, bent'-hen', *p.* touching. *Pro.*

Bearach, ber'-ăch, *n. f.* dog, fish, gobag.

Bearn, byârn, *n. f.* a small gap or breach; a fissure; *v.* notch, hack.

Bearnach, byărn'-ăch, *a.* having broken teeth, notched, hacked, full of gaps; *n. f.* a female with broken teeth.

Bearr, byărr, *v.* shave, crop, *B.*; taunt, gibe, jeer.

Bearra byarr'-a, a spear, a dart. *Sh.*

Bearradair, byarr'-a-'dăr, *n. m.* a barber, *B.*; *a.* giber, a taunting fellow.

Bearradaireachd, byărr'-a-'dăr'-achg, *n. m.* the occupation of a barber; gibing, jeering, taunting, criticising.

Bearradh, byărr'-X, *n. m.* the brow of a hill; a precipice; na shuidhe air a' bhearradh ad, *sitting on the brow of yonder hill.*

Bearraideach, byărr'-ăj-ach, *a.* flighty, light-headed, giddy; nimble.

Bearraideachd, byarr'-ăj-ăchg, *n. f.* flightiness, giddiness; light-headedness.

Beart, byart, *n. m.* deed, act; chum a *bhearta* iongantach a dheanamh aithnichte do chlann na daoine, *to make known his wonderful acts to the sons of men. Bible.*

Beath, bā'-ă, *n. m.* a birch tree; birch written *beith* also.

Beatha, bé'-ă, *n. f.* life, food, livelihood; welcome, salutation; is amhuil aislinn 's ar beatha, *our life is like a dream*; gheibh e'*bheatha, he will get his livelihood*; bhur *beathsa*, a ghaisgich, *you are welcome, O heroes!* dean a *bheatha, welcome him;* se slàinte do *bheatha, you'r quite welcome to it*; fad làithean a *bheatha, all the days of his life*; bhur *beatha* an dùthaich, *you are welcome to the country, you are welcome home*; an e mo *bheatha, am I welcome?* bheir duine *beatha* air éigin ach cha d' thoir e rath air éigin, *a man may force a livelihood, but cannot force success* or *prosperity. P.*

Beathach, bé'-ach, *n. m.* and *f.* an animal, a beast, a brute; term of contempt for a person.

Beathachadh, bé'-ăch-X, *n. m.* livelihood, sustenance, maintenance; a benifice; fhuair am ministir òg *beathachadh, the young clergyman got a living* or *a benifice*; *p.* supporting, maintaining, feeding.

Beathaich, bé'-èch, *v.* feed, nourish, maintain, support, cherish, feed; *bheathaich* e chuid eile, *he fed the rest*; *beathaich* mo chaoraich *feed my sheep, B.*;

beathaich thusa mise an diugh, is *beathachaidh* mise thusa am màireach, *feed you me to-day and I will feed you tomorrow. A. B.*

Beathaichte, béa'-èch-tya, *p.* fed, nourished, supported, maintained.

Beathalachd, béa'-hal-achg, *n. f.* vitality

Beathannan, bé'-ann-un, *pl.* victuals.

Beathail, bé'-'hal, *a.* vital, living, pertaining to life.

Beic, bāèchg, *n. m.* courtesy, obeisance; *v.* courtesy; dean do *bheic*, *make a courtesy, make your obeisance.*

Beiceis, bāèchg'-ăsh, *n. f.* hopping, bobbing, skipping, frisking; *beic* leumnach, *prancing.*

Beiceasach, bāèchg'-ăsh-ăch, *a.* fond of hopping, bobbing; frisky.

Beiceil, bāèchg'-al, *n. f.* and *p.* courtesying, hopping, frisking, prancing.

Beilbheag, bāl'-uv-ăg, *n. f.* a corn poppy.

Beile, bāl'-lyà, *n. m.* bit of bridle.

Beilean, bāl'-lyăn', *n. m.* a prating mouth, a little mouth.

Beileanach, bāl'-an'-ach, *a.* prating; *n. f.* a prating, garrulous female; loquacious, talkative.

Beileanachd, bāl''-an'-achg, *n. f.* half-impertinent prattle, *or* prating.

Beileach, bāly''-ach, *n. f.* a muzzle for a horse, *or* any other brute; in Lewis, *beileag*; in other places, *meileag.*

Beileich, bāly''-èch, *v* muzzle, stop impertinent talk.

Beileag, bāly'-ag, *n. f.* a muzzle; the outer coating of a birch tree. *H.*

Beilleach, bāll''-ach, *a.* blubber-lipped, (borrach,) having thick lips. *H.*

Beimcheap, bām'-chyāp, *n. f.* a whipping stock. *M. L.*

Being, bāng, *n. f.* a bench plank of a bed.

Beingidh, bāng'-è and -èch, *n. f.* the front plank of a bed; a bank. *Is.*

Beinn, bānn', *n. f.* a mountain, a hill, a pinnacle; mar an ceò thall air a *bheinn*, *as the distant mist on the hill. O.*

Beinneal, bān2'-nyal, *n. m.* binding of a sheaf of corn. *H.*

Beir, bār'2, *v. n. irreg.* bear; lay hold of, capture, overtake, get out of sight with; agus *beiridh* tu mac, *and thou shalt bear a son*; agus *beiridh* i mac agus *bheir* thu Iosa, mar ainm air; oir soaraidh e a shluagh féin o 'm peacaibh, *and she shall bring forth a son, and thou shalt call his name* Jesus; *for he shall save his people from their* sins; agus *rug* e air ann an sliabh Ghilead, *and he overtook him in the mount of Gilead*; *beir* uam e! *beir* uam e! *away with him! away with him!* feuch bithidh maighdean torrach agus *beiridh* i mac, *behold a virgin shall be with child and bring forth a son*; mur *beirear* duine a ris cha fheud (fhoad) e rioghachd dhé fhaicinn, *unless a man is born again, he cannot see the kingdom of God*; *beir* air an uan, *catch*, or *lay hold of the lamb*; *rug* sinn orra ma leth an rathaid, *we overtook them about half way*; 'nuair chi thu bean oileanach *beir* urra, *beir* urra, oir, mar *beir* thusa urra, *beiridh* fear eile urra, *when you see an accomplished lady (female) take her, take her; for unless you will, another will take her. B. A.* &c.

Beirbh, bār'-uv, *n. f.* Copennagen; baile mòr Lochlainn, *the chief city, capital*, or *metropolis of Denmark.*

Beirm, bār'-um, barm; deasgnain. *Ar.*

Beirte, bār''-tyà, *p.* born, brought forth.

Beist, bāshj, *n. m.* and *f.* a beast, a brute a beastly person; *béist* dubh *béist* donn, *an otter*; *beisd* mhaol, *a sea calf. H.*

Beistealachd, bāshg'-ăll-ăchg, *n. f* beastliness, brutality, brutishness.

Beisteag, bāshj'-ag, *n. f.* an earth worm.

Beisteil, bāshj'-ăl, *n.* beastly, brutish.

Beith, bā2'-à, *or* bā, the second letter of the alphabet; birch.

Beithir, bā'-hyur', *n. f.* a prodigiously large serpent. There are most surprising stories about such large serpents in the Highlands. *See* Nathair; in *Lw.* a thunder-bolt; a very large skate, *M. L.* a bear. *Ar.*

Beitir, bā'-tyur, *a.* tidy, neat, clean. *Mf.*

Beo, byô, *a.* lively, active; tha e gu math *beo*, *he is pretty lively*, or *brisk*; living, alive; air gaoith chithear suinn nach *beò*, *on the wind are seen heroes that are not, that are no more, are dead, O.*; ma bhitheas mi *beò*, *if I live*; mar is *beò* mise, cha 'n 'eil tlachd agamsa ann am bàs a pheacaich, deir an Tighearn, *as I live, saith the Lord, I have no pleasure in the death of the wicked*; *n. c.* life time, the living; ri d' *bheò*, *during your life time*; cha'n fhaic thu ri d' *bheò* e, *you shall never see him*; nach *beò* e, *is he not living?* am bheil e *beò*, *is he living?* am *beò* dhuit, a Dheirg, *are you living*, or *are you alive, O Dargo!* gu ma fad *beò* an righ, *long live the king! B. O.*; am *beò* e, *is he living?* am *beò* 's na mairbh, *the living and the dead*; neas is *beo* mi, *during my life time, while I live*; ann an tìr nam *beò*, *in the land of the living*; thoir *beò*, *bring alive*; *beo-leatromach, quick with child*; *beo-dhùil, a living creature*; *beo-iobairt, a living sacrifice*; *beò-ghlac, take alive.*

Beothachan, byŏ'-ach-an, *n. m.* a little fire.

Beoir, byoer, *n. f.* beer; *beoir* laidir, *strong beer*; *beòir chaol, small beer.*

Beolach, byô'-llăch, *n. f.* ashes with living embers, hot ashes.

Beo-shlainte, byŏl'-hlàent'-tyå, *n. f.* liferent; tha '*beo-shlainte* aice dheth, *she has a life-rent of it*; livelihood; gabh do *beò-shlainte* dheth, *take your livelihood of it.*

Beothach, byò'-ăch, *n. c.* a beast, a brute.

Beothachadh, byŏ'-ăch-X, *n. m.* and *p.* reanimation, refreshment; reanimating; kindling as a fire; enlivening; quickening.

Beothachail, byŏ'-ăch-al, *a.* having a reanimating *or* quickening influence.

Beothaich, byŏ'-èch, *v.* kindle; reanimate, revive, quicken.

Beothail, byŏ'-al, *a.* lively, active, brisk.

Beothalachd, byŏ'-all-achg, *n. f.* liveliness, smartness, briskness; agility, activity.

Beuban, băb'-an, any thing mangled. *See* Eubainn, eu- and -bainne, a starvling,

Beubanaich, băb'-an-èch, *v.* mangle.

Beuc, bèuchg, *v.* yell, bellow; *n. m.* a yell, an outcry, a bellow.

Beucail, bèuchg'-ul, *n. m.* and *p.* yelling, bellowing; roaring.

Beud, bă'd, *or* băd', *n. m.* harm, hurt, mischief, pity, nothing; cha 'n 'eil *beud* air, *there's nothing the matter with him*; 's mòr am *beud* e, *it is a great pity*; cha d' éirich *beud* da, *no harm has happened to him*; duan gun *bheud, a poem without blemish, O.*: cha d' fhuilinn e *beud, he sustained no loss*; druidear beul nam *beud, iniquity shall shut her mouth*; cha bhi *beud* ort, *nothing will be wrong with you.*

Beudach, bă'd'-ăch, *a.* hurtful, blemished, guilty; fatal; is *beudach* borb am buille, *fatal and fierce is the blow*; am fear a bhios *beudach*, cha sguir e dh' éigneachadh chàich, *he that is guilty himself, tries to involve others. Os. Ar.*

Beudachd, bă'd''-ăchg, *n. f.* harm, hurt.

Beul, béul *or* bè'l, *n. m.* a mouth; is tobar beatha *beul* an fhìrein, *the mouth of a righteous man is a well of life, B.*; air *bheul* a bhi deas, *nearly prepared*, or *ready*; *beul* an latha, *dawn of day*; *beul* na h-oidhche, *dusk of the evening*; an taobh *beòil, the fore-part*, or *front*; *beul* ri, *about, near*; *beul* ri tri mìosa, *about three months. Bible, Arm.*

Beulach, béul'-ach (*not* bă'-lach), *a.* fawning, fair-spoken, plausible, prating.

Beul-chrabhadh, béul'-chrâv-ăt, hypocrisy, lip-religion; *beul* ghràdh, *lip-love, flattery dissimulation*; cuir, a Thighearna, faire air mo bheul; gléidh dorus mo bhilean, *set, O Lord, a watch before my mouth, keep the door of my lips. B.*

Beulachas, bĕul'-ăch-us, *n. f.* fawning, flattering, artful speaking.

Beulag, bèul'-ăg, *n. f.* a gap, a fissure, *N.*; a fore tooth.

Beul-aithris, bèul'-ăĕr-èsh, *n. f.* tradition; *beul aithris* nan seanar, *the tradition of the elders. Bible.*

Beulaobh, bèul'-hăov, *n. m.* front, foreside, presence; written more correctly *beulthaobh. See* Dr. N. M'Leod's Col. *beul* phurgaid, *a gargle.*

Beulstoc, bèul'-stŏchg, *n. m.* a gunwale, *Islay*; in some places of Argyle, beulmòr.

Beulthaobh, béul'-haŏv, *n. m* front, presence; *beulthaobh* an tighe, *the front of the house*; air mo *bheulthaobh, in my presence*; cuir air a *bheulthaobh* e, *set it before him.*

Beum, băm, *n. m.* a cut, a gash, a stroke, a sarcasm *or* taunt; cha ruig tha leas *beum* a thoirt, *you not need taunt* or *gibe me*; *v.* strike; taunt; ring.

Beumach, băm'-ăch, *a.* sarcastic, bitter, destructive; mar theine *bheumach, like a destructive fire, Os. Ar.*; aineolach *beumach, ignorant and sarcastic. M. A.*

Beumnach, băm'-nach, *a.* sarcastic, reproachful; bilean *beumnach, reproachful lips, B.*; destructive; buillean cothromach *beumnach, well-aimed destructive blows. O. A.*

Beum sgeithe, băm'-skă-å, *n. m.* a striking the shield, the usual mode of giving challenge, or of sounding an alarm among the old Caledonians; le *beum sgéithe* ghlaoidh iad comhrag, *with a blow on the shield they called to battle*; bhuail Treunmor *beum sgéithe, Treunmor sounded an alarm, Oss. Arm.*; a severe sarcasm, a sly insinuation. *Is.*

Beum-sul, băm'-sûl, *n. m.* a blasting of the eye, an optical delusion. *Arm.*

Beur, bărr, *n. m.* a pinnacle; *beur* àrd, *a lofty pinnacle. Ossian, Arm. See* bearradh,—wit.

Beurla, bărr'-llå, *n. f.* the English tongue; *gnathbheurla* na h-Eirionn, *the vernacular dialect of the Irish*; *beurla* Albannach, *the Anglo Scottish*; a' *bheurla* leathan a' *bheurla* mhòr, *the broad Scotch*; Shassunnach, *pure English. H. S.*

Beurlach, bărr'-llăch, *a.* well versed in the English language, belonging to the English language.

Beurra, bărr'-å, *a.* eloquent and witty, well-spoken—genteel. *Arm.*

Beurrach, bărr'-ach, *a.* witty, eloquent. *n. f.* prating female.

Beurrachd, bārr'-ăchg, eloquence, wit, waggery. *Is.*

Beurradair, bārr'–ă'dăr', *n. m.* a wit, a wag; a satirist.

Beurran, bārr'-an, *n. m.* a witty, prating, garrulous, little fellow.

Beuradh-theine, bār'-ur'-hān'-nyȧ, *n. f.* a meteor, a falling star.

Beus, bās, *n. m.* and *f.* moral quality; manners; character; fo dheadh *bheus, under a good character*; fo dhroch *bheus, under a bad character*; conduct, doings; aithneachar leanabh le *'bheus, a child is known by his manners, B.A.*; virtue; righ na *beusa* mòra, *the king of lofty virtues, O.*; custom, habit, practice, use and wont; gheibh thu *beus* is gnàth na dùthcha, *you shall get what the use and wont of the country sanction,* or *what use and wont sanction, Islay*; *beus* na tuath air am bithear is e a nithear, *the habits* or *customs of your associates (farmers) you must follow; beus* an àite anns am bìtear 's e nìtear, *the use and wont of the place you dwell in, must be conformed to.* P. sub.

Beusachd, bās''-achg, *n. f.* moral rectitude, modesty; manners, morals; inoffensive conduct.

Beusaichead, bās3'-ėch-ud, *n. m.* degree of moral purity *or* modesty.

Beusail, bās3'-al, *a. See* Beusach.

Beusan, bās3'-un, *n. m.* morals, manners; deadh *bheusan, good morals*; droch *bheusan, bad morals.*

Beutal, bāt''-al, *a.* a cow; kine. *Ar. Fren.*

B'fhearr, bbyârr, *(for* bu fheàrr) it were better, it is preferable; *b'fhearr* leam, *I would prefer*; *b'fhearr* dhuit, *it were better for you*; *b'fhearr* dhomh, *it would be,* or *it were better for me*; *b'fhearr* dhoibh, (dhaibh, ghīv) *it were better for them.*

Bh', uv, for bha, before a word beginning with a vowel; as, an duine a *bh'* ann, *the man that was*; a bh' ann is pronounced, uv'-vhann. *Is.*

Bha, vvhâ, *pret. ind.* of bi, was, were, wert; an duine a *bha, the man who was*; *a bha* is thus pronounced uv'-vhâ, which is the reason for doubling the v.

Bhac, vvhăchg, as *f.* of bac, to hinder; *bhac* e an duine, *he prevented the man.*

Bhagair, vvhăg'-ur, *pret. a.* of bagair, to threaten.

Bhaird, vvhârj, as *f.* of bard, a poet; mac a *bhàird*, măchg uv'-vhârj, *the poet's son,* or *the son of the poet.*

Bharr, fârr, *pre.* off, from off; *bhàrr* na talmhainn, *from off the earth.*

Bharrachd, (*a.*) vvhârr' achg, as *f.* of barrachd, moreover, besides; a *bharrachd* air a cheud ghorta, *besides the first famine*; *pro.* uv'-vhărr-ăchg.

Bheachd, vvhechg, as *f.* of beachd, an opinion; a réir mo *bheachdsa, according to my opinion*; mo *bheachd, pro.* muv' vhechg.

Bheag, vvhĕug, as *f.* of beag, little; cha d' fhuair iad a *bheag, they got little or nothing*; uv'-vhĕug.

Bheairt, bhyart', as *f.* of beart.

Bhean, vvhen, as *f.* of bean, a woman; a bhean, uv'-vhen, *his wife,* or, *O woman!*

Bheannaich, vvnyănn'-ėch, *pret. a.* of beannaich; an tì a *bheannaich* thu, *the one that blessed you*; uv-vhyănn'-ėch.

Bheir, vvhārr, *f. a.* of thoir, to give, grant, bestow; cò *bheir* comhrag, *who is he that will give battle? O.*

Bhinn, vvhēnn, of binn, melodious; and binn, a sentence, a decision; thoir *binn* a mach, *give a decision, pronounce sentence.*

Bhlais, vvhlăsh, *pret. a.* of blais, to taste; *bhlais* mi, *I tasted.*

Bho, vō, *pre.* this is the way all the Islanders pronounce the *pre.* O, whether single or compounded; thus, bhuam, vvhŭăm, from me; bhuait, vvhŭăet, from you, at a distance from you; bhuainne, vvhŭăėn'-nyȧ, from us, at a distance from us; bhuaibh, vvhŭăėv, from you, at a distance from you. Dr. Smith uses bho in his ancient Celtic Poems; but modern authors prefer O, uam, &c.

Bhobh, vvhō'-uv, *int.* O dear! strange; O *bhobh, O dear! strange, pro.* ōv'-vō-uv.

Bhos, vvhȯs, *pre.* this side, on this side; oftener a bhos, *pro.* uv'-vhȯs; thall 's a *bhos, here and here, hither and thither.*

Bhur, vur, more often ăr, *poss. pro.*; spiorad *bhur* n-inntinn, *the spirit of your minds*; gu'm fosglair *bhur* sùilean, *that your eyes shall be opened.* B

Bi, bē, the *verb* to be, be thou *or* you; *p.* tha; *tha* gu dearbh, *yes, indeed, it is so indeed*; *bithidh, shall be*; *bithidh* iad an sin, *they shall be there*; *bhithinn, I would be*; *bithibh, be ye* or *you. See* Gram.; *bithidh* cron duine cho mòr ri beinn ma'n léir dha féin e, *a man's fault will be as huge as a mountain before he himself can perceive it*; *bithidh* na gobhair bodhar 'san fhobharradh, *the goats are deaf in harvest.*

B'i, bē, (for bu i) it was she; am *b'i* bha siod, *was it she that was yonder.*

B' iad, béud and (bēăd, *No.*) for bu iad, it was they; *b' iad* am feagar agus a mhadainn an ceud là, *the evening and the morning were the first day.*

Biadh, bĕă′-gh′, *v.* feed, nourish, maintain; agus gu'm *biadhar* e ann am fearann duine eile, *and it shall be fed in another man's field, (land,) B.*; *v. n. biadh* orra e, *dole it out in small equal quantities,* as *short provision.*

Biadh, bĕă′-gh′, *n. m.* food, provision, meat; duibhse *bithidh* e mar *bhiadh, to you it shall be for food*; *gen. bìdh* and *bidhith, pro.* bè′-ėch; some places, bāē; *biadh* is aodach, *food and clothing.*

Biadhadh, bĕă′-Ă, *n. m.* feeding, doling out piece-meal.

Biadhadh, bĕă′-aŏ-gh′, *p.* feeding, doling out piece-meal, *or* in small quantities, as short provisions, &c.

Biadhchar, bĕăch′-chur, *a.* productive; síol *biadhchar, substantial,* or *productive corn, corn that produces a good deal of meal.*

Biadhcharachd, bĕăch′-char′-ăchg, *n. f.* productive quality, substance.

Biadhta, bĕă′-tyȧ, *p.* fed, fattened.

Biadhtach, *n f.* a kitchen.

Biadhtachd, bĕăt′-ăchg, *n. f.* hospitality, entertainment; 's bochd a *bhiadhtachd* so, *this is a poor entertainment.*

Biadhtaiche, bĕăt″-ėch-a, *n. m.* and *f.* an entertainer, a host, *or* hostess; tha e na dheadh *bhiadhtaiche, he is a liberal host* or *landlord. Is.*

Biadhtaich, bĕăt′-ėch, feed, share.

Biadhaid, bĕă′-ăj, *n. f.* a pantry.

Bian, bĕăn, *n. m.* a wild animal's skin.

Bianadair, bean′-ad'-ar', *n. m.* a currier.

Biasgach, bĕăsg′-ăch, *n.* niggardy. *N.*

Biast, bĕăst, *n. m.* and *f.* a beast; béist.

Bibh, bēuv, for bithibh, be ye. *Po.*

Bibhidh, bē′-vhė, *n. m.* a very large fire, *Is.*; from *bith.*

Biceir, bēchg′-ar', *n. f.* a small wooden dish.

Bicheanta, bēch′-chyannt-ȧ, *a.* common, frequent, general, numerous. *Islay.*

Bicheantachd, bēch′-chyannt-ăchg, *n. f.* frequency, generality, commonness.

Bid, bēj, *n. f.* a chirp; *v.* pinch, nip. *Lw.*

Bideach, bēj′-ach, *a.* little, small. *North.*

Bideachd, bēj′-achg, *n. f.* littleness, smallness.

Bideag, bėj′-ag, *n. f.* a small portion of any thing.

Bidean, bėj′-an', a point, a tip, a pinnacle, *Is.*; a hedge, a fence. *Stewart.*

Bideil, bēj′-ull, *n. f.* chirping; bigeal.

Bidh, bē′-gh', bė′-ėch, *gen.* of Biadh, meat.

Bidse, bėj′-shȧ, *n. f.* a bad woman.

Big, bēgg, *v.* chirp, be bickering

Big, bėgg, *n. m.* a chirp; *int.* mode of calling to chickens, big! big! *n. pl.* of *beag,* little, small, the young.

Bigeil, bėgg′-ul, *n. f.* chirping.

Bigh, bē′-gh, *n. m.* a post; a pillar; eadar dà *bhìgh* an doruis, *between the posts of the door*; eadar dà *bhìgh* a' gheata, *between the portals* or *pillars of the gate.*

Bile, bėl′-ȧ, *n. m.* a lip; a margin; a rim, brim, edge; do bhrìgh gur fearr do caoimhneas, gràidh na beatha, bheir mo *bhilean* cliù dhuit, *because thy loving kindness is better than life, my lips shall praise thee, Ps.* 63.; *bile* nan sruthan uaigneach, '*the margin of the lonely brooks, Sm.*; *bile* na h-ata, *the brim* or *rim of the hat.*

Bileach, bėl′-ach, *a.* bordered, edged, having a margin; *bileach* choigeach, *marigold. H.*

Bileag, bėl′-ag, *n. f.* a leaflet, a blade; *bileag* fheòir, *a blade of grass*; *bileag* bhaite, *water-lily.*

Bilearach, bėl′-ăr-ăch, *n. f.* sweet, *or* sea-grass; on con. of Argyle, *bileanach.*

Bileil, bėl′-al, *a.* labial, belonging to the lips.

Bilistear, bėll′-asht-ar', *n. m.* a mean fellow.

Billeachd, bėll2′-ăchg, *n. f.* poverty.

Bim, and b'im, *or* bē'm, *or* bēum, for *bithidh,* I shall be in poetry. *Ross. Ps.*

Binealta, bēn′2-alt-a, *a.* fine, elegant.

Binn, bēnn' *a.* melodious, harmonious, musical; *n. f.* sentence, decision; bi sin a' *bhinn* a thug e mach, *that was the decision he gave*; a chionn nach 'eil *binn* an aghaidh droch oibre 'ga cur an gnìomh gu luath, uime sin tha cridhe chloinn nan daoine làn shuidhichte air son olc a dheanamh, *because sentence against an evil work is not speedily executed, therefore the heart of the sons of men is fully set in them to do evil. So.* 8-11.

Binndeach, bēnj′-ăch, *a.* coagulation.

Binndeachadh, bēnj′-ăch-Ă, *n. m.* and *p.* making cheese; curdling; coagulating.

Binndeal, bēnj′-jăl, *n. m.* a head dress.

Binndich, bēnj′-ėch, *v.* make cheese, curdle, coagulate.

Binne, byėn′-nyȧ, *n. f.* melody, music.

Binneach, bēnn′-ach, *a.* light-headed, pointed, pinnacled, high-topped.

Binnean, bėnn'-an', *n. m.* pinnacle, point; *binnean* an teampuill, *the pinnacle of the temple. B.*

Binnead, bēnn″-ud, *n. f.* degree of melody.

Binnid, bėn′2-ėj, *n. f.* runnet, stomach.

Binnideach, bėn''-ėj-ach, *a.* like runnet.
Biobhuan, bėv'-vun *or* vuan, *a.* lasting; eternal.
Biobhuantachd, bėv'-vuant-ăchg, *n. f.* eternity; quality of lasting long.
Biobull, bēbb'-ull, *n. m.* the Bible.
Biobullach, bēbb'-ull-ach, *a.* Biblical.
Biod, bė'd *or* bėud, *v. n.* pique, gall, vex.
Biod, bēdd, *v.* bicker; canker.
Biodag, bėud'-ag, *n. f.* a dirk, a dagger. It is impossible to pronounce this word; the *e* short and *u* shut pronounced quick.
Biodan, bēdd'-an, *n. m.* bickering fellow.
Biodanach, bēdd'-ăn-ăch, *a.* bickering, cankering; *n. f.* a bickering, eternally scolding, *or* complaining female.
Biodh, bĕaŏgh, 3 *per. sing. v.* bi for bitheadh.
Biog, byúg, *v.* gripe; start.
Biogadh, byúg'-Ă, *n. m. p.* a griping; a starting, a sudden emotion, a whim.
Biogail, byúg'-al, *a.* lively, active, smart.
Biogarra, bėgg'-úrr-a, *a.* mean, churlish.
Biogarrachd, bėgg'-ur-achg, *n. f* meanness, churlishness, inhospitality.
Bioirlinn, byúr'-llyėnn, *n. f.* a pleasure-boat. *Is.*
Biolair, byúl'-ur', *n. f.* cresses, water-cresses.
Bior, bėrr, *n. m.* a pointed small stick, a prickle; *v.* prick; gall, vex.
Biorach, bėrr'-ăch, *a.* pointed; sharp; *n. f.* a heifer, *Is.*; in *Sk.* a colt, loth; an instrument to prevent calves from suckling, *M. L.* cròcach.
Bioraich, bėrr'-ėch, *v. n.* make sharp; look steadfastly, stare most wonderful.
Bioraichead, bėrr'-ėch-ud', *n. m.* pointedness, degree of sharpness *or* pointedness.
Bioran, bėrr'-an, *n. m.* a little stick.
Bioranach, bėrr'-ăn-ăch, *a.* full of little sticks, prickled, full of prickles.
Bioran deamhainn, berr'-an-dyŏv'-ėnn, *n. m.* a pink, a minnow; (in Islay, *breac deamhainn. H.*)
Bioras, bėrr'-as, *n. f.* water lily. *M. L.*
Biorchluasach, bėrr'-chlŭăs-ăch, *a.* sharp-eared.
Biorg, byúr'-ug, *v.* tingle, thrill, feel a tingling sensation.
Biorgadaich, byúrg'-ad-ėch, *n. f.* a thrilling *or* tingling sensation *or* feeling.
Biorganta, byúrg'-ănt-ă, *a.* thrilling.
Biorgantachd, byúrg'-ănt-ăchd, *n. f.* degree of thrilling *or* tingling sensation; entanglement. *M.*
Biorguinn, byúrg'-gŭenn, *n. f.* rending pain. *H.*
Biorraid, byúrr'-aj, *n. f.* a cap with a scoop on it, a head piece; an osier twig.
Biorraideach, byúrr'-aj-ach, *a.* scooped, conical.
Biorshuileach, byėrr'-hŭll-ăch, *a.* sharp-sighted.
Biorsamaid, byúr'-sa-măj, *n. f.* a Roman balance for weighing small quantities; a steel-yard. *M. L.*
Biota, bėtt'-a, *n. m.* a churn. *Skye.*
Biotailt, bėtt'-ăllt[2], *n. f.* victuals.
Bir, bērr, *n. m.* the alarm note of the sol. and geese when attacked. *Martin.*
Birlinn, bērr'-lyėnn, *n f.* a barge *or* pleasure boat. *H. S.*
Bith, bė, *n. f.* existence, being.
Bith, bē, *n. m.* gum, tar, *N.*; *a.* quiet; bi cho *bìth* ri uan, *be as quiet as a lamb.*
Bith-bhuan, bė-vŭăn', *a.* eternal. *B.*
Bith-bhuantachd, bė-vŭănt'-achg, *n. f.* eternity, perpetuity. *B.*
Bitheanta, bė'-ant-a, *a.* frequent. *M. L.*
Bitheantachd, bė'-ant-achg, *n. m.* frequency.
Bithis, bē'-ėsh, *n. f.* vice, screw. *Inver.*
Buitheas, bū'-as, *n. m.* libel, defamation of the worst kind and degree—fame.
Buitheasach, bū'-ăs-ăch, *a.* defamatory, libelous in the highest degree possible.
Buitheasachd, bū'-ăs-ăchg, *n. f.* defamatory *or* libelous nature *or* quality. *Arg.*
Blabhdair, blăv'-ud-ăr', *n. m.* a babbler; yelling, howling, babbling. *D. M. L.*
Blad, blăd', *n. m.* an enormous mouth.
Bladach, blăd''-ăch, *a.* wide-mouthed; *n. f.* a female with a large mouth.
Bladaire, blăd''-ur-ȧ, *n. m.* a babbler.
Bladairt, blăd''-ărt[2], *n. f.* babbling.
Bladh, blaŏ-gh', *n. f.* substance, meaning pith, energy.
Bladhail, blaŏgh''-al, pithy, substantial.
Bladhar, blaŏ-gh'-ghur, *a.* substantial, full of meaning, substance, *or* importance.
Blaigh, blĭĕ-'yh', and blaŏė-yh, *n. f.* a part, a portion, a fragment, a small share.
Blaighdeach, bllij'-dyach, *n. f.* part, a portion, an instalment; *a.* in smalls, in portions.
Blaighdeachas, bllij'-dyach-us, *n. f.* the act *or* state of being cut into small portions.
Blaighlin, blĭĕ-gh'-llēn', *n. m.* a sheet.
Blaighdeachadh, bllij'-dyach-Ă, *p.* cutting asunder, *or* into fragments *or* small portions. *Is.*
Blaighdich, blij'-dyėch, *v.* cut asunder *or* into small portions.
Blais, blăėsh, *v.* taste, try; 'nuair a *bhlais* e am fion, *when he tasted the wine. B.*
Blaiseamachd, blăsh'-am-ăchg, *n. f.* smacking with the lips.
Blaiseamaich, blăsh'-ăm-ėch, *v.* smack with the lips; taste, try.

Blaithe, blă-è, *deg.* of blath, warm, affectionate, kind; ni 's *blaithe, more warm, more affectionate.*

Blaithteachadh, blâêt2'-tyach-Ă, *n. m.* a warming; feeling affection for; *p.* warming. *B.*

Blaithtich, blăêt'-tyèch, *v.* warm, heat.

Blanndaidh, blănnd'-è, *a.* stale as milk.

Blanndar, blannd'-ur, *n. f.* dissimulation.

Blaom, blāom, *v. n.* stare with the greatest surprise, as when taken unawares, start.

Blaomadh, blāom'-Ă, *p.* a wonderful stare; *p.* staring, starting; foolish excitement. *H.*

Blaomair, blāom'-ur', *n. m.* a fellow that stares like a fool; a fellow easily frightened; nonsensical talk. *H. S.*

Blaomaireachd, blāom'-ur'-ăchg, *n. f.* a habit of staring foolishly; starting.

Blaomannach, blāom'-ann-ăch, *a.* inconstant, variable, talking inconsistently.

Blar, blâr, *n. f.* a battle, engagement; battle-field; a cheud *bhlàr* a chuir iad, *the first battle they fought*; a' dol sìos do'n *bhlàr, going down to the battle-field*; fraoch nam *blàr, the rage of battle, O.*; ground, plain; a muigh air a *bhlàr, out on the ground*; na shìneadh air a' *bhlàr, stretched on the ground*; chaidh e feadh a *bhlàir, it spilled on the ground*; sgeadachair na *blàir, the plains shall be covered* or *clothed*; réith a *bhlàir, the plain of battle, M. L.*; thoir am *blàr* ort, *away! go about your business*; *blàr* mòna *or* mòine, *a peat-moss*; *blàr* gealachaidh, *a bleach-field*; a cow with a white spot on the face; cuir a stigh a' *bhlàr, put in the cow with the white face*; a white spot in the face, as a cow, a horse, &c. a white face; tha *blàr* na h-aodann, *she has a white spot on her face*; *a.* white-faced, having a white spot in the face; an t-each *blàr, the white-faced horse.*

Blas, bllăss, *n. m.* taste, savour, relish; a particle, the least part; am bheil *blas* air gealagan uibhe, *is there any taste in the white of an egg? Job*; cia milis leam' *blas* do bhriathran, ni's milse tha iad na mil do m' bheul, *how sweet are thy words unto my taste! yea, sweeter than honey to my mouth, P.* 119-103; is dona am *blas* a th' air, *it has a very bad taste*; cha 'n' eil *blas* deth an so, *there is not a bit* or *a particle of it here*; tha *blas* na meal air do phògan, *the taste of honey is on thy kisses*; do bheul air *bhlas* an t-siùcair, *thy lips are as sweet as sugar. Sgs.*

Blasad, bllăss'-ud', *n. m.* taste, a tasting; gun am *blasad, without tasting them. O.*

Blasadh, blăs'-Ă, *p.* tasting; *n. m.* the act of tasting.

Blasardaich, bllăss'-ard'-èch, *n. f.* smacking the lips, tasting with relish.

Blasda, blăsd''-ă, *a.* delicious, sweet, savoury, tasteful; agreeable; eloquent; agus dean domh biadh *blasda, and make unto me savoury meat*; briathran *blasda, agreeable* or *eloquent words,* or *talk. B. Sg.*

Blasdachd, bllăssd''-ăchg, *n. f.* deliciousness, sweetness, savouriness, agreeableness.

Blasmhor, blăss'-vur, *a. See* Blasda.

Blasphog, blăss'-ffŏg, *n. f.* a sweet kiss.

Blath, bllhâ', *n. f.* bloom, blossom; flowers; ged nach d' thoir an crann-fige uaith *blàth*; ged nach fàs air an fhìonain cinneas, &c.; gidheadh ni mise gàirdeachas anns an Tighearna; ni mi aoibhneas ann Dia mo shlàinte, *although the fig-tree shall not blossom; neither shall fruit be in the vine; yet I will rejoice in the Lord, I will joy in the God of my salvation, Hab.* iii, 17; fo làn *bhlàth, in full bloom*; thig e mach mar *bhlàth, he shall come forth as a flower, Job*; consequence; effects; bithidh a *bhlàth* ort, *the consequence* or *effects will be seen in your case*; is léir a *bhlàth* ort, *the consequences are obvious in your case*; *a.* affectionate, tender, warm; is *blàth* anail na màthar, *affectionate is the breath of a mother*; tha e glé *bhlàth, he is affectionate enough.*

Blathach, bllhâ'-ach, *a. n. f.* buttermilk.

Blathaich, blhâ'-èch, *v.* warm.

Blathas, blhâ-us, *or* blâ'-ăs, *n. m.* warmth, kindliness, affectionate disposition.

Blathmhaiseach, blhă'-vhăsh-ach, *a.* in the bloom of youth.

Blathobair, blhâ'-ôb-èr', *n. f.* embroidery; blàthoibrich, *embroider. H. S.*

Bleachdair, blèchg'-ur', *n. m.* a flattering fellow.

Bleathghluineach, blā2'-ghlŭèn-ach, *a.* in-kneed, knock-kneed.

Bleid, blàj, *n. f. a.* importunity, sly kind of impertinent begging.

Bleideil, bllàj'-al, *a.* intrusive, begging in a sly way, troublesome.

Bleidir, bllàj'-èr *v.* beg in a genteel way, tease, importune, trouble.

Bleidire, bllāj'-èr-ă, *n. m.* genteel beggar, a mean obtrusive fellow.

Bleidireachd, blāj'-èr'-ăchg, *n. f.* importunity; genteel begging.

Bleith, bllhā, *v.* grind; *n. f.* grinding; gabh na clacha muilinn agus *bleith* min, *take the millstones and grind meal*; fuaim na *bleith, the sound of grinding B.*

Bleithte, bllhā'-tyă, *p.* ground.

Bleodhainn, bhlyȯ′-ėnn. *v.* milk, squeeze out of; also bleothainn.

Bleodhan, bhlyȯ′-an, *n. m.* a wheel-barrow. *N. H.*

Bleodhann, bhlyȯ′-un, *n. m.* milking, the act of milking cattle.

Bliadhna, bhlĕă′-nhȧ, *n. f.* a year; is buaine *bliadhna* na nollaig, *a year is more lasting than Christmas. M In.*

Bliadhnach, bhlĕă′-nnach, *n. m.* and *f.* a year old, a yearling.

Bliadhnachd, blhĕăn′-năchg, *n. f.* an annuity.

Bliadhnail, bhlĕăn′-nal, *a.* yearly.

Blian, blĕăn, *n. f. m.* the groin, the belly; *v.* bask, as fish, &c. *Skye*; tarr-geal. *W. N.* meagre, lean; insipid.

Bligh, blhė, *v.* milk; 's ann as a ceann a *bhlighear* a bhò, *you milk a cow just as you feed her.*

Bliochan, bleúch′-an, *n. f.* marigold. *H.*

Bliochd, bleuchg, *n. m.* milk. *Welsh,* blith, strippings, athtoirt.

Bloigh, blaŏĕgh′, *n. f.* a part. *b. Ir.*

Bloighdich, blaŏĕj′-jech, *v.* cut into pieces.

Bloinigeach, blŏėn′-ėg-ach, *a.* plump, fat, soft.

Bloinigean, blŏėn″-ėg-an′, *n. c.* a fat child.

Blonag, blon′-ag, *n. f.* lard, fat.

Blosg, blŏsk, *v.* sound a horn. *Glen M. M.*

Bo, bō, *int.* to frighten children; *a.* strange.

Bo, bō, *n. f.* a cow; *gen. sing.* boine; *plu.* bò, (*pro.* baw.)

Bobug, bōb′-ug, *n. m.* a fellow.

Boc, bōchg, *n. m.* a he-goat, a roe-buck; *v.* leap, skip, as a buck. *M. L.*

Boc, bôchg, *v.* swell, inflame.

Boch, bŏch, *n. m.* ecstacy, great happiness, joy, rejoicing;—peculiar to the Islands.

Bochail, bŏch′-al, *a.* happy, overjoyed.

Bochalachd, bŏch′-ăl-ăchg, *n. f.* extreme happiness *or* joy; *a.* liveliness.

Bochd, bŏchg, *a.* poor, needy, necessitous; ni làmh na leisg bochd, *the hand of laziness maketh poor*; tha neach ann a leigeas air a bhi *bochd,* agus mòr shaibhreas aige, *there is that maketh himself poor, yet hath great riches*; coinnichidh am beairteach agus am *bochd* a chéile, is e'n Tighearna a rinn iad gu léir, *the rich and the poor meet together, the Lord is the maker of them all*; sad, melancholy; is *bochd* an gnothuch e, *it is a sad affair, it is a melancholy circumstance*; is *bochd* nach d' f huair sinn e, *it is a pity we did not get it*; dear; an duine *bochd, the dear creature,* or *good creature*; is *bochd* a thachair dha, *it has sadly happened to him*; tha e gu *bochd, he is not well, he is sick*; lean, lank; crodh *bochd, lean cattle*; *n. m.* and *f.* the poor, the parish poor; cuid do *bhochdaibh* na tìre, *some of the poor of the land. B.*; a' roinn airgiod nam *bochd, distributing the poor's funds*; am *bochd* 's an nochd, *the poor and naked*; is fearr a bhi *bochd* na bhi breugach, *it is better to be poor than a liar—than be false*; leagh aidh am bròn am bochd anam, *affliction* or *sorrow melts (dissolves) the wretched soul. O. A.*

Bochd, bôchg, *v.* swell, puff, get turgid.

Bochdainn, bŏchg′-ėnn, *n. f.* extreme poverty, poverty, distress, affliction, trouble, mischief, mishap; old Nick *or* old Pluto; chuir sin e gus a *bhochdainn, that reduced him to poverty*; thàinig e gu *bochdainn, he was reduced to extreme poverty*; 's ann air a tha blàth na *bochdainn, he has every sign of extreme poverty about him*; thig am misgear, agus geòcair gu *bochdainn, the drunkard and the glutton shall come to poverty, B.*; chaidh a' *bhochdainn* uile ort an nios, *you have gone to extremes now altogether*; thàinig *bochdainn* an rathad an teaghlaich, *the family was visited with affliction* or *sickness*; dé a' *bhochdainn* a rug ort, *what the mischief came over you!* mar bha *bhochdainn* an dan domh, *as misfortune* or *bad luck would have it.*

Bochdan, bôchg′-an, *n. m.* a hobgoblin, a scare-crow, an apparition.

Boc-roin, bòchg-rôėn, *n. m.* a prawn, a shrimp.

Bodach, bòd″-ach, *n. m.* an old man, a churl *or* niggardly fellow; cha 'n 'eil e 'na *bhodach, he is not a churl*; a mutchkin; *bodach* uisge bheatha, *a mutchkin of whisky*; *bodach* ruadh, *a codling*; a hobgoblin, a spectre; beiridh na *bodaich* ort, *the hobgoblins will lay hold of you, will catch you*; churlishness, meanness of spirit, niggardliness; 's e chuireadh am *bodach* a fear a bhiodh teann, *it (whisky) would drive meanness* or *niggardliness out of a miser* or *churl. M. In.*

Bodhag, bō′-hăg, *n. f.* a sea-lark. *M. L.*

Bodachail, bòd″-ăch-al, *a.* churlish.

Bodhaig, bòh′-hăg, *n. f.* the human body. *See* Boghainn.

Bodhan, bò′-han, *n. m.* the ham, thigh. *M. L.*

Bodhair, bò′-hyur′, *v.* deafen, stun with noise; cha mhòr nach do *bhodhair* an t-òlach mi le 'raibheiceil (raoiceil as it is corrupted), *the fellow almost stunned me with his roaring*; na *bodhair* mi le d' dhrabhluinn, *do not deafen* or *stun me with your absurdity.* Some pronounce drabhluinn, *draoluinn* and *drowluinn,* but in Islay we never murder a Gaelic word. *Scotch,* bother and bather.

Bodhar, bò′-hur, *a.* deaf, dull of hearing.

ach mar dhuine *bodhar* cha chluinn mise, *but as a deaf man I do not hear*; the deaf; tha na *bodhair* a cluinntinn, a ta na mairbh air an dùsgadh, agus tha an soisgeil air a shearmonachadh do 'na bochdaibh, *the deaf hear, the dead are raised up, and the poor have the gospel preached unto them, B.*; cluinnidh am *bodhar* fuaim an airgid, *even the deaf hear the clink of silver (money)*; *bodhar* fhead, *a dull, heavy sound, as of whistling wind*; *b dhar* fhuaim, *a dull, heavy, hollow sound*; cò a rinn am *bodhar, who made the deaf. B.*

BODHRADH, bōh'-rĂ, *n. m.* and *p.* deafening, tha thu air mo *bhòdhradh, you deafen* or *stun me with your noise* or *importunity.*

BOG, bògg, *a.* soft, miry, moist, damp; aite *bog, a place where a person* or *beast is apt to sink*; soft, timid, spiritless; cha 'n 'eil ann ach duine *bog, he is only a simple, timid, chicken-hearted, spiritless fellow*; *v.* wag, bob, shake; tha 'n cù a' *bogadh* urbaill, *the dog wags his tail*; is fhearr an cù a *bhogas* urball na cù a chuireas dreang air, *the dog that wags his tail is better than the one that girns*; move *or* excite; 'nuair *bhogadh* an dram air, *when the whisky would excite him.*

BOGACHADH, bŏg'-ach-Ă, *n. m.* and *p.* softening; steeping; moistening; getting more soft.

BOGADAICH, bògg'-ad'-èch, *n. f.* waving, tremour from heat *or* passion. *H.*

BOGADAN, bògg'-ad-an, *n. m.* waving, wagging, heaving; tha chraobh a' *bogadan, the tree waves*; wagging, bobbing.

BOGADH, bògg'-Ă, *p.* moistening, softening; *n. m.* the state of sticking fast in the mire; chaidh a' bhò am *bogadh, the cow stuck fast in the mire.*

BOGAICH, bògg'-èch, *v.* soften, moisten, steep; *bogaich* an leathrach, *steep the leather.*

BOGAICHTE, bògg'-èch-tyå, *p.* softened, moistened.

BOGANACH, bògg'-ăn-ăch, *n. m.* a soft, simple, booby-like fellow.

BOGARSAICH, bòg'-ar-ssèch, *n. f.* waving; wagging; bobbing.

BOGBHUINE, bògg'-vvhŭèn-nyå, *n. f.* a bulrush.

BOG-CHRIDHEACH, bògg'-chrè-ăch, *a.* chicken-hearted, faint-hearted.

BOGHA, bò'-ha, *n. m.* a bow, a bend, an arch; a sunk rock at sea; the wave, called a heaver; *bogha* saighead, *an archer's bow*; tha *bogha* air, *it has a bend* or *bow*; *bogha* na drochaid, *the arch of the bridge*; tha *bogha* mòr air a' bhalla, *the wall has a great bow or bulge*; fear *bogha, an archer*; *boghadaireachd, archery*; mar *bhogha* air ghleus, *like a bow on the stretch*; *bogha* na fiodhlach, *the fiddle-bow*; tha *bogha* air a' ghéig, *the branch has a bend*; bogh-braoin, *bogha* frois, *a rain-bow*; mar *bhogha* braoin a soillseachadh, *as a rain-bow shining, O.*; *v.* bow, bend, bulge; tha e '*boghadh* a mach, *it bulges out.*

BOGHADAIR, bòh'-hăd-ăr', an archer.

BOGHADAIREACHD, bòh'-ha-dăr'-ăchg, *n. f.* archery.

BOGHAINN, bo'-hyènn, *n. m.* the human body, person; is ciatach a *bhoghainn* dhuine e, *he is a handsome person*; nach ann aig a tha *bhoghainn, what a handsome body he has.*

BO GHAMHNA *or* GHAMHNACH, bō-ghàv'-na *or* -nach, *n. f.* a farrow cow.

BOGHAN, bò''-han, *n. m.* the calf of the leg, the ham.

BOGHSDAIR, bòs'-ddar[2], *n. m.* a bolster.

BOGLACH, bògg'-llăch, *n. m.* a marsh, a quagmire, any place where a beast is apt to stick fast.

BOGAINN, bògg'-ènn, *n. m.* a marsh. *North.*

BOGLUACHAIR, bògg'-lŭăch-ar', *n. f.* bullrush.

BOGLUASGACH, bòg'-llŭăsg-ăch, *a.* waving, floating; softly moving.

BOICEANN, bŏèchg'-ann, *n. m.* a goat-skin, a skin of any kind.

BOICEANNACH, bŏèchg'-ann-ăch, *n. f.* the small-pox, *Suth.-shire*; in *Lw.* the shingles or herpes; an deilginneach, *Islay.*

BOICNEACHADH, bŏèchg'-nyach-Ă, *n. m.* and *p.* belabouring most furiously; beating till the skin blisters.

BOICNICH, bŏèchg-nnyèch, *v.* belabour till the skin blisters; beat with all your might.

BOID, bōèj, *v.* solemnly vow or promise; *n. f.* a solemn vow; *gen.* of the *Bòd, the Island of Bute*; cha 'n ann am *Bòd* uile tha 'n t-olc, ach an Cumradh bheag tha làmh ris, *it is not in Bute alone that the mischief is, but in little Cumra just near it.*

BOIDEACH, bōèj'-ăch, *a.* pertaining to a vow.

BOIDEAN, bōj'-un, *pl.* of bòid, vows; *bòidean* baistidh, *baptismal vows.*

BOIDHEACH, bôe'-yhach, *a.* pretty, beautiful, comely, handsome, neat.

BOIDHEACHD, bôèch'-achg, *n. f.* beautifulness, handsomeness, elegance.

BOIDHCHE, bôèch'-chå, *n. f.* beauty, degree of beauty, extreme beauty; 's e do *bhoidhche* a leòn mi, *it is thy excessive beauty that has wounded me*; *comp.* &c.

deg. more beautiful; is ise is *boidhche, she is the more* or *most beautiful.*

BOIDHCHEAD, bôěch'-chyud, *n. f.* degree of beauty; increase in beauty.

BOIDHRE, bôěr'-rå, *deg. comp.* more *or* most deaf *or* dull of hearing, more commonly *buidhre.*

BOIDHREAD, bŏěr'-ud, *n. f.* degree of deafness.

BOIDICH, bōj'-ěch, *v.* vow, promise; foreswear solemnly; *bhòidich* thu bòid do'n tighearn, *thou hast solemnly vowed unto the Lord; thou hast vowed a vow; bòidcan* chiaraig ris na fearaibh is bòid nam fear uile ri ciarag, *like the swarthy maid who foreswore the men, as she had been foresworn by them. G. P.*

BOIDSEAR, bŏjsh'-ăr', *n. m.* a blockhead, a stupid fellow.

BOIDSEARACHD, bŏjsh'-ăr2-ăchg, *n. f.* stupidity, the conduct of a blockhead.

BOIL, bu'l, *n. f.* madness in the extreme, rage, fury; highest degree of passion, frenzy; c'arson a ghabh na cinnich *boil, why did the heathen rage, P.*; a chridhe laiste, le *boil* chatha, *his soul highly inflamed with the fury of battle, S.*; tha e air *boil, he is furiously mad, he is under the influence of the greatest passion*; fear na *boile, the passionate man, Bible*; 's ann á tha thu air *boil, you are quite mad*; 's ann orra a siod a bha *bhoil, how mad* or *enraged those were.*

BOILICH, bô'll'-ěch, *n. f.* ostentation, boasting, romancing; gasgonading; telling fibs; tha e cho làn do *bhòilich* is a tha 'n ubh do'n bhiadh, *he is so full of romancing as the egg is of substance, (meat;)* thoir thairis do d' *bhòilich, be done of your romancing* or *gasgonading.*

BOILLSG, bull'-ěshg, *n. f.* prattling. *M. L.*

BOILLSG, bull'-ěshg, *v.* flash, gleam, shine with great lustre *or* glitter; *n. f.* effulgence, glitter.

BOILLSGEACH, bull'-ěshg-ach, *a.* flashing, gleaming, shining with effulgence.

BOILLSGEADH, bull'-ěshg-Ă, *n. m.* effulgence; *p.* gleaming, shining; beaming.

BOILLSGEANTA, bull'-ěshg-annt-a, *n. f.* gleaming, flashy, gaudy; fond of dress.

BOILLSGEANTACHD, bull'-ěshg-annt-achd, *n. f.* gaudiness; effulgence, flash.

BOILLSGEIL, bull'-ěshg-al, *a.* flashing, gleaming, gaudy, effulgent.

BOINE, bòn''-nyå, *gen.* of *bo*, a cow; laogh na *boine, the cow's calf.*

BOINEID, bŏěn'-ăj, *n. f.* a bonnet.

BOINEANTA, bŏěn'-nyant-a, *a.* mild, gentle; stout, handsome. *M. In.*

BOINEANTACHD, boin'-nyant-ăchg, *n. f.* mildness, gentleness, handsomeness.

BOINN, baŏinn, *pl.* of *bann*, hinge, &c.

BOINNE, bŏěn'-nyå, *n. m.* a drop; *boinne* taig, *a drop of rain. Dr. M'Leod.*

BOINNEALAICH, bŏin'-nyal-ěch, *n. f.* dropping of rain before a shower.

BOIR, bŏěr, *n. m.* an elephant. *Irish.*

BOIRCHE, bŏěrch'-chå, *n. m* an elk, a buffalo; a thick edge.

BOIREAL, bŏěr'-al, *n. m.* a joiner's brace.

BOIREAM, bôer'-um, *n. m.* a rumour, a surmise, creating a hubbub. *Islay.*

BOIREAMAIL, bôěr'-um-al, *a.* spreading as a rumour *or* surmise; creating great interest.

BOIRIONN, bŏěr''-unn, *a.* female, of the feminine gender; feminine, belonging to a female.

BOIRIONNACH, bŏěr-unn-ăch, *n. f.* a female; *boirionnach* bòidheach, *a pretty female*; firionnach is *boirionnach, a male and a female, a man and a woman*; *boirionnach* eireachdail, *a handsome female.*

BOIRG, bŏer' ěg, *n. m.* a little screwed-up mouth.

BOIRGEACH, bŏer'-ěg-ach, *a.* having a little prating mouth; *n. f.* a prating female.

BOIRGIRE, bŏer'-ěg-ěr-å, a fellow with a little screwed mouth, a tattler.

BOISCEAL, baŏěsh'-kyal, *n. m.* and *f.* a savage man *or* woman. *Ar.*

BOISE, bŏěsh'-å, *gen.* of *bas*, the palm of the hand.

BOISEAG, bŏsh'-åg, *n. f.* a palm full of water; a blow with the palm *or* on the palm.

BOISEID, bŏsh'-ěj, *n. f.* a budget, a belt, a girdle. *H. S.*

BOISG, baŏěshk, *v.* flash, gleam, dart, shine with effulgence.

BOISGEACH, baŏeshk'-ăch, *a.* flashing, shining, gleaming, effulgent; sparkling.

BOISGEALACHD, baŏěshg'-ăl-ăchg, *n. f.* effulgence, radiance, glitter, brightness.

BOISGEANTA, baŏěshg'-annt-a, flashing.

BOISGEANTACHD, baŏěshg'-annt-ăchg, *n. f.* luminousness, brightness; gleaming.

BOISGEIL, boaěshg'-al, *a.* bright, gleaming, beaming.

BOITEAL, bŏět''-al, *n. m.* pride. *Arm.*

BOITEAN, bŏět''-an', a bundle *or* truss of straw *or* hay; some places, *boiteal.*

BOITEANAICH, bŏět''-an'-ěch, *v.* make into bundles *or* trusses.

BOITIDH, bŏět'-ě, *n. m.* a sow; *int.* boitidh! boitidh! *Skye*; in *Argyle*, duradh! duradh!

BOITH, bŏych, *n. f.* a hut, a mean cottage.

BOLADH, bŏll'-Ă, *n. m* smell, stink; *boladh* gràiniel, *an abominable smell.*

BOLANNTA, boll'-annt-å, *a.* excellent.

BO-LAOIGH, bō'-lāoěgh', *n. f.* a cow with a calf, a milch cow.

Bolb, bol′-ub, *n. f.* a sort of worm. *Ir.*

Bolg, bŏll′-ug, and bal′-ag, *n. m.* a pair of bellows; a womb; séid am *bolg, blow the bellows*; a *bolg* na maidne, *from the womb of the morning, S.*; *bolg* saighid, *a quiver*; *a blister*; *a big belly*; *v.* bulge, swell, puff, blister.

Bolgach, bŏll′-ug-ach, *a.* bulging, jutting, having a large belly; *n. f.* corpulent female.

Bolgaire, bŏll′-ug-ur′-à, *n. m.* a man with a big belly; a glutton.

Bolgam, bŏll′ ug-um, *n. m.* a mouthful of any liquid; *bolgam* bainne, *a mouthful of milk*; *bolgam* uisge, *a mouthful of water.*

Bolgan, boll′-ag-an, *n. m.* the calf of the leg; a little blister. *D. M.*

Bolg-losgainn, boll′-ug-llòsg-ēnn, *n. m.* a mushroom.

Bolgan-beucan, boll′-ăg-an-bèuchg-an, *n. m.* a fuzz-ball.

Bolla, bòll′-à, *n. m.* a net *or* anchor-buoy; a boll; *bolla* mine, *a boll of meal*; *bolla* buntata, *a boll of potatoes.*

Bollsg, bòll′-usg, *v.* bluster, babble.

Bollsgach, bòll′-usg-ach, *a.* blustering, boasting; *n. f.* a blustering curious female.

Bollsgaire, bòll′-usg-ur-à, *n. m.* blustering, swaggering, bullying fellow.

Bollsgaireachd, bòll′-usg-arr-ăchg, *n. f.* a habit of blustering or swaggering.

Bollsgannta, bòll′-usg-annt-a, blustering, swaggering; bullying.

Boltrach, bŏll′-ttrach, *n. f.* smell, perfume, *H.*; a volume *or* bolt of smoke and fire, ashes, &c. *Is.*

Boltrachas, bŏll′-trach-us, *n. f.* perfumery, fragrance.

Bomanach, bòm′-an-ach, *a.* blustering. *D. M.*

Bonn, bōn′n, *n. m.* a sole, a foundation, a piece of money; bottom *or* base; bomb of a sail; *bonn* leth chruin, *a half-crown piece*; *bonn* na bròige, *the sole of the shoe*; thug e na *buinn* air, *he took to his heels*; cha ′n ′eil mi *bonn* ann ad eisimeil, *I am not the least in your reverence, I do not care a straw for you*; thoir na *buinn* ort, *make off! be off as fast as you can! take to your heels!* fichead *bonn* airgid, *twenty pieces of silver*; *bonn* na beinne, *the foot* or *base of the mountain*; fo *bhonnaibh* ur cas, *under the soles of your feet.*

Bonnach, bŏnn′-ăch, *n. m.* a cake.

Bonnachair, bonn′-ach-ur, *n. m.* a wandering greedy beggar.

Bonnanta, bŏnn′-annt-a, *a.* firm, stout.

Bonn-a-se, bōn′n′-é-shè, and shĕă, *n. m.* a halfpenny; lit. a piece out of six.

Bonnchart, bōn′n′-chărt, balk; cnàimh crìche; near Inverary, *cnocaid.*

Bonntach, bōn′n′-ttach, *n. f.* the thickest part of a hide for soles.

Borb, bŏrr′-ub, *v.* inflame; get enraged; *bhorb* a′ chas, *his foot inflamed*; *bhorb* i ′na aghaidh, *she got enraged against him.*

Borb, bŏrr′-ub, *a.* turbulent; of a turbulent disposition; fierce, savage, cruel, boisterous; o′n iorguill *bhorb, from the fierce contest, S.*; th′ am fuaim mar an geamhradh *borb, their sound is like the boisterous winter*; nochd a sluagh *borb* caoimhneas nach bu bheag dhuinn, *the barbarous people shewed us no small kindness*; is *borb* an duine e, *he is a passionate man*; *buirbe,* fierceness, cruelty, turbulence; also more *or* most fierce *or* furious.

Borbachd, bŏrr-ub′-ăchg, *n. f.* turbulence, savageness, cruelty, fierceness.

Borbadh, bŏrb′-Ă, *p.* inflaming, as a limb; enraging, getting furious.

Borbas, borb′-us, *n. f.* strictness, rigour.

Borbbhriathrach, borr-ub-vvhrĕărr′-ăch, *a.* fierce speaking; furious.

Borbhan, borv′-vhan, *n. m.* a murmur; *a.* the purling of a streamlet; more often *mhorbhan.*

Borbhanaich, borv′-vhăn-ěch, *n. f.* murmuring; gurgling; muttering.

Borbnaich, borr-ub′-nyèch, *v.* enrage, heave with anger. *See* Borb.

Borbsmachdail, bŏr′-ub-smăchg-al, *a.* imperious, arbitrary.

Borc, bŏrk, *v.* blossom, sprout.

Bord, bôrd′d, *n. m.* table, board; plank; ma′n *bhòrd, about the table*; aig ceann a′ *bhùird, at the head of the table*; sgoil *bhùird, a boarding-school*; *bùirdeasach, a boarder*; cuir air ′*bhòrd* e, *send him to a boarding-house, board him*; chaidh iad air *bòrd, they went on board the vessel*; air *bòrd, on board*; thig air *bòrd, come on board*; am *bòrd* uaine, *the green table*; *bòrd* urchair, *or* an urchair, *the mould board of a plough*; in *H. S. bòrd* ùrchrainn; am *bòrd* mòr, *the first service*; tha e fo′n *bhòrd, he is dead.* This phrase is peculiar to a part of Perthshire, but is quite common in Ireland; originating from a practice that obtains, among the lower classes there, of placing the corpse when coffined under a table; groaning under bottles, tobacco, &c. *Friend.*

Bord, bôrd′d, *v.* board; *bhord* iad an long, *they boarded the ship*; tack. *H. S.*

Borlum, bôr′-llum, *n. m.* a sudden evacuation; a ridge of land. *Skye.*

Borr, bôrr, *n. m.* a curled upper lip, a blubber lip, *Is.*; *v.* scent as a dog.

Borrach, borr'-ăch, *a.* blubber-lipped; *n. m.* mountain grass. *Skye.*

Borradh, bŏrr'-X, *n. m.* scent, smell.

Borran, bŏrr'-an, little blubber-lip.

Bosd, bôsd, *v.* boast, vaunt; *n. m.* boasting, vaunting, vain-glory; a trunk.

Bosdail, bôsd''-al, *a.* boastful, vain, vaunting, boasting, inclined to boast.

Bosdalachd, bôsd'-ăl-ăchg, *n. f.* boastfulness, vain-glory; romance, swaggering.

Bosdan, bôsd'-an, *n. m.* a small trunk *or* box.

Bosdair, bôsd'-ar', *n. m.* a swaggerer.

Bot, bōt, *n. f.* a vote; *v.* vote.

Bot, bŏt, *n. f.* a house, bank of a river.

Both, bŏ, *n. m.* a plash, a hut. *H.*

Bothan, bŏ'-han, *n. m.* a hut, a booth, a tent; *bothan* an am fasgadh nam fuar bheann, *a hut in the shelter of the bleak mountains*; rinn e *bothain* da spréidh, *he made booths for his cattle*; mar *bhothan* a ni am fear coimhead, *as a booth that the keeper maketh. B. A.*

Botramaid, bot'-ram-ăj, *n. f.* a slatern.

Botuinn, bôt''-ėnn, *n. f.* a boot.

Botuinneach, bot'-ėnn-ėch, *a.* booted.

Brabhd, brăv'-ud, *n. f.* a bandy-leg; in Lochaber, browd.

Brabhdach, brăv'-ud-ăch, *a.* bandy-legged; *n. f.* a bandy-legged female.

Brabhdair, brăv'-ud-ăr, *n. m.* a bandy-legged man; a boaster. *Ar.*

Brach, brăch, *n. m.* bear; *v.* malt.

Brachadair, brăch'-a-dăr', *n. m.* a maltman.

Brachadh, brăch'-X, *p.* malting; fermenting, putrifying.

Brachd, brăchg, *n. m.* any thing fermented, rubbish.

Bradach, brăd'-ăch, *a.* thievish, stolen, roguish; tha thu cho bhreugach is a tha luch cho *bhradach*, *you lie as the mouse pilfers, M. In.*; measar sin mar ni *bradach*, *it shall be reckoned as stolen goods. Ar.*

Bradag, brad'-ag, *n. f.* a thievish female.

Bradaidh, brăd'-ė, *n. m.* a thief, *D. M.*; *North*, the devil.

Bradaidheachd, brad'-ė-ăchg, *n. f.* theft, trickiness. *D. M. L.*

Bradalach, brăd'-al-ăchg, *a.* haughty, thievish. *Arm.*

Bradan, brăd'-an, *n. m.* a salmon; a swelling in a person's skin.

Bradh, brâ, *n. f.* a quern, a hand-mill; is fheairrde *bràdh* a breacadh gu'n a bristeadh, *pick a quern, but do not break it*; *a quern is the better of being picked, without being broken.*

Bradhadair, bră'-ăd-ăr', *n. m.* a large fire. *Skye.*

Bragh, bră'-gh, *n m.* a burst. *H.*

Braghad, brâăd, *n. m.* neck, throat, the upper part of the neck; a *bràghad* gu séimh a soillseadh, *her neck softly shining*; ruisgidh brù *bràghad*, *the belly will strip the neck*; losgadh *bràghad*, *the heart-burn. C. G. Ar.*

Braghadach, bràăd'-ăch, *a.* belonging to the neck.

Braghadaich, bră'-ad-ėch, *n. m.* crackling; bursting; noise. *D. M.*

Bragsaidh, brăg'-sė, *n. m.* disease in sheep.

Braich, brăėch, *n. f.* malt, (from brach, *v.*) *gen.* bracha.

Braid, brīj, *n. f.* a horse collar, *Arm.*; *bràid*-chluaisean, *a pair of hems.*

Braid, brăj, *n. f.* theft; luchd *braid*, *thieves, rogues.*

Brag, *v.* be infected with an epidemic *or* contagion; fag; boast. *Belgic.*

Braigh, brī'-yh', *n. m.* top, summit; a *bràigh* an tighe, *on the top of the house* *bràigh* na beinne, *the summit of the hill* *bràigh* a chroinn, *the mast head*; *bràigh* a' ghlinne, *the head* or *uppermost part of the glen*; *bràigh* na leapa, *the top of the bed*; am *bràigh* na dùthcha, *in the higher parts of the country*; a cable. *M. L.*

Braigh, brăė'-yh', *v.* give a crackling sound, as wood burning; crackle; burst explode; crash.

Braigheadh, brī'-X, *n. m.* report, an explosion, crackling; a blow.

Braigheardaich, brī'-ărt-ėch, *n. f.* crackling; blustering; swaggering.

Braighe, brī'-hă, }
Braighdean, brīj'-dyan, } *n. m.* and *f.* hostages, captives, pledges.

Braighdeach, brăj'-dyach, *n. m.* a horse collar. *D. M. L.*

Braighdeanas, brīj'-dyăn-us, *n. m.* bondage; the state of having a halter about the neck, lit.

Braigheach, brī-gh''-ăch, *n. m.* a mountaineer, one that inhabits the mountains.

Braigheachd, brī'-gh-ăchg, *n. f.* imprisonment, constraint, confinement.

Braighdean, brīj'-dyan', *n. m.* a calf's collar.

Braighghill, brī-gh'-yėll, the goal, the ascendant, *or* pre-eminence; thug thu *braigh-ghill* air na chualadh mi riamh, *you surpass every thing I have ever heard*; tha sin a' toirt *braigh-ghill* air na h-uile ni, *that excels* or *exceeds every thing*; fhuair e *braigh-ghill* ort, gun taing dhuit, *he got the ascendant* or *pre-eminence, in defiance of you.*

Braighleach, brrăė'-llyach, *n. m.* the breast. *Lw.*

Braigh-chrann, brī-chrann, *n. m.* a topmast.

Braighid, brīj², *or* brī'-ėj, *n. f.* a pair of hems; a collar about a thief's neck. *Islay.*

Braighleab, brī-gh''-lleb, *n. m.* wood-roof of a house; sarking. *Sc.*

Braighleag, brrīėl'-ag, *n. f.* a whortleberry.

Braighlich, brīl-lyėch, *n. f.* noise, crackling; blustering, swaggering; *v.* make noise, crackle; bluster, swagger.

Braigh-sheol, brī'-hhyôll, *n. m.* a topsail.

Braigh-shlat, brī'-hhlăt, a topsail-yard *See* Long, *a ship*

Braight, brījt, *n. f.* an enormous large fire; a bon-fire; in old times, the fire that the Druids had on the top of mountains, (braigh-aite.) This word must be the true etymon of the English word *bright.* It is peculiar to Islay and other two of the islands. *See* Dr. MacLeod's Collection; also *Druidh.*

Braightseal, brījsht'-shyăl, *n. m.* a fire on the top of a hill, as a beacon, (*old*;) now used for a large fire of any kind, particularly in time of rejoicing; a volley; a broadside; a billingsgate, *or* a terrible scolding of ladies; s ann agaibh a th' am *braightseal* ciatach, *what a fine blazing fire you have*; a cheud *bhraightseal* a leig iad, *the first broadside* or *volley they fired*; 's iad siod a thug am *braightseal, what a billingsgate those (ladies) had.*

Brailis, brăl'-ėsh, *n. f.* worts.

Brainn, brīėnn, *n. f.* the belly; a bulging.

Brais, brăsh, *n. f.* a fit, a convulsion; tha na *braisean* tric, *the fits return often.*

Braisd, brôshj and brâshj, *n. m.* a broach.

Braise, brăsh'-ȧ, *n. f.* impetuosity; keenness; rashness.

Braisead, brăsh'-ad, *n. f.* degree of impetuosity; rashness; impetuosity, fervour, ardour; wantonness; forwardness.

Braiseil, brăsh'-al, *a.* keen, impetuous, forward.

Braisgeul, brash-skéul', *n. m.* a romance.

Braithrearchas, brâr''-hyur'-ach-us, *n. m.* brotherhood, friendship, partiality.

Bran, brăn, *n. m.* the name of Fingal's dog, the name of several rivers in the Highlands.

Branna, brănn'-a. *gen.* of brainn, the belly.

Brannach, brănn'-ach, *a.* corpulent, having a big belly; *n. f.* a corpulent female.

Brannaire, brann'-ăr'-ȧ, *n. m.* a corpulent male.

Brannamh, bran'-nuv, *n. m.* a coat of mail.

Branndair, brannd'-ăr', *n. m.* a sort of a gridiron.

Braoileag, brāŏėl'-ag, *a.* whortleberry.

Braoisg, brāoėshg, *n. f.* a grin, a distortion of the mouth, as in contempt.

Braoisgeach, brāoėshg''-ăch, *a.* grinning, gaping; having broken teeth, notched; *n. f.* a female with broken teeth; a grinning female.

Braoisgeil, brāoėshg'-ėl, *n. f.* prating, prattling.

Braoisgire, brāoeshg'-ėr'-ȧ, *n. m.* a grinning fellow, one that distorts his mouth in contempt.

Braon, brāon, *n. m.* drop; gach *braon,* da fhuil, *every drop of his blood*; drizzling rain; le *braonaibh* na h-oidhche, *with the drops of night*; *braon* nan sìon, *the drizzling of the blast, Am.*; light shower; *v.* drizzle, distill.

Braonach, brāon'-ăch, *a.* showery, drizzling; rainy; dewy; 'sa mhadainn *bhraonaich, in the dewy morning, M. L.*; an duibhre *braonach, the dewy gloom*; falling in gentle showers.

Braonachd, brāon'-ăchg, *n. f.* drizzling rain; genial showers; showery weather.

Braonan, brāon'-an, *n. m.* an earth-nut; *braonan* nan con, *dog carmillion. H. S.*

Bras, brăss, *a.* keen, rash, impetuous, fervent, ardent, incautious; inconsiderate; *bras* le d' bheul, *rash with thy tongue*; sruth *bras, an impetuous current* or *torrent*; each *bras, a mettlesome horse*; mar steud shruth *bras, like an impetuous torrent, O. A.*; *bras*-bhuileach, *ready in dealing blows*; *bras*-chaoin, *quick and pleasant*; *bras* chomhrag, *tournament.*

Brasailt, brăsh'-ăėlt, *n. m.* a panegyric, eulogy.

Brat, brăt, *n. m.* hair cloth for a kiln, an apron, *Is.*; a covering, a mantle, a veil; crochaidh tu am *brat, thou shalt hang the veil, B.*; *brat* ùrlair, *a carpet*; *a garment*; agus ghabh Shem agus Iaphet *brat, and Shem and Japhet took a garment.*

Brat broin, brat'-brôėn, *n. m.* a mortcloth.

Bratach, brăt'-tach, *a.* banner, flag, colours, ensign; a' *bhratach* mhòr aig righ nan lann, *the great banner of the king of swords*; *bratach* aluinn righ nam magh, *the beauteous banners of the king of fields. O.*

Bratag, brăt'-ăg, *n. f.* the rough, *or* caterpillar.

Brataich, brăt'-ėch, *v.* kindle. *North.*

Brath, brhă, *n. m.* knowledge, information; pursuit of information; advantage by unfair means; ghabh e *brath* orm, *he took the advantage of me*; bi air *brath, be in pursuit of information*; am bheil *brath* agad c'àit' am bheil e, *have you any idea* or *information where he is?* 's ann a tha *brath* amadain agad air, *you take the advantage of him as if he was a fool*; an d' fhuair thu a *bhrath, did you get any information of him?* 's ann aig Dia tha *brath, God alone knows*; tha mhiann air *brath* ort, *he means to inform against you*; a' *brath* tighinn, *intending* or *meaning to come*; bha e a' *brath* mo bhualadh, *he was on the eve of striking me*; tha e air *bhrath, he is to be found*; cha bhi am bàrd air *bhrath, the bard shall not be found.*

Brath, brhă, *v.* betray, deceive, inform against; agus an sin gabhaidh mòran oilbheum, agus *brathaidh* iad a chéile, *and then shall many be offended and shall betray one another*; esan a *bhrath* e, *he that betrayed him. B.*

Brath, brâch, conflagration, destruction; gu *bràth, for ever*; na tréig mi gu buileach na gu *bràth, do not forsake me utterly* or *for ever*; gu la *bhràth* cha n éirich Oscar, *Oscar shall never rise*; *literally, till the day of conflagration,* (buidealaich) *the day when the world is burnt up*; cha'n fhaic thu e gu *bràth, you shall never see him*; seachd bliadhna roimh'n *bhràth*, thig muir thar Eirinn re aon trà, *seven years before the last day, the day of conflagration, the sea at one tide shall cover Ireland, Oss.*; cha ghluais e gu cruadail gu *bràth, he shall never move to the perils of war. Oss. H.*

Brathadair, brhâ'-ad'-ăr', *n. m.* a traitor, a betrayer, a knave, an informer.

Brathadh, brhă'-ӑ, *p.* betraying, informing; *n. m.* treachery, deceit.

Brathair, brhâ'-hyur, *n. m.* a brother; *brathair* athar, *a paternal uncle*; *brathair* màthar, *a maternal uncle*; *brathair* céile, *a brother-in-law*; *bràthair* bochd, *a friar.*

Brathaireachas, brhâ'-hyur-ăch-us, *n. m.* brotherhood, fraternity; partnership.

Brathairealachd, brhă'-hyur-hyăl-ăchd, *n. f.* brotherhood, brotherly attachment, fraternity, unanimity, harmony.

Brathaireil, brhâ'-hyur-al, *a.* brotherly, affectionate; agus nach do chuimhnich iad an comhcheangail *brathaireil, and that they have not remembered the brotherly covenant, Amos*; *bràthair* mhort, *fratricide.*

Brath-foille, bră-faòél'-lyȧ, *n. f.* disguise, deceit.

Breab, brrăb', *v.* kick, stamp with the foot; *n. m.* a kick, a prance, a start.

Breabardaich, brrăbb'-ărt-ėch, *n. f.* kicking, prancing, stamping, raging.

Breabadair, brrăbb'-ăd-ar', *n. m.* a weaver. *Skye.*

Breabail, brrăbb'-ăl, *see* Breab.

Breabadh, brrăbb'-ӑ, *p.* stamping, kicking.

Breaban, brăbb-an, *n. m.* a heel piece. *Is.*

Breac, brechg, and brrúchg, *a.* pie-bald• each *breac, a pie-bald horse*; bò *bhreac, a party-coloured* or *speckled cow*; fear *breac, a man marked with the small pox*; cù *breac, a spotted* or *party-coloured dog*; *breac* le neònainibh, *chequered with daisies.*

Breac, brechg, *or* brúchg, *v.* pick a millstone, bespangle, chequer, speckle; *n. f.* the small-pox; *breac* nam bò, *breac* a' chruidh, *the cow-pox*; *breacadh* seunain, *freckles on the face*; *breac* a mhuilinn, *that modification of cloud called cirro-cumulas, Ar.*; *breac* otrach, *(the dung-hill-pox,) the shingles* or *herpes.* It is hoped that no person will style this disease in such a manner after this. *Deilgginneach* is the proper and the Islay name for it; *breac* an t-sìl, *the white and grey wag-tail*; *breac* beadaidh, *the fish called loach.*

Breac, brechg, *or* brúchg, *n. m.* a trout.

Breacadh, brechg-, *or* brúchg'-ӑ, *p.* getting freckled; getting black and white; picking a millstone; *breacadh* teine, *shin-freckles*; *breac*-luirgneach, *shin-freckled*; *breach* shìth, *livid spots on the shin, hives*; *breacadh* rionnaich, *a dapple sky.*

Breacag, brechg'-ag, *or* brúchg'-ăg, *n. f.* a pan-cake.

Breacair, brechg'-ar', *n. m.* the engraver's tool.

Breacan, brechg'-an, *or* brúchg'-an, *n. m.* tartan, tartan plaid, a Highland plaid; a parti-coloured dress, used by the Celts from the earliest times. The *breacan* of the Highland king had seven different colours; the Druidical tunic had six; and that of the nobles four; *breacan* an fhéilidh, *the belted plaid*; consisting of twelve yards of tartan, worn round the waist obliquely across the breast and over the left shoulder, and partly depending backwards.

Breachdan, brechg'-an, *n. m.* a custard, *M. L.*

Breacarsaich, brúch'-ăr-ssėch, *n. f.* twilight; middle state, particularly of health.

Breacnaich, brechg'-nyėch, *v.* chequer, mix.

Breacta, bryéchg'-tya, *p.* picked as a millstone; spotted; carved.

Breagh, brè *or* brya; *No.* brĕă, *a.* handsome, beautiful, fine; nighean *bhreagh, a handsome young woman*; latha *breagh, a fine day*; surprising; is *breagh* nach d' thàinig thu dhachaidh an àm, *it is surprising you did not come home in time*; gu *breagh* anan och, *pretty late in the evening.*

Breaghachd, brya'-'hăchg, *n. f.* handsomeness; beauty, elegance; degree of beauty.

Breaghaich, brya'-'hèch, *v.* adorn.

Breaghchaid, brya'-chyud', *n. f.* degree of beauty, superiority in beauty.

Breamain, bryèm'-ăn', *n. m.* tail, train.

Breamaineach, bryem'-ăn'-ăch, *a.* tailed, as a tail *or* train.

Breamas, bryem'-as, *n. m.* a blunder, mishap; misfortune; cha leighis aithreachas *breamas, repentance cannot remedy a blunder*; 's ann duit a dh'éirich am *breamas, what a mishap has befallen you.*

Breamasach, brem'-as-ach, *a.* unfortunate, unlucky; blundering; bungling.

Breamasachd, brem'-ăs-ăchg, *n. f.* unfortunate state *or* condition, fatality, misfortune.

Breath, brheyă, *n. f.* a row, a rank. *B.*

Breathach, bră'-hhach, *n. m.* Welshman.

Breathal, bryaŏh'-hal, *n. f.* raving, confusion of mind, terror, flurry.

Breathanas, bryaŏh'-hyan-us, *n. m.* judgment, decision, retributive justice; from breith.

Breathas, braŏh'-as, *n. m.* fury, frenzy.

Breatunn, brrăt'-ttunn, *n. m.* Britain.

Breatunnach, brră'-ttunn-ach, *a.* British; *n. m.* a Briton.

Breathnachadh, bren'-nach-Ă, *n. m.* apprehension; conception, imagination.

Breathnaich, bren'-nèch, *v.* conceive, apprehend, suppose. *Islay.*

Breid, brrăjj, *n. m.* a kerchief, a napkin, a piece of cloth of any kind, a woman's head dress, consisting of a square of fine linen, neatly pinned on the head; generally put for the female badge of marriage; *v.* spread peats. *North.*

Breideach, bryăjj'-ach, *a.* like a kerchief, a woman wearing the bréid *or* badge of marriage.

Breigchiabh, brrăg'-chĕăv, *n. f.* a wig. *H.*

Breigchiabhadair, brrăg-chĕăv'-a-dar', *n. m.* a wig-maker.

Breigriochdaich, brăg'-rrúchg-èch, *v.* disguise, disfigure.

Breilleis, brăll'-èsh, *n. f.* confusion of mind, raving, delirium. *Dr. M'Leod.*

Breine, brrăèn'-nyă, *n. f.* turbulence, a turbulent disposition; stink, stench.

Breinead, brrăen'-ad, *n. f.* degree of turbulence, turbulence; rottenness, stench.

Breineag, brrăn'-ăg, *n. f.* a turbulent female.

Breinean, brăn'-an, *n. m.* a turbulent man.

Breisleach, brăsh'-llyach, *n. f.* raving, delirium, confusion of mind; chuir e 'm *bhreislich* mi, *he quite confounded me*; chaidh mi am bhreislich, *I was confounded, I got quite bewildered*; distraction of mind.

Breisleachail, brrăsh'-lyach-al, *a.* confusing, confounding; delirious, causing delirium.

Breislich, brăèsh'-llèch, *v.* confuse, confound, rave, talk inconsistently *or* incoherently.

Breith, brrhă, *n. f.* judgment, decision, sentence; *breith* air a phobull bheir thu, *thou shalt judge the people;* gu cinnteach tha Dia ann a tha toirt *breith* air an talamh, *verily there is a God that judgeth in the earth*; na h-aingidh anns a' *bhreith, the wicked in the judgment*; interpretation, meaning, signification; dé's *breith* do m' bhruadar, *what is the interpretation of my dream*; thoir *breith* air mo bhruadar, *interpret my dream*; birth; a dol air seacharan o'm *breith, going astray from their birth*; O *bhreith* gu bàs, *from birth to death, from the cradle to the grave*; sguir i '*bhreith* cloinne, *she left off child-bearing*; overtaking, laying hold of, capturing, seizing; *breith* buidheachas, *thanksgiving*; air *breith* buidheachas, *after giving thanks*; *breith* luath lochdach, *a rash unfair judgment*; *breith* air éigin, *a child scarcely alive when born*; *deforcement.*

Breith, brrhă, *p.* bearing, seizing, carrying away, catching; a' *breith* air làimh orm, *seizing me by the hand*; cha b' fhad bha sinn a' *breith* orra, *we soon overtook them*; a' *breith* air a chéile, *seizing each other, laying hold of each other*; tha i a' *breith* cloinne, *she is bearing children*—a' *breith* uibhean, *laying eggs*; a' *breith* searraich, *casting a foal*; a' *breith* laoigh, *calving*; a' *breith* uain, *yeaning*; a' *breith* oircean neo, thoircean, *farrowing*; a' *breith* chuileanan, *whelping*; a' *breith* phiseag, *kittening.*

Breitheach, bră'2-ach, *a.* judicial, exact.

Breitheil, bră'-ul, *n. f.* raving, delirium.

Breitheamh, bră'2-uv, *n. m.* a judge; an umpire; nach dean *breitheamh* na talmhainn uile ceartas, *shall not the judge of all the earth do justice?*

Breitheanas, brhă'-an-us, *n. m.* a judgment; decision, sentence; a just retribution for one's sins; thàinig *breitheanas* ort, *a judgment came upon you*; thàinig sin mar *breitheanas* ort, *that came your way as a just retribution for your sins*;

oir seasaidh sinn gu léir am fianuis caithir *breitheanais* Chrìosd, *for we shall all stand before the judgment-seat of Christ*; is fìrinn *breitheanais* an Tighearna; tha iad gu h-iomlan cothromach. Ni's mò ran iarraidh tha iad na'n t-òr, seadh, na mòran do'n òr fhìorghlan, agus ni's milse na a' mhil, seadh, na ciribh mheala, *the judgments of the Lord are true and righteous altogether. More to be desired are they than gold, yea, than much fine gold; sweeter also than honey and the honey comb.*

Breitheanasach, brā'-an-as-ach, *a.* retributive, as a just judgment.

Breith-dhitidh, brhà'-yhèjt-ė, *n. f.* sentence of condemnation.

Breithneachadh, brā'²-nyach-ă, *n. m.* apprehension, idea. *High. So.*

Bbeithnich, brā'²-nyèch, *v.* conceive.

Breitich, brā'-ttyèch, *v.* swear. *H. S.*

Breo, bryò, *n. m.* a fire, a flame. *H. S.*

Breochaid, *n. m.* any tender or fragile thing, *Skye*; spreòchdainn.

Breoc, bryôchg, *v.* patch. *H. S.*

Breoite, bryô'-tyȧ, *a.* frail, weak, feeble, infirm, sickly, indisposed.

Breoiteachd, bryô'-ttyȧchg, *n. f.* infirmity, weakness, debility, frailty, feebleness; tha mi *breòite* tinn, *I am weak, feeble and sickly. Sm.*

Breolaid, bryôl'-lăj, *n. m.* dotage. *M. L.*

Breoth, bryō², *v.* putrify, rot, corrupt.

Breothadh, bryō²'-ă, *n. m.* corruption, beginning to corrupt, *or* get useless; rotting.

Breug, brèug, (not brāg) *gen.* bréig, *pro.* brāg, *n. f.* a lie, a falsehood, an untruth; saor m' anam o bhilean nam *breug, deliver my soul from lying lips*; fhuaradh 'sa *bhrèig* e, *he was found out in a lie*; ann an dòchas na beatha maireannaich a gheall Dia do nach comasach *breug* a dheanadh roimh chruthachadh an t-saoghail, *in hope of eternal life, which God, that cannot lie, promised before the world began*; *v.* pacify, lull, flatter, entice; *breug* am pàisde, *pacify, lull,* or *soothe the child*; *breug* leat e, *flatter* or *cajole him away with you*; 'ga *bhreugadh* mar gu 'm biodh leanabh ann, *cajoling, soothing,* or *caressing him as if he was a child.*

Breugach, brèug'-ach, *a.* lying, false, deceitful; tha e cho *bhreugach* is a th' an cat cho bhradach, *he is as great a liar as the cat is a thief*; tha thu *breugach, you are a liar*; nach *breugach* thu, *how much you lie*; *n. f.* a lying female.

Breugadh, brèug'-ă, *p.* cajoling, flattering, lulling, pacifying, soothing, caressing.

Breugaich, brè'g'-èch, *v.* belie, falsify, give the lie, disprove, gainsay; *n. f.* thug e a' *bhreugaich* dhomh, *he belied me to the face*; *bhreugaich* e mi, *he belied me*; *breugaich* e, *belie him.*

Breugaire, brèug'-ur'-ȧ, *n. m.* a liar; is fearr duine bochd na *breugaire, a poor man is better than a liar*; éisdidh am *breugaire* ri teanga an aimhleis, *a liar giveth ear to a naughty tongue, P.* 17-4; is feairrde *breugaire* fianuis, *a liar requires a voucher, one that is belied* or *contradicted is the better of a witness.*

Breugaireachd, brèug'-ur'-ăchg, *n. f.* the habit *or* vice of telling lies; the practice of belying *or* contradicting.

Breugan, brèug'-un, *n. p.* lies, falsehoods.

Breug-chrabhadh, brèug'-chrâv-ă, *n. m.* hypocrisy, pretensions to religion; breug-chrábhach, hypocritical, deceitful.

Breuglaich, brèug'-llèch, *v.* foreswear, perjure, gainsay. *Armstrong.*

Breugnachadh, breug'-nnach-ă, *p.* belying, falsifying, contradicting.

Breugnaichte brèug'-nnèch-tyȧ, *p.* belied, falsified, contradicted.

Breugriochdaire, brèug'-rryúchg-ur'-ȧ, a disguiser, a pretender, a traitor.

Breugriochd, breug'-rryúchg, *n. f.* disguise.

Breun, brrānn, *a.* of a turbulent, boisterous disposition; bold, indelicate, as a female; putrid, filthy, *lobh, grod.*

Breunadh, brrānn'-ă, *p.* becoming putrid.

Breunach, brrānn'-ach, *n. f.* a turbulent, indelicate, *or* immodest female.

Breunachd, brrānn'-ăchg, *n. f.* turbulence, indelicacy; rottenness, putridness.

Breunair, breānn'-ur', *n. m.* a turbulent man.

Briagh, brēă, *prov.* for breagh.

Brian, brēănn, the name Brian.

Briathar, brhrēăr'-ur, *n. m.* a word, a verb; a saying, an assertion; dh'iarr an searmonaiche *briathra* taitneach fhaotainn; agus bha a ni sgrìobhadh ceart, briathra na fìrinn, *the preacher sought out acceptable words; and that which was written was upright, even words of truth*; tha *briathra* na daoine glice mar bhioraibh, *the words of the wise are as goads, Exc.*; (brigh-athar,) *the essence of the father. M. L.*

Briathrach, brēăr'-ăch, *a.* wordy, talkative, verbose, loquacious.

Briathrachas, brēăr'-răch-us, *n. m.* wordiness, wit, eloquence, verbosity.

Briathradan, brēăr'-ad-an, *n. f.* a vocabulary.

Briathradair, brēăr'-ad-ăr', *n. m.* a dictionary, a lexicon.

Briathradairachd, brĕăr′-ad′-ar-ăchg, *n. f.* lexicography; a lexicographer's work.

Briathraich, brĕăr′-rèch, *v.* affirm, assert, maintain. *H. S.*

Briathrail, brĕăr′-al, *a.* verbal, in a word.

Brib, brēbb, *n. m.* a small sum of money, a dribblet, an item; am bheil thu brath am *brìb* sin a phaidheadh, *are you going to pay that trifling sum? Is.*; a bribe; *brìb* nach do ghabh, *who has not received a bribe. B.*

Bribearachd, brēb′-ar′-ăchg, *n. f.* payment in small sums, trifling sums of money.

Bric, brēchg, *gen.* of breac, *plu.* of breac, a trout.

Bricean, brèchg′-an′, *n. m.* a sprat, *or* small trout; *bricean* baintighearn, *a wagtail*; *bricean* beithe, *a linnet. H. S.*

Bride, brrējj′-à, contraction of brighide; Brighit, latha fhèill *brìde, Candlemas, St Bridget's days.*

Brideag, brrējj′-ăg, *n. f.* the jaws of a brute.

Brideach, brējj′-ach, *a.* a dwarf; cha *bhrìdeach* air an fhaich e, *he is not a dwarf on the battle-field. Old Song. Arm.*

Bridean, brējj′-an′, *n. m.* the sea-piet; cho luath ris a *bhrìdean* 'san traigh, *as swift as the sea-piet on the sea-shore.*

Brig, brēgg, *n. f.* a heap, a pile; *v.* pile, build as a pile of peats, &c.; a' *brìgeadh* na mòna, *building the peat-stack. Mul.*

Brigh, brē′-yh′, *n. f.* substance, essence, elixir, juice, sap; chaill na h-ùbhlan am *brìgh, the apples lost their juice* or *sap*; feoil gun *bhrìgh, beef without substance*; meaning, interpretation; briathran gun *bhrìgh, words without meaning*; innis domh *brìgh* mo bhruadair, *tell me the interpretation of my dream*; a' caitheadh mo *bhrìgh, dissolving my substance, Job*; is deacair *brìgh* do sgeoil, *sad is the substance (subject) of thy tale, O.*; b'e so a bu *bhrìgh* d'an dàn, *this was the substance of their tale, Sm.*; caitheidh cumha gun *bhrìgh, mourning consumes without avail, Arm. O.*; do *bhrìgh*, a *bhrìgh, by virtue of, because, Bible*; pith, energy; thuirt triath Eirinn bu mhòr *brìgh, said Ireland's chief of mighty energy. Oss.*

Brighealachd, brēyh″-all-ăchg, *n. f.* substance, vigorousness, juiciness, pithiness.

Brigheamh, bhrē′-uv, *n. m.* a judge; from *brìgh, interpretation.*

Brigheil, brē′-gh′-al, *a.* substantial, juicy, pithy, full of meaning, sap *or* energy.

Brigis, brēgg′-èsh, *n. f.* breeches. *M. Int.*

Brighinn, brē′-hyùnn, *n. f.* seasoning, any fat; delicacies, dainties.

Brighinneachadh, brē′-hyun-ăch-Ă, *n. m.* the act of seasoning; the act of feeding with dainties *or* delicacies.

Briog, brègg, *v.* stab, thrust, *N.*; cut round; *n. m.* confinement, restraint. *D. M'L.*

Briogach, brègg′-ach, *a.* mean, miserly, spiritless, avaricious, sordid.

Briogachd, brègg′-achg, *n. f.* sordidness, meanness, want of spirit, shabbiness.

Briogadaich, brègg′-ad-èch, *n. m.* sordidness, avarice, meanness; ludicrous capering. *D. M'L.*

Briogaid, brègg′-aj, *n. f.* a little, elderly, morose, miserly female.

Briogaideach, brègg′-ăj-ăch, *a.* elderly, little and mean, as a female.

Briogaire, brègg′-ur-à, *n. m.* a sordid, shabby fellow; a miser; a churl.

Briogaireachd, brègg′-ur-ăchg, *n. m.* sordidness, meanness, avarice, want of spirit.

Brioghas, brú′-gh′-us, *n. f.* fervour of passion, dalliance; fondness.

Brioghasach, brúgh′-as-ach, *a.* fond.

Brioghmhoireachd, brhé′-vur-ăchg, *n. f.* substantiality; the state of being full of meaning.

Brioghmhor, brē′-gh′-′vur, *a.* full of substance, *or* meaning, *or* energy.

Briolag, brúl′-lag, *n. f.* an illusion. *D. M.*

Brionglaid, brreug′-llăj, *n. f.* a bickering sort of squabble; wrangling, disagreement.

Brionglaideach, bryung′-llăj-ăch, *a.* squabbling, bickering, wrangling, quarrelsome.

Brionnach, bryunn′-ăch, *a.* party-coloured and shining, *or* glittering; pretty; flattering; lying. *A. D. M.*

Brionnachd, bryunn′-ăchg, *n. m.* variety of colours, glitter; flattery, falsehood. *D. M.*

Brionnel, bryunn′-al, *n. f.* flattery, fawning, *Sm.*; toying, caressing, flirting.

Brionshuileach, bryunn′-hŭl ăch, *a.* having a bright shining quick eye.

Brios, brèss, *n. m.* the state of being half intoxicated; mockery. *A. M. D.*

Briosaid, brrèss′-aj, *n. f.* a girdle, a belt. *Arm.*; a witch, a sorceress. *Ir.*

Briosaideach, brrèss′-ăj-ach, *a.* belted.

Briosg, brrèsg, *v.* start, jerk; move, *or* come alive, as a child in the womb; oir, feuch, co luath as a thàinig fuaim do bheannachaidh am chluasaibh, *bhriosg* an naoidhean, le h-aoibhneas am bhroinn, *for, lo, as soon as the voice of thy salutation sounded in mine ears, the* BABE LEAPED *in my womb for joy*; move, as the flesh of an animal immediately after being slaughtered; crumble.

Briosgail, *n. f.* sudden start *or* movement.

the state of coming alive; *p.* moving, starting, coming alive.

Briosgadh, brrēssg'[2]-X̆, *p.* jerking, starting, moving.

Briosgaid, brrēssg'[2]-ăj, *n. f.* a biscuit.

Briosgannta, brrēssg'[2]-annt-à, *a.* apt to start, move, jerk, *or* start.

Briosgardaich, brrèssg'-ard-èch. *n. f.* starting *or* jerking movement, as the flesh of an animal after being flayed; starting, moving.

Briosuirneach, brèss'-urn-ach, *a.* ludicrous, *H.*; ait, dhrabhluinneach.

Briot, brrètt, } *n. m.* the language
Briotal, brrètt'-al, } of birds, a flock of wild fowls, in pursuit of the fry of fish; a meeting *or* company where every one is speaking; nonsensical talk; chit-chat, tattle, chattering; flattery.

Bris, brrēssh, *v.* break, fracture.

Brisd, brrēshj, *v.* break, fracture, become insolvent, *or* a bankrupt; splinter.

Brisdeach, brrēsshj[2]'-ach, } *a.* apt to
Bristeach, brrēssht'-ăch, } break, brittle, interrupted, confused, unsettled, as weather; uair *bhrisdeach, unsettled weather.*

Brisdeadh, brrēsshj[2]-X̆, *n. m.* a break, a breach, a fracture; an eruption; an outbreaking; *p.* breaking, fracturing; *brisdeadh* cridhe, *a heart-break*; *brisdeadh* céile, *derangement*; *brisdeadh* a mach, *an eruption, an outbreaking, a rebellion, an insurrection.*

Brisg, brrēsshg, *v.* brittle, apt to break; as flesh—tender, fine; as a horse, mettlesome; as a person—ready, not stingy, active, lively, brisk.

Brisge, brrèsshg'-à, *n. f.* readiness, aptness, activity; tenderness; brittleness.

Brisgeachd, brrèshg'-achg, *n. f.* brittleness, readiness, aptness; tenderness, activity, cleverness.

Brisgead, brrēsshg'[2]-udd, *n. f.* brittleness, degree of brittleness, tenderness; briskness, &c.

Brisgean, brrèsshg'[2]-ăn', *n. m.* the part of tripe called the brisket *or* gristle; the root of wild tansy *or* silver weed; moor grass, garbhlach, fineach.

Brislean, brrèssh-llyan', *n. m.* wild tansy, *pr.*

Brist, brrèsshjt, *v.* break, fracture. *Pr.*

Briste, brrèssht'-à, *p* broken, made a bankrupt, insolvent, bruised; tha mo chridhe *briste, my heart is broken*; is dlùth an Tighearn dhaibhsan a tha *briste* nan cridhe; agus saoraidh e iadsan, a tha brùite 'nan spiorad, *the Lord is nigh unto them that are of a broken heart, and saveth such as be of a contrite spirit*; is iad iobairtean Dhé spiorad *briste*; air cridhe *briste* agus brùite, a Dhé, cha dean thusa tair, *the sacrifice of God is a broken spirit*; *a broken and a contrite heart, O Lord, thou wilt not despise.*

Britinneas, brrējt'-èn-nus, *n. f.* the measles. *Ir.*

Brobh, brŏv, round rooted, basdard cypress. *Ir.*

Broc, brŏchg, *n. m.* a badger; *gen.* bruic.

Brocach, brŏchg'-ăch, *a.* marked with the small pox; speckled in the face; greyish, like a badger.

Brocail, brôchg'-èll, *v.* mangle. *North.*

Brocaire, brŏchg'-ur'-à, *n. m.* a fox-hunter, a destroyer of vermin in the Highlands.

Brocaireachd, brŏchg'-ur-ăchg, *n. f.* the occupation of fox-hunter, &c. *H. S.*

Brochaill, brŏch' all, *n. m.* the name of the Banner of Gaul, the son of Morni. *Ar. Ir.*

Brochan, brŏch'-an, *n. m.* porridge, pottage; deoch *bhrochain, gruel*; sodar *brochan, thick gruel*; *brochan* bainne, *milk-pottage*; a phoite *bhrochain, the pottage* or *porridge pot*; *brochan* do ghall-pheasair, *pottage of lentiles*; agus bhruich Iacob *brochan, and Jacob sod pottage. Bible.*

Brochanach, brŏch'-an-ăch, *a.* well-supplied with porridge *or* pottage; bi gu curaiceach, brògach, *brochanach* 'sa gheamhradh, *be thou well capped, well shod, and well supplied with gruel in winter. G. P.*

Brochlach, brŏch'-lăch, *n. f.* a woman. *H.*

Brochlaid, broch'-llăj, *n. m.* trash. *Arm.*

Brochlainn, broch'-llènn, *n. f.* a badger's den; any stinking place.

Brod, brŏd'd, *n. m.* the choice part of any thing, the choice quality of any thing; *brod* an t-sìl, *the best part of the oats*; a lid; *brod* na poite, *the lid of the pot*; *a box* or *ladle handed round in church for collecting alms*; *a small board*; *brod* gheadh, *a goose that has a brood, a dam*; *v.* level *or* smooth land with the spade after the first ploughing; poke, probe, rouse.

Brodadh, brŏd'-X̆, *p.* levelling land, poking.

Brod, brôd, *n. m.* pride, arrogance, haughtiness; *M.* land *Arg.* a brood, a crowd.

Brodail, brôd'd'-al, *a.* proud, haughty, arrogant; tha e cho *bhròdail* ris a mhacmhalachd, *he is as proud as Lucifer*, or *old Pluto*, or, *as he is called in the North, Ian.*

Brodalachd, brôd'-al-ăchg, *n. f.* arrogancy, haughtiness, extreme pride.

Brod-iasg, brŏd'd'-ëăsg, *n. m.* needle-fish.

Brodunn, brŏd'd-ènn, *n. m.* a goad, a staff.

Brog, brŏgg[2], *n. m.* a probe, a poker; *v.*

n. poke, probe, stir, stimulate; bestir yourself.

Brog, brôg'g, *n. f.* a shoe; cuir ort do *bhrògan, put on your shoes*; hoof; *bròg* an eich, *the hoof of the horse*; evil consequence; buailidh e *bròg* ort fathast, *you will will feel the bad effects of that hereafter*; bhuail an t-earrach so *bròg* oirnn, *we have felt the sad effects of this untoward spring*; *bròg* fhiodh, *a clog, a sandal*; *bròg* na cuthaig, *butter-wort*; *a.* sorrowful. *H. S.*

Brogach, brôg'g'-ach, *a.* well shod; strong-hoofed.

Brogach, brog'g'-ăch, *n. m.* a boy, a lad. *North.*

Brogaich, brôg'g'-ėch, *v.* shoe; approach.

Brogail, *see* Broigeil.

Brogaire, brôg'g'-ur'-å, *n. m.* a cobbler, a shoe-mender.

Brogaireachd, brôg'g'-ur-ăchg, *n. f.* shoe-mending, cobbling.

Broid, brôėjj, *v* embroider. *O. R.*

Broidireachd, brôėjj'-ėrr-ăchg, embroidering.

Broigealachd, brŏėg'-al-ăchg, *n. f.* activity, liveliness, as an old man *or* woman.

Broigeil, brŏėg'-al, *a.* tho old, stout, lively, and active; hale, hearty, applied to old people always.

Broigeanta, brŏeg'-annt-ă, *a.* active, lively, spirited, sturdy.

Broigeantachd, brŏėg'-annt-ăchg, *n. f.* liveliness, activity, sturdiness, alacrity.

Broigheal, broy'-ghyal, a cormorant, sgarbh.

Broighlich, braŏėll'-ėch, *n. f. prov.* for braighlich, the crackling of wood on fire; swaggering; *braigh, the top,* the place where the Druids had their bon-fires, and the consignative, la 'lich, &c. to make, to make noise; the Irish pronounce ai, for the most part aŏe, but the Highlanders pronounce it ĭė; hence, dhoibh in place of dhaibh; broinn instead of brainn; broighlich in place of braighlich, (brrĭėl'-ėch.)

Broilean, brŏl'-an', *n. m.* manyplies *or* king's hood in an animal, (braigh'-la.)

Broileanach, brŏėl'-ăn'-ach, *a.* manyplied.

Broilleach, brrŏėl'-llyăch, *n. m.* the breast, the bosom; front; a *broilleach* mar chobhar nan stuadh, *her bosom like the foam of the waves, (mountain-high waves;)* an urrainn duine teine a ghabhail 'na *bhroilleach* agus gun eudach a bhı air a losgadh, *can a man take fire in his bosom and his clothes not be burnt? Prov.*; 'na *bhroilleach, in his bosom, Exd.*; folachaidh an leisgein a làmh na *bhroilleach*; uiread as chum a bheòil cha tobhair e i, *a slothful man hideth his hand in his bosom, and will not so much as bring it to his mouth again.*

Broin, brôėn, *gen.* of bròn, mourning; *v.* mourn, lament, deplore.

Broineach, brŏėn'-ăch, *n. f.* a ragged woman, a ragged garment *or* vesture; *a.* ragged, tattered.

Broineag, brŏėn'-ăg, *n. f.* a rag, a tatter, a shred.

Broineagach, brŏen'-ăg-ăch, *a.* ragged, tattered.

Broinn, *prov.* for brainn, a belly.

Broisde, brôshg'-å, *n. m.* a braoch. *Is.*

Broisg, brŏėshg, *v.* excite. *Arm.*

Broit, brŏėt, *n. f.* bosom; cuir ad *bhroit*, e, *put it in thy bosom. North H.*

Brollach, brŏll-ăch, *n. m.* breast. *Irish.*

Brollachan, brŏll'-ach-an, *n. m.* any thing entangled *or* entwined.

Brolluinn, brŏll'-ėnn, *n. m.* steam, stench; meeting of currents. *North.*

Bromach, brŏm'-ach, *n. m.* a colt. *N.*

Bron, brôn, *n. m.* mourning, sorrow, wailing, weeping; grief, lamentation; mourning dress *or* habiliments; 's e so fàth mo *bhròin, this is the cause of my lamentation* or *sorrow*; fo *bhròn, sorrowing, lamenting*; is beannaichte iadsan a tha ri *bròn* oir gheibh iad sòlas, *blessed are they that mourn for they shall be comforted, M.* 5-4; thionndaidh thu dhomhsa mo *bhròn* gu dabhsadh, *thou hast turned for me my mourning into dancing, P.* 30-11; oladh aoibhneas an àite *bròin, the oil of joy for mourning*; tha iad am *bròn, they are wearing mournings*; is fear dol do thigh a' *bhròin*, na dol do thigh na cuirme; oir 'se sin crioch na uile dhaoine; agus gabhaidh am beò g' a chridh' e, *it is better to go to the house of mourning, than to the house of feasting; for that is the end of all men; and the living will lay it to his heart.*

Bronach, brôn'-ach, *a.* sad, mournful, melancholy, grievous, sorrowful; mean.

Bronag, bròn'-ag, *n. f.* a sorrowful woman.

Bronbhrat, bròn'-vvhrăt, *n. m.* a mort-cloth.

Bronnag, brŏn'n'-ag *n. f.* a gudgeon.

Brosdan, brŏsd''-an, *n. m.* a spunk, little sticks to kindle the fire.

Brosg, brŏsk, *v.* bestir yourself, excite.

Brosgadh, brŏsg'-Ă, an exhortation, an excitement.

Brosglach, brŏsg'-llach, *a.* lively, active, brisk.

Brosglaich, brŏsg'-llėch, *v. n.* excite, bestir yourself; flatter, coax, cajole.

Brosguil, brosg'-ėl, *v.* flatter, coax.

Brosgul, brŏsg′-ul, *n. m.* flattery. *Skye.*

Brosnachadh, brŏs′-nnach-Ă, *n. m.* incitement, provocation, exhortation; also a piece of Highland music; encouragement; *pt.* spurring, exciting.

Brosnachail, bross′-nach-al, *a.* instigating, encouraging.

Brosnaich, bross′-nnèch, *v.* excite, provoke, bestir, encourage; gu cinnteach cha'n fhaic iadsan am fearann a mhionnaich mi d' an aithrichibh, ni mò a chi neach air bith dhiubhsan a *bhrosnaich* mi, *surely they shall not see the land which I swear unto their fathers, neither shall any of them that provoked me see it.*

Brot, brŏtt, *n. m.* broth; *a.* fat. *North.*

Broth, brrhŏ, *n. m.* an eruption on the skin.

Brothlainn, brrhŏ′-llènn, *n. f.* heat and stink; disagreeable heat.

Bru, brrû, *n. f.* a big belly, as a woman with child; a belly, a bulge; tha *brù* air a' bhalla, *the wall bulges*; a womb.

Bruach, brŭăch, *n. m.* a bank, a border, edge, brim, a steep, a precipice; *bruach* an uillt, *the bank of the river*; air na *bruachan* so *about these borders*; ma na *bruachaibh* so, *about these borders*; *bruach* dhuine, *a boor of a fellow, a stupid fellow*; a small rising ground.

Bruachaire, bruach′-ar′-à, *n. m.* a sullen fellow; a hoverer.

Bruadair, brŭăd″-dăr′, *v.* dream, see a vision; *bhruadair* mi an rair, *I dreamed last night*; *bhruadair* mi gu'm faca mi, *I dreamed that I saw.*

Bruadar, brŭăd′-ar, *n. m.* a dream, a vision; agus air faotainn rabhaidh o Dhia ann am *bruadar, and being warned of God in a dream. Bible.*

Bruadaraiche, brŭăd′-ar-èch-à, *n. m.* a dreamer.

Bruadrach, brŭăd″-rrach, *a.* visionary.

Bruaillean, brŭăly″-lyan, *n. m.* disturbance, noise, tumult, trouble, offence; cò a tha cur *bruaillean* ort, *who is troubling* or *offending you*; duine gun *bhruaillean, an inoffensive man*; 's mòr am *bruaillean* a dhùisg thu, *you have created a tumult*; mar *bhruaillean* thonn air driom a chuain, *as the tumult of waves on the height of the ocean*—tha *bruaillean* air aghaidh nan tom, *there is boding gloom on the face of the bushes. H. S.*

Bruailleanach, brŭăly″-an′-ăch, *a.* troublesome, riotous, tumultous; noisy, disturbing; causing disturbance; annoying, grieved, vexed.

Bruailleanachd, brŭăly′-an′-ăchg, *n. f.* troublesomeness, the state of giving trouble *or* being troubled.

Bruan, brŭăn, *n. m.* short-bread, a cake made with butter, &c. to keep children quiet; a crumb, a morsel; *v.* crumble, pulverise, crush.

Bruanachd, brŭăn′-ăchg, *n. f.* continued breaking *or* smashing; fragments.

Bruanag, brŭăn′-ag, *n. f.* a little cake.

Bruansgail, brŭăn′-skul, *v.* make a deep crashing, crushing noise; make a grating noise; crumble, break into fragments.

Bruansgal, brŭăn′-skal, *n. f.* a crumbling noise; a grating noise.

Bruanspealt, brŭăn′-spyălt, *n. m.* splinter; *v.* smash, hack, hew.

Brucach, brŭchg′-ăch, *a.* speckled in the face, as a sheep; gloomy, lowering, as weather; latha *brucach, a gloomy lowering day*; coara *bhrucach, a speckled sheep, a black-faced sheep.*

Brucachd, brŭchg′-ĕchg, *n. f.* gloominess.

Brucanaich, brŭchg′-an-èch, *n. f.* peep of day, the dawn; bi an so 'sa *bhrucanaich, be here at peep of day. Is.*

Bruchd, brûchg, *n. m.* a disruption, *or* rushing forth, as a multitude; a bulge; a sudden rushing forth, a belch, a rift; rinn e *brùchd, he belched* or *rifted*; thàinig *brùchd* do na daoine a mach, *a rush of the people came forth*; a heap, *or* great quantity; thuit *brùchd* do 'n mhòine, *a great quantity of the peats fell*; a rush, a gush; thàinig *brùchd* do 'n uisge a mach, *a gush of the water came forth.*

Bruchd, brûchg, *v.* rush forth, sally bulge, belch, rift; *bhrùchd* na daoine a mach, *the men rushed forth*; tha e, *brùchdail, he is belching,* or *rifting*; gush; *bhrùchd* 'f huil a mach, *his blood gushed* or *poured out.*

Bruchdadh, brûchg′-Ă, *p.* rushing; bulging; belching; rifting; gushing.

Bruchdail, brûchg′-al, *n. m.* rushing; belching; rifting; a gush.

Bruchlag, brŭch′-llag, *n. f.* a mean hovel.

Bru-chorc, brŭ-chŏrk′, } *n. m.* stool-
Bru-chorcan, brŭ′-chŏrk-an, } bent, *or* dirk grass.

Bruthaiste, brŭ′-ăsht-à, brose, brothas. *Inver.*

Bru-dhearg, brû′-yhyèrg, *n. m.* robin redbreast.

Bruich, brŭèch, *v.* boil, seethe, simmer, sod; *a.* boiled, seethed, simmered; *n. f.* boiling; the state of being boiled; the act of boiling; *bruich* e, *boil it*; tha e *bruich, it is boiled*; is dona a' *bhruich* a th' air, *it is not well boiled*; *p.* boiling; tha e 'ga *bhruich, he is boiling it.*

Bruicheil, brŭèch′-al, *a.* sultry, warm. *H.*

Bruid, brŭj, *n. f.* captivity; chaidh thu

suas ionad ard; thug thu *bruid* am braighdeanas, *thou hast ascended on high, thou hast led captivity captive, Ps.* lxxviii, 18; anguish; great anxiety; tha thu 'gam chumail ann am *bruid, you keep me in great anxiety,* or *anguish*; *v.* give the hint, by touching, touch; *bhruid* e mi, *he gave me the hint,—he touched me*; poke, probe; a' *bruideadh* fo'n bhruaich, *probing under the bank of the river.*

Bruid, brûj, *n. m.* a brute, a beast, a brutal person.

Bruidealachd, brûj'-ăl-ăchg, *n. f.* brutality; brutishness, beastliness; coarseness.

Bruideil, brûj'-al, *a.* brutal, beastly.

Bruideadh, brŭj'-Ă, *n. m.* touch, by way of a hint; a hint; *p.* stabbing, thrusting; poking; probing.

Bruidhinn, brúĕ'-ênn, *n. f.* talk, speech, report; conversation; tha mi a' cluinntinn *bruidhinn, I hear a talk or conversation*; *bruidhinn* mhòr, *loud talk*; tha leithid sin do *bhruidhinn* a measg dhaoine, *there is such a report among people*; chualadh mi *bruidhinn* fada uam, *I heard talking at a great distance*; *v. n.* speak, say, talk; *bruidhinn* ris, *speak to him*; *bhruidhinn* mi ris, *I spoke to him, I talked to him*; bha mi a' *bruidhinn* ris, *I was talking to him*; com' am b' fhiach leat *bruidhinn* ris, *why would you condescend to speak to him?* cha 'n 'eil agad ach a bhi '*bruidhinn, talk on as long as you like, blab on*; *p.* talking, speaking; a' *bruidhinn* r'a chéile, *speaking to each other.*

Bruidhne, brúe'nyȧ, *gen.* of bruidhinn; fear na mòr *bhruidhne, the talkative man. Bible.*

Bruidhneach, brúenn'-nyach, *a.* talkative, blabbing; loquacious; 's e siod am fear *bruidhneach, what a garrulous talkative fellow he is*; sgathaidh an Tighearn na bilean miodalach uile, agus an teanga *bhruidhneach, the Lord shall cut off all flattering lips, and the tongue that speaketh proud things. P.* xii, 3.

Bruidhneachd, brúenn'-nyăchg, *n. f.* talkativeness, garrulity, loquaciousness.

Bruidlich, brùĕj'-llêch, *v.* stir up. *H. S.*

Bruilleadh, brûêll'-Ă, *p.* bruising; crushing; *n. m.* a crush, a squeeze, a bruising.

Bruilidh, brŭll'-ê, a man of clumsy figure, and of awkward unwieldy motion.

Bruill, brûêll, *v.* crumble, bruise, crush; *brùillidh* mi do chnàmhan, *I will crush your bones to atoms*; squeeze.

Bruineard, bruen'-ard, *a.* high-crested *Ar.*

Bruinne, brŭĕnn-ȧ, breast, waist. *R. M.*

Bruite, brût'-tyȧ, *p.* (of bruth) bruised, broken, oppressed, sad, crushed; daoine *brùite* truagh, *poor oppressed men, Ps.* carson osnaich *bhrùite* ad chliabh, *why the sad sigh from thy bosom, O.*; iadsan a tha *brùite* 'na spiorad, *they who are contrite in their spirit, B.*; fuil *bhrùite, extravasated blood*; tha m' anam *brùite* am chom, *my soul is oppressed within me. Ps.*

Bruth, brrhŭ, *n. m.* the dwelling of fairies in a hill; a house half under the surface; a cave.

Bruth, brhû, *v.* bruise, crush, pulverise; pound; agus cuiridh mi naimhdeas eadar thusa agus a' bhean agus eadar do shìolsa agus a sìolsa; agus *bruthaidh* esan do cheann agus *bruthaidh* tusa a shail-san, *and I will put enmity between thee and the woman, and between thy seed and her seed, it shall bruise thy head, and thou shalt bruise his heel.*

Bruthach, brhŭ'-hach, *n. m.* an acclivity, ascent, a steep, a hill side, a precipice; a' dol a suas am *bruthach, ascending the acclivity* or *ascent*; thoir am *bruthach* ort, neo thoir na buinn ort, *take to your heels, be off!* thug e am *bruthach* air, *he took to his heels*; le *bruthach, downwards*; ri *bruthach, ascending, upwards*; fo chreig a *bhruthaich, under the rock of the steep*; ruithidh an taigeas féin le *bruthach, the haggis itself will run downwards. Ossian, A. S. B.*

Bruthachail, brhŭ'-ach-al, *a.* steep, full rising grounds *or* eminences

Bruthadair, brhŭ'-ha-dar', *n. m.* a pounder, a pestle; a bruiser *or* crusher.

Bruthadh, brhŭ'-Ă, *n. m.* a contusion, a bruise; *p.* bruising, crushing; pounding.

Bruthainn, brhŭ'-ênn, *n. f.* sultry heat.

Bruthainneach, brhŭ'-ênn-ach, *a.* sultry; warm; aimsir *bhruthainneach, sultry weather.*

Bruthainneachd, brhŭ'-enn-achg, *n. f.* sultriness.

Bu! bû, *int.* a sound to excite fear in children.

Bu, baŏ, *pret. indic.* of the verb to be; *bu* i, *bu* e, *bu* iad, contracted b'i, b'e, b' iad, *it was he, it was she, it was they,* pronounced bbē, bè, bèud *or* bĕăd; it is always contracted before *f* aspirated; as, *b'* fhearr leam, *b'* fhasa, *I would prefer, it would be easier*; pronounced byârr, bbăsȧ; *b'* fhearr a bhi gun bhreith na bhi gun teagasg, *it would be better not to have been born than to want instruction*; *b'* fhearr gun toiseachadh na sgur gu'n chrìochnachadh, *it would be better not to* *begin than to stop without finishing*; b' fhearr a bhi gun fhàine na fàine luachrach, *better to be without a ring, than wear a rush-ring*; *d, g, m, p,* are aspipirated after *bu*; as, *bu* dhana e, *how daring he was*; *bu* gheur e, *how sharp it was*, &c.; *bu* mhiosa e, *it was worse, he was worse*; *bu* phailt iad, *they were plentiful*; *b, m, p, l,* take a double sound in these cases; thus, bu phailt, buv'-fhăĕlt; bu mhiosa, buv-vhèss'-â; bu bhochd, buv'-vhŏchg; bu leathan, bul'-lă-hun; a laoich an sòlas-nam fleagh *bu* mhòr (buv'-vhōr) 's an am cruadail, *hero, who wast great in the joy of feasts, and in time of trial. Oss.*

Buabhaill, bŭăv''-all, *n.f.* a cow-stall. *Ir.*

Buabhull, buav'-vul, *n. m.* a unicorn; ach mar adharc *buabhuill*, àrdachaidh tu m' adharcsa, *but my horn shalt thou exalt, as the horn of a unicorn, Ps.* 92-10; a cornet, a wind instrument; le h-iolach agus le fuaim a *bhuabhuill, with shouting, and with the sound of the cornet.*

Buac, bŭăchg, *v.* work lime and gravel into mortar; work clay, &c.; in Irish, unbleached linen cloth. *See* Buaichd.

Buacadh, bŭăchg'-ă, *p.* working lime, clay, &c.

Buachaile, bŭăch'-èlly'-â *n. m.* a cowherd, a herd.

Buachailleachd, bŭăch'-èlly'-ăchg, *n. f.* herding, tending cattle, the occupation of a herd.

Buachaillich, bŭăch'-èlly'-èch, *v.* tend, herd, watch, *or* keep cattle.

Buachar, bŭăch'-ur, *n. m.* cow-dung, dung.

Buachair, bŭăch'-èrr, *v.* bedaub with dung.

Buadh, bŭă'-gh', *gen. plu.* of buaidh.

Buadhach, bua'-gh'-ach, *a.* victorious, triumphant; highly gifted; having inherent qualities to effect something wonderful.

Buadhachadh, bŭăgh''-ach-ă, *n. m.* the act of gaining the ascendant; *p.* succeeding well in any thing; conquering, overcoming.

Buadhachail, bŭă-gh''-ăch-al, *a.* triumphant, victorious, overcoming, subduing.

Buadhachas, bŭă-gh''-ach-us, *n .m.* the ascendancy, and superiority; success, victory.

Buadhaich, bŭă-gh'-èch, *v.* overcome, gain the victory, prevail, subdue, overthrow, subject, triumph.

Buadhaiche, bua'-gh'-èch-â, *n. m.* a victor.

Buadhail, bŭă-gh''-al, *a.* victorious, triumphant.

Buadhalachd, bŭă-gh''-al-ăchg, *n.* superiority, ascendant, mastery.

Buadhmhoireachd, bŭăv'-vur-ăchg, *n. f.* the mastery, ascendant, superiority; victoriousness.

Buadhmhor, bŭăv'-vur, *a.* triumphant, victorious, successful, gaining the ascendant.

Buaghair, bua'-har, *n. m.* a herd; thachair orra *buaghair* bhò, *a cow-herd met them. Legend. Arm.*

Buaghallan, bŭă-gh'-ghallan, *n. m.* groundsel, ragwort, *or* ragweed, *buaghallan buidhe.*

Buaic, bŭăèchg, *n. f.* the wick of a candle *or* lamp.

Buaiceach, bŭăèchg'-ach, *a.* giddy. *M. L.*

Buaichd, bŭăèchg, *n. f.* cow dung, with which green linens are steeped preparatory to bleaching.

Buaidh, bŭăè'-gh', *n. f.* victory, conquest, success, palm; thugadh *buaidh* am f hianuis 'sa bhlàr; thog gaisgich an ruaig is lean, *victory was obtained in my presence on the battle-field*; *heroes took up the pursuit and followed, Oss.*; endowments, qualifications, talents, accomplishments; deadh *bhuaidheanan* naduir, *excellent, natural endowments* or *talents*; deadh *bhuaidheanan* inntinn, *excellent mental endowments* or *talents*; virtue, attribute; tha *buaidh* air an uisge bheatha, *whisky has a virtue in it*; faigh, neo thoir *buaidh, obtain the victory,* or *conquer*; a bhuidhinn *buaidh* 'sa comhstri, *who gained the victory in the strife*; beannachd do t' anam is *buaidh, a blessing to your soul and success, Oss.*; fear nam *buadh, the man of talents* or *accomplishments*; ma gheibh sinn *buaidh, if we triumph* or *obtain the victory*; *buaidh* chaithream, *a triumphant shout* or *song of triumph*; a deanamh *buaidh* chaithream, *triumphing. Bible.*

Buaidhear, bŭăè'-yuhăr[2], a conqueror, a victor.

Buaidhearachd, bŭăe'-yhyar'-ăchg, triumph, victory; coming off victoriously.

Buaigheal, bŭăè'-ghyall, *n. f.* a cowstall. *Is.*

Buail, bŭă'l, *v. n.* strike, beat, smite; *bhuail* e mi, *he struck* or *smote me*, thrash, as sheaf corn; beetle, as lint; tha iad a *bualadh* 'san t-sabhal, *they are thrashing in the barn*; tha iad a' *bualadh* an lìn, *they are beetling the lint*; attack, fall to, belabour; *bhuail* iad oirnn, *they attacked us*; *bhuail* thuige Deargo, *Dargo rushed* or *moved towards him*; *bhuail* iad thun na beinne, *they rushed towards the mountain, they betook themselves to the mountain*; *bhuail* e chruaidh na taobh, *he thrust his steel into her side*; *buailibh* clarsach, *strike up the harp*; a cheud fhear a *bhuail* an tìr, *the first man that touched the land*, Oss. *A.*; *bhuail* iad thun a chéile, *they attacked each other*; *bhuail* iad thun a chladaich, *they rushed towards the shore*; knock; *buail* an dorus, *knock at the door.*

Buaile, bŭă′-llà, *n. f.* a fold for black cattle; a bhò a's miosa a tha 'sa *bhuaile* s i a's airde geum, *the worst cow in the fold gives the loudest low*; *buailtean* spréidhe, *herds of cattle*; ba 'sna *buailtean*, *cows in the folds. Bible.*

Buaileach, bŭăl′-ăch, *a.* belonging to a fold.

Buailte, buaèl″-tyà, *p.* struck, thrashed.

Builteach, bŭăèl′-tyăch, *a.* subject to, liable to; *buailteach* do iomadh cunnart, *subject to*, or *liable to many dangers*; apt to strike, *or* quarrelsome; cha 'n 'eil e 'na dhuine *buailteach*, *he is not a quarrelsome fellow*; gun bhi *buailteach*, *not given to strike. B. A.*

Buailteach, bŭăèl′-tyach, *n. m.* booth, *or* huts for shealings; bothagan airidh.

Buailtean, bŭăĕl′-tyan′, *n. m.* that part of a flail that strikes the corn, (sùist.)

Buailtear, bŭăèl′-tyăr′, *n. m.* a thrasher.

Buain, bŭăèn, *n. f.* reaping, harvest; a' dol thun na buana, *going to the reaping* or *harvest*; a' *bhuain* eòrna, *barley harvest, B.*; am na *buana*, *harvest time*, or *reaping time*; cut, pull; a' *buain* na mòna, *cutting the peats*; a' *buain* shlat, *cutting twigs*; a *buain* chnù, *pulling* or *gathering nuts. Is.*

Buain, bŭăèn, *v.* reap, shear, cut, hew, pluck, pull; cha *bhuain* thu gu buileach, *thou shalt not wholly reap, Ruth.*; am fear nach dean cur ri là fuar, cha dean e *buain* ri là teth, *he that will not sow on a cold day, will not reap on a warm one*; *buain* a' chraobh so, *hew* or *cut down this tree.*

Buaine, bŭăĕn′-nyà, *comp. deg.* of buan, lasting, durable; lasting; is *buaine* na gach ni an nàire, *shame is more lasting than any thing else*; durability, durableness; *buaine* an ni so, *the durableness* or *perpetuity of this thing.*

Buainead, bŭăèn′-ad, *n. m.* degree of durability *or* lastingness; durability.

Buainte, bŭăèn′-tya, *a.* shorn, reaped, cut, pulled.

Buair, bŭăèr, *v.* trouble *or* make muddy, as water; *bhuair* thu 'n t-uisge, *you have made the water muddy*; tempt, allure, provoke, annoy, tease, disturb; 'nuair a *bhuair* bhur n-aithrichean mi, agus a dhearbh iad mi, *when your fathers tempted me and provoked me. Ps.*

Buaireadair, bŭăer′-ad-ăr′, *n. m.* and *f.* a tempter.

Buaireadh, bŭăèr′-ă, *n. m.* a temptation, provocation, disturbance, annoyance; severe trial; an diugh ma dh' éisdeas sibh r'a ghuth, na cruaidhichibh bhur cridhe, mar anns a chonsachadh, mar ann an là a' *bhuairidh* anns an fhàsach, *today if ye will hear his voice, harden not your hearts, as in the provocation, and as in the day of temptation in the wilderness.*

Buaireanta, bŭăr″-ant-à, *a.* tempting.

Buaireas, bŭăèr′-as, *n. m.* tumult, an uproar, confusion, disturbance, trouble, ferment; fo *bhuaireas*, *troubled, annoyed*; a' cur *buaireas* a measg na daoine, *creating a disturbance* or *tumult among the people*; confusion of mind; fìon a *bhuaireis*, *wine that disturbs the mind. On.*

Buaireasach, bŭăèr′-ăs-ăch, *a.* annoying, disturbing, creating a tumult; inflaming the passions, tumultous, provoking; deoch *bhuaireasach*, *drink that inflames*, or *maddens*; duine *buaireasach*, *a man that annoys* or *disturbs, a tumultuous fellow.*

Buaireasachd, bŭăèr′-ăs-ăchg, *n. f.* turbulence of temper *or* disposition; tumultuousness; turbulence, boisterousness; storminess.

Buairte, bŭăèrt′-tyà, *p.* disturbed, confused; troubled *or* made muddy, as water; tempted, enraged, provoked.

Bualadh, bŭăl′-ă, *n. m.* thrashing, beetling; *p.* striking, beating, knocking.

Bualaidh, bŭăl′-è, *n. f.* cow-stall. *N. H.*

Bualachd, bŭăl′-ăchg, *n. f.* a drove.

Bualtrach, bual′-trach, *n. f.* cow dung.

Buamasdair, bŭăm′-ăsd′-ăr′, *n. m.* a blockhead, a turbulent fellow.

Buamasdaireachd, bŭăm′-ăsd-ăr′-ăchg, *n. f.* stupidity; turbulence; boasting. *H.*

Buan, bŭăn, *a.* lasting, durable; cruaidh măr am fraoch, *buan* mar an giuthas, *hard as the heather, lasting as the pine, or fir-tree*; tedious; rathad *buan*, *a tedious road* or *way.*

Buanachadh, buan′-ăch-ă, *n. m.* and *p.* perseverance, continuing, persevering; lasting; 'n am brosnachadh nach 'eil mo shùil a' *buanachadh*, *in their provocation, doth not mine eye continue? Job.*

Buanaich, bŭăn′-èch, *v.* continue, abide, endure, last, persevere.

Buanaiche, bŭăn′-èch-à, *n. m.* and *f.* a shearer, a reaper.

Buanas, bŭăn′-as, *n. m.* durability.

Buanna, bŭăn′-nà, *n. m.* a billet-master; an idler, a straggler; sè *buannachan* deug Mhic Domhnuill, *MacDonald of the Isles' sixteen billet-masters*; Trad. in the islands. *See* Domhnull.

Buannachail, bŭăn'-năch-al, *a.* beneficial, gratis, as a billet; useful.

Buannachas, bŭăn'-năch-us, *n. f.* free quarters of soldiers, in place of rent.

Buannachd, bŭăn'-năchd, *n. f.* benefit, profit, gain, emolument.

Buannachdach, bŭăn'-năchg-ăch, *a.* profitable, beneficial, useful.

Buannachdail, bŭăn'-năchg-al, *a.* beneficial, profitable, useful.

Buannaich, bŭăn'-nnèch, *v.* gain, profit, acquire, win, reap benefit from.

Buantas, bŭănt'-as, *n. f.* duration.

Buar, bŭăr, *n. m.* cattle, kine. *Bible.*

Buarach, bŭăr'-ăch, *n. f.* cow's fetters; shackles on the hind legs of a cow while milking.

Buath, bŭă, *n. m.* madness, rage. *M. Lach.*

Bub, bûbb, *v.* blubber, as a child; weep in a most melancholy way.

Bubail, bûbb'-ăl, *n. f.* blubbering.

Bubaire, bûbb'-ur'-ă, a person that blubbers.

Bubaireachd, bûbb'-ur'-ăchg, *n. f.* blubbering.

Bubarsaich, bubb'-ăr-ssèch, *n. f.* blubbering.

Bucach, bŭchg'-ăch, *n. m.* a boy. *N. H.*

Bucaid, bŭchg'-ăj, *n. f.* a pimple; a bucket.

Bucaideach, bŭchg'-ăj-ăch, *a.* full of pimples.

Buchd, bûchg, *n. m.* bulk, size; the cover of a book. *H. S.*

Buchainn, bŭch'-èn', *a.* melodious, binn.

Buchallach, bŭch'-al-ăch, *a.* nestling.

Bucull, bŭchg'-al, *n. m.* a buckle.

Buigire, bŭèg'-èr-ă, *n. m.* the puffin. *St. Kilda.*

Budhailt, bŭ'-ăèlt, *n. f.* recess in a wall; a wall press in a cottage.

Bughall, bbŭ'-all, *n. m.* a pot-hook.

Buicean, bŭèchg'-an², *n. m.* a pimple, a pustule; a little buck.

Buiceanach, bŭèchg'-an²-ăch, *a.* full of pimples *or* pustules; breaking out in pimples.

Buideal, bŭjj'-ăll, *n. m.* a cask, an anker, *North,* a bottle; mar *bhuideal* anns an toit, *as a bottle in the smoke. R. Ps.*

Buidealaich, bŭjj'-all-èch, *n. f.* a conflagration; a blaze; 's ann an sin a tha *bhuidealaich, what a conflagration is there*; chaidh e 'na *bhuidealaich, it blazed.*

Buidealair, bŭjj'-al-ăr', *n. m.* a butler. *Bible.*

Buidealaireachd, bŭjj'-all-ăr'-ăchg, *n. f.* the office of a butler; butlership.

Buidhe, bhŭ'-è, *a.* yellow, of a gold colour falt *buidhe*, yellow hair; glad; *adv.* fain, gladly; bu *bhuidhe* leis na ruisg itheadh, *he would fain eat the husks* or *peelings.*

Buidheach, bŭè'-ăch, *a.* pleased, satisfied, contented; grateful, thankful; cha 'n 'eil e *buidheach, he is displeased*; bi *buidheach, be grateful* or *thankful*; bu choir dhuit a bhi *buidheach, you should be grateful*; tha mi *buidheach, I am satisfied.*

Buidheach, bûĕ-yh'-ach, *n. f.* the jaundice.

Buidheachas, bŭè'-ăch-as, *n. m.* thanksgiving, gratitude; thanks; thoir *buidheachas, return thanks, express your gratitude*; ach *buidheachas* do Dhia a tha toirt dhuinne na buadha, tre ar Tighearna Iosa Criosda, *but thanks be to God, who giveth us the victory, through our Lord Jesus Christ*; the state of being bought, but the bargain not concluded abeyance; fo *bhuidheachas,* neo ann an *buidheachas, in abeyance.*

Buidheag, bŭĕ'-ăg, *n. f.* a goldfinch.

Buidheagan, buĕ'-ag-an, *n. m.* the yolk of an egg.

Buidheann, bŭĕ'-yhyunn, *n. f.* a company, a troop, a gang, band, a party; *buidheann* shaighdearan, *a company* or *party of soldiers*; *pl.* buidhnear, buidhnichean, parties, &c.; rinn na Caldeanaich tri *buidhnean, the Chaldeans made out three bands.*

Buidhinn, bhŭè'-ènn, *n. m.* gain, profit, emolument; quarrying stones; is dona a *bhuidhinn* a th' air na clachan sin, *these stones are not properly quarried.*

Buidhinn, bhŭĕ'-ènn, *v. n.* gain, win, acquire, get the better of; *bhuidhinn* sinn bàir, *we gained a game*; quarry.

Buidhinneach, bŭĕ'-ènn-ăch, *n. f.* a quarry.

Buidhne, bŭĕ'-nyă, *gen.* of buidhinn, gain; a troop, a band.

Buidhneach, bhŭèn'-nyach, *a.* in troops *or* companies; numerous; na laoich *bhuidhneach,* mhòr, *the high-minded, numerous heroes. Mt. H. S.*

Buidhnich, bŭèn'-nnèch, *v.* arrange into companies.

Buidhre, bŭĕ'-rră, *deg.* more *or* most deaf; *n. f.* deafness, degree of deafness.

Buidseach, bŭjsh'-ach, *n. m.* and *f.* a witch, a wizard; is *buidseach* i, *she is a witch*; is *buidseach* e, *he is a wizard.*

Buidseachas, bujsh'-ăch-us, *n. m.* witchcraft, sorcery.

Buidseachd, bŭjsh'-ăchg, *n. f.* witchcraft, sorcery.

Buige, bŭĕg′-ă, *n. f.* softness; humidity; effeminacy; *deg.* of bog; ni's *buige, softer, more effeminate.*

Buigead, buĕg′-ud, *n. f.* degree of softness, softness.

Buigileag, bŭĕg′-ė-llăg, *n. f.* a crab after casting the shell; a soft unmanly person; *North*, a quagmire, suil-chrith.

Buil, bŭ'l, *n. f.* consequence, effect, result; bithidh a *bhuil* duit, *the consequence* or *result must be obvious in your case*; is léir a *bhuil, the result is obvious*; *buil* gach aon taisbein, *the effect of every vision*; tha a *bhuil* sin air, *the effect of that is obvious on him* or *it*; an rud a nìthear gu ceart chitear a *bhuil, when a thing is properly done, the result must tell*; use, application, completion, end; a thoirt gu *buil* fhacail, *to complete* or *fulfil his word*; a bheir a dhroch innleachdan gu *buil, who will bring his wicked devices to pass. Bible*; dean deadh *bhuil* deth, *make good use of it, apply it properly*; *buil* cheart a dheanadh dheth, *to make proper improvement* or *application of it.*

Buileach, bŭ'l′-ăch, *a.* complete, whole, total, entire; gu *buileach, entirely, completely, wholly*; *adv.* wholly, entirely, completely; is *buileach* a dh' fhairslich e ort, *it has most completely defied you*; is *buileach* a chaidh thu dholaidh, *you are entirely ruined.*

Buileachadh, bŭ'l′-ăch-Ă, *pt.* bestowing; granting; improving; finishing completely; a' *buileachadh* ort, *bestowing on you.*

Builg, bu'l′-ėg, *v.* bubble, blister, rise, as fish in the water; rise to the fly; a *builgeadh, bubbling*; *pl.* of bolg, bellows; distemper in cattle. *N. H.*

Builgeadh, bŭl′-ėg-Ă, *p.* bubbling, blistering.

Builgeag, bu'l′-ėg-ag, *n. f.* a blister, a bubble.

Builgeagach, bu'l′-ėg-ach, blistered.

Builgean, bu'l′-ėg-ăn', *n. m.* a blister. *D. M. L.*

Builich, bu'l′-ėch, *v. n.* grant, bestow, improve; gach ni a *bhuilich* Dia ort, *every thing God hath bestowed on thee*; finish completely; *builich* an latha, *finish the day completely.*

Builionn, bu'l′-unn, *n. f.* a loaf.

Builionnaiche, bu'l′-unn-ėch-ă, *n. m.* a baker.

Buille, bŭlly″-ă, *n. m.* a stroke, blow, a knock; *buille* air son *buille, blow for blow. B.*

Builleach, bŭlly′-ăch, *a.* apt to strike.

Buillsgean, bŭlly″-skyan', *a.* the heart-middle, the centre· am *buillsgean* an teine, *in the heart-middle, or centre of the fire.*

Buimealair, bŭėm′-al-ar, *n. m.* a booby, a blockhead, a clumsy fellow.

Buin, bŭĕn and bŏėn, *v. n.* touch, handle, be related to, belong to; meddle; na *buin* da sin, *do not touch that*; *buinidh* iad da chéile, *they are related to each other*; 's ann do Dhia a *bhuineas* slàinte, *to God belongs salvation, B.*; 's ann do 'n Tighearn Dia a *bhuineas* an t-slighe o'n bhàs, *and to the Lord God belongs the issues from death, P.* lxviii, 20; deal with; tear from; *buin* gu caoimhneil ri m' ghoal, *deal gently with my love*; cha *bhuinte* bho 'gaol i, *she could not be torn from her love, Oss. Ar.*; cò dha a *bhuineas* so, *to whom does this belong?* cha *bhuin* e dhuitse, *it does not belong to you*; comhairle clag Scàinn, an rud nach *buin* duit na *buin* da, *the advice of the bell of Scoon,—the thing that does not belong to you, meddle not with.*

Buinne, bŭĕn′-nyă, *n. m.* the meeting of many currents, confluence; a pool in a river; air *buinne* réidh, *on a smooth pool. Mt.*

Buinne, bûėn″-nyă, *n. m.* a statue, a bust; one that stands stock-still; is tu am *bùinne, you stand stock-still, like a statue. Islay. See* Domhnull.

Buinneach, bŭĕn′-nyăch, *n. f.* a diarrhœa, dysentery; a flux; *a.* contemptible, abominable; duine *buinneach, a contemptible person.*

Buinnire, bŏĕn′-nyur-ă, a footman. *H. S.*

Buinnteach, bŭėnnt′-tyach, *n. f.* leather for soles; the thickest part of a hide.

Buir, bûer, *v.* bellow, as a bull; roar.

Buirbe, bŭėr²′-ub-ă, *n. f.* turbulence, a fierce, boisterous temper; boisterousness; rage, fury.

Buirbeachd, bŭėr′-ub-ăchg, *n. f.* turbulence, extreme degree of rage *or* wrath, boisterousness, savageness.

Buirbein, bŭėr′-ub-ėn, *n. m.* a cancer. *Ir.*

Buird, bûrjj, *plu.* of bord, tables.

Buirdeiseach, bŭrjj′-ash-ăch, *n. m.* and *f.* a boarder, an idler, *Is.*; a burgess, a citizen, *H. S.*; an inhabitant; *buirdeisich* sgiathach nan speur, *the winged inhabitants of the sky. Md. Ar.*

Buire, buireadh, bŭer′-Ă, *n. m.* a rutting place of deer; burst of grief, a wailing; bhrist uaith *bùire, she broke a loud burst of grief. Oss.*

Buirich, bŭėr′-ėch, *n. f.* roaring as a bull, bellowing; wailing.

Bul, bûll, *n. m.* a pot-hook. *M.*

Bun, bŭnn, *n. m.* a stock, a stump; root; bottom; *bun* na craoibh, *the root* or *stump of the tree*; *bun* na beinne, *the* *bottom of the hill*; *bun* an urbaill, *the rump*; *bun* na h-àltrach, *the foot of the altar*; spìon as a' *bhun* e, *root it out*; dependance, trust, confidence; na dean *bun* a gàirdean feòla, *place no dependance* or *confidence in an arm of flesh*; dean *bun* a Dia, *place your confidence in God*; cha 'n fhàg e *bun* na barr, *he will leave neither root or branch, B.*; *bun* as cionn, *upside down, topsy-turvy*; am *bun* an tighe, *taking care of the house*; an *bun* nan caorach, *tending* or *taking care of the sheep*; asad a rinn ar sinnsir *bun, in thee our father's placed confidence*; *bun* eich, *an old stump of a horse.*

BUNACH, bŭn'-ach, *n. m.* coarse tow.

BUNACHAR, bŭn'-ach-ur, *n. m.* dependance, confidence, trust; na dean *bunachar* sam bith a sin, *place no dependance on that*; cha 'n 'eil *bunachar* eile agam, *I have nothing else to depend on. Islay.*

BUNACHAINNT, bun'-a-chăènnt, *n. f.* etymology.

BUNACHAS, bun'-ăch-us, *n. f.* principle. *H.*

BUNADAS, bun'-a-das, *n. m.* origin, foundation, stòck.

BUNAICH, bun'-èch, *v. n.* depend on; found.

BUNAILT, bun'-ălty', *n. f.* constancy, steadiness, inflexibility; firmness.

BUNAILTEACH, bŭn'-ălty2-ach, *a.* stationary, fixed in one place; established, sure, steady; am bheil e *bunailteach* 'san aite sin, *is he stationary* or *established in that place?* attentive; *bunailteach* aig' a ghnothuch, *attentive to his business.*

BUNAILTEACHD, bun'-alty'-ăchg, *n. f.* constancy, firmness, steadiness; fixedness; inflexibility.

BUNAIT, bŭn'-ăjt, *n. f.* foundation.

BUNAITEACH, bŭn'-ăjt-ach, *a.* stationary, fixed, steadfast, immoveable.

BUNAITEACHD, bŭn'-ăjt-ăchg. *See* Bunailteachd.

BUNAITICH, bun'-ăjt-èch, *v.* settle, fix your abode, inherit, inhabit.

BUNAMAS, bŭn'-am-us, *n. m.* discernment.

BUNAMHAS, bŭn'-a-vvhăs, *n. m.* a buttock.

BUNANTA, bun'-ant-a, *a.* strong, stout, firm, well set, having a good foundation.

BUNASACH, bun'-as-ach, *a.* steady, firm.

BUNCHIALL, bun-chĕăll', *n. m.* a moral meaning; *bun* dubh, *the bottom of a corn stack.*

BUN-LUCHD, bŭn'-luchg, *n. p.* original inhabitants.

BUNNDAIST, bunn'-'dăsht, *n. f.* a perquisite, a bounty; grassum, *M. L.*; *North*, fee, wages.

BUNTATA, bŭn-tâ'-ttà, *n. m.* potatoes; supposed to signify bun-taghta; literally, a choice root.

BURABHUACHAILL, bŭr'-a-vhŭăch-ĕll, *n. f.* the sea-bird called the Holland auk; more properly murabhuachaill; literally, sea-herd.

BURACH, bûr'-ăch, *n. m.* searching *or* turning up the earth; delving, digging.

BURAICH, bûr'-àch, *v.* dig lightly and irregularly.

BURAICHE, bûr'-èch-à, *n. m.* a hoe a mattock; a delver, a digger.

BURAIDH, bûr'-è, *a.* mouldy, as land; easily dug *or* delved.

BURAIDHEACHD, bûr'-è-ăchg, *n. f.* mouldiness.

BURBAN, bur'-ub'-an, *n. m.* wormwood.

BURD, bûr'd, *n. m.* a hum.

BURDAN, bûr'd'-an, *n. m.* a humming noise, grumbling, muttering.

BURDANACH, bûr'd'-ăn-àch, *a.* humming, grumbling, muttering, prone to grumble.

BURMAID, búr'm-ăj, *n. m* wormwood. *B.*

BURN, bŭr'n, *n. m.* fresh water; sàil is *burn, salt water and fresh water*; ni *burn* salach làmhan glan, *foul water makes clean hands. Gaelic Proverbs.*

BURNACH, bŭrn'-ach, *a.* watery.

BURRAIDH, bŭrr'-è, *n. m.* a blockhead, a fool.

BURRAIL, bûrr'-a'l, *v.* romp, as children; play rudely.

BURRAIS, bŭrr'-ash, *n. m.* a caterpillar. *Bible.*

BURRALADH, bûr'-al-À, *n. m.* and *p.* romping; rude play, noisy play.

BURRALL, bŭrr'-all, *n. m.* a deep-toned howl, *or* weeping; wailing, burst of grief.

BURRALACH, bŭrr'-al-ach, *a.* crying; apt to whine *or* howl.

BURRALAICH, bŭrr'-al-èch, *n. f.* continued howling, wailing, *or* lamentation.

BURRACAID, bŭrr'-ăchg-ăjj, *n. f.* a stupid female; a silly woman.

BURT, bŭrtt', *n. m.* mockery, sport. *No.*

BUS, bŭss, *n. m.* a mouth of a beast; a mouth with very large lips; a large mouth.

BUSACH, bŭs'-ăch, *a.* blubber-lipped; *n. f.* a female having large lips.

BUSAG, bŭs'-ăg, *n. f.* a ludicrous name for a smacking kiss; a smacking kiss.

BUSACHD, bus'-ăchg, *n. f.* the deformity of blubber-lips.

BUSAIRE, bŭs'-ăr'-à, *n. m.* a man having blubber-lips a sullen fellow.

BUSG, bŭsg, *v.* thread a fishing hook. *Bute*, Scotch.

BUSGADH, busg'-À, *n. m.* threading *or* tying a hook.

BUSGAID, bŭsk'-ăj. *n. m.* bustle. *H. S*

Buisinn-iall, bŭsh'-enn²-ĕall, *n. m.* a horn for holding tallow.

Buta, bŭt'-å, *n. m.* a bird; difference in price; difference, surplus; *Dutch*, banta; *Sax.* bota.

Buth, bhû, *n. m.* a shop, *Is.*; a tent; a cot; shuidhich e *'bhùth, he pitched his tent*; chomhnuich iad am *bùthaibh, they dwelt in tents, B.*; sròl as a' *bhùth, crape from the shop*; *North.* an ant-hill.

Buthainn, bhu'-hyèn', *n. m.* long straw used for thatch; *v.* thump, beat lustily. *N.*

C

C, c, the third letter of the alphabet; called call, *or* caltuinn, the hazel tree; or, as the Irish pronounce it, coll, *or* coltuinn. It has a peculiar influence on the article; thus, an cù, *the dog*, pronounced ung'-kû; an caman, *the shinty*, pro. ung'-kăm-an; nan con, *of the dogs*, pro. nang'-kŏn.

C sounds like kk often; ending a syllable, for the most part, sounds chg; as, tac, rac, pro. tăchg, răchg.

C' for cia, ca, *pron. interr.*; thus, *c'aite, where? c'aite* am bheil thu, *where art thou? c'* ainm a thoirt, *what is your name? for* cia e an t'aite, &c.

Ca, kkâ, *adv.* where; *ca'm* bheil thu, *where art thou? cà* an d' thoir mi e, *where shall I bring it? cà* an d' fhuair thu e, *where did you get it? cà* nis am bheil do ghath, *where now is thy sting?*

Cab, kăbb, *v.* notch, as the edge of a bladed weapon; hack, indent; *chab* thu an sgian, *you have notched the knife.*

Cab, kabb, *n. m.* a mouth with broken teeth, *or* ill set with teeth; a notch, a gap.

Cabach, kăbb'-ăch, *a.* having broken teeth; notched, gapped; *n. f.* a female with broken teeth.

Cabadh, kăbb'-Ă, *p.* indenting, notching; indenting the edge.

Cabag, kâbb'-ăg, *n. f.* a cheese; *Scotch*, kebboch; *Ir.* càbag.

Cabag, kăbb'-ăg, *n. f.* a female with broken teeth; a hacked instrument, as a knife, &c.; a tattling, prating female.

Cabaire, kăbb'-ur'-å, *n. m.* a fellow with broken teeth; tattler, a prating fellow.

Cabaireachd, cab'-ăr'-ăchg, *n. f.* the practice of tattling or prating.

Cabais, kăbb'-ăsh, *n. f.* the prating, prattling, *or* babbling.

Caball, kâb'-all, *n. m.* a cable; Arabic, kebl, a rope, a cord; Hebrew, cabal, to be tied.

Cabar, kăbb'-ăr, *n. m.* a rafter on the roof of a house; an antler *or* a deer's horn; *cabar* féidh, *the antler of a deer, Song*; gu *cabarach, well supplied with antlers, Mackint.*; Scotch, keabar; Com. keber; Arm. ceibir. *Arm.*

Cabarach, kabb'-ăr-ăch, *a.* well supplied with antlers *or* rafters; *n. pl.* deer; an déigh *chabarach, in pursuit of deer, Oss.*; a thicket; mar astar dall an *cabarach, as a blind man's progress through a thicket. Proverbs.*

Cabh, kavf, *v. n.* drift; tha cur is *cabhadh* ann, *it is snowing and drifting.*

Cabhadh, kavf'-Ă, *n. m.* the drift; *pt* drifting; an sìobadh.

Cabhachan, kavf'-ach-an, *n. m.* the bird, cuckoo-titterer.

Cabhag, kavf'-ag, *n. f.* haste, hurry, speed, strait, difficulty.

Cabhagach, kavf'-ăg-ach, *a.* hasty; fast-speaking; hurried, impatient, abrupt, sudden.

Cabhagachd, kăvf'-ăg-ăchg, *n. f.* hastiness.

Cabharnach, kav'-arr-nach, *n. f.* a wicket, (cachladh) a bar-gate, gate-way. 30.

Cabhlach, kav'-llach, *n. f.* a fleet; na *chabhlach* dhorcha, *in his dark fleet. Oss.*

Cabhlaiche, kavf'-llĕch-å, *n. m.* an admiral.

Cabhruich, kav'-roèch, *n. f.* flummery; in Scotch, sowens; continent of Argyle, *Cowry.*

Cabhsaidh, kav'-ssè, *a.* snug, comfortable.

Cabhsaidheachd, kav'-sse-achg, *n. f.* snugness, too much fondness for comfort.

Cabhsair, kav'-ssar', *n. m.* pavement, a causeway, paved path *or* walk. Cowsair, *C. A.*

Cabhsaireachd, kav'-sar'-achg, *n. m.* the business of making pavements *or* causeways.

Cabhsairiche, kav'-săr'-èch-å, *n. m.* a paver.

Cabhsannta, kav'-sannt-a, *f.* fond of comfort, effeminate, unmanly.

Cabhtair, kav'-tăr', *n. f.* an issue in the body; in some places cowtair.

Cabhuil, kav'-ul, *n. m.* a creel for catching fish, a hose net: àbh.

Cablaid, kâb'-llăj, *n. f.* turmoil, tumult.

Cablaideach, kâb'-llăj-ăch, *a.* tumultuous.

Cabrach, kab'-rrach, *a.* belonging to Lochaber; bràdh *chabrach, a Lochaber quern*; *n. f.* a bold masculine female; a thicket; *n. m.* a deer; *cabrach* nan cnoc, *the deer of the hill. Sm.*

Cac, kăchg, *n. m.* excrement, ordure; *v.* void, go to stool; *a.* filthy, dirty.

Cach, kâch, *pron.* the rest; àrd ro *chàch, high above the rest, Oss.*; *càch* a chèile, *each other*; thoir do *chàch* e, *give it to the rest*; thàinig e ro *chàch, he arrived before the rest*; a measg *chàch, among the rest.*

Cadadh, kad''-ă, *n. m.* tartan for hose; còta do *chadadh* nam ball, *a coat of the spotted tartan. Mackintyre.*

Cadal, kăd''-ăl, *n. m.* sleep, slumber; is sèimh do *chadal, gentle is thy sleep, O.*; tha e 'na *chadal, he is sleeping*; an *cadal* duit, *are you sleeping?* chaidh iad a *chadal, they went to sleep, they went to bed*; cha do *chadail* mi neul, *I have not slept a wink*; *cadal* deilgneach, *the tingling sensation in a torpid limb.*

Cadaltach, kăd''-alt-ăch, *a.* sleepy.

Cadaltachd, kăd''-ălt-ăchg, sleepiness.

Cadaltaiche, kad''-ălt-èch-ă, *n. m.* and *f.* a dormant creature, such as the serpent, &c. &c.

Cadh, kă, *n. m.* an entry, a pass, a partition. *C. A.*

Cadhag, kă'-ăg, *n. f.* a wedge; gein. *Sk.*

Cagail, kag'-èl', *v.* cover fire, to keep it from extinguishing, *Arran,* (smàll); neo *cagail* an teine, *secure the fire*; improperly used for save, spare, *coamhainn.*

Cagailt, kăg'-èlty', *n. f.* the hearth; corra-*chagailt, the sulphurous hue seen in ashes on a frosty night.*

Cagainn, kăg'-ènn. *v.* chew, champ, gnaw, masticate.

Cagar, kag'-ur, *n. m.* a whisper, secret.

Cagarsaich, kag'-ar-ssèch, *n. f.* whispering.

Cagair, kăg'-èr, *v.* whisper, listen.

Cagnadh, kag'-nĂ, *n. m.* mastication; *pt.* chewing, champing, gnawing.

Caibe, kaŏèb'-ă, *n. m.* a mattock, a spade.

Caibeal, kīb'-al, *n. m.* a tomb, a chapel; a family burying place.

Caibhtinn, kăĕf'-tyènn, *n. m.* a captain.

Caibideal, kēb'-èj-al, *n. m.* a chapter.

Caidil, kăj'-èl, *v.* sleep, repose.

Caidir, kaj'-èr, *v.* embrace, hug; indulge in, fondle, caress, cherish, *Ps.*; olc ni 'n *caidir* thu, *thou shalt not indulge in iniquity. Ps.*

Caidreamh, kaj'-rruv, the embrace, the bosom; ann an *caidreamh* a chéile, *in the embrace or bosom of each other*; fondling; familiarity.

Caidreamhach, kăj'-ruv-ăch, *a.* mutually embracing, familiar, social; *n. m.* and *f.* a friend, a companion, a bosom friend.

Caigean, kăĕg'-an, *n. f.* a brace, two tied together, a couple, a pair; a group.

Caignich, kăĕg'-nnyèch, *v.* join two and two.

Cail, kâ'l, *n. m.* constitution, energy, strength, pith; tha a *chàil* air falbh, *his constitution wears away*; gun *chàil, without strength* or *energy*; *power of motion*; 's an tigh chaol gun *chàil, in the narrow house, without power of motion, lifeless*; mo *chàil* a' trèigsinn, *my constitution* or *strength failing, Oss. Ar.*; chàill iad *càil* an claisteachd, *they lost their sense of hearing, Md.*; cha'n 'eil *càil* do bhiadh agam, *I have no appetite for food, H.*; chum molaidh gleusaibh binn ar *càil, to praise, attune your voice. D. B.*

Cailc, kăĕlk *n. f.* chalk; *v.* chalk line.

Caileabh, ka'l'-av, *n. m.* partition, *R. M. D.* In Islay, caileadh, partition.

Caile, ka'l-ă, *n. f.* a girl, a vulgar girl; *caile* bhalach, *a romp.*

Caileachd, kà'l'-ăchg, *n. f.* endowments.

Caileag, ka'l-ăg, *n. f.* a girl, a lassie.

Caileiginn, kà'l'-è-gènn, *n. m.* some, somewhat, something, a small matter; tha *cailiginn* do mhaith air, *it is worth something.*

Caileil, kă'l'-ăl, *a.* quean-like.

Cailidear, ka'l'-èj-ar, *n. m.* Rheum, snot. *Sh.*

Cailinn, ka'l'-ènn, *n. f.* a damsel, a maid; *cailinn* ro mhaiseach, *a very handsome damsel*; chum beathachadh do *chailinn, for the maintenance of thy maidens. Bible. Ir.*

Caill, kăĕlly', *v.* lose, suffer loss; forfeit; (a testicle obs.); hence Caillteanach. *Armstrong.*

Cailleach, kăĕly'-lyăch, *n. f.* a nun, an old woman; the last handful of standing corn in a farm; the circular wisp on the top of a corn-stalk; *cailleach* oidhche, *an owl, a spiritless fellow*; *cailleach* dhubh, *a nun.*

Cailleachail, kăĕlly'-ăch-ăl, *a.* old-wifish.

Cailleachanta, kăĕlly'-ăch-ănnt-a, *a.* old-wifish.

Cailleag, kăĕl'-ag, *n. f.* a cockle, husk of lint.

Caillte, kăĕly''-tyă, *pt.* lost, ruined, damned.

Caillteach, kăĕlly'-tyăch, *a.* ruinous, losing; causing loss.

Cailtleachd, kăĕlly'-tyăchg, *n. f.* ruination, degree of loss *or* detriment, loss.

Caillteanach, kăĕly'-tyan-ach, *n. m.* a eunuch.

CAIMDEAL, kaemj'-jal ,*n. f.* tedious way of speaking; an objection (fadtharainneachd).

CAIMDEALACH, kaemaj'-ja-lach, tedious, drawling.

CAIME, kăĕm'-â, *n. m. n. f.* crookedness, degree of crookedness; blindness of an eye.

CAIME, kăĕm'-â, *deg.* more *or* most crooked; tha am bata ni's *caime, the staff is more crooked.*

CAIMEAN, kăĕm'-an' *n. f.* a mote; dùradan. *Is.*

CAIN, kàĕn, *v.* traduce, revile, dispraise, backbite, slander, satirise; *càineam* is aoiream a' bhaoibh rinn an t-òran, *let me revile, lampoon,* or *satirise the fury that composed the song; n. f.* a fine; payment in kind, given to a blacksmith; chuir iad *càin* air, *they fined him*; *a.* white, fair; cu *càin, a white dog, tribute*; dh' òladh e *chàin* a bh' aig Parraig air Eirinn, *he would drink the tribute that Ireland paid St. Patrick.*

CAINEAB, kăĕn''-ub, *n. f.* hemp, (*Is.*) canvas, *M. L.*; written more often and properly, *caineab.*

CAINEABACH, kăĕn'-ub-ach, *n. f.* rope-yarn.

CAINEADH, kàĕn''-Â, *n. m.* traducing, slandering; *pl.* scolding, traducing, slandering, back-biting.

CAINEAL, kăĕn'-al, *n. m.* cinnamon.

CAINGIS, kăĕng'-ėsh, *n. f.* Pentecost, Whitsuntide.

CAINNEAG, kàĕn'-ăg, *n.f.* a hamper(cisean), *Sk.*; mote, *H.*

CAINNT, kăĕnnty', *n. f.* talk, language; speech; conversation, discourse; *pt.* saying, speaking, talking; conversing; discoursing.

CAINNTEACH, kăĕnty'-ăch, *a.* loquacious, talkative.

CAINNTEAL, kăĕnty'-al, *n. m.* a press, a crowd. *H.*

CAINNTEAR, kăĕnty''-ar', a speaker, an orator. *H.*

CAIR, kâry', *n. f.* a grinning expression of countenance; the ripple of the sea; a gum; an image, *M. L.*; *v.* mend, repair; *air* a charadh, *mended.*

CAIRBH, kăĕr'-uv, *n. f.* carcase, a dead body (*closach*); *cairbh* spréidhe neoghloinn, *the carcase of unclean cattle.*

CAIRBHINN, kăĕr'-vvėnn, *n. f.* the carcase of a person; *cairbhinn* an righrean, *the carcases of their kings. Bible.*

CAIRBHEISTE, kaer'-asht-â, *n. f.* baggage, luggage (*Lewis*); rent-service (borlanachd, *West H.*) *Sk.*; flogging. *N.*

CAIRC, kăĕr'k, *n. f.* strait predicament, *Is.*; 's e bha 'na *chairc, he was in a curious predicament*; *hurry-burry.*

CAIRD, kârjj, *n. f.* cont. for cairdeas, gun chàird, without partiality, without lenity, *Ps. Metre.*; kindness; fasgadh is *caird, shelter and kindness. Sg.*

CAIRDEACH, kârjj'-ăch, *a.* related, connected; tha iad *cairdeach* da chéile, *they are connected* or *related to each other*; do na h-uaislean tha thu *cairdeach, you are related to the gentry. Sg. A.*

CAIRDEALACHD, kârjj'-ăll-ăchg, *n. f.* friendliness, benevolence, kindness, goodness, good-will.

CAIRDEAN, kârjj'-unn, *n. m.* and *f. pl.* friends, relations; in the shape of *cousins, bad.*

CAIRDEAS, kârjj'-us, *n. m.* friendship, relationship, connexion, fellowship.

CAIRDEIL, kârjj'-al, *a.* friendly, kind, tender; related, connected; gu *càirdeil, kindly.*

CAIREAN, kâry''-an', *n. m.* the gum, palate; tha caithlean am *chàirean, there is a seedling in my gum*; do m' *chàirean* ni's milse, *to my palate sweeter. Bible.*

CAIRFHIADH, kăĕr'-ĕă-gh', *n. m.* a hart, stag.

CAIRGE, kăr'-ėg-â, *dat.* of carraig, a headland, a natural quay; tha am bàta tighinn thun na *cairge, the boat is coming to point.*

CAIRICH, kâr'-ėch, *v.* mend, repair, order, lay to one's charge; sooth, cajole; inter, bury; *cairich* an altair, *repair their altar*; na *cairich* am peacadh oirne, *lay not their sins to our charge, Bible*; *cairich* r' an taobh e, *place it aside them*; *cairich* air falbh e, *cajole him away*; *chairich* iad 's an uaigh e, *they laid him in the grave, they interred him.*

CAIRIDH, kăr'-ė, *n. f.* a weir; *cairidh* a caradh an éisg, *a weir to deceive the fish Song.*

CAIRMEAL, kăry''-mal, *n. m.* wild liquorice; corra-meille, *wild pease.* Dr. ARMSTRONG says, that we, the Islanders, were accustomed to make mead of it. *Pennant.*

CAIRNEACH, kărry''-nyach, *n. f.* a quarry, *or* any place like it; scàirneach, *a deserted quarry,* or *place like an old quarry. Obs. ospray. Shd.*

CAIRNEAN, kăĕrn'-an', *n. m.* egg-shell. *Arm.*

CAIRT, kărty', *n. f.* a cart; roth na *cartach, the cart wheel*; bark, chart; *cairt* dharaich, *the bark of an oak tree*; *v.* tan, cart; *cairt* an leathrach, *tan the leather*; *cairte, tanned, carted*; leathrach *cairte, tanned leather*; cleaned tha bhathaich *cairte, the byre is cleaned*; a card; ag iomairt air na *cairtean, playing at cards.*

CAIRTEAL, kărty′′-al, *n. m.* a quarter. *N.*

CAIRTEALAN, kaert′-al-un, *n p.* lodgings; more properly *cairsealan, places for temporary residence.*

CAIRTEAR, kaert′-ăr′, *n. m.* a carter, a waggoner.

CAIR-THALMHAINN, kăĕr-hav′-vhĕnn, *n. f.* millfoil, yarrow.

CAIRTIDH, káĕrt′-e, *a.* swarthy, tawny, bark-coloured, tanned.

CAIRTIDHEACHD, kaert′-e-ăchg, *n. f.* swarthiness.

CAIS, kăsh, *v.* twist, twine; *cais* an t-sreang, *twist the line* or *string*; *caiste, twisted, twined.*

CAISBHEART, kash′-art, *n. m.* shoes, stockings, boots, &c.

CAISE, kâsh′-shå, *n. m.* cheese; pailteas do dh' ìm is do *chàise, plenty of butter and cheese.*

CAISE, kăsh′-å, steepness; *caise* a bhrúthaich, *the steepness of the ascent*: shortness of temper; 'se do *chaise* féin a's coireach, *it is your own crossness that is the cause*; impetuosity, rapidity; *caise* an t-sruith, *the impetuosity of the current*; shortness of time, haste; cha d'thig e an *caise, he will not come in a hurry*; *deg.* more *or* most rapid, passionate, &c; tha 'n sruth ni's *caise, the stream* or *current is more* or *most rapid.*

CAISEACH, kâsh′-ach, *a.* well supplied with cheese.

CAISEAD, kash′-ud, *n. m.* degree of rapidity; passion; steepness, impetuosity, &c.

CAISEAL, kăsh′-al, *n. m.* bulwark. *Shd.*

CAISEAMACHD, kăsh′-ăm-ăchg, *n. f.* beating time to music with the foot. *Islay.*

CAISEAN, kash′-ăn′, *n. m.* and *f.* a short-tempered person; a curl *or* dewlap, *H. S.*; *caisean* uchd, *breast-stripe of a sheep, roasted at Christmas, and smelled by all in the house, to keep away fairies for the rest of the year, H. S.* In Islay, any time, but never for the sake of fairies.

CAISEANACHD, kăsh′-ăn′-ăchg, *n. f.* fretfulness, peevishness, bickering, shortness of temper.

CAISEARBHAIN, kăsh′-ar-vhon, *n. m.* the herb dandelion.

CAISFHIONN, kăsh′-un, *a.* white-footed.

CAISG, kâeshg, *n. f.* Easter, the passover; di-dònaidh *càisg, Easter Sunday*; a feast.

CAISG, kăĕshg, *v.* restrain, check, stop, still, quiet; *caisg* an cù, *stop* or *restrain the dog*; staunch; *caisg* an fhuil, *staunch the blood.*

CAISIAL, cash′-ĕăl, *n. m.* shoemaker's strap.

CAISLEACH, kăsh′-lyăch, *n. m.* a ford, a foot-path, a smooth place. *H. S.*

CAISLEACHADH, kash′-lyăch, *n. m.* and *pt.* stirring up a feather bed, shaking; dubbing.

CAISLICH, kăsh′-lyĕch, *v.* shake, stir, rouse.

CAISMEACHD, kash′-măchg, *n. f.* the quick part of a tune on the bag-pipes; an alarm to battle; a war-song.

CAISREABHACHD, kăsh′-ruv-ăchg, *n. f.* juggling. *Ld.*

CAISREAG, kăsh′-rrăg, *n. f.* a ringlet, a curl.

CAISREAGACH, kăsh′-rrăg-ăch, curled.

CAISTE, kăsh′-tyå, *pt.* twisted, curled, twined; snath *caiste, sewing thread.*

CAISTEAL, kăsh′-tyål, *n. m.* a castle, a garrison, a tower; a turreted mansion.

C'AITE, kâty′, *ad.* where, in what place; *c'ait* an robh thu, *where have you been? c'àite* am bheil e, *where is he? c'àite* an d fhuair thu e, *where got you it?*

CAITEAG, kăty′′-ag, *n. f. a.* a basket for trouts, *Is.*; a leather pot, *Sh.*; a small bit, *H.S.*; a place to hold barley, &c. in, a barn, *D. M. L.*; (in Islay, cat). Cat eòrna, sìl, buntata, &c.

CAITEAN, katy′′-an′, *n. m.* shag, *or* nap of cloth; *caitean* air an aodach, *the cloth is shaggy*; the ripple of the sea; a ruffled surface.

CAITEANACH, kăty′′-ăn-ăch, *a.* nappy, shaggy, ruffled, rough with a slight breeze.

CAITEAS, kăty′′-us, *n. m.* caddice; scrapings of linen, applied to wounds.

CAITH, khăĕ, *v.* spend, waste, wear, consume, exhaust; squander; *chaith* e 'shaibhreas, *he squandered his wealth*; *chaith* e 'aodach, *he has worn his clothes*; a' *caitheadh* casaig, *wearing a long coat*; *chaith* a' choinneal, *the candle is consumed*; *chaitheadh* e, *it is exhausted*; casting, shooting; a' *caitheadh* chlach, *casting stones at*; a' *caitheadh* air comharra, *shooting* or *aiming at a mark.*

CAITH, kâĕch, *n. f.* seeds *or* husks of corn; *gen.* catha; sugh na *càtha, the juice of the seeds for making flummery* or *sowens.*

CAITH, khâĕ, *v.* winnow corn; more often cath.

CAITHEACH. *See* Caithteach, prodigal, wasteful.

CAITHEADH, khăĕ′-aăgh′, *pt.* spending, wearing; *n. m.* consumption, wasting, dying by inches.

CAITHEAMH, khăĕ′-uv, *n. m.* consumption. *Prov.*

CAITHE-AIMSIR, khăĕ′-å-ém-shur, *n. m.* pastime.

Caithe-beatha, khăĕ'-bhé-à, *n. m.* moral conduct, conversation; behaviour; conduct, mode of living.

Caithear, kăĕ'-hur, *a.* well bestowed, just. *N. H.*

Caithleach, ka'l'-ăch, *a.* husks, chaff. *Bib'e.*

Caithlean, ka'l'-ăn', seedling; *caithlean* 'na fhiachail, *a seedling between his teeth.*

Caithleanach, ka'l'-an'-ach, *a.* seedy, husky; min *caithleanach, meal full of seedlings.*

Caithream, căr'-um, *n. f.* beating, as a drum, at regular intervals, *Is.*; joyful sound, shout of triumph and rejoicing; chum *caithream* a dheanamh ann ad chliù, *to rejoice in thy praise*; a loud shout of any kind; is *caithream* bròin am beul ar bàird, *and the shout of death in the mouth of our bards. Sm. H.*

Caithreamach, kăĕr'-um-ăch, *a.* beating at regular intervals; shouting for grief or joy.

Caithris, kăĕr''-ěsh, *n. f.* excessive fatigue from watching incessantly; the state of being exhausted and worn out by watching; watching.

Caithriseach, kaer'-ěsh-ach, *a.* fatigued by continual watching; restless; wanting regular rest; worn out by watching.

Caithrinn, kar''-ěnn, *n. f.* refuse of straw taken out of corn after being thrashed.

Caithrinnach, kăĕr'-enn-ěch, *v.* shake straw before bundling it, or making it into trusses.

Caithte, kăĕ'-tyà, *pt.* spent, worn out, consumed, exhausted, lean, lank.

Caithteach, kăĕ'-tyàch, *a.* apt to wear or waste one's strength; *caithteach* air duine, *apt to exhaust* or *wear one down soon*; wasteful, lavish, prodigal, profuse; duine *caithteach, a wasteful* or *prodigal person.*

Caithteachd, kăĕ'-tyachg, *n. f.* liability to be worn out; state of wearing or exhausting; waste, prodigality, profusion.

Caithtiche, kăĕ'-tyěch-à, *n. m.* a spendthrift.

Cal, kâll, *n. m.* cole-wort, greens, cabbage; (Scotch) kail; *càl* ceannan, *a dish of potatoes and greens mashed together*; *càl* ceairsleach, *cabbage*; *càl* colaig, *collyflower.*

Cala, kall'-à, *n. m.* land in the distance, as at sea; thog sinn *cala, we descried land*; a harbour, a haven, a port; cha d'thug thu do long gu *cala* fhathast, *you have not brought your ship into harbour yet*; thog sinn *cala* air an treas là, *we descried land on the third day*; *cala*-dhìreach an long, *slack-sheet*; written caladh also.

Cala-dhireach, kăll'-a-yhēr-ăch, *adv.* slack-sheet; right before the wind; in a secondary sense, in a straight line; *ca'a dhìreach* an aghaidh a chéile, *diametrically opposite.*

Calaich, kăl'-ěch, *v.* moor, anchor.

Calaman, kăl'-ăm-ăn, *n. m.* a dove, a pigeon.

Calanas, kăl'-ăn-us, *n. m.* spinning; working at wool, flax, hemp, &c. manafacturing.

Calbh, kăl'-uv, *n. m.* a twig, an osier, headland; gushing of water, *N. A.*; bald. *Irish.*

Calbhair, kal'-uv-ur, *a.* greedy of food. *Suth. Sh.*

Calc, kălk, *v.* caulk, drive, ram, push violently.

Calcadh, kalk'-Ă, *n. m.* caulking, cramming; *pt.* cramming, caulking, driving.

Calcaire, kălk'-ur-à, *n. m.* a caulker, a rammer.

Calg, kăl'-ag, *n. m.* awn, refuses of lint, beard of barley; a spear; bristles of pigs, &c.

Calgach, kal'-ug-ach, *a.* prickly, bristly.

Calg-dhireach, kal'-ug-yhēr'-ach, *adv.* straight. *Ir.*

Call, kăli, *n. m.* loss, detriment, damage, privation; is mòr mo *chall* ris, *great is my loss by it*; *much have I lost by it*; *pt.* losing, dropping; a' *call* air, *losing by it*; a' *call* airgid, *dropping money.*

Callag, kâll'-ag, *n. f.* the bird called the diver; the guillemot; eun dubh a' chrudlain.

Callaich, kâll'-ěch, *v.* tame, domesticate.

Callaid, kăll'-ăj, *n. f.* a partition; a hedge; an ti a bhriseas *callaid*, teumaidh nathair e, *he that breaketh a hedge, a serpent shall bite him, Bible*; (loitidh nathair e); a wig, *Mf.*; *a.* a fence.

Callaideach, kăll'-ăj-ach, *a.* surrounded, fenced.

Callaidh, kâll'-ě, *a.* domesticated, tame; beathaichan *càllaidh, domesticated animals.* In Irish, active, agile, beothail.

Callaidheachd, kâll'-ě-achg, *n. f.* tameness.

Callan, kăll'-ăn, *n. m.* noise, absurd hammering at any thing; hardness of the hands from working with spades, oars, &c; callosity; a corn.

Callda, same as Callaidh.

Calldach, kâll'-dach, *a.* losing, ruinous: *n. f.* loss, damage, detriment.

Calldachd, kalld'-ăchg, *n. f.* loss, damage.

Calm, kal'-um, *n. m.* a pillar, a thick-set stout-built person; a prop.

Calma, kal'-um-à, *a.* thick-set, brawny.

Calmachd, kal'-um-ăchg, *n. f.* stoutness.

Calmarr, kal'-um-ărr, *n. m.* one of Fingal's heroes.

Calmarra, kal'-um-arr-a, *a.* brawny, thick-set, well-made.

Calp, kăl'-up, *n. m.* the calf of the leg; the principal at interest; *calp* is riadh, *principal and interest*; a hawlyard.

Calp, kal'-up, *n. f.* a rivet nail.

Cam, kăm, *a.* blind of an eye; tha e *cam*, *he is blind of an eye*; crooked, bent; maide *cam*, *a crooked* or *bent stick*; *n. f.* a female blind of an eye; *v.* bend; curve *cham* thu am maide, *you bent the stick*; make crooked.

Camacag, kăm'-ăchg-ăg, *n. f.* a trip; casbhacaig.

Camag, kăm'-ăg, *n. f.* a curl, a ringlet, a crook, clasp; the temple; bhuail e 'sa *chamaig* e, *he struck in the temple*; a comma in writing.

Camag-gharraidh, kam-ăg-gharr'-ê, *n. f.* the hollow above the temple; the temple.

Caman, kam'-an, *n. m.* a shinty, a club for golf *or* cricket; golf-club.

Camanachd, kam'-ăn-ăchg, *n. f.* playing at golf *or* shinty.

Camart, kam'-ărt', *n. f.* a wry-neck. *N.*

Camh, kăv, *n. m.* the dawn. *Bible Ref.*

Camhanach, kav'-an-ach, *n. m.* the dawn. *Bible.*

Camp, kâmp, *n. m.* a camp. *Teut. Bible. T. Basq.*

Campachadh, kâmp'-ach-X, *pt.* encamping; tha aingeal Dè a' *campachadh*, *the angel of the Lord encamps*, *Ps.*; *n. m.* encampment.

Campaich, kamp'-ėch, *v.* encamp, surround.

Campar, kămp-'ur, *n. m.* vexation, uneasiness, grief; na cuireadh sin *campar* ort, *let not that vex you.*

Camparach, kamp'-ur-ach, *a.* galling, vexing, sad.

Camshron, kam'-hrŏn, *n. f.* a crooked nose.

Camshronach, kam'-hron-ach, *a.* having a crooked nose; *n. m.* and *a.* Cameron, Cameronian.

Camas, kam'-as, *n. m.* a bay, a creek, the space between the thighs; a'n *camas* Chluba nan ioma stuadh, *in the bay of Cluba of many waves*; a mould for making bullets. *Arab.*

Can, kan, *v.* say, affirm, speak, express, sing; *canaibh* òran, *sing a song. B.*

Cana, kăn'-a, *n. f.* a little whale. *Skye, &c.*

Canabhas, kan'-a-vas, *n. m.* canvas, sackcloth. *Lat.*

Canach, kan'-ach, *n. m.* moss-cotton, down; mountain-down; a sturgeon.

Canach', kân'-ach, *gen.* of Càin; a' pàigh na *cànach, paying the fine* or *tribute.*

Canain, kàn'-ăn', *n. f.* language, speech, dialect.

Canainiche, kạn'-an-ėch-à, *n. m.* a linguist.

Cangluinn, kăng'-llun', *n. f.* vexation, aimheil.

Canna, kănn'-à, *n. m.* a can; *cantharus*, *Latin.*

Cannach, kănn'-ăch, *n m.* sweet-willow, myrtle.

Canntaireachd, kănnd'-ar'-ăchg, *n. f.* humming a tune; chanting, singing; warbling.

Canran, kàrr'-an, *n. m.* bickering, scolding, and reflecting incessantly; grumbling.

Canranach, kan'-ran-ach, *a.* bickering, fretful.

Caob, kùb, *n. m.* a lump, as in thread; a bite, and also a nip, *N. H.*; *v.* bite; nip, crim.

Caoch, kāoch, *a.* void, hollow; falamh.

Caochag, kāoch'-ag, a nut without the kernal; blind man's buff; *falach fead.*

Caochail, kāoch'-ėlly, *v.* change, alter; putrefy; *chaochail* e a ghnùis, *he changed his countenance*, *B.*; expire, die, give up the ghost; *chaochail* e, *he yielded up the ghost. B.*

Caochan, kāoch'-an, *n. m.* fermented worts; in Scotch, wash; tosgaid *chaochain, wash vat*; a gurgling streamlet; a purling rill, purling noise, like worts fermenting.

Caochlach, kāoch'-llach, *a.* changeable.

Caochladh, kāoch'-llă, *n. m.* change, alteration; *pt.* changing, putrefying.

Caochlaideach, kāoch'-llăj-ăch, *a.* changeable, variable; uair *chaochluideach, changeable* or *variable weather*; fickle, inconstant, whimsical; duine *caochlaideach, a fickle* or *inconstant person.*

Caochlaideachd, kāoch'-llăj-ăchg, *n. f.* changeableness, variableness; inconstancy, mutability, fickleness.

Caog, kāog, *v.* wink, connive.

Caogad, kāog'-ad, *n. f.* for coigead, fifty

Caogadh, kāog, *n. m.* a wink; *pt.* winking; a' *caogadh* sùl 'na biom, *let me not wink with the eye. Ross. Ps.*

Caoidh, kúė-yh", *v.* lament, weep, wail for loss of; *n. m.* lamentation, wailing, weeping; *pt.* lamenting, wailing, weeping.

Caoile, kāoėl'-à, *n. f.* want of fodder for cattle, leanness, dearth; bhàsaich an crodh leis a' *chaoile, the cattle starved for want of fodder*; narrowness, straitness, slenderness.

CAOILEAD, kāoěl'-ud, *n. f.* degree of narrowness, smallness; fineness, as linen, yarn, &c.

CAOILLEAN, kāoěll'-an', *n. m.* a twig, slatag. *N. H.*

CAOILTEAN, kāoěl'-tyun, *pl.* of caol, a sound, a strait, a narrow; a' seòladh thro na *caoiltean, sailing through the sounds* or *straits.*

CAOIMHEACH, kúėv'-ach, *a.* kind; *n. m.* a friend.

CAOIMHNEALACHD, kaŏěn'-nyal-ăchg, *n. f.* kindness; courteousness; agreeableness to the touch.

CAOIMHNEAS, kaŏěn''- *or* kāŏěv'-nyas, *n. m.* kindness, mildness; affability; a kind turn.

CAOIMHNEIL, kaoen'-nyal, *or* kaŏěv'-nyal, *a.* kind, mild, affable, courteous, benevolent.

CAOIN, kāoěn, *v. n.* weep, lament, mourn, deplore, wail; regret; *a.* kind, tender; seasoned, as hay, sheaf-corn, fish, &c. *n. f.* sward; *caoin* uaine, *green sward*; rhind; bhrisd e *caoin* an leathraich, *he broke the rhind of the leather, Is.*; the right side; *caoin* is as-*caoin, the right and wrong side. Sk.*

CAOINEACHADH, kāoin'-ăch-X, *n. m.* seasoning *or* drying hay, fish, &c.; exposure to the sun's heat for the purpose of drying.

CAOINEADH, kāoėn'-X, *n. m.* and *pt.* weeping, wailing, mourning; lamenting, lamentation.

CAOINEAR, kaŏěn'-ur, *n. m.* sheer indifference.

CAOINEARACH, kaŏėn'-ăch, *a.* indifferent, careless.

CAOINEIS, kaŏěn'-as, *n. m.* taking off, gibing, jeering.

CAOINEISEACH, kaŏěn'-ash-ach, *a.* indifferent, apt to gibe, jeer, *or* take off.

CAOINEISEACHD, kaŏěn'-ash-achg, *n. f.* assumed indifference; fastidiousness; foolish pride.

CAOINICH, kāoėn'-ėch, *v.* dry, season, expose to dry, as hay, fish

CAOIN-SHUARACH, kāoėn-hŭăr-ăch, *a.* indifferent

CAOIN-SHUARACHD, kāoėn'-huar-ăchg, *n. f.* indifference.

CAOINTEACH, kāoėnt'-ach, *n. f.* a female fairy *or* water-kelpie, whose particular province it was to forewarn her favourite clans of the approach of death in the family, by weeping and wailing opposite the kitchen door; *a.* weeping, mourning; bha acain *caointeach, his moan was mournful. Sm.*

CAOIR, kāoir, *n. f.* a foam with sparks of fire in it, as in a stormy sea; a flame, accompanied with noise; a fiery flame; na tonnan na *caoir, the waves like flame. Oss. C.*

CAOIREALL, kaŏir'-all, *n. m.* one of Fingal's bards; loud and continual speaking.

CAOIRTHEACH, kāoir'-hach, *a.* flaming, fiery; sruth *caoirtheach* bho chruaich nam beann, *a fiery stream from the brow of the mountain. Oss.*

CAOL, kāoll, *a.* slender, thin; lean, lank, attenuated; narrow; *n. m.* a narrow; a sound, a strait, a frith; *caol* Ila, *the sound of Islay*; an *caol* Muileach, *the sound of Mull*; the small parts; *caol* an droma, *the small of the back, the spine*; *caol* an dùirn, *the wrist*; *caol* na coise, ceangail a' chaoil, *bind him hand and foot*; an tigh *caol, the narrow house, the grave.*

CAOLACH, kāol'-ach, the worst part of corn; the herb, fairy flax. *Ir.*

CAOLAICH, kāol'-ėch, *v.* make narrow, taper.

CAOLAN, kāol'-an, *n. m.* gut, tripe.

CAOLAS, kāol'-as, *n. m.* a sound, a strait.

CAOMH, kùv, *a.* kind, mild, beloved, meek, gentle; labhair e gu *caomh* ris a ghruagaich, *he spoke kindly to the damsel*; cha *chaomh* leam e, *he is not dear to me, I do not like him*; a dearly beloved person; an tog mi mo shiuil 's gun *chaomh* am fagus, *shall I hoist my sails without a friend being near, Sm.*; kindness, hospitality; *caomh* mo theach, *the hospitality of my house. D. B.*

CAOMHACH, kùv'-ăch, *n. m.* a friend. *Sm.*

CAOMHACHAS, kùv'-ach-us, *n. m.* chambering; sensuality, dalliance.

CAOMHALACHD, kùv'-ăl-ăchg, *n. f.* kindness of disposition; kindness; urbanity.

CAOMHAIL, kùv'-al, *a.* kind, friendly.

CAOMHAINN, kùv'-ėnn, *v.* spare, save, economise, reserve; *caomhainn* e gus an màireach, *reserve it till to-morrow*; na *caomhainn* e, *do not spare it.*

CAOMHANTACH, kùv'-ant-ach, *a.* sparing, economical, frugal, saving; stingy.

CAOMHANTACHD, kùv'-ant'-ăchg, *n. f.* economy, frugality; a saving disposition, parsimony.

CAOMHNADH, kùv'-nX, *n. m.* economy, frugality, parsimony; *pt.* saving, sparing, reserving.

CAOR, kāor, *n. f.* a fiery wave, as in a storm; the berry of the mountain ash.

CAORA, kāor'-à, *n. f.* a sheep; caoirich, more than one sheep; *gen.* caorach; ri taobh na *caorach, at the side of the sheep*; berries; *caora* bada miann, *the stone brambles*; *caora* feullain, *ivy berry*; *caora* madaidh, *dog-berry*; *caora*-fiadhag, *crow-berries*; *caora* dromain, *elder berries.*

CAORAN, kāor′-an, *n. m.* a fragment of peat.

CAORNAG, kāorn′-ag, *n. f.* a wild hive, a battle, a fray, a squabble.

CAORUNN, kāor′-unn, mountain ash *or* rowan tree; rowan berries; the wood of the mountain ash.

CAOTHACH, kāo′-ăch, *n. m.* madness, insanity; confounded with cuthach, *hydrophobia.*

CAPALL, kap′-ull, *n. f.* a mare, in some places a horse, a colt. *Dr. Stew. Dirg.*

CAPAL-COILLE, kap′-ull-kaŏll-lyȧ, *n. m.* the great cock of the wood; caperkailly.

CAR, kâr, *n. m.* for Caraid in poetry; mossy soft ground; a reub an *càr* (caraid) dha 'n robh' ghràdh, *that tore the friend whom she loved*; Latin, carus dear.

CAR, kăr, *prep.* during, for the space of; *car* tiotaibh, *for a moment*; *car* oidhche, *for the space of a night*; *car* uair, *for a time*; *car* miosa, *for a month*; *car* greais, *for a while*; *car* ùine bhig, *for a short time.*

CAR, kăr, *n. m.* a turn, a twist, a bend; meandering; an *car* a bhios 'san t-sean mhaide is duilich a thoirt as, *the bend* or *twist that is in an old stick, is not easily made straight*; trick, fraud, deceit; gach *car* a th' ann is cleas, *all his wiles and tricks, Ps.*; thug e an *car* as am, *he cheated me, he outwitted me*; *car* a mhuiltean, *a sommerset*; *car* air char, *topsy-turvy*; contact, direction; gach ni a thig ad *charaibh, every thing that comes your way,* or *direction*; an *caraibh* a chéile, *in contact with each other, in mutual contact*; thug thu mo *char* is mo leth *char* asam, *you have cheated me in earnest, to all intents and purposes*; aom 'na *caraibh, bend in their direction, in their way*; an *caraibh* a bhrocluinn, *in the direction of its den, Is. Oss.*; motion, movement; na cuir *car* dheth, *do not move it*; gun aon *char* a chur deth, *without movement, without stirring it*; a string of beads, pearls, &c.; *car* chneap, *a string of beads; car* neamhuinn, *a string of pearls.*

CAR, kâr, *n. m.* a mossy plain, a fen; mar channach *càir, like the moss cotton Song.*

CARA, kăr′-a, for caraid; gu cluinn mi mo *chàra, that I may hear my friend.*

CARACH, kăr′-ach, *a.* deceiving, deceitful; tha 'n soaghal so *carach, this world is deceitful*; fear *carach, a deceitful person*; cho *carach* ris a mhadadh ruadh, *as wily as a fox*; whirling, circling; measg osnaich *charach, amid the circling breeze. Oss.*

CARACHADH, kăr′-ăch-Ă, *pt.* moving, stirring.

CARACHD, căr′-ăchg, *n. f.* wrestling, sparring; deceitfulness; *carachd* an t-saoghail so, *the deceitfulness of this world.*

CARADH, kâr′-Ă, *n. m.* condition, state; is truagh mo *chàradh, sad is my condition*; is dona an *càradh* a dh' fhàg thu air, *you have left him in a sad condition*; *pt.* mending, repairing, dressing; placing.

CARADH, kăr′-Ă, *pt.* cheating, deceiving.

CARAICH, kăr′-èch, *v.* move, stir, turn; na *caraich* e, *do not stir it*; cha *charaich* thu as an so, *you shall not move hence; charaich* iad, *they moved.*

CARAID, kăr′-ėj, *n. m.* a male friend *or* relation; banacharaid, *a female friend or relation.*

CARAID, kàr′-ăj. *n. f.* a pair, a brace, a couple, a married couple.

CARAIDICH, kâr′-ăj-ėch, *v.* join together in pairs *or* couples.

CARAMASG, kăr′-a-măsk, *n. m.* confusion.

CARBAD, kârb′-ud, *n. f.* a chariot; araon *carbad* is marc-shluagh, *both chariot and horsemen, B.*; a bier.

CARBAD, kărb′-ad, *n. m.* a jaw bone; buail am balach air a *charbad* is buail am bàlgair air an t-sròin, *strike the clown on the jaw, and the dog on the nose. G. P.*

CARBADAIR, kărb′-ad-air, *n. m.* a charioteer.

CARBH, kărv, *n. f.* a ship *or* boat, built after a particular fashion. *Is.*

CARBHAIDH, karv′-ė, *n. f.* caraway.

CARBHANACH, karv′-ăn-ăch, *n. m.* a carp. *Is.*

CARCAIR, kark′-ur, *n. m.* a prison, *Bible*; Latin, a sink, *or* sewer. *North Highlands. Inn. W.*

CARD, kârd′, *n. f.* a card; *v.* card wool, &c.

CARD, kârd, *n. m.* an English gallon, *or* two Scotch pints; a quarter of a yard.

CARDAIR, kârd′-ăr′, *n. m.* carder.

CARDAIREACHD, kard′-ăr-ăchg, *n. f.* carding.

CARLAS, kâr′-lus, *n. f.* excellence. *Smith's Poems.*

CARN, kârn, *n. m.* a heap of stones; kairn raised over the tombs of heroes; cuiridh mise clach ad *charn sa, I will befriend you yet*; *pl.* cùirn; *v.* heap, pile, accumulate; a *carnadh* airgid, *accumulating silver* or *wealth.*

Carn, karn, *n. m.* a horning. *Irish.*

Carnach, kărn′-ăch, *n. f.* a stony place, *a.* rocky.

Carnadh, kărn′-X, *pt.* heaping, piling; *charnadh* le Daorghlas an t-seilg, *the game was piled up by Dorglas.*

Carnag, karn′-ag, *n. f.* a small fish, *Sk.*; a she terrier. *N.*

Carnaid, kărn′-ăj, *n. f.* flesh colour. *Mack.*

Carnanaich, kărn-an-ėch, *p.* Highlanders. *Arm.*

Carr, kârr, *n. m.* the scurvy, scab, mange; duine aig am bheil *càrr, a man that has the scurvy, Bible*; scall *or* leprosy; plàigh 'na *carra, the plague of the leprosy, Bible*; a dray, a sledge; each anns a' *chàrr, a horse in the dray* or *sledge.*

Carrach. kărr′-ach, *a.* scorbutic, itchy, mangy; having an uneven surface; am fear a bhios *carrach* 'sa bhaile so, bithidh e *carrach* 'sa bhaile ad thall, *he that is scabby* or *mangy in this town, will be mangy every where*; crustacious, as potatoes.

Carrachan, kărr′-ăch-an, *n. m.* a little, old fashioned fellow; the fish called the lump, frog-fish, *or* chub, *greasaiche*; *carrachan* cnuacach, *rock fish* or *conger-eel.*

Carragh, kărr′-a, *n. m.* an erect stone, raised as a monument; a monument; a pillar; far an d'ung thu an *carragh, where thou didst anoint the pillar. Bible*; thamhaisg nan *carragh, ye spectres of the rock. Oss.*

Carraid, kărr′-ăj, *n. f.* fatigue and anguish from watching a sick person dear to one; conflict, trouble; *carraid* nan sìon, *the conflict of the elements, O.*; le *carraid* ghéir, *with sore distress* or *fatigue. Sm.*

Carraideach, kărr′-ăj-ach, *a.* fatigued and sorely distressed from watching a sick person; grieved and fatigued; troublesome; afflicting.

Carraideachd, kărr′-ăj-ăchg, *n. f.* fatigue.

Carraig, kărr′-ėg, *n. f.* a headland, a cliff, a rock jutting into the sea, serving as a quay *or* fishing station; a rock; *carraig* mo neart, *the rock of my strength, Sm.*; mar thuinn ma *charraig, as waves round a cliff, Oss.* In common speech never used for *creig.*

Carran, kărr′-an, *n. m.* scurvy grass.

Carran-creige, kărr-an-krāg′-ȧ, *n. m.* fish called a lump.

Carrsan, kârr′-san, *n. m.* a wheezing in the throat, catarrh.

Carrsanach, kârr′-săn-ach, *a.* subject to catarrh, wheezing, hoarse.

C'arson, kăr-son′, *adv.* why, wherefore; *c'arson* a ghabh na cinnich boil, *why did the heathen rage.*

Cart, kârt, *n. m.* a quart, a quarter, a lippy. *North H.*

Cart, kărt, *v.* clean, as stable, &c.

Cartadh, kărt′-X, *n. m.* act of cleaning a stable, byre, stye, &c.; tanning.

Cartan, kărt′-an, *n. m.* a heath-mite.

Carthannach, kărr′-han-ăch, *a.* kind, polite.

Carthannachd, karr′-hann-ach, *n. f.* politeness.

Carthanta, karr′-hant-a, *a.* kind, polite.

Carthantachd, kărr′-han-tachg, *n. f.* politeness.

Car-tuathail, kărr′-tūă-al, *n. m.* a wrong turn; unprosperous course.

Cas, kăs, *v. n.* twist, wreathe, bend, curl; a' *casadh* an t-snàth, *twisting the thread*; *chas* e ma làimh e, *he wreathed it about his hand*; gnash, girn, gape; make mouths; *chas* e 'f hiachlan, *he gnashed with his teeth*; *chas* e bheul, *he gaped with his mouth, Bible*; near, approach; a *casadh* air a' bhaile, *approaching the town*; be angry with, enrage; *chas* e ris, *be enraged against him, he got angry with him*; brandish; *chas* e 'shleagh, *he brandished his spear. O.*

Cas, kás, *n. f.* foot, leg, stem, haft, handle, shaft; taobh do *choise, the side of your foot; cas* na sgine, *the haft of the knife; cas* an ùird, *the shaft* or *handle of the hammer*; aig *cois* na beinne, *at the foot of the hill*; *a.* short-tempered, irritable, passionate; duine *cas, an irritable* or *passionate man*; headlong; steep; abrupt; sruth *cas, a headlong stream, an impetuous or rapid current*; *cas* air a chéile, *close upon each other*; bruthach neo aonach *cas, a steep* or *headlong acclivity* or *ascent*; eager; *cas* gu comhrag, *eager for battle*; gu *cas, quickly, Sm. Oss.*; curled; cùl faineach *cas, curled, wreathed hair, Gil.*; *deg.* caise.

Cas, kâs, *n. m.* dilemma, predicament; hardship; distress, difficulty, emergency; anns gach *càs, in every emergency;* cha 'n e an *cas, it is not the difficulty;* 's ann dhuit is lèir mo *chàs, thou seest my distress.*

Casach, cäs′-ăch, *n f.* the outlet of a lake, (in *Su.* òs); a ford; a hook-line.

Casachdaich, kăs′-ăchg ėch, *n. f.* cough; casf huachdaich. *Islay.*

Casad, kas′-ad, *n. f.* a cough; *v.* cough.

Casadaich, kas′-ăd-ėch, *n. f.* cough; gripes in cattle, making them strike the belly with their feet.

Casadh, kăs′-X, *n. m.* and *pt.* grinning, twisting, approaching; gnashing; gaping.

Casag, kăs′-ag, *n. f.* a long coat.

Casaid, kăs′-aj, *n. f.* complaint, accusation; *v.* accuse, complain, lodge a complaint; chasaid e orm, *he lodged a complaint against me*; a' *casaid, lodging a complaint.*

Casaideach, kas′-ăj-ăch, *a.* prone, *or* apt to complain.

Casair, kas′-ur, *n. f.* sea drift. *Sk.*

Casan, kas′-an, *n. m.* a path, a walk.

Casbhrat, kas′-vhrat, *n. m.* a carpet.

Cas-chrom, kăs-chrōm′, *n. f.* a plough of a curious make, like a spade. *Skye.*

Casgadh, kăsg′-X, *pt.* stopping, staunching; a' *casgadh* 'na fola, *staunching the blood*; an f huil a ruith gun luibh 'ga *casgadh, the blood flowing without an herb to staunch it.*

Casgair, kăsg′-er, butcher, slaughter.

Casgairt, kasg′-ărt′, *n. m.* massacre, slaughter; *casgairt* ort féin, *may death take you.*

Casgradh, kasg′-rX, *n. f.* slaughter; mheasadh sinn mar choaraich chum a *casgraidh, we were esteemed as sheep for the slaughter*; *Bible*, (slad).

Casgoil, kâsk′-ēl′, *n. f.* dilemma, predicament; ann an *càsgoil, in a dilemma. Is.*

Caslach, kăs′-llach, *n. f.* a tribe. *Irish.*

Casnaid, kas′-năj, *v.* split wood. *Id.*

Caspanach, kăsp′-an-ach, *a.* parallel. *Ir.*

Casruisgt, kăs′-rŭsht, *a.* barefooted.

Cat, kat, *n. m.* and *f.* a cat; faodaidh an *cat* amharc air an righ, *a cat may look at a king*; Gr. kata; Lat. catus; Teut. katt; heap of potatoes, corn, &c. *N.* catag.

Cataich, kât′-ėch (tàlaich), *v.* tame. *Lw.*

Cath, kkă, *n. m.* a battle, a fight; struggle; chuir iad *cath* ris, *they struggled against him, Sm.*; an teichinn féin o'n *chath, should I myself desert the battle.*

Cath, kâ, *v.* winnow, fan; a' *càthadh* san t-sabhal, *winnowing in the barn*; in many parts of the continent of Argyle, a gréidheadh 'san t-sabhal; *n. m.* seeds, (caith).

Cathach, kă′-ăch, *n. m.* a warrior; seachd *cathaich, seven warriors. Tradition.*

Cathachadh, kă′-ach-X, *p.* fighting, struggling; a' *cathachadh* riut, *struggling against you.*

Cathag, kă′-ag, *n. f.* a daw, a jackdaw.

Cathaich, ka′-ėch, *v.* fight, contend, struggle.

Cathair, kă′-hyur′, *n. f.* a chair, a gig, *Islay*; a city, a town, a throne; *cathair* an righ, *the king's throne*; *gen.* cathrach; each na *cathrach, the gig horse*; *cathair* breathanais, *judgment seat, tribunal.*

Cathan, kă′-ăn, *n. m. abb.* yarn on the warping machine, crann-dealbh.

Cathmhor, kâ′-vhur, *a.* husky, chaffy; 'se am fobharadh gaothmhor a ni an coirce *cathmhor, it is the windy harvest that makes the oats husky.*

Cat-luch, kăt′-lŭch, *n. m.* a mouse-trap. *Lw.*

Catran, kat′-ran, *n. m.* the fourth of a stone of cheese, butter, wool, &c. *Is.*

Ce, kā, *int. pron.* who, which, what; *adv.* c'e do lamh, *shew me your hand, reach me your hand.*

Ce, kā, *n. m.* the earth; an cruine *cè, the globe, the earth, the world.*

Ceabhar, kèv′-ur, a slight *or* gentle breeze; the state of being slightly intoxicated.

Ceach, kech, *int.* expression of dislike.

Cead, kād², *n. m.* leave, permission, license, liberty; farewell, adieu; iarr *cead, ask liberty* or *leave*; gun do *chead* a' ghabhal, *without asking your permission*; an d' f huair thu *cead, have you got liberty?* thoir dhomh *cead, give me leave*; le'r *cead, with your permission*; tha le'r *cead, yes, sir* or *madam*, or *with your permission*; thoir a *chead* da, *set him about his business; cead* dol dachaidh, *permission to go home*; *cead* fuireachd, *liberty to remain*; gun *chead, without permission.*

Ceadachail, kād²′-ach-ăl, *a.* allowable, permissible, permissive.

Ceadaich, kăd′-ėch, *v.* permit, allow, grant, give permission; na *ceadaich* dha, *do not permit him*; am bheil thu *ceadachadh, do you permit? do you grant liberty? ceadaichte, permitted, granted, permissive.*

Ceadha, kā′-à, *n. m.* quay, part of a plough.

Ceaird, kyùrj, *or* kyârj, *n. f.* trade, occupation, handicraft, employment; dè's *ceaird* duit, *what is your occupation? B.*

Ceairdealachd, kyùrj′-ăl-ăchg, *n. f.* skillfulness; tradesman-like manner.

Ceardeil, kyùrj′-al, *a.* mechanical, tradesman-like, business-like.

Ceaird, kyârj, *gen.* of ceard, a tinker.

Ceairsle, kyărsh′-llâ, *n. f.* a clew.

Ceairsleach, kyărsh′-lyach, *a.* like a clew.

Ceairslich, kyarsh′-llich, *v.* make clews, wind, form into clews, coil.

Ceal, kyè'll, *n. m.* hue of the countenance; is bochd an *ceal* a th' ort, *you have a miserab'e expression of countenance.* In Irish, death.

Cealaich, kyèll′-ėch, *v.* eat, *Kirk. Ps. Ir*

CEALAIDEACH, kyè'll'-ăj-ach, *n. m.* and *f.* a miserable looking person.

CEALG, kyăll'-ag, *n. f.* hypocrisy; *prov.* for ceilg.

CEALGACH, kyăll'-ug-ach, deceitful, hypocritical, treacherous, cunning, crafty, wily.

CEALGAIR, kyall'-ug-ar', *n. m.* a hypocrite, a cheat, a rogue, a deceiver.

CEALGAIREACHD, kyăll'ug-ăr'-achg, *n. f.* hypocrisy, treachery, deceit, dissimulation; roimh gach ni, bithibh air ar faicill o thaois ghoirt nam Pharasach, eadhan *cealgaireachd, first of all, beware ye of the leaven of the Pharisees, even hypocrisy;* basachaidh dòchas a *chealgair, the hope of the hypocrite shall perish.*

CEALL, kyăll, *n. f.* a church. *Irish.*

CEALLAIRE, kyall'-ăr-à, *n. m.* head *or* superior of a church *or* monastery. *Ir.*

CEALLTAIR, kyăll'-lt-ăr', *n. m.* gray cloth. *No.*

CEANALTA, kyen"-ălt-à, *a.* docile, tractable, amiable, kind, mild, pleasant, urbane, polite.

CEANALTACHD, kyén"-alt-achg, *n. m.* docility, tractableness; mildness of disposition, urbanity, politeness.

CEANALTAS, kyen"-alt-us, *n. m.* same as ceanaltachd.

CEANFHIONN, kyén"-unn, *a.* gray-faced, as a beast; grayish.

CEANGAIL, kyéng'-ël', kyén'-nyàl, *v.* tie, bind, fetter, fasten, restrain; (from ceann and iall) ceangailte, bound; restrained; tied, fastened.

CEANGAL, kyéng'-al, &c. *n. m.* tie; fastening; obligation, a bond, a knot; *ceangal* posaidh, *betrothment*; ni thu *ceangal* posaidh, *thou shalt betroth a wife, Bible*; fo *cheangal* aig duine sam bith, *under restraint to any one*; am fear a *cheanglas* a's e a shiubhlas, *he that ties his bundle fast may walk without stopping*, G. *P.*; *pl.* ceanglaichean and ceangaltaichean.

CEANGLAICHE, kyéng'-llèch-à, *n. m.* a binder.

CEANN, kyănn, *n. m.* a head, point; end, limit; period, expiration; extremity; genius, ingenuity; chief, master, commander, attention; headland; hilt; thog tuinn an *cinn, waves reared their head*; sleagh is géire *ceann, a spear of the sharpest point*; *ceann* nan laoch, *the chief of the heroes*; an *ceann* bliadhna, *at the expiration of a year*; an *ceann* dà latha, *at the expiration of two days*; ma *cheannaibh* nan crann, *about the top of the trees*; bi ad *cheann* mhath dha, *be kind to him* (*be good to him*); 'na dhroch *cheann* duit, *very bad for you*; is dona an *ceann* sin duit, *that is against your health*; bha e na dhroch *cheann* da, *he behaved very ill to him, he used him ill, he was a bad master to him*; a' dol air *cheann* gnothuich, *going on business*; cha 'n eil an droch *cheann* aige, *he is not destitute of genius*; air *cheann* da tighinn dachaidh, *preparatory to his coming home*; an *ceann* a sè deug, *at long last*; an *ceann* a chéile, *mixed, assembled*; an *ceann* thri mìosan, *at the expiration of three months*; 's ann agad a tha 'n *ceann, how shrewd you are*! shiubhail mi Ila bho *cheann* gu *ceann, I travelled Islay, from one extremity to the other*; na cuir *ceann* na leithid sin, *do not attempt such a thing*; thoir an *ceann* deth, *be head him*; a chur *ceann* air stri, *to conclude the strife, O.*; am a bheir ar n-amhghar gu *ceann, a time that will bring our troubles to a close, M. L.*; *ceann* 'na ciche, *the nipple*; an *ceann* t otaibh, *in a little while*; an *ceann* tacain, *in a little while*; *ceann* nan lann, *the hilt of the sword, O.*; dè an *ceann* a rinn e ruit, *what attention did he show you*? gus an liath do *cheann, tell you are grey-headed*; liath thu mo *cheann, your conduct has made my head grey*; ghabh e an saoghal ma *cheann, he took the range of the wide world*; as *ceann* an athair, *above the firmament*; an *ceann* shìos, *the fàrthest off extremity*; an *ceann* shuas, *the upper end* or *extremity. Oss. B. Arm. Is. C.*

CEANNABHARD, kyann"-a-vhărd, *n. m.* and *f.* commander-in-chief, commander, a leader; *ceannabhard means, literally,* the mean bard, the BARDS formerly being among the commanders of armies; *see* M'Dhomhnaill; *ceannard* must be a corruption of *ceannabhard.*

CEANNACH, kyănn'-ach, *n. m.* a present, a reward, compensation; a bribe; *ceannach* geal nuair thig an sneachd, *a white present when the snow comes*; cha *cheannach* air an ubh an gog, *the egg is no compensation for the noise (cackling)*; *pt.* purchasing, buying; a *cheannach* fiodh, *to purchase timber.*

CEANNACHD, kyann'-ăchg, *n. f.* merchandise, commerce, traffic; agus ni sibh *ceannachd* 'san tìr, *and ye shall traffic in the land*; oir is fhearr a *ceannachd* na *ceannachd* airgid, *for her merchandise is better than the merchandise of silver. Bible.*

CEANNAICH, kyann'-èch, *v.* purchase, buy, redeem; traffic; a *cheannaich* sinn cho daor, *which we so dearly purchased*; *ceannaichte, purchased, bought.*

CEANNAICHE, kyann'-èch-à, *n. m.* a purchaser, a buyer, *West*; *North*, a merchant (marsanta).

CEANN-AIMSIR, kyann-em'-shèr, *n.m.* term, period; epoch, date, era.

CEANNAIRC, kyann'-ăĕrk, *n. f.* rebellion, sedition, mutiny, insubordination.

CEANNAIRCEACH, kyann'-ăĕrk-ach, *a.* rebellious, seditious, mutinous; perverse; stubborn.

CEANNAIRE, kyann'-ar'-â, *n. m.* a horse-driver, *Lw.*; a hammer. *Shaw.*

CEANN-AOBHAIR, kyann-ăov'-ur, *n. f.* a prime *or* first cause.

CEANNAODACH, kyann'-aŏd-ach, *n.m.* head-dress.

CEANNARD, kyann'-ard, *n. f.* a lofty head, also a commander, a leader, a chief.

CEANNARDACH, kyann'-ard-ach, *a.* high-headed.

CEANNARDACHD, kyann'-ărd-ăchg, *n.f.* arrogance; superiority, chieftainship. *D. M. L.*

CEANNAS, kyann'-as, *n. f.* superiority, pride. *M. L.*

CEANNASACH, kyann'-ăs-ăch, *a.* proud, aspiring.

CEANNASACHD, kyănn'-as-ăchg, *n. f.* ambition, pride.

CEANNASG, kyann'-ăsg, *n. f.* hair-lace. *Irish.*

CEANNLAIDIR, kyann'llăj-er, *a.* stubborn, mulish, headstrong, self-willed.

CEANN-CINNE, kyann'-kyènn-è, *n. m.* a chieftain; also keann-feadhna, ceann-finne, a chieftain.

CEANNSACHADH, kyănn'-săch-X, *pt.* subduing; subjecting; keeping under authority.

CEANNSACHD, kyann'-ssăchd, *n. f.* subordination, authority, government; temperance.

CEANNSAICH, kyann'-ssèch, *v.* subdue; conquer, quell, train; ceannsaichte, subdued, quelled.

CEANNSAL, kyănn'-sal, *n. f.* subjection.

CEANNSALACH, kyann'-sal-ach, *a.* authoratative.

CEANNSALACHD, kyann'-săl-ăchg, *n. f.* sway.

CEANN-SIMID, kyann-shēm"-ėj, *n. m.* tadpole.

CEANN-TIRE, kyann-tyēr'-â, *n. m.* a peninsula, headland, promontory, land's end; Kintyre.

CEANN-TOTA, kyann'-tot'-a, *n. m.* bench-piece.

CEANN-UIDHE, kyann'-ŭĕ, *n. m.* journey's end, destination; hospitable landlord. *Mt.*

CEAP, kāp[2], *n. m.* a last; a clog *or* stumbling-block on a beast's foot; the stocks; a snare; do leag iad *ceap, they laid a snare, Ps.*; *v.* intercept, stop, obstruct; *ceap* e, *intercept* or *stop him*; carp.

CEAP, kepp, a cap; Chaldee, ceip, a cap.

CEAPADH, kāp'-X, *pt.* intercepting, catching, carping; a *cheapadh* chuileag, *catching flies.*

CEAPAIRE, kāp'-ur'-â, *n. m.* bread covered with butter; and sometimes overlaid with cheese.

CEAPANTA, kāp'-ant-â, *a.* carping; snatching, carping.

CEARB, kerb, *or* ker'-ub, *n. f.* a skirt, corner; a rug e air *chirb, he laid hold of a skirt*; a defect, a blemish; òran gun *chearb, a song without blemish* or *defect.*

CEARBACH, ker-ub'-ăch, *a.* ragged, imperfect, unfortunate; is *cearbach* nach robh thu so, *it is a pity you were not here*; is *cearbach* an gnothuch e, *it is an unfortunate affair.*

CEARBAN, ker'ub-an, *n. m.* the sail-fish; *cearban* feoir, the plant crow-foot.

CEARC, kerk, *n. f.* a hen; cearcan, hens; *cearc* fhrangach, *a turkey hen*; *cearc* fhraoich, *moor hen*; *cearc* thomain, *a partridge.*

CEARCALL, kerk'-ăll, *n. m.* a hoop; circumference; *cearcall* fuileach rè 's i làn, *the bloody circumference of the full moon. Oss.*; gad chuireadh tu *cearcall* air Albainn, *though you should include all Scotland.*

CEARCALLACH, kerk'-all-ach, *a.* hooped.

CEARD, kyârd', *n. m.* a tinker; a blackguard; *ceard* airgid, *silversmith*; *ceard* òir, *goldsmith*; *ceard* staoin, *tinsmith*; *ceard* umha, *coppersmith.*

CEARDACH, kyârd'-ach, *n. f.* a smithy; forge.

CEARDAIL, kyârd'-al, *a.* tinker-like.

CEARDALACHD, kyard'-al-ăchg, *n. m.* shameful conduct; ingenuity. *A m.*

CEARDAMAN, kyârd'-am-an, *n. m.* a hornet; a dung-beetle.

CEARN, kyârn, *n. m.* corner; quarter; region; *cearnan* iomallach, *remote corners*; sluagh bho gach *cearn, people from every quarter*; co an *cearn* do 'n t-saoghal am bheil e, *in what quarter of the globe is he?*

CEARNACH, kyârn'-ach, *a.* angular, cornered, square; victorious, *Ir.*; *n. m* a pane of glass.

CEARR, kyărr, *a.* wrong, awkard; an taobh *cearr, the wrong side*; chaidh e *cearr, he went wrong*; *adv* improperly; is *cearr* a fhuaradh thu, *you have acted very improperly.*

CEARRA, kyărr'-â, *n. f.* impropriety, wrongfulness.

Cearrach, kyârr′-ach, *a.* dexterous, *H.S.*; *n. m.* a gamester.

Ceart, kyart, *a.* right, just, upright, proper, fair, correct; tha thu *ceart, you are quite correct*; bha Noah 'na dhuine *ceart* agus iomlan, *Noah was a just man and perfect*; exact, precise; very, identical; a *cheart* duine, *the very man, the identical man*; an *ceart* ni a bha dhì orm, *the very thing I wanted*; an 'sa *cheart* là, *on the very same day*; an *ceart* uair, *this moment*; *adv.* equally, just; exactly, precisely; *ceart* cho math neo maith, *equally well*; *ceart* mar thuirt thu, *exactly as you said, precisely as you said*; *ceart* mar sin, *just so, precisely so*; *ceart* mar nach d' thugadh Dia fainear, *just as if God did not observe*; is *ceart* cho math leam, *I like equally well*; *ceart* mar gu'm bitheadh, *just as if it were*; *n. m.* justice, propriety; is rinn 'se an *ceart, and he executed justice, Isl. Oss. B. Ps.*; cur *ceart, put to rights, rectify, correct, adjust.*

Certachadh, kyărt′-ach-X, *n. m.* amendment; *pt.* rectifying, correcting, amending, putting to rights; adjusting, trimming; *ceartaichean*, little domestic jobs.

Ceartachail, kyărt′-ach-al, *a.* rectifiable.

Ceartachair, kyart′-ăch-ur′, *n. m.* a rectifier, adjuster, corrector, regulator.

Ceartaich, kyart′-èch, *v.* rectify, adjust, amend, put in order, *or* to rights.

Ceartaiche, kyart′-èch-å, *n. m.* a corrector.

Ceartas, kyărt′-us, *n. m.* justice, equity; dean *ceartas, decide* or *give sentence impartially*; is siad *ceartas* agus breitheanas àite tàimh do righ chaithreach, *justice and judgment are the habitation of thy throne*; do bheir se *ceart* breith air do shluagh, *he shall pronounce a righteous judgment upon thy people. B. Ross.*

Ceartchreideamh, kyart′-chraŏj′-X, *n. m.* soundness of faith, orthodoxy; *ceartchreideach, orthodox, sound in the faith.*

Ceartair, kyart′-ar′ (ceart′-uair), *adv.* this moment.

Ceasach, kās[2]′-ăch (stair *or* staoire), a temporary bridge *or* foot-path over bogs. *Is.*

Ceasad, kās[2]′-ad, *n. m.* repining, grumble at your lot *or* your share of any thing; discontent; confounded with (casaid); *a' ceasad, repining, grumbling.*

Ceasadach, kās′-ăd-ach, *a.* repining, whining, discontented, displeased with one's share; (quite different from casaideach).

Ceasnachadh, kās′-nnăch-X, *n. m.* an examination; *pt.* examining, interrogating, catechising.

Ceasnachail, kās′-nach-al, *a.* interrogatory; inquisitive; impertinent.

Ceasnaich, kās′-nnèch, *v.* examine; catechise, interrogate, question; *ceasnaichte*, catechised.

Ceathach, kĕ′-ăch, *n. m.* mist, fog (ceò); an *ceathach* a seòladh, *the mist gliding*; mar *cheathach* (ceo) air beanntaibh, *as mist on the hills. Ossian.*

Ceathairne, kyaŏ′-ăern′-å, peasantry, (Tuath).

Ceathairneach, kaŏ′-ăĕrn-ach, *n. m.* a sturdy fellow; a freebooter, a robber, a hero.

Ceathairneachd, kaŏ′-ăĕrn-achg, *n. f.* heroism.

Ceathramh, ker′-ruv, *a.* the fourth; an *ceathramh* mìosa, *the fourth month*; an *ceathramh* bhliadhna, *the fourth year.*

Ceathrar, kĕrr′-ur, *a.* four; *ceathrar* mac, *four sons*; *ceathrar* nighean, *four daughters*; *n. m.* and *f.* four; thàinig *ceathrar* a stigh, *four came in.*

Ceig, kāĕg[2], *n. m.* a kick; *v.* kick, clot. *No.*

Ceigean, kāĕg′-ăĕn, *n. m.* a squat fellow; a turd. *Ar.*

Ceil, kā′l, *v. n.* conceal, hide, screen, shelter; ma *cheileas* sinn fhuil, *if we conceal his blood. Bible.*

Ceile, kā′l′-å, *n. m.* and *f.* a spouse; a match; husband; a wife; *céile* a h-òige, *the husband of her youth*; a *céile, her husband, her spouse*; a *chéile* cadail, *the wife of his bosom*; as match, it is never used but with *per. pronouns*; as a *chéile, asunder, disjoined*; a chum a *chéile, towards each other*; dh' fhuathaich iad a *chéile, they hated each other*; miadhail m' a *chéile, fond of each other*; cuir r'a *chéile* iad, *join them, make them fight*; bho *chéile, asunder, separate*; tha trocair agus firinn a' comhlachadh a *chéile, mercy and truth meet each other*; tha ceartas agus sìth a' pògadh a *chéile, justice and peace have kissed each other*; a' brosnachadh a *chéile, mutually urging each other*; thoir bho *chéile* iad, *separate them*; cum bho *chéile* iad, *keep them separate*; mar chìr mheala silidh do bhilean, a *chéile, as the honey-comb, thy lips drop, O spouse! Bible*; a' gabhal da *chéile, belabouring each other*; thar a *chéile, at variance*; across; ameasg a *chéile, mixed, confused, huddled*; chaidh iad am badaibh a *chéile, they fought tooth and nail.*

Ceilear, kā′l′-ar, *n. m.* warble, warbling.

Ceilearach, kā′l′-ăr-ach, *a.* warbling

CEILEIR, kā'l'-ėr, *v.* warble, sing sweetly; mar smeòrach a' *ceilearadh, warbling like a mavis*; cluinnidh Goll an *ceileir* 'na cheò, *Gaul shall hear their warbling in amazement.*

CEILEIRICHE, ka'l'-ėr-ėch-å, *n. m.* a warbler.

CEILICH, kā'-lėch, *v.* participate, eat, *Ross. Ps.*

CEILIDH, kā'-lė, *n. f.* visit; air *chèilidh, on a visit*; gossiping; cha robh *cèilteach* nach robh bradach, *there never was a person fond of gossiping, but would steal*; pilgrimage, sojourning; neas a bhios tu an *cèilidh* an t-saoghail, *while your earthly pilgrimage lasts.*

CEILTICH, kā'l'-tyech, *n. p.* Celts, Gaidhil.

CEILTINN, kā'l'-tyėnn, *n. f.* and *pt.* concealing, hiding.

CEILTIDH, kālly²'-tė, *a.* wise, sober, (bad). *S. D.*

CEILTE, kālly'-tyå, *pl.* concealed, hid, secret.

CEILTEACH, kāly''-tyach, *a.* fond of gossiping *or* visiting; *n. f.* a gossiping female.

CEIN, kāėn', *a.* distant; fad air falbh.

CEIR, kāėr, *n. m.* wax; *v.* seal, wax; *cèir* an litir, *seal* or *wax the letter.*

CEIREACH, kāĕr'-ach, *gen.* of céir, *a.* waxen.

CEIREAN, kāėr'-an', *n. m.* a wafer.

CEIREAN, kaėr²'-an, *n. f.* a plaster, poultice.

CEIRSLE, for ceairsle, a clew.

CEIRTE, kāėr'-tyå, *pt.* sealed, waxed.

CEIS, kāsh, *n. m.* a case, hamper. *North.*

CEIS-CHRANN, kēsh'-chrann, herb, polypody.

CEISD, kāshjj, *n. f.* a question, doubt, anxiety; agus cha robh a mhisneach aig neach air bith o sin suas *ceisd* a chur air, *and no man after that durst ask him any question, Mark* xii. 34; tha gun *cheisd, yes, undoubtedly, yes, indeed;* a beloved object, darling; tha, a *cheisd, yes, darling.*

CEISDEILACHD, kāshjj'-al-achg, *n. f.* questionableness.

CEISDEIL, kāshjj'-al, *a.* questionable, beloved.

CEISDLEABHAR, kāshjj'-llov'-ăr, *n. m.* catechism.

CEITEAN, kājt'-an', *n. m.* month of May beginning of summer, *W.*; *North,* fair weather, a favourable season; *ceitean* na h-òinsich, *from April 19th to May 12, H. S.*; *a.* belonging to May, &c.

CEITEANACH, kājt'-an'-ach, *n. m.* the size larger than a cuddy of the coal-fish.

CEITHEARRAMHACH, kā'-hyur-rav-ach, *a.* four-oared; *n. f.* a quadrereme, *or* four-oared boat; sgioba na *ceithearramhach, the crew of the four-oared boat,* or *quadrereme.*

CEITHIR, kā'-hyur', *a.* four.

CEITHIRCHASACH, kā'-hur-chas-ach, *a.* four-footed, quadruped; *n. c.* a quadruped, *or* four-footed animal.

CEITHIR-CHEARNACH, kā'-hyur-chyarn-ach, quadrangular, quadratic.

CEITHIR-DEUG, kā'-hyur-jāg *or* dyāg, *a.* fourteen.

CEITHIR-FILLTE, kā'-hyur-fēljt-tya, *a.* fourfold.

CEITHIR-OISINNEACH, kā'-hyur-osh-ėnn-ach, *a.* square, quadrangular, having four squares.

CEITHIR - SHLISNEACH, kā'-hyur-hllēsh-neach, *a.* four-sided, quadrilateral.

CEO, kyô, *n. m.* mist, fog; amazement; chaidh e 'na *cheò, he got quite amazed*; Goll 'na *cheo, Gaul in his cloud,* lit. *mist. Sm.*

CEOB, kyôb, *n. m.* drizzly rain; *N.* a nook.

CEOBAN, kyôb'-an, *n. m.* drizzly rain.

CEOBANACH, kyôb'-an-ach, *a.* drizzling, misty.

CEOBHAINNE, kyô'-vhan'-nyå, *n. m.* drizzling rain.

CEODHAR, kyô'-yhur, *a.* misty, foggy, obscure.

CEOL, kyôll, *n. m.* music, melody, harmony.

CEOLAN, kyôl'-an, *n. m.* a hum-drum of a person; one quite bewildered; a tender strain of music. *Oss.*

CEOL-CHUIRM, kyôll'-chūrm, *n. m.* a concert.

CEOLMHOIREACHD, kyôl'vhŭr-achd, *a.* melodiousness, harmony, harmoniousness.

CEOLMHOR, kyôl'-vhur, *a.* tuneful, harmonious, melodious.

CEOLRAIDH, kyôll'-rrė, *n. f.* the muses.

CEOTHMHOIREACHD, kyô'-vhur-ăchg, *n. f.* mistiness.

CEOTHMHOR, kyô'-vhur, *a.* misty, foggy.

CEOTHRAGACH, kyô'-rrăg-ăch, *v.* a drizzling rain; *a.* drizzly, misty, foggy.

CEOTHRAGACH, kyôr'-ag-ach, *n. f.* drizzliness.

CEOTHRANACH, *see* Ceothragach.

CEUD, kěăd, *n. m.* a hundred; a first hundred; *ceud* fear, *a hundred men*; a *cheud* fhear, *the first man.*

CEUDACH, kěăd'-ăch, *a.* centuple, in hundreds.

CEUDAMH, kěăd'-uv, *a.* the hundredth.

CEUDBHILEACH, kěăd'-vhill-ach, *a.* the herb centuary; lus nan ceud bhile.

CEUDFAITHNE, kyěad'-fà-nya, *n. m.* first principles; *a.* sense, faculty.

CEUDNA, kĕăn′ na,and kyeud′.na, *adv.* also; mar an *ceudna, also*; the one formerly mentioned, the same; an duine *ceudna, the same man, the identical man*; mar an *ceudna*, an duine so, *likewise this man*; air an dòigh *cheudna, in like manner.*

CEUDNACHD, kĕăd′-nachg, sameness, identity.

CEUD-TARRUINN, kĕăd′-tar-ènn, *n. m.* first drawing. singlings.

CEUD-THOISEACH, kĕăd′-hosh-ach, *n. m.* first principles, commencement.

CEUM, kām, *n. m.* a step, a pace, a degree; *v.* step, walk, pace; move; tri *cheum-anan, three paces; cheum* e gu mòr ma cuairt, *he walked majestically about, M'Lach. Ar.*; tha e *ceum* ni's fhaide mach, *he is a degree farther removed in connection.*

CEUS, kās, *v. a.* crucify, torture.

CEUSADAIR, kās′-ad-ar′, a tormentor.

CEUSADAIREACHD, kās′-ad-ar′-achg, *n. f.* crucifying.

CHA, bhâ, *neg. part.* not; *cha* bhuail mi, *I shall not strike*; *cha* dean mi, *cha* dean thu, *I will not do, thou wilt not*; *cha* d' èisd mi, *I did not listen.* Takes 'n before *f* aspirated and a vowel; *cha* 'n fhaod thu, *you must not*; *(pro.)* chănn′-āod-û; *cha* 'n iarr mi, *I will not ask*; *(pro.)* chan′-nĕăr-mē; *cha* 'n 'eil eadar an t-amadan agus an duine glic ach tairgse mhaith a ghabhail, 'nuair a gheibh e i, *there is no difference between the wise man and the fool, but to accept a good offer when in his power*; *cha* mhac mar an t-athair thu, *you are not a son worthy of your father*; after *cha, b, m, f, g,* and *t,* are aspirated; *cha* d' thèid e dhachaidh, *will not go home*; *cha* d' thig fuachd gu h-earrach, cruaidh chàs, na droch cheannach, *cold, hardships, and bad bargains come not till spring*; *f* takes 'n and d'; *cha* 'n fhidir an sathach an seang; 's mairg a bhiodh na thraill do 'n bhroinn, *the satiated will not sympathise with the starvling*; *wo to him who is a slave to his belly*; *cha* 'n fhiach duine gun sibht gun seòltachd, *a man without thrift and ingenuity is good for nothing*; *cha* 'n 'eil ann ach bò mhoal odhar agus bò odhar mhaol, *it is only a cow without horns that is dun, and a dun cow without horns—six of the one, and half a dozen of the other*; *cha* mhòr nach do mharbh e mi, *he almost killed me.*

CHAGAINN, chăg′-ènn, *part.* of caigainn, did chew.

CHAIDH, chăĕ′-yh′, *pt.* of theirig, go; theirig dhachaid, *go home*; *chaidh* e dhachaidh, *he went home*; theid e dhachaidh, *he shall go home.*

CHAILL, chăĕll, *pt. chaill* e, *he lost.*

CHAIN, chàĕn, *pt. chàin* e, *he traduced.*

CHAIRICH, châĕr′-èch, *pt.* did mend *or* repair.

CHAISG, chăĕshg, *pt.* did stop *or* appease.

CHAITH, chăĕ, *pt.* did spend *or* consume.

CHAOCHAIL, chāoch′-èlly′, *pt.* did change *or* die.

CHAOMHAINN, chāov′-ènn, *pt.* did spare.

CHAS, chăs, *pt.* did twist; gape *or* gnash.

CHEADAICH, chyād²′-ech, *v.* did permit *or* allow.

CHEANA, chyena, *adv.* already, before, now; rinn e sin *cheana, he did that already*; am fear a mharbh a' mhàthair *cheana*, bheireadh e beò a nis i, *he who killed his mother a little ago, would fain have her alive now. Pro.*

CHEILE, chyăll′-â, *asp. fem.* of céile; mo *chéile, my spouse*; *pron.* both; rinn sin le *chéi'e, both did that*; as a *chéile, asunder. See* Céile.

CHI, chē, *fut. ind.* of faic, see, behold; *chi* mi triuir, *I shall see three.*

CHINNTE, chènnt′-â, *as. f.* cinnte; air *chinnte, most assuredly, decidedly so.*

CHIONN, chyúnn, *prep.* because, as; *chionn* gun do bhoin e ruinn gu fiall, *because he dealt bountifully with us*; *chionn* nach do chreid iad, *as they did not believe. Bible.*

CHO, chō², *adv.* so, as; *cho* dalma, *so presumptuous*; *cho* chruaidh ris an stailinnn, *as hard as steel*; cha robh mi *cho* brònach 's *cho* dall, *I was not so mournful and blind. Ossian.*

CHOIDHCHE, chúĕ′-chă, *adv.* for ever, never; cha till e *choidhche, he shall never return*; a so suas *choidhche, henceforth and for ever.*

CHOINNICH, chōn′-nèch, *pt.* met; *choinnich* iad cheana, *they met already.*

CHUALA, chual′-â, *pt.* heard, did hear.

CHUIR, chŭĕr, *pt. chuir* sinn siol, *we sowed corn*; *chuir* e sneachd, *it snowed*; *chuir* sinn iad, *we invited them*; *chuir* sinn an so e, *we placed it here*; *chuir* sinn air folbh (*or* falbh, if you please) e, *we sent him off.*

CHUM, chûm, *pt.* come; *chum* sinn iad, *we kept* or *detained them*; *chum* an soitheach e, *the dish contained it.*

CHUM, chum, *prep.* for, towards; in order that; *chum* an duine, *to* or *towards the man*; *conj.* for the purpose of, in order that; a *chum* mo sgrios, *for the purpose of killing me,* or *destroying me*; more often and properly, thun.

CIA, kā², *int. pron. cia* aois thu, *how old are you? cia* b'e air bith do d' sheirbhisich aig am faighear e, *with whomsoever of thy servants it may be found, Bible cia* as duit, *whence? cia* minig, *cia* tric, *how often? cia* mheud, *how many? cia* mheud a th' ann, *how many are there of them?*

CIABH, kĕăv, *n. f.* lock of hair, tress; thuit i is sgaoil a *ciabh* air làr, *she fell, and her locks spread on the ground, Oss.*; *v.* tease, gall, vex; tha e 'gam *chiabadh, he is teasing me.*

CIABHACH, kĕăv'-ach, *a.* having ringlets, tressy.

CIABHAG, kĕăv'-ag, *n. f.* a lock, *or* tress of hair.

CIAL, nonsense, for ciobhal, a cheek, a brim.

CIALL, kĕăll, *n. m.* sense; meaning; prudence; as a *chéill, out of his senses, mad, deranged*; duine gun *chiall, a madman, a senseless fellow*; ceann na *céille, the prudent man*; *a* darling; a *chiall* mo chridhe, *my darling*; a *chiall* do 'na fearaibh, *my beloved of all men*; glac *ciall, be easy, do not forget yourself*; dè 's *ciall* duit, *what do you mean?* de's *ciall* do na daoine, *what do the people mean?* dè's *ciall* da sin, *what is the meaning of that?* de's *ciall* do m' aislinn, *what is the interpretation of my dream?* understanding, wisdom; tha e dhì *céille, he lacks understanding*; air bheag *céille, possessing little understanding, Bible*; 'se an *ciall* ceannaichte is fhearr, *bought wisdom is best*; *wisdom gained by experience is best*; air call a *chéille, losing his senses, doting. B.*

CIALLACH, kĕăll'-ach, *a.* sensible, sedate, prudent, rational; dean do ghnothuch gu *ciallach, do your business rationally*; ceilidh duine *ciallach* masla, *a prudent man covereth shame. B.*

CIALLACHAIL, kĕăll'-ach-al, *a.* significant.

CIALLAICH, kĕăll'-èch, *v.* signify, mean; dè tha sin a' *ciallachadh, what does that mean?*

CIALLRADH, kĕăll'-ră, *n. m.* a full sentence. *Ir.*

CIAN, kĕăn, *n. m.* long time; is ioma *cian* o nach robh e 'n so, *it is a long time since he was here, C.*; gu *cian* nan *cian, for ever, from all eternity*; *a.* tedious, long, dreary; is *cian* an oidhche, *tedious* or *dreary is the night*; bu *chian* leinn guin am buillean, *painful was the noise of their blows,* &c.; *adv.* as long as, while, whilst; *cian* a bhios mi beò, *while I live. S.*

CIANAIL. kĕăn'-al, *a.* solitary, dreary, tedious, forlorn; sad, lamentable, mournful.

CIANALACHD, kĕăn'-ăl-ăchg, *n. f.* tediousness, dreariness, loneliness· solitariness; sadness.

CIANALAS, kĕăn'-ăl-us, *n. m.* dreariness, sadness, melancholy; a' cur dhinn air *cianalas, banishing dreariness,* or *melancholy,* or *sadness.*

CIAR, kĕăr, *a.* dun, sable; roan; dusky, dark, brown; sléibhte nan earba *ciar, the hills of the dusky roes*; *n. m.* dusk, gloominess; *ciar* nan carn, *the gloom of the rocks, Oss. Ar.*; *v.* grow dusky; am feasgar a' *ciaradh, the evening getting dusky. O.*

CIARADH, kĕăr'-Ă, *n. m.* and *pl.* dusk of the evening, growing dusky; 'sa *chiaradh, in the dusk.*

CIARALACH, kĕăr'-ăl-ach, *a.* quarrelsome.

CIAT, kĕăt, *n. m.* pleasure, love; *ciat* mhòr, *great pleasure* or *love. Smith.*

CIATACH, kĕăt'-ăch, *a.* handsome, goodly, seemly; personable; beautiful; luach (pris) *chiatach, goodly price, B.*; duine *ciatach, a handsome person*; a Chonnail *chiataich, ye handsome Connal.*

CIATAICH, kĕătt'-èch, *n. f.* love; delight; pleasure; cha 'n 'eil *ciataich* sam bith aig e dheth, *he has no great affection for him* or *it.*

CIATAICHEAD, kĕăt'-èch-ad, *n. f.* handsomeness, degree of beauty, elegance, *or* beauty; a' dol an *ciataichead, improving in elegance, beauty, &c.*

CIBH, kē, *n. m.* a wreath of snow. *Sk.*

CIBHEAR, kēff'2' ur, *n. m.* drizzle, drizzling rain.

CIBHRINN, kēv2'-rrènn, *n. m.* counterpane, coverlet; in Skye, Ciobhraig.

CICHE, kèch'-ă, *gen.* of a pap, breast ceann na *ciche, the nipple.*

CIDHIS, kē'-yhès, *n. m.* a mask. *Ir. Arm.*

CILEAN, kēl'-an', *n. m.* a large cod. *Skye.*

CILL, kēlly', *n. f.* a church-yard, a burying-ground; in *H. S.* a cell, a church.

CILLE, kēlly'2'-ă, *gen.* of Cill; prefixed to places signifying burying-places; Cille-bhride, *Kilbride,* &c. before a vowel *or* fh, Cill, as Cill-fhinn.

CILLTEAN, kēlly'-tyun, *pl.* burying grounds.

CINN, kēnn', *n. pl.* heads; *v. n.* grow, increase; vegetate, multiply; result from, happen, grow taller.

CINNEADAIL, kēnn2'-ad-al, *a.* clannish.

CINNEADALACHD, kènn2'-ad-al-ăchg, *n. f.* clannishness, attachment to one' clan.

CINNEACH, kēnn2'-ach, *n. m.* a heathen nation.

CINNEADH, kēnn2'-nyĂ, *n. m.* clan, kin, tribe; surname; kindred; fear *cinnidh, a namesake*; (bean chinnidh, also.)

CINNEAS, kēnn'2'-as, *n. m.* growth; vegetation; produce, crop, production; increase; fruit.

Cinneasach, kènn2′-äs-ach, *a.* productive, germinative; vegetative; fruitful.

Cinneasachd, kēnn2′-as-ăchg, *n. f.* fruitfulness, vegetativeness; vegetation, growth.

Cinnseal, kēnn2′-shall, *n. m.* contact; a' dol an *cinnseal* gàbhaidh, *getting in contact with danger*; is coma leam dol 'na *chinnseal, I do not like to get in contact with it*; origin, commencement.

Cinnte, kēnnt′-à, *n. f.* assurance, certainty; cha 'n 'eil *cinnte* nam beul, *there is no certainty in their lips, Smith*; air *chinnte, certainly, most assuredly, decidedly so.*

Cinnteach, kēnn′-tyăch, *a.* certain, positive, assured, confident; unerring; exact; plain, evident, obvious; chò *chinnteach* ris a' bhàs, *as sure as death*; saighide cò *cinnteach* 's am bàs, *arrows as sure as death, Oss.*; nach *cinnteach* a làmh, *how unerring his hand is*; am bheil thu *cinnteach, are you quite sure?* tha mi làn *chinnteach, I am completely certain.*

Cinnteachd, kēnn2′-tyachg, *n. f.* unquestionableness, sureness of aim; positiveness; assurance; demonstration; confidence, reliance.

Cinnteadair, kyēnnt″-ad-ar', an insurer.

Cinntealas, kyenn′-tyal-us, *n. f.* certainty.

Cinntinn, kyēnn2′-tyènn, *p.* growing, increasing.

Ciob, kēbb, *n. m.* moor-grass, *Mt.*; *North,* tow; in *Is.* sponge; *a.* spongy, porous; moine *chìob, spongy* or *porous peats* or *turf*; *v.* bite. *H.*

Ciobhal, kē′-ull, *n. m.* jaw-bone, *Argyle*; jaw-bones, ciobhlan.

Ciobair, kēbb′-ăr', *n. m.* a shepherd.

Ciobaireachd, kēb′-ăr'ăchg, *n. f.* herding sheep.

Cioch, kē'-ch, *n. f.* pap, breast of a woman; *cìoch* a mhuineil, neo bhraghaid, *the uvula*; *cìoch* an t-sluigein, *the sac that propels the food into the gullet.*

Ciocrach, kē'chg-rach, *a.* longing as a female; greedy, voracious.

Ciocras, kē'ch′-rus, *n. m.* absurd longing of a female; earnest longing, greediness.

Ciod, (Latin, quid) kud, *int. pro.* what; dè, which is ten hundred times more common in the Highlands, is a few thousand years older.

Ciogailt, kyúg′-alt', *n. f.* tickling.

Ciogailteach, kyúg′-alty'-ach, *a.* ticklish, critical; gnothuch *ciogailteach, a critical affair.*

Ciolam, kyul′-um, *n. f.* an Irish vessel.

Ciom, kēm. *n. f.* a wool card. *Armstrong*

Ciomach, kēm′-ach, *n. m.* a prisoner, a captive. *Bib.*

Ciomachas, kēm′-ach-us, *n. m.* captivity. *Bible. Ir.*

Ciombal, kēmb′-al, *n. m.* a cymbol; a bed. *Ps. Ar.*

Ciomboll, kēmb′-oll, *n. m.* a bundle of straw. *Skye.*

Cion, kyun, *n. m.* want, defect; also *corr.* of gion; *cion* lèirsinn, *want of sight, defect of vision*; *cion* faobhair, *bluntness.*

Cionn, kyunn, mispronunciation of ceann, air mo *chionn, waiting me*; air *chionn* da tighinn dachaidh, *waiting him when he comes home*; as do *chionn, above you, over your head.*

Cionnas, kyunn′-us, *inter. pro.* how? by what means? a dh' fhaicinn, *cionnas,* a a dh' ainmicheadh e iad, *to see how he would name them. Bible.*

Cionfa, kyun-fâ′, *n. m.* cause, reason. *Sm.*

Ciont, kyunt, *n. m.* fault, guilt, crime.

Ciontach, kyunt′-ach, *a.* guilty, criminal, at fault, sinful; gun *chionta, blameless.*

Ciontach, kyunt′-ach, *n. m.* and *f.* a defaulter.

Ciontachadh, kyunt′-ach-X, *n. m.* and *pt.* transgressing, sinning; le *ciontachadh* am aghaidh, *with trespassing against me.*

Ciontachd, kyunt′-ăchg, *n. f.* degree of guilt, guiltiness; sinfulness.

Ciontaich, kyunt′-èch, *v.* sin, transgress; *chiontaich* iad am aghaidh, *they sinned against me. B.*

Ciora, kyēr′-à, *n. f.* a pet sheep. *Skye.*

Ciorram, kyur′-um, *n. m.* a maim, a defect in a person's body.

Ciorramach, kyurr′-am-ach, also kérr′-um-ach, *a.* maimed, deformed, mutilated; *H. S.* painful.

Ciosnachadh, kēss′-nnach-X, *pt.* subduing, conquering; appeasing; oppressing.

Ciosnachail, kēss′-nach-al, *a.* overpowering, made to pay tribute.

Ciosnaich, kēss′-nnèch, *v.* subdue; overpower, conquer.

Ciotach, kĕ'tt′-ach, *a.* left-handed, defective.

Ciotachd, ke'tt′-ăchg, *n. f.* left-handedness.

Ciotag, kĕ'tt′-ag, *n. f.* the left hand.

Cipean, kĕ'p′-an' *n. m.* a tether-stake.

Cir, kēr', *n. f.* a comb; part of a key; the cud; tha bhò a' cnàmh a *cìr, the cow is chewing the cud*; a honey-comb; *v.* comb; curry; tease, as wool.

Cirean, kyēr2′-an', *n. m.* crest, cock's comb.

Cireanach, kyēr′-an'-ach, *a.* crested.

Cis, kēsh, *n. f.* tax, tribute; thoireadh Cu

chulin dhomh *cìs*, *let Cuchulin yield me tribute.*

Cisean, kēsh^2'-an', *n. m.* a hamper. *Is.*

Cisire, kēsh'-ėr-ȧ, *n. m.* tax-gatherer.

Cisireachd, kēsh'-ėr-achd, *n. f.* tax-gathering.

Cis-leagadair, kēsh-llāg^2'-ad-ăr', an assessor.

Cis-mhaor, kēsh'-vhāor, *n. m.* a tax-gatherer.

Ciste, kēsh'-tyȧ, *n. f.* a chest; a coffin.

Cith, kē, *n.* fury; *Oss.* (fearg) particle. *Suths.*

Citheach, kē^2'-ach, *a.* furious. *Ossian.*

Ciucharan, kyûch'-ar-an, *n. m.* a low-voiced lamentation; plaintive moaning.

Ciuin, kyūėn, *a.* mild, gentle; amiable, meek; agus bha 'n duine Maois ro-*chiùin*, *and the man Moses was very meek*; still, calm, quiet; feasgar *ciuin*, *a still* or *calm evening*; smooth, agreeable to the touch; (aodach *ciuin*, *smooth cloth, North*); *Per. v.* calm.

Ciuine, kyūen'-ȧ, mildness, meekness, gentleness; *deg.* ni's *ciùine*, *more* or *most meek, gentle,* &c.

Ciuineachadh, kyūėn'-ach-X, *p.* calming, appeasing, pacifying, quieting.

Ciuineachd, kyūėn'-ăchg, *n. f.* mildness, &c. calm.

Ciuineas, kyūėn'-us, *n. m.* mildness, meekness, gentleness.

Ciuinich, kyūėn'-ėch, *v.* pacify, appease, assuage, still, calm; *chiùinich* e, *he stilled* or *calmed*; *ciùinichte, stilled, calmed, appeased.*

Ciuirteach, kyūr'-tyach, *a.* extremely painful, agonizing; torturing the mind.

Ciurr, kyūėrr, *v.* torture, agonize, *Is.*; hurt. *Bible.*

Ciurrail, kyūrr'-al, painful in the extreme.

Clab, klăb, *n. m.* an enormous mouth.

Clabach, klăb'-ach, *a.* having a large mouth; *n. f.* a large-mouthed female.

Clabaire, klăb'-ăr'-ȧ, *n. m.* a babbler.

Clabar, klab'-ar, *n. m.* a mill-clapper.

Clabar, klâb'-ur, *n. m.* a puddle; mire, dirt.

Clabastar, klab'-ast-ar', *n. m.* a brawler; *clabastair* clocharain, *the frog-fish*; greasaiche. *Sk.*

Clach, clach, *n. f.* a stone; a stone weight; *gen.* cloiche; *dat.* chloich. In Irish, cloch; *v.* stone, punish by stoning; *clach*-bholg, *a rattle*; *clach*-chinn, *a head grave stone*; *clach*-fhaobhrachaidh, *a hone, a sharping* or *whet-stone*; *clach*-mheallain, *hail.*

Clachach, clach'-ach, *a.* stony, rocky, pebbly.

Clachair, clach'-ăr, *n. m.* a mason.

Clachaireachd, clach'-ăr'-achg, *n. f* masonry, mason-work, architecture.

Clachan, clach'-an, *n. m.* stepping-stones a village, a hamlet, where a church is; said to have been Druidical places of worship.

Clacharan, clach'-ar'-an, *n. m.* a wagtail; a stone-chatterer, *Is.*; stepping-stones. *Dr. M'L.*

Clach-bhuaidh, clach'-vhuae-yh', an amulet, a charm; a gem.

Clach-bhrath, chlach-vhră', *n. f.* rocking-stone.

Clach-chrich, clach-chrēch', *n. f.* march-stone; cnaimh, cnaimh-crìch.

Clach-fhuail, clach'-ŭăėl, *n. f.* gravel-stone.

Clach-gheurachaidh, chlăch-yhgār'-ach-e, *n. f.* a hone, a whet-stone, sharping-stone.

Clach-ghuiteir, clach-yhŭet'-ār', kennel-stone.

Clach-ghluin, clăch'-ghlūėn, *n. f.* an amulet.

Clach-inne, clach'-ėnn'-ȧ. *n. f.* a kennel-stone.

Clach-liobhaidh, clach-lēv'-ė, *n. f.* grind-stone, a polishing-stone; *Persh.* clach leanraidh.

Clach-mhile, clach-vhēl'-ȧ, *n. f.* a mile-stone.

Clach-mhuilinn, clach'-vhŭ'l-ėn', *n. f.* mill-stone.

Clach-mhullaich, clach'-vhull-ėch, *n. f.* top-stone.

Clach-na-cineamhuinn, clach'-nna-kėn-uv-ėnn, *n. f.* fatal-stone, the stone on which the ancient Caledonians inaugurated their kings. *Armstrong.*

Clach-na-sul, clach-na-sûl', *n. f.* the apple of the eye.

Clach-neart, klach-nyert', *n. f.* putting-stone.

Clach-oisean, klach-ōsh'-an', *n. f.* corner-stone.

Clach-smior, klach'-smyúr, *n. f.* emery.

Clad, klăd, *n. m.* a wool-card; *v.* card wool. 10.

Cladach, klad'-ach, *n. m.* shore, beach, stony shore, *or* beach; any thing scattered; cha shuaicheantas còrr air *cladach*, *a heron on the shore is no novelty. P.*

Cladan, klà^4'-dan, *n. m.* a flake of snow; bur.

Cladanach, klàd^4'-an-ach, *a.* flaky, like burs.

Cladh, klaŏ'-gh', *v.* spawn, as fish; tha na bradain a' *cladh*, *the salmon are spawning*; *n. m.* the act of spawning; church-yard.

Cladhach, klaŏ'-ach, *pt.* digging, delving,

poking; a' *cladhach* fo'n bhruaich, *poking under the bank of the river*; *n. m.* act of digging.

CLADHAICH, klaŏ-gh''-êch, *v.* dig, delve, poke.

CLADHAIRE, klaŏ-gh'-ăr'-â, *n. m.* a coward; gu'n robh còta dubh air cealgair na còta dearg air *cladhaire, may a hypocrite never wear a black coat, nor a coward a red one*; a hero formerly, the one superintending the burying of soldiers in an army; now, grave-digger.

CLADHAIREACHD, klaŏ'-ăr'-ăchg, *n. f.* cowardice.

CLADRACH, klad''-rrach, *n. m.* any thing scattered.

CLADRAICH, klad''-rêch, *v.* scatter.

CLAG, kllăg'-g, *n. m.* a bell; a crash.

CLAGARSAICH, klăgg'-ar-sich, *n. f.* crashing, crashing noise; dangling, waving.

CLAG-THIGH, klagg'-hăêgh, *n. m.* a belfry, steeple.

CLAIDEAN, klăj'-ăn', *n. m.* an absurd hammering at any thing; dangling.

CLAIDHEAMH, kllī'-yhêv, *n. m.* a sword; murdered into kllê'-ê, in many places; *pl.* claidhmhichean, kllīv'-êch-un, swords; *claidheamh* mor, *a broad sword*; *claidheamh* crom, *a sabre*; *claidheamh* coal, *a small sword*; cha 'n 'eil fhios dè'n *claidheamh* a bhios 'san truaill gus an tairnear e, *it is not known what sword is in the sheath* or *scabbard, till it is drawn.*

CLAIDHEAMHAIR, cllīv'-vhăr', *n. m.* swordsman.

CLAIDHEAMHAIREACHD, kllīv'-var-ăchg, *n. f.* swordsmanship; more correctly, claidhmhaireachd.

CLAIDREACH, klăj'-rach, *a.* fatiguing.

CLAIDRICH, klaj'-rêch, *v.* fatigue, shatter.

CLAIGEACH, klăêg'-ach, *n. m.* a steeple. *Irish.*

CLAIGIONN, klăĕg'-unn, *n. m.* a skull, scalp; the best field of arable land in a farm.

CLAIGIONNACH, klăĕg'-unn-ach, *a.* headstall of a bridle, halter, &c.; best arable land of a district.

CLAIR, kllăĕr, *n. m. p.* lids.

CLAIS, kllăsh, *n. f.* a furrow, a trench.

CLAISIRE, klash'-êr-â, *n. m.* trencher.

CLAISDEACHD, klăshj'-achg, *n. f.* sense of hearing, hearing; ann am *chlaisdeachd, in my hearing,* (cluas èisdeachd); chaill e a *chlaisdeachd, he lost his sense of hearing.*

CLAISEACH, klash-ach, *a.* furrowed, trenched.

CLAISTINN, klàsh'-tyenn, *pt.* hearing. *North.*

CLAMBAR, klamb'-ăr, litigiousness, wrangling; evil report, private slander.

CLAMHAIR, kláv'-ăr, *v.* scratch, shrug.

CLAMHAS, klav'-us, *n. m.* clamour, unfounded report, clatter; brawling.

CLAMHASAIL, klav'-ssal, *a.* brawling, clattering.

CLAMBRACH, klamb'-ar-ăch, *a.* litigious, fond of law; wrangling, slandering.

CLAMHRADH, klav'-rĂ, *pt.* scratching, shrugging.

CLAMHUINN, klav'-enn, *n. m.* sleet, flinne. *D. B.*

CLANN, klan'n, *n. m.* and *f.* children, offspring, descendants; a clan; cha robh duine *cloinne* aice, *she had no children, B.*; a *chlann* nan sonn, *ye descendents of heroes*; *clann* an TOISICH, *the Mackintoshes*; *clann* Rànnail, *the clan* RANALDS; *clann* diolain, *bastard children*; *clann* an *cloinne, their children's children*; (Teutonic, klein); a curl, a ringlet; na *clannaibh, in curls, in ringlets, Song*; *v.* curl.

CLANNACH, klann'-ach, *a.* fruitful; curled, in ringlets; Anna *chlannach, Anne, with the many ringlets. Song.*

CLANNAICH, klann'-ech, *v. n.* beget children.

CLAOIDH, klúe'-yh', *v.* cloy, exhaust, overfatigue; fag; overcome with fatigue; mar *chlaoidheas* teine coillteach, *as fire overcomes wood, Sm.*; *n. m.* fatigue, excessive fatigue; *pt.* fagging, fainting; mortifying; *claoidhibh* ar buill, *mortify your members. Bible.*

CLAOIDHTE, klúêly''-tya, *pt.* exhausted with fatigue.

CLAOIDHTEACH, klúety'-tyach, *a.* exhausting one's strength; fatiguing, fagging, fainting, overcoming; spending.

CLAOIDHTEACHD, klúêty''-tyăchg, *n. f.* exhaustion, fagging *or* exhausting; fatigue.

CLAOINE, klăoên'-â, *n. f.* inclination, squintness.

CLAON, klăon, *v.* incline, go aside, rebel; *chlaon* iad uile, *they have all gone aside*; move aslant *or* obliquely; mar a' ghriana tha *claonadh* 'sa ghleann, *like the sun that moves aslant in the glen, Oss.*; *a.* squint, oblique, slanting; meandering; linne a tha *claon* 'sa ghleann, *a pool* or *stream that is meandering in the valley, Oss.*; squint-eyed; fear *claon, a man that squints*; (Lat. et Gr. clino).

CLAONADH, klăon'-Ă, *n. m.* and *pt.* squinting, slanting, meandering, inclining, bending; mar sgàile a *claonadh* sios, *like a shadow declining, Sm.*; *a.* inclination; oblique motion.

CLAONBHAIGH, k'äon'-vhâe-yh', *n. f.* partiality. *B.*

CLAONBHORD, klāon'-vhŏrd, *n. f.* desk, inclined plain, a sloping table.

CLAONBHREITH, klāon'-vhrrā², *n. f.* partiality, an unfair judgment *or* decision.

CLAR, klâr, *n. m.* lid of a chest; stave of a cask, harp, &c. *Oss.*; *Bible,* plank, table. *v. n.* maintain, contradict, oppose; a *claradh* orm, *contradicting* or *maintaining stoutly*; 's ann tha e a' *claradh* orm, *he stoutly contradicts me.*

CLARACH, klâr'-ach, *n. f.* clumsy female.

CLARAG, klâr'-ag, *n. f.* a fore *or* front-tooth; frame of a fishing line; clarag dorgh. *Lewis.*

CLARAICH, klâr'-ech, *n. f.* wooden partition *or* floor.

CLARSACH, klâr'-ssach, *n. m.* a harp; cho caoin ri *clarsaich, as melodious as a harp.*

CLARSACH-URLAIR, klâr'-sach-ûr-llar, *n. f.* an old woman in gentlemen's families, kept for the purpose of telling stories; a witch.

CLARSAIR, klâr'-sar', *n. m.* a harper, minstrel.

CLARSAIREACHD, klâr'-săr'-achd, *n. f.* harping, music.

CLEACHD, klechg, *v.* practise, accustom, inure, habituate, use; *chleachd* mi a bhi, *I was accustomed to be*; *chleachd* mi mòran deth f haotainn, *I was accustomed to get much of it*; habit, *Oss.*; curl. *B.*

CLEACHDACH, klechg'-ach, *a.* customary, practised; habitual; curled; clearcach rather.

CLEACHDUINN, kllechg'-ènn, *n. f.* habit, practice, custom; is dona a *chleachduinn* sin, *that is a bad practice* or *custom*; deadh *chleachduinn, a good custom* or *practice.*

CLEACHDTA, *or* CLEACHDTE, klechg'-tya, *pt.* accustomed, practised, inured; trained; used; *cleachdta* ri olc, *accustomed to do evil.*

CLEAMHNAS, kllev'-nus, *n. m.* sexual intercourse, carnal connexion; confounded shamefully with CLIAMHUINNEAS, consanguinity, relationship by marriage.

CLEARC, klerck, *n. f.* a curl, a ringlet, a lock of hair; *v.* curl, make into ringlets, arrange.

CLEARCACH, klerk'-ach, *a.* curled in ringlets.

CLEAS, kllāss², *n. m.* trick, craft, feat, gambol; a stratagem; Cuchullainn nan *cleas, Cuchullin full of stratagems. Oss.*

CLEASACH, kllas²'-sach, *a.* playful, full of tricks.

CLEASACHD, klāss'-ăchg, *n. f.* play, sport, diversion, as jugglers, legerdemain, sleights; ri *cleasachd, playing, sporting*; dh' éirich iad gu *cleasachd, they rose up to play*; *cleasachd* dhaoine, *the sleights of men. Bible, Arm.*

CLEASAICHE, klās²'-èch-á, *n. m.* a juggler, a cunning fellow; a conjuror.

CLEASANTA, klās'-ănt-a, *a.* tricky, playful.

CLEASANTACHD, klas²'-ant-ăchg, *n. f.* frolicsomeness.

CLEATHA, klā²'-ha, *n. m.* a club *or* clumsy stick, a goad, a rib, a stake.

CLEID, kllăj, *n. f.* a flake, a clot.

CLEIDEACH, kllăj'-ach, *a.* clotted, shaggy.

CLEIDEAG, klăj'-ag, *a.* clot, a flake.

CLEIDEAGACH, klăj'-ăg-ach, *a.* clotted, shaggy, ragged, full of clots *or* tatters.

CLEIR, klār', *n. f.* the clergy; a presbytery. Welsh, clèr; Arm. cloer; Spanish, clero.

CLEIREACH, klār''-ach, *a.* a clerk; a beadle, *or* church officer. *Argyle.*

CLEIREANACH, klār'-ăn-ăch, *a.* sword. *Per. Arm.*

CLEIT, klăjt, *n. m.* a ridge *or* reef of sunk rocks, *Isl.*; a quill, a feather, *Skye*; eaves, *Arm.*; a rocky eminence. *H. Society.*

CLEITH, kllhā, *v.* conceal, hide; *n. m.* concealment, secrecy; cha 'n 'eil *cleith* air an olc ach gun a dheanadh, *the best way to conceal evil is not to commit it, P.*; (Hebrew, *chele,* Chall *klei*).

CLEOC, klley'-ôchg, *n. m.* a cloak, a mantle.

CLI, kllē, *n. m.* strength, energy; locomotion, vigour, pith; gun *chli, without power of motion*; duine gun *chli, a man without energy* or *vigour*; force; chunnaic e ghaoth gun *chli, he saw the wind without force. Oss.*

CLI, kllē, *a.* left, left-handed; slow, awkward; feeble; an taobh *clì, the left side*; a dh' ionnsaidh na laimhe *clì, to the left side*; *clì* 'sa comhrag, *lame* or *feeble in the strife*; labhair *clì, speak humbly. Oss.*

CLIABH, klĕăv, *n. m.* a strait-jacket, a strait-vest of wicker-work, for a madman; hence, 's ann a tha 'n t-òlach ann an *cliabh, the fellow is mad,* said to people who have bad Gaelic; in a secondary sense, a creel *or* hamper; the chest, the breast; a taomadh ma *chliabh, pouring it on his breast*; *cliabh* guthainn, *boddice of a gown.*

CLIABHACH, klĕăv'-ach, *a.* like baskets, chested; belonging to the chest.

Cliabhsgeithreach, kleav′-skăr′-ach, a vomit.

Clia-lu, klĕă′-llû, *n. m.* all the fingers in motion playing on the bagpipes.

Cliamhuinn, klĕăv′-eun, *n. m.* a brother-in-law, *Isl.* In the Bible, a son-in-law; (cliabh-dhuine, *Arm.*)

Cliamhuinneas, klĕăv′-un-nyŭs, *n. m.* relationship by marriage; consanguinity, friendship.

Cliar, klĕăr, *n. m.* a poet; a brave man; fuil nan *cliar*, *the blood of the brave.*

Cliaraiche, klĕăr′-ėch-à, a singer. *Md.*

Cliata, klĕat′-a, a meadow, *N.*; a burr. *Lw.*

Cliath, kllĕă, *n. f.* a harrow, a hurdle, as when fulling cloth; a latice *or* casement, *B.*; a worm in distillation; stann *cleith, worm vat*; a shoal of fish; *cliath* sgadan, *cliàth* bhradan, *cliath* phiocach, *a shoal of herrings, a shoal of salmon, and a shoal of coal-fish*; some style, *shoal,* a creel of herrings, &c. (bravo, Parraig &——!) darning of stockings, (Armstrong says); weir for salmon. *Lw.*

Cliath, klhĕă, *v.* harrow; tread, as the male, in poultry; a' *cliathadh* nan cearc, *treading the hens*; darn. *Armstrong.*

Cliathach, klleu′-ach, *n. f.* the side of any thing; ri *cliathach* na luinge, *at the side of the ship*; ri d' *cliathaich, at your side.*

Cliath-sheanachais, klĕă-hen′-ach-ush, *n. f.* a genealogical table. *Lewis.*

Clibish, klĕb′-ėsht, *n. f.* a misadventure.

Clibisteach, klĕb′-ėsht-ach, *a.* awkward.

Clichd, klĕchg[2], *n. m.* a hook; a bad trick.

Cliob, klĕbb, *n. m.* an excrescense.

Cliobag, klĕbb′-ag, *n. f.* a filly. *Irish.*

Cliobain, klĕbb[2]′-an′, *n. m.* an excrescence, a dew-lap; any thing dangling.

Cliobaire, klĕbb′-ăr′-a, *n. m.* a clumsy person; a simpleton.

Cliospach, klĕsp′-ach, *a.* lame, not active.

Clip, klĕpp, *n. m.* a large hook, a hand-hook, for taking large fish, too heavy for the line into a boat; a stratagem, deceit, cunning; *v. n.* hook, pilfer; snatch, steal.

Clis, klĕsh, *a.* quick, active; lively, nimble, agile, speedy, clever, handy; *v.* leap.

Cliseach, klĕsh[2]′-ăch, *n. f.* a wicket.

Clisbeach, klĕsh′-byach, *a.* unsteady.

Clisg, klĕshg, *v.* start, startle, leap through fear; *chlisg* e, *he startled.*

Clisgeach, klĕshg′-ach, *a.* skittish, apt to startle, timid, fearful.

Clisgeadh, klĕshg′-Ă, *n. m.* a startle, a start; *pt.* starting, leaping; bi an so an *clisgeadh, be here instantly*; *chlisg* féidh is earba 'san f hraoch, *deer and roe startled in the heath. Oss.*

Clisneach, klĕsh′-nyach, *n. f.* a wicket, (cachladh;) a mouth never at rest. *MacIntyre.*

Cliu, kllū, *n. f.* praise, renown; fame, reputation; character; fo dheadh *chliù, under a good character*; cha 'n éireadh mo *chliù* na bhàs, *my fame would suffer by his death, my praise would not be enhanced by his death, Ossian.* Welsh, clod; Greek, kleos.

Cliuchd, kllūchg, *n. f.* a stratagem, a hellish trick, deceit; *v.* mend nets. *Lewis.*

Cliuchdach, kllūchg′-ach, deceitful, cunning, *Is.*; *n. f.* a deceitful female.

Cluichdaire, klūchg′-ur-à, *n. m.* a stratagist, a cunning fellow; mender of nets.

Cluichdaireachd, klūchg′-ar′-ăchg, *n. f.* deceitfulness, cunningness; mending nets. *Lewis.*

Cliud, kllūd′d, *n. f.* a small trifling hand.

Cliudan, kllūd′-an, *n. m.* a trifling stroke *or* blow.

Cliuiteach, kllū′-tyach, *a.* praise-worthy, laudable, commendable; famous, celebrated, renowned, extolled; praised; Finghall *cliùiteach, celebrated Fingall*; is *cliùiteich* an onair na 'n t-òr, *honour is more comendable than gold.*

Cliuthachadh, klū′-ach-Ă, *pt.* praising, extolling, celebrating, lauding, renowning, exalting.

Cliuthaich, klū′-ėch, *v.* praise, laud, extol, commend, exalt; celebrate.

Cliumhor, klū′-vur, praise-worthy.

Cliu-thoillteannach, klū-hŏelly″-tyánnăch, *a.* praise-worthy, commendable.

Clo, kllō, *n. m.* cloth, home-made cloth.

Clo, kllô, *n. m.* a slumber, dozing, lethergy; sometimes clò-cadail.

Clobha, klō′-à, *n. m.* a pair of tongs.

Clo-bhuail, klô′-vvŭăėl, *v.* print (bad).

Cloca, klôchg′-à, *n. m.* a cloak, mantle; better than cleoca.

Clocaire, klôchg′-ur′-à, *n. m.* a rogue, a deceitful fellow, a dissembler; pretender.

Clocaireachd, klôchg′-ur′-achg, *n. f.* dissimulation.

Cloch, klŏch, *n. f.* a goggle-eye, *Isl.*; stone. *Ir.*

Clochar, klŏch′-ur, *n. m.* wheezing in the throat.

Clocharra, klŏch′-urr-a, *a.* goggle-eyed.

Clo-cadail, klô-căd-ėl, *n. m.* slumber, dozing.

Clod, klod′, *n. m.* a clod; *v.* clod (Teutonic.)

CLODHADAIR, klō′-ad-ăr′, *n. f.* printer.

CLODHADAIREACHD, klō′-ad-ar′-achg, *n. f.* printing.

CLOGAD, klŏg′-ad, *n. m.* a helmet, a cap, a head-piece. In *H. S.* a cone, a pyramid.

CLOGAIS, klog′-ash, *n. f.* a wooden shoe.

CLOIMH, klŏĕ-yh′, *n. f.* scab, mange, itch.

CLOIMH, klò′-ė, *n. f.* down, feathers, plumage; in some places, wool.

CLOIMHTEACH, klò′-tyach, *n. f.* down, feathers.

CLOIS, klŏsh, *n. f.* march weed.

CLOS, klŏss, *n. m.* rest, repose, stillness, quietness; gabh *clos, rest, be still,* or *quiet.*

CLOSACH, klos′-ach, *n. f.* a carcass, carrion.

CLOSAICH, klos′-ėch, *v.* get lank or gaunt, as a half-starved brute.

CLOSAID, klôs′-ăj, *n. f.* a closet, a study.

CLUAIN, klŭăĕn, *n. f.* pacification, quietness; cuir *cluain* air an leanabh, *pacify the child, appease the child.*

CLUAIN-LIN, klŭăĕn-llēn′, *n. f* corn-spurry.

CLUAINTEAR, klŭăĕn′-tyar, *n. m.* a flatterer, a cajoler, a hypocrite, a cunning fellow.

CLUAINTEARACHD, klŭăĕn′′-tyar′-achg, *n. f.* fawning; cajoling, flattery, hypocricy, intrigue.

CLUAISEAN, klŭàsh′-an, *n. m.* a blow on the ear; porringer.

CLUANAG, klŭăn′-ăg, *n. f.* an islet in a river, a small piece of choice pasture, a meadow.

CLUARAN, klŭăr′-an, *n. m.* a thistle, fountain; a spunge, còs, cìob.

CLUARANACH, klŭăr′-ăn-ăch, *a.* thistly, fungous.

CLUAS, klŭăs, *n. f.* an ear; handle of a dish.

CLUASACH, klŭăs′-ăch, *a.* eared, having handles.

CLUASAG, klŭăs′-ăg, *n. f.* pillow, pin-cushion.

CLUAS-CHIUIL, klŭăs′-chū′l, *n. m.* a musical ear.

CLUAS-LIATH, kluas′-lĕă, *n. f.* herb, colt's foot.

CLUD, klûd, *n. m.* patch, a rag, clout; *v.* patch.

CLUDADH, klûd′-Ă, *pt.* patching, mending.

CLUDAIR, klûd′-ăr′-ȧ, *n. m.* patcher, cobler.

CLUICH, klŭéch, *n. m.* play, sport, game, school vacation; *v.* play, sport.

CLUICHEADAIR, klŭĕch′-ad-ar, *n. m.* a player.

CLUICHEALACHD, klŭĕch′-al-ăchg, *n. f.* playfulness.

CLUICHEIL, klŭĕch′-al, *a.* playful, sportive.

CLUIGEAN, klŭĕg′-ăn′, *n. m.* an ear-ring, or pendant, a cluster; any thing dangling.

CLUINN, klúėnn, *v.* hear, listen, hearken, attend; an tì a shuidhich a' chluas, nach *cluinn* e, *he that planted the ear, shall he not hear?* an sin *cluinnidh* mise, *then shall I hear*; *chuala* mi, *I hea d*; nach *cluinn* thu, *do you not hear*; *cluinnidh* sinn, *we shall hear.*

CLUINNTE, klŭĕn′-tyȧ, *pt.* heard, attended to.

CLUINNTINN, klŭĕnn′-tyenn, *pt. pres.* hearing.

CLUIP, klŭĕp, *n. f.* deceit. *See* Cuip.

CLUPAID, klup′-ėj, *n. f.* swollen throat in cattle.

CNAC, krăchg, *or* kun′-ăg, *v.* crack. *Teutonic.*

CNAG, krág, *n. f.* a peg, a pin, a knob; hold-pin of a boat (putag), *Skye; v.* thump, knock, rap.

CNAGACH, kunăg′-ăch, *a.* knotty, knobby.

CNAGACHD, kunag′-achg, *n. f.* knobbiness, knottiness.

CNAGAID, krăg′-ăj, *n. f.* an old maid; an old cow with stumps of horns.

CNAGAIRE, krag′-ŭr-ă, *n. f.* a gill, a noggin, *No.*; a gill; in Lewis, Frangach, *i. e.* a Frenchman.

CNAID, kréj, *v.* scoff; *n. f.* a jeer, a scoff, magadh.

CNAIMH, krīĕv, *n. m.* a bone; bones, cnàmhan; *cnàimh* an droma, *the spine, the back bone*; *cnàimh* na lurga, *the shin bone*; *cnàimh* a ghobhail, *the share bone*; *cnàimh* criche, and *cnaimh, a balk,* or *land-mark, Is.* also a matter of dispute.

CNAIMHEACH, krìv′-ach, a rook, ròcaideach.

CNAIMHTEACH, knáv′-tyăch, *a.* digestive, corrosive.

CNAMH, kràv, *v.* chew, ruminate, digest; a' *cnàmh* a chìr, *chewing the cud*; *chnàmh* e a bhiadh, *he digested his food*; corrode, consume; *chnàmh* an t-iarrunn, *the iron corroded*; *chnàmh* an gealbhan, *the fire consumed or wasted*; *genitive plu.* of cnaimh; ri taobh nan *cnàmh, at the side of the bones.*

CNAMHACH, kráv′-ach, *a.* bony, having large bones; corrosive, consuming.

CNAMHAG, kráv′-ăg, *n. f.* refuse of any thing, any thing deprived of its substance; corn spoiled by cattle.

CNAMHAIRNEACH, kráv′-ăr′-nyach, *n. f.* a transparant small fish, found on all the coast of the islands; sprats of the mackerel, a skeleton; a raw-boned fellow.

CNAMHAN, kráv′-an, *n. m.* unceasing bickering.

CNAMHARLACH, kráv'-ar-lach, *n. m.* a hard boned, cadaverous person; a stalk. *H.*

CNAP, krápp, *n. m.* a lump, a knob, a potato, a thump; *v.* thump; 'gam *chnapadh, thumping me.*

CNAPACH, kráp'-ach, *a.* lumpy, knobby.

CNAPAIRE, kráp'-ur-à, *n. m.* a thumper; a stout article; a stout fellow.

CNAPAN, kráp'-an, *n. m.* a little lump.

CNAPANACH, kráp'-an-ach, *a.* lumpy.

CNAPARRA, kráp'-ărr-à, *a.* stout, sturdy; falling with a thumping noise.

CNAP-STARRA, kráp'-starr-à, obstruction; ball on the end of a spear.

CNATAN, knat'-an, *n. m.* a cold, cough, *N. H.*; more properly, cneatan.

CNEAD, kréd, *n. f.* a sudden sign *or* moan, as when one gets a blow unexpectedly; nothing; cha bhi *cnead* ort, *nothing will be wrong with you*; cha 'n 'eil *cnead* air, *nothing is wrong with him*; *v.* sigh, moan.

CNEADAIL, kréd'-ul, *pt.* sighing and moaning heavily and quickly.

CNEADH, more properly creidh, a wound.

CNEAMH, krév, *n. m.* wild garlick; *cneamh* muc fiadhaich, hart's tongue; elecampane; written, creamh.

CNEAP, krépp, *n. m.* a button; cneapan, buttons.

CNEAPADAIR, krépp'-a-dăr, *n. m.* button-maker.

CNEAS, kréss, *n. m.* bosom, breast, waist.

CNEASDA, krés'-d-á, *a.* humane; moderate.

CNEASDACHD, krés'-dăchg, *n. f.* humanity; piety.

CNEASNAICH, krés'-nyéch, *v.* squeeze and shake a person.

CNEASNAIDH, krés'-nnė, *a.* delicate, slender.

CNEASNAIDHEACHD, krés'-nnė-ăchg, *n. f.* delicacy.

CNEATAN, krétt'-an, *n. m.* a cold, coughing.

CNEATAS. *See* Cneidsinn, knitting, tape.

CNEIDH, kréė'yh', *n. f.* wound, hurt.

CNEIDSINN, kréjsh'-ėnn, *n. m.* knitting, tape.

CNO, for Cnú, *a.* a nut, a filbert.

CNOC, krŏchg, *n. m.* a knoll, an eminence.

CNOCACH, krŏchg-ach, *a.* hilly, rugged.

CNOCAID, krŏchg'-ăj, *n. f.* a land-mark, balk.

CNOCAIRE, krŏchg'-ar', *n. m.* a loiterer, saunterer.

CNOCAN, krŏchg'-an, *n. m.* a hillock, a knoll.

CNOC-FAIRE, krŏchg'-făr'-à, *n. m.* an alarm post.

CNOD, krŏd, *n. m.* a patch; *v.* patch.

CNOID, krŏj, *n. m.* a splendid present. *Skye.*

CNOIDH, króėyh, *n. f.* great pain. *Skye.*

CNOIDHFHIACHALL, krŏė'-yh-ĕăchg-all, *n. f.* gum-boil.

CNOIMH, krőė'-yh', cruiyh, *n. f.* a maggot.

CNOIMHEAG, knő'-ăg, *n. f.* a maggot; niggardly female.

CNOMHAGAG, *Sk.* (conachag, a conch) guth-le-gúg. *Luing.*

CNOT, krótt, *v.* husk barley, oarslip. *Sk.*

CNOTAG, krott'-ăg, *n. f.* husking mortar.

CNU, krû, *n. f.* a nut, a filbert; *cnu*-f hrangach, *a walnut*; *cnu*-dharaich, *an acorn*; *cnu*-bhachair, *a mulacca nut.*

CNUACHD, krŭăchg, *n. f.* a lump; *v.* thump.

CNUACHDACH, krŭăchg'-ăch, *a.* lumpy; shrewd.

CNUACHDAIRE, krŭăchg'-ar'-à, *n. m.* shrewd man.

CNUAS, krŭăs, *v.* gather eatables; quash.

CNUASACHD, kruas'-achg, *n. m.* gathering eatables.

CNUASAICH, kruas'-ěch, *v.* gather, ponder

CO, kō, *int. pro.* who; *cò* an so, *who is this?* *cò* e, *who is he?* *cò* i, *who is she?* *adv.* as; *cò* mòr, *so big*; *cò* bheag, *as little*; *cò* leathann, *as broad*; used for comh; as, co-aontaich, yield assent, consent, admit, permit.

CO-AONTACHADH, kó-āon'-tach-ă, *n. m. p.* consent, acquiescence, agreement, consenting, agreeing.

CO-AONTAICH, kó-āon'-ttěch, *v.* acquiesce, yield.

COB, kōb, *n. m.* plenty, pailteas. *Irish.*

COBHAIR, kō[2]'-ėr, *n.* relief; *v.* relieve, aid, help.

COBHAN, koff'-an, (I think,) a chest, coffin. *B.*

COBHAR, kò'-ur, *n. m.* froth, foam, sillabub.

COBHARTACH, kò'-art-ach, *n. m.* any property coming on shore, supposed by every genuine Celt to be a God-send; *a.* helping.

COC, kŏchg, *v.* cock; hold up in defiance; *coc* do bhonnaid, *cock your bonnet. Teutonic*

COCA, kawchg'-à, *conj.* or *pro.* whether, which of the two; *còca* a dh' f holbhas na dh' f hanas tu, *whether you go* or *stay.*

COCAIRE, kawchg'-ur'-à, *n. m.* & *f.* a cook, *Ger.* coch; is math an *cocaire* an t-acras, *hunger is a good cook.*

COCHULL, còch'-ull, *n. m.* husk, skin of a snake.

COCHULLACH, còch'-ull-ach. *a.* capsular, husky.

CODACH, kod'd'-ach, *gen.* of cuid; air son mo *chodachsa* dheth, *for my part of it.*

CODHAIL, kau'-al, *n. f.* meeting, reproach; am *chodhail, to meet me*; thoir *codhail* da, *reproach him.*

COG, kògg, *v. n.* war, fight; jibe, jeer;

ch g iad, *they warred, Bible*; tha e a' *cogadh* air, *he jibes* or *jeers him.*

COGADH, kògg'-Ă, *n. m.* war, warfare: *pt.* warring; jibing; thun *cogaidh, for war.*

COGALL, kŏg'-ull, just cockle, peasair chapull.

COGAIS, kŏgg'-ăsh, *n. f.* a prodigious large, red, carbuncled nose (like a boiled lobster,) *St. Kilda, Rum, Egg, Canna, Mull, Coll, Jura, Islay, Giogha*; also the cog of a wheel; a ludicrous name for a large pinch of snuff, *ib.*; in Skye, just a nose; in Lewis, the nasal canal; in Ross-shire and Caithness, the cork of a bottle; in Inverness, a huge frog; in some parishes of the Continent of Argyle and Perthshire, conscience.

Note.—In the shape of conscience, it is only applied to the male sex. The consciences of all Highland ladies, whether M——— or not, is universally COIMHSEAS. In Arran, it signifies the throttle.

COICHEID, kŏĕch'-ăj, *n, f.* an objection, obstruction; cò chuir *coicheid, who objected?*

COICHEIDEACH, coych'-ăj-ach, *a.* objective, hindering.

COIDHEAS, kŏĕ'-yheas, more frequently pronounced and written Coingeis, tha mi coingeis, I do not care; it is no matter to me.

COIG, kōĕg, *a.* five; *còig*-deug, fifteen. In many outlandish places, oi is frequently pronounced, or rather mispronounced, ŭĕ; hence SUD instead of siod, (shĕdd;) druim, in place of driom, (ddrēm) the back; but in the islands of Argyle, every word is pronounced just as ADAM spoke it.

COIGEACH, kòĕg'-ach, *n. f.* a hand; from còig. *MSS.*

COIGEAD, kòĕg'-ud, *n. m.* fifty; *a.* fifty.

COIGEAMH, kòĕg'-uv, *a.* the fifth.

COIGEAR, kòĕg'-ur, *n. m.* & *f.* five persons.

COIGNEAR, kòĕg'-nyur, *n.* five persons.

COIGREACH, kòĕg'-ryach, *n. m.* stranger, foreigner.

COIGREACHAIL, kŏĕg'-rryach-al, *a.* strange, foreign.

COIG-SHLISNEACH, kòĕg'-hllĕsh-nyach, *a.* pentagonal, pentilateral; coig-thaobhach, more properly.

COILCEADHA, kŏelg'-kyănn-ă, *n. p.* bed materials. *Oss.*

COILEACH, kull'-ach, *n. m.* a cock; *coileach* frangach, *a turkey cock*; *coileach*-coille, *wood cock*; *coileach* dubh, *a black cock*; *coileach* fraoich *heath cock*; *coileach* tomain, *a cock partridge*; *coileach* ruadh, *a red grouse cock.*

COILEACH-GAOITH, kull'-ach-gäoĕch, *n. m.* weather-cock, a vane.

COILEAR, kŏll'-ăr', *n. m.* a collar, neck. *French,* &c.

COILEID, koll'-ăj, *n. f.* noise, stir, hubbub. *Skye.*

COILLE, kaŏly"-lyȧ, *n. f.* wood, forest; coiltean, *woods.*

COILLEANTA, kaŏly"-lyannt-ȧ, *a.* tall, straight, and slender.

COILLEARNACH, kuly'-ar-nach, *a.* shrubbery.

COILLTEACH, kaŏlly'-tyach, *n. f.* woodland, a celt, a wild.

COILLTEACHAIL, kaŏlly'-tyăch-al, *a.* woody; savage, wild; sylvan uninhabited.

COILLTEAR, kaŏly"-tyăr', *n. m.* a saunterer, wanderer.

COILLTEIL, kaŏly'-tyal, *a.* wild, woodland.

COIMEAS, koym'-ăs, *n. m.* comparison, parable, an equal, a match; gun a *choimeas* ann, *without his equal* or *match*; *a.* like.

COIMEAS, koym'-ĕss, *v. n.* compare, liken.

COIMEASG, koym'-ĕsg, *v.* mix, mingle.

COIMH, kóĕ, a prefix, answering *con.* and *com.* in English, placed before words beginning with the two vowels *e* and *i*, unless when the pronunciation requires it.

COIMHEACH, kóe'-ach, *a.* foreign, strange, shy, unkind; duine *coimheach, a strange person,* or *a shy person*; terrible; gnothuch *coimheach, a terrible affair*; *n.* a stranger; aig na *coimhich, with strangers.*

COIMHEAD, kói'-údd, *v.* see, look, *Lochaber*; preserve, keep; watch; *n. m.* preserving inspection; a weaver's laze. *Islay.*

COIMHEARSNACH, kóĕ'-ar-snach, *n. m.* a neighbour.

COIMHEARSNACHD, kŏĕ'-ar-snăchg, *n. f.* neighbourhood, vicinity; vicinage; neighbourly conduct.

COIMHEICHEAS, kóĕ'-ĕch-us, *n. f.* estranged affection, want of hospitality, sourness of disposition.

COIMGHEALL, kóĕ'-ghyall, *v.* fulfil an engagement, perform your promise.

COIMGHEALLADH, kóĕ'-ghyăll-Ă, *n. m.* performance of one's promise, fulfilment.

COIMHIDEACHD, kóĕ'-ĕj-ăchg, *n. f.* accompanying, escorting; attending; luchd-coimhideachd, an escort, a suite, a levee, a retinue.

COIMHLEAPACH, kóĕ'-llepp-ach, *n. m.* and *f.* a bed-fellow.

Coimhseas, kŏev''-shas, *n. f.* conscience, (comhaois-f hios *or* fhàs.)

Coimhseasach, kŏev2'-shăs-ach, *a.* conscientious, conscionable.

Coimhseasachd, koev'-shas-ăchg, *n. f.* consciousness.

Coimhlion, cóé'-llèn, *v.* fulfil, fill up, accomplish, perform a promise.

Coimhlion, kŏèl'-lyan, *a.* and *adv.* as often as, as many as; equal in number.

Coimhthional, cóé'-heun-al, *n. m.* assembly, gathering, collecting; collection.

Coimpire, kóèm'-pèr-à, *n. m.* and *f.* an equal in rank.

Coimpireachd, kóèm'-pèr-ăchg, *n. f.* equality in rank, a commonwealth, commonweal.

Coin, kóén, *n. m. pl.* dogs; *coin*-f hodair, *fleas.* We must not tell the island where this word is used, otherwise our M—— friends would kill us.

Coin-bhraghad, kóèn-vhrâd', *n. pl.* king's evil.

Coinean, kŏĕn'-an', *n. m.* a rabbit, a coney.

Coingeis, kóèng'-ăsh, *a.* indifferent, quite careless; tha mi *coingeis, I am quite indifferent, I do not care*; is *coingeis* còca, *it is no matter*; is *coingeis* dhuit, *it is no matter to you, it is all the same to you*; an *coingeis* cò aca a bheir mi leam, *is it indifferent which of them I take?*

Coingheall, kŏèn'-nyall, *n. m.* a loan.

Coinghealach, kóèn'-nyall-ăch, *a.* accommodating, lending, helping, kind, ready to lend.

Coingheallaich, kóèn-nyall-èch, *v.* lend, accommodate.

Coinigin, kóèn'-ê-gin, *n. f.* a rabbit warren.

Coinne, kòen'-nyà, *n. f.* meeting, assignation, reproach; cha 'n f haigh mi *coinne* air son m' athar, *I will never be reproached on account of my father*; picnic party, *North*; *v.* imitate, follow the example of; an ann a' *coinne* riumsa a tha thu, *is it imitating me you are?*

Coinneach, kōèn'-nyach, *a.* fog, moss, còinnteach.

Coinneal, kaŏn'-nyall, *n. f.* a candle; *pl.* coinnlean.

Coinnealaich, kŏèn'-nyal-èch, *v.* brandish, flourish, *coinnealaich* bata, *brandish a stick.*

Coinneal-bhath, kun'-nyal-vhâ, *v.* excommuniecte; Irish, cuir a mach a comunn.

Coinneamh, kòèn'-uv, *n. f.* meeting, assembly.

Coinnich, kòèn'-nyèch, *v.* meet, assemble, oppose.

Coinnlean bianain, teine-thionnachain.

Coinnleir, kaŏély''-lyar', *n. m.* a candlestick.

Coip, koyp, *n. f.* a heap of foam *or* froth.

Coir, kôer, *a.* decent; easy minded, worthy; duine *còir, a decent* or *worthy man.*

Coir, kôèr, *n. f.* right, equity, justice, integrity, honesty; propriety; a' cumail na *corach* rium, *doing justice to me*; maintaining my right; rinn thu *chòir, you have acted with propriety*; charter; *coirichean* an f hearainn, *the charter of the land*; proximity, nearness, contiguity; a' *chòir* a' bhaile, *near the town*; na d' thig am *chòir, do'nt come near me*; mar bu *chòir* dhuit, *as you ought*; *còir*-bhreith, *birth-right*; authority; le *còir, with authority.*

Coirb, kŏèrb, *v.* corrupt; coirbte, abandoned.

Coirce, kŏèrk'-à, *n. m.* oats.

Coirceag, a bee-hive; caornag properly.

Coire, kur''-à, *n. m.* blame, fault, defect, wrong, hurt, harm; sin, guilt, crime.

Coire, kŏèr''-a, *n. m.* a cauldron, kettle, a place resembling a cauldron; a dell, whirlpool; *coire*-bhreacain, *the Jura whirlpool.*

Coireach, kur''-ăch, *a.* in fault, blameable; *n.* a defaulter; criomachair an *coireach, blame the defaulter*; the guilty.

Coireaman, kur'-am-an, *n. m.* coriander

Coirich, kur'-èch, *v.* blame, reprove.

Coireal, kur'-al, *n. m.* loud tone of voice, as a person scolding, *or* in a passion.

Coirneach, kŏĕr'-nyach, the bird kingfisher.

Coirneal, kôèrn''-all, *n. m.* colonel.

Coisbheart, kosh'-art, *n. m.* greaves, shoes, &c.

Coise, kòèsh'-à, of a foot.

Coiseachd, kòsh'-ăchg, *n.f.* pedestrianism, walking; travelling on foot.

Coisg, kŏshg, *v.* staunch; quiet, still; caisg.

Coisich, kòsh'-èch, *v.* walk, travel on foot.

Coisiche, kòsh'-èch-à, *n. c.* a traveller, pedestrian.

Coisinn, kòsh'-ènn, *v* gain, earn, win; deserve.

Coisrig, kòsh'-règ, *v.* consecrate, sanctify; coisrigte, *consecrated*; uisge *coisrigte, holy water.*

Coiste, kŏshj'-tyà, *pt.* spent, exhausted, worn.

Coite, kŏèjt'-à, *n. f.* a punt, *or* small boat; hut.

Coitcheann, kŏejt'-chyann, *a.* public exposed to many callers, as a house near the highway.

COITCHEANNAS, kŏĕjt′-chyann-as, *n. f.* exposure, state of being subject to many calling; a public situation, as a house.

COITEACHADH, kōjt′-ach-a², *pt.* pressing to accept any thing; contending, as in an argument.

COITEAR, kŏejt′-ar′, a cottager, cotter.

COITICH, kōĕt′-ėch, *v.* press, contend, maintain.

COL, koll, *n. m.* incest; *v.* restrain, hinder.

COLBH, kŏll′-uv, *n. m.* front of a bed; plank, pillar; our àigeach friends murder it, calbh.

COLG, koll′-ug, *n. m.* fierce, determined look; confounded with calg often.

COLGARRA, koll′-ug-urr-à, fierce-looking, stern.

COLGARRACHD, kŏll′-ug-urr-achg, *n. f.* sternness; new-year's eve; an absurd hammering at any thing.

COLLAINN, kŏll′-ènn, *n. f.* new year's eve, &c.

COLLUNN, koll′-unn, *n. f.* the body, the trunk.

COLPACH, kŏlp′-ach, *n. f.* heifer; biorach.

COLTACH, kŏll′-tach, *a.* like, probable, likely.

COLTAIR, kŏllt²′-ur, *n. m.* a coulter.

COLTAS, kŏllt′-as, *n. m.* appearance, resemblance.

COM, kōm, *n. m.* the trunk of the body, chest, the region of the viscera.

COM', kōm, *n. m. adv.* why, wherefore; *com'* am b'fhiach leat, *why would you condescend?—never mind.*

COMA, kōm′-à, *a.* indifferent, not caring; disagreeable, hateful; is *coma* leam thu, *I hate you, you are disagreeable to me*; nach *coma* leatsa, *what is that to you—never you mind*; is *coma* dhomhsa còc, *it is no matter to me—I am quite indifferent*; is *coma* leis an righ Eòghan, is *coma* le Eòghan co dhùibh, *the king hates Hugh, and Hugh does not care a straw for that.*

COMAIN, kōm′-an′, *n. f.* obligation, favour received; tha mi mòran ad *chomain, I am much obliged to you*; cha 'n 'eil mi ad *chomain, I am not obliged to you*; cha b'e do *chomain* e, *I did not deserve that at your hand*; *comain* do làimh fèin, *tit for tat*; fogh *chomain* agadsa, *under obligations to you*; *comain* an uilc a ni, *reprisals, evil for evil. Sm.*

COMAITH, kōm′-ėch, *n. f.* messing, mess; eating out of the same dish.

COMANACHADH, kòm′-ăn-ăch-Ă, *n. m.* sacrament; communion; celebration of the Lord's supper; luchd *comanachaidh, communicants.*

COMANAICH, kòm′-an-ėch, *v.* communicate.

COMARADH, kŏm′-ar-Ă, *n. m.* any thing thrown on the shore; booty.

COMARAICH, kōm′arr-ėch, *n. f.* protection. *Mf.*

COMAS, kòm′-us, *n. m.* ability, capability, permission; authority, power; virility; orra-chomais, an amulet to deprive a person of his virility; power, licence.

COMASACH, kòm′-as-ach, *a.* able, capable, powerful; in good worldly circumstances.

COMASACHD, kòm′-as-achg, *n. f.* capability.

COMEIRCE, kom′-erk-a, *n. m.* dedication. *Irish.*

COMH, kó, for *con.* and *com.* in English; written often co, and signifies equality, fellowship; air *chomh*-bidhich is leapa riumsa, *having the same meat and bed as I have*; *comh*-aigne, *fellow-feeling.*

COMHAIMSIREACH, kó-ém′-shėr-ach, *a.* at the same time; contempory; *n. c.* a contempory.

COMHAIMSIREIL, ko-ém′-shėr-al, *a.* contempory.

COMHAIR, kó′-ėr, *n. m.* direction, tendency; an *comhair* a chinn, *headlong, forward*; an *comhair* a chuil, *backwards.*

COMHAIRLE, kó′-urly²-à, advice, counsel.

COMHAIRLICH, kó′-urly′-ėch, *v.* advise, counsel, admonish, put on one's guard.

COMHAIRLICHE, kó′-url-ėch-à, *n. m.* an adviser, admonisher, monitor, counsellor.

COMHAIB, kó′-aŏėb, *n. f.* contention about rights; *v.* contend about rights, *or* time to do something.

COMHAOIS, kó′-aŏsh, *n. m.* and *f.* eelings, a contemporary; one of the same age.

COMH-AONTAICH, kó-ùnt′-ėch, *v.* yield assent, agree, accede, accord.

COMHARRA, kó′-urr-ă, *n. m.* mark, sign, token, symptom; sexual mark.

COMHARRAICH, kó′-úrr-ėch, *v.* mark, observe, point out; comharraichte, singular, noted.

COMHARTAICH, kó′-art-ėch, *n. f.* barking, tabhunn.

COMH-BHANN, kó-vhann′, *n. m.* bond.

COMH-BHUAIL, kó′-vhŭăĕl, *v.* strike mutually.

COMH-CHOMUNN, ko′-chòm-unn, *n. m.* fellowship.

COMH-CHRUINNEACHADH, kó′-chrŭĕn-nyach-Ă, collection, assembly, congregation.

COMH-CHRUINNICH, kó′-chrŭĕn-nėch, *v.* gather, assemble, collect, congregate.

COMH-CHUDTHROM, kó′-chŭd-hròm, *n. m.* equiponderance, equilibrium, equal weight.

COMHDACH, kó'-ddach, *n. m.* clothing, dress; a proof, evidence; mar *chomhdach* air sin, *as a proof of that*; dè 'n *comhdach* bh' air, *what dress had he on?*
COMHDAICH, kó'-ddèch, *v.* dress, cover, clothe, shelter; prove, witness.
COMH-DHAINNICH, kó'-ghénn-èch, confirm.
COMHDHALTA, kó'-ălt-a, *n. c.* foster-brother *or* sister; a Highland cousin.
COMHDHALTAS, kó'-allt-us, *n. m.* relationship of fosterage; sucking the same breast.
COMH-DHEUCHAINN, kó-ghèch'-ènn, *n. f.* competition, rivalry, trial of valour.
COMHDHUIN, kó'-ghŭn, *v.* conclude, close, end.
COMHDHUNADH, kó'-ghun-X, *n. m.* conclusion.
COMH-EIGNICH, kó'-āèg-nnèch, *v.* force, compel.
COMHEUD, kuv'-vhèdd, *adv.* how many.
COMHFHARPAIS, kó'-arp-ash, *n. f.* competition, emulation; gibing, jeering, taking off.
COMHFHARPAISEACH, kó-arp'-ash-ach, *a.* imitative.
COMH-FHOGHAR, kó-aŏ'-ur, *n. m.* a consonant; mutual stroke and sound, resound.
COMH-FHREAGAIR, kó-rrăg'-ur', *v.* suit, re-echo; *chomh-fhreagair* gach tulm is cnoc, *every hill and knoll resounded, re-echoed. Sm.*
COMHFHREAGAIRT, kó-rrăgg'-ărty', *n. f.* a re-echo, correspondence, uniformity, agreement.
COMHFHREAGARRACH, kó-rrăg'-arr-ach, *a.* correspondent.
COMHFHUILINN, kó-ŭll'-ènn, *v.* sympathize.
COMHFHULANNAS, kó-ŭll'-unn-us, *n. m.* fellow-feeling, sympathy, fellow-suffering.
COMHFHURTACHD, kó'-urt-ăchg, *n. m.* comfort, consolation; aid, help.
COMFHURTAICH, kó'-urt-èch, *v.* comfort, aid.
COMHFHURTAIR, kó'-urt-ăr', *n. m.* a comforter.
COMH-GHAIR, kó'-ghàèr, *n. f.* conclamation.
COMH-GHAIRDEACHAS, kó'-ghârj-ach-us, *n. f.* congratulation, mutual joy.
COMH-IOMLAID, kó'-ém-lăj, *n. f.* commutation.
COMH-IONNAN, kó'-ĕŭn-un, *a.* equal, same.
COMH IONNANAS, kó'-ĕun-ann-us, *n. f.* equality.
COMHLA, kó'-lla, *ad.* together, along with, in company; thigibh *comhla, come together*; falbh *comhla* riumsa, *come along with me.*
COMHLACH, kò'-llach, *n. f.* straw, fodder.
COMHLAICH, kò'-llèch, *v.* meet, intercept.
COMHLADH, kó'-llà, *n. f.* door, shutter.
COMHLANN, kó'-llann, *n. f.* duel, combat.
COMHLORG, kó'-llòrg, *n. m.* result, effort
COMHLUADAIR, kó'-lŭăd-ar, *n. m.* conversation.
COMH-MHOTHAICH, kó-vhó'-èch, *v.* sympathize; comh-mhothachadh, sympathy, sympathising.
COMHNADH, kó'-na[2], *n. m.* help, assistance.
COMHNADALACH, kó'-na-dull-ach, *a.* conversable; duine còir *comhnadalach, a decent conversable man.*
COMHNADAIL, kó'-na-dull, *n. m.* conversation, conference, dialogue, talking together; (comhna-dail.)
COMHNARD, kó'-nârrd, *a.* level, plain, even; rathad *comhnard, a level* or *even road* or *surface*; *n. m.* a plain.
COMHNUICH, kó'-nnèch, *v.* dwell, inhabit, reside; more often, gabh comhnuidh.
COMHNUIDH, kó'-nnè, *n. m.* habitation, a residence; an *comhnuidh, habitually.*
COMH-OBAIR, kó-ōb[2]'-ur', *n. f.* same employment.
COMH-OIBRICH, kó'-aŏèb-rèch, *v.* co-operate.
COMH-OIBRICHE, kó'-aŏĕb-rrèch-à, *n. m.* co-operator, coadjuator; fellow-labourer.
COMH-OIGHRE, kó-aŏĕ'-rrà, *n. m.* co-heir.
COMHPHAIRT, compairt, partnership.
COMHRADH, kó'-rră, *n. m.* conversation, dialogue.
COMHRAG, kó'-ragg, *n. m.* fight, as bulls, &c.
COMHRAIG, kó'-règg, *v.* fight, as black cattle.
COMHSAICH, kó'-sèch, *v.* contend, dispute.
COMH SGOILEAR, kó'-skŏll-ăr', *n. m.* schoolfellow.
COMH-SHEIRM, kó-hārum', *n. m.* harmony.
COMH-SHEOMRAICHE, kó-hyôm'-rrèch-à, *n. m.* a room companion *or* chum.
COMH-SHINTE, kó-hyēnn'-tyà, *a.* parallel.
COMH-SHIORRUITH, kó-hē[2]'-rruèch, *a.* coeternal.
COMH-SHRUTH, kó-hrrû', *n. m.* confluence.
COMH-SHUIRICH, kó'-hŭèr-èch, *n. f.* rivalship.
COMH-SHUIRICHE, kó-hŭèr''-èch-a, a rival.
COMHSPAID, kó'-spăj, *n. f.* a quarrel.
COMHSPAIDEACH, co'-spajj-ach, *a.* quarrelsome, contentious; ill-natured.
COMH-SPAIRN, kó-spâĕrn', *n. f.* emulation.
COMHSTACH, kó'-stach, *a.* obliging, accom

modating, useful, convenient; *n. f.* a concubine, a whore

Comhstath, kó'-sta, *n. m.* a loan, an accommodation, obligation, favour.

Comh-stri, ko'-strêv, *n. f.* strife; emulation, rivalry, mutual striving.

Comh-thruas, kó-hrŭăs', *n. m.* sympathy, pity.

Comh-thulgadh, kó-hŭlg'-X, *n. m.* agitation.

Companach, kómp'-an-ach, *n. m.* companion.

Companachd, kómp'-an-achg, *n. f.* companionship.

Compairt, kómp'-ârty', *n. f.* partnership.

Compairteach, komp'-ărty'-ach, partaking.

Compairteachd, ko'mp-arty'-achg, *n. f.* participation.

Compairtich, komp'-arty'-êch, *v.* participate, partake.

Companas, komp'-an-us, *n. f.* partnership, society, friendship, fellowship; intercourse.

Comunn, kòm'-unn, *n. m.* society, club, company; fellowship, intercourse, association.

Comunnaich, kòm'-unn'-êch, *v.* associate.

Cona, kòn'-a, *n. m.* moss crops.

Conablach, kón'-abb-lach, *n. m.* any thing mangled.

Conablaich, kón'-abb-llêch, *v.* mangle, disfigure, lacerate; conablachadh, mangling, &c.

Conachag, kón'-ăch-ag, *n. f.* a conch. (Greek.)

Conachair, kŏn'-ăch-aêr, *n. c.* a sick person, who neither gets better or worse in health.

Conairt, kón'-ărty', *n. f.* barking of many dogs; scolding on a high key.

Conaltrach, kon'-alt-rach, *a.* convers able.

Conaltradh, kon'-alt-rX, *n. m.* conversation, talk.

Conan, kon'-an, *n. m.* one of the Fingalians; peevish person.

Conanachd, kon'-an-ăchg, *n. f.* venery *Lochaber.*

Conas, kon'-us, *n. m.* furze, whins; strife, 1.

Conasach, kon'-us-ach, *a.* fretful, peevish, short-tempered, apt to take offence.

Conasg, kon'-ask, *n. m.* whins, furze.

Condasach, kond'-as'-ach, *a.* furious; *air boil.*

Condrachd, kónd'-drachg, *n. f.* mischief, mishap; *condrachd* ort, *mischief take you!*

Condual, cón'-dŭăl, *n. m.* embroidery. *Ir.*

Confhadh, kon'-X, *n. m.* the raging of the sea; fury, the greatest rage.

Conghair, kón'-a-ghăêr, *n. f.* uproar fury.

Conlach, Irish pronunciation of Comhlach.

Conn, kōnn2, *n. m.* water-band of a hank of yarn; da-*chonn, heer-band,* band for two cuts of yarn. In Skye, principle; duine gun *chonn, a man without principle* or *sense.*

Connadh, kōnn2'-X, *n. m.* fuel, firewood, cuall *chonnaidh, a faggot of firewood.*

Connsaich, for Comhsaich, co-sathaich, quarrel, dispute, contend.

Connspaid, for Comhspaid, dispute.

Connspeach, konn'-spech, a wasp.

Connspunn, konn'-spunn, *n. f.* hero, *gaisgeach.*

Conntraigh, konn''-trăĕ-yh', *n. f.* neaptide.

Connuibh, kŏnn''-ŭĕv, *n. m.* hornet, ceardaman.

Cop, kōp, *v.* capsize; *n. m.* a cup.

Copadh, kōp'X, *pt.* capsizing.

Copagach, kōp'-ag-ach, *n. f.* the herb, dock.

Copan, kōp'-an, *n. m.* a cup; the pan of the head; any thing curved.

Copar, kop'-par, *n. m.* copper.

Cor, kŏr, *n. m.* condition, state, situation; is truagh mo *chor, sad is my condition*; dè's *cor* da, *what is become of him?* air na h-uile *cor, by all means*; cò a dh' f hidireas mo *chor, who will feel for my condition, who will sympathize with me?* s'e sin mo *chor, that is my condition*; air *chor, so that*; custom; *cor* na talmhainn, *the custom of the land*; cha dean mi e air *chor* sam bith, *I will not do it on any account*; air *chor* air bith, *anywise, by no means*; air *chor* is gun d' thig thu, *on condition that you come.*

Cora, kòr'-ă, more befitting; bu *chòra* dhuit dol dachaidh, *it is more befitting that you should go home.*

Corach, kòr'-ach, *gen.* of Còir, of right, justice, rectitude; slighe na *còrach, the path of rectitude* or *justice.*

Coracha, same as Còra, more befitting.

Corc, kŏrk, *n. f.* a butcher's cleaver *or* knife; Scotch whittle.

Coram, kŏr'-um, *n. m.* a faction *or* association; a bad set of people.

Corc, kŏrk, *n. m.* a fairy bull, a water bull; laogh corcach, *a calf having small ears, like his father the* corc, (ominous of evil); *n. f.* hemp, caineab.

Corcan-coille, kŏrk'-an-kully'-a, *n. m.* bullfinch.

Corcur, kŏrk'-ŭr, *n. m.* crimson, scarlet.

Cord, kôrd'd, *v.* agree, settle, accord, adjust, arrange; used for Sginnich too.

Cordadh, kôrd'-X, *n. m.* agreement, settlement, good terms *or* understanding.

CORN, kôrn, *n. m.* a bale of cloth; a drinking-horn; *v.* fold cloth.

CORNADH, kôrn′-Ă, *pt.* folding cloth.

CORNAIRE, kŏrn′-ăr'-ȧ, *n. m.* a folder.

CORN-CAISIL, kôrn′-kash-ėl, *n. m.* wall penny wort.

CORON, kor′-on, *n. m.* a crown, a chaplet.

CORP, korpp, corpse, the body.

CORPANTA, korp′-annt-ȧ, *a.* corpulent, bulky.

CORPANTACHD, kŏrp′-ănnt-achg, *n. f.* corpulence.

CORPARRA, kŏrp′-urr-a, corporeal, not spiritual.

CORP-SHNASAIR, kŏrp′-hunăs-ar'-ȧ, a body polisher; a statuary.

CORP-SGIAN, korp′-skĕăn, *n. f.* a scalpel, *or* doctor *or* dissector's knife.

CORP-SGIANADAIR, kŏrp′-skĕăn-ăd-ar', *n. m.* a dissector, an anatomist, a doctor.

CORP-SGIANADAIREACHD, kŏrp′-skĕăn-ad-aer-achg, anatomy, dissection, fear-rannsachaidh cuirp; also, corp-rannsachair.

CORR, kôrr, *n. m.* odds, excess, surplus, overplus, remainder; thoir dhomhsa an *còrr, give me the surplus*; a heron, a stork, a hern; *còrr* air cladach, *a heron on the sea shore*; also, *corra* chrithich, *corra* bhàn, a heron, &c.; *adj.* singular, extraordinary, odd; bliadhna *chòrr, an extraordinary year*; duine *còrr, a singular person, an eminent person.*

CORRA-BEAGA, corr′-a-beug-ȧ, tiptoe; *North*, corra-bìod.

CORRA-CHAGAILT, kŏrr′-a-chag-alty', *n. f.* sulphureous hue in dying embers, salamander.

CORRACH, kŏrr′-ach, *a.* steep, precipitous; àite *corrach, a steep place*; passionate.

CORRACH, kŏrr′-ach, *n. f.* fetters; Lang-aid. (Irish.)

CORRACHEANN, kŏrr′-a-chyann, *n. m.* a giddy head.

CORRACHEANNACH, korr′-a-chyann-ach, light-headed, giddy, inconstant.

CORRAG, kŏrr′-ag, *n. f.* fore-finger; left-hand stilt of a plough.

CORRA-MARGAIDH, kŏrra′-mărg-ė, *n.* the rabble, the offscouring of the people. *B.*

CORRA-MAOTHAR, kŏrra′-maŏ-har, *n. m.* the sea-pike, seòrsa éisg. *Islay.*

CORRAN, korr′-an, *n. m.* a shearing-hook *or* sickle; semi-circular bay; point of land, like a hook *or* sickle.

CORRANACH, kŏrr′-an-ach, *n. f.* funeral-cry. *Ir.*

CORRA-CHEOSACH, kŏrr′-a-chyôs-ach, *n. f.* cheslip.

CORRA-MEILLE, kŏrra′-măly'-a, *n. m.* wild liquorice.

CORRAMHEUR, kŏrr′-a-vhérr, *n. f.* little finger.

CORRALACH, kŏrr′-a-lach, *n. m.* remainder, excess, surplus, overplus, odds.

CORR-SHUGAN, korr′-hûg-an, *n. f.* twist-handle.

CORRUICH, korr′-ėch, *n. f.* offence, rage, anger, ire, wrath; tha *corruich* air, *he is offended*; na gabh *corruich, be not offended.*

CORSA, kôr′-sȧ, *n. m.* coast; air *còrsa* na Frainge, *on the coast of France.*

CORSAIR, kôr′-săr, *n. f.* a coaster, cruiser.

CORSAIREACHD, kôr′-săėr-achg, *n. f.* coasting, cruising.

COR-SHIOMAIN, kŏr-hēmm′-an^3, *n. f.* twist-handle.

COS, an Irish foot, ditto, with a lump on it, coich.

COS, kōs, *n. m.* a sponge, *I.*; crevice, hole. *O.*

COSACH, kōs′-ach, *a.* spongy, porous.

COSACHD, kōs′-achg, *n. f.* sponginess, porousness.

COSAICHE, kōs′-ėch-ȧ, *n. f.* degree of sponginess, &c.

COSAIL, kŏs′-al, *a.* likely, like, similar.

COSALACHD, kŏs′-al-achg, *n. f.* likeliness, similarity.

COSD, kŏsdd, *v.* spend, waste, wear. *Teu.*

COSDAIL, kosdd′-al, *a.* expensive, extravagant.

COSDALACHD, kŏsdd′-ăl-ăchg, *n. f.* expensiveness.

COSDAS, kosdd′-us, *n. f.* expense, expenditure, cost; waste, profuseness.

COSLAS, kos′-las, *n. m.* appearance, likeness.

COS-NABUIDH, kŏs′-nnà-bė, *n. m.* walking companion. *No.*

COSAMAL, kōs^2′-a-mal, *n. f.* refuse of meat, straw, &c.

COSNACH, kōs^2′-nach, *n. c.* a labourer, hired servant.

COSNADH, kŏs′-nĂ, *n. m.* earning, winning.

COTA, kaut′-ȧ, *n. m.* coat, petticoat. (Teut.)

COTA-BAN, kaut′-a-bàn, *n. m.* groat, fourpence; fourpence land; leirtheas, two of them; ochdamh, four; ceithrea, eight.

COTA-MOR, kôt′-a-mòr, a great coat.

COTHAICH, kō^2′-ėch, *v.* maintain, contend, strive.

COTHLAM, kŏ′-hllám, *v.* mix different sorts of wool, as black and white.

COTHLAMADH, kŏ′-hllám-Ă, *n. m.* mixture of wools.

COTHONNACH, kō^2′-hŏnn-ach, *n. f.* froth, spray, foam; comh-thonn, beating of waves together; hence the surname Colquhoun.

COTHROM, kŏr′-um, *n. m.* justice, fair play; a dol a dh' ionnsuidh a *chothrom, going to seek justice*; opportunity; a cheud *chothrom* a gheibh mi, *the first opportunity I get*; thoir *cothrom* na Féinne dhomh, *give me fair play*; comfortable circumstances; tha e ann an *cothrom* math, *he is in comfortable circumstances*; weights. *Loch.*

COTHROMACH, kŏrr'-um-ach, just, honest, *B.*; parallel, even with, of the same size; rich, wealthy; duine *cothromach, a just man,* or *a man in easy circumstances.*

COTHROMAICH, kŏr'-um-ēch, *v.* make even with; make of the same size; a *cothromachadh* na scleata, *sizing the slates*; a *cothromachadh* nam bròg, *paring the shoes*; weigh, tomhais. *Lochaber.*

COTA-IOCHDAIR, kŏtt-ēchg'-ėr, *n. m.* under petticoat.

CRABHACH, krâv'-ach, *a.* very religious, very devout, very pious, austere.

CRABHADAIR, krâv'-a-dăr', *n. m.* a monk, an austere religionist, devotee.

CRABHADH, krâv'-Ă, *n. m.* monkish piety.

CRABHAT, krăv'-att, *n. m.* a cravat; Fr. cravate.

CRACAIREACHD, krachg'-ar-achg. *n. f.* conversation. *Sc.*

CRADH, krâ'-gh', *n. m.* torment, torture; *v.* torture; rè a laithean uile *cràdhar* an t'aingidh, *the wicked man travaileth with pain (shall be tortured) all his days.*

CRADHGHEADH, krâ'-yhè, *n. m.* shell-drake, a shell-duck.

CRADHSHLAT, krâ'-hllat, *n. f.* a sort of pillory *or* tread-mill, used by the old Gael; anguish, torment; O, mo *chradhshlat! alas, my torment,* (common.)

CRAG, krâgg, *n. f.* a large hand; also, cròg.

CRAICEANN, kraīchg'-unn, *n.m.* skin, hide; murdered into CROICEONN.

CRAINN, kràènn, *n. f.* the queen of the hive; an ugly old woman, *Islay*; a pig. *No.*

CRAITEACH, krâ'-tyach, *a.* intensely painful, torturing, tormenting; causing great pain.

CRAITEACHD, krâ'-tyăchg, *n. m.* painfulness.

CRAMBAID, kramb'-ăj, *n. m.* a cramp; objection.

CRALAIDH, krâ'-llī, *v.* crawl, sprawl; craladh, crawling, sprawling, (cràdh-laidh.)

CRANN, krann, *n. m.* a plough; cuir na h-eich 'sa *chrann, yoke the horses in the plough*; bar, bolt; cuir an *crann* air an dorus, *bolt the door*; a mast; *crann* na luinge, *the ship's mast*; full of a barrel of fresh herring; in the shape of a tree (obsolete); a lot; chance, risk, ballot; thàinig an *crann* air, *he was chosen by ballot*; cha 'n 'eil cuid na *crann* agad 'sa ghothuch so, *you have neither part nor lot in this affair, Bible, Islay*; side, partiality, interest; tha Dia Jehovah air mo *chrann, the Lord, Jehovah is on my side, is in my interest*; cò bhios air do *chrann, who shall be your friend*; ma bhios tusa air mo *chrann, if you befriend* or *side me*; gabh cuid do *chroinn, take your chance*; ma s'e sin do *chrann, if that be your lot*; *crann*-mòr, neo, meadhoin, *main-mast of a ship*; *crann*-uisge, spreoid dall, *a bowsprit*; *crann* deiridh, *mizen-mast*; *crann*-fige, *fig-tree*; *crann*-fiona, *a vine.*

CRANN, krann, *v.* bar, bolt, barricade wither, decay, wear off; wind; a' *crannadh, withering, dying by inches*; *crann* an dorus, *bolt* or *bar the door.*

CRANNAG, krann'-ag, *n. f.* pulpit; cross-trees.

CRANNALACH, krann'-al-ach, *n. f.* a wreck; chaidh i' na *crannalach, she was wrecked, (as a ship)*; ruins of any thing.

CRANN-ATHAIR, krann'-á-hur, the constellation called the bear; the seven stars in it; crann-arair. *Mull.*

CRANNCHUR, krann'-ach-ur, *n. m.* lot, ballot; fate, destiny, predestination; casting of lots, choosing by ballot; ma s'e sin mo *chrannchur, if that be my fate* or *destiny*; cuir *crannchur, refer to the lot.*

CRANN-COTHROMACHAIDH, krann-kór'-am-ăch-ė, meidh, balance.

CRANNDAIDH, krannd'-ė, *a.* excessively cold and withering, as weather in the spring of the year.

CRANNDAIDHEACHD, krannd'-ė-achg, *n. f.* cold withering weather, the withering blast.

CRANN-DEALBH, krănn-dyal'-uv, *n. m.* weaver's warp, *or* warping machine.

CRANNTACHAN, krann'-tach-an, *n. m.* churn-stick.

CRANN-TARA, krann'-tar-a, *n. m.* a beam of gathering, as a signal for battle.

CRANNTARRUNN, krann'-tarr-unn, *n. f.* a tree-nail, *or* the wooden pegs in ship-building.

CRANNTARSUINN, krann'-tars-ènn, *n. m.* diameter.

CRANN-TOISICH, krann-tôsh'-ēch, *n. m.* fore-mast.

CRAOBH, krāov, *n. f.* a tree; globules *or* bells on whisky, *or* any other liquid; *v.* spread, gush out and ramify at the same time; 'fhuil a' *craobhadh* ma thalamh, *his blood gushing and ramifying*; propagate, shoot forth.

CRAOBHACH, krāov'-ach, *a.* full of trees in ramifying gushes, as blood; 'fhuil *chraobhach, his streaming blood.*

Craobhaidh, krāov′-ė, *a.* tender, nervous. *N.*

Craobharnach, krāov′-arn-ach, a shrubbery, a hedge of thorn, whins, &c.

Craobh-ealp, kraov′-ĕălp, *v.* ingraft, graft.

Craobh-ealpaire, krāov′-yalp-ar à, *n. m.* an ingrafter, fear ealpaidh chraobh.

Craobh-sgaoil, kraov′-skāŏėl, *v.* branch, ramify, spread, propagate.

Craobh-sgaoileadh, krāov′-skāoėl-a², *n. m.* propagation; *pt.* publishing, spreading.

Craos, krāos, *n. m.* an enormous mouth.

Craosach, krāos′-ach, *a.* wide mouthed; voracious; *n. f.* a wide-mouthed female.

Craosaire, krāos′-ar'-à, *n. m.* wide-mouthed fellow.

Craosnach, kraos′-nnach, *n. f.* particular kind of spear, (sleagh.) *Dr. Smith.*

Crasgach, krâsg′-ach, *a.* crawling *or* walking, as a person feeling torturing pain; branching, as stamped cloth.

Crasgaoil, krâ′-sgăŏėl, *v.* spread hands and feet, as a person feeling torturing pain; *n. f.* sprawling, crawling; torture.

Crath, krahă, *v.* shake, agitate; *crath* do cheann, *shake your head*; tremble, quiver, brandish, flourish; *chrath* e a bhata, *he flourished his staff*; coinnealaich; *v. n.* besprinkle, sprinkle, wave; *crath* uisge air, *besprinkle it with water*; wave; *crath* ris, *wave to him*; a *crathadh*, shaking, brandishing, waving.

Cre, krā, *n. m.* the body; keel. *M. L.*

Creabhaichean, krév′-ėchg-ăn', *n. m.* a bandy.

Creach, krech, *v.* harrow a nest, rob birds of their young; despoil, plunder, rob, ruin, pillage; *chreach* thu mi, *you have ruined me*; *n. f.* pillage, spoil, plunder, ruination, devastation; mo *chreach*, mo *chreach*, *my complete ruination!* alas! and alas!

Creachadair, krech′-a-dăr, *n. m.* despoiler, pillager, freebooter, depredator, robber.

Creachan, krech′-an, *n. m.* a large, ribbed cockle, a drinking shell; far an nall an t-slige *chreachain, hand over the drinking shell.*

Creadh, krè, *n. f.* clay, (*No.* crĕă); plaster with clay; bedaub.

Creagach, krrăgg′-ach, *a.* rocky, craggy, rough, cliffy; from creig; *gen.* creige.

Creagag, krăgg′-ăg, *n. f.* sea perch; *creagag* uisge, *a water perch*; never conger.

Creamh, krév, *n. m.* garlick, leeks.

Crean, krén′, *v. n.* suffer for; cò a *chreanas* air sin, *who shall suffer for that? creante*, dearly bought *or* suffered for. *Isles.*

Creanaich, krén′-ėch, *v.* tremble, shiver, start, feel a tremour *or* thrilling.

Creangan, kreng′-an, *n. m.* a deep wound.

Creapal, kremp′-all, hinder. *H. S.*

Creathall, krā²′-all, *n. f.* a cradle.

Creatrach, krā²t′-rach, *n. f.* wilderness, fàsach.

Creic, krāėchg², *v.* sell, dispose of; trade.

Creid, krāojj, *v.* believe, rely; be convinced.

Creideach, krăŏjj′-ach, *n. m.* a believer.

Creideadh, krāojj′-aŏ-gh', *n. m.* faith, belief, persuasion, religious tenets, *Argyle*; in Ireland, creideamh.

Creideas, kraŏjj′-as, *n. m.* credit, esteem.

Creideasach, kraŏjj′-as-ach, *a.* respectable; responsible, creditable; in good repute, credible.

Creidte, kraojj′-tyà, *pt.* believed; confirmed.

Creig, krăgg, *n. f.* a rock; taobh na *creige, aside the rock*; a precipice, quarry.

Creim, krām, *v.* pick, nip, nibble, gnaw.

Creameartaich, *n. f.* picking; *pt.* picking.

Creis, krāėsh, *v.* grease; *n. f.* grease.

Creithire, for Greighire, a gnat; from greigh, uncommon heat of the sun.

Creoth, kryô *n.* hurt, wound. *Skye.*

Creoithtiche, kryô′-tyėch-à, *n. m.* an invalid *or* sick person, getting well one day, and worse the next.

Creothar, krô′-ar, *n. m.* a woodcock. *Irish.*

Creothluinn, krôl′-llėnn, *n. f.* a bier, 20; sickly person. *Is.*

Creubh, krāv, *n. m.* body; *v.* dun, (not *English.*)

Creubhach, krāv′-ach, *n. m.* withered wood *or* branches; fire-wood; dry sticks.

Creubhag, krāv′-ag, *n. f.* a beloved little female.

Creuchd, krāchg, *n. m.* wound; *v.* hurt.

Creuchdach, krāchg′-ach, *a.* full of sores, wounded, hurtful, sore distressed.

Creuchdaire, krāchg′-ur-à, *n. m.* an invalid.

Creud, krādd, *int. pron.* how, *Irish*; *n. m.* a creed, belief; tha barrachd a's *chreud* is a phaidir aige, *he knows more than his creed and rosary, he has had intercourse with the devil, he is a wizard.*

Creutair, krătt′-ăr', *n. c.* a creature, a being.

Criathair, krĕăr′-ėr, *v.* sift, sieve; examine.

Criathar krĕăr′-ar, *n. m.* a sieve.

Criathrach, krĕăr'-ăch, *n. f.* marshy ground.

Criathrachail, krĕăr'-rach-all, *a.* marshy.

Criathradh, krĕăr'-Ă, *n. m.* the process of sifting; *pt.* sifting; shrugging.

Cridhe, krrē²'-à, *n. m.* heart; presumption; dè a' *chridhe* bh' agad, *how dare ye presume!* cha 'n 'eil a *chridhe* agad, *you dare not*; a chiall mo *chridhe, my dearest dear*; a mhic *cridhe, my dear, Sir!* a n'ic *cridhe, my dear, Madam!* literally, the son and daughter of my heart; fhir mo *chridhe, my dear fellow*; cha 'n 'eil a *chridhe* neo dh' anam agad, *you dare not for your life*; cha dean *cridhe* misgeach breug, *the drunken soul tells no lies*; nach ann aige tha an *cridhe, how hardened he is!* bha mi mar mo *chridhe* airson sin, *I did my utmost for that*; bha e mar a *chridhe, he was very keen for it.*

Cridhealas, krhrė'-al-us, *n. m.* kind *or* hearty reception, as a host; state of being touched with drink.

Cridheil, krhė'-al, *a.* hearty, kind, cheerful.

Crinbhriathrach, krēn'-vhrėăr-ach, *a.* silly. *MSS.*

Crine, krē'-nyà, *n. m.* excessive littleness, meanness; also, more *or* most trifling *or* diminutive.

Crinlein, krėn'-lyėn, *n. m.* small writing-desk. *Ir.*

Crioch, krē'ch, *n. f.* boundary, frontier, land-mark; ma na *crìochan, about the borders* or *boundaries*; end, conclusion, close; cuir *crìoch* air, *finish it, kill him*; tha 'n lath' a tighinn gu *crìch, the day comes to a close*; intention, design.

Criochnach, krhrē'-nnach, *a.* come to the years of maturity *or* discretion. *Is.*

Criochnaich, khrė'-nėch, *v.* finish, close; expire, die; *chriochnaich* e an ràir, *he expired last night*; conclude.

Criodhdaich, krēdd'-ėch, *v.* pat *or* stroke affectionately.

Criom, krēmm, *v.* nip, pick, nibble.

Criomag, krėm'-ag, *n. f.* a very small bit.

Criomagaich, krėmm'-ag-ėch, make very small bits; nip, nibble, tease, gall.

Criomb, krēmb, *v.* nip; make small bits.

Criombanta, krēmb'-ant-à, *a.* niggardly mean.

Criombantachd, krēmb'-ant-achg, *n. f.* meanness, niggardliness, want of spirit.

Criombaire, krēmb'-ăr'-a, *n. m.* a miser, churl.

Crion, krēn, *a.* very little *or* diminutive, very trifling; *v.* wither, fade; *chrìon* e, *it faded.*

Crionach, krēn'-ach, *n. m.* withered branches, fire-wood; cual *chrìonaich, faggot of fire-wood.*

Crionna, krēnn'-a, } attentive to the
Crionnta, krēnnt'-à, } minutest articles of gain; wise, prudent.

Crionnachd, krēnn'-achg, } wisdom, pru-
Crionntachd, krēnn'-achg, } dence, minuteness, sagacity.

Criopag, krēpp'-ag, *n. f.* a clew of yarn.

Crios, krėss, *n. m.* girdle, belt, strap, zone; the waist; *v.* gird, belt.

Criosadair, krrėś'-ad-ar, *n. m.* belt-maker

Criosraich, krėss'-rrėch, *v.* gird, bind, swathe.

Criosd, krēssdd, *n. m.* Christ, our Saviour.

Criosdachd, krēssdd'-achg, *n. f.* Christianity, Christendom; feadh na *Criosdachd, throughout Christendom*; benignity.

Criosdail, krēssd'-al, *a.* Christian-like.

Criosdalachd, krēssd'-al-achg, *n. f.* a Christian behaviour and disposition.

Criosduidh, krēssd'-ė, *n. m.* a Christian.

Crios guailne, kress'-gŭăėl-nyà, *n. m.* shoulder-belt.

Crioslach, krėss'-llach, *n. m.* a girdle, belt.

Crioslaich, krėss'-llėch, *v.* gird, tighten, bind.

Crios-muineil, krėss'-mŭėn-al, *n. m.* necklace.

Crios-neimhe, krėss'-nyėv-a, *n. m.* the zodiac.

Criot, krėtt, *n. m.* an earthen vessel. *N.*

Criothach, krė'-ach, *n. m.* the aspen *or* trembling poplar.

Criothnaich, krė'-nnėch, *v.* tremble.

Crioth-thalmhainn, krė'-hhal-vėn, *n. f.* an earthquake.

Criothunn, kre'-unn, *n. m.* poplar-tree.

Crioplach, krėŭp'-lach, *a.* cripple, a decrepid person; *Teut.* cruppal.

Crioplaich, krėŭp'-lėch, *v.* cripple.

Crith, krhė, *v.* tremble, be in a tremour; *n. f.* a tremour, ague; trembling.

Crith-cheol, krhė'-chyôl, *n. f.* quavering.

Crith-chreideadh, krhė'-chraŏjj-Ă, *n. m.* & *f.* Quakerism; crith-chreideach, a Quaker.

Critheanach, krhė'-an-ach, *a.* tremulous, trembling; am fiabhrus *crithcanach, the ague.*

Crith-reothadh. *See* Liathnach, hoar *or* hair frost.

Cro, krrō, *n. m.* a fold; *crò*-chaorach, *a sheep-fold*; a hut; the eye of a needle.

Croc, krôchg, *n. p.* antlers of deer; *v.* pound. *N.*

Crocach, krôchg'-ach, *a.* antlered; *n. f.* an antlered machine, to keep calves from sucking.

Croch, krôch, *n. m.* saffron red, dearg.

Croch, krŏch, *v.* hang, suspend; depend; *chroch* iad e, *they hanged him*; *croch* an còta, *suspend the coat*; an *crochadh* ris, *depending on it.*

Crochadair, krŏch-a-dăr, *n. m.* a hangman.

Crochaire, krŏch-ar'-å, a villain, rogue.

Crodh, krò-gh, *n. p.* black cattle, kine; in Perthshire, plural of bò, cows, ba.

Crodha, krò'-å, *a.* valiant, gaisgeil.

Crodhan, krŏ'-an, *n. m.* parted hoof.

Crog, krôgg, *n. f.* a large hand; a paw.

Crogach, krôg'-ach, *a.* having large hands *or* paws; *n. f.* a female having large hands.

Crogaid, krŏgg'-ăj, *n. f.* a beast having small horns.

Crogair, kròg'-ėr, *v.* handle awkwardly; bungle.

Crogaire, krôg'-ăr'-å, *n. m.* a man having large hands; a bungler.

Crogairsich, krôg'-ar-sėch, *n. f.* rough handling; bungling, spoiling.

Crogan, krŏg'-an, *n. m.* a little dish.

Crogan, krogg'-an, *n. f.* a little horn.

Croic, krŏėchg, *n. f.* difficulty, hardships, a hard task; cha *chròic* sin air, *that is no task to him*; foam, froth.

Croich, kroych, *n. f.* a gibbet, gallows, cross.

Croid, krojj, *n. m.* a handsome present.

Croidh, kròė'-yh', *v.* house corn; pen *or* fold cattle; a *croidheadh* an arbhair, *housing the corn*; (in Harris,) a' dluitheadh an arbhair; a *cròidheadh* nan caorach, *penning* or *folding the sheep.*

Croidhfhionn, krŏe-yh''eunn, *a.* white-hoofed.

Croidhleon, krŏĕ'-yh'-llyon, *n. m.* a ring *or* circle of children; game of touch.

Croinn, krăoėn, *n. p.* masts; ploughs, &c.

Croinnach, krăoėnn-ach, *n. f.* gibbe, *or* old worn-out animal.

Crois, krŏsh, *n. f.* a yarn reel; a misfortune, a mishap; *v.* reel *or* wind yarn.

Croisgileid, krojsh'-gėl-aėj, child's head-dress. *N.*

Croislin, krosh'-llėn, the line that measures a circle across; diameter. *Irish.*

Crois-tarra, krŏsh-tăr'-ă, *n. m.* a signal of defiance, before commencing battle

Croit, krŏėt', *n. f.* a hunch-back; eminence.

Croit, kraŏėt, *n. f.* a croft, a pendicle of land.

Croitear, kraŏėt'-ăr', *n. m.* crofter.

Cro-leaba, krô-leb'-å, *n. f.* a bier to carry a wounded person.

Crom, krōm, *v.* bend, stoop, decline; descend, bow; tha a' ghrian a' *cromadh, the sun descends*; *crom* do chean, *bend or bow your head*; *a.* bent, crooked, sloping, curved, not straight; *n. m.* a circle. *Ossian.*

Cromadh, krōm'-,ă *n. m.* roof; fo *chromadh* an tighe, *under the roof of the house*; *pt.* bending, stooping, bowing.

Cromag, krŏm'-ag, *n. f.* a peg *or* catch, a tache, a hook to hang on.

Crom-aisinn, krŏm'-ash-ėnn, *n. f.* little rib.

Croman, krŏm'-an, *n. m.* a hawk; kite the *S* of a plough; hip-bone; hoe; *crom an* donais, *a bungler, dolt.*

Crom-nan-gad, krŏm'-na-gad'd, *n.m.* a sort of lazy plough.

Crom-leac, krōm'-llechg, *n. f.* a druidical altar; flag supported by three pillars.

Cron, krŏn, *n. m.* fault, defect, harm, blame, imputation of wrong.

Cronaich, krŏn'-ėch, *v.* hurt with an evil eye; reprove, chide, check, reprimand; *chronaich* e mi, *he reprimanded me.*

Cronail, kron'-al, *a.* offensive, hurtful.

Cronalachg, kron'-al-achg, *n. f.* offensiveness, hurtfulness; perniciousness.

Cronan, kròn-an, *n. m.* purling of a streamlet; purring of a cat; murmuring noise.

Cronanach, kròn'-an-ach, *a.* purring, purling.

Cronanaich, kròn'-an-ėch, *n. f.* a continued slow, gurgling, humming, buzzing, purring sound; a dirge; a bass.

Cron-seanachais, krŏn'-shen-ach-ėsh, *n. m.* anachronism.

Cros, kross, *v.* forbid, go across; air a' *chrosadh, forbidden, set round.*

Crosag, kross'-ag, *n. f.* frame of a fishing-line.

Crosanach, kross'-an-ach, *a.* perverse.

Crosanachd, kross'-ăn-ăchg, *n. f.* bickering, picking a quarrel, as children.

Crosda, krossd'-a, *a.* perverse, fretful; froward, peevish, ill-natured, cankering.

Crosdachg, krosd'-ăchd, *n. f.* fretfulness, perverseness, ill-nature.

Crosgach, krosg'-ach, *a.* traverse, across, diagonal, put cross-ways.

Cruach, krŭăch, *n. f.* a stack of hay *or* peats; heap above the brim of a vessel; pile *or* heap; *v.* pile, heap; 'ga *chruachadh, heaping it, making into stacks.*

Cruachan, krŭăch'-an, *n. m.* the hip; os ceann a' *chruachain, above the hip*; a conical hill; a hill in Argyle.

Cruadal, krŭăd'd'-al, *n. f.* hardship, distress, difficulty; hardihood; never virtue.

Cruadalach, kruad'd'-al-ach, *a.* hardy, capable of enduring hardship *or* pain; duine *cruadalach, a hardy, energetic*

person, distressing, moving, ni *cruadalach, a distressing thing.*

Cruadalach, krăŭd'd''-all-achg, *n. f.* hardship, hardihood; endurance, bravery.

Cruadhach, krăŭ'-ach, *gen.* steel.

Cruadhaich, krau'-ėch, *v.* harden, dry; a *cruadhachadh, hardening, drying.*

Cruadhas, krau'-as, *n. m.* hardness, rigour.

Cruadhlach, krŭăl'-ăch, *n. m.* hard bottom; (boglach, soft bottom); rocky place. *H. S.*

Cruaidh, krŭăė'-yh', *a.* hard, firm; àite *cruaidh, a hard* or *firm place*; distressing, woeful, painful; ni *cruaidh, a distressing thing*; scarce, hard; bliadhna *chruaidh, a scarce year*; narrow-minded, niggardly, parsimonious; duine *cruaidh, a niggardly, parsimonious,* or *narrow-minded person.*

Cruaidh, krŭăė-yh', *n. f.* steel, anchor; *cruaidh* agus dearg, *steel and fire, straw and fire used to light a torch. M. L.*

Cruaidh-ghleachd, kruaĕ'-yh-ghlechg', *n. f.* agony.

Cruas, krŭăs, *n.m.* hardness; niggardliness; hardship; difficulty. *Cont. of* Cruathas.

Crub, krûb, *v.* crouch, cringe, squat, sit; *n. f.* a lame foot; nave; part of a mill; a halt.

Crubach, krûb'-ăch, *a.* lame of a leg.

Crubaiche, krûb'-ėch-å, *n. f.* lameness; a halt.

Cruban, krûb'-an, *n. m.* a crab-fish; cringing or crouching attitude.

Crudha, krû'-a, *n. f.* horse-shoe, hoof.

Cruidh, krŭĕ'-yh', *v.* shoe, as a horse *or* wheel of a cart, coach, &c.

Cruidhte, krŭĕ'-yh'-tya, *pt.* shod as a horse.

Cruime, krŭĕm'-å, *n. f.* a bend, curvation, crookedness; more *or* most bent.

Cruimeal, krŭĕm'-al, *n. c.* a tall bent person.

Cruinn, krŭĕnn, *n. m.* a circle; *a.* round, globular, circular, rotund; maide *cruinn, a round stick*; tha'n saoghal *cruinn, the world is globular*; assembled, collected, gathered, as people; tha'n pobull *cruinn, the people are assembled*; scant, somewhat scant *or* short; tha 'm bàrr gu math *cruinn, the crop is somewhat scant* or *short.*

Cruinne, krŭĕn'-nyå, *n. m.* roundness, rotundity, circularity; the globe, the world; gu crìch na *cruinne, to the ends of the earth*; cha' n' eil do leithid 'sa *chruinne, your match is not on the face of the globe.*

Cruinne-ce, krun-nya-kā', *n. m.* the globe, the world, the universe.

Cruinneachadh krŭĕn'-nyăch-Ă, *n. m.* an assembly, a gathering; *pt.* gathering, collecting, adding.

Cruinneachd, krŭĕn'-nyachg, *n.m.* wheat.

Cruinneadair, krŭĕnn'-ă-dăĭr, *n. m.* a geometrician, fear tohmhais a chruinne.

Cruinneadaireachd, krŭĕnn'-a-dăr'-achg, *n. f.* geometry, spherics, geography.

Cruinneag, krŭĕn'-nyăg, *n. f.* a neat, tidy female.

Cruinnean, krŭĕn'-nyan, *n. m.* all the fingers put together; the quantity the fingers can hold.

Cruinnealas, kruinn'-ăl-ăs, *n. m.* tidiness, economy.

Cruinneil, krŭĕnn'-al, *a.* tidy, economical.

Cruinnich, krŭĕn'-nyėch, *v.* gather, collect; assemble, accumulate, convene draw close, round.

Cruinnichte, krŭĕnn'-ėch-tyå, *pt.* collected.

Cruinnire, krŭĕnn'-ăr-å, *n. m.* a turner. *H.*

Cruinnleum, krŭĕnn'-lyām, *n. m.* a bound.

Cruinte, krŭn'-tyå, *pt.* crowned, finished.

Cruisgean, krŭĕshg'-an', *n. m.* a lamp.

Cruisle, krŭĕsh'-llå, *n. m.* a mausoleum. *Sm.*

Cruit, krŭĕt, *n. f.* a harp; hunch-back, a cringing attitude; *cruit* chiuil, *musical instrument.*

Cruitire, krŭit'-ĕr-å, *n. m.* a hunch-backed person; a harper, musician.

Cruithear, krŭĕ'-ar, *n. m.* a creator.

Cruithneach, krŭĕn'-ach, *n. m.* a Pict.

Cruitheachd, krŭĕ'-achg, *n. m.* the universe, the exact figure, the identity of a person.

Crun, krûn, *n. m.* a crown, five shillings, crown of the head; a garland of flowers.

Crunadh, krûn'-Ă, *n. m.* coronation; *crùnadh* an righ, coronation of the king. *pt. crowning.*

Crun-easpeig, krûn-ās'²-pėg, *n. m.* a mitre.

Crunluadh, krŭn'-lŭă, *n. m.* a quick measure in highland music, a seal.

Crup, krŭp, *v.* contract, shrink.

Crupadh, krŭp'-Ă, *n. m.* contraction; *pt.* contracting; *crupadh*-feithe, *a spasm.*

Cruth, krŭ, *n. m.* shape, form, appearance, expression of countenance.

Cruthach, krŭ'-ăch, *a.* identical, exactly, like, resembling; cho *chruthach, so identical.*

Cruthachadh, krŭ'-ăch-Ă, *n. m.* the creation, the universe; *pt.* creating.

Cruthadair kru'-a-dăr, *n. m.* a creator

CRUTH-ATHARRAICH, krù-ă'-harr-êch, *v.* change shape, transform, transfigure; *cruth-atharrachadh,* transformation, transfiguration; *pt.* transforming.

CRUTHLACH, kru'-llach, *n. c.* a tall bent person; a ghost, a fairy.

CU, kû, *n. m.* a dog; dogs, coin; of the dog, a' choin; nan con, *of the dogs*; *cù* eunaich, *a pointer* or *spaniel*; *cù* luirge, *a blood-hound, a beagle*; *cù* uisge, *a Newfoundland dog.*

CUACH, kŭăch, *n. f.* a Norwegian wooden cup; a drinking cup, bowl of a nest; *cuach* pharaig, plantain, a fold, plait; *v.* plait, fold.

CUACHACH, kŭăch'-ăch, *a.* curled, plaited.

CUAILEAN, kŭăl''-an, *n. m.* a cue, plaited hair.

CUAILLE, kŭăl'-lyâ, *n. m.* a club, bludgeon.

CUAIN, kŭăên, *n. f.* a litter of pigs, whelps, &c.

CUAIRSG, kŭăershg, *v.* roll, wrap, fold.

CUAIRSGEACH, kŭăĕrshg'-ach, *n. f.* a wrapper.

CUAIRT, kŭăirt, *n. f.* a circuit, a round, a circle, a circumference; luchd faire air *chuairtibh,watchmen on their rounds*; a cheud *chuairt, the first round*; pilgrimage, sojourn; cha 'n 'eil annainn ach luchd *cuairt* air thalamh, *we are only sojourners on the earth*; fear-*cuairt, sojourner, a pilgrim*; a trip, a tour, an excursion; chaidh sinn air *chuairt* do'n ghalltach, *we went on an excursion to the Low Country*; circumlocution, cainnt gu'n *chuairt, language without circumlocution*; (Macl.) circulation; *cuairt* na fola, *the circulation of the blood*; theirig ma'n *cuairt, go round, get round about*; ma'n *cuairt* do dheich bliadhna, *about ten years*; (*has an obscene meaning in song-books*).

CUAIRTEACH, kuaerjt'-ach, *a.* surrounding; circumambient, circuitous, circulating.

CUAIRTEAR, kŭăērt'-ăr', *n. m.* a tourist, a sojourner, a pilgrim.

CUAIRTICH, kŭăĕrjt'-êch, cuartaich.

CUAIRT-GHAOITH, whirlwind. (bad, bad).

CUAIRTLINN, kŭăĕrjt'-llyen, *n. f.* a whirlpool.

CUAIRT-RADH, kŭăĕrjt-rrâ', *n. f.* circumlocution.

CUAL, kŭăl, *n. m.* a faggot, *cual* chonaidh, *a faggot of fire-wood.*

CUALA, kŭăll'-â, part of cluinn; an *cuala* thu, *heard you!*

CUALAG, kŭăll'-ag, *n. f.* a hard task, a burden; cha *chualag* sin air, *that is no task to him*; burden.

CUALLACH, kŭăll'-ach, *n. f.* herding; agus e a *cuallach* na spréidhe, *and he tending* or *herding the cattle*—a corporation, society; family. *H. S.*

CUAN, kŭăn, *n. m.* an ocean; an *cuan*-t-siar-siar, *the Atlantic Ocean,* or *Western Ocean*; an *cuan* deas, *the Southern Ocean* an *cuan*-sèimh, *Pacific Ocean*; an *cuan* tuath, *the Northern Ocean.*

CUANAL, kŭăn'-al, a social band; a group of children living on the best of terms; a choir.

CUANNA, kŭănn'-a, *a.* snug, comfortable.

CUANTAICHE, kŭăn'-ttêch-â, *n. m.* a rover.

CUARAN, kuar'-an, *n. m.* a sandal, a bandage on a wounded finger, &c.

CUARSGAG, kuarsk'-ag, an eddy; a curl.

CUARTAG, kŭărt'-ag, *n. f.* an eddy, curl.

CUARTAICH, kuart'-êch, *v.* surround, enclose, encompass, environ, go about, circumnavigate, circumvolve; a *cuartachadh, surrounding, encircling,* &c.

CUB, kûb, *v.* feel the utmost torment of mind; coop, cringe.

CUBA, kŭb'-â, a bed; *cuba*-chuil, bedroom. *N. H.*

CUBAID, kûb'-ăj. *n. f.* a precentor's desk—in the North, a pulpit, Crannag.

CUBAIR, kûb'-ar', *n. m.* a cooper.

CUBHAG, kŭ'-ag, *n. f.* a cuckoo, guthag.

CUBHAIDH, kŭ'-ê, *a.* hereditary, having a just claim to; cha bu *chubhaidh* dhuit, *you have no family right to it*; tha thu mar bu *chubhaidh* dhuit, *you are just as one would expect from the offspring of such parents*; decent, fit, beseeming; mar bu *chubhaidh* do mhnàthan pòsda, *as befitting married women.* (Bible).

CUBHRAIDH, kû'-rrê, *a.* fragrant; fàile *cubhraidh* do t'anail, *a fragrant flavour of thy breath; giving a pleasant smell.*

CUBHRAIDHEACHD, kû'-rê-ăchg, *n. f.* fragrance.

CUCHAILTE, kŭch'-ajlte, *n. m.* residence.

CUCHAIR, kŭch'-êr, a hunter, sealgair.

CUDAINN, kŭd'-ênn, *n. f.* sprat of coal-fish six months old; a tub.

CUDTHROM, kŭd'-hröm, *n. m.* weight, heaviness, importance.

CUDTHROMACH, kŭd'-hröm-ăch, *a.* weighty, important, momentous; 's ann a tha sin gnothach *cudthromach, that is a momentous affair.*

CUDTHROMACHD, kŭd'-hrôm-achg, *n. m.* weighing.

CUIBH, kŭĕv[2], *a.* muzzle-bar *or* splinter; *cuibh*-mhòr, *one for four horses*; gearra-*chuibh, one for two horses*; (Islay, Lochaber, Cowal—Mainland of Argyle), Amall.

CUIBHEAS, kwees, *n. m.* moderation; cha 'n eil sin na *chuibheas, that is beyond all bounds, all moderation*; cha 'n 'eil thu ad *chuibheas, you are not easily dealt with*; (more expressive,) *ye'r nae canny.*

CUIBHEASACH, kwees'-ach, *a.* easily dealt with.

CUIBHREACH, kŭĕr'-ryach, *n. m.* bondage, trammels; harness of a plough horse; from *cuibh.*

CUIBHRICH, kŭĕv''-rėch, *v.* trammel, entangle, put in bonds *or* irons; discommode.

It is proper to note here, that every word ending ich and inn, is pronounced, in many parts of the Highlands, ig; even on the continent of Argyle, inn and ann are half murdered ing and ang, which when contracted, is ag and ig; the Islanders of Argyle, however, never mangle or murder a single Gaelic word.

CUIBHRIONN, kŭĕv²'-runn, *n. f.* a lot of land; a portion, share; allotment, (from cuibh and roinn).

CUID, kŭjj', *n. c.* part, portion; property, share; 'se so mo *chuidse, this is mine; this is my property*; a' *chuid* a 's mò, *the greater part, the majority, the generality*; *cuid* do chroinn, *your chance, your lot*; mò *chuidse* dheth, *my part of it*; *cuid* oidhche, *a night's entertainment, night's lodging*; *cuid* an tràth, *what serves for a meal of meat*; mo *chuid* do'n t-saoghall, *my all, my part and portion*; *gen.* codach; air son mo chodachsa, *for my part of it*; *cuid* duine chloinne, *the share of one of a family*; cha d' thoir muir na monadh a' *chuid* o dhuine sona, *dangers by sea or land cannot deprive a fortunate man* of his lot; used for his, her: a *chuid* mac, *his sons*; a *cuid* mac, *her sons*; used as an *indef. pro. cuid* do na daoine, *some of the men*; a' *chuid* eile, *the rest*;—*privates.*

CUIDEACHADH, kŭjj'-ach-Ă, *n. m.* assistance, aid, succour, help; *pt.* assisting, aiding, succouring, relieving.

CUIDEACHD, kŭjj'-achg, *n. f.* company, society; am *chuideachd, in my company* or *society*; intercourse; *a company, a society*; *cuideachd* shaighdearan, *a company of soldiers.*—CUIDE-RI, a bawdy word.

CUIDEACHD, kŭjj'-achg, *conj.* also, likewise; thàinig esan *cuideachd, he came also*; *adv.* in company, accompanying; *cuideachd* rium, *along with me.*

CUIDEACHDAIL, kŭjj'-ăchg-al, *a.* social.

CUIDEALAS, kujj'-ăl-ăs, *n. m.* conceitedness.

CUIDEIL, kŭjj'-al, *a.* conceited, prim.

CUIDHEAL, kŭĕ'-gh'-al, *n. f.* a wheel, coil.

CUIDHILL, kŭĕll, *v.* wheel, lash lustily; coil, roll, make a coil.

CUIDHTE, kŭĕ'-tya, *a.* quits, rid of.

CUIDHTICH, kŭĕ'-tyėch, *v.* quit, abandon.

CUIDHTICHTE, kŭĕ'-tyėch-tya, *pt.* forsaken, quit of.

CUIDICH, kŭjj'-ėch, *v.* assist, aid, help, succour; *cuidichte,* helped, assisted, aided.

CUIDREACH, kŭjj'-rojach, *a.* in partnership.

CUIFEIN, kŭėff'-an', *n. m.* wad of a gun.

CUIG, còig, murdered hollow.

CUIGEAL, kŭĕg'-al, *a.* distaff; *cuigeal* is feairsid, *distaff and spindle*; *cuigeal* nan losgan, neo nam ban sith, *the herb, reedmace.*

CUIL, kû'l', *n. f.* a corner, a nook, niche.

CUILBHEART, kŭ'l'-a-vhyart, *n. f.* wile, deceit.

CUILBHEARTACH, kŭ'l'-a-vhyart-ach, *a.* wily.

CUILBHEARTACHD, ku'l'-a-vhyart-achg, *n. f.* wiliness.

CUILBHEIR, kŭ'l'-e-văr', *n. f.* a gun, fowling piece.

CUILC, kŭlėg, *n. f.* reed, cane.

CUILCEARNACH, kŭlėg'-ar-nach, *n. f.* a place overgrown with reed *or* bulrushes.

CUILE, kŭ'l'-a, *n. f.* a store-room. *N.*

CUILEACHAN, ku'l'-ach-an, basket. *North.*

CUILEAG, ku'l'-ag, *n. f.* a fly.

CUILEAN, ku'l'-an', *n. m.* whelp, cub, pup, used by some blockheads for MY DEAR.

CUILTHINN, ku'l'-ėnn, *a.* handsome. *Ir.*

CUILGEAN, kŭlėg'-an, *n. m.* particle of awn.

CUILGEANACH, kulėg'-an-ach, *a.* prickly.

CUILIDH, ku'l'-ė, and ėch, *n. f.* a press, a lockfast place; cellar; cha bhi e an àird na 'n ìseal, nach faic sùil an Ilich; is cha bhì e an cùil na 'n *cuilidh,* nach faic sùil a' *Mhuilich; there cannot be any thing in the sky or earth, but the Islay men's eye can behold*; *nor can any thing in a corner* or *lockfast place, escape the eye of a Mullman*—Ullumh Ileach.

CUILIONN, ku'l'-unn, *n. m.* holly; craobh *chuilinn, a holly-tree*; *cuilionn* mara, *sea-holly*; some places—tragha.

CUILLIDH, kŭlly''-ė, *n. m.* a horse; cuir an *cuillidh* 'san f hèin, *yoke the horse in the cart,* Strathtay.

Dr. Armstrong, an excellent, if not the best of judges, says the people of this district speak the purest Gaelic; Feun, used in Scripture for cart, is not used so (excepting Arran) in Argyle.

CUILTEACH, kŭly''-tyach, *a.* dark, dismal, full of ugly nooks; *n. f.* a skulking female; in *Irish,* a bed, a bakehouse, and a Culdee.

CUILTEAR, kûly''-tyar, *n. m.* smuggler,

skulker, *cuiltearachd*, skulking, smuggling.

Cuime, kŭëm′-å, *int. pro.* of whom? about whom? respecting whom? about what?

Cuimhne, kŭĕv2n′-nå, *n. f.* memory, recollection, remembrance; an *cuimhne* leat, *do you recollect?* is *cuimhne* leam, *I distinctly recollect*; cha *chuimhne* leam, *I do not recollect*; ma's *cuimhne* leat, *if you recollect*; ma's math mo *chuimhne*, *if I recollect aright*; a rèir *cuimhne* dhomhsa, *to the best of my recollection*; cum ad *chuimhne*, *keep in remembrance*.

Cuimhneach, kŭĕv2n′-ach′, *a.* mindful.

Cuimhneachail, kŭĕv2n′-ach-al, *a.* keeping in mind; cò e an duine gu 'm bitheadh tusa *cuimhneachail* air, *what is man that thou shoudlst be mindful of him?*

Cuimhneachan, kŭĕv2n′-ach-an, *n. m.* a memorial; token of respect *or* gratitude.

Cuimhnich, kŭĕv2n′-ėch, *v. n.* remember, bear in mind, recollect, be mindful.

Cuimhniche, kŭĕv2n′-ėch-å, *n. m.* a remembrancer, a recorder, a chronicler.

Cuimir, kŭĕm′-ėr′, *a.* tidy, trim, neat, as a female; equally filling, exactly of the same size, well proportioned; short, concise.

Cuimireachd, kŭĕm′-ėr-achg, *n. f.* neatness, symmetry; proportion, same size.

Cuimrich, kŭĕm′-ėr-ėch, *v.* size, as slate; make of the same size; pare, as shoes.

Cuimse, kŭĕmsh′-a, *n. f.* moderation; ni gun *chuimse*, *a thing without moderation*; dean *cuimse* air siod, *aim at that*; sufficiency, enough, tha *cuimse* agamsa, *I have enough* or *sufficiency*.

Cuimseach, kŭĕm′-shach, *a.* moderate, indifferent, tha e *cuimsheach* 'na leoir, *he is but very indifferent indeed*; befitting, suitable to one's case; is *cuimseach* dhuit sin, *it is but proper that you should be so*.

Cuimsich, kŭĕm′-shėch, *v.* aim, hit; a' *cuimseachadh* air comharra, *aiming* or *shooting at a mark*, or *object*.

C'uin, *or* more properly **Cuin**, kŭĕn′, *adv.* when? at what time?

Cuing, kŭėng, *n. f.* the asthma, *or* shortness of breath; tha e làn *cuing*, *he is quite asthmatic* (N. *cuing*-analach,) tyranny; fa *chuing* agadsa, *under your tyrannical sway*; bondage.

Cuingeach, kueng′-ach, asthmatic.

Cuingeil, kŭĕng′-al, *a.* tyrannical, arbitrary.

Cuinge, kŭėng′-å, *a.* more *or* most narrow *or* narrow-minded; *n. f.* exceeding narrowness, *cuing*-fhuail na uisge, stranguary.

Cuingead, kŭĕng′-ad, *n. m.* narrowness.

Cuingich, kŭĕng′-ech, *v.* tyrannize, straiten.

Cuinn, kûĕnn′, *v.* coin.

Cuinneadh, kûĕnn′-a2, *a.* coin; *p.* coining.

Cuinneag, kŭĕnn-ag′, *n. f.* water-pitcher; in Scotch, a water stoup; in Kintyre, a churn.

Cuinnean, kŭĕnn′-an′, *n. m.* nostril.

Cuinnlean, kŭĕnn′-lyan′, *n. m.* stubble.

Cuinnsear, kuenn′-shăr, *n. m.* a sword.

Cuinnte, kûĕnnt′-å, *pt.* coined.

Cuip, kŭĕp, *v.* whip, lash; *n. f* a whip, a stratagem, *or* trick, deceit.

Cuir, kŭĕr′, *v.* sow, snow; tha iàd a' *cur*, *they are sowing*; tha e a' *cur* is cabhadh, *it is snowing and drifting*; put, place, lay; *cuir* an sin e, *lay* or *place it there*; send, despatch; *cuir* fios, *send word*; *cuir* an umhail, *cuir* an amharus, *suspect*; *cuir* amach air, *set at variance*, *be at variance*; *cuir* feadh a' chéile, mix; *cuir* seachad, lay by, hoard; *cuir* an cèill, declare, profess; *cuir* air folbh, *send*, *send away*; *cuir* air aghaidh, *send forward*, *forward*; *cuir* as da, *kill him*; *cuir* as, *extinguish*; *cuir* umad, *put on*, *dress yourself*; *cuir* dragh air, *put him to inconvenience*; molest, trouble; cuiridh mise riut, *I can manage* or *master you*; cha *chuir* e air, *it will not in the least annoy him*; *cuir* dreang ort, girn; cò a tha' cur ort, *who molests you?* *cuir* amach leobhar, *publish a book*; *cuir* dàil, *delay*, *prorogue*; *cuir* an suarachas, *slight*, *make light of*; *cuir* air laidhthuige, *make the ship lie-to*; *cuir* campar, *ruffle*, *vex*; *cuir* 'sna casan, *take to your heels*; *cuir* am mearachd, *put wrong*, misadvise, misdirect; *cuir* am fiachaibh, *bind one to act in a given manner*; *cuir* mar fhiachaibh, *make one believe*, *pretend*; *cuir* alladh air, *libel him*; cò a tha' *cur* ort, *who annoys* or *accuses you?* *cuir* am mothadh, *render useless*, *ruin the well being of*; *cuir* stad air, *stop him* or *it*; *cuir*, *invite*; *cuir* e, *invite him*; cò a *chuir* thu, *who invited you?*

Cuir, kŭĕr, *gen.* of car; also *pl.* twist, tumble; na *cuir* a *chuir* a dheth, *the tumbles he got*.

Cuircinn, kŭĕrk′-einn, *n. m.* head-dress. *H. S.*

Cuireadh, kŭĕr′-a2, *n. m.* an invitation; thig gun *chuireadh*, *obtrude*; thoir *cuireadh* dhaibh; *invite them*.

Cuireall, kŭĕr′-al, *n. m.* a kind of pack-saddle. *H.*

Cuireid, kŭĕr′-ăj, *n. m.* a wile, stratagem, as a girl; coquettish conduct.

Cuireideach, kŭĕr′-ăj-ach, *a.* coquettish, wily; *n. f.* a coquette; a flirt *or* wily girl.

Cuireideachd, kŭĕr′-ăj-achg, *n. f.* flirtation.

Cuirm, kŭėrm, *n. f.* a feast, banquet.

Cuirmire, kŭĕrm′-ŭr-å, *n. m.* an entertainer, a host, *or* one that gives a feast.

Cuirneachadh, kûĕrn′-ăch-ă, *n. m.* an envelope, a cover; *pt.* covering.

Cuirnean, kûĕrn′-an′, *n. m.* the head of a pin, (*Islay*); a dew drop, a heap, *H.*

Cuirnich, kŭĕrn′-ėch, *v.* cover, envelope.

Cuirp, kŭėrp, of a corpse; dead people.

Cuirt, kûĕrt, *n. f.* a court, palace, privilege, honour, favour; fhuair e *cùirt* air, *he has gained favour* or *privilege*; area, yard; *cùirt* ma choinneamh an tighe, *an area opposite the house.*

Cuirte, kŭrtj′-å, *pt.* planted, sowed, set.

Cuirtealachd, kûĕrt′-ål-achg, *n. f.* courtliness.

Cuirtear, kûĕrt′-ar, *n. m.* a courtier.

Cuirteis, kŭĕrt′-ash, *n. f.* currying favour, ceremony; gallantry.

Cuirteiseach, kûĕrt′-ash-ach, *a.* ceremonious.

Cuirteil, kûĕrt′-al, *a.* courtly; petted.

Cuirtinn, kûĕrt′-ėnn, *n. f.* a curtain.

Cuis, kûsh, *n. f.* the side which one takes in a game, particularly in playing at golf or cricket; case, cause, matter, point discussing, or subject of dispute; cha 'n e sin a' *chùis, that is not the case, that is not the matter in dispute,* or *the subject of discussion, the point at issue*; millidh tu *chùis, you will spoil the business, affair* or *matter*; bithidh, e air *cùis* na còrach, *he will support the cause of right* or *humanity*; *cùis* a h-aislinn, *the subject of her dream, Sg.*; fate; bu *chùis* dhomh anart is uaigh, *my fate would be the winding-sheet and the grave; cuis*-dhìtidh, *ground of condemnation*; *cùis* ghearain, *ground of complaint*; *cùis* fharmaid, *an object of envy, an enviable object.*

Cuisire, kûsh-ur″-å, *n. m.* a client, one that employs a lawyer, casuist.

Cuiseach, kŭsh′-ach, *n. m.* rye-grass.

Cuiseag, kŭsh′-ag, *n. f.* a stalk of ryegrass.

Cuisle, kŭsh′-lå, *n. f.* a vein, a layer of ore, as in a mine; an artery; rapid stream *or* current in the sea.

Cuisleach, kŭsh′-lach, *n. f.* a lancet, lance.

Cuisleanach, kŭsh′-lyan-ach, an Irish piper.

Cuisnich, kûsh′-ĭ ėch, *v.* freeze, reodh. *Ir.*

Cuith, kŭĕ, *n. m.* a wreath of snow; pit.

Cul, kûll, *n. m.* the back of any thing; hair of the head; *cùl* buidh dualach, *yellow curled hair*; air do chùl, *behind you*; bithidh mise air do *chùl, I will be behind you,* i. e. *ready to support you*; gu *cùl, thoroughly, completely*; is tu an cù gad *chùl, you are a dog every inch of you*; cuir *cùl* ris, *reject him,* cuir *cùl* rithe, *reject her*; *cùl* ri *cùl, back to back.*

Culach, kŭl′-ach, *a.* fat, plump, *N.*

Culag, kûl-′ag, *n. f.* grinder *or* backtooth, a peat.

Culaidh, kŭll′-ė, *n. f.* materials, apparatus; na biodh a' *chulaidh* agam, *were I to have the materials*; condition; clothes, (*Bible*); subject, object; *culaidh* magaidh, *an object,* or *subject of merriment*; *culaidh* bhùird, *a butt.*

Cularan, kul′-ar-an, *n. m.* a cucumber. *Shaw.*

Cul-chain, kŭl-chàėn′, *v.* backbite, detract, slander; *cùl-chàineadh,* detraction, calumny.

Cul-chuideachd, kûll-chŭjj′-achg, *n. m.* rearguard, reserve, company to assist.

Cullach, kull′-ach, *n. m.* a boar, *I.*; a polecat (Mull); a stirk, eunuch. *S. D.*

Cullaich, kŭll′-ech, *v.* line, as a boar.

Cul-sgriobh, kûll′-skrēv, *v.* direct, address, as a letter; *cùl-sgrìobhte, addressed* or *directed; cùl-sgrìobhadh, direction.*

Cul-shleamhnaich, kûl-hlev′-nėch, *v.* backslide, apostatize.

Cul-taic, kull-tăĕchg′, *n. m.* support, prop, a patron; patronage, support.

Culthaobh, kûll′-hāov, *n. m* back, back parts; *prep.* behind; *culthaobh* an tighe, *behind the house*; *culthaobh* is beulthaobh, *back and front, front and back part.*

Cul-tharruinn, kŭll-hărr′-ėnn, *n. f.* a sly insinuation, *I.*; retraction. *H.*

Cum, kûm, *v. n.* keep, hold; *cum* so, *hold* or *keep this*; contain, as a dish; *cumaidh* an soitheach so e, *this dish will contain it*; withhold; *cum* uaith a thuarasdal, *withhold his wages*; refrain; *cum* o 'n òl, *refrain from drinking*; *cum* air do laimh, *restrain thy hand*; *cum* a mach, *hold forth, maintain, contend*; *cum* ris, *keep up to him, do not yield to him; celebrate* or *observe, as holidays*; a *cumail* latha a féill, *celebrating holidays*— shape, frame, on continent of Argyle; but in the Islands, (CUNN;) detain, obstruct.

Cuma, kum′-å, *n. m.* shape, form, figure, pattern, more properly *cunna.*

Cumachdail, kŭm′-achd-al, *a.* well-shaped.

CUMAIL, kŭm′-al, *n. f.* detention, maintenance; keeping; *p.* celebrating.

CUMAN, kŭm′-an, *n. m.* milking pail.

CUMASG, kŭm′-ask, *n. f.* a tumult, ùtaig.

CUMHA, kŭv2′-â, *n. m.* an elegy, eulogy *or* poem in praise of the dead, also an epic poem; mourning, lamentation; *cumha* fir Arais, *the elegy of the Chief of Aros.*

CUMHACHD, kŭv2′-achg, *n. m.* power, might, strength, energy, ability, authority, commission, permission, influence.

CUMHACHDACH, kuv′-achg-ach, *a* powerful, having great sway *or* influence; duine *cumhachdach, a man of great influence* or *sway*; mighty, strong, able.

CUMHACHDAIR, kum′-achg-ăr′, *n. m.* a commissioner, a delegate, agent.

CUMHANN, kŭv2′-unn, *a.* narrow, strait, narrow-minded; contracted; *n.* strait.

CUMHASAG, kuv2′-as-ag, *n. f.* an owl; cailleach oidhche, also chumhachag.

CUMHNANT, kùv2′-nant, *n. m.* a covenant, a league, bargain, contract; an engagement; compact, agreement; a réir ceannaibh a' *chumhnant, agreeable to the terms of engagement*; an *cumhnant* rinn e riutha, *the covenant, contract* or *compact he made with them.*

CUMHNANTACH, kûv′-nant-ach, *a.* stingy, unaccommodating; duine cruaidh *cumhnantach, a niggardly, stingy fellow.*

CUMHNANTAICH, kuv2′-nant-èch, *v.* covenant.

CUMHRADH, kûv′-rĂ, *n. m.* a good bargain.

CUNG, kŭng, *n. f.* a medicine, drug; droch *chungan, bad medicine.*

CUNGAIDH, kŭng′-è, *a.* medicine, materials; na biodh a *chungaidh* agam, *if I had the materials*; ingredients; means.

CUNGAISICH, kŭng′-ash-èch, *v.* subdue, conquer, subjugate, overcome.

CUNGLACH, kŭng′-lach, *n. m.* narrow place *or* range, a narrow defile.

CUNN, kŭnn, *v.* shape, frame, count; *cunn* an còta, *shape the coat.*

CUNNA, kunn′-a, *n. f.* shape, form, figure; construction. *Islands.*

CUNNABHALLACH, kunn′-a-vhall-ach, *a.* well shaped, well formed, well proportioned, as a person; affording means of support.

CUNNABHALLACHD, kŭnn′-a-vhall-achg, *n. f.* proportion of limbs; handsomeness.

CUNNARACH, kŭnn′-ar-ach, *n. m.* cheap bargain; (has an obscene meaning).

CUNNART, kŭnn′-art, *n. m.* danger, risk, jeopardy; cuir an *cunnart, risk, endanger, take chance.*

CUNNARTACH, kŭnn′-ărt-ach, *a.* dangerous.

CUNNRADH, kûnn′-rĂ, *n. m.* cheap bargain.

CUNNT, kŭnnt, *v.* count, enumerate.

CUNNTAIR, kunnt′-ĕr, *n. m.* counter, an arithmetician; enumerator, accountant.

CUNNTAS, kŭnnt′-as, *n. m.* number, arithmetic; tha e *cunntas, he is working at arithmetic*; an account; paidh do *chunntas, pay your account*; a' *cunntas, settling, numbering.*

CUNNAIL, kŭnn′-al, *n. f.* an objection.

CUP, an English cup, cop, copan.

CUPLAICH, kŭp′-lèch, *v.* couple, &c.

CUPULL, kŭp′-ull, *n. f.* a pair.

CUR, kŭr, *n. m.* sowing; am a *chuir, seedtime*; a fall of snow; *cur* is cabhadh, *a fall of snow and drift*; *pt. snowing, sowing;* tha e a' *cur, he is sowing,* &c.

CURA, kûr′-a, *n. m.* a protector, a guardian; protection, guardianship; bithidh e 'na *chùra* orra, *he will be a protector to them,* (Latin cura, care).

CURACH, kŭr′-ach, *n. f.* a canoe, coracle.

CURACHD, kŭr′-achg, *n. f.* the quantity sown, *or* to be sown, seminary.

CURADAIR, kûr′-a-dăr, *n. m.* curator.

CURAIDH, kŭr′-è, *n. m.* a hero, champion.

CURAINN, kûr′-ènn, *n. f.* plaiding, (felt).

CURNAICH, kûrn′-ech, *v.* cover, envelope.

CURAM, kûr′-am, care, anxiety, charge, responsibility; air mo *chùramsa, under my charge*; na biodh *curam ort, never you mind*; is beag mo *chùram,* air a shon sin, *I feel no uneasiness on that score*; bithidh iad fo *chùram, they will feel anxiety* or *anxious.*

CURAMACH, kûr′-am-ach, *a.* careful, solicitous, anxious; attentive.

CURANTA, kur′-ant-a, bold, heroic.

CURANTACHD, kŭr′-ant-achg, *n. f.* bravery.

CURR, kûrr, *n. m.* corner, site, pit. *H. S.*

CURRACHD, kurr′-achg, *n. m.* women's cap *or* head-dress; *curraichdean, caps,* &c.; *currachd* na cubhaig, *hare-bell, blue-bottle.*

CURRACHDAG, kŭrr′-achg-ag, *n. f.* peat-heap.

CURRAN, kŭrr′-an, *n. m.* a carrot; *currain* bhuidh is *currain* ghealla; *carrots and parsnips; horse panniers for corn,* &c.

CURRACAG, kurr′-achg-ag, *n. m.* lapwing *or* pee-wee, sagharcan.

CURSA, kûr′-sa, *n. m.* course; seòl do *chùrsa, steer your course*; career, layer; *cursa* ma seach, *layer about.*

CUS, kŭs, *n. m.* enough; superfluity; many. *N.*

CUSP, kŭsp′, *n. f.* a kibe, chilblain.

CUSPACH, kŭsp′-ach, *a.* kibed, as a heel.

CUSPAIR, kusp′-ar′, *n. m.* a mark to aim at, an object of any kind.

Cuspaireachd, kŭsp′-ăr′-achg, *n. f.* intermeddling, officiousness; aiming, marking.

Cuspairich, kŭsp′-ăr-ėch, *v.* meddle, aim.

Cuspuinn, kŭsh′-ėnn, *n. f.* custom, tribute, import, tigh-*cuspuinn, Custom-house.*

Cut, kŭt, *v.* gut, as fish.

Cutach, kŭt′-ach, *a.* bob-tailed, curtailed, docked; *n. f.* little woman.

Cutaich, kŭt′-ėch, *v.* curtail, dock.

Cutag, kŭt′-ag, *n. f.* a short spoon, *or* tobacco pipe.

Cutag, kût′-ag, *n. f.* a circular kiln.

Cuthach, kŭ′-ach, *n. m.* hydraphobia.

D

D, d, the fourth letter of the Gaelic alphabet, denominated by the Irish dair, (pronounced ddaŏir,) the oak-tree; hence darach, the wood of an oak-tree.

D', for do, thy, or your, used before words beginning with a vowel or fh-; as, *d'* each, *thy horse*; *d'* fhear, *thy husband,* always pronounced, and very often written T'; as, *t'* athair, *t'* fhear, *your father, your husband*; 2*d*, *d'* for do, to; *do* chloinn, *to children*; 3*d*, sign of pret.

Da, dă, to him; thoir *dà* e, *give it to him*; thoir dhaibh, *give it to them*; 2*d*, d'a, for do a; as, *d'a* mhathair, *d'a* leanabh, *to his mother, to his child.*

Da, dâ, *adj.* two; *dà* bhean, *two women, two females*; *dà* sheachdainn, *two weeks*; *dà*-adharcach, *two-horned, bicornous*; *da*-cheannach, *two-headed, becipitous*; *da*-chorpach, *bicorporal.*

Dabhach, dăv′-ăch, *n. f.* a mashing-tun, or vat; Fingall's mother; a huge lady; urchair an doill m' an *dabhaich, a throw, or blow at a venture.*

Dabhan, dăv′-an, *n. m.* pitcher. *Ir.*

Dabhasg, dav′-usg, *n. m.* a deer. *H. S.*

Dabhd, dav′-ud, *n. m.* sauntering.

Dabhdail, dăv′-ud-ul, *n. m.* and *part.* prowling, sauntering, loitering.

Dabhliadhnach, dâv′-*vh*lĕăn-ach, *n. c.* a two year old beast; used of cattle, murdered in some parts—dô′-*vh*lĕăn-ach.

Dabhoch, dăv′-ŏch, *n. f.* a farm, capable of pasturing three hundred cattle. *Skye.*

Dacha, dàch′-a, more likely, for dòcha.

Dachaidh, dăch′-ė, *n. f.* a home, dwelling place; residence, domicil; ga *dhachaidh* fhein, *to his own home*; *adv.* homewards; a dol *dachaidh, going homewards, going home.*

Dachasach, dâ′-chăs-ăch, *a.* two-footed; *n. c.* a biped; gach *dàchasach* a th' agam, *every biped I have.*

Dad, dădd′, } any thing, aught, no
Dadum, dădd′-um, } thing; cha 'n 'eil *dad* maith air, *it is not worth any thing*; dè th' ort, *what is wrong with you*? cha 'n 'eil *dad, nothing is wrong with me*; dad a's leatsa, *aught of thine.*

Dadhas, dă′-us, *n. m.* a fallow deer.

Daga, dagg′-â, *n. f.* a pistol; *daga* dioll-aid, *a holster, a blunderbush. Saxon.*

Daibh, ddīv, to them; thoir *daibh, give them*; near Inverary, ddī

Daibhair, ddīv′-ėry′, *adj.* adverse, destitute; *daibhir* na saibhir gu'n robh mo chor, *let my fate be either prosperous or adverse*; *n. m.* the common, or worst pasture of a farm; *Innis,* the best pasture.

Daibheid, ddév′-aj, *n. m.* self-command, circumspection; daibheideach, *self-denying.*

Daibhreas, ddīv′-rus, *n. m.* poverty.

Daichalachd, dâėch′-all-ăchg, *n. f.* plausibility, false appearance.

Daicheil, dâėch′-al, *a.* plausible, like a hero, but a coward; is minig a bha an Donas *daicheil, the Devil has been found often plausible.*

Daighneach for dainneach, from dainn, a rampart.

Dail, dăl, *n. f.* a field—collar *Nasg. H. S.*

Dail, dà'l, *n. f.* delay; preparation; interval, intermediate space; thig gun *dàil, come without delay*; *dàil* eadar an dà làmhnain, *the intermediate space of the couples*; trust, credit; *dàil* shè mìosan, *credit for six months*; contact; is coma leam dol 'na *dhàil, I don't like to get in contact with him,* or *to have any thing to do with it*; feumaidh sinn rudaiginn an *dàil* an dònaich, *we must have something in preparation for the Sabbath*; cuir *dàil, delay, procrastinate*; thoir *dàil, give on trust,* or *credit.*

Dail-chuaich, dă'l′-chŭăěch, *n. f.* an herb.

Daimh, ddīv², *n. pl.* oxen, bullocks.

Daimh, dàėv, *n. f.* connexion, affinity, relationship; dlùth an *dàimh, nearly connected*; fada mach an *dàimh, distantly related*; dàimhich, *blood relations.*

Daimhalachd, dàėv′-all-ach, *n. f* relationship, kindred spirit, habits, and disposition.

Daimheil, dàėv′-al, *a.* kindred, fond of relations, affectionate; nearly related.

Dainn, dáėnn, *n. f.* a rampart, barrier; hence, dainneach, a fort, fortification; and dannarra, not easily prevailed upon.

Daingneach, dèng′-nyach, } *n. f.* a for-
Dainneach, dènn′-ach, } tress, a fort, castle.

DAINGEANN, DAINNIONN, dàènn'-unn, *adj.* firm, strong, unmoveable, tight.

DAINNICH, DAINGNICH, dàèn'-nyèch, *v.* fortify, confirm, establish, tighten.

DAINNEACHAS, dáénn'-ach-as, *n. m.* assurance, confirmation, perfect security.

DAIR, dàèr, *n. m.* the state of being lined as a cow; air *dàir, a-bulling.*

DAIR, daŏèr, *or* dáèr, *v.* line, as a bull; dàirte, *lined, in calf.*

DAIS, dăsh, *n. m.* a mow in a barn of sheaf corn, *or* a pile of seasoned fish; *v.* mow, pile as seasoned fish.

DALL, dăll, *a.* blind; *n.* blind person; *v.* blind, dazzle; 'gam dhalladh *blinding me.*

DALLAG, dăll'-ăg, *n. f.* a young dog-fish—a shrew-mouse, a leech. *H. S.*

DALLANACH, dăll'-an-ach, *n. f.* a large fan; a volley *or* broadside; blindness from excessive drinking; air an *dallanaich,* (blin' fu',) *completely intoxicated;* leig iad *dallanach, they fired a volley* or *broadside.*

DALLARAN, dăll'-ar-an, *n.* a bewildered person.

DALLTA, dăll'-tà, *n. m.* the very same case, *or* way, *or* method; *adv.* in the way, very same manner; *dallta* sheumais, *just as James would have acted; dallta* an fhir nach mairean, *just as he that is no more would have done.*

DALMA, dăllm'-ă, *adj.* audacious, bold.

DALMACHD, dăllm'-ăchg, *n. f.* audacity, presumption, impertinence, forwardness.

DALTA, dăllt'-ă, *n. c.* a foster child, stepson, step-daughter, god-son.

DAM, dám, *n. m.* mill-dam (linne mhuilinn,) reservoir, conduit. *Teutonic.*

DAMAIN, dăm'-ènn, *v.* damn, curse—*Bible;* damainte, *accursed, most abandoned.*

DAMH, dáv, *n. m.* an ox, bullock; stag; a mast. *Oss.*; a joist; *damh* suirn, *a kiln-joist. Is.; a Gaelic Doctor. H. S.; damhan*-eallaich, *a spider;* lìon an *damhain*-eallaich, a *cobweb.*

DAMHAIS, dáv'-èsh, *v.* dance, caper.

DAMHSA, dàv'-sá, *n. m.* dancing, a ball.

DAMHSAIR, dáv'-săry, *n. m.* a daneer, caperer.

DAMNADH, dăm'-nX, *n. m.* damnation, *pt.* damning; *damnar* e, *he shall be damned. B.*

DAN, dàn, *adj.* resolute, intrepid; presumptuous; cha *dàn* leam innseadh dhuit, *I do not think it presumptuous in me to tell you;* cho *dàn* is a chaidh e air 'aghaidh, *he went forward so resolutely.*

DAN, dàn, *n. m.* destiny, fate, decree, predestination; ma tha sin an *dàn, if that be ordained;* bha sin an *dàn* domh, *that was my fate; song, poem;* sean *dàin* le H-Ossian, *Ossian's ancient poems;* is duilich cuir an aghaidh *dàn, to oppose fate* or *destiny, is difficult;* ma tha e an *dàn* domh a bhi beo, *if it be destined for me to live.*

DANACH, dàn'-ach, *a.* poetical, of poetry.

DANACHD, dàn'-achg, *n. f.* poetry; boldness.

DANADAS, dàn'-add'-as, *n. m.* presumption, familiarity; audacity, boldness, assurance; agus mar an ceudna o pheacadh *danadais* cum t-oglach air 'ais, *and also from sins of presumption keep back thy servant. Psalms.*

DANAICH, dàn'-èch, *v.* defy, dare. *Arm.*

DANNARRA, dănn'-arra, *a.* mulish, stubborn, obstinate, contumacious, opinionative.

DANNARRACHD, dănn'-arr-achg, *v. f.* stubbornness, obstinacy, boldness, resolution.

DANTACHD, dànt'-ăchg, *n. f* fatalism.

DAOCH, dāoch, *n. f.* disgust; dèis'hinn.

DAOI, ddúè, *a.* wicked; foolish. *Smith.*

DAOIMEAN, daŏè'-mon, *n. m.* diamond. *Eng.*

DAOINE, dāoèn'-à, *n. f.* men, people; mòran *dhaoine, many people;* ameasg 'nan *daoine, among the people.*

DAOINEACHD, dāoèn'-achg, *n. f.* population.

DAOIRE, dāoèr'-à, more *or* most dear; *n.* extreme dearness; ni's *daoire, dearer.*

DAOL, dāol, *n. f.* a chafer, beetle.

DAOLAG, dāol'-ag, *n. f.* little chafer.

DAONNA, dāon'-na, *a.* human; humane, an cinne *daonna, mankind.*

DAONNACHD, dāon'-năchg, *n. f.* humanity; fear na *daonnachd, the humane man. St.*

DAONNAN, dāonn'-an, *adv.* always, continually, habitually, at all times.

DAOR, dāor, *a.* high priced, dear, costly; scant, scarce; bliadhna *dhaor, a year of scarcity;* also, most abandoned; complete, corrupted; *daor* shlaoightire, *a most abandoned rascal; daor* mheairleach, *a most abandoned thief; daor* bhodach, *a complete churl; daor* bhalach, *a complete boor.*

DAORSA, dāor'-sà, *n. f.* famine, dearth; bondage, captivity; ar clann ann an *daorsa, our children in bondage or captivity. Bible.*

DA-PHEIGHINN, dâ-ffă'-ènn, *n. f.* two pence Scots; ancient coin.

D'AR, dăr, *pre.* and *pro.*; do ar; into our; *d'ar* cloinn, *to our children.*

D'AR-RIGHRIBH, dăr-rē-ry''-uv, *adv.* in earnest; seriously: an ann *d'ar righribh* a tha thu, *are you serious? are you in earnest? you are not joking?* literally, *is it to our kings you are speaking?* (*daridheadh* is nonsense.)

Dara, dar′-ă, *a.* second; the second; an *dara* uair, *the second time.*

Darach, dă′-rach, *n. m. oak timber.*

Darag, dar′-ăg, *n. f.* stump of a tree.

Dararach, dar′-ar-ach, *n. f.* a volley; stunning noise.

Darna, dăr′-na, *a.* second; either the one or the other; an *darna* cuid, *either of the two*; an *dara* té, *the second woman.*

Dasan, dâs′-un, *pre.* and *pro.* to him; thoir *dàsan* e, *give it to him.*

Dath, dă, *v.* colour, tinge, dye; *n. m.* dye, colour, tinge.

Dathadair, dă′-add-ăr, *n. m.* dyer.

Dathadaireachd, dă′-ădd-ăr-ăchg, *n. f.* the process of colouring; trade of a dyer.

Dathail, dă′-al, *a.* well-coloured.

De, jjā, *or* dyā, *int. pro.* what? used in all the Oriental languages as an interrogative, or a personal pronoun; *dè* sin, *what is that?* *dè* b'aille leat, *what is your will?*

Dee, jjā, *or* dyā, *gen.* of *Dia*, God.

De, jjā, *adv.* an *dè*, yesterday.

Deacaid, jjechg′-aj, *n. f.* corsets; boddice.

Deacair, dyechg′-ur, *a.* difficult, sore.

Deacaireachd, dyechg′-ur-ăchg, *n. f.* difficulty.

Deach, dyech, *pret. int.* of *v.* theirig; an *deach* e dhachàidh, *has he gone home?* more often deachaidh.

Deachamh, dyèch′-uv, *n. m.* tythe, tenth.

Deachd, dyechg *or* dyúchg, *v.* indite, dictate, inspire, *B.*; make completely certain; assure positively, *Islay*; *deachdta, completely certain*; gu *deachdta, most certainly, most assuredly.*

Deachdair, dyechg′-urr-a, *n. f.* dictator, &c.

Deadh, dyāo, *a.* very good, excellent; placed always before the noun it qualifies; *deadh* bheusan, *excellent morals,* &c.

Deadhainm, dyaŏ′-én-um, *n. m.* good name.

Deagal, dyā^{2}g′-ul, twilight. *Irish.*

Deal, dyal, *n. f.* a leech, teat ballan (*Is.* gioll); *a.* keen, eager; more properly *deil*; cho *deil* is a tha e aig' a ghnothuch, *so enthusiastic at his business.*

Dealachadh, dyal′-ach-Ă, *n. m.* separation, divorce; a division, *pt.* separating, divorcing.

Dealachail, dyal′-ach-al, *a.* causing separation; that may be separated, separable.

Dealaich, dyăl′-ěch, *v. n.* separate, divide, part with; cha *dhealaich* mi ris, *I will not part with it.*

Dealan, dyal′-an, *n. m.* cross-bar on a door.

Dealan-de, dyal-an-jjā′, *n. m.* a butterfly.

Dealanach, dyal′-an-ach, *n. m.* lightning.

Dealas, dyal′-as, *n. m.* the keenness of a woman spinning *or* in household affairs.

Dealasach, dyal′-as-ach, *a.* keen, eager.

Dealbh, dyal′-uv, *n. m.* warping, abb; figure, image, form; ghoid Rachel na *dealbhan, Rachel had stolen the images;* shape, form, conformation; agus bha'n talamh gun *dealbh, and the earth was without form;* order, arrangement; gnothuch gun *dealbh, an absurd thing;* is beag *dealbh* a th' air, *it is out of order* or *arrangement*; cuir air *dealbh* neo cuir *dealbh* air, *arrange, adjust, put in order.*

Dealbh, dyal′-uv, *v.* warp, make abb of; form, shape; ma'n do *dhealbh* thu an talamh agus an cruinne, *ere thou hadst formed the earth and the world*; devise, plot, contrive; glacar iad 'sna innleachdan a *dhealbh* iad, *let them be taken in the devices they have imagined*; tha i a' *dealbh, she is warping* or *making abb.*

Dealbhach, dyall′-ach, *a.* handsome, well-shaped; likely, probable; *n. f.* abb; snàth air crann-*dealbh* figheadair, 12.

Dealbhadair, dyall′-vadd-ar, *n. m.* deviser, framer, former; warper.

Dealbhadaireachd, dyall′-vadd-ar-ăchg, *n. f.* warping; delineation, framing, shaping.

Dealbhadh, dyall′-Ă, *p.* delineating, forming, shaping, contriving.

Dealbh-chluich, dyal′-uv-chlŭech, *n. f.* play, stage-play, drama. *H. S.*

Deal-each, dyal′-ech, *n. f.* horse-leech; gioll-tholl.

Dealg, dyal′-ag, *n. f.* stocking-wire, a skewer, a bodkin; hair-pin, a prickle.

Dealgach, dyallg′-ach, *a.* prickly, thorny.

Dealgan, dyall′-ug-an, *n. m.* collar-bone; (in Bible, spindle, fearsaid.)

Dealrach, dyall′-rach, *a.* shining, brilliant, refulgent, resplendent, radiant, bright.

Dealradh, dyall′-rĂ, *n. m.* effulgence, refulgence, splendour, lustre, radiance; *pt.* gleaming, shining, beaming.

Dealair, dyall′-ur′, *v.* shine, beam, gleam.

Dealraich, dyall′-rrěch, *v.* shine, beam, gleam, glitter, flash, emit rays.

Dealt, dyăllt, *n. m.* rain glittering on the grass; dew, drizzle.

Dealtair, dyāly′-tăr′ *v.* glitter, gild.

Dealtradh, dyalt′-rĂ, *n. m.* glitter, besprinkling; *pt.* bedropping; varnishing.

Deamhan, dyŏv^{2}′-an, *n. m.* devil, demon.

Deamhas, dyév′-as, *n. m.* sheep-shears.

Dean, dyèn, *v.* make, do, act, perform; suppose, imagine, think; *dean* urnuigh, *pray; dean* deifir. *hasten, make haste;*

dean gu rèidh, *do at leisure*; *dean* moill, *delay, stop*; *dean* fuasgladh, *deliver, release*; *dean* gàirdeachas, *rejoice*; *dean* uaill, *boast, brag*; *dean* strì *or* strìobh, *try, strive, compete*; *dean* rèite, *make peace, reconcile*; tha mi a *deanadh, I suppose*; am bheil thu *deanadh, do you suppose*; *dean* domh, *make for me*; *dean* fastath, *hire yourself*; *dean* iomlaid, *exchange*; *dean* faighidinn, *wait a short time, have patience.*

Deanachdach, dyén'-ăchg-ăch, *a.* vehement, keen, incessant; uisge *deanachdach, vehement rain*; as speech, *emphatic*; labhair e gu *deanachdach, he spoke emphatically* or *with great emphasis.*

Deanachdachd, dyén'-achg-achg, *n. f.* emphasis, vehemence, violence of rain.

Deanadach, dyèn'-add-ăch, *a.* industrious, persevering, laborious, diligent.

Deanadas, dyèn'-add-as, *n. m.* industry, diligence, perseverance, activity.

Deanadh, dyèn'-Ă, *pt.* doing, making, supposing; imagining.

Deanas, dyèn'-as, *n. m.* an act, result of one's industry *or* labour.

Deanasach, dyèn'-as-ach, *a.* industrious.

Deanasachd, dyén'-as-achg, *n. f.* industry.

Deann, dyann, *n. f.* a small quantity of any thing, like meal, snuff; cha 'n 'eil *deann* snaoisean agam, *I have not a particle of snuff*; a rush *or* dash towards any thing; thàinig e stigh 'na *dheann, he rushed in*; *full speed*; an t-each 'na *dheann, the horse at full speed.*

Deannag, dyann'-ag, *n. f.* a very small quantity of snuff, meal, &c.

Deannal, dyănn'-al, *n. m.* a spell *or* a little while at any thing with all one's might,—conflict; shot; hurry.

Deantag, see Feantagach, nettle.

Deanta, dyèn'-tyă, *pt.* done, made.

Deantanas, dyèn'-tăn-as, *n. m.* an act.

Dearbadan-de, dealan'-dè, butterfly.

Dearbh, dyérv, *v.* prove, confirm, try; *dearbh* sin, *prove that*; *adj.* sure, certain, very identical; an *dearbh* ni a bha dhì orm, *the very thing I wanted*; an *dearbh* dhuine, *the identical man*; tha gu *dearbh, yes, indeed*; *adv.* truly, really, certainly; is *dearbh* gu'm bheil, *it is truly* or *positively so.*

Dearbhach, dyerv'-ach, *a.* confirmatory.

Dearbhachd, dyerv'-achg, *n. f.* demonstration.

Dearbhadas, dyerv'-ad-as, capability of proof; way of leading a proof.

Dearbhadh, dyer'-Ă, *n. m.* proof, confirmation; evidence; *pt.* proving, confirming, demonstrating; mar *dhearbhadh* air sin, *as a proof of that*; a' *dearbhadh* na cùise, *confirming the fact*; *proving the case.*

Dearbhann, dyerv'-ann, *n. m.* axiom. *Ir.*

Dearbhta, dyĕrv'-tyă, *pt.* proved, established; confirmed, demonstrated.

Dearc, dyerk, *n. f.* a berry; a grape; fàgaidh tu *dearcan, thou shalt leave grapes, B.*; *v.* look steadfastly and piercingly, fix the mind on intensely; *dearcam* ort do gnàth, *I will make thee the subject of my meditations continually. Ps.*

Dearc-aitinn, dyerk-ajt'-ènn, *n. f.* a juniper berry, (dearc iùbhair); *dearc* dharaich, *an acorn*; *dearc* fhrangach, *a currant*; *dearc* fhìona, *a grape.*

Dearc-luachair, dyerk-lŭăch'-èr, *n. f.* a lizard *or* asp.

Dearcnach, dyerk'-nach, *a.* handsome. *Irish.*

Dearcnachadh, dyerk'nach-Ă, *n. m.* marking *or* criticising, scrutinising keenly.

Dearcnaich, dyerk'-nnèch, *v.* criticise look steadfastly and keenly.

Dearg, dyerg, *or* dyer-ug', *adj.* red; most abandoned, notorious *or* complete; *dearg* amadan, *a complete fool*; *dearg* mheairleach, *a notorious thief*; *dearg* strìopach, *a most abandoned strumpet*; *dearg* mar fhuil, *red as blood*; air an *dearg* chaothach, *stark mad.*

Dearg, dyerg, *n. m.* red colour, crimson; *v.* redden, make red, make an impression; cha *dearg* e air, *it makes no impression on him* or *it.*

Deargan, dyerg'-an, *n. m.* red stain; *deargan* doirionn, *a nebula*; *deargan* àllt, *a kestril hawk.*

Deargann, dyerg'-unn, *n. f.* a flea; *deargann* tràgha, *a multipede.*

Dearg-las, dyerg-llăss', *v.* blaze.

Deargnaidh, dyerg'-nè, *a.* unlearned. *Ir.*

Dearlan, see Earlàn, brimful.

Dearmad, dyer'-mad, *n. m.* an omission.

Dearmadach, dyer'-mad-ach, *adj.* forgetful; negligent, careless.

Dearmadachd, dyer'-mad-achg, *n. f.* extreme forgetfulness *or* negligence.

Dearmaid, dyer'-mè, *v.* omit, forget.

Dearn, dyârn, *n. f.* palm of the hand.

Dearnadair, dyârn'-ad-ăr', *n. m.* a palmist.

Dearnadaireachd, dyâr'-add-ar'-achg, *n. f.* palmistry, divination by the palm of the hand.

Dearnagan, dyârn'-ag-an, *n. m.* a cake. *B.*

Dearras, dyărr'-as, *n. m.* keenness, enthusiasm.

Dearrasach, dyarr'-as-ach, *a.* keen, eager.

Dearrs, dyârs, *v.* shine, beam, emit rays, gleam, radiate, burnish.

Dearrsach, dyarr'-sach, *a.* shining, radiant.

Dearrsadh, dyârr'-sX, *n. m.* a gleam, a ray.

Dearrsnaich, dyârrs'-nèch, *v.* polish, gild.

Dearrsnaiche, dyârrs'-nèch-å, *n. m.* a polisher.

Dearrsanta, dyârr'-sannt-a, *a.* radiant, effulgent, gleaming, beaming.

Deas, dyās[2], *n. m.* the south; bho 'n *deas, from the south*; *adj.* south; gaoth *deas, south wind*; proper, right; rinn thu sin gu *deas, you have done that properly*; well-shaped, handsome; duine *deas, a well-shaped, personable individual*; ready, prepared; am bheil thu *deas, are you prepared*; easily accomplished; bu *deas* domh sin a dheanadh, *I could easily accomplish that*; bu *deas* domh mo lamh a' ghacail, *I could easily engage* or *close a bargain*; an lamh *dheas, the right hand.*

Deasach, dyās''-ach, *n. m.* a West Highlander; Tuathach, *a North Highlander.*

Deasachadh, dyās''-ach-X, *n. m.* the act of baking; a bake; *pt.* baking, preparing.

Deasaich, dyās''-ech, *v.* prepare, bake, gird; *deasaich* do chaidhimh, *gird your sword. Ps.*

Deasbair, dyās''-bèr, *v.* argue, dispute.

Deasbaire, dyāsb''-ur-å, *n. m.* a disputant.

Deasbaireachd, dyās[2]'-bar'-achg, *n. f.* disputation, dispute, wrangling, reasoning.

Deaschainnt, dyās[2]'-chăènnt, *n. f.* eloquence.

Deaschainntach, dyās'-chăènnt-ach, *a.* eloquent, witty, ready in replying.

Deasgainnean, dyāsg[2]'-unn-unn', *n. pl.* barm, yeast, runnet, lees.

Deaslamhach, dyās[2]'-láv-ach, *a.* dexterous.

Deasmaireas, dyās[2]'-mar-us, *n. f.* curiosity. *N.*

Deat, dyāt[2], *n. m.* a year old unshorn sheep; cosail ri *deata, like an unfleeced year old sheep. Skye.*

Deatach, dyett'-ach, *n. m.* smoke on the eve of getting into a flame; gas.

Deatam, dyāt[2]'-um, *n. m.* keenness, eagerness. *Sk.*

Deatamach, dyāt'-am-ach, *a.* necessary; needed, *Is.*; eager, keen for the world. *Skye.*

Deatamas, dyāt'-am-as, *n. m.* a requisite; a family necessary *or* want.

Deathach, dyé'-ach, *n. f.* smoke (toit). *P. S.*

Dee, jjā, *n. p.* gods; more properly *deidh.*

Deibh, deibhinn, dyāv'-ènn *pre.* about; concerning. *Irish.*

Deich, dyāèch[2], *n. f.* ten; *a.* ten.

Deich-filte, dyāèch[2]'-fēlly-tyå, *a.* ten fold.

Deichmhios, dyāèch-vhēss', *n. m.* December.

Deichnear, dyāèch'[2]-nur, *n. c.* ten persons.

Deich-roinn, dyāèch-raōènn', *n. m.* a decimal.

Deich-shlisneach, } dyāèch'-hlesh-nyach
Deich-thaobhach, } dyāèch'-hāov-ach, *n. m.* a decagon.

Deideadh, dyājj'-X, *n. m.* the toothache.

Deidh, dyāè-yh'', *n. f.* great propensity; a *dheidh* air òl, *his great propensity for drink*; *keen desire, longing*; tha e an *deidh* urra, *he is very fond of her*; na *dheidh* sin, *after that*; na *deidh, after her*; nar *deidh, after us*; mar *deidh, about, concerning us.*

Deidhealachd, dyāè'-yhall-achg, *n. f.* extreme *or* degree of desire *or* propensity.

Deidheil, dyāè'-yhal, *a.* very fond of, *or* addicted to; *dèidheil* air an uisge bheatha, *fond of*, or *addicted to, whisky.*

Deifir, dyāff[2]'-èr', *n. f.* speed, expedition; (more properly deiffir,) haste, hurry.

Deifreach, dyāff'-ryach, *a.* requiring expedition; gnothuch *deifreach, an affair requiring the utmost expedition*; *hasty, hurried.*

Deifrich, dyāff'-rèch, *v. n.* hasten, expedite; *deifrich* ort, *be quick*, or *clever.*

Deigh, dyā, more fit; (eigh, ice, *Sk.*)

Deigh-laimh, dyāè-yh'-làè'v, *adv.* too late, afterwards; after-hand.

Deighlean, dyā'-lyăn, *n. m.* quire of paper. *Irish.*

Deil, jāl, *n. m.* lath. *Irish.*

Deil, jjēl[2], *a.* enthusiastic, keen; cho *deil* aig a gnothuch, *so keen* or *enthusiastic at his business*; indefatigable, persevering, industrious.

Deile, (dè'-eile) jāl[2]'-å, *inter. pro.* what else? *deil'* a th' air t' fhaire, *what else do you mean*? *deil'* a dheanainn, *what else could I do*? *deile* a dhean e, *what else did he do*?

Deile, jjēl'[2]-å *n. f.* enthusiasm, industry.

Deile, jāl'-å, *n. f.* a deal, plank.

Deileann, dyāl'-unn, *n. m.* barking. *North.*

Deimhinn, dyév'-ènn, *a.* certain, sure, of a truth; gu *deimhinn, verily*; gu *deimhinn*, gu *deimhinn*, tha mi ag radh riut, *verily, verily, I say unto you. Bible.*

Deimhinneachd, dyév'-ènn-ăchg, *n. f.* complete certainty *or* proof.

Deimhinnich, dyév'-ènn-èch, *v.* verify, confirm, ascertain, demonstrate.

Deine, dyān''-å, *a.* more keen, more certain; *n. f.* eagerness, keenness.

DEINACHD, dyāèn'-ăchg, *n. f.* ardour.

DEINEIS, dyān'-ash, *n. f.* faint attempt to be diligent *or* eager; keenness.

DEIR, jjār', *v.* say, affirm; a' *deirim, I say*; a *deir* esan, *says he. Ir.*

DEIR, jàr, *n. f.* shingles, an ruaidh. *Ir.*

DEIRC, jāèrk, *n. f.* alms, charity.

DEIRCEACH, jāèrk'-ach, *n. c.* beggar.

DEIRCIRE, jāèrk'-ur-à, *n. m.* beggar; an almoner.

DEIREADH, dyār'-â2, *n. m.* end, conclusion; *deireadh* a ni so, *the conclusion of this thing*; stern of a boat, &c.; *deireadh* na luinge, *the stern of the ship*; *deireadh* cuaich, *a round stern*; rear; *deireadh* poite, lees; air *deireidh, behind, in the rear*; ma *dheireadh, at last*; toiseach tighinn is *deireadh* falbh, *first to come and last to go.* (Gaul's motto.)

DEIREANNACH, dyār'-ann-ach, *a.* last, hindermost, hindmost, latter; 'sna laithean *deireannach, in the latter days*; last; an neach *deireannach, the last individual.*

DEIREAS, dyār'-as, *n. m.* requisite, a convenience; dearasan, *domestic necessaries* or *convenience*; tha mi gun *deireas, I am quite well.*

DEIREASACH, dyār'-ās-ach, *a.* very requisite, needful, defective.

DEIRGE, dyērg'-à, redness, red; more *or* most red; also deirgead.

DEIS, dyāsh, *adv.* an *dèis, after.*

DEIS, dyāsh, *v.* skelp the breech.

DEISEAG, a little skelp on the breech.

DEISE, dyāsh2'-à, *n. f.* suit of clothes; symmetry of the body; shapeliness; proportionable parts,—more or most fit; shapely, proportioned. *See* Deas.

DEISCIOBUL, dyās'-kèb-ul, *n. m.* a disciple.

DEISEAD, dyāsh'-ad, *n. f.* degree of symmetry, handsomeness, elegance of person, &c.

DEISEALANN, dyash'-al-ann, *n. m.* slap on the cheek, box on the ear.

DEISEARACH, dyāsh'-arr-ach, *a.* conveniently situated, applicable; *deisearach* air an sgoil, *near the school, &c.*

DEISEARACHD, dyāsh'-arr-achg, *n. f.* convenience in point of situation, applicability.

DEISEIL, dyāsh'-al, *a.* toward the south, southward; neas 'sa bhios a' ghrian a' dol *deiseil, while the sun goes southwards.*

DEISINN, more properly deisthinn, disgust at the conduct *or* consequence of skelping the breeches.

DEISTINN, dyāsh'-tyènn, *n. f.* disgust; see dèisthinn, (dèis and tinn, sick).

DEISTHINN, dyāsh'-hyènn, *n. f.* disgust, squeamishness, abhorrence.

DEISTHINNEACH, dyāsh'-hyènn-ach, *a.* disgusting, causing squeamishness.

DEISTHINNEACHD, dyāsh'-hyenn-achg, *n. f* disgustfulness, extreme disgustfulness.

DEO, dyô, *n. f.* breath, the vital spark, the ghost; spark of fire; ray of light; gun *deò, breathless*; cha 'n 'eil aige na chumas an *deò* ann, *he has not what will keep the vital spark in him*; tha e an imf hios an *deò* a chall, *he is on the eve of giving up the ghost*; thug Abraham suas an *deò, Abraham gave up the ghost*; cha 'n 'eil *deò* gaoith ann, *there is not a breath of wind*; *deò* gealbhain, *a spark of fire*; *deò* soluis, *a ray of light*; cha d' thig *deò* do 'n ghrèin a stigh, *a single ray of the sun cannot enter*; neas a bhios an *deò* annad, *while you breathe*; gun *deò* leirsinn, *without a ray of vision, stone-blind*; glacaibh mo *dheò, lay hold on my departing spirit—on my ghost*; *deò*-greine, *sun-beam,* standard of Fingal.—*Ossian.*

DEOCAN, dyŏchg'-an, *n. m.* noise in sucking, &c.

DEOCH, dyōch, *n. f.* a drink, draught, liquor; thoir dhomh *deoch, give me a drink*; thoir *deoch* as, *take a draught out of it*; *deoch*-eiridinn, *a potion*; *deoch* an doruis, *a stirrup-cup*; *deoch* slàinte, *a toast, a health*; dat. dibh, deochannan, *spirits, all sorts of drinks, liquors*; *deoch*-eolais, *the first glass drunk to a stranger*; *deoch* m' eolais ort, *may we be better acquainted.*

DEOIGH, dyôè'-yh', *adv.* fa *dheoigh, at last.*

DEOIN, dyôèn, *n. f.* will, pleasure, acquiescence, assent; am *dheòin*-sa, *with my assent* or *concurrence*; le *deòin* Dia, *God willing*; a *dheòin* neo dh' aindeòin, *whether he wishes it or not*; cha b' ann am *dheòin* a rinn mi e, *I did not do it intentionally* or *on purpose—I was forced to it.*

DEOIR, dyōir, *n. pl.* tears; deur, *a tear.*

DEOIRID, dyôir'-èj, *n. c.* a broken-hearted, tearful person; also deoirideach.

DEONACH, dyôn'-ach, *a.* willing; *adv.* most willingly, voluntarily; is *deònach* a dheanainnse e, *most willingly would I do it.*

DEOINICH, dyôn'-ĕch, *v.* grant, give consent, vouchsafe; *deònaich* dhuinn gàirdeachas do shlàinte, *vouchsafe unto us the joys of thy salvation. B.*

DEORACHD, dyôr'-achg, *n. f.* affliction.

DEOTHAIL, dyō'-èll, *v.* suck, extract; fut. *deothlaidh, shall suck, extract, &c.*

DEOTHAL, dyô'-ăll, *n. m.* sucking, suck as infants *or* young of any kind.

DEOTHAS, dyō'-as, *n. m.* longing *or* eagerness of a calf for its mother; lust; this abominable word is used by indelicate WRITERS often very improperly.

DEOTHASACH, dyô'-as-ach, *a.* keen as a calf; very lustful as a person.

DETH, dyhé, (pro. *et* pre.) of him, of it, off; thoir *dheth* a' phoite, *take off the pot.*

DEUBH, jjāv, *n. f.* fetters for the fore feet of a horse; (1) deubh-leum, (4) deubh-ann, (Lewis), Mainland, gad.

DEUBH, dyāv, *v.* leak, chink as a dish; tha chuinneag air deubhadh, *the water-pitcher is leaking* or *chinking.*

DEUBHOIL, dyā'-v*h*yèl, *n. f.* enthusiasm, eagerness; *adj.* keen, enthusiastic, (dee·bhoil.) *Islay.*

DEUCH, dyèch, *v.* taste, try, sort.

DEUCHAINN, dyèch'-ènn, *n. f.* trial, taste, experiment, essay, distress; fhuair mi *deuchainn* deth, *I got a taste* or *trial of it.*

DEUCHAINNACH, dyèch'-ènn-ach, *a.* trying.

DEUD, dyādd, *n. m.* set of teeth; teeth.

DEUDACH, dyādd-ach, *n. f.* tooth-brush.

DEUG, dyāgg, *n. pl.* teens; used only in composition; còig-deug, *fifteen.*

DEUR, dyèrr, jèrr, a drop, a tear; a sileadh nan *deur, shedding tears*; cha'n'eil *deur* an so, *there is not a drop here*; a deòir a' snitheadh, *her tears trickling.*

DEURACH, dyèrr'-ach, *a.* tearful, sorrowful; *n. f.* a burning pain. *North Highlands.*

DEURSHUILEACH, dyerr'-hû'l-ach, *a.* blear-eyed.

DH', gh', aspirated form of d' *for* do.

DH', gh', do, sign of the *past,* used before fh and a vowel; as, *dh'* fhàg e i, *he abandoned her, he left her*; *dh'* aithnich mi, *I understood, I recognised.*

DHA, yhâ, asp. of *dà,* two; *dha* neo tri, *two or three*; also, for do e, thoir sin *dà* or *dhà, give him that*; thoir sin *daibh* or *dhaibh, give that to them*; *dhomh, to me*; *dhuinn, to us. See* Grammar.

DHACHAIDH, dhach'-ė, asp. form of dachaidh, home; also *adv. dhachaidh, dhachaidh, away home, home.*

DH'AINDEOIN, ghén'-nyăn, *adv.* in defiance, spite of; in spite of.

DHEIBHINN, yhāv'-ènn, *pre.* concerning; ma *dhèibhinn* sin, *concerning that.*

DHI, yhė, to her; thoir *dhi, give her.*

DHOMH, ghóv², *to me*; innis *dhomh, tell me*; thoir *dhomh, give me*; dean *dhomh, do for me,* or *to me.*

DI, jē, *n. m.* a day; *di*-luain, *Monday*; *di*-màirt, *Tuesday*; *di*-ciadain, *Wednesday*; *dior*-daoin, *Thursday*; *di*-thaoine, *Friday*; *di*-sathuirne, *Saturday*; *di*-domhnuich, *Sunday.*

DIA, dyēā, *n. m.* God, the Almighty, a god, dèidh, gods.

DIABHLUIDH, dyéávll'-ė, *a.* devlish, hellish.

DIABHLUIDHEACHD, jjĕāll'-ė-achg, *n. f.* devilishness.

DIABHOLL, dyĕāv²'-ul, *n. m.* Satan; the devil.

DIACHADAICH, jjĕāch'-ad-ėch, *adv.* especially. *N.*

DIADHACHD, jjĕā-gh''-achg, *n. f.* divinity, godliness, theology; diadhaidheachd.

DIADHAICH, jjĕāgh'-ėch, *v.* deify, adore.

DIADHAIDH, dyèā-gh'-ė, *a.* godly, holy.

DIADHAIR, dyĕā'-ghar', *n. m.* a divine.

DIADHAIREACHD, dyea'-ghăr-ăchg, *n. f.* divinity.

DIADHALACHD, dyĕā-gh''-al-achg, *n. f.* godliness.

DIA-DHEANADH, dyĕā-yhèn'-Ă, *n. m.* deification.

DIALL, dyĕāll, *n. m.* attachment, fondness, continuance; 's mòr an *diall* a th' aige air an uisge, *there is a great continuance of rain, v.* attach, get fond of, as a child, dog, &c.

DIALTAG, dyĕālt'-ag, *n. f.* a bat.

DIAMHALLAICH, dyĕā-vhŏll'-ėch, *v.* blaspheme.

DIA-MHASLACH, dyĕā-vhas'-lach, *a.* blasphemous.

DIA-MHASLADH, dyĕā-v*has*'-lă, *n. m.* blasphemy.

DIAN, dyĕān, *a.* keen, impetuous, eager, vehement, violent, furious; nimble; often used before the noun qualified *dian* fhearg, *fiery indignation*; *dian* ruaig, *close pursuit*; oppression; *adv. dian* iarr, *importune*; *dian*-loisg, *burn vehemently*; *dian* theth, *intensely hot*; *dian*-mhear, *furiously lustful.*

DIAS, dyĕās, *n. f.* an ear of corn.

DIASACH, dyĕās'-ach, *a.* luxuriant as a crop.

DIASAG, dyĕās'-ag, *n. f.* ludicrous name for a carper, *or* satirist's tongue.

DIASAIR, dyĕās'-ur, *v.* glean; dioghloim.

DIORDAOIN, dyĕrr-dāoėn', *n. m.* Thursday.

DI-SATHUIRNE, dyē-sa''-hurn-à, *n. m.* Saturday.

DIBH, dyėv, *dat.* of deoch, liquor, drink.

DIBHE, dyėv'-à, *gen.* of deoch, of drink.

DIBHEACH, dyėv'-ach, *n. m.* an ant; seangan.

DIBLIDH, dyēb'-llė, *a.* very mean *or* abject.

DIBLIDHEACHD, dēb'-llė-achg, *n. f.* abjectness.

DICHEANN, dyē-chyann', *v.* behead.

DICHIOLL, dyēch'-chyal, *n. m.* utmost endeavour; a forlorn effort; diligence.

DICHIOLLACH, dyēch'-ull-ach, *a.* struggling with disadvantages; diligent, endeavouring.

DI-CHRANNAICH, dyē-chrann'-ėch, *v.* dismast.

DI-CIADAOIN, dyē'-kĕādd-an², *n. m.* Wednesday.

DIDEANN, dyējj'-ann', *n. m.* rampart, protection, refuge; more correctly dighdion.

DID, dyējj, *v.* peep, *N.*; *a.* worse, *Is.*; is beag a's *dìd* thu sin, *you are little the worse for that.*

DIG, dyēgg, *n. f.* a fen, a ditch, a drain; (*N.* wall of loose stones;) *v.* dress *or* trench, as potatoes; furrow, drain.

DIGIRE, dyēgg′-ur-à, *n. m.* a ditcher.

DIGH, dyē, *n. f.* a conical mound built by the Danes; a rampart; an abode of fairies; *digh* mhòr Thallanta, *a noted one in Islay*; hence dideann, *a place of refuge.*

DIL, dyėl, *a.* diligent, persevering, zealous. *Is.*

DILE, dyē′-là, *n. f.* flood, deluge; an *dìle* ruadh, *the general flood,* or *deluge.*

DILE, dyël′-à, *a.* more *or* most diligent *or* persevering; *n. m.* love, *Ir.*; an herb.

DILEAB, dyēl′-ub, *n. f.* a legacy, a bequest.

DILEABACH, dyel′-ab-ach, *n. c.* a legatee.

DILEABAICHE, dyēl′-ub-ėch-a, } *n. c.* a testator, feartiomnaidh.
DILEABAIR, dyēl′-ub-ăėr, }

DILEAS, dyēl[2]′-us, *a.* loyal, favourable, faithful; nearly connected *or* related; bì *dìleas* do'n righ, *be loyal* or *faithful to the king*; *dìleas* domh, *nearly connected with me*; *dìleas* do d' mhaighstir, *faithful to your master*; ni's *dìlse, more loyal.*

DILINN, dyēl′-ėnn, *n. f.* deluge, eternity, age; gu *dìlinn*, ever, never; *adv.* never, ever; cha *dìlinn* a thig e, *he shall never come* (through all eternity); gus an caillear ann *dìlinn* aois, *till age is lost in the flood of time*; gu *dìlinn* cha dùisg thu, *you shall never awake. Oss.*

DILLEACHDAN, dyēlly″-achg-an, *n. c.* an orphan; *dìleachdach, fatherless. MSS.*

DILLSE, dyėlly′-shà, *n. f.* relationship, faithfulness; more *or* most nearly related.

DILLSEACHD, dyēlly″-shăchg, *n. f.* degree of kindred; faithfulness, connection.

DI-LUAIN, dyė-llŭăėn′, *n. m.* Monday.

DI-MAIRT, dyė-màrty′, *n. m.* Tuesday.

DIMEAS, dyēm′-mėss, *n. m.* disrespect, contempt, reproach.

DIMEASACH, dyēm′-mėss-ach, *a.* disrespectful, contemptible, despicable, mean.

DIMEASAIL, dyēm′-méss-al, *a.* disrespectful.

DING, jjėng, a wedge, geinn. *Irish.*

DINN, dyēnn, *v.* press down, ram, stuff.

DINNEADH, dyēnn′-Ă, *pt.* pressing down, cramming, stuffing; *n. m.* act of pressing.

DINNEAR, dyēnn[2]′-ar′, *n. f.* dinner. *French.*

DINNIRE, dyēnn[2]′-ur-à, *n. m.* ramrod.

DINNSEAR, dyēsh′-ur, *n. m.* ginger; wedge.

DINNTE, dyėnt′-tyà, *pt.* packed, pressed; closely packed *or* stuffed; crammed.

DIOBAIR, dyēbb′-ėr, *v.* extirpate, root out; *dhìobair* mi an fheanntagach, *I have extirpated the nettle;* depopulate, banish; forsake, abandon.

DIOBAIRT, dyēbb′-arty′, *n. f.* extirpation, depopulation; *pt.* forsaking, leaving.

DIOBARACH, dyēbb′-ar-ach, *n. c.* an outcast; a deserted person; an exile *dìobaraich* Israel, *the outcasts of Israel. Bible.*

DIOBHAIL, dyēv′-al, *n. f.* want; *dìobhail* misnich, *want of courage*; defeat.

DIOBHAIR, dyēv′-ėr, *v.* vomit, puke; in Lochaber, dyŭr *or* jû-er.

DIOBHAIRT, dyēv′-ărty′, *n. f.* vomiting.

DIOCAIL, dyēchd′-ėl, *v.* abate, as rain.

DIOCHUIMHN, dyē′-chyŭėnn, *n. f.* forgetfulness; *diochuimh*neach, forgetful.

DIOCLA, dyėchg′-la, *n. m.* abatement of rain; uisge gun *dìocla, incessant rain. Isds.*

DIOD, jjėdd, *n. f.* a drop, spark. *Is.*

DIOG, jj'úg, *n. m.* a word, a syllable; nan h-abair *diog, say not a word.*

DIOGAIL, dyúg′-ėll, *v.* tickle; diogailt, *tickling*; cuir *diogailt* ann, *tickle him.*

DIOGAILTEACH, dyúg′-alty-ach, *a.* ticklish.

DIOGHAIL, dyú′-ėll, revenge, retaliate.

DIOGHAILTE, dyu′-allty′ *a. pt.* revenged, avenged.

DIOGHALTACH, dyú′-alt-ach, *a.* vindictive, revengeful, requiring much.

DIOGHALTAIR, dyúll′-tyar, *n. m.* an avenger.

DIOGHALTAS, dyúlt′-tyas, *n. m.* vengeance.

DIOGHLOIM, dyùl′-ėm, *v.* glean after shearers; cull, gather minutely; *n. m.* diogh lom, gleanings, the thing gathered.

DIOL, dyēll, *v.* recompense, requite; *dhìol* thu sin, *you have recompensed that*; *n. m.* condition, state; is boidheach a *dhìol, he is in a pretty condition*; satiety, satisfaction, abundance; tha mo *dhìol* agamsa, *I have my satisfaction* or *abundance*; a *dhìol* ùine aige, *he has plenty of time*; complement, proportion; clach chàis le a *dìol* do dh'ìm, *a stone of cheese with its complement of butter.* (*Lw.*)

DIOLAIN, dyēll′-ên, *a.* illegitimate; mac *dìolain, an illegitimate son* or *bastard.*

DIOLANAS, dyēll′-an-as, *n. f.* bastardy, illegitimacy, fornication; rugadh an *dìolanas* e, *he was born in fornication.*

DIOLLAID, dyēll′-ajj, *n. f.* a saddle.

DIOLLADAIR, dyēll′-ad-ăr, *n. m.* saddler; diolladaireachd, *saddler's business.*

DIOMB, jēmb[2], *n. f.* indignation, offence, resentment, displeasure; na toill *diomh* duine 'sam bith, *incur not the displeasure of any person.*

DIOMBACH, jjēmb[2]′-ăch, *a.* indignant, dissatisfied, offended at, displeased.

DIOMBACHD, jēmb[2]′-achg, *n. f.* indignation

DIOMBUAIN, dyēm′-ăn′, *a.* fading, transitory, fleeting, transient; more properly diomain, the b being changed into m, which often happens.

Diombuanachd, dyēm'-an'-achg, *n.f.* transitoriness, evanescence, short duration.

Diombuanas, same as above.

Diombuil, dyėmb'-bŭl, *n.f.* misapplication.

Diomhair, dyēv'-ur', *a.* secret, mysterious, private; gnothach *dìomhair*, a private affair; lonely, solitary.

Diomhaireachd, dyēv'ăr'-achg, *n. f.* privacy, mystery; solitude.

Diomhanach, jjēv'-an'-ach, *a.* idle, lazy; in vain; vain; is *dìomhanach* dhuit teannadh ris, *it is idle, it is in vain for you to attempt such.*

Diomhanas, jjēv'-an-as, *n. f.* idleness, laziness; labour in vain; emptiness, vanity.

Diomol, dyēm'-ol, *v.* dispraise, libel, depreciate, undervalue, disparage.

Diomoladh, dyēm'-ol-X, *n. m.* dispraise, disparagement; abuse; *pt.* dispraising, undervaluing, abusing.

Dion, dyēn, *n. m.* shelter, covert, defence; fo *dhìon* do sgèith, *under the covert of thy wing* or *shield*; airson mo *dhìon, for my defence, for my protection*; state of being wind and water tight; tha *dìon* san tigh, *the house is wind and water tight*; *v.* protect, defend, shield, save; shelter, guard; *dìon* thu fhèin, *defend yourself*; *dìon* mi le d' sgèith, *defend me with thy shield*; *dion* àite, *a place of refuge.*

Dionach, dyēn'-ach, *a.* water-tight, airtight; not leaky as a vessel; tigh *dìonach, water-tight house*; long *dhìonach, a ship without a leak*; safe, secure.

Dionachadh, dyēn'-ach-X, *n. m.* security, caution, bail.

Dionachd, dyēn'-achg, *n. m.* security.

Dionadair, dyēn'-add-ėr, *n. m.* a fender, a defender, protector.

Dionaich, dyēn'-ėch, *v.* secure.

Dionag, dyēn'-ag, *n. f.* a two-year old sheep *or* goat. (jēăn-ag. *N.*)

Dion-bhreid, jēn'-vhrāj, *n. m.* apron.

Diong, jung, a hillock; *v.* join, *H.* match; *diongamsa* righ Innescon, *let me match the king of Innescon. Oss.*

Diong, jung, *a.* worthy, unmoveable.

Diongalta, jung'-alt-ȧ, *a.* firm, secure, efficient, completely certain.

Diongaltas, jung'-ălt-as, *n. f.* security, complete certainty, efficiency, sufficiency, tightness; also diongaltachd.

Dioras, jērr'-as, *n. m.* tenacity, pertinacity; childish efforts.

Diorasach, jērr'-as-ach, *a.* tenacious, pertinacious; opinionative, striving in vain.

Diorasachd, jērr'-as-achg, *n. f.* extreme pertinacity *or* tenacity.

Diosg, jjēssg, *v.* creak as hinges, gnash as teeth; *n. m.* state of being without milk, as a female; a dish. *North.*

Diosgail, dyēsg'-al, *n. m. pt.* creaking.

Diot, dyēăt, *n. f.* diet, meal.

Dipinn, dyēp'-ėnn, *n. f.* deepening of a net, a certain quantity of net.

Dir, dyērr, *v.* ascend, go up; a *dìreadh* a' bhruthaich, *ascending the acclivity* or *steep.*

Direach, dyērr'-ach, *a.* straight; an ni sin a tha cam, cha ghabh e dheanadh *dìreach, that which is crooked cannot be made straight, B.*; *adv.* directly, exactly so; *dìreach* mar thuirt thu, *just as you said*; dìreach! dìreach! *just so! just so!* upright, is *dìreach* Dia, *God is upright.*

Direachan, dyēr'-ach-an, *n. f.* perpendicular.

Direadh, dyērr'-X, *n. m. pt.* ascending; ceò a' *dìreadh* aonaich, *mist ascending a hill.*

Dirich, dyērr'-ėch, *v.* make straight, mount, climb; cha *dìrich* thu am fireach, *thou shalt not climb the steep, Oss. dhìrich* e an carbad, *he mounted the chariot, M'L.*; am fear nach *dìrich* a dhriom, *he that will not be at the trouble of raising his head, straightening his back. Maclachlan.*

Dis, dyēsh[2], *a.* fond of the fire; susceptible of, *or* not capable of bearing cold; *n. m.* a Celtic Deity, a God.

Di-sathuirne, dyē-sa'-hurn-ȧ, *n. m.* Saturday.

Disinn, dyēsh'-ėnn, *n. m.* a die, dice; *gen.* disne, ag iomairt air dìsnean, *playing at bagammon*; a cube, a wedge, as in the shaft of any thing.

Disle, another form of dillse, more nearly connected.

Dit, dyējt, *v.* condemn, sentence; co a *dhìteas* iad, *who shall condemn them, Sm.*; reproach, despise; na *dìt* mi airson sin, *reproach me not for that. C.*

Diteadh, dyējt'-X, *n. m.* condemnation; 'se so an *dìteadh* gu d' thàinig an solus do 'n t-saoghail, *and this is the condemnation, that light is come into the world. Bible.*

Dith, dyē, *n. f.* want, deficiency; *dìth* cèille, *want of sense*; cha 'n 'eil *dìth* air, *he wants for nothing*; dè tha *dhìth* ort, *what do you want?* is mòr a tha *dhìth* orm, *I want much*; chuir thu *dhìth* orm, *you deprived me of this*; is mòr a tha sin a *dhìth* orm, *I want that very much*; is beag a tha sin a *dhìth* ort, *you stand very little in need of that*; thèid iad a *dhìth* orm, *I shall be deprived of them*; a *dhìth* fasgaidh, *for want of shelter*; tha mòran a *dhìth, there is a great deficiency.*

Dith, dyė, *n. f.* a layer, a course, a streak;

dith ma seach, *a layer about*; *dithean* saille, *layers* or *streaks of fat*, as in beef; a vein, as in a mine; *ditheanan* luaidh is airgid, *veins of lead and silver ore*; *v.* press, squeeze. *N.*

DITHEACH, dyḗ-ach, *n. c.* a beggar.

DITHEAN, dyē'-an', *n. m.* the herb darnal.

DITHICH, dyē'-èch, *v.* extirpate, root out; *dìtheachaidh* mi an ìomhaighean, *I will root out their images; dhìthich* mo chàirdean, *my friends have failed. B. O.*

DITHIS, dyè'-èshj, more properly dithisd.

DITHISD, dyè'-èshj, *n. c.* two; a brace; pair; thàinig *dithisd, two came*; *adj. dithisd* fear, *two men;* na *dithisdean, in pairs*; *dithisd* do gach seorsa, *two of each species.*

DITH-LATHRAICH, dyè-llàr'-èch, *v.* utterly destroy, annihilate.

DIMHILLTEACH, dyē'-vhělly'-tyach, *n. m.* a destroyer; a miserable person.

DITHREABH, dyē'-ruv, *n. f.* wilderness; fàsach, *B.;* higher grounds. *North.*

DIU, jū, *a.* due; French deu.

DIU, jū, *n. m.* refuse; the worst; roghainn is *diù, pick and choice;* an object of contempt; cha *diù* idir, *it is no object of contempt.*

DIUBH, jū, *pre.* and *pro.*, of them; cuid *diubh, some of them*; aon *diubh, one of them*; also diùbhsan.

DIUBHAIL, jūv''-al, *n. f.* calamity, distress; destruction, ruin; mo *diùbhail, my ruination*; is mòr an *diùbhail, it is a thousand pities*; differs from *dìobhail,* want, deficiency.

DIUBHALACH, jū'-al-ach, *a.* calamitous, distressing; heart-rending.

DIUBHALAICH, jū'-al-èch, *v.* recompense, compensate; make up deficiencies; *diùbhalachadh, compensation.*

DIUCHD, jjūchg, *n. m.* duke, (Latin dux).

DIUG, jūgg², *inter.* chuck.

DIUGH, jŭ'-gh, *adv.* an diugh, to-day; an *diugh* fhèin, *this very day.*

DIUID, jjūj, *a.* timid, diffident, fearful, bashful, awkward, sheepish.

DIUIDE, jjūj'-à, *n. f.* timidity, diffidence, sheepishness; more *or* most timid.

DIUIDEACHD, jjūjj'-ăchg, *n. f.* extreme diffidence; backwardness, timidity.

DIULACH, jjūll'-ăch, *n. m.* a hero; a handsome brave man.

DIULT, dyūlt, *v.* refuse, reject.

DIULTADH, dyūllt'-Ă, *n. m.* refusal, denial; *pt.* refusing, rejecting, denying.

DIUNANAICH, jjūnn'-an-èch, *v.* wallop; drub; 'ga dhuinanachadh, *wallopping* or *drubbing him.*

DIUNLACH, dyūn'-llăch, *n. m.* handsome man.

DIURR, jùrr, *n. f.* vital spark; cha'n'ei *diùrr* ann, *he is quite dead.*

DIURRAIS, jjùrr'-èsh, *n. f.* a secret a mystery; an *diurrais, as a secret.*

DIURRAISACH, jjùrr'-èsh-ach, *a.* secret, private; requiring secrecy.

DIUTHA, dyūch'-à, *pre.* and *pro.* of them; cuid *diùtha, some of them. Is.*

DLAGH, dloă'-gh, *n. m.* what the hand can grasp in shearing corn; natural order; as a *dhlagh, out of its natural order* or *arrangement.*

DLEAS, dllăss², *n. m.* right, due, merit, desert; mo *dhleas* fhèin, *my own due* or *right*; *adj.* due, deserved, merited; is *dleas* sin da, *that is due to him*; ma tha sin *dleas* duit, *if that be due to you*; incumbent; in duty bound; an *dleas* dhomh sin a dheanadh, *is it incumbent on me to do that*; *v.* owe, extort, procure; na *dleas* ni do dhuine sam bith, *owe no man any thing, Bible*; *dleasaidh* airm urram, *arms procure respect. G. Proverbs.*

DLEASNACH, dlăss'-nnach, *a* dutiful.

DLEASNAS, dlăss²'-nas, *n. m.* duty; filial duty; affection; rinn mi mo *dheasnas, I did my duty*; obligation.

DLIGH, dllè, *v.* owe; ma *dhligheas* mi ni sam bith, *if I owe any thing. Bible.*

DLIGHE, dllè'-à, *n. m.* duty; right; due; 'se so mo *dhlighe, this is my due. Bible.*

DLIGHEACH, dllè'-ach, *a.* rightful, lawful; legitimate; oighre *dligheach, rightful heir*; clann *dhligheach, lawful children* due; ma's *dligheach* dhuit sin, *if that be due you.*

DLOGH, dllò'-ghd, *n. m.* a wart; handful of half-thrashed corn.

DLOGHAINN, dllò'-ènn, *n. f.* sheaf-corn half-thrashed, given to cattle when fodder is scarce.

DLUITH, dllûèch *and* dlûè, *a.* near, approach, draw near; house-corn (Harris); *dlùith* rium, *draw near me*; *dhlùith* iad ris a' bhaile, *they approached the town*

DLUTH, dllhû, *a.* near, nigh, close to; *dlùth* air an latha, *near day-light*; *dlùth* air a' chéile, *close upon, near each other*; related, nearly connected.

DLUTH, dl'û-gh, *n. m.* warp of cloth; na leoir do *dhlùth* is fuigheal innich, *abundance of warp,* and *remainder of woof*; enough and to spare, something to go and come upon. *Prov.*

DLUTHADH, dlû'-a', *and* dlûch'-Ă, *pt.* approaching, nearing, drawing near.

DLUTHAICH, dlu'-èch, *v.* same as dluith.

DLUTH-LEAN, dlû'-llen, *v.* stick close to.

DLUTH-THEANN, dlû'-hyann, *v.* press; near.

DO, daŏ, (du, when before a consonant); *prep.* to; *do* 'n duine, *to the man*; pronounced dun duine; takes often dh' before vowels; *do* dh' Eirinn, *to Ireland*; pronounced daŏ-y*hār*''-ènn,*do* d'mhàthair, *to thy mother*, pronounced dud-v*hà'*-hyaĕr, *to thy mother*; *do* is wholly IRISH. The Celtic preposition, in common with the old French and Teutonic, being du, the u pronounced as in gu; it is the case joined to the pronouns—thus, duinn, *to us*; duit, *to thee*; duibh, *to you*; excepting domh and daibh, or, as the Irish spoil the latter doibh, *to them.*

N. B.——Some of our dòbhliadhnach friends pronounce daibh, daŏĕv, and dà, *to him, dò.*

DO, *and* du, daŏ, *pro.* thy; *do* mhathair, *thy mother*, pronounced duv'-vhàhyĕr—often changed before vowels into t'; as t'athair, *thy father*; as, in the French, the initial consonant is always joined to it; *do* làmh, dull'-làv, *thy hand*; *do* fhreagairt, dur'-răg²-ărty', *thy answer*; *d* is always written dh' after it; *do* dhamh, daŏ y*háv*, *thy ox*; sign of the past *inter.*; as an do fhreagair e, *did he or it answer?* used adverbially, or as a negative before words thus—*do*-fhulann, *difficult to endure*; *almost impossible to endure.*

DO-AIREAMH, dò-âr''²-uv, difficult to count, innumerable.

DOBHAIDH, dô'-vè, *a.* boisterous; oidhche *dhòbhaidh, a boisterous night;* terrible.

DOBHARCHU, dō²'-ur-chŭ, *n. m.* a kind of otter which has no existence but in DONALD's imagination; the price of his skin which can heal all diseases, is its full of pure gold, when made into a bag—a chimera.

DO-BHEAIRT, dò'-vhyărty', *n. f.* vice.

DOBHRAN, dōr'-an, *n. m.* an otter; ball *dobhrain, a freckle on the skin, mole.*

DOBHRON; see Dubh-bhròn, dejection.

DOCAIR, dŏchg'-ur', *n. f.* uneasiness, trouble, annoyance; *a.* uneasy, not settled; àite-suidh *docair, an uneasy seat*; socair neo *docair, either easy* or *uneasy,* or *difficult.*

DOCHA, dŏch'-a, *a.* comp. of toigh; is toigh leam thusa ach 's *docha* leam esan, *I like you, but he is more dear to me*; I love you, but I love him more.

DOCHA, dôch'-à, *a.* comp. of dogh; is dogh gu'm bheil, *probably it is so*; 'se so a's *dòcha, this is more probable,* or *likely.*

DOCHAINN, doch'-ènn, *v.* injure, hurt.

DOCHAIR, dŏch'-ur, *n. m.* hurt; *v.* hurt.

DOCHANN, doch'-unn, *n. m.* hurt, harm, damage, mischief; agony; a *dochann* bàis, *from the agony of death. Smith*; fhuair e *dochann, he got a hurt*; thaobh *dochann, on account of damage. Bible.*.

DOCHANNACH, dŏch'-ann-àch, *a.* hurtful, injurious, noxious.

DOCHARACH, doch'-ar-ach, *a.* uneasy; 'se an suidhidh *docharach*, sa tigh-òsda is fhearra, *the uneasiest seat in the alehouse is the best.*

DO-CHARACHADH, dò'-char-ach-à, *a.* not easily moved, unmoveable.

DOCHAS, dôch'-as, *n. m.* expectation, hope, trust, confidence; tha mi an *dòchas, I fondly hope*; gun *dòchas, without hope*; an *dòchas* do theachd, *in expectation of thy coming, Oss*; conceit, notion, presumption; do *dhòchas, your conceit, your presumption.*

DOCHASACH, dôch'-as-ach, *a.* conceited, vain, presumptuous; 'se fear *dochasach* e, *how conceited* or *presumptuous he is*; hoping, confident, confiding.

DOCHASACHD, dôch'-as-achg, *n. f.* confidence, hopefulness, conceitedness.

DOCHASG, dō-chasg', *a.* unquenchable.

DO-CHEANNSACHADH, do-chyănn'-sach-à, *a.* not easily managed, invincible.

DO-CHIOSNACHADH, dò'-chēss-năch-à, *a.* unconquerable, invincible.

DO-CHLAOIDH, dò'-chlùè-yh', *a.* indefatigable.

DO-CHLAOIDHTEACHD, *n. f.* dò'-chlùè-yhtyachg, *n. f.* invincibility, insuperability.

DO-CHOMHAIRLEACHADH, dò'-chŏm-urly'-ach-à, *a.* incorrigible, untameable.

DO-CHREIDSINN, dò'-chraŏjj-shènn, *a.* incredible; do may be prefixed to almost any word,—it signifies not easily accomplished.

DOD, dōd², *n. m.* a huff; see Sdod.

DODACH, dōd²'-ach, *a.* pettish, peevish.

DO-DHEANADH, dò'-ghèn-à, impossible.

DOG, ddŏg, *n. m.* a junk; a short thick piece of any thing; thickset person; *dog* bùill, *a junk of a rope, &c.*

DOGANTA, dog'-ănt-à, *a.* thickset, stumpish,—fierce. *North.*

DOGH, dô, *n. m.* opinion; 'mo *dhòghsa* gu 'm bheil, *in my opinion it is so*; *a.* like, probable; is *dogh* nach 'eil, *it is probably not so*; 'sè so is *dòcha, this is more probable*—sometimes doigh.

DOIBH, for daibh, ddìv, to them.

DOICHEALL, dòèch'-ull, *n. m.* act of grudging, churlishness; *pt.* grudging.

DOICHEALLACH, dòèch'-all-ach, *a.* churlish, grudging, inhospitable.

DOICHILL, dòèch'-èll, *v.* begrudge, grudge; cha 'n ann 'ga *dhoicheall* a tha mi, *I am not grudging it to you*; be churlish.

DOID, dŏjj, *n. f.* a croft, a pendicle.

DOIDIRE, dŏjj'-ur-à, *n. m.* a crofter, a cottager.

DOIDEACH, ddŏjj'-ach, *a.* frizzled. *North.*

DOIDEAG, dŏjj'-ăg, *n. f.* a celebrated Mull

witch who caused the DESTRUCTION of the Spanish Armada ! ! !

DOIGH, dôe-yh, *n. f.* method, manner, way, means; air an *dòigh* so, *in this manner*; condition, state; dè an *dòigh* a th' ort, *how are you?* cùir air *dòigh, arrange, adjust, put in order*; confidence, trust; cuiridh mi mo *dhòigh* an Dia, *I will put confidence in God, Bible.*; gun *dòigh, out of order, absurd.*

DOIGHEIGINN, dŏe'-yh'-ê-gènn, *adv.* somehow or other, somehow.

DOIGHEALACHD, dôĕ-yh''-al-achg, *n. f.* excellent arrangement, capability of adjustment.

DOIGHEIL, dôè'-yh'-al, *a.* well arranged, in good trim *or* condition; systematic, in proper train.

DOILEAS, dól'-as, *n. f.* difficulty, hardship.

DOILGHEAS, do'l'-ghès, *n. m.* sorrow, affliction.

DOILGHEASACH, do'l'-ghês-ach, *a.* sorrowful.

DOILLE, ddaŏl'-lyå, *n. f.* blindness, darkness, stupidity; more blind *or* stupid, ignorant.

DOILLEARACHD, dòl'-lyar'-achd, *n. f.* stupidity, darkness, obscurity.

DOILLEIR, dòl'-lyar, *a.* dark, stupid; duine *doilleir, a stupid person*; (do-leir.)

DOILLEIRICH, dòl'-lyar'-èch, *v.* obscure, dim.

DOIMH, dóèv', *a.* galling, vexing; gross, clumsy; gu dùmhail, *doimh*, mar bhiòs màthair fhir an tighe an rathad na cloinne, *bulky and clumsy, as the husband's mother is in the way of the children. Prov.*

DOIMHEADACH, dóè'-ad-ach, *a.* vexing, galling; is *doimheadach* an ni e, *it is a vexing thing.*

DOIMHEADAS, dŏè'-ad-as, *a.* vexation, grief.

DOIMHNE, dóè'-nyå, *n. f.* depth, the deep, the ocean; *doimhne* a' gairm, air *doimhne, deep calling into deep*; air gnùis fhoisneach na *doimhne, on the still face of the deep, Sm.*; na's *doimhne, deeper, more profound.*

DOIMHNEACHD, dóè'-nyachg, *n. f.* depth, deepness, profundity; deep water; 'san *doimhneachd, in deep water*; air an tanalach, *in shoal water.*

DOIMHNEAD, dóèn'-nad, *n. m.* degree of depth, deepness, profundity.

DOIMHNICH, dóèn'-nyèch, *v.* deepen, hollow.

DOINION, dŏèn'-un, storm; more properly doirionn, do-rìon; (rian, *North.*)

DO-INNSE, dō-ënn'-shå, *a.* unaccountable.

DO-IOMCHAIR, dò-èm'-ach-ur, *a.* intollerable.

DO-IOMPACHADH, dò-ēmp'-ach-Ă, *a.* perverse.

DOIRB, dóèr'-ub, *n. f.* a minnow; breac deamhain, *a reptile. Arms.*

DOIRBH, dóèr'-uv, *a.* difficult; ceisd *dhoirbh, a difficult question*; stormy, boisterous; oidhche *dhoirbh, a boisterous night*; wild, ungovernable; duine *doirbh, a turbulent incorrigible person*; grievous, intolerable; mo reachdsa cha 'n 'eil *doirbh, my law is not grievous. Bible.*

DOIRBHE, dóer'-å, *a.* more difficult, &c. *n. f.* difficulty, boisterousness, indocility, &c.

DOIRBHEACHD, dóerv'-achg, *n. f.* difficulty.

DOIRBHEAD, dóèr'-ad, *n. f.* degree of difficulty, boisterousness, storminess, hardship.

DOIRBEADAS, dóèr'-ad-as, *n. f.* ungovernableness, peevishness, turbulence.

DOIRBHEAS, dóèr'-as, *n. f.* difficulty, &c. grief, anguish, distress, boisterousness; latha an *doirbheis, the day of adversity*; a' dol gu *doirbheas, getting obstreperous, unmanageable.*

DOIRCH, dóèrch, dór'-èch, *n.* get dark; *dhoirch* an oidhche dhuinn, *we were benighted, the night got dark on us.*

DOIRCHE, dór'-èch-å, darker, *n. f.* extreme darkness.

DOIRE, ddŏer''-å, *n. m.* a grove, a thicket, a species of tangle, (in *Skye*, stamh); shuidhich Abraham *doire* chraobh, *Abraham planted a grove of trees*; gach coille is gach *doire, every wood and grove.*

DOIREACH, daŏĕr'-ach, *a.* woody, wild.

DOIRIONN, dóèr'-unn, *n. f.* inclemency, stormy weather; thàinig *doirionn* a gheamhraidh, *the inclemency of winter has come*; storminess; (doirbh *or* do-rìon.)

DOIRIONNACH, dóèr'-unn-ach, *a.* stormy.

DOIREANNACHD, dóèr'-unn-achg, *n. f.* storminess.

DOIRLINN, dôèr'-lyènn, an islet to which one can wade at low water; (*Mainland*), peebly *or* stony part of a shore; (*Islands*), an isthmus.

DOIRNEAG, dŏèrn'-ag, *n. f.* a pebble.

DOIRNEAGACH, dŏèrn'-ag-ach, *a.* pebbled.

DOIRT, dōèrty', *v.* pour, spill, shed, rush forth; stream, gush; scatter; *dhòirt* e 'fhuil, *he shed his blood*; *dhòirt* e ma cheann e, *he poured it on his head*; *dhòirt* iad thun a chladaich, *they rushed towards the shore. Ossian.*

DOIRTEACH, dōèrty''-ach, *a.* apt to spill; *n. f.* flood, a sudden pour of rain.

DOIRTEALL, dōèrty''-all, *n. m.* a sink, a drain.

DOITE, dô'-tyå, *pt.* dogh, singed, seared.

DOITEACHAN, dô'-tyach-an, *n. m.* a miserable singed looking person.

DOL, dòll, *n. m.* condition, state; is boidheach an *dol* a th' air, *it is in a pretty condition*; an *dol* a dh' fhàg thu air, *the condition in which you left it*; *dol* an t-saoghail, *the state of the world*; *dol* as *escape*; cha 'n 'eil *dol* as aige, *he has no way of escape.*

DOL, dòll, *pt.* of theirig; theirig dhachaidh, *go home*; a' *dol* dachaidh, *going home*; *dol* fodha na gréine, *going down of the sun*; a' *dol* iomrol air a chéile, *missing each other*; a' *dol* as, *escaping, extinguishing as fire, light*; a' *dol* sìos, *going down, descending*; a' *dol* suas, *ascending.*

DOLACH, dōl'-ach, *a.* indifferent; duine dona *dòlach, a bad, or at least, an indifferent person.*

DOLAIDH, doll'-ê, *n. f.* harm, ruination, mischief; cuir a *dholaidh, ruin, destroy the well-being of*; is beag an *dolaidh, it is no great harm*; dè an *dolaidh* a rug ort, *what the mischief came over you?*

DOLAS, dō'-las, *n. m.* harm; grief; (doleas.)

DOLASACH, dô'-las-ăch, *a* grieved, hurtful.

DO-LEASACH, dò-llās²'-ach, *a.* irreparable.

DO-LEIGHEAS, dò-llā'-us, *a.* irremediable.

DO-LEUBHADH, dò'-lāv-Ă, *a.* illegible, inexplicable, ill to explain.

DO-LUBADH, dò-lûb'-Ă, *a.* inflexible.

DOLUM, dō'-um, *n. m.* wretchedness, ill.

DOLUMACH, dō'-um-ach, *a.* wretched.

DO M', dumm, to my, *or* mine; *do m'* mhàthair, *to my mother*; for do mo.

DOM, dōm, *n. m.* gall bladder.

DOMAIL, dōm²'-al, *n. m.* injury, harm, damage, particularly damage by cattle, as corn.

DOMBLAS, dōm'-las, *n. m.* gall; more often domlas-sàth, gall-bladder.

DOMHAIL; see Dumhail, bulky.

DOMHNALL; see Macdhomhnaill.

DOMHNALL-DUBH, dòn'-all-dūgh', *n. m.* Old Nick, Old Pluto, Aul' Mahoun. *N. Ian.*

DOMHAN, dov²'-un, *n. m.* the universe, the globe, the whole world; an *domhan*'s na bheil ann, *the universe and all it contains*; an *domhan* ma 'n iadh grian, *the globe which the sun surrounds.*

DOMHNACH, dôv²'-nach, *n. m.* Sunday, the Sabbath; *dòmhnach* càisg Paschal Sunday, Easter.

DOMLAS, dōm²'-las, *n. m.* the gall.

DON, don, *n. m.* want; *don* bidh ort, *ill betide thee, may you want food*; *v.* make worse, deteriorate.

DONA, dŏn'-à, *a.* bad, evil, vile; na 's miosa, *worse*; is miosa, *the worst.*

DONADAS, don'-ad-as, *n. m.* evil, badness; a' dol an *donadas, deteriorating.*

DONADH, dŏn'-Ă, *n. m.* evil, injury. *Ossian.*

DONAS, don'-as, *n. m.* the Devil; evil, mischief; harm, hurt, badness.

DONN, dōnn, *a.* brown, dun, sable, brown-haired; Diarmaid *donn, brown-haired Dermid*; nighean *donn, a nut-brown girl*; each *donn, a bay horse*; indifferent, bad; cha 'n 'eil ann ach duine *donn, he is only a man so and so, an indifferent man*; *v.* make brown, imbrown, bronze 'nuair a' *dhonnadh* na speuran, *when the heavens were darkened. Ossian.*

DONNAG, donn'-ăg, *n. f.* a young ling.

DONNAL, dōnn²'-all, *n. m.* a howl, bawl.

DONNALAICH, dŏnn'-al-êch, *n. f.* continued howling, *or* slow drawling barking; *v.* bark.

DONN-RUADH, donn-rūă-gh'', *a.* chesnut-coloured.

DORCH, dorăch, *or* dorch, *a.* dark, somewhat dark; obscure, mysterious.

DORCHADH, dŏr'chĂ, *pt.* getting dark *or* obscure, mystifying; doirch.

DORCHADAS, dŏrch'-ad-as, *n. m.* darkness; a bhròn a' *dorchadh, his sorrow darkening. Ossian.*

DO-REIR, dò'-rrār', *prep.* according to; do rèir t'iarrtais, *according to,* or *agreeable to your request.*

DORGH, dŏrgh', *n. m.* hand-line drogh, *Lewis.*

DORLACH, dôr-llăch, *n. m.* considerable quantity; confounded with dornlach, hilt, &c.

DORN, dŏrn'n, *n. m.* a fist, a box, the hold of an oar; *v.* box; *dorn* e, *box him.*

DORNADAIR, dorn'-ad-ăr', *n. m.* boxer, pugilist.

DORNADAIREACHD, dorn'-ad-ăr'-achg, *n. f.* boxing, pugilism, thumping.

DORNLACH, dŏrn'-llach, *n. f.* hilt of a sword, quiver, handful.

DORNAN, dorn'-an, *n. m.* handful of lint.

DORRAMAN, dōrr'-a-man, *n. m.* a person alone, a hermit, a recluse. *Islay.*

DORRAMANACHD, dōrr'-am-an-achg, *n. f.* hermitage, living *or* dandering alone, seclusion.

DORRAN, dŏrr'-an, *n. m.* offence at a trifling cause; vexation, slight offence.

DORRANACH, dŏrr'-an-ach, *a.* vexing, galling.

DORSACH, dŏrr'-sach, *a.* exposed to the blast, as a house, a field of corn, &c.

DORSAICHE, dŏrr'-sêch-à, *n. f.* exposure to the blast; exposed situation.

DORSAIR, dŏrr'-săr', *n. c.* a door-keeper, porter.

DORSAIREACHD, dōrs'-ăr'-achg, *n. f.* office of a door-keeper, porterage; b' fhearr leam bhith *dorsaireachd, I had rather be a door-keeper. Bible.*

DORTACH, dŏrt'-ach, apt to spill, not tight, *or* keeping, *or* retaining.

Dortadh, dŏrt'-X, *n. m.* shedding, spilling; *dortadh* fola, *bloodshed*; *an issue of blood.*

Do-ruigsinn, dò-rŭeg'-shènn, *a.* unattainable.

Doruinn, dôr'-ènn, *n. f.* pain, anguish.

Doruinneach, dôr'-ènn-ăch, *a.* painful, excruciating, tormenting; much pained.

Doruinneachd, dôr'-ènn-ăchg, *n. f.* painfulness; extreme painfulness.

Dorus, dor'-us, *n. m.* door-way; dùin an *dorus, shut the door*; an opening, *or* orifice, as of a wound; neasgaid làn *dhorsan, an ulcer full of orifices.*

Dos, dŏss, *n. m.* a plume *or* cockade; a thicket; one of the drones of a bagpipe; a tassel; a forelock; a bush; *dos* do'n t-sìoda, *a tassel of silk*; *gen.* and *pl.* duis.

Dosgach, dŏsg'-ăch, *a.* calamitous; liable to accidents *or* damage; unfortunate.

Dosgaich, dŏsg'-èch, *n. f.* misfortune; loss of cattle; accident; damage; liability to damage *or* misfortunes.

Do-sgrudadh, dò-sgrûd'-è, *a.* unscrutable.

Dosguinn, dŏsg'-ènn; see Dosgaich.

Do-sheachanntach, dò-hech'-ănnt-ăch, *a.* inevitable, unavoidable.

Do-smachdachadh, do'-smachg-ăch-X, *a.* incorrigible, untractable, obstinate.

Dosrach, dŏss'-rrach, *a.* luxuriant, flourishing, as corn, trees, &c.; tufted, bushy; a' cinntinn gu *dosrach, growing* or *flourishing luxuriantly*; plumed.

Dosraich, dos'-rèch, *n. f.* luxuriance, branching appearance.

Do-thuigsinn, do'-hŭĕg-shènn, *a.* unintelligible.

Note—Do does not convey the idea of impossibility, but difficulty, as a prefix.

Drab, drăb, *n. f.* a slattern, a slut. *Teut.*

Drabaire, drăb'-ur-à, *n. m.* a sloven.

Drabasda, drăb'-ăsd-à, *a.* filthy, obscene, smutty; indecent in words.

Drabasdachd, drab'-asd-achg, *n. f.* obscenity of language; smuttiness.

Drabh, drăv, *n. m.* draff; grain.

Drabh, drâv, *v.* scatter, as a multitude; bulge, as a wall.

Drabh, drâv, *n. m.* ruination, ruin; chaidh e *dhràibh, it* or *he has gone to pigs and whistles*; *he is gone to ruin.*

Drabhadh, drâv'-X, separating, as a crowd; bulging, as a wall.

Drabhag, drâv'-ag, *n. f.* a market thinly attended; a scattered multitude.

Drabhas, drăv'-as, *n. m.* filth. *Irish.*

Drabhloinn, drăv'-llaŏèn, *n. f.* absurdity; sheer nonsense; (*dràbh*, ruin, and *loinn*, propriety); pronounced on continent of Argyle, drow-lunn.

Drabhloinneach, drăv'-llaŏèn-ach, *a.* absurd; very nonsensical; an absurd person. *Islands.*

Drabhloinneachd, drăv'-llaŏènn-achg, *n. f.* sheer absurdity; absurd conduct.

Dragh, draŏ'-gh, *n. m.* trouble, annoyance; na cuir *dragh* air, *don't trouble him*; *v.* drag, tug; ga *dhraghadh, dragging it.*

Draghail, draŏ-gh'-al, *a.* troublesome.

Draghaire, draŏ'gh-ur-a, *n. m.* a dray.

Draghaistich, draŏ'-asht-èch, *v.* drag, in an absurd *or* childish way.

Draghalachd, draŏ'-gh-al-achg, *n. f.* troublesomeness; annoyance.

Dragon, drâg'-on, *n. m.* a dragon.

Draigh, drrĭ'gh', *n. f.* thorn-tree.

Draighearnach, drĭ-ghur'-nach, a hedge of thorn; thicket of thorn.

Draighionn, drrĭ'-unn, *n. m.* thorn, wood of the thorn generally.

Draighneach, draŏè'-nyach, *n. f.* lumber; absurd detention. *Islay.*

Draing, dréng, *n. f.* a snarl; grin.

Draingeis, dréng'-ăsh, *n. f.* snarling, carping; childish bickering.

Draingeiseach, dreng'-ash-ach, *a.* girning, snarling; bickering.

Drann, drănn, *n. m.* a hum; a word; a syllable; cha d' fhuair sinn *drann, we have not got a word.*

Dranndan, drannd'-an, *a.* hum; buzzing of bees; a bickering, querulous complaint; grumbling, teasing.

Dranndanach, drannd'-an-ach, *a.* querulous; humming; buzzing.

Dranndanachd, drannd'-an-achg, *n. f.* querulousness; gurgling noise.

Drannadh, drann'-X, *n. m.* word.

Draoidheachd, draŏè'-yhyachg, *n. f.* enchantment; state of being spell-bound.

Draosda, drāosd'-à, *a.* obscene, smutty.

Draosdachd, drāosd'-achg, *n. f.* obscenity; smuttiness; lewdness; filthiness of speech.

Draoth, drāo, *n. c.* a good-for-nothing person; a humdrum.

Drathais, dră'-èsh, *n. f.* an old pair of trowsers; patched one.

Dreach, drech, *n. m.* colour *or* hue of the complexion; form, image, probability, seemliness; *v.* colour, paint.

Dreachadair, drech'-ad-ăr', *n. m.* painter.

Dreachail, drech'-al, *a.* handsome, good-looked; comely, personable.

Dreachalachd, drech'-al-achg, *n. f.* comeliness, handsomeness, personableness.

Dreachmhor, drech'-ur, *a.* handsome.

Dreag, drāg[2], *n. f.* a meteor, supposed to portend the death of a great personage, particularly the **Laird**, (draoidh-eug.)

Dreall, dryall, *n. m.* a blaze; a torch.

Dreallag, dryall′-ag, *n. f.* a swing, swinging machine; absurdity.

Dreallaire, dryăll′-ăr-å, *n. m.* loiterer.

Dreallsach, dryall′-sach, *n. f.* a blazing fire; the face blazing with liquor.

Dream, drèm, *n. m.* race of people; a tribe.

Dreamag, drrém-ag, *n. f.* handful of sheaf-corn, used as a decoy for a horse; a little sheaf-corn.

Dreamluinn, in Skye for drabhloinn.

Dreang, dréng, *n. f.* a snarl, girn; a girning expression of countenance; *v.* snarl, grin.

Dreangaire, dréng′-ar′-å, *n. m.* a snarler.

Dreangais, dréng′-ash, *n. f.* snarling.

Dreas, drāss², *n. f.* a bramble, brier; of a brier, dris.

Dreasail, drāss′-al, *a.* prickly.

Dreasarnach, drāss′-ăr-năch, *n. f.* a thicket of brambles *or* briers.

Dreathann, dré′-unn, *n. m.* a wren.

Dreochdam, dryôchg′-um, *n. m.* purring.

Dreodan, dryāod′-an, a little louse.

Dreolan, dryôl′-an, *n. m.* a wren.

Dreos, dryôss, *n. m.* a blaze. *Mackintyre.*

Dreollunn, dryôll′-unn, *n. m.* an old name for the island of Mull.

Driamlach, drĕăm′-llach, *n. m.* a fishing-line; tall, ugly fellow.

Dril, drēl, *n. m.* a drop of dew; state of being slightly drunk.

Drilleachan, drēlly²′-ach-an, *n. m.* the bird, sand-piper.

Drillseach, drēlly′-shyăch, *a.* glimmering.

Drillsean, drēlly″-shyan, *n. m.* a glimmer; glimmering fire; rush-wick; rush-light.

Drillseanach, drēlly″²-shan-ach, *a.* glimmering, sparkling as fire.

Drimneach, drēm′-nyach, *a.* striped, streaked; party-coloured; pie-bald.

Driobhail-drabhail, drèv′-ul-drav′-ul, *adv.* hurly-burly.

Driod-fhortan, drèdd′-ort-an, *n. m.* an anecdote; a mishap; ag innseadh *dhrìod-fhortan, relating anecdotes.*

Driodshuileach, drèdd′-hŭ′l-ach, *a.* having a twinkling eye.

Driothlunn, dryúll′-unn, *n. f.* a ray of light.

Driothlag, dryúll′-ag, *n. f.* a glimmering fire.

Drip, drēp², *n. m.* predicament; hurry-burry; snare meant for another, but ensnaring the author of it.

Dripeil, drēp″-al, *a.* embarrassed; confused.

Driucan, dryūchg′-an, *n. m.* beak, *Ir.*; an incision under one of the toes. *Islay.*

Driuch, drĕūch, *n. m.* activity, energy; cuir *druich* ort, *bestir yourself.*

Driuchail, drüéch′-al, *adj.* active, lively.

Driuchan, drĕūch′-an, *n. m.* a stripe, as in cloth; *driuchean* geal is dubh, *a white and black stripe.*

Driuchanach. dryûch′-an-ach, *a.* striped.

Driuchd, dryūchg, *n. m.* dew. *Provin.*

Driuchdan, dryùchg′-an, *n. m.* a dew-drop.

Drobh, drōv², *n. m.* a market (Lewis); a crowd; a drove, *Co.* The etymon of drove in English.

Drobhair, drôv′-ăr′, *n. m.* a drover cattle-dealer; a man at a market.

Drobhaireachd, drôv′-ăr′-ăchg, *n. f.* cattle-dealing; sauntering at market.

Droch, drŏch, *a.* bad, evil; *droch* bhean, *droch* fhear, *a bad woman*; *a bad man*; used always before the noun.

Drochaid, drŏch′-ăj, *n. f.* a bridge.

Drochbharail, droch-v*h*ar′-al, *n. f.* a bad opinion; a prejudice.

Droch-chreideadh, droch′-chraŏjj-X̆, *n. m.* heresy; *droch-chreideach, a heretic.*

Drochmhuint, droch′-vhŭĕnt, perverse.

Drochmhunadh, droch′-vhŭn-X̆, malice.

Drogaid, drōg′-ăjj, *n. f.* drugget; any thing spoiled by being mixed.

Drogha, drō²′-å, *n. m.* a hand fishing-line.

Droineach, drŏĕn′-ach, *n. f.* a ragged garment.

Droineap, drŏĕn′-ap, a ragged person; any thing ragged.

Droing, drŏĕng, *n. f.* a race; tribe.

Drola, drōl′-å, *n. m.* pot-hook; bughall.

Drolabhaid, drol′-a-vaj, *n. m.* lumber.

Drolabhan, drol′-a-vin, *n. m.* a good-for-nothing fellow.

Droll, drōll, *n. m.* back of a beast; rump; high dudgeon.

Drollach, drōll″-ach, *a.* apt to take great, great offence.

Droma, drŏm′-a, of back; cnaimh an *droma, the back bone, spine.*

Dromach, drom′-ăch, *n. f.* backbone. *P.*

Droman, for druman, alder.

Dromannan, drŏm′-ăn-ăn, *n. p.* backs.

Dronn, drŏnn, *n. f.* back, rump.

Dronnag, dronn′-ag, *n. f.* a hunch.

Drothanach, drŏ′-an-ach, *n. m.* a light breeze, a gentle breeze.

Druaip, drŭăĕp, *n. f.* debauchery, drinking in bad company; a debauchee.

Druaipeil, drŭăĕp′-al, *a.* debauched.

Druaipire, drŭăĕp′-ur-a, *n. m.* a tippler.

Druchd, drûchg, *n. m.* dew, tear; *v.* ooze, emit drops.

Drudhadh, drù′-X̆, *n. m.* impression, influence; cha d' rinn e an *drùdhadh* a bu lugha air, *it has not made the smallest impression on him*; *pt.* pouring out the last drop, penetrating to the skin; oozing.

Drudhag, dru′-ag, *n. f.* a small drop.

Druid, drŭėjj, *v.* shut, close.

Druideadh, drŭĕjj′-Ă, *pt.* closing, shutting; *n. m.* a conclusion, close.

Druidh, drùė′-yh, *v.* penetrate to the skin, impress, make an impression, influence, ooze; *dhrùidh* e orm, *the rain has penetrated to my skin*; 'san mar sin a *dhrùidh* e air, *that is the way it impressed him*, or *he felt it*; *v. n.* pour forth the last drop; *dhrùidh* e an soitheach, *he poured forth the last drop in the dish.*

Druidh, drúĕ′-yh, *n. m.* a magician, a sorcerer, a philosopher; dh'innis e sin do na *drùidhean, he to'd that to the magicians.*

Druidheachd, drúe′-yhachg, *n. f.* magic, sorcery, witchcraft.

Druidhteach, drûėt′-ach, *a.* impressive, emphatic, penetrating; cainnt *dhrùidhteach, impressive* or *emphatic language.*

Druidte, drŭėjt′-ă, *pt.* shut, closed.

Druim, for driom, back, keel, &c.

Druin, drûėn, *v.* shut, close.

Druinnean, drŭĕn′-nyån′, *n. m.* the lowest part of the back.

Druis, drûsh, *n. m.* lust.

Druisealachd, drûsh′-al-achg, *n. f.* moisture.

Druiseil, drûsh′-al, *a.* lustful.

Druisire, drûsh′-ur-a, *n. m.* fornicator.

Druma, drŭm′-a, *n. f.* a drum.

Drumach, drŭm′-ach, *n. f.* ridge-band of a cart horse, &c.

Drumaireachd, drŭm′-ar′-achg, *n. f.* drumming; absurd hammering; noise.

Drunadh, drûn′-Ă, *pt.* shutting, closing; *n. m.* conclusion

Druth, drû, *n. f.* a harlot. *Irish.*

Du, dû, *a.*; see Dûth.

Duaichneachd, dŭăĕch′-nyachg, *n. f.* ugliness, deformity.

Duaichnidh, dŭăėch′-nė, *a.* ugly, gloomy, any thing but pretty.

Duaichnich, dŭăĕch′-nėch, *v.* make ugly.

Duairc, dŭăĕrchg, *n. f.* surliness.

Duairceil, dŭăĕrchg′-al, *a.* unamiable.

Duais, dŭăsh, *n. f.* a reward, premium, present; in Perthshire, wages, fees.

Duaisire, dŭăsh′-urr-ă, *n. m.* a rewarder.

Dual, dŭăll, *n. m.* a fold, *or* ply of a rope, *or* any thing twisted; a plait; also corruption of duthail, hereditary; *v.* plait, fold, ply.

Dualach, dŭăll′-ăch, *a.* plaited as hair.

Duan, dŭăn, *n. f.* a poem.

Duanachd, dŭăn′-achg, *n. f.* poetry, versification, making poems.

Duanag, dŭăn′-ag, *n. f.* a sonnet, a ditty, a catch, a canto, a little poem.

Dubailte, dûb′-alyt-a, *pt.* double, double-minded; (French, Spanish, &c.); duine *dubailte, a double minded person.*

Dubailteachd, dûb′ ălyt-ăchg, *n. f.* dissimulation, double dealing; deceit.

Dubh, dŭ-gh, *a.* black, dark, lamentable, disastrous; more properly dugh; *v.* blacken.

Dubh, dŭgh′, *n. m.* the pupil of the eye; ink, blackness, darkness.

Dubhach, dŭ′-ach, *n. m.* blackening; *dubhach* bhròg, *shoe blackning*; *dubhach* cobhain, *lamp-black.*

Dubhach, dŭ′-ach, *a.* very sad, very sorrowful, melancholy, disastrous, mournful.

Dubhachas, dŭ′-ach-as, *n. m.* melancholy, sorrow, sadness.

Dubhadan, dŭ′-ad-an, *n. f.* ink-holder.

Dubh-aigean, dŭgh′-ăĕg-ĕn′, *n. m.* abyss.

Dubhailc, dŭv″-ăėlk, *n. f.* vice.

Dubhan, dŭ′-an, *n. m.* a hook, particularly a fishing hook, a claw, a clutch; ad *dhubhain, in thy clutches.*

Dubhair, dŭv2′-ėr, *v.* darken, shade.

Dubhar, dŭv″-ur, *n. m.* shade; tha anam an righ mar *dhubhar* na h-uaighe, *the soul of the king is like the shade of the grave*; darkness.

Dubharach, dŭv2′-ar-ach, *a.* shady, shadowy, opaque, dusky.

Dubharachd, dŭv2′-ar-achg, *n. f.* a shady *or* dusky place; opacity, an eclipse of the sun or moon.

Dubharaich, dŭv2′-ar-ėch, *v.* shade, eclipse.

Dubh-bhron, dŭ-vhrôn′, *n. m.* overwhelming grief; dubh-bhrònach, *disconsolate.*

Dubhchaile, dŭ-chal′-ă, *n. f.* a trollop.

Dubhchasach, dŭ-chas′-ach, *n. f.* maiden hair.

Dubh-chis, dŭ-chyēsh′, *n. f.* blackmail.

Dubhdhearg, dû-yherg′, *a.* dark red.

Dubhdhonn, dû-yhŏrn′, *a.* drab, dun.

Dubh-ghall, dû-ghăll′, *n. c.* a lowlander, a foreigner. *Islay.*

Dubhghlas, dû-ghlăss, *a.* dark grey; also the surname Douglas

Dubhghorm, dû′ ghŏrm, *a.* very blue.

Dubhghrain, dŭ-ghràėn′, *n. f.* complete disgust.

Dubh-ghrainich, dŭ-ghràėn′-ėch, *v.* detest.

Dubhlachd, dûb-lachg, *n. f.* cold and storm in season; wintry weather, depth of winter.

Dubhlachdail, dûl′ lachg-al, *a.* wintry.

Dubhlaidh, dûll′-ė, *a.* darkish; wintry.

Dubhlaidheachd; dûll′-ė-achg, *n. f.* darkishness, dark-blue.

Dubhlan, dŭll-un, *n. m.* hardihood, capability of bearing cold, hardship, and want; the quick. [illegible] nce, challenge; cuir ga *dhubh*[illegible] *him to the quick, defy, challenge*; 'nuair thèid duine ga *dhubhlan, when a person is touched to the quick.*

Dubhlanach, dŭll'-unn-ach, *a.* capable of bearing cold and fatigue, hardy; brave, defying, challenging.

Dubhlanachd, dŭll'-unn-achg, *n. f.* hardihood, degree of bravery, fearlessness.

Dubhliath, dŭl'-llĕă, *n. f.* the spleen.

Dubhloisgte, dû-llōshg²-tyâ, *pt.* burnt to a cinder; dùbhloisg, *burn to a cinder.*

Dubh-ogha, dû'-â-a, *n. m.* the great grandson's grandson. *H. S.*

Dubhradh, dûrr'-ă, *n. m.* a dark object in the distance, darkness.

Dubhradan, dŭrr'-a-dan, *n. m.* a mote.

Dubhruadh, dû'-rŭăgh, *a.* auburn.

Dubh-shiubhlach, du-hŭl'-ach, *n. f.* a strolling female or gypsy.

Dubh-thrath, dŭ-hrâ, *n. m.* the dusk.

Dublachadh, dŭb'-lach-ă, *n. m.* distilling the second time; *pt.* act of doubling.

Dublaich, dûb'-llèch, *v.* double, distill.

Dud, dûdd, *n. m.* a hollow sound.

Dud, dŭdd, *n. m.* a small lump.

Dudach, dûdd'-ach, *n. f.* a trumpet, a bugle, a war-horn.

Dudaire, dûdd'-ur-â, *n. m.* trumpeter.

Duibh, dŭĕv, to you, (do sibh.)

Duibhe, dŭĕ'-â, *n. m.* blackness; more *or* most black; ni's *duibhe, blacker.*

Duibhre, dŭr'-â, darkness, shade. *Smith.*

Duibhse, dŭĕv'-shâ, to you, *emph.* form.

Duibreac, dŭ'-bréŭchg, *n. m.* a spirling.

Duil, dû'l, *n. f.* expectation, hope, belief; supposition; tha *dùil* againn, *we expect*; tha mi 'n *dùil*, *I hope, I suppose, I expect, I imagine*; am bheil *dùil* aga, *do you suppose?* an *dùil* ra theachd, *in expectation of his coming*; thug sinn ar *dùil* deth, *we lost all expectation of him*; am bheil *dùil* agadsa, *do you suppose?* is beag *dùil* a bh'agamsa, *little did I expect*; tha *dùil* agam ris, *I expect him*; am bheil *dùil* agaibh ris, *do you expect him?* chàill sinn ar *dùil* deth, *we lost all expectations of him.*

Duil, dû'l, *n. m.* a creature, nature, the elements; gach *dùil* bheo, *every living creature*; na *dùile* leaghaidh, *the elements shall melt. Smith.*

Duil, dû'l, *v.* hoop *or* thread as a hook. *P. shire.*

Duile, dû'l'-â, *n. m.* a poor creature, a little *or* diminutive person; also dùileag.

Duileachd, dŭ'l'-achg, *n. f.* doubt, suspicion, as of a child; ga chur an *duileachd, suspecting that the child is not your own*; dubh shliochd.

Duileann, dŭl'-unn, *n. m.* a perquisite, a present; mòran *dhuilleannan* eile, *a great number of other perquisites*; a tribute. *Ir.*

Duileum, dŭĕl'-lyăm, *n. m.* a bound, leap.

Duileasg, dŭ'l'-usg, *n. m.* dilse, sea weed.

Duilich, dŭ'l'-èch, *a.* difficult, hard; ceisd *dhuilich, a difficult question*; sorry, grievous; is *duilich* leam, *I am sorry*; is *duilich* leis, *he is sorry*; is *duilich* dhuit fhàgal, *it is a pity for you to leave him*; sgeul a bu *duilich* leinn, *news for which we are very sorry*; is *duilich* leam gur fìor, *I am sorry it is too true*; na's *duile, more difficult.*

Duilichinn, dŭ'l'-èch-ènn, *n. f.* sorrow, grief, vexation; tha e fo mhòran *duilichinn, he is very sorry, he is much grieved*; is beag *duiliehinn*, a th' ort, *you seem, not to be the least sorry for it.*

Duille, dŭ'lly'-â, *n. f.* a leaf of any kind.

Duilleach, dŭlly''-ach, *n. m.* foliage.

Duilleachan, dŭlly''-ach-an, *n. m.* a pamphlet.

Duilleag, dŭèlly'-ag, *n. f.* a leaflet; a leaf of any kind; taobh *duilleig, a page*; *duilleag* comhla, *leaf of a door*; *flap of the breast*; *duilleag* bhàite, *white water li'y.*

Duilleagach, dŭ'lly'-ag-ach, *a.* leafy.

Duillich, dŭ'lly''-èch, *v.* sprout, flourish.

Duin, dûèn, *v. n.* shut, enclose, close, button, lace, darken, obscure; *dhùin* ceò bhliadhna air a dheàrrsa, *the mist of years has shrouded his splendour, Ossian*; *dùin* an dorus, *shut the door.*

Duine, dŭ'n'-â, *n. m.* a person; body; a man; an individual; an *duine, the landlord*; an *duine* agamsa, *my good man, my husband*; am bheil *duine* a's tigh, *is there any body in?* is fhearra *duine* na doaine, *a proper person is better than many men. G. P.*

Duineachan, dŭ'n'-ach-an, *n. m.* a manikin.

Duinealachd, dŭĕn'-all-achg, } *n.m.* manliness; decision of character.
Duinealas, dŭĕn'-all-as, }

Duineil, dŭĕn'-al, *a.* manly; like a man.

Duinn, dŭènn, to us; thoir *dhuinn, give us.*

Duinne, dŭĕnn'-â, *a.* more *or* most brown.

Duinte, dŭĕn'-tyâ, *pt.* shut; closed.

Duintean, dŭĕn'-tyăn, *n. pl.* heaps; fortification, forts.

Duire, dûèr'-a, *a.* more obstinate; more untractable; *n.* obstinacy, stiffness, indocility.

Duiseal, dŭsh'-al, *n. f.* a whip. *North.*

Duisg, dûèhsk, *v.* awake; *duisgte, awakened.*

Duit, dŭĕty', to you; also *dhuit.*

Dul, dŭll, *n. m.* a noose; slipping noose.

Dul, dûll, *gen.* of Dùil, Dia nan *dùl*, the God of nature.

Duldaidh; see Dùbhlaidh.

Dumhail, dûv2′-al, bulky; thick.

Dumhlachadh, dûll′-ăch-X, *pt.* crowding; growing more dense; thickening.

Dumhladas, dûll′-ad-us, *n. m.* bulk, bulkiness, crowdedness, clumsiness, denseness.

Dumhlaich, dûll′-èch, *v.* crowd; get more dense; press as a multitude.

Dun, dûn, *n. m.* a heap, a fortress, a castle, a fortification, a fort.

Dunadh, dûn′-X, *n. m.* conclusion; close; *pt.* shutting, closing.

Dunaich, dŭn′-ăĕch, *n. f.* mishap, mischief; dè'n *dunaich* a thàinig ort, *what the mischief came over you?*

Dunan, dûn′-an, *n. m.* a dung-hill.

Dun-eidion, dûn-ājj′-un, Edinburgh; from dùn, *fort*, and èidion, *want of proper ramparts* or *defence*.

Dun-lios, dûn′-llĕss, *n. m.* palace-yard.

Dunt, dŭntt, *n. m.* a thump.

Duntail, dŭntt′-al, *n. f.* et *part.* thumping.

Dur, dûrr, *a.* indocile, untractable; stubborn, stiff; (water, *obsolete.*)

Durachd, dûrr′-achd, sincere intention *or* wish; sincerity, earnestness; am bheil e ann an *dùrachd* math dhuit, *has he good intentions towards you? does he mean well?*

Durachdach, dûrr′achg-ach, *a.* sincere; very sincere *or* earnest; neodhùrachdach, *careless.*

Duradan, dûr′-ad-an, *n. m.* a mote; particle of dust; chaidh *dùradan* am shùil, *a mote stuck in mine eye.*

Duraichd, dûrr′-èchg, more often dŭèrchg; *v.* sincerely hope; fain hope; sincerely wish.

Durd, dûrd, *n. m.* a hum, buzz; *v.* hum, buzz.

Durdail, dûrdd′-al, *pt.* buzzing, humming; *n. f.* continued buzzing, humming, murmuring.

Durdan, dûrd′-an, *n. m.* grumbling, teasing.

Durdanach, dûrd′-an-ach, *a.* querulous.

Durdanaich, durd′-an-èch, *n. f.* querulousness.

Durradh, dŭrr′-X, *n. f.* a pig, sow; *durradh! durradh!* grumphy! grumphy!

Durrag, dŭrr′-ag, *n. f.* a little pig; worm.

Dus, dŭss, *n. m.* dust, smithy ashes.

Dusal, dûs′-al, *n. m.* slumber. *Bible.*

Dusan, dŭs′-an, *n. m.* a dozen. French, douze

Dusgadh, dûsg′-X, *n. m.* awakening; excitement; *pt.* rousing, exciting.

Duslach, dŭs′-lach, *n. m.* dust; miln-dust.

Duslachail, dŭs′-llach-al, *a.* dusty; dusail.

Duslainn, dŭs′-llènn, *n. m.* dust; dark place.

Duth, dû, *a.* due, hereditary, fit; what circumstances warrant; befitting one's case; cha *dùth* dha sin, *that cannot be expected from him*; tha e mar is *dùth* dha, *he is just as you would expect*; an *dùth* dhomhsa sin, *can that be expected of one similarly situated with me?* is *dùth* dha gu'm bheil e mar sin, *it is befitting his case that he should be so.*

Duth, dû, *n. m.* complement, proportion; equitable share; proportionate quantity *or* number; tha mo *dhùth* fhèin agamsa, *I have my own proportion*; clach ime le a *dùth* do chàise, *a stone of butter, with its complement of cheese*; na faighinn mo *dhùth* fhèin, *were I to get my own equitable share*; tha *dhùth* sin a *dhùth* orm, *I want a proportionate quantity* or *number*; *there is the equal to that deficient.*

Duthail, ddŭ′-al, *a.* hereditary; giving just grounds to anticipate *or* expect; quite natural; reasonable; is *dùthail dùthchas* ìm ùr a bhith air blàthaich, *it is quite natural that new-churned milk should produce fresh butter.*

Duthaich, (dùth′-fhaich,) dû-èch, *n. f.* country; air an *dùthaich*, *on the country*; muinntir mo *dhùthcha*, *my country folk.*

Duthaich, dŭ′-èch, *n. f.* large gut; the anus.

Duthchas, dûch′-us, *n. m.* hereditary, failing, *or* propriety of conduct; nativity.

Duthchasach, dûch′-chăs-ach, *a.* hereditary; bu *dùthchasach* sin dà, *that was hereditary in his family*; *n. c.* a native; an aboriginal; 'nuair a' thrèigeas na *dùthchasaich* Ila, beannachd le sìth Albainn, *when the natives forsake* Islay, *farewell to the peace of* Scotland; St. Collumbus, a Huge Reformer.

Duthchasachd, dûch′-chăs-achg, *n. f.* hereditary right, *or* privilege, *or* failing; nativity.

E

E, e, ā, the fifth letter of the alphabet, named eubh, the aspen-tree; it has various sounds; e, the personal pronoun, sounds like e in there; in rè, *during*; cè, *the earth* ā, as a in fame,—at the end of a word, particularly participles, it sounds like u in gun, pronounced quick, without touching the n; as,

E, è, personal pronoun, he, him, and it, both accusative and nominative; when it precedes e the accusative, *or* fèin, *self,* it is written 'sè, as, mharbh *'se* e, *he killed him*; marbh *'se* e fèin, *he killed himself.*

E, ā! *inter.* ay! è! è! ay! ay!

Ea-, å, *or* ā, *neg. part.* improperly used for eu, which is also very stupidly confounded by respectable people, though miserable Gaelic scholars, with ao-,—as, eugasg for aogasg, *appearance, &c.*

Eabair, å'-băr2, *v.* make slimy, as mud, by continual tramping; roll in the mud.

Eabar, å'-bur, *n. m.* slimy mud, mire.

Eabhra, ĕăv'-rrå, *or* yyav'-ra, *n. f.* Hebrew, the Hebrew language or tongue.

Eabhrach, yyav'-rach, *n. m.* a Hebrew, a Jew; *adj.* Hebrew, Jewish; na h-*eabhraich, the Jews*; a chainnt *Eabhrach, Hebrew.*

Eabrach, åb'-rrăch, *a.* miry, slimy.

Eabradh, åb'-rĂ, *n. m. pt.* a wallowing, &c. a chum a h-*eabradh* 'san làthaich, *to her wallowing in the mire. Bible.*

Each, ech, (in one parish in Islay, yyăch,) *n. m.* a horse, a brute; horses, eich; eich mheamnach, *mettlesome horses*; *each* marcachd, *a riding horse*; *each* ceannaich, *a post horse*; *each* buidh, *a cream-coloured horse*; *each* breac, *a piebald horse*; *each* saibhd, *each* fuadain, *a stray horse*; *each* cartach, *each* fèin, *a cart horse*; *each* odhar, *a dun horse*; *each* donn, *a brown horse*; *each* beilichte neo *each* meileige, *a muzzled horse*; *each* gorm, *a dapple-grey horse*; *each* geal, *each* bàn, *a white horse.*

Eachach, ech'-ach, *a.* well supplied with horses.

Eacharnach, ech'-arn-ach, *n. f.* park for horses. *Islay.*

Eachan, ech'-an, *n. m.* swifts; smooth cockle.

Each-aodach, ech'-āod-ach, *n. m.* caparison.

Eachdair, echg'-ur, *n. f.* history. *Ossian.*

Eachdaire, echg'-ar'-å, *n. m.* a historian, a chronicler, a recorder; *eachdair'* ar comhraig, *the historian of our battle, Os.* from euchd, a feat treubhas.

Eachdaireachd, echg'-ur'-ăchg, *n. f.* historiography, history, chronicles.

Eachdraiche, echg'-rèch-å, *n. m.* a historian. *Islay.*

Eachdraich, echg'-rèch, *or* -rè, *n. f.* history.

Eachdraidheachd, echg'-rè-achg, *n. f.* historiography, chronicles, history.

Eachlair, ech'-llăr', *n. m.* a brutish fellow.

Eachlaireachd, ech'-lar-achg, *n. f.* brutish conduct

Eachlais, ech'-lash, *n. f.* a passage, entry.

Eadail, corruption of feudail, wealth in cattle; m' *fheudail, my treasure.*

Eadailt, corruption of an Fheadailt, Italy; 's an Fheadailt, *in Italy*; the aspiration of f is the cause.—see 1st page.

Eadar, å'-ddăr, *prep.* between; *eadar* mise agus tusa, *between us*; among; *eadaruibh* f hèin, f huaradh e, *among yourselves it was found*; both; *eadar* bheag is mhòr, *both great and small*; *eadar* long is lamruig, *between the cup and the lip,* lit. *between the ship and the quay*; *eadar* f heala-dhà is d' ar rìghibh, *between jest and earnest*; *eadar* mhaith is olc, *both good and bad*; *eadar* am bogha is an t-sreang, *with much ado,* making both ends meet with great difficulty; *eadar* da lionn, *between wind and water, between sinking and swimming.*

Eadar-dhealachadh, å'-ddar-yhyăl-ach-Ă, *n. m.* distinction, difference; *pt.* distinguishing; separating.

Eadar-dhealaich, å'-ddur-yhyal-èch, *v.* distinguish, separate, divide.

Eadar-ghuidh, å-ddar-ghue-yh'', *v.* intercede, make intercession.

Eadar-ghuidhe, eå-ddar-ghŭ'-ė, *n. f* intercession, mediatory prayer.

Eadar-ghuidhear, å-ddăr-ghŭĕ'-yhyar, *n. m.* an intercessor, a mediator.

Eadar-mheadhonach, å-ddar-vhé'-un-ach, *a.* intercessory; indifferent, middling.

Eadar-mheadhonaich, å'-ddar-vhé-un-èch, *n. f.* middling state; tha e 'sa *eadar-mheadhonaich, he is but very indifferent.*

Eadar-mheadhonair, å-ddar-vhé'-un-ăr', *n. m.* an intercessor, a mediator, an arbiter; eadar-mheadhonaireachd, *mediation, intercession.*

Eadar-mhineachadh, å-ddar-vhēn''-ach-Ă, *n. m.* annotation, interpretation, explanation.

Eadar-mhineachair, å-ddar-vhēn''-ach-ăr, *n. m.* interpreter, annotator, explainer.

Eadar-mhinich, å-ddar-vhēn''-èch, *v.* explain.

Eadar-sgar, å-ddar-skar', *v.* separate.

Eadar-sgarachdainn, å-ddar-skăr'-achg-ènn, *n. f.* separation, divorce; *pt.* divorcing.

Eadar-shoillse, å-hăoelly''-shå, *n. f.* dawn.

Eadar-shoillsich, å-ddar-haŏèll'-shèch, *v.* dawn.

Eadar-sholus, å-ddar'-hol-us, *n. m.* twilight, dawn.

Eadar-theangachaidh, å-héng'-ach-Ă, *v.* translation, interpretation; *pt.* translating, interpreting.

Eadar-theangaich, å-ddăr-héng′-êch, *v.* translate.

Eadar-theangair, å-ddăr-héng′-ărr, *n. m.* translator.

Eadh, eaŏ-gh′, *adv.* yes; an *eadh, is it so?* cha 'n *eadh*, ni h-*eadh, it is not so.*

Eadhain, yú- *or* ėú′-yhăn′, *adv.* to it, namely; bheir mise, *eadhain* mise, dìle uisgeanna air an talamh, *and I, even I, will bring a flood of waters upon the earth.*

Eadradh, ä′-ddrĂ, *n. m.* noon; ma *eadradh, about noon*; time of day for milking cattle.

Eadraiginn, å′-ddrė-gėnn, *n. f.* interposition to separate two combatants; act of separating; is minig a fhuair fear na h-*eadraiginn* buille, *often has the queller of strife been struck*; interference.

Eadruinn, å-ddrŭėnn, between us; a' cur *eadruinn, causing us to disagree*; thaing rudaiginn *eadruinn, we disagreed about something.*

Eag, āgg′², *n. f.* a nick, notch, *or* hack.

Eagach, āgg′-ach, *a.* notched, indented.

Eagachadh, āgg′²-ach-Ă, *pt.* indenting, hacking.

Eagaich, āgg′-ėch, *v.* indent, notch, imbed.

Eagal, āgg′-ăll, *n. m.* fear, dread, terror; dè s *eagal* duit, *no harm will happen to you*; ni h-*eagal* leam, (*P. S.*) *I am not afraid*; tha *eagal* orm, *I fear, I am afraid*; is mòr m' *eagal, I am much afraid, I fear very much*; cò a chuireas *eagal* orm, *who shall make me afraid?* is beag m' *eagal, I am not the least afraid, I little fear*; tha *eagal* a chridh air, *he is terrified out of his wits*; an *eagal* domhsa do chruth, *am I afraid of your form——spectre, Oss.*; cha 'n *eagal* duit, *there is no fear of you*; superstition; chuir an t-*eagal* as da, *superstition deprived him of his senses.*

Eagalach, āgg²′-al-ach, *a.* fearful, dreadful, superstitious; ni *eagalach, a dreadful thing*; duine *eagalach, a terrible* or *superstitious person*; tha e *eagalach, he is superstitious.*

Eagalachd, āgg′-al-ăchg, *n. f.* terribleness, dreadfulness, superstitiousness.

Eagar, ägg²′-ur, *n. m.* regular building, as peats, hewn stone; (*M'L.*) order, rank; *Bible.*

Eagair, āgg²′-ėr, *v.* build as peats; gnìomh.

Eaglais, āgg²′-llėsh, *n. f.* a church, temple; *eaglais* chathach, *church militant*; *eaglais* neamhaidh, *church triumphant*; *eag'ais* na Roimh, *Catholic Church*; (French, eglise,) almost all other languages.

Eaglaiseil, āgg²′-llash-al, *a.* ecclesiastical.

Eaglaisear, āgg²′-llash ar, *n m.* a churchman.

Eagnach, āgg′-nyach, *a.* careful about little things, as a housewife; prudent.

Eagnaidh, āg²′-nyė, *a.* attentive to nignags; extremely careful; more properly eignidh.

Eagnaidheachd, agy²′-nyė-ăchg, *n. f.* pointedness about the minute articles of gain; prudence.

Eairleis, ĕăr′-llėsh, *n. f.* earnest-penny.

Eairleig, earr′-llyėg, *n. f.* strait for want of money; from *earr*, the chime of a cask, and *leig.*

Eairleigeach, ĕărr′-llyèg-ach, *a.* urgent.

Eairlinn, eărr′-llyėnn, *n. m.* keel; driom. *St.*

Eala, ĕăll′-a, *n. f.* a swan; Tighearn Loch nan *eala, Lochnell*; *the proprietor of Lochnell.*

Ealachain, ĕăll′-ach-ăėn, *n. f.* the furnace, particularly of a distillery; a hearth; a gauntree, fulcrum.

Ealaidh; see callaidh, (eun-laidh.)

Ealain, eall′-ăny′, *n. f.* trade, profession, occupation; dè'n ealain a tha e leantainn, *what profession does he follow? what is his trade* or *occupation?*

Ealamh, eăl′-uv, *a.* quick, expert.

Ealamhachd, ĕăll′-uv-achg, *n. f.* expertness, quickness.

Ealanta, ĕăl′-ant-a, ingenious.

Ealantachd, eal′-ant-achg, *n. f.* ingenuity.

Ealbhuidh, eal′-a-vhŭĕ, *n. f.* St. John's wort; seud challum chille. *Mackintyre.*

Ealg, ĕăll′-ug, *a.* noble, expert. *O. G.*

Ealla, eăll′-a, *n.* gabh *ealla* ris, gabh *iolla* ris, *look on it, and have nothing to do further with it.*

Eallach, eăll′-ach, *n. m.* burden, charge.

Eallachail, eall′-ach al, *a.* hard, grievous.

Ealt, eăllt, *n. m.* flight of birds, flock.

Ealtainn, eal′-ton, *n. m.* razor; lann-smig; also a flock of birds. *H. Society.*

Eanach, eăn′-ăch, *n. f.* dandriff ceanna-ghalar, hat *or* scarf; down, wool. *North.*

Eanchainn, eúch′-ach-ėnn, *n. f.* brains; impudence, audacity, ingenuity.

Eandagach; see Feandagach, nettle.

Eang, eng, *n. m.* the twelfth of an inch; mesh of a net; a gusset, a tract.

Eangach, eng′-ach, *n. f.* a large fishing-net; a chain of nets.

Ear, er, *n. f.* the east; an ear, from the east; gaoth an *ear, east wind.*

Earail, err′-al, *n. f.* exhortation, guard; *v. n.* caution; dh' *earail* mi air, *I cautioned him.*

Earailt, err′-alyty′, *n. f.* exhortation; caution.

Earailteach, err′-alyty′-ach, *a.* circumspect.

Earailteachd, err′-allyty′-achg, *n. f.* cautiousness.

Earalachadh, err′-all-ach-X, *pt.* cautioning, exhorting, putting on one's guard.

Earalaich, err′-al·ėch, *v.* caution, warn, guard against; exhort, entreat.

Earar, err′-ur, *n. m.* the day after to-morrow.

Eararadh, err′-ar-X, *n. m.* parched corn; parching of corn in a pot for the mill.

Earassaid, err′-as-ăjj, *n. f.* a sort of surtout worn long ago by Highland ladies; a frock; a shawl of tartan.

Earb, erb, *v. n.* confide, rely, depend, hope; *earbam* ris, *I will confide in him*; *earbam* riut, *I entrust in you*; na h-*earb* as a sin, *depend not on that*; *n. f.* a roe; mhosgail an *earb, the roe awoke. P.*

Earbach, er′-bach, *a.* full of roes.

Earbail, erb′-ull, *n. f.* trust. *North H.*

Earbais, erb′-ash, *n. f.* inhibition. *N.*

Earball, erb′-all, *n. m.* a ludicrous name for a tail *or* train.

Earbsa, erb′-sa, *n. f.* complete trust, dependence, reliance, *or* confidence.

Earbsach, erb′-sach, *a.* fully depending, confident, relying, trusting.

Earbsachd, erb′-sachg, *n. f.* complete confidence, fullest assurance *or* trust.

Eargnaich, erg′-nech, inflame; feargnaich.

Earlaid, ĕâr′-llajj, *n. f.* trust. *Stewart G.*

Earnach, ĕârn′-ach, *n. f.* murrain; bloody flux in cattle.

Earr, ĕărr, *n. m.* lowest extremity; tail; glac air a h-*eàrr* i, *catch her by the tail*; extremity of a barrel.

Earrach, eărr′-ach, *n. m.* the chink of a dish, where the edge of the bottom enters; lower extremity; the chime.

Earrach, eărr′-ach, *n. m.* the spring.

Earrachail, ėărr′-ach-al, *a.* spring-like; *n. m.* loss of cattle in spring. *Skye.*

Earradh, ėărr′-X, *n. m.* dress. *Ossian.*

Earradhreas, ėărr′-a-ghrăs², *n. f.* dog-brier.

Earradhudh, ĕărr′-ghŭ, *n. m.* wane; 'sa *earradhudh, in the wane*; geallach *earradhuidh, the waning moon.*

Earraghloir, ĕărr′-a-ghlôėr, *n. f.* gibberish.

Earraghaidhiell, ĕărr′-a-ghâĕ-ėll, *n. m* Argyle.

Earragheall, ĕărr′-a-ghyall, seorsa eoin, nygarg.

Earraid, ĕărr′-ajj, *n. m.* king's messenger; maor-righ.

Earraig, ĕărr′-ĕg, *n. f.* the last shift; great deal ado; greatest strait.

Earraigeach, ĕărr′-ėg-ach, *a.* straitened.

Earraigh, ĕărr′-ė, *n. m.* a captain. *H. S.*

Earrann, ėărr′-ann, *n. f.* share; section of land; division; portion; a paragraph.

Earrannach, ĕărr′-ann-ach, *n. f.* fleece; wool.

Earrannaich, ĕărr′-ann-ėch, *v.* share. divide.

Earras, ĕărr′-as, *n. m.* goods; portion; Helen 'sa h-*earras* thèid dhachaidh, *Helen and her marriage-portion shall go home*; the person secured, *or* the principal; cha'n fhearr an t-urras na t-*earras, the security is not a whit better than the principal, the one secured*; property; gun òr gun *earras, pennyless, and without property*; wealth, treasure.

Earrasach, ĕărr′-as ach, *a.* wealthy, rich.

Earr-fhighe, ĕărr-ė′-ă, *n. m.* weaver's tenter. *Skye.*

Eas, ās², *n. m.* a waterfall, cataract, cascade; gach coille, gach doire is gach *eas, every wood, grove, and waterfall. O.*

Eas, ās², prefix, signifying in, un, &c.

Easach, ās²′-ach, *a.* full of cascades; *n. f.* a cascade.

Eas-aontachd, ās²-āont′-achg, *n. f.* discord, factiousness, disagreement, disobedience.

Eas-aontaich, ās′-āont-ėch, *v.* disagree; secede.

Easaontas, ās²′-āont-as, *n. m.* transgression.

Easaraigh, ās²′-ār²-ė, *n. f.* state of requiring much attendance and service without moving from your seat; boiling of a pool where a cascade falls; tumult, noise.

Easbalair, āsb²′-ul-ar, *n. m.* a trifling, tall, slender, good-for-nothing fellow.

Easbhuidh, ās′-vė, *n. m.* want, defect; dè tha *easbhuidh ort, what do you want?*

Easbuig, ās²′-bėg, *n. m.* a bishop.

Easbuigeach, ās²′-bėg-ach, *a.* episcopal.

Easbuigeachd, ās²′-bėg-achg, *n. f.* bishopric.

Eascain, ās²′-kan'², *n. f.* imprecation. *Sm.*

Eascairdeach, ās²′-kărj-ach, *a.* inimical, hostile.

Eascairdeas, ās²′-karjj-as, *n. f.* enmity, hostility.

Eascaoin, ās²′ kan', *n. m.* unsoundness, as meal, grain; *a.* unsound, as grain. *I.*

Easg, āsk², *n. f.* a ditch formed by nature; a fen, a bog; an eel. *Ar.*

Easgach, āsk²′-ach, *a.* full of ditches.

Easgaid, āsk′-ăjj, *n. f* the hough; the ham.

Easgaideach, āsk′-ăjj-ach, *a.* having a slender hough; *n. c.* term of contempt for a slender, tall person.

Easgaidh, ėsg′-ė, *a.* willing to serve, quick, nimble to do a thing you have no right to do, but neglectful of duty; is *easgaidh* an droch ghille air chuairt, *the lazy servant is active from home*; officious, too ready.

EASGAIDHEACHD, èsg'-è-ăchg, *n. f.* officiousness, excessive readiness of a lazy person to do what he has no right to do.

EASGANN, āsg'2-unn, *n. f.* an eel; more correctly easgfhionn,——easg, a ditch where eels come alive, and fionn, a hair, the thing from which they breed.

EASGANNACH, āsg'2-ann-ach, *a.* supple, lively.

EAS-IONRACAS, ās2-ĕúr'-achg-us, *n. m.* dishonesty.

EAS-IONRAIC, ās'-eún-rég, *a.* dishonest, bad.

EASLAIN, ās'2-lăĕn', *a.* infirmity, sickness.

EASLAINNT, ās'2-láĕnnt, *n. f.* sickness; luchd *easlainnt, invalids, sick people. B.*

EASLAINNTEACH, ās'2-láėnt-ach, sickly, infirm.

EASLAN, ās'2-lan, *a.* sickly, invalided.

EAS-ONAR, ās2-ŏn'-ar, *n. f.* dishonour.

EAS-ONARAICH, ās2-ŏn'ăr-ėch, *v.* dishonour.

EAS-ORDUGH, ās2-ŏrd'-aŏgh, *n. m.* anarchy.

EASDRADH, ās'2-drǍ, *n. m.* ferns; froinneach. *Skye.*

EAS-UMHAIL, ās2-ŭv'-ăl, *a.* disobedient, irreverent; *eas-umhail* do pharantan, *disobedient to children. Bible.*

EAS-UMHLACHD, ās2-ûv'-lachg, *n. f.* disobedience, insubordination, disloyalty, rebelliousness, irreverence; luchd na h-*eas-ùmhlachd, the insubordinate.*

EAS-URRAM, ās2-ŭrr'-am, *n. f.* disrespect, contempt.

EAS-URRAMACH, ās-ŭrr'-am-ach, *a.* disrespectful.

EAS-URRAMAICH, ās-ŭrr'-am-ėch, contemn.

EATHAR, ā'2-ur, *n. f.* a boat, a skiff.

EATORRA, ătt'2-urr-a, between *or* among them.

EATORRAS, ătt'2-urr-as, *n. f.* mediocrity, middle state of health; deamar tha thu, *how do you do?* tha mi an *eatorras, I am tolerably well, in tolerable health.*

EIBH, āv', *n. f.* the death-watch, a tingling noise in the ear, portending sudden death; tha an *èibh* am chluais, gu 'n gleidheadh Dia na 's caomh leam, *the death-watch is in my ear, may God watch over all who are dear to me*; a long-continued swelling cry, as when women hear of some disastrous catastrophy; *èibh* nam ban Muileach is iad a' caoineadh 'sa tuireadh, *the lamentation of the Mull women mourning for the dead*; *èibh* a bhàis, *the lamentable cry of death, Oss.*; *v.* cry in a slow swelling manner.

EIBHINN, āv'-ènn, *a.* very happy, ecstatic, overjoyed, odd, curious; is *èibhinn* thu fhèin, *you are an odd fellow.*

EIBHLE, āv'-ul, *n. f.* an ember *eibhlean, embers.*

EIBHLEAG, āv'2-llag, *n. f.* a small ember.

EIBHNEACH, āv'-nyach, *a.* in raptures, in transports of joy, rapturous.

EIBHNEAS, āv'-nyus, ecstacy, raptures.

EIBHRIONN, āv'2-runn', *n. m.* a castrated he-goat; in Lochaber, eibhrionnach.

EICEART, ă'-cyart, *n. f.* injustice; *a.* unjust.

EID, ājj', *v.* accoutre, put on your uniform, dress; mount, as with silver, or as swingles, (Grealagan) 'ga *èideadh* fhéin, *putting on his accoutrements, dressing.*

EIDEADH, ājj'-Ǎ, *n. m.* uniform, the Highland garb, armour; na *èideadh* soillse, *in his armour of light, Oss.*; ar *èideadh* cuirp, *our body garments*; gun *èideadh* gun each, *without horse* or *armour*; nuair rachadh tu t' *èidheadh, when in full dress, when in your Highland garb* or *uniform, Oss. Sm. T*; *èideadh* calpa, *greaves*; *èideadh* uchd, *breast plate*; *èideadh* bròin, *mournings, mourning dress*; *èideadh* muineil, *a gorget*; *èidhadh* gaidhealach, *Highland garb*; *èideadh* droma, *back-piece.*

EIDHEANN, ā'2-unn, *n. m.* ivy, (*Islay*); spìon an t-*eidheann* bho 'craoibh, spìon an fhiolair bho ciar chreach, spìon an leanabh bho 'mhàthair ghaoil—ach na spìon o m' ghaol mis', *tear the ivy from its twigs, tear the eagle from her dun prey, tear the babe from its fond mother, but never tear me from my* LOVE.

EIDHEANNACH, ā'2-ann-ach, } in Islay, ice,
EIDHEANTACH, a'2-ann-tach, } in Arran, ivy.

EIFEACHD, āff'-ăchg, *n.* effect, avail, consequence; gun *éifeachd, without effect. Bible.*

EIFEACHDACH, āff'-achg-ach, *a.* effectual.

EIGE, āg'2-à, *n. f.* a web; eigeachan, *webs.*

EIGEACH, āg'2-ach, *n. f.* abb, snàth air crann-dealbh figheadair, 20.

EIGEANNACH, āg'-unn-ach, *a.* requiring every kind of shifts, indispensable; (from èiginn.)

EIGEANTAS, ā'2-gyunt-us, *n. m.* miserable shifts; state of requiring every kind of shifts.

EIGINN, ā'-gènn, *a.* some; cuideiginn, *some person*; fearaiginn, *some man*; rudaiginn, *something*; te-eiginn, *some female* or *woman.*

EIGINN, ā'-gènn, *n. f.* rape, violence; thug e a h-*èiginn, he committed rape, he forced* or *violated her*; distress, difficulty, strait; tha e 'na *èiginn, he is distressed, he is straitened*; thog e air *èiginn* a shùil, *he raised his eye with difficulty*; beò air *èiginn, just alive and that is all*; air *èiginn, with much ado, scarcely.*

Eiginneach, ā′-gènn-ăch, *a.* indispensable.

Eignich, āg′-nèch, *v.* force, ravish; agus dh' *èignich* na h-Amoraich clann Dhain, *and the Amorites forced the children of Dan, Bible*; ag *èigneachadh, forcing, ravishing, violating.*

'Eil, āl′, (for bheil,) cha 'n 'eil, *no, not.*

Eilde, āl′2-jà, gen. of Eilid, a hind.

Eildeach, āl′2-jach, *a.* abounding in hinds.

Eile, ā′-là, *pro. indef.* another, other; duine *eile, another person*; ni *eile, another thing*; neach *eile, another individual*; agus rud *eile* dheth, *and another thing of it, more than that*; co *eile, who else?*

Eileach, ā′-llach, *n. m.* mill-dam; linn-muilinn.

Eilean, ā′-llăn2, *n. m.* an island.

Eileanach, ā′-llan′-ach, *a.* insular; *n. c.* an islander, inhabitants of an island.

Eileanachd, ā′-llăn′-achg, *n. f.* insularity.

Eilear, ā′-llăr′, *n. f.* a deer's walk, desert.

Eilgheadh, ā′-ghλ, *n. m.* first ploughing.

Eilid, ā′-llèjj, *n. f.* a hind; laidh an *eilid* air an fhuaran, *the hind lay at the spring well.*

Eilidriom, ā′2-e-drèm, *n. f.* a bier, hearse, (*Skye*); snaoimh, *West Highlands.*

Eilthireach, āl′-hĕr-ach, *n. c.* foreigner.

Eirbheart, ār″-art, *n. m.* locomotion, power of motion; tha comas *eirbheirt* aice, *she is able to move about*; *pt.* seeking.

Eirbheir, ār′-ar, *v.* seek in an indirect way; cò a th' ag *eirbheirt* sin ort, *who asks that of you? insinuates that?*

Eire, ār′-à, *n. f.* burden; ealach.

Eireachd, ār″-ăchg, *n. f.* for eireachdas.

Eireachdail, ār″-ăch-al, *a.* handsome, fine, beauteous, graceful; fit to appear in company with, as dress.

Eireachdas, ār″-ăchg-ăs, *n. f.* decency, suitableness to appear in company with, seemliness, handsomeness; company; a' dol a dh' *eireachdas* leis, *appearing in company with it.*

Eireag, ār″-ag, *n. f.* a pullet, a young hen.

Eirearaich, ār″-ar-èch, *n. f.* parched corn hastily made for the hand-mill.

Eirich, ār″-èch, *v.* rise, get up; *èirich* moch 'sa mhaidinn, *rise early in the morning*; *èiridh* mi, *I shall rise.*

Eiridinn, ār″-è-jjènn, *n. f.* nursing a sick person; *pt.* nursing the sick; *v.* nurse or attend a sick person or patient; deoch *eiridinn, a potion.*

Eiridinneach, ār″-èjj-ènn-ach, *n. c.* a patient.

Eiridnich, ăr″ èj-nyèch, *v.* nurse the sick.

Eirig, ār″-èg, *n. f.* ransom, mulct for bloodshed, reparation; an *èirig* m' anama, *in ransom for my soul*; ann an *èirig* a ghràidh, *in return for his love. Bible.*

Eirigeach, ār″-èg-ach, *a.* as a ransom, *n. m.* a heretic, a captive, a bondsman; duine a tha na *èirigeach, a man that is a heretic. Bible.*

Eirigh, ār″-è, *n. f.* rebellion, rising.

Eirinn, ār″-ènn, *n. f.* Ireland, patland; Dr. Armstrong calls it Iar-fhonn, Westland; the Irish, I-iaruinn, the Iron island.

Eirionnach, āèr′-unn-ach, *n. m.* an Irishman; *adj.* Irish; im *Eirionnach, Irish butter*; castrated he-goat, Lochaber, *i. e.* Eibhrionnach, more properly Eibhrionn.

Eirthir, ār″ hyèr, *n. m.* links; fighdean, fighdeach.

Eis, āsh, *n. f.* want, obstruction. *Lewis.*

Eisd, āshjj, *v.* listen, hear, hearken, hark; *èisdibh* uile shluagh, *hearken all ye people.*

Eisdeachd, āshjj′-achg, *n. f.* hearing, listening, hearkening; attention; luchd *èisdeachd, hearers, auditory, audience*; an tì bheir *èisdeachd, he that hears* or *listens.*

Eiseach, āsh′-ach, } *n. f.* a crupper, *Jura*
Eisleach, āsh′-lach, } and *Mainland.*

Eiseamplair, āsh-ampl′-ăr, *n. m.* example, pattern, ensample, model; eiseamplaireach, *exemplary*; gu 'n robh sibh na'r *eiseamplairibh, that you were examples.*

Eisg, āshg, } a satirist; èisgearachd,
Eisgear, āshg′-ār′, } *satire, a satirical turn.*

Eisgeil, āshg′-al, satirical, flippant.

Eisglinn, āshg′-llènn, *n. f.* fish pond.

Eisiomail, āsh2′-èm-al, *n. f.* reverence, dependence, power; cha 'n 'eil mi t-*eisiomail, I am not in your rev. rence*; gun *èisiomail,* gun umhlachd, *without reverence,* or *dependence*; ni mi e gun *eisiomail, I can do it without being in the reverence of any person for help*; cha 'n 'eil mi bonn ad *eisiomail, I am not a whit in your reverence*; written eiseimeil also.

Eisiomalach, āsh′-mal-ach, a dependent.

Eisiomalachd, āsh′-mal-achg, *n. f.* dependence, state of dependence, poverty.

Eisir, āsh′-èr, *n. f.* an oyster; eisrean, *oysters.*

Eislean, āsh′-lyan′, *n. m.* drowsiness.

Eisleanach, āsh′-lyan-ach, *a.* dull, drowsy.

Eiteach, ājt′-ach, *n. f.* burnt heath. *Arm.*

Eitean, ājt′-an, *n. m.* kernel; *eitean* chnù, *kernel of nuts*; itean properly. *Bible.*

Eitheach, ā′2-ach, *n. f.* perjury, false oath; thug e mionnan *eithich, he perjured himself*; luchd *eithich, perjurers. Bible.*

Eithear, ā′2-hyur, *n. f.* a boat, barge. *Oss.*

Eitich, āty′-èch, *v.* refuse, deny. *Arm.*

Eitidh, ā′2-tyè, *a.* dismal, ugly. *Oss.*

Eitridh, ājt″-rè, *n. f.* for sèitrich. *Ossian*

Eoin, ĕòèn, *gen.* of eun—also birds—also John in Bible—more often Iain.

Eol, eòll, *n. m.* knowledge; is eòl dhomh, *I know*; seldom used. *Provin.*

Eolach, ĕòll'-ach, *a.* acquainted, knowing, intelligent, expert, skilful; tha mi *eòlach* air, *I am acquainted with him*; *I know him*; am bheil thu *eòlach* air, *do you know him?* duine *eòlach*, *a man well acquainted, an intelligent man.*

Eolas, ĕòll'-as, *n. f.* acquaintance, intelligence, knowledge; dìth *eòlais*, *ignorance*; ann an tìr m' *eòlais*, *in the country where I am acquainted, in my own country*; chaidh e air' *eòlas*, *he strayed to the place where he was formerly*—said of cattle; cuir *eòlas* air, *get acquainted with him*; skill, science, an enchantment or spell; *eòlas* nan sùl, *a spell to get free of a mote in the eye.*

Eorna, ĕòrn'-à, *n. m.* barley; *eòrna* agus lìon, *barley and flax*; *eòrna* fo dhèis, *barley in ear*; a cur *eòrna*, *sowing barley.*

Eornach, ĕòrn'-ach, *n. f.* barley-land.

Eorpa, ĕòrp'-a, *n. f.* Europe; shiubhail mi an Roinn *Eòrpa*, *I travelled the whole of Europe.*

Esan, ess'-un, *pron.* he, him, himself.

Eubh, āv, *n. f.* Eve, first woman; Adhamh agus *Eub*, *Adam and Eve*; aspen-tree.

Eucail, ā'-kal, *n. f.* disease, distemper; neart m' *eucalach*, *the strength of my disease*; gach *eucail*'na aoraibh, *every disease or distemper in his constitution. B. J.*

Eucaileach, ā-kal'-ach, *a.* diseased, distempered.

Eucaileachd, ā-kal'-achg, *n. f* state of disease; infectiousness, distemper.

Euchd, āchg, *n. f.* exploit *or* achievement; cuimhne *euchd* neo treubhais, *memory of*; exploit *or* achievement. *Oss.*

Euchdach, āchg'-ach, } heroic, chivalrous,
Euchdail, āchg'-al, } brave, daring; doaine treubhach *euchdail*, *heroic, chivalrous people*; Bàs a ghaisgich *euchdail*, *the death of the chivalrous hero*, (Oss. song); *euchdalachd*, *degree of heroism, bravery.*

Eud, èdd, *n. m.* jealousy; malice at an other's success; zeal; *eud* do theachdsa, *the zeal of thine house*; tri nithe gun iarraidh, *eud*, farmad is eagal, *three things that come without seeking*, (in defiance,) *jealousy, malice, and fear*—superstitious fear.

Eudach, èdd'-āch, *n. m.* jealousy between man and wife; ag *eudach* rithe, *accusing her of being unfaithful to his bed*; also provincial for aodach, *clothes, dress.*

Eudachail, èdd'-ach-al, *adj* jealous.

Eudaich, èdd'-èch, *v.* watch zealously. *Arm.*

Feudal for feudal, wealth in cattle.

Eudann, èdd'-ann, for aodann, face.

Eudmhoireachd, èdd'-vhurr-achg, *n. f.* jealousy; degree of jealousy, *or* zealousness.

Eudmhor, èdd'-vhur, *a.* jealous, zealous.

Eu-dochas, āò-dôch'-as, *n. m.* despair, despondency, dejection; see Aodòchas, &c.

Eug, āg, *n. m.* death; suain an *èig*, *sound sleep of death*; *v.* die, perish; dh' *eug* i, *she died*; an dòigh 'san d' *eug* i, *the manner in which she perished.*

Eugach, āg'-ach, *a.* death-like; deadly; buille eagalach *eugach*, *a terrible deadly blow.*

Eugas, āg'-us, *n. m.* likeness, for eugmhais, *eugas*, &c.; see Aogmhais, Aogais, &c. &c. being the same.

Eugsamhluich, āg-sáv'-llèch, *v.* vary, change; (seldom used.)

Eugsamhuil, āg'-sáv-èl, *a.* various, different; dathan *eugsamhuil*, *various colours*, *Bible*; mournful; ceòl *eugsamhuil*, *mournful music. Ossian.*

Eun, èn, *n. m.* a bird, chicken; eoin, *birds*; an t-*eun*-fionn, *the hen-harrier*; *eun*-siubhail, *a bird of passage, a straggler*; cu-*eunaich*, *a pointer.*

Eunadair, èn'-add-ăr', *n.m.* fowler, gamekeeper, bird-catcher; O lìon an *eundadair*, *from the fowler's snare*; *eunadair eachd*, *game-keeping.*

Eunadan, èn'-ad-an, *n. m.* a bird-cage. *Bible.*

Eunan, èn'-an, *n. m.* a humming bird

Eunbhrigh, én'-vhrè, } soup; chicken-
Eunruith, én'-rèch, } broth; cha'n'eil aon a dh'itheas pàirt da sheanmhair nach fhaod pàirt da h-*eunruith* òl, *he that eats a slice of his grandmother, may, with great propriety, sip the soup that is made of the same. Prov.*

Eunlaidh, èl'-llī, *v.* creep; sneak as a bird-catcher *or* fowler.

Eunlaith, èn'-llèch, *or* èll'-èch, *n. f.* fowls; birds; eallt *eunlaith*, *a flight of birds*; *eunlaith* a-rèir an gnè, *fowls after their kind. Bible.*

Eur, èr, *v.* refuse, (obsolete). *Ossian.*

Eutrom, āot'-trōm[2], *a.* light; see Aotrom.

F

F, f, styled Fearn by the Irish, is the sixth letter of the alphabet. It has the same sound as in other languages. Fh is always silent, which is the cause of many corruptions; dh' fhuirich mi, *I staid*; neo-fhasanta, *unfashionable*, (nyó-[illegible]-ănt-à.)

Fa, fã, *prep.* on account, upon. *Smith*; *fa*-dheoigh, *at last*; *fa*-leith, *apart.*

Fabhd, făv′-ud, (foud,) fault; *Perthshire. Lewis.*

Fabh, faff, / **Fabhachd**, fav′-achg, } *n. m.* a thick cake; thick bread.

Fabhor, fâv′-ur, *n. m.* favour, interest, friendship.

Fabhorach, fav′-ur-ach, *a.* favourable, kind.

Fabhorachd, fav′-ur-achg, *n. f.* favourableness; a friendly disposition; kindliness.

Fabhra, fav′-ra, *n. m.* an eye-lid, (rosg); a fringe; a flounce. *Bible.*

Facal, fachy′-al, *n. m.* word; solemn oath; thoir t' *fhacal, swear, make oath, a solemn appeal*; mispronounced and written in one county in Ireland *focal*, but never so in the Highlands; *fòcal* is a pole-cat.

Fa-chomhair, fa-chó′-ėr, *pre.* before, opposite to him; *fa-comhair, opposite to her*; m'am choinneamh ma coinneamh, properly speaking.

Faclach, fachg′-llach, *a.* wordy, verbosė.

Faclair, fachg′-laėr, *n. m.* a vocabulary.

Fad, fădd, *n. m.* length, distance, talness; *fad* is leud an tighe, *the length and breadth of the house*; cheann *fada, at long distance of time*; a' dol am *fad, getting longer*; bho cheann *fada, long ago*; *fad* finn foinneach an latha, *the live-long day*; *prep.* during, over, throughout; *fad* an t-saoghail, *throughout the world*; cha d' thig e gu ceann *fada, he will not come for a long while*; air *fad, altogether, wholly*; air *fhad, lengthways, longitudinally*; *fad* làithean mo bheatha, *throughout my whole life.*

Fada, fădd′-a, *adj.* long, distant; o thìr *fhada, from a distant country. Oss.*; rathad *fada, a long way*; *fada* bhuam, *far from me*; *fada* air falbh, *far off, at a great distance; adv.* long, tediously; is *fhada*, a dh' fhan thu, *you staid long.*

Fadadh, fad′-ă, *n. m.* fire place of a kiln; pan of a gun; *part.* inflaming, kindling a fire; a' *fadadh* gealbhain, *kindling a fire*; a' *fadadh* bhur ana-mianna, *inflaming your lusts. Bible.*

Fadaich, fad′-ėch, / **Fadaidh**, fad′-ī-yh′, } kindle, inflame, lengthen; *fadaichte, kindled.*

Fadal, fadd′-all, *n. m.* longing, thinking, tedious; na gabh *fadal, do not think it too long*; tha *fadal* orm, *I think it long.*

Fadalach, *a.* dreary, tedious, longsome; oidhcheachan *fadalach, dreary* or *tedious nights, Bible*; slow, tardy.

Fadcheannach, fad′-chyann-ach, *adj* long-headed, sagacious, shrewd.

Fadcheumach, fad′-chyām-ach, *a.* striding, bounding, bouncing.

Fadchluasach, fad′-chlŭās-ach, *a.* long-eared.

Fadfhulann, fad-ŭll′-unn, *n. m.* long-suffering, forbearing, longanimity.

Fadfhulannach, fad-ŭll′-unn-ach, *a.* long-suffering, forbearing, patient.

Fadh, fâ′-gh, *gen. plu.* of faidh; na bith eadh fios nam *fàdh* agam, *had I the gift of prophecy?*

Fadhairt, faŏ′-ărty′, *n. f.* temper of a knife, hatchet, &c.; gun fhadhairt, *blunt.*

Fadhairtich, fao′-arty′-ėch, *v.* temper.

Fadlamhach, fad′-láv-ach, *a.* long-handed; disposed to pilfer, thievish.

Fadshaoghalach, fad′-hāol-ach, *a.* long-lived; living a long life.

Fadtharruinn, fad′-harr-ėnn, *n. f.* dilatoriness, procrastination, drawling; *fad tharruinneach, dilatory, procrastinating.*

Fag, fàg · leave, quit, abandon, forsake, relinquish; *fàg* sin, *leave that*; dh *fhàg* e i, *he forsook her*; *he abandoned her*; outrun, outstrip; dh' *fhàg* am bàta an tè eile, *the one boat outstripped the other*; render, make, effect; dh'fhagadh tu am buamasdair treubhach, *thou wouldst render the blockhead heroic*; *v. n.* father upon, accuse of, lay to the charge; dh' *fhàg* iad sin air, *they fathered that upon him, they laid that to his charge*; dh' *fhàg* iad am pàisde air, *they fathered the child on him*; *fàg* m' fhianuis, *get out of my presence*; cackle as a duck.

Fagail, fâg′-al, *pt.* leaving, forsaking; rendering, abandoning; *n. f.* a curse, a fatality, destiny; tha '*fhàgail* fhéin aig' gach neach, *every one has his own peculiar destiny* or *fate*; is bochd an *fhàgail* a th' agad, *there is a sad fatality following you.*

Fagaire, fàg′-ur-å, *n. m.* a wag; a wit, though nothing like such; fàgaireachd, *waggery* or *witticisms of a person from whom nothing of the kind is to be expected.*

Faganta, fâg′-annt-å, *adj.* slow, drawling, yet witty and waggish.

Faghail, fa′-al, *pt.* getting, gaining.

Fagus, fag′-us, / **Fagusd**, fag′-usd, } near, nigh, near hand, nearly related; *fagus* oirnn, *near* or *nigh us*; *fagus* air bhi deas, *nearly ready*; na 's *fhaisge, nearer.*

Faibhle, fiv′-lå, *n. m.* beech-wood.

Faic, fáėchg, *v.* see, behold, observe; *faiceam* do làmh gheal, *let me see your fair hand*; *faic* mo dheoir, *observe my tears*; *inter.* see! behold! lo!

Faich, fīch, *n. f.* a field where soldiers are reviewed; a plain, a meadow, a green.

Faiche, fīch'-ê, *n. f.* the burrow of shell-fish; *faiche* giomaich, *a lobster's burrow.*

Faicheachd, fīch'-achg, *n. f.* training, drilling of soldiers, parading.

Faicheil, fīch-al, *a.* neat, trim, tidily and cleanly dressed as soldiers, and at same time proud of such; stately in gait.

Faicill, } **Faichill**, } fīch'-ėlly', *n. f.* caution, pre-caution; *faichill* ort, *take care, be on your guard*; be upon the watch; (faich-chiall.)

Faichilleach, } **Faicilleach**, } făĕch'-ėlly'-ach, *adj.* cau-tious, circumspect, watchful.

Faichilleachd, făĕch'-chyėlly'-ăchg, *n. f.* chariness, cautiousness, circumspection, watchfulness, observance.

Faicinn, făĕchg'-ėnn, *n. f.* observation; leig 'fhaicinn domh, *shew me*; *pt.* seeing, observing, viewing, attending to.

Faicsinneach, făĕchg'-shėnn-ach, *adj.* visible, conspicuous, notorious; an eaglais *fhaicsinneach, the visible church*; very observant.

Faicsinneachd, făĕchg'-shėnn-achg, *n. f.* visibleness, conspicuousness, clearness.

Faid, făj, *n. m.* a prophet, faidh. *Ir.*

Faide, făjj-å, *deg.* longer, longest; a 's *fhaide* gu mòr, *longer by far*; length.

Faidh, fâe'-yh', *n. m.* a prophet, seer; tha 'm *fàidh* breugach, *the prophet is a liar*; fàidhean, *prophets.*

Faidheadaireachd, fâd'-dăer-achg, prophecy.

Faidheil, fâė'-yhal, *a.* prophetic.

Faidhir, fī'-ăr, *n. f.* market, fair.

Faidse, fajsh'-å, *n. m.* lump of bread.

Faigh, féė'-yh', *v.* get, acquire, obtain, find; gheibh (yhō) sinn, *we shall get*; fhuair sinn, *we have found*; *faigh* a mach, *find out.*

Faigse, făėg'-shå, *n. m.* nearness; *deg.* more *or* most near; a 's *fhaigse, is nearer.*

Fail, fă'l, *n. f.* mark, print, trace; *fail* do laimhe, *the print of your hand*; *fail* do choise, *the print of your foot, Argyle*; ring. jewel, ouch, *Bible*; *fail*-chon, *dog-kennell*; *fail*-mhuc, *a pig sty*; *v.* get rotten; air *faileadh, rotting, loosening as wool from a skin*; *adv.* where.

Fail, fà'l, *n. f.* a peat-spade; ring. *B.*

Failbhe, fa'lv'-å, for Failmhe, the firmament; from Fallamh, empty.

Failbheag, fa'lv'-ag, *n. f.* a ring, a bolt-ring for a rope; *fàilbheagan* òir, *gold rings*; ceithir *failbheagan* òir, *four gold rings. Bible.*

Failc, făĕlk, for Falc, bathe.

Failceach, făĕlk'-ach, *n. f.* a bath, bathing; *failceach* do iubhar beinne, *bath of the juice of juniper, a sovereign remedy for the head-ache.* Old Wives.

Failcean, făĕlk'-ăn, *n. m.* the rotula *or* whirl-bone of the knee, *Arm.*; (Failmean, *Is.*)

Faile, } **Faileadh**, } fâll'-aŏgh, *n. m.* smell, flavour; droch *fhàileadh, bad smell*; the air, the draught; tha 'm *fàileadh* fuar, *the air is cold.*

Faileag, fa'l'-ag, and a'l'-ag, *n. f.* hiccup; tha 'n an *fhaileag* orm, *I have the hiccup.*

Faileas, fa'l'-as, *n. m.* shadow, reflected image; mar *fhaileas* ar làithean, *our days are like a shadow—spectre.*

Faileasach, fa'l'-as-ach, *a.* shadowy.

Failinn, fà'l'-lyėnn, *n. m.* fainting fit; failing; thàinig *failinn* air, *he fainted.*

Failinneach, } **Failneach**, } fàel'-nyach, *a.* faint, delicate, wanting; fallible, frail.

Faillean, fă'ly'-ån, *n. m.* drum of the ear; a chluás o'n *fhaillean, the ear from the root*; branch, tender twig.

Failmean, faŏ'l'-myaen', *n. m.* pan of the knee.

Failmhe, faluv'-å, *n. f.* firmament, a void.

Failnich, fàeln'-nyêch, *v.* fail, faint, decay, fall off; a' *fàilneachadh, decaying, failing, fainting, wearing away.*

Failte, fàly''-tyå, *n. f.* salutation, welcome, a salute, hail; chuirinn *fàilte, I would hail* or *salute*; ceud *fàilte*, a righ, *a hundred welcomes, O king! fàilte* shìth, *salutation of peace, Ossian*; cuir *fàilte* air, urra, *welcome* or *salute him, her.*

Failteach, fàly''-tyach, *a.* kind, hospitable.

Failteachas, fà'ly'-tyach-as, *n. f.* hospitality; kind reception, salutation.

Failteachail, see Fàilteach, hospitable.

Failtich, fàly''-tyêch, *v.* salute, hail.

Faim, fīm, *v.* hem, border; *n. f.* a hem, a border; a' *faimeadh*, aodaich, *hemming his garments*; circumspection; cuir *faim* air do theanga, *be circumspect in what you say.*

Fainich, see Aithnich, recognise, know.

Fainne, fàen''-nyå, *n. m.* a ring; thug iad leo *fàinneachan, they brought rings.*

Fainneach, fàen'-nyach, *a.* in ringlets, in curls; a cùl *fàinneach, her curled locks.*

Fair, fáėr, *v.* watch at night, keep guard, keep awake; *fair* thusa an nochd, *keep you guard to-night.*

Faire, făėr'-å, *n. f.* guard, watch; cuir *faire* air, *set a watch* or *guard on it* croc *faire, a watch-tower*; a wake; tigh na *faire, the wake-house*; *faire* chlaidh, *church-yard watch*; dawn; bristeadh na *faire, the dawn*; attention, circumspection; dè th' air t' *fhaire, what do you mean?* thoir an *fhaire, take care, be cir* *cumspect, be upon the watch*; cum t' *fhaire* air sin, *advert* or *attend you to that*; 'sè sin a bh'air m' *fhaire, that is what I had in view.*

FAIRC, făĕrk, *n. f.* a link, *or* land sometimes covered by the sea, *Bute Is.* hole; *v.* bathe. *North.*

FAIRCEALL, făĕrk'-all, *n. m.* lid, (brod) *Sk.*

FAIRCHE, făĕrch'-à, } *a.* mallet, rammer, hammer.
FAIRCHEAN, făĕrch-ăĕn, }

FAIRDINN, farjj'-ènn, *n. f.* a farthing; bonn a sè is *fairdinn, three farthings.*

FAIRE! FAIRE! făĕr'-à-faer'-à, *inter.* ay! ay! my conscience! what a pother!

FAIREACH, făĕr'-ăch, *a.* watchful.

FAIREACHADH, făĕr'-ach-Ă, *pt n. m.* waking; am bheil thu t' *fhaireachadh, are you awake?* eadar cadal is *faireachadh, between sleeping and waking.*

FAIREACHAIL, făĕr'-ach-al, *a.* attentive.

FAIREAG, făĕr'-ag, *n. f.* a gland, a hard lump between flesh and skin.

FAIRGE, fărėg'-à, the sea, an ocean; 'sa *fhairge, in the sea*; thar *fairge, cross the sea*; fairgeachan, *seas, oceans.*

FAIRICH, făĕr'-èch, *v.* watch, feel, perceive; dè dh' *fhairich* thu, *what do you feel? what do you mean? fairich* as do shuain, *awake from your profound sleep, Smith.*; *n. f.* a parish, *Arm.*

FAIRSLICH, } fărs'-llyèch, *v. n.* defy, worst;
FAIRTLICH, } dh' *fhairslich* e ormsa, *he* or *it defied me, he worsted me.*

FAISG, fâshg, *v.* press, wring, squeeze by twisting; 'ga *fhàsgadh* eadar a làmhan, *compressing it in his hands*; *n. m.* cheese press, chesit; (fiodhan,) *Irish*; fàisgte, wrung, squeezed, pressed, compressed.

FAISGE, făshg'-à, *n. f.* nearness, proximity; *'fhaisge* air a' bhaile, *his proximity* or *nearness to the town*; *faisge* air fichead bliadhna, *near twenty years*; *deg.* nearest, nearer; is esan a's *fhaisge, he is the nearest* or *nearer.*

FAISGEACH, fâshg'-ach, *n. f.* spunge, a press.

FAISNEACHD, fâsh'-nyachg, *n. f.* prophecy, soothsaying; fàisneach, prophetic, from fàisinnis, secret hint.

FAISNICH, fàsh'-nnyèch, *v* prophecy, foretell, divine, forebode; a' *fàisneachadh*, aislinnean brèige, *prophesying, false dreams. Bible.*

FAISNEAS, fàsh'-nyas, *n. m.* a friendly or secret hint; secret intelligence. *Islay.*

FAITEACH, făjty''-ach, *a.* delicate, timid, shy.

FAITCHEAS, } făjty''-us, *n. m.* delicacy of
FAITEAS, } sentiment, timidness, shyness; cha ruig thu leas *faiteas* sam bith a bhi ort, *you need not feel the least delicacy.*

FAITHILTEAR, făĕ-ėly'-tyar, *n. m.* broker.

FAL, fâll, *n. f.* sythe, (speal,) peat-spade bow; a fold, a hedge, *Arm.*; *v.* sythe, mow, cut peats. *Arm.*

FALA, fal'-a, *or* fol'-a, of blood.

FALACH, fah'-ach, *n. m.* concealment, a place of concealment; tha e am *falach, he* or *it is concealed*; a veil, covering; *falach* fead, *bo-peep, hide and seek.*

FALACHD, fal, *or* fŏl'-achg, *n. f.* a feud, a family quarrel *or* grudge; more often folachd; *folachd* eadar chàirdean, *feuds among friends. Oss.*

FALADAIR, fàl'-ad-ăr', *n. m.* a mower, (spealadair) *fàladaireachd, mowing*; (Cowal, *P. S.*)

FALAICH, fal'-èch, *v.* hide, veil, conceal.

FALAIRE, fàl'-ur-à, *n. m.* an ambler, prancing horse; fàlaireachd, *cantering, prancing.*

FALAMH, fal'-uv, *a.* empty, void; in want, unoccupied; tigh *falamh, unoccupied house*; soitheach *falamh, an empty dish*; air àite *falamh, in a void space*; is fhearra fuine thana na bhi uile *falamh, a thin batch is better than to want bread altogether.*

FALAMHACHD, fal'-uv-ăchg, *n. f.* void, gap.

FALBH, falv, *v.* go, begone, depart, retire, away with you; *falbh* romhad, *go about your business*; more often folbh, *n. m.* gait, motion.

FALBHAN, fălv'-an, *n. m.* continual motion.

FALC, falchg, *v.* bathe; 'ga *fhalcadh, bathing*; falcaire, *a bather.*

FALLAID, făll'-ėj, *n. f.* sprinkling of meal.

FALLAINE, făll'-ăĕn-à, *deg.* more *or* most healthy; 's esan is *fallaine, he is more healthy*; also healthiness, soundness.

FALLAINEACHD, fall'-ăn'-achg, *n. f.* soundness, healthiness, wholesomeness, salubriousness; *fallaineachd* am fheoil, *soundness in my flesh. Ps.*

FALLAN, făll'-an, *a.* healthy, sound; duine *fallan, a healthy man*; wholesome; biadh *fallan, wholesome food*; fàileadh *fallan, salubrious air.*

FALLSA, fall'-sa, *adj.* false, (Latin,) deceitful, treacherous; measg bhràithrean *fallsa, among false brethren. B.*

FALLSACHD, fall'-sachg, *n. f.* falseness, treacherousness; false philosophy, sophistry.

FALLSAIRE, fall'-săr'-a, *n. m.* a sophist, false philosopher; *fallsaireachd, sophistry.*

FALLSAIL, fall'-săl, *a.* false, deceitful.

FALLSANACH, fall'-san ach, *n. m.* sophist.

FALLSANACHD, fall'-san-achg, *n. f.* sophistry.

FALLOISG, fall'-llòshg, *n. f.* moor-burn—burnt heath, (from *fal*, mark, and *loisg*, burn.)

Falluinn, fall′-enn, *n. f.* mantle, cloak.

Fallus, fall′-us, *n. m.* sweat, perspiration; tha mi 'm lòn *falluis, I am over head and ears in perspiration*; *fallus* do ghnùis, *the sweat of thy brow. B.*

Fallusail, fall′-us-al, *a. n.* sudorific.

Falm, falum, *n. m.* alum.

Falm, falum, *n. f.* helm, rudder; elm-tree; the letter A; mucaga *failm, elm-berries*; glac an *fhalm, take your turn at the helm*, steer.

Falmadair, fălum′-ăd-ăr, *n. m.* a tiller.

Falt, făllt, *n. m.* hair of the head; *gen. fuilt, a single hair of the head*, fuiltean; *'fhalt* òr-bhuidh, *his golden locks. Oss.*

Faltan, falt′-an, *n. m.* a snood, hair-belt.

Famh, fáv, *n. m.* a mole.

Famhair, fáv′-ăĕr, *n. m.* a giant; bann-*fhamhair, a giantess*; *famhairean, giants.*

Famhaireachd, fáv′-ăĕr-achg, *n. f.* giganticness; prowess of a giant.

Fan, fan, *v. n.* wait, stay, stop, continue, remain; *fan* an so, *remain here*; *fan* ort, *stop, wait a little, not so fast*; dh' *fhan* sinn, *we staid*; *fanaidh* bhur mnaoi, *your wives shall stay*; *fanaibhse* an so, *tarry ye here*; *fan* agad *fhèin, keep by yourself, keep your distance, come not near me.*

Fanachd, fan′-achg, *n. f.* waiting; *pt.* staying, tarrying, remaining, residing.

Fanaid, făn′-ăj, *n. f.* mockery, ridicule.

Fanaideach, fan′-aj-ach, *a.* mocking.

Fanas, fàn′-us, *n. m.* an opportunity; a sly kind of undue advantage; a void.

Fang, făng, *n. f.* a vulture; (feitheid) sùil na *fainge*, (feitheide,) *the vulture's eye, B.*: *n. m.* a fank, durance, custody; ann an *fang, in durance, in custody.*

Fann, fănn, *a.* weak, feeble, faint; duine *fann, a feeble person*, *v.* fish while the boat is rowing slowly. *Is.*; while stationary. *Skye*; a' *fannadh, fishing with the artificial fly while the boat rows slowly—while sailing under great weigh*, sìob-ladh.

Fannaich, fann′-èch, *v.* get faint, debilitate, make feeble; tha e a' *fannachadh, he is getting more feeble*, or *making more feeble.*

Fantalach, fant′-al-ach, *a.* dilatory.

Fantainn, fant′-ènn, *n. f.* et *pt.* waiting.

Faob, fùbb, *n. m.* a lump; a large one.

Faobairneach, fùb′-ar′-nyach, *n. m.* a large one of any thing.

Faobhar, făov′-ur, *n. m.* edge of a tool, as knife; air *fhaobhar, edgewise.*

Faobhraich, făov′-rréch, *v.* edge, sharpen, whet, hone; *faobhraich* an sgian, *hone the knife, whet the knife*; *faobhraichte, honed, whetted, sharpened.*

Faoch, făoch, *a.* periwinkle, whirlpool *faochag, a little wilk* or *whirlpool.*

Faochadh, făoch′-ă, *n. m.* a favourable crisis of a disease; alleviation; fhuair i *faochadh, she got a favourable crisis*; gun *fhaochadh* fad an latha, *without the slightest alleviation the live-long day.*

Faochainn, făoch′-ènn, *v.* entreat most earnestly; urge earnestly.

Faochnach, făoch′-nach, *adj.* urgent, earnest in requesting; nì *faochnach, an urgent affair.*

Faochnadh, făoch′-nă, *n m.* a most urgent request *or* petition; *pt.* urging; a *faochnadh* orm dol leis, *vehemently urging me to go along with him.*

Faochnaich, făoch′-nnèch, *v.* urge, entreat perseveringly; be not refused. These words, peculiar to Argyle, has reference to a mode of expression quite common—chuir e liugha car dheth is a chuir am biadh 'san fhaochaig, d'fheuch an rachainn leis, *he tried all manner of means, to see if I would go along with him*—literally, he used as many wiles as there are twists in the kernel of the wilk, &c.

Faodhail, faŏ′-ul, *n. f.* a river through a strand; *a.* a strait *or* narrow, through which one can wade at low water.

Faoghaid, faŏ′-ăj, *n. f.* a chase, a hunt; tha *faoghaid* a bhaile na dèigh, *all the dogs in the village are in pursuit of her.*

Faoghar, faŏ′-ur, *n. m.* a sound, a vowel.

Faoil, făoĕl, *n. m.* profuse hospitality.

Faoileann, făoel′-unn, *n. f.* sea-gull, mew.

Faoilidh, făoĕl′-è, *a.* profusely liberal.

Faoilleach, făolly′-ach, **Faoilteach**, făolly′-tyach, } *n. m.* the storm-days, first fortnight in spring and last in winter; the opposite of iuchar, *the worm-month*; smeuran dubha 'san *fhaoilteach, ripe bramble-berries in the storm-days—a great rarity.*

Faoilte, nonsense, for fàilte.

Faoin, făoèn, *a.* silly, trifling, light, idle; nì *faoin, a trifling affair*; is *faoin* duit, *it is idle for you, it is unavailing for you*; duine *faoin, a silly fellow*; tha thu *faoin* ad bharail, *your opinion is ill-founded.*

Faoineachd, făoèn′-achg, *n. f.* extreme silliness *or* vanity; silly manner.

Faoineis, făoèn′-ash, *n. f.* trifling consideration *or* conduct; vanity, idleness.

Faoisg, făoèshg, *v.* chink, as a dish; unhusk, as nuts.

Faoisgnich, făoèshg′-nèch, *v.* chink, gape as a dish; tha chuinneag air *faoisgneadh, the water-pitcher chinks* or *leaks.*

Faol, făoll, *n. m.* wolf; madadh-gala.

Faosad, fāos'-ad, *n. m.* confession to a priest; dean d' *fhaosad, confess to the priest.*

Faondrach, fāond'-drach, *a.* neglected.

Faondradh, fāond'-râ, *n. m.* neglect, unsettled state; air *faondradh, neglected, unattended to.*

Faotuinn, fāont'-ènn, *pt.* getting, finding; faigh so, *get this*; a' *faontuinn, getting.*

Far, far, *adv.* where; *far* a bheil e, *where he is*; *v.* freight; *far* am bàta, *freight the boat*; hand, reach, bring; *fàr* (fâr) a nall an t-searrag, *hand* or *reach here the bottle*; *far* for *where*, is less often used than *fail*; fail a bheil e, *where it is.*

Faradh, fàr'-Ă, *n. m.* a ladder; shrouds.

Faradh, făr'-Ă, *n. m.* freight, fare; paidh am *faradh, pay the fare* or *freight*; henroost *or* cock-loft; air an *fharadh, on the cock-loft.*

Faraich, far'-èch, *n. f.* cooper's wedge.

Farasda, far'-asdă, *a.* merry, solid, solemn, softly; gu *farasda* fòil, *solemnly and softly. Ossian.*

Farasdachd, far'-asd-achg, *n. f.* composure.

Farbhail, far'-vhul, *n. f.* a lid. *H. Society.*

Farbhalla, see Barrabhalla.

Farchachan, far'-ach-an, *n. m.* a mallet.

Farcluais, fark'-klash, *n. f.* eaves-dropping, listening thievishly, overhearing.

Fardach, fàrd'-ach, *n. f.* house; lodging; *fardach* oidhche, *nights' lodgings.*

Fardal, fard'-al, *n. m.* delay, detention.

Fardath, fard'-dă, *n. m.* lye, or any colour in liquid; *fàrdath* gorm, *liquid blue.*

Farleus, fâr'-llès, *n. m.* skye-light.

Farmad, făr'-mad, *n. m.* envy; cùis *farmaid, an enviable object*; gabh *farmad* ris, *envy him*; a grudge at another's success; malice.

Farmadach, farm'-ad-àch, *a.* envious.

Farmail, far'-mal, large pitcher. *North.*

Farpais, farp'-ash, *n. f.* meddling, contention

Farradh, fârr'-a', *n. m.* litter in a boat.

Farraid, farr'-èj, *v.* inquire; *n. f.* inquiry.

Farran, farr'-ân, *n. m.* slight offence.

Farrusg, fărr'-usg, *n. m.* inner rhind, *or* skin.

Farspach, farrsp'-ach, *n. f.* sea-gull. *Lew.*

Farsuinn, farrs'-ènn, *a.* wide, capacious.

Farsuinneachd, fărs'-ènn-achg, *n. f.* wideness

Farsuinnich, fărrs'-ènn-èch, *v.* widen.

Farum, far'-um, *n. m.* sound of the trampling of horses; clangour, clashing, rustling; *farum* an stailinn, *the clangour of their steel*; *farum* an duillich sheargte, *the rustling of their withered foliage, Oss.*; merry.

Farumach, far'-um-ach, *a.* noisy, merry; a' dol air aghaidh gu *farumach, going forward merrily*; beating at regular intervals.

Fas, fâs, *n. m.* growth, vegetation, increase, produce; *fàs* an fhuinn, *the produce* or *increase of the land*; cha 'n 'eil *fàs* aig ni sam bith, *there is no vegetation of any thing*; *pres. part.* growing, increasing; *adj.* unoccupied, uncultivated, vacant, hollow, void; tigh *fàs, an unoccupied house*; fearann *fàs, waste* or *uncultivated land*; ni thu e *fàs, thou shalt make it hollow*; rinn mi *fàs* an sràidean, *I have laid their streets waste* or *desolate, Bible*; cuir *fàs, lay waste*; false, hollow; thug e ceum *fas, he gave a false step.*

Fas, fâs, *v.* grow, increase, become, rise, dh' *fhàs* e mòr, *he grew tall*; dh' *fhàs* slèibhte ceò air an fhàirge, *mountains of mist rose on the sea*; *fàs* ramhar, *get fat*; dh' *fhàs* an t-eòrna, *the barley grew, vegetated.*

Fasach, fâs'-ach, *n. f.* wilderness, desert, desolation; *fàsach* fhiadhaich, *terrible wilderness.*

Fasaich, fâs'-èch, *v.* desolate, lay waste, depopulate; dh' *fhàsaich* e an duthaich, *he laid waste* or *depopulated the country.*

Fasail, fâs'-al, *adj.* desolate, solitary, sruthan *fàsail, a lonely brook, dry brook.*

Fasan, fâs'-an, *n. m.* refuse of grain.

Fasan, fas'-an, *n. m.* fashion; 'sa *fhasan, in fashion*; as an *fhasan, out of fashion.*

Fasair, fâs'-ur', *n. f.* harness; pasturage.

Fasanta, fas'-annt-â, *a.* fashionable.

Fasantachd, fas'-ant-achg, *n. f.* fashionableness, adherence to custom *or* fashion.

Fasbhuain, fas'-vhŭăĕn, *n. f.* stubble.

Fasdadh, fasd'-Ă, *n. m.* hiring, engagement, as a servant; *part.* hiring, binding.

Fasdaidh, fasd'-ie-yh', *v.* hire, engage.

Fasg, făsg, *v.* search for vermin.

Fasgach, fasg'-ach, *a.* well sheltered; àite *fasgach, a well sheltered place.*

Fasgadh, fàsg'-Ă, *n. m.* search for vermin.

Fasgath, fasg'-ă, *n. m.* shelter, refuge ('Fo, under, and Sgath, shade.)

Fasgnag, fasg'-nag, *n. f.* winnowing fan.

Faslach, fàs'-llach, *n. f.* a hollow, a void.

Fath, fâ, *n. m.* cause, reason; *fàth* mo dhuilichinn, *the cause of my sorrow*; opportunity, seasonable time; gabh *fàth* air sin, *watch an opportunity for that.*

Fathamas, fă'-am-as, *n. m.* indulgence, lenity, partiality; gun *fhathamas* do dhuine seach duine, *without partiality to one man more than another*; mitigation.

Fathast, fa'-ăst, *adv.* yet, still; thig e *fhathast, he sha'l come yet.*

Fathunn, fa'-unn, (babhd,) sort of report.

Fe, fè, *n. f.* dead, calm; thàinig *fè* oirnn, *we were becalmed*; trà thig an *fhè, when the calm comes*; tha 'n oidhche na *fè, the night is dead calm. Oss.*

Feabhas, (can't pronounced this,) provincial for feobhas, superiority, degree of goodness.

Feachd, fechg, *n. m.* forces, troops, war, an army; bliadhna an *fheachd* (1745,) *Prince Charles' year*; warfare, a host; làthaibh cath 'is *feachd, in the days of fight and warfare*; *feachd* nan sonn, *the battle of the brave*; *v.* yield, swerve; ceannabhard nach gabhadh *feachd, a chief who would not yield, Mack. Sm.*; esan a dh' *fheachd* o'n chòir, *he that swerved from the path of rectitude. Maclachlan.*

Feachdaire, fechd'-ăr'-ă, *n. m.* a warrior.

Fead, fā²d, *n. f.* whistle; hissing noise as of wind; *fead* an aonaich, *the hissing of the wind on the heath*; dean *fead, whistle*; ni e *fead, he shall whistle*; *v.* whistle; hiss; *feada*-coille, *sorrel* (samh).

Feadag, fā²d'-ag, *n. f.* a plover; binn *fheadag* is an coileach ruadh, *the shrill plover and grouse-cock*; flute. *Bible.*

Feadailich, fā²d'-ul-ēch, } *n. f.* continued whistling *or* hissing.
Feadaireachd, fā²d'-ur'-achg, }

Feadailt, fā²d'-alyty', *n. f.* Italy; *adj.* feadailteach, *belonging to Italy*; also an Italian man.

Feadan, fā²d'-an, *n. m.* an oaten-pipe, fife, discharge of a still, a spout; water-pipe; *feadan* taomaidh, *a pump*; chanter of bagpipes.

Feadanach, fā²d' an-ach, *a.* piped, well supplied with fifes, flageolets, &c.

Feadh, fyaŏ-yh', *prep.* among, amid, during, through; *feadh* ghleanntan fàsail, *through desert valleys, Ossian*; *feadh* gach tìr, *throughout every land*; *feadh* an làtha, *during the day time*; sometimes, air feadh; *adv.* while, whilst, so long as; *feadh* 'sa beò mi, *while I live*; an *fheadh* 'sa mhaireas an ruaig, *while the chase lasts*; *feadh* is a bha mise a' tighinn, *while I was coming.*

Feadhachan, fe'-ăch-an, *n. m.* gentle breeze.

Feadhainn, fyaŏdh-, fyāgh''-ènn, *n. c.* folk, people; some, others; those; *feadhainn*, a thàinig a stigh, *people that came in*; *feadhainn* diutha, *some of them*; *feadhainn* eile, *others*; an *fheadhainn* a dh' fhàg sinn, *those we left*; an *fheadhainn* diutha a thig, *those of them who mean to come*; cuid 'na *feadhnach* so, *the property of those*; ceann-feadhna, *chieftain.*

Feadraich, fā²d'-rēch, *n. f.* whistling.

Feaird, fyârjj, degree of math and maith; is *fheaird* thu sin, *you are the better for that*; cha 'n *fheaird* thu stugh e, *you are nothing the better for that.*

Fairdeachd, fyârjj'-achg, improvement, convalescence; superiority, excellence; cha 'n fhaic mi fhèin *feairdeachd* sam bith air, *I don't see any symptom of convalescence* or *improvement.*

Feairt, fyarjt, *n. f.* answer, attention, notice; na d' thoir *feairt* air, *don't answer, pay no attention to him.*

Feall, fyăll, *n. f.* deceit; *a.* false.

Fealla-dha, fyall-a-ghâ', *n. f.* a joke; thèid an *fhealla-dhà* gu fealla-trì, *joking will soon end in serious earnest.*

Feallan, fyal'-an, *n. f.* itch; sgrìobach. *B.*

Feall-lighiche, fyall'-llē-èch-ă, *n. m.* a quack.

Feallsaimh, fyall'-sév, } *n. m.* a sophist; false philosopher. *Bible.*
Feallsanach, fyall'-san-ach, }

Feallsanachd, fyall'-san-ăchg, *n. f.* sophistry; false philosophy *or* learning.

Fealltach, fyallt'-ach, *a.* false. *Bible.*

Fealltair, fyall'-tar', *n. m.* a quack.

Feam, fem, } *a.* dirty tail *or* train, dirt, filth.
Feamain, fem'-aèn, }

Feamainn, fem'-ènn, *n. f.* sea-weeds, cast-ware; *v.* manure with sea-weeds; 'a feamnadh an *fhearainn, manuring the land.*

Feann, fyănn, *v.* skin, flay; a' *feannadh, flaying* or *skinning a beast*; dean *feannadh* builg, *flay as a hare.*

Feannag, fyann'-ag, *n. f.* a Royston *or* hooded crow; as a ridge, nonsense.

Feanndagach, fyann-, and fyúnnd'-ag-ach, *n. f.* nettle; sometimes, places where nettles grow.

Fear, fer, *n. m.* a man, a husband, a goodman; any object of the masculine gender; *fear* saoraidh, *a saviour*; *fear* an tighe, *the landlord*; *fear* aisig, *a fe ryman*; *fear* baile, *a tenant of a whole farm*; *fear* bainnse, *a bridegroom*; *fear* brataich, *an ensign*; *fear* ciuird, cèird, ceàird, *a tradesman, a mechanic*; *fear*-cinnidh, *a kinsman, namesake*; *fear*-ciuil, *a musician*; *fear*-cuiridh, *an inviter*; *fear*-cùirn, *an outlaw*; *fear*-faire, *a guard, a watchman*; *fear*-fuadain, *a straggler*; *fe r*-labhairt, *a speaker*; *fear*-sotail, *a flatterer*; *fear*-obair, *a workman*; *fear*-lagh, *a lawyer*; luchd-lagh, *lawyers*; *fear*-tagraidh, *a pleader*; *fear*-pòsda, *a married man*; *fear*-suirich, *a sweetheart, a wooer*; plural, *fir* or luchd; as, luchd-ciuil, *fir*-chiuil, *musicians*; *v.* follow, as a chieftain, claim kindred with; a dh' aindeoinn cò dh' *fhearas* ort, *in defiance of any person* *that will take your part*; *fear*-amhairc, *an overseer.*

FEARACHAS, fer'-ach-as, } *a.* act of
FEARACHDAIN, fer'-achg-enn, } claiming kindred, *or* siding with; following, as a chief, kindred, &c.

FEARAIL, fer'-al, *a.* manly, masculine.

FEARALACHD, fer'-al-achg, *n. f.* manliness.

FEARANN, fer'-unn, *n. m.* land, earth, ground, country; *fearann* àlluinn na h-Eirinn, *the fair country of Ireland*; *fearann* tioram, *dry land.*

FEAR-BOGHA, fer'-bò-à, *n. m.* archer, bowman.

FEARDHA, fyar'-gha, *a.* brave—Macdonald.

FEAR-EADRAIGINN, fer'-ā²-drè-gènn, *n. m.* reconciler.

FEAR-FEOIRNE, fer'-fyôrn-à, *n. m.* chessman.

FEARG, ferg, *n. m.* anger, wrath, fury, passion; *fearg* dhoirionnach, *stormy wrath, Sm.*; a' cur *feirg* air, *irritating, provoking*, or *enraging him*; ann am *feirg*, *in a passion*, furious; a passionate person.

FEARGACH, ferg'-ach, *a.* passionate, angry, furious, enraged, irritated, outrageous, raging; 'san doirionn *fheargaich*, *in the raging storm*; an dà righ *feargach*, *the two kings outrageous*, in a passion; nuair a thraoghas '*fhearg*, *when his passion subsides.*

FEARGACHD, ferg'-achg, *n. f.* passionateness.

FEARGAICH, ferg'-èch, *v.* enrage, fret, vex, gall, get outrageous, provoke.

FEARN, fyârn, *n. m.* the alder-tree; letter F.; alder-wood; a shield; leis am bristear gach *fearn*, *by whom every shield shall be broken. Ar.*

FEARR, fyârr, *deg.* of math and maith, better, best, preferable; is *fhearr* dhuit falbh, *you had better go*; an *fhearra* dhomh falbh? is *fhearr*, *had I better be going? yes*; b' *fhearr* leam bhi dorsaireachd, *I would prefer being a door-keeper*; *I had rather be a door-keeper.*

FEARRASAID for earrasaid, mantle.

FEARRSAID, fyarrs'-sèj, *n. f.* a spindle.

FEAR-SARAICHAIDH, fer-sâr'-ăch-è, *n. m.* an oppressor; *fear*-seolaidh, *fear*-stiùraidh, *a guide*; *fear*-rùin, *a confidant*; bean rùin, *a confidante.*

FEART, fyart, *n. f.* a virtue, an attribute; a virtue to effect something; wonderful qualities; *feartan* buairidh, *tempting qualities. Ml.*; Dia nam *feart*, God *of many attributes*; *feartach*, *having many virtues*; substantial; toradh *feartach*, *substantial* or *productive crops.*

FEARTAIL, fyart'-al, *a.* having good qualities.

FEART-BHRIATHAR, fyărt'-vrĕăr, *n. m.* an adjective.

FEARTHUINN, fer'-hûnn, *n. m.* rain. *Smith.*

FEASD, fāsd², *adv.* never; ever, for ever; cha d' thig e am *feasd*, *he shall never come*; an do sguir a ghràs am *feasd*, *has his grace ceased for ever?*

FEASGAR, fāsg²'-ur, *n. m.* evening, afternoon.

FEATH, fĕă, *n. f.* calm weather; dead calm; more properly *feuth*, eu being always long, prevents the è being marked.

FEATHAIL, fè'-al, *a.* calm, quiet, still.

FEATHALACHD, fè'-al-achg, *n. m.* calmness.

FEIDH, fā'-yh', *gen.* and *pl.* deers, roes.

FEILD, fālyj, *n. m.* philosopher. *Irish.*

FEILE, fā'l'-à, *n. f.* generosity, hospitality; cridhe na *fèile*, *the liberal soul. Is.*

FEILEADH, fā'l'-Ă, *n. m.* kilt; *feile*-beag, *the kilt in its modern shape.*

FEILL, fālly', *n. f.* market day; holyday; a' cumail latha *féill*, *observing* or *holding a holyday* or *festival*; a feast; an *fheill*-brìde, *Candlemas*; an *fheill*-màrtainn, *Martinmas*; *feill*-mìcheil, *Michaelmas.*

FEILTIRE, fāly'-tyèr'-à, *n. f.* an almanack.

FEIN, fēin, self; *pron.* used in compounds; mi-*fhèin*, *myself*; thu *fhèin*, *yourself* or *thyself*; sibh *fhèin*, *yourselves*; the proper orthography is "PHEIN." In Argyle generally we hear sibh *pèin.*

FEINEALACHD, fān'-al-achg, *n. f.* selfishness.

FEINEIL, fān'-al, *a.* selfish, self-interested.

FEIN-FHIOSRACH, fān-ēs²'-rach, *a.* conscious.

FEIN-FHIOSRACHADH, fān-ēs²'-rach, *a.* consciousness; experience of self; *fein*-fhoghainteach, *self-confident*; *fein*-ghluasadach, *self-moving* or *automical*; *fèin*-ìriseil, *condescending.*

FEIN-MHORT, fān-vhort', *n. f.* self-murder; suicide.

FEIN-MHORTAIR, fān-vhŏrt'-ăr', *n. c.* a suicide.

FEINN, fānn', the Fingalians; the country of the Fingalians; the Highlands; the Irish militia; troops, forces.

FEIN-SPEIS, fān'-spāsh', *n. f.* self-conceit, conceit.

FEIN-SPEISEIL, fān'-spāsh-al, *a.* self-conceited.

FEISD, fāshjj, *n. f.* an entertainment, festival, banquet; a feast.

FEISDIRE, fāshjj'-èr-à, *n. m.* an entertainer.

FEITH, fā, *v. n.* wait upon, wait; *feith* ris, *wait for him*; *feith* air, *attend him*; *n. f.* a short respite *or* crisis of a disease; fhuair e *feith*, *the fever abated a little.*

FEITH, fā, *n. f.* a sinew, a tendon; an *fhèith* a chrup, *the sinew which shrank*; a fen, a bog, a morass; (easg) a fear bhios 'san *fhèithe* cuiridh gach duine a chas air, *every one has a kick at him who sticks in the mud.*

Feitheach, fā'-ach, *a.* sinewy, muscular.

Feitheadh, **Feitheamh**, } fā'-ă, *n. m.* and *pt.* waiting, attending; a' *feitheadh* ortsa, *attending you.*

Feitheid, fā²'-aj, *n. c.* a bird *or* beast of prey, a vulture; thug na *feitheidean* leo e, *the vultures have taken it away, the birds of prey*; in Mainland, thug na fithich leo e, (ravens.)

Feitheideach, fā²'-aj-ach, *a.* like a bird *or* beast of prey; *n. c.* a person ready to pounce on any thing, like a vulture or bird of prey.

Feith-ghaire, fè'-ghăĕr-à, *n. m.* a smile.

Feobhas, fyō², and fyōv²'-us, *n. f.* excellence, superiority, improvement; a' dol am *feobhas, getting better, improving*; cha 'n fhaic mi *fheobhas, I cannot see its superiority*; an duine d'a *fheobhas, man in his best estate*; airson *fheobhas, for its superiority*; air *'fheobhas* gu'm faighear thu, *let you exert yourself ever so much*; tha'n duine tinn a' dol am *feobhas, the invalid* or *sick person is convalescent,* is getting better.

Feodar, fyôd'-ar, *n. m.* pewter.

Feodaire, fyôd'-ar-à, *n. m.* a pewterer.

Feoil, fyô'll, *n. f* flesh; muilt-*fheoil, mutton*; *feoil*-dhathach, *carnation colour.*

Feoil-ithach, fyôll-èch'-ach, *a.* carnivorous.

Feoirlinn, fyôr'-llinn, *n. f.* a mite, *or* the twelfth part of a penny, turn-odhar.

Feoirne, fyôer'-nà, *n. m.* chess.

Feoirnean, fyoenn'-an, *n. f.* blade of grass.

Feoladair, fyôl'-ad-ăr', *n. m.* a butcher.

Feolmhoireachd, fyôl'-vur-achg, *n. f.* lust.

Feolmhor, fyôl'-vhur, *a.* lustful.

Feorag, fyôr'-ag, *n. f.* squirrel.

Feoraich, fyôr'-èch, *v.* inquire, ask; *n. f.* an inquiry; asking, inquiring.

Feuch, fèch, *v. n.* try, taste, shew; *inter.* behold! lo! see!

Feuchadair, fèch'-ad-ăĕr, *n. m.* a tester, competitor, rival—witch, wizzard. *H. S.*

Feuchainn, fèch'-ènn, *n. f.* trial, taste; *pt.* trying, tasting; striving, competing; a' *feuchainn* a chèile, *competing with each other.*

Feuchainneach, fèch'-ènn-ach, *a.* trying.

Feud, fèd, may, can, for **Faod**.

Feudail, fād'-al, *n. f.* wealth in cattle, treasure, dearest object; tha *'fheudail, yes, my dearest of earthly objects.*

Feudar, fād'-ur, I must, *Is.*; is *fheudar* domh, *I must*; ma's *fheudar* duit, *if you must.*

Feum, fām, *v. imp.* it behoves, requires, must, must needs; *feumaidh* mi falbh, *I must needs go*; dh' *fheumadh* tu dol dachaidh, *you would require to go home*; *it behoves me to go home*; *n. m.* urgent need; dire necessity *or* poverty; 'sè am *feum* a thug air sin a' dheanadh, *dire necessity* or *sheer want made him do that*; need, worth, use, occasion; dè 's *feum* da, *what is the use of it?* cha 'n 'eil *feum* sa chruinne agam air, *I have no earthly use for it*; is beag *feum* a th' ort, *there is little occasion for you,* you are quite useless, there is no necessity for you, time of need; distress; ann am *fheum, in my distress in time of need.*

Feumail, fām'-al, *a.* needful, requisite.

Feumalachd, fām'-al-achg, *n. f.* what occasion requires, what serves one's purpose; fhuair mi m *'fheumalachd, I have got what serves my purpose*; utility; *feumalachd* an ni so, *the utility of this thing.*

Feumannach, fām'-ann-ach, *n. c.* the needy, the poor, the destitute, the beggar—overseer, *North*; cuid an *fheumannaich, the portion of the poor.*

Feun, fān, *n. f.* cart, (cairt), wain, *Bible*; *Strath Tay, Arran,* feunadair, *waggoner.*

Feur, fèrr, *n. m.* grass, pasture, herbage, hay; *feur* tioram, *hay*; crauch *fheoir, hay-rick*; *v.* pasture, feed cattle in choice pasture; dh' *fheur* e an t-each, *he grazed the horse.*

Feurach, fèrr'-ach, *a.* grassy; *n. m.* pasture.

Feuraich, fèrr'-ech, *v.* feed, graze.

Feuran, fèrr'-an, *n. m.* sives.

Feur-itheach, fèrr-èch'-ach, *a.* graminivorous; beathaichean *feur-itheach, graminivorous beasts*; beathaichean nach ith ach feur.

Feurlochan, fèrr'-loch-an, *n. m.* morass, marsh.

Feusag, fès'-ag, *n. f.* beard.

Feusagach, fès-ag-ach, *a.* bearded, hairy.

Feusgan, fèssg'-an, *n. m.* a mussel.

Fhuair, hŭăĕr, *part.* of faigh, did get.

Fiabhras, fĕăv'-ras, *n. m.* a fever.

Fiabhrasach, fĕăv'-ras-ach, *a.* feverish.

Fiacaill, fĕăchg'-èlly', *n. f.* a tooth, a jag, as in a saw, file, rasp, comb, or any other dentated instrument; fiaclan, *teeth, jags, prongs.*

Fiach, fĕăch, *n. m.* worth, value; *fiach* shè sgillinn, *sixpence worth*; an *fhiach* e, *is it worth, is it good?* cha 'n *fhiach* e, *it is not good, it is worthless*; an d' fhuair thu *'fhiach, did you get its value*; coma am b' *fhiach* leat labhairt ris, *why would you condescend to speak to him, why would you* *stoop so low as to speak to him*; cha b' *fhiach* leam e, *I would scout it, I would scorn it, I would spurn at the idea*; debt, incumbent duty, solemn charge, inviolable obligation; am bheil sin mar *fhiachaibh* ormsa, *is that my incumbent duty, am I under obligations to do that*; am bheil e am *fiachaibh* ortsa so a' dheanadh, *is it incumbent on you, is it obligatory on you, to do this*; cuiream mar *fhiachaibh* oirbh, *let me charge you*; tha e cuir mar *fhiachaibh* ormsa, *he would fain make me believe, he pretends*; b' àill leis a' chur mar *fhiachaibh* ormsa, gur càise mo shròn, *the fellow would fain make me believe that my nose is cheese.* In this last sense fiacham is used—tha e cuir mar *fhiacham* orm, *he pretends to me, he assumes as taken for granted.*

FIACH, fĕăch, *a.* worth, worthy, respectable, important, valuable; cha 'n *fhiach* so, *this is not worth, this will not do*; ma 's *fhiach* an duine a tha do gnothuch ris, *if you have to do with a respectable person*; an *fhiach* dhuit do shaoir, *is it worth your trouble, your while*; ma 's *fhiach* an teachdaire, is *fhiach* an gnothuch, *if the bearer is respectable, the message is important, Prov.*; cha 'n *fhi ch* sin idir, *that is not proper at all*; ma 's *fhiach* leat, *if you condescend to such*; (ironically).

FIACHAIL, fĕăch -al, *a.* worthy, respectable, valuable, important; duine *fiachail, a respectable* or *worthy man*; ni *fiachail, an important affair.*

FIACHAN, fĕăch'-an, *n. m.* value; debt.

FIACHAM, fĕăch'-am, *n. m.* pretension; cuir mar *fhiacham, pretend, assume.*

FIACLACH, fĕăchg'-lach, *a.* toothed, jagged, pronged.

FIACLAICH, fĕăchg'-llèch, *v.* girn, bicker and gape; indent, notch, make jags.

FIADH, fĕă-gh', *n. m.* deer; fèidh, *deers.*

FIADHACH, fĕă-gh'-ăch, *a.* full of deer.

FIADHACHD, fĕă-gh'-achg, *n. f.* deer-hunt.

FIADHAICH, fĕă'-èch, } *a.* wild, terrible, savage, as weather,
FIADHAIDH, fĕă'-ê, } boisterous; fiadhaidheachd, *terribleness, savageness.*

FIADHAIR, fĕărr, ley-land; fiar.

FIAL, fĕăl, *a.* kind; *n. m.* bounty.

FIALACHD, for fialaidhachd.

FIALAIDH, fĕăl'-ê, *a.* profusely liberal.

FIALAIDHEACHD, fĕăl'-ê-achg, *n. f.* hospitality, liberality to profusion.

FIAMH, fĕăv, *n. f.* a tinge, tincture, hue; *fiamh* dhearg, *a tinge of red*; *fiamh* ghorm, *a tincture* or *hue of blue*; a degree *or* tinge of fear, slight fear; *fiamh* ghaire, *a smile*, literally, *a tinge of a laugh*; awe, reverence.

FIAMHACHD, fĕăv'-achg, *n. f.* modesty. *Sg.*

FIANN, fĕănn, *n. m.* a Fingalian, a giant; na *Fiantan, the giants*; fianntachan, *a dwarf of the Fingalians*—about the size of the celebrated SAM MACDONALD.

FIANAIS, fĕăn'-êsh, *n. f.* testimony, record, evidence; thog iad *fianais* na aghaidh, *they bore testimony against him*; mar fhianais air sin, *as evidence of that*; witness; aon do na *fianaisean, one of the witnesses*; presence; mach am *fhianuis*! *get out of my presence, go about your business*! tog *fianuis, bear record, give evidence.*

FIANAISEACH, fĕăn'-ĕsh-ach, *a* capable of bearing testimony; *n. c.* a witness; is *fianaiseach* thusa air sin, *you are able to give evidence in this instance*; aon do 'na *fianuisich, one of the witnesses.*

FIAR, fĕăr, *adj.* and *adv.* oblique, aslant, awry, cross, inclining, meandering, fluctuating; cuir *fiar* e, *place it obliquely, crossways*; mar bhogha *fiar, as a slanting bow*; ann an gleanntaibh *fiar, in meandering valleys*; perverse, froward, unjust; duine a tha *fiar* na shlighe, *a man that is perverse* or *froward in his way. Bible.*

FIAR, fĕăr, *v.* pervert; a' *fiaradh* na fìrinn, *perverting the truth, the Bible, (Paul)*; sheer, go obliquely, as a ship, beat against the wind; squint.

FIARSHUILEACH, fĕăr'-hŭ'l-ach, *a.* squint-eyed.

FICHEAD, fèch'-ud, *n.* and *adj.* twenty.

FICHEADAMH, fèch'-ud-uv, *a.* twentieth.

FIDEAG, fĕjj'-ag, *n. f.* fife, whistle, herb.

FIDHLE, fĕ'll'-â, *gen.* of a fiddle.

FIDHLEAR, fĕll'-ar', *n. m.* a fiddler; fidhleireachd, *playing on the violin* or *fiddle*; more properly fiodhlair.

FIDIR, fĕjj'-èr, *v.* sympathise, inquire minutely; cha 'n *fhidir* an sàthach an seang, *the satiated will not sympathise with the starvling*; weigh, consider well.

FIDRICH, fejj'-rrech, *v.* inquire into minutely.

FIGH, fè-yh', *v.* weave, plait, knit; *figh* an eige, *weave the web*; *figh* na stocaich, *knit the stocking*; *figh* an t-sreang, *plait the cord.*

FIGHDEAN, fĕjj'-un, } *n. c.* links, *or* land
FIGHDEACH, fejj'-ach, } sometimes covered by the sea; in Cow. gabht, marfhaichean, Ml.—*fighdean* Lite, *Leith Links.*

FIGHE, fè²'-â, *n. f.* state of being woven, plaited, &c.

FIGHEADH, fe'-Ă, *pt.* weaving, knitting.

FIGHEADAIR, fè'-ad-ăr', *n. m.* weaver, knitter.

FIGHTE, fè'-tyâ, woven, &c.

FILE, fè'-lâ, *n m.* a bard, a poet. *Ossian.*

Fileachd, fé'-achg, *n. f.* poetry, poesy.

Fileannta, fèl'-annt-à, *a.* eloquent, fluent.

Fileanntachd, fèl'-annt-ăchg, *n. f.* eloquence, flow of language, fluency.

Fill, fĕlly', *v.* fold, imply, plait; *fill* an t-aodach, *fold the cloth*; tha sin a' *filleadh* a stigh, *that implies.*

Filleadh, fĕlly'-X, *pt.* folding, implying; *n. m.* a fold, a ply; trì filltean, *three plies* or *folds*; fillte, *implied, folded, plaited.*

Fine, fĕn'-à, *n. f.* a tribe, a surname, a clan, kindred; na *fineachan* gaidhealach, *the Highland clans*; an *fhine* againne, *our clan.*

Fineachas, fĕn'-ach-us, *n. f.* kindred.

Fineag, fēn'-ag, *n. f. a cheese-mite.*

Fineagach, fēn'-ag-ach, *a.* full of mites.

Finealta, fēn'-ăllt-a, *a.* fine, polite.

Finealtachd, fēn'-alt-achg, *n. f.* fineness, eloquence, polished manners, politeness.

Finichd, fēn'-èchg, } *n. f.* jet; cho dubh
Finiche, fēn'-èch-à, } ri *finichd, as black as jet.*

Finid, fēn'-ăj, *n. f.* end, finale; cuir ceann *finid* air, *bring it to a close, finish it.*

Finne, fènn'-à, *n. f.* a maid, a maiden.

Finnean, fēnn'-an', *n. m* a buzzard.

Fiodh, feú-gh', *n. m.* wood, timber; an t-sail as an *fhiodh, the log out of the timber*; *fiodh*-ghual, *charcoal.*

Fiodhag, feú-gh'-ag, *n. f.* a fig, bird-cherry.

Fiodhlair, fè'l'-ar', *n. m.* a fiddler.

Fiodhrach, fēúr'-ach, *n. m.* timber; *fiodhrach* a thoirt do Loch-chabar, *to bring timber to Lochaber, bringing coals to Newcastle*; *fiodhrach*-tarsuinn, *ribs of a boat* or *ship.*

Fiodhull, fè'-ull, *n. f.* fiddle, violin.

Fiolann, feúl'-unn, *n. f.* an earwig.

Fiolair, feúl'-ur', *n. f.* an eagle.

Fion, fē'n, *n. m.* wine; òl *fìon, drink wine.*

Fionan, fē'n'-an, *n. m.* vine, vineyard, vinery; gàrradh-*fìon*, *fìon*-lios—*fìon*-dhearc, *a grape*; also *fìon*-chaor; *fìon*-amar, *wine press.*

Fion-fhasgaire, fēn'-âsg-ur-à, *n. m.* wine press; literally a wine squeezer.

Fionn, f'yúnn, *n. m.* Fingal; cataract on the eye; *adj.* pale, lilac, wan, a lady of the masculine gender!!! a degree of cold; *v.* flay, skin. *P. S.*

Fionnachd, feúnn'-achg, *n. m.* cool, coolness; am *fionnachd* an fheasgair, *in the cool of the evening.*

Fionna, fēúnn'-à, *n. m.* fur, pile in beasts, hair, the grain; 'ga tharruinn an aghaidh an *fhionna, pulling it against the grain.*

Fionnag, fēúnn'-ag, *n. f.* the fish whiting.

Fionnairidh, fēúnn'ar'-ê, *n. f.* watching.

Fionnar, } fēúnn'-ur, *a.* coldish, cool,
Fionnfhuar, } piercing cold.

Fionnarachd, féúnn'-ar-achg, *n. f.* coolness; in Kintyre, feannarachd.

Fionnaraich, feunn'-ar-èch, *v.* cool.

Fionnogh, fēún'-ò, *n. c.* great-great-grandchild; see Ionnogh.

Fior, fēr, *a.* true, genuine, real, just, upright; true enough, sterling; am bheil e *fìor, is it true*? is *fìor* e, *true enough*; very; *fìor* ghrund an loch, *the very bottom of the lake*; duine *fìor, a just man*, *adv. fìor* bhochd, *very poor*, or *poorly*; *fìor* chosail, *very probable*; *fìor* mhath, *just so, very well, perfectly so*; *fìor* shlaoightire, *a complete villain*; is *fìor* an seanfhacal, *the proverb holds true*; *fìor* dhìleas, *very nearly connected*; *fìor*-chreideach, *orthodox*; *fìor*-chreideadh, *orthodoxy.*

Fiorghlan, fēr'-ghlăn, *a.* transparent, pure.

Fioruisg, fēr'-ŭshg, *n. m.* spring-water.

Fios, fēs[2], *n. m.* word, information, message, invitation, intelligence, notice; fhuair mi *fios, I got word, I got notice*; thoir *fios, inform, give notice*; fhuair sinn droch *fhios, we received sad intelligence*; am *fios* duit, *do you know? are you aware*? tha *fios* 'am, *I know, am aware*; c'uin a fhuair thu *fios, when got you information*? a rèir' *fios* dhomhsa, *to the best of my knowledge*; a's *fios* do'n bheò, *the living know*; g'a *fios*-se, *to her knowledge*; g'a *fhios, to his knowledge*; thàinig e stigh gun *fhios* da, *he came in unknown to him, without his knowledge*; gun *fhios* nach d' thig e, *not knowing but he may come, lest he should come*; gun *fhios* dè nì mi, *not knowing what to do*; gun *fhios* c'arson, *not knowing why* or *wherefore, B. Sm. O.*; thàinig *fios* ort, *a message came for you*; *fios* an tòrraidh, *an invitation to the funeral*; *fios* fuadain, *a flying report*; *fios* nam fàdh, *foreknowledge, prophet's knowledge*; a *fios* a bu lugha, *the slightest hint*; *fios* air an fhios, *repeated information, an urgent invitation*; is beag *fios* domhsa, *little do I know.*

Fiosachd, fès'-achg, *n. f.* fortune-telling, divination, augury, sorcery, soothsaying.

Fiosaiche, fēs[2]'-èch-à, *n. m.* soothsayer wizzard.

Fiosrach, fès'-rach, *a.* intelligent, conscious; tha mi *fiosrach, I am conscious*; is *fiosrach* mi, *I am fully aware*; duine *fiosrach, an intelligeut man*; am *fiosrach* thu air sin, *are you aware of that, are you apprised of that*; mar is fhiù is mar is *fhiosrach* mi, *to the best of my knowledge and belief.*

Fiosrachadh, fès'-rach-X, *pt.* inquiring,

experience; o m' fhèin *fhiosrachadh, from my own experience*; a' *fiosrachadh* a mach, *ascertaining*.

FIOSRACHAIL, fès'-rach-al, *a.* intelligent.

FIOSRAICH, fès'-rèch, *v.* enquire, ask, enquire into, enquire after, ask after, examine.

FIR, fĕr'2, *n. f.* men, husbands; *gen.* of man.

FIR-BHOLG, fĕr''-vholug, *n. pl.* the Belgæ, old Irish.

FIR-CHLIS, fĕr'2'-chlèsh, } streamers,
FIR-CHLISNEACH, fĕr'2'-chlēs-nyach, } Northern lights, aurora borealis; in Broad Scotch, merry dancers.

FIREACH, fĕr''-ach, *n. m.* moors, hill-land.

FIREAN, fĕr'-ăèn, *n. c.* the righteous, the just.

FIRINTEACHD, } fĕr'-ènnt-tyachg, *n. f.*
FIREANTACHD, } righteousness, integrity.

FIREUN, fĕr''-èn, *n.m.* the eagle, the real bird.

FIRINN, fĕr'-ènn, *n. f.* the truth, a truth: *fìrinn* shuidhichte, *an aphorism, an established fact*.

FIRINN, fèr'-ènn, *a.* girl, maiden; an *fhirinn, the girl, Brae-Mar.*

FIRINNEACH, fĕr'-ènn-ach, *a.* true, righteous.

FIRINNICH, fĕr'-ènn-èch, *v.* justify, excuse.

FIRINTEACHD, fĕr'-ennt-tyachg, *n. f.* righteousness.

FIRIONN, fèr''-unn, *a.* male, masculine.

FIRIONNACH, fèr'-unn-ach, *n. m.* a male, a man.

FIRIONNACHD, fĕr'-unn-achd, *n. f.* manhood.

FITHEACH, fè'-ăch, *n. m.* a raven, vulture.

FITHRIACH, fē'-rĕăch, *n. m.* dilse duileasg.

FIU, fū, *a.* worthy, estimable; cha'n *fhiù*, e dad, *it is not worth any thing*; cha'n *fhiù* e air, *he is not deserving of it*; cha'n *fhiù* e mise, *he is not worthy of me*; *n. m.* knowledge, value; is beag t' *fhiù, you are worth little*; mar is *fhiù* is mar is fhiorrach mi, *to the best of my knowledge and belief.*

FIUBHAIDH, fū'-ve, *n. m.* an arrow. *Maclach.*—a prince, a chief. *High. Society.*

FIUGHAIR, fú'-uèr, *n. m.* earnest expectation, hope; cha'n 'eil *fiughair* ris, *there is no expectation of it*; bha *fiughair* againne, *we expected.*

FIUGHANTACH, fū'-annt-ach, *a.* liberal, benevolent, giving profusely; brave.

FIUGHANTACHD, fū'-annt-achg, *n. f.* liberality, generosity, benevolence, bravery.

FIUGHANTAS, fū'-annt-as, *n. f.* liberality.

FIURAN, fūr'-an, *n. m.* a sapling, stripling.

FLAICHE, flì-è, *n. m.* gust of wind. *Irish.*

FLAITHEAS, flăĕ'-us, } *n. m.* Heaven,
FLAITHEANAS, flăĕ'-un-us, } region of bliss, (flath-innis.)

FLANN-BHUINEACH, flann'-vūnn-ach, flux.

FLATH, fla, *n. m.* a prince, a hero. *Ossian.*

FLATHAIL, fla'-al, *a.* stately, princely, gay

FLEAGH, flyaŏ'-gh, *n. f.* a banquet, feast; *fleagh* do m' rèir, *feast worthy of me. Ossian.*

FLEASG, flăsg2, *n. m.* crown, chaplet, wreath; *fleasg* òir, *a crown of gold. B.*

FLEASGACH, flăsg'-ach, *n. m.* a bachelor, a hero, a youth; nur a bha thu ad *fhleasgach* òg, *when you were a stripling.*

FLEISDEAR, flăsg2'-ar, *n. m.* an arrow-maker; Mac an *fheisdeir, the surname Fletcher* or *Leslie.*

FLEOG, flyóg, *n. m.* a sole, bradan leathan.

FLICHE, flèch'-à, *n. f.* witness, fluiche.

FLICHNE, flich'-nyà, *n. f.* sleet (Cow. Coll.)

FLICHNEACH, flèch'-nyach, *a.* sleety.

FLINNE, flēnn'-à, *n. m.* sleet. *Islay.*

FLICHNEACHD, flich'-ny-achg, } sleety wea-
FLINNEACHD, flènn'-achg, } ther; cold raw weather.

FLIODH, flyú'-gh', *n. m.* chicken-weed; wen. *B.*

FLIUCH, flĕŭch, *v.* wet, make wet; *fliuch* e, *wet it*; *adj.* wet, rainy; latha *fliuch, a wet day, rainy day*; 'ga *fliuchadh, wetting it.*

FLIUCHBHORD, fluch'-vŏrd, *n. m.* keel-board. *North.*

FLIUCHALACHD, fluch'-al-achg, *n. f.* wetness.

FLIUICHE, fyluèch'-à, *n. m.* wetness; more wet, &c.

FLOD for plod, float; *a* fleet.

FLUR, flûr, *n. m.* flour. *B.*; French.

FO, fō, (before consonants, before a vowel, foidh); under, beneath, below, at the foot of; *fo* chìs, *tributary, paying tribute*; *fo* bhròn, *mournful*; *fo* leòn, *wounded, mentally wounded*; *fodham, under me*; tha tighinn *fodham, I feel inclined.*

FOBHAILE, fo'-val-à, *n. m.* a suburb.

FOCAL, fôchg'-al, *n. m.* a pole-cat; faoghaid an *fhòcail, chase of the pole-cat*; *fòcalan, the kitten of a pole-cat.*

FOCHAID, fŏch'-aj, *n. f.* mocking, scoffing.

FOCHAIDEACH, fŏch'-ajj-ach, *a.* derisive.

FOCHAR, foch'-ar, *n. m.* contact, presence, conjunction; dithisd na *fochar, two in contact with them, near them.*

FOCHANN, foch'-ann, *n. m.* blade; corn in the blade; fo *fhochann, in blade.*

FOCALAN, fôchg-al'-an, *n. m.* pole-cat's kitten.

FOD, fôd, *n. m.* land, country, cold clammy earth; gus an càrar mi fo'n *fhòd, till I am placed under the clammy earth*; o'n thàinig e do'n *fhòd, since he came to the country. Mull Song.*

FODAR, fŏd'2-ur, *n. m.* fodder, provender.

Fodraich, fōd'2-rêch, *v.* give provender.

Fogair, fôg'-ur', *v.* banish, expel; gach eagal *fograidh, shall banish every fear.*

Fogairt, fôg'-aërt, *n. m.* banishment, expulsion; *pt.* driving away, expelling.

Fogarrach, fôg'-urr-ach', *n. c.* an exile, a vagabond, an outlaw, a fugitive.

Foghail, *for* othail gun àrdan gun othail, *without pride* or *blustering.*

Foghainn, fŏ'-ènn, *v. n.* be sufficient, suffice; *fòghnuidh* so, *this will suffice, this is sufficient*; do for, finish, kill; *foghnuidh* mi dhuit, *I will do for you, I will finish your days.*

Foghannas, fŏ'-unn-us, } *n. f.* sufficiency,
Foghantas, fŏ'-unnt-us, } quite enough; tha m' *fhoghantas* agamsa, *I have quite enough, I have sufficiency.*

Foghainteach, fogh'-ènnt-ach, *a.* sufficient, fit; co tha' *foghaintiach* air son na nithe so, *who is sufficient for these things? Bible*; brave, valorous; duine *foghainteach, a brave, valorous person.*

Foghar, faŏ'-ur, *n. m.* a resound, a re-echo; a blow that causes a sound; vowel.

Fobhar, } faŏ'-ur, *n. m.* autumn, harvest;
Foghar, } meadhon an' *fhobhair, mid-autumn.*

Fobharradh, } faov'-urr-Ă, *n m.* autumn,
Fogharradh, } harvest; meadhon an' *fhobharraidh, middle of autumn*; (fo bhàrr.)

Foghlainteach, fô'-llàénty'-ach, *n. m.* an apprentice.

Foghluim, fôhl'-èm, *v.* learn, educate.

Foghlum, fôl'-um, *n. m.* learning, intelligence; *pt.* learning, acquiring; a' *foghlum* gliocais, *learning wisdom. B.*

Foghlumadair, fôlt'-mad-ar', *n. m.* a professor, teacher.

Foghlumaid, fôll'-um-aj, *n. f.* a college, a university; (foghlum and àite,) *a place of learnimg.*

Foghlumach, fôll'-um-ăch, *n. m.* learner, novice.

Foghnadh, fōn'-Ă, *n. m.* enough; use.

Fograch, fôg'-rach, *n.m.* an exile, fugitive.

Fogradh, fôg'- Ă, *pt.* banishing, exiling.

Foi', for foidh.

Foicheall, foich'-al, *n. m.* day's hire. *N.*

Foid, fōjj, *n. m.* a peat, a turf, a sod, clod.

Foidh, fŏĕ, fŏĕ'-yh, *prep.* under; cuir *foidh, put under*; mispronounced in many places, fuidh.

Foighid. *See* Foighidinn.

Faighidinn, } fī'-ėjj-enn, *n. f.* patience,
Foighidinn, } forbearance, long-suffering.

Faighidinneach, } fī'-ėjj-nyach, *a.* pa-
Foighidinneach, } tient; fuirich gu *foighidinneach* ri Dia, *wait patiently on God.*

Foighneachd, faŏen'-achg, *n. f.* inquiry, inquire, ask, question.

Foighnich, făoen'-êch, *v.* inquire, ask.

Foil, fŏ'l, *v.* roast *or* broil hurriedly on embers; a' *foileadh* bonnaich, *toasting a cake in a hurried manner*; *foileachan, the cake so toasted* or *roasted.*

Foil, fôėl, *a.* solemn in gait, stately.

Foill, faŏėlly', *n. f.* deceit, treachery.

Foill, fôelly', *n. m.* composure, ease. *N.B.*

Foillealachd, faŏėlly''-al-achg, *n. f.* falsehood, deceitfulness, treachery.

Foilleil, fŏăėlly''-al, *a.* false, treacherous, unfair, fraudulent, deceitful.

Foillsich, faŏelly''-shêch, *v.* reveal, publish, disclose, discover, manifest, lay open, declare; a' *foillseachadh,* manifesting, declaring.

Foinne, fŏënn'-ă, *n. m.* a wart; foinneamh.

Foinnich, fŏēn'-nyêch, *v.* temper. *Armst.*

Foir, fŏër, *v.* help, aid; *v.* help, aid.

Foirbheach, fŏërv'-ach, *a.* come to years of discretion *or* maturity; *n. m.* an elder in the church; one come to years of discretion; forbhidheach.

Foirbheachd, foerv'-achg, man's estate; eldership; tha e aig *foirbheachd, he is come to man's estate.*

Foirbhidh, fŏërv'-ė, *a.* come to man's estate; come to years of maturity; duine *foirbhidh, a full grown man, complete.*

Foirbhriathair, fŏër'-vrĕăr, *n.* adverb

Foirdhealbh, fŏër'-yhyalv, *n. f.* scheme.

Foirdhorus, fŏër'-ghŏr-us, *n. m.* a vestibule.

Foireiginn, foer'-āg2-ènn, an ineffectual effort to force a door; force, violence; *v.* try to force ineffectually.

Foireignich, fŏër'-āg-nyêch, *v.* force.

Foirfe, mispronunciation of foirbhidh.

Foirichean, fŏër'-êch-un, *n. pl.* borders, suburbs; ma 'na *foirichean* so, *about these borders*; *foirichean* a bhaile, *the suburbs of the city.*

Foiriomal, fŏër'-ēm2-al, *n. f.* oiriomal.

Foirlion, fŏër'-lēn, *n.* crew, sgioba.

Foirm, fŏërm, *n. f.* pomp, ostentation, display; thàinig e stigh le *foirm, he came in with pomp, with ostentation.*

Foirmealachd, fŏĕm'-al-achg, *n. f.* pomposity.

Foimeil, fŏĕm'-al, *a.* pompous, forward.

Foim, fŏĕm, *v.* intrude. *Irish.*

Foirneart, fôër'-nyert, *n. m.* violence, force, oppression, fraud.

Foirneartach, fŏĕrn'-nyart-ăch, *a.* violent.

Fois, fŏsh, *n. f.* rest, respite, quietness, leisure; gabh gu *fois, take to rest*; *fois* do t' aman, *peace to thy soul*; *fois* d'a bhonn a choise, *rest for the sole of his* *foot*; gabh gu *fois, take rest*; is beag *fois* a fhuair e, *little rest did he get.*

FOISDIN, fŏshj′-ènn, *n. f.* quietness.

FOISDINNEACH, fŏsh′-jèn-àch, *a.* at rest.

FOISICH, fŏsh′-èch, *v.* rest, remain.

FOLA, fŏl′-a, *gen.* of fuil, blood.

FOLACH, foll′-ăch, *a.* for falach.

FOLACHD, fol′-achg, *n. f.* a feud, grudge, extraction; àrd am *folachd, of noble extraction*; iseal am *folachd, of a base extraction*—such as every person that is not HIGHLAND!!!!!

FOLAIS, fōl²′-ash, *n. f.* publicity, public view; a thoirt gu *folais, to give it publicity*; state of being well known.

FOLAISEACH, fōl²′-ash-ach, *a.* public, exposed to public view; quite public.

FOLAISEACHD, fōl²′-ash-achg, *n. f.* publicity, state of being public; clearness.

FONN, fŏnn, *n. m.* land, region; cha'n eil a leithid 'sa *fhonn, his match is not in the land*; humour, frame of mind; dè n *fonn* a th'ort, *how do you do? in what frame of mind are you?* tha *fonn* ciatach air, *he is in a grand key, glee,* or *humour*; air, tune; òran air *fonn* Bhèinn Dorain, *a song, to the air of Ben Doran.*

FONNAR, } fŏnn′-ur, *a.* cheerful, gay,
FONNMHOR, } gleesome, musical; àite *fonnar, a cheerful situation*; inclined.

FONNARACHD, } fŏnn′-ur-achg, *n. f.*
FONNMHORACHD, } cheerfulness, gaiety, hilarity.

FOIRABUIDH, fòr′-ab-è, *adj.* premature.

FONNSAIR, fŏnn′-sar′, *n. m.* trooper.

FONNTAN, fonnt′-an, *n. m.* a thistle.

FORAIL, for′-al, *n. m.* command. *H. S.*

FORAIM, for fairainm, nickname.

FORAS, for′-as, *n. m.* assumed importance, *or* airs of a trifling person; a denomination.

FORASACH, for′-as-ach, *a* assuming airs.

FORC, fork, push with the feet, as a person dragged against his will; also fork, (Welsh, forc; Lat. furcá; Teut. vorcke); pitch with a fork; (sgorr. *Is.*)

FORLACH, fôrl′-àch, *n. m.* leave of absence to a soldier; furlough.

FORN, fŏrn, *n. m.* furnace; shop-work. *Ir.*

FORTAIL, fort′-al, *a.* strong. *H. Society.*

FORTAN, fŏrt′-an, *n. m.* fortune.

FORTANACH, fort′-an-ach, *a.* fortunate.

FORTANTANACHD, fort′-an-ach, *n. f.* extreme good luck, *or* good fortune.

FOS, fôs, *adv.* moreover, yet, still, also; ma'n do ghineadh *fòs* na cnuic, *before ere yet the hills were formed*; *fòs* tamul beag, *yet a little while. B.*

FOS, fòs, *v.* rest, respite; *fòsadh*, a respite; *fòsadh*-comhraig, *cessation of a ms. Macdonald*; foiseadh properly.

FO-SCRIOBH, fo-skrēv′, *v.* subscribe.

FO-SCRIOBHADH, fo-skrēv′-Ă, *n. f.* postscript.

FOSGAIL, fōsg²′-èl, *v.* open, unbolt, disclose, unlock; *fosgail* an dorus, *open* or *unbolt,* or *unlock the door*; *fosgailte, opened, unbolted, unbarred.*

FOSGAILTEACHD, fōsg′-alyty′-achg, *n. f.* openness, candour, fairness.

FOSGLADH, fōsg′-llĂ, *n. m.* an opening, act of opening; *pt.* opening, discharging.

FOSAIR, fŏs′-èr, *v.* labour awkwardly in dressing food—pound bark. *N. H.*

FOT, fôt, *n. m.* rotten earth.

FOTAS, fôt′-as, *n. m.* rotten pus, refuse.

FOTHACH, fŏ′-ach, *n. m.* glanders in horses.

FRADHARC, fraŏ′-ark, *n. m.* eyesight, vision, sight, view.

FRAG, frâg, *n. f.* a kind wife. *H. Society.*

FRAIGH, frē-yh, *n. f.* partition wall; a roof, a shelf, *fraigh* shnighe, *rain oozing through a wall, M'F.*; is duilich beanastaighe a dheanadh fo na *fraighibh* falamh, *it is hard to keep house with empty cupboards, G.P.*; a border of a country. *Armstrong.*

FRAIGHNICH, frēn′-èch, *n. f.* moisture oozing through the wall of a house.

FRAINGEALAS, frang′-a-las, *n. f.* tansy. *M'L.*

FRAING, fréng, *n. f.* France.

FRAINGEIS, fréng′-èsh, *n. f.* French, gibberish.

FRANGACH, frang′-ach, *adj.* French; *n. m.* a Frenchman, a Frank; gill. *Lw.*

FRAOCH, frăoch, *n. m.* heath, heather; anger, a girning expression of countenanee, ripple.

FRAOCHAG, frăoch′-ag, *n. f.* whortle-berry.

FRAOCHAIL, frăoch′-al, *a.* furious, fretful.

FRAOCHAN, frăoch′-an, *n. m.* shoe toe-bit.

FRAOCH-FRANGACH, frăoch′-frang-ach, *n. m.* cat-heather; mionnfhraoch, fraoch meangain.

FRAOIGHLICH, frăoĕ′-lèch, *n. f.* blustering, as one in liquor.

FRAON, frăon, *n. m.* shelter in a hill.

FRAS, frăs, *n. f.* a shower; *n. m.* seed, small shot; *fras* feoir, *grass seed*; *fras* 'sa ghunna, *small shot in the gun*; *fras* lìn, *flax seed*; *v. n.* shower, scatter, dash; 'ga *fhrasadh* ma chluasan, *dashing* or *scattering it about his ears.*

FRASACH, fras′-ach, *a.* showery.

FRASACHD, fras′-achg, *n. f.* showery weather.

FREACADAN, for freiceadan.

FREAGAIR, frā²′-gur, *v.* answer, reply; *freagair* an duine, *answer the man*; reply, suit, fit; am *freagair* an còta, *will the coat suit?*

FREAGAIRT, frăg′-arjty′, *n. f.* an answer, a reply; *pt.* answering, suiting, fitting.

Freagarrach, frāj²′-arr-ach, *adj.* answering, answerable, suitable, fitting.

Freagarrachd, frāg′-arr-achg, *n. f.* answerableness, suitableness, fitness.

Freagarraich, frāg′-arr-ėch, *v.* suit, fit.

Freasdail, frāsd²′-ėl, *v.* attend, wait on; *freasdail* do 'n bhord, *attend the table, wait at table*; *v. n.* assist, relieve; cò a *fhreasdail, who relieved*; helped, aided, attended ?

Freasdal, frāsd²′-al, *n. m.* providence; *freasdal* Dè, *God's providence*; attendance, service; visitation, charge; choimhead do *fhreasdal, thy visitation has preserved*; *freasdal* Dè, *the charge of God.*

Freasdalach, frāsd²′-al-ach, *a.* attentive, serviceable, providential.

Freacadain, frāėchg²′-ad-ăėn, *v.* watch narrowly and slyly.

Freiceadan, frāėchg′-ad-an, *n. m.* watching most attentively and slyly, watching narrowly.

Freiceadanach, frāėchg²′-ad-an-ach, *a.* watching narrowly, and very attentively.

Freimeiseanta, frem′-ėsh-ant-a, *adj.* hale, hearty, though very old.

Freimseadh, frém-shĂ, *n. m.* a great huff, *or* offence, for no, or slight cause.

Freimseil, frém′-shall, *a.* hale, hearty, though an old person, jolly.

Freiteach, frāty″-ach, *n. m.* a vow to refrain from any thing, interdictory resolution to keep from drinking, &c.

Freitich, frāty″-ėch, *v.* vow, resolve to keep from something, as temperance society folk, &c.

Freumh, frèv, *n. m.* root, stock, stem, lineage; *v.* take root, establish.

Freumhach, frēv′-ach, *n. m.* root, fibre.

Freumhach, frèv′-ach, *a.* fibrous, rooted.

Freumhachd, frèv′-achg, *n. f.* an original cause; etymology.

Freumhaich, frèv′-ėch, *v.* take root.

Freumhail, frèv′-al, *a.* radical.

Fri, frē, } **Frid**, frēj, } *prep.* through; 't'ar m' onam gu'n deach e *frìd* a' bhealaich mhòir, (say the Irish) that is, *'pon conscience he took leg-bail, he took to his heels.*

Frid, frējj, } **Frideag**, frējj′ag, } *n. f.* a letter, ringworm, flesh-mite.

Fridiomb, frējj′-ėmb, *n. m.* the use of another man's house for a limited time, as your own; kindliest hospitality; hence the Belgic and English word freedom, and fer-dimb, (frì-diomb.)

Fridiombach, frējj′-emb-ach, *a.* quite at home, under no restraint in another man's house.

Fridh, frē-yh', *n. f.* a forest, *Bible*; frìdhire, *forester. R. S.*

Friochd, frèúchg, *v.* lance, prick, pierce, *or* probe quickly as with an awl, pin, &c —half-glass whisky after a sgailc, a bumper. *N. H.*

Friochdadh, freúchg′-Ă, *n. m.* a quick stab; *pt.* stabbing quickly and painfully.

Friogham, frĕú′-gh'-an, *n.m.* sows' bristles.

Frioghanach, frĕú-gh'-an-ach, *a.* bristly.

Frionas, frĕún-as, *n. m.* fretfulness.

Frionasach, fréún-as-ach, *a.* fretful.

Frionasachd, frĕún-as-achg, *n. f.* fretfulness, peevishness, cholericness, impatience.

Frioth, frė², *adj.* and *prefix*, small, slender; used before words whose first vowel is a, o, *or* u; frith, before e and i. It is always used before the noun qualified.

Friothailt, frė′-alyt, *n. f.* attendance on a woman in child-bed.

Friothainbheach, frė′-env-ach, *n. m.* arrears, trifling debts, remainder of a debt.

Frioth-bhuail, frė′-vŭăėl, *v.* palpitate, vibrate.

Friothfhroineach, } **Friothfhraineach**, } frė′-rŏėn-ach, *n. f.* dwarf-fern.

Friothgharradh, frė′-ghar-Ă, *n.m.* an old *or* small fence; aig taobh an *fhrioth-gharraidh, aside the old fence.*

Friothradhad, frė′-râd, *n. m.* a foot path.

Frith, frė, *a.* little—before e and i.

Frith, frē, *n. f.* an encantation to find whether people at a great distance or at sea be in life, *Islay*; gain, profit, part of.

Frithealadh, frė′-al-Ă, *pt.* attendance on women in child-bed; *pt.* attend such, *Islay*; minister, *Bible*; bean *fhritheal-aidh, a midwife*; fear-*frithealaidh, a man attending a woman in child-bed, accoucheur.*

Fritheàrr, frė′-urr, *a.* peevish, whimsical.

Fritheil, frė′-aely, *v.* attend a woman in child-bed; *Bible*, minister, attend.

Frog, frôg, *n. f.* a dark dismal hole *or* crevice, an ugly place or cranny.

Frogach, frôg′-ach, *a.* full of ugly crannies, having ugly sunk eyes.

Frogan, frŏg′-an, *n. m.* degree of tipsiness.

Froganta, frŏg′-annt-ȧ, *a.* merry, lively.

Froineach, frŏėn′-ach, *n. f.* ferns.

Froinse, frŏėn′-shȧ, *n. f.* fringe. *H. S.*

Frois, frŏsh, *v.* spend, as standing corn; come off as thread, untwine yarn from a clue, scatter.

Froiseach, frŏsh′-ach, *a.* apt to spend, as corn, scattering, shaking.

Fromh, frȯv, *n. m.* hoarseness, a cold.

Fromhaidh, frȯv′-e, *adj.* hoarse; guth *fròmhaidh, a hoarse voice, deep-toned.*

Fuachd, fŭăchg, *n. m.* a cold, *or* obstructed perspiration; coldness.

Fuadach, fŭăd′-ach, *a.* the driving a vessel out of her course; estrangement of affections, as a person, abalienation; *pt.*

driving out of the course *or* destination; estranging the affections; air ar *fuadach* do dh' Eirinn, *weather-beaten into Ireland*; 'ga *fhuadach* air an tigh, *scaring him from the house.*

Fuadaich, fuad'-èch, *v. n.* drive out of the proper course *or* channel; estrange the affections.

Fuadan, fŭăd'-an, *n. m.* carrying clandestinely, as a horse; state of straggling; is coma leam fear *fuadain* is e luath a' labhairt, *I hate a talkative straggler, G. Proverbs*; naigheachd *fuadain, a side-wind story.*

Fuadachd, fŭăd'-ăchg, *n. f.* estrangement, abalienation, banishment.

Fuadh, fŭă-gh, *n. m.* a horrid sight, ghost. *Lewis.*

Fuaidreag, fŭăjj'-rag, *n. f.* the eel *or* natural fly used in fishing. *Islay.*

Fuaigh, fŭăe-yh', *v.* sew, stitch, seam *or* nail as planks in boat-building; fuaighte, *sewed, seamed, nailed, pegged.*

Fuaigheal, fŭăĕ-gh'-al, *n. m.* and *pt.* sewing, stitching.

Fuaigheil, fŭăĕ'-yhĕlly', *v.* sew, a seam, nail, peg.

Fuaim, fŭăĕm, *n. m. f.* a noise, echo; *v.* sound, give a sound, re-echo.

Fuaimeil, fŭăĕm'-al, *a.* resounding.

Fuaimneach, fŭăĕm'-nyach, *a* sonorous.

Fuaire, fŭăĕr''-â, *deg.* colder, coldest.

Fuairead, fŭăĕr'-ad, *n. f.* degree of coldness.

Fual, fŭăll, *n. m.* urine; galar-*fuail, the stone.*

Fuar, fŭăr, *a.* cold, cool, stingy; *v.* get ahead; get before the wind of another ship *or* boat; get to windward of a point; feuch am *fuar* thu a charraig, *see and weather the point, try to get the weather-board of the point* or *ship.*

Fuaradh, fŭăr'-Ă, *n. m.* the weather-gage, the starboard, on your starboad, air *fuaradh* ort; on your larboard, *leis ort, neo leis dhit*—also, air taobh an fhuaraidh is *air an taobh leis*; *pt.* weathering, beating, as a ship, gust before a shower.

Fuarachadh, fŭăr'-ăch-Ă, *n. m.* relief; *pt.* cooling.

Fuarag, fŭăr'-ag, *n. f.* mixture of cold water, *or* cold milk and meal; hasty pudding, Scotch crowdy.

Fuaraich, fŭăr'-èch, *v.* cool, become cool.

Fuaran, fŭăr'-an, *n. m.* a perennial spring.

Fuar-chrabhadair, fŭăr'-chrâv-add-ăĕr, *n. m.* a hypocrite; fuăr-chràbhadh, *hypocrisy.*

Fuarlit, fŭăr''-lyèjt, *n. m.* cataplasm, poultice, (fuar-lite.)

Fuarrachd, fŭăr'-achg, *n. f.* dampness, chill.

Fuarraidh, fŭărr'-è, *adj.* dampish, damp.

Fuas, fŭăs, contraction of fuathas.

Fuasgaill, fŭăsg'-èlly', *v.* loose, untie; *fuasgaill* an t-sreang, *loose the cord*; unriddle, guess; *fuasgaill* an toimhseagan, *guess the meaning of the riddle*; *v. n.* relieve, aid, assist; *fuasgaill* air, *relieve him.*

Fuasgailte, fŭăsg'-aljt-â, *pt.* and *adj.* loose, untied, free; unrestrained, active, nimble, loosed.

Fuasgailteach, fŭăsg'-altj-ach, *a.* loose, active.

Fuasgailteachd, fŭăsg'-alyty'-achg, *n. f.* nimbleness; freedom, activity, unconstraint, free use of limbs.

Fuasgladh, fŭăsg'-llĂ, part, loosing, freeing; 'ga *fhuasgladh, loosing* or *freeing him* or *it*; relieve; a *fuasgladh* air, *relieving him*; *n. m.* relief, redemption; thug e *fuasgladh* dhà, *he gave him relief, succour* or *aid*; *fuasgladh* na cèisd, *the answer of the riddle* or *dark question.*

Fuath, fŭă, *n. m.* hatred, aversion, hate.

Fuathach, fŭă'-ach, *a.* hating, loathing.

Fuathachail, fŭă'-ach-al, *a.* loathsome.

Fuathachd, fŭă'-achg, *n. f.* loathsomeness.

Fuathaich, fŭă'-èch, *v.* hate, loath, detest; *fuathaichte, hated, abhorred, detested.*

Fuathas, fŭăs, *n. m.* a prodigy, a spectre, terrible sight; choinnic iad *fuathas, they saw an apparition* or *spectre*; great number *or* quantity; *fuathas* dhaoine, *fuathas* èisg, *a vast number of people, a vast quantity of fish.*

Fuathasach, fuas'-ach, *adj.* terrible, horrid, prodigious, wonderful, astonishing.

Fuathmhor, fua'-vur, *a.* horrifying; hateful.

Fuc, fûchg, *v. n.* press against.

Fucadair, fûchg'-ad-ăĕr', *n. m.* fuller; muillear-luaidh.

Fudar, fûd'-ur, *n. m.* powder, gunpowder.

Fudaraich, fûd'-ar-èch, *v.* powder; urge on to mischief; instigate; is tusa a dh *fhudaraich* e, *it is you that instigated, that urged him to it.*

Fuich! **Fuich**! fŭĕch! fŭĕch! *adv.* fie! fie! pshaw!

Fuidh, fŭĕ, mispronunciation of foidh, under; why not, fudhainn, fudhad, *if you mean to be consistent.*

Fuidir, fûjj'-èr, *v.* fumble, besprinkle.

Fuidreadh, fûjj'-ryĂ, *n. m.* sprinkling; *pt.* fumbling.

Fuidse, fûjj'-sha, *n. m.* craven; poltroon-cock.

Fuidheag, fŭĕ'-ăg, *n. f.* a thrum; fuighealag.

Fuiffean, fueff′-an2, *n. m.* a blister on the breech.

Fuigheal, fŭĕ′-al, *n. m* remainder, refuse.

Fuighleach, fŭĕl′-ach, *n. m.* remains.

Fuil, fŭĕl, *n. f.* blood, bloodshed; extraction; a' doirteadh fola, *shedding blood*; rinn iad *fuil, they made bloodshed*; o'n *fhuil* rioghail gun smal, *from the royal extraction uncontaminated*; *fuil* bhrùite, *extravasated blood*; gu *fuil* is gu bàs, *to bloodshed and death. Ossian.*

Fuilchiont, fŭĕl′-cheúnt, *n. f.* blood-guiltiness

Fuileach, fŭĕl′-ach, *a.* bloody, sanguinary, cruel; comhrag *fuileach, a bloody battle*; a righe a's *fuiliche* lann, *ye kings of the most sanguinary sword. Ossian.*

Fuileachd, fŭĕl′-achg, *n. f.* bloodiness.

Fuileachd, fŭĕl′-achg, *n. m.* extraction.

Fuileachdach, fŭĕl′-achg-ach, *adj.* bloody, sanguinary, ravenous; duine *fuileachdach, a bloody man*; an eunlaith *fhuileachdach, the ravenous birds. B.*

Fuileamain, fŭĕl′-am-ăĕn, *n. m.* a blister on the toe; on the breech, fuiffean.

Fuilich, fŭĕl′-ėch, *v.* bleed; let blood; dh' *fhuilich* e gu bàs, *he bled to death.*

Fuilig, fŭĕl′-ėg, } *v.* suffer, permit,
Fuilinn, fŭĕl′-ênn, } bear, admit; *fuilinn* domh, *permit me*; cha'n *fhuilinn* an gnothach e, *the circumstance will not admit of it*; cha'n *fhuilinn* mi dhuit, *I will not suffer you.*

Fuil-mios, fŭĕl-mēss′, *n. f.* menstrual discharge.

Fuilteach, fŭĕlt′-ach, *a.* bloody, cruel.

Fuilteachas, fŭĕl′-tyach-us, *n. f.* bloodiness, slaughter, cruelty; extreme cruelty.

Fuiltean, fŭĕljt′-ăĕn′, *n. m.* a single hair of the head.

Fuin, fŭĕn, *v.* bake, knead, make bread; a' fuine 'na taois, *baking the dough. B.*

Fuine, fŭĕn′-à, *n. f.* a batch, a bake; *pt.* baking, kneading; fuinte, *baked, kneaded.*

Fuineadair, fŭĕn′-ad-ar′, *n. m.* a baker.

Fuireach, fŭĕr′-àch, *n. m.* stay; *pt.* staying.

Fuireachd, fŭĕr′-achg, *n. f.* stay; dè 'n *fhuireachd* a nì thu, *what stay will you make? pt. staying.*

Fuirich, fŭĕr′-ėch, *v. n.* stay, remain, reside, abide, stop, reside; take up your abode.

Fuirleach, *n. f.* a parchment *or* skin to cover a milk dish.

Fuirm, fŭĕrm, *n. pl.* stools; also *gen.*

Fuirneis, fŭĕrn′-ash, *n. f.* furnace; household furniture.

Fuirneisich, fŭĕr′-nash-ėch, *v.* furnish.

Fulang, } fŭl′-unn, *n. m. pt.* suffering, ca-
Fulann, } pability of suffering; forbearance, patience, hardihood.

Fulannach, ful′-ann-ach, *adj.* hardy, patient.

Fulannachd, full′-unn-achg, *n. f.* passiveness.

Fulangas, } full′-unn-us, *n. f.* endu-
Fulannas, } rance.

Fulasg, fŭl′-asg, *v.* moving, turamain.

Fulmair, the bird fàsgadair. *English.*

Furachail, fŭr′-ach-al, *adj.* attentive; carefully observing; looking keenly.

Furacharas, fur′-ach-ar-as, *n.f.* vigilance; extreme attention to the business in hand.

Furail, fŭr′-al, *adj.* command; offering.

Fur, fŭr, **Furan**, fŭr′-an, joy at meeting; fawning, courtesy, courteous reception.

Furanach, fŭr′-an-ach, *a.* joyful at meeting.

Furanachd, fŭr′-an-achd, complacency.

Furas, fŭr′-us, *n. m.* leisure; am bheil *furas* ort, *have you leisure?* a cheud **fhuras** a bhios orm, *the first leisure I get.*

Furas, fur′-us, **Furasda**, fŭr′-asd-a, easily accomplished; not difficult to accomplish.

Furasdachd, fŭr′-ăsd-ăchg, *n. f.* facility; easiness in doing *or* accomplishing.

Furbhailt, furv′-aljty′, *n. f.* kindly reception, complacency, urbanity.

Furbhailteach, fŭrv′-aljty′-ach, *adj.* courteous, complaisant, polite, affable; (fur, kindness, and failte, f being changed into bh, i, e, hospitable reception.)

Furbhailteachd, fŭrv′-aljt-ach, *a.* courteousness, affability; extreme complacency; a Highland welcome.

Furm, fûrm, *n. m.* a stool, seat.

Furtach, fŭrt′-ach, *n. f.* relief, aid, help.

Furtachail, fŭrt′-ach-al, *a.* giving relief.

Furtachd, fŭrt′-achg, *n. f.* comfort, relief, aid, consolation; *furtachd* aige an Dia, *consolation with God.*

G

G, g, the seventh letter of the Gaelic alphabet, named Gort *or* Gart, a garden *or* vineyard; (obsolete except in names of farms, in this sense); it has the same sound as in English, except before e and i.; see gh.

'G, 'g, for, ag *and* aig; as, tha mi 'g iarraidh, (ag iarraidh), *I seek, I want*; before consonants never used; 2d, *comp. pro.* (for aig), with whom *or* which, to whom *or* to which; 'g am bheil an cridhe briste, *who has the broken spirit*; i. e. *to whom there is a broken spirit*; 3d, *prep.* for gu, to; 'ga céiltinn 'ga cheann, *concealing it to his head*; *'ga* bhrògan, *to his very shoes.*

'G'A, gă, (for ag a,) at him, at her, at it; *'ga* leadairt, *drubbing him*; *'ga* loireadh, *wallowing him*; 2d, (for aig a,) *'ga* bheil cinnte air gach ni, *who has complete certainty about every thing*; 3d, (for gu a,) to him, to her, to its; *g'a* cheann, *to his head*, or *to its extremity*; *g'a* ceann, *to her head*, or *its extremity.*

GAB, gabb, *n. m.* a mouth never at rest; (almost in all languages,) a tattling mouth.

GABACH, gabb'-ach, *a.* garrulous; *n. f.* tattling female.

GABAIRE, gabbar'-à, *n.m.* a garrulous fellow.

GABH, gav, (murdered by some, gow *and* gaw,) *v. n.* accept, receive, take, accept of; *gabh* so, *take this, accept of this*; kindle, burn; *ghabh* an t-ainneul, *the fire kindle*; conceive, be in the family way; *ghabh* i ri cloinn, *she conceived*; assume, pretend; *gabh* ort gu'm fac thu mise, *pretend that you saw me*; betake, repair; *gabh* thun a mhonaidh, *betake yourself to the hill, repair to the hill*; go, proceed; *gabh* air t'aghaidh, *proceed, go on*; *gabh* romham, *lead the way, guide* or *lead me*; *gabh* seachad, *pass by*; *gabh* thun an doruis, *be off! leave my presence!* enlist, engage; *ghabh* e 'san arm, *he enlisted in the army*; *gabh* agamsa, *engage with me*; *gabh* mo leithsgeul, *excuse me, apologise for me*; contain, hold; *gabhaidh* so tuilidh, *this will contain* or *hold more*; beat, belabour; *gabh* air, *beat* or *belabour him*; *gabh* comhairle, *be advised, take advice*; *gabh* òran, *sing a song*; *gabh* rann, *deliver an oration*; *gabh* naigheachd dheth, *inquire after news from him*; *gabh* ris a' phàisde, *father the child*; ferment; an caochan a' *gabhail, the wash fermenting*; be infected; *ghabh* e bhreac dheth, *he was infected of the small-pox by him.*

GABHADH, gâv'-Ă, *n. m.* a jeopardy, peril; great danger; *gabhadh* cuain, *perils by sea*; an *gàbhadh* gach uair, *in jeopardy at all times.*

GABHADHBHEIL, gâv'-a²-vhell, *n. m.* a druidical ordeal; literally the jeopardy of Bel, the god of the Druids.

Note—The Druids used the ordeal of fire in cases where the innocence of a person could not be otherwise ascertained; and hence Dr. Smith thinks it probable, that St. Paul, who might have seen this engine of torture, when passing through the nations which he travelled, alludes to it in 1 Cor. iii. and 15.

GABHAIDH, gâv'-è, *a.* austere, stern, tyrannical; duine *gàbhaidh, an austere* or *tyrannical fellow*; boisterous, inclement; uair *ghàbhaidh, inclement* or *boisterous weather*; perilous, dangerous; amanan *gàbhaidh, perilous times*; dreadful.

GABHAIDHEACHD, gâv'-è-achg, *n. f.* austerity, tyrannical manner, tyranny; inclemency, boisterousness; dreadfulness, terribleness.

GABHAIL, găv'-ul, *n. f.* a portion of land done by cattle in ploughing; a lease, a farm; *pt.* taking, accepting, fermenting; fathering; a tack, as a ship; a course; air a *ghabhail* so, *on this tack*; mol a' *ghabhail, keep a sharp look out*; a chum-as a' *ghabhail* gun dad luasgain, *which preserves her course without jumbling. Macd.*; taking as fish, rising to the fly; chuir thu as mo *ghàbhail* mi, *you have disappointed me*; na cuir as a *ghabhail* e, *do not disappoint him.*

GABHALTACH, gav'-ălt-ach, *a.* infectious, contagious; galar *gabhaltach, an infectious* or *contagious disease, contagion.*

GABHALTACHD, găv'-ălt-achg, *n. f.* contagiousness, infectiousness, capaciousness.

GABHALTAICHE, găv'-alt-èch-à, *n. m.* a renter, farmer; *deg.* more *or* most infectious *or* contagious.

GABHALTAS, găv'-alt-us, *n. m.* a tenement, leasehold, a farm; conquest. *N. M.*

GABHAR, ga'-ar, *n. f.* a she-goat. *Perthshire*; in Argyle universally gobhar; *gen.* goibhre; *gabhar*-athair, *a snipe, Skye*; meanbhaghuthrag; *gabhar*-bhreac, *a buck-snail, shell-snail.*

GABHD, gav'-ad, *n. f.* a hellish stratagem.

GABHDACH, gav'-ad-ach, *a.* hellishly crafty *or* cunning; *n. f.* a shrew, a coquette.

GABHDAIRE, gav'-ad-ăr', *n. m.* a hellish stratagist.

GABHDAIREACHD, găv'-ad-ăr'-achg, *n. f.* low stratagem, mean artifice, low cunning.

GABHT, gowt, *n. m.* links. *Cowal.*

GABHTA and **GABHTE**, gav'-tyà, *pt.* taken.

GACH, găch, *adj.* every, all, each; *gach* coille, *gach* doire, 's *gach* eas, *every wood, each grove, and each cataract. Ossian.*

GAD, găd, *conj.* although, though; in Irish, ged; *n. m.* a wythe; goid, *wythes*; *gadrach, wythe-twigs*; *gad* do chrochte mi, *though I were hanged.*

GADACHD, gad'-achg, *n. f.* theft, roguery.

GADHAR, gaŏ'-ur, *n. m.* a lurcher-dog; more proper than gaothair, **AO** being always long.

GADMUNN, gad'-munn, *n. m.* a nit, mote, insect. *H. S.*

GADUICHE, găo'-èch-à, *n. m.* a thief, robber.

GAEL, see Gaidheal, *a.* a Highlander.

GAG, gàg, *n. f.* a chink; impediment of speech; *v.* chink, cleave.

GAGACH, găg′-ăch, *a.* stuttering, stammering; *n. f.* a stuttering *or* stammering female.

GAGACHD, gag′-achg, } *n. f.* impediment
GADAICHE, găg′-ėch-a, } of speech; a stammer, a stutter; *gagaire,* a stammerer.

GAID, gaŏejj, *v.* steal; more often, and less properly goid.

GAIDHEAL, găė′-al, *n. m.* a Highlander; an ancient Gaul; Highlandmen, *gaidheil, Highlanders.*

GAIDHEALACH, găėl′-ach, *adj.* Highland.

GAIDHEALTACHD, găĕlt′-achg, *n. f.* Highlands of Scotland; feadh na *gaidhealtach, throughout the Highlands.*

GAIDHLIG, gà′-llėg, *n. f.* the Gaelic language.

GAILBHEACH, ga′l′-ach, *a.* boisterous, as weather; enormous, as price; austere, as a person; terrible.

GAILL, (gàill), surly look; storm.

GAILLEACH, gàelly′-ach, *n. m.* seam of shoe-uppers.

GAILLEART, găĕlly²′-art, *n. f.* masculine woman.

GAILLIONN, ga′lly″-unn, *n. f.* storm, tempest.

GAILLIONACH, găĕlly′-unn-ach, *a.* wintry.

GAILLSEACH, gaŏĕlly′-shyach, *n. f.* earwig, (friothlunn.)

GAINEAMH, găĕn′-uv, } *n. f.* fine sand;
GAINEACH, găĕn′-ach, } *gaineach*-shùigh, *quick-sands.*

GAINEAMHAN, găĕn′-uv-an, *n. m.* sand-bottom, (sea.)

GAINNE, gaŏĕn′-nyȧ, *n. f.* scarcity; more scarce.

GAINNTIR, gáėnn′-tyėr, *n. m.* a prison, jail.

GAIR, gâėr′, *v.* laugh; *n. f.* a drawling, melancholy din of many voices, as women drowning.

GAIRBH, gaŏėrv, *n. m.* deer's stomach.

GAIRBHE, gaŏrv²′-ȧ, *n. f.* roughness; degree of garbh; na's *gairbhe, more rough, most rough.*

GAIRBHEAD, găŏĕr′-ad, degree of roughness.

GAIRBHEAL, gaŏĕr′-al, *n. m.* free-stone. *B.*

GAIRBHEIL, gaŏar′-al, *adj.* rough tempered.

GAIRDEACH, găĕrj′-ach, *a.* joyful, glad.

GAIRDEACHAIL, gâĕrjj′-ach-al, *a.* congratulatory, joyous, joyful, glad.

GAIRDEACHAS, gâĕrj′-ach-as, *n. m.* congratulation, joy, rejoicing, gladness.

GAIRDEAN, gâĕrjj′-an′, *n. m.* an arm.

GAIRDEANACH, gâĕrjj′-an-ach, *adj.* brawny.

GAIRDICH, gâėrjj′-ėch, *v.* rejoice.

GAIRE, găĕr′-ȧ, *n. m.* a laugh—near. *N.*

GAIREACH, gâĕr′-ach, *a.* laughing.

GAIREACHDAICH, gâĕr′-achg-ėch, *n. f.* laughter; continued bursts of laughter.

GAIREAS, gaŏėr′-as, *n. f.* convenience.

GAIREASACH, gur″-as-ach, *a.* convenient.

GAIRGE, gaŏėrg′-ȧ, *n. m.* tartness; more tart.

GAIRICH, gâĕr′-ėch, *n. f.* continued wailing.

GAIRISINN, gaŏėr′-ėsh-ėnn, *n. f.* disgust.

GAIRISNEACH, } gaŏĕrsh′-nyach, *a.* dis-
GAIRSINNEACH, } gusting, horrible, detestable.

GAIRM, gaŏĕrm, *v.* proclaim banns in church; crow as a cock; call on beasts, as hens, &c.; *n. f.* proclamation of banns; a call to do something; calling.

GAIRMEADAIR, gaoerm′-ad-ăĕr, *n. m.* proclaimer.

GAIRNEAL, gyârn′-nyal, *n. f.* a large chest.

GAIRNEALAIR, gârn′-al-ăr′, *n. m.* gardener.

GAIS, gash, *v.* daunt; shrivel up. *Ml.*

GAIS, gâsh, *n. f.* a surfeit. *Islay*; torrent. *High. Society.*

GAISE, gash′-ȧ, *n. f.* daunt; cha do chuir e *gaise* air, *it did not daunt him in the least*; boldness. *High. Society.*

GAISGE, gashg′-ȧ, *n. f.* heroism, valour, feats, achievements; do *ghaisge* féin, *your own valour.*

GAISGEACH, gashg′-ach, *n. m.* a hero, a champion.

GAISGEACHD, gashg′-achg, *n. f.* heroism.

GAISGEANT, găshg′-annt, *adj.* heroic.

GAISGEALACHD, gashg′al-achg, *n. f.* heroism.

GAISGEIL, gashg′-al, *a.* heroic, brave.

GAL, gal, *n. m.* wailing; *v.* wail; *pt.* wailing; 'a *gal* is a' caoinidh, *wailing and weeping.*

GALAD, găl′-ad, *n. f.* term of kindness to a girl.

GALAN, gal′-an, *n. m.* youth; a sapling.

GALAR, gal′-ăr, *n. m.* disease, distemper.

GALC, galk, full cloth; (luaidh.) *N.*

GALL, gâll, *n. m.* a Low countryman; gaill, *Low countrymen*—also, of a Low countryman.

GALLAN-GREANNACH, gall-an-gren′-ach, *n. m.* colts foot: *gallan* mòr, *butterwort.*

GALL-CHNU, gall-chrû′, *n. f.* walnut.

GALLDA, galld′-ȧ, *a.* Low country, foreign.

GALLDACHD, galld′-achg, *n. f.* the Low country of Scotland, stinginess.

GALL-DRUMA, gall-drŭm′-a, *n. f.* kettle-drum.

GALL-SHEILEACH, gall-hāl′-ach, *n. m.* cooper's willow.

GAMHAINN, gáv′-ėnn, *n. m.* stirk, year old calf; a stupid fellow; *gamhainn* tairbh, *year old bull*; a yearling.

GAMHLAS, gav′-llas, *n. m.* malice, grudge.

GAMHLASACH, gáv′-las-ach, *a.* vindictive.

GAMHNACH, gáv′-nach, *a.* farrow; *n. f.* a farrow cow; tha i *gamhnach, she is farrow.*

GANGAID, gang′ ajj, *n. f.* deceit, giddy girl. *H. S.*

Gann, gănn, *a.* scarce, scant, limited; bliadhna *ghann, a year of scarcity*; *adv.* scarcely, hardly, scarce; 's *gann* a ràinig mi, *I scarcely arrived*; 's *gann* a nì e feum, *it will hardly do*; rare; few, small; nì *gann, a scarce thing*; mic an anma *ghainn, sons of the pusillanimous souls*; gun iongantas *gann, with no small wonder.*

Ganntachd, gannt'-achg, *n. f.* scarcity.

Ganradh, gàn'-rX, *n. m.* a gander.

Ganraich, gàn'-rèch, romping, screeching.

Gaog, gúg, *n. m.* lump, as in cloth.

Gaoid, gāoèjj, *n. f.* blemish, flaw, particularly in cattle; defect; gun *ghaoid* gun ghalar, *without blemish* or *disease.*

Gaoir, gāoèr, *n. f.* noise of steam escaping; buzzing of liquors fermenting; continuous drawling, moaning; the spigot of a cask; thoir a' *ghoair* as a' bhuideal, *take the spigot out of the cask*; *gaoir* chath, *the din of arms*; *gaoir* theas, *a flickering sheet of cobwebs, seen on the grass in autumn, portending rain.*

Gaoiseach, gāoèsh'-ach, *n. f.* a gun-bolt.

Gaoisid, gāosh'-èjj, *n. f.* coarse hair, horsehair.

Gaoisideach, gāosh'-èjj-ach, *a.* hairy.

Gaoisneach, gāosh'-nyach, *a.* hairy, rough.

Gaoith, gāoèch, *n.* sometimes the nominative, and always the genitive of gaoth, wind.

Gaoithseach, gaŏè'-shyach, a sheaf put as thatch on a little shock.

Gaol, gāol, *n. m.* love, affection, fondness, a darling; a *ghaoil, my darling*; a mhic mo *ghaoil, my beloved son*; am fac thu mo *ghaol, saw you my beloved*? clann mo mhàthar *ghaoil, the children of my beloved mother*; a nighean mo *ghaoil, girl of my affections, M'L.*; my beloved girl; thug mi *gaol* d'ar rìghribh dhuit, *I loved you most truly.*

Gaolach, gaol'-ach, *n. c.* beloved person, a darling; *adj.* beloved, affectionate, dearly beloved; Ardar *gaolach, beloved*; Ardar *gaolach* am bròn, *affectionate in grief*; tha, a *ghaolach, yes, my darling*!

Gaorr, gùrr, *n. m.* gore; *v.* tap, gore.

Gaorran, gùrr'-an, *n. m.* big belly.

Gaorsach, gāor'-sach, *n. f.* a most abandoned strumpet, one that lies down in the kennel.

Gaorsachd, gāor'-sachg, *n. m.* prostitution.

Gaort, gúrt, *n. m.* saddle-girth.

Gaoth, gāo, *n. f.* the wind, flatulency; *gaoth* tuath, *north wind*; *gaoth* deas, *south wind*; *gaoth* 'niar, *west wind*; *gaoth* 'n ear, *east wind.*

Gaothair, gāoèr, *n. f.* wind-piece of a bagpipe.

Gaothar, gaŏ'-ur, *n. m.* lurcher, gadhar.

Gaothar, } gāo'-ur, *adj.* windy; as a
Gaothmhor, } person flatulent.

Gaotharachd, } gāo'-ur-achg, *n. f.* flatulency,
Gaothmorachd, } windiness.

Gaothran, gāo'-ran, *n. m.* a giddy fellow.

Gar, găr, *v.* warm; *gar* thu fhéin, *warm yourself*; *garaidh* 'se e féin, *he shall warm himself.*

'G'ar, (for ag ar,) găr, *pre.* and *pro.* *'g'ar* toirt, *bringing us*; *g'ar* lèireadh, *tormenting us.*

Garadh, gar'-X, *n. m.* den of quadrupeds; warming of the body with fire; *pt.* warming; dean do *gharadh, warm yourself*; tha *garadh* aig na sionnaich, *the foxes have dens. B.*

Garail, găr'-al, *a.* snug, comfortable.

Garalachd, găr'-al-achg, *n. f.* snugness.

Garbh, gărv, *adj.* rough, thick, not slender, rugged; harsh; brawny; maide *garbh, a thick stick*; duine *garbh, a harsh* or *a brawny man*; casan *garbh, brawny legs*; àite *garbh, a rough* or *rugged place*; hoarse; stormy, boisterous; coarse; guth *garbh, hoarse voice*; anart *garbh, coarse linen*; oidhche *gharbh, a boisterous night*; *garbh* 'na chàint, *harsh in his expressions*; a' *gharbh* chuid diutha, *the majority, the generality of them, the bulk of them*; more or most harsh, gairbhe;—nì a's *gairbhe* na leasraidh, *what is thicker than the loins, Bible*; *n. m.* thick; an *garbh* is an caol, *the thick and thin.*

Garbhag, garv'-ag, *n. f.* the plaise, *or* spotted kind of flounder;—*North,* sprats of herring, sgadan gearr.

Garbhan, garv'-an, *n. m.* coarse ground meal, *Islay*; gills of fish, (giùran,) *N.*

Garbhbhallach, gărv'-vall-ach, *a.* brawny.

Garbhchramhach, garv'-chràv-ach, *a.* raw-boned.

Garbhchriochan, garv'-chrĕch-an, *n. pl.* rough boundaries, part of Scotland.

Garbhghucag, garv'-ghuchg-ag, *n. f.* first-shot, *or* what comes first from the still.

Garbhlach, garv'-lach, *n. m.* rank moor-grass; (fineach, *Lew.*) rugged country.

Garg, gărg, *a.* fierce, harsh, turbulent; duine *garg, a turbulent person*; tart, bitter, acrid, pungent; blas *garg, a pungent* or *tart taste*; is *gairge, more tart.*

Garlach, gârl'-ach, *a.* spoiled child; a most impertinent fellow, (gàrr.)

Garluch, gar'-luch, *n. f.* a mole *H S.*

Garmainn, garm'-ènn, *n. f* weaver's beam; *garmainn* bhall, *a windlass.*

Garr, gàrr, *n. f.* a gorbelly, the belly of a spoiled child, *or* starvling.

Garrach, gărr'-ach, *n. m.* a gorbellied child, a most impertinent fellow.

Garradh, gàrr'-ă, *n. m.* a garden, a fence *or* dike, wall-fence.

Garradair, gàrr'-ad-aer, *n. m.* a gardener.

Garrag, gàrr'-ag, young crow.

Gart, gart, *n. m.* standing corn, vineyard.

Gartan, gart'-an, garter.

Gart-eun, gart-èn', *n. m.* a quail.

Gartghlainn, } gart'-llăĕnn, *v.* weed,
Gartlainn, } free from noxious weeds.

Gartghlan, } gart'-lann, *n. m* weeds;
Gartlann, } (gart *and* lann, weed-hook.)

Garthaich, see Sgathruith.

Gas, găs, *n. m.* stalk, stem, particle, a broom; *gas* a sguabadh an tighe, *a broom to sweep the house*; *gas* càil, *a stock of coleworts*;—gach *gas*, *every particle*;—*Mainland*, *gen.* gois.

Gasair, gas'-ėr, *v.* line as a bitch.

Gasar, gas'-ar, *n. m.* pert fellow.

Gasda, gasd'-a, *adj.* fine, well-shaped; ni *gasda*, *a fine thing*; duine *gasda*, *a well-shaped* or *handsome person.*

Gasdachd, gasd'-achg, *n. f.* fineness, handsomeness, beauty, expertness, *H.*

Gasg, găsg, *n. m.* tail, *H. Society.*

Gat, gât, *a.* bar of iron; a stalk; *gàt* siabuinn, *a bar* or *stalk of soap*; *gàt* siùcair duibh, *a stalk of black sugar.*

Gath, gă, *n. m.* a sting, a dart, a beam, *or* ray; *gath* an t-seillein, *the sting of the bee*; *gath* na grèine, *sun beam*, also *Fingal's banner*; inner row of sheaves in a corn stack; *gath* dubh, *foundation sheaves.*

Gath-cuip, gă'-kŭĕp, *n. m.* medical tent.

Gath-muigh, gă'-mûė-y', *n. m.* a mane, gath-muing.

Ge, gā, *pro. indef.* whatever, whoever; *ge* b'e neach, *whatever person*; *conj.* though.

Gead, gyā'd, *n. f.* a bed in a garden *or* small ridge of land; star in a horse's head; *v.* clip, *H. S.*

Geadas, gyād2'-ăs, *n. m.* coquettry; the fish, pike.

Geadasach, gyād2'-as-ach, *a.* coquettish, flirting.

Geadh, gè-aŏgh'', *n. m.* a goose, lump of the finest part of meal, made by children, tailor's goose.

Geadh, gé, *v.* pole *or* shove a boat by means of a boat-hook *or* pole.

Geadha, gé-à, *n. m.* a pole, a boat-hook.

Geadhach, gé-ach, *n. f.* goose quill, ite.

Geadhachail, gyaŏ'-ach-al, *n. pl.* domestic jobs *or* messages.

Geadhail, gye'-ul, *n. f.* a field, park.

Geal, gyal, *adj.* white, fond of, clear, bright; cha 'n 'eil e *geal* da, *he is not fond of it* or *him, he has no great affection for him*; *n. m.* white of any thing; *geal* na sùile, *the white of the eye.*

Gealach, gyăl'-ăch, *n. f.* the moon.

Gealachadh, gyal'-ach-ă, *n. m.* bleaching, a bleach; *pt.* bleaching; blàr *gealachaidh*, *bleachfield.*

Gealag, gyal'-ag, *n. f.* a grilse, bànag *gealag* bhuachair, *a bunting*, *H. Society.*

Gealagan, gyal'-ag-an, *n. m.* the white of an egg.

Gealaich, gyal'-ėch, *v.* bleach, whiten.

Gealbhan, gyalv'-an, *n. m.* a common fire.

Gealbhonn, gyalv'-onn, *n. m.* a sparrow.

Geall, gyăll, *n. m.* a pledge, bet, *or* wager, mortgage; thoir dhomh *geàll*, *give me a pledge*, *Bible*; cuir *geàll*, *lay a bet*; mo gheàllsa nach faic thu e, *I pledge my word you shall not see him*; great fondness; tha e an *geàll* urra, *he is excessively fond of her*; *v.* promise, pledge, vow; *geallaidh* iad *gealladh*, *they shall vow a vow*, *Bible*; tha e an *geall* na's fhiach e, *every thing he has is at stake.*

Geallachas, gyall'-ach as, *n. m.* prospect, success.

Gealladh, gyall'-ă, *n. m.* a promise, a vow, a mortgage; *gealladh* gun a choghealladh, *a promise without performance*; gheall mi, *I promised*; *gealladh-pòsaidh*, *betrothment.*

Gealltainn, gyâll'-ttėnn, *pt.* promising.

Gealltannach, gyallt'-unn-ach, *a.* promising, auguring well, promissory, hopeful.

Gealltanas, gyâllt'-an-as, *n. m.* pledge.

Geallshuil, gyâll'-hŭėl, *n. f* moon-eye.

Geallshuileach, gyâll'-hŭėl-ach, *a.* moon-eyed.

Gealtach, gyallt'-ach, *a.* cowardly.

Gealtachd, gyăllt'-achg, *n. f.* cowardice.

Gealtair, gyăllt'-āer', *n. m.* a coward.

Geamha, gé'-a, *n. m.* pledge, compensation; cha bu *gheamha* leam, *I would not for, it would be no compensation to me*; am bu *gheamha* dhomhsa air an t-saoghail, *would the whole world be a compensation to me?*

Geamhd, gyév-ud, *n. m.* a junk, thick-set person.

Geamhlag, gyév'-lag, *n. f.* a crow, lever, bar.

Geamhrach, gyav'-rach, *n. f.* a winter park.

Geamhrachail, gyáv'-rach-al, } *a.* wintry,
Geamhradail, gyáv'-rad-al, } stormy, cold.

Geamhradh, gyáv'-ră, *n. m.* winter.

Geamhraich, gyáv'-rėch, *v.* winter; feed during winter, furnish provender geamhraichte, *wintered.*

Geamhrail, gyav'-ral, *adj.* wintry, cold.

Gean, gyen, *n. m.* good humour.

Geanail, gen'-al, *adj.* cheerful, gay.

Geanm, gėnum, *n. f.* chastity.

Geanmnaidh, genum'-nnė, *adj.* chaste.

Geannaire, gyann'-ăr-à', *n. m.* a hammer, rammer; ri *geannaireachd, hammering.*

Geanta, gè'nt'-a, abstemious; modest, chaste.

Geantachd, gè'nt'-achg, *n. f.* abstinence, modesty, self-command, continence; *gèantachd* na faollainn, *the abstinence of the sea-mew*—which eats a full grown fish at a gulp, and makes three portions of the sprat.

Gearain, ger'-áèn, *v.* complain, appeal.

Gearan, ger'-an, *n. m.* complaint, appeal, accusation, supplication, application for redress; dean do *ghearan* ris, *apply for redress,* or *appeal to him*; cha ruig thu leas a bhi *gearan, you need not complain*; fuilinn domh mo *ghearan* a dheanadh riutsa, *permit me to appeal to you*; cha 'n 'eil stàth dhuit a bhi *gearan* ris, *it serves no end to appeal to him*; rinn iad *gearan, they murmured*; ri *gearan, complaining*; wailing, moaning; bha e a' *gearan* feadh 'na h-oidhche, *he was moaning through the night.*

Gearanach, ger'-an-ach, *a.* plaintive, sad, apt to complain, querulous; sgeul ma 'n *gearanach* daoine, *news about which men are apt to complain.*

Gearr, gyârr, *v.* cut, geld, satirize, describe as a circle; *adj.* short, of short continuance; ann an ùine *ghearr, in a short time*; *n. m.* an abridgement; *geàrr* a ghnothuich, *the abridged statement of the affair*; an còrr 's an *geàrr, the short and the long of it*—the odds and ends—the two extremes. A hare, (gearraidh,) weir, for fish, (caraidh,) *Provincial.*

Gearrach, gyârr'-ach, *n. f.* flux, dysentery.

Gearrachuibh, gyărr'-a-chŭĕv', *n. f.* a muzzle-bar for two horses; cuibh-mhòr, *for four horses. Islay.*

Gearrabhodach, gyarr'-a-vōd^{2}-ach, *n. m.* a young middle-sized cod.

Gearrabhonn, gyărr'-a-vōnn^{2}, *n. m.* a half sole.

Gearradair, gyărr'-ad-ăĕr, *n. m.* cutler.

Gearradh, gyarr'-ă, *n. m.* a cut, shape; a severe taunt, *or* sarcasm; bowel complaint, flux.

Gearraidh, gyarr'-ĭ-yh', *n. m.* a hare. *Is.*

Gearraiseach, gerr'-èsh-ach, *n. f.* swingle-chain. *North.*

Gearran, gyărr'-an, *n. m.* a gelding; time from 15th March to April 11th, inclusive.

Gearr-fhiadh, gyârr-ĕăŏgh', *n. m.* short deer, a hare.

Gearrsgian, gyarr'-skĕăn, *n. m.* a dirk, biodag.

Gearrshaoghlach, gyărr'-hul-ach, *a.* short-lived.

Gearsum, gyar'-sum, *n. m.* entry money; difference in money.

Geartach, gyărt'-ach, *n. f.* a trip, an excursion; *geartach* do 'n Ghalldachd, *a trip* or *excursion to the Low country*; a short time.

Geas, gāss^{2}, *n. f.* metamorphosis, enchantment; nighean righ fo *gheasaibh, a princess metamorphosed*; chaidh e fo *gheasaibh, he was metamorphosed*; a solemn engagement, *or* charge; tha mi a' cur mar *gheasaibh* ort, *I solemnly charge you*; sorcery.

Geasadair, gās^{2}'-ad-ăĕr, *n. m.* an enchanter, a charmer; geasadaireachd, *enchantment, sorcery, witchcraft.*

Geata, gāt^{2}'-à, *n. m.* a gate; sort of play, a stick; dhùin iad an *geata, they shut the gate. Bible.*

Geill, gyălly', *v.* yield assent, admit, submit; tha mi a' *gèilleachdainn* da sin, *I admit that, that is granted, I concede that point*; dha 'n *géill* mòr ghaillion, *to whom yields the great tempest, Oss.*; *n. f.* submission, homage, concession, admission; na d' thoir *géill* da leithid sin, *yield assent to no such thing, make no concession*; tha e a' cur an *géill, he is manifesting, holding forth, strenuously maintaining*; a *géilleachdainn* da reachd, *yielding assent to his law, admitting the uprightness of his law. Ps.*

Geilt, gyălty'^{2}, *n. f.* terror, dread, awe.

Geimheal, gév'-ul, *n. f.* chain, fetter.

Geimhlich, gyév'-lyèch, *v.* chain, fetter.

Geinn, gyā^{2}nn', *v.* a wedge, any thing firm.

Geinneanta, gyānn^{2}'-annt à, *adj.* firm, stout.

Geir, gyăr^{2}, *n. f.* tallow, grease, (suet, saill)

Geire, găr''-à, *adj.* more sharp, &c. sharpness.

Geiread, gyăr''-ud, *n. f.* degree of sharpness, *or* acuteness.

Geireas, găĕr'-ash, *n. f.* witticisms.

Geireanachd, găĕr'-an'-achg, *n. f.* a satirical turn, bickering sort of wit.

Geisg, see Gìosg.

Geob, gyòb, *n. m.* a gaping mouth, a little mouth; *v.* gape with the mouth, as fish when losing the vital spark.

Geobail, gyòb'-al, *n. m.* a gape; *pt.* gaping.

Geoc, gyòchg, *n. f.* gluttony.

Geocach, gyòchg'-ach, *n. m.* a glutton, gormandiser.

Geocail, gyôchy'-al, *a.* gluttonous.

Geocair, gyôc'-ăr', *n. m.* a glutton, a gormandiser; geocaireachd, *gluttony, gormandising.*

Geodha, gyô'-à, *n. m.* a narrow creek, *or* cove between impending rocks.

Geosgail, gyŏsg'-ul, *n. f.* blustering talk.

Geola, gyol'-a, *n. f.* a yawl, a small boat.

Geolach, gyol'-ach, *n. f.* a bier, shoulder-belt. *Armst.*

Geon, gyòn, *n. m.* avidity, keenness.

Geonail, gyòn'-al, *a.* keen, with avidity.

Geotan, gyôt'-an, *n. m.* a driblet, *or* trifling sum *or* debt, an item, a small quantity; a' cruinneachadh *gheòtan, collecting trifling debts*; a pendicle.

Geuban, gāb'-an, (sgròban) crop. *Bible.*

Geug, gā'g, *n. f.* a branch, a sapling; a young superfine female; barr-*geug*, a belle, lasdaire, a beau.

Geugach, gā'g'-ach, *a.* branchy, ramifying.

Geum, gā'm, *n. m.* lowing of cows, calves, &c. *v.* low.

Geumnaich, gā'm'-nyèch, *n. f.* continuous lowing.

Geur, gè'r, *a* sharp, sharp pointed, sharp edged; mentally acute, shrewd, ingenious; acute of vision; sgian *gheur, sharp knife*; duine *geur, a shrewd, acute,* or *ingenious fellow*; suil *gheur, a keen eye*; claidheamh *geur, a sharp-edged sword*; acrid, bitter, tart; blas *geur, acrid, bitter,* or *tart taste*; severe, harsh, keen; tha e tuilidh is *geur, he is too severe* or *keen*; sleagh *gheur, sharp-pointed spear*; bainne *geur milk of an acrid taste*; fion *geur, sour wine.*

Geurach, gār'-ach, *n. f.* the herb agrimony.

Geuraich, gèr'-èch, *v.* sharpen, hone, whet; a' *geurachadh* na sgine, *sharpening, honing,* or *whetting the knife*; sour, embitter; am bainne a' *geurachadh, the milk souring*; *adv.* sharply, keenly; a *geur* amharc, *looking keenly*; *geuraichte, sharpened, whetted, honed.*

Geurchuis, gàr'-chŭsh, *n f.* acuteness, penetration, ingenuity, mental energy.

Geurchuiseach, gūr'-chūsh-ăch, *adj.* acute, penetrating, sharp, ingenious, subtle, inventive.

Geur-lean, gār'-llen, *v.* persecute, harass.

Geur-leanmhuinn, gèr'-len-vhènn, *n. f.* persecution; *geur-leanmhuinn,* na gort, *persecution* or *famine.*

Gheibh, y*h*ō^{2}, *fut. aff.* of faigh; faigh aon, *get one*; *gheibh* mi, *I shall get*; fhuair mi, *I have got,* or *I got.*

Gheibheadh, y*h*ōv^{2}'-ă, would get.

Gheibhear, y*h*ōv^{2}'-ur, shall *or* will be got.

Gheibhinn, y*h*ōv^{2}'-enn, I would get.

Gial, gĕăl, *n.m.* gum; ciobhall, contracted and corrupted, a jaw-bone.

Gibneach, gēb^{2}'-nyach, *n. m.* cuttle-fish.

Gidheadh, gė-yhaŏgh', *conj.* yet, nevertheless.

Gighis, ge'-yhē, *n. m.* a masquerade.

Gilb, gēlb, *n. f.* a chisel; *gilb*-thollaidh, *gough.*

Gile, gēl^{2}'-â, *n. f.* whiteness, clearness, fairness; degree; na's *gile, whiter, fairer*; *gile* a'n anairt, *whiteness of the linen*; also gilead.

Gille, gėlly^{2}'-â, *n. m.* servant man; a young man; a lad; *gille*-each, *a groom*; *gille*-coise, *footman*; *gille*-ruith, *a courier*; *gille*-fionn and -fiondrain, *a small white periwinkle*; *gille*-greasaidh, *a postilion*; also *gille*-marcachd; *gille*-gnothuich, *one that runs messages*; *gille*-mirein, *a tee-totum, a whirligig*; *gille*-guirminn, corn-sgabious, *gille*-sguain, *train-bearer*; *gille*-copain, *cup-bearer*; leanabh-*gille, a male child, a man child.*

Gilm, gem, *n. m* a buzzard.

Gin, gēn^{2}, *v.* beget, gender, conceive, produce; o'n a ghineadh e, *since he was conceived*; ma'n do ghineadh na cnoic, *before the hills were produced*; ghin an crodh, *the cattle gendered*; ginte, *begotten*; *n. m.* one, individual, one, any, nobody; 'na h-uile *gin, every one, all*; cha'n'eil *gin* agam, *I do not possess a single one*; cha d'thainig *gin, none came, nobody came*; am bheil *gin* agadsa, *have you any*?

Gineal, gēnn^{2}'-al, *n. f.* offspring, race, lineage; do *ghineal, your offspring*; a *ghineal* dhubh, *the black race*; growth of corn in the stack *or* shock.

Ginealach, gēnn^{2}'-al-ach, *n f.* a race. *B.*

Ginealaich, gēnn^{2}'-al-ach, *v.* grow as corn in shocks.

Gineamhuinn, gēn'-uv-ènn, *n. m.* conception.

Giob, gē'b^{2}, *n. f.* shag, hairiness.

Giobach, gē'b^{2}'-ach, *adj.* shaggy, hairy.

Giobag, gē'b^{2}'-ag, *n. f.* a handful of lint.

Giobaiche, gēb^{2}'-èch-â, *n. f.* shagginess.

Giobairneach, gēb^{2}'-ăr-nyach, *n. m.* cuttle-fish.

Gioball, gēb^{2}'-all, *n. m.* mantle, shawl; *n. c.* an odd fellow, *or* lady.

Giobarsaich, gēb'-ars-èch, *n. f.* shagginess.

Giog, gē'g, *v.* peep, steal a look at; cringe, crouch, fawn; ghiog e stigh air an uinneig, *he peeped in at the window*; cha *ghiogainn* do dhuine, *I would not cringe to any man.*

Giogaire, gē'g'-ar'-â, *n. m.* a cringer, fawner.

Giol, geúl, *n. f.* a leech; *giol*-tholl, *horse-leech.*

Giolc, gĕúlk, *v.* bend, stoop, aim at; *giolcom* ort, *let me try to hit you*; make a sudden movement.

Giolla, for gille.

Giollachd, gĕúll- *or* gè'll'-achg, *n.f.* and *pt.* manufacturing, preparing, dressing, improving; a' *giollachd* leathraich, *dressing* *or* manufacturing leather; a' *giollachd* buntàta, *dressing potatoes in the fields.*

Giollaichd, geúll'-èchg, *v.* dress, manufacture, as leather, &c.; a' *giollachd* lìn, *dressing* or *manufacturing lint.*

Giomach, gēm²'-ach, *n. m.* a lobster.

Giomanach, gēm²'-an-ach, *n. m.* a masterly fellow in any thing; *gìomanach* a ghunna, *the masterly marksman* or *shooter.*

Giomlaid, gēm²'-llajj, *n. f.* gimlet.

Gion, gĕún, *n. m.* excessive love *or* desire; appetite; tha mo *ghion* ort, *I am excessively fond of you, I love you with all my heart.*

Gionach, gĕún'-ach, *adj.* appetised, keen.

Giorag, gĕúr'-ag, *n. m.* panic, great fear.

Gioragach, gĕúr'-ag-ach, *a.* panic-struck.

Giorra, gĕúrr'-a, *n. f.* shortness, fewness; *giorra* làithean neo, *giorra* shaoghail, *fewness* or *shortness of days* or *life*; abridgement, degree of geàrr *and* goirid, na's *giorra, shorter, more limited.*

Giorrach, gĕúrr'-ach, *n. f.* short heath *or* hair. *H.*

Giorrachd, gĕúrr'-achg, *n. f.* shortness, abridgment, compendium, abbreviation.

Giorraich, gĕúrr'-ēch, *v.* shorten, abbreviate, abridge, curtail, epitomise.

Giorruinn, gĕúrr'-ènn, *n. f.* a barnacle (giorra-eun), it being a bird of passage.

Giosg, gēssg, *v.* creak; a' *gìosgail, creaking*; *n. m.* a creak; *gìosg* fhiaclan, *gnashing of teeth.*

Girlinn, gérr''-lyènn, *n. f.* a barnacle; (giorra-linn), a bird of passage.

Gis, gèsh, *n. m.* enchantment; gisreag.

Gisreagach, gèsh'-rag-ach, *a.* superstitious; fond of charms *or* enchantment.

Giugach, gyūg'-ach, *a.* cringing, drooping the neck in a cringing position; (from giuig.)

Giuig, gĕūĕg, *n. f.* a crouch; cringing, drooping position of the head, as a person sheltering himself from rain; *v.* cringe, droop.

Giuigire, gyūèg'-ėr-à, *n. m.* cringer.

Giuir, gyūèr, *n. f.* same as giuig.

Giuirideach, gyūr''-ejj-ach, *n. c.* a cringing, drooping, miserable looking person.

Giulain, gēūl'-dèn, *v.* carry, behave, conduct; *giùlain* an gunna so, *carry this gun*; *giùlain* thu féin, *conduct* or *behave yourself*; bear, suffer, permit; cha urra mi sin a' *ghùilan, I cannot suffer* or *bear that*; *I cannot support* or *endure that.*

Giulan, gyūl'-an, behaviour, conduct; do *ghiùlan* fhéin, *your own conduct* or *behaviour*; *pt.* carrying, permitting, enduring, tolerating.

Giulla, giúll'-a, for Gille.

Giubhas, } geū'-us, *n. m.* fir, pine; the
Giuthas, } banner *or* armorial ensign of the Macalpines, (kidnapped by others); ga ba shuaicheantas *giubhas, whose armorial ensign is the fir-crop. Song.*

Giuran, gyūr'-an, *n m.* gills of fish; a sort of herb.

Glac, glăchg, *v.* seize, lay hold of, catch, grasp, embrace, take prisoner; *ghlac* iad a' phoite ruadh, *they seized the still*; *ghlac* iad e, *they took him prisoner*: *n. f.* a valley, a defile, a dell, a hollow; 'sa *ghlaic* so, *in this hollow, a grasp* or *hollow of the hand*; embrace; *glac* na beinne, *the defile of the mountain*; fuar *ghlac* a bhàis, *the cold embrace* or *grasp of death. Hom.*; is gann a chìtear tom na *glac, scarcely could hill* (bush,) or *dell be seen*; an *glacaibh* a chéile, *embracing each other*; handful.

Glacach, glachg'-ach, *n. f.* swelling in the hollow of the hand; palmful; *adj.* full of dells.

Glacadair, glachg'-ad-ăĕr, *n. m.* catcher seizer.

Glacaid, glachg'-aj, *n. f.* handful.

Glacadh, glachg'-a, } *n. f.* seizure; *pt.*
Glacail, glachg'-al, } seizing, catching.

Glag, glăg, *n. m.* a crash; a horse-laugh.

Glagaid, glag'-aj, *n f.* blustering female.

Glagaire, glag'-ar-à, *n. m.* a blusterer.

Glagarsaich, glag'-ar-sech, *n. f.* crashing, clangour, blustering, horse-laughter.

Glaim, gláėm, *n. f.* a large mouthful; *v.* seize upon voraciously; usurp.

Glaimsear, gláėm'-shaėr, *n. m.* a fellow that wishes to monopolise booty; a usurper.

Glaine, gllinn'-à, for gloine. *North.*

This certainly, is the proper pronunciation and orthography (from glan). *West,* gloine.

Glais, glăsh, *v.* lock, embrace, secure.

Glaise, glăsh'-à, *n. f.* greyness. *H. S.*; a strait.

Glaiseach, glash'-ach, *n. f.* foam; cothar, lockfast place.

Glaisean, glăsh'-aèn, *n. m.* a coal-fish.

Glaisleun, glash'-lèn, *n. f* spearwort.

Glaisnealach, glash'-néll-ach, *adj.* pale, wan.

Glaisrig, glash'-rēg, *n. f.* a female fairy, half-human, half-beast; a gorgon.

Glaiste, glasht'-à, *pt.* locked, secure.

Glam, glàm, *v.* handle awkwardly; lay hold of voraciously.

Glamair, glam'-us, glam'-ėr, *and* -us, *n.m.* smith's vice; chasm.

Glan, glan, *v.* clean, wipe, cleanse, wash, purify; *glan* so, *clean this*; free from scandal, purge, biaze, brighten, beam; *ghlan* solus an aodann an righ, *light* *beamed on the face of the king, Ossian; glanaidh* e 'beul, *he shall wipe her mouth. Bible.*

Glan, glăn, *adj.* clean, cleansed, purged *or* freed from scandal; pure, radiant, clear; *glan* mar a ghrian, *clear as the sun*; is *glaine* a measg nam ban, *purest among women, Oss.*; *adv.* thoroughly, wholly, completely; *glan* mharbh, *completely dead; glan* ruisgte, *wholly bare.*

Glanadair, glan'-ad-aer, *n. m.* a cleanser, purifier.

Glaodh, glăo-gh, *n. m.* a cry, a shout.

Glaodhaich, glăo'-èch, *n. f.* incessant crying.

Glaogh, glăo'-gh, *n. m.* a glue; *v.* glue.

Glaoghan; see Laoghan.

Glaoidh, glăo'-ėyh', *v. n.* cry, bawl, shout, proclaim, call; *glaoidh* air, *call to him.*

Glas, glas, *n. f.* a lock; *glas*-chrochta, *padlock*; *glas*-ghuib, *a muzzle, a gag*; chuir mi a' *ghlas*-ghuib air, *I muzzled him, I gagged him*; a *ghlas*-mheur, *a masterpiece of bagpipe music.*

Glasach, glas'-ach, *n. f.* ley-land. *North.*

Glasadh, glas'-Ă, *pt.* looking, securing.

Glasdaidh, glasd'-ė, *adj* greyish.

Glas-lamh, glass'-làv, *n. f.* handcuff, manacles.

Glasraich, glas'-rèch, *v* convert into meadow.

Glastalamh, glas'-tal-uv, *n. m.* unploughed *or* pasture land.

Glastarriunn, glas'-tarr-ènn, *v.* remove sheaf-corn when cut; *n. f.* act of removing such.

Gle, glă, *adv* enough, sufficiently; *glè* gheall, *white enough*, or *sufficiently white.*

Gleachd, glechg, *n. f.* sparring, sparring-match; a struggle, a conflict; agony; a fight; a' *gleachd* ris a bhàs, *in the agonies of death*; le mòr *ghleachd, with many a struggle*; *pt.* struggling, striving, endeavouring.

Gleachd, glechg, *v.* strive; properly gleichd.

Gleachdair, glechg'-ăr'-à, *n. m.* a sparrer.

Gleadh, glaŏ, an onset, exploit. *H.*

Gleadhar, glaŏ'-ur, *n. m.* a noisy blow.

Gleadhrach, glyaŏr'-ach, *n. m.* sea-weed. *North.*

Gleadhraich, glăor'-ėch, *n. f.* clangour; a rattling rustling noise.

Gleadhran, glăor'-an, *n. m.* a rattle.

Gleang; see Gliong.

Gleann, glyann, *n. m.* a valley, a dell, a dale; *glinn* and *gleanntan*, glens, valleys.

Gleannan, glyann'-an, *n. m.* a dale.

Gleannach, glyann'-ach, *a.* full of dales.

Gleanntail, glyant'-al, *adj.* haunting *or* fond of roaming in glens.

Gleidh, glāe-y', *v.* keep, preserve, retain hold, protect; *gleidhte, kept, protected,* &c.

Gleidheadh, glā²'-Ă, *pt.* preserving, keeping; *n. m.* preservation; a good turn.

Gleidhteach, glā-y''-tyach, *a.* careful, frugal; in safe custody *or* keeping; tha sin *glèidhteach, that is in safe keeping*; duine *glèidhteach, a careful* or *frugal man.*

Gleidhteachd, glā-y''-tyachg, *n. f.* safe custody; state of preservation *or* keeping.

Gleo, glyò, *n. m.* a dazzling kind of haziness about the eyes, as a person losing sight, *or* threatened with a cataract.

Gleodhadh, glyô'-Ă, *n. m.* tipsiness.

Gleog, glyóg, *n. f.* a blow, a slap. *H. S.*

Gleogair, glyog'-ar', *n. m.* stupid fellow.

Gleoid, glyôjd, *n. f.* bewildered female.

Gleoidseach, glyòjsh'-ach, *n. f.* stupid woman.

Gleoidsear, gly'-ôjsh-ăr', *n. m.* a stupid man.

Gleodhaman, glyó-am-an, *a.* silly man.

Gleorann, glyô'-rann, *n. m.* cresses; biollair.

Gleosg, glyosg, }
Gleosgaid, glyosg-'aj, } *n. f.* a silly blustering humdrum of a female.

Gleus, glās, *v.* tune, attune, put in trim, prepare; *gleus* an fhìodhull, *tune the fiddle* or *violin*; *gleusaibh* bheir cridheachan gu ceòl, *attune your hearts to music*; *ghleus* iad na h-eich, *they trimmed* or *harnassed the horses. Maclachlan.*

Gleus, glās, *n. m.* trim, order, condition; lock of a gun; screw of a spinning-wheel; gamut in music; preparation; dè an *gleus* a th'ort, *how do you do, how are you?* readiness for action; tha iad air *ghleus, they are in trim, in readiness for action*; cuir air *ghleus, prepare, make ready*; trim; thug aois dhiom *gleus, age deprived me of my trim* or *readines for action, Ossian*; chaidh e air *ghleus, he put himself in preparation. Maclachlan.*

Gleusadair, glās'-ad-ar', *n. m.* tuner, trimmer.

Gleusda, glāsd'-ă, *a.* in trim, ready, clever well exercised; well accomplished, is *gleusda* a gheibhear e, *he does well, he is clever*; keen.

Gleusdachd, glāsd'-achg, *n. f.* expertness, cleverness; attention and success in business.

Glib, glip, glĕpp, *n. f.* weather in which sleet and showers of hail prevail alternately; raw weather.

Glibeil, glĕpp'-al, *a.* sleety and showery with hail now and then.

GLIBHEID, glēv′-aj, *n. f.* weather in which a curious mixture of rain, sleet, and hail prevails.

GLIBHEIDEACH, glēv′-ăj-ach, *a.* rainy, sleety, thawing.

GLIC, glēchg[2], *a.* wise, prudent; na's *glice, wiser,* or *most wise,* or *prudent,* or *sagacious.*

GLIDICH, glėjj′-ėch, *v.* move, stir. *Perth.*

GLINN, glĕnn, *n. pl.* glens, valleys.

GLIOCAS, glĕuchg′-as, *n. m* wisdom, prudence.

GLIOCAIRE, glėuchg′-ăer-ă, } *n. m.* a wise
GLIOCASAIR, glėuchg′-ăs-ăr′, } man, a philosopher, in a good sense, a sage.

GLIOG, glĕug, *n. m.* motion: cha d' thoir e *gliog* as, *he cannot stir or move it.*

GLIOGARSAICH, glēg′[2]-ar-sėch, *n. m.* dangling and tingling; also gliogartaich.

GLIOMACH, glēm′-ach, *n. m.* an enormous man's ———.

GLIONG, gleung, *n. m.* clang, tingle, jingle; *v.* tingle, jingle, clash, as metals.

GLIONGARSAICH, } gleung′-art-ars-ėch, *n. f.*
GLIONGARTAICH, } a continuous tingling, ringing noise.

GLIUCHD, glĕŭchg, *n. m.* a bumper, a gulf; a blubbering and sobbing.

GLOC, glochg, *n. m.* a large wide throat *or* mouth; the bung of a cask; clucking of hens; a' *glocail, clucking.*

GLOCAN, glochg′-an, *n. m.* a bird cherry; bung.

GLOG, glŏg, *a.* sudden, hazy calm *or* sleep.

GLOGACH, glog′-ach, *a.* soft, lubberly.

GLOGAID, glog′-aj, *n. f.* a lubberly female.

GLOGAINN, glog′-ėnn, *n. f.* a sudden, hazy kind of calm, with sometimes puffs of soft wind; stupor, dozing slumber.

GLOGAIRE, glŏg′-ar′, *n. m.* a lubber.

GLOGLUINN, glog′-llėnn, *n. f.* rolling of the sea; a calm. *H. S.*

GLOICHG, gloėchg, *n. f.* a stupid female.

GLOICHDEIL, glŏėchg′-al, *a.* idiotical, as a female, stupid, senseless.

GLOINE, glaŏn′-a, *n. m.* glass, drinking glass, a bumper, a pane of glass.

GLOIR, glôėr, *n. f.* glory, state of bliss; treun thar *glòir, powerful beyond praise.*

GLOIREIS, glôėr′-ash, *n. f.* prating nonsense.

GLOIRIONN, glôr′-unn, *adj.* of an ugly drab colour.

GLOIRMHOR, gloer′-vur, *a.* glorious. *Bible.*

GLOMAINN, glôm′-ėnn, *n. f.* twilight, dawn.

GLOMHAR, glov′-ar, *n. m.* a gag in beasts; thàinig an *glomhasas, he is ungagged.*

GLOMHAS, glôv′[2]-us, *n. m.* a horrible chasm.

GLOMNAICH, glôm′-nėch, *v.* dawn.

GLONN, glŏnn, *n. m.* feat, qualm. *H. S.*

GLUAIS, glŭăĕsh, *v.* move, bestir, stir, make a motion, get up; *gluais* as an so, *move out of this*; *gluais* gu blàr, *bestir yourself to the battle-field*; *ghluais* o'n ear a mhaidinn ghlan, *radiant morn advanced from the east, Oss.*; affect, agitate; *ghluaiseadh* an righ, *the king was affected* or *agitated*; *ghluais* iad thun a bhaile, *they proceeded towards the town, Oss. Bible,* &c.; an ni nach cluinn cluas cha *ghluais* e cridhe, *what does not reach the ear cannot affect the heart*; *ghluais* e an t-ùisge, *he agitated the water*; *gluaiste, moved, agitated.*

GLUASAD, glŭăs′-ad, *n. m.* motion, movement, agitation, conduct, behaviour; gun *ghluasad, without motion*; ann ad *ghluasad, in your behaviour, in your bearing*; *gluasad* sèimh, *unostentatious behaviour*; gesture, gait, carriage; tha *gluasad* mna uaillse aice, *she has the gait of a lady*; *pt.* moving, stirring.

GLUG, glug, *n. m.* rumbling noise, as fluids; a rumbling stutter *or* stammer; *v.* stammer.

GLUGACH, glug′-ach, *a.* rumbling noise *or* stammer; *n. f.* stammering female.

GLUGAIRE, glŭg-ăĕr-ă′, *n. m.* rumbler.

GLUINEACH, glŭėn-ach′, *a.* in-kneed, having joints, as reeds; jointed; *n. f.* in-kneed female; large-kneed female.

GLUINEAN, glŭėn-an′, *n. m.* a garter. *Skye.*

GLUM, glum, *n. f.* large mouthful of liquids. *H. S.*

GLUN, glûn, *n. m.* a knee, a joint in reeds; *glùin,* glùintean, *knees*; bean *ghlùin, midwife*; an t-aon nach teasgaisgear ris a' *ghlùn,* cha fhòghlumar ris an ullainn, *the child that is not taught at the knee, cannot be taught at the elbow*; *glun*-lubadh, *genuflexion.*

GLUT, glŭt, *n. m.* a gulp, a glut; *v.* gulp, glut.

GLUTAIRE, glŭt′-ăr′-ă, *n. m.* glutton.

GNAITHSEACH, grà′-shach, *n f.* arable land under crop.

GNAITHSEAR, grà′-shar, *n.m.* husbandman.

GNATH, grà, *n. m.* custom, habit, manner, practice; mar bu *gnàth* leis, *as his practice* or *manner was*; talla do'n *gnàth* na cuirm, *halls where feasting* (hospitality,) *was the fashion* or *frequent. Oss.*; an, do, or a *ghnàth, always, habitually*; *adj. gnàth* obair, *constant work*; *gnàth* chleachdainn, *habitual practice.*

GNATHACH, grà′-ach, *a.* customary.

GNATHACHADH, grà′-ach-Ă, *n. m.* behaviour, conduct, custom, practice; do dhroch *ghnathachadh, your own bad habits* or *behaviour, your evil conduct.*

GNATHAICH, gnàith, gràėch, *v. n.* use, make a practice of, behave: gnàith nec *gnàthaich* thu fhéin gu ceart, *behave yourself properly*; a' *gnàthachadh* tombaca, *using tobacco*; is dona a *ghnàthaich*, e i, *he behaved very ill to her, he conducted himself very ill towards her.*

GNATHFHACAL, grà ăchg-al, *n. m.* a proverb, an aphorism, a wise saying.

GNATHTA, grà'-tyă, *adj.* arable; talamh *gnathta, arable land.*

GNE, grè, *n. f.* expression of countenance, complexion; a slight degree of the nature of any thing; a tinge, *or* tincture; in the Bible, species, kind, sort; is dona a *ghnè* a th' air, *his expression of countenance does not bespeak any thing good, his physiognomy is greatly against him*; ainfhir a bu mhìne gnè, *a virgin of the mildest complexion, Oss.*; *gnè* chreadha, *a slight degree of clay*—clayish, (as soil); *gnè* dheirge, *a tinge,* or *tincture of red*; gach creutair a réir an *gnè*, *every beast after its kind, B.*; nature, quality.

GNEIDHEALACHD, grè'-al-achg, *n. f.* state of having much of the milk of human kindness; tenderness, good nature.

GNEIDHEIL, grè'-al, *adj.* humane, kindly, tender, urbane.

GNIOMH, grēv, *n. m.* work, action, a deed; office; a farm stewart, *or* overseer; the seventh sheaf as payment to the hinds that work the farm of tenants or landlords; the building of a peat stack, *or* hewn stones; droch *ghnìomh, bad deed*; *gnìomh* mnà-ghlùin, *the office of a midwife*; phàidh an *gnìomh* mi, *the overseer paid me*; *v.* build or pile as a peat stack, or wall of hewn stones; *gnìomh* duine, *the office or work of any man*; an exploit.

GNIOMHACH, grēv'-ach, *adj.* active, busy, making great or good deeds.

GNIOMHACHAS, grēv'-ach-as, *n. f.* industry; office of an overseer.

GNIOMHARRAN, grēv'-arr-an, *n. f.* deeds, &c.

GNOG, grog, *v.* knock down, kill; knock against; a' *gnogadh* an cinn, *knocking their heads against each other.*

GNOGACH, grŏg'-ach, *a.* sulky, peevish.

GNOIG, grŏĕg, *n. f.* a surly old-fashioned face on a young person; sulks.

GNOIGEIS, grŏĕg'-ash, *n. f.* peevishness, sulks.

GNOIGEISACH, grŏĕg'-ash-ach, *adj.* peevish, sulky as a young person; grim.

GNOIMH, grŏĕv, *n. f.* a grin, greann.

GNOIN, gróen, *v.* shake and scold a person at the same time; a' *gnoineadh, scolding and shaking a person at the same time.*

GNOMH, grŏff, *v.* grunt like a pig.

GNOS, gros, *n. m.* snout of a beast.

GNOSAIL, gros'-al, *n. f.* a grunt; *pt.* grunting.

GNOTHACH, } GNOTHUCH, } gró'-ach, *n. m.* business, message, matter.

GNUGAG, grûg'-ag, *n. f.* sulky female.

GNUGACH, grug'-ach, *a.* surly, sulky.

GNUGAIR, grûg'-ăr, *n. m.* a surly fellow.

GNUIG, grûĕg, *n. f.* a surly lowering expression of countenance.

GNUIS, grûsh, *n. f.* countenance, face.

GNUIS-BHRAT, grûsh'-vrat, *n. f.* a veil.

GNUISFHIONN, grûsh'-unn, *a.* white-faced.

GNUISFHIOSACHD, grûsh'-ēs-achg, *n. f.* physiognomy.

GNUSAD, grus'-ad, *n. m.* low moan by a cow before lowing; also, gnòsad, gnùsadaich, a continuous moaning.

GO, gô, *n. m.* guile, deceit; duine gun *ghò*, *a guileless man*; dà reith gun *ghò*, (ghoaid,) *two rams without blemish. B.*

GOB, gob, *n. m.* a bill *or* beak of a bird.

GOBACH, gob'-ach, *a.* beaked; *n. f.* a scold.

GOBAG, gob'-ag, *n. f.* a dog-fish.

GOBAIRE, gob'-ur-ă, *n. m.* trifling prater.

GOBHA, GOBHAINN, gō2'-ă, *n. m.* blacksmith; *gobha* dubh, *water ousel.*

GOBHALL, gȯ'-ull, *n. f.* props, support; pair of compasses; *n. m.* space between the legs.

GOBHAR, gŏ'-ur, *n. f.* a she goat; in Perth a sort of branching river, and therefore, gobhar is pronounced gă'-ur.

GOBHLACH, gōll'-ach, *adv.* astride; *adj.* forked, pronged, long-legged.

GOBHLAN, gō2-ll'-an, *n. m.* a fork.

GOBHLAN-GAOITH, gȯll-an-gāoèch', *n. m.* swallow; gobhlan-gainich, *sand martin.*

GOBHLAISGEACH, gōll'-ashg-ach, *n. c.* a long-legged person.

GOC, gochg, *n. m.* a fawcet; *v.* bristle.

GOCAICH, gochg'-èch, *v.* cock, bristle.

GOCAM-GO, gŏchg-am-gô', *n. m.* a spy, scout, a fellow perched on any place.

GOCAMAN, gochg'-am-an, a domestic sentinel, one on the look-out in a mast, &c.

GOD, god, *v.* toss the head; cha'n e *godadh* nan ceann a ni an t-iomram, *tossing the head will not make the boat row.*

GOG, gog, *v.* cackle as a hen; toss.

GOGAID, gog'-aj, *n. f.* light-headed girl.

GOGAIDEACH, gog'-ăj-ach, *a.* light-headed.

GOGAIDEACHD, gog'-ajj-achg, *n. f* giddiness.

GOGAN, gog'-an, *n. m.* wooden dish.

GOGCHEANNACH, gog'-chyann-ach, *a.* lightheaded.

GOIBHNEACHD, gŏĕn'-achg, *n. f.* blacksmith's trade.

GOIBHRE, goyr'-ă, *gen.* she goat.

GOIC, gŏĕchg, *n. f.* a wry-neck, in despite.

GOICEIL, gŏĕchg'-al, *adj.* disdainful.

GOID, gŏĕjj, *v.* steal, pilfer; sneak, slip; also *plur.* of gad, wythes; *goid* a stigh, *slip in*; *pt.* stealing.

GOIL, gaŏ'l, *v.* boil as liquid, *pt. n. f.* boiling; air *ghoil, at the boiling point.*

GOILE, gul'-ă, *n m.* stomach, appetite.

GOILEACH, gul′-ach, *a.* boiling as liquids, hot, at the boiling point.

GOILEADAIR, gul′-ad-ar′, *n. m.* a kettle.

GOILEAM, gŏl′-um, *n. m.* incessant, high-toned, chattering *or* prattle.

GOILEAMACH, gŏl′-um-ach, *adj.* prating.

GOILL, gōělly′[2], *n. f.* blubber-cheek, expression of discontent, *or* sullenness in the face.

GOILLEACH, gŏělly′[2]′-ach, *adj.* blubber-cheeked.

GOILLEAG, gō[2]lly″-ag, *n. f.* slap on the cheek.

GOILLIRE, gō[2]lly″-ur-a, *n. m.* blubber-cheeked fellow; in Lewis, a sea bird that comes ashore only in January; (blubber-cheeked female, goilleach.)

GOIMH, gŏěv, *n. f.* a pang; malice, grudge.

GOIMHEIL, gŏěv′-al, *adj.* venemous; inflicting pangs; bearing a grudge *or* malice.

GOINEIDEACH, gŏěn″-aj-ach, *n. c.* person hurt with an evil eye, *or* bewitched, (from gon.)

GOINOLLANN, gŏen′-ŏl-unn, *n. f.* bad kind of wool next the skin of a sheep.

GOINTE, góenty′-á, *pt.* hurt with an evil eye, piqued, galled to the core.

GOIR, gaŏěr, *v.* crow as a cock; sing as the cuckoo; to apply it to a person is not good *or* polite.

GOIREAS, goăěr′-as, *n. m.* family necessary, *Is.*; a tool, apparatus; (acfhuinn,) *H. S.* written also, gaireas.

GOIREASACH, găŏěr′-as-ach, *adj.* useful, needful.

GOIRSINN, gaŏěr′-shènn, *n. f.* cock-crowing, singing as a cuckoo; *pt.* crowing, &c.

GOIRT, gŏěrty′, *adj.* sore, painful; severe, sour, acid; salt; cas *ghoirt, sore foot*; deuchainn *ghoirt, severe trial*; baine *goirt, sour* or *acid milk*; sgadan *goirt, salt herring.*

GOIRTEAD, gōěrty′[2]′-àd, degree of soreness.

GOIRTEAN, gōěrty′[2]′-an, *n. m.* a field of arable land, an inclosure, a park.

GOIRTEAS, gŏirty′[2]′-us, *n. m.* soreness; saltness, painfulness; sourness, acidity.

GOIRTICH, gōěrty″-èch, *v.* hurt, pain, gortaich.

GOISINN, gōsh[2]′-ènn, *n. m.* a trap. *H. Soc.*

GOISDIDH, gōshjj[2]′-è, *n. m.* gossip; godfather.

GOISDEACHD, gōěsh[2]′-achg, *n. f.* office, *or* duty of a godfather; ri *goisdeachd, assuming the office of a god-father.*

GOMAG, gòm′-ag, *n. f.* a nip, criomag, miogag.

GON, gŏn, *v.* hurt with an evil eye; pique *or* gall to the core; a *ghon* thu, *that galled you*; a′ *gonadh, hurting* or *galling intensely.*

The Arabs pray that an evil eye may not hurt their favourite horses; and hence, the learned Dr. Clarke argues, that the Irish and Scotch Gael must have carried this superstitious practice from the East. *Clarke's Travels.*

GORACH, gôr′-ach, *a.* silly, foolish.

GORAICH, gôr′-èch, *n. f.* folly; mo *ghòraich* 's coireach rium, *my own folly is the cause. Sm.*

GORAG, gôr′-ag, *n. f.* silly female; young she-crow; goracan, *a young he-one,* or *silly fellow.*

GORM, gŏrm, *adj.* blue, azure; also, green, as grass; feur *gorm, green-grass*; each *gorm, dark grey horse*; aodach *gorm, blue cloth*; *v.* and *pt.* dye blue, make blue; a′ *gormadh, dyeing blue*; *n. m.* blue colour; an *gorm* is an dubh, *the blue and black.*

GORMAN, gŏrm′-an, *n. m.* a wood, a plant.

GORMGHLAS, gorm′-ghlăs, *a.* sea-green.

GORN, gŏrn, *n. m.* an ember, eibhleag. *H. S.*

GORT, gŏrt, *n. f.* famine, starvation, letter *g.*

GORTACH, gŏrt′-ach, *a.* hungry; miserly.

GORTACHD, gŏrt′-achg, *n. f.* starvation, extreme degree of famine *or* hunger.

GORTAICH, gôrt′-èch, *v.* hurt, get sour, &c

GOTH, gŏ, *v.* toss the head contemptuously, *or* giddily; gothail, *airy, giddy.*

GRAB, grab, *v.* obstruct, restrain, intercept, hinder, prevent, impede, stop, molest.

GRABADH, grab′-Ă, *n. m.* obstruction, hindrance, impediment; *pt.* hindering, detaining.

GRABAIRE, grăb′-ăr[2]-a, *n. m.* obstructer.

GRABH, grâv, *v.* engrave; *n. m.* horrid thing. *North.*

GRABHALTAIR, grâv′-alt-ăr′, *n. m.* engraver.

GRAD, grad, *adj.* quick, nimble; irascible, irritable, very quick in motion; *adv.* uncommonly quick *or* agile; cho *ghrad* is a dh′ èirich e, *he rose so suddenly, so nimbly*; *ghrad* chlisg e, *he quite of a sudden started.*

GRADAG, grad′-ag, *n. f.* hurry, extreme haste, jiffy; cha d′ thig e an *gradaig, he will not come in a hurry*; bi an so an *gradaig, be here instantly.*

GRADCHARACH, grad′-chăr-ach, *a.* very agile.

GRADCHARACHD, grad′-char-achg, *n. f.* agility.

GRADH, grâ-gh′, *n. m.* extreme love *or* affection; a dearest dear, *or* loveliest of darlings; da d′ thug m′ anam *gràdh, whom my soul excessively loved*; a *ghràidh, my dearest dear, my darling*; charity, humanity. *Bible.*

GRADHACH, grâ-gh′-ach, *adj.* dearest, greatly loved.

Gradhachd, grà-aŏhg''-achg, *n. f.* extreme love.

Gradhaich, grâgh'-èch, *v.* love to distraction, love in the highest degree; *gràdh* dhaoine, *philanthropy.*

Gradhmhor, grâ-gh''-var, *a* greatly beloved.

Graide, grajj'-à, *n. f.* quickness, quicker.

Graideachd, grajj'-achg, *n. f.* degree of quickness.

Grain, gràèn, *n. f.* disgust, loathing.

Graineag, gràn'-ag, *n. f.* a hedge-hog.

Grainealachd, gràèn'-al-achg, *n. f.* abomination, abominableness, detestableness, loathsomeness.

Graineil, gràèn'-al, *a.* disgusting.

Graing; see Sgraing, dreang.

Grainich, gràèn'-èch, *v. n.* detest, loathe, impress with disgust; aversion *or* loathing.

Grainne, gràn'-nà, } *n. f.* a grain; a
Grainnean, gràèn'-nyan, } pellet of shot; a small number *or* quantity of any thing, particularly granulated substances.

Grainneanaich, gràèn'-nyan-èch, *v.* granulate; make into small grains.

Grainnseach, gràènn'-shyach, *n. f.* a granary; confounded with gnàithseach, land under cultivation.

Grainnseag, gràènn'-shag, *n. f.* bearberry.

Graisg, grâèshg, *n. f.* rabble, mob, low people.

Graisgealachd, grâèshg'-all-achg, *n. f.* vulgarity, blackguardism, turbulence.

Graisgeil, gràèshg'-al, *a.* vulgar, low, mean, blackguardish.

Graitinn, grà'-tyènn, *pt.* saying, affirming, hence; mor-ghràitinneach, beag-*ghràitinn, babbling, taciturn, fashionably,* ràidhtinn, see abair 'ag radh.

Gramaich for greimich.

Gran, gràn, *n. m.* kiln-dried grain.

Granabhall, gran'-a-vull, *n. f.* pomegranate; seorsa do *ubhall* mhòr. *Bible.*

Granna, grànn'-à, *adj.* ugly, shameful; causing shame; murdered, grada, grannda, &c.

Grannachd, grànn'-achg, *n. f.* ugliness.

Grapa, gràp'-à, *n. m.* dung-fork.

Gras, grâs, *n. m.* grace, favour; grace in the soul; free love.

Grasail, gràs'-al, *adj.* gracious.

Grasalachd, gràs'-al-achg, *n. f.* graciousness.

Grasmhor, gràs'-vur, *adj.* gracious.

Grasamhorachd, gràs'-vur-achg, *n. f.* graciousness, benignity, gloriousness.

Grath, gră, *adj.* fearful, ugly. *North.*

Grathunn, gră'-unn, *n. f.* a long *or* considerable time; a while—short while.

Gread, grād²'-v, drub, whip lustily; dry.

Greadadh, grăd²'-ă, *n. m.* drubbing, whipping lustily; *pt* drubbing.

Greadan, grăd²'-an, *n. m.* a considerable time with all your might at any thing, parched corn, nome made snuff.

Greadh, gryaŏgh', *n. f.* joy, happiness; stud of brood mares; stud of horses.

Greadhaire, gryaŏgh'-ăr'-à, *n. m.* a stallion; stone-horse; an entire horse. *Islay*; in Lochaber, a groom; in Perth, a brutish fellow.

Greadhnach, gryāon'-ach, *adj.* joyful, cheerful, merry; from greadhuinn.

Greadhnachas, gryāon'-ach-us, *n. m.* joy, festivity, pomp; august appearance.

Greadhuinn, gryaŏ'-ènn, *n. f.* a convivial party, a festive group, a happy company.

Greaghlain, gryaŏgh'-lyan, *n. m.* an old starved horse; a donkey; an old sword.

Greallach, gryall'-ach, *n. f.* entrails; *a.* dirty.

Greallag, gryăll'-ag, *n. f.* a swing, swingle; ann an *greallag, in a swing*; *greallagan* a chroinn, *the plough's swingles.*

Greann, gryann, *n. f.* a grim, angry, surly look; appearance of rage; a head having the hair standing on end, and the hair dry and withered; a bristling of hair, as on an angry dog; ripple on the surface of water; *greann* air an fhairge, *the sea has a rippled scowling aspect.*

Greannach, gryann'-ach, *adj.* having a dry bristled hair; claigionn *greannach* cruaidh, *a hard dry-haired scalp. Ps.*; as a person crabbed-looking, irascible; diune *greannach, an irascible* or *fiery person, as weather lowering and gloomy*; feasgar *greannach, a lowering windy evening*; *threatening evening.*

Greannaich, gryánn'-èch, *v.* bristle, get angry with; *ghreannaich* e rium, *he bristled, he enraged against me.*

Greannar, greannmhor, gryánn'-vur, *adj.* lively, active, pleasantly droll, *or* facetious.

Greas, grās², *v. n.* hasten, urge, drive on, mend your pace; *greas* ort, *make haste.*

Greasachd, grās²'-achg, *n. f.* hastening, quickening, urging; also greasadh.

Greasad, grās²'-ud, *n. m.* act of hastening.

Greidlean, grăjj'-lyen, stick for leavening bread; in baking, bread-stick.

Greidh, grāè'-yh', *v.* toast as bread; a *grèidheadh* an arain, *toasting bread*; cure as fish; a *grèidheadh* an éisg, *curing the fish*; a' *grèidheadh* san t-sàbhail, *winnowing in the barn. Jura*; (a' cathadh.)

Greidheadh, gră'-a², *pt.* dressing, curing,

toasting, winnowing; *n. m.* act of curing or state of being cured, toasting, &c.; *grèidhte*, cured, toasted, winnowed.

Greigh, grā'-y'^{2}, *n.f* uncommon heat of the sun after bursting out from under a cloud; also greighinn.

Greighire, grā^{2}'-ĕr-à, *n. m.* gnat, gad-fly.

Greim, grām, *n. m.* a piece bread; stitch in sewing; a stitch, *or* pain; a bit, *or* bite; a hold, custody; *greim* biodhaich, *a morsel of food*; *greim* san aodach, *a stitch in the cloth*; tha 'n deadh *greim* aige, *he has a firm hold*; tha e an *greim*, *he is in custody, as a horse, employed*; cha 'n 'eil *greim* agad air, *you have no hold of him* or *it*.

Greimeadas, grām'-ad-as, *n. m.* a hold, tenement.

Greimealas, grām'-al-as, *n. m.* firmness of hold, *or* capability of holding well.

Greimich, grām'-ĕch, *v. n.* hold fast, cleave to, cling to; *n. m.* a flesh-hook; vice, glamus.

Greimir, grām'-ur', *n. m* pincers, turcais.

Greine, grān'-à, *gen.* of sun, grian.

Greis, grāsh^{2}, *n. f.* a while, space of time.

Greus, grās, *n. f.* embroidery; *v.* embroider.

Greusaich, grès'-ĕch, *n. m.* a shoemaker; frog-fish, *or* chub, *or* lump.

Greusachd, grès'-achg, *n. f.* shoe-making.

Grian, grĕăn, *n. f.* the sun.

Grianach, grĕăn'-ach, *a.* sunny, warm.

Grianachd, grĕăn'-achg, *n. f.* sunshine.

Grianair, grĕăn'-ar, *v.* bask in the sun, also grianaich 'ga *grianradh* fhèin, *basking himself in the sun.*

Grianan, grĕăn'-an, *n. m.* a drying place for any thing, particularly peats.

Grian-chrios, grĕăn'-chrès, *n. m.* zodiac.

Grid, grējj, a very keen penurious female-quality, substance. *H. Society.*

Grideil, grejj'-al, *adj.* very keen *or* industrious.

Grinn, grēnn, *adj.* very kind, very polite; *n. f.* fine as linen, &c.; duine *grinn*, *a very kind person*; anart *grinn*, *very fine linen*; a's *grinne*, *kinder, politer, finer*; *adv.* very kindly *or* politely; *n. f.* a girning expression of countenance.

Grinneach, grēnn'-ach, *n. m.* stripling. *H.*

Grinneas, grēnn'-as, *n. m.* kindness, extreme kindness *or* politeness; fineness, neatness.

Grinnich, grēnn'-ĕch, *v.* polish, finish.

Griob, grēb, *v.* nibble, moibeil. *H. S.*

Griobh, grēv, *n. m.* a pimple, guirean.

Griobhach, grēv^{2}'-ach, *n. f.* the measles; mispronounced grū'-ach; see page 23.

Griobhag, grēff'-ag, *n. f.* hurry-burry in a neat manner; genteel hurry.

Griobhagach, grēff^{2}'-ag-ach, *a.* in a hurry-burry about trifles, *or* nothing at all.

Griobharsgaich, grēv'-arsg-ĕch, *n. f.* a rush of pimples through the skin; lichen, *or* a kind of scum on water.

Griobhlach, grūl'-ach, measles. *Skye.*

Griobhrach, grūr'-ach, measles. *Inverness.*

Grioch, gre'ch', *n. m.* a lean deer. *H.*

Griochaire, grēch'-ur-a, *n. m.* an invalid.

Griogag, grēg'-ag, *n. f.* a small cheese, *Is.*; a bead *or* pebble. *Lewis, Lochaber.*

Grioglachan, grēg'-lach-an, *n. m.* the plough *or* constellation of seven stars.

Grios, grēss, *v.* blaspheme; entreat by every thing that is holy, beseech.

Griosadair, grēs'-ad-ăr', *n. m.* a blasphemer; ri *griosadaireachd*, *blaspheming.*

Griosach, grēss'-ach, *n. f.* fire of embers.

Grioth, grè, *n. f.* a gravel pit, pebble.

Griothalach, grè'-al-ach, *n. f.* gravel. *Is.*

Gris, grēsh, *n. f.* perspiration *or* sweat produced by the idea of horror; great horror; horrified expression *or* appearance; the horrors; thug e *gris* orm, *he put me in the horrors*: heat.

Griseach, grēsh'-ach, *adj.* shivering, fond of the fire, *North*; *West*, dis.

Grisfhionn, grēss'-unn, *adj.* brindled.

Griuthach, for griuthach, griulach; see Griobhach.

Grob, grôb, *v.* groove, sew awkwardly, cobble; *n. m.* a groove; a' *gròbadh*, *grooving, &c.*

Grobag, grŏb'-ag, *n. f.* a broken tooth, a little female with broken teeth.

Groc, grôchg, *v.* threaten in order to frighten children; croak; gròcail, *croaking.*

Grod, grŏd, *adj.* rotten, putrid; *v.* rot, get putrid, become putrid, cause to rot; a *grodadh*, *becoming putrid, rotting*; iasg *grod*, *putrid fish.*

Grodair, grŏd'ur-a, *n. m.* a stinking fellow, *or* a putrid fish.

Grogach, grôg'-ach, *adj.* awkward.

Grogaire, grôg'-ur-à, *n. m.* a bungler, awkward fellow.

Groig, grôèg, *v.* bungle, botch.

Groigean, see Grogaire.

Groigealais, grôèg'-al-ash, *n. f.* unhandiness.

Groigeil, grôèg'-al, *adj.* awkward, unhandy.

Groiseid, grôsh'-ăjj, *n. f.* a gooseberry; Scotch Groset.

Gruag, grŭăg, *n. f.* hair of the head, wig.

Gruagach, grŭăg'-ach, *n. f.* damsel, a bride's maid of honour; a supposed household goddess; *adj.* having a beautiful head of hair.

Gruagaire, grŭăg'-ur-à, *n. m.* wig-maker.

Gruaidh, grŭăè'-yh', *n. f.* the profile, cheek.

Gruaigean, grŭăĕg'-an', *n. m.* birses; muirlinn, 10.

Gruaim, grŭăĕm, *n. f.* gloom, sullenness.

Gruamach, grŭăm'-ach, *adj.* gloomy, sulky, morose, sullen; *a.* a forbidding face.

Gruamachd, grŭăm'-achg, *n. f.* gloominess, sullenness, surliness; unhappy temper.

Gruan, grŭăn, *n. m.* liver of a person, *or* four-footed beast; of a fish, àithne; *a deep moan.*

Grudaire, grûd'-ărr-å, *n. m.* brewer, distiller, mashman, a publican.

Grugach, grûg'-ach, *adj.* sullen, having a gloomy surly face; *n. f.* a surly female.

Grugaire, grûg'-ur-å, *n. m.* morose man.

Gruid, grûjj, *n. f.* lees, dregs, grounds.

Gruig, grûég, *n. f.* a morose, cast-down, sullen countenance, a sullen look *or* expression.

Gruigh, grŭègh, *n.m.* a dish of curds dressed with butter, &c.

Grunn, grûnn, *n. m.* a crowd, a group; *grunn* dhaoine, a crowd of people, ground, bottom; *grunnan, a little group* or *crowd. Prov.*

Gruitheam, grŭĕ'-y'am, *n. m.* curd-pie.

Grullagan, grŭll'-ag-an, *a.* constellation *or* circle; a ring of people.

Grunnaich, grŭnn'-èch, *v.* sound the bottom; touch the bottom, as of the sea; deuch an *grunnaich* thu, *see if you touch the bottom of the water.*

Grunnasg, grŭnn'-ăsg, *n. m.* groundsel.

Grunnd, grûnnd, *n. m.* ground, attention, economy; dean le *grunnd* e, *pay attention to it, do it carefully*; decision of character; duine gun *ghrunnd, a man without decision of character.*

Grunndail, grŭnnd'-al, *adj.* very attentive and punctual; economical.

Grunndalachd, grŭnnd'-al-achg, *n. f.* attention to business; decisive character.

Gruth, grŭ-gh, *n. m.* curds.

Gu, gaŏ, *prep.* to; *gu* fichead, *to twenty*; also *sign of adverb*; *gu* fìor, *truly*; *gu* sìoruith, *gu* suthainn, *for ever*; *gu* minig, *often*; *gu* léir, *altogether.*

Guag, gŭăg, *a.* splay-foot; giddy fellow. *H.*; *guagaire, splay-footed fellow.*

Guailleach, gŭăèlly''-ach, **Guaillinneach**, gŭăèlly''-ènn-ach, *n. f.* shoulder-chain *or* strop of a horse.

Guaillean, gŭăèlly''-an', *n. m.* a cinder.

Guaillfhionn, gŭălly''-unn, *a.* white-shouldered.

Guaim, gŭăĕm, *n. f.* economy; attention to minute articles of gain; prudence.

Guain, gŭăèn, *n. f.* giddiness, lightness.

Guairne, gŭăĕny2'-å, *n. f.* an unshapely, unmannerly female.

Gual, gŭăl, *n. m.* coals; *v.* gall, pain most intensely; (lit.) burn to a cinder.

Gualadh, gŭăll'-X, *pt. n. m.* torturing, torture; greatest pain; tormenting.

Guallann, gŭăll'-unn, *n. f.* shoulder, mountain projection; stamina.

Guamach, gŭăm'-ach, *a.* economical, snug.

Guamachd, gŭăm'-achg, *n. f.* degree of economy.

Guanach, gŭăn'-ach, *a.* giddy, light-headed.

Guanag, gŭăn'-ag, *n. f.* light-headed girl.

Guanach, gŭăn'-ach, *adj.* giddy, light.

Guanalais, gŭăn'-al-ash, *n. f.* giddiness.

Gucag, gŭchg'-ag, *n. f.* a bud, a sprout; bell.

Guda, gûd'-å, a gudgeon.

Gug, gûgg, *n. m.* cluck as poultry.

Guidh, gŭĕ'-y', *v.* pray, entreat, beseech, wish earnestly; *v. n.* imprecate.

Guidhe, gŭĕ'-å, *n. f.* entreaty; a curse, an imprecation; *pt.* beseeching.

Guidhidinn, gŭi' dyènn, *n. f.* an injunction; a strict injunction *or* entreaty; *v.* enjoin; tha mi a' cur mar *ghuidhidinn* ort, *I enjoin, I lay you under an injunction, I entreat most earnestly.*

Guil, gŭĕl, *v.* weep, wail; *pt.* weeping.

Guilbearnach, gŭèl'-ăĕrny-ach, } a curlew.
Guilbneach, gŭĕlb'-nyach, *n. f.* }

Guileag, gŭĕl'-ag, *n. m.* a drawling screech, supposed to resemble the swan's note.

Guin, gŭĕn, *n. f.* a pang, dart; *v.* pain.

Guineach, gŭèn'-ach, *adj.* venomous, fierce.

Guir, gŭèr', *v.* hatch; watch strictly.

Guirean, gŭĕr''-an', *n. m.* a pimple; pustule.

Guirme, gŭĕrm'-å, degree of gorm; na's *guirme, bluer*; *n. f.* blueness.

Guirminn, gŭĕrm'-ènn, *n. m.* indigo.

Guirminnich, gŭèrm'-ènn-èch, *v.* tinge with blue, as linen; give a blue hue *or* tinge.

Guiseid, gŭsh'-ăj, *n. f.* a gusset of a shirt.

Guit, gŭty', *n. f.* fasgnag, a fan; Kintyre, giot.

Guitear, gŭĕty''-ar', *n. m.* kennel, sewer.

Gul, gŭll, *n. m.* weeping; *pt.* wailing.

Gun, gun, *prep.* without; *gun* eòlas, *ignorant*; *gun* fhiòs dè a nì mi, *not knowing what to do.*

Gun, gŭ'-ann, gùn, *n. m.* a gown; more properly gughann, gughann sìota, a silk gown.

Gunna, gŭnn'-å, *n. f.* a gun; *gunna*-mòr, *a cannon*; *gunna-glaic, a fusee*; *gunna* coal, *a fowling-piece*; *gunna* barraich, *or* sgailc, *a pop-gun*; *gunna*-dìollaid, *a holster.*

Gur, gŭr, *n. m.* a brood, a hatch, *or* an incubation; mar chearc a nì *gur, as a* *nen that hatcheth. B.*; *pt.* a' *gur, hatching, breeding, watching strictly.*

GURADAN, gŭr'-ad-an, *n. m.* a crouching attitude.

GURRACH, gŭrr' ach, *n. m.* a huge stupid fellow; a great blockhead; also gurraiceach.

GURRAICEIDEACH, gŭrr'-èchg-ajj-ach, a dotterel.

GUS, gus, (gas) *adv. conj.* and *prep.* until, till, into, to, in order that, as far as, so that; *gus* an till iad, *until they return*; *gus* am faic mi thu, *till I see you*; *gus* am bì mi, *till I be*; *gus* an am so an athbhliadhna, *till this time twelve-month, till this time next year*; a sheachduinn *gus* an dè, *yesterday se'ennight*; *gus* nach cluinnte e, *so that he could not be heard*; *gus* an so, *as far as this*; *gus* nach d' thigeadh e stigh, *so that he* or *it could not come in*; *gus* am b' fhearra dhomh, *so that it was better for me.*

GUSG, gŭsg, *n. m.* a bumper; fhuair thu fhéin a cheud *ghusg* dheth, *you yourself, got the first bumper of it.*

GUSGAN, gŭsg'-an, *n. m* a swig, a draught.

GUSGAL, gŭsg'-al, *n. f.* blubbering. *Macf.*

GUTH, gŭ-gh, *n. m.* a voice, a word, a syllable, a mention, report; chluala e *guth, he heard a voice*; dean *guth* rium, *speak a word*; cha chluala mi *guth* air riamh, *I never heard the slightest mention of it*; dh' aithnich mi a *ghuth, I recognised his voice*; na d' thoir *guth* air a leithid sin, *never mention such a thing*; *guth* caointeach, *a plaintive voice*; a warning, *or* secret hint from the dead; thàinig *guth* a dh' ionnsuidh, *a voice from the dead warned him.*

GUTHACH, gŭ'-ach, *a.* vocal; *n. f.* cuckoo.

GUTHAID, gu'-ăjt, *n. f.* place of an oracle; an oraculum. *Bible.*

H

H, h, this letter is not acknowledged in our Alphabet; but to keep the Gaelic in character with us, the Highlanders, who are THE BRAVEST and *most singular* people in the WHOLE WORLD, (as the SCOTS TIMES says,) it is used, not only in every word, but almost in every syllable expressed or understood.

I

I, i, the eighth letter of the Gaelic alphabet; styled Iubhar, the yew-tree. It has many sounds; i, sounds like ee in sheer; as, sìr, shēr, continually:—short; as, dis, dyĕsh.

I, ē, *pro.* she, her, it; *n. f.* an isle, Iona.

Iad, èd, *or* ĕăd, *pron.* they; *iad* fhéin, *they themselves*; in *Argyle* it should be written eud.

IADH, ĕaŏ-gh, *v.* surround; an saoghail ma 'n *iadh* grian, *the sun which surrounds the world.*

IADSAN, èd'-sun, *pro.* they, themselves.

IADHSHLAT, ĕă'-hlat, *n. f.* honey-suckle, woodbine; an t-eidheann, an fheulainn.

IAL, ĕăll, *n. f.* moment; gach *ial, every moment. Sm.*

IALL, ĕăll, *n. f.* a thong, leather strop.

IALLACH, ĕăll'-ach, *adj.* in strings.

IALTAG, ĕălt'-ag, a bat, beathach.

IAR, ĕăr, *n. f.* the west; an *iar, westward*; an *iar* is an *iar*-dheas, *west by south*; *adv.* westerly.

IARGAIN, ĕăr'-găĕn, *n. f.* the evil effects of any thing, lees of whiskey, (iarguinn.)

IARGAINEACH, ĕărg'-ăĕn-ach, *adj.* afflictive.

IARGALTA, ĕărg'-alt-ă, *adj.* turbulent.

IARGALTACHD, ĕărg'-alt-achg, *n. f.* turbulence, a turbulent disposition; also iargaltas.

IARLA, ĕărl'-ă, *n. m.* an earl, iarfhlath.

IARLACHD, ĕărl'-achg, *n. f.* earldom.

IARNAICH, ĕărn'-èch, *v.* iron, smooth with a hot iron as linen; ag *iarnachadh, smoothing, ironing as linen.*

IARNAIDH, ĕărn'-è, *adj.* iron like, very forbidding in features, hard, miserly.

IAROGH, ĕăr'-ō2, *n. c.* great-grandchild.

IARR, ĕărr, *v.* seek, ask; search for; pain *or* search as medicine; probe.

IARRAIDH, ĕăr'-è, *n. f.* a search, petition.

IARRTAS, ĕărrt'-as, *n. f.* petition, request.

IARRTASACH, ĕărrt'-as-ach, *adj.* soliciting, frequently asking *or* seeking.

IARTHUATH, ĕăr'-hŭă, *n. f.* the north-west.

IARUNN, ĕărr'-unn, *n. m.* iron, an iron.

IASACHD, IASAD, ĕăs'-achg, ĕăs'-ad, *n. f.* a loan.

IASG, ĕăsg, *n. m.* a fish, fishes, èisg.

IASGACH, IASGACHD, ĕăsg'-ach, *or* -achg, *n. m.* fishing, a take of fish; act *or* art of fishing.

IASGAICH, ĕăsg'-èch, *v.* fish, angle.

IASGAIR, ĕăsg'-ăr', *n. m.* fisher, fisherman.

IBH, ēv, *v.* drink; *n. f.* a drink.

IC, ēchg2, *v.* affix; *n. f.* an affix, appendix.

IDIR ĕjj'-èr', *adv.* at all; cha 'n 'eil *idir, not at all*; cha d' thig e *idir, he will not come at all*; cha 'n e *idir, that is not it at all.*

IFRINN, ĕff2'-runny', *n. m.* hell, Ifrionn

IFRINNACH, IFRIONNACH, ĕff'2'-runn-ach, *adj.* hellish, fiendlike; *n. m.* a fiend, demon.

Igh, ē-yh', *n. f.* tallow, geir. *H. S.*

Ila, ēll'-a, *n. m.* Islay, an island of Argyle, a Danish princess.

Ileach, ēl'-ach, *a.* belonging to Islay; an Islayman; ceann-*ileach*, *particular kind of sword made by smiths of the name of Maceachern*.

Illse, ēlly"-shă, *n. f.* lowness; *deg.* lower.

Illsich, elly"-shēch, *v.* lower, abase.

Im, ēm, *n. m.* butter.

Imcheist, ēm2'-chyăsht', *n. f.* perplexity, anxiety, distraction; an *imcheist*, *perplexed.*

Imcheisteach, ēm2-chyăst-ach, *adj.* perplexing, perplexed, distracting, distracted.

Imeachd, ēm2'-achg, *n. f.* travelling, departure, the very spot, distinction; ma'n *imeachd* so, *hereabouts*; dè 'n *imeachd* ma'n d' fhàg thu e, *whereabouts did you leave it.*

Imfhios, em"-ēss, *n. f.* hesitation, eve; an *imfhios* dol fodha, *almost sinking*, literally, hesitating whether to sink or swim; an *imfhios* teicheadh, *on the eve of scampering, hesitating whether to decamp*; an *imfhios* a chiall a' chall, *almost losing his senses, on the eve of losing his senses.*

Imire, ēm'-ēry'-ă, *n. m.* a ridge of land; *v. n.* behove, need: *imiridh* mi falbh, *I must go, it behoves me to go, I must be off.*

Imirich, ēm2'-ėr-ech, *v.* walk in ranks *or* procession, march.

Imireachadh, em'-ear'-ach-X, *pt.* walking in ranks, *or* procession; *n. m.* a procession; *imearachadh* an tòrraidh, *the funeral procession. Islay.*

Imir-chuimir, ēm2-ēr'-chūēm"-ėr, *adv.* wholly and solely, most completely *or* thoroughly; tha iad mar sin *imir-chuimir*, *they are so wholly and solely, thoroughly.*

Imleach, 2ēml"-ach, *n. m.* a licking.

Imlich, 2ēml'-ėch, *v.* lick with the tongue.

Impich, **Iompaich**, 2ēmp'-ėch, *v.* convert, persuade; dh' *impich* mi e dh' fhalbh, *I persuaded him to go*; dh' *iompachadh* e, *he was converted.*

Impidh, 2ēmp'-ē, *n. f.* prayer, persuasion, supplication.

Impis, ėmp'-ės, same as imfhios.

Imrich, ēm'-rėch, *n. f.* flitting, removing from one residence to another; *v.* remove residence, (iomairc.)

Inbh, ĕn'v', ėnn'a, *n. f.* eve, condition, rank, perfection, maturity as a person, state of advancement, progression, progress; dè an *inbh* a bheil thu, *how far have you advanced? what progress have you made?* tha mi an *inbhe* mhath, *I have made a considerable progress*; tha mi deas gu h-*inbhe* deich, *I am prepared, within ten*; bha mi an *inbh* is an dorus a dhùnadh, *I was on the eve of shutting the door, I was hesitating whether to shut the door*; am bheil iad an *inbhe* a bhi deas, *are they near a close.*

Inbheach, ēnv'-ach, *a.* mature, ripe, of a mature age; of rank.

Inbhidh, 2ēnv"-ē, mature, ripe, of a mature age; duine *inbhidh*, *a man come to the age of discretion*; perfection.

Inbhidheachd, 2ēnv'-ė-achg, *n. f.* perfection, maturity, years of discretion. *Islay.*

Inbhir, 2ēnn'-vėr', *n. f.* a cove *or* creek at the mouth of a river; meeting of the sea and river, confluence; hence, Inbhir-Aoradh, Inbhir-nis, Inbhir-lochaidh; Inverary, the mouth *or* confluence of the river Aoradh; Inverness, the confluence of the river Ness; the confluence of the river Lochy—(pronounced generally ēnn-ėr'); invhir a ghualaidh, *a haven in Jura.*

Inne, 2ēnn'-a, *n. f.* nail of the finger.

Inne, 2ēnn'-ă, *n. f.* the kennel, the gutter, a common sewer; tha t' aodann cho dubh ri clachan na h-*inne*, *your face is so black as the kennel stones*; in the Bible, entrails, mionnach.

Inneach, 2ēnn"-ach, *adj.* black, dirty, having nails; *n. m.* woof, (snath-cuir.)

Inneachas, ēnn"-ach-as, *n. m.* a scramble.

Inneal, 2ēnn"-all, *n. m.* machine, an engine, instrument, means, apparatus; *inneal*-ciuil, *musical instrument*; *inneal*-coise, *foot-step of a spinning wheel*; na bitheadh an t-*inneal* agam, *had I the means*; *inneal*-stoith, neo-toitlinn, *steam engine*; *inneal*-tarruinn, *a capstan*; *inneal*-buill, *a windlass.*

Innealta, 2ēnn'-alt-ă, *a.* ingenious.

Innealtachd, 2ēnn"-alt-achg, *n. f.* ingeniousness, ingenuity, fitness, aptness.

Innean, 2ēnn"-ăĕn', *n. f.* smith's anvil.

Inneanadh, 2ēnn"-an-X, *n. m.* deficiency of yarn in weaving.

Innear, 2ēnn"-ăr', *n. f.* cattle's dung, (from inne.)

Innich, ēnn"-ėch, *v. m.* scramble, struggle

Innidh, 2ēnny"-ė-ēch, *adj.* expert, clever, smart; gille *innidh*, *a clever, active young man.*

Innidheachd, 2ēnny"-ė-achg, *n. f.* expertness.

Innil, 2ēnn"-ėl, *v.* prepare, equip.

Innis, 2ēnn"-ėsh, *n. f.* choice pasture, an inclosure for cattle, choice place, *Islay*; *innis* nam bò laogh 's na fiadh, *choice place for milk cows and deer*; (Moladh na Lanntair,) *a resting place for cattle, an island, a headland*; (as in Craignish, Toirninish, &c.

Innis, ²ēnn′-ėsh, *v. n.* relate, tell, inform.

Innisg, ²ēnn′-ėshg, *n. f.* a libel, calumny, defamation, reproach; a tilgeadh *innisgean, defaming, reproaching, libelling.*

Innisgeach, ²ēnn″-ĕsk-ach, *adj.* reproachful, defamatory, disgraceful.

Innleachd, ēnn″-lyachg, *n. f.* invention, device, a stratagem; ingenuity, contrivance, power of invention, expedient; cha'n'eil e am *innleachdsa* sin dheanadh, *I cannot devise an expedient to serve you that way, it is not within the power of my invention to do that*; dealbhmaid *innleachdan, let us devise devices. B.*; ni airc *innleachd, a strait is the mother of invention*; am bheil e ad *innleachd* misc a leigeil air falbh, *is it within the compass of your invention to let me go?*

Innleachdach, ēnn″-lyachg-ach, *adj.* inventive, ingenious, fit to devise ways and means.

Innleachdair, ēnn″-lyachg-ar, *n. m.* inventor.

Innleag, ²ēnn′-lyag, *n. f.* a child's doll. *Ir.*

Innlinn, ēnn″-llyēnn²′, *n. f.* the third part of the straw left by the tenant removing for the one entering a farm, for bedding to the cattle to help manure; (inne, kennel, and lìon *or* linn, a proportionate quantity,) *Argyle*; in the Bible, provender, forage, fodder.

Innis-gaidheil, ²ēnn″-ėsh-găĕ-ėl, *n. f.* the Hebrides,—choice place of Highlanders.

Innse, ēnn″-shȧ, *n. f.* information, intelligence, report, sign; is dona an *innse* ort, *it is a very bad sign of you, report of you.*

Innseach, ²ēnn′-shyach, *adj.* insular; prone to inform against, tattling.

Innseag, ²ēnn′-shag, *n. f.* an eight *or* islet in a river; an isle.

Innsean, ēnn′-shan, *n. pl.* the Indies; *innsean* na h-aird' an ear is an iar, *the East and West Indies.*

Innseanach, ēnn′-shyan-ach, *n. m.* an Indian; *adj.* belonging to India.

Innte, ²ēnnjt′-tya, *pro.* and *prep.* within her *or* it.

Innteart, ²ēnnty″-ărjt, *n. f.* entry, beginning, also inntreadh, commencement.

Inntinn, ²ēnnty″-²ēnn′, *n. f.* mind, intellect, intention, intent, purpose, will, pleasure.

Inntinneach, ²ēnn″-tyėnn′-ach, *adj.* sprightly, lively, animated, elevated, elated, jolly, intellectual, sportive, merry, hearty, high-minded.

Inntir, ²ēnnty″-ėr, *v.* enter, introduce.

Inntrinn, ²ēnnty″-rēnn², *v.* enter, inntrig.

Iob, ēbb, lump of dough, uibe.

Iobair, ēbb′-ėr, *v.* sacrifice; dh' *iobair* iad uan, *they sacrificed a lamb. B.*

Iobairt, ēbb′-arjty′, *n. f.* sacrifice, offering

Iobartan, ēbb′-art-an, *n.* means to do evil.

Iobradh, ēb′-rae, *pt.* sacrificing.

Ioc, ēchg, *v.* pay; *n. m.* medicine; pay. *Ir.*

Iocshlaint, ēchg′-hláēnty′, *n. f.* balm, medicine, cordial, balsam; bheirinn mar *iocshlaint*, bainne mo chìochan do m' ghoal, *as a cordial I would give the milk of my breast to my love. Sm.*; b'e sin an *iocshlaint, that was the cordial. C.*

Iocshlainteach, ēchg′-hláēnty′-ach, *a.* balsamic, cordial as medicine; soothing, alleviating, salutary.

Iochd, ĕúchg, *n. m.* mercy, clemency, kindness, humanity, generosity, compassion; dean do ghearan ri fear gun *iochd* is their e, tha thu bochd, *complain to a man without compassion, and he shall say thou art poor!*

Iochdar, ēchg′-ur, *n. m.* the bottom, the lowest part; an *iochdar* dheth, *under, worsted, cheated*; *iochdar* is uachdar, *top and bottom.*

Iochdaran, ēchg′-aran, *n. m.* a subject, an underling, an inferior.

Iochdrach, ēchg′-rach, *adj.* nether, lowest, lowermost, nethermost; a chlach mhuilinn *iochdrach, the nether millstone*; ifrinn *iochdrach, the lowest hell.*

Iochdmhoireachd, ĕúchg′-vur′-achg, *n. f.* mercifulness, kindness, humanity, compassionate regard.

Iochdmhor, éŭchg′-vur, *adj.* compassionate, humane; merciful, compassionate.

Ioclus, ēchg′-lŭs, *n. f.* medicinal herb.

Iodhal, ĕú-gh′-ăll, *n. m.* an idol, image; luchd *iodhal* aoraidh, *worshippers of false gods, idolators, worshippers of images.*

Iogan, ēgg′-an, *n. m.* deceit, guile.

Ioghnadh, ĕùn′-nX̆, *n. m.* cause of surprise, curiosity, wonder; an exhibition of curiosities; show, play; surprise; cha bhitheadh *ioghnadh* orm, *I would not be surprised.*

Iol, ĕúl, an Irish prefix, signifying many, seldom *or* never used in Gaelic.

Iollag, ĕúll′-ag, *n. f.* a skip, trip; gu h-*iollagach, on the light fantastic toe.*

Iolla, ėúll′-a, *n. f.* sight, view; gabh *iolla, just look at it*;—fishing-station. *Skye.*

Iom, ²ēm, prefix, signifying many; im before e and i.

Iomach, ²ēm′-ach, *n. f.* various in colours; party-coloured; various; of various kinds. *Lw.*

Ioma-chomhairle, ēm′-a-chóv²-urly′-ȧ, *n. f.* perplexity, doubt, suspense.

Ioma-chruthach, ²ēm-a-chrŭ′-ach, *a.* having many forms *or* shapes; various, multiform.

Iomachain, ēm′-ach-ăn′, *n. f.* anxiety, solicitude.

Iomachaineach, ²ēm′-ăch-an′-ach, *a.* anxious.

Iomachuimhn, ²ēm′-a-chŭenn, *n. f.* anxiety, solicitude; tha e fodh *iomachuimhn, he is anxious* or *solicitous.*

Iomachuimhneach, ²ēm′-a-chŭĕnn-ach, *adj.* very anxious, very solicitous.

Iomachuinge, ²ēm′-ă-chŭėng-a, *n. f.* narrowness, extreme narrow-mindedness.

Iomachumhann, ²ēm′-a-chŭ-ann, *adj.* very narrow; very narrow-minded, *or* niggardly.

Iomad, ²ēm′-ad, *a.* many, various, divers; *iomad* seòl, *various ways, divers manners.*

Iomadh, ²ēm′-Ă, *n. m.* various, many, divers.

Iomadach, ēm′-ad-ach, *a.* many; *iomadach* uair, *often*; *iomadach* tè, *many a female*; *iomadach* fear, *many a man.*

Iomadaich, ²ēm′-ad-ėch, *v.* multiply.

Iomadaidh, ²ēm′-ad-ė, *n. f.* many; great number.

Iomadail, ēm′-ad-al, *adj.* multiplicable.

Iomadalachd, ²ēm′-ad-al-achg, *n. f.* multiplicity, plurality; oir thig aislinnean le *iomadalachd* ghnothaichean, *for dreams come through multitude of business. B.*

Iomadathach, ²ēm′-ad-ach, *a.* of many colours.

Iomagain, } ²ēm′-ag-aĕn′, *n. f.* anxiety,
Iomaginn, } great solicitude; fo *iomagain, solicitous.*

Iomagaineach, ²ēm′-găĕn-ach, *adj.* solicitous.

Iomaghaoith, ²ēm′-a-ghaŏėch, } *n. f.* eddy-
Iomaghaoth, ²ēm′-a-ghaŏ, } wind; in bad Gaelic, whirlwind.

Iomain, ²ēm′-ăĕn′, *n. f.* a drove of cattle; play at golf, *or* cricket, *or* shinty; *pt.* driving; fear-*iomain, a driver, drover*; *v.* drive, play at shinty; ag *iomain, playing at shinty, striking as with the foot.*

Iomair, ²ēm′-ėr′, *v.* row, pull, play at cards, backgammon, &c.; *iomair* Eachainn, dean fodha, a Ruaraidh, *pull* or *row, Hector—make back-water, Rory*; ag *iomairt* air chairtean, *playiag at cards*; ag *iomairt* air a' bhall-speil, *playing at hand-ball*; is dona a dh' *iomair* thu do chairtean, *you played your cards very ill*; *imp. v.* behove, must.

Iomairc, ²ēm′-ăĕrk, *n. f.* removal; *v.* remove.

Iomairt, ²ēm′-arjt, *n. f.* play, game, conflict, danger, hurry-burry, confusion; 'san orra a bha'n *iomairt, they were greatly confused*; ciuin, tlà ann a h-*iomairt, mild and gentle in danger,* distress; *pt.* playing, gaming, betting.

Iomairteach, ²ēm′-arjty'-ach, *adj.* betting, laying wagers; lavish.

Iomall, ²ēm′-all, *n. m.* outskirts, limit, border, refuse, remainder; an *iomall* na dùthcha, *in the outskirts of the country*; *iomall* a bhaile, *the outskirts* or *suburbs of the city*; aon *iomall* a bhìos aca, *any refuse they may have.*

Iomallach, ²ēm″-all-ach, *adj.* remote, distant; aiteanan *iomallach, remote* or *distant places, uttermost, farthest off*; a chuid a b' *iomallaiche* do 'n t-sluagh, *the uttermost of the people. B.*

Iomarbhuidh, ²ēm′-ur-v*h*ė, *n. f.* hesitation; confusion about what to do, or how to proceed.

Iomarcach, ²ēm′-arck-ach, *adj.* in many straits; in distress, distressed, (airc.)

Iomasgaoil, ²ēm′-a-skăoėl, *v.* slack, slacken, loosen, untighten.

Iomasgaoilte, ēm′-ask-aŏėl-tyȧ, *pt* loose, slack, slackened, loosened.

Iomasgaoilteachd, ēm′-ask-sgaŏėty'-achg, *n. f.* slackness, looseness, freedom.

Iomchair, ²ēm′-chăėr, *v.* bear, carry.

Iomchar, ²ēm′-char. *n. f.* bearing, carrying

Iomchoir, em′-chŏėr, *n. f* reflection; a cur *iomchoir* ormsa, *reflecting on me.*

Iomchuidh, ²ēm′-ach-ė, *a.* proper, fit, befitting; is *iomchuidh* sin duit, *that is be fitting your case*; mar chì thusa *iom chuidh, as you see proper*; is *iomchuidh* dhuit dol dachaidh, *it is highly proper that you should go home.*

Iomchuidheachd, ²ēm′-chŭĕ-achg, *n. f.* fitness, suitableness, propriety.

Iomdhruid, ²ēm′-a-ghrŭjj, *v.* inclose.

Iomfhuasgail, em′-ăŭsg-ėl, *v.* trade, relieve; loosen, slacken.

Iomfhuasgladh, ²ēm′-ŭăsg-lĂ, *n. m.* traffic, trade, something to trade with.

Iomhaigh, ēm′-ē²y*h*′, *n. f.* image, likeness, similitude, statute, expression of countenance; na *iomhaigh* féin, *in his own likeness.*

Iomhaigheachd, ēvv′-ē-achg, *n. f.* imagery, imagination; gach fear ann an seòmraichibh *iomhaigheachd* fhéin, *every one in the chambers of his own imagination.*

Iomlag, ²ēm′-llag, *n. f.* navel, nave.

Iomlaid, ²ēm′-llajj, *n. f.* exchange, course, duration; *v.* exchange; dean *iomlaid, exchange, barter*; ann an *iomlaid* dà latha, *in the course of two days, during two days.*

Iomlaideach, ²ēm′-llajj-ach, *adj.* fluctuating, tossing as a sick person, restless, tossing.

Iomlaideachd, ²ēm′-llajj-achg, *n. f.* unsteadiness, fickleness, changeableness.

Iomlaine, ²ēm′-láėn-ȧ, *deg.* of iomlan.

Iomlanachd, ėm′-lan-achg, } *n. f.* per-
Iomlaineachd, ²ēm′-lláėn-achg, } fection, integrity, maturity, completeness.

Iomlan, ^{2}ēm'-llan, *adj.* perfect, complete, full, sound, duine *iomlan, a perfect man.*

Iomluaisg, ^{2}ēm'-a-lŭăshg, *v.* disorder, confuse, toss, tumble.

Iomluasgadh, ^{2}ēm'-lŭăsg-X̆, *n. f.* confusion, commotion; *pt.* putting out of order, deranging.

Iom-oiseanach, ^{2}ēm'-ōsh-an'-ach, *a.* multtangular.

Iompachadh, ^{2}ĕmp'-ach-X̆, *pt.* converting, persuading; *n. f.* conversion, persuasion.

Iompaich, ēmp'-ėch, *v.* convert, impich.

Iompaidh, ēmp'-ī, *n. f.* means, medium, instrumentality, as a person to do good; persuasion.

Iomradh, ^{2}ēm'-ră, *n. m.* report, fame, renown, mention; tha t' *iomradh* feadh na tìre, *your fame* or *renown is spread throughout the land*; na d' thoir *iomradh* air, *never mention it*; tha leithid sin do *iomradh* measg dhaoine, *there is such a report among people.*

Iomraich, ^{2}ēm'-rėch, *v.* tell, bear.

Iomraiteach, ^{2}ēm'-rājt-ach, *a.* notorious, pub ic, far spread; ni *iomraiteach, a notorious thing*; eminent, far-famed, renowned; do cliù *iomraiteach, your fame is well known*; dh' fhàs iad na daoine *iomraiteach, they became men of renown, Bible*; written iomraidhteach also.

Iomrall, ^{2}ēm'-rrăll, *n. m.* an error, entanglement, entwining; chaidh e *iomrall* orm, *it was mislaid, I missed it, I went wrong, I erred,* ioma-roll.

Iomram, Iomramh, ^{2}ēm'-ram, *n. m.* rowing.

Ion, ĕŭn, *adv.* having great *or* fit reason *or* cause; *adj.* fit, befitting; is *ion* duit teicheadh, *you have great reason to scamper*; cha 'n *ion* dhomhsa ach bhi ga d' moladh, *it is befitting indeed that I should praise thee*; cha 'n *ion* ni sam bith a dhiùltadh, *nothing is proper to be refused, Bible*; a prefix, signifying worthy, befitting.

Ionad, eun'-ad, *n. m.* place, situation; *ionad* naomh, *a holy place, a sanctuary.*

Ionaltair, ^{2}ēnn'-alt-ăr', *v.* graze, pasture, as cattle.

Ionaltradh, ēnn^{2}'-alt-rX̆, *n. m.* pasture, pasturage; *pt.* pasturing, feeding, grazing.

Ionann, ĕŭn'-unn, *adv.* and *adj.* just so, all the same, equally well, in like manner, in a suitable manner; is *ionann* sin is mar a thachras dhuit, *just so shall happen you*; is *ionann* sin, *that is all the same*; is *ionann* iad, *they are all the same, they are identical*; cha 'n *ionann* daibh, *they are not the same*; cha 'n *ionann* a fhreagaras dà làtha màrgaidh, *two market days do not correspond*; cha 'n *ionann* a thig an cota fada do na h-uile fear, *the long coat does not suit every one alike, equally well.*

Ionannachd, ĕŭn'-ann-achg, *n. f.* equality; identity, similarity, sameness; equalization.

Ionga, ĕúng'-å, *n. f.* the nail, the quick; chaidh am prìnne 'san *ionga, the pin touched the quick.*

Iongantach, éúng-unnt-ach, *adj.* wonderful, surprising, strange, extraordinary.

Ionganntas, ĕúng'-ant-as, *n. m.* wonder, surprise, miracle, astonishment, marvelousness.

Iongar, ĕúng'-ur, *n. m.* pus, purulent matter.

Iongarach, ĕúng'-ur-ach, *a.* purulent.

Iongarachadh, ĕŭng'-ar-ach-X̆, *pt.* suppurating, getting purulent; *n. m.* suppuration.

Iongaraich, eug-ur-ėch, *v.* suppurate; dh-*iongaraich* a chas, *his foot suppurated*; *cont.* iongraich.

Ionghnadh, Iongnadh, ĕún'-nX̆, *n. m.* surprise, astonishment; cha 'n *ionghnadh* leam, *I am not at all surprised*; gu m' *ionghnadh, to my astonishment.*

Iongmhas, ĕún'-nas, *n. m.* treasure, riches.

Iongmhasach, ĕŭn'-nas-ach, *a.* wealthy, rich.

Ionmhasair, eun'-nas-ar', *n. m.* a treasurer.

Ionmholta, ĕŭn'-vōlt-ă, *a.* praiseworthy.

Ionmhuinn, ĕŭn'-vėn^{2}, *a.* dearly beloved; a mhac *ionmhuinn, his dearly beloved son*; hence the surname Mackinnon, *a dearly beloved son*; mar a b' *ionmhuinn* leis, *as he greatly desired*; is *iomhuinn* le gach neach a choslan, *every one is fond of his equal, birds of a feather flock together.*

Ionnal, see Ionnlaid, wash, bathe.

Ionnas, Ionns, ĕúnns, *conj.* and *adv.* so that, insomuch; so much so; *ionns* gu 'n do theich e, *so much so, that he decamped, he took French leave.*

Ionnaraidh, ĕúnn'-ăr'-ė, *n. f.* watch, night watching.

Ionndrainn, ĕŭnd'-rráėn, *v.* miss; *n. f.* the thing amissing; object amissing; am faca tu m' *ionndrainn, saw you the object amissing*; sometimes ionndraichinn; co tha thu ag *ionndraichinn, whom do you miss?*

Ionnlad, ĕún'-lad, *n. m.* bathing.

Ionnlaid, ĕún'-llėjj, *v.* bathe, wash.

Ionnsachadh, éŭn'-sach-X̆, *n. m.* learning, scholarship, education; *pt.* learning, educating, teaching.

Ionnsaich, ĕúnn'-ssēch, *v.* learn, teach.

Ionnsaidh, ĕúnn'-sė, *n. f.* attack, assault, a rush *or* dash; thug e *ionnsuidh* orm, *he assaulted me, he dashed* or *rushed towards me.*

Ionnracan, ĕúnn′-rachg-an, *n. m.* the just, the righteous, the honest man; 'nuair a throideas na meairlich thig an t-*ionnracan* g'a chuid, *when the thieves cast out, the honest man gets his own.*

Ionnraic, ĕún- *or* ĕúr′-rėg, *adj.* honest, just, upright; duine *ionraic, an honest man.*

Iorguill, ĕúrg′-ėll, *n. f.* a fray, a quarrel; uproar, skirmish; also iorghuill.

Iorguilleach, ĕūrg′-ėlly'-ach, *a.* uproarous, quarrelsome, fond of battles.

Iorram, ĕúrr′-am, *n. f.* an oar-song; boat-song.

Iorna, ērrn′-a, *n. m.* hank, skein.

Iornalais, ērn-, *or* ēúrn′-al-ash, *n. f.* lumber.

Iosa, ēss′-å, *n. m.* our Saviour Jesus.

Iosail, ēss′-ŭl, *a.* low, mean; can't pretend to pronounce it properly; same as ìseal.

Ioslaich, ēss′-lėch, *v.* lower; degrade.

Ire, ²ēr″-å, *n. m.* earth, condition, state.

Irich, er′-ėch, *v.* rise, get out of bed.

Iriosail, ²ēr″-²ēsh-ul, *a.* humble, unpresuming, unpretending. *Bible.*

Irioslaich, ēr″-us-lėch, *v.* humble.

Iris, ēr″-ėsh, *n. f.* hamper-strop; braces; Ireland; the Irish language; (I-ris, the exposed isle.)

Iriseal, ēr″-ėsh-al, *a.* humble, retiring, unpretending, unostentacious.

Iriseileachadh, ēr″-esh-lyach-Ă, *n. m.* humiliation, debasement, degradation.

Irislich, ēr″-ėsh-llyėch, *v.* debase, humble, lower, degrade, humiliate.

Is, us, *s. conj.* and wisely spelt thus to prevent the u being sounded like u in full, which is uniformly the case in first syllables; contraction of agus.

Is, *pres.* of *indict. verb,* to be; *is* e, *is* i, *is* mi, *it is he, it is she*; *I am,* &c.

Isbeann, ²ēsh′-byann, *n. f.* sausage; samhsair.

Ise, ēsh′-å, *pro.* emphatic form, she; *ise* fhèin, *she herself.*

Iseal, ēsh′-al, *adj.* low, humble.

Isean, ēsh′-an', *n. m.* gosling; a brat.

Isle, ēsh′-lyå, *n. f.* lowness, meanness, degree; more *or* most humble *or* low.

Isleachadh, ĕsh′-lyach-Ă, *pt.* lowering, abasing, degrading; *n. f.* humiliation.

Isleachd, ēsh′-lyachg, *n. f.* degree of lowness.

Islead, ēsh′-lyud, *n. f.* degree of lowness.

Islean, ēsh′-lyan, *n. pl.* lower classes.

Islich, ēsh′-lyėch, *v.* lower, humble.

Isneach, ēsh′-nyach, *n. f.* rifle-gun.

Ist, ēsht, *inter.* hush! hist!

Ite, ²ējty″-å, *n. f.* quill, feather; *itean* èisg, *fins of fish*; *itean* geoidh, *goose-quills.*

Iteach, ²ējty″-ach, *n. f.* plumage, fins.

Iteachan, ējty'-ach-an, *n. m.* bobbin.

Iteagaich, ėjt′-ag-ėch, *v.* fly like a bird.

Iteagh, ath′-teogh, hemlock.

Itealaich, ²ējty″-al-ach, *n. f.* fluttering

Ith, ėch, *v.* eat, corrode.

Itheanaich, ėch′-an'-ėch, *n. f.* damage done by cattle; something to eat.

Ithte, ėch′-tyå, *part.* eaten, consumed.

Iubhar, ĕūv²′-ur, *n. m.* juniper; yew-tree.

Iubhrach, ėū′-rrach, *n. f.* wherry, a barge.

Iuchar, ĕūch′-ur, *n. m.* dog-days; worm-month.

Iuchair, ėūch′-ėr, *n. f.* key; roe of fish.

Iudas, ĕūd′-as, *n. m.* Judas; traitor.

Iul, ĕūl, *n. f.* guidance, land-mark, way.

Iulmhor, ĕūl′-vur, *adj.* learned, wise.

Iursach, ĕūrs′-ach, *n. f.* a girl. *Irish.*

L

The ninth letter of the Gaelic alphabet, named Luis, the quicken-tree. It has a double sound in many cases; as, an long un llōnng. See Abridgement of Grammar.

La, llâ, poetical contraction of latha.

Lab, llâb, *n. m.* day's labour; mud.

Labaire, llâb′-ur-a, *n. m.* labourer.

Labh, llăv, *n. m.* word, lip.

Labhair, llăv′-ėr, *v. n.* speak, say on.

Labhairt, llav′-ărjt, *n. f.* speech, delivery, *or* style of language; is math an *labhairt* a th' aig, *he has an excellent delivery* or *style of language*; *pt.* speaking.

Labharra, llăv′-urr-a, *adj.* boastful, noisy, loquacious, talkative.

Labharrachd, llav′-ar-achg, *n. f.* loquacity, noisy boasting; in poetry, contracted labhrachd.

Labhra, llab′-ră, } *adj.* loquacious,
Labhrach, llav′-rach, } speechifying,
boastful; cho *labhra* ris a ghaoith, *as noisy in speech as the* (storm) *wind*; *labhra,* cealgach, *loquacious and cunning. Ossian*; *Ar.*

Labhradair, llăb′-rad-ăr', } *n. m.* orator,
Labhraiche, llav′-rėch-å, } speaker; *labhradair* pongail, *distinct orator, interpreter, translator.*

Labhras, lăv′-rus, *n. f.* laurel-tree.

Lach, llăch, *n. f.* a widgeon, duck; a horse-laugh; a burst of laughter; (Teut. lach, *a loud laugh*); *lach* lochanach, *a dunter-goose*; *lach* ceann-ruadh, *the herb celindine*; *lach* uaine, *a mallard. Armst.*

Lach, llach, *n. m.* a reckoning at a wedding. *North.*

LACHARDAICH, llach'-ard-ech, } a loud con-
LACHANAICH, llăch'-ăn-èch, } tinued laughter, *or* repeated bursts of laughter.

LACHDUNN, llăchd'-unn, *adj.* dun, swarthy.

LADAR, lăd'-ăr, *n. m.* a ladle.

LADARNA, llăd'-ărr-ă, *adj.* audacious, bold.

LADARNACHD, llad'-arn-achg, *n.f.* audacity.

LADARNAS, ladd'-arn-us, *n. m.* audacity.

LADHAR, lao'-ar, *n. f.* toe, prong, claw.

LADHRACH, lāor'-ach, *a.* pronged, clawed.

LAG, llag, *n. f.* hollow, cavity; *adj.* feeble, faint; 'san *lag, in the hollow*; duine *lag, a faint person*; *v. n.* faint, weaken; *lag* air, *he failed*; *lag*-mhisneachail, *lag*-chridheach, *faint-hearted, chicken-hearted.*

LAGAICH, llag'-èch, *v.* faint, weaken.

LAGAN, lag'-an, *n. m* a dimple, little hollow; meal-receiver in a mill; leumhann.

LAGAN, llâg'-an, *n. f.* flummery; cabhruich,

LAGH, llaŏ'-gh', *n. m.* law, right, order, method; see Laight, mould, shape.

LAGHACH, llaŏgh'-ach, *a.* fine, decent, kind; duine *laghach, a decent, kind man*; nì *laghach, a fine* or *convenient thing*; is *laghach* a fhuaradh e, *he did pretty well, he did surprisingly*; is *laghach* an duine e, *he is a fine* or *kindly man.*

LAGHADAIR, llaŏgh'-ad-ar', *n. m.* spoon-mould.

LAGHAIL, llaŏ'-ghal, *a.* lawful, litigious; nì *laghail, a lawful thing*; duine *laghail, a litigious person.*

LAGHALACHD, laŏgh'-al-achg, *n. f.* lawfulness, legality; litigiousness.

LAGLAMHACH, llăg'-lăv-ach, *a.* weak-handed.

LAIB, lìèb, *n. f.* mire; slimy mud *or* clay.

LAIBEIL, lìèb'-al, *adj.* miry, dirty, filthy.

LAIDH, lăe'-y', *v. n.* lay, recline, couch; go, stretch, go to sleep; set as the sun; urge, importune; *laidh* an cù, *the dog couched*; *laidh* e air an làr, *he stretched himself on the ground*; *laidh* iad, *they went to bed*; *laidh* i leis oirnn, *she stretched to leewards of us*; *laidh* e orm gus an d'thug e orm a dheanadh, *he importuned me till he made me do it*; *laidh* a' ghrian, *the sun set*; *laidhe*-thuige, *lie-to.*

LAIDH, lăĕ'-è, *n. f.* lay, position, attitude; tack *or* stretch, as of a ship; crouching; setting of the sun.

LAIDIONN, lăjj'-unn, *n. f.* the Latin.

LAIDINNICH, lăjj'-ènn-èch, *v.* Latinize.

LAIDIR, lâjj'-èr, *adj.* strong, robust, powerful, fortified; potent, ardent, intoxicating; duine *làidir, a strong* or *powerful man*; deoch *laidir, potent* or *intoxicating liquor*; dùn *laidir, a well-secured fort*; surprising, wonderful; 's ann is *làidir* a gheibhear thu, *you act, do,* or *behave surprisingly well*; a's treise, *stronger, more powerful.*

LAIDIREACHD, llăjj'-èr'-achg, *n. f.* strength

LAIDRICH, llâjj'-rèch, *v.* strengthen.

LAIGE, laŏg'-a, *adj.* weaken.

LAIGHT, laŏjty', *n. f.* shape, mould; chuir thu m' ata as a *laight, you put my ha out of its shape*; natural order, method; cuir na *laight* e, *put it in its natural or der*; bogha air *laight, a bow on th stretch.*

LAIGSE, laŏèg'-shà, *n. f.* a fainting fit weakness, debility, feebleness, infirmity chaidh e an *laigse, he fainted*; do *laigse, your weakness.*

LAIMH-RI; see Lamh-ri, near to.

LAIMHRIG, } láem'-rrèg, *n. f.* landing place,
LAIMRIG, } natural quay, *or* pier.

LAIMHSEACHADH, láèv'-shyach-Ă, *pt.* handling; *n. m.* trade, management; *laimhseachadh* an nì sin, *the management of that affair*; am bheil *laimhseachadh* sam bith aige, *has he any dealings among hands*; discussion, treatment of an argument.

LAIMHSICH, láèv'-shèch, *v.* handle, manage, finger, treat, deal.

LAINE, lláèn'-à, } *n. f.* fulness, degree
LAINEAD, lláèn'-ad, } of fulness, *or* completeness.

LAINNIR, see Lannair, fish-scales, glitter.

LAIPHEID, llì'-ffăj, *n. f.* spoon-mould.

LAIR, lâèr, *n. f.* a mare.

LAMH, làv, *n. f.* a hand, a sailor, a handle, an attempt, *or* attack; thug e *làmh* air, *he attacked him, he almost lay violent hands on him, he attempted it*; cuir do làmh leinn, *lend us a hand*; mo *làmhsa* dhuitse, *there is my hand, I can assure you*; *làmh* air làimh, *hand in hand, hand in glove*; rug se air *laimh* urra, *he shook hands with her*; a' cumail làimh rithe, *paying his addresses to her, keeping her in hopes of marriage*; tha e an làimh, *he is in custody, he is in a strait*; gabh as *làimh, undertake, assume*; tha iad ag iomairt a làmhan a cheile, *they understand each other, there is a collusion between them.*

LAMHACH, làv'-ach, *adj.* dexterous, masterly; *n. m.* report of guns, gleaming.

LAMHAINN, làv'-ènn, *n. f.* a glove; lamhadair, *a glover, glove-maker.*

LAMHAIRC, lăv²'-ăèrk, *n. f.* right-hand stilt of a plough; corag, the left hand stilt.

LAMH-ANART, searadair, hand-towel.

LAMHCHLAG, làv'-chlag, *n. m.* a hand-bell.

LAMHCHAR, làv'-char, *adj.* dexterous.

LAMH-CHRANN, làv'-chrann, *n. f.* hand staff of a flail, the strikes, buailteanan.

LAMH-GHLAIS, làv'-ghlash, *v.* handcuff.

LAMH-LAIDIR, lav'-llăj-er, *n. f.* oppression.

Lamhnain, làv²′-ăěn, *n. f.* couple of a house, a pair; *làmhnain* phòsda, *a married couple.*

Lamh-uisge, làv-ûshg′-ă, *n.f.* sluice-handle.

Lan, làn, *adj.* full, perfect; satiated; *n. m.* a full, fulness, repletion; the tide, flood-tide; pique; cha ruig tha leas a leithid do *làn* a ghabail as, *you need not pique yourself so much on that*; *adv.* completely, wholly, quite; tha *làn* fhios 'am air sin, (*làn* mhath,) *I know that quite well*; *làn* cheart, *quite right*; rug an *làn* oirnn, *the tide overtook us*; *làn*-ùghdaras, *full authority, plenipotentiary's authority*; *làn* dhearbh, *demonstrate, make completely certain*; *làn* fhiosrach, *fully certain*; *làn* dhamh, *a full grown stag* or *hart*; *làn* chothrom, *ample justice, best opportunity*; *làn* chumhachd, *discretionary power, full authority*; *làn* fhoighinteach, *fully equal to*, or *capable of, fully competent.*

Lanachd, làn′-achg, *n. f.* fulness, full.

Lanadair, làn′-ad-ăr′, smith's mould-piece.

Langa, láng′-a, *n. f.* a ling.

Langaid, lăng′-ăj, *n. f.* fetters for the hind and fore feet of a horse or mare. *Islay.*

Langan, láng-an, *n. m.* drawling bellowing, *or* lowing of deer *or* cattle.

Langanaich, láng′-an-èch, *n. f.* continued bellowing *or* lowing of deer, &c.

Langar, láng′-ar, *n. m.* a sofa, fetters; *langar* ileach, *a lamprey. H. Society.*

Lann, lánn, *n. f.* a blade, a sword, scales of fish, an enclosure, as land; *lannan* is itean an èisg, *the scales and fins of the fish*; *lann* na sgine, *the blade of the knife* (or *sword*); lann-smig, *a razor*; lann-chuilse, *a lancet*; *v.* scale, take scales off fish, &c.

Lanntair, lánnt′-ėr, a landscape, beautiful side of country full of wood and arable land facing the sea; " moladh na *lanntair*," *description of the landscape.* D. Campbell, Esq.

Lannair, lánn′-ėr, *n. f.* the phosphoric glitter of scales of fish in the dark, radiance, glitter of swords, &c. gleam.

Lannrach, lánn′-rach, *adj.* gleaming, shining.

Laoch, lāoch, *n. m.* Fingal's aid-de-camp, *or* right hand man in battle; a hero, a companion; hence, a *laoch*-fhinn, contracted laochan, *term of endearment*; tha, a *laochain, yes, my dear fellow!*

Laochraidh, lāoch′-rė, *n. f.* a band of heroes; corps of reserve for emergencies.

Laogh, lāo-gh′, *n. m.* a calf; a friend.

Laoghan, lāo-gh′-an, *n.m.* pulp, as of potatoes or wood, a glutinous substance; pith of wood.

Laoidh, lùė-y′, *n. f.* a hymn, an anthem.

Laoir, lùėr′, *v.* drub most lustily

Laom, lāom, *v.* lodge, as corn; *n.m.* a blaze.

Laosboc, lùs′-bŏchg, *n.f.* eibhreann, gelded he-goat.

Lapach, lap′-ach, *a.* slim; *n. m.* a slim.

Lapachas, lăp′-a-us, *n. m.* pliability.

Lapaich, lap′-ėch, *v.* flap, flag, lag.

Lar, lâr, *n. m.* a floor, ground floor, ground; air *làr, on the ground, on the floor*; dol ma *làr, going to nought*; cuir ma *làr, abrogate*; *adj.* complete; *làr* bhurraidh, *a complete blockhead.*

Larach, làr′-ach, *n. f.* stand *or* site of a building; a building in ruins, a ruin; battle-field.

Las, las, *v.* kindle, enrage, flash, sparkle.

Lasag, las′-ag, *n. f.* little flame, *or* blaze.

Lasaich, lăs′-ėch, *v.* flag, lag.

Lasair, lăs′-ėr, *n. f.* a flame, a flash.

Lasan, las′-an, *n. m.* slight passion, spark.

Lasanta, las′-ant-a, *a.* passionate, fiery.

Lasantachd, lăs-ant-achg, *n. f.* fieriness.

Lasdaire, lasd′-ur-ă, } *n. m.* a beau, a
Lasgaire, lasg′-ur-a, } spark, a fop, a dandy.

Lasgarra, lasg′-urr-a, *adj* beauish, brave

Lasrach, las′-rach, *adj.* flaming, blazing.

Lasraich, las′-rėch, *n. f* conflagration.

Latha, la′-ă, *n. m.* a day; *adv.* once.

Lathailt, lă′-alytj, *n. f.* mould, shape, way.

Lathair, lâ′-ėr, *n. f.* presence, existence, company, sight; na d' thig an *làthair, do present yourself*; mach as mo *làthair, get out of my presence!* am bheil e a *làthair, is he in existence? is he alive?* neas is a bhios mise an *làthair, while I am present, while I live*; an *làthair* a chèile, *face to face, before each other*; cum as an *làthair, keep out of sight*; am fear nach eil ann *làthair, he that is no more, he that is absent*; an robh e an *làthair, was he present? adj.* present, living, remaining; ghuil na bha *làthair, all that were present* or *remaining wept, Oss.*; laithreachd, *presence*; uile-làithreachd, *omnipresence*; gun bheag na mhòr *làthair, without a particle remaining.*

Le, llā², *pre.* with, along with, by means of, in estimation of, in company; in the interest of, together with; bhuail e i *le* clach, *he struck her with a stone*; tha e *le* 'r càirdean, *he is along with, in the interest of*, or *belongs to our friends.*

Leaba, lyab′-ă, *n. f.* a bed, couch; leapa, *of a bed*; leapaichean, *beds*; na *leaba, in his bed.*

Leabag, } lĕ'b′-ag, *n. f.* a flounder; *North*
Leubag, } lĕăb-ag; leabagan, *flounders.*

Leabhar, lyō′-ur, *n. m.* a book, volume; from leubh, read; *leabhar* Eoin, *a book full of receipts for witchcraft and incantation.*

LEABHAR-LANN, lyō²'-ur-lann, *n. f.* library.

LEABHAR-REICEADAIR, lyô'-ur-rāēchg-adar', *n. m.* a bookseller, a retailer of books.

LEABHODACH, lyāv²'-vòd-ach, *n. m.* half-a-mutchkin; half-a-pint.

LEABHRACH, lyō'-rach, *n. f.* a library, *adj.* bookish.

LEABHRADAIR, lyōr'-ad-ăr', *n. m.* a publisher, an editor, an author.

LEABHRAICHE, lyōv'-ēch-à, *n. m.* a librarian, a bookseller; leabhar-reiceadair.

LEABHRAN, lyōr'-an, *n. m.* a pamphlet.

LEABHRATHAIR, lyā²'v-vrāĕr, *n. m.* half-brother.

LEABHRUADAR, lyā²v'-vrŭăd-ar, *n. m.* vision.

LEABHRUICH, lyāv'-vrŭēch, *v.* parboil; *a.* purboiled.

LEABHRUTHACH, lyā²v'-vrŭăch, *n. m.* a gentle slope, *or* declivity, *or* inclination.

LEAC, lyek, lyechg, lyúchg, *n. f.* a flag, slate, slab, tombstone; taobh no lice, *at the side of the tombstone.*

LEACACH, lyechg'-ach, *a.* granite, in flags.

LEACAID, lyech'-aj, slap on the cheek. *Pr.*

LEACAICH, lyechg'-ech, *v.* pave with flags.

LEACANN, lyechg'-unn, *n. f.* a sloping side of a hill or country.

LEACANAICH, lyechg'-nyēch, *v.* get inseparably fond of, as a child to a nurse, &c.

LEACANTA, lyechg'-ant-à, *adj.* stiff, formal.

LEAFHACAL, lyā'-achg-al, *n. m.* a hint; the slightest hint.

LEACHLACH, lyā -chlăch, *n. f.* half-a-stone.

LEACHAS, lyăch'-chăs, *n. f.* one foot; air a *leachois, on one foot, getting backwards in worldly circumstances.*

LEACHAR, lyā²ch'-chăr, *n. m. adv.* somewhat, in some measure, in some degree.

LEACHRUN, lyăch'-chrŭn, *n. m.* half a crown.

LEACLACH, lyechg'-llach, *n. f.* granite.

LEAD, lā'dd', *n. m.* beautiful head of hair.

LEADAIR, llā'-dur', *v.* lay hold of a person's hair in one hand, and belabour him masterly with the other, drub; leadairt, *a masterly drubbing in this style.*

LEADAN, lyād'-an, *n. m.* a little pretty head of hair, a note in music; the herb teazle.

LEADANACH, lyā'd'-an-ach, *adj.* adorned with a beautiful head of hair, melodious.

LEADARRA, lyā²d'-urr-a, *a.* melodious. *Mt.*

LEAG, lyā²g, *v.* put *or* throw down as a wrestler; place *or* lay; pull down, fell; he pulled down the house, *leag* e an tigh, *leag* e mi, *he put me down*; *leag* e a chlach steigh, *he laid the foundation-stone.*

LEAGADH, lyăg'-Ă, *n. m.* a fall; *pt.* putting down, pulling down; also leagail.

LEAGH, lyaŏ'-gh', *v.* melt, liquify.

LEAGHACH, lyaŏ'-ach, *adj.* soluble.

LEAGHADAIR, lyaŏ'-ad-dăr', *n. m.* smelter.

LEALAMH, lyāl²'-láv, *n. f.* the one hand.

LEALAMHACH, lyāl'-láv-ach, *a.* unaided.

LEAM, lyăm. *pro.* and *prep.* (le mi) with me, having property in; is *leamsa* so, *this is mine*; along with me: thalla *leamsa, come along with me*; by my means, by me; rinneadh *leamsa* sin, *that was made by me, by my means*; in my interest, on my side: agus thuirt e co tha *leamsa, and he said, Who is on my side? B.*; is mòr *leam, I think it too much*; is beag *leam*, I THINK IT TOO LITTLE; is coma *leam, I am indifferent, I dislike*; is duilich *leam, I am sorry*; is fhad a *leam, I think too long*; is doirbh *leam* a chreidsinn, *I can hardly believe it*; is soirbh *leam* sin a chreidsinn, *I can easily believe that*; is math *leam* sin, *I am glad of that*; their *leam, I should suppose, I think*; leig *leam, let me alone, let go with me*; leig *leam* i, *let her accompany me.*

LEAMH, lyév, *a.* vexing, galling; bu *leamh* leam, *I thought it galling*; a nis bha so *leamh, now this was galling*—impudent, *N. H.*; pertinacious. *M'I.*

LEAMHADAS, lév'-ad-us, *n. m.* vexation.

LEAMHAN, léa'-an, *n. m.* the elm; elm-tree.

LEAMHAS, lya²v'-vas, *n. f.* one buttock.

LEAMHNACH, lev'-nachg, *n. f.* tormenting.

LEAMHRAGAN, lev'-rag-an, *n. m.* a stye.

LEAN, lyen, *v. n.* follow, pursue, chase; *lean* sinn iad, *we followed them*; stick to, adhere to, cleave to, continue, persevere; *lean* e ri m' lamhan, *it adhered to my hands*; *leanadh* mo theanga ri mo chiobhall, *let my tongue cleave to the roof of my mouth*; ma *leanas* an uair tiorram, *if the weather continue fair*; *lean* mar sin, *persevere so*; na *lean* orm ni's fhaide, *don't importune me farther.*

LEANA, lyèn'-a, *n. f.* a plain; green leuna.

LEANABH, lyen'-uv, *n. m.* a child; infant.

LEANABACHD, lyén'-ab-achg, *n. m.* childhood, childishness, dotage; leanabaidh.

LEANABAIDH, lyén'-ub-ē, *adj.* childish, silly; na aois *leanabaidh, in his dotage.*

LEANABAIL, lyén'-ab-al, *adj.* child-like. spoiled.

LEANABANTA, lyen'-ab-anta, *adj.* puerile.

LEANABANTACHG, *n. f.* puerility.

LEANACHD, lyén'-achg, *n. f.* pursuit, following, consequence.

LEANAILTEACH, lyen'-ălly-tyach, *a.* persevering, adhering; see Leantalach.

LEANMHUINN, lyén'-vhyènn, *pt.* following a person, as a chief claiming kindred, pursuing; *n. f.* kindred, clanship, bond of connection *or* tie of friendship; tha *leanmhuinn* a thaobhaiginn, eatorra, *there is some bond of connection* or *clan-*

ship between them; tha iad a' *leanmhuinn* air an teàghlach sin, *they have some family claim on that house*; tha e a' *leanmhuinn* ormsa so, *he claims this from me, he insinuates his claim to this from me*; a luchd-*leanmhuinn, his followers* or *kindred, his vassals, minions.*

LEANMHUINNEACH, lyen'-vhènn-ach, *adj.* following, consequent, adhering, having kindred claims.

LEANN, lyann, *n. m.* ale, beer; *leantan, humours of the body*; droch *leantan, bad humours.*

LEANNAICH, lyănn'-èch, *v.* suppurate; more often lionnaich.

LEANNAN, lyann'-an, *n. c.* a lover, sweetheart.

LEANNANACH, lyann'-an-ach, *a.* amorous.

LEANNANACHD, lyann'-an-achg, *n. f.* courtship, gallantry, blandishments, dalliance.

LEANN-DUBH, lyan'-dŭgh, *n. m.* a settled melancholy, *or* depression of spirits; sadness, lowness of spirits.

LEANTAIL, lyent'-al, *pt. adj.* sticking, following.

LEANTACH, lyènt'-ach, *n. f.* country of plains; a place abounding in plains; an extensive plain, leuntach.

LEANTALACH, lyen'-tal-ach, *adj.* adhesive, cohesive, persevering; *leantalach* air obair, *persevering at his work*; tha 'n glaogh *leantalach, the glue is adhesive.*

LEANTALACHD, lyen'-t-al-achg, *n. f.* adhesiveness, adherence; ability to persevere unremittingly; *leantalach* air an uisge, *raining incessantly.*

LEAPA, lyep'-a, *gen.* of leaba, a bed.

LEAPAICH, lyep'-èch, *v.* imbed; lodge, as water, &c.; tha an t-uisge a *leapachadh* an so, *the water is lodging here*; a' *leapachadh* am f heoil, *embedding in my flesh.*

LEAPACHAS, lyep' ach-us, *n m.* lodgement.

LEAPHUNND, lyā'-fŭnnd, *n. m.* half-a-pound.

LEAR, lyer, *n. f.* the sea; an fhàirge. *Oss.*

LEARACH, lyer'-ach, *n. f.* larch-tree.

LEARG, lyerg, *n. f.* the rain-goose; sloping face of a hill, *or* sloping place exposed to the sun and sea.

LEAS, lyăs², *n. m.* interest, advantage; 'se a bh'air do *leas, it is he that had your interest in view*; cha'n e mo *leas* a bh'air t' fhaire, *it is not my interest you had in view*; na bitheadh e air do *leas, if he had your interest at heart.*

LEAS, lless, (*a.*) cha ruig thu *leas, you need not*; *n. f.* thigh; deasaich do chlaidhimh air do *leas, gird your sword on your thigh. Sm.*

LEASACH, lyās²'-ach, *n. m.* manure. *Loch. a.* trifling, sheep-shanked.

LEASACHADH, lyās²'-ach-ă, *pt.* manuring, improving; a' *leasachadh* an fhearainn, *manuring the land*; a' *leasachadh* a' gnothaich, *ameliorating* or *improving the thing*; *n. m.* dung, manure; a' cur amach an *leasachaidh, carting dung,* or *laying out manure*; *n. m.* melioration, amends, reparation; cha *leasachadh* air sin a ni sin, *that is no improvement of,* or *reparation for that affair.*

LEASACHAIL, lyā²s'-ach-al, *adj.* making amends, ameliorating, repairing; caustic escharatic.

LEASAICH, lyās'-èch, *v.* improve, repair, make up deficiencies; *leasaich* a ni sin, *improve* or *amend that thing*; manure, dung, cultivate; *leasaich* am fearann, *manure* or *cultivate the land.*

LEASAINM, lyās²'-ènum, *n. m.* a nickname.

LEASDAIR, lyās²'-dăr', *n. m.* a lamp; crùisgean.

LEASAN, llyās²'-an, *n. m.* a lesson.

LEAT, llétt', *prep.* le, and thu *pro.*, in thee, with thee, in your company—same as leam, &c.

LEATH, llyā², half, used before words beginning with a, o, u, as a prefix; thus, *leathbhodach, half-a-mutchkin*; *leathchrun, half-a-crown*; more properly leabhodach leachrun, the TH being left out before two consonants, as leatrom, *pregnancy,* but retained when preceding vowels—*leathamadan, a fellow that is an idiot*; *leathamaid, a woman that is an idiot*—divided by a hyphen when the accent is not on *leath,* as leatrom, leathad; *leath*-chudthrom, *a preponderance*; leith before e and i, as leiphinnt, *half-a-pint*; *leith* and *pinnt* pronounced llā'-ffēnty'; in some districts, leth, llé, the é sounding like the e in there, but the ea and ei in Argyle sound like ā in fame.

LEATHA, llé'-a *and* lèch'-â, *prep. pron.* along with her; with her; see Leam; also Leathasa.

LEATHACHAS, lyā²'-ash-as, *n. m.* partiality, unfairness, injustice; na dean *leathachas* sam bith air, *show him no partiality.*

LEATHAD, llé'-udd, *n. m.* a slope, a declivity; a dol le *leathad, declining, descending*; half-ridge.

LEATHAN, LEATHANN, lyā'-unn, *adj.* broad; na's leithne, neo na's leatha, *broader.*

LEATHAR, lyé'-ur, *n. m.* tanned leather.

LEATHRACH, lyaŏ'-rach, *n. m.* tanned leather.

LEATHUILINN, lyā'-ŭll-ènn, *n. f.* one elbow; air a *leathuilinn, declining, going down hill.*

LEATHUNNSA, lyā'-ŭs-â, *n. m.* half ounce.

LEATRATH, lyāt²'-tră, *n. m.* half rations; milking once a-day, half-allowance.

LEATROM, lyāt'-trŏm, *n. m.* pregnancy, state of being pregnant, a burden. *Bibl-*

Leatromach, lyāt′-tròm-ach, *adj.* pregnant, with child, in the family way burdensome.

Leathamadan, lyā²′-am-ad-an, *n m.* an idiot.

Leathamaid, lyā′-am-ėjj, *n. f.* an idiot.

Leathoir, lyă′-²ōėr′, *n. f.* suburb, border.

Leathoireach, lyā′-ōėr-ach, *a.* remote, lonely.

Leibh, llāv, *pron. prep.* along with you, by means of you; see Leam.

Leibhliadhna, lyāv²′-vhlĕăn-â, *n. f.* half a year.

Leibhreac, lyāv′-ryăchg, *n. m.* exact patern, the like, equal, match, fellow; *leibhreac* so, *the exact patern of this*; *leibhreac* siod, *the exact model of that*; mo *leibhreac* fhèin, *my own equal, my compeer*; *leibhreacan* a chèile, *the exact patern* or *fellows of each other*; cha 'n 'eil do *leibhreac* r'a fhaotainn, *your match is not to be found*; (leith bhreac tha iad cho chosail ri dà bhreac, *they are so identical, so like each other as two trouts.*——common saying.

Leibid, lyāb′-ėjj, *n. f.* a paltry female, or, consideration, term of contempt.

Leibideach, lyāb′-ėjj-ach, *adj.* paltry, trifling.

Leibideachd, lyāb′-ėjj-achg, *n. f.* paltriness.

Leicheathra, lyā′-chér-a, *n m.* two ounces, half-a-quarter, one flank of a beast.

Leidir, lyajj, *v.* drub most lustily.

Leig, lyē²g, *v.* permit, allow, let be, let run; urge a dog to the chase, broach, fire; lance, commence raining; *leig* dhà falbh, *permit him to go*; *leig* dhomh, *let me alone*; *leig* an linne, *let the water run from the reservoir*; *leig* fuil, *let blood*; *leig* urchair, *fire with the gun, draw the trigger*; *leig* an lionnachadh, *lance the suppuration, the tumour*; milk; *leig* an crodh, *milk the cattle*; tha an latha a' brath leigeil fodha, *this day is likely to rain*; *leig* am buideal, *broach on the cask*; *leig* tamh domh, *let me alone*; *leig* air 'aghaidh, *don't restrain him, permit him to go forward*; *leig* thun a' cheile iad, *let them fight it out*; *leig* na coin ann, *set the dogs to him.*

Leigeadh, llyėg′-ă, *pt.* permitting, urging, &c.

Leigeil, lyėg′-al, *n. f. pt.* letting, permitting, &c.

Leigh, lyāē-y′, *n. f.* medicine.

Leigh, lyāē-y′, *n. m.* a physician, surgeon, doctor; 's esan is *lèigh* anama agus cuirp, *he is (the Almighty) the physician of soul and body. O. W.*

Leigheas, lyā′-us, *n. m.* a cure, remedy, medicine; *pt.* healing, curing, remedying.

Leigheasach, llyā′-us-ach, } *adj.* medicinal, curing, remedial.
Leigheasail, llyā′-as-al, }

Leighis, lyā′-êsh, *v.* cure, heal, remedy.

Leighiste, llyā′-êshj-â, *pt.* healed, cured.

Leigh-loisg, lyā′-llòshg, *v.* cauterise.

Leigte, llyēg²′-tyâ, *pt.* lanced, running, &c.

Leine, lān′-â, *n. f.* a shirt; *leine*-bhàis, *shroud, winding-sheet*; *leine*-chreis, *a privy counsellor, a confidant.*

Leinn, lāènn, *prep. pron.* along with us, in our company, alone; leig *leinn, let us alone*; thalla *leinn, come along with us.*

Leinteach, llyān′-tyach, *n. f.* shirting.

Leiphiuthar, lyā²f-fū²-ur, *n. f.* half-sister.

Leir, lārr, *adj.* obvious, evident, *imp. v.* see, behold, perceive, understand; cha *leir* domh, *I cannot see, it is not obvious to me*; is *lèir* a bhuil, *the result is sufficient proof, the result is obvious, is quite evident to me,* I can perceive or understand it; mar a's *leir* dhomh, *as far as I can see*; is math is *lèir* dhomh, *I can see well*; am bheil thu a' leirsinn, *do you see? can you see? do you perceive?* cha *lèir* dhomh sin, *I cannot perceive that*; cha *lèir* dhomh do dhearas, *I cannot perceive your want* or *deficiency*; the proper orthography of this word and its derivatives is leur, as is obvious from the pronunciation of leirsinn, (lārr′-ssènn, and not lyār′-shyènn); give the most agonising pain, torture, torment; 'gam *leireadh, torturing me, tormenting me, giving me the most acute pain.*

Leir, lyāry′, *adj.* whole, all, every; gu *lèir, wholly, altogether, completely, utterly.*

Leireadh, lyārr′-ă, *pt.* tormenting, torturing; *n. m.* the severest mental pain, inward torture.

Leir-sgrios, lyar′-skrès, *v.* utterly ruin; *n. f.* utter destruction, utter ruination, devastation.

Leirsinn, lyār′-sènn, *n. m.* eye-sight, vision, sight, perception, clear conception; *pt.* perceiving, understanding, seeing.

Leirsinneach, lyār′-sènn-ach, *adj.* capable of perceiving, sharp sighted, decerning.

Leirsinneachd, lyār′-sènn-achg, *n. f.* perfection of vision, quick perception, intelligence.

Leis, lyāsh, *gen.* of leas, of thigh.

Leis, llāsh, *adj.* lee, leeward, larboard, air an taobh *leis, on the larboard side* am fearann *leis, the land to leewards, lee land, leeward land*; leig *leis! slacksheet! let go before the wind!* *leis* oirnn, *to leeward of us*; cum *leis* oirnn, *keep to leeward of us.*

Leis, llāsh, *pro. prep.* along with, with him, with it, in his company, being his property or right; by means of, with what, down hill, down the stream; a' dol leis, *going along with him*; *leis* fhèin, *all alone, without any assistance, by by means of his own energies*; *leis* an t-sruth, *down the stream*; ciod *leis* a glan an t-òganach, uile shlighe féin, *by what means shall a young man purify all his ways?* belonging to; cò *leis* thu, *whose son* or *daughter are you?* tha mi leatsa ma cheannaicheas tu mi, *I will be yours, if you bribe me well*; is *leis* an duine so mi, *I am the son* (or *daughter*) *of this gentleman*; co *leis* a nì thu e, *with what (means) shall you do it?* cò *leis* a théid thu, *with whom shall you go?* leatsa, *a-long with you*; *leis* an dithisd so, *by means of these two*; on account of; *leis* a chabhag, *on account of the hurry*; is aithreach *leis, he regrets*; cò *leis* a tha thu, *on whose side are you? in whose interest are you? leis* a' ghaoth, *with the wind, on account of the wind*; *leis* a' bhruthach, *down the hill*; leig e *leis, he fainted, fagged, he permitted him.*

Leiscioball, lāsh'-kēb-all, *n. c.* a minion, vassal; a creature.

Leisdear, llyāshj'-ar', *n. m.* an arrow-maker.

Leisg, llyāshg, *adj.* lazy, indolent, slothful; loath, reluctant, unwilling; duine *leisg, a lazy, indolent* or *slothful person*; is *leisg* leam, *I am loath*; is *leisg* leam cuir a mach air, *I feel reluctant to cast out with him*; is *leisg* leis sin a dheanadh, *he feels reluctant to do that*; *n. f.* laziness, sheer indolence, sloth, slothfulness; 's e an *leisg* a thug ort sin a dheanadh, *sheer indolence made you do that*; cha dean làmh na leisge beairteas, *the hand of sloth maketh not rich.*

Leisgear, } **Leisgean**, } llyāshg'-ar', *n. m.* a sluggard; imich chum an t-seangain, a *leisgein, go to the ant, thou sluggard.*

Leisgeul, (leith-sgeul, or rather leisg-sgeul,) llāēshg²'-al, *n.m.* excuse, apology; gabh mo *leisgeul, pardon me, apologize for me*; pretence; cha 'n 'eil ann ach *leisgeul, it is only a pretence.*

Leisgeulach, lyāshg'-skyal-ach, *adj.* shuffling, evasive, pretending; excusable.

Leisgeulachd, lyashg'-skyal-achg, *n. f.* habits of pretending or evading, evasiveness.

Leith, lyhā², *n. f* the half; side, share, interest, charge; *leith* mar *leith, share and share alike*; chaidh e as mo *leith, he sided with me, he took my part*; chuir iad sin as a *leith, they laid that to his charge*; air leith, *apart, separately*; *leith* slighe, *half way, midway, half the voyage*; troidh gu *leith, a foot and a half*; a *leith* a's mò, *the majority, the bulk, the greater part*; somewhat; *leith* chruinn, *somewhat round*; leith gheur, *somewhat sour*; leith chosail, *somewhat like*; leith fhìor, *somewhat true.*

Leithid, lyā²-èjj, *n. c.* match, equal, like, compeer, a fellow; is annamh a *leithid, his match is seldom met with*; leithidean a cheile, *the very paterns of each other.*

Leithne, lyān'-nyà, **Lethe**, lé-à, degree of leathann; na's *leithne, broader*;—broadness.

Leitir, lyāty''-ēr, *n. f.* side of a hill, an extensive slope or declivity.

Leo, lyō, *pro. pre.* along with them; their *leo, they thought, they should think.*

Leob, lyāob, *n. f.* an ugly slice or piece of any thing; *v.* tear unmercifully into shreds.

Leobhar, lyō'-ur, properly a book.

Leog, lyôg, *v.* fag on the stomach; *n. f* a marsh; also leoig, *a ditch, morass.*

Leogach, lyôg'-ach, *adj.* marshy.

Leoghann, } **Leomhann**, } lyô-gh'-unn, *n.m.* lion; bann-*leòghann, lioness.*

Leointe, lyôin'-tyà, *pt.* wounded, painful.

Leoir, lyôēr, *n. f.* sufficiency, enough, a bellyful; fhuair mi na *leoir, I have got enough.*

Leom, lyôm, *n. f.* drawling pronunciation.

Leomach, lyôm'-ach, *adj.* drawling in talk.

Leomann, lyāom'-ann, *n. f.* a moth.

Leon, lyôn, *v.* wound, gall, pique, grieve; *n. m.* wound, grief, vexation.

Leor, lyôr, same as leoir.

Lesan, lā'-sun, *prep. pron.* (for leis esan,) along with him, accompanying him, in his opinion; is leoir *lesan, he thinks it enough*; is beag *lesan, he thinks it too little.*

Leth, llé, *n. m.* provincial for leith.

Leubh, lyāv, *v.* read, lecture, explain; cha 'n 'eil math dhomh a bhi *leubhadh* sin duitse, *it serves no end to explain that to you*; a leubhadh a chall is a chumhnart, *expatiating on his loss and danger.*

Leubhadair, lyāv'-ăd-ār', *n. m.* reader.

Leubhadh, lyāv'-Ă, *n. m.* reading, lecturing; *pt.* reading, explaining, expounding, expatiating.

Leud, lèdd, *n. m.* breadth; *leud* ròine, *hair's breadth*; air fad is air *leud, in length and breadth.*

Leudaich, lèdd'-èch, *v.n.* widen, expatiate.

Leug, lyāg, *n. f.* lye, or ashes and water for bleaching; in some places a jewel, precious stones.

Leugach, *a.* drawling, sleugach.

Leugh, lyāv, see Leubh.

Leum, llyām, *v. n.* jump, spring, leap,

frisk, skip, start, fight, quarrel; *leum* iad air a cheile, *they fought, they quarrelled*; *n. m.* a jump, leap, spring; animal semen, an emission.

Leumadair, lām′-ad-ăr′, *n. m.* the size of salmon, between the grilse and full grown salmon, *Is.*; dolphin, *Shaw*; a small whale, *H. Society*; *leumdair* feoir, *a grasshopper*; also *leumadair* uaine.

Leumhann, lyāv′-ānn, *n. m.* meal-receiver.

Leumraich, lyām′-rrēch, *n. f.* frisking, skipping; also leumnaich.

Leum-uisge, lyām′-ūshg-å, *n. m.* water-fall.

Leus, llās, *n. m.* blink, glimmer, ray of light; cha 'n 'eil *leus* soluis an so, *there is not a blink* or *ray of light here*; a torch for poaching fish on rivers; a blister; mil air do bheul gad robh *leus* air do theanga, *honey on your lips, though there should be a blister on your tongue. Prov.* a cataract or speck on the eye. *M. P.*

Leusaich, llyès′-ėch, *v.* blister, raise blisters.

Leus-teine, lyès′-tyen-å, *n. m.* firebrand.

Liagh, lĕă, *n. f.* a ladle, an oar-blade.

Liath, lĕă, *v.* lilac, grey-haired, grey-headed, mouldy; *v.* make grey-headed, make grey, turn grey, mould, get mouldy; aran air *liathadh, bread getting mouldy*; *liath* e, *his head got grey.*

Liathchearc, llĕă′-chyerk, *n. f.* female of the black grouse *or* blackcock.

Liathfail, lĕa′-fâ′l, *n.f.* the stone on which the ancient kings of Scotland used to be crowned, now in Westminster Abbey. *Smith.*

Liathghlas, lhĕă′-ghlas, *adj.* greyish.

Liathghorm, lĕă′-ghŏrm, *adj.* light-blue, lilac.

Liathlus, lĕăl′-lūs, *n. m.* mugwort.

Liathnach, lĕăn′-nach, *n.m.* hare- *or* hoar-frost. *Islay*; in some places liath-reothadh.

Liaththrosg, lĕă′-hrŏsg, *n. m.* bird fieldfare. *H. S.*

Lid, llėjj, *n. m.* a word, syllable.

Lighe, llé′-å, *n. f.* flood. *H. Society.*

Lighich, lé′-ėch, *v.* doctor, lance, let blood.

Lighiche, lyé′-ėch-å, *n. m.* a physician, a doctor, a surgeon; lighichean, *doctors.*

Linn, lyēnn, *n. f.* a generation, age, ministration, incumbency or time in office, race, offspring; family; day; ri *linn* do sheanmhair, *during the time* or *age of your grandmother*,—long, long ago; anns na *linntean* deireanach, *in the latter days*; ri *linn* Mhaighstir Alastair, *during the ministration* or *incumbency of the Rev. Mr. Alexander*; ri m' *linn, in my day, while I was in office, while I was there*; ri d' *linn*-se, *during your incumbency*; cogadh o *linn* gu *linn, war from generation to generation*; ri d' latha is ri d' *linn, during your day and generation*; *linn* Dhiarmaid o'n Tuirc, *the family of Diarmed from Turkey, Lg.*; o *linn* gu *linn, from one generation to another*; gu *linn* nan linntean, *from generation to generation*; ri *linn* duit dol dachaidh, *at the period you may go home*; eadar da *linn, between wind and water, between sinking and swimming.*

Linne, lyėnn′-å, *n. f.* a pool, a mill-dam, a lake, a sound, a channel; a' dol thar na *linne, crossing the channel*; an *linne* Rosach, *the Sound of Jura*; lit. *the channel of disappointment, it being very ill to navigate.*

Linnich, lyėnn′-ėch, *v.* line, as clothes; sheath, as a vessel; *n. f.* layer; a lining, sheathing; a line, a note, a card in writing; a *linnich* phòsaidh, *marriage-line*; cuir *linnich* a dh'ionnsuidh, *drop him a card*; *linnich* ma seach, *layer about*; a brood *or* dozen of eggs; linig. *N.*

Linnseach, lènn′-shyech, *n. f.* shrouds, canvass.

Liob; see Sliop, a blubber-lip.

Liobasta, see Sliobasta, slovenly, clumsy.

Liobh, lēv, *n. f.* slimy substance like blood on the surface of water—hence Glenlyon, from a memorable battle fought by the Romans there.

Liobhair, lyēv′-ér, *v.* deliver, hand over, resign; in Lochaber, lèū′-ér.

Liobhairt, lēv′-ărty′, *n. f.* delivery, resignation.

Liobhragach, lēv′-rag-ach, *n. f.* kind of sea-lichen, *or* sea-weed of a greenish colour.

Liod, lyėdd, *n. m.* a lisp, stammer.

Liodach, lyēd2′-ach, *adj.* stammering.

Liodaiche, lēd2′-ėch-å, *n. m.* stammerer, stutterer, lisper; impediment of speech.

Liomh, lēv, *v.* put to the grinding-stone; polish, burnish; clach *liomhaidh* neo *liomhain, a grindstone*; clach lionraidh, *in some places.*

Liomharra, lēv′-urr-a, *a.* glossy, polished.

Lion, llēn, *n. m.* lint, flax; a net, a snare; proportionate quantity *or* complement; a bualadh an *lin, beetling the flax*; *lion* lan èisg, *net full of fish*; biadh le a *lion* do ainleann, *food, with its complement*, or *proportionate quantity of condiment*; *v.* fill, satiate, replenish, completely please *or* satisfy; flow as the tide; *lion* an soitheach, *fill the dish*; cha'n'eil so 'gam *lionadh, this does not entirely please me*; thra e *lionadh, the tide is coming in.*

Lionadair, lēn′-ad-ăr, *n. m.* filler.

Lionadh, lēn′-Ă, *n. m.* the reflux of the tide; *pt.* filling, flowing, answering expectations replenishing, satiating.

Lionmhoireachd, lēn′-vur′-achd, *n. f.* numerousness, multiplicity, great abundance.

Lionmhor, lē′-vur, *a.* numerous.

Lionn, lyúnn, *n. m.* humour, (ale.)

Liontach, lēn′-tach, *a.* satiating.

Liontachd, llēnt′-achg, *n. m* satiety; quality of filling by eating but little.

Lios, lēss, *n. m.* garden; fìon lios, *vineyard*; *a fuller*, or *printer's press*; *mangle.*

Liosadair, lèss′-ad-ăr, *n. m.* gardener; a printer, a pressman.

Liosair, lèss′-èr, *v.* press, as cloth; print, mangle, drub most heartily; *liosairte, smoothed, pressed.*

Liosda, lèssd′-a, *adj.* getting more intrusive the more one gets of bounty—importunate, lingering. *H.*

Liosdachd, lèssd′-achg, *n. f.* greed, importunity; tediousness, slowness. *H. S.*

Lip, lyeep, *n. m.* lip. *H. S.*; *Armst.*

Lit, lyėjt′, *n. f.* porridge; fuairlit, cataplasm.

Litir, lyėjt′-èry′, *n. f.* a letter; an epistle.

Litrich, lyėjt′-rèch, *v.* letter, print.

Liug, lyūg, *n. f.* a lame hand. *Arg.*; foot.

Liugach, lyūg′-ach, *a.* lame of hand; *n. f.* an unhandy female; a drab.

Liugaire, lyūg′-ur-a, *n. m.* an unhandy fellow; one with a lame hand.

Liugha, lyū′-a, } *adj.* and *adv.* fre-
Liughad, lyū′-ad, } quent, many; cia *liughad* uair is a thàinig e, *as often as he came*; cia *liugha* uair a dh'innis mi sin duit, *how often have I told you that?*

Lobair, lob′-er, *v.* draggle in the mire.

Lobrogan, a drenched, smeared fellow.

Lobh, lò, *v.* rot, putrify; *adj.* rotten, putrid.

Lobhar, lò′-ar, *n. m.* a leper. *Bible.*

Lobhta, lòt′-a, *n. f.* loft, gallery.

Locair, lochg′-èr, *n. f.* a plane; *v.* plane.

Locradh, lochg′-rĂ, *pt.* planing.

Loch, lòch, *n. f.* a lake; arm of the sea.

Lochan, lòch′-an, *n. m.* a pool; pond.

Lochd, lochg, *n. m.* harm, hurt, mischief, crime, evil, fault; a momentary sleep.

Lochlannach, loch′-llann-ach, *adj.* Danish; *n. m.* a Dane; *n. f* a widgeon.

Lochlainn, lŏch′-llènn, *n. f.* Denmark, Scandinavia; also the Baltic sea; Righ *Lochlainn, the King of Denmark.*

Lochlein, loch-llèn′, *n. f.* the groin; flank of a beast.

Lochran, lôch′ ran, *n. m.* latern. *Bi.*; *Oss.*

Lod, lôd, *n. m.* a load, a broadside, a volley; cargo, lading, burden; pool, puddle.

Lodaich, lod′-èch, *v.* lade, burden.

Lodail, lôd′-al, *a.* clumsy, bulky.

Lodan, lōd2′-an, *n. m.* water in one's shoe.

Lodrach, } lôd′-rech, *n. f.* baggage, lug-
Lodraich, } gage; a great company.

Logais, lŏg′-ash, *n. f.* a slipper; patched shoe.

Logh, lo, *v.* pardon, (not good.)

Loineag, lōėn′-ag, *n. f.* fleece of very fine wool.

Loinean, lŏėn′-an, *n. c.* a greedy gut.

Loineid, lóėn′-ėj, *n. f.* a froth-stick.

Loineis, lŏėn′-ash, *n. f.* fast-speaking.

Loingeas, **Luinneis**, lóènn′-us, *n. f.* shipping, ships; *loingeas* chogaidh, *ships of war*; *loingeas* mharsantachd, *merchant-ship*; *loingeas*-spuinnidh, *pirates, privateers.*

Loinn, loăenn, *n. f.* propriety, ornament, decorum, elegance, grace; dean le *loinn* e, *do it gracefully, do it with propriety*; cha bhi *loinn* ach far am bi thu, *there is no decorum* or *elegance but where thou art*; good state, thriving condition; is beag *loinn* a bhios air do gnothach, *your business cannot be in a thriving condition*; chuir thu bho *loinn* e, *you have spoiled it*; dh'fhalbh, *loinn* an tighe leis, *the ornament*, or *elegance*, or *propriety of the house went with him*; cha mhòr a *loinn, its consequence is not very promising.*

Loinneil, laŏenn′-al, *adj.* handsome, elegant, fine, splendid; duine *loinneil, a splendid fellow, a proper one*; ceòl *loinnei′, fine music*; tigh *loinneil, an elegant house.*

Loir, lŏer, *v.* roll in the mire; drub.

Loirc, lŏérk, *n. f.* wonderfully short foot.

Loirceach, lŏerk′-ach, *adj.* short-footed; *n. f.* a woman whose feet can hardly keep her body from the mire.

Loircire, lŏérk′-èr-ă, *n. m.* a short-footed man, one whose body is almost on the ground.

Loireanach, lŏér′-an-ach, *n. m.* a bespattered dirty little fellow.

Loiseam, lôesh′-um, *n. m.* assumed pomp.

Lois, **Loiseunn**, losh′-ènn, *n. f.* the groin.

Loisg, lōshg, *v.* burn, consume, fire.

Loisgeach, lōshg′-ach, *a.* inflaming, fiery.

Loisgeanta, loshg′-ann-tă, *adj.* very keen, fiery; loisgeantachd, *fieriness.*

Loit, lŏėjt, *v.* sting as a bee *or* snake

Loite, lòjty″-ă, *pt.* stang, stung, bit.

Lom, lōm, *v.* bare, make bare, ill clad, defenceless; bare, clip, pillage, make bare, shave.

Lomadair, lom′-ad-ăėr, *n. m.* a shaver, parer.

Lomadh, lōm′-Ă, *pt.* baring, pillaging; *n. m.* utter ruin, devastation, ruination.

Lomair, lōm′-er, *v.* fleece, shear sheep.

Lomairt, lōm2′-ărty′, *n. f.* a fleece; *pl.* fleecing.

Lomartair, lōm2′-ărt-ăr′, *n. m* sheep-shearer.

Lomhainn, ló-ènn, *n. m.* pack of hounds, a string that ties a pack of hounds.

Loma-lan, lòm′-a-làn, *adv.* quite full.

Loma-luath, lŏm2′-a-lŭă, *adv.* immediately; cho *loma-luath* 's a chì thu e, *as soon as you behold him* or *it*.

Lomnochd, lòm′-nochg, *a.* bare; *n. m.* nakedness.

Lompair, lŏmp′-ăr′, *n. f.* a common.

Lomrach, lŏm′-rach, *a.* fleecy.

Lon, lŏn, *n. m.* voracity, as cattle.

Lon, lŏn, *n. f.* a dub, a marsh, morass, blackbird; also lon-dubh, *a blackbird*; *an elk*.

Lon, lòn, *n. m.* food, provisions—a rope. *St. Kilda*.

Lonach, lŏn′-ach, *a.* voracious; *n.f.* a garrulous voracious female.

Lonaire, lon′-ar′-à, *n. m.* a voracious man.

Long, lŏng, *n. f.* a three masted vessel, ship.

Longphort, lŏng′-fŏrt, *n. m.* a harbour, haven; long mharsantachd, *a merchant-ship*; long chogaidh, *sloop of war*; long-aisig, *a transport*; long spùinnidh, *a pirate*; long dhìon, *a convoy, guard-ship*.

Lonn, lŏnn, *a.* strong, powerful.

Lorg, lôrg, *n. f.* shepherds staff; a trace in links, the sand, &c.; thog mi air luirg e, *I followed his track*; consequence, footsteps; ann an *lorg* a ghnothaich so, *as the consequence of this thing, consequent on this affair*; *v.* search for information, forage, trace; a' *lorg* lòin, *foraging provision*.

Lorgaich, lôrg′-èch, *v.* trace out, track.

Lorgaire, lôrg′-ar-a, *n. m.* a tracer, spy.

Losgadh, losg′-Ă, *n. m.* burning, firing; *pt.* burning, firing, act of burning.

Losgann, lŏsg′-unn, *n m.* a frog, sledge.

Lot, lŏt, *v.* wound, hurt; *n. m.* a wound.

Loth, lŏ, *n. f.* a filly; in *Irish*, cliobag.

Lothail, lŏ′-al, *n. m.* brooklime.

Luach, lŭăch, *n. m.* worth, value.

Luachair, lŭăch′-ar, *n. f.* rushes; *luachair* bhog, *bull-rushes*.

Luachmhor, lŭăch′-ar, *a.* precious, valuable.

Luachmhoireachd, lŭăch′-ur-achg, *n. f.* preciousness, valuableness, worthiness.

Luadh, lŭă-gh, *pt.* mentioning, laying to the charge; *n. c.* a beloved object; mo *luaidh, my dearest dear*!

Luadhadair, lŭă′-ad-ar, *n. m* fuller, waulk-miller.

Luadhadh, lŭă′-Ă, *pt.* waulking, fulling; *n. m.* the act of waulking or fulling cloth, charging, *or* laying to the charge.

Luaidh, lŭăĕ-y′, *v. n.* full, *or* waulk cloth, lay to the charge, mention; *luaidh* an t-aodach, *full the cloth*; na *luaidh* a leithidsin riumsa, *lay not such a thing to my charge*, or *mention not such a thing in connection with my name*; *n. f.* lea , shot, plummet for sounding *or* sinking; na *luaidhibh* dèe eile, *mention not other gods*; stàilinn is *luaidh, steel and lead*; dear object; a luaidh, *my dearest*!

Luaim, lŭăim, *n. f.* restlessness, giddiness.

Luaimneach, lŭăĕm′-nyach, *adj.* restless.

Luain, lŭăĕn, *n. f.* restlessness, giddiness.

Luaineach, lŭăĕn′-ach, *adj.* giddy, restless, changeable, inconstant, volatile—traveller. *H. Society*.

Luaineachd, lŭăĕn′-achg, *n. f.* changeableness, volatility, inconstancy, fickleness; luaineis, *fickle conduct*.

Luaisg, lŭăshg, *v.* wave, swing, rock.

Luaith, lŭăĕch, *n. f.* ashes; *luaith* fhroinnich, *fern ashes*.

Luaithe, lŭăĕ-à, *deg.* luath, faster.

Luaithir, lŭăĕr, *v.* toss in the ashes.

Luaithre, lŭăĕr′-à, *n. f.* see Luaith, ashes.

Luaithreadh, lŭăĕr′-Ă, *pt.* tossing in ashes.

Luaithreach, lŭăĕ′-ryach, *adj.* early, as seed; siol *luaithreach, early oats*, or *seeds*; fobharradh *luaithreach, an early harvest. Islay*.

Luaithreachd, lŭăĕr-achg, *n. f.* earliness

Luaithrich, lŭăĕr′-èch, *v.* make earlier, hasten, expedite.

Luamh, lŭáv2, *n. f.* the lesser paunch.

Luan, lûán, *n. m.* moon, Monday, paunch

Luas, for luathas.

Luasaich, for lughasaich, allow.

Luasgach, lăŭsg′-ach, waving, undulating, oscillating, rocking hither and thither.

Luasgadh, lŭăsg′-Ă, tossing, rocking, tumbling, waving, oscillation.

Luath, lŭă, *adj.* fast, swift, fleet, nimble, quick, speedy, early; each *luath, a fleet horse*; is *luath* a thàinig thu, *you came early*.

Luatha, lŭă′-à, *gen.* of luaith, ashes.

Luathaich, lŭă′-èch, *v.* hasten, quicken.

Luathas, lŭăs, *n. f.* fleetness, speed, fastness, quickness, swiftness of foot; earliness; *luathas* an fhobhair, *the earliness of the harvest*.

Luathbheulach, lŭăv′-véll-ach, *adj.* blabbing, fond of gossipping stories.

Luathlamhach, lŭăl′-láv-ach, *adj.* thievish, tar-fingered; apt to strike.

Lub, lûb, *n. f.* a bend, fold, curvature, loop, noose, cunningness, trick; meander, maze; *v. n.* yield, meander, assert, be deceived by; *lùb* an t-slat, *bend the switch*; tha an abhainn a *lùbadh, the river meanders*; *lùb* i leis, *she was deceived by him, she yielded to his embraces*; na *lùib, in its fold, in contact with*; an *lùib* an domhnuich, *in contact with the Sabbath, in preparation for the Sabbath*.

Luba, lŭb′-ȧ, *n. f.* a dub, marsh, pool.

Lubach, lûb′-ach, *a.* deceitful, meandering;—a loop, a hinge. *H. Society.*

Lubach, lŭb′-ach, *a.* marshy, full of pools.

Lubag, lûb′-ag, *n. f.* a hank of yarn; a little twist *or* meander.

Lubair, lŭb′-ėr, *v.* paddle, draggle.

Lubaire, lûb′-ăr-ȧ, *n. m.* a deceitful person.

Lubairt, lŭb′-arjt, *n. f.* paddling, draggling.

Lunarsaich, lûb′-ar-sėch, *n f.* contortions, serpentine motion, as eels, &c.

Lub-ruith, lŭb-rúėch′, *n. f.* a running noose.

Luch, lŭch, *n. f.* a mouse.

Luchairt, lûch′-ărjty′, *n. f.* palace, castle, an establishment.

Luchd, lŭchg, *n. m.* cargo, load; *luchd* an t-soithich, *the ship's cargo*; also people, folk; also used a sign of the plural; as, *luchd* àiteachaidh, *the husbandmen, cultivators, inhabitants*; *luchd* eolais, *acquaintances, the literati*; *luchd* èisdeachd, *hearers*; *luchd* amhairc, *overseers, superintendants, supervisors, spectators*; *luchd*-leanmhuinn, *followers, adherents, relations*; *luchd* fiosachd, *wizards, witches, soothsayers, sorcerers*; luchd dìon, *luchd* faire, *a watch, watchmen*; *luchd*-mìoruin, *malicious people, haters*; *luchd*-turais, *travellers.*

Luchdaich, lŭchd-ėch, *v.* load, lade; di-*luchdaich, discharge a cargo, unship.*

Luchdail, lŭchg′-al, } *adj* capacious,
Luchdmhor, lŭchg′-ur, } capable of containing much.

Ludhaig, see Lughasaich, permit, allow.

Lug, lûg, *n. f.* a bandy-leg, brabhd, *Harris.*

Luga, lŭg′-ȧ, *n. f.* sea sand-worm.

Lugach, lûg′-ach, *adj.* bandy-legged.

Lugh, lŭ, *n. m.* a joint; as cionn an *luigh, above the joint*; sgion-*luigh, clasp-knife.*

Lugh, lû-*gh*′, *n. m.* power of a limb; tha chas gun *lùgh, his foot is powerless*; chàill e *lùgh* a laimhe, *he lost the power of his arm*; locomotion, power of motion; chàill e *lùgh, he lost his power of motion, locomotion.*

Lugh, lŭ, *a.* blaspheme; a' *lughadh* na Trianaid bheannaichte, *blaspheming the holy Trinity.*

Lugha, lú′-ȧ, *deg.* beag, little, less, least; is *lugha, less, least*; more *or* most disagreeable; is *lugha* orm thu na sneachd, *you are more disagreeable to me than the snow.*

Lughad, lú-ud, *n. f.* littleness, degree of littleness.

Lughadair, lŭ′-ad-ăr′, *n. m.* blasphemer.

Lughadaireachd, lŭ′-ad-dry-achg, *n. f.* blasphemy; ri *lughadaireachd, blaspheming*; *blasphemy.*

Lugh dh, lŭ′-Ă, *pt.* blaspheming; *n. m.* blasphemy, profanation, swearing, profaning.

Lughadrach, lugh′-ad-rach, *a.* blasphemous.

Lughaide, lú′-ăj-ȧ, *adv.*; also *deg.* of beag; cha *lughaide* e sin, *it is not the less for that*; cha *lughaide, perhaps.*

Lugharr, } lû′-ghurr, *adj.* swift of foot;
Lughmhor, } fleet, nimble, brisk, strong.

Lugharrachd, } lû′-ghurr-achg, *n. f.*
Lughmhoireachd, } agility, fleetness, nimbleness.

Lughasachadh, lŭ′-as-ach-Ă, *pt.* ordaining, decreeing, allowing, permitting; 'na tha Dia a' *lughasachadh* dhomh, *what God decrees for me*; an *lughasaich* thusa dhomhsa, *do you allow* or *permit me? n. m.* allowance, permission, decree, ordination.

Lughasaich, lŭ′-ăs-ėch, *v.* allow, permit, advise, ordain, decree, line out; am bheil thu a' *lughasachadh* dhomhsa so a' dheanadh, *do you allow* or *advise me to do this? lughasaich* Dia clann da, *God ordained that he should have offspring.*

Lughchleas, lŭ-gh′-chlăs[2], *n. m.* slight-of-hand, legerdemain, jugglery; *lughchleasach, juggling, expert in slight-of-hand* or *legerdemain.*

Lughchleasachd, lŭ′-gh-chlăs[2]-achg, *n. f.* slight-of-hand; activity, agility, juggling.

Lughdachadh, lùd′-ach-Ă, *pt.* lessening, diminishing; *n. m.* diminution, subtraction, decrease.

Lughdag, lùd′-ag, *n. f.* the little finger.

Lughdagan, lud′-ag-an, *n. m.* pivot of a hinge; also lughdallan.

Lughdaich, lùd′-ėch, *v.* diminish, lessen, decrease, subtract, undervalue.

Lughdalann, lú′-gh-al-ann, *n. m.* hinge-pivot.

Lughdarna, lŭd′-arn-ȧ, } heavy, clumsy,
Lughdarra, lŭd′-urr-a, } unwieldy, stupid.

Lughdarnachd, lŭd′-arn-achg, *n. f.* clumsiness; a drawling, unseemly gait; untidiness.

Luib, lŭėb, *n. f.* a bay, creek; a fold, corner.

Luibeach, lŭĕb′-ach, *adj.* meandering, serpentine; full of creeks *or* corners.

Luibh, } lŭĕ′-yh′, *n. f.* an herb, a plant.
Luigh, }

Luid, lŭjj, *n. f.* a rag, a tatter.

Luideach, lŭjj′-ach, *adj.* ragged, tattered.

Luideag, lŭjj′-ag, *n. f.* a rag, tatter.

Luideagach, lujj′-ag-ach, *adj.* ragged; is màirg a bheireadh droch mheas air gille *luideagach* is air loth pheallagach, *a ragged boy and shaggy colt should never be despised.*

Luidealach, lujj′-al-ach, *n. c.* a ragged person, *or* shaggy beast; lazy fellow. *H. S*

Luidh, lûė, *v.* lie down, settle, perch; same as laidh.

Luidhe, lú'-ė, *n.f.* lying, perching; *laidhe*, shùibhladh, *child-bed, parturition.*

Luidir, lŭjj'-ėr, *v.* roll in the mire *or* mud; paddle through water, besmear, bedaub.

Luidhear, lŭė'-yhar, *n.m.* a vent, chimney.

Luidreach, lŭjj'-ryach, *n.f.* a ragged garment; ragged, clumsy person.

Luidreadh, lŭjj'-ră, *n. m.* rolling in the mire, puddling; *pt.* rolling, puddling, besmearing.

Luidse, Luidseach, lŭjj'-sha, *and* -shach, *n. c.* a clumsy, awkward, dull, stupid person.

Luig, lŭėg, *n. f. gen.* lag; thun a luig, *towards the hollow* or *glen.*

Luigh, lŭė'-yh', *n. f.* an herb, a plant; *luigh* na macraidh, *wild thyme*; *luigh* na tri beann, *trefoil*; sometimes written luibh, but uniformly pronounced lŭė'-yh'.

Luigheachd, lŭĕ'-yhyachg, *n. f.* reward.

Luigheadair, lŭĕ-yhyead'-ăr', *n. m.* herbalist, botanist.

Luigheanach, lŭĕ'-yhyan-ach, } *n.f.* noxious
Luighearnach, lŭĕ'-yharn-ach, } weeds;—botanist. *H. S.*

Luim, lŭĕm, *n. f.* shift, resource, invention; leig ga *luim* f'héin, *leave him to his own resources*, or *his own shifts*; *gen.* of lom.

Luime, lŭĕm'-ă, *n. f.* sheer poverty, bareness, smoothness; 's i an *luime* a thug air a dheanadh, *sheer poverty forced him to it*; also more *or* most bare, (lom.)

Luinn, lŭėnn, *plu.* of lunn; also *gen.*; also the island of Luing.

Luinneach, lŭėnn'-ach, *a.* belonging to Luing; *n.m.* an inhabitant of Luing.

Luinneag, lŭnn'-ag, *n. m.* a ditty, sonnet; mournful voice *or* sound; a chorus.

Luinneanachd, lŭėnn'-an2-achg, *n. f.* paddling; sailing for pleasure about quays.

Luinneas, lŭėnn'-us, *n. f.* shipping.

Luinnseach, lŭėnn'-shyach, *n. c.* a very tall, slim, bowed-down fellow.

Luir, lŭėr, *v.* torture, torment; give most acute pain, drub most lustily; 'gam *lùireadh, torturing me.*

Luireach, lûr''-ach, *n. f.* a coat of mail.

Luirgneach, luėrg'-nyach, *a.* sheep-shanked.

Luirist, lŭėr'-ėshj, *n. c.* a tall, slender, slovenly, pithless, good-for-nothing person.

Luis, lŭsh, *n. pt* herbs; also *gen.* lus.

Lunasda, lûn'-usd-a, } *n. m.* Lammas,
Lunasdal, lûn'-usd-al, } 1st of August.

Lunn, lŭnn, *n. m.* a heaving billow; a heaver that does not break; a bier, a spoke *or* lever; the mid-part of an oar.

Lunnainn, lŭnn'-ėnn, *n. m.* London, —*lunn*-inne, i. e. *resting-place of waves.*

Lunnainneach, lŭnn'-ėnn-ach, *n. m.* a Cockney; *adj.* Cockney.

Lunndach, lŭnnd'-ach, *a.* very indolent.

Lunndachd, lŭnnd'-achg, *n. f.* extreme indolence *or* laziness; lounging.

Lunndaire, lŭnnd'-ar'-ă, *n. m.* a lounger, a loung; indolent fellow.

Lunndaireachd, lŭnnd'-ar-achg, *n. f.* lounging, sheer indolence, sluggishness.

Lunntair, lŭnnt'-ėr, *v.* put down and thump; box and kick with all your might.

Lunntairt, lŭnnt'-arty', *n. f.* a most complete thumping, boxing, and kicking.

Lupaid, lŭp'-ėjj, *n. f.* St. Patrick's sister.

Lur, lŭr, *n. m.* a gem, a jewel, a treasure, delight; tha, a *lur, yes, my jewel! my darling!*

Luradair, lur'-ad-ăr', *n. m.* a jeweller.

Lurach, lŭr'-ach, *adj.* exquisitely beautiful; gem-like, jewel-like, grand, superb.

Luraicheas, lŭr'-ėch-as, *n. f.* surpassing beauty; elegance, neatness.

Lurg, lŭrg, *n.f.* shin, shank, stem, *or* stalk, as of an herb; shaft; also *lurgann, lurg* an f'heoir, *the stem of the grass.*

Lus, lŭs, *n. m.* an herb, plant; *lus* a bhalla, *pellitory*; *lus* a bhaine, *milkwort*; *lus* a choire, *coriander*; *lus* a chàlmain, *columbine*; *lus* a chorrain, *spleenwort*; *lus* a chinn, *daffodill*; *lus* a chrùbain, *gentian*; *lus* an t-sleugaire, *laveage*; *lus* an t-siùcair, *succory*; *lus* bealtainn, *marigold*; *lus* na fola, *yarrow, milfoil*; *lus* na (*or* lus-rìgh) macraidh, *wild thyme*; *lus* an t-samhraidh, *gilly-flower*; *lus* mhic cruiminn, *cummin*; *lus*-crè, *speedwell*; *lus* garbh, *goose-grass*; *lus* a phìobaire, *dittany*; *lus* na miall, *scorpion-grass*; *lus* na fearnaich, *sun-dew*; *lus* nan cnàmh, *samphire*; *lus* nan dearc, *blackberry plant*; *lus* nan gnàithseag, *whortleberry plant*; *lus* nan meall, *mallow*; *lus* nan laoch, *rosewort*; *lus* nan laogh, *golden saxifrage*; *lus* nan leac, *eye-bright*; *lus* nan sìbhreach, *loose-strife*; an trì-bhileach neo lus nan trì-bilean, *valerian.*

Lusach, lŭs'-ach, *a.* botanical; full of herbs.

Lusadair, lŭs'-ad-ăěr, *n. m.* a botanist, herbalist.

Lusadaireachd, lŭs'-ad-ăėr-achg, *n.f.* botany; study of botany.

Lusarnach, lus'-arn-ach, *n.f.* weeds.

Lusrach, lŭs'-rach, *adj.* full of herbs; *n.f.* herbage; a place well supplied with herbs; *lusrach* a' searg air beinn, *herbage withering on a hill. Sm.*

Luth, provincial for lùgh; pronounced lû'-*gh*.

M

M, m, the tenth letter of the alphabet; muin, the vine; gives a peculiar nasal sound to a, and e, ending words; ràmh, tàmh, ròmach, neamh, pronounced and marked in the key ràv, tàv, ròm-ach, nèvv; at the beginning of words, sounds v*h*.; as, mhean, v*h*én.

'M, m, for am, art; after words ending with a vowel; as, tu '*m* balach, *thou art a boor.* 2d, for ann am, in the, in a, (pre and am, art); as, e '*m* fonn nam beò, (ann am fonn &c.) *he in the land of the living*; taobh na creige '*m* blàs (for ann am blàs) na grèine, *aside the rock in the warmth of the sun.* 3d, for am, *relative pro.*—as, ma '*m* bi iad ag ràdh, *about whom they assert.* 4th, for *interog. pro.* and *interog. conj.*—as, '*m* bheil tuigse aig neach, *has any understanding?* 5th, for am, their; as, le '*m* beul is le '*m* bilibh, *with their mouth and with their lips, B.* 6th, for am, *inter. part.*; as, am bheil e, *is he?* gus '*m* bu mharbh iad, *till they died, while they lived*; see Am in all its variations, page 10.

M' for mo, my—used before vowels; as, *m'* athair, *m'* anam, *my father, my soul.* 2d, for ma, (or if fond of nonsense MU,) *prep. ma* fhichead, *about twenty*; *ma* cheud, *about a hundred*; (*Welsh,* ma and am.)

M'A, for ma a; as, *m'a* cheann, *about his*; (ma a cheann,) *about his head*; *m'a* casan, *about her feet*; (ma a casan.)

MA, mhă, *conj. if*; *ma's* aille le neach 'sam bith tighinn am dhèigh-sa, àicheadh 'se e fèin, *if any man will come after me, let him deny himself*; *ma's* e agus, *if so be*; *ma* 's e 's gu 'm bi, *if so be that it be*; *ma* 's urrainn mi, *if I can.*—*Heb.* mah, if; also *Arm.* ma, if.

MAB, mab, *n. m.* stutter, a lisp, stammer; *v.* abuse, vilify, reproach, *H. S.*; tassel; see Pab.

MABACH, mab-ach, *adj.* lisping, stuttering; *n. f.* stuttering *or* stammering female.

MABACHD, mab'-achg, *n. f.* stammering.

MABAIRE, mab'-ur-à, *n. m.* stammerer.

MAC, machg, *n. m.* son, a darling, used for the young of any animal, and almost in the names of all the Highlanders; *mac* brathar athar, *a paternal cousin german*; *mac* brathar, *nephew, brother's son*; *mac* peathar, *nephew by the sister*; *mac* brathar mathar, *maternal cousin german*; *mac* brathar seanar, *a paternal grand uncle's son*; *mac* brathar seanmhar, *a maternal grand uncle's son*; *mac* an dogha *bur dock*; *mac* an luinn, *Fingal's sword*; *mac* samhuilt, *match, like, equal*; *mac* sgal, *an echo*; bheireadh e *mac*-sgal a creagan, *he would make the very rocks re-echo*; also, *mac* tallamh—*mac* mallachd, *Old Pluto, Old Nick*; *mac* meamnadh, *a whim, imagination*; *mac* làmhaich, *Sea Devil*, greusaiche.

MACABH, machg'-uv, *n. pl.* an accomplished hero.

MACAIL, machg'-al, *adj.* filial.

MACANTA, machg'-ant-a, *adj.* meek.

MACANTACHD, machg'-ant-achg, *n. f.* meekness, urbanity; na daoine *macanta, the meek. Bible.*

MACANTAS, machg'-ant-us, *n. f.* meekness.

MACH, măch, *adv.* outside, without, out; thugaibh a *mach, take out*; a *mach* 'sa mach, *wholly, thoroughly, altogether*; bithibh cinnteach gu faigh bhur peacadh a *mach* sibh, *be sure that your sins shall find you out*; thug an Tighearna *mach* clann Isreal a tigh na daorsa, *the Lord brought out the children of Israel out of the house of bondage*; *mach* air a chèile, *at variance*; *int.* out! get out! *conj.* except, but; *mach* o h-aon, *but one, except one.*

MACHAIR, mach'-èr, *n. f.* an extensive beach, a plain; seldom used for any thing else in common speech but *beach.*

MACLACH, mach'-lach, *n. f.* womb.

MACNUS, machg'-nus, *n. m.* lust.

MACNUSACH, machg'-nus-ach, *a.* lustful.

MADACHAIL, mad'-ach-al, *a.* doggish.

MADADH, mad'-Ă, *n. m.* a dog; the hold for the flint in a gun; *madadh*-ruadh, *a fox*; *madadh* gal, neo alluidh, *a wolf.*

MADAR, mâd'-ur, *n. m.* madder.

MADRAIDH, mad'-rè, *n. pl.* dogs, pack of dogs.

MADUINN, mad'-ènn, *n. f.* morn, morning in Argyle maidinn. *French,* matin. *Italian,* matìna.

MADUINNEAG, mad'-ènn-ag, morning star.

MAG, mâg, *n. f.* a soft plump hand; a paw; air a *mhàgan, he on all-fours*; arable land, *N.—W.* a very broad ridge of land.

MAG, măg, *v.* scoff, deride; magadh, *deriding, ridiculing, mocking, scoffing.*

MAGACH, mâg'-ach, *adj.* having short feet and broad, as a cow, pawed; having soft large plump hands; a frog.

MAGAIL, mag'-al, *adj.* derisive, mocking.

MAGAILL, mâg'-èlly', *v.* paw; *pt.* pawing.

MAGAIR, mâg'-èr, *v.* creep slyly, paw.

MAGAIRE, mag'-ar'-à, *n.m.* scoffer, mocker.

MAGAIRT, mâg'-arjty', *n. f.* pawing.

MAGAIRLE, mag'-arly'-à, *n. f.* scrotum, testicle.

MAGH, magh, *n. f.* a field, plain.

Maghar, maŏ′-ar, *n. m.* artificial fly.

Maide, májj′-ậ, *n. m.* a stick; *maide* milis, *root of sea grass, called liquorice.*

Maidealag, maŏdjj′-al-ag, *n. f.* a small shell, *Lewis*; (paindeag,) part of a spinning-wheel.

Maideannas, n ăjj′-unn-us, *n. m.* morning-dram.

Maidinn, mèjj′-ènn′, *n. f.* morning.

Maidinneach, mejj′-ènn′-ach, *adj.* early.

Maidne, mejj′-nyâ, *gen.* of morning.

Maidneach, mejj′-nyàch, *n. f.* morning-star.

Maidse, májj′-shâ, *n. m.* a turd; smàidse.

Maidsear, mèjj′-shar, *n. m.* a major in the army. *H. Society.*

Maigh, mī′-yh, *n. m.* May, Macdonald.

Maighdean, maŏèjj′-un, *n. f.* a virgin, a maid, maiden; *maighdean*-mhara, *a mermaid.*

Maighdeanas, maŏejj′-unn-us, *n. f.* virginity.

Maigheach, moy′-ach, *n. m.* a hare.

Maighstir, mīèsht′-èr, *n. m.* master.

Maighstireachd, mīèsht′-èr-achg, *n. f.* mastery, superiority; superintendance, superiority; assumed authority, officiousness, rule.

Maighstirealachd, māèsht″-èr′-al-achg, *n. f.* assumption of undue authority, masterliness.

Maighstireil, māèshty″-er-al, *adj.* lordly, authoritive, dogmatical, arbitrary.

Maileid, mâl′-ăj, *n. f.* a wallet, budget; pack; in derision a gorbelly.

Maileideach, mâl′-ăj-ach, *adj* gorbellied.

Maille, măly2′-â, *n. f.* delay; *maille* ri, *along with*; *maille* ris an sin, *together with that*; comhla ris an sin, *rather.*

Mailleach, màly′-ăch, *n. f.* coat-of-mail.

Maim, maŏèm, *n. f.* a panic, horror.

Mainnir, máènn″-èr, *n f.* sheep-fold, pen.

Mair, măèr, *v.* last, live, endure; neas a *mhàireas* an ruaig, *while the pursuit lasts*; cha *mhair* iad leith an là, *they shall not live half their days*; *mairidh* tròcair Dhè, gu sìor, *God's mercy shall endure for ever.*

Mairbh, maŏèrv, *gen.* of marbh; na *mairbh*, *the dead*; am beò 'sna *mairbh*, *the living and the dead.*

Mairc, măèrk, *n. f.* objection, subject of regret; cò chuir *mairc* ort, *who objected to you*? cha do chuir mise *mairc* sam bith air, *I did not oppose him* or *it.*

Maireach, màèr′-ach, *n. m.* next day; an diugh is a *màireach*, *to-day and to-morrow.*

Maireachdainn, Mairsiunn, măèr′-achg-ènn, marsh′-ènn, *part.* enduring, lasting, continuing.

Maireann, măèr′-unn, *n. m.* life-time; *adj.* living, in the land of the living; ri d' *mhaireann*, *during your life-time*; cha *mhaireann* e, *he is not living*; am fear nach *maireann*, *he that is not living, he that is no more.*

Maireannach, măĕr″-unn-ach, *adj.* everlasting, eternal; a' bheatha *mhaireannach*, *everlasting life.*

Mairg, màrèg, *n. m.* great pity, object, *or* subject of regret; cha *mhàirg* tè a fhuair e, *she is no subject of regret that has got him, got it*; is *màirg* dhuit a rinn e, *it is a great pity you did it*; is *màirg* dhuit nach d' thigeadh, *it is a pity you would not come*; *adj.* deplorable, pitiable, silly; sonn nach *màirg*, *a hero that is not to be pitied*; is *màirg* a loisgeadh a thiompan duit, *silly is he that would burn his harp to warm you.*

Mairiste, màèr′-èshty′-â, *n. m.* match, marriage; fhuair i an deadh *mhairiste*, *she got an excellent match*; a' deanadh a suas a' *mhairiste*, *making up the match.*

Mairisteach, maèr′-èshj′-ach, *adj.* marriageable.

Mairneal, màèr′-nyal, *n. m.* detention; slow, drawling manner, dilatoriness; procrastination.

Mairnealach, màèr″-al-ach, *adj.* dilatory, tardy, tedious, drawling in manner; procrastinating.

Mairnealachd, màèrn′-al-achg, *n. f.* procrastination, dilatoriness, dilatory manner.

Mairsinn, măr′-shyènn, *adj.* lasting, living.

Mairtfheoil, maerty″-ĕŏl, *n. f.* beef.

Mairtireach, màrty′-er-ach, *n. m.* martyr. *Bible.*

Maise, măsh′-â, *n. f.* ornament, great beauty, elegance; chuireadh tu *maise* air baile, *you would prove an ornament to a city*; *maise* nam ban, *the ornament of women. Bible.*

Maiseach, măsh′-ach, *adj.* ornamental; very elegant *or* handsome; fair; is *maisich* thu na clan na daoine, *thou art fairer than the sons of men. Sm.*; nighean *mhaiseach*, *an elegant female.*

Maiseachd, măsh′-achg, *n. f.* superiority in beauty, handsomeness, elegance, fairness.

Maisealachd, măsh′-achg, *n. f.* elegance.

Maiseil, măsh′-al, *adj.* ornamental.

Maistir, măèshjty″-èr, *n. m.* stale urine.

Maistir, măshty′-èr, } *v.* churn, agitate as liquids.
Maistrich, mash′-trèch, }

Maistreadh, mashj′-rĂ, *pt.* churning, agitating; also the quantity of butter taken off a churn.

Maiteach, màèty′-ach, *adj.* ready to forgive.

Maith, maech*or* măĕ, provincial for math; also *gen.* of math, good, well; *v.* forgive.

Maithean, măĕ'-un, *n. p.* magistrates, aldermen, nobles; thàinig maithre is *maithean* bhaile-chliabh mach 'na coinneamh, *the Lord Mayor and magistrates of Dublin came out to meet them*; *maithean* na Féinne, *the nobles* or *chiefs of the Fingalians.*

Maitheas, măĕ'-us, (from maith, *gen.*) mercy, goodness, bounty of God.

Mal, màl, *n. m.* rent, tribute.

Mal-ios, mal'-ēs, *n. f.* portmanteau.

Mala, màl'-à, *n. f.* bag of a pipe; budget; dà *mhàla, two bags. Bible.*

Mala, mall'-à, *n. f.* eye-brow.

Malach, mal'-ach, *adj.* having large brows; surly, sulky, forbidding.

Maladair, màl'-ad-ăr', *n. m.* a sub-tenant who pays rent in kind; renter, tenant.

Malairt, măl'-arjt, *n. f.* exchange, barter, space; *v.* exchange, barter, traffic, trade.

Malairteach, màl'-arjty"-ach, *a.* exchangeable, mutual, reciprocal; fit to exchange.

Malairtich, mal'-ărjty'-ėch, *v.* barter.

Malairtear, mal'-ărjty²-ar', *n.m.* barterer.

Malc, mălk, *v.* begin to rot *or* putrify.

Malda, màld'-à, *adj.* modest, gentle.

Maldachd, màld'-achg, *n. f.* gentleness, diffidence.

Mall, mâll, *adj.* slow, tardy, late; bitheadh gach duine ealamh chum éisdeachd *mall* chum labhairt, *mall* chum feirge, *let every man be quick to hear, slow* (or diffident) *to speak*; calm; feasgair *mall* is na h'eoin a' séinn, *a calm evening, and the birds warbling.* (*Smith's Poems.*)

Mallachadh, mall'-ach-Ă, *pt.* cursing; it is written mollachadh—always pronounced so.

Mallachd, mŏll'-achg, *n. f.* malediction.

Mallaich, mŏll'-ėch, *v.* curse, imprecate.

Mam, màm, *n. m.* an extensive moor, gently rising and not pointed; a palm full of meal, &c. a bile in the arm-pit, *or* palm of the hand; mother.

Mamaidh, mam'-ė, *n. f.* mamma.

Mam-sic, mam'-shēchg², *n. m.* rupture, hernia.

M'an, măn, (for ma an,) m'an d'fhuair e bàs, *before he died.*

Manach, see Mann, Mannach, monk.

Manadh, măn'-Ă, *n. m.* omen, sign, apparition, enchantment; choinnic e *manadh, he saw an apparition*; tha e a' cuir air *mhanadh* dhomh, *he prophesies to me.*

Manas, màn'-us, *n. m.* a farm in the natural possession of a proprietor. *H. S.*

Mandrag, mănd'-rag, *n. f.* mandrake. *B.*

Mang, măng, *n. f.* a fawn, deer.

Mannd, mannd, *n m.* a lisp, stammer.

Manndach, mănnd'-ach, *a.* lisping.

Manran, mànr'-an, *n. m.* dandering, humming a tune to banish vexation.

Manrain, manr'-ăėn, *v.* dander; *manrain* thusa air t' aghaidh, *dander you forward.*

Maodal, māod'-ul, *n. f.* paunch, maw.

Maodalach, māod'-al-ach, *a.* having a large belly, clumsy; a clumsy corpulent female in contempt, (in some parts a servant girl.)

Maoidh, mòėyh', *v. n.* threaten, cast up favours bestowed, upbraid; tha e *maoidheadh* orm, *he threatens me*; tha e *maoidheadh* gu 'n do rinn e siod is so dhomh, *he casts up that he did this and that for me.*

Maoidheadh, māoėyh'-Ă, *n m. pt.* a threat, upbraiding; casting up favours bestowed, reproaching; ma tha aon neach agaibh a dh' uirbheasbhuidh gliocais, iarradh e o Dhia, a bheir do gach neach gu pailt agus nach *maoidh, if any of you lack wisdom let him ask of God, who giveth all men liberally and upbraideth not. Apostle James.*

Maoidhean, múe'-an, *n.* supplication. *B.*

Maoidhseig, mòsh'-ag, *n. f.* fastidiousness.

Maoile, māoil'-à, *n. f.* baldness; an aite fuilt bitheadh *maoile, instead of hair, baldness. B.*

Maoilead, māoėl'-ud, *n. f.* degree of baldness.

Maoim, māoėm, *n. f.* panic, wild expression of countenance; biodh *maoim* air do naimhdean, *let your enemies be in a panic*; a burst, expressions of fear; *v.* horrify, terrify.

Maoim-sleibhe, maŏėm-slyāv'-à, *n. f.* a water-spout *or* plump of rain all of a sudden.

Maoin, māoėn, *n. m.* a hoard, hoarded wealth; wealth worshipped; goods, *Cat. R.*

Maoirne, māoėrny"-à, *n. m.* a little one, as potatoes; in *North*, a bait.

Maoirnean, maoern"-an, *n. m.* little potato.

Maois, mùsh, *n. m.* Moses; hamper, a heap of sea weed on the shore, *North*; in *Argyle*, five hundred fresh herrings in time of fishing.

Maoiseach, māosh'-ach, } a roe *or* doe,
Maoisleach, māosh'-llyach, } a she deer.

Maol, māol, *n. f.* Mull, *or* chief headland, *or* cape of land; Maol-chintire, *Maol* na h-ò, *the Mull of Kyntire, Mull of Kinnouth*; a head polled, *or* cropped; cow without horns;—a holy man's servant. *Obs. v.* blunt.

Maolachadh, maol'-ach-Ă, *pt.* blunting; laying down the ears as a horse.

MAOLAG, māol′-ag, *n. f.* a dish for milk—stocking wanting the head. *North.*

MAOLAICH, māol′-ēch, *v.* blunt, deprive of edge; *mhaolaich* an sgian, *the knife got blunt*; lay down the ears as horses, hares, *or* does.

MAOLCHLUASACH, māol′-chlūās-ach, *adj.* blunt, dull, stupid, dull of hearing.

MAOLCHLUASAICH, māol′-chlūās-ēch, *n f.* stupidity, dulness, lifelessness.

MAOLOISEAN, maol′-ōsh-an′, *n. m.* high-temple.

MAOLOISEANACH, maol′-ōsh-an′-ach, high-templed, as a person.

MAOR, māor, *n. m.* messenger, an officer, *maor*-baile, *an under bailiff*; *maor* coille, *a wood-ranger*; *maor*-siorram, *a sheriff officer*; *maor* Rìgh, *a messenger at arms, King's messenger*; *maor*-cìse, *a tax gatherer, assessor*; *maor*-strìopach, *a pimp, pander*; *maor*-rinndeil, *a ground-officer*—a great man formerly.

MAORACH, māōr′-ach, *n. m.* shell-fish; a bait or allurement for fishing.

MAORSUINNEACHD, māor′-senn-achg, *n. f.* office of a messenger; officiousness, meddling.

MAOTH, mù, mùgh, *adj.* tender, soft; of a tender age; delicate; muirichinn *mhaoth, a large family slenderly provided for, of a tender age.*

MAOTHAG, mù′-ag, *n. f.* premature egg.

MAOTHAICH, mù′-ēch, *v.* soften, alleviate.

MAOTHAIL, mù′-al, *adj.* emolient.

MAOTHALACHD, mù′-al-achg, *n. f.* delicacy, tenderness, softness; a thaobh mùirn agus *maothalachd, on account of tenderness and delicacy.*

MAOTHAN, mù′-an, *n. m.* cartilage, a twig.

MAOTHAIN, mù′-ăen, *n. pl.* abdomen, a disease of young persons arising from raising burdens.

MAOTH-BHLATH, mù-bhlâ′, *a.* lukewarm.

MAOTH-BHLATHAS, mù-v*h*làs′, *n. f.* lukewarmness, half indifference.

MAOTHRAN, mùr′-an, *n. m.* an infant, child.

MAOTHRANACH, mùr′-an-ach, *a* infantile

MAR, măr, *conj.* as, just as, even as, like, in the same manner; *mar* theicheas iad, *as they scamper*; *mar* rinn mise, *just as I did*; rinn e mar sin, *he did so, in like manner*; *mar* bu mhiann leis, *just as he would wish*; *mar* gu 'm b'ann, *just as it were*; *mar* sin, *in that manner.*

MARA, măr′-à, *gen.* of muir, sea.

MARACHD, măr′-achg, *n. f.* seafaring life, navigation; ri *marachd, following the sea.*

MARAG, măr′-ăg, *n. f.* pudding, thick person.

MARAICHE, mar′-ēch-à, *n. m.* seaman, marine.

MARAON, mar′-ùn, *adv.* together, in concert.

MARASGAIL, már′-asg-ēl, *v.* manage, trade.

MARASGAL, mar′-ask-ul, *n. m.* managing.

MARASGLADH, már′-ăsg-lÅ, *n. m.* management, superintendance, supervision, traffic.

MARASGLACHD, măr′-ăsg-lachg, *n. f.* see above.

MARASGLAICH, mar′asg-lēch, *v.* superintend, guide, oversee, rule, trade with. *Is.*

MARBH, mârv, *adj.* dead, lifeless, dull; *v.* kill, slay, slaughter; *n.* the dead.

MARBHADH, măr′-Å, *n. m.* and *pt.* killing.

MARBHANACH, marv-an-ach, *n. c.* person almost dead, one pretending to be dead.

MARBHANTA, mărv′-ant-à, *adj.* inactive.

MARBHANTACHD, mărv′-ant-achg, *n. f.* dulness, inactivity, stupor, marbhantas.

MARBHPHAISG, marv′-făshg, *n. m.* a coffin, used as hearses are now; it was very ingeniously constructed, having a slider in the bottom, and otherwise formed so as to prevent the body being seen till covered by the earth—afterwards it was conveyed to the church, till another occasion—hence, marbhphaisg ort, *may you slip into your grave without a coffin.*

MARBHRANN, marv′-rănn, *n. f.* an elegy; a funeral oration; also rann-mairbh.

MARBHSHRUTH, marv′-hrŭ, *n. m.* slack-water.

MARC, mărk, *n. m.* charger, steed, a horse; *marc* uaibhreach, ard-cheumach, *a proud, high-bounding horse* or *charger. Smith.*

MARCACHD, mark′-achg, *n. f.* a ride, act of riding, equestrianism, (from marc.)

MARCAICH, mark′-ēch, *v.* ride.

MARCAICHE, mărk′-ēch-à, *n. m.* rider, equestrian; also marcair, marclann, stable.

MARCAID, mark′-aj, *n. m.* market. Cow. S. Tay.

MARCSHLUAGH, mark′-hlua-gh′, *n. f.* cavalry, horsemen.

MARG, mârg, *n. m.* a merk, 13½d.

MARGADH, mărg′-Å, *n. m.* market, sale.

MARGAIL, mârg′-al, } *adj.* marketable,
MARGADAIL, mârg′ad-al, } saleable, disposable.

MARGADALACHD, mârg′-ad-all-achg, *n. f.* saleableness.

MARL, mârl, *n. m.* the clay, marl.

MARMHOR, marv′-ur, *adj.* marble. *Bible.*

MAR-RI, bawdy-word.

MARR, màrr, *v.* obstruct, hinder. *Gen.*

MARRACH, mârr′-ach, *n. f.* enchanted castle, entering which, none could find his way back till the spell was removed; a thicket to catch cattle in; a labyrinth.

MARSANTA, mars′-ant-à, *n. m.* merchant.

MARSANTACHD, mars′-ant-achg, *n. f.* merchandise, wares, trade, traffic, dealing.

Mar so, mar'-shŏ, *adv.* in this way.

Mar siod, măr'-shědd, and shŭdd, *adv.* in that way, in that manner *or* method.

Mart, mârt, *n. m.* seed-time, March, the throngest time at any thing, throng; great haste.

Mart, mărt, *n. f.* a cow, cow to kill.

Martair, mârt'-ar', *n. m.* a cripple. *Arm.*

Ma's, (ma, and is,) măs, if; *ma's* e agus, *if so be*; *ma's* e agus gu, *if so it be that*; *ma's* e 's nach, *if so be that not*; *ma's* fhìor e fhèin, *in his own belief, if he judges aright*

Mas, màs, *n. m.* buttock, hip; do *màsan*, *your buttocks*; bottom of dish; *màs* cuinneig, *pitcher's bottom.*

Masach, màs'-ach, *adj.* large-hipped, having large hips; *n. f.* a large-hipped female.

Masaire, mās'-ur'-ȧ, *n. m.* large-hipped man

Masan, măs'-an, *n. m.* dilatoriness.

Masanach, mas'-an-ach, *adj.* dilatory.

Ma seach, ma'-shech, *adv. prep.* time about, alternately; uair *ma seach, time about, one by one*; deanaibh *ma seach* e, *do it alternately.*

Ma seadh, ma'-shyaŏgh, *conj.* if so be, then.

Masg, măsg, *v.* infuse, as tea, mash as malt.

Masgadh, masg'-Ă, *pt.* mashing, infusing; *n. m.* a mash; an infusion.

Masgaire, masg'-ăr'-ȧ, *n. m.* mashman.

Masgall, masg'-all, *n. m.* flattery. *H.*

Maslach, mas'-llach, *adj.* disgraceful, ignominious, reproachful; slandering.

Masladh, măs'-llĂ, *n. m.* disgrace.

Maslaich, măs'-llèch, *v.* disgrace, taunt, degrade; maslaichte, *disgraced, slandered.*

Mata, ma-tâ', *inter.* then! oh! *adv.* and *conj.* indeed, nevertheless, then, if so, truly, really.

Math, mhá, *v.* pardon, forgive; *math* dhuinn ar peacadh, *pardon our sins.*

In Perthshire, it is thought that Argylemen pronounce this word mī; on the other hand, it is thought in Argyle that maith is peculiar to Perth, whereas (the *gen.*) it is not used anywhere in the kingdom, saving a part of a parish in the latter County. It gives great offence every where; and, therefore, Dr. Armstrong has searched many of the cognate dialects, to show that it should be written math; *Irish*, math; *Arab.* madi; *Box. Lex.* mad; *Welsh* and *Cornish*, mat; *Armoric*, mat, *and* ma, good; *Hebrew* and *Chald.*, matach and mata.—See *Armstrong.*

Math, mhá, *n. m.* interest, end, purpose, kindness, wish, inclination; s'ann air do *mhath* fhéin a tha mise, *it is your own interest I have in view*; *math* an aghaidh an uile, *good for evil*; cha'n 'eil *math* 'sam bith an sin duit, *that serves no end to you*! dè am *math* th'ort, *what is the good of you*? am *math* leat sin, *do you wish that, do you consider that a good thing*? am *math* 's an t-olc, *the good and bad*; *adv.* well, pretty well, considerably; is *math* a labhair thu, *you spoke well*; is *màth* a chì thu, *you see well*; is *math* a fhuaradh thu, *you have done pretty well, you behaved cleverly*, masterly.

Math, mhá, *adj.* good, wholesome, considerable; duine *math, a good man*; astar *math* air falbh, *a considerable distance off*; ithibh na nithe a tha *math*, eat, *that which is good*, (wholesome); happy, glad; is *math* leam sin, *I am happy at that, I am glad of it*; is *math* dhuit, *it is happy for you*; am *math* leat mise a-dheanadh so, *is it your wish that I do this? do you wish that I should do this?* kind, favourable; bha e *math* dhuinn, *he was kind to us*; valid, legal, rightful; is *math* mo choir air, *I have a legal right to it, I have a valid claim to it*; correct, accurate; ma's *math* mo bheachdsa, *if I form a correct* or *accurate idea of it*; fhuair sin cuid *maith* dheth, *we have got a considerable quantity* or *number of it*; valuable, useful; is *math* an salann, *salt is valuable* or *useful. Bible*; ready, expert, dexterous; tha e *math* air na h-uile nì, *he is dexterous at every thing*; prosperous, successful; làithean *maith* fhaicinn, *to see prosperous days*; cho *math* 's a bha iad, *so prosperous as they were*; is *math* an nì dhuit fhaicinn, *you can hardly see it*; latha *math* dhuit, oidhche *mhath* dhuit, *good day to you, good night to you*; is *math* leam sin, *I am happy of it, I am glad of it.*

Mathachadh, mhá'-ach-Ă, *pt.* cultivating, improving; *n. m.* improvement, cultivation; a' *mathachadh* an fhearainn, *improving the land*; manure, manuring.

Mathaich, mhá'-èch, *v.* manure, cultivate.

Mathair, mhà'-hyėr, *v.* mother; mo *mhàthair, my mother*; dam; cha bhruich thu meann ann am bainne *mhathair, thou shalt not seethe a kid in the milk of its dam, mother*; cause, source; *màthair* aobhair, *primary cause, first cause, efficient cause*; *mathair* chéile, *mother-in-law*; *mathair*-ghuir, *cause of suppuration, the queen of the hive*; *mathair* na lughdaig, *ring-finger*; *mathair*-mhort, *matricide*; *mathair*-mhortair, *a matricide.*

Mathairealachd, màĕr'-al-achg, *n. f* motherliness, kindliness, tenderness.

Mathaireil, màèr′-al, *adj.* motherly, kind.

Mathair-uisge, máěr′-ŭshg-à, *n. f.* reservoir, conduit, source of a river.

Mathanas, má′-an-us, *n. m.* pardon, forgiveness; written maitheanas, mī′-an-us;

Mathanasach, má′-un-as-ach, *adj.* forgiving, lenient, not harsh.

Mathas, má′-us, *n. m.* benevolence, charity, humanity; benefit, bounty; *maitheas, goodness of God.*

Mathasach, má′-us-ach, *adj.* benevolent, humane, tender, kind, bountiful, beneficial.

Mathasachd, ma′-us-achg, *n. f.* bountifulness, charitableness; munificence, benevolence.

Mathghamhainn, mà′-ghàv-ènn, maghamhainn, a bear.

Mathroinn, măr′′-ènn, *n. f.* disposal, risk; fag air a *mhathroinn* e, *leave it to his risk*; air mo *mhathroinnsa, at my disposal, at my risk.*

Meacan, mechg′-an, *n. m.* root, offspring.

Meach, méch, *adj.* mild, modest. *Sm.*

Meachair, mech′-ėr, *adj* having a countenance uncommonly white, tinged with light red; very fair *or* beautiful, as a female; delicate.

Meachaireachd, mech′-ăr′-achg, *n. m.* beautiful countenance; beautiful mixture of colours in the face; sweetness of expression of countenance.

Meachannas, mech′-ann-us, *n m.* lenity, indulgence, mitigation, partiality; gun *meachannas* do dhuine seach duine, *without indulgence* or *partiality to any one. Argyle.*

Meachnasach, mech′-nnus-ach, *adj.* indulgent, lenient, partial.

Meachran, mech′-ran, officious person; see its compound, Smeachranachd, &c.

Meachuinn, mech′-uènn, *n. f.* abatement, lenity, partiality; discretionary power; is màirg a rachadh fo d' *mheachuinn, I pity him that depends on your will.*

Meadar, med′-ur, *n. m.* small ansated wooden-dish; milk-pail.

Meadhail, myaŏ′-al, *n. f.* exstacy, transports, raptures, overjoy; an uncommon and unaccountable burst of joy, on the eve of getting some distressing news; cha robh *meadhail* mhòr riamh gun dubh-bhròn na déigh, *there never was an extravagant burst of joy without the most afflicting news in its train. Ullamh Ileach.*

Meadhon, mé′-un, *n. m.* medium, middle, centre, heart; biodh mo chaomhaich ait am *meadhon* mo chàirdean, *let my acquaintance, my bosom friends, be glad in the centre of my friends, relations. Sm.*; waist; ma d' *mheadhon, about your waist*; means, as regards things, (never of persons); smaointicheadh e air *meadh on-aibh, let him devise means. Bible*; dean *meadhonan, strike a medium.*

Meadhonach, mé′-un-ach, *adj.* centrical, intermediate; àite gu math *meadhonach, a pretty centrical situation*; indifferent, in a tolerable *or* middle state, as of health; dè mar tha thu, *how are you? meadhonach, tolerable, in a middle state, middling well, indifferent enough.*

Meadhonaich, mé′-un-ăch, *n. m.* middle state, in point of situation *or* health.

Meadhon-latha, ménn-lā′-à, *n. m.* mid day, noon; an déigh *mheadhon-latha, in the afternoon.*

Meadhonoidche, mén′-ùėy2-chyà, *n. m.* midnight.

Meadhrach, myāor′-ach, *adj.* lustful, merry.

Meadhrachas, myāor′-ach-us, *n. f.* lust, joy.

Meadhradh, myāor′-Ă, *pt.* drawn into lust. *B. n. m.* lust.

Meag, mègg, *n. m.* whey; *gen.* mìg, meug.

Meal, myal, *v.* enjoy, possess; *meal* is caith e, *may you enjoy and wear it*, use it; na'n na *mheal* thu e, *may you never enjoy it—may you not live to wear it.*

Mealag, Mealg, myal′-ag, *n. f.* melt of fish.

Mealanan, myal′-an-un, sweet-meats.

Mealbhac, myall′-vachg, *n. m.* a melon.

Mealbhag, pollan buidh, a poppy.

Meall, myall, *n. m.* a lump, knob, bunch; *meall* luaidhe, *a lump of lead*; *meall* f hìgean, *not good*, for bad, *a bunch*; bad f hìgean, *bunch of figs*; *v.* deceive, cheat, entice, defraud; mar am *meall* thu 'm bharail mi, *unless you deceive me in my opinion—unless I am mistaken*; *mheall* thu mi, *you deceived* or *defrauded me*; *mheall* e stigh mi, *he cajoled* or *enticed me into the house*; *mheall* an nathair Eubh, *the serpent beguiled* Eve.

Meallach, myall′-ach, *adj.* lumpish.

Mealladh, myăll′-Ă, *pt.* deceiving, beguiling, cajoling, enticing, cheating, alluring, *or* disappointing; *n. m.* deception; mar bheil mi air mo *mhealladh, unless I am deceived, if I am not much mistaken.*

Meallshuil, myall′-hûèl, *n.f.* goggle-eye; *meallshuileach, goggle-eyed, having a deceiving eye.*

Meallta, myăll′-tà, *pt.* cheated, enticed.

Mealltach, myallt′-ach, *adj.* deceptive.

Mealltachd, myallt′-achg, *n. f.* imposture.

Mealltair, myăllt′-ăèr *n. m* impostor

deceiver, a cheat; fraudulent person; *mealltaireachd, imposture, fraudulence, deceitfulness*; *mealltaireachd* a pheacaidh, *the deceitfulness of sin. Bible.*

MEALTAINN, myalt-ènn, *pt.* enjoying; math a *mhealtainn* 'na shaothair, *to enjoy good in his labour. Bible.*

MEAMBRANA, mem′-bran-a, parchment. *B.*

MEAMNA, mem′-nà, *n. m.* a sensation about the lip or elbow, supposed to portend a sudden death, &c.; imagination, whim; gladness, joy; mettle.

MEAMNACH, mem′-nach, *adj.* mettlesome, as a horse; lustful, courageous, brave, as a person.

MEAMNACHD, mem′-nachg, *n. f.* courage, mettlesomeness, energy, high spirit.

MEAN, men, *adj* little, mionn.

MEANAN, mēn′-an, *n. m.* a yawn.

MEANANAICH, mèn′-ăn′-èch, *n. f.* continuous yawning, ever yawning.

MEANAIDH, men′-è, *n. m.* shoemaker's awl.

MEANBH, men′-uv, *adj.* diminutive, very small, slender *or* little; duine *meanbh, a diminutive person.*

MEANBHAIDH, menv′-è, *adj.* diminutive.

MEANBHBHITH, menuv′-è, *n. m.* animalcule.

MEANBHCHRODH, men′-uv-chrŏ, *n. m.* such as stirks, calves, sheep, goats, &c.

MEANBHCHUILEAG, mēna′-chŭil-ag, *n. f.* midge.

MEANBHLACH, men′-a-llach, *n. m.* small potatoes, &c. or the refuse of such.

MEANBH-PHEASAIR, mén′-uv-fās-èr, *n. f.* millet.

MEANG, méng, *n. m.* fault, blemish; gun *meang, faultless, without blemish*; see Miong, *v.* lop.

MEANGACH, méng′-ach, *n. m.* the plant, cinquefoil.

MEANGALACHD, méng′-al-achg, *n. f.* faultiness.

MEANGAIL, méng′-al, *adj.* faulty, blemished.

MEANGAN, méng′-an, *n. m.* a branch, twig.

MEANGANAICH, méng′-an-èch, *v.* lop, prune, lop.

MEANN, myănn, *n. m.* a kid, young roe.

MEANN-ATHAIR, mén′-ă-èr, *n. f.* snipe.

MEANNT, mint, cartal.

MEAIRLE, myàrly′-à, *n. f.* theft, roguery.

MEAIRLEACH, myàrly″-ach, *n. c.* rogue, a thief, cut-throat.

MEAR, mer, *adj.* lustful, in high glee, joyful, joyous, *B.*; very joyous; le suilibh *mear, with lustful eyes.*

MEARACHD, mer′-achg, *n. m.* mistake, error, wrong; chaidh thu 'm *mearachd, you have gone wrong, you erred*; tha thu am *mearachd, you are mistaken*; mar bheil mi am *mearachd, unless I am mistaken*; cò tha gun *mhearachd, who is faultless?* na h-abair ma choinneamh an ainneil gu 'm bu *mhearachd* e, *thou shalt not say before the angel that it was an error. Bible.*

MEARACHDACH, mer′-achg-ach, *adj.* in error, wrong, in fault, erroneous, culpable.

MEARACHDACHD, mer′-achg-achg, *n. f.* erroneousness, faultiness, culpability.

MEARACHDAICH, mer′-achg-èch, *v.* wrong.

MEARAICHE, mer′-èch-a, *n. m.* merry-Andrew.

MEARAIL, mer′-al, *n. m.* error, mistake.

MEARCACH, mer′-kach, *adj.* confident. *Sm.*

MEARCHUNN, mer′-chunn, } *v.* miscalculate, cheat by misreckoning.
MEARCHUNND, mer′-chunnd, }

MEARCHUNNAS, mer′-chŭnn-us, } cheating one with his eyes open, miscalculation, misreckoning.
MEARCHUNNDUS, mer′-chunnd-us, }

MEARGANTA, merg′-ant-a, *adj.* brisk. *Ross.*

MEARLA, for meàirle, theft.

MEARRACHDAS, myarr′-achg-us, *n. m.* wantonness, indelicate romping, nearly wanton joy.

MEARS, mèrs, *v.* march, English.

MEAS, mēss², *n. m.* respect, fruit, respectability, estimation, esteem, public notice; le *meas* is miadh, *with respect and approbation*; thoir gu *meas, bring to notice*, is beag *meas* a bh' agadsa air, *you lightly esteemed him, you had little respect for him*; cha robh *meas* aig air Cain, *he had no respect for Cain*; ma chall a *mheas, about the loss of his fame, reputation*; a rèir do *mheas, according to your estimation*; valuation, estimate, appraisement; *meas* nan tighean, *the appraisement*, or *valuation of the houses, the estimate of the houses*; gun *mheas* gun mhiadh, mar Mhànus, *without respect* or *approbation, like Magnus*; fruit; *meas* nan craobh, *the fruit of the trees*; *v.* value, estimate, reckon, count, regard; *measar* an t-amadan fhèin, 'na dhuine glic 'nuair bhìos e 'na thosd, *even the fool is esteemed* or *regarded a wise man when he holds his peace*; *mheas* iad am bàrr 's na tighean, *they appraised* or *valued their crop and steadings*; *pt.* esteeming, regarding; tha mi a' *meas, I regard, I esteem.*

MEASACH, mēss²′-ach, fruitful. *Macf.*

MEASADAIR, mēss²′-ad-ăr′, *n. m.* appraiser, valuator; measadaireachd, *estimating, valuing, appraising.*

MEASADH, used improperly for meas, *pt.*

MEASAIL, mēss²′-al, *adj.* respectable, worthy; duine *measail, a respectable individual*; esteemed, valued, respected; *measail* aig uaislibh is islibh, *respected by high and low, by the great and humble.*

Measair, mēss²′-ėr′, *n. f.* a dish, measure.

Measalachd, mēss²′-al-achg, *n. f.* respectability, merit, dignity, regard, esteem.

Measan, mēss²′-an, *n. m.* a lapdog, puppy.

Measarra, mēss²′-urr-a, *adj.* temperate, abstemious, sober, moderate, frugal; uime sin bithibh *measarra, therefore be sober. Bible.*

Measarrachd, mēss²′-arr-achg, *n. f* moderation, sobriety, temperance, frugality; ann am *measarrachd, in moderation.*

Measg, mēssg², *n. m.* a mixture; am *measg, among,* i. e. *in the mixture*; *prep.* among, amidst, midst; *measg* bheannta fàsail, *among desert mountains*; *measg* tamhaisg a shluaigh, *amidst the spectres of his people*; *measg* na strìobh, *in the midst of battle*; nar *measg*-ne, *in our middle, among us*; nam *measg, among them*; *v.* mix, mingle, stir about; mharbh i a feòl, *mheasg* i a fuil, *she hath killed her beasts, (flesh,) she hath mingled her blood. Bible, Ossian, &c.*

Measgadh, mēssg²′-ă, *pt.* mixing, mingling; *n. m.* a mixture, admixture.

Measgan, mēssg²′-an, *n. m.* butter-crock.

Measgte, mēssg²′-tyā, *pt.* mixed, mingled.

Measgnaich, mēssg²′-nnėch, *v.* mix, *Macl.*

Measraich, mėss′-rėch, *v.* think. *H.*

Meat, } mėtt′-a, *adj.* timid, chicken
Meata, } hearted, easily abashed, cowardly; sìol *meata, a timid race, O.*; cha bhuadhaich am *meata* gu bràth, *the chicken-hearted shall never conquer,* or *prosper. Proverb.*

Meatachadh, mėtt′-ach.ă, *n. m.* benumbing, daunting, damping the spirits; thug sin *meatachadh* mòr as, *that daunted him greatly*; a' *mheatachadh, his being benumbed*; *pt.* benumbing; daunting, starving of cold.

Meatachd, mėtt′-achg, *n. f.* timidity, delicacy of feeling, *or* sentiment; cowardice; sheas Fionn air leirg gun *mheatachd, Fingal stood on a declivity undauntingly.*

Meataich, mėtt′-ėch, *v.* damp, daunt, intimidate; starve of cold, benumb; *mheataich* siod gu mòr e, *that daunted* or *damped his spirits greatly.*

Meath, mhé, *v.* fade, decay, fail; *mheath* a' chraobh, *the tree faded, Is.*; *v.* taunt, damp; a' toirt meathadh dhomhsa, *taunting me, Islay*; *n. m.* consumption, failing, fading; *mheath* i gach cridhe, *she damped every spirit. Smith.*

Meathadh, mhé′-ă, *pt.* decaying, fading, failing; damping, discouraging; *n. m.* taunt, jeer, gibe; cha ruig thu leas a bhi toirt *meathadh* dhomhsa, *you need not taunt me on that account.*

Meath-challtuinn, mé′-challt-ėnn, *n. f.* southern-wood. *Macdonald.*

Meath-chridheach, mé′-chrė-ach, *adj.* faint-hearted, chicken-hearted, timid.

Meidh, mē-yh′, *n. f.* a balance; pronounced in the Mainland, mé, *v.* weigh.

Meidheach, mé′-ach, *a.* mild. *Ossian*

Meidheadair, mē′-yă-dăr′, *n. m.* balancer.

Meidhis, mē′-ėsh, *n. f.* an instalment; phàidh sin air *mheidhisean* e, *we paid it by instalments*; a cheud *mheidhis, the first instalment*; na *mheidhisean, by instalments.*

This word is peculiar to Argyle, and has reference to the ancient mode of payments, i. e. by weight, (from meidh)—pronounced on the Mainland, mé-ėsh, and confounded often there, with minis, a degree *or* set portion; ni sinn na *mhinisean* e, *we shall do it by degrees* or *allotted portions*

Meidhichean, méyh′-ėch-an, *n. pl.* hip-joints; as na *meidhichean, the hip-joint dislocated, the spine hurt.*

Meidhisich, mé′-ėsh-ėch, *v.* graduate.

Meig, méėg, *n. f.* a protuberant chin, the snout of a goat.

Meigeadaich, méig′-ad-ėch, } *n. f.* bleat-
Meigeardaich, méig′-ard-ėch, } ing of goats.

Meigeil, meig′-ėl, *v.* bleat as a goat.

Meil, mėll, *v.* bleat as a sheep.

Meil, mā²′ll, *v.* grind, meal, mill; *meileadh* mo bhean do neach eile, *let my wife grind to another, Bible*; pound, pulverise; a chailc air a *meileadh, the chalk pulverised.*

Meile, mā²l′-ă, *n. m.* mill-staff.

Meileachd, mā²ll′-achg, *n. f.* multure.

Meileadair, mā²ll′-ad-ăr′, *n. m.* grinder.

Meileag, mā²ll′-ag, muzzle, beileag.

Meileartan, mā²ll′-ărt-an, *n. pl.* flesh-mites, generally under the toes.

Meilich, mėll′-ėch, *n. f.* bleating of sheep, querulousness; *mèilich* nan caorach, *bleating of sheep*; *mèilich* mhaoth, *soft bleating. M'F.*

Meilich, méll′-ėch, *v.* bennmb.

Meiligeag, mā²l′-ėg-ag, *n. f.* pea-husk.

Meiltir, mālly′-tyėr, see Meildreach.

Mein, mèin, *n. f.* ore, metal, bullion; *mèin* airgid, *silver ore*; *mèin* òir, *gold metal.*

Meineadair, mèin′-ad-ar′, *n. m.* miner, mineralogist, student of ores.

Meineadaireachd, mèin′-ad-ăr-achg, *n. f.* mineralogy, the occupation of a miner.

Meinire, mèėn′-ėr-ā, *n. m.* mine-sieve.

Meinn, mèinn, *n. f.* expression, features; is dona a *mhèinn* a th'ort, *your expression of countenance does not betoken any thing good*; cia mordha a *mhèinn, how majestic* *her countenance, Maclachlan*; mercy, clemency, discretion, discretionary power; fàg na *mhèinn* fhèin e, *leave it to his own discretion*; tha e ad *mhèinn, it is left to your own clemency*; am *mèinn* na gaoith, *to the mercy of the wind*; duine air fhàgail g'a *mhèinn* féin, *man left to his own shifts* or *prudence*; native energy, *or* quality; talamh a bheir bàrr o a *mhèinn* fhèin, *land that can produce crops from its own nature* or *native energy, Macdonald.*

Meinnealachd, mèènn'-al-achg, *n. f.* productive quality; tenderness, as grass, tallow, &c.

Meinneil, mèènn'-al, *adj.* tender, productive, prolific, as a female; native; flexible as metals; substantial, sappy.

Meirbh, mārv, *adj.* slender; *v.* digest.

Meirg, mārėg, *n. f.* rust; *v* rust, corrode.

Meirgeach, mārėg'-ach, *adj.* rusty; as a person, cadaverous, ill tempered.

Meirgeal, mārėg'-al, *n. m.* a cadaverous person.

Meirghe, māryh"à, *n. m.* a banner. *Irish.*

Meirgich, mārėg'-ich, *v.* grow rusty.

Meirle for **Meairle**, theft.

Meoir, myòėr, *n. pl.* fingers; also *gen.* of meur, a finger.

Meomhair, myó'-ėr, *n. f.* memory, recollection; faigh air do *mheomhair, get by rote, get by heart*; gleus do *mheomhair, excite your memory. M'L.*

Meomhrach, myór'-ach, *n. f.* memorandum.

Meorachadh, myòr'-ach-À, *pt.* meditating, pondering; observing attentively; *n. f.* meditation.

Meoraich, myór'-ėch, *v.* meditate, ponder.

Meoraich, myòr'-ėch, *v.* meditate, ponder, calculate, reconsider, study; literally, count your fingers, a mode of calculation not altogether extinct; notice, note.

Meud, mèdd', mēdd, *n. m.* size, bulk, dimensions, extent, magnitude, greatness; *meud* an tighe, *the size of the house*; air *mheud* gu 'm bheil e, *let him* or *it be ever so great*; ma 'n *mheud* siod, *about that size*; *meud* do ghàirdean, *the greatness of thy arm*; *meud* a bhròin, *the magnitude of his grief*; dè a *mheud, what is his stature* or *its size*? *meud* a' ghoirtean, *the extent of the field*; as many as, number, quantity; co *mheud* a th' ann, *how many are there*? agus a' *mheud* agus a bhoin ris, leighis e iad, *and as many as he touched, he healed*; a *mheud*'s a tha lathair, *as many as are present, as many as there are alive* or *surviving*; a' *mheud* agus gu d' rinn thu sin, *inasmuch, in so much as, in as far as you have done that*; co *meud* a fhuair thu, *how many* or *what quantity did you get*? a' dol am *meud, growing in size*, or *stature*, or *extent.*

Meudachadh, mèdd"-ach-À, *pt.* increasing, augmenting, multiplying; *n. m.* an enlargement, augmentation, increase, growth.

Meudachd, medd"-achg, *n. f.* size, stature, magnitude, dimensions, extent, bulk; is ioghnadh leam a *mheudachd, I am surprised at its dimensions. O.*; duine do *mheudachd* mhòir, *a man of great size* or *stature*; agus thàinig Iosa air 'aghaidh ann an gliocas is ann am *meudachd, and Jesus grew in wisdom and stature. B.*; is ionghnadh leam fhèin a *mheudachd, I am surprised at its bulk. Sm.*

Meudaich, mèdd'-ėch, *v.* increase, enlarge, multiply, add, abound, grow in size, improve, augment; *meudaichaidh* mi do dhoilghios, *I will multiply thy sorrow*; *meudachaidh* tu a luach, *thou shalt increase its value. Bible*; am fear nach *meudaich* an carn, gu'm *meudaich* e a' chroich, *he that will not add to the cairn, may he add to the dignity of the gibbet. Prov.*; far an do *mheudaich* am peacadh bu ro-mhò a *mheudaich* gràs, *where sin abounded, grace did much more abound*; Rom. v. and 20.; *meudaichte*, increased, &c.

Meudd-bhrann, *or* **-bhronn**, mèd'-vrănn *n. f.* dropsy.

Meug, mègg, *n. m.* whey.

Meugach, mègg'-ach, } *adj.* serous, like
Meugail, mègg'-al, } whey, of whey.

Meunan, mén'-an, *n. m.* a yawn, gape.

Meunanaich, mèu'-an-ėch, *n. f.* yawning; thòisich e air *meunanaich, he began to yawn.*

Meur, mèrr, *n. f.* a finger, branch, prong, knot of wood, toe; thum an sagairt a *mheur, the priest dipped his finger*; na casan agus am meoir, *the feet and their toes*; *meur* a ghràpa, *the prong of the fork*; *meur* do'n teàghlach sin, *a branch of that family*; tha *meoir* san fhiodh, *the wood is knotty*; a slight degree; *meur* do'n chaithidh, *a slight degree of consumption*; *meur* a ghiomaich, *the claw of the lobster.*

Meurach, mèrr'-ach, *adj.* fingered, pronged, knotty; full of knots *or* bumps.

Meuradan, mèrr'-ad-an, *n. m.* a delicate, slender, weak person.

Meuradanach, mèrr'-ad-an-ach, *a.* delicate.

Meuradanachd, mèrr'-ad-an-achg, *n. f* the conduct of a delicate person; eating *or* dealing with, gently.

Meurag, mèrr'-ag, *n. f.* little finger.

Meuragaich, mèrr'-ag-ėch, *v.* finger, fidget; also meuraganaich, and meuraich.

Meuraich, mèrr′-èch, *v.* prong, finger.

Meuran, mèrr′-an, *n. m.* a thimble.

Meuranta, mèrr′-annt-a, *a.* delicate.

Meurantachd, mèrr′-annt-achd, *n. f.* delicacy of constitution, silliness of person.

Mh, v*h*, aspirated form of m.

Mhain, v*h*àèn, *adv.* only, alone; is tusa a *mhàin* Iehobhah, *thou art alone, Jehovah*; cha'n e sin a *mhàin, that is not all,* or *alone.*

Mi, mē, *per. pron.* I; is *mi, it is I*; bithidh *mi, I shall be*; 2d, *neg. part,* signifying not, and answering to in, un, il, &c., in English; sometimes signifies evil, the worst.

Miadh, mĕā′-gh', *n. m.* demand, call; cha 'n'eil *miadh* sam bith air crodh, *there is no demand for cattle*; honour, approbation; meas agus *miadh, respect and approbation*; gun *mhiadh*, gun bhàigh, *without honour* or *affection.*

Miadhalachd, mĕā′-ghal-achg, *n. f.* degree of demand; preciousness, respectability, fondness, rareness.

Miadhail, mĕā′-gh'-al, *adj.* in great demand; precious, valuable, fond of, very fond of; tha buntàta *miadhail, the potatoes are in great demand*; *miadhail* m'a chloinn, *dotingly fond of his children*; gnothach *miadhail, precious* or *valuable thing.*

Miag, mĕăg, *n. m.* a mew of a cat; caterwauling; *v.* mew, caterwaul, as a cat.

Miagail, mĕăg′-al, *n. f.* mewing, caterwauling.

Mial, mĕăl, *n. m.* a louse; *mial* spàgach, *a crab-louse*; *mial*-mòna, *peat-louse*; *mial*-caorach, *a tick,* (seòlann properly.)

Mialach, mĕăl′-ach, *adj.* lousy.

Mialachd, mĕăl′-achg, *n. f.* lousiness.

Mialchu, mĕăl′-chŭ, *n. m.* greyhound.

Mi-altrum, mē-alt′-rum, *n. m.* bad nursing; cinnidh mac o *mhi-altrum* ach cha chinn e o'n aog, *a son may grow from bad nursing, but cannot escape the grave. G. Proverbs.*

Miann, mĕănn, *n. m.* intention, desire, inclination, will, purpose, love, delight, appetite; dè tha *mhiann* ort a dheanadh, *what do you mean to do*? am *miann* leat blàr, *is your intention battle*? an sàsuich thu *miann* na leòghuinn òig, *wilt thou fill the appetite of the young lion*? a shluagh gun chiall, thug *miann* do'n òr, *ye senseless people that bestowed your affections on gold*; tha '*mhiann* sin orm, *I mean* or *purpose to do that*; dè tha *mhiann* ort a dheanadh, *what do you mean to do*? tha '*mhiann* air teicheadh, *he means to desert, to decamp*; *miann* nan aingidh, *the desire of the wicked*; bàs mo naimhde cha *mhiann* leam, *the death of my foes I do not desire*; tha *mhiann* orm, *I mean, I intend*; ma tha *mhiann* ort dol dachaidh, *if you purpose* or *intend going home*: cha n eil am *miann* san sàsaichte, *their appetite is not appeased*; am *miann* leat sìth, *do you wish for peace*? an absurd longing of a woman in the family way; mole on the child in consequence of that desire not being satisfied; complete satisfaction, entire approbation; rinn e gad' *mhiann, he did it to your entire satisfaction,* or *approbation*; tha *miann* air 'aodann, *there is a mole on his face*; *miann* fìon, *a mole of the colour of wine.*

Miannach, mĕănn′-ach, *a.* desirous, keen.

Miannachadh, mĕănn′-ach-Ă, *pt* coveting, desiring; am *miannàchadh* cuid duine eile, *coveting another's property*; a'*miannachadh* gu mòr fhaicinn, *longing* or *desiring greatly to see him.*

Miannaich, mĕănn′-èch, *v.* desire, covet, lust after, fix one's heart on, wish greatly.

Miannar, **Miannmhor**, } mĕănn′-ur, *adj.* desirous, covetous, greedy.

Miaogus, mē-ŭog′-us, *n. m.* unseemliness.

Miapachd, mĕăp′-achg, *n. f.* cowardice.

Miapadh, mĕăp′-Ă, *n. m.* bashfulness, cowardice, pusillanimity; also miap.

Miapaidh, mĕăp′-ê, *adj.* cowardly.

Mias, mĕăs, *n. f.* dish, platter, charger, plate; ceann Eòin bàistidh air *mèis, the head of John the Baptist on a charger,* (*on a plate.*) *Bible.*

Mi-bhaigh, mē-v*h*ī′-y', *n. f.* unkindness.

Mi-bhail, mē-vha'l′, *n. f.* profusion. *H. S.*

Mi-bhanail, mē-vhăn′-al, *a.* immodest.

Mi-bhanalachd, mē-vhan′-al-achg, *n. f.* immodesty.

Mi-bheus, mē-văs′, *n. f.* vice, immorality.

Mi-bheusach, mē-văs′-ach, *a.* immodest.

Mi-bheusachd, mē-văs′-achg, *n. f.* immorality, immodesty, unpoliteness, bad manners.

Mi-bhlasda, mē-v*h*lăsd′-a, *a.* insipid.

Mi-bhlasdachd, mē-v*h*lăsd′-achg, *n. f.* insipidity.

Mi-bhoidheach, mē-vòê′-ach, *adj.* unhandsome.

Mi bhreathnaich, mē-vren′-èch, *v.* misconceive.

Mi-bhreith, mē-vhrā′, *n. f.* wrong judgment.

Mi-bhuaireasach, mē-vŭăr″-as-ach, *a.* good tempered.

Mi-bhuaidh, mē-vŭă-y″, *n. f.* defeat.

Mi-bhuidheach, mē-vŭē-y″ ach, *a.* dissatisfied, displeased, discontented.

Mi-bhuil, mē-vŭĕl, *n. f.* misapplication, profusion; rinn thu *mi-bhuil* deth, *you misapplied it, you made bad use of it, you wasted it.*

MI-BHUILICH, mē-vūĕl′-ėch, *v.* misapply, misimprove, waste, squander; *mhi-bhuilich* thu t-ùine, *you misapplied your time*; mi-bhuilichte, *misapplied, misimproved, wasted.*

MI-BHUNAILTEACH, mē-vŭn′-aljt-ach, *adj.* unstationary, inconstant, unsettled.

MI-CHAIDREACH, mē-chăjj′-ryach, *a.* unsociable, disaffected, unfriendly.

MI-CHAIRDEAS, mē-chărjj′-us, *n.m.* unkindness.

MI-CHAIRDEIL, mē-chârjj′-al, *a.* unfriendly.

MI-CHALMARRA, mē-chalm′-urr-a, *a.* feeble.

MI-CHAOIMHNEIL, mē-chaŏėn′-al, *a.* unkind.

MI-CHAOIMHNEAS, mē-chaŏėn′-as, *n. m.* unkindness.

MI-CHAOIMHAINN, mē-chùv′-ėnn, *v.* misspend.

MI-CHAOMHNADH, mē-chùv′-nĂ, *n. m.* profusion.

MI-CHEART, mē-chyart, *adj.* unjust, evil.

MI-CHEARTAS, mē-chyart′-us, *n. m.* injustice.

MI-CHIALL, mē-chĕăll, *n. m.* insanity, folly.

MI-CHIALLACH, mē-chĕăll′-ach, mad, insane.

MI-CHIAT, mēch′-chĕăt, *n. f.* dislike.

MI-CHINNT, mē-chyĕnjt, *n. f.* uncertainty.

MI-CHINNTEACH, mē-chyĕnjt′-ach, *a.* uncertain.

MI-CHION, mē-chyun, *n. m.* aversion.

MI-CHIUIN, mē-chyūėn, *a.* boisterous.

MI-CHLIS, mē-chlėsh, *a.* inactive.

MI-CHLEACHD, mē-chlechg, *v.* abrogate, disuse, render obsolete.

MICHLIU, mē′-chlū, *n. f.* disgrace, infamy, reproach, bad fame *or* character.

MICHLIUITEACH, mē-chlūjt″-ach, *a.* disgraceful, infamous, reproachful, dishonourable.

MI-CHREASDA, mē-chresd′-a, *adj.* cruel.

MI-CHREASDACHD, mē-chrest′-achg, *n. f.* cruelty.

MI-CHOLTACH, mē-chŏlt′-ach, *a.* improbable, unlikely; unlike, dissimilar.

MI-CHOLTACHD, mē-chŏlt′-achg, *n. f.* improbability, dissimilarity, unlikeliness.

MI-CHOMPANTA, mē-chŏmp′-ant-à, *adj.* unsocial, unsociable, distant.

MI-CHOMPANTACHD, mē-chŏmp′-ant-achg, *n. m.* unsociableness, distant manner.

MI-CHORD, mē-chôrd′, *v.* disagree, dissent.

MI-CHORDADH, mē-chôrd′-Ă, *pt.* disagreeing, dissenting; *n m.* disagreement.

MI-CHOTHROM, mē-chor′-um, *n. m.* unfairness, disadvantage, injustice.

MI-CHOTHROMACH, mē-chor′-um-ach, *adj.* uneven, rugged; unfair, unjust.

MI-CHREID, mē-chraŏj, *v.* disbelieve.

MI-CHREIDEACH, mē-chraŏjj′-ach, *a.* distrustful; *n.m.* unbeliever, infidel, heretic.

MI-CHREIDEADH, } mē-chraoj′-Ă, *n. m.* unbelief, heresy, want of faith; air son am *mi-chreideadh, for their unbelief. Bible.*
MI-CHREIDEAMH, }

MI-CHREIDEAS, mē-chraojj′-as, *n. m.* want of confidence, disrespect, distrust.

MI-CHREIDEASACH, mē-chraojj′-as-ach, *adj.* disrespectful, distrustful.

MI-CHRIDHEIL, mē-chrē²′-al, *a.* heartless.

MI-CHRUINNEALAS, mē-chrŭĕnn′-al-us, untidiness, profusion.

MI-CHRUINNEIL, mē-chrŭĕnn-al, *adj.* untidy, uneconomical, profuse.

MI-CHUIMHNEACH, mē-chŭĕn′-ach, *a.* forgetful.

MI-CHUIS, see Miochuis, jilting, smirking.

MI-CHUMACHDAIL, mē-chum′-achg-al, } *adj.* unshapely, ill-shaped.
MI CHUNNADAIL, mē-chunn′-ad-al, }

MI-CHURAM, mē-chûr′-um, *n. f.* negligence.

MI-CHURAMACH, mē-chûr′-am-ach, *a.* careless.

MI-DHAICHEALACHD, } mē-*gh*âėch′-al-achg *n. f.* absurdity.
MI-DHAICHEALAS, }

MI-DHAICHEIL, mē-*gh*âėch-al, *a.* absurd, improbable, unlikely, nonsensical.

MI-DHEALBH, mē-y*h*yalv, *n. m.* absurdity.

MI-DHEALBHACH, mē-y*h*yal′-ach, *a.* absurd.

MI-DHEAS, mē-y*h*yās², *a.* unprepared, wrong.

MI-DHIADHACHD, mē-y*h*ėaŏ-gh″-achg, *n. f.* ungodliness, unholiness, irreligion.

MI-DHIADHAIDH, mē-*gh*eaŏ-gh″-ė, *a.* unholy.

MI-DHILEAS, mē-y*h*ēl′-us, *a.* unfaithful.

MI-DHILLSEACHD, mē-y*h*ělly″-shachg, *n. f.* disloyalty, unfaithfulness, treachery.

MI-DHLEASNACH, mē-*gh*lās²′-nach, *a.* undutiful, disloyal, unfaithful.

MI-DHLEASNAS, mē-*gh*lās²′-nas, *n. m.* undutifulness.

MI-DHIGHE, mē-*gh*le-ă *n. f.* unlawfulness.

MI-DHIGHEACH, mē-ghlė′-ach, *a.* not due.

MI-DHLIGHEIL, mē-*gh*lė′-al, *a.* unlawful.

MI-DHOCHAS, mē-*gh*ôch′-us, *n. m.* despair.

MI-DHOCHASACH, mē-ghôch′-as-ach, *adj.* despondent; diffident, unpretending, retiring.

MI-DHOIGH, mē-ghôe′-y′, *n. f.* want of method, awkwardness, absurdity.

MI-DHOIGHEIL, mē-ghŏĕ-y″-al, *adj.* disarranged, immethodical, absurd.

MI-DHREACH, mē′-*gh*rech, *n. m.* deformity.

MI-DHREACHMOR, mē-*gh*rech′-ur, *a.* ugly.

MI-DHURACHD, mē-*gh*ûr′-achg, *n. m.* insincerity.

MI-DHURACHDACH, mē-*gh*ûr′-achg-ach, *a.* insincere, indifferent, careless, negligent.

MI-EARBSA, mē-erb′-sà, *n. f.* distrust.

MI-EARBSACH, mē-erb′-sach, *adj.* distrustful, suspicious, despondent, despairing.

MI-EIFEACHD, mē-āf′-achg, *n. f.* inefficacy

MI-EARACHDAIL, mē-ār''-achg-al, *a.* unseemly.

MI-EARACHDAS, mē-ār''-achg-us, *n. m.* ungentility.

MI-FHAICHILL, mē-ìch'-ėlly', *n. m.* negligence, unguardedness; *mi-fhaichilleach,* uncautious.

MI-FHAIGHIDINN, mē-ìy''-ė-jėnn, *n. f.* impatience, greed, keenness.

MI-FHAIGHIDINNEACH, mē-ēy''-ejj-ėnn-ach, *adj.* impatient, too impetuous, too keen.

MI-FHEUM, mē'-ām, *n. m.* misapplication, uselessness, bad use.

MI-FHREAGARRACH, mē-rāg'-arr-ach, *a.* unsuitable, unanswerable, unbefitting.

MI-FHREASDALACH, mē-rāsd'-al-ach, *adj.* inattentive, heedless, improvident.

MI-FHURACHAIL, mē-ŭr'-ach-al, *a.* inattentive, careless, unguarded.

MI-FHURASD, mē-ŭr'-asd, *a.* difficult.

MI-GHIULAN, mē-ghû'l''-an, *n. m.* misconduct.

MI-GHLIC, mē-ghlēchg', *adj.* unwise.

MI-GHLIOCAS, mē-ghlēúchg'-us, *n. m.* folly.

MI-GHNATHACHADH, mē-ghrâch'-Ă, *n. m.* abuse, misconduct, misapplication.

MI-GHNATHAICH, mē-ghrà'-ėch, *a.* abuse.

MI-GHRASAIL, mē-ghrâs'-al, *a.* reprobate.

MI-GHRUNND, mē'-ghrûnnd, *n. m.* indifference.

MI-GHRUNNDAIL, mē-ghrûnnd'-al, *a.* care less.

MI-IOMCHUIDH, mē-ēm'-ach-ė, *a.* unfit.

MI-IOMCHUIDHEACHD, mē-ēm'-ach-ė-achg, *n. f.* impropriety, unfitness, indecency.

MI-IOMRADH, mē-ēm'-rā, *n. m.* evil report.

MI-IONRAIC, mē-ēŭn'-rėg, *a.* dishonest.

MIL, mėl, *n. f.* honey; cìr-mheala, *honey-comb*; do phòg air bhlas na meala, *your kiss has the taste of honey. Stew.*

MI-LABHRACH, mē-llăv'-rach, *a.* taciturn.

MI-LAGHAIL, mē-llaŏgh'-al, *a.* unlawful, illegal, illicit, prohibited.

MIL-CHEO, mėl'-chyô, *n. m.* mildew.

MI-DHEOIN, mē-y*h*yòėn', *n. f.* reluctance.

MI-DHEONACH, mē-y*h*yòn'-ach, *a.* reluctant.

MILE, mēl'-ă, *n. m.* a mile, a thousand; *mìltean, thousands.*

MILEACHADH, mėl'-ach-Ă, *n. m.* benumbing, starving of cold.

MILEAMH, mēl'-uv, *adj.* thousandth.

MILEANTA, mėl'-annt-ă, *adj.* sweet-lipped. *Is.*; heroic, brave. *Macd.*; stately. *M'F.*

MILICH, mėl'-ėch, *v.* benumb.

MILIDH, mėl'-ė, *n. m.* champion. *Smith.*

MI-LIOSDA, mē-llėsd'-a, *adj.* unobtrusive.

MILIS, mėl'-ėsh, *adj.* sweet, savoury.

MILL, mĕlly', *n. pl.* lumps; *meall, one*; *v.* spoil, hurt, mar, disarrange; *mhill* thu e, *you spoiled it—N.* starve of cold.

MILLEADH, mĕlly''-Ă, *pt.* spoiling, ruin.

MILLEACH, mĕlly''-ach, *n. m.* tender, sappy grass.

MILLSE, mĕlly''-shă, *n.* degree of sweetness.

MILLSEAD, mĕlly'-shad, *n. f.* deg. of sweetness.

MILLSEACHD, mĕlly''-shachg, *n. f.* sweetness.

MILLSICH, mĕlly''-shyėch. *v.* sweeten.

MILLTE, mĕlly'-tyă, *pt.* spoiled, ruined.

MILLTEACH, mĕlly'-tyach, *adj.* ruinous.

MILLTEACHD, mĕlly'-tyachg, *n. f.* destructiveness.

MILLTEAG, mĕlly'-tyăg, *n. f.* battle of thatch.

MILLTEAR, mĕlly²'-tyăr, *n. m.* spendthrift; a prodigal person; mar an ceudna, esan a tha leisg na obair, is bràthair e do'n *mhìlltear* mhòr, *also he that is slothful in his work, is brother to him that is a great waster.*

MI-LOINN, mē'-lăŏėn, *n. f.* ungracefulness.

MI-LOINEIL, mē laŏėn'-al, *adj.* awkward.

MI-MHAISE, mē-mhăsh'-ă, *n. f.* deformity.

MI-MHAISEIL, mē-văsh'-al, *a.* deformed.

MI-MHEAS, mē'-v*h*ĕss, *n. m.* disrespect.

MI-MHEASAIL, mē-v*h*ĕss'-al, *a.* disrespectful.

MI-MHEASARRA, mē-vĕss'-arr-ă, *adj.* intemperate, immoderate, dissolute, incontinent.

MI-MHINICH, mē-vēn'-ėch, *v.* disinterpret, misconstrue, mis-expound.

MI-MHISNEACH, mē-vēs²h'-nyach, *n. f.* discouragement, irresolution, shiness, diffidence, damp.

MI-MHISNEACHAIL, mē-vēs²h'-nyach-al, *a.* faint-hearted, disheartening, cowardly, backward.

MI-MHISNICH, mē-vēsh'-nyėch, *v.* discourage, dishearten, dismay; damp the spirits.

MI-MHODH, mē-v*h*ō², *n. m.* rudeness.

MI-MHODHAIL, mē-vhō²'-al, *a.* rude, unpolite, unmannerly, ungentlemanly.

MIN, mēn, *adj.* smooth, agreeable to the touch; soft, delicate, tender; mìn bhasan bàna, *delicate, soft, fair hands. Mt.*; aodach *mìn, smooth cloth—cloth agreeable to the touch*; clacha *mìne* a'n t-sruith, *smooth stones from the stream*; gentle, mild, quiet, inoffensive; an gille *mìn,* an ighean *mhìn, the gentle, inoffensive young man,—the gentle inoffensive maid*; pulverised, ground small; fine; *min* mhìn, *fine meal*; *meal ground* or *pulverised too fine.*

MIN, mėn, *n. f.* meal; *min* eorna, *barley-meal*; *min* chruinneachd, *flour, wheat-meal*; *min*-eararaidh, *parched-meal*; *min* sheaguil, *rye-meal*; *min*-pheasair, *pease-meal*; *min* phònair, *bean-meal.*

MI-NADUR, mē-nàd'-ur, *n. m.* ill nature.

MI-NADURRA, mē-nàd'-urr-a, *adj.* preter

natural, unnatural; void of natural affection.

MI-NAIRE, mē-nàėr′-à, *n.f.* impudence.

MI-NAOMH, mē-nùv′, *a.* unholy, profane.

MI-NAOMHACHADH, mē-nùv′-ach-Ă, *pt.* profaning; *n.m.* profanation; act of profaning.

MI-NAOMHACHD, mē-nùv′-achg, *n.f.* profanation, unholiness.

MI-NAOMHAICH, mē-nùv′-ėch, *v.* profane unhallow; a *mhi-naomhaich* an t-sàbbaid, *that profaned* or *unhallowed the Sabbath.*

MIN-BHRIST, mēn′-vrėsjj, *v.* pulverise.

MINEACH, mēn″-ach, *n. m.* tender grass.

MINEACHD, mēn′-achg, *n. m.* softness, delicacy, fineness; *minead, deg. of fineness.*

MINEACHADH, mēn′-ăch-Ă, *pt.* expounding, interpreting, explaining, simplifying; *n. m.* exposition, explanation, interpretation; a' *mineachadh* na h-earrann so, *explaining* or *expounding this passage*; *mineachadh* a' Bhìobuill, *exposition* or *explanation of the Bible, annotations of the Bible.*

MINICH, mēn′-ėch, *v.* interpret, explain, illustrate, expound, simplify; *minich* so dhomh, *explain this to me*; *mhìnich* iad slighe Dhè na bu coimhlionta, *they expounded the way of God more perfectly. Bible.*

MINICHE, mēn′-ėch-à, *n. m* interpreter.

MINID, mėn′-ėj, *n. f.* runnet; binid.

MINIDH, mėn′-ė, *n. m.* awl; meanaidh.

MINIG, mėn′-ėg, *adj.* and *adv.* frequent, often; is *minig* a thachras a leithid sin, *the like of that often happens*; nì *minig, frequent thing.*

MINISTIR, mēnn″-ėshjt-ėr, *n. m.* minister, clergyman; ionns gu'm bithinn a'm *mhinistir* aig Iosa Criosda, *so that I might be a minister of Jesus Christ. B.*

MINISTREIL, mēn2′-ėshjt-ral, *a.* ministerial.

MINISTREILEACHD, mēn2′-ėshjt-ral-achg, *n. f.* ministration, clerical function, incumbency; *ministreileachd* an fhacail, *ministration of the Word. Bible.*

MINIS, mēn′-ėsh, *n. f.* a degree *or* portion; nì sin air *minisibh* e, *we will do it by degrees, by little and little*; a cheud *mhinis* deth, *the first portion* or *part of it.*

MINMHEAR, mėn′-vhėr, *n. f.* hemlock. *Ir.*

MINN, mēnn, *n. pl.* kids; *gen.* of a kid.

MINNEAN, mēn′-aėn, *n. m.* kidling.

MINNICEAN, mēnn′-ėchg-ăn, *n.m.* kid-skin.

MIO, mē, prefix for mi-, before a, o, u.

MIOCHUIS, mēch′-chūsh, *n. f.* flirtation, pretended indifference, coquettry, leer.

MIOCHUISEACH, mē′-chūsh-ach, *adj.* coquettish, flirting, as a prude, leering with the eye; *n. f.* a coquette, flirt.

MIOCHUISEACHD, mē′-chūsh-achg, *n. f.* flirtation, coquetry; assumed indifference.

MIODAL, mėd′-al, *n. m.* flattery.

MIODALACH, mēd′-al-ach, *a.* fawning.

MIODAR, mēdd″-ur, *n. m.* meadow, good grass *or* pasture.

MIODHAIR, mē-ur′, *n. m.* churl, niggard; *adj.* pitiful, paltry.

MIOFHORTAN, mē′-ŏrt-an, *n.m.* misfortune.

MIOFHORTANACH, mē′-ŏrt-an-ach, *adj.* unfortunate, misfortunate, disastrous, unhappy.

MIOG, mēgg, *n. f.* a wanton leer, *or* eye, *or* look; mìogshuil, *laughing eye, an ogling, wanton, leering eye.*

MIOGSHUILEACH, mēg′-shŭŭl-ach, *adj.* having a leering wanton eye.

MIOLARAN, mėúl′-ar-an, *n. m.* fawning of a dog, expression of joy.

MIOLASG, mėúl′-ăsg, *n. m.* skittishness, skit of a horse.

MIOLASGACH, mėúl′-asg-ach, *adj.* skittish.

MIOLASGACHD, mėúl′-asg-achg, *n. f.* skittishness.

MIOMHAIL, mēv′-al, *adj.* impertinent.

MIOMHALACHD, mēv′-al-achg, *n. f.* impertinence.

MION, mėún′, *adj.* small; buntàta *mion, small potatoes*; *adv.* minutely; am bheil thu *mion* eòlach air, *are you minutely acquainted with him?* an do *mhion* rannsuich thu e, *did you search it minutely*

MIONACH, mėn′-ach, *n. m.* entrails, bowels.

MIONAN, mėn′-an, *n. m.* sheep, *or* dove-dung.

MIONACRACH, mėn′-achg-rach, *a.* eating but little at a time, but often trying meat, as an invalid, when convalescent.

MIONAID, mėn′-aj, *n. f.* minute, moment.

MIONAIDEACH, mėn′-ăj-ach, *adj.* minute; iarr gu *mionaideach, search minutely.*

MIONN, mėúnn, *n. f.* an oath, a vow, declaration on oath, curse; beul nam *mionn, the cursing lips*;—also, crown of the head, (obsolete.)

MIONNAICH, mėúnn′-ėeh, *v.* swear, curse, make oath, make a solemn appeal to God; *mionnaich* dhòmhsa air Dia, *swear unto me by God, Bible*; *mionnaichte, sworn, bound by-an-oath*; tha e *mionnaichte* ris gu cuir e as dhuit, *he is fully resolved, is bound by an oath to finish your days.*

MIONORAICH, mē-ŏn′-ar-ėch, *v.* dishonour.

MIORAILT, mēr′-aljt, *n. f.* miracle.

MIORAILTEACH, mēr′-aljty′-ach, *adj.* miraculous, past comprehension, incomprehensible.

MIORAILTEACHD, mēr′-ăljty-achg, *n. f* miraculousness, incomprehensibility, wonderfulness.

Miorbhuil, mērv′-ùl, *n. f.* miracle.

Miorbhuileach, mēr′-vŭly′-ach, *adj.* miraculous, marvellous, wonderful.

Miorbhuileachd, mēr′-vŭly-achg, *n. f.* wonderfulness, marvelousness, miraculousness.

Miorun, mēr′-rŭn, *n m.* malice, ill will, spite.

Miorunach, mēr′-rŭn-ach, *a.* malicious, malevolent.

Miorunachd, mēr′-rŭn-achg, *n. f.* maliciousness, malevolence, ill will, spitefulness.

Mios, mēss, *n. m.* a month ; b' fhaide gach *miosa* na bliathna, *every month seemed longer than a whole year. Smith.*

Miosa, mės′-à, *deg.* of dona, worse, worst, inferior ; bithidh staid dheireanach an duine sin na 's *miosa* na a thoiseach, *the last state of that man shall be worse than the first, the beginning.*

Miosach, mēss′-ach, *adj.* monthly, menstrual ; an galar *miosach, menstrual courses, Arm.* ; *n. f.* herb, the purging-flax.

Miosail, mēss′-al, *a.* monthly.

Miosadair, mēss′-ad-ăr, *n. m.* an almanack, kalendar.

Miosgan, mėsg′-an, *n m.* butter-kit.

Miosguinn, mėssg′-ėnn, *n. f.* malice. *H. Society.*

Miotag, mėt′-ag, *n. f.* worsted glove.

Miothaird, mē′-ārj, *n. f.* unprotection, state of not being looked after.

Miothlachd, mē′-hlăchg, *n. m.* offence, displeasure, resentment ; a' toiltinn *miothlachd* duine sam bith, *incurring the displeasure,* or *resentment of any person.*

Miothlachdar, mē′-hlachg-ur, *adj.* displeasing, disagreeable, vexing, galling.

Mir, mėr, *n. f.* fury, rage, mad play, *or* romping ; tha e air *mhir, the man is stark mad* ; *v.* sport, skip, frisk.

Mir, mēr, *n. m.* bit, particle ; cha 'n 'eil *mir* agam, *I have'nt a particle* ; na h-uile *mir, every bit, every particle* ; a subdivision, a portion ; *mir* mòna, *a subdivision of a peat-stack* ; *mir* fearainn, *a patch of ground. Bible.*

Mire, mėr′-à, *n. m. pt.* sport, sporting, levity, fury, rage, frenzy ; dh' éirich iad suas gu *mire, they rose up to play, B.* ; *mire*-chath, *rage* or *fury of battle* ; also the degree of mear, merry, wanton ; na's *mire, more merry* or *wanton.*

Mireag, mėr′-ag, *n. f.* frisking, skipping.

Mireannach, mēr′-ann-ach, *n. m.* bridle-bit.

Mi-reuson, mē-rĕăs′-un, *n. m.* repartee.

Mi-reusonta, mē-rĕăs′-ant-à, *a.* irrational.

Mi-reusontachd, mē-rĕăs′-unt-achg, *n. f.* unreasonableness, unconscionableneness.

Mi-riaghailt, mē-rĕă′-aljty′, *n. f.* misrule, disorder, quarrel, confusion, turmoil.

Mi-riaghailteach, mē-rĕă′-aljty'-ach, *adj.* unruly, confused, unreasonable, quarrelsome.

Mi-rian, mē-rēnn, *n. m.* want of humour, *or* order.

Mi-rioghail, mē-rē-yhal, *adj.* disloyal ; unbecoming a king, unprincely ; *v.* misrule.

Misd, mėshj, **Misde**, mėshj′-à, degree of olc, dona, adv. &c. ; cha *mhisde* mi siod, *I am not a grain the worse for that* ; dè 's *misde* thu e, *what are you the worse for it ?*

Misdeachd, mėshj′-achg, *n. f.* inferiority, deterioration, tear.

Mi-stiuir, mē-styūėr, *v.* misdirect, misadvise.

Mise, mėsh′-à, *pron.* I myself, me myself.

Misg, mėshg, *n. f.* drunkenness, a debauch, intoxication, inebriety ; thugaibh an f haire dhuibh féin air eagal uair air bith gu'm bith bhur cridheachan fodh uallach le geòcaireachd agus le *misg, take heed unto yourselves, lest at any time your heart be overcharged with surfeiting and drunkenness, Luke* xxi, 34. ; air *mhisg, drunk* ; uair air *mhisg*, is uair air uisge, *one day drunk, and another day drinking water. G. Proverbs.*

Misgeach, mėshg′-ach, *adj.* drunken, intoxicated, cha dean cridhe *misgeach* breug, *a drunkard often tells (reveals) the truth. Prov.*

Misgear, mėshg′-ăr', *n. m.* drunkard.

Misgearachd, mėshg′-ăr'-achg, *n. f.* drunkenness, potations ; ri *misgearachd, at potations.*

Misgeil, mėsg′-al, *adj.* intoxicating.

Mi-sgeinm, mē-skenm′, *n. f.* slovenliness, indecorum, indecency, untidiness.

Mi-sgeinmeill, mē-skénm′-al, *a.* untidy.

Mi-sgeul, mē-skė'll, *n. m.* evil report.

Mi-sgiobalta, mē-skēb′-alt-à, *adj.* clumsy untidy, unwieldy, awkward in dress.

Mi-sgiobaltachd, mē-skēb′-alt-achg, *n. f* untidiness, awkwardness in gait or dress.

Mi-sgoinn, mē-skaŏėn, *n. f.* indecency.

Mi-sheadh, mē-hyaŏ-gh', *n. m.* absurdity.

Mi-sheadhail, mē-haŏ-ghal, *a.* absurd.

Mi-sheilbh, mē-hālv, *n. f.* misfortune.

Mi-sheirc, mē-hăėrk′, *n. f.* disaffection.

Mi-sheirceil, mē-hăėrk-al, *adj.* surly.

Mi-sheol, mē-hyôl, *v.* mislead, misguide.

Mi-sheolta, mē-hyôlt′-a, *adj.* unhandy.

Mi-sheoltachd, mē-hyôlt′-achg. *n. f.* unskilfulness, unhandiness, inexpertness.

Mi-shiobhalta, mē-hēv′-alt-a, *adj.* uncivil.

Mi-shiobhaltachd, mē-hēv′-alt-achg, *n. f.* uncivility, rudeness, unpoliteness, turbulence.

MI-SHOCAIR, mē-hochg′-ėr, *a.* uneasy, unsettled, uncomfortable, troubled, disturbed; *n. f.* disquietude, unsettled state, *or* case of.

MI-SHONA, mē-hŏn-â, *adj.* unfortunate.

MI-SHONAS, mē-hŏn-us, *n. f.* bad luck.

MI-SHUAIMHNEACH, mē-hŭăėv′-nyach, *adj.* restless, disquieted, disturbed, annoyed, distressed.

MI-SHUAIMHNEAS, mē-hŭăėv′-nyas, *n. m.* disquiet.

MI-SHUAIRC, mē-hŭăėrk, *a.* unpolite.

MI-SHUGHAR, mē-hû-ghar, *a.* sapless.

MI-SHUIM, mē-hûėm, *n.f.* heedlessness, indifference, inattention, carelessness.

MI-SHUIMEIL, mē-hŭėm′-al, *adj.* careless.

MISIMEAN, mėsh′-ėm-ăėn, *n. m.* bog-mint, (cartal,) *Irish.*

MISNEACH, mėsh′-nyach, *n. f.* courage, spirit; manliness; cheer, encouragement; biodh deadh *mhisneach* agaibh, *be of good cheer, Bible*; glac *misneach, pluck up courage*; le dìth *misnich, for want of courage*; is beag *misneach* a tha sin a' toirt domhsa, *that affords but slender encouragement to me*; cum suas do *mhisneach, keep up your spirits*; thoir *misneach* mhaith dha, *keep him in spirits*; cum am *misneach* mhath e, *keep him in good hopes*; fear na *misnich, the man of courage, the brave man*; chaill e *mhisneach, he is quite disheartened,* or *dispirited.*

MISNEACHAIL, mėsh′-nyach-al, *a.* courageous, manly, brave, intrepid, undaunted.

MISNICH, mėsh′-nyėch, *v.* encourage, exhort.

MI-STATH, mē-stha, *n. m.* idleness, vanity.

MI-STEIGHEALACHD, mē-styăē-yhal-achg, *n. f.* unsteadiness, fickleness, giddiness.

MI-STEIGHEIL, mē-styăė-′yhal, *adj.* unsteady.

MI-STIUIR, mē-styŭėr, *v.* mislead, misguide.

MI-STIUIREADH, mē-styŭr′-Ă, *pt.* misleading, seducing; *n. m.* unmanageableness, seduction.

MI-STUAMA, mē-stŭăm-â, *adj.* unguarded.

MI-STUAMACHD, mē-stŭăm-achg, *n. f.* unguardedness, intemperance, immodesty.

MI-THABHACHD, mē-hâv′-achg, *n. f.* inefficiency.

MI-THAING, mē-háėng, *n. f.* ingratitude.

MI-THAINGEIL, mē-háėng′-al, *a.* ungrateful

MI-THAITINN, mē-hăjt″-ėnn, *v.* disagree with, displease, give offence, offend; agus an uair a rinn an sluagh gearan, *mhithaitinn* e ris an Tighearn, *and when the people complained, it displeased the Lord.*

MI-THAITNEACH, mē-hăėjt′-nyach, *a.* disagreeable.

MI-THAITNEAS, mē-hăėjt′-nyas, *n. m.* offence.

MI-THAIRBE, mē-hăėr′-â, *n. f* disadvantage.

MI-THARBHACH, mē-hav′-ach, *adj.* unprofitable, unsubstantial, unproductive.

MI-THARBHACHD, mē-hărv2′-achg, *n. f.* unprofitableness, unproductiveness, unfruitfulness.

MITH, mhė, *n. m.* low person. *Macdonald.*

MI-THEIST, mē′-hāsht, *n. f.* bad report.

MI-THEISTEIL, mē-hāsht′-al, *adj.* disreputable.

MI-THEISTNEAS, mē-hāsht′-nyas, *n. f.* ill-repute.

MITHICH, mē′-yėch, *n.f.* fit time, high time, nick of time; is *mithich* dhuinn folbh, *it is high time that we should be off*; is *mithich* dhuibh èiridh, *it is time that you should get out of bed*; cha'n uair romh a *mhithich* e, *it is not an hour before the proper time*; properly meidhich, from meidh; air *mheidh* a dhol dachaidh, *on the eve of going home.*

MI-THLUSAR, mē-hlŭs′-ur, *adj.* cold in affections; as clothes next the skin, uncomfortable.

MI-THLUSARACHD, mē-thlŭs′-ur-achg, *n.m.* coldness of manner; uncomfortableness, as clothes.

MI-THOGARRACH, mē-hȯg′-arr-ach, *a.* a verse.

MI-THOGRADH, mē-hŏg′-rĂ, *n. m.* lust; aversion.

MI-THOIL, mē′-hŏ'l, *n. f.* reluctance.

MI-THOILEACH, mē-hŏ'l′-ach, *a.* averse.

MI-THOILICH, mē-hŏ'l′-ėch, *v.* displease.

MI-THOILICHTE, mē-hŏ'l′-ėch-tyȧ, *pt.* displeased, dissatisfied, discontented, unsatisfied.

MI-THROCAIR, mēhrôchg′-ėr, *n. f.* cruelty.

MI-THUIG, mē′-hŭėg, *v.* misunderstand.

MI-THUIGSEACH, mē-hŭėg′-shyach, *adj.* senseless, stupid, dull, absurd.

MI-UAIBHREACH, mē-ŭăėv′-rach, *adj.* humble.

MI-UASAIL, mē-ŭăs′-al, *adj.* ignoble, mean.

MI-UAISLE, mē-ŭăsh′-lȧ, *n. f.* meanness.

MI-UMHAIL, mē-ŭv2′-al, *a.* disobedient.

MI-UMHLACHD, mē-ûv2′-lachg, *n. f.* disobedience, rebelliousness, disloyalty.

MI-URRAM, mē-ŭrr′-um, *n. f.* disrespect.

MI-URRAMACH, mē-ŭrr′-am-ach, *adj.* disrespectful.

MNA, mrà, *gen.* of bean, a wife, woman

MNAI, mràė, *pl.* of bean, women, wives.

MNAOIDH, mrùė, *dat.* of bean, to a woman, to a wife.

MNATHAN, mrà′-an, *n. pl.* wives, women.

MO, maŏ, *pass. pro.* my, mine; *mo* cheum, *my footsteps*; *mo* nighean, *my daughter*; MU, properly.

MO, mò, poetical contraction of momha, greater, &c.; is esan is *momha, he is greater*; cha *momha* orm thu 's an cu, *I do not value you more than a dog*; dè 's *momha* orms thu, *what do I care for you*! cha *mhomha* a nì mi e, *neither will I do it*; is *momha* e na sin, *it is greater than that*; cha *mhomha* leam dè their thu is beagan, *I care miserably little for what you say*; o'n aon a's lugha gus an aon is *momha*, *from the least to the greatest*; is *momha* e na gach aon, *he is greater than all*; cha *mhomha* orm thu is an cù, *I care as little for you as for a dog*.

Moch, mŏch, *adj.* early; o dhùsgadh na maidne *moich*, *from the awakening of early morn*. *Sm.*; *adv.* early, betimes, soon; éirich *moch*, *rise early*; *moch* an dè, *early yesterday*; is *moch* a dh'èirich thu, *you rose early*; *moch* is anamoch, *early and late*; *moch* am màireach, *early to-morrow*; *n.m.* dawn, morn; o *mhoch* gu dubh, *from the dawn till the dusk*; is *moiche*, *earlier*.

Mochd, mŏchg, *v.* yield. *Gill.*; *H. S.*

Mochairidh, mŏch-ăr'-ė, *n. f.* } waking,
Mochfhairich, mŏch'-ăr'-èch, } *or* rising early; is tu a rinn a *mhochairich*, *how early you are afoot*! *mochairich* is ionairich, *rising early, and late sitting*; bi subhach, sunntach, *mochairEach*, *be cheerful, lively, and an early riser*; rinn iad *mochairidh*, na *mochairich*, *they rose early*.

Mochrath, mŏch'-hră, *n. m.* dawn; 'sa *mhochrath*, *in the dawn*; *adv.* very early; bha e so *mochrath*, *he was here early*; anns a *mhochrath*, *early in the morning*, (moch and trath.)

Mod, mòd, *n.m.* court of justice; a' dol do 'n *mhód*, *going to the court of justice*; an assembly, meeting.

Modh, mò'-gh, *n. m.* politeness, good manners, good breeding; duine gun *mhodh*, *an ill-bred man,—a man without good breeding*; manner, method; air a *mhodh so*, *by this method, in this manner*; *v.* tame.

Modhalachd, mò'-al-achg, *n.f.* good manners, politeness, good breeding, modesty.

Modhar, mò'-ghar, *a.* soft, modest, silly, gentle; an gleann *mòdhar* nan sruthan lùbach, *in the still vale of the meandering streamlets*.

Mog, mòg, *n.f.* plump hand.

Mogach, mòg'-ach, *adj.* soft-handed; pawed.

Mogan, móg'-an, *n. m.* old stocking; a stocking without a foot; oat-whisky. *Sk.*

Moglaich, móg'-llèch, *v.* husk nuts.

Mogull, móg'-ull, *n. m.* husk of a nut.

Moibill, moyb'-ėlly', *v.* gnaw, mumble, mutter, half-chew.

Moibleadh, moyb'-llĂ, *pt.* mumbling muttering, half-chewing; *n. m.* gnawing, mutter.

Moiche, moych'-â, *adj.* earlier, earliest; *n. f.* earliness, soonness; degree of earliness.

Moid, mòjj, *n.f.* greatness. *Gillies.*

Moide, mòjj'-â, *deg.* of mòr, great; cha *mhòid*, or momhaide, *perhaps*; cha *mhòide* e sin, *it is nothing the greater for that*; uime sin bu *mhòide* a dh' iarr na h-Iùdhaich a mharbhadh, *therefore the Jews sought the more to kill him*; bu *mhòid'* a ghlaoidh e, *the more he cried*.

Moidreag, mójj'-ryag, *n. f.* a plump girl; a fat, plump, good-natured female child.

Moilean, mól'-ăèn, *n. m.* fat, plump male child; a plump man.

Moileanach, mól'-ăĕn-ach, *n. m.* a plump young man; *adj.* plump.

Moill, māoėlly', *n. f.* delay, detention.

Moine, mòėn''-a, *n.f.* peats, moss, morass.

Moineis, móėn'-ash, *n. f.* false delicacy.

Moineiseach, móėn'-ash-ach, *adj.* low, diffident, dilatory, fastidious.

Moinig, mòėn'-ėg, *n. f.* fastidiousness, nicety, boasting of favours conferred.

Moinigeil, móėn'-ėg-al, *adj.* fastidious, assuming indifference; making nice.

Mointeach, mòėn'-tyach, *n. f.* moss-land, moor-land; *adj.* mossy.

Mointeachail, mòėn'-tyach-al, *adj.* mossy.

Mointidh, mòėn'-tyė, *adj.* mossy.

Moirear, mór'-ăĕr, *n. m.* a lord, nobleman; *morair* properly, (mòr-fhear.)

Moireachd, móėr'-achg, *n. f.* lordship, title, dignity, greatness.

Moirneas, mòėrn'-ash, *n. f.* great cascade, volcano; mar *mhòirneas* do theine theintich, *as a volcano of lava*; melted metal. *Old Song*; *Armstrong*.

Moit, mòjt, *n. f.* pretended indifference about a thing one is very keen for; fastidiousness; nicety about a thing one is fond of; shiness, airs, foolish pride.

Moitealachd, móėjt'-al-achg, *n.f.* state of assuming airs of importance; fastidiousness.

Moiteil, mŏėjt'-tyal, *adj.* assuming airs; pretending indifference; excessively nice.

Mol, mól, *v.* praise, laud, eulogise, exalt, extol, magnify; *moladh* m' anam Dia, *let my soul praise God*; recommend, exhort, advise; *mholainn* duit dol dachaidh, *I would recommend to you to go home*; *mholainn* dhuit na buinn a thoirt ort, *I would recommend to you to take to your heels—to take French leave*, or *leg-bail*.

Molach, mól'-ach, *adj.* rough, hairy.

Molachas, mól'-ach-us, *n. f.* hairiness.

Moladh, mól'-Ă, *pt.* praising, eulogising, applauding, recommending; *n.m.* praise, eulogy, commendation: cha dean mi tuilidh *moladh* ort, *I will not speak more in thy praise*; cha *moladh* do *mholadh, your eulogy is no praise.*

MOLL, mŏll, *n. m.* chaff; mar *mhòll* air 'fhuadachadh le gaoith, *as chaff driven by the wind*; leaba *mhùill, chaff-bed.*

MOLLTE, moll'-tyă, *pt.* praised, lauded.

MOLT, móltt, *n. m.* wedder; *muilt*, wedders.

MOLTACH, molt'-ach, *adj.* praiseworthy.

MOLLTAIR, bolltair, multure, mill-dues.

MOMHA, mó'-a, *deg.* greater, greatest; cha *mhomha* na thu fhèin a gheibheadh e, *none but a friend like yourself would get it—no less important a person than yourself would get it.*

MOMHAIDE, mó'-ėjj-ă, *deg.* mòr, cha *mhomhaide*, perhaps; cha *mhomhaide* e sin, *it is not greater for that*; cha *mhomhaide* gun dh' thig e, *perhaps he will not come*; contracted mòide.

MONADH, món'-Ă, *n. m.* moor, heath.

MONADAIL, món'-ad-al, *adj.* moorish, hilly.

MONAR, món'-ar, *n. m.* refuse, contemptible person *or* object; tha 's, cha b'e *monar* e, *yes, and it is not the refuse—yes, and he is not the contemptible person, he is a great man* or *person.*

MONMHOR, mòn'-vur, *n. m.* murmur. *B.*

MOR, mōr *and* môr, *adj.* great, of great size; tall; and important; duine *mòr, a great man, a tall man, considerable personage*; great, numerous; sluagh *mòr, a great* or *numerous people* or *multitude*; important, weighty, considerable; nì *mòr, an important* or *weighty affair*; mighty, overbearing, self-important; cho *mhòr* as fhèin ris a mhac-mhallachd, *as self-important as Lucifer*; familiar, intimate, much attached, gracious; tha iad *mòr* aige a chèile, *they are great chums*; tha iad cho *mhòr* aige chèile is urrainn iad, *they are as gracious as can be—they are as familiar as possible*; much valued, esteemed much, thought much of; bu *mhòr* aca fhèin e, *it was much valued by themselves—they thought much of it themselves*; much, great in degree; is *mòr* a dh' fhuilneas cridhe ceart ma'm brist e, *a well-regulated heart suffers much ere it break*; *adv.* and *n. m.* much, many; is *mòr* leam, *I think it too much*; is *mòr* leam sin a dheanadh, *I think it too much to go that length*; is *mòr* a dh' fhuilinn mi, *greatly did I suffer*! tha e ra-*mhor, it is too big, it is too much*; cha *mhòr* a chì e, *few shall see it*; cha *mhòr* math a th' air, *it is not worth much*; am *mòr* leat na dh' itheas e, *do you grudge what he eats? do you think him a gormandiser*? is momha esan, *he is greater* or *taller*; cha *mhòr almost*; cha *mhòr* nach do bhual e mi, *he almost struck me*; the great, the mighty, the chivalrous, the renowned, the famous; cò tha coltach ri *mòr* nan cliù, *who is like the mighty of renown*? am beag is am *mòr, both great and small, the mighty and the feeble-handed*; great number, great deal.

MORACHD, môr'-achg, *n. f.* greatness, mightiness; majesty, dignity, rank.

MORAIL, môr'-al, *adj.* majestic, magnificent.

MORAN, môr- *or* mōr-an, *n. m.* great deal, great number, many, great quantity; *mòran* aca ag radh, *many of them assert*; *mòran* eile, *many more*; *mòran* nithe, *many things*; *mòran* cuideachd, *a great company*; *moran* èisg, *great quantity of fish*; *mòran* nighean, *great number of daughters*; *adv.* by a great deal; *mòran* na 's fhaisge, *by a great deal nearer*; *mòran* eile, *great number of others.*

MORCHUIS, mōr'-chŭsh, *n. f.* ambition, pomp, pageantry, magnificence.

MORCHUISEACH, mōr'-chŭsh-ach, *adj.* ambitious, pompous, splended, high-minded.

MORCHUISEACHD, mōr'-chŭsh-achg, *n. f.* ambitiousness, splendour, pomposity.

MORROINN, mōr'-raŏènn, *n. f.* province. *B.*

MORT, mŏrt, *n. m.* murder, massacre; *v.* murder, slay; *mort* Ghlinne-Chomha, *Glencoe-massacre.*

MORTACH, mŏrt'-ach, } *adj.* murderous,
MORTAIL, mŏrt'-al, } murdering.

MORTAIR, mŏrt'-ăr', *n. m.* murderer, killer, assassin; am *mortair, the murderer.*

MORTAIREACHD, mort'-ar'-achg, *n. f.* massacre.

MORTHIR, môr'-hèr, *n. f.* mainland.

MORTHIREACH, môr'-hyèr-ach, *n. c.* person belonging to the mainland; *a* belonging to a continent.

MOR-UAISLE, mōr-ŭăèsh'-lyă, *n. m* nobility.

MOSACH, mŏs'-ach, *adj.* filthy, nasty; nì *mosach, a filthy thing*; mean, inhospitable, not liberal; is tu a tha *mosach, how inhospitable you are!*

MOSAG, mos'-ag, *n. f.* filthy or dirty female; parsimonious niggardly female.

MOSAICHE, mŏs'-ėch-ă, } *n. f.* filthiness,
MOSRAICHE, mos'-rėch, } niggardliness.

MOSG, mŏsg, } *n. m.* dry-rot; *a.*
MOSGAIN, mŏsg'-ăėn, } having dry-rot, as wood.

MOSGAILL, mosg'-ėly', *v.* arouse, rouse.

MOSGALACH, mŏsg'-al-ach, *adj.* watchful.

MOSGALACHD, mŏsg'-al-achg, *n. f.* vigilance.

MOSGLADH, mosg'-lĂ, *pt.* rousing, awaking; *n. m.* rouse, rousing.

MOSRAICHE, mŏs'-rèchă, *n. f.* smuttiness.

MOTHACHADH, mŏ'-ach-Ă, *n. m.* feeling,

sensation; chaill e *mhothachadh, he lost all sense of feeling, all sensation, all sensibility*; muinntir air dhaibh am *mothachadh* a chall, *people who being past feeling, B.*; *pt.* feeling, observing, noticing, attending.

MOTHACHAIL, mŏ-ach-al, *adj.* sensible, observant, considerate, kind.

MOTHAICH, mŏt′-ėch, *v.* feel, perceive; *mothaich* so, *feel this*; *mhothaich* sinn 'ga threigsinn a ghuth; *mhothaich* gun lugh a mheoir, *we perceived his voice forsaking him*; *we perceived his fingers becoming feeble*; observe, notice; an do *mhothaich* thu e a' dol seachad, *did you observe* or *take notice of him passing*.

MOTHAR, mhó′-hur, *n. m.* a deep-toned, unearthly voice *or* sound, as a person in a cave or cauldron; thug e *mothar* as, *he gave a most appalling cry*; chuala sinn *mothar, we heard a most unearthly voice* or *sound*. In Dr. N. Macleod's Glossary, a sweet melodious sound.

MU, for ma, which see.

MUC, mŭchg, *n. f.* a sow, a pig, a large ball of snow—heap, *North*; *muc*-mhara, *a whale*; *muc*-steallain, *muc*-bhiorach, *porpoise*.

MUCACH, mŭchg′-ach, } *adj.* swinish, dirty,
MUCAIL, mŭchg′-al, } surly, stupid.

MUCAG, mŭchg′-ag, *n. f.* a hip; *mucagan* is sgeachagan, *hips and haws*.

MUCAIRE, mŭchg′-ăr′-à, *n. m.* swine-herd.

MUC FAILM, mŭchg-faŏėl′-um, *n. f.* dog brier berry, *or* hip.

MUCH, mûch, *v.* smother, quench.

MUCHADAIR, mûch′-ad-ăr′, *n. m.* extinguisher.

MUCHADH, mûch′-Ă, *pt. n. m.* smothering, quenching, extinguishing.

MUG, mûg, *n. m.* a snuffle through the nose.

MUGACH, mûg′-ach, *adj.* snuffling, gloomy; *n. f.* a snuffling female.

MUGAICHE, mûg′-ėch-à, *n. f.* snuffle, gloom.

MUGAIRE, mûg′-ăr′-à, *n. m.* snuffler.

MUGH, mŭ, and mû-gh, *v.* change, as money, begin to rot, decay, deteriorate; a' dol am *mùghadh, decaying, perishing*; do bhrathair lag am *mùghadh, thy weak brother perishing, Bible*; in Argyle, an mothadh—*mùghadh* puinnd, *the change of a pound*; fhuair mi *mughadh, I have got change. Argyle.*

MUGHADH, mú′-gh-Ă, *pt. n. m.* change, decay; *pt.* changing, decaying.

MUGHAIRN, mu-gh′-ăėrn, *n. m.* ankle. *Is.*

MUGHAIRNEACH, mu′-ăėr-ach, *adj.* large-ankled, having large ankles.

MUICFHEOIL, muėchg′-ėôl, *n. f.* pork.

MUIDH, mŭe-y′, *n. m.* the mane of a horse, lion, leopard, &c.; gath-muidh.

MUIG, mûėg, *n. f.* discontented expression of countenance, frown, gloom; cuir *mùig* ort, *frown*; *v.* frown.

MUIGEAN, mŭėg′-aėn, } *n. m.* a surly dog of
MUIGIRE, mŭėg′-ėr-a, } a fellow, frowner.

MUIGEIS, mŭėg′-ash, *n. f.* snuffling, surliness.

MUIGH, mŭė-y′, *n. m.* the outside, surface; am *muigh, on the outside*; superficially; a chum am *muigh* is am mach, *that, by all means, on all accounts, completely, wholly, out and out*; abair ris a bhith an so, am màireach *muigh* is a mach, *tell him to be here, by all means, to-morrow*.

MUIGH, mûė-y′, *n. m.* churn. *Arg.*

MUIGHTEACH, mŭe′-tyach, *a.* changeable.

MUIL, mŭ′l, *n. c.* mule, all Languages.

MUILE, mŭ′l′-à, *n. m.* Isle of Mull.

MUILEACH, mŭ′l′-ach, *n.* Mull-man; *a.* of Mull.

MUILEANN, mŭ′l′-ann, *n. m.* grist-mill, mills, muillean and muilnean; *muileann*-sàbhaidh, *a saw-mill*, or *machine*; *muileann*-càrdaidh, *carding-machine*; *muileann*-luaidhe, *waulking-machine*, or *mill*; *muilean*-lìn, *lint-mill*; *muileann* laimh, *a hand-mill*.

MUILEAD, mŭėl′-aj, *n. m.* mule, mùil. *B.*

MUILICHINN, mŭėl′-ėch-ėnn, *n. m.* sleeve.

MUILICHINNEAN, mŭėl′-ėch-ėnn-unn, *n. pl.* see Muirlinn, birses; gruaigean Mull, &c. *sort of edible-sea weed, like gloves*.

MUILLEAR, mŭėll′-ăr′, *n. m.* miller; muilcarachd, *the office* or *occupation of a miller*.

MUILL, mûėlly′, *gen.* of moll, chaff.

MUILLEAN, mûėlly″-ăėn, *n. m.* particle of chaff *W.*; a bundle or truss of straw, boitean, *North*.

MUILLEARACHD, mŭėlly″-ăėr-achg, *n. f.* office, *or* occupation of a miller.

MUILLION, mŭėlly″-unn, *n. m.* million. *B.*

MUILT, mŭėljt, *n. pl.* wedders.

MUILTFHEOIL, mŭėljt′-ĕŏl, *n. f.* mutton.

MUIME, mŭėm′-à, *n. f.* step-mother; nurse

MUIN, mûėnn, *v.* piss, make water.

MUIN, mŭėn, *n. m.* back, top; thog e air a *mhuin* an loach, *he raised the herc on his back*, muinn.

MUINCHILL, mŭėn′-chėlly, *n. f.* sleeve, muilichinn.

MUINEAL, mŭėn″-al, *n. m.* neck of a person.

MUINEALACH, mŭėn″-al-ach, *a.* long necked

MUING, mŭėng, *n. m.* mane of a horse more properly, muidh.

MUINIGHINN, } mŭėn′-ėnn, *n. f.* fort, de-
MUINNINN, } pendance, fortress, trust, stay, confidence; ann am *muinninn* neo *muinighinn* a chosnaidh, *depending on his daily labour*; is tu mo *mhuinighinn* threun, *thou art my strong tower, my chief confidence*; from muinn-inne.

Muinn, mŭènn, *n. f.* back, top.
Muinne, mŭèn-nyà, *n. f.* tallow-tripe.
Muinninn, mŭènn'-ènn, *n. m.* dependence, trust.
Muinntir, mŭènn'-tyer', *n. f.* people, relations, inhabitants; thàinig e a dh'ionnsuidh a dhùthcha féin is cha do ghabh a *mhùinntir* fhéin ris, *he came into his own country, and his own (friends,* or *relations,) received him not, B.*; *mùinntir* a bhaile so, *mùinntir* an tighe so, *the inhabitants of this town, the inhabitants of this house*; in some places, a' *mhuinntir* bheaga, a' *mhuinntir* mhòra, for na feadhainn bheaga, *the little ones, &c.*; do *mhuinntir, your people, your relations*; do *mhuinntir* chéile, *your spouse's people*.
Muinntireach, mŭènn'-tyèr'-ach, *n. c.* an acquaintance, follower; sean *mhuinntireach, an old acquaintance.*—servant. *N.*
Muinntireachd, mŭènn'-tyèr'-achg, *n. f.* acquaintance, dealings, correspondence; sean *mhùinntireachd, old acquaintance,* or *correspondence.*
Muinntireas, mŭenn'-tyèr'-us, *n. f.* correspondence, dealing, communication—service, servitude. *North.*
Muir, mŭer, *n. f.* sea, ocean, wave.
Muire, mŭer'-à, *n. f.* hurry; leprosy. *N.*
Muirichinn, mŭèr'-èch-ènn, *n. f.* a young, throng, ill-provided-for family; hurry-burry, a hard task *or* burden.
Muirichinneach, mŭèr'-èch-ènn-ach, *adj.* hurried, hard-pressed; having a large family, *or* young, ill-provided-for family.
Muirichlinn, mŭèr'-èch-lyènn, **Muirlinn**, mŭèr'-lyènn, *n. f.* edible sea-weed, called birses; in some places gruaigean.
Muirn, mûèrn, *n. f.* a respectful, tender reception, *or* genuine Highland hospitality; sann rompa a bha *mhùirn, how respectfully and hospitably they were received!* entertainment with excessive tenderness *or* fondling, as of children; caressing; le furbhailt is *mùirn, with complacency and hospitality*; tigh na *mùirn, the home of hospitality. Islay*; delicateness, tenderness; le *mùirn, on account of delicacy.*
Muirneach, mûèrn'-ach, *adj.* dearly beloved, excessively fondled, almost spoiled, as a child; tender, delicately received and entertained; hospitable; mac *mùirneach, dearly-beloved son*; *mùirneach* uime, *caressing him, almost killing him with Highland hospitality.*
Muir-robainn, mŭèr'-rrŏb-ènn, *n. f.* piracy; also muir-spùinneadh.
Muirsgian, mŭr'-skĕăn, *n m.* razor-fish.
Muir-spuinneadair, mŭèr-spûènn'-ad-ăr', *n. m.* a pirate, sea-robber, plunderer.
Muir-titheachd, mŭèr'-tyē-achg, *n. f.* sea-blubber *Skye*; sgeith-ròin. *Argyle.*
Muiseall; see Smuiseall, muzzle of a plough.
Muiteach, mùighteach, changeable.
Mulachan, mul'-ach-an, *n. m.* a cheese giùlain am *mulachan, carry the cheese.*
Mulad, mŭl'-ad, *n. m.* sadness, grief.
Muladach, } mŭl'-ajj-ach, *adj.* sad, melancholy; distressing;
Mulaideach, } naigheachd *mulaideach, melancholy* or *distressing intelligence.*
Mulaideachd, mŭl'-ăjj-achg, *n. f.* distressing nature, *or* circumstances of a case.
Mulan, mŭl'-an, *n. m.* stack of corn—(never of hay); a large conical wave *or* billow.
Mulart, mŭll'-art, *n. m.* dwarf-elder. *Ir.*
Mulc, mŭlk, *n. m.* a lump, a dive, a duck; *v.* ram, push suddenly, dive, duck.
Mulcach, mŭlk'-ach, *adj.* lumpish.
Mulcadh, mŭlk'-Ă, *pt.* diving, pushing.
Mullach, mŭll'-ach, *n. m.* roof, top, ridge, apex; height, eminence; the very essence; *mullach* na beinne, *the top* or *ridge of the hill*; air *mullach* an tighe, *on the roof of the house*; *mullach* an t-shlaoightire, *a most complete rogue—a rogue in earnest.*
Mult; see Molt, wedder.
Mu'm, mu'n, see ma'm, ma'n.
Mun, mûn, *n. m.* urine, piss; *pt.* pissing, drawing water.
Mun, mûn, *v.* instruct *or* school in lessons of politeness *or* good-breeding; rear; *pt.* teaching.
Munadh, mûn'-Ă, *pt.* instructing in good morals and manners; *n. m.* good morals, good manners *or* breeding.
Munloch, mŭn'-loch, *n. f.* puddle. *H. S.*
Mur, mur, *conj.* except; *mur* dean thu, *except you do*; *mur* dean sibhse aithreachas, sgriosar sibhse uile *mar* an ceudna, *except ye repent, ye shall be all destroyed also*; *mur* bhiodh gu'n, *were it not*; *mur* bhiodh gu'n do thog e chuis, *were it not that he had appealed. Bible.*
Mura-bhith, mar-a-vè', *n. f.* excuse, pretence, exception; gun *mura-bhith* sam bith, *without any exception* or *pretension*; without were-it-not.
Mur, mûr, *n. m.* wall of a rampart. *Ir.*
Murach, mûr'-ach, *n. f.* a down *or* sandhill on the sea-shore; in Coll, meàllach, feadh na *mùraichean, through the Downs,* or *sand-hills.*
Muran, mŭr'-an, *n. m.* bent, down-grass.
Mura-bhuachaill, mŭr'-a-vhŭăch-èlly', *n. m.* a Holland auk; bura-bhuachaill in some parts.
Murlach, mûr'-lăch, *n. m.* king-fish.
Murlach, mûr'-lăch, *n. f.* fishing-basket, *Mull*; in some parts murluinn, murla—a female having an ugly head of hair. *Is*

MURLAN, mŭr′-llan, *n. m.* an ugly head of hair; dirty, matted hair.

MURRACH, mŭrr′-ach, *a.* able. *Provincial.*

MURRACHD, mŭrr′-achg, *n. f.* ability. *Pro.*

MURRAICHD, mûrr′-èchg, *n. f.* handsome present; spoil on the sea-shore.

MURT, mŭrt, *for* mort, murder.

MUSG, mûsg, *n. m.* eye-rheum; ugly eye.

MUSG, mŭsg, *n. f.* a musket.

MUSGACH, mûsg′-ach, *n. m.* rheum-eyed.

MUTAN, mût′-an, *n. m.* stump of a finger; in some places worsted gloves.

MUTH, *for* mugh, mû′-gh′, to change.

MUTHACH, mû′-ach, *n. m.* a herd; buachaile caillear bò an droch *mhùthaich* seachd bliadhna romh am mithich(meidhich,) *the bad herd's cow is lost seven years before the time. Highland Society.*

N

N, n, the eleventh letter of the alphabet, called by the Irish, Nùin. It has various sounds, for which you are referred to the Grammar and Key.

N for an, (art), after words ending with a vowel; thus, dh'òl iad do'*n* fhìon, *they drank of the wine*; 2d, (for an), their, *pro.*; le'n làmhan is le'n casan, *with their hands and with their feet*; 3d, for whom, (*rel. pro.*) ma'n d' thubhairt iad, *of whom they assert*; 4th, for contraction of ann an; '*n* tigh, (for ann an tigh,) *in a house*; 5th, *inter. part,* '*n* d' fhàg thu mi, *have you left me*? used so, often in poetry; 6th, for an, *part. expl.*; as, a chionn gu'*n* robh eagal orra, *because they were afraid*; 7th, *n-*, before ar, *our*, bhur, *your*, '*nar*, *in our*—when the noun following, begins with a vowel; ar *n*-aithrichean,'nar *n*-oige, bhur *n*-igheanan, *our fathers, in our youth, your daughters.*

NA, nă, *nom. pl. art.* as, *na* mnàthan, *the women*; 2d, for ann an; as, '*na* d' shuain, *in thy profound sleep*; 3d, *gen. sing. fem.* of *art.* an, *of the*; as, fo ghruaim *na* h-oidhche, *under the gloom of the night*; also *dat. plu.* of the *art.*; as, 'air *na* beanntaibh, *on the mountains*; 4th, *comp. adv.* or *conj.* than, as, *na's* fhearr, *na's* miosa, *better, worse*; 5th, *rel. pro. sing.* and *plu.* in all cases, including often the antecedent in itself; as, all, all those, what, what number, those who, those which; *na* thàinig, *all that came—all those that came*; *na's* urrainn mi, *all that I can*; ma *na* thubhairt e rium, *concerning all that he said to me*; ma *na* nithe so, *about these things*; *na* dh' fhanas, *all those that may remain*; 6th, *conj.* than; *na's* fhearr *na* esan, *better than he is*; *inter. part. na* (for an do); 'n a thuit thu 'n cadal trom, *hast thou fallen into profound sleep*? 7th, *adv.* not, let not, either, or; a h-'aon *na* dhà, *either one* or *two*; *na* d'thig an so, *do not come here*! 8th, for ann a '*na*, *he being a* or *as*; '*na* choigreach, *he being as a stranger*, or *a stranger.*

NABAIDH, nà′-bè, *n. c.* neighbour, *North*; in the *West*, a North Highlander.

NABAIDHEACHD, nà′-bè-achg, *n. f.* neighbourhood.

NACH, nach, *neg. rel. pro.* who not, whom not, what not, that not; an t-aon *nach* d' thig, *the individual who will not come*; suinn *nach* beò, *heroes that are not living*; feadhainn *nach* d' thig, *people that will not come*; 2d, *inter.* and *neg. part. nach* truagh leat mi, *do you not pity my case? nach* math e, *is it not very good? nach* d' thig thu, *do you not come? nach* 'eil fhios agad, *do you not know*? 3d, *conj.* and *adv.* that not, in that not; a' chionn *nach* 'eil an righ a' toirt fògarraich air an ais, *in that the king does not restore the banished, the fugitives.*

NAD, nonsense for, ann ad.

NADUR, nàd′-ur, *n. m.* and *f.* the work of nature; obair *naduir, the work of nature*; disposition, temper, inclination; do dhroch *nàdur, your bad temper* or *disposition*; the sinful disposition of mankind; nature.

NADURRA, nàd′-urr-à, *adj.* natural, affectionate; nighean *nàdurra, an affectionate daughter.*

NADURRACHD, nàd′-urr-achg, *n. f.* the course of nature; natural affection; also, bent of inclination; instinct.

NADURRAIL, nàd′-urr-al, *adj.* natural, &c.

NAID, năjj, *n. f.* lamprey, seòrsa èisg.

NAIGHEACHD, năè′-yachg, *n. m.* news, tidings, intelligence; dè do *naigheachd, what is your news*? droch *naigheachd* dhuitse, *bad intelligence for you.*

NAILE, nàèl′-à, *n. m.* (an naile,) *adv.* the name of a Celtic saint; hence, a Naile thà, *yes, indeed! forsooth, it is so! by St. Neill, it is so!* an *Naile* fhèin, *ay, indeed! by my troth, you are a fine fellow*!

NAIMHDE, naév′-ja, *gen.* of nàmhaid, foe.

NAIMHDEAN, név′-jjăn, *pl.* foes, enemies.

MAIMHDEACH, név′-jach, *a.* virulent, hostile.

NAIMHDEIL, név′-jal, *a.* hostile; venomous, malicious, inimical, keen, eager to revenge.

NAIMHDEAS, név′-jus, *n. m.* enmity, hostility, malice, vindictiveness, resentment.

Naimhdealachd, név′-jăl-achg, *n. f.* revengefulness, vindictiveness, resentment.

Naimhdealas, név′-jăll-us, *n. f.* see above.

'Naird, nârj, (for ann an aird,) *adv.* aloft, upwards, up; chaidh e *'n aird, he went aloft, he mounted, went up!*

Naire, nàer′-à, *n. f.* sense of shame; disgrace, ignominy; gabh *nàire, feel ashamed*; gun *nàire* gun athadh, *without shame or a blush, confusion of face.*

Naisg, náèshg, *v.* deposite money, pledge; *naisg* thusa an t-airgead an làmhan an duine uasail so, agus théid mise am bannaibh dhuitse gu'm faigh thu e, *deposite you the money in the hands of this gentleman, and I will be bound that you shall get it.*

Naisgte, năèshg′-tyà, *pt.* deposited, pledged.

Naisinn, nàsh′-ènn, *n. f.* a deep and over-delicate sense of duty; an excessive sense of gratitude, particularly in matters of hospitality; hospitality that puts to inconvenience; na biodh *nàisinn* 'sam bith ort air mo shonsa, *don't put yourself to any inconvenience on my account*; is beag *nàisinn* a th'ormsa air a shon sin, *I do not feel any excessive sense of propriety to return that favour*; a native; *nàisinn* an àite, *the natives of the place.* In Mull, *nàistinn.*

Naisneach, nàesh′-nyach, *adj.* feeling a deep sense of obligation; perseveringly at work from a sense of duty (to a fault); shewing excessive hospitality and decency to a stranger from a delicate sense of the laws of such; in some places, nàistinneach.

Naisneachd, nàesh′-nyachg, *n. f.* deep sense of duty *or* propriety of the observance of hospitality; too much keenness at work from the same feeling; shamefacedness, bashfulness; le *nàisneachd* agus stuaim, *with shamefacedness and sobriety*; gun sgeadachadh fèin le *nàisneachd, adorning themselves with shamefacedness. Tim. Bible*—(seldom used in this sense.)

Naitheas, náè′-hus, *n. m.* hurt. *H. S.*

Nall, nnăll, *adv.* to this side, hither, toward us, in our direction; an nunn is a *nall, hither and thither, across and back again.*

Nam, năm, *conj.* if; *nam* biodh, *if it were*; *nam* biodh mo chliù-sa cho maireann, *were my fame so lasting*; 2d, *gen. pl.* of an, *art.* as, glac *nam* beann, *the gorge of the hills—pass of the hills*; used before b, f, m, p.

'Nam, năm, (for ann am, *or* ann mo, contracted); *'nam* meadhon, *in the midst of them*; that is, ann am meadhon; used as above before b, f, m, p; 2d, for ann mo, *in my*; as *'nam* fhearann, *in my land.*

Namh, nàv, *n. m.* enemy. *Ps. Smith.*

Namhaid, nàv′-èjj, *n. m.* enemy, foe, adversary; naimhdean, naimhde, *foes, &c.*

Nan, nan, *gen. pl. art.* an, used before all letters except b, f, m, p,; see an, page 9.

'Nan, năn, same as 'nam, used as above.

'Nann, nănn, *inter. part.* *'n ann* mar sin a dh' àithn' mi dhuibh, *is it thus that I commanded you*? *'n ann* mar sin, *is it so*?

Naoidh, núè-y', *n. m.* and *adj.* nine; an ceann *naoidh* mìosan, *at the expiration of nine months*; *naoidh* fir, *nine men.*

Naoidh-deug, núèy″-jūg, *n. m.* and *adj* nineteen; naoidh fir dheug, *nineteen men*; so *naoidh-deug, here nineteen.*

Naoidhean, núè′-yhăèn, **Naoidheachan**, núè′-ach-an, *n. c.* a little child, an infant, babe.

Naoidheanachd, núe′-an'-achg, *n. f.* infancy.

Naoimh, nùèv, *n. pl.* and *gen.* of naomh, saints.

Naomh, nùv, *adj.* holy, sacred, consecrated, sanctified; *n. c.* a saint, holy person; na *naoimh, the saints*; na's *naoimhe, holier.*

Naoitheamh, nùè′-uv, *adj.* ninth.

Naomhachadh, nùv′-ach-Ă, *pt.* sanctifying, consecrating; *n. m.* sanctification, consecration.

Naomhachd, nùv′-achg, *n., f.* holiness, sanctity; *naomhachd* na sàbaid, *sanctity of the Sabbath.*

Naoimhaich, nùv′-èch, *v.* consecrate, sanctify, hallow; gu *naoimhaichear* t' ainm, *hallowed be thy name*; *naomhaich* e, *he sanctified.*

Naomh-cheannachd, nùv-chyann′-achg, *n. f.* simony, purchasing holy things by money.

Naomh-ghoid, nùv-ghaŏj′, *n. f.* sacrilege.

Naomh-oran, nùv-ōr′-an, *n. f.* anthem.

Naomh-threig, nùv-hrāg′, *v.* apostatise.

Naom-threigire, nùv-hrāg′-èr-à, *n. m.* apostate.

Naomh-threigsinn, nùv-hrāg′-shènn, *n. f.* apostacy, infidelity, hypocrisy.

Naonar, nùn′-ur, *n. f.* nine persons.

Naontach, nùn′-tach, *n. f.* ninety.

Naosg, nùsg, *n. f.* snipe; meanbhghuthrag.

Nar, năr, *adv.* may not, let not; *'nar* leigeadh Dia, *God forbid*; more often *'nan* na leigeadh Dia, *God forbid.*

Nar, năr, (for ann ar); *'nar* cadal, *in our sleep*; *'nar* meadhon, *in the midst of us*

Narach, nàr′-ach, shameful, disgraceful, ignominious; nì *nàrach, an ignominious thing*; easily abashed, bashful; tha an duine *nàrach, the man is bashful.*

Narachadh, nàr′-ach-ă, *pt.* putting to shame; abashing, disgracing.

Naraich, nàr′-êch, *v.* shame, put to shame; disgrace; *nàraichte, disgraced.*

Nasg, nnăsg, *n. m.* cow-tie, *or* collar; deposit, pledge; tha an t-airgead an *naisg, the money is left in pledge—is deposited as security.*

Nasgadh, nnăsg′-ă, *pt.* pledging, depositing.

Nasgaidh, } nnăsg′-êch, *n. f.* pledge, depo-
Nasgaich, } sit; gift; a *nasgaich, out of pledge*; free, gratis; fhuair mi a *nasgaich* na *nasgaidh* e, *I got it gratis, I got it without price*; free; a *nasgaidh* fhuair sibh, a *nasgaidh* thugaibh uaibh, *freely ye have received, freely give. B.*; thug e dhomh a *nasgaidh* e, *he gave it me as a gratuity.*

Nasgaidheachd, năsg′-ê-achg, *n. f.* freeness, unconditional freeness; gratuity, gratuitousness.

Natar, nàt′-ur, *n. m.* nitre. *Bible—Jerim.*

Nathair, n*há′*-êr, *n. f.* serpent, viper, snake, adder; (in Lewis, rìghinn,) mheall an *nàthair* mi, *the serpent beguiled me*; beithire, *an enormous serpent* or *boa-constrictor.*

There are wild stories about these large serpents in the Highlands, as having destroyed a whole fleet of shipping, &c. The print or bed that one of them made in the earth, is pointed out in Islay; and, if the history be correct, the monster could not have been less than fifty feet long, and its chest like a PUNCHEON!!!

Nathrach, nár′-ach, *gen.* of a serpent, adder, &c.

Nathraichean, nár′-êch-unn, *pl.* serpents.

Neach, nyach, *n. c.* an individual, person, one; *neach* sam bith, *any one*; *neach* eile, *another person* or *individual*; gach *neach, every one.*

Nead, nyéd, *n. f.* nest, nid, nests; of a nest.

Neadaich, nyed′-êch, *v.* nestle, bed, embed; an *neadachadh* am fheoil, *imbedding in my flesh.*

Neagaid, nyég′-aj, *n.f.* a little sob *or* sigh, oft repeated, as a person before *or* after weeping; suppressed sighing *or* sobbing.

Neamh, nèv, *n.m.* Heaven, region of bliss; the sky, firmament; *nèamh* nan speur, *the starry heavens*; proper orthography, *neumh*, preventing the E being marked.

Neamh, nyev, *n. f.* venom, keenness of air; wicked keenness; confounded with nimh, virus, *poison.*

Neamhalachd, név′-al-achg, *n. f.* venomousness, greediness in wickedness, piercing coldness.

Neamhail, név′-al, *adj.* venomous; venomously cold; keenly wicked.

Neamhach, nèv′-ach, *n. m.* an angel.

Neamhachd, nèv′-achd, *n. f.* heavenliness.

Neamhaidh, nèv′-ê, *adj.* heavenly, divine.

Neamhaidheachd, név′-ê-achg, *n. f.* heavenliness, holiness, solemnity, blessedness.

Neamhain, nèv′-ênn, } *n. f.* a pearl, gem,
Neamhnaid, nèv′-năj, } jewel. *Bible.*

Neapaiginn, nèp′-ê-gyênn, *n. m.* napkin.

Nearachd, nyèr′-achd, *n.f.* happiness, fortunateness; is *nèarachd* an duine a smachdaicheas Dia, *happy is the man whom God correcteth. Job.*

In Lewis, and the Bible, nèarachd; in Argyle, meurachd.

Neart, nyert, *n. m.* force, pith, power, might, energy, vigour; le'd t-uile *neart, with all your might*; cuir do *neart* ris, *apply to it with your whole vigour, with all your force*; vast quantity, number, superabundance; *neart* airgid, *a vast quantity of money, Bible*; *neart* buntàta, *neart* èisg, *a vast quantity of potatoes, enormous quantum of fish*; Righ Bhreatainn le a *neart, King of Britain and all his forces*; cha'n'eil *neart* aige air son sin, *he has not force sufficient to accomplish that.*

Neartaich, nyert′-êch, *v.* strengthen, invigorate; infuse strength, vigour, *or* energy into.

Neartalachd, nyert′-al-achg, *n. f.* vigourousness, pithiness; energy of character.

Neartail, nyert′-al, *a.* powerful, robust, vigorous; also neartmhor, *or* neartar.

Neartmhoireachd, nyert′-vur-achg, *n. f.* powerfulness, energy, vigorousness.

Neas, nyess, *n. f.* a weazle.

Neas, nyess, nyăss[2], *adv.* while, whilst; *neas* 'sa beò mi, *while I live*; *neas* a bha e air folbh, *while he was away*; *neas* a chì mi, *while I see.*

Neip, nèp; in broad Scotch, turnip.

Neo, nyó, *adv.* or, nor, neither, either, else, otherwise; *neo* is traugh mo chàradh, *else sad is my condition*; *neo* teichidh mi, *otherwise I will decamp*; thusa *neo* mise, *either you or I*; dhà *neo* trì, *either two or three*; *neo* thèid mi dhachaidh, *otherwise I will go home*; also *neg. part.* as *neo*-ghlic, *unwise*; *neo*-amadaideach, *any thing but foolish.*

Neo-abuidh, } nyò-ab′-ê, *a.* unripe, prema-
Neo-abuich, } ture, abortive.

Neo-aire, nyó-ăêr′-ă, *n.f.* inattention, unguardedness.

Neo-airsnealach, nyo-ărsh′-nyel-ach, } *a.*
Neo-airtnealach, nyo-arjt′-nyel-ach, } cheerful, gay.

Neo-amhalach, nyo-àv'-al-ach, *adj.* slily and without attention; gu *neo-amhalach, unawares, slily*; thàinig e stigh gu *neo-amhalach, he came in without my being aware of it, unawares.*

Neo-amharas, nyo-àv'-rus, *n. m.* unsuspiciousness; want of suspicion.

Neo-amhrasach, nyo-àv'-rus-ach, *a.* unsuspicious, undubitable, unquestionable.

Neo-aoibhneach, nyó-aöév'-nyach, *a.* surly, cheerless, gloomy.

Neo-aoibheil, nyo-aöév'-al, *a.* cheerless.

Neo-aoibhneas, nyo-aöév'-nyus, *n. f.* gloom.

Neo-bhaigheil, nyo-vhï'-al, *a.* harsh, unkind.

Neo-bheairteach, nyò-v*h*yarjt'-ach, *a.* poor.

Neo-bheothail, nyó-vyó'-al, *a.* lifeless.

Neo-bhrigh, nyó'-vrè, *n. f.* inefficacy, no effect; chuir sibh an *neo-bhrigh* àithne Dhè, *you have made of none effect the command of God.*

Neo-chaochlaideach, nyó-chāoch'-laj-ach, *adj.* unchangeable, immutable.

Neo-chaochlaideachd, nyó-chāoch'-lăj-achg, *n. f.* unchangeableness, immutability.

Neo-charraideach, nyó-chărr'-ăj-ach, *adj.* quiet, peaceable, without toil.

Neo-cheadaich, nyó-chād'-èch, *v.* prohibit.

Neo-cheadaichte, nyó-chād'-èch-tyà, *pt.* prohibited.

Neo-chealgach, nyo-chyalg'-ach, *a.* candid.

Neo-chealgachd, nyó-chyalg'-achg, *n. f.* candour, unfeignedness, fairness.

Neo-cheangail, nyó-chéng'-èl, *v.* untie.

Neo-cheangailte, nyó-chéng'-aljt-à, *pt.* unbound, free, disengaged, at liberty.

Neo-cheannsuichte, nyó-chyann-sèch'-tyà, *pt.* unconquered, unsubdued.

Neo-chearbach, nyó-chyerb'-ach, *a.* efficient.

Neo-cheart, nyó'-chyart, *adj.* not true, unfair, ill-founded; unhandsome.

Neo-chiallach, nyó-chēăl'-ach, *a* mad.

Neochinnt, nyó'-chyenjt, *n. f.* uncertainty, fickleness, whimsicality.

Neo-chinnteach, nyó-chyènnjt'-ach, *adj.* uncertain, problematical, fickle.

Neochiont, nyó'-chĕŭnt, *n. f.* innocence.

Neochiontach, nyó-chĕŭnt'-ach, *adj.* innocent, free from blame, unblameable.

Neochiontachd, nyó-chĕŭnt'-achg, *n. f.* innocence, innocency, uprightness.

Neo-chlaon, nyó'-chlāon, *a.* upright.

Neo-chleachd, nyó'-chlechg, *v.* abrogate, discontinue the practice of.

Neo-chleachdainn, nyó-chlechg'-ènn, *v.* discontinuing the practice of; abrogation.

Neo-chleachdta, nyó'-chlechg-tyà, *a. pt* unaccustomed to, unusual, unpractised.

Neo-choimheach, nyó-chóè'-ach, *adj.* free, not stingy, not surly; kind.

Neo-choimhicheas, nyó-chóè'-èch-us, *n. f.* making one's self at home; freedom, kindness.

Neochoireach, nyó-chur'-ach, *adj.* unblameable, innocent, blameless.

Neochoireachd, nyó-chyur'-achg, *n. f.* blamelessness, innocence.

Neo-chomas, nyo-chòm'-as, *n. m.* impotence.

Neo-chomasach, nyo-chòm'-ur-ach, *adj.* impossible, unable, impotent.

Neo-chomasachd, nyó-chòm'-as-achg, *n. f.* impossibility, incapability.

Neo-chompanta, nyó-chŏmp'-ant-à, *adj.* unsocial, not companion-like.

Neo-chompantas, nyó-chŏmp'-ant-as, *n. m.* unsociableness, unamiableness.

Neo-chosallachd, nyó-chŏs'-al-achg, *n. f.* improbability, unlikelihood, dissimilarity.

Neo-chosail, nyó-chŏs'-al, *adj.* unlikely, unlike, dissimilar, improbable.

Neo-chorthromach, nyó'-chór-um-ach, *adj.* uneven, rough; unfair, unjust.

Neo-chrabhach, nyó-chráv'-ach, *adj.* not austere in religious matters.

Neo-chreideach, nyó-chraŏj'-ach, *adj.* unbelieving, unholy, infidel.

Neo-chriochnach, nyó-chrēch'-nach, *adj* endless, infinite, everlasting, unlimited.

Neo-chronail, nyó-chrŏn'-al, *a.* harmless.

Neo-chruadalach, nyó-chrŭăd'-al-ach, *adj.* unhardy, soft, effeminate, lubberly.

Neo-chubhaidh, nyó'-chŭè, *adj.* having family right, not hereditary; unmerited, unfit.

Neo-chuimhne, nyó-chŭèn'-à, *n. f.* forgetfulness, negligence, want of memory.

Neo-chuimhneach, nyó-chŭèn'-ach, *a.* forgetful.

Neo-chruinnichdte, nyó-chrŭènn'-èch-tyà, *pt.* uncollected, ungathered; not gathered.

Neo-chruthaichte, nyó-chru-ĕch-tya, *pt.* uncreated.

Neo-chuimhseach, nyó-chŭèmsh'-ach, *adj.* immoderate, vast, exorbitant; of a bad aim.

Neo-chuirteil, nyó-chûèrjt'-al, *a.* uncourtly.

Neo-chumhanta, nyó-chunn'-ant-a, *adj* uncommon, rare, novel, unusual.

Neo-chumhantachd, nyó-chŭnn'-ant-achg, *n. f.* uncommonness, rareness, novelty.

Neo-churam, nyó-chûr'-am, *n m.* carelessness, negligence, neglect, indifference.

Neo-churamach, nyó-chûr'-am-ach, *adj.* careless, negligent, prodigal, indifferent.

NEO-DHAICHEIL, nyó-ghâêch'-al, *adj.* unlikely, absurd, nonsensical;—ungenteel. *Highland Society.*

NEO-DHAICHEILACHD, nyó-ghâêch'-al-achg, *n. m.* unlikelihood, absurdity,—ungentility.

NEO-DHIADHUIDH, nyó-ghyĕăgh'-ė, *adj.* unholy, profane, ungodly, impious.

NEO-DHIADHUIDHEACHD, nyó-ghyĕaŏgh'-ė-achg, *n. f.* ungodliness, impiety, irreligion.

NEO-DHILEAS, nyó-ghēl'-as, *adj.* unfaithful, faithless, disloyal, undutiful.

NEO-DHILLSE, nyó-ghĕlly''-sha, *n. f.* disloyalty.

NEO-DHIONGALTA, nyó-yhung'-alt-ă, *adj.* insecure, insufficient, precarious, uncertain.

NEO-DHIONGALTACHD, nyó-yhung'-ălt-achg, *n. f.* infirmness, insecurity, uncertainty.

NEO-DHLEASNACH, nyó-ghlās'-nach, *adj.* undutiful, disobedient to parents; disaffected.

NEO-DHLIGHEACH, nyó-ghlė'-ach, *a.* unlawful, not hereditary, not rightful; undue.

NEO-DHUINE, nyó-ghŭn'-ă, *n. m.* a decrepid person, a useless person; ninny.

NEO-DHUINEIL, nyó-ghŭn'-al, *adj.* unmanly.

NEO-DHURACHD, nyó-ghûr'-achg, *n. m.* insincerity, heedlessness, negligence.

NEO-DHURACHDACH, nyó-ghûr'-achg-ach, *adj.* insincere, negligent, careless.

NEO-EAGALACH, nyó-ā'-gal-ach, *a.* fearless.

NEO-EALANTA, nyó-ĕăl'-ănt-a, *adj.* inexpert.

NEO-EALANTACHD, nyó-ĕăl'-ant-achg, *n. f.* awkwardness, unskilfulness, want of art.

NEO-EIFEACHD, nyó-āf'-achg, *n. f.* inefficacy.

NEO-EIFEACHDACH, nyó-āf'-achg-ach, *adj.* ineffectual, inefficient, inefficacious.

NEO-EOLACH, nyó-ĕôl'-ach, *a.* unacquainted.

NEO-FHABHORACH, nyó-av'-ur-ach, *a.* unfavourable, unfair; not fair, as wind; impartial.

NEO-FHAICSINNEACH, nyó-éêchg'-shyènnach, *adj.* not visible, invisible; not to be seen properly.

NEO-FHALLAN, nyó-ăll'-an, *adj.* unsound, unhealthy; as food or air, unwholesome.

NEO-FHALLSA, nyó'-alls-a, *adj.* candid, fair.

NEO-FHASANTA, nyó'-as-ant-ă, *adj.* unfashionable, uncommon, out of fashion.

NEO-FHASANTACHD, nyó-ăs'-ant-achg, *n. f.* unfashionableness, oddness, rareness.

NEO-FHEUMAIL, nyó-ām'-al, *adj.* needless, useless, unavailing, unnecessary.

NEO-FHIOR, nyó-ērr', *adj.* untrue, false.

NEO-FHIOS, nyó-ės', *n. m.* ignorance.

NEO-FHIOSRACH, nyó-ės'-rach, *adj.* unintelligent, ignorant, unacquainted, unconscious.

NEO-FHIRINTEACH, nyó-ēr'-ênjt-ach, *adj.* unrighteous, unjust, wicked, bad.

NEO-FHOGHAINTEACH, nyó-o'-ênjt-ach, *adj.* ineffectual, inefficacious, cowardly.

NEO-FHOGHLUIMTE, nyó-ôll'-um-tyă, *a.* untaught.

NEO-FHOILLSICHTE, nyó-aŏělly-shèch-tyă, *a.* unrevealed.

NEO-FHOIRBHAIDH, nyó-orv'-ė, *a.* in nonage.

NEO-FHOISNEACH, nyó-ōsh'-nyach, *adj.* restless, unquiet, annoyed, disturbed.

NEO-FHOISNEACHD, nyó-ōsh'-nyachg, *n. f.* restlessness, disquietude, disturbance.

NEO-FHREAGARRACH, nyó-răg'-arr-ach *a.* unanswerable, unsuitable, unfit, inapplicable.

NEO-FHREAGARRACHD, nyó-răg'-ărr-achg, *n. f.* unfitness, unanswerableness, unsuitableness.

NEO-FHREASDALACH, nyó-răsd'-al-ach, *adj.* inattentive, careless, improvident.

NEO-FHURAS, nyó-ŭr'-as, *n. m.* impatience.

NEO-FHURASACH, nyó-ŭr'-as-ach, *a.* impatient.

NEO-FHURASDA, nyó-ŭr'-asd-a, *adj.* difficult.

NEO-GHEALTACH, nyó-ghyalt'-ach, *adj.* fearless.

NEO-GHEALTACHD, nyó-ghalt'-achg, *n. f.* fearlessness, intrepidity, boldness.

NEO-GHEUR, nyó-ghār', *a.* blunt, not sour, dull, stupid.

NEOGHLAN, nyó-ghlan', *a.* impure, unclean.

NEO-GHLIC, nyo-ghèchg', *adj.* unwise, foolish.

NEOGHLOIN, nyó-ghlaŏėn', *n. f.* impurity.

NEO-GHLUAISTE, nyó-ghlŭăsh'-tyă, *pt.* unmoved.

NEO-GHNAITHTE, nyó-ghràèch'-tyă, *adj.* unaccustomed, unpractised, abrogated, unusual.

NEO-GHOIREASACH, nyó-ghaŏr'-as-ach, *adj.* unnecessary; inconvenient, unfit, unmeet.

NEO-GHRAD, nyó-ghrad', *adj.* sluggish, unapt.

NEO-GHRASMHOR, nyó-ghrâs'-ur, *adj.* ungracious, unmerciful, graceless.

NEO-GHRINN, nyó-ghrènn', *adj.* unkind, coarse, inelegant, unmannerly.

NEO-GHRINNEAS, nyó-ghrènn'-as, *n. m.* unkindness.

NEOIL, nyòėl, *n. pl.* clouds; *gen.* of a cloud; *neoil* a seòladh, *clouds gliding, sailing.*

NEO-INBH, nyó-ēnv'-ė, *adj.* premature, unripe, abortive; under age.

NEO-INBHEACH, nyó-ēnv'-ach *adj.* premature, unripe, abortive; torraicheas *neo-inbheach, a premature* or *abortive conception*; not come to the years of maturity; tha e *neo-inbheach, he is not of age, he is minor.*

NEO-INBHEACHD, nyó-ēnv'-achg, *n. f.* prematurity, abortiveness, non-age; contracted for neo-inbhidheachd.

NEOINEAN, nyó ăēn', *n. m.* daisy.

NEONEANACH, nyó-ăēn''-ach, *adj.* bespangled *or* speckled with daisies.

NEO-IOCHDMHOR, nyó-ĕúchg'-ur, *adj.* unmerciful, inhuman, merciless.

NEO-IOCHDMOIREACHD, nyó-ĕúchg'-ur'-achg, *n. f.* unmercifulness, inhumanity, cruelty.

NEO-IOMCHUIDHE, nyó-ēm-ach-è, *adj.* improper, unfit, unmeet, unbecoming.

NEO-IOMCHUIDHEACHD, nyó-ēm'-ach-è-achg, *n. f* unfitness, impropriety, unmeetness

NEO-IOMLAINEACHD, nyó-ēm'-láèn'-achg, *n. f.* imperfection, incompleteness.

NEO-IOMLAN, nyó-ēm'-lan, *a.* imperfect.

NEO-IOMPAICHTE, nyó-ēmp'-èch-tyà, *pt.* unconverted, unpersuaded.

NEO-IONNAN, nyó-éún'-un, *adj.* dissimilar; unlike each other.

NEO-IONNANACHD, nyó-éúnn'-un-achg, *n. f.* dissimilarity, inequality, unlikelihood.

NEO-IONMHUINN, nyó-éúnn'-vhènn, *a.* unbeloved.

NEO-IONNSIUCHTE, nyó-ĕūnn'-sèchty'-à, *pt.* unlearned, unskilful, ignorant, inexpert.

NEO-LAGHALACHD, nyó-llaŏ'-ghall-achd, *n. f.* unlawfulness, illigitimacy; illegality.

NEO LAGHAIL, nyó-laŏgh'-al, *a.* unlawful.

NEO-LEASAICHTE, nyó-llās'-èch-tyà, *pt.* unmanured, undunged; unamended.

NEO-LOCHDACH, nyó-llŏchg'-ach, *adj.* harmless, inoffensive, innocent, uncontaminated.

NEO-LUAINEACH, nyó-lŭăēn'-ach, *a.* sedate.

NEO-LUCHDAICH, nyó-lŭchg'-èch, *v.* discharge, unship, unload; neo-luchdaichte, *disburdened.*

NEO-MHAITHTEACH, nyó-mha'-tyach, *adj.* unforgiving, unrelenting.

NEO-MHEADHONACH, nyó-vhé'-un-ach, *adj.* not centrical; awkward in point of situation; out of place.

NEO-MHEALLTACH, nyó-vhyall'-tach, *adj.* fair, candid, undisguised, sincere, honest.

NEO-MHEARACHDACH, nyó-vhĕr'-achg-ach, *adj.* unerring, infallible, true, wise.

NEO-MHEANGAIL, nyó-véng'-al, *a.* unblemished, sound, healthy, whole.

NEO-MHEASARRA, nyó-vēss'-urr-a, *adj.* intemperate, immoderate, debauched.

NEO-MHEASARRACHD, nyó-vēss'-arr-achg, *n. f.* intemperance, debauchery, glut.

NEO-MHEASGTE, nyó-vēsg'-tyà, *pt.* unmixed.

NEO-MHEASAIL, nyó-vēss'-al, *adj.* disrespectful.

NEO-MHEATA, nyó-vét'-à, *adj.* daring.

NEO-MHISGEALACHD, nyó-vēshg'-al-achd, *n. f.* sobriety.

NEO-MHISGEIL, nyó-vēshg'-al, *adj.* sober.

NEO-MHOTHACHALACHD, nyó-vó'-ach-al-achg, *n. f.* insensibility, stupidity, want of feeling.

NEO-MHOTHACHAIL, nyó-vó'-ach-al, *adj* senseless, stupid, void of sense *or* feeling.

NEONACH, nyòn'-ach, *adj.* novel, rare, curious, strange; ni *neònach, a novel* or *curious thing*; eccentric, droll; duine *neònach, a droll, eccentric,* or *magòtty fellow*; strange, unusual, surprising; is *neònach* leam, *I am surprised, I think it strange*; is *neònach* leis, *he thinks it strange.*

NEONACHAS, nyòn'-ach-as, *n. m.* surprisingness, curiosity; *neònachas* an nì so, *the oddity* or *curiosity of this thing*; eccentricity, drollness, strangeness; tha *neònachas* orm, *I am surprised, it is a matter of curiosity to me.*

NEONI, nyón'-è, *n. m.* nothing, non-entity, a ninny; thig iad gu *neoni, they shall come to nothing*; 'nuair chuala *neoni* guth a bheoil, *when chaos heard the voice of his mouth. Buchannan*

NEONITHEACH, nyón'-èch-ach, *adj.* trifling, inconsiderable, insignificant.

NEONITHEACHEACHD, nyòn'-èch-ach-achg, *n. f.* nothingness, insignificance, inconsiderableness.

NEO-OILEANAICHTE, nyó-ul'-áèn-èch-tyà, *pt.* not well bred, unmannerly, impatient.

NEO-ONARACH, nyó-ŏn'-ar-ach, *a.* ignoble, dishonourable, mean, low.

NEO-PHRIS, nyó-frēs, *n. f.* contempt.

NEO-RIAGHAILTEACH, nyó-rĕă'-ăljt-ach, *adj.* irregular, anomalous, turbulent, quarrelsome.

NEO-RIAGHAILTEACHD, nyó-rĕă'-aljt-achg, *n. f.* irregularity, anomaly, turbulence.

NEO-SGAIRTE, nyó skar'-tyà, *a.* inseparable

NEO-SGAIRTEIL, nyó-skarjt'-al, *a.* spiritless.

NEO-SGATHACH, nyó-skâ'-ach, *a.* fearless.

NEO-SGEADAICH, nyó-skăd'-èch, *v* undress.

NEO-SGITHICHTE, nyó-skĕ'-ěch-tyà, *a.* unfatigued.

NEO-SGOINNEIL, nyó-sgaŏènn'-al, *a.* drabbish.

NEO-SHALACH, nyó-hal'-ach, *a.* unpolluted.

NEO-SHANNTACH, nyó-hănnt'-ach, *adj.* unambitious, not covetous, indifferent.

NEO-SHARACHAIL, nyó-hâr′-ach-al, *adj.* indefatigueable, unconquerable, keen.

NEO-SHARAICHTE, nyó-hâr′-ėch-tyȧ, *a.* unoppressed, unfatigued, indefatigueable.

NEO-SHEARGTE, nyó-herg′-tyȧ, *pt.* undecayed.

NEO-SHEASACH, nyó-hyās′-ach, *a.* unsteady

NEO-SHOCAIR, nyó-hŏchg′-ėr, *a.* uneasy.

NEO-SHOCAIREACHD, nyó-hŏchg′-ăĕr-achg, *n. f.* uneasiness, unsettledness, restlessness.

NEO-SHNASAR, nyó-nás′-ur, *a.* inelegant, unpolished, ill-finished, untidy.

NEO-SHOILLEIR, nyó-hŏelly′-ăĕr, *a.* darkish, indistinct, not clear *or* evident.

NEO-SHOIRBHEACHALACHD, nyó-hŏĕrv′-ach-al-achg, *n.f.* unsuccessfulness, unpromising state.

NEO-SHOIRBHEACHAIL, nyó-hŏerv′-ach-al, *adj.* unsuccessful, unprosperous.

NEO-SHOLASACH, nyó-hôl′-as-ach, *adj.* joyless, discomfortable, uncomfortable.

NEO-SHUAIMHNEACH, nyó-hŭăĕv′-nyach, *adj.* restless, any thing but quiet *or* easy.

NEO-SHUBHACH, nyó-hŭ′-ach, *a.* joyless.

NEO-SHUIDHICHTE, nyó-húe′-ėch-tyȧ, *adj.* unsettled.

NEO-SHUILBHIR, nyó-hŭĕl′-vėr, *a.* cheerless.

NEO-SHUNNTACH, nyó-hŭnnt′-ach, *adj.* drowsy.

NEO-SMIORAIL, nyó-smur′-al, *a.* spiritless.

NEO-SPEISEIL, nyó-spāsh′-al, *a.* unloving.

NEO-SPORSAIL, nyó-spôrs′-al, *a.* humble.

NEO-SPRAICEIL, nyó-sprāĕchg′-al, *a.* dull.

NEO-STRAICEIL, nyó-strâĕchg′-al, *a.* unconceited.

NEO-STRUIDHEIL, nyó-strúey″-al, *a.* frugal.

NEO-THABHACHD, nyó-hâv′-achg, *n. f.* futility.

NEO-THABHACHDACH, nyó-hâv′-achg-ach, *adj.* fu̇tile.

NEO-THAITINN, nyó-hăĕjt′-ėnn, *v.* displease

NEO-THAITNEACH, nyó-hăĕjt′-nyach, *a.* unpleasant.

NEO-THARBHACH, nyó-hâv′-ach, *a.* unproductive.

NEO-THEAGAISTE, nyó-hăg′-ashj-tyȧ, *a.* untaught.

NEO-THEARUINTE, nyó-hėr′-ėnjt′-ȧ, *a.* insecure.

NEO-THEARUINTEACHD, nyó-hėr′-ėnjt-achg, *n. f.* insecurity, uncautiousness.

NEO-THEOM, nyó′-hyăom, *adj.* inexpert.

NEO-THIMCHEALL GHEAR, nyó-hēm-chyall-ghear′, *v.* uncircumcise; *neo-thimcheall-ghearadh, uncircumcision. Rom.*ii.and 25.

NEO-THOGARRACH, nyó-thōg$^{2\prime}$-arr-ach, *a.* reluctant as a person, uninviting as weather.

NEO-THOILEACH, nyó-hŏl′-ach, *a.* reluctant.

NEO-THOILEALACHD, nyó-hŏl′-al-achg, *n.f.* reluctance, disinclination, aversion, disgust.

NEO-THOILICH, nyó-hŏl′-ech, *v.* dissatisfy.

NEO-THOILICHTE, nyó-hŏl′-ėch-tyȧ, *a.* dissatisfied.

NEO-THOILLTINNEACH, nyó-haŏėjll′-tyėnn ach, *adj.* undeserving, unworthy, unmeriting.

NEO-THOILLTINNEAS, nyó-haŏlly′-tyann us, *n.f.* unworthiness, demerit, bad desert.

NEO-THOINISGEIL, nyó-hŏėn′-ėshg-al, *a.* stupid.

NEO-THOIRT, nyó′-hŏėrty, *n.f.* indifference.

NEO-THOIRTEIL, nyó-hŏėrty′-al, *a.* indifferent.

NEO-THORACH, nyó-hŏr′-ach, *a.* unfruitful.

NEO-THORACHD, nyó-hŏr′-achg, *n. f.* unproductiveness, unfruitfulness, unsubstantialness.

NEO-THORRACH, nyó-hŏrr′-ach, *a.* barren.

NEO-THORRAICHEAS, nyó-hŏrr′-ėch-us, *n.f.* barrenness, infecundity, abortiveness.

NEO-THRAIGHTEACH, nyó-hrâĕ′-y′-tyach, *adj.* inexhaustible, unexhausted, infinite.

NEO-THRATHAIL, nyó-hrâ′-al, *a.* late.

NEO-THROCAIREACH, nyó-hrôchg′-ăĕr-ach, *adj.* unmerciful, merciless, cruel, relentless.

NEO-THROCAIREACHD, nyó′-hrôchg-ur′-achg, *n.f.* unmercifulness, relentlessness.

NEO-THRUACANTA, nyó-hrŭăchg′-ant-ȧ, *adj.* pitiless, unrelenting, unfeeling, cruel.

NEO-THRUACANTACHD, nyó hrŭăchg′-ant-achg, *n. f.* unfeelingness, uncompassionateness.

NEO-THRUAILICHTE, nyó-hrŭaėly′-ėch-tyȧ, *pt.* undefiled, pure, unadulterated.

NEO-THRUAILLIDH, nyó-hrŭălly′-ė, *adj.* liberal.

NEO-THUIGSE, nyó-hŭėg′-shȧ, *n. f.* stupidity.

NEO-THUIGSEACH, nyò-hŭėg′-shyach, *adj.* senseless.

NEO-THUILLSEACH, nyó-hullysth′-ach, *adj.* infallible.

NEO-THUILLSEACHD, nyó-hullysh′-achg, *n. f.* steadiness, infallibility, stability, firmness.

NEO-THUITEAMACH, nyó-hŭėjty′-am-ach *a.* infallible, unerring, steady, sure.

NEO-UASAIL, nyó-ŭăs′-al, *adj.* ignoble.

NEO-UIDHEAM, nyó-ŭĕ′-y′-am, *n. f.* dishabille.

NEO-UIDHEAMAICHTE, nyó-ŭĕ′-y′-am-ėch-tyȧ, *pt.* unprepared, undressed; in disabille.

NEO-ULLAMH, nyó-ŭll′-uv, *a.* unprepared.

NEUL, nyėll, *n. m.* a cloud; mar a' ghrian is *neul* 'ga sgàileadh, ***as the sun and a cloud overshadowing it. Sm.***; a nap *or* wink of sleep; cha d' fhuair mi *neul* cadail, *I have not got a wink of sleep*; tinge, hue, slight appearance; *neul* bainne, *slight tinge* or *hue, of the colour of milk*; tha *neul* deoch air, *he has a slight appearance of drink*; a trance *or* swoon; chaidh e ann an *neul, he was in a trance, he fainted, he swooned.*

NEULACH, nyàll'-ach, *a.* cloudy. *Bible.*

NEULADAIR, nyèll-ad-aèr, *n.m* astrologer.

NEULADAIREACHD, nyèll'-ăd-ăèr-achg, *n.f.* astrology, astronomy; astrological knowledge.

NEULAR, nyèll'-ur, *a.* well-coloured.

NI, nyē, *n. m.* cattle, thing, circumstance, affair, matter; aon *ni, one thing, matter*, or *affair*; nithe *and* nithean, *things, affairs, &c.*

NI, nnē, *fut. v.* dean; dean so, *do this*; *ni* mi sin, *I will do that.*

NIAG, nĕăg, *n. f.* squint eye. *H. Society.*

NIAGACH, nĕăg'-ach, *adj.* surly, squint-eyed.

NIC, nēchg, *cont.* for nighean mhic; *nic* Ailpean, *nic* Dhomhnuil, *a female of the name of Macalpine or Macdonald.*

NIC-CRIDHE, nēchg-crē'-ă, *n.f.* term of endearment to a female; tha *nic-cridhe, yes, my dear madam! my dear lassie!*

NID, nyèjj, *n. pl.* nests; also *gen.* of a nest.

NIGH, nè-h', *v.* wash, lave, cleanse, purify; *nigh* do chasan, *wash your feet. Bible.*

NIGHEADAIR, nè'-h'-ăd-ăèr, *n. m.* washer, cleanser.

NIGHEADAIREACHD, nè'-ăd-ăèr-achg, *n. f.* washing of clothes particularly; cleansing.

NIGHEADH, nè'-Ă, *pt.* washing, cleansing.

NIGHEAN, nyè'-un, *n.f.* a daughter, a girl.

NIGHNEAG; see Nioghnag, girly, lassie.

NIGHTE, nyè'-tyă, *pt.* washed, bathed.

NIMH, nyèv, *n. f.* virus, venom.

NIMHEIL, nyèv'-al, *a.* venomous, keenly wicked.

NIOGHNAG, nnē'-nag, *n. f.* a daughter, a girl.

NIOMSA, nè'-um-să, for ni mise, *I will do.*

NIOR, nēr, *adv.* not. *Ross.*

NIOS, nnēss[2], *n. m* top, summit; thoir an *nìos, bring up, bring to the top*, literally; a sìos is a *nìos, up and down*, literally *to the top and bottom.*

NIS, nyēsh, *adv.* now, AT THIS TIME; *nis* bha so mar sin, *now, this was that way*; thig a *nis, come along now*; a *nis* is a rithisd, *now and then, at this time and afterwards*; *nis* is fheudar dhomh innseadh dhuit, *now I must plainly tell you.*

NITHE, nèch'-ă, **NITHEANAN**, nèch'-an-an, *n.f.* things, matters, affairs.

NITEAR, nnēt'-ur, **NITHEAR**, nnè'-ur, *fut. pass.* of dean, *shall be done*; *nìthear*, neo *nithear* sin, *that shall be done.*

NIUC, nyèŭchg, *n.f.* a corner, nook.

NOCHD, nŏchg, *v.* present, reveal, table shew, discover; *nochd* an t-airgead, *table the money*; *nochdaidh* mi dhuit, *I will shew you*; ni maith, co a *nochdas* dhuinn a nis, *who will shew us any good? n. m.* nakedness; chomhdaich iad *nochd* an athar, *they covered the nakedness of their father. Bible*; mo *nochd* is mo nàire, *my nakedness and shame! adj.* bare, nochta.

NOCHD, nŏchg, *n. f.* night; an *nochd, to-night*; an d'thig e *nochd, will he come to-night?*

NOCHDADH, nnŏchg'-Ă, *pt.* shewing, tabling, uncovering, revealing, discovering.

NOCHTA, nnŏch'-tyă, *pt.* shewn, tabled; bare; shabby, ill-dressed.

NODAN, nnŏd'-an, *n. m.* short sleep.

NOIG, noèg, *n. f.* old-fashioned face;—a podex *or* anus. *Macdonald.*

NOIGEAN, nyŏèg'-aèn, *n. m.* Scotch noggie, *or* wooden-dish, with one handle *or* ear.

NOIGEISEACH, nŏèg'-ăsh-ach, *a.* snuffy.

NOIN, nòèn, *n. m.* noon. *Latin*; *North.*

NOLLAIG, nŏll'-èg, *n f.* a feast; Christmas; latha *nollaig, Christmas-day*; an *nollaig* bheag, *New-year's day*; *nollaig* mhòr, *Christmas.*

NOMHA, nŏv[2]'-a, *adj.* quite new; ùr *nomha, quite new*; duine *nomha, a new man.*

NOS, nòs, *n. m.* custom; bainne nùis, *beastings.*

NUADH, nŭă, *adj.* new, fresh.

NUADHACHD, nŭă'-achd, *n.f.* newness.

NUAG, nŭăg, *n f.* sunk eye.

NUAGACH, nŭăg'-ach, *a.* sunk-eyed, surly.

NUAIR, nŭăèr, *adv.* when, at the time.

NUALL, nŭăll'-an, *n. m.* a long drawling howl, as a lion *or* wild-cat; horrid howl *or* yell.

NUALLANACH, nŭăll'-an-ach, *adj.* horridly yelling *or* howling; drawlingly howling.

NUALLANAICH, nŭăll'-an-èch, *n. f.* a continuous, drawling howl, *or* yelling.

NUAS, nŭăs, *n.f.* bottom, ground; thig an *nuas, come down*; a suas is an *nuas, up and down.*

NUIG, nŭèg, *n.f.* extent; gu *nuig, to. Ross.*

NUIMHIR, nimhir, number. *M'F.*

NUIN, nŭèn, *n. f.* ash-tree; also letter N. *Irish.*

NULL, nŭnn, *n. m.* the other side; *adv.* hither, thither, across; theirig an *nunn, go across, go over, go thither.*

NUR, nur, *adv.* when, at the time; supposed, on very slender grounds, to be a contraction of nuair.

NUS, nûs, *n. m.* milk *or* chyle, used by the fœtus in the womb; bainne *nùis, beastings*; bheir e *nùs* a mhàthar as a ròin, *he will make the chyle drop from his nose.*

O

O, o, the twelfth letter of the Gaelic alphabet, called òir, *furze*; (conas *or* conasg); *n. m.* also water, *obs.*

O, ò, for *adv.* or *conj.* on, since; *o* thàinig e as a bholg, *since he was born. B.*; 2d, *o*, vō for bho, *prep.*; *o* laimh mo bhràthar, *o* laimh Esau, *from my brother's hand, from the hand of Esau*; 3d, O, ō, *inter.* ò dhuine! *O man!*

Ob, ōb, *n. m.* creek, haven; also óban.

Ob, òb, *v.* refuse, reject, object.

Obag, òb'-ag; see Ob-obagail.

Obainn, òb'-ènn, *adj.* pert, meddling, sudden.

Obainneachd, òb'-ènn-achg, *n.f.* pertness, impertinence, suddenness, *or* readiness in things not your own.

Obair, ōb'-èr, *n.f.* labour, work, employment, occupation; intermeddling, workmanship; *obair* do mhcuran fein, *the workmanship of thy own hands*; *obair*-uchd, *parapet*; *obair* theine, *fire-work*; *obair*-dhìon, *rampart, bulwark*; *obair*-shnàthaid, *needle-work*; *obair*-lìn, *net-work*; *obair*-uisge, *water-work*; *obair* ghloine, *glass-work*; a dh' aon *obair*, *purposely, intentionally, on purpose*; also meeting of two rivers—hence, *obair*-feallaidh, *obair*-raighuinn, Aberfeldy, Aberdeen; confluence.

Ob-obagail, òb-òb'-ag-ul, *n. f.* flutter.

Obh, obh, ōv, ōv, *inter.* och! ay! O dear!

Obunn, see Obainn. *Bible.*

Ocar, ŏchg'-ur, *n. f.* interest, riadh.

Och, òch, *inter.* och! *alas! my conscience!* oh heu! also, ochan! och nan och is och eile! *my conscience, thrice over!!!*

Ochanaich, ŏch'-an-èch, *n. f.* sighing, sobbing.

Ochd, ōchg[2], *adj.* and *n.* eight; ochd-oisneach, *having eight sides* or *angles*; rifle gun, *H. S.*; ochd-shlisneach, also.

Ochdamh, ŏchg[2]'-uv, *adj.* the eighth; *n.m.* also eight groats land; an octave. *Islay.*

Ochdamhach, ŏchg'-uv-ach, *adj.* octangular; *n. f.* an octagon, or figure having eight sides.

Ochd-deug, ŏchg-dyāg', *n. f.* eighteen.

Ochdar, ŏchg[2]'-ur, } *n. c.* eight persons
Ochdnar, ŏchg[2]'-nur, } *or* things.

Och-thon, òch-hŏn', *inter.* O dear! alas!

Od, ŏdd, *inter.* tut! no! ay!

O'd, ōd', for o do; *o d'* cheann, *from thy head*; *o d'* sheanair, *from your grandfather.*

Odhar, ŏ'-hur, *adj.* drab, dun, dapple, sallow; *odhar*-liath, *dapple-coloured.*

Odhraich, ōr'-èch, *v.* make dun.

Ofrail, ōeff'-rral, *n. f.* offering. *Bible*

Og, òg, *adj.* young; *n. c.* the young.

Oganach, ôg'-an-ach, *n.m.* young man.

Ogha, ŏ'-hà, *n. c.* grandchild.

Oghum, ò-um, *n. f.* ocult sciences. *Ir.*

Oglach, ôg'-llach, *n. m.* young man, lad.

Ogluidh, ŏg'-lè, *adj.* awful, terrible. *B.*

Og-mhios, ôg'-vhēs, *n. m.* June.

Oibre, aŏèb'-rà, *gen* obair, of work.

Oibreachadh, ŏèb'-rach-ă, *pt.* working, labouring; fermenting; an caochan ag *oibreachadh, the wash fermenting, mixing*; ga *oibreachadh, mixing it.*

Oibrich, aŏèb'-rèch, *v.* work, ferment, mix; oibrichte, *wrought, fermented.*

Oide, aŏj'-à, *n. m.* foster-father, god-father.

Oideachd, oăj'-achd, *n. f.* instruction from evil *or* familiar spirits, occult science.

Oidhche, úëy''-chà, òèch'-à, *n. f.* night.

Oidheam, ŏë'-um, properly foidheam, (fodh-ainm,) a secret *or* hid meaning, inference; nuair a dh' fhosgail e an *fhoidheam, when he expounded* or *unriddled the meaning. Maclachlan*—translated by a blockhead, *when he opened the book*; 'se sin an *fhoidheam* thug mise as, *that is the inference I drew, that is the meaning I made of it, but I may be wrong*; gnothach gun *fhoidheam, a thing without meaning*; co is urrainn *foidheam* sam bith a thoirt as, *who can bring any sense out of it?*

Oidheamach, ŏë'-um-ach, ideal.

Oidhirp, aŏèr'-up, *n. f.* attempt, essay.

Oidhirpeach, aŏèrp'-ach, *a.* diligent.

Oidhirpich, oăèrp'-èch, *v.* attempt, essay.

Oid-ionnsachaidh, ujj-éúnns'-ach-è, *n. m.* a familiar spirit, instructor in the occult sciences.

Oifig, ŏèf'-èg, *n. f.* office, occupation.

Oifigeach, ŏèf'-èg-ach, *n. f.* officer.

Oige, ôèg'-à, *n. f.* youth, youthfulness.

Oigeach, ôèg'-ach, *n. m.* an entire horse.

Oigead, òèg'-ad, *n. f.* youth, degree of youth.

Oigear, òèg'-ar', *n. m.* young man.

Oigealachd, ôèg'-al-achg, *n. f.* youthfulness.

Oigeil, òèg'-al, *adj.* youthful, young-looking.

Oigh, òë-y'. *n. f.* virgin, maiden.

Oigheachd, òë-yhyachg', *n. f.* virginity.

Oigheannach, òë-yhyann'-ach, thistle. *P. shire*; froinneach, *Arg.*

Oighre, aŏèr'-à, *n. m.* an heir; beiridh bean mac, ach se Dia ni *oighre, a woman may bear a son, but God alone can make an heir. G. P.*

Oighreachd, aŏèr'-achg, *n. f.* heirship,

inheritance, possession, freehold, free-land.

Oigridh, òĕg'-re, *n. f.* youth, young folk.

Oil, ull, *v.* rear, instruct in politeness; mar dh' *oil* i a clann, *as she brought up her children. Bible.*

Oil, ŏ'l, *n. f.* offence, cause of regret *or* offence; cha 'n *oil* leamsa gad a robh thu air do chrochadh, *it is no offence to me though you were hanged*; dè chuir gu b' *oil* leamsa, *why should it offend me*? mas *oil* leat sin, na dean a rìthisd e, *if that be an offence to you, don't do it again.*

Oilbheum, ŏl'-vām, *n. m.* offence, (oil.)

Oileamh, ul'-uv, *n. m.* Doctor of Laws, L.L.D.; murdered by Shaw and other ———, ollamh.

Oileamhaid, ul'-uv-ăjj, *n.f.* university. *M.*

Oileadair, ul'-ad-aėr, *n. m.* professor.

Oileamhach, ul'-uv-ach, *n. f.* university.

Oilean, ul'-aėn, contraction of oileamhain, instruction, breeding; household instruction *or* discipline; droch *oilean, bad breeding, want of politeness.*

Oileanach, ul'-aėn-ach, *adj.* polite, well-bred.

Oileanaich, ul'-aėn'-ėch, *v.* instruct in politeness, bring up well; *n. m.* scholar, student, pupil.

Oileanta, ul'-ant-ȧ, *adj.* well-bred, polite.

Oileid, ul'-aj, *n. f.* college; (oil-aite,) *Iona Leg.*

Oilearach, ul'-ur-ach, *n. f.* nursery. *Arm.*

Oilire, ul'-ur-ȧ, *n. m.* professor.

Oillt, oăeljt, *n. f.* greatest horror, detestation; dluth-chrith air gach cnàimh le h-*oillt, every bone shaking with horror.*

Oillteachadh, oăėlljt'-ach-X, *pt.* horrifying in the highest degree, horror-struck; *n. m.* the highest degree of horror *or* detestation, horrification.

Oilltealachd, oăėly'-tyally'-achg, *n. f.* horrific nature *or* quality; horrificness, dreadfulness.

Oillteil, oăėly'-tyal, *adj.* horrifying, horrific, terrible in the highest degree; disgusting in the highest degree.

Oilltich, oăėlly'-tyėch, *v.* horrify.

Oillthigh, ul'-haŏėy', *n. m.* seminary.

Oilthir, ul'-hyėr, *n. f.* beach, shore.

Oilthireach, ul'-hyėr-ach, *n. c.* stranger.

Oin, òėn, *n. f.* agony of death, great mental distress; in Mull, omhain.

Oinnseach, òėnn'-shyach, *a. n. f.* idiot.

Oinnseachail, òėn'-shach-al, *a.* foolish, as a female, like a foolish female.

Oir, óėr, *conj.* for, because that; *oir* chuimhnich iad, *for they remembered*; *oir* is fhearr leam, *because that I prefer.*

Oir, òėr', *n. f.* hem, border, edge, margin; *oir* an aodaich, *the hem of the cloth*; *oir* an t-sruthain, *the margin of the brook* gun *oir, without a border.*

Oir, ôėr, in Irish, the letter o *gen.* of òr.

Oirbh, ŏėrv, *pro. pre.* (air sibh,) on you, owed by you; the matter with you; you under the necessity; dè tha a' cur oirbh, *what is wrong with you*? bheir mi *oirbh, I will force you, I will lay you under the necessity*; dè tha a' cur ort, *what ails you, what is wrong with you*? dè th' aig *oirbh, how much is owed by you to him*?

Oirbheart, oirbheas, good deed.

Oirbheas, ór'-as, *or* -vās², *n. f.* act of charity; bu *oirbheas* dhuit a' dheanadh, *it were an act of charity in you to do it*; cha 'n *oirbheas* 'sam bith dhuit a leithid a dheạnadh, *it would be no act of charity in you to do it.*

Oirbheasach, óėr''-vă̈s²-ach, *a.* charitable.

Oirbhse, óėrv'-shȧ, *emph.* of oirbh.

Oircean, oėrk'-aėn, *n. m.* pigling.

Oirchis, oėr'-chėsh, *n. f.* act of charity.

Oirde; see Ord, junk of salmon, &c.

Oirdhearc, } or'-yhyerg, *adj.* famous, su-
Oirdhearg, } perb, *lit.* the redness of gold.

Oirdhearcas, òėr'-yhyerg-us, *n. f.* superiority, excellency, superbness, pre-eminence.

Oirfeid, óėr'-fėjj, *n. m.* music; na uile *oirfeid* na crìosdachd, *than the whole melody of Christendom. M'D.*

Oirfeideach, òėrf'-ėjj-ach, *n. m.* musician; *adj.* musical.

Oirleach, òėr'-lyach, *n. m.* an inch.

Oirnn, óėrnn, *pre. pro.* (for air sinn,) on us, upon us, owed by us, matter with us; see Oirbh, &c.

Oirre, for urra, on her, owed by her, &c.

Oirthir, òėr'-hyėr, *n. f.* beach, border.

Oirthireach, òėr'-hyėr-ach, *n. m.* borderer; *adj.* maritime.

Oiseach, for òinseach, female idiot.

Oiseann, ōsh²'-aėnn', *n. m.* corner, angle, nook; *gen.* oisinn, of a corner, nook, &c.

Oiseannach, ōėsh²'-aėnn-ach, *a.* angular.

Oisg, òėshg, for othaisg.

Oiteag, ōėty'²'-ag, *n. f.* light squall, gust.

Oiteagach, ōėty'²'-ag-ach, *adj.* squally.

Oitir, ōjty''-ėr, *n. f.* reef of sand, *or* bar in the sea, a shallow, *or* shoal in the sea.

Ol, ôll, *n. m.* drink, potations, drunkenness, inebriety, habitual potations; tha trom air an *òl, he is tedious at his potations, he is a hard drinker*; 'se an t-*òl* a chuir an dunaich ort, *drunkenness put you to the mischief*; *pt.* drinking spirituous liquors, drinking; *v.* drink, slacken thirst; dh' òladh tu is cha phaidheadh tu, *you shine in drinking and skulk in time of paying*; sip; ag *òl* brochain, *sipping* *porrage*; in some places, òl snaoisean, *take snuff*!!

Ola, ŏl′-â, *n. f.* ointment for medicinal purposes; never oil, ùilleadh, *lamp oil.*

Olach, ôll′-ach, *n. m.* a gentleman deprived of all his —— for adultery,—a punishment not peculiar to Celts, a very odd fellow; is éibheinn an t-*òlach* thu, *you are an odd fellow indeed.*

Olachd, òl′-achg, *n.f.* castration wholesale of a fellow for adultery.

Olann, ōl2′-unn, *n. f.* wool; *gen.* olla.

Olar, ôll′-ur, *adj.* addicted to drink.

Olc, ŏlk, *n. m.* mischief, evil, wickedness, apparition; *adj.* evil, bad, wicked; *adv.* wickedly, very ill; is *olc* a fhuara thu, *you behaved very ill*; duine *olc*, *a bad* or *wicked man*; chaidh e thun an uilc, *he went to the mischief*; *deg.* is miosa, is uilce; seachainn, an t-*olc* is seachnaidh an t-*olc* thu, *avoid evil and evil will avoid you*; gu h-*olc*, *sick, very ill, badly.*

Olcas, olk′-us, *n. m.* badness, ——, sickness; air *olcas* 's am bheil e, *let it* or *him be ever so bad*; olcad, degree of badness, inferiority, &c.

Olla, ōll2′-â, *gen.* of ollann, of wool.

Ollach, ōll2′-ach, *a.* woolly, fleecy.

Olladh, } **Ollamh**, } ŏll′-uv, *n. m.* Doctor, for oil-eamh, a Dr. of Laws, L.L.D.

Ollamhrachd, ŏll′-uv-rachg, *n. f.* professorship.

Ollaodach, ōll2′-aŏd-ach, *n. m.* woollen cloth.

Omar, ôm′-ur, *n. m.* amber, ombar.

Omhar, ó-ur, *n. m.* milk, froth.

On, ōn, *conj.* since, since it is so.

Onair, ŏn′-aĕr, *n. f.* honour, dignity; na bitheadh m' *onair*-sa air a h-aonadh, *let not mine honour be united*; gun *onair, without honour.*

Onfhadh, ŏn′-a-gh, *n. m.* rage, raging of the sea; fury; see Confhadh.

Onarach, ŏn′-ăr-ach, *adj.* honourable.

Onaraich, ŏn′-ăr-ėch, *v.* honour, revere.

Onnchonn, ŏnn′-chunn, *n. m.* ensign. *Ir.*

Onrachd, òn- *or* òrr′-achg, *n. f.* solitude, solitariness; a fhèin 'na *onrachd, he himself alone*; agus cha bhi mi am *ònrachd* tuilidh, *I will not be solitary longer*; ann an *ònrachd* an rathaid, *in the solitude of the place.*

Onrachdach, òn′-rachd-ach, *a.* solitary.

Onrachdan, órr′-achg-an, *n. c.* hermit, a person left alone, *or* deserted person, recluse.

Onrachdanach, òrr′-ach-an-ach, *a.* solitary.

Onrachdanachd, òrr′-achg-an-achg, *n. f.* loneliness, solitariness, seclusion, solitude.

Or, òr, *n. m.* gold; *v.* gild, burnish, òir.

Orachd, òr′-achg, *n. f.* hoarding gold.

Orachd, ŏr′-achg, *n.f.* fictitious ornament, fantasies, fantastic dress *or* ornaments; tuilidh is a chòir do *orachdan, too many fantastic ornaments* or *assumed airs.*

Or-thigh, òr-haŏê-y', *n. m.* treasury.

Oraid, òr′-ăj, *n. f.* oration, speech. *Bible.*

Oraideach, òr′-ăj-ach, *a.* oratorical.

Oraidear, or′-ăj-ăĕr, *n. m.* orator.

Orail, òr′-al, *adj.* golden.

Oran, ōr′-an, *n. m.* song, glee, catch; a' gabhail *òrain, singing songs.*

Orair, òr′-aĕr, *n. m.* porch. *Irish.*

Or-bhuidh, òr′-vŭé, *a.* golden-coloured; nighean *òr-bhuidh, a golden-haired lass.*

Orcheard, òr′-chyărd, *n. m.* goldsmith.

Ord, ôrd, *n. m.* sledge-hammer; a junk *or* round piece of salmon, &c.;—conical hill, *H. S.*; hammers, junks, ùird, also *gen.* of a hammer, &c.

Ordachadh, ôrd′-ach-ă, *pt.* ordering, directing; officiously interfering; ordaining, decreeing, predestinating.

Ordag, ôrd′-ag, *n. f.* thumb, great toe.

Ordaich, ôrd′-ėch, *v.* order, direct; decree, ordain; dh' *òrdaich* Dia, *God ordained.*

Ordail, ôrd′-al, *a.* well-arranged, orderly, decent, becoming, regular.

Ordagh, } **Ordugh**, } ôrd′-aŏgh, *n. m.* order, command, injunction, instruction; decree, edict; *ordugh* o'n tigh-chuspainn, *a decree* or *edict from the custom-house*; cuir an *ordugh, put in order, arrange*; gun *ordugh, without instruction* or *direction, deranged*; ann an *ordugh*-cath, *in battle array—ordinance, Sacrament of the Lord's Supper. North.*

Orm, ŏrm, *pre. pron.* on me, owed by me; wrong with me; dè a th' aig *orm, what do I owe him*? dè th' ort, *what is wrong with you*? *what ails you*? a' cur *orm, dressing—dressing myself*; also ormsa.

Orra, ŏrr′-a, *pre. pro.* on them, &c.; see above; (air iad) dè th' *orra, what is wrong with them*? *how much do they owe*? *how are they dressed*? *n. f.* amulet *or* enchantment, to effect something wonderful; *orra*-ghràidh, *an amulet to provoke unlawful love*; *orra*-sheamlachais, *an amulet to make a cow allow the calf of another cow, to suck her*; an imposture of any kind; *orra*-chomais, *an amulet to deprive a man of his v-r-l-ty, particularly on the marriage-night, by way of vengeance,* (a fine thing to cure blackguards); *orra*-na-h-aoine, *an amulet to drown a foe*; orra-an-donais, *one to send one's foe to the mischief*; *orra*-ghrùdaire, *an amulet to make every drop of the wash to overflow the wash-tuns*; an *orra*-bhalbh, *an amulet to prevent* *one's agent to make defence in a court of justice*; *orra* nan oileamh, *an amulet to prevent d——s to succeed in any publication, such as a Gaelic Dictionary*, &c. &c. &c. When a genuine Celtic — — — or — — is thus spell-bound, instead of styling BABACHD, (from bab,) human ex-c—m—t, the uniform interpretation is, SWEETNESS AND INNOCENCE, &c. &c.

ORRADH; see òradh, burnishing, gilding.

ORRAIS, ôrr'-êsh, *n. f.* nausea, water-brash, squeamishness, *or* gnawing at the stomach; chuireadh tu an *orrais* air mathgamhainn, *your conduct would make a bear squeamish*; bha'n *òrrais* ri m' fhiacail, fad an latha, *the water-brash annoying me, the live-long day.*

ORT, ŏrtt, *prep. pro.* on thee, upon thee, owed by thee; wrong with, *or* ailing thee; dè a th'aig *ort, how much owest thou him?*

OS, ŏss, *n. f.* an elk; lean thusa an *os* bhallach, *pursue thou the spotted elk. Sm.*

OS, ōs, *n. m.* outlet of a lake *or* river. *Lew.*; a sand-bar (oitir, west). *North.*

OSAG for oiteag, light squall *or* blast.

OSAN, ōs2'-an, *n. m.* a hose, *or* tartan stocking, the leg of trowsers.

OSANN, ŏs'-ann, *n. f.* a deep sob *or* sigh.

OSANNAICH, ŏ 2'-ann-êch, *n. f.* continuous sighing *or* sobbing; heavy blasts *or* gusts of wind.

OS-AIRD, òs'-ărj, *adv.* openly, (not the thing); gu follaiseach.

OS-BHARR, ŏs'-bhârr, *adv.* besides, moreover, (properly a' bhàrr a' bharrachd.)

OSCAR, ŏs'-kăr, Fingal's best beloved son.

OSCARRA, ŏsk'-arr-ă, *a.* fierce, bold; unfeminine, masculine, as a female; indelicate.

OSCARRACHD, ŏsk'-arr-achg, *n. m.* fierceness; masculineness, as a female; indelicateness.

OS-CIONN, as ceann, above.

OSD, ôsd, *n. m.* an inn; drink; a bhean *òsd, the landlady of the inn*; air dhuinn a bhith 's tigh-*òsd, having happened to meet in the inn.*

OSDAIR, ôsd'-ăêr, *n. m.* a host, landlord of an inn; also fear-*òsd, innkeeper.*

OS-ISEAL, ôs-ēsh'-al, *adv.* privately; gu dìomhair, an diùbhrais.

OSNACH, ŏs'-nach, *a.* blustering, as wind; blubbering, as a person.

OSNAICH, ŏs2-nnĕch, *n. f.* continued sighing, *or* blustering, *or* blubbering, &c.

OSP, ŏsp2, *v. n.* gasp, sob quickly.

OSPAG, ŏsp2'-ag, *n. f.* a gasp; quick, deep sob.

OSPAGAIL, OSPAIL, } ŏsp'-ag-al, ŏsp'-ul, *n. f.* continuous gasping, *or* quick sobbing; *pt.* sobbing, sighing.

OSPAIRN, OSPAIRNICH, ŏsp2'-ăêrn, ŏsp'-ăêrn-êch, *n. f.* same as above, gasping quickly.

OTH, ō2, *n. m.* water; large body of water; Loch-*otha, Loch-awe, in Argyle*; cha leithne Loch-*otha* a nunn na nall, *Loch-awe is equally broad, whether you cross it hither or thither. Proverbs.*

OTHAIL, ō2'-u'l, *n. f.* hurry-burry; tumult, confusion; a' bhanais a bha CIOSTALL-ODHAR, cha robh *othail* chòir urra, *there was no decent hurry-burry at the* (genteel) *wedding in Keestallohar*!!!

OTHAINN, òh'-ènn, *n. f.* the largest kind of rivers; *abhainn, a secondary river*; (from otha, water, and inne, channel). *Is.*

OTHAISG, ò'-êshg, *n. f.* a yearling ewe; a soft, lubberly person; a blockhead.

OTRACH, ŏt'-răch, *n. c.* dung-hill. *Buch.*; in Islay, a drabbish, very fat female.

OTRACHAIL, ŏt'-rach-al, *a.* drabbish, filthy.

P

P, p, the thirteenth letter of the Gaelic alphabet, named Beith-bhog, that is, soft B; sounds like p in English uniformily.

PA, pâ, *inter.* and *n. m.* pappa.

PAB, pab, *n. f.* a tassel, knob; paban an òir, *golden tassels. Arg.*; shag. *N.*

PABACH, pab'-ach, *adj.* tasselled, tufted, shaggy.

PABAG, pab'-ag-ach, *n. f.* little tassel.

PABAGACH, pab'-ag-ach, *adj.* tufted.

PABHAIL, păv'-all, pavement. *Ir.*; *Welsh.*

PAB-CHEANN, pab'-chyann, *n. m.* shaggy-head. *H.*

PAC, pachg, *v. n.* pack up, get out of the house, get about your business; *n. m.* a pack, a vile crew *or* set of people; a *phaca, ye vile crew! ye sad set!* (*Teut.* and *Belgic.*)

PACAID, pachg'-aj, *n. f.* a packet, (*Fr.* and *Ger.*); a female tell-tale *or* tattler.

PACAIRE, pachg'-êr-ă, *n. m.* one that packs.

PACARRAS, pachg'-arr-as, *n. m.* trash, refuse.

PAGANACH, pâg'-an-ach, *n. m.* a heathen, a pagan; *adj.* heathenish, pagan.

PAGANACHD, pâg'-an-achg, *n. f.* heathenism.

PAGANTA, pâg'-ant-ă, *adj.* heathenish.

PAGHADH, pă'-Ă, *n. m.* thirst; tha *paghadh* orm, *I am thirsty*; am bheil *paghadh*, ort, *are you thirsty? paighteach, thirsty.*

PAIDH, pâê'-yh', *v. n.* pay, suffer for, remunerate, atone, make amends; *paidhidh* tu sin fhathast, *you shall suffer for that yet,* (*French.*)

PAIDHEADH, pûè-yhy-ă, *n. m.* payment, pay; *pt.* paying, remunerating, suffering for.

PAIDHEAR, pâè'-yhyar', *n. m.* payer, sufferer.

PAIDHIR, pī'-ėr', *n. f.* pair, brace, couple.

PAIDHNEACHAS, paŏèny''-ach-as, *n. m.* penalty, pledge; ann an *paidhneachas* fichead punnd sasannach, *under the penalty of twenty pounds sterling.*

PAIDHNAICH, paŏèn'-ėch, *v.* bind under penalty.

PAIDHRICH, pâèr''-ėch, *v.* pair, as birds, &c.

PAIDHRICHTE, păèr''-ėch-tyà, *pt.* paired.

PAIDHTE, pâè'-y^2-tyà, *pt.* paid, remunerated.

PAID, păjj, *n. m.* } cluster, string of beads; Lord's prayer; rosary, *or* the string of beads used by Catholics.
PAIDIR, păjj'-ėr', }

PAIDREAN, pajj'-ryan, *n. m.* cluster of grapes, &c.; posy, string of any thing, as beads, shells, &c.

PAIDRICH, pâjj'-rich, *v* string together.

PAIGHTEACH, pâ'-tyach, *adj* thirsty, bibacious.

PAIGHTEACHD, pâ'-tyachg, *n. f.* bibacity, thirstiness.

PAIL; see Peula, a pail, (*Spanish.*)

PAILIOS, pèl'-ės, *n. f.* palace, (*Latin.*)

PAILLEART, pally''-art, *n. m.* a box on the ear; in Irish, a tune *or* air on a bagpipe.

PAILLINN, pâll'-ėnn, *n. f.* tent, tabernacle, pavillion; deanamaid tri *pàillinnean, let us make three tabernacles. Bible.*

PAILM, paŏèl'-um, *n. f.* palm-tree. *Bible.*

PAILT, păljty', *adj.* plentiful, abundant.

PAILTEACHD, paljty''-achg, *n. f.* plentifulness.

PAILTEAS, palyjty''-as, *n. m.* plenty, abundance.

PAIND, PAINDEAG, pénj, penj'-ag, *n. f.* pebble.

PAINDEALACH, pénj'-al-ach, *n. c.* a person laced up like a dandy; article of dress too strait.

PAINNSE, pensh, *n. f.* tripe, (*Scotch.*)

PAINNTIR, penjt'-er, *n. f.* trap, snare. *Ross.*

PAIPEAR, pīp'-ăėr', *n. m.* paper, advertisement.

PAIPRICH, pīp'-rėch, *v.* cover with paper.

PAIRC, pâėrk, *n. f.* a park, (*Sax.*)

PAIRILIS, downright nonsense for paralais; in Latin, PARALYSIS.

PAIRT, parjty', *n. f.* part, share, portion, interest, connection, some; *pàirt* deth, *some of it*; ghabh e '*phàirt, he enlisted in his interest, he took his part*; cha bhith cuid na *pàirt* agam deth, *I will take no manner of connection with it*, (*Latin.*)

PAIRTEACH, pârjt'-ach, *a.* liberal, sharing.

PAIRTEACHAIL, pârjt'-ach-al, *a.* divisible.

PAIRTICH, pârjt'-ėch, *v.* participate, share.

PAISDE, pâshj'-à, *n. m.* child, infant, babe.

PAISDEIL, pâshj'-al, *a.* infantile, childish.

PAISG, păeshg, *v.* fold, wrap, imply; *phaisg* si i fèin, *she wrapt herself. Bible*; *paisg* an t-aodach, *fold up the cloth*; *n. pl.* parcels, bunches, as of keys; *gen.* of *pasg, a parcel* or *bunch.*

PAISGTE, pashg'-tyà, *pt.* folded, wrapt.

PAIT, pajt, *n. m.* a bump, *or* thump on the head; a smart blow on the head, producing a bump to a phrenologists' complete content.

PAITEACH, pajt'-ach, *adj.* phrenological.

PAITIRE, pajt'-ėr-a, *n. m.* a PHRENOLOGIST, thumper.

PAITIREACHD, pajt'-ėr-achg, *n. f.* phrenology, thumping.

The sublime science of PHRENOLOGY has been in use, in the *Highlands*, for time immemorial, though the inhabitants of Edinburgh, piqued themselves on its discovery.

PAP, pâp, *n. m.* the POPE.

PAPANACH, pâp'-an-ach, *n. m.* a papist; *a.* popish.

PAPANACHD, pâp'-an-achg, *n. f.* popery.

PARACAS, par-âchg'-as, *n. m.* a rhapsody.

PARALAIS, păr'-al-ach, *n. f.* a slight stunning *or* swoon; palsy.

PARANT, pâr'-ant, *n. c.* a parent. *Latin.*

PARLAMAID, pärl'-ăm-ajj, *n. f.* parliament.

PARLAMAIDEACH, párl'-ăm-ăj-ach, *a.* parliamentary.

PARRA, pârr'-a, } *n. m.* Peter *or* Patrick; *parra* ruadh nan cearc, *a hen-harrier* or *hawk. Arm.* (The Doctor must have meant some other Peter or Patrick.)
PARRAIG, pârr'-ėg, }

PARRAIST, par'-asht, parish, *North*; sgìorachd, *West.*

PARRAS, pârr'-as, *n. m.* Paradise.

PARTAN, part'-an, *n. m.* crab; in Skye, portan.

PASG, pasg, *n. m.* bunch, bundle, parcel, faggot; *pasg* iùchraichean, *a bunch of keys*; *pasg* aodaich, *a parcel of cloth*; *pasg* shlat, *faggot of twigs.*

PASGACH, pasg'-ach, *n. f.* a wrapper.

PASGADH, păsg'-ă, *pt.* folding, wrapping.

PASGAN, pasg'-an, *n. m.* little bundle, &c.

PASMUNN, pas' munn, *n. m.* expiring pang. *Highland Society.*

PEABAR, pāb^2'-ur, *n. m.* pepper, (*Greek*; *Ger.*)

PEABRAICH, pāb^2'-rėch, *v.* pepper, season.

PEACACH, pechg'-ach, *a.* sinful; *n. c.* sinner.

PEACACHADH, pechg'-ach-ă, *pt.* sinning, erring; *n. m.* transgression.

PEACAICH, pechg'-ėch, *v.* sin, commit sin.

PEACAIDHEACHD, pechg'-e-achg, *n. f.* sinfulness.

PEALL, pyall, *n. m.* horse; bunch of matted hair, &c. *Irish*; *v.* clot, mat, as wool; tha 'ghruag air *pealladh, his hair is clotted* or *matted.*

Peallach, pyall'-ach, *a.* matted; paltry, trifling.

Peallag, pyall'-ag, *n. f.* a mat of straw; bass; sort of under pack-saddle.

Peallaid, pyall'-ăjj, *n. f.* a sheep-skin. *Ir.*; paltry female. *Islay.*

Peálltag, pyallt'-ag, *n. f.* patched cloak. *N.*

Peanas, pen'-as, *n. m.* punishment, penance.

Peanasach, pen'-as-ach, *a.* penal; annoying.

Peanasaich, pen'-as-ėch, *v.* punish, annoy.

Peanasaiche, pen'-as-ėch-å, *n. m.* punisher.

Peann, pyann, *n. m.* a pen; Latin, penna.

Peanntair, pyannt'-ėr, *v.* scribble, scrawl.

Peanntaireachd, pyannt'-ėr-achg, *n. f.* a scribbling, scrawling.

Pearluinn, pārl'-ėnn, *n. f.* muslin. *M'F.*

Pearsa, pers'-å, *n. c.* person, any body. *B.*

Pearsanta, pers'-annt-a, *adv.* personally. *Is.*; *adj.* handsome, personable, portly.

Pearsantachd, pers'-annt-achg, *n. f.* personality.

Pears-eaglais, pers-āg -llėsh, *n. m.* clergyman.

Peasair, pās2'-ėr, *n. f.* pease.

Peasan, pās2'-an, *n. m.* impertinent person.

Peasanach, pās'-an-ach, *adj.* petulent.

Peasanachd, pās2'-an-achg, *n. f.* impertinence.

Peasanta, pās2-ant-å, *adj.* petulent, pert.

Peasg, pāsg2, *n. f.* a gash, as in the skin; crevice, as in wood; *v.* gash, chink, notch; chop, as hands.

Peasgach, pāsg'-ach, *adj.* gashed, chinked.

Peasrach, pās'-rach, *gen.* of peasair.

Peata, pāt'-å, *n. m.* a pet; spoiled child.

Peatarnachd, pāt'-arn-achd, *n. f.* fondling.

Peathar, peh'-ur, *gen.* of piuthar.

Peathraichean, per'-ėch-un, *n. f.* sisters.

Peic, pāėchg, *n. f.* a peck; measure.

Peighinn, pā'-ėnn, *n. f.* penny, coin, stiver; cha 'n 'eil *peighinn* agam, *I have not a stiver*; na h-uile *peighinn, every coin*;—Fiscal denomination of land, equal to *cota bàn*, groat land, *Mull*; round bit, or any thing like a shilling; 'ga ghearradh na *pheighinnean, cutting it in round bits.*

Peighinneach, pā'-ėnn-ach, *a.* spotted. *H. Society.*

Peighinnich, pā'-ėnn-ėch, make round bits, as a shilling or sixpence.

Peighinn-rioghail, pā'-ėnn-rrė-ghål, *n. f.* penny-royal; am bearnan-bride is *pheighinn-rioghail, the dandelion and the penny-royal. Mackintyre, Ar.*

Peilear, pāl'-aėr, *n. m.* a bullet, a ball.

Peileastar, pā2l'-ast-ur, *n. m.* a quoit. (*Lat.*)

Peileid, pā2l'-ăj, *n. m.* young porpoise, *Argyle*; a blow, *or* slap, *or* sheep skin, *North.*

Peilic, pā2l'-ėchg, *n. f.* a booth, pit. *Irish.*

Pein, pāėn, *n. f.* pain of body, agony,

Peinngilleachd, peng'-ėly'-hyachg, *n. f.* tyranny.

Peinnt, penjt, *n. f.* } a small pretty shell
Peinnteag, penjt'-ag, } or pebble; in Lewis, maidealag.

Peinnteal, penjt'-al, *n. f.* a mare, *Ir.*

Peinntealach, pėnjt'-al-ach, *n. c.* a slender tightly laced dandified person: a strait article of dress, as coat, trowsers.

Peirceall, pāėrk'-al, *n. m.* a lantern-jaw, a lean, large, lank jaw.

Peirceallach, pāėrk'-al-ach, *n. c.* a lean, lank, lantern-jawed person; *a.* lantern-jawed.

Peireid, pār'-ăj, *n. f.* a ferret.

Peirigill, pār'-ėg-ėly', *n. f.* agonies of death, excruciating mental tortures *or* torment. *Is.*

Peiriglich, pār'-ėg-lėch, *v.* torture, torment.

Peirean, pār'-ån, *n. m.* buttocks, *Skye*; see Peuran, and hence peursa, f—ting in a certain mode.

Peislear, pāsh'-lyar', *n. m.* a trifling person.

Peitean, pājt'-ăėn, *n. m.* woollen shirt, jacket.

Peithire, pā2'-ėr-å, *n. m.* a message boy; peithireachd, *running messages,* or *making domestic jobs.*

Peuc, pāchg, *n. m.* pea-hen; also peucag.

Peucail, pāchg'-al, *a.* trim, neat, cleanly.

Peuc-choileach, pāchg'-chul-ach, *n. m.* peacock.

Peula, pā'l'-å, *n. m.* milk-pail, (*Spanish.*)

Peur, pār, *n. f.* a pear—buttock. *Skye.*

Peurd, pėrdd, *v.* first-card; *n. f.* a flake of wool when giving the first carding · peurdag, *Islay.*

Peurs, pārs, *v.* f—t drawlingly.

Pian, pĕān, *n. f.* infliction of pain by way of punishment; torture, torment; *v.* pain, torture; *phian* e mi, *he tortured me.*

Pianadair, pĕăn'-ad-ăėr, *n. m.* tormentor.

Pianail, pĕăn'-al, } *adj.* excruciating;
Piantach, pĕănt'-ach, } also piantachail.

Piantaiche, pĕănt'-ėch-å, *n. m.* overwrought person, an ill-used *or* distressed person.

Pibhinn, pėv'-ėnn, *n. m.* lapwing, sadharcan.

Pic, pĕchg, *n. f.* a warlike pike, pike-axe; niggardliness, churlishness.

Pic, pėchg, *n. f.* pitch; comhdachaidh tu

a stigh is a muigh le *pìc, thou shalt cover it within and without with pitch. B.*

PIC, pēchg, *n. f.* churlishness, niggardliness

PICEAR, pēchg'-ăĕr, *n. m.* a niggard, churl.

PICILL, pēckg'-ėly', *n. f.* pickle, brine.

PIGE, pėgy''-å, *n. m.* a jar, earthen jar.

PIGEAN, pėg''-aėn, *n. m.* gorbelly, *or* a little gorbellied person.

PIGIDH, pėg'-ė, *n. m.* robin-red-breast, (bruideargan,) *H. Society's Dict.*

PIGHINN, pė'-ėnn, *n. m.* pye. *Irish.*

PILL, pėlly', *n. f.* a sheet, cloth; *pill*-chuir, *a sheet holding seed-corn when sowing*; fold; *v.* fold, put one in his winding-sheet; also an unique refinement on the Irish verb fill; fill e dachaidh, the Irish, for thill e dachaidh, *he returned home.*

PILLINN, pėly''-ėnn, *n. f.* saddle-cloth; shovel. *H. S.*

PINN, pėnn', *n. pl.* pens; *gen.* of a pen.

PINNE, pėnn''-nyå, *n. m.* a pin, a peg.

PINNICH, pėnn'' ėch, *v.* pin, peg, fasten.

PINNT, pėnnjt, *n. f.* a pint, half a gallon.

PIOB, pēbb, *n. f.* pipe, bag-pipe; smoke.

PIOBADAIR, pēbb'-ad-ăĕr, *n. m.* pipe maker.

PIOBAIRE, pēbb'-ur-å, *n. m.* a piper; a' *piobaireachd, playing at bag-pipes, squalling.*

PIOB-SHIONNAICH, pēbb-húėnn'-ėch, } *n. f.*
PIOB-THEANNAICH, pēbb-hyann'-ė, }
Irish pipes, *or* bellows' pipe.

PIOC, pėúchg, *n. m.* a nip, a pick, nibble; *v.* pick, nibble; a' *piocadh, picking, nibbling, nipping. Teut.*

PIOCACH, pėúchg'-ach, *n. m.* coal-fish in its third and fourth year; first year, céiteanach.

PIOCAID, pėúchg'-ăj, *n. f.* pick-axe.

PIOCAIRE, pėúchg'-ur-å, *n. m.* nibbler.

PIOGHAID, pė'-ăj, *n. f.* a magpie.

PIOCH, pēch, *v.* wheeze.

PIOCHAN, pēch'-an, *n. m.* wheezing.

PIOCHAIR, pēch'-ėr, *v.* line as cats; air *phìochradh, salacious as a cat.*

PIOLLACH, pėúll'-ach, *a.* fretful, and curious looking, contemptible.

PIORRABHUIG, pēr²'-a-vŭėg, *n. f.* periwig, *French.*

PIORR, pėúrr, *v.* stab, make a dash at in order to probe or stab.

PIORRADH, pėúr'-ă, *pt.* keen gust of wind; *pt.* dashing at, stabbing quickly.

PIOS, pēss, *n. m.* a piece, patch, *B. A. L.*; *v.* cut into shreds, lascerate, tear.

PISEAG, pėsh'-ag, *n. f.* kitten.

PISEACH, pėsh'-ach, *n. m.* increase, progeny, offspring; *piseach* air do phiseach agus piseach ann ad bhrainn, *may you see your offspring's offspring and have a young progeny yourself*; prosperity, success; *piseach* ort, *success to you*! am bi *piseach* orra, *shall they prosper?* le *piseach* a bhilean, sàsaichear e, *by the increase of his lips, shall he be filled. Bible.*

PISEACHAIL, pēsh'-ach-al, *adj.* successful.

PIUTHAR, pėŭ'-ur, *n. f.* a sister; *gen.* peathar.

PIUTHRAG, pėŭr'-ag, *n. f.* female fellow gossip.

PIUTHRAGACH, pėŭr'-ag-ach, *a.* gossiping.

PIUTHAR-ATHAR, pūr-ar'-ur, *n. f.* paternal aunt.

PIUTHAR-CHEILE, pūr'-chāl-å, *n. f.* sister-in-law; piuthar-màthar, *maternal aunt*; piuthar-seanar, *paternal grand-aunt*; piuthar-seanmhar, *maternal grand-aunt.*

PLAB, plab, *v.* make soft noise.

PLABARTAICH, plabb'-art-ėch, *n. f.* rumbling noise in speech. *N.*

PLACAID, plăchg'-aj, *n. f.* fat, broad, good natured female,—dish. *M'F*; *Ir.*

PLAID, plajj, *v.* drill potatoes, lay out ground in plots, plant as greens *or* colewort.

PLAIDE, plajj'-å, *n. f.* a plot of ground. *Is.*; blanket, Mainland of Argyle.

PLAIDE-LAIDHE, plajj'-a-lă-ėy-ė, *n. f.* an ambush, (from plaide,) *Bible.*

PLAIGH, plâė-y', *n. f.* plague, pestilence.

PLAIGHEIL, plâė'-yhal, *a.* pestilential.

PLAM, plăm, *n. f.* fat blubber-cheek.

PLAMACH, plăm'-ach, *adj.* fat-cheeked, fair-haired, and pale-faced.

PLAMAIC, plam'-ėchg, *v.* fumble, mix, handle awkwardly.

PLANG, pláng, *n. m.* plack. (*Scotch*); *or* a third of a penny.

PLANGAID, plăng'-ăj, *n. f.* blanket, the price of which was formerly a plack.

PLANNT, plă-ănt, *n. m.* a plant.

PLANNTAICH, plă'-ant-ėch, *v.* plant.

PLANNTAR, plannt'-ur, *n. m.* choice corn for seed, choice quality of oats.

PLAOISG, plāoėshg, *v.* husk, peel.

PLAOSG, plāosg, *n. m.* husk as of nuts, egg-shell.

PLAOSGACH, plaosg'-ach, *a.* husky, shelly.

PLAOSGAID, plāosg'-aj, *n. m.* soft, stupid woman.

PLAOSGAIRE, plāosg'-ăėr-å, *n m.* soft, stupid fellow.

PLASD, plâsd, *n. m.* a plaster, cataplasm, poultice; *v.* plaster, daub, spread awkwardly.

PLAT, plat, *n. f.* straw-cloth, peallag, *North*; *v.* thurst in, clap upon; *phlat* e 'lamh air, *he clapped his hand on it. Islay.*

PLATH, plă, *v.* puff, blow upon.

PLATHADH, plă'-ă, *n. m.* puff of wind; thàinig *platha* oirnn, *a puff came on us*; a' *platha* marn-aodann, *puffing* or *plashing about our faces*; glimpse, moment; ann am *platha, in a moment, Bible*; fhuair sin *platha* dheth, *we got a glimpse of it.*

PLEADAIRT, plăd'-ărjt, *n f.* an importunate petition, begging earnestly and humbly.

Pleadhag, plé'-ag, *n. f.* a paddle, dibble.

Pleasg, plèsg, *n. f.* noise. *Irish.*

Pleat, plètt, *v.* patch, mend.

Pleat, plett, *v.* plait, braid, fold; *n. f.* a plait, braid, tress, fold.

Pleata, plètt'-a, *n. m.* a patch, a piece.

Pleath, plè, *v.* beg a thing to be paid for.

Pleathainn, ple'-ènn, *n. f.* the act of begging a thing you are to pay for; *pt.* begging humbly a thing you must pay for, earnestly begging.

Pleideir, plăjj²'-èr, *v.* plead, *or* beg importunately, beg humbly and incessantly, (*French* plaider.)

Pleisg, plăshg, *v.* revile *or* abuse with all your might.

Pleisgeadh, plăshg'-ă, *pt.* reviling; *n. m.* a scold in a calm, sarcastic manner.

Pleod, plyôd, *v.* make milk-warm, warm slightly.

Pleodag, plyôd'-ag, *n. f.* soft, simple female.

Pleoisg, plyôshg, *n. m.* a booby. *Irish.*

Pliadh, plĕă, *n. f.* splay-foot, *and* bandy-leg; *v.* swagger.

Pliadhach, plĕă'-ach, *n. f.* splay-footed female; *adj.* splay-footed and bandy-legged

Pliadhair, plĕă'-ăèr, *n. m.* splay-footed, *and* bandy-legged man.

Pliodair, plĕdd''-èr, *v.* cajole, seduce by flattery, cradle into acquiescence, *Arg.*

Pliodaire, plĕdd'-ur-à, *n. m.* cajoler.

Pliodairt, plĕdd'-arjt, *n. f.* cajoling, caressing; *pt.* cajoling, caressing a person, as if a child, in a soothing fawning manner.

Pliut, plèŭt, *n. f.* a splay-foot on one side of the foot; pliutach, *having such a foot*; *n. f.* a female having such feet.

Pliutaire, pleŭt'-èr-à, *n. m.* half-splay-footed fellow.

Ploc, plochg, *n. m.* any round mass; junk of a stick; potato-masher, large clod, a very large head; *v. n.* ram against, mash as potatoes, greens, &c.; a' *plocadh* a' bhuntàta, *mashing the potatoes.*

Plocach, plochg'-ach, *adj.* having a large head, *or* lumps; galar-*plocach*, *quinsy, the mumps.*

Plocach, plŏchg'-ach, *n. m.* boy. *H. Soc.*

Plocanta, plŏchg'-ant-a, *adj.* stout, sturdy

Plod, plŏdd, *n. m.* a fleet of shipping; carnage; damage; *plod* mòr loingeas, *a large fleet of vessels*; siad a rinn am *plod*, *what carnage* or *damage they have made*! *v.* float, cause to float; air *phlod*, *afloat*: tha i air *phlod*, *she is afloat*; ma 'n do *phlod* i, *before she floated*; half scald as a pig, in order to loosen the pile; a' *plodadh* na muice, *scalding the pig.*

Plodach, plodd'-ach, *a.* luke-warm, *or* milk-warm.

Plodachd, plod'-achg, *n. f.* milk-warmness.

Plodh, pllô, *n. c.* any thing put temporary together; a sick person that dies, on getting the slightest cold or injury; a man *or* any thing, hardly hanging together.

Plodhaisg, plŏ'-èshg, *n. c.* } bumpkin,
Plodhaman, plo'-a-man, *n. m.* } a booby, a hum-drum.

Plodraich, plodd''-rèch, *n. f.* carnage, havoc, state of lying here and there uncared for.

Ploide, plòjj'-à, *n. f.* a tartan blanket.

Ploideag, plòj'-ag, *n. f.* a shawl; good-natured female.

Plosg, plŏsg, *v.* palpitate, throb, pant, sob; a' chridhe a' *plosgail, his heart palpitating* or *panting, throbbing, &c.*; *n. m.* a throb, palpitation, pant; gun *phlosg* air dèile, *without a throb* or *gasp on the stretching board.*

Plosgail, plosg'-al, *pt.* throbbing, palpitating.

Plosgartaich, plŏsg'-art-èch, *n. f.* throbbing, palpitating, panting, gasping.

Plub, plŭbb, *v.* plump, plunge, make noise as in water; blubber, *or* speak indistinctly; *n. m.* a clumsy lubberly person; noise made by any thing falling into water, plump, plunge, soft lump.

Plubach, plŭb'-ach, *adj.* soft and clumsy; *n. f.* a soft lubberly female.

Plubaire, plub'-ŭr-à, *n. m.* lubber, blubberer.

Plubairt, plŭb'-arjt, *n. f.* plunging, plumping; *pt.* plunging, blubbering, plumping.

Plubartaich, plŭb'-art-èch, *n. f.* plunging always; floundering, blubbering.

Plubraich, plŭb'-rèch, *n. f.* gurgling.

Pluc, plûchg, *n. m.* lump, bump, jumble of a sea; *v.* lump, thump, jumble.

Plucach, plŭchg'-ach, *adj.* lumpish, jumbling.

Plucan, plŭchg'-an, *n. m.* little jumble of a sea; plucanach, *with a little jumbling of a sea.*

Pluch, plûch, *v.* squeeze slowly, compress slowly and gradually, but tightly.

Pluchadh, plûch-ă, *pt.* squeezing slowly and lastly tightly; *n. m.* a squeeze.

Pluic, plŭèchg. *n. f.* a blub-cheek.

Pluiceach, plŭèchg'-ach, *adj.* blub-cheeked; *n. f.* the toothache. *H. S. N.*

Pluidse, plûjj'-shà, *n. m.* big lumpish fellow *or* beast.

Pluidseach, plûjj'-shyach, *n. f.* lumpish female.

Plum, plûm, *n. m.* dead-calm; hum-drum.

Plumaich, plŭm'-èch, *v.* coagulate without yeast, as milk; stagnate.

Plumb, plûmb, *n.f.* heavy shower. *Stew.*

Plundair, plŭnd′-ėr, *v* plunder, pillage.

Plundrainn, plund′-rėnn, *n.f.* plunder, pillage, spoil; *pt.* plundering, pillaging, spoiling, robbing.

Plur, properly flùr; a flower; flour. *Fr.*

Pobull, pōb′-ull, *n. m.* people, congregation.

Poca, pôchg′-ȧ, *n. m.* pocket *or* pouch.

Poca, pōchg′-ă, *n. m.* a bag, a short bag.

Pocaich, pōchg″-ėch, *v.* pocket, poke.

Pocaich, pōchg′2-ėch, *v.* bag, put into a bag.

Pocan, pòchg′-an, *n. m.* a little squat fellow; little bag.

Pog, pôg, *v.* kiss; *n. f.* a kiss; *pògan*, kisses.

Pogach, pôg′-ach, *adj.* fond of kisses; *n. f.* a blandishing female, offerer of kisses.

Pogaire, pôg′-ar-ȧ, *n. m.* a kisser.

Poiblidh, poyb′-lė, *gen.* pobull, of people.

Poibleachd, poyb′-lachg, *n. f.* commonwealth.

Poit, pôjt, *n. m. pt.* potations, tippling.

Poite, pŏjt′-ȧ, *n. f.* a pot; *poite*-ruadh -dhubh, *a still*; *poite* fheòla, *flesh-pot*; *poite*-mhùin, *a jordan, a chamber-pot.*

Poitear, pôjt′-ăėr, *n. m.* a tippler, drinker; *pòitearachd, habitual drinking*, or *potations.*

Poll, pōll2, *gen.* puill; *n. m.* mud, mire; pond; nostrils; *poll*-iasgaich, *fish-pond, fishing-station*; pit, a hole; *poll*-mòna, *peat-pit.*

Pollag, poll′-ag, *n. f.* a little pit, nostril; the fish guigniad *or* gweniad.

Ponaidh, pōn′-ė, *n. m.* a docked horse.

Pong, pong, (*gen.* poing,) point; a quibble in law; chuir thu as mo *phoing* mi, *you disappointed me, you defeated my intention* or *purpose*; tha e làn *phongan, he is full of quirks* or *quibbles*; air a *phoing* sin, *on that point.*

Pongaid, pòng′-aj, *n.f.* a hellish quirk, quibble, *or* stratagem; làn do *phongaidean, full of quibbles,* or *quirks,* or *stratagems.*

Pongaideach, pŏng′-aj-ach, *adj.* stratagistical; full of quirks and quibbles, *or* tricks.

Pongalachd, pòng′-all-achg, *n.f.* pointedness, exactness, punctuality; great attention.

Pongail, pông′-al, *adj.* pointed; particularly punctual; business-like in every thing.

Por, pôr, *n. m* seed of any sort; grain, a clan, a progeny; droch *phòr, bad seed*; am *pòr* dubh, *the black set, the wicked race*; *pòr* Dhiarmaid, *the race of Dermid*; i. e. the Campbells; pore of the body, (*Poros. Greek*); mo *phòran* air stopadh, *my pores stopped, perspiration*; obtructed.

Porach, pòr′-ach, *adj.* seminal.

Port, pŏrt, *n.m.* a port, a haven, harbour (Latin, portus); a tune on any musical instrument; ri *port, storm-staid, windbound*; favourable opportunity; gabh *port* air, *watch your opportunity.*

Portair, pŏrt′-ăėr, *n. m.* a ferryman.

Portan, pŏrt′-an, *n. m.* a crab. *Skye.*

Portas, pŏrt′-as, *n. m.* mass-book. *Macd.*

Pos, pôs, *v.* marry, wed, get married.

Posachail, pôs′-ach al, *adj.* marriageable.

Posadh, pôs′-Ă, *n. m. pt.* marrying, wedding; wedlock, matrimony; bonds of wedlock.

Posda, pôsd′-ȧ, *pt.* married, wedded.

Posgheall, pôs′-ghyall, *v.* betroth; *posghealladh, betrothment, promise of marriage.*

Post, pŏst, *v.* tramp, as a woman does clothes in washing; tread; *post* an làthach, *tread the clay. B.*; *n. m.* a post, portal, pillar. *B.*; a letter-carrier, puist, pillars; *postaichean, letter-carriers.*

Postachg, pŏst′-achg, *n. f.* letter-carrying.

Postanach, pŏst′-an-ach, *n. m.* thick-set child that just begins to walk.

Prab, prăb, *n. f.* rheum on the eye;—*v.* unfit. *H.*

Prabach, prăb′-ach, *adj.* rheum-eyed, contemptible; *n. f.* contemptible female.

Prabaire, prăb′-ur-ȧ, *n. m.* contemptible man.

Prabar, prâb′-ur, *n. m.* rabble; little people.

Prabardaich, prăb′-ard-ėch, }
Prabearsaich, prăb′-ars-ėch, } *n.f.* a smattering; slight knowledge; *prabarsaich* leubhaidh, *smattering of reading*; *prabarsaich* chunntais, *smattering of arithmetic*; lit. *the rabble language* or *acquirements.*

Prabshuil, prab′-hŭėl, *n f.* blear-eye.

Prabshuileach, prab′-hŭėl-ach, *a.* bleareyed.

Prac, prâchg, *n. m.* tithes. *Skye*; *Lewis.*

Pracas, prâchg′-as, *n.m.* dispute not easily settled; nonsensical difference; hotch potch.

Praib, prīb, *n. m.* rabble. *North.*

Praingealais, préng′-al-ash, *n. f.* gibberish.

Prainn, *gen.* of prann; hence the above.

Prainnseag, prénn′-shag, *n. f.* minchcollops.

Prais, prash, *n.f.* a pot; cas na *praise* tighinn an uachdar, *the stump* or *foot of the pot coming on the surface,* (said Donald, seeing the porpoise tumbling.)

Praiseach, *n. f.* a whore, *or* concubine; *athphraiseach, a harridan,* or *old whore.*

Pradhainn, pră′-ènn, *n. f.* press of business, throng, throngness; flurry. *Isl.*

Pradhainneach, pră′-enn-ach, *adj.* hurried, pressed for time, throng, flurried.

Pramh, pràv, *n. f.* melancholic dullness; dosing, slumbering, half-sleeping.

Pramhail, pràv'-al, *adj.* sad, sleepy.

Prann, pránn, *v.* pound, mash, bray, bruise; *phrann* mi e, *I pounded it, I brayed it*; mutter; dè 'm *prannadh* a th'ort, *what are you muttering about?* hence, *praingealais*, and *prainnseag*, and why mispronounced *pronn?* You may as well write seoladh, and not sealadh; leom, and leum, and not leam, and a thousand other absurdities, found in the mouths of those that pronounce it so.

Pranntair, prannt'-ėr, *v.* scribble, mutter.

Pras, prâs, *n. m.* brass.

Prasach, prăs'-ach, *n. f.* a manger.

Prasaire, prâs'-ur-à, *n. m.* a brasier.

Preach, prèch, *n. f.* a bog, a marsh, a morass; chaidh a' bhò 'sa *phrèach, the cow stuck in the marsh,* (*Lewis*); in Argyle, chaidh a bhò am bogadh, but preachan is applied to a little fen; *v.* preach *or* speak, like a bittern.

Preachaire, prèch'-ur-à, *n. m.* a croaking preacher, a miserable orator; am *preachaire* granna bodaich, *the old, ugly, croaking orator.*

Preachan, prèch'-an, *n. m.* the moss-bittern; a little peat-pit; mean orator; *preachan* ìnneach, *a vulture, Bible*; *preachan* gearr, *a buzzard*; *preachan* ceannann, *an osprey, O'B.*

Preachanach, prèch'-an-ach, *adj.* querrulous croaking; as a place, full of little pits.

Preas, prās², *n. f.* a bush, shrub, thicket, a wrinkle, a plait; thilg i an leanabh fodh aon do na *preasan, she threw the child under one of the shrubs*; ann am *preas, in a bush* or *thicket, Bible*; tha *preasan* 'na aodann, *his face is wrinkled* or *corrugated, Argyle*; *v.* wrinkle, corrugate; air *preasadh, corrugated*; gun *phreas* gun small, *without wrinkle* or *spot.*

Preasach, prās²'-ach, *a.* wrinkled, corrugated.

Preasadh, prās'-X, *pt.* wrinkling, corrugating; gun small gun *phreasadh, without spot* or *wrinkle. Bible.*

Preasarnach, prās²'-ărn-ach, *n.f.* a shrubbery, brushwood, thicket.

Preasantan, prās'-unt-án, *n. pl.* hens' eggs given to landlords by tenants as part of rent; in Irish, a wedding-present; *preasannta, a hen so given.*

Prine, prēn'-à, *n. m.* a pin for clothes.

Prinich, prēn'-ėch, *v.* pin, tuck.

Priob, prėbb, *v.* wink; twinkle as the eye.

Priobadh, prėb'-X, *pt.* winking, twinkling; *n. m.* a wink, a twinkling, glimpse, moment; bi an so am *priobadh, be here in a twinkling, in a jiffy*; cha do *phriob* mo shùil, *I did not sleep a wink.*

Priobairneach, prėbb'-ăern-ach, *n. f.* arousing. *H. S.*

Priobshuil, prėbb'-hŭel, *n. f.* twinkling-eye.

Priomh, prēv, *a.* first, main, chief, principal.

Priomh-bhaile, prēv'-vha'l'-à, capital, metropolis; *prìomh-sheòl, main-sail. Skye*; *prìomh-athair, patriarch, progenitor*; *prìomh-chlèireach, notary, secretary*; *prìomh* chrann, *main-mast*; *prìomh* easbuig, *archbishop*; *prìomh-long, first rate ship,* &c.; thog iad am *prìomh-sheòl, they raised the main-sail. Bible.*

Prioghainn, prė'-ėnn, sauce *or* seasoning in viands; choice food.

Prioghainnich, prė'-ăenn-ėch, *v.* season, as viands; feed with choice food, (brìgh.)

Priomhlaid, prėv'-lăj, *n. m.* a prelate. *Ir.*

Prionnsa, prėúnn'-sa, *n. m.* a prince.

Prionnsail, prėúnn'-sal, *a.* princely.

Priosan, prēs'-un, *n. m.* prison, (*French,* prisan.)

Priosanach, prēs'-un-ach, *adj.* very confined, within narrow bounds; *n. c.* a prisoner.

Priosanaich, prēs'-un-ėch, *v.* imprison, incarcerate; a' *prìosanachadh, narrowing, keeping confined,* or *in bondage*; *n. m.* imprisonment, incarceration.

Pris, prēsh, *n. f.* price, value, esteem; great demand, estimation; dè 's *prìs* dà? *what is its price?* ga chur am *prìs, raising it in estimation*; tha e am *prìs, it is in high estimation, there is a vast demand for it*; *conj.* and *adv.* so much as; *prìs* na circe, *so much as a hen*; *prìs* an fhrìne, *so much as a pin,* (*Fr.* prìs. *Welsh*; *Arm.,* &c. &c.)

Prisealachd, prēsh'-al-achg, *n. f.* preciousness.

Priseil, prēsh'-al, *adj.* valuable, precious.

Prisich, prēsh'-ėch, *v.* price, value.

Procadair, prŏchg'-ad-ăėr, *n. m.* law-agent, (*Latin*); procurator, man of business.

Proinn, praŏėnn, *n.m.* dinner. *Arm.*; *M'F.*

Prois, prôėsh, *n. m.* a neat, punctilious, little female; a prude. *Islay*; pride. *Sk.*

Proisealachd, prôėsh'-al-achd, *n.f.* punctilious prudery, neatness; pridefulness.

Proiseil, prôėsh'-al, *adj.* neat, little, and punctilious; uppish, like a prude; proud.

Proitseach, projtsh'-ach, *n. m.* a good lump of a fellow *or* boy. *Is.*; stripling. *High. Society.*

Pronn, mispronunciation of prann.

Prop, prop, *n. m.* a support, prop; *v.* support, prop, (*Belgic.*)

Propanach, prop'-an-ach, *n. m.* a boy well built, beginning to run about.

Prothaist, prŏ'-asht, *n. m.* provost. *Fr.*

Puball, pŭb'-ùll, *n. m.* a tent. *Ross.*

Puc, pûchg, *v.* fumble, ram, cram.

Puic, pûèchg, *n. f.* a bribe; *v.* bribe, ram secretly. *Is.*; fhuair e *pùic, he has been bribed.*

Puiceach, pûèchg'-ach, *adj.* giving bribes, bribing; *n. f.* a female that bribes.

Puicear, pûéchg'-aèr, *n. m.* a briber.

Puinsean, pùèsh'-un, *n. m.* poison, virus.

Puinseanach, pûèsh'-un-ach, *adj.* poisonous, venomous, vindictive; revengeful.

Puinseanaich, pùèsh'-un-èch, *v.* poison.

Puinseantas, pùèsh'-ant-â, *n. m.* poisonousness, venomousness, vindictiveness; resentment.

Pulag, bullag, *n. f.* large round stone.

Punc for poing, a point, a quirk.

Pund, pŭnd, *n. m.* a pound of any thing.

Punnd, pŭnnd, *n. m.* a place for securing stray cattle, *or* cattle trespassing; *v.* secure cattle.

Punndainn, pŭnnd'-èng, *n. f.* bad usage in being confined in a damp place; starvation, benumbing; the state of being confined to a cold place.

Purgaid, pŭrg'-aj, *n. f.* a purge, a purgative; aperient medicine; *purgaideach, aperient, laxative, purging.*

Purgadair, pŭrg'-ad-ăèr, *n. m.* purgatory, tormentor; the greatest anxiety to get freedom, *or* permission to shift quarters.

Purp, pŭrp, *n. m.* the faculties of the mind; full possession of mental powers; chaill e *phurp, he lost his faculties, he is under mental aberration*; neas a bhios mo *phurp* agam, *while I possess my faculties*; gun *phurp, uncollected.*

Purpalachd, pŭrp'-al-achg, *n. f.* collectiveness; full possession of faculties; punctuality.

Purpail, pŭrp'-al, *adj.* collected; in one's senses; punctual, pointed, sound in mind.

Purpur, pŭrp'-ur, *n. m.* purple.

Purr, pŭrr, *v.* stab, thrust, push, jostle.

Purradh, pŭrr'-Ă, *n. m.* a shove, jostle, dash at, as a bull; *pt.* pushing, jostling, shoving; a' *purradh* le 'adharcaibh, *butting with his horns*; an reith a *purradh, the ram butting. Bible.*

Puis, pŭsh, *n. f.* a cat.

Put, pŭtt, *v.* push, shove, jostle.

Puta, pût'-a, *n. m.* a trout. *North*; young moor-fowl. *C.*

Putadh, pŭt'-Ă, *pt.* pushing, shoving, jostling, butting; *n. m.* a push, a shove, a jostle; check. *H. S.*

Putag, pŭt'-ag, *n. f.* a hold-pin of an oar; in Irish, Kintyre, a pudding;—a ring of land. *Highland Society.*

Puth, pŭ, *n. f.* a puff; *v.* puff; chuir e *puth* as a shròin, *he puffed through his nose.*

Puthar, pŭ'-ar, *n. m.* power, authority; (*French,*) Mackintyre, the poet.

R

R, r, the fourteenth letter of the Gaelic alphabet, named Ruis, the alder-tree.

'R, for ar, *pro.* le '*r* cinn, *with your heads*; 2d, for bhur, your; le '*r* cead, *with your permission.*

R' for ri; *r*'a taobh, *at her side*; *r*'a cois, *at her foot*; *r*'a chois, *at his foot.*

Ra, ră, *adv.* too, too much, very, exceeding, quite; *ra*-mhòr, *too large, very great*; is tu an Dia *ra*-mhòr, *thou art a very great God, Smith's Psalms.*—Since the curious rule was introduced into Gaelic, " that he who writes the greatest nonsense is always the best Gaelic scholar," this word has been written *ro*-mhor, *ro*-bheag, *too great, too little,* or *very great, very little*; *ra*-mhath, *very well! too good*; cha 'n 'eil mi *ra*-chinnteach, *I am not very sure*; tha e gu *ra*-bhochd, *he is very sick*; cha 'n 'eil e *ra*-thogarrach, *he is not excessively willing.*

Rabach, râb'-ach, *a.* litigious. *Irish.*

Rabaire, râb'-ur-â, *n. m.* quarrelsome fellow.

Rabh, răv, *v.* warn, guard.

Rabhacaire, rav'-achg-ur-â, *n. m.* a nonsensical rhapsodist, haranguer, *or* proser.

Rabhacaireachd, răv'-achg-ur-achg, *n. f.* rhapsody, prosing, haranguing, talking nonsense.

Rabhachail, răv'-ach-al, *a.* admonitory.

Rabhadair, rav'-ad-ăèr, *n. m.* a beacon, a warner, a spy, a scout.

Rabhadh, răv'-Ă, *pt.* warning; *n. m.* a friendly hint, *or* information, caution; thoir *rabhadh* dha, *inform, tell, put him* or *her on the alert.*

Rabhairt, răv'-ărjt, *n. f.* spring-tide, a person that goes furiously to work; murdered in many places reobhart.

Rabhoil, râv'-ul, *n. m. n. f.* rhapsody delivered in a drawling manner, mad saying; drawling in manner or gait.

Rabhd, rav'-ud, *n. f.* nonsensical, *or* idle talk.

Rabhdaire, răv'-ad-ăèr, *n. m.* rhapsodist.

Rabhadaireachd, răv'-ad-ăèr-achg, *n. f.* rhapsody, prosing, verbiage, haranguing.

Rabhdail, răv'-ad-al, *n. f.* prosing, coarseness.

Rac, râchg, *n. m.* in the North, a drake; (trachd,) a rake, (rallsa,) in Ireland, a king; West, discordant, disgusting music *or* oratory.

Racaid, ràchg'-aj, *n. f.* a drawling female.

Racaire, râchg'-ur-à, *n. m.* a drawling, croaking orator, *or* piper, a croaker of a preacher.

Racaireachd, râchg'-ăĕr-achg, *n. f.* croaking, discordant oratory, *or* music.

Racan, rachg'-an, *n. m.* a bandy *or* crooked stick.

Rach, rach, *v. irreg.* go, proceed; *rachaibh* dhachaidh, *go ye home*; théid sinn dachaidh, *we shall go home*; na d' theirig dhachaidh, *go ye not home*; chaidh sinn dhachaidh, *we went home*; an deachaidh e dhachadh, *has he gone home?* rachainn, *I would go*; *rachadh* e, *let him go*; racham, *let me go.*

Rachd, nonsense, for reachd.

Radan, răd'-an, *n. m.* a rat, cunning person.

Radh, râ, *n. m.* saying, assertion, word; tha 'n *ràdh* ad fior, *that assertion* or *saying is true*; *pt.* saying, asserting, affirming, expressing; (see Abair); tha mi ag *radh, I say, I assert, &c.*

Radharc, raŏ'-ark, for fradharc, eye-sight.

Rag, răg, *a.* stiff; *n. f.* a rag; starch. *H. S.*

Ragaire, râg'-ur-à, *n.m.* extortioner, *Kirk.*

Ragaireachd, râg'-ăĕr-achg, *n. f.* oppression. *Smith.*

Ragh, râ-gh', *n. m.* a row, a rank; *ràgh* shaighdearan, *rank of soldiers*; a raft of wood. *Islay.*

Rag-mhuinealach, rag-vùèn'-al-ach, *adj.* stiff-necked, stubborn; rag-mhuinealachd, *contumacy, stubbornness.*

Raibheic, rīv'-èchg, *and* rev'-èchg, *n. f.* the roar that a cow gives when gored by another; most unconscionably murdered by the best Gaelic scholars **raoichd**, (from rabh, *and* beuc.)

Raideil, rajj'-al, *a.* inventive. *Bible.*

Raidh, râe-y', *n. f.* arbitration, decision, appeal; good will; leig gu *ràidh* na daoine so e, *submit it to the arbitration of these gentlemen*; tha mise, a dhaoine uaillse, leigeil a' ghnothaich so, g'ar *ràidhse, I appeal unto you, gentlemen, I appoint you arbitrators*; fear-*ràidh, an arbiter, arbitrator*; competition; a *ràidh* air a chéile, *competing with each other, trying each other's metal*; also nonsense, for raith, răĕch, *a quarter of a year.*

Raidheil, răĕ'-al, *adj.* challenging, fond of challenging, boasting.

Raidseach, răjj'-ach, *n. f.* a chief witch.

Raidseachas, rajj-ach-us, *n. m.* witchery; enchantment; prating. *North.*

Raignich, reg'-nyèch, *v.* stiffen, benumb; tha mo làmhan air *raigneachadh, my hands are benumbed, are getting stiff.*

Raimhe, rév'-à, *n. f.* fat, suet, fatness; *raimhe* a bheothaich, *the fatness of the beast*; *raimhe* 'sa phoite, *the suet in the pot*; high-water, *or* full spring tide, *Is.*; *deg.* of ramhar, stupidly written reamhar, more fat, thick, corpulent, &c.

Raimhead, rév'-ad, same as the above.

Raimisg, ram'-èshg, *n. c.* coarse vulgar person.

Raineach, ren'-ach, *n. f.* fern, froinneach.

Rainig, rràèn'-ėg, *pret. v.* ruig, reach; *ràinig* sinn, *we reached, we arrived.*

Raip, răĕp, *n. f.* debauchery, filth. *H.*

Raisinn, rāsh'-ènn, *n. f.* goat's tail. *North.*

Raite, râjt'-à, saying. *Smith.*

Raiteach, râjt'-ach, *a.* verbose; mor-*ràiteach, babbling*; beag-*ràiteach, taciturn, quiet.*

Raiteachail, ràjty'-ach-al, *adj.* challenging, boasting of feats, *or* bravery.

Raiteachas, ràjty'-ach-as, *n. f.* competition, emulation, trial of strength; a *ràiteachas* air a chéile, *competing, emulating each other from ostentatious motives*; arrogance, pride.

Raith, raĕch, *n. f.* quarter of a year.

Raitheil, răech'-al, *a.* quarterly.

Raitinn, rájt'-ènn, *pt.* saying.

Rair, rīr, *n. f.* last night; an *rair, last night.*

Ralls, râlls, *v.* rake, as grass, &c.

Rallsa, râlls'-à, *n. m.* a rake.

Rallsadh, ralls'-Ă, *pt.* raking; *n. m.* rough handling; the act of raking.

Ramair, răm'-ăĕr, *n. c.* a romp, a vulgar coarse fellow; *ramaireachd, romping.*

Ramalair, rám'-al-air, *n. m.* a coarse vulgar humorist, a humorous fellow.

Ramallag, ram'-all-ag, *n. f.* a puddle.

Ramasg, ram'-asg, *n. m.* tangle, doire.

Ramh, ràv, *n. m.* an oar; *raimh*, oars.

Ramhach, ràv'-ach, *a.* oared; *n. f.* a galley.

Ramhachd, ràv'-achg, *n. f.* rowing, pulling.

Ramhaiche, ràv'-ėch-à, *n. m.* a rower.

Ramhadair, ràv'-ad-aėr, *n. m.* a rower.

Ramhar, ráv'-ur, *a.* fat, thick, corpulent.

Ramhlong, ràv'-long, *n. f.* a galley.

Ramhraich, ráv'-rrėch, *v.* fatten, come to high water, as spring-tide; beat till one's body swells.

Ran, ràn, *n. f.* a drawling, dissonant roar *or* cry; melancholy cry; *v.* roar.

Ranach, ràn'-ach, a cave that gives an echo; a large ill-furnished house.

Ranaich, ràn'-ėch, *n. f.* drawling crying.

Ranail, ràn'-ul, *n. f.* same as above.

Rann, ránn, *n. m.* an oration in poetry.

Rann, ràn, *n. f.* a verse, a distich.

Ranna, ránn'-à, *gen.* of rainn *or* roinn, a peninsula; *rannach*, belonging to a peninsula.

Rannadhail, rann'-a-ghál, *n. f.* rhapsody, rant, ranting, (approach to rhyme, *literally.*)

Rannadhaileach, rann'-a-ghál-ach, *adj.* rhapsodical; nonsensical in oratory.

Rannaire, ránn'-ur-a, *n. m.* a poet, orator; a divider, divisor; distributer.

Ranndachd, ránnd'-achg, *n.f.* versification, poetry;—extent of territory. *N. M'L.*

Rannsachadh, ránn'-sach-ă, *pt.* searching minutely, inquiring into; *n. m.* search, scrutiny.

Rannsachair, ránn'-sach-aėr, *n. m.* searcher.

Rannsaich, rann'-sėch, *v.* search, scrutinize, examine minutely, explore.

Rannsaiche, rann'-sėch-â, *n. m.* searcher.

Ranntair, ránnt'-ur, *n. f.* a range, a sphere *or* extent of territory; tha'n *ranntair* iomachumhann, *the range is limited*; a' tighinn a stigh air an *ranntair* againne, *encroaching on our territory. Is.*

Ranntrach, rannt'-rach, *adj.* extensive.

Raoic, absolute nonsense for raibheic.

Raoir, rāoėr, *n. f.* (rair), last night.

Raoit; see Ruit, a rakish female.

Raon, rāon, *n. m.* plain; mossy plain.

Raonach, rāon'-ach, *n. f.* plain country.

Rap, răp, *n. m* a bad halfpenny.

Rapaire, rap'-ur-â, *n. m.* a worthless fellow.

Rapaire, râp'-ur-a, *n. m.* a drawling fellow.

Rapais, rap'-ėsh, *n. f.* a drab, a careless female, (*Hebrew*, rapish, mire.)

Rapal, ràp'-ul, *n. f.* nonsensical talk.

Rasan, râs'-an, *n. m.* a tedious highway, *or* bickering, *or* grating noise, *or* smell.

Rasanach, râs'-an-ach, *a.* tedious, drawling,—full of brushwood, *North.*

Rasdal, răsd'-al, *n. m.* rallsa, rake.

Rath, ră, *n. m.* prosperity, increase, use, profit, advantage; is beag *rath* a bhios ort, *your success will be very precarious*; is beag *rath* a rinn e dhomhsa, *it did very little good to me*; chaidh e bho *rath*, *he is gone to pigs and whistles.*

Rath, ràgh; see Ràgh, a row, rank.

Rathad, ra'-ud, *n. m.* a road, method, highway.

Rathaich, ră'-ėch, *v.* bless, prosper.

Rathan, ră'-ăn, *n. m.* surety, security; thèid mise an *rathan* ort, *I can assure you. North*;—thèid mise an urras ort, thèid mise am bannaibh dhuit, bàirnidh mise thu, *I can assure you. Islay.*

Rath-dorcha, ră-dŏrch'-â, *n. m.* the wane.

Re, rā, *prep.* during; *ré* an latha, *during the day*; *n. f.* moon; *ré* nuadh, *the new moon, B.*; duration, interval; fad mo *rè* is mo là, *during my day and generation. Sm.*

Reachd, rechg, *n. m.* law, statute, ordinance; *reachd* ùr a thàinig a mach, *a new statute* or *ordinance that has been issued*; èisdibh ri m' *reachd, listen to my law, B.*; deep sense of sorrow, expression of grief, great sorrow; bhrist *reachd* air, *he gave expression to his grief* or *sorrow*; substance, productiveness, as corn.

Reachdaich, rechg'-ėch, *v.* enact.

Reachadair, rechdj'-ad-aėr, *n. m.* lawgiver.

Reachdar, } rech'-ur, *adj.* luxuriant,
Reachdmhor, } productive as corn, *or* crop full of substance as corn; seachd diasan *reachdmhor* agus math, *seven ears rank and good. Bible.*

Reachdmhorachd, rechg'-ur-achg, *n. f.* rankness, productiveness, as corn.

Reamhar, rav'-ar, for ramhar; from ramh, fat, plump, fleshy, thick.

Reamhraich, rav'-rech, *v.* fatten.

Reang, reng, *n. f.* a wrinkle, a fibre, as in one's face; *v.* starve. *H. S.*

Reangach, reng'-ach, *adj.* full of wrinkles or fibres; full of strings.

Reas, rās[2], *n. m.* a head of dry curled hair.

Reasach, rās'-ach, *a.* having dry curled hair.

Reasan, rās'-an; see Reas.

Reasgach, riasgach, from riasg.

Reic, rāėchg[2], *n. f.* sale, traffic; *v.* sell dispose of; *pt.* selling, disposing of; a *reic, selling.*

Reiceadair, rāėchg'-ad-aėr, *n. m.* seller.

Reicte, rāech'-tyâ, *pt.* sold, disposed of.

Reidh, rā, *adj.* plain, level, cleared; àite *rèidh, a plain* or *cleared place*; exempt, free from, done of; tha mi *rèidh* 's e, *I am done of it, I will have nothing more to do with him or it*; reconciled, at peace; tha iad *rèidh* a nis, *they are at peace now*; *also they have finished*; *rèidh* ri Dia, *at peace with God. B.*; ready, prepared; am bheil thu *rèidh, are you prepared?* gu h-ŏrdail *rèidh, well-ordered, and harmoniously*; gu *rèidh, at leisure! avast!* smooth, plain; fiodh *rèidh, smooth-wood*; *n. m.* a plain, a level; gabh *rèidh* a bhlàir, *betake yourself to the plain, to fair field.*

Reidheachd, rā'-achg, *n. f.* smoothness.

Reidheas, rāsg, *n. f.* peace; faigh le *rèidheas* e, *get it in peace, without disturbance.*

Reidhlean, rāl'-àėn, *n. m.* a plain, a green, a bowling-green; air an *réidhlean, on the plain*; thun an *réidhlean, to the plain.*

Reilig, rāl'-ėg, *n. f.* a crypt *or* burying-place under a church; stone-chest where the bones, dug out of the graves, are placed; bithidh dùil ri fear fairge, ach cha bhi dùil ri fear *reilig, there may be hopes of a person at sea, but none of one in the grave.*

Reim, rām, *n. m.* power, authority. *Irish.*

Reir, rāėr, *n. f.* accord, agreement; do *rèir*,

according to, like as; do *réir* a chéile, *they upon an agreeable footing, on the best of terms, on a friendly footing.*

REIS, rāĕsh, *n. f.* a race *or* running-course; a span; ruith e '*rèis, he ran his course*; *rèis* d'a theangaidh, *a span of his tongue.*

REISIMEID, rāsh'-am-aj, *n. f.* a regiment.

REITE, rājt'-å, *n. f.* harmony, agreement, reconciliation; dean *réite, be reconciled, be friends, effect a reconciliation*; atonement, expiation; a dh'fheuchainn an dean mi *rèite* air son bhur peacaidh, *to try if I shall make an atonement for your sins. B.*; a marriage-contract. *Is.*

REITEACH, rā'-tyach, *n. m.* } disentanglement,
REITEACHADH, rājt-ach-Ă, } putting in order, as a house; a smattering; *pt.* disentangling, unravelling; reconciling, agreeing.

REITH, rà^2, *n. m.* a ram; *reith*-cogaidh, *battering-ram. Bible.*

REITHICH, rā^2'-ėch, *v.* rut, line, as a ram.

REITICH, rājt'-ech, *v.* put in order, adjust; *rèitich* an tigh, *put the house in order*; determine, adjust; *rèiteachar* a chèist, *the question shall be determined. B.*; *rèitich* thu àite fa chomhair, *thou preparest a place for him. Sm.*; betroth, settle on terms of marriage; disentangle; *rèitich* an snàth, *disentangle the thread*; *rèitichte, disentangled, determined, adjusted*; *rèitich* an rathad, *clear the way.*

REODH, ryō^2, *v.* freeze, frost, as a foot.

REODHADH, ryō^2'-Ă, *n. m.* frost; *pt.* freezing.

REODHTE, ryō'-tyå, *pt.* frozen.

REOTHART, rav'-arjt, rabhairt, spring-tide.

REUB, rèbb, *v.* gore, as a bull; tear, as with a shearing-hook, *or* any other jagged instrument; lacerate, pain intensely.

REUBADH, rèbb'-Ă, *pt.* goring, tearing.

REUBAIRE, rèbb'-ur-å, *n. m.* tearer.

REUBALLACH, rābb'-al-ach, *n. m.* a rebel.

REUDAN; see Riuidean, wood-moth.

REUL, räll, *n. f.* a star; a belle.

REULACH, räl'-ach, *a.* starry, starred.

REULADAIR, räl'-ad-äĕr, *n. m.* an astronomer; *reuladaireachd, astronomy.*

REUL-BHAD, räll'-väd, *n. f.* } a constellation, a
REUL-BHUIDHINN, räll'-vú-ėn, } bunch of stars, literally.

REULTACH, räll'-trach, *adj.* starry.

REULTAIR, räll'-tar', *n. m.* astrologer.

REULTAIREACHD, räll'-täer-achg, *n. f.* astrology.

REUSAN, rĕäs'-an, *n. m.* reason, cause.

REUSANACH, rĕäs'-an-ach, *a.* reasonable.

REUSANAICH, rĕäs'-an-ėch, *v.* reason, argue.

REUSANTA, rĕäs'-ant-a, *adj.* reasonable, rational, endowed with reason and sense, just.

REUSANTACHD, rĕäs'-ant-achg, *n. m.* reasonableness, rationality, justness, just grounds.

RI, rė, *prep.* to, into, during, like to, of concerning; chò mhìn *ri* minicean, *as soft* or *smooth as kidskin*; *ri* d' chluas, *to your ear*; exposed to; as, *ri* gréin, *exposed to the sun*; ascending, going up; *ri* bruthach, *ascending the declivity*; against, in opposition; a cogadh *ri* gaisgach, *fighting, opposed to*, or *against a hero*; against, in contact with; bhuail e chas *ri* cloich, *he dashed his foot against a stone*; occupied in, employed in; *ri* saorsainneachd, *occupied* or *employed as a house carpenter*; see Ris, Rithe Riutha.

RIABHACH, rĕä'-ach, *adj.* drab, greyish, brindled, grizzled; bò *riabhach, a grizzled* or *brindled cow*; *n. m.* louse-wort. *H.*

RIABHAG, reab'-ag, *n. f.* a lark.

RIABHAICHE, rĕä'-ėch-å, *n. f.* greyishness.

RIADH, rĕaŏ-gh, *n. m.* interest of money, usury; tigh-rèidh, *a bank*; *v.* lend another's property from house to house, without bringing it back to the owner.

RIADHADAIR, rĕä'-ad-äĕr, *n. m.* usurer.

RIAGHAILL, rĕä'-ėly', *v.* rule, govern; *riaghalaidh* lamh an dìcheallaich, *the hand of the diligent shall govern. Prov. B.*; more properly rioghail, from righ.

RIAGHAILT, rĕä'-aljt, *n. f.* a rule of any kind; a law statute; is math an *riaghailt* sin, *that is a good law*; sense, judgment; chaidh e as a *riaghailt, he lost his senses* or *judgment.*

RIAGHAILTEACH, rĕä'-aljt-ach, *adj.* regular, sober, decent, orderly.

RIAGHAILTEACHD, rĕä'-aljt-achg, *n. f.* regularity, orderliness, sobriety, sedateness.

RIAGHAILLTEAR, rĕä'-aljt-äĕr, *n. m.* regulator.

RIAGHAILTICH, rĕä'-aljt-ėch, *v.* arrange, adjust, regulate, put to order.

RIAGHLADAIR, rĕä'-lad-ar, *n. m.* governor.

RIAGHLAIR, rĕäll'-äĕr, *n. m.* governor.

RIALLS, rĕälls, *v.* handle roughly, *or* unseemly, as a female.

RIALLSADH, rĕälls'-Ă, *pt.* handling roughly *or* improperly; *n. m.* such a handling.

RIAMH, rĕäv, *n. f.* a drill of potatoes, turnips, &c. *Sk.*, *H. S.*;—duration; *v.* drill.

RIAMH, rĕäv, *adv.* ever, used only of past time; an robh *riamh, was there ever*? always; bha e *riamh* mar sin, *he was always so*; (with nach, never,) mar *nach* robh *riamh* a leithid ann, *such as never was the like.*

RIAN, for rioghn, *or* rion, method, order.

RIAR, rĕär, *n. m.* approbation, satisfaction, will, inclination, pleasure; agus nì thu mo *riar, and thou shalt do my desire or will, B.*; dean mo *riar*-sa, *act up to my pleasure* or *approbation*; word of honour; mo *riar* fhèin, *upon my word of honour*; ma ni thusa a *riar*, *if you act up to his approbation*; dean thusa mo *riar-sa*, *study you to please me*; mo *riar-sa* nach d' thig e nochd, *forsooth, he will not come to-night*; mo *riar*-sa nach 'eil, *upon my word it is not so!* cha 'n 'eil e soirbh a *riar* a dheanadh, *it is not easy to please him, to answer his wishes.*

Riarachadh, rĕăr'-ach-Ă, *pt.* distributing, attending at table, *or* distributing at a funeral; pleasing, satisfying; *n. m.* distribution of elements at a sacrament; satisfaction, pleasure; *riachachadh*-inntinn, *self-satisfaction, mental pleasure.*

Riarachas, rĕăr'-ach-as, } satisfaction;
Riarachd, rĕăr'-achg, *n. f.* } distribution.

Riaraich, rĕăr'-ĕch, *v.* distribute, dispense the sacrament, *or* ordinance of the supper; satisfy, please; *riaraich* orra e, *distribute it among them.*

Riaraichte, rĕăr'-ĕch-tya, *pt.* served, supplied; satisfied, pleased; distributed.

Riasg, rĕăsg, *n. m.* land that cannot be ploughed or dug, on account of dirk-grass; land so hid with this sort of grass; (bruth-chorcan,) *that it cannot be cultivated*; dirk-grass; indocility, stubbornness.

Riasgach, rĕăsg'-ach, *a.* turbulent.

Riasgail, rĕăsg'-al, *a.* that cannot be taught, indocile, untractable, mulish.

Riasglach, rĕăsg'-lach, *n. f.* land that cannot be cultivated; mangled carcase. *N.*

Riasgalachd, rĕăsg'-al-achg, *n. f.* turbulenee, indocility, untractableness.

Riasan, rĕăs-un, *n. m.* reason; improperly written *reuson*, cause.

Riastair, rĕăst'-ĕr, *v.* wander, entangle.

Riataidheachd, rĕăt'-ĕ-achg, *n. f.* fornication, *North*; wantonness, *Macdonald.*

Riatanas, rĕăt'-an-as, *n. f.* necessity. *N.*

Rib, rĕbb, see Riob.

Ribh, rŭĕv, *pro. pre.* to you, with you, against you; molesting you; mastering you; a' bruidhinn ribh, *speaking to you*; a' gleichd *ribh*, *sparring with you*; cò tha *ribh*, *who molests you*? a' cur *ribh*, *mastering you, sorting you.*

Ribinn, rĕb'-ĕnn, *n. m.* ribband; *Fr.* ruben.

Ribleach, rĕb'-lyach, **Rioblach**, rĕb'-llach properly, fringe, shagginess.

Ribheid, rĕv2'-ăj, *n. f.* reed of a pipe, barb of a hook; properly riobhaid.

Rideal, rhĕjj'-ul, *n. f.* a riddle.

Ridill, rĕjj'-ĕly', *v.* riddle, winnow.

Ridire, rejj- *or* rhúejj'-ur-ă, *n. m.* a knight; *ridire* nan spleagh, *a knight-errand, a sort of Highland Roderick Random* or *Don Quixotte, whose foot served in place of a draw-bridge to ferry his soldiers across arms of the sea*!!! *Legends.*

Ridireil, rĕjj'-ur-al, *a.* knightly.

Ridireachd, rĕjj'-ar-achg, *n. f.* knight-hood.

Righ, rhē, *n. m.* a king, governor; *righ* nan dùl, *the governor of the elements*; *righ* nan gràs, *the dispenser of sovereign grace*, *Inter.*, *oh king! would to God!*

Righ, rhĕ, *v.* stretch on a death-bed; dress *or* shroud as a corpse; a *righ*, nach robh thu air do righeadh, *I wish to goodness, you were shrouded.*

Righe, rhĕ'-ă, *n. f.* the arm; thog e è air ceannaibh a *righe*, *he raised it on the bend of his arms*; bac na righe, *the bend of the arm.*

Righinn, rhĕ'-ghyĕnn, *n. f.* a princess, a nymph, a belle; in Lewis, a serpent, from a tradition that it is a princess metamorphosed.

Righinn, rrĕú'-ĕnn, *adj.* tough; dilatory; more properly ruighinn.

Righich, rhĕ'-ĕch, *v.* reign, rule, govern, lord; *rìoghachaidh* an Tighearn gu saoghal nan saoghal, *the Lord shall reign for ever and ever. Bible.*

Righil, rĕ'-ul, *n. m.* a reel, armoric.

Righleadh, rhĕl'-Ă, *pt* reeling, floundering

Righ-mhort, rhĕ'-vŏrt, *n. m.* regicide.

Righ-mhortair, rhĕ'-vort-ăĕr, *n. m.* a regicide.

Righ-nathair, rhĕ-nhá'-ĕr, *n. f.* cockatrice. *Bible.*

Righne, rhĕ'-nyă, *deg.* of righinn; na's righinn neo na's ruighne, *more tough.*

Righnich, rúĕn'-ĕch, *v.* get tougher.

Righ-theachdaire, rhĕ-hechg'-ur-ă, *n. m.* an ambassador, an envoy, plenipotentiary.

Rinn, róĕnn, *past v.* dean; dean so, *do this*; *rinn* iad sin, *they did that.*

Rinndeal, rĕnnjj'-dyal, *n. m.* sphere, extent, limits, boundaries, territory; tha an *rinndeal* iomachumhann, *the boundaries are limited, the sphere is circumscribed*; leabhar an *rinndeal*, *the rental or stent-book*; dè an *rinndeal* fearainn a th' agad, *what extent of land do you possess*? a cheart *rinndeal*, *the very extent or sphere*; on the Mainland, ringeal, a circle, sphere, &c.

Rinniche, rĕnn'-ĕch-ă, *n. m.* engraving chissel.

Riob, rĕbb, *v.* ensnare, try to take away a person that is guest with another.

Rioba, rĕbb'-ă, *n. m.* a hair, a snare to catch fish, a double rope to keep a mad bull; shag.

Riobach, rĕbb'-ach, *a.* hairy, shaggy; cold.

Riobachd, rĕbb'-achg, *n. f.* hairiness.

Riobag, rĕbb'-ag, *n. f.* a little hair, lock of wool, lint, *or* any such thing.

Riobagach, rĕbb'-ag-ach, *adj.* hairy.

Riobalach, rèbb′-al-ach, *n. m.* hairy, curious-looking ragged person.

Rioblach, rèbb′-llach, *n. m.* a fringe, any thing hairy *or* entangled.

Rioblaich, rèbb-llèch, *v.* fringe, make hairy *or* entangled.

Rioch, rēch, *v.* graze, plough along the skin, cut as when flaying a beast; *rìoch* e air mo chraiceann, *it grazed on my skin.*

Riochd, rèúchg, *n. m.* shape, form, metamorphose; chaidh i an *riochd* gearaidh, *she metamorphosed herself into a hare, she assumed the shape of a hare*;* interpretation, meaning, exposition; dè 's *riochd* do m' aislinn, *what is the interpretation of my dream?* an *riochd* mairbh, *in the shape of a dead man, a skeleton* or *miserable looking person*; in the Bible, proportion.

Riochdaich, rèúchg′-èch, *v.* personate.

Riochd-ainm, rèúchg-én′-um, *n. m.* pronoun.

Riochdail, rèúchg′-al, *adj.* actual, real, positive; gu *riochdail* glan, *actually and really so, positively so*; dh innis e dhomhsa e gu *riochdail* glan, *he told it me as a positive fact.*

Riochdall, rèúchg′-all, *n. c.* skeleton, poor looking person.

Riochdair, rèúchg′-aèr, *n. m.* a substitute, representative, delegate, plenipotentiary.

Rioghach, rhé′-ach, *n. f.* a pinion, *or* string to tie the arms of a prisoner; an *rìoghach* air an òlach, *may the fellow be pinioned, the deuce take the fellow*; the pink of Gaelic writers, styles this an **riadhach**, i. e. *may the dun cow be on the top of you!! Parr.*

Rioghachadh, rhē′-ach-Ă, *pt.* reigning.

Rioghachd, rhēúchg, *n. f.* a kingdom, realm, dominion, empire; is farsuinn do *rìoghachd* 's gur fial, *extensive is thy dominion and hospitable. M'L.*

Rioghaich, rè′-èch, *v.* pinion, tie.

Rioghail, rhē′-ghal, *adj.* loyal, kingly.

Rioghaire, rhē′-ghur-à, *n. m.* a loyalist—a Whig or a Tory as occasion requires.

Rioghalachd, rhē′-ghal-achg, *n. f.* royalty, loyalty, dignity of port and character.

Rioghthach, rhé′-hach, *n. f.* felloe of a wheel.

Riolluinn, rèúll′-ènn, *n. m.* cloud. *Sm. H.*

Riomb, rēmb, *or* rāmb, *n. m.* a wheel, *N.*

Riomba, rēmb′-à, *n. m.* a semicircular bay *or* beach.

Riomball,* rēmb′-all, *n. m.* a circle, a halo; *rìomball* ma 'n ghealaich, *a halo about the moon*; gearr *rìomball*, *describe a circle.*

Riomballach, rēmb²′-all-ach, *adj.* circular, circuitous, like a circle.

Riomballachd, rēmb²′-all-achg, *n. f.* circularity, roundness, circuitousness.

Riomh, rēv, *n. m.* a costly jewel; in Irish, a counting, reckoning.

Riomhach, rēv′-ach, *a.* gaudy, fond of.

Riomhachas, rēv′-ach-us, *n. f.* gaudiness.

Riomhadh, rēv′-Ă, *n. m.* gaudery, finery.

Riomhair, rēv′-aèr, *n. m.* dandy; counter.

Rion, rēn, *n. m.* good order *or* arrangement, *Lewis*; mispronounced rian, in some places.

Rionadair, rēn′-ad-aèr, *n. m.* governor, supercargo, representative, ruler.

Rionnach, rèúnn′-ach, *n. m.* a mackerel.

Rionnag, rèúnn′-ag, *n. f.* glimmering starlet; rionnagach, *bespangled* or *studded with glimmering starlets.*

Riostal, rēst′-ul, *n. m.* a lame plough, *Lewis.*

Rireadh da'ridheadh, absolute nonsense for *d'ar righibh*; an ann *d'ar righibh* a tha thu, *are you serious, are you in earnest!* literally, *are you telling the truth, just as if speaking to our kings*—hence, the loyalty of Highlanders.

Ris, rèsh, *adj.* exposed to view; tha e *ris*, *it is exposed to view*; casan *ris*, *bare-footed*; leig *ris*, *expose, devulge, reveal your mind to*; *prep.* and *pron.* (ri-esan,) cum *ris*, *do not yield to him* or *it*; is math a tha thu cumail *ris*, *you wear out well, you match him well*; na bi *ris*, *do not molest him, do not use* or *practise*; using, in the practice of, in the habit of; *ris* an tombaca, *ris* an t-snaoisean, *using tobacco, using snuff*; to him, to it, matching him, equal to it; abair *ris*, *say to him*; theirig *ris*, *fight him, try him*; sìn *ris*, *be seduced by him, yield to his embraces*; try and make a bargain with him; against him *or* it; employed at, engaged in; dè do ghnothach *ris*, *what is your business with him? why do you middle with him* or *it?* dè a tha thu a' cur *ris*, *how are you employed*, or *what are you engaged in? ris* a chlachaireachd, *employed as a mason, engaged at mason work*; thig mi *ris*, *I will do for him, I will finish him*; thig e *ris*, *it will please him*; cuir *ris*, *master him, add to it.*

---

* Ladies in the Highlands are very fond of these pranks, and the most effectual way of killing them, is to put a sixpence into a gun instead of a bullet; but, from the scarcity of the *ammunition*, the experiment has never been tried by any of those whose lot it was to see the *old* wives milking their neighbours' cattle in the shape of *HARES!*

* Assaulted by ghosts or hobgoblins at any time in the Highlands, you have only to describe a circle, within which, you are as safe, as if aside your mother at the fireside—the moment the cock crows, your tormentors will scamper !!

RIS, risd, rēsh, rēshj, poetical contraction for rithìs, *and* rithisd, again.

RISEAN, rèsh'-un, *emphatic* form of ris, to him, &c.

RITHE, rrēch'-chà, (*pre. pron.*) against her, molesting her, to her; na bi *rithe, do not molest her*; na h-abair *rithe, say not unto her*; cuir *rithe, master her.*

RITHIS, rè'-èsh, } *adv.* again, a second
RITHISD, rè'-eshj, } time; cha mhallaich mi *rithisd* an talamh, *I will not again curse the earth*; an dràsd is *rithisd, now and then*; a choigrich, guil *rithisd, stranger, weep again. Ossian.*

RIU, RIUTHA, riù, rûch'-chà, *prep. pro.* to them, against them; cuir *riù, manage them, add to them*; cum *riù, keep up to them, supply them, do not yield to them*; na bi *riù, do not molest them, do not annoy them.*

RIUIDEAN, rūjj'-äèn, *n. m.* a knuckle; moth, *or* dry-rot in wood.

RIUIDEANACH, rūjj'-äèn-ach, *a.* dry-rotten.

RIUIDEANAICH, rūjj'-äèn-èch, *v.* dry-rot.

RIUM, rūm, *pro. pre.* against me, to me; thùirt e *rium, he said unto me*; cum *rium, keep up to me, supply me as I want, hold up to me*; thig e *rium, it will please me*; na bi *rium, do not molest me, do not meddle with me*; abair *rium, say to me*; comhla *rium, along with me.*

RIUT, rūt, *prep. pron.* to thee, towards thee, with thee; maille *riut, along with thee*; an d'thig e *riut, will it please you?* comhla *riut, along with thee*; a iomall na talmhainn, eibhidh mi *riut, from the ends of the earth, I will cry unto thee. Bible*

RIUTHA, rūch-cha, emphatic of riù; dè thig *riutha, what will become of them?*

RO, the Irish way of pronouncing RA; *ro*-bheag, *ro*-mhath, *too little, very well.*

RO, rô, *n. m.* romance, gasconading; thà e chò làn *rò* is a theachdas e, *he is as full of romancing as he can hold—he draws a long bow.*

ROB, rŏb, *v.* rob, steal, (*old French*);—*n. m.* shag. *N. H.*

ROBACH, rŏb'-ach, *a.* shaggy and filthy.

ROBAG, rob'-ag, *n. f.* a slut, a drab.

ROBAIR, rob'-äèr, *n. m.* robber, (*Fr.*; *It.*; *Teutonic*); *robaireachd, robbery, house-breaking.*

ROBAIRNEACH, rob'-ăèrn-ach, *n. m.* smart, *or* clever boy. *H. Society.*

ROBH, rò, *pret. inter. ineg.* and *part.* of the, *v.* bi; an *robh* thu, *were you?* cà an *robh* thu, *where were you?* cha *robh* mi, *I was not.*

ROC, rôchg, *n. m.* a sunk-rock; any thing that entangles a fishing-hook; an entanglement; cuiridh tu do cheann ann an *roc, you will involve yourself—you will entangle yourself*; a wrinkle, *or* plait, *or* corrugation, particularly in cloth-waulking; *v.* wrinkle.

ROC, rôchg, *n. m.* hoarse voice; a haw.

ROCAIDEACH, rôchg'-ăj-ach, *n. m.* a rook. *Islay.*

ROCANAICH, rôchg'-an-èch, *n. f.* hawing, hemming; also ròcail.

ROCHAILT, rŏch'-aljt, *n. f.* a blustering female.

ROD, rôd, *n. m.* sea-weed, foam. *North*; also nonsense for ràd; poetical contraction for rathad, (*French* and *Teutonic*, &c., râde, ràd); also, a rood of mason-work; a perch of land, ditch, &c.; *v.* scarify; *ròd* do chas, *scarify your foot*; a' *ròdadh, scarifying. Islay.*

RODAIDH, rŏd'-è, *adj.* ruddy.

RODAIDHEACHD, rŏd'-è-achg, *n. f.* ruddiness.

ROG, rôg, *n. f.* roguery, sliness, theft. *Lew.*

ROGAIRE, rôg'-ur-à, *n. m.* a rogue; *rogaireachd, roguery, downright villainy.*

ROGHA, raŏ'-à, *n. m.* choice, the best; *rogha* is tagha gach bidhich is dibhe, *pick and choice of eatables and drinkables*; theirig do *rogha* beallach, *go where you will*; *rogha* do sheudar, *the best of cedar*; tharruinn i sreang le *rogha* beachd, *she drew the string with her best aim*; *rogha* nam ban, *the best of women*; *rogha* céile, *the best of husbands* or *wives.*

ROGHALACHD, rô'-ghal-achg, *n. f.* romancing disposition; gasconading inclination.

ROGHAIL, rô'-ghal, *adj.* fond of romancing.

ROGHAINN, raŏ'-ènn, *n. f.* choice, selection, option; gabh do *roghainn, take your choice*; air fhàgal gu d' *roghainn, left in your option*; cò do *roghainn, which is your choice?* tha diugh is *roghainn* ann, *there is pick and choice among them*; *roghainn* an t-sealgair, *the best of marksmen*; preference, eligibleness; a *roghainn* air sin, *in preference to that*; dean do *roghainn* ris, *make a kirk or a mill of it.*

ROGHNACH, rāon'-ach, *a.* eligible; *roighneach* a ni a's *roighniche* leat, *what you think preferable*; an *roighniche* leat so, *do you prefer this?* is *roighniche, yes!*

ROGHNAICH, provincial for roighnich, choose.

ROI, róè, *prep.* for roimh, before; before him.

ROIB, royb, *n. m.* } a circle of grease
ROIBINN, royb'-ènn, } about the lips; also pubes, *or* circle of hair; beard.

ROIBHE, royv, *n. m.* sneezewort. *Irish.*

ROIBHNE, royv'-nyà, *n. m.* dart, lance. *Ir.*

ROIC, rôèchg, *n. f.* sumptuous feasting of boorish people; superabundance of the good things of life, without any of the refined manners of genteel society.

ROICEALACHD, rôèchg'-al-achg, *n. f.* luxuriousness, a sort of brutish luxury *or* gluttony.

ROICEIL, rôèchg'-al, *adj.* luxurious, epicurean.

ROID, rŏjj, *n. f.* a race before a leap; a little while *or* time; a rush *or* bounce; thug e *roid* a stigh, *he bounced in, he rushed* or *popped in*; a' dol *roid* do 'n-bhaile ad thall, *going a little while to yonder town*; leum *roid, a leap after a race*; cruinleum, *a bound.*

ROID, rojj, ROIDEAGACH, rojj'-ag-ach, *n. f.* wild *or* Dutch myrtle; the sweet-gale; *gen.* of rod.

ROIDEIS, rŏjj'-ash, *n. f.* bounding, skipping.

ROIGHNEACH, raŏèn'-ach, *adj.* preferable, eligible; 'se so is *roighniche* leam, *I think this is preferable,* or *more eligible*; c'a b'a 's *roighniche* leat, *whichsoever you may choose.*

ROIGHNICH, raŏèn'-èch, *v.* choose, make choice; select, make a selection; elect.

ROILEISG, rŏl'-èshg, *n. f.* confused joy, *or* person.

ROILIG, ró'l'-èg, *n. c.* a frolicsome person.

ROILIGEACH, rŏ'l'-èg-ach, *adj.* frolicsome.

ROIMH, rhóè, *prep.* and *pron.*; also *adv.* for, *or* of him, *or* it; before him *or* it; before, *or* formerly; choinnic mi *roimh* thu, *I saw you before*; ghabh e eagal *roimh, he was afraid of him, he took fright at him*; in preference to, rather than; *roimh* na h-uile ni, *in preference to every thing, rather than any thing*; *roimh* na h-uile nì, mo bhràithre, *above all things, my brethren. B.*; gabh *romhad, go about your business, begone*! cuir *romhad, determine, resolve, purpose, intend*; tha thu a' cur *romhad* cur as da, *you are determined to finish him*; chuir mi *romham* dol dachaidh, *I was determined to go home*—used by Smith for throimh; chuir e *roimh* chéile iad, *he disturbed them, he confused* or *mixed them*; *adj.* former, other; an latha *roimh, the other day, a few days ago*; co *roimh* a bhiodh eagal orm, *of whom should I be afraid*; *roimh* sgrios théid uabhar, *before destruction goes pride*; am bheil *romhad* dol dachaidh? *do you mean to go home?*

ROIMH, róèv, *n. f.* the city of Rome; chaidh e do'n *Roimh, he went to Rome.*

ROIMH-ORDUICH, ro'-ôrd-èch, *v.* fore-ordain.

ROIMHIBH, róèv, (*prep. pro.*) before you; in preference to you; standing *or* walking before you.

ROIMHID, rhóè'-èj, *adv.* before, formerly, previously; choinnic mi *roimhid* thu, *I saw you previous to this time, before,* or *prior to this time.*

ROIMPE, róèp'-à, (*pre. pro.*) before her, &c.

ROIN, ròèn, *n. f.* a hair; leud *ròine, a hair's-breadth*; *n. pl.* seals, *or* sea-calves.

ROINEACH, róèn'-ach, *adj.* full of hairs, as meat, &c.

ROINEAG, róèn'-ag, *n. f.* a small hair.

ROINN, raŏèn, *n. f.* a pair of compasses; a share, proportion, distribution, division; mo *roinn* fhèin, *my own share*; an *roinn* a rinne orra, *the distribution* or *division he made of them*; a peninsula; an *Roinn* ìleachd, *the Rhynns of Islay, the peninsula of Islay*; *gen.* Ranna, ann an ìochdar na Ranna, *in the farthest-off parts of the Rhynns*; an *Roinn* Ghallaibh, *Rhynns of Galloway*; (*Welsh,* Rhyns); *roinn* mhìc is athar, *share and share alike, equal distribution*; the part distinct from the point of a sword; *v.* divide, share, distribute, impart; *roinn* orra e, *distribute* or *divide it amongst them*; *roinneadh* esan aig am bheil dà chòta, *let him that has two coats, impart, Bible*; *pt.* dividing, distributing, sharing, imparting; a' *roinn* orra, *distributing among them.*

ROINNEADAIR, raŏnn'-ad-aèr, *n. m.* divider.

ROINNICH, raoènn'-èch, *v.* sharpen. *H. S.*

ROINNTE, raŏènn'-tyà, *pt.* divided, distributed.

ROISEAL, rôsh'-shyal, *n. f.* pomp; display of ability; le *ròiseal, with an ostentatious display*; (also, *roisealadh*); *v.* display; make a pompous display; (from rò, romancing, and seal, sight, *or* short glimpse.)

ROISEALACH, rôsh'-shyall-ach, *adj.* pompous, ostentatious; fond of displaying one's feats, *or* ability.

ROISEALACHD, rôsh'-shyall-achg, *n. f.* pomposity, ostentatious display; ostentation.

ROISEID, ròsh'-aj, *n. f.* rosin.

ROISEIDEACH, rôsh'-ăj-ach, *adj.* resinous.

ROISGEUL, rôshg'-skyall, *n. m.* a romance.

ROISGEULACH, rôshg'-skyall-ach, *a.* romancing.

ROIST, rôshjj, *v.* roast; *ròiste, roasted.*

ROITHLEAN, ro'l'-ăèn, *n. m.* shave of a block, *or* pulley; (rothail, *contracted,*) *n. f.* worm-wood, gall. *Irish.*

ROITHLEAR, rŏ'l'-ăèr, *n. m.* a roller, ruler.

ROL, rŏl, *n. m.* volume *or* book; a roll, *Bible*; (rothal, contracted.)

ROL, rôl, *v.* roll, wheel; (rothail.)

ROLAG, rŏl'-ag, *n. f.* the thing of wool the Scotch call Rowan; swathe of grass.

ROM, rôm, *n. f.* a ——, pubes, shag.

ROMACH, rôm'-ach, *adj.* hairy, shaggy.

ROMAICHE, rôm'-èch-à, *n. f.* hairiness.

ROMH, ró, *prep.* and *adv.* before, previous to, prior to; *romh* an am, *previous to before*, or *prior to this time*; in preference to; *romh* ghin, *in preference to any*.

ROMHAD, ró′-ad, *pre. pro.* before thee *or* you, previous to you, in your contemplation *or* intention; at you, of you, *or* with you; is beag eagal a th' aig *romhad, little does he dread you*; dé a tha thu a' cur *romhad, what do you mean to do?* tha mi cur *romham* sin a dheanadh, *I have it in contemplation to do that*, or *I am determined to do that*; gabh *romhad, go about your business, begone!* abair *romhad, say on*; am bheil *romhad* thu fhèin a mhilleadh, *do you mean to ruin yourself.*

ROMHAIBH, ró′-èv, *pre. pro.* before you, &c. (romh-sibh,) tha *romhaibh, you are determined.*

ROMHAM, ró′-um, *pre. pro.* before me, (romh-mi); see Romhad.

ROMHAINN, ró′-ènn, *pre. pro.* before us, (romh-sinn.)

ROMPA, rómp′-a, before them; see above.

RON, ròn, *n. m.* a seal, *or* sea-calf; ionad falaich na *ròn* slapach, *the hiding-place of the splashing seals*, or *sea-calves. Sm.*; near Inverary, fetters for the fore feet of a horse, (deubh); hair. *N.*

RONACH, ròn′-ach, *n. f.* seal-hunt. *Skye.*

RONG, rŏng, *n. f.* a bandy, vital spark; lounge.

RONGACH, rong′-ach, *a.* lounging, cadaverous.

RONGAICHE, rông′-èch-å, *n. f.* lounging.

RONGAIRE, rông′-ur-å, *n. m.* a lounge.

RONGAIREACHD, rông′-ăèr-achg, *n. f.* tedious, drawling, lounging manner, *or* habits

RONGAIS, rông′-èsh, *n. f.* a bandy, a bludgeon.

RONN, rōnn, *n. f.* a slaver, ropy spittle.

RONNACH, rônn′-ach, *a.* viscous, ropy, glutinous; *n. f.* slavering, dirty female.

RONNAICH, rônn′-èch, *v.* become viscid.

RONNAIR, rônn′-ur-å, *n. m.* a slavering man.

ROP, rŏp, *v.* gore; let out the viscera with a knife; tear open a bag with a knife; (*Dan.* raffle.)

ROP, rōp, *n. m.* an auction; *v.* roup. (*Fr.*)

ROPACH, rôp′-ach, *adj.* viscous, glutinous.

ROPADAIR, rôp′-ad-ăer, *n. m.* rope-maker.

RORAM, rôr′-um, *n. m.* the quality of dealing out extensively among a family, as provisions; the quality of being able to stand fatigue; liberality, with a deal of ostentation; hospitality; rò-rum.

RORAMACH, rôr′-am-ach, *adj.* liberal, highly liberal; lasting long, and being capable of dividing well in a family, as provisions.

RORAMACHD, rôr′-um-achg, *n. f.* liberality, extensive usefulness in a family.

ROS, rôs, *n. m.* a rose; erysipelas; (rosa, *Latin*; also *Spanish, French*, &c. &c.)

ROS, rŏs, *v. n.* defeat, miscarry; *ros* e orm, *it miscarried, I have been disappointed in it*; *ros* an làr bracha so orm, *this floor of malt went wrong, miscarried*;—also for frois, spend as corn. *North*; *n. m.* disappointment; a promontory *or* peninsula; an *ros* Muileach, *the promontory of Mull*; (Rudha Muileach.)

ROSACH, rŏs′-ach, *adj.* disappointing, defeating; an Linne *Rosach, the channel of disappointment, the Sound of Jura*, (truly so); *n. m.* one of the name of Ross; also a Ross-shire man.

ROSAD, ros′-ad, } *n. m.* disappointment,
ROSADH, ros′-ă, } misfortune, mischief; dè 'n *rosad* a rug ort, *what misfortune*, or *the mischief came over you?*

ROSADACH, ros′-ad-ach, *a.* untoward.

ROSG, rosg, *n. m.* an eye-lid, eye-lash; prose.

ROSP, rôsp, *n. f.* a blear eye.

ROST, rôst, *n. m.* a roast; piece of beef.

ROTACH, rŏt′-ach, *n. m.* a circle of filth on one's clothes. *Islay*; a rush at starting, (sigheadh); a hand-rattle, (clach-bholg).

ROTAIR, rott″-ur-å, *n. m.* a sloven.

ROTH, ró, *n. m.* wheel of a cart, &c.; halo; tha *roth* ma'n ghealaich, *there is a halo round the moon.*

ROTHA, rò′-å, *n. m.* a roll of tobacco. *Islay.*

ROTHADAIR, ró′-ad-aěr, *n. m.* wheel-wright.

ROTHAICH, ró′-èch, *v.* twine, roll.

RUADH, rŭă′-gh, *a.* red-haired, reddish *n. m* reddish colour, redness; a hind, deer.

RUADHAG, rŭă′-ghag, *n. f.* young roe.

RUADHAN, rŭă′-an, *n. m.* mineral scruff.

RUADHBHUIDH, rŭă′-vŭè, *a.* auburn.

RUADH-CHAILC, rŭă′-chăèlk, *n. f.* ochre.

RUAGADH, rŭăg′-ă, *pt.* driving away, pursuing.

RUAGAIRE, rŭăg′-ur-å, *n. m.* pursuer, lock-bar; an outlaw, a wanderer; swan-shot.

RUAIDH, rŭă′-èy′, *n f.* the disease called the herpes, *or* shingles, caused by nausea. (*West*); the rose. (*Lewis*); erysipelas. *Ir.*

RUAIG, rŭăèg, *n. f.* pursuit, persecution; thog iad am *ruaig, they took up the pursuit*; defeat, flight, hunt, chase; chuir sinn an *ruaig* orra, *we put them to flight, we defeated them*; ghabh iad an *ruaig, they took to flight*; *ruaig* an tuirc, *the boar-hunt. Ossian*; has an obscene meaning; *v.* drive away, pursue, chase; 'ga *ruagadh, driving him away, pursuing him.*

RUAIM, rŭăèm, *n. f.* flush of anger; line.

RUAIMILL, rŭăèm′-èly′, *v.* rumble; agitate water.

RUAIMLEADH, *pt.* rumbling; *n. m.* water lily, fuller's-earth, muddiness of water.

RUAIMHSEANTA, rŭá′-shant-a, *adj.* jolly hale; hearty, though very old. *Islay.*

Ruaimhseantachd, rŭáėsh′-ant-achg, *n.f.* an old person s heartiness, vigour.

Ruaimneach, rŭăėm′-nyach, *a.* strong. *N.*

Ruamh, rŭav, *n.f.* a spade. *Shaw.*

Ruamhair, rŭá′-aėr, *v.* delve, dig.

Ruamhar, rŭá′-ar, *n. m.* delving, digging.

Ruais, rŭăsh, *n. f.* and *c.* rhapsody; a senseless flow of language; rhapsodist.

Ruaiseil, rŭăsh′-al, *adj.* rhapsodical.

Ruapais, rŭăp′-ėsh, *n. f.* rigmarole.

Rub, rhŭb, *v.* rub, (rhub, *Brit.*)

Rubadh, rhŭb′-ă, *pt.* and *n. m.* rubbing, friction.

Rubail, rûb′-ul, *n. f.* a tumult, rumbling.

Rubair, rŭb′-aėr, *n. m.* a rubber, scraper.

Ruc, rŭchg, *n. m.* a rick of hay, peats, &c.; *v.* make ricks, build peats into small stacks.

Rucas, rŭchg′-as, *n. m.* jostling kind of fondness.

Ruchd, rûchg, *n. m.* a retch, grunt, ructation; *v.* retch groaningly, (*Lat.* ructa.)

Ruchdail, rûchg′-al, *n. f.* retching, belching; *pt.* retching.

Rud, raŏd, *n. m.* a thing; pudendum; agus *rud* eile dheth, *more than that, moreover.*

Rudainnte, raŏd′-anjt-å, *pt.* done; *adj.* particular, somewhat odd.

Rudanach, raŏd′-an-ach, *a.* particular.

Rudanaich, raŏd′-an-ėch, *v.* dress.

Rudha, rŭ-ă, *n. m.* a point of land in the sea, promontory; deuch am fuar thu 'n *rudha, see, and weather the promontory*; a turn; cuiridh so *rudha* seachad, *this will serve for our turn, it will serve for this time.*

Rudhag, rŭ′-ăg, *n. m.* crab *N.*; partan.

Rudhagail, rŭ′-ag-ul, *n. f.* thrift, shift; tha e gu math *rudhaglach, he is pretty thrifty*; g'a *rudhagail* fhéin, *to his own thrift.*

Rudhaglach, rŭă′-ag-lach, *adj.* thrifty.

Ruga, rŭg′-a, *n. m.* rough cloth, *or* female (*Swedish* rugg.)

Rugaid, rŭg′-ăj, *n. f.* an old cow, *or* worthless female.

Rug, rrŭg, *past, v.* bare; *rug* iad clann, *they bore children*; *rug* i uan, *she yeaned*; *rug* i meann, *she kidded*; *rug* i piseagean, *she kittened*; *rug* i cuileanan, *she whelped,* or *cubbed*; *rug* i searrach, *she foaled*; *rug* i ugh, *she laid an egg*; *rug* i oirceanan, *she farrowed*; *rug* sinn urra, *we overtook her*; *rug* e air bhuam, *he laid hold of it out of my hands.*

Rugaire, rûg′-ur-å, *n. m.* drunkard. *N.*

Rugha, rŭ′-ă, } *n. m.* a blush; ni mò
Riugha, reaŏ-y″-å, } a bha *rugha* air an gruaidh, *neither was their a blush on their cheek. Bible.*

Ruideal, rŭjj′-al, *n. f.* a riddle; *v.* riddle.

Ruideis, rûjj′-ash, *n. f.* skipping, frisking.

Ruideiseach, rûjj′-ash, *adj.* frisky, lively

Ruig, rûėg, *v. n.* reach, extend; *ruig* air so, *reach at this, extend your hand to this*; ràinig mi air, *I reached at it*; arrive, come to, attain to; an *ruig* e nochd, *shall he arrive to-night*? cia fhada a *ruigeas* tu, *how far wilt thou go*? cha *ruig* mi air, *I cannot attain to it, B.*; need, must needs; cha *ruig* thu leas a bhi aig do dhragh, *you need not be at the trouble*; properly riog.

Ruige, rûėg′-å, *n. m.* place, point; gu *ruige* so, *to this point, to this place*; gu *ruige* an tigh, *to the house, as far as the house.*

Ruighe, for righe, the arm.

Ruigheachd, rė′-achg, *n. f.* arrival; air dhuinn *ruigheachd, on our arrival*; *pt.* reaching, attaining, stretching: a' *ruigheachd* or *rioghachd* air, *stretching his hand towards it.* (from righe.)

Ruin, rûėn, *gen.* and *plur.* of rùn.

Ruinn, rŭėnn, *pre. pron.* to us, against us, meddling with us; thuirt e *ruinn, he said to us.*

Ruinnse, rŭėsh′-shå, *n. m.* an enormous ——; any thing long; *v.* ———.

Ruinnsear, rĕŭnnsh′-aėr, *n. m.* scourer.

Ruintean, rûėnjt′-un, *n. pl.* intentions, &c.

Ruisg, rûshg, *n. pl.* fleeces, peelings; *gen.* of rosg, of eye-lids; *v.* peel, make bare, disclose; gall, denude, unsheathe; *rùisg* am buntàta, *peel the potatoes*; *rùisg* a' chraobh, *strip the tree*; *rùisg* do claidheamh, *unsheathe thy sword*; *rùisg* e ghàirdean, *he made bare his arm*; na *rùisg* do dhearas do d' nàimhaid, *reveal* or *disclose not, your defects to your enemy.*

Ruisgte, rûshg′-tyå, *pt.* peeled, unsheathed, stript, made bare; disclosed, revealed

Ruit, ruėjt, *n. f.* a rakish female.

Ruiteach, } ruėch′-tyach, *adj.* florid,
Ruithteach, } ruddy, apt to run, slippery, as small shot; flushing and blushing; apt to blush; bha e *ruiteach, he was florid. Bible.*

Ruitear, rùėjt′-åėr, *n. m.* a rake, abandoned man.

Ruith, ruėch, *v.* run; flow as a stream; *ruith* e, *he ran*; *ruith* an fhuil, *the blood flowed*; melt, as lead, *or* suet; speak fast; chase, distill, flow, overrun, *or* go over superficially; *ruith* e as mo dhèigh, *he chased me*; a' *ruith* ceudtarruinn, *distilling low wines*; *ruith* orra, *run superficially over them, adjust* or *serve them once*; *ruith* a mach, *be exhausted,* or *expended*; *pt.* chasing, running, distilling, adjusting.

Ruith, ruėch, *n. f.* a race, a rate, full speed; esan na *ruith, he at full speed*; air an *ruith* cheudhna, *at the same rate*;

air a' cheart *ruith, at the same rate precisely*; dyssentery; fast speaking *or* talking; *ruith*-fhola, *hemorrhoids, Bible*; treatment, slight arrangement; line, parallel, the same way; thoir an aon *ruith* dhaibh, *give them the same treatment*; thoir *ruith* orra, *give them a slight adjustment, put them in somewhat of order*; air *ruith* an tighe so, *in a line with this house, parallel with this house*; thoir *ruith* cladaich dhith, *run her aground*; *ruith* na teanga, *a complete scold*; thoir an aon *ruith* dhaibh, *serve them all alike, make no distinction.*

RUM, rûm, *n. m.* room, space, place, *Teut.*

RUMACH, rŭm'-ach, RUNNACH, rŭnn'-ach, } *n. f.* a slimy tough kind of marsh or puddle.

RUMALACHD, rŭm'-all-achg, *n. f.* spaciousness.

RUMAIL, rŭm'-al, *adj.* spacious, roomy.

RUMP, rŭmp, *n. m.* the rump. *Teutonic.*

RUN, rhûn, *n. m.* secret intention, mystery, secret; tha *rùn* an Tighearn aig an dream d'an eagal e, *the secret of the Lord is with them that fear him*; inclination, secret resolution, disposition, intention; dè tha d' *rùn, what do you mean?* dè n *rùn* am bheil e dhuit, *how is he disposed towards you?* tha e an *rùn* nan tuadh dhomh, *he would wish to cut me down, (with the Lochaber axe,* lit.); na innis do *rùn* do nàmhaid ghorach na do charaid glic, *disclose not your purpose to a foolish foe, or a wise (cunning) friend*; *Welsh,* rhin; a beloved object; tha a *rùn, yes, my love!* mo *rùn* a tighinn, *my love coming*; *rùn*-phairteach, *communicating secrets*; *rùn*-phàirtich, *communicate secrets.*

RUNACH, rûn'-ach, *adj.* loved, secret.

RUNAICH, rûn'-èch, *v.* intend, mean.

RUNAIRE, rûn'-ăer-à, *n. m.* secretary.

RUNRACH, rûn'-rach, *n. m.* a search.

RUNRAICH, rûn'-rèch, *v.* search, explore.

RUSG, rhûsg, *n. m.* peeling, rind, skin, fleece.

RUSGACH, rûsg'-ach, *a.* fleecy, husky.

RUSGADH, rûsg'-Ă, *pt.* peeling, stripping, fleecing, making bare; driving thatch of.

RUSGAIRE, rûsg'-ur-à, *n. c.* a strong brawny person, that does a deal of work coarsely.

RUT, rûtt, *v.* rust, corrode. *Arran.*

RUTA, rût'-a, *n. m.* a ram, reith, *Arran.*

RU, rû, *n. m.* herb, rue, *Fren.*; *Teutonic.*

S

S, s, the fifteenth letter of the Gaelic alphabet; named by the Irish Sail, *or* Suil, the willow-tree.

'S, contraction of agus, *or* is, and; *'s* their thu, *and thou shalt say*; *'s* mòr t-fhacal, *and ostentatious is thy word*; 2d, for anns; *'s* a cheò, (for anns a cheò,) *in the mist, in amazement*; 3d, for *verb,* am, art, is, &c.; *'s* i s è, *'s* esan, *it is she, it is he, it is he himself*; 4th, *'s* contraction of the prefix *ais*; as, braigh, aisbraigh, *i. e.* spraigh, burst, &c.

SA, sà, *emphatic adjective,* (for so, se,) used thus, dhomh-*sa,* dhith-*se, to me myself, to her herself*; 2d, used with verbs, dh'innsinn-se dhuibh, *I would have told you*; 3d, *cont.* for anns a, in the; as, *'sa* ghleann, (for anns a ghleann,) *in the glen*; 'sa', for the same before an aspiration; *'sa'* mhaidinn, *in the morning*; 4th, (for anns a,) in his, in her, in it.

SABAID, for tabaid, fray, row. *Skye*; *Lw.*

SABAID, sâb'-ăj, *n. f.* the sabbath, sunday.

SABAIDEACH, sâb'-ăjj-ach, *adj.* sabbatical.

SABH, sâv, *v.* saw, cut with a saw; *n. m.* a saw; *sabh*-dùirn, *hand-saw*; *sabh*-mòr, *whip-saw*; salve, ointment; *sabh*-shùl, *eye-salve. Bible.*

SABHADAIR, sâv'-add-àèr, *n. m.* a sawyer; ri *sàbhadaireachd,* a' sàbhadh, *sawing, cutting.*

SABHAILL, sâv'-ăly', *v.* save, preserve.

SABHAILTE, sâv'-alyt'-à, *adj.* safe, preserved

SABHAILTEACHD, sâv'-alyt'-achg, *n. f.* safety, a saving disposition, safe state *or* condition.

SABHALL, săv'-ull, *n. m.* a barn, barns; saibhlean, pronounced sev- *or* ssìv'-llun; murdered, saŏèl'-un.

SABHALADH, sâv'-al-Ă, *pt.* saving, rescuing; retrenchment; is mòr an *sabhaladh* sin, *that is a great retrenchment,* or *saving.*

SABHD, sâv-ud, *n. m.* straying; cù *saibhd, stray dog*; chaidh e air *sabhd, he strayed away*;—a lie. *North.*

SABHADAIRE, săv'-ud-ur-à, *n. m.* stroller; —liar. *North.*

SABHS, săvs, *n. m.* a sauce, fish-sauce, *sabhs* èisg; *gravy, juice of meat.*

SABHSAIR, săv'-săèr, *n. m.* a sausage.

SAC, săchg, *n. m.* a sack; load; (all Lang.)

SACAICH, săchg'-èch, *v.* press in a bag, load.

SACANTA, sachg'-annt-a, *adj.* thickset, squat.

SACHASAN, sach'-as-an, *n. f.* sand-eel, (siolag.) *North.*

SACRAMAID, sâchg'-ram-ăj, *n. f.* sacrament

SAD, sad, *v.* dash upon, as dust; 'ga *sadadh* am shuilean, *dashing it in my eyes*; *n.* dust, dislike.

SADACH, sad'-ach, *n. m.* meal-dust.

SAGART, SAGAIRT } sag'-ărjt, *n. m.* a Roman, *or* any priest.

SAGAIRTEACHD, săg' arjt-achg, *n. f.* priesthood.

Sagairteil, săg′-arjt-al, *adj.* priestly.

Saibhear, sīv′-ăr, *n.f.* a common sewer.

Saibhir, ssīv′-ėr′, *adj.* plentiful; rich, opulent, pretty full, as clothes; còta *saibhir, a coat pretty full,* or *easy coat*; bliadhna *shaibhir, a plentiful year*; duine *saibhir, a wealthy* or *rich man.*

Saibhlean, ssīv- *or* sev′-llun, *n.f.* barns.

Saibhreas, ssīv′-rus, *n. m.* plenty; wealth.

Saidealach, săjj′-al-ach, *a.* bashful. *Ir.*

Saidh, saŏe-yh′, *n. f.* part of any instrument that is in the handle; post; *saidh*-dheiridh, *stern-post*; *saidh*-thoisich, *bow-post.*

Saidse, săjjsh′-ȧ, *n. m.* a crash, fall, noise.

Saidseach, săjjsh′-ach, *n.f.* beggars' mattle.

Saidsear, săjj′-er, *n.m.* a heavy clumsy man

Saigean, săėg′-aėn, *n. m.* squat fellow.

Saigeanach, sâėg′-ăėn-ach, *adj.* fat, thick-set, and little; *n. m.* man so conditioned.

Saigh, ssī-y′, *n. f.* a bitch; (galla,) *North*; *n. m.* coal-fish; *saighean* mòr, *coal-fish, next in size to ugsa,* stenlock.

Saighd, ssījj, *v.* dart, pop, bolt, *or* dash in, *or* forward; inflict pain, *or* pang; thug e *saighdeadh* ad a stigh, *he bolted* or *popped, darted in.*

Saighde, ssījj′-ȧ, *n. pl.* arrows, of an arrow.

Saighdeach, saŏjj′-ach, *a.* piercing, arrowy.

Saighdear, saŏjj′-ăėr, *n. m.* soldier, arrower; a hero; is tu an *saighdear, thou art the hero*! *saighdear*-coise, *a foot soldier, an infantry man*; *saighdear*-fairge, *a marine*; *Welsh,* sawdwr.

Saighdearachd, sījj′-ar′-achg, *n. f.* soldiery; heroism.

Saighdearail, saŏjj′-ar-al, *adj.* military, brave.

Saighead, sī²′.ud, *n. f.* an arrow; a stitch.

Sail, sa′l, *n. f.* a log of wood, joist.

Sail, sâ′l, *n. m.* salt water.

Sail, sâ′l, *n. f.* a heel; sàiltean, *heels.*

Sail-bhuinn, să′l′-vŭėnn, *n. f.* groundsel.

Sailche, sul′-ėch-ȧ, *n. f.* dirtiness; more dirty.

Sail-ghille, sâ′l′-ghėlly′-ȧ, *n. m.* footman.

Saileag, sâ′l′-ag, *n. f.* a heel-step.

Saill, saėly′, *v.* salt, season with salt; *n f.* suet, fat; *sàill* nan dubhan, *fat of the kidneys.*

Sailleach, saėlly′-ach, *adj.* fat, full of suet.

Sailleadair, săėlly′-ad-ar′, *n. m.* salter, curer.

Saillear, săėlly″-aėr, *n.m.* a salt, salt-dish.

Saillte, săėlly′-tyȧ, *pt.* salted, seasoned.

Saillteachd, săėlly″-tyachg, *n. f.* saltness.

Sailm, saŏl-um, *n. m.* a decoction, *Irish*; *n. pl.* psalms; also *gen.* of salm, a psalm.

Saimh, sīv, *n f.* luxury, ease.

Saimh, săėv, *n. pl.* twins, a pair. *Irish.*

Saimheachd, săėv′-achg, *n. f.* gross indulgence.

Sainnseal, senn′-shal, *n. m.* a handsel.

Saith, sâėch, *n. f.* belly-full, satiety. *Islay.*

Saitheachd, săėch′-achg, *n. f.* satiety.

Saiste, sashj′-ė, *n. m.* the herb, sage. *N.*

Sal, săll, *n. m.* wax of the ear, slimy dirt.

Salach, sal′-ach, *adj.* dirty, nasty, foul, poxed.

Salachadh, săll′-ach-ă, *pt.* polluting, defiling.

Salachar, săll′-ach-ar, *n. m.* dirt, filth, ordure.

Salaich, sal′-ėch, *v.* defile, pollute, pox; soil; *shalaich* thu am paipear, *you soiled the paper.*

Salaichte, sal′-ėch-tyȧ, *pt.* defiled, poxed.

Salann, sall′-unn, *n. m.* salt; *gen.* salainn.

Salltair, sâllt′-ėr, *n. f.* chalder, 16 bolls.

Salm, sal-um, *n. f.* a psalm, anthem.

Salmach, sal′-um-ach, *adj.* psalm tune.

Salmadair, sal′-um-ad-ăėr, *n. m.* psalmist.

Salmair, sal′-um-aėr, *n. m.* precentor.

Saltair, săllt′-ėr, *v.* trample, tread.

Saltairt, sallt′-ărjt, *n. f.* act of treading, *or* trampling; *pt.* treading, trampling, walking upon.

Samh, sáv, bad smell arising from a sick person, or a dirty hot place; sorrel; ag itheadh *saimh, eating sorrel*;—a savage, *Mackenzie.*

Samhach, sàv′-ach, *adj.* quiet, still, calm; feasgar *sàmhach, a calm,* or *still evening*; bithibh *sàmhach* agus tuigibh gur mise Dia, *be still and know that I am God, Bible*; fan *sàmhach, keep settled, keep quiet.*

Samhach, sáv′-ach, *n. f.* an axe, *or* hatchet, (tuadh,) *Sk.*; *Lew.*; the haft of such. *B.*

Samaircean, sáv′-aerk-aėn, *n. m.* primrose. *Ir.*

Samhanach, sáv′-an-ach, *n. m.* a savage; chuireadh tu eagal air na *samhanaich, you would frighten the very savages. Is.*

Samhan-aithrich, sáv-an-ăėr′-ėch, *n. m.* skin rubbed off in one's sleep; cause, *or* object of regret.

Samhchair, sáv′-chăr′, *n. m.* quietness.*Sm.*

Samhlach, sáv′-lach, *adj.* typical.

Samhlachadh, sáv′-lach-ă, *pt.* likening; laying something bad to one's charge.

Samhlachail, sáv′-lach-al, *a.* emblematical.

Samhlachas, sáv′-lach-as, *n. m.* comparison.

Samhlachd, sáv′-lachg, *n. f.* comparability.

Samhladh, sáv′-lă, *n. m.* type, form, proverb.

Samhlaich, sáv′-llėch, *v.* compare, liken *v. n.* lay to one's charge; na *samhlaich* a leithid sin riumsa, *don't lay such things* *to my charge*; as the Scotch say, "don't even such to me."

Samhna, sáv'-nà, *gen.* of samhainn.

Samhnag, } sav'-nag, *n. f.* a bon-fire, on **Samhnach**, } the 12th of November.

Samhnach, sáv'-nach, *n. f.* Macdonald of the Isles, deer-park; winter-park.

Samhnaich, sáv'-nnèch, *v.* winter.

Samhnachan, sáv'-nach-an, *n. m.* a trout.

Samhrach, sáv'-rach, *a.* } relating to **Samhrachail**, sáv'-rach-al, } summer; summer-like.

Samhail, sáv'-ul, *n. m.* likeness. *B.*

Samhailt, sáv'-aljt', *n. m.* likeness, like; do mhac *samhailt, your precise resemblance—the son of your likeness*, literally.

Samhuinn, sáv'-ènn, *n. f.* Hallow-tide, the feast of All Souls; o Bhealltainn gu *samhuinn, from May day to Hallow-day.*

Sampuill, sàmp'-ull, *n. m.* example; bithidh tu ad bhall-*sampuill, you will be an example. B.*

San, sán, (for anns an); '*san* tigh, (for anns an tigh), *in the house*; 2d, emphatic *pron. his, her, its*; as, a chuid-san, *his share* or *property*; a cuid-se, *her property*; eich-*san, his horses.*

Sanas, sán'-us, *n. m.* a friendly hint, *or* warning; bheir e *sanas* le 'chois, *he will give a hint with his foot*; (bruididh e le a chois); mar *shanas* do gach tìr, *as a warning to every country. Bible.*

Sanasail, sán'-as-al, *adj.* giving warning.

Sannt, sánnt, *n. m.* greed, covetousness, lust; esan a dh' fhuathaichias *sannt, he that hates covetousness*; inclination, desire; ma tha' *shannt* sin air, *if he has a desire for that.*

Sanntach, sánnt'-ach, *a.* greedy, covetous.

Sanntachd, sánnt'-achg, *n. f.* covetousness.

Sanntaich, sánnt'-èch, *v.* covet, lust after, incline; ma *shanntaich* tu, *if you incline* or *please*; a' *sanntachadh, coveting, lusting after.*

Sanntaire, sannt'-èr-à, *n.m.* covetous man.

Saobh, sãov, *n. m.* hypocrisy; *v.* err; *saobh* shruth, *eddy-tide*; *shaobh* iad, *they erred*; *adj.* erroneous, eddying.

Saod, sãod, *n. m.* a prosperous train, condition; good humour; cuir *saod* air, *put it in a likely* or *prosperous train*; dè 'n *saod* a th'ort, *how do you do?* gun *saod* air dol as, *without an expedient to escape*; feumaidh sinn *saod* a chur air, *we must devise an expedient to accomplish it.*

Saodaich, sãod'-èch, *v.* drive cattle to pasture, &c.; coax away in good humour.

Saodar, *a.* } sãod'-ur, in good humour, on **Saodmhor**, } good terms; well-planned.

Saoghal, são'-ul, *n. m.* the world, universe, life, lifetime; feadh an t-*saoghal, throughout the world*; fad do *shaoghail, during your lifetime*; *saoghal* fad dhuit, *long may you live*; droch *shaoghal, bad times*; mo chuid do'n t-*saoghal, my all! my dearest dear!* ma gheibh mi *saoghal, if I live*; gu *saoghal* nan *saoghal, henceforth and for ever*; an *saoghal* salach, *the deceitful world!* air son an t-*saoghail, for the whole universe.*

Saoghalach, são'-al-ach, *a.* long-lived.

Saoghalachd, são'-al-achg, *n. f.* long life.

Saoghalta, são'-ăltt'-à, *adj.* worldly-minded.

Saoghaltachd, são'-alt-achg, *n. f.* worldliness.

Saoibhir, sãoèv'-èr, *n. m.* St. Kilda skate; also a mispronunciation of saibhir ssìv-èr.

Saoidh, sùe'-y', *n. m.* a hero, warrior; *saoidhean* Mhanuis, *the warriors of Magnus*; *adj.* brave.

Saoidhean; see Saigh, coal-fish.

Saoil, são'l, *v.* suppose, think, imagine, seem; *shaoil* mi, *I thought* or *imagined*; an *saoil* thu, *think you? do you imagine? shaoil* e gun nàmhaid a bh'ann, *he thought he was an enemy*; nach *saoil* thu, *do you not think? shaoil* mise, *I supposed*; an *saoil* sibhse, *do ye suppose? shaoileadh* duine, *one should suppose*; ma *shaoileas* tusa, *if you judge*, or *think.*

Saoilsinn, são'l'-shènn, } *part.* suppos- **Saoiltinn**, sao'l'-tyènn, } ing, imagining, thinking, judging.

Saoire, sãoèr'-à, *deg.* saor, na's *saoire, cheaper*; *n. f.* preference in cheapness; cheapness.

Saoiread, sãoèr'-ud, *n. f.* degree of cheapness.

Saoirthrich, sãoèv'-èch, *v.* toil, be at pains put yourself to the trouble; an ni a *saoithrich* mi air a shon, *what I toiled for*; *shaoithrich* mi a nuas, *I put myself to the trouble of coming down*; thug thu orm *saoithreachadh, you put me to the trouble of coming*; *saoithrich* am fearann, *labour the ground. Bible.*

Saoithreach, sãory''-ach, *gen.* of saothair; *adj.* fatiguing; at great pains; gu *saoithreach, at pains*; also saoithreachail.

Saor, sãor, *adj.* cheap, a good bargain; buntàta *saor, cheap potatoes*; free, at liberty, not enslaved; clann na mnà *saoire, the children of the free woman*; exempt, free, not guilty; *saor* o'n mhionnan, *exempt from the oath*; free from expense, clear of blame *or* aspersion; *saor* o'n aladh sin, *free,* or *clear of that aspersion*; bheir mise a mach *saor* thu, *I shall take you out free of expenses*; bheir mi dhà gu *saor, I shall give him freely*;—clach *shaor, free-stone. N.*; *v.* free of aspersion *or* calumny; purge; *saor* am boirreannach so, *free* or *clear this woman from scandal*; save, absolve, acquit; cha *saor* mi thu, *I will not acquit* or *absolve you. B.*; *conj.* except, save; *saor* o dhithisd, *except two, save two*; as an *adj.* used generally before the noun; *saor*-thobhartas, *free-offering.*

Saor, sãor, *n. m.* a carpenter, house-carpenter; Mac an t-*saoir, the carpenter's son—the surname, Mackintyre*; *saor*-bhàtan, *a boat-builder*; *saor*-mhuileann, *mill-wright*; *saor*-luinneas, na loingeas, *ship-carpenter*; *saor*-chuidhlean, *wheel-wright*; tuadh an lamh an t-*saoir, an axe in the hand of the carpenter. B.*

Saoradh, sãor′-Ă, *pt.* freeing, exempting; *n. m.* absolution, freedom, liberation.

Saoranach, sãrr′-an-ach, *n. m.* a freeman.

Saorsa, sēars′-â, *n. f.* freedom, liberty; *saorsa* o'n olc, *freedom from sin*; cheapness; *saorsa* an nì so, *the cheapness of this thing*; is mòr an t-suim air an do cheannaich mise an t-*saorsa* so, *great is the sum for which I purchased this freedom. B.*

Saorsachd, sãors′-achg, *n. f.* abatement.

Saorsainneachd, sãor′-sènn-achg, *n. f.* carpenter's trade; working with carpenter's tools.

Saothair, são′-èr, *n. f.* toil, pains, labour, work; le mòran *saothair, with great pains* or *toil*; deanaibh *saothair, labour* or *toil*; gabh *saothair, bestow pains, toil for it*; luach saoithreach, *what is worth one's while* or *pains*; cha'n fhiach dhuit do *shaothair, it is not worth your while, worth your pains*; air bheagan *saothair, easily, without much pain*; tàileamh mo *shaoithreach, the result of my toil*; ann an *saothair, in great travail*; *saor*-chloinne, *travail, labour of childbed*; a dh'aindeoin do *shaoithreach, after all your labour*, or *pains.*

Saothraich, sãor′-èch, *n. m.* labourer. *B.*

Saiphir, saff′-èr, *n. m.* sapphire. *Bible.*

Sar, sâr, *n. m.* a true hero, a brave warrior; cha robh eagal air *sàr* riamh, *a true hero never feared the face of clay*; chualas le *sàr* a ghuth, *a hero heard his voice*; a *shàir, thou hero*! *Oss.*; a tick, *or* sheep-louse; oppression. *H. S.*; *adj.* complete, wholly, completely abandoned; *sàr* ghaisgeach, *a complete hero*; *sàr* chù, *a dog every inch of him*; *sàr* shlaightire, *a most abandoned villain*—placed always before the nouns.

Sarachadh, sâr′-ach-Ă, *pt.* oppressing, wronging, annoying, distressing, harrassing; 'gam *shàrachadh, oppressing* or *harassing me*; *n. m.* oppression.

Sarachail, sâr′-ach-al, *a.* oppressive, distressing, harassing, burdensome.

Saraich, sâr′-èch, *v.* distress, oppress, burden, harass; overcome, wear out, fatigue, deal unjustly with, do violence to, use ill.

Saraichte, sâr′-èch-tyâ, *pt.* oppressed, exhausted, over-fatigued, overcome, beat.

Sardail, sârd′-al, *n. m.* sprat sgadan-gearr.

Sas, sâs, *n. m.* bondage, custody, durance; tha e an *sàs, he is in custody, he is captivated*; air dhà a bhi an *sàs, having happened to be in durance*; cause, means; is math an *sàs* thu fhéin air sin, *you are a fit cause* or *means for that yourself,* (never used otherwise); *v.* lay hold of. *H. S.*

Sasag, săs′-ag, *n. f.* straw-chair. *North.*

Sasachd, săs′-achg, *n. f.* satiety. *Bible*; (sath.)

Sasaich, sâs′-èch, *v. n.* satiate, attack, fix; a' *sàsachadh* na feòla, *satisfying the lusts of the flesh*; *shàsaich* e orm, *he attacked me tooth and nail.*

Sasda, sâsd′-a, *adj.* saucy, contemptuous.

Sasdachd, sâsd′-achg, *n. f.* sauciness, pride.

Sasunn, sas′-unn, *n. m.* England.

Sasunnach, săss′-unn-ach, *n. m.* an Englishman; *adj.* English, belonging to, *or* of England.

Sath, sâ, **Saith**, sâèch, *n. f.* bellyful, plenty, abundance, enough; cha'n ith a *shàith* ach an gù, *none but a dog eats a bellyful, to satiety.*

Sath, sâ, *v.* transfix, fix, thrust; *shàth* e dhubhain annam, *he transfixed his clutches in me*; *shàth* e ann e, *he thrust it into it* or *him*; *sàthar* sleagh throimh, *he shall be pierced through, with a spear*; *sath* a stigh i, *push it in.*

Sathach, sâ′-hach, *adj.* satiated, filled.

Sathadh, sâ′-Ă, *n. m.* a thrust, push, shove, thug e *sàthadh, he gave a thrust*; *pt.* thrusting, pushing.

Sb, sc, for most words thus beginning, see Sp, sg.

Scorr, sbairn, see Sgòrr, spàirn.

Se, shè, *per. pron.* he; tha *sè, he is*; 2d, *n. c.* and *adj.* six; *sè* daoine, *six men.*

Sea, shēă, see Sè, six.

Seabh, **Seubh**, shèv, *v.* stray.

Sheabhaltrach, shév′-alt-rach, *n. m.* straggler.

Seabhach, shév′-ach, *a.* trim. *H. S.*

Sheabhag, see Seobhag.

Seac, shyúchg, shechg, *v.* wither, decay; *sheac*-mharbh e i, *he killed her outright*; tha e air *seacadh, it is withered.*

Seacachd, shyúchg′-achg, *n. f.* withered state, *or* condition of any thing.

Seacaich, shyúchg′-èch, *v.* wither, fade.

Seach, shyach, *n. m.* turn; gach aon ma *seach, each in his turn, each alternately*; *adv. conj.* past, gone by, away, aside; rather than, rather than that; besides, beyond; *seach* an dorus, *past the door* cha d' theid e *seach* so, *he will not pass this*; *seach* aon eile, *rather than any one else*; *seach* leigeil dà dol *seachad, rather than that he should pass by*; do dh' aon *seach* aon, *to the one more than to another*; *seach* a chèile, *one from another*; fear *seach* fear, *one man more than another*; cha n-aithne dhomh aon *seach* a chéile, *I know not one from the other*; *seach* innseadh air, *rather than inform against him*; *seach* a chéile, *one past the other*; cha d' théid e *seach* am baile so, *he will not go beyond this vil'age*; in preference to; *seach* e fhéin a mhilleadh, *in preference to spoiling himself*; chaidh e ma *seach* orm, *I missed it—it did not occur to me.*

Seachad, shyach'-ad, *adv.* aside, by, out of the way; along, onward, forward; a dol *seachad, passing by,* or *along*; an latha air dol *seachad, the day passing*; a' cur *seachad,* na h'ùine, *passing the time*; cuir *seachad* so, *lay this bye*; *seachad* oirnn, *by us*; na cuir *seachad* ormsa e, *do not put it by me*; cuir *seachad* airgead, *hoard money*; theirig *seachad, pass by*; beyond, more; cha'n'eil *seachad* air fichead ann, *there is not beyond twenty in it altogether—more than twenty*; is math *seachad* e, *it is good to have it by, to be done of it*; a dol *seachad,* air t-ais is air t-aghaidh, *not calling, passing and repassing*; labhair, 'san dol *seachad, speak, when passing,* en passant; *seachad* air mìle, *more than,* or *beyond, a mile,* or *a thousand*; *Inter. seachad*! *seachad*! *by with you*! *away with you*!

Seachainn, shyech'-ênn, *v.* avoid, shun, keep at distance from; *seachainn* an t-olc, *avoid evil*; dispense with, spare; an *seachainn* thu so, *can you spare,* or *dispense with this*? mholainn duit mise a *sheachnadh, I would recommend to you, to keep at arm's-length from me.*

Seachanta, shyech'-ant-a, *adj.* to be avoided; latha *seachanta* na bliadhna, *Childermas-day.*

Seachantach, shyech'-ant-ach, *adj.* avoidable, guarded against; *seachantach* air òl, *guarded against drunkenness* or *debauchery.*

Seachantachd, shyech'-ant-achg, *n. f.* avoidableness; continual precaution to avoid.

Seachd, shyăchg, *n. c.* and *adj.* seven; *seachd*-fillte, *seven-fold*; *seachd*-thaobhach, *heptagon*; *adj.* heptagonal; an t-*seachd*-reultach, *the pleiades.*

Seachamh, shyăchg'-uv, *adj.* seventh.

Seachd-deug, shyăchg'-dyāg, *n. a.* seventeen.

Seachd-mhios, shyăchg'-vhēs, *n. m.* September.

Seachdar, shyachd'-ar, *n.c.* } seven people,
Seachdnar, shyachg'-nar, } *or* any thing.

Seachduinn, shyăchg'-ênn, *n. f.* a week, (seachd-ùine); *seachduinn* bho 'n diugh, *this day se'enight*; *seachduinn* bho 'n dè, *yesterday se'enight*; uair s'a t-*seachdainn, once a-week*; *seachduinn* ma seach, *a week about, a week in rotation*; gach darna *seachduinn, every alternate week.*

Seachlach, shyech'-llach, *n. f.* cow that calves only once in two years, *Lewis*; uairneach; a barren heifer of age to have a calf. *North.*

Seachlaimh, shyech'-lév, *a.* in store.

Seachnach, shyech'-nach, *adj.* shunning.

Seachnadh, shyech'-nĂ, *pt.* avoiding, shunning; *n. m.* sparing, act of avoiding *or* sparing.

Seachran, shyech'-ran, *n. m.* wandering, act of going astray; air *seachran, going astray, getting out of the proper path.*

Seachranach, shyech'-ran-ach, *adj.* wandering; reulta *seachranach, wandering stars, B.*; erring, straying; causing to err.

Seadh, shyaŏ-gh, *adv. inter.* yes, yea? just so, as you say; *seadh,* a Thighearna, *yea, Lord*! *yes, my Lord*! *seadh* gu dearbh, *yes, just so*! seadh! seadh! *just so*! *just so*! *truly*! *really*! *n. m.* meaning, interpretation; import, sense, purport; dè *seadh* dha, *what is the import* or *purport of it*? *seadh* na lice so fheòraich, *to inquire into the purport of this tombstone.*

Seadhach, shyaŏ'-ghach, } *adj.* containing
Seadhail, shyaŏ'-ghal, } much meaning *or* sense; important, weighty; seadhmhor, also.

Seagull, shyāg'-ull, *n. m.* rye; *g.* seaguill.

Seal, shyal, *n. m.* glimpse, spot, time.

Sealbh, shyâlv, *n. f.* possession; thugaibh dhomh *sealbh, give me possession. Bible.*

Sealbhach, shyalv'-ach, *adj.* lucky.

Sealbhachadh, shyălv'-ach-Ă, *pt.* possessing, enjoying, acquiring; winning.

Sealbhadair, shyav'-ad-ăer, *n. c.* possessor.

Sealbhag, shyalv-ag, *n. f.* sorrel, samh.

Sealbhaich, shyălv'-êch, *v.* possess, inherit.

Sealbhaichte, shyălv'-êch-tya, *pt.* possessed, inherited.

Sealbhanaich, shyalv'-an-êch, *v.* throttle. *North.*

Sealbhar, shyalv'-ur, *adj.* possessing, lucky.

Sealg, shyălg, *v. n.* hunt, lay wait for, watch narrowly; *n. f.* a hunt, a chase, seilg.

Sealgair, shyălg'-ăer, *n. m.* a hunter, sneaker; sealgaireachd, *hunting, watching narrowly.*

Seall, shyall, *v.* see, behold, look.

Sealladh, shyall'-ă, *n. m.* vision, eyesight; chaill e a *shealladh, he lost his eyesight*; view, sight; fad mo *sheallaidh, the extent of my view*; a dol as an t-*sealladh, getting out of sight*; spectacle, apparition; a leithid do *shealladh, such a spectacle*; a réir an t-*sealladh* so uile, *according to all this vision. Bible.*

Sealltainn, shyall'-ttènn, *pt.* seeing, viewing.

Seam, shyèm, seum, *n. f.* an entreaty; an earnest petition; is ioma *seum* a thug mise air, *many an earnest request I made*; forbid, (seun.) *Lewis.*

Seama-guad, shém'-a-gŭăd, *n. m.* a quibble

Seamair, shém'-ĕr, *n. f.* wild clover; shamrock; breac le *seamair* is neoineanan, *bespangled* or *chequered with clover and daisies*; also seamrag.

Seamasan, shem'-as-an, *n. m.* stupid evasion, a quibble, *or* quirk, shuffling, sham.

Seamasanach, shem'-as-an-ach, *a.* evasive, tricky, absurd in the extreme.

Seamasanachd, shem'-as-an-achg, *n. f.* evasiveness, habits of shuffling, *or* quirking, quibbling, shamming.

Seamasanaich, shém'-as-an-èch, *v.* sham, shuffle, evade, coax one out of his right; 'gam *sheamasanachadh* air an dòigh sin, *quibbling* or *shamming me in that style.*

Seamh, shév, *n. f.* an enchantment to make one's friends prosper.

Seamhas, sév'-us, *n. m* good luck, prosperity.

Seamhsail, sévs'-ăl, *a.* lucky, fortunate.

Seamhsalachd, sévs'-al-achg, *n. f.* luckiness.

Seamsan, shéms'-an, *n. m.* sham, quibble to gain good time, *or* ends; a silly evasion; for seamasan, *i. e.* seumfhasan.

Seamlach, shem'-llach, *n. f.* a cow that allows another cow's calf to suckle her;—one that gives milk without a calf; a dupe, silly person; (from seum.)

Seamlachas, shem'-lach-as, *n. m.* an imposture.

Seamlaich, shem'-llèch, *v.* dupe, impose on; 'gam *sheamlachadh*-sa, *duping me, making a fool of me*; chuir thu an orra-*sheamlachais* orm, *you charmed me out of my wits, you duped me.*

Sean, shén, *adj.* old, aged, ancient; carson a bhios na h-aingidh beò, a dh'fhàsas iad *sean*, agus a bhios iad àrd ann an cumhachd, *wherefore do the wicked live, become old, and are high in power? Job* xxi. 7.; an *sean* sruthan sin, *that ancient stream*; o *shean, anciently, of old.*

Seanachaidh, shén'-ach-ė, *n. m.* reciter of tales; recorder; bha e 'na *sheanachaidh, he was recorder. Bible.*

Seanachd, shén'-achg, oldness. *Bible.*

Seanachar, shén'-ach-ar, *a.* old-fashioned. *Stew.*

Seanachas, shén'-ach-as, *n. m.* tradition; conversation, *or* talk of old stories, *or* ancient history; history, ancient history *or* biography.

Seanachasach, shén'-as-ach, *a.* conversible, having tales; traditionary; relating tales.

Seanadh, shén'-ă, *n. m.* a synod, senate.

Seanachrionta, shén'-a-chrènt-à, *a.* old fashioned, too wise for one's years.

Seanaighille, shen'-à-ghèlly-à, *n. m.* bachelor.

Seanair, shen'-aèr, *n. m.* grandfather, senator, elder; a *sheanairean* glic, *his senators wise. Bible.*

Seanaireachd, shén'-ar'-achg, *n. f.* presbytery. *Bible.*

Seanalair, shen'-a-lar', *n. m.* a general.

Seandachd, shénd'-achg, *n. f.* aged appearance, *or* look, agedness, oldness.

Seandaidh, shénd'-ė, *adj.* oldish, aged.

Seandaidheachd, shénd'-ė-achg, *n. f.* oldishness, agedness.

Seanfhacal, shén'-achg-al, *n. m.* proverb, adage, bye-word.

Seanfhaclach, shén'-achg-llach, *a.* proverbial.

Seang, shèng, *adj.* lank, slender; a choin *sheang, his lank dogs*; hungry looking.

Seangachd, shéng'-achg, *n. f.* slenderness.

Seangaich, shèng'-èch, *v.* get slender, *or* lank.

Seangan, shéng'-an, *n. m.* pismire, ant, emmet; an *seangan* beag, *the little pismire, emmet*, or *ant. Bible.*

Seangarra, shéng'-urr-à, *adj.* withered in person.

Seanghir, shéng'-hér, *n. m.* child in old age.

Seanmhair, shén'-văĕr, *n. f.* grandmother.

Seansgeul, shén'-skéll, *n. m.* legend.

Seansgeulach, shén'-skéll-ach, *a.* legendary.

Seantalamh, shén'-tal-uv, *n. m.* waste land, new land.

Seap, shèp, *v.* slink, sneak away, drag off, stealth; *sheap* e air falbh, *he slank off*; *n. m.* a tail hanging down, *H. S.*; skulking *or* sneaking out of battle.

Seapach, shèp'-ach, *adj.* slinking, sly; *n. f.* a sly, slinking female.

Seapaire, shèp'-ur-à, *n. m.* a sly, sneaking fellow; a poltroon, deserter.

Seapaireachd, shèp'-ăĕr-achg, *n. f.* slinking.

Searach, shèr'-ach, *n. m.* six month old beast.

Searamhach, shèr'-ráv-ach, *adj.* six-oared; *n. f* a six-oared galley, a felucca.

Searbaid, sherb′-aj, *n.m.* boat-thwart, tota.

Searbh, sherrv, *adj.* sour, tart, bitter; measan *searbh, bitter fruits*; pungent, acrid; tha e *searbh, it is pungent* or *acrid*; disagreeable, disgusting; gnothach *searbh, a disagreeable business*; tha mi *searbh* dheth, *I am disgusted with it*; 'nuair a bu *shearbh* leam éisdeachd ris, *when I found it intolerable to listen to him.*

Searbhachd, sherv′-achg, *n. f.* bitterness.

Searbhadas, sher′-ad-as, *n. m.* disgust, dislike.

Searbhag, sherv′-ag, *n. f.* refuse of liquids, acid.

Searbhdaich, shèrd′-ėch, *v.* disgust, tease, embitter; *shearbhdaich* e mi, *he teased* or *disgusted me*; *shearbhdaich* iad mi, *they annoyed* or *teased me, they embittered my life*; searbhdaichte, *teased, embittered.*

Searbhanta, sherv′-ant-a, *n. f.* servant-maid. *French.*

Searbhantachd, sherv′-ant-achg, *n. f.* service, office of a maid.

Seardair, shèrd′-àèr, *n. m.* hand towel, drudge; a' brath *seardair* a' dheanadh dhim, *meaning to make me his slave* or *drudge.*

Searg, shergg, *v.* wither, decay, fade, shrivel; *v. n.* pine away; *shearg* na lusan, *the flowers* or *herbs faded,* or *withered*; tha an duine sin a *searg* air falbh, *that man is pining away*; *n. m.* a shrivelled *or* decayed person. *H.*

Seargach, shergg′-ach, *a.* evanescent, fading

Seargaire, shergg′-ur-à, *n m.* pining person

Seargadh, shergg′-Ă, *pt.* fading; pining.

Seargte, sherg′-tyå, *pt.* withered, faded.

Searmoin, sher′-mènn, *n. f.* a sermon, discourse, lecture, pleading; *N.* searmaid.

Searmonaich, sher′-mènn-ėch, *v.* preach, lecture, discourse; deliver a discourse.

Searmonaiche, sher′-mun-ėch-à, *n. m.* preacher.

Searr, shyàrr, *n. m.* a shearing hook, sickle; corran, *Macdonald*; colt, *Sh.*; *v.* reap, cut, hash.

Searrach, shyarr′-ach, *n. m.* foal, colt.

Searrag, shyarr′-ag, *n. m.* a bottle. *Arg.*

Searraigh, shyārr′-ė, *n f.* colewort. *Irish.*

Seas, shās², *v.* stand, stop; an *seas* thu am fhainuis, *shalt thou stand in my presence?* maintain, endure, support; cò a *sheasas* tu, *who shall support you? seas* an còir, *maintain their rights, B.*; a dh' aindeoin cò a *sheasadh* tu, *in defiance to all that will take your part*; cha 'n urrainn mi so a *sheasadh, I cannot endure this*; *seasaidh* mise thu an còir 'san eucòir, *I will support you, whether in the right or wrong*!!! (THE STERLING, OLD HIGHLAND CHIEFTAINS' CREED.)

Seasach, shăs′-ach, *adj.* steadfast, firm.

Seasadh, shās²′-Ă, } *n. m.* standing posture; 'na *sheasamh, he standing*; 'na *seasamh, she standing*; *pt.* enduring, maintaining, &c.
Sheasamh, shās²′-uv, }

Seasaireachd, shās′-aėr-achg, *n.f.* penance in church.

Seasg, shăsg, *adj.* without milk, as a female; barren, unprolific; ni 'sam bith *seasg* ad thìr, *any thing barren in thy land, B.*; *n. m.* barrenness, sedge, water-sedge; a' buain *seasg, cutting sedge.*

Seasgach, shăsg′-ach, *n. m.* farrow cattle.

Seasgaire, shăsg′-ur-à, *n. m.* lazy person.

Seasgaireachd, shăsg′-ur′-achg, *n. f.* indulgence in ease; quietness, peace.

Seasgar, shăsg′-ur, *adj.* quiet, comfortable, at ease, as weather, settled; bi *seasgar, be quiet*; fan *seasgar, keep quiet.*

Seasglach, shăsg′-llăch, *n. f.* a barren cow

Seasmhach, shās′-ach, *a.* steady, settle.

Seasmhachd, shās′-achg, *n. f.* firmness, settled state, as of weather; stability, steadiness.

Seathadh, shé′-Ă, *adj.* the sixth.

Seathnar, shèn′-ar, *n. c.* six persons *or* kinds.

Seic, shăėchg, *n. f.* manger, *North*; see Seich.

Seiceal, shăchg′-ul, *n. f.* heckle. *Scotch.*

Seiche, shăch′-à, *n. f.* a hide; *v.* skin.

Seicheadair, shăch′-ad-aėr, *n. m.* a currier, skinner.

Seichearnach, shăch′-arn-ach, *n. f.* tan-work.

Seiceil, shăchg′-ėl, *v.* dress flax; beat *or* scold lustily.

Seiclear, shăchg′-laėr, *n. m.* flax-dresser.

Seid, shăjj, *n. f.* plethora, tympany, swelling in a person from luxurious living and deep potations; nach ann a tha 'n t-*sèid, how the fellow is puffed up with good living! v.* blow, become a storm; *shéid* e, is *shéid* e, *it blew and it blew, it blew into a hurricane*; instigate, prompt to evil, puff; is tusa a tha 'ga *shéideadh, it is you that instigate him*; breathe; *shéid* e an cuineinibh a shròine anail na beatha, *he breathed into his nostrils the breath of life. B.*

Seid, shăjj, *n. f.* a complete bellyful, surfeit; fhuair e a *sheid, he got his bellyful*; pallet, couch; na laidhe air *seid, sleeping,* or *lounging on a pallet.*

Seideadh, shăjj′-Ă, *pt.* blowing, puffing; *n. m.* storm.

Seidhir, shăr, *n. f.* a chair, *North.*; (*Fr.*)

Seidire, shăjj′-ėr-a, *n. m.* a swell, puffed fellow.

Seidrich, shăjj′-rėch, *n. f.* hissing of serpents, &c.

Seidte, shăjj′-tyå, *pt.* blown, puffed.

Seilbh, shālv, *n. f.* possession; a beast *or* living creature in possession; gach *seilbh* a th' agam, *every living creature I possess*; fhuair e *seilbh, he has got possession*; fad-*seilbh, infeoffment*; thoir fad-*seilbh, infeoff.*

Seile, shāl'-à, *n. f.* spittle; glaise-*sheile, water-brash.*

Seileach, shāl^2'-ach, *n. m.* the willow.

Seilear, shāl'-àėr, *n. m.* a cellar; *seilear* làir, *a vault*; *seilear*-dibhe, *spirit-cellar.*

Seileastar, shāl'-ast-ar, *n. m.* water-flags.

Seilg, shālėg, *n. f.* what is hunted *or* killed; *gen.* of sealg, a hunt, chase.

Seilicheag, shāl'-ė-chăg, *n. f.* snail, slug.

Seillean, shāly''-aėn, *n. m.* a heath-bee; a teasing repetition *or* request.

Seilleanach, shāly'-àėn-ach, *adj.* teasing, in request, importunate; full of bees.

Seimh, shèv, *a.* mild, gentle, calm, placid; 'na 's *séimhe, milder, more placid*; properly seumh, having no need of a marked *è*; *n. f.* mildness.

Seimheachd, shèv'-achg, *n. f.* mildness, placidity, gentleness, calmness, docility, good temper.

Seimheanachd, shèv'-aėn-achg, *n. f.* indulgence in ease, chambering, effeminate conduct.

Seimhich, shāv'-ėch, *v.* become calm, *or* gentle, abate as a storm, sooth.

Seineach, shen'-ech, *n. m.* a pad, donkey; cha mò orm thu, na 's mò air *seineach* a mhàthair, *I care as little for you as an old horse cares for his mother, (dam.)*

Seinilear, see Siomlair, Siomlainn, a chimney.

Seinn, shāėnn, *v.* sing, chant, warble; na h-eoin a' *sèinn, the birds warbling*; play upon a musical instrument; *shèinn* e an fhiodhull, *he played upon the violin*; air clàrsach, *on the harp*; ring a bell; *sèinn* an clag, *ring the bell*, (*Inverness*); gliong an clag, *ring the bell*, (*Argyle*); report, propagate a story; air a *shèinn* feadh na dùthcha, *reported ding-dang through the country*; *n. m. pt.* singing, art of singing, *or* playing on an instrument, melody, church music; droch *shèinn, bad church music* or *instrumental music.*

Seipinn, shāp^2'-ėnn, *n. f.* choppin, quart.

Seirbhe, shār''-à, *deg.* searbh, more tart, *or* disagreeable; *n. f.* tartness, bitterness; also seirbhead.

Seirbheachd, shār'-achg, *n. f.* bitterness, tartness, disagreeableness; discordance.

Seirbhis, shārvv''-ash, *n. f.* service, hire work.

Seirbhiseach, shārvv'-ăsh-ach, *n. c.* a servant.

Seirbhisich, shārv'-ăsh-ėch, *v.* serve, attend upon.

Seirc, shāėrk^2, *n. f.* affection, kindness.

Seircealachd, shā^{2}ėrk'-al-achg, *n. f* kindliness.

Seirceil, shāėrk^2'-al, *a.* affectionate, kind.

Seircire, shàerk'-àr-à, *n. m.* kindly person.

Seirgneach, shāe^{2}rg'-nyach, *n. c.* skeleton.

Seirm, shāė^{2}rm, *n. f.* tune, tone; tune of church-music; trim; cuir air *seirm, attune, tune, trim*; am bheil a' chlarsach air *seirm, is the harp in tune.*

Seirmeadair, shāėrm'-ad-àėr, *n. m.* precentor, tuner.

Seirmeil, shārm'-al, *a.* in trim, tuned, attuned; in a business-like manner.

Seirs, shèrs; see Seurs, charge, brandish.

Seisd, shāshjj, *v.* besiege; *n. m.* a siege; *séisd* a Dhoìre, *the siege of Londonderry*; air, tune; òran air an t-*séisde* cheudhna, *set to the same tune—a song set to the same air.*

Seisdeadh, shāshjj'-Ă, *pt.* besieging.

Seise, shāsh^2'-a, *n. m.* a match *or* equal in strength *or* valour; tha do *sheise* an taice riut, *you have your match in valour in contact with you—you have your match to do with*; barrachd 's a *sheise, more than his match.*

Seiseach, shāsh'-ach, *n. f.* a sofa. *North.*

Seisean, shāsh'-un, *n. m.* a session, season.

Seisear, shāsh'-ur, *n. f.* six persons.

Seisich, shāsh^2'-ėch, *v.* satisfy, (sathaich).

Seobhag, shyō'-ag, *n. f.* a hawk. *Bible.*

Seoc, shyôchg, *n. f.* plume or a helmet; veil; *seòc* air aghaidh, *a plume* or *veil on his face. Ossian.*

Seocalachd, shyôchg'-al-achg, *n. f.* portliness and tallness.

Seocail, shyôchg'-al, *adj.* portly and tall, having the port *or* gait of a gentleman *or* lady.

Seocair, shyôchg'-aėr, *n. f.* portly fellow.

Seod, shyôd, *n. m.* a hero; *seoid, heroes.*

Seoid, shóėj, *n. f. gen.* of seòd; heroes.

Seol, shôl, *v.* sail, direct, guide; *sheòl* iad an dè, *they set sail yesterday*; *seòl* e, *direct* or *guide him*; *n.m.* a sail; siuil, *sails*; thog iad an siùil, *they hoisted their sails*; method, expedient, manner, mode; air *seòl* eile, *by another method*; gun *seòl* air dol as, *having no expedient to escape*; an *seòl* ceart, *the proper mode*; *seòl*-labhairt, *mode of speech, idiom*; *seòl* toisich, *fore-sail*; *seol*-meadhoin, prìomh-*sheòl, main-sail*, also *seol*-mòr; *seòl*-cinn, *gib*; braigh-*sheòl, top-sail*; choinnic sinn *seòl, we descried a sail.*

Seoladair, shôl'-ad-aėr, *n. m.* sailor, seaman.

Seoladaireachd, shôl'-ad-àėr-achg, *n. f.* navigation, sailing, navigating, seafaring life.

Seoladh, shôl′-ă, *pt.* sailing, navigating, directing, guiding; 'gam *sheòladh, directing* or *leading me.*

Seol-mara, shôl′-mar-a, *n. m.* a tide.

Seolta, shyôl′-tà, *adj.* ingenious, wise, prudent; gu *seòlta, ingeniously, wisely, prudent.*

Seoltachd, shyôl′-ttachg, *n. f.* ingenuity, skill.

Seomar, } **Seombar**, } shòmb′-ar, *n. m.* apartment, a room, chamber—(just the French chamber, shàmb′-èr); *seombar-*cùl, *back-room*; *seombar-*aghaidh, *front-room*; *seòmbar-*cadail, *bed-room*; *seòmbar-*biadhtachd, *guest* or *dining-room*; *seombar-*suidhe, *sitting-room, parlour*; *seombar-*stuidearachd, *study*; *seombar-*dìomhair, *consulting-room*; *seombar-*mansantachd, *shop, ware-room*; *seombar-*gnothaich, *business-room, office*; *seombar-*moid, *court-room, court of justice*; *seombar-*èididh, *dressing-room, wardrobe*; *seombar-*cuideachd, *drawing-room*; *seombar-*cloinne, *nursery*; *seòmbraichean, rooms, apartments, parlours,* &c.

Seombradair, shômb′-rad-aèr, chamberer, a chamberlain; *i. e.* seumalair, properly.

Seonaid, shyôn′-ăj, *n. f.* Janet.

Seonaidh, shyôn′-è, *n. m.* a Lewis deity.

Seorsa, shyôrs′-a, *n. m.* kind, sort, species.

Seorsaich, shyôrs′-èch, *v.* sort, classify.

Seot, shyot, *v.* sprout, as greens; pick the best, (*Belgic*; *Scotch*); *sheot* an càl, *the greens sprouted*; *n.* worst beast; na *sheotaichan, the worst beasts,* or *any thing*; in Skye, a short tail.

Se-shlisneach, shè-hlēsh′-nyach, } **Se-thaobhach**, shè-hāov′-ach, *a.* } hexagonal; *n. f.* hexagon.

Seubhas, shèv′-as, *n. m.* wandering as beasts.

Seud, shădd′, *n. m.* a jewel. *Bible*; thing, nothing; cha'n'eil *seud* mhaith air, *it is not worth any thing*; *seud-*challum-chille, *St. John's wort*; gach *seud* a th' agam, *every thing I have*; cha bhi *seud* ort, *nothing will be wrong with you.*

Seudaich, shăd′-èch, *v.* adorn, garnish.

Seudaire, shădd″-ur-a, *n. m.* jeweller.

Seul, sāl, *n. m.* a seal for marking; *v.* seal.

Seum, shèm, *n. f.* an earnest entreaty *or* injunction; an earnest petition; is ioma *seum* a thug mise air, *many an earnest injunction I laid him under.*

Seumadair, shèm′-ad-ăèr, *n. m.* a petitioner.

Seumaich, shèm′-èch, *v. n.* petition earnestly; charge, enjoin solemnly.

Seumalair, shèm′-all-ăèr, *n. m.* chamberlain.

Seun, shèn, *n. m.* an amulet to render a warrior invulnerable; a charm; *v.* shun, refuse; cha ghabh mi *seunadh* na àicheadh, *I will not be either refused* or *denied.*

Seunadair, shèn′-ad-aèr, *n. m.* charmer.

Seunadh, shèn′-ă, *pt.* refusing; *n. f.* refusal.

Seunas, shèn′-as, *n. m.* beauty-teeth.

Seurs, shèrs, *v.* charge, brandish.

Seusar, shās′-ur, *n. m.* acme, perfection, height, *or* utmost point. *Islay*; an a *seusar* a chluiche, *in the heart-middle of the thing, of the play.*

Seusrach, shās′-rrach, *adj.* mettlesome, as a horse; in high condition.

Sgaball, skab′-all, *n. f.* a helmet. *O'R.*

Sgad, sgăd, *n. m.* mishap, misfortune. *N*

Sgadan, sgadd′-ăn, *n. m.* a herring.

Sgadarlach, skadd′-arl-ach, *n. m.* any thing scattered.

Sgaffaire, sgăff′-ăèr-à, *n. m.* scolding man.

Sgaffart, skaff′-art, *n. f.* a scolding female.

Sgaffall, skaff′-all, *n. m.* scaffolding. *Fr.*

Sgaffanta, skaff′-annt-à, *a.* vehement in speech, venomous in scolding; emphatically speaking.

Sgaffantachd, skaff′-annt-achg, *n. f.* vehemence of speech; the quality of scolding keenly.

Sgag, skăg, *v.* chink, chop, crack.

Sgagach, skăg′-ach, *adj.* chinked, cracked.

Sgagaire, skăg′-ur-à, *n. m.* a poltroon, great coward; one that chinks at the slightest appearance of danger.

Sgagaireachd, skăg′-ur-achg, *n. f.* cowardice; unfounded fear.

Sgaift, sskĭfjt, *v.* burst in consequence of eating too much; *n. f.* a notorious bellyful.

Sgail, skâ′l, *a.* cover, veil, sprinkle; approach, near; cha *sgàil* so air, *this will not come near the thing*; cha dean e *sgàile* air, *it will not do near it*; *n. m.* a cover, shade; fo *sgàil* do sgéith, *under the shadow of thy wing—under the covert of thy wing. Smith.*

Sgaileadh, ska′l′-à, *n. m.* a sprinkling: *sgàileadh* a's lugha, *the least sprinkling* or *shade.*

Sgailc, skăèlk, *n. f.* a smart blow *or* pelt; the crown of the head without hair; bumper; *v.* pelt, beat in a masterly manner.

Sgailcire, sgăèlk′-èr-à, *n. m.* a bald-headed man.

Sgailcanta, skaèlk′-ant-a, smart in blows.

Sgaileach, skâe′l′-ach, *n. f.* a veil, curtain.

Sgaileachd, skâ′l′-achg, *n. f.* sprinkling.

Sgailleag, skăly′-ag, *n. f.* smart slap on the cheek.

Sgain, Sgainn, skàènn, a complete bellyful *or* surfeit; *v.* burst, burst asunder, cause to burst; *sgàinne, he burst asunder*

Sgainte, Sgainnte, skàènnjt′-à, *pt.* burst.

Sgainneal, skáènn′-al, properly scannal.

Sgainnir, skâènn′-èr, *v.* stroll. *H. S.*

Sgainnteach, skåénnjt′-ach, *n. f.* rheumatism.

Sgainnteachail, skàénnjt′-ach-al, *a.* rheumatic.

Sgair, skăěr, *n. f.* a seam, a stitch.

Sgaird, sgâěrjj, *n. f.* flux; geàrrach. *N.*

Sgaireach, skâěr′-ach, *a.* cold, somewhat windy, and threatening rain, as weather.

Sgaireap, skăěr′-up, *n. f.* weather with whistling wind, threatening rain; a sudden squeel, as bagpipes.

Sgaireapail, skăěr′-up-al, *adj.* whistling, gusty, and threatening rain, as weather.

Sgairn, skăěrn, *n. f.* noise of stones.

Sgairneach, skâěrn′-ach, *n. f.* a deserted quarry; a great number of stones like an old quarry on a hill.

Sgairt, skăjrt, *n. f.* energy, business appearance, authority; a smart breeze; dean do gnothach le *sgairt, do your business manfully, with energy*; le *sgairt* do ghaoth tuath, *with a smart breeze of northerly wind*; in *Irish*, a cry; in the *Bible*, caul, sgamh-chridhe.

Sgairtealachd, skarjt′-al-achg, *n. f.* liveliness, vigourousness; half-stormy weather.

Sgairteil, sgărjt′-al, *adj.* clever, active, energetic; duine *sgairteil, an energetic person*; breezy; an latha *sgairteil, the half-stormy*, or *blowy day.*

Sgaiteach, sgăjt′-ach, *adj.* energetic, sarcastic, *or* cutting in words; very keen.

Sgaiteachd, skăjt′-achg, *n. f.* sharpness.

Sgaithte, skăjt′-a, *adj.* lopped off; pruned.

Sgal, skăl, *n. f.* sudden, quick cry; *v.* shriek suddenly, cry suddenly; squeel.

Sgalach, skal′-ach, *adj.* shrill and sharp.

Sgalag, skal′-ag, *n. c.* servant, (bad, bad.)

Sgalan, sgâl′-an, *n. m.* scale of a balance.

Sgalais, sgăl′-ash, *n. f.* jeering, gibing, continuous jeering. *Smith.*

Sgalartaich, sgăl′-art-ěch, *n. f.* yelling, *or* sharp howling.

Sgald, nonsense for sgàll.

Sgaldach, skâld′-ach, *a.* scalding.

Sgall, skâll, *v.* scald; gall, pain;—baldness, bald head. *North.*

Sgalla, skăll′-a, *n. f.* an old hat.

Sgalla, skâll′-a, *n. f.* large wooden dish cut out of a tree. (*Danish.*)

Sgamal, skám′-al, *n. f.* scale. *B. B.*

Sgamh, sgáv, *n. f.* lobe of the lungs; lights.

Sgamhainn, skáv′-ènn, *v.* build corn. *N.*; dais an t-arbhar. *W.*

Sgamhan, sgáv′-an, *n. m.* lungs, lights.

Sgamhanach, sgáv′-an-ach, *adj.* roan, drab, having the colour of lights; aodach *sgamhanach, roan-coloured cloth.*

Sgamhanaich, sgáv′-an-ěch, *n. f.* break of day, grey of the morning; bha e an so, 'sa *sgamhanaich, he was here in the grey of the morning, in the dawn*—(Islay has six words for this.)

Sgann, skănn, *n. f.* hand, membrane. *Sh.*

Sgannal, skann′-al, *n. f.* scandal, calumny.

Sgannalach, skann′-al-achg, *adj.* scandalous.

Sganr, skàrr, *v.* scare; scatter, as cattle, geese, &c.

Sganradh, skàrr′-Ă, *pt.* dispersing, scattering, frightening cattle; *n. m.* dispersion. The n is put into this word, and similar ones, to give it the nasal sound—thus, in mànrach, màrrach, mànrain, màrran, &c.

Sgaog, skăog, *n. f.* foolish, giddy female.

Sgaoil, skāo′l, *v.* extend, stretch, spread; *sgaoil* e a làmhan, *he spread* or *extended his hands*; disperse, scattered; *sgaoil* iad feadh an t-saoghail, *they dispersed throughout the world*; dismiss, send away; *sgaoil* e an *sgoil, he dismissed the school*; expand, distend, widen, loosen, untie; *sgaoil* an t-sreang, *untie the cord*; divulge, reveal; *sgaoil* e an naighachd, *he divulged the secret*; *n. m.* liberty, freedom; mar *sgaoil, at liberty, having freedom*; cuir mar *sgaoil, set sail, unfurl your sails, weigh anchor.*

Sgaoileadh, skāo′l′-Ă, *pt.* spreading, untying, dismissing; *n. m.* dispersion, dismission.

Sgaoilte, skāo′l′-tyâ, *pt.* scattered, spread.

Sgaoilteach, skāo′l′-tyach, *adj.* wide-spread, scattered; unguarded, imprudent; cainnt *sgaoilteach, imprudent* or *unguarded expressions.*

Sgaoilteachd, skāo′l′-tyachg, *n. f.* scattered state.

Sgaoim, skaŏěm, *n. f.* terror from false alarm; skittishness, as a horse, *or* a beast.

Sgaoimealachd, skaŏěm′-al-achg, *n. f.* terror; aptness to take alarm at nothing almost.

Sgaoimeil, skāoěm′-al, *adj.* skittish, feared.

Sgaomaire, skāom′-ur-a, *n. m.* coward.

Sgaoth, skhāo, *n. m.* a swarm; great number.

Sgap, skăp, *v.* hash, hack; a' *sgapadh* càise, *hacking down cheese*; distribute profusely, scatter, disperse. *Ossian.*

Sgapadair, skăp′-ad-ăěr, *n. m.* hasher.

Sgapadh, skăp′-Ă, *pt.* hacking, hashing.

Sgar, skăr, *v.* separate *or* disjoin by force *or* violence; *n. f.* seam, *or* joint, as in a boat; tàirnean-*sgair, seaming nails,—knot on the surface of wood. N.*

Sgarach, skăr′-ach, *a.* separating asunder.

Sgarachdainn, skar′-achg-ènn, *pt.* separating, tearing asunder; *n. m.* separation by force.

SGARADH, skăr'-X, *pt.* tearing from an object of affection; ruin, separation; mo *sgaradh, my ruin!*

SGARBH, skarv, *n. m.* a cormorant; *Scotch* scart.

SGARLAID, skârl'-aj, *n. f.* scarlet. *French.*

SGARTHANAICH, skăr'-han-èch, *n. f.* dawn, grey of the morning; twilight.

SGAT, skat, *n. m.* a skate, a sea fish.

SGATH, skhâ, *n. m.* shelter; *sgàth* an tighe, *shelter of the house*; slight fear, *or* dread; shade, protection; tha *sgàth* orm, *I feel somewhat afraid*; fo *sgàth* do sgéith, *under the covert of thy wing, under the shadow* or *protection of thy wing*; account, sake; air *sgàth* sgoinne, *for decency's sake*; 'na dh' fhuilinn e air mo *sgàth*-sa, *what he suffered on my account*; gun *sgàth, without dread.*

SGATH, skă, *v.* lop off; chop, prune; *sgath* an ceann deth, *chop off his head*; *sgath* na meanglain, *chop off the twigs*; *n. m.* damage by cattle; short part of lint, called by the Scotch, brairds.

SGATHACH, skâ'-hach, *adj.* skittish; tha 'n t-each a bhuailear 'sa cheann *sgàthach, the horse struck in the head is ever after easily frightened*, or *is skittish.*

SGATHACH, skă'-ach, *n. f.* a hurdle, *or* a great bundle of twigs to serve as a portable porch at a Highlandman's door; *N.* sgath.

SGATHADAIR, skâ'-ad-aèr, *n. m.* lopper, cutter.

SGATHAIRE, skhă'-ur-à, *n. m.* hewer, lopper.

SGATH-THIGH, skâ-haŏè-y'', *n. m.* a porch.

SGE, for sgéidh, *or* sgeith.

SGEACH, SGEACHAG, skech'-ag, *n. f.* a haw.

SGEADACHADH, skād²'-ach-X, *pt.* clothing, dressing, adorning; *n. m.* clothes, dress, garments.

SGEADAICH, skād'-èch, *v.* clothe, dress.

SGEADAICHTE, skād'-èch-tyà, *pt.* clothed, dressed.

SGEADACH, skād'-ach, *n. f.* ornament.

SGEALB, skyalub, *n. f.* a splinter, long piece of wood; *v.* splinter, dash to pieces.

SGEALLAN, skyall'-an, *n. m.* wild mustard.

SGEALP, skyâlp, *n. m.* a lively tall man.

SGEALP, skélp, *n.* shelf. *Scotch.*

SGEAMH, skév, *n. m.* speck on the eye, thin skin, membrane, *or* in Irish, polypody.

SGEAMHAG, skéff'-ăg, *n. f.* small slice.

SGEAMHAIRE, skéff'-ur-à, *n. m.* a satirist.

SGEAMHALTRACH, skév'-alt-rach, *n c.* a person that does any thing furiously.

SGEAMHLA, skév'-là, *n. m.* keen appetite.

SGEAN, skyén, *n. m.* squint; *v.* squint, look awry.

SGEANN, skyenn, *n. f.* cleanliness.

SGEANNAIL, skyenn'-al, *a.* neatly clean.

SGEARACH, skĕr'-ach, *n. m.* any thing scattered.

SGEARAICH, skèr'-èch, *v.* scatter.

SGEAP, skāp, *n. m.* bee-hive; *v.* pass over.

SGEIG, skăĕg, *n. f.* mockery, derision, jeering.

SGEIGEIL, skăĕg'-al, *adj.* jeering, jibing.

SGEIGEIS, skăĕg'-ash, *n. f.* buffoonery, waggery.

SGEIGIRE, skăĕg'-èr-à, *n. m.* derider, wag.

SGEIGIREACHD, skăĕg'-èr-achg, *n. f.* waggery.

SGEILM, skèlum, *n. f.* a thin-lipped mouth, a prater's mouth; vain glory.

SGEILMEACH, skèlum'-ach, *adj.* prating; *n. f.* a prating, vain silly woman.

SGEILMEIL, skyèlum'-al, *adj.* having a prater's contemptuous mouth; prating.

SGEILMIRE, skèlum'-ur-à, *n. m.* a prater.

SGEILMIREACHD, skèlum'-urr-achg, *n. f.* an impertinent prattle *or* garrulity.

SGEILMSE, skèlum'-shà, *n. f.* an attack. *N.*

SGEILP, skālp, *n. f.* cliff, *or* shelf of a rock.

SGEILPEACH, skālp'-ach, *n. f.* shelvy, cliffy; provincial for sgilp, *or* sgiolp.

SGEIMH, nonsense for sgiamh.

SGEINM, skén'-um, *n. f.* decency; propriety

SGEINMEIL, sken'-um-al, *n. f.* proper; decent.

SGEIR, skā²èr, *n. f.* a rock surrounded by the sea; a rock sometimes under the water; peat-bank.

SGEIRMSE, skārmsh, *n. f.* panic, skirmish.

SGEITH, skā, *n. m.* matter thrown from the stomach; *v.* vomit; overflow as a river, spread as water;—cut off, cut to shape. *North.*

SGEITHTE, sgā'-tyà, *pt.* vomited, overflowed.

SGEITHREACH, skā'-rach, *n. f.* a vomit.

SGEOD, skyôd, *n. f.* corner, angular piece.

SGEOGAIRE, skyŏg'-ur-à, *n. m.* silly fellow.

SGEOB, skyôb, *n. m.* aperture, wry-mouth.

SGEUL, skè'll, *n. m.* news, intelligence; de do *sgeul, what is your news?* narrative, narration; *sgeul* m' an Fhéinn, *a narration, narrative about the Fingalians*; droch *sgeul, bad intelligence*; information, tidings; bi air *sgeul, be in pursuit of information*; am bheil e air *sgeul, is he* or *it to be found* or *forthcoming*; a dh' innseadh *sgeoil, to tell the result.*

SGEULACHD, skè'll'-achg, *n. f.* vague reports.

SGEULAICHE, skèll'-èch-à, *n. m.* relater, narrator.

SGEULTACH, skèll'-tach, *adj.* fond of telling tales; running from house to house with reports; *n. f.* a female tell-tale, *or* gossip.

SGEULTACHD, skè'llt'-achg, *n. f.* tradition, legendary lore; *sgeultachd* m'an Fhéinn, *tradition of the Fingalians*; *sgeultachd* nan seanar, *tradition of the elders*, or *sages*, or *wise men*.

SGEULTAIR, skèllt'-ăėr, *n. m.* a narrator.

SGIAB, skĕăb, *n. m.* start, snatch; *v.* start.

SGIAMH, skĕăv, *n. f.* a squeel, mew; *v.* squeel, shriek *or* mew, caterwaul.

SGIAMH, skĕăv, *n. f.* wild expression of countenance; a degree of beauty *or* decency.

SGIAMHACH, skĕăv'-ach, *adj.* pretty, decent

SGIAMHAIL, skĕăv'-al, *pt.* squeeling, mewing.

SGIAMHAIL, skĕăv'-al, *adj.* seemly, decent.

SGIAN, skĕăn, *n. f.* a knife; sgeanan, *knives*; air son na *sgine*, (*gen.*) *for the knife*; *sgian*-pheann, *pen-knife*; *sgian*-lughaidh, *clasp-knife*; *sgian*-bhùird, *table knife*; *sgian*-fhola, *a lancet*; *sgian*-phrannaidh, *a chopping-knife*.

SGIADH, SGIATH, skĕă-aŏgh', *n. f.* wing; shield, buckler, target; fo d' *sgéidh*, *under thy wing*; le a *sgiadh* is le a chlogad, *with his shield and helmet*; *gen.* sgéidh.

SGIATHACH, skĕă'-ach, *a.* winged, white-sided.

SGIATHAIRE, skĕă'-ur-ȧ, *n. m.* flutterer, idler.

SGIATHLAICH, skĕăl'-ėch, *n. f.* fluttering.

SGID, skėjj, *n. m.* little excrement.

SGIDEAN, skėjj'-aen, *n. m.* little contemptible man.

SGIL, skė'l, *n. f.* skill, knowledge, expertness, dexterity. *Islandic.*

SGILEAR, SGILEIL, skėl'-ur, skėl'-al, *adj.* skilful.

SGILLINN, skėly'-ėnn, *n. f.* a penny; Fiscal denomination of land; *sgillinn*-shassanach, *a shilling sterling*, literally, *an English shilling*.

SGILM, skėl'-um, *n. m.* a razor-lipped mouth; or expression of countenance, indicating a scolding, pert, prating, impertinent disposition.

SGILMEIL, skėlm'-al, *adj.* having a pert, prating, officious mouth, *or* expression of countenance.

SGIMILEAR, see Sgiomalair.

SGILP, skėl'p, *n. f.* cliff, clift.

SGINN, skyėnn, *verb* } squeeze or force out of its skin or socket.
SGINNICHD, skėnn'-ėchg, } squeeze or force out of its skin or socket.

SGINNICH, skĕnn'-ėch, *n. f.* cord, twine; sgiùrsair do *sginnich* chaol, *a scourge of small cords*; *v.* cord, tie with twine.

SGIOB, skėbb, *n. f.* a Dutch-built boat; *v.* man; air a *sgiobadh* le gille sgairteil, *manned with right fellows*.

SGIOBA, skėbb'-a, *a.* a ship *or* boat's crew; fo làn *sgioba*, *having full complement of crew*.

SGIOBAIR, skėbb'-ăėr, *n. m.* a captain, skipper, shipmaster, commander of a boat.

SGIOBAIREACHD, skėbb'-ăėr-achg, *n. f.* navigating, navigation; command of a ship

SGIOBAILT, skėb'-a!jt, *n. f.* touch, the play, touch-and-begone; Scotch tig.

SGIOBAL, skėbb'-al, *n. m.* barn. *Ross*; *H.S.*

SGIOBALL, skėbb'-all, *n. f.* fold, *or* loose part of a garment; cuir ad *sgioball* e, *put it in the fold of your coat.*

SGIOBALTA, skėbb'-alt-a, *a.* tidy; portable.

SGIOBALTACHD, skėbb'-alt-achg, *n. f.* tidiness, trimness, portability; snugness.

SGIOBLAICH, skėbb'-lėch, *v.* tuck up your dress, truss; make tidy, trim, *or* neat.

SGIOL, skeúl, *v.* shell corn, unhusk, loosen, as the pile of a beast.

SGIOLADH, sgėúl'-Ă, *n. m.* shelling; *pt.* baring.

SGIOLC, skėúlk, *v.* slip in, or out.

SGIOLCARRA, skeulk'-urr-a, *adj.* clever in motion, very apt to slip out or in.

SGIOLTA, SGIOLTE, sgėúl'-tyȧ, *pt.* shelled; nimble *or* eloquent, as one's tongue.

SGIOM, skēm, *n. m.* fat sticking to dishes; scum, on the surface of water; (*Danish*, schum.)

SGIOMLAIR, sgēm'-laėr, *n. m.* an instrument to take suet off a pot; a mean person that steals out of pots; an intruder.

SGIOMLAIREACHD, skėúm'-lăėr-achg, *n. f.* mean habits of popping in upon people at meals; living and doing nothing about gentlemen's kitchens.

SGIORR, skėúrr, *v.* slip in, fall, happen.

SGIORRADH, skėúrr'-Ă, hurtful, disastrous accident.

SGIORRAIL, skėúrr'-al, *adj.* hurtful, in consequence of an accident; disastrous.

SGIORT, sgiuirt, *a.* skirt. *Bible.*

SGIOS, skēss, *n. m.* fatigue, weariness; leig do *sgìos*, *rest yourself*; ag obair gun *sgìos*, *working indefatigably*; cìa mòr an *sgìos* e, *what a weariness it is*; toil, lassitude; a chlann na *sgìos*, *ye sons of toil*, *Oss.*; le *sgìos*, *on account of lassitude.*

SGIOT, skėtt, *v.* scatter. *H. S.*; *North.*

SGIREACHD, skēr"-achg, *n. f.* a parish (sgire, *N.*) ministir-*sgireachd*, *parochial minister.*

SGIREACHDAIL, skēr"-achg-al, *a.* parochial.

SGITEAL, skėjt'-al, *n. m.* plash of water. *N.*

SGITH, skhē, *adj.* tired, fatigued, weary.

SGITHEACH, skhė'-ach, *n. m.* thorn, hawthorn.

SGITHEACHADH, skhė'-ach-Ă, *pt.* fatiguing.

SGITHICH, skhė'-ėch, *v.* weary, fatigue, tire.

SGIUCH, skyŭch, *n. f.* activity, cleverness.

SGIUCHAIL, skyŭch'-al, *adj.* active, clever.

SGIUCHAN, skyŭch'-an, *n. m.* moor-hen's note.

Sgiuird, skyùrjj, *v.* squirt; *n. f.* the flux.

Sgiuirdire, skyùrjj'-ėr-à, *n. m.* a syringe.

Sgiuirt, skeúrjt, *n. f.* skirt, corner.

Sgiut, skyùt, *v.* dart, *or* dash forward; slip by.

Sgiunach, skyūn'-ach, *n. f.* a charm *or* enchantment to enable its possessor to get all the fish about a boat or headland, while his less fortunate neighbours stare with amazement; amulet to excel in any thing;—a shameless, bold woman. *H. S.*

Sgiurs, skyûrs, *v.* scourge, whip, afflict; *sgiùrsaidh* iad sibh, *they shall scourge you. Bible.*

Sgiursach, skyûrs'ach, *n. f.* a whore, scourge. *Islay.*

Sgiursachas, skyûrs'-ach-us, *n. f.* whoredom.

Sgiursadh, skyûrs'-Ă, *pt.* scourging, lashing; *n. m.* a scourge, *or* scourging; pain.

Sgiursair, skyûrs'-ăėr, *n. f.* whoremonger, whip.

Sgiuthadh, skyŭ'-Ă, *n. f.* a lash. *North.*

Sgabhart, skaff'-art, *n. m.* box on the ear.

Sglaim, skláėm, *n. f.* a great deal of the good things of life, got in a questionable shape; booty; *v.* to usurp wealth *or* property; monopolise, usurp.

Sglaimire, skláėm'-ur-à, } *n. m.* a usurper;
Sglamaire, sklàm'-ur-à, } one who is wise to appropriate booty *or* any such to himself.

Sglamaireachd, sklâm'-ur-achg, *n. f.* monopoly, usurpation, voracity, glut.

Sglaimsear, skláėm'-sh-ar', *n. m.* usurper.

Sglamh, skláff, *v.* eat voraciously, glut; eat, as a hungry dog; scold, of a sudden, *or* furiously.

Sglamhadh, skláff'-Ă, *pt.* eating voraciously; attacking and scolding at a terrible rate.

Sglamhaire, skláff'-ur-à, *n. m.* glutton; terrible scolder; a voracious fellow.

Sglamhair, skláv'-uėr, *v.* claw awkwardly.

Sglamhradh, skláv'-rĂ, clawing *or* scratching one's skin voraciously; bad itch.

Sgleamacair, sklém'-achg-ur-a, *n. m.* dauber; a mean, low, worthless fellow.

Sgleamaic, sglém'-ėchg, *v.* plaster, *or* flatten awkwardly; daub filthily.

Sgleamaid, sklém'-ăjj, *n. f.* horrid snotters.

Sgleap, sklėp, *n. m. v.* flatten, spoil the shape; draw down your under-lip, wag your head, and stare at a person most astonishingly; *sglèapaire, a fellow that does so*; *sgleàpaid, a silly female that does so*; foolish, boorish starers—applied to silly children, brought up in remote corners, where they have seldom seen strangers; *n. f.* low meanness, under the guise of liberality.

Sgleapaid, sklèp'-ăg, *n. f.* see Sgleàp.

Sgleapaire, sglèp'-ur-à, *n. m.* see Sgleàp.

Sgleapaireachd, sglèp'-ur-achg, *n. f.* foolish, unmannerly, staring, *or* boasting.

Sgleat, sklètt, *v.* slate, as a house.

Sgleata, sklètt'-à, *n. f.* a slate, (*Scotch*, sclate.)

Sgleatach, sklètt'-ach, *n. f.* granite, slate-quarry.

Sgleatair, sklètt'-ăėr, *n. m.* a slater.

Sgleataireachd, sklètt'-ăėr-achg, *n. f.* slating; the occupation of a slater, *or* slate-quarrier.

Sgleo, sklhyô, *n. m.* disease of the eyes, glare about the eyes; amazement, misapprehension; romancing of one who sees imperfectly, and consequently misrepresents facts; romancing, gasconading.

Sgleoid, sklyôjj, *n. c.* silly person.

Sgleothail, sklyô'-al, *adj.* romancing.

Sgleothaire, sklyô'-ur-à, *n. m.* romancer.

Sgliomair; see Sgiomlair, Sliomair.

Sgliurach, sklėūr'-ach, *n. f.* newly-fledged crow *or* sea-gull; an untidy female.

Sgloid, sklŏjj, *n. f.* a heavy, clumsy, lifeless female. *Islay*; filth, dirt. *North.*

Sglong, sklong, *n. f.* a horrid snotter.

Sglongach, sklŏng'-ach, *adj.* dirtily viscous.

Sglongaid, sklong'-ăj, *n. f.* horrid snot.

Sglongaideach, sklong'-ăj-ach, *a.* mucous.

Sgob, skòb, *v.* snatch, nibble lightly.

Sgobadh, skòb'-Ă, *pt.* snatching, nibbling; *n. m.* a short while; *sgobadh* bho 'n bhaile, *a little while from home*; *sgobadh* dheth, *a short while of it.*

Sgoch, skoch, *v.* gash, make an incision; *n. f.* a gash, incision; first-shot from a still. *Perthshire.*

Sgod, skôd, *n. m.* corner of cloth; sheet, sheet-rope; *sgòd* an t-siuil mheadhoin, *main-sheet*; *sgòd* an t-siùil thoisich, *the foresail-sheet*; *sgòd* an t-siùil-chinn, *the gib-sheet*; blemish. *Mainland.*

Sgog, skòg, *n. m.* a fool, an idler. *H. S.*

Sgog, skòg, *v.* hesitate, waver.

Sgogarsaich, skòg'-ars-ėch, *n. f.* hesitation.

Sgoid, skòėj, *gen.* of Sgòd.

Sgoideis, skòjj'-ash, *n. f.* vain show.

Sgoil, skŏ'l, *n. f.* school, seminary, education, (Latin schola); am bheil *sgoil* aige, *has he education*; a' dol do 'n *sgoil, going to school*; science, literature; *sgoil* fhairge, *the science of navigation*; *sgoil*-speur, *sgoil* reul, *astronomy*; *sgoil* mharsantachd, *the science of book-keeping*; *sgoil*-fhearainn, *the science of land-surveying*; *sgoil* rìomball, *spherics*; *sgoil*-fhionnsaireachd, *the science of fencing*; *sgoil*-dhorn, *the science of boxing*; *sgoil*-chlaidheamh, *sword-exercise*; cha 'n 'eil *sgoil* agam air. *I know nothing of it I am quite ignorant* *of it*; *sgoil*-chruinne, *geography*; *sgoil*-àitean, *topography*; *sgoil*-lusan, *botany*; *sgoil*-mhulcach, PHRENOLOGY; *sgoil*-chiuird, *mechanics*; *sgoil*-dhamhsaidh, *dancing-school, the sublime science of waltzing*; *sgoil*-chreig, *geology*; *sgoil*-eun, *ornithology*; *sgoil*-fhacal, *sgoil*-fhreumhachd, *etymology*; also faclaireachd; *sgoil*-mharcachd, *riding-school*; *sgoil*-leubhaidh, *reading-school*; *sgoil*-sgrìobhaidh, *writing-school*; *sgoil*-dhiadhaireachd, *theology*; *sgoil*-eachdraidh, *historiography*; *sgoil*-mhiotailt, *mineralogy*; *sgoil*-chogaidh, *military academy*; *sgoil*-uisge, *hydrostatics*; neo uisgearachd: *sgoil*-dhreag, *meteorology*; neo dreagaireachd; *v.* school, teach; *sgoil*-inntinn, *intellectual philosophy*; *sgoil*-bhùird, *a boarding-school*; *sgoil*-dhubh, *the philosophy of Satin.*

SGOILEAM; see Sgoilm.

SGOILEAR, sko'l-ăĕr, *n. m.* a student, pupil, scholar, a learned man, disciple, school-boy.

SGOILEARACH, sko'l'-aĕr-al, *adj.* scholastic, learned.

SGOILEARACHD, sko'l'-aĕr-achg, *n. f.* scholarship, learning; erudition, learning, education, intelligence.

SGOILM, skó'lum, *n. f.* razor-bill; mouth *or* face expressive of scolding disposition; high key in scolding.

SGOILMEACH, sko'lum'-ach, *adj.* venomous in scolding; *n. f.* a shrew, a scold, *or* scolding female.

SGOILMEIS, sko'lum'-ash, *n. f.* a biting severe scold.

SGOILLT, skòolljt, *v.* cleave, split, separate.

SGOILLTE, skō²lljt'-à, *pt.* cleft, split, chinked.

SGOILLTEAN, skòlljt'-áèn, *n. m.* a split, half; half of a square neckerchief; a billet of wood.

SGOINN, skăŏènn, *n. f.* decency, taste, propriety; dean le *sgòinn* e, *do it tastefully*; air sgàth *sgòinne, for decency's sake*; rinn mi e air sgàth *sgòinne, I did it for decency's sake*; is beag *sgoinn* a bhìos air do ghnothach, *your business must be done with little propriety*; neatness.

SGOINN, skŏènn, *a.* check *or* reprove, *or* scold keenly *or* bitterly.

SGOINNEIL, skăoènn'-al, *adj.* decent, tasteful.

SGOINNEACH, skŏènn'-ach, *adj.* bitter in scolding; *n. f.* bitter scolding female.

SGOIRM, skŏèrm, *n. f.* the throat. *H. S.*—brow of a hill; an draigheann gorm air *sgoirm* nan carn, *the green brier on the brow of the hills*, (*cairns*), *Ossian.*

SGOITICHE, skŏejt'-èch-à, *n. m.* a quack.

SGOLB, skŏl'b, *n. f.* a wattle, *or* spray for fastening thatch; splinter, split;—thorn.

SGOLBACH, skŏl'b'-ach, *a.* prickly, thorny.

SGOLBANTA, skŏl'b'-ant-à, *a.* sharp, prickly

SGOLL, skôll, *n. m.* ugly scum, as on proud flesh.

SGOLL, skŏll, *v.* skull a boat, (*Danish*); brush off, rinse off, (*Macdonald*); scolding on a high key, sgollan.

SGOLLACHAN, skôll'-ach-an, *n. m.* an unfledged bird.

SGOLTADH, skŏl²'-ttĂ, *pt.* splitting, cleaving, riving asunder, chinking; *n. m.* a cleft, a chink, a rent, a rift; a *sgoltadh* cheann, *to cleave heads.*

SGONN, skŏnn, *v. n.* gulp, glut, eat in large mouthfuls; 'ga *sgonnadh* air, *gulping it up, eating it up in large mouthfuls*; *n. f.* a large mouthful, a gulp, *or* glut; a block of wood; a huge unshapely person.

SGONNAIRE, skŏnn²'-ur-à, *n. m.* a gulper, boor.

SGOR, skŏr, *v.* fork peats *or* hay, lay out peats to dry; gash, hack, scarify, *H. S.*; *n. f.* a fork; sgian agus *sgor, a knife and fork*; a gash, a notch.

SGORADH, skŏr'-Ă, *pt.* forking; gashing; *n. m.* laying out or forking of peats.

SGORAG, skŏr'-ag, *n. f.* scollop, a waving edge.

SGORAGAICH, skŏr'-ag-èch, *v.* scollop, cut the edge of cloth, &c. in a waving line.

SGORNACH, skôrn'-ach, SGORNAN, skôrn an, *n. m.* the throttle, *or* gullet, *or* windpipe; tha 'n *sgòrnan* fosgailte mar uaigh, *their throat is an open sepulchre. Sm.*

SGORR, skôrr, *n. f.* a peak, *or* cliff, sharp point, a conical sharp rock; a bucktooth.

SGORRABHEINN, skôrr'-a-*vh*ăènn, *n. f.* a cliff, *or* peaking, cliffy, conical mountain; a mountain in the island of Islay, Argyleshire.

SGORRACH, skôrr'-ach, *adj.* pronged, peaked, cliffy, having a buck-tooth, conical.

SGOT, skot, *n. f.* a small farm or village.

SGOTBHAILE, skŏt'-v*h*a'l-à, *n. m.* a village, *Islay.*

SGOTH, skhó, *n. f.* a Norway skiff.

SGOTHLONG, skól'-lŏng, *n. f.* a yacht.

SGRABAIRE, skrab'-ur-à, *n. m.* Greenland dove. *Mn.*

SGRAIBHSE, skraosh, *n. f.* hand-saw. *Irish.*

SGRAID, skrăoèjj, *n. f.* a hag, *or* old mare, *or* cow.

SGRAIDEAG, skrâjj'-ag, *n. f.* little potatoe, *or* any thing.

SGRAILL, skrâly', *v.* revile, abuse terribly.

SGRAILLEADH, skrâly'-Ă, *pt.* reviling, scolding terribly; *n. m.* the greatest abuse, worst language.

SGRAING, skrèng, *n. f.* a scowl; a scowling *or* forbidding countenance, *or* aspect.

SGRAINGEALACHD, skrèng'-all-achg, *n. f.*

sullenness, surly morosity, *or* countenance.

Sgraingeil, skréng'-al, *adj.* scowling, sullen.

Sgraingire, skrèng'-ur-à, *n. m.* a scowler.

Sgrath, skhră, *n. f.* a thin sod, (divot); what covers the kiln of grain;—scum; rind. *H.*

Sgrathaire, skrá'-ur-à, *n. m.* skeleton.

Sgrathall, skră'-all, *n. pl.* small ones of any thing, rubbish, refuse of any thing.

Sgreab, skrāb[2], *n. f.* a scab, blotch.

Sgreabach, skrāb[2]'-ach, *adj.* scabbed, blotched.

Sgreabaire, skrāb'-ur-à, *n. m.* mean fellow.

Sgread, skrād[2], *v.* screech; *n. f.* screech, gnash.

Sgreadag, skrād'-ag, *n. f.* an acid, any thing sour.

Sgreadail, skrād'-al, *n. f.* screeching, gnashing.

Sgreadaire, skrād'-ur-à, *n. m.* screecher.

Sgreag, sgrāg[2], *v.* parch; see Sgreath.

Sgreamh, skrév, *n. f.* slight nausea, disgust; thin scum *or* rind, *or* ugly skin.

Sgreamhaich, skrév'-èch, *v.* loathe, abhor.

Sgreamhail, skrév'-al, *adj.* loathsome.

Sgreamhladh, skrév'-llĂ, *n. f.* a thick wettish rush through the skin.

Sgreat, skrātt[2], *n. f.* great horror, *or* disgust.

Sgreatachd, skrāt'-achg, *n. f.* horrifying nature *or* quality of any thing; sgreataidheachd.

Sgreataidh, skrāt'-è, *adj.* horrifying, disgusting.

Sgreataich, skrāt'-èch, *v.* horrify, highly disgust.

Sgreath, skrā[2], *v.* parch, *or* dry hurriedly the outside, without entering into the inner part.

Sgreoth, skhyrò, *v.* parch as cloth.

Sgreothainn, skryò'-ènn, *n. f.* straw used in place of hair-cloth on a kiln—straic. *P.*

Sgreuch, skrèch, *v.* and *n. m.* screech in a croaking drawling manner.

Sgreuchail, skrèch'-al, *n. f.* screeching; *n. m.* a continuous croaking screeching.

Sgreuchaire, skréch'-ur-à, *n. m.* screecher

Sgribhinn, skrēv'-ènn, *n. f.* rocky side of a hill.

Sgrid, skrèjj, *v.* breathe your last in consequence of laughing or weeping; *n. m.* breath, gasp; cha 'n 'eil *sgrid* ann, *there is not a breath in him.*

Sgriob, skrēbb, *n. f.* a scrape, the rut of a plough, or it's swathe of earth; a trip, an excursion; *sgrìob* do 'n ghalldachd, *an excursion or trip to the Low country*; stroke of a saw; *sgrìob* an t-saibh-mhòir, *the stroke of the whip-saw*; *v.* itchiness about the lip, portending a kiss, *or* a swig of whisky!!!

Sgriob, skrēbb, *v.* scrape, drag, *or* dredge for fish or oysters; snatch, *or* sweep away; *sgrìob* leat e, *sweep* or *snatch it away with you*; a *sgrìobadh* 'sa phort, *dredging in the port*; a' *sgrìobadh* buntàta, *scraping potatoes.*

Sgriobach, skrēbb'-ach, *n. f.* itch,—the Scotch, *or* Highland fiddle! murdered in many places, skreūb'-ach!!

Sgrioban, sgrēbb'-an, *n. m.* long line.

Sgriobaire, sgrēbb'-ur-à, *n. m.* a dredge, a scraper, scratcher; curry-comb.

Sgriobh, sgrēvv, *v.* write, compose a book; *sgrìobh* a dh' ionnsaidh, *write to him*; a' *sgrìobhadh* leobhair, *writing* or *composing a book.*

Sgriobhadair, skrēvv'-ad-ăèr, *n. m.* writer.

Sgriobhadaireachd, skrēvv'-ăd-ăèr-achg, *n. f.* a writer's business; writing; sgriobh thigh, *writer's office.*

Sgriobhadh, skrēvv'-Ă, *pt.* writing, composing; *n. f.* hand-writing, manuscript, writing.

Sgriobhte, sgrēvv'-tyà, *pt.* written, composed.

Sgriobtur, skrup'-tur, *n. m.* the scripture; nach do leubh sibh an *scrioptuir*, *have ye not read the scripture*; scrioptural, *scriptural.*

Sgriodan, skrēdd'-an, *n. m.* stony ravine.

Sgrios, skrēss, *v.* destroy, ruin, annihilate; *sgriosaidh* mi an duine, *I will destroy* (or *annihilate*) *the man. B.*; scrape, *or* sweep off the surface; a' *sgriosadh* an leathraich, *sweeping off the rind of the leather*; *n. f.* destruction, ruin, ruination; mo *sgrios, my destruction* or *ruination*; bheir thu *sgrios* oirnn, *thou shalt annihilate us*; sweeping away of surface, *or* scraping rind;—stumble, slip, *Arm.*

Sgriosach, skrèss'-ach, } *adj.* destructive,
Sgriosail, skrèss'-al, } ruinous, detrimental, pernicious.

Sgriosadair, skrèss'-ad-áèr, *n. m.* destroyer, pillager.

Sgriotachan, skrètt'-ach-an, *n. m.* a child that is likely to die; little squalling infant.

Sgrioth, (sgriothan), skrē, *n. m.* gravel. *Is.*

Sgriubh, skrèū, *n. f.* a screw; *v.* screw. *French, Teutonic, Danish, &c.*

Sgrob, skrôb, *v.* scratch with the nails, *or* claws of a cat; *sgrobadh, a scratch, scratching,* (scrobben, *Belg.*)

Sgroban, skrôb'-an, *n. m.* little crop of a bird, craw; gizzard; cha d'theid mir ad *sgroib, not a particle will enter your gizzard* or *crop.*

Sgrobh, skrov, *n. f.* a screw. *N.*; a sod.

SGROCH, skrôch, *v.* scratch with nails, &c.
SGROCHAILL, skrôch'-ėly', scrawl, scribble.
SGROCHLADH, scrôchl'-lĂ, *pt.* scrawling, scribbling; *n. m.* a scrawl, a scribbling.
SGROG, skrŏg, *v.* bite, as a horse; *n. f.* the head in ridicule; *n. f.* a bite, a mouthful; *sgrog* e mi, *he bit me*; *v. n.* also tighten quickly your head-dress; *sgrog* do bhonaid ort, *tighten your bonnet on your head*; *doff.*
SGROGAID, sgrŏg,-ājj, *n. f.* an old hat *or* cap.
SGROGAIRE, sgrŏg'-urr-å, *n. m.* biter, carper.
SGROLL, skrŏll, large wide piece, *obsolete.*
SGROILLEAG, skrôlly''-ag, *n. f.* large piece of skin *or* any peeling scraped off.
SGROTH, skrô, *n. f.* large thick sod.
SGRUB, skrŭb, *v.* hesitate, delay. (*Teut.*)
SGRUBAIL, skrŭb'-al, *adj.* hesitating, scrupulous, (*Lat.* scrupulus); niggardly parsimonious. (*Teut.*)
SGRUBAIRE, skrŭb'-ŭr-å, *n. m.* a churl, niggard.
SGRUBAIREACHD, skrŭb'-aėr-achg, niggardliness.
SGRUBANTA, sgrŭb'-ant-å, *adj.* scrupulous; parsimonious; *sgrubantachd, scrupulosity, niggardliness.*
SGRUD, skrûdd, *v.* scrape thoroughly, search minutely, scrutinize, examine minutely.
SGRUDADH, skrŭdd'-Ă, *pt.* searching; *n. m.* utmost scraping of any thing in a dish.
SGRUDAIRE, skrŭdd'-ur-a, *n. m.* scrutinizer.
SGRUIGEAN, skrŭėg'-ăėn, *n. m.* neck of a bottle.
SGRUIDTE, skrûjj'-tyå, *pt.* cleared out *or* wholly searched; scrutinized, perfectly freed *or* cleared.
SGRUIT, skruėjt, *n. f.* an old decayed person. *North.*
SGUAB, skŭăb, *n. f.* a sheaf of corn; a besom, broom, brush; *v.* sweep, sweep away.
SGUABACH, skŭăb'-ach, *n. f.* a brush, broom.
SGUABADH, skŭăb'-Ă, *pt.* sweeping, cleaning; *n. m.* art of sweeping *or* cleaning.
SGUABANTA, skŭăb'-ant-a, *adj.* portable, trim.
SGUAB-LION, skŭăb'-lēn, *n. f.* a sweep-net.
SGUCH, skŭch, *v.* strain, sprain. *North.*
SGUDALL, skŭdd'-al, *n. m.* trash, offals.
SGUDALAIR, skŭd'-al-aėr, *n. m.* a scullion, drudge; a mean fellow. *North,* sguidealair.
SGUGACH, skŭg'-ach, *n. m.* a soft boorish fellow.
SGUIDS, skŭjsh, *v.* dress flax, switch, drive.
SGUIDSEACH, skŭjsh'-ach, *n. m.* a tall, slender, young girl;—prostitute, stripling. *N.*
SGUIDSEADH, skujsh'-Ă, *pt.* dressing, lashing.
SGUIDSEANACH, skŭjsh'-ăėn-ach. *n. m.* a very tall, slender, very young man.
SGUIR, skŭėr, *v.* cease, stop, give over, desist; *sguir* dheth, *stop, desist, cease, be done of it.*
SGUIT, skúejtt, *n. pl.* skates, foot-board.
SGULAN, skûll'-an, *n. f.* large basket. *N.*
SGULAIR, skûll'-ăėr, *n. f.* a large old hat.
SGUM, skûm; see Sgiom, scum.
SGUR, skŭr, *n. m.* cessation, stop; buidheachas gun *sgur, thanks without ceasing*; *pt.* ceasing, desisting, leaving off; stopping; ma'n do *sgur* sinn, *ere we desisted,* or *ceased,* or *left off*; gun *sgur, unceasingly, incessantly.*
SGUR, skûr, *v.* scour, burnish, rub up; *sgùradh* nan iarran, *burnishing the fire-irons.*
SGURACHDAINN, skŭr'-achg-ėnn, *pt.*; see Sgur.
SGURAINN, skûr'-ėnn, lye, *or* ley; any trash of liquor in contempt; toplash.
SGURR, skûrr, *n. m.* a large conical hill.
SGURT; see Sgiut, scud, sweep away.
SHABH, hâv, *part. verb* sàbh; *shàbh* e, *he sawed.*
SHABHAIL, hâv'-al, *p. v.* sàbhail; *shàbhail* e, *he saved, he escaped, he preserved,* or *kept clear.*
SHAIBHIR, hīv'-ėr, *asp. f.* saibhir, plentiful, &c.
SHAIL, há'l, *asp. f.* sail, heel; a *shàil, his heel.*
SHAILL, hăėly', *past,* saill; *shaill* e, *he salted.*
SHALACH, hâl'-ach, *gen.* sail, of the heel.
SHAMHACH, hàv'-ach, *asp.* of sàmhach, quiet, still.
SHANNT, hănntt, *as. fo.* covetousness, greed.
SHANNTAICH, hănnt'-ėch, *v.* I coveted, envied.
SHAOIL, hāo'l, *p. v.* I supposed, *or* imagined.
SHAOR, hāor, *p. v.* I freed, absolved, &c.
SHARAICH, hâr'-ėch, *p. v.* I oppressed, hurt.
SHE, hè, *asp.* form of sè, six; a *shè* fhèin, *his six.*
SHEAC, hechg, *asp.* form, I withered, decayed.
SHEACHD, hechg, *a.* 'sheachd fir, his seven men; also of seven.
SHEALG, hyalg', *asp.* a shealg, his hunting.
SHEALL, hyall, *p. v.* sheàll mi, I beheld, saw.
SHEAP, hyèp, *p. v.* shèap e, he sneaked.
SHEARG, hyerug, *p. v.* shearg ise, she withered.
SHEAS, hās, *p. v.* sheas e, he stood, he sustained.
SHEID, hājj, *p. v.* blew; *shèid* oiteag o'n aonaich, *a blast from the hill blew.*
SHEINN, hăėnn, *v. p.* sheinn e, he sang.

SHEOL, hyôll, *p. v.* sheòll I, she sailed; guided.

SHIAN, hě..n, *p. v.* shian e, he drawling cried.

SHIN, hěnn, *p. v.* shìn sinn, we stretched, put off.

SHIOL, hhěll, *asp. f.* a shìol na leirg, ye children of the coast; d'a *shìol, to his oats* or *offspring.*

SHIOS, hěss, *adv.* down, downwards, hither.

SHIR, hèr, *p. v.* shir sinn e, we sought it.

SHIUBHAIL, hěū'-al, *p. v.* shiubhail e, he died, &c.

SHLAINTE, hlàènjt'-a, *asp. f.* a shlàinte, his health; chaill e *shlàinte, he lost his health.*

SIA, shěă, *n. adj.* sè. *N. Highlands.*

SIAB, ssěăb, *v.* breathe away dust; *siab, to angle with a fishing-rod*; fish.

SIABADH, shěăb'-Ă, *pt.* breathing away.

SIABH, shěăv, *n.* stewed winkles. *Skye.*

SIABHAIR, shěăv'-ěr, *v.* tease, weary out.

SIABUNN, shěăb'-unn, *n. m.* soap.

SIAD, (for se iad), shèdd, it is they.

SIAD, shěăd, *v.* sheer, go obliquely.

SIADAIRE, shěăd'-ur-ă, *n.m.* a sly, skulking fellow; a shuffler; stinkard; *v.* slink.

SIADAIREACHD, shěăd'-ăer-achg, *n. f.* slinking, shuffling, sly, roguish conduct.

SIAN, shěăn, *n. f.* a drawling scream, *or* squeel; *v.* squeel, cry, scream tediously, raising your voice gradually;—pile of grass. *Macdonald.*

SIANAIL, shěăn'-al, *n.f.* drawling squeeling.

SIAR, shěăr, *v.* lurch, go obliquely; *adv. adj.* west, westward; *siar* ort, *to the westward of you.*

SIBH, shěv, *pro.* ye *or* you; SIBH-SE, shěv'-shă, you, yourself; dè 'n ni *sibh, what will ye do*? *sibh* fhèin, *ye, yourselves, you, yourself.*

SIBHREACH, shěvv'-ryach, *n. c.* a fairy, a spectre, an apparition; (sìth-bhruthach.)

SIBHREACHAIL, shěv'-ryach-al, *adj.* fairy-like.

SIBHT, shěvjt, *n. f.* shift, expedient.

SIBHTEIL, shěvjt'-al, *adj.* inventive, thrifty.

SIC, shěchg, *n. f.* the inner skin that is next the viscera in animals; bhrist an t-*sic, the inner skin broke*; màm-*sic, rupture, hernia.*

SICHD, sěchg, *n.* dash to lay hold of. *Ar.*

SICIR, shěchg'-ěr, *adj.* prudent, steady. *Arm.*

SID, shějj, *n. f.* abatement of a storm; mood *or* humour; abatement of rage; 'nuair a nì e *sìd, when the storm abates*; dè n t-*sìd* a th'ort, *in what humour are you*? am bheil *sìd* air a nis. *has his rage abated*?

SIDEIL, shějj'-al, *adj.* more moderate, as wind; in good humour, as a person; na ' *sìdeiliche, more moderate, more calm.*

SIGEACH, shěg'-ach, *a.* slim, slimy.

SIGEANN, shěg'-unn, *n. f.* pleasant countenance.

SIGEANTA, shěg'-unt-a, *adj.* cheerful.

SIGEANTACHD, shěg'-unt-achg, *n. f.* cheerfulness, complacency, affability.

SIGH, shhė, *v.* glide, skip, dash forth, dart; a' *sigheadh* air mullach nam beann, *skipping on the top of the mountains*; *shigh* i seachad, *she glided by. Bible.*

SIGHEADH, shhė'-Ă, *p.* gliding, vanishing, skipping; thug e an *sigheadh* ad, *he made such a bolt.*

SIGHIDEACH, shhė'-ăj-ach, *n. f.* spectre, fairy, a person taken away by the fairies.

SIL, shė'l, *v.* rain, drop, drip, *shil* e, *the rain has commenced*; a *sileadh* o 'n tigh, *dripping from the house*; man *sil* e, *ere it rain*; a' *sileadh* nan deur, *shedding tears.*

SILE, for seile, a spittle.

SILEADH, shė'l'-Ă, *pt. n. m.* raining, dropping, dripping; mar shìor-*shileadh* uisge, tha aimhreitean mnà, *as the continual dropping of waters, are the contentions of women*; dispensation, economy; fo *shileadh* an t-soisgeil, *under the gospel dispensation*; fo *shileadh* an t-Sean-tiomnaidh, *under the Mosaic economy, under the Old Testament dispensation*; drop, drip; gach *sileadh, every drop.*

SILEAN, shė'ly'-aėn, *n. m.* single grain.

SILE-REUM, shėl-a-răm', *n. m.* salivation.

SILTEACH, shėly'-tyach, *a.* dropping; tearful; sùil *shilteach, tearful eye*; often raining; uair *shilteach, weather in which rain prevails*; *n. f.* an issue, running of an issue; ma dhùinear a suas 'fheoil o '*shilteach, if his flesh be stopped from his issue*; discharge; làithean a *siltich, the days of her discharge*; air son a *shiltich, on account of his issue. Bible.*

SILTEACHD, shily$^{2'}$-tyachg, *n. f.* raininess; state of being subject to issues, &c.

SIMID, SIMIDEAN, shěm'-ėj, *n. m.* a mallet, beetle; ceann-*simid, beetle.*

SIMILEAR; see Siomlainn, chimney.

SIMPLIDH, shěmp'-llė, *a.* single-hearted.

SIMPLIGHEACHD, shėmp'-lė-achg, *n* simplicity.

SIN, shėn, *adj. pron.* that, those; na daoine *sin, those men*; an duine *sin, that man*; *inter. adv. conj.* well done! there now! sin! sin! enough! enough! avast! *sin*-thu, a laochain, *well done, my good fellow*! as an *sin* thu, *be off with you*! *sin* agad *sin, there is for you*! *sin* agad e, *there it is for you*! *there he is for you*! O *sin, since*; an t'am *sin, that time*; mar *sin, in that manner*; *sin* r'a ghràdh, *that is to say*; *sin* thu fhèin, *that is your sort, well done yourself*! an *sin, on that occasion—there, in that place*; an *sin* fhèin, at *that very time* or *place*; *sin* mar thàinig e, *in that manner he came*; mar *sin, just so*; mar *sin* sìos, *and so on.*

Sin, shēn, *v. n.* stretch, reach, hand; *sìn* domh *sin, hand me that*; *sìn* do lamh, *stretch your hand*; *sìn* do làmh dha, *reach out your hand*, or *drub him*; lean; extend, prolong, grow in stature; tha e *sìneadh, he is growing*; ma *shìneas* Dia mo làithean, *if God prolong my days*; pursue, chase, with all your might, fall to; shìn *sinn* orra, *we pursued them with all our might*; an deigh *sìneadh, having commenced*; *shìn* i ris, *she was seduced by him*; *sìn* air, *chase him*; act of leaning *or* lounging on a bed; tha e 'na *shìneadh, he is leaning*; he is leaning on a bed *or* sofa.

Sine, shén'-à, *deg.* sean, old; is *sine, older, elder*; co dhiutha a 's *sine, which is the elder*; *n. f.* oldness, agedness; a *shine, his agedness.*

Sinead, shén'-ad, *n. m.* seniority, degree of age; air a *shinead, let him be ever so old.*

Sineadh, shēn'-Ă, *pt.* stretching, reaching; *n. m.* length, stretch; pursuit, pursuing; prolongation; *sìneadh* làithean, *length of days.*

Sinn, shénn, *pers. pro.* we, us; rinn *sinn, we made*; their *sinn, we shall say.*

Sinn-sheanair, shénn-shen'-ar, *n.m.* great-grandfather; *sìnn-sìnn-sheanair, great-great-grandfather*; *sìnn*-seachad-*sìnn-seanair, great-great-great-grandfather.*

Sinnsear, shénn'-shur, *n. pl.* ancestors, fathers.

Sinn-seanmhair, shēnn'-shen-va-hyar, *n. f.* great-grandmother; *sìnn-sìnn-seanmhair, great-great-grandmother*; *sìnn*-seachad-*sìnn-seanmhair, great-great-great-grandmother.*

Sinnsearachd, shēnn'-shar-achg, *n. f.* genealogy, forefathers, ancestors, ancestry.

Sinte, shēnjt'-à, *pt.* stretched, reached, fetched; *sìnte* r' a thaobh, *stretched by his side.*

Sinteach, shēnjt'-ach, *n. f.* plough-trace, also sìnte, *adj.* straight, extended, prostrate.

Siob, shēbb, *v.* drift, as snow; angle *or* fish; a' cur is a *sìobadh, snowing and drifting*; angling.

Siobail, shēb'-èl, *v.* fish, and the boat under sail; angle.

Sioblach, shēbb'-lach, *n. m.* a long streamer; a long person.

Siobladh, shēbb'-lĂ, *pt.* fishing, and the boat under sail; *n. m.* time of tide suiting fishing.

Siobhach, shéff'-ach, *n. m.* rye-grass.

Siobhag, shéff'-ag, *n. f.* straw, pile of rye-grass.

Siobhalt, shēvv'-allt', *adj.* civil, obliging, affable, kind, urbane, polite, courteous.

Siobhaltachd, shēvv -alt-achg, *n. f.* civility.

Siobhaltas, shēvv'-alt-as, *n. f.* common civility.

Sioch, shē'ch, *v.* strain, sprain, hurt; *n. f.* peace, quiet, repose, comfort.

Siochadh, shē'ch'-Ă, *n. m. pt.* a sprain, spraining, a strain, straining, as foot, &c.

Siochalachd, shē'chal'-achg, *n. f.* peacefulness.

Siochail, shē'chal, *adj.* peaceful, quiet, *B.*

Siochaint, shēch'-cháènjt, *adj.* peace, repose.

Siochainteach, shēch'-cháènjt-ach, *adj.* peaceful, quiet, undisturbed, unmolested.

Siochainteachd, shēch'-cháènjt-achg, *n. f.* peacefulness, quietude, happy repose, and peace.

Siochaire, shēch'-ur-a, *n. m.* a fairy-like person; a trifling ninny.

Siochaireachd, shēch'-ur-achg, *n. f.* trifling conduct, quantity, *or* consideration.

Siod, shédd, *and* shŭdd, *Dem. pro.* yon, that there; *siod* an duine, *yonder is the man, yonder is the hero*; *adv.* an *siod* is an so, *here and there*; *siod* e, *yonder he is*; *siod* agad *siod, there is for you, there is your match, more than your match for you!!* *siod* fhèin, *for every reason, because I thought it proper*; mar *siod* is mar so, *this way and that way*; *siod* an t-àite, *yonder is the place for you!* dè bha *siod, what was that?* carson *siod, why yon way? why so?* an d thèid thu an *siod, will you go yonder?* chaidh e an *siod, he went yonder*; *siod* mar dh' iomair e 'chluiche, *yon is the manner in which he played his cards*; yon place; an deach thu an *siod, did you go yonder, to yon place?* *siod* an lamh a thogas an t-sleagh, *there is the hand that can play vengeance with the spear!* *siod* mar chìteadh an greugach, *so was the Grecian seen*; *siod* mar thacair dhuinn, *so it happened us.*

Sioda, shēdd'-à, *n. m.* silk; also of silk.

Siod-choimh, shēdd'-chróè, *n. f.* silk-worm

Siog, shēg, *n. f.* cadaverous appearance.

Siogach, shēg'-ach, *a.* greasy, slimy.

Siogaid, shēg'-aj, *n. m.* lank person. *N.*

Siol, shē'll, *n. m.* oats; *siol*-gruind, *seed-oats*; race, offspring; *sìol* Dhiarmaid, *the race* or *offspring of Dermid*; seed, semen; *Inter.* mode of calling geese.

Siola, shúll'-a, *n.m.* gill; ceathra bhodaich.

Siolach, shēll'-ach, *n. m.* breed, brood, offspring; particularly applied to cattle, birds, &c.

Siolachadh, shēll'-ach-Ă, *p.* propagating, engendering, breeding; *n.m.* propagation.

Siolachan, shēll′-ach-an, *n. m.* strainer, filterer.

Sioladh, shēll′-ă, *pt.* subsiding; straining, filtering; a' *sìoladh* a bhainne, *straining the milk*; tha a ghaoith a *sìoladh*, *the wind is subsiding*; tha'n t-uisge a' *sìoladh*, *the sediments in the water are subsiding, the water is filtering*; *n. m.* a syllable, propagation.

Siolag, shēll′-ag, *n. f.* sand-eel; *pl.* sìolagan,—in Perth, a breeding sow.

Siolaich, shēll′-ēch, *v.* breed, propagate, multiply; *shìolaich* iad, *they increased, multiplied*; *siolaichibh* is fàsaibh lìonmhor, *be fruitful and multiply, Bible*; o Dhiarmaid *shìolaich* clann nach gann, *from Dermid sprang a numerous offspring.*

Siolaiche, shēll′-ēch-ă, *n. m.* propagator.

Siolaidh, shēll′-ēy′, *v.* subside, strain, filter; *shìolaidh* an soirbheas, *the wind subsided.*

Siolc, shéúlk, *v.* snatch, seek, tiolp.

Siol-cuir, shēll′-kūĕr, *n. m.* seed corn.

Sioll, shĕúll, *n. m.* turn, rotation; *sioll* ma seach, *time about, in rotation, alternately*; 'sè so mo *shiollsa*, *this is my rotation*; an d' thàinig do *shioll-sa* stigh fhathast, *is your rotation* or *turn come round yet.*

Siolmhor, Siolar, shēll′-ur, *adj.* prolific, fertile; as corn productive, substantial.

Siolmhoireachd, shēll′-uėr-achg, *n. f.* fecundity, productiveness, fertility.

Siolt, shéúlt, *n. m.* the bird, teal.

Sioltaich, shéúlt′-ēch, *n. m.* bird, goosander.

Sioltaiche, shēlt′-ēch-ă, *n. m.* stallion, *Arran*; breeder, propagator.

Siomaidean, shēm′-aj-aen, *n. m.* a mallet.

Siomain, shēm′-an′, *n. m.* rope, sùgan.

Siomlachd, shēm′-llachg, *n. f.* chicken-heartedness, sheepishness, great cowardice.

Siomlaidh, shēm′-llē, *adj.* chicken-hearted, sheepish, spiritless, heartless.

Siomlag, shēm′-llag, *n. m.* great coward.

Siomlair, shēm′-llaėr, } *n. m.* a chimney
Siomlainn, shēm′-llēnn, } vent; ceann-*siòmlainn, chimney-stalk*; thromh 'n t-*siomlainn, through the vent.*

Sion, shēnn, *n. m.* thing, particle, nothing; cha 'n 'eil *sìon* agam, *I have nothing*; gach *sìon* a th' agam, *every particle I possess*; cha 'n 'eil *sìon* mhaith air, *it is worth nothing*; climate, element, air, atmosphere; blast, drift; a' dol an aghaidh an t-*sìon, going against the blast*; an *sìon* na chùlthaobh, *the blast, the drift of the rain in his back*; tha na *sìontan* air atharrachadh, *the climate has changed*; fom' *shìontan* dùthchasach, *under my native climate, in my native atmosphere*; mar chritheach 'san t-*sìon, like the aspen in the blast, Oss.*; tamhasg air éideadh le *sìontaibh, a spectre shrouded with the elements.*

Sionnach, shúnn′-ach, *n. m.* pipe-reed; a fox

Sionnsair, shúnn′-săr′, *n. m.* pipe-chanter.

Sior, shērr, *n. m.* time; circle of time; gu *sìor, for ever*; *adv.* and *adj.* continually, continual, perpetual, perpetually; used always before the noun or verb qualified; a' *sìor*-amharc orm, *eternally staring at me*; *sìor*-atharrachail, *ever-variable, ever-changing*; *sìor*-bhualadh, *eternally striking, thrashing*; *sìor*-iarrtach, *importunate*; *sìor*-mhagadh air, *eternally, perpetually*, or *continually jeering* or *gibing him.*

Siorr, shéurr, *v.* scud *or* slip in or out.

Siorradh, shurr′-ă, *pt.* darting, dart;—in Perthshire, sheriff, siorram.

Siorram, sheurr′-am, *n. m.* a sheriff.

Siorramachd, shurr′-am-achg, *n. f.* county, shire; sheriffdom. *Argyle.*

Siorruith, shūrr′-rúėch, *adj.* eternal, everlasting; gu *sìorruith, eternally*; (sìor, continually, and ruith, running, ever-running.)

Siorruitheachd, shērr′-ēch-achg, *n. f.* eternity.

Sios, shēss, *n. m. adv.* bottom; a *sìos, down, downward*; a' dol *sìos, going down, setting, sinking*; o shiùbhail *sìos* agus suas, *from going up and down. Bible.*

Siosar, shēss′-ur, *n. m.* pair of scissors.

Siota, shētt-a′, *n. m.* a blackguard, a pet.

Sir, shēr, *n. m.* a knight; *Sir* Seumas, *Sir James*; *v.* seek, ask, search; *sir* e, *seek it*; want; dè tha thu *sireadh, what do you want?* esan a *shireas*, gheibh, *he who seeks, shall find. Bible.*

Siris, Sirist, shēr′-ēsh, shēr′-ēshj, *n. f.* cherry; the island of Tyree.

Siristeach, shēr′-ēshjj-ach, *adj.* belonging to Tyree; *n. m.* a shelty, pony; a Tyree man.

Sitearn, shējt′-arn, *n. f.* a harp.

Sith, shhe, *adj.* spiritual; daoine *sìth, fairies*; bean, neo leannan *sìth, a familiar spirit, Bible*; *n. f.* peace, truce; cogadh na *sìth, either war or peace*; quietness, tranquillity; an *sìth, in quietness.*

Sith, for sigh, shēgh, skip, dart.

Sitheach, shē′-ach, *n. m.* a fairy, *Mainland*; *Argyle.*

Sitheil, shē′-al, *adj.* peaceful, quiet.

Sithionn, shē′-unn, *n. f.* venison.

Sith-mhaor, shē-vāor′, *n. m.* a herald.

Sith-shaimh, shē-háėv, *n. f.* delightful, quiet.

Sitir, shējt′-ēr, *v.* neigh; *n. f.* a neigh.

Sitreach, shəjt′-ryach, *adj.* neighing.

Sitrich, shəjt′-rrēch, *n. f.* continuous neighing.

Siubhail, shū²′-ul, *v.* go, proceed, walk; *siùbhlaidh* sinn le 'n anam do 'n àraich, *we shall accompany their souls to the battle field, Oss.*; traverse, search; *shiubhail* mi am baile, *I traversed* or *perambulated the whole city*; die, depart this life; *siùbhlaidh* sinn gu lèir, *we shall all die,*

Siubhal, shū′-al, *pt.* traversing, perambulating, searching; a' *siubhal* a' bhaile, *traversing the town*; dying, act of dying; tha e *siubhal, he is dying*; time, course, trip; so mo *siubhalsa, this is my time*; marsanta-*siubhail, a pedlar, packman, hauker*; luchd *siubhail, travellers*; tha i air *shiubhal, she (the mare) is salacious*; time, trip; air an t-*siubhal* so, *at this time*; *siubhail* eile, *at another time*; bithidh fios do sheud do *shiubhail* agamsa, *I shall know the object of your pursuit* or *journey*; *adv.* once, at a time; *siubhal* a chaidh mi do'n ghalldachd, *once I went to the Low country*; an dubh-*shiubhlach, the street-walker*; air gach *siùbhal, at every trip*; bean-*shiùbhla, woman in child-bed*; laidhe-*shiùbhla, confinement at,* or *before child-birth.*

Siubhlach, shūl′-ach, *a.* nimble; traversing.

Siuc, shŭchg, way of calling horses in Lewis.

Siucar, shûchg′-ar, *n. m.* sugar, (*Fr.*sucre).

Siuch, shèŭch, *n. m.* a drain, sewer. *Scotch.*

Siud, shŭdd′, *v.* fall to; swing.

Siudadh, shŭdd′-ă, *n. m.* commencement.

Siudan, shūd′-an, *n. m.* oscillation, swinging; a *siùdan* a nunn is nall, *oscillating this way and that way*; ri *siùdan, vibrating, swinging, oscillating.*

Siudanach, shūd′-an-ach, *adj.* swinging, rocking, oscillating, vibrating.

Siug, shŭg, *inter.* mode of driving away hens.

Siuil, shū'll, *gen. pl.* seòl, sails, &c.

Siursach, shūrs′-ach, *n. f.* a whore.

Siursachd, shūr′-achg, *n. f.* whoredom.

Siuthad, shŭ′-ad, *v.* say away, fall to, commence; swing; contracted Siùd.

Slabhacan, slâv′-achg-an, *n. m.* sea-edible weed, styled by the Scotch Slogue.

Slabhag, slav′-ag, *n. f.* a horn-pith.

Slabhraidh, -**raich**, slav′-rēch, *n. f.* a chain; *slabhraich* òir, *gold chain*; pot-hanger; gen *slabhraich*; hence Maclauran, from a most singular tradition about a sea-nymph.

Slabhradair, slav′-rad-aèr, *n. m.* chair-maker.

Slachd, slăchg, *v.* beat, thrash; *n. m.* mallet.

Slachdanaich, slăchg′-an-èch, *v.* beetle.

Slachdraich, slachg′-rēch, *n. f.* incessant hammering.

Slad, slădd′, *n. m.* havoc, carnage; 's iad a rinn an *slad, what havoc they have made*! 's ann an sin a bha an *slad, that was the awful place for carnage*! *v.* cause to fag, fag, deprive of strength; *shlad* sin seachad iad, *that made them fag*; it palled on their stomach; *shlad* e mo chlì bhuan, *it deprived me of my strength*;—robbing, rob. *Macdonald.*

Slaight, slaŏėjt, *n. f.* roguery, knavery, villainy; *v.* sneak *or* steal by; *shlaight* e seachad, *he sneaked* or *stole by*; better than *slaoight*, because ao is always long and marked thus, āo; short aŏ in the key.

Slaightear, slaŏėjt′-ăer, *n. m.* rogue, villain, knave.

Slaightearachd, slaŏėjt′-ar-achg, *n. f.* roguery, villainy, sneaking.

Slaighteil, slaŏėjt′-al, *adj.* roguish, sneakish.

Slaim, sláèm, *n. f.*; see Sglaim.

Slaine, slàèn′-à, more *or* most healthy.

Slainte, slàenjt′-á, *n. f.* health, salvation; mar chìr mheala, tha briathra taitneach, milis do 'n anam, agus n' an *slàinte* do na cnàmhan, *pleasant words are as an honey-comb, sweet to the soul, and health to the bones*; chionn gun do dhìochuimhnich thu Dia do *shlàinte, because thou hast forgotten the* God *of thy salvation*; toast; thoir dhuinn *slàinte, give us a toast*; dh' òl sinn do dheoch *slàinte, we drank to your health*; air do *shlàinte, to your good health*; *slàinte* agadsa, *thank you, Sir,* or *Madam.*

Slaintealachd, slàènjt′-al-achg, *n. f.* healthiness.

Slainteil, slàènjt′-al, *a.* healthy, solitary.

Slais, slăsh, *v.* last, drub; *n. f.* a lash; a great quantity *or* number; *slais* èisg, *great number of fish*; fhuair iad *slais, they got a great quantity.*

Slamb, slămbb, *n. m.* jam, jelly;—lock. *Ir.*

Slamban, slámb′-an, *n. m.* curds and cream.

Slan, slàn, *adj.* healthy, in good health, sound; whole, perfect, unbroken; am bheil thu *slàn, art thou in good health*? thoir dhomh *slàn* e, *give it me whole*; *slàn* leat, *fare thee well! farewell*! gu 'm a *slàn* gu 'n till thu, *may you return in health*; an *slàn* duit, *art thou well*? a nighean nan òr-chleachd, an *slàn* duit, *maiden of the golden locks, art thou well*? tha i gu *slàn* fàllan, *she is perfectly well, she is hale and sound*; òighean bhoidheach, *slàn* leibh, *ye pretty maids, farewell! Oss. Ar.*; gu'm a *slàn* a chì mi thu, *well may I see you.*

Slanach, slàn′-ach, *a.* convalescent.

SLANAICH, slàn'-èch, *v.* heal, make whole.

SLAN-LUS, slàn'-lus, *n. m.* ribwort.

SLANAIGHEAR, slàn'-è-ar, *n. m.* saviour.

SLAOD, slāod, *v.* drag, haul, pull along; 'ga *shlaodadh, trailing* or *hauling it*; *n.m.* a lounge, a great quantity; raft, float.

SLAODACH, s'lāod'-ach, *a.* lounging, lazy.

SLAODADH, s'lāod'-X, *pt.* dragging, trailing.

SLAODAIL, s'lāod'-al, *adj.* clumsy, lazy.

SLAODAIRE, s'lāod'-ur-a, *n. m.* lounger.

SLAODANACH, s'lāod'-an-ach, *n.* heavy fellow.

SLAODRAICH, s'lāod'-rèch, *n. f.* great haul of fish; trailing continually *or* always.

SLAOIGHTIRE, slāoèjt, &c.; see Slaightire.

SLAOP, s'lāop, *v.* parboil *or* boil slowly, as shell-fish for fish-bait; boil slightly.

SLAOPAIRE, slāop'-ur-a, *n. m.* a drawler, trailer.

SLAP, s'lăp, *n. m.* a flap, flapping; *v.* flap, fling; a' *slapail* ma'm' chluasan, *flapping about my ears.*

SLAPCHAIL, slăp'-cha'l, *n. m.* spinage.

SLAPAIRE, s'lap'-ur-à, *n. m.* dangler.

SLAPAICH, s'lăp'èch, *v.* get flappish, get soft and pliant, as greens heated.

SLAT, s'lat, *n. f.* a wand, a yard of any kind, a switch, rod, *or* twig; thog e an t-*slat, he lifted the rod*; *slat* air fad, *a yard long*; *slat*-iomain, *a goad*; *slat*-mharcachd, *rider's whip* or *switch*; *slat*-shiùil, *sail-yard*; *slat*-shuaicheantais, *a sceptre, mace*; *slat*-dhraoidheachd, *mace, rod of office*; *slat*-thomhais, *a wand*; *slat*-sgiùrsaidh, *a lash, scourge*; *slat*-rìoghail, *a sceptre*; *slat*-mhara, *tangle*; *slat* ghlas do 'n chritheach, *a green rod of poplar*; *slat*-iasgaich, *fishing-rod*; *slat*-reul, *an astrolobe*; *slat*-bheoil (beulstoc properly) *gunwale*; *v.* do so and so. *Per.*

SLATAIRE, slăt'-ur-à, *n. m.* debauchee. *P.*

SLATAIREACHD, slat'-ur-achg, *n. f.* v——, *Perthshire*; in Lochaber, Conanachd; in Argyle, Cleamhnas.

SLEAGH, slyaŏgh, *n. f.* spear, lance, javelin; biodh ar *sleagh* mar theachdaire a bhàis, *let your spears be as the messengers of death*; thog sinn *sleigh, we lifted spears. Ossian.*

SLEAGHACH, slyaŏgh'-ach, *a.* armed with spears.

SLEAGHAIRE, slyaŏgh'-eir-à, *n. m.* spearman.

SLEAMHNA, slév'-nà, *adj.* more slippery.

SLEAMHNACHADH, slév'-nach-X, *pt.* sliding, slipping; retrograding, getting worse.

SLEAMHNAICH, slev'-nnèch, *v.* slide, slip.

SLEAMHUINN, slev'-ènn, *adj.* slippery.

SLEIBH, slyāv, *gen.* sliabh, mountains.

SLEIBHTE, **SLEIBHTEAN**, slyāv'-tya, slyāv'-tyan, *n. pl.* sides of hills, hills; mossy plains.

SLEIBHTEACH, slyāv'-tyach, *adj.* mountainous.

SLEISDE, slyāshj'-à, *n. gen.* sliasaid.

SLEOG, slyôg, *v.* pall on the stomach.

SLEOGACH, slyôg'-ach, *adj.* apt to pall on the stomach; slimy.

SLEUG, slè'g, *v.* sneak, drawl.

SLEUGACH, slègg'-ach, *n. f.* a sneaking, sly, drawling female; *adj.* sly and slow.

SLEUGAIRE, slègg'-ur-a, *n. m.* sly, drawling, sneaking fellow; a sneaker, drawler.

SLEUCHD, slyèchg, *v.* go on your knees, prostrate; *sleuchdamaid, let us kneel, prostrate.*

SLEUCHDADH, slyèchg'-X, *pt.* prostration.

SLIABH, slĕăv, *n. m.* the face of a hill, a heath; an extensive tract of dry moorland, a hill; *slèibhtean, faces of hills, hills.*

SLIABHAIRE, slĕăv'-ur-a, *n.m.* mountaineer

SLIASAID, slĕăs'-ējj, *n. f.* a thigh; *pl.* sléisdean, *part of a boat near the stern.*

SLIBIST, sliobast, clumsy, unhandy.

SLIGE, slèg'-à, *n. f.* a shell; *slige* creadha, *a potsherd, Bible*; *slige*-chreach, *a scollop-shell*; hull of a ship *or* any vessel.

SLIGEACH, slèg'-ach, *adj.* a shelly; *n. f.* a wreck; crustacious surface.

SLIGIRE, slèg'-ur-à, *n. m.* conchologist.

SLIGHIREACHD, slèg'-ur-achg, *n. f.* conchology.

SLIGHE, slè'-à, *n. f.* a way, craft; journey.

SLIGHEACH, slè'-ach, *a.* crafty, wily, cunning.

SLINN, slènn, *n. f.* weaver's reed *or* sleay.

SLINNEAN, slènn'-ăèn, *n. m.* shoulder-blade.

SLINNEANACH, slènn'-ăèn-ach, *a.* broad shouldered.

SLINNEANACHD, slènn'-ăèn-achg, *n. f.* a sort of augury by inspecting gigots of an animal, by eating the flesh without touching the bone with a tooth *or* nail.

SLIOB, slèbb, *v.* stroke gently. *H. S.*

SLIOBASTA, slèbb'-ast-a, *a.* clumsy.

SLIOBASTACHD, slèbb'-ast-achg, *n. f.* clumsiness.

SLIOCHD, slèùchg, *n. m.* offspring, progeny, descendants, posterity; *sliochd* Dhiarmaid, *the offspring of Dermid*; track, print, rut; *sliochd* na roithean, *the track or rut of the wheels*; *sliochd* a mheur, *the print of his fingers.*

SLIOG, slĕgg, *v.* stroke gently, cajole.

SLIOGAIRE, slĕgg'-ur-a, *n.f.* stroker, cajoler.

SLIOGACH, slĕgg'-ach, *adj.* sleeky, slim.

SLIOM, slĕm[2], *adj.* sleeky, smooth.

SLIOMAIR, slĕm'-ăèr, *n. m.* a mean, low, flattering, fawning fellow.

SLIOP, slĕpp[2], *n. f.* a hanging under-lip.

SLIOPACH, slĕpp[2]'-ach, *adj.* blubber-lipped.

SLIOPAIRE, slépp'-ur-à, *n. m.* a sulky, surly, blubber-lipped fellow.

Slios, slêss, *n. m.* side; gentle declivity.
Slis, slèsh, *v.* slice; *n. f.* a chip, shave.
Slisneach, slèch′-nyach, *adj.* having sides.
Slochd, slòchg, *n. m.* den, pit, dungeon; *slochd*-guail, *coal-pit*; *slochd*-sàibhaidh, *saw-pit.*
Slochdach, slochg′-ach, *a.* full of pits.
Slochdaich, slochg′-ach, *v.* hollow, dig.
Sloinn, slaŏ′-ènn, *v.* name, bestow a surname; *sloinnidh* e féin air ainm Israil, *he shall surname himself by the name of Israel. B.*
Sloinneadh, slaŏènn′-X, *n. m.* surname.
Sloinntear, slaŏènn′-tyar, *n. m.* genealogist.
Sloinntearachd, slaŏènn′-tyar-achg, *n. f.* genealogy.
Sloinnteil, slaŏènjt′-al, *adj.* genealogical.
Sloisir, slosh′-ėr, *v.* dash against. *H. S.*
Sluagh, slŭă′-gh, *n. m.* multitude, people.
Sluaigheach, slŭaĕ′-y-hach, *n f.* an expedition. *Ir.*
Sluaisdir, sluashj′-ėr, *v.* draggle, poke.
Sluasaid, slŭăs′-ėjj, *n. f.* a shovel.
Slug, slŭg, *n. f.* a miry puddle.
Slug-pholl, slŭg′-fòll, *n. f.* whirlpool. *Ir.*
Sluichd, slŭèchg, *n. pl.* pits; *gen.* of a pit.
Sluig, slŭėg, *v.* swallow, devour.
Sluigean, slŭėg′-ăėn, *n. m.* the gullet.
Sluigte, slŭėg′-tya, *pt.* swallowed, devoured.
Smachd, smăchg, *n. m.* authority, control; fo'd' *smachd*-sa, *under your authority* or *control*; correction, discipline; cuir *smachd* air, *correct him, control him, discipline him.*
Smachdaich, smăchg′-ėch, *v.* correct, check, discipline; keep in order, chastise, reprove.
Smachdail, smachg′-a'l, *adj.* authoritative.
Smachdalachd, smăchg′-al-achg, *n. f.* authoritativeness, firmness of character.
Smad, smâdd, *v.* revile terribly, abuse.
Smadadh, smâd′-X, *pt.* abusing; *n. m.* abuse.
Smadail, smâdd′-al, *adj.* abusive in the extreme; very abusive.
Smag, smág, *n. f.* a paw, large hand.
Smag, smâg, for smàig, the ascendant.
Smagach, smâg′-ach, *n. m.* a toad. *North.*
Smaig, smâėg, *n. f.* tyranny, the upper-hand, the ascendant; fo d' *smàig*, *under your tyranny, arbitrary sway, despotism.*
Smaigealachd, smăėg′-al-achg, *n. f.* extreme despotism, great degree of tyranny.
Smaigeil, smâėg′-al, *adj.* despotic, arbitrary.
Smaigean, smâėg′-aėn, *n. m.* a toad. *P. S.*
Smaigire, smâėg′-ėr-á, *n. f.* tyrant, despot.
Smaigireachd, smâėg′-ėr-achg, *n. f.* tyranny, despotism, tyrannical conduct.
Smal, smâll, *v.* snuff a candle, dash to pieces; *smàl* e as a chéile iad, *he dashed them to pieces, he smashed them*; *n. f.* snuff of a candle, ashes.
Smal, smal, *n. m.* dust covering any thing; spot; *smal* air an òr, *the gold became dim. B.*; stain, spot. *B.*
Smaladair, smâll′-ad-aėr, *n. m.* pair of snuffers.
Smaladh, smâll′-X, *pt.* snuffing, smashing, dashing to pieces; *smàlaidh* mi an t-ionnachainn asad, *I will dash out your brains.*
Smalag, smăl′-ag, *n. m.* coal-fish; céiteanach; *n. f.* smacking kiss.
Smalan, small′-an, *n. m.* slight melancholy.
Smaoin, smùėn, *n. f.* a thought, idea.
Smaoinich, } smùėnjt′-ėch, *v.* think, ima-
Smaointich, } gine, conceive, ponder, meditate.
Smaoitinn, smùėnnjt′-ėnn, *n. f.* idea, thought; *pt.* thinking, conceiving, pondering, imagining. *Argyle.*
Smarach, smar′-ach, *n. m.* a large, large louse.
Smeach, smech, *v.* make a fillip with the fingers; *n. m.* smart, quick blow; a fillip; in Irish, chin.
Smeachan, smech′-an, *n. m.* chin-bit, *or* cheek-band of a bridle. *Islay.*
Smeacharra, smech′-urr-a, *adj.* lively, brisk.
Smeacharrachd, smech′-urr-achg, *n. f.* liveliness.
Smeachran, smech′-ran, *n. m.* too much liberty with edged tools; tampering.
Smeachranachd, smech′-ran-achg, *n. f.* bandying civilities with your betters; officious interference, using too much liberty with people, *or* dangerous weapons.
Smealach, smel′-ach, *a.* having a beautiful eye and engaging countenance; *n. m.* offals. *N.*
Smeid, smèjj, *v. n.* beckon, wave to;—aim.
Smeideadh, smèjj′-X, *pt.* beckoning, waving; *n. m.* a wink, *or* beckoning; aim; slight tinge, *or* degree; cuir *sméideadh* mar so e, *put it a slight degree this way*; *sméideadh* eile, *another touch*; *sméid* air, *wave to him, beckon to him.*
Smeoirn, smyôėrn, *n. m.* end of an arrow.
Smeorach, smyôr′-ach, *n. f.* mavis, thrush.
Smeur, smèr, *n. f.* a bramble-berry; *v.* smear, (smiùr, properly in the latter sense.)
Smeuraich, smèr′-ech, *v.* grope for vermin; used for smùraich, more properly.
Smid, smėjj, *n. f.* syllable; na h-abair *smid, mum! hush! open not your lips.*
Smig, smèg, smigead, smėg′-ad, *n. f.* chin.
Smigeal, smėg′-ul, *n. f.* smirking, smiling.
Smiolamas, smeúl′-am-as, *n. m.* refuse of a feast.

SMIOR, smèûr, *n. m.* marrow, the best, hero, energy; *smior* an t-sìl, *the best of the oats*; duine gun *smior, a man without energy*; *smior*-chailleach, *the spinal marrow.*

SMIORAIL, smèûr'-al, *adj.* brisk, energetic.

SMIORACH, smèûr'-ach, *n. m.* a lively louse.

SMIORALAS, smeúr'-al-us, *n. m.* energy, life.

SMIOT, smètt, *v.* throw in the air with one hand, and strike with the other; strike smartly; a' *smiotadh, thus striking*; also smart blow.

SMIUR, smèûr, *v.* smear, *or* grease.

SMIURADH, smèûr'-ă, *pt. n. m.* smearing.

SMOD, SMODAN, smod'-an, *n. m.* drizzling rain.

SMODAL, smod'-al, *n. m.* smattering, refuse.

SMODANACH, smod'-an-ach, *adj.* drizzling.

SMODANACHD, smod'-an-achg, *n. f.* drizziliness.

SMOG, smôg. *N. H.*; see Smàg.

SMOGAIRNEACH, smôg'-arn'-ach, *n. m.* a large-pawed squat fellow, *or* beast.

SMUAIN, smŭăèn, *n. f.* thought. *Perthshire.*

SMUAINICH, smŭăĕn'-èch, *v.* think, imagine.

SMUAIREAN, smŭăèr'-áèn, *n. m.* slight offence, dejection, *or* grief, *or* melancholy.

SMUAIREANACH, smŭăĕr'-ăèn-ach, *adj.* grieved, dejected, somewhat melancholy.

SMUAIS, smŭăèsh, *n. f.* substance of bones.

SMUCH, smûch, *n. f.* nasal sound; *v.* purr.

SMUCHAIL, smûch'-ul, *adj.* nasal, purring through the nose; *pt.* speaking through the nose.

SMUCHAN, smŭch'-an, *n. m.* half-smothered fire.

SMUDAN, smûd'-an, *n. m.* smoke raised for signal;—a kiln; music of birds. *N.*

SMUG, smŭg, *n. f.* spittle, phlegm, snot.

SMUGAID, smŭg'-èjj, *n. f.* spittle, phlegm.

SMUGAIDEACH, smŭg'-èjj-ach, *a.* phlegmatic.

SMUID, smûjj, *n. f.* column of smoke; smoke; *v.* smash, dash, to pieces; *smùid* e as a chéile e, *he dashed it to pieces*; curse.

SMUIDEADH, smûjj'-ă, *pt.* dashing, smashing; swearing terribly, cursing.

SMUIDREACH, smûjj'-ryach, *n. f.* bolt of smoke.

SMUILC, smŭelk, *n. f.* a curled nose.

SMUILCEACH, smŭèlk'-ach, *adj.* curl-nosed.

SMUIRNEAN, smûèrn'-ăèn, *n. m.* a mote • dust.

SMUR, smûr, *n. m.* dust, dross, rubbish.

SMURACH, smûr'-ach, *n. m.* dust; groping among dust with the hands; *pt.* groping.

SMURAICH, smûr'-èch, *v.* grope in dust.

SMUT, smutt, *n. f.* pug-nose, snout.

SMUTACH, smŭtt'-ach, *a.* pug-nosed, snoutish

SNA, snă, (for anns an, *and*, is na), in the; and not; *'sna* h-oidhcheachan, *in the nights*; folbh *'sna* fan, *go and wait not.*

SNAG, snag, *n. f.* a smart, little, audible knock.

SNAG, snàg, *pt.* sneaking, creeping.

SNAGAIRE, snàg'-ur'-ă, *n. m.* creeping, sly fellow; sneaking fellow.

SNAGAN, snág'-an, *n. m.* a deep drink.

SNAGAN, snàg'-an, *n. m.* creeping slily.

SNAGARDAICH, snág'-ard-èch, } *n. f.* gnashing of teeth.
SNAGARSAICH, snág'-ars-èch, }

SNAIDH, snáè'-y', *v.* reduce by cutting with a knife; hew stones; clachan *snaidhte, hewn stones*; pine away; tha e a' *snaidheadh* as, *he is pining away.*

SNAIDHEADAIR, snáè'-ad-ăèr, *n. m.* hewer, cutter.

SNAIDHEADH, snáè'-yă, *pt. n. m.* cutting, slicing, hewing, pining away; art of hewing, &c.

SNAIDHTE, snăè'-y[2]-tyă, *pt.* cut down, hewn; dressed, as a stick.

SNAIG, snàèg, *v.* creep, crawl, sneak.

SNAIM, snàèm, *n. f.* knot, tie; snaom.

SNAITH, snàè, *v.* thread a hook. *Suthl.*

SNAITHEAN, snáèch'-áèn, *n. m. pt.* a single thread.

SNAMH, snàv, *n. m.* swimming; *v.* swim, air *snàmh, swimming, afloat, skim over*; tha m'anam a' *snàmh* an ceò, *my soul swims in mist. Sm.*; cuir air *snàmh, cause to float*; deluging; a' cur an tighe air *snàmh, deluging the house*; cuirear an tìr air *snàmh, the land shall be deluged*; soaked. *Bible*; *pt.* swimming, floating, soaking, deluging.

SNAOIS, snùsh, *n. f.* a slice; boat-prow. *Sk.*

SNAOISEAN, snùsh'-áèn, *n. m.* snuff, pinch; thoir dhomh *snaoisean, give me a snuff a pinch*; a huff.

SNAOISEANACH, snùsh'-áèn-ach, *a.* snuffy.

SNAOIDH, snúèy', } *n. f.* a bier; air an t *snaoidh, on the bier.*
SNAIMH, snúèv, }

SNAOIM, snùm, *n. f.* a knot, tie; *v.* tie a knot.

SNAOTH, snú, *v.* jerk, twitch.

SNAOTHADH, snú'-ă, *pt. n. m.* jerking; a jerk.

SNAP, snap, *v.* snap; trigger; *n. m.* morsel.

SNAS, snás, *n. m.* regularity, elegance, seemly appearance, decency; dean le *snas* e, *do it decently*; gnothach gun *snas, an absurd thing—business without any degree of elegance* or *propriety*; polish; *v.* polish, ornament; also snasaich.

SNASAR, } snás'-ur, *adj.* elegant, polished, neat.
SNASMHOR, }

SNASMHORACHD, snás'-ur-achg, *n. f.* elegance.

SNATH, snhá, *n. m.* thread, yarn.

SNATHAD, snà'-ud, *n. f.* a needle.

SNATHAINN, snà'-ènn, snaithean; thread.

SNATHAINNEACH, snà'-ăèn-ach, *a.* ropy.

SNATH-CUIR, snhà'-kŭèr, *n. m.* waft.

SNEACHD, snechg, *n. m.* snow.

SNEADH, sné, *n. f.* a nit; sneomh.

SNEOGHAN, snḗ-an, *n. m.* ant; seangan. *N.*

SNEOMH, snyóv², *n. f.* nit, louse-egg.

SNICHD, SNICHDEAN, snhéchg'-áén, *n. m.* a stitch of a needle; a thread; gach *snichdean* a th' agam, *every stitch I have.*

SNIDH, snhė, *v.* drop, shed tears; bheireadh do ghnáthachadh air na clachan *snidheadh, your conduct would make the very stones shed tears.*

SNIDHE, snhė'-ă, *pt.* oozing through the roof of a house; shedding tears; a ghruaidh a' *snidhead, his cheek shedding tears.*

SNIDHEACH, snhė'-ach, } *adj.* not water-
SNIDHTEACH, snhė'-tyach, } tight, as a house; tearful.

SNIOMH, snēv, *v.* spin, twist, twine; *shnìomh* na mnathan, *the women spun*; *shnìomh* e á m' laimh e, *he twisted it out of my hand*; *n. m.* spinning; the art of spinning, *or* twisting; *pt.* spinning; *shniomh* e an t-sleagh a làimh, *he twisted the spear out of his hand. Oss.*; *shniomh* e an ceann deth, *he wrung his head off. Bible.*

SNIOMHAIN, snhėv'-áėn, *n. m.* twisted, spiral, helical; falt *snìomhain, hair in ringlets.*

SNIOMHTE, snhēv'-tyȧ, *pt.* spun, twisted.

SNIOMHADAIR, snēv'-ad-ăėr, *n. m.* spinner.

SNOD, snôdd', *n. f.* fishing-line.

SNOID, snôėjj, *v.* hoop *or* thread a hook.

SNOIDEAN, snôjj'-aėn, *n. m.* snuff; an òl thu *snòidean, will you take* (drink) *a snuff*?—downright nonsense for an gabh thu *snaoisean*, (must not tell.)

SNOIG, snóėg, expression of countenance of a testy *or* snuffy person.

SNOIGEIS, snóėg'-ash, *n. f.* huff, testiness.

SNOIGEISEACH, snóėg'-ash-ach, *a.* huffy, testy.

SNOMHACH, snóv'-ach, *n. f.* foliage, verdure, (the compound of nomhach, *or* nomha,) under skin.

SNOT, snŏtt, *v.* snuff the wind, suspect. *H.S.*

SNUADH, snŭă'-gh, *n. m.* visage, hue, colour of the face; beauty, complexion, aspect; bheir thu air a *shnuadh* caitheadh mar leòmainn, *thou shalt make his beauty to consume as a moth. B.*; is gruamaiche *snuadh, of the gloomiest aspect.*

SNUADHAR, *adj.* } snua'-ghur, good-look-
SNUADMHOR, } ing, having a fair complexion; *snuadhar* treun, *pleasant to behold, and valiant. Oss.*; duine *snuadhar, a comely person. B.*

SO, shó, *nem. pron.* this, these; an duine *so, this man*; an nighean *so, this girl*; na nigheanan *so*, na daoine *so, these girls, these men*; *adv.* mar *so, in this manner, thus*; rinn mi mar *so, I acted thus, I did this way*; an *so*, ann an *so, here*; *so, so, come, come, here, here*; c'arson *so, why so*? gluais as an *so, leave this place, be off*! mar *so*, is mar siod, *this way and that way*; gus an *so, till this time, till now*; gus an *so* bu treun e, *till now he was valiant*; o'n àm *so, henceforward, hence*; *so* agad e, *here you have him* or *it*; thoir a *so* e, *take him hence, take it away*; *so* mar a ni thu, *thus you will do*; an *so* 'san sìod, *here and there.*

SO, sō², *adv.* easily, (used always before the participle qualified); *so*-aireamh, *easily counted, computable, numerable*; *so*-cheannsachadh, *conquerable*; *so*-leubhadh, *legible, readable, easily read*; *so*-aithneachadh, *easily recognised, conspicuous*; *so*-lùbadh, *flexible, seducible*; *so*-aimsir, *good weather*; *do*-aimsir, *bad weather.*

SOBHRACH, *n. f.* } sōr'-ach-an, *n. m.* prim-
SOBHRACHAN, } rose; sort of clover.

SOC, sōchg², *n. m.* ploughshare.

SOC, sŏchg, *n. m.* snout of a pig; beak.

SOCACH, sŏchg'-ach, *a.* snouttish; *n. f.* pert female; certain extent of arable land. *N. Highlands.*

SOCAIR, sŏchg'-ėr, *n. f.* ease, quiet, rest, leisure; gabh *socair, take ease*; am bheil thu air do *shocair, are you at leisure*? *socair* a dhuine so, *at leisure, my dear sir*? settled state of weather, abatement of a storm; a cheud *socair* a thig, *the first abatement of the storm*; prop, fulcrum, peace, tranquillity; gun *socair* oidhche na latha, *without peace night or day*; *adj.* easy, comfortably situated, *or* seated, at rest; tranquil, peaceable; tha mi *socair, I am well seated, I am at peace*; mild, moderate, settled; tha'm feasgair *socair, the evening is mild, is more moderate*; *Int.* avast! avast!

SOCHAR, soch'-ur, *n. m.* benefit, advantage; cha *sochar* 'sam bith sin domhsa, *that is no advantage to me*; immunity, *or* privilege; *socharan* chlann Dhè, *the privileges of the children of God.*

SOCHARACH, sŏch'-ar-ach, *adj.* simple, easily imposed upon, silly; duine *socharach, a weak* or *simple person*; o'n a bha mi cho *socharach, since I was so simple, so silly*; c'arson a bha thu cho *socharach, why were you so silly* or *simple*?

SOCHARACHD, sŏch'-ar-achd, *n. f.* gullability.

SOCHARAICH, sŏch'-ar-ėch, *n. f.* simplicity, too compliant a disposition, silliness, want of suspicion; 'si an t-*socharaich*, a thug orm a dheanadh, *pure simplicity made me do it.*

SOCRACH, sochg'-rach, *adj.* easy, moderate.

SOCRAICH, sŏchg'-rėch, *v. n.* settle, establish, fix, appease; *shocraich* am feasgar, *the evening settled, got moderate*; *shocraich* e fichead pund sassannach urra 'sa bhliadhna, *he settled an annuity of twenty pounds on her*; *shocraich* e chridhe air sin, *he fixed his heart on that*; appease, assuage; *shocraich* 'fhearg, *his rage subsided*; arrange, adjust; *shocraich* e an gnothach sin, *he adjusted that business, arranged that affair*; level, make even; *socraich* an t-àite so, *level* or *make even this place.*

SOCRAICHTE, sŏchg'-rèch-tyà, *adj.* settled, arranged, &c.; made level, *or* even; established, fixed upon; a chridhe *socraichte* air peacadh, *his heart fixed,* or *bent on sin*; tha'n t-àite sin *socraichte, that place is levelled, made even.*

SOD, sòd, *n. m.* steam. *N.*; stout person.

SODAN, sòd'-an, *n. m.* complaisance, expression of happiness by gesture at meeting; air son *sodain* riutsa, *out of sheer complaisance to you*; fawning; rinn an cù *sodan* ris, *the dog fawned upon him.*

SODANACH, sod'-an-ach, *adj.* complaisant.

SODAR, sòd'-ur, *n. m.* trotting horse. *H. Society.*

SODARBHROCHAN, sod'-ur-vhrŏch-an, *n.* thick gruel.

SOG, sŏg, *n. m.* good humour; na biodh *sog* air, *were he in good humour?* merriment. *H.*

SOGH, sô'-gh', *n. m.* luxury, delicious fare.

SOGHALACHD, sôgh'-al-achg, *n. m.* luxuriousness, sumptuousness, deliciousness.

SOGHAIL, sô'-ghal, *a.* delicious, luxurious.

SOGHAR, sô'-ghur, *adj.* luxurious, delicious.

SOILLEARACHADH, sòelly''-ar²-Ă, *pt.* getting clear *or* dawning; elucidating, manifesting; *n. m.* elucidation, dawn; anns an t-*soillearachadh, about the dawn;* an latha a' *soillearachadh, the day dawning.*

SOILLEARACHD, sòelly''-aèr'-achg, *n. f.* brightness, shrewdness, conspicuousness, clearness.

SOILLEIR, sòelly'-aèr, *adj.* clear, evident, plain; tha sin *soilleir, that is evident* or *obvious*; latha *soilleir, clear day*; limpid, transparent, conspicuous; *soilleir* mar chriostal, *clear as crystal. Bible*; sruth *soilleir, limpid stream*; a' deanadh *soilleir* a' ghnothaich, *making the business conspicuous*; shrewd, clear-sighted.

SOILLEIRICH, sòelly'-aèr-èch, *v.* elucidate, manifest, make evident, explain; a' *soilleireachadh* a ghnothaich so dhomh, *elucidating,* or *making this affair evident to me.*

SOILLSE, saŏèllsh'-shà, *n. f.* flash of light; a luminary; light of the sun; light from heaven.

SOILLSEACH, saoèllsh'-ach, *a.* bright; *n. f* eye-bright.

SOILLSEACHADH, saŏellsh'-shech-Ă, *pt.* enlightening, gleaming; *n. f.* elucidation, explanation.

SOILLSICH, saŏellysh'-èch, *v.* enlighten, dawn.

SOILLSIRE, saŏellsh'-ur-a, *n. m.* a lantern.

SO-IOMCHAR, so'-em-ach-ur, *a.* easily borne.

SOIR, sòer, *n. m.* bag. *M'F.*; *adv. adj.* east, eastward. *N.*

SOIRBH, sŏèrvv, *adj* easily accomplished, easy; ni *soirbh, an easy thing, a thing easily accomplished*; gentle, good-natured, docile; duine *soirbh, tractable, docile,* or *a good-tempered person*; kind; urbane. *Gillies.*

SOIRBHE, sŏer'-a, *n. m.* easiness; *deg.* easier, &c.

SOIRBHEACHADH, sŏerv'-ach-Ă, *pt.* succeeding, prospering; *n.m.* success, prosperity; *soirbheachadh* math leat, *great success,* or *prosperity to you.*

SOIRBHEACHD, sŏerv'-achg, *n. f.* easiness.

SOIRBHEAS, sŏèr'-as, *n. m.* wind; easiness, quietness, gentleness, docility, success.

SOIRBHICH, sŏèrv'-èch, *v. n.* succeed, prosper; deamar a *soirbhich* leat, *how did you succeed? shoirbheachaidh* leis gach ni a ni e, *every thing he doth shall prosper.*

SOIRE, sòer'-à, *n. m.* vessel, womb. *Bible.*

SOIREANN, sŏer'-unn, *n. f.* calm weather.

SOIS, sŏsh, *adj.* fond of ease, snug.

SOISE, shāoèsh'-à, *n. f.* a bolis, *or* ball of fire, moving majestically in the heavens, and often near the earth.*

SOISEALTA, sŏsh'-allt-a, *adj.* fond of ease, effeminate, unmanly.

SOISEALTACHD, sŏsh'-allt'-achg, *n. f.* indulgence in ease *or* effeminacy.

SOISGEUL, saŏèsh'-skèll, *n.m.* gospel; (from *sois,* a meteor, *or* bolis, and *sgeul,* tidings, *i. e.* the history of the star in the horizon.)

SOISGEULACH, saŏèsh'-skell-ach, *a.* evangelical; bringing good news *or* tidings; evangelical.

SOISGEULAICHE, saoèsh'-skèll-èch-à, *n. m.* evangelist.

---

* These are very common in the Highlands, and are supposed to presage the death of some personage, or the fall of some nation. Soise Tragh-Ghrunairt was a remarkable one, being seen in the vicinity of the place where the memorable battle of "Latha-Tragh-Ghrunairt" was fought—so decisive of the fate of the Macleans, in their struggle for the ascendant, against MACDONALD OF THE ISLES, the nephew of "LACHLAN-MOR," the leader of the conquered party.—See FEUDS OF THE CLANS

Soisich, saŏêsh′-êch, *v.* flash, gleam, enlighten, explain, elucidate, illustrate.

Soisinn, sòènn″-unn, *n. f.* taste, decency.

Soitheach, saŏ′-ach, *n. f.* a dish, vessel.

Soitheach, saŏ′-ach, *n. f.* a ship, vessel.

Soitheamh, } sŏê-êv, *adj.* tractable, do-
Soithibh, } cile; gentle, mild; duine *soithibh, a tractable* or *docile person*; easily prevailed upon *or* entreated; easily done *or* accomplished.

Soithibheachd, sŏê′-êv-achg, *n. f.* docility; ease.

Sol, sŏll, *adv.* ere that, *Ross*; *n. m.* delight.

Solach, sōl′-ach, *adj.* highly delighted.

Solair, sŏl′-aèr, *v.* cater *or* provide provisions, purvey; provide accommodation; do *sholair* nead dhith féin, *she provided a nest for herself*; a' *solar* lòin, *purveying* or *catering provisions.*

Solar, sol′ar, *n. m. pt.* purveying, providing; provisions provided.

Solarach, sŏl-ar-ach, *a.* making provision.

Solas, sôll′-as, *n. m.* solace, (*French*); calm, luscious pleasure *or* delight, comfort, consolation.

Solasach, sôl as-ach, *adj.* affording calm continued pleasure, highly gratifying *or* comfortable.

Solasaich, sôl′-as-éch, *v.* give continued soothing joy.

So-leirsinn, sò-llăr′-shènn, *a.* very visible

So-lubachd, sò-llûb′-achg, *n. m.* elasticity.

So-lubadh, sò-llûb′-Ă, *pt.* flexible, elastic.

Solus, sòll′-us, *n. m.* light of any kind; moon; an *solus* ùr, *the new moon*; a *solus* so chaidh, *the last moon*; atharrachadh an t-*soluis, the change of the moon.*

Solusdach, sò′ll′-usd-ach, *a.* luminous.

Somalta, som′-alt-a, liberal, sonnalta.

Son, sŏn, *n. m.* stead, purpose, account, preparation; sake, reason; air mo *shon-sa, on my account, as for me, for my sake*; air-*son, as for, on account, for the sake, for the purpose of, as a reward for, in order to, for, for any thing*; air *son* mo chodach-sa dheth, *for my part of it*; air *son* tighinn dachaidh, *for the purpose of coming home, preparatory to coming home, as a reward for coming home*; air *son* dithisd, *as for two, for two, for the matter of two*; air *son* teicheadh, *for the purpose of decamping, as a reward* or *punishment for deserting*; car *son, why? wherefore? on what account? for what reason?* air a *shon*-sa, *on his account*; air a *son*-se, *on her account*; air an *son*-san, *on their account* or *sake, in preparation for them*; air-*son* dithisd na triuir, is coma leam còc, *as for two or three, I don't care*; air *son* sin deth, *as to that matter, as for that*; car-*son, why?* siod fhéin, *for every reason, because I judged it right*; air *son* falbh, *as a reward for going, in order to go*; car-*son* so, *why so? on whose account is this?* dh' fhalbh é air mo *shon*-sa, *he went on my account. he went in my place* or *stead*; air mo *shon* féin, *for myself, for my own part, as for me*; air *son* so uile dheth, *for all this*; air a *shon* sin, *nevertheless*; air na h-uile *son, for every reason*; air-*son* sgillinn, *for a penny, as to a penny.*

Sona, sŏn′-a, *adj.* lucky, fortunate; is fearra a bhi *sona* na éiridh moch, *luck is better than early rising, luck outstrips industry*; happy, in happiness; *sona* bithidh tu agus éiridh gu math dhuit, *happy shalt thou be, and it shall be well with thee, B.*; 's *sona* a bhithinn-se, *and happy would I be*; gu *sona* sòlach, *happy and quite contented.*

Sonas, sŏn′-us, *n. m.* luck, success, fortune; happiness, bliss felicity; *sonas* is àdh ort, *success and prosperity to you*; mo *shonas* fhéin, *my own happiness*; vexation, grief, *Gillies*; *sonas* na donas, *success* or *misfortune,* (*mischief*).

Sonn, sōnn, *n. m.* a hero; uamh an t-suinn, *the hero's cave*; (in Islay), courier;—bait, fishing-bait. *M'F.*; *v.* press.

Sonnalta, sōnn²′-allt-à, *adj.* liberal, handsome, very generous.

Sonnaltachd, sōnn²′-allt-achg, *n. f.* liberality.

Sonrachadh, sòrr′-ach-Ă, *pt.* particularizing, specifying; pointing out; appointing.

Sonraich, sòrr′-êch, *v.* appoint, ordain; individualize; neach a *shònraich* Dia na ìobairt-réitich, *one whom God set forth, a propitiation*; 'gam *shonrachadh*-sa, *individualizing me, pointing me out as a mark*; *v. n.* make a tool *or* a butt of.

Sonraichte, sòrr′-êch-tyà, *adj. pt.* particular, special; notable, certain, remarkable; gnothach *sònraichte, a particular business*; peculiar, noted, notorious; sluagh *sònraichte, a peculiar people*; duine *sònraichte, a certain* or *notorious man.*

Sop, sōp², *n. m.* a single straw; a wisp of thatch; *sop* as gach seid, *straw from every pallet*—said of those that court every one; *sop*-reic, *tavern sign. Ir.*

Soplach, sōp′-llach, *n. m.* refuse of straw.

Sor, sŏr, *v.* hesitate. *Provincial.*

Soradh, sŏr′-Ă, *pt. n. m.* hesitating, hesitation.

Soraidh, sŏr′-ê, *n. f.* compliments, blessing; success, farewell; *soraidh* slàn do'n ghàidheil ghasda, *success and health to the handsome Highlander*; *soraidh* leat, a ghràidh, *farewell, my beloved! Ossian*; thoir mo *shoraidh* le 'dhùrachd, *bring* *my best respects* or *compliments, my sincere blessings.*

Sorch, sôrch, *n. m.* a pedestal, gauntree.

Sorchan, sôrch'-an, *n. m.* a little one, also place for ball or cricket.

Sorn, sorn, *n. f.* a kiln; damh-*sùirn, a kiln-joist, lantern of a kiln.*

Sornan, sŏrn'-an, *n. m.* fish, thorn-back; young skate. *Islay*; little chin. *North.*

Sos, sŏs, *n. m.* unseemly mixture of food. *North.*

Sotal, sòt'-all, *n. m.* flattery, fawning.

Sotalach, sòt'-all-ach, *adj.* flattering.

Sotalachd, sòt'-all-achg, *n. f.* flattering disposition, *or* fawning nature *or* quality.

Sotail, sòtt'-uèl, *v.* fawn, flatter.

So-thaomadh, sò'-hāòm-a, *pt.* exhaustible.

So-theasgasg, sò'-hăg-ask, *adj.* docile, teachable.

So-thuigsinn, sò'-hŭēg-shènn, *a.* very intelligible.

Spad, spădd, *v.* knock down at a blow; knock the brains out at a blow; kill; *a.* flapping, hanging down; *spad*-chluasach, *having flappy ears.*

Spad, spâd, *n. f.* a spade; (*Saxon*, spad). *Islay*; (*German*, spade; *Swedish*, spàd.)

Spadag, spad'-ag, *n. f.* terrible oath; fillip. *Macfarlan*; in Islay, smeach, fillip.

Spadaire, spăd'-ur-à, *n. m.* terrible swearer.

Spadchas, spad'-chas, *n. f.* splay-foot.

Spadchluas, spăd'-chlŭăs, *n. f.* hanging, flapping ear.

Spadh, spaŏ'-gh, *v.* jerk, twitch.

Spadhadh, spaŏ'-Ă, *pt. n. m.* jerking, twitching; a jerk, *or* sudden pull; twitch. *Islay*;—swathe of grass. *N.*; stagh.

Spad-thinneas, spăd'-hyènn-us, *n. m.* apoplexy, epilepsy; tinneas-tuiteamach.

Spag, spâg, *n. f.* club-foot, paw, claw.

Spagach, spâg'-ach, *n. f.* club-footed female; *adj.* clawed, pawed; club-footed.

Spagaire, spâg'-ur-a, *n. m.* club-footed man.

Spagloinn, spăg'-laŏènn, *n. f.* the attitude of having the hand akimbo, and the foot stretched out; fools' pride.

Spagloinneach, spăg'-laŏènn-ach, *a.* conceited.

Spaid, spâj, *gen.* of spàd. *Prov.* spade.

Spaidhir, spi'-yhèr, *n. f.* pocket-hole of a petty-coat; flap of trowsers, breeches, &c.

Spaideil, spâjj'-al, *adj.* conceited, proud.

Spaidir, spăjj'-èr, *v.* scatter carelessly.

Spaidreach, spăjj'-ryach, *n. f.* thing scattered, *or* the state of lying here and there.

Spaig, spâègg, *n. f.* wry mouth. *H. S.*

Spaillichd, spally''-echg, *n. f.* vain-glory.

Spailp, spa'lp, *n. f.* the foot stretched out, as a self-important fellow does; airs of importance; great consequence in one's own eyes; cha riog thu leas a bhi cur *spailp* ort riumsa idir, tha mi am mhac math ar is athar cho math riut fhéin, *you need not assume such airs in my presence at all,—I am just as good a man as yourse'f,—the son of parents as good as yours.*

Spailpeil, spa'lp'-al, *adj.* self-conceited.

Spailpeis, spa'lp'-ash, *n. f.* self-importance.

Spaipean, spa'lp'-aèn, } *n. m.* a conceited
Spailpire, spa'lp'-èr-a, } fellow; the Irish, spalpeen.

Spailpireachd, spa'lp'-èr-achg, *n. f.* self-importance; airs of importance of a silly person.

Spain, spàèn, *n. f.* a spoon; (spàintean, spoons); also *spain*, (shaped like a spoon.)

Spainteach, spàèn'-tyach, *adj.* belonging to Spain; *n. f.* rifle, a gun; spoonful; *spàinteach* ime, *spoonful of butter*; *n. m.* a Spaniard.

Spairn, spâèrny', *n. f.* effort, great exertion, hard task; cha *spàirn* sin orm, *that is no hard task for me*; nì mi sin gun *spàirn, I can manage that without an effort*; *spàirneag* bàirneach, *a limpet*; *spàirneil, requiring struggles* or *efforts.*

Spairis, spăèry'-èsh, *n. f.* (spaidhiris); *n. f.* the conduct *or* attitude of having the hands in the flaps of the trowsers; conceitedness, foppishness.

Spairiseach, spaèr''-ach, } *adj.* foppish,
Spairiseil, spaèr' èsh-al, } beauish, gaudy.

Spairt, spăèrjt, *n. f. gen.* spart;—clod. *H.*; drop; *v.* spatter, bespatter.

Spairte, spàrjt'-à, *pt.* bolted, thrust, jammed.

Spairteach, sparjt'-ach, *adj.* thick, as cream.

Spaisd, spăshjj, *v.* walk. *O'Brien.*

Spaisdir, spăshjj'-èr, *v.* walk for pleasure.

Spaisdreach, spăshjj'-ryachg, *n. f.* a walk; a walk in a garden; promenade.

Spaisdreachd, spăshjj'-ryachd, *n. f.* walking for exercise *or* pleasure; promenade; written sometimes Spaisdireachd, &c.

Spaisdrich, spashjj'-ryèch, *v.* walk, saunter.

Spal, spâll, *n. f.* weaver's shuttle.

Spalan, spâll'-an, *n. m.* pea-cod.

Spalpaire; see Spailpire.

Spang, spàng, *n. f.* thin plate of metal.

Spann, spánn, *v.*; see Spannaich.

Spannach, spann'-èch, *n. f.* a splinter *spannach*-anguill, *bone of contention.*

Spannaich, spánn'-èch, *v.* splinter, dash.

Spaoil, spāo'l, *v.* tie tightly, swathe.

Spaoile, spāo'l'-à, *n. m.* a spindle of yarn.

Spaoilte, spāo'l'-tyĂ, *pt.* swathed, swaddled.

Spard, spârd, *n. m.* roost; hen-roost.

Sparr, spărr, *n. m.* thrust in, wedge in, clap upon; *spàrr* e 'lamh innte, *he thrust his hand into it*; *sparr* air e, *clap it on it*; a' crannadh is a' *spàrradh* an doruis, *bolting and wedging the door*; enforce by argument, inculcate; a' *sparradh* an ni so oirnn, *inculcating this thing on us*; *n. f.* a cross-beam of a couple; a large nail.

Sparrach, spărr'-ach, *n. f.* a sheath, truaill, *Leg.*

Sparradh, spărr'-Ă, *p.* thursting; inculcating.

Sparrag, spărr'-ag, *n. f.* bridle-bit, mìreannach. *Bible.*

Sparraich, spărr'-èch, *n. pl.* household furniture, particularly beds, tables, chairs, &c.—there are four words for household furniture in Islay.

Sparranan, spărr'-an-an, *n. pl.* spasms.

Spart, spărt, *n. m.* essence, quintessence; *spart* an uachdair, *the essence of cream, the best of cream*; *spart* cabhrach, *the ferina of the sowens without the liquid part.*

Spathall, (spòll), spá'-alt, *n. f.* a limb. *North.*

Speach, spech, *n. f.* a wasp; a smart clever blow, a bite; *v.* bite, strike smartly.

Speachanta, spech'-ant-a, *adj.* waspishness.

Speacharra, spech'-urr-a, *adj.* clever, active.

Spead, spā'd', *n. f.* a wonderfully small foot *or* leg.

Speadach, spā'd''-ach, *adj.* sheep-shanked; *n. f.* sheep-shanked female.

Speadaire, spā'd'-ur-à, *n. m.* a sheep-shanked man *or* gentleman.

Speal, spyal, *n. f.* a scythe; *v.* scythe, mow.

Spealadair, spyall-ad-aèr, *n. m.* a mower.

Spealadaireachd, spyall'-ad-aèr'-achg, *n. f.* mowing.

Spealg, spyallg, *v.* splinter, split; *n. f.* splinter.

Spealgach, spyallg'-ach, *n. f.* splinter; *a.* in splits.

Spealgaire, spyallg'-ur-a, *n. m.* a splinterer.

Spealt, spyallt, *n. m.* a tall person; *v.* splinter.

Spealtaire, spyallt'-ur-a, *n. m.* cleaver, cutter.

Spearrach, spyărr'-ach, *n. f.* a sort of cross-fetters for sheep—for goats. *N.*

Spearralach, spyarr'-al-ach, *n. f.* ham-string.

Spearralaich, spyarr'-al-èch, *v.* ham-string.

Speic, spèèchg, *n. f.* a spike; spoke.

Speid, spājj, *n. f.* expedition; preparation; order; cuir *spéid* ort, *bestir yourself*; cuir *spéid* air siod neo so, *prepare this or that*; activity; (*Belg.* spoid).

Speideil, spajj'-al, *a.* clever, business-like.

Speil, spā'l, *n. pl.* cattle, *Ir.*; herd, *or* drove, *North*; *v.* climb, *Is.*; slide, skait, *North*; *speileadaireachd, climbing, sliding.*

Speileanachd, spā'l'-an-achg, *n. f.* sliding. *North.*

Speileanta, spā'l'-ant-a, *adj.* eloquent.

Speileantachd, spā'l'-ant-achg, *n. f.* eloquence.

Speilg, spā²'lèg, *n. f.* a sheep-shank.

Speilgeach, spā²'lèg'-ach, *adj.* sheep-shanked; *n. f.* a sheep-shanked lady *or* female.

Speilgire, spā²'lèg'-èr-à, *n. m.* a sheep-shanked man, a trifling-looking fellow.

Speir, spāèr'², *n. f.* hoof, ham; gach *speir* a th'agam, *every hoof I possess.*

Speirbh, spāèv, *n. f.* a very slender leg *or* foot.

Speirbheis, spāèv'-ash, *n. f.* a sheep-shanked female.

Speireach, spāèr'-ach, *adj.* slender-limbed; *n. f.* cross-fetters.

Speireag, spāèr'-ag, *n. f.* sparrow-hawk.

Speirid, spāèr''-èjj, *n. f.* energy; speed, expedition.

Speirideil, spāèr'-èjj-al, *adj.* active, expeditious.

Speis, spāsh, *n. f.* love, affection, regard, attachment; thoir *spèis, regard, bestow affection*; ma bheir mi *spèis* do dh'aingidheachd, cha 'n éisd an Tighearna rium, *if I regard iniquity, the Lord will not hear me, B.*; tha *speis* aige dhith, *he is attached to her.*

Speisealta, spāsh²'-allt-a, *adj.* cleanly, as a cook *or* housewife; neatly dressed, tasteful.

Speisealtachd, spāsh'-allt-achg, *n. f.* cleanliness, as cook *or* housewife; tastefulness.

Speiseil, spāsh'-al, *adj.* fond of, attached to.

Speuc, spèchg, *v.* to diverge, divaricate.

Speuclair, spāchg'-llăèr, *n. m.* pair of spectacles; an object of surprise *or* wonder.

Speuclaireachd, spāchg'-llăèr-achg, *n. f.* opticians' trade, speculation *or* surprise.

Speur, spār, *n. m.* a star, the sky, *or* firmament; climate; the heavens; nèamh nan *speur, the starry heavens*; mar theine *speur, like the star-light, the fire-ball. Oss.*; nochdaidh na *speura* gniomh a làmh, *the firmament sheweth forth his handywork. Ps.*

Speur, spār, spèr, *v.* blaspheme, swear by the heavens—peculiar to Islay.

Speurach, spār′-ach, *adj.* celestial, etherial.

Speuradh, spèr′-Ă, *n. m.* blasphemy; a horrid oath; *a* an oath by Heaven.

Speuradair, spār′-ad-āer, *n. m.* astrologer.

Speuradair, spèr′-ad-āer, *n. m.* blasphemer.

Speuradaireachd, spār′-ad-aer-achg, *n. f.* astrology, astronomy, star-gazing, oaths.

Speur-ghorm, spār′-ghŏrm, *a.* azure-green.

Spid, spējj, *n. f.* contempt; the utmost contempt; tyranny; a′ caitheadh *spìd* orm, *using me contemptuously*; fo d′ *spìd*, *under your contemptuous sway* or *tyranny*; (spiote. *Belgic*); spite. *N.*

Spidealachd, spējj′-all-achg, *n. f.* contemptuous conduct *or* disposition; spitefulness.

Spideil, spējj′-all, *adj.* very contemptuous; in the North, in good health.

Spiligean, spēl′-ėg-ăen, *n. m.* single grain.

Spioc, spēchg, *n. f.* niggardliness, meanness.

Spiocach, spēchg′-ach, *a.* dastardly, mean.

Spiocaid, spėúch′-ajj, *n. f.* spigot; gaoir.

Spiocaire, spēchg′-ur-a, *n. m.* mean fellow.

Spiocaireachd, spēchg′-ăer-achg, *n. f.* dastardliness, meanness, shabbiness, parsimony.

Spiod, spėdd, *v.* tug *or* pull slightly. *Islay.*

Spiodadh, spėdd′-Ă, *pt.* tugging; *n. m.* quick pull *or* tug; a hint.

Spiol, spėul, *v.* pluck, tug; pick in a childish way; as cattle, browse; as egg, unshell.

Spioladair, speul′-add-aėr, *n. m.* picker, plucker.

Spioladh, speul′-Ă, *pt.* tugging, picking.

Spiolg, spėulg, *v.* unhusk, shell; *spiolgadh* nam faochag, *shelling the winkles.*

Spiolgaire, spėúlg′-ur-a, *n. m.* an husker.

Spion, spēn, *v.* pull, tug, root, tear from by force *or* violence; ach na *spìon* o'm' ghaol mise, *but tear me not from my love. Oss.*; *spìon* as a bhun e, *eradicate, extirpate, root it out.*

Spionnadh, spėúnn′-Ă, *n. m.* strength, vigour.

Spionndach, speúnnd′-ach, *adj.* strong, vigorous.

Spiontach, spēúnt-ach, *n. f.* skin wool. *Perthshire*; marbhchan. *Argyle.*

Spiontachan, spėúnn′-tach-an, *n. m.* a person like a plucked fowl.

Spiontag, speunt′-ag, *n. f.* a currant. *M'F.*

Spiorad, spėr′ ad, *n. m.* a spirit; spirituous liquors; an apparition, spectre; heart.

Spioradail, spėr′-ad-al, *adj.* spiritual.

Spioradalachd, spėr′-ad-al-achg, *n. f.* spirituality, spiritedness, liveliness.

Spiosrach, spēs′-rach, *n. f.* spicery.

Spiosraich, spēs′-rėch, *v.* spice, season.

Spiris, spėr′-ėsh, *n. f.* a spire; hen-roost.

Spitheag, spė′-hag, *n. f.* pebble, small stone.

Splaidse, splăjsh′-shå, *v.* fall with a crash; shut with a crash; *n. m.* a crash, noise.

Splang, splàng, *n. f.* a sparkle; *v.* sparkle.

Spleadh, splhaŏ, *n. m.* an enormous splay-foot, a large foot to serve for a bridge; a romance; see Ridire nan *spleadh, Don Quixotte*; cum a stigh do *spleadhan*, *keep in your ugly toes*, or *feet.*

Spleadh, splė-aŏ, *v.* fall with a crash.

Spleadhach, splėaŏ′-ach, *adj.* romantic, incredible, having enormous feet, having ugly feet.

Spleadhachas, splėaŏ′-ach-as, *n. f.* wonder, surprising nature *or* quality of any thing.

Spleadhadh, splé′-Ă, *pt. n. m.* a fall, crash, falling.

Spleadhaire, spleaŏ-ur-å, *n. m.* a romancer.

Spleadhrach, spleāor′-ach, *adj.* romantic. incredible, enormous; gasgonading, romancing.

Spleadhraich, splėāor′-ėch, *n. f.* romance.

Spleuc, splèchg, *v.* flatten awkwardly, open your mouth and eyes and stare like a fool.

Spleucach, splèchg′-ach, *adj.* flat, ugly as stamped cloth, *or* print.

Spleucaid, splèchg′-ăj, *n. f.* a foolish starer

Spleucair, splèchg′-aėr, *n. m.* a foolish gazer.

Spliuc, spleūchg, *n. f.* fluke of an anchor.

Spliucan, splėūchg′-an, *n. m.* a tobacco-pouch.

Spliug, splėūgg, *n. f.* a blubber-lipped person's mouth, a most unmanly phis, *or* expression of countenance.

Spliugaid, splėūg′-åj, *n. f.* a blubbering female.

Spliugaire, splėūg′-ur-å, *n. m.* a blubberer.

Spliut, splėūtt, *n. f.* a splay-foot; *v.* gash.

Spliutaire, spleutt′-ur-a, *n. m.* splay-footed man; a splay-footed female, spliutach.

Spoch, spoch, *n. f.* a sudden attack *or* assault, as a cat does; *v.* attack angrily.

Spochanach, spoch′-an-ach, *a.* fond of picking quarrels.

Spochanachd, spoch′-an-achg, *n. f.* picking quarrels, as a feeble ill-natured person.

Spog, spôg, *n. f.* a paw, claw, flat foot.

Spogach, spôg′-ach, *a.* clawed, pawed.

Spoinnich, spòėnn′-ėch, *v.* bristle against.

Spoithte, spò′-tya, *pt.* gelded, castrated, prepared for thatch, as straw; very bare, as a measure.

Spoll, spôll, *n. f.* a quarter, leg, as of a sheep, fowl; *v.* quarter, tear.

Spong, spòng, *n. m.* a tinder, meanness.

Spongaire, spōng′-ur-å, *n. m.* churl, niggard.

Spongaireachd, spŏng'-ur-achg, *n. f.* churlishness, niggardliness, mean disposition.

Spor, spŏr, *n. f.* a spur, talon of a cock, gun-flint; *v.* incite, instigate, spur.

Sporan, spòr'-an, *n. m.* a purse, dew-lap.

Sporg, spŏrg, *v.* ruzzle, struggle without effect.

Sporgail, spŏrg'-ul, *n. f.* ruzzle, ruzzling noise; *pt.* ruzzling, struggling without effect.

Sporraich, spŏrr'-ēch, *v.* bristle; *sporraich* e rium, *he bristled up to me.*

Spors, spôrs, *n. f.* diversion, play, fun; gheibh sinn *spòrs*, *we shall get some sport* or *fun*; pride, disdain; 'si an *spòrs* thug ort sin a dheanadh, *sheer pride made you do it.*

Sporsail, spôrs'-al, *a.* proud, disdainful.

Sporsalachd, spôrs'-al-achg, *n. f.* pridefulness, disdainfulness, sheer haughtiness.

Spot, spŏt, *n. f.* a spot; (spotte, *Flem.*)

Spotagach, spŏtt'-ag-ach, *a.* spotted.

Spoth, sphò, *v.* geld, castrate; fit straw for thatch.

Spothadair, sphò'-ad-aėr, *n. m.* gelder.

Spothadh, sphò'-Ă, *pt.* gelding, castrating.

Spraic, sprăēchg, *n. f.* an angry, authoritative tone of voice, and attitude; cleverness.

Spraiceil, sprăēchg'-al, *adj.* authoritative. commanding, lively, active, energetic.

Spraigh, sprăē'-y', *v.* burst, (ais-braigh.)

Spraigheadh, sprăē'-y-Ă, *pt. n.* burst, bursting.

Spreidh, sprāē'-y', *n. f.* cattle of all sorts.

Spreig, sprā²ēg, *v.* divulge any thing you are enjoined to keep secret;—reprove. *B.*; blame, reprove. *Highland Society.*

Spreigeadh, sprā²ēg'-Ă, *n. m.* pith, energy; mòine gun *spreigeadh*, *pithless peats*; *pt.* divulging a secret. *Islay*; chiding, reproving, inciting, instigating. *Bible*; *Highland Society.*

Spreigeil, sprā²eg'-al, *a.* lively, energetic.

Spreill, sprălly', *n. f.* the tongue hanging out in contempt, *or* from discontent.

Spreochainn, spryôchg'-ėnn, *n. f.* a person *or* thing hardly hanging together;—feebleness, want of pith. *H. Society.*

Spreod, spryôd, *n. m.* sprit;—beam. *H. S.*

Sprochd, sprŏchg, *n. m.* dejection, sadness, lowness of spirits, melancholy.

Sprog, **Sprogan**, sprog'-an, dewlap.

Sprogaill, sprŏg'-ally', *n. m.* dewlap. *N.*

Spruan, sprŭăn, *n. m.* short-bread, brushwood.

Sprudhan, *n. m.* fragments, crumbs.

Spruileach, sprŭ'l'-ach, *n. m.* fragments.

Spruiseil, sprŭsh'-al, *a.* neat, trim. (*All Languages.*)

[S]pu[a]cadh, spŭăchg'-Ă, *pt.* daubing awkwardly; plastering any thing against mightily.

Spuaic, spŭăēchg, *n. f.* a bruise, a maul, callosity; a tumour on the side of the head; *spuaic* theanga, *disease in cattle*; *v.* maul, bruise, plaster awkwardly with all your might.

Spuill, spûėlly' *v.* plunder, spoil, prey.

Spuinn, spûėnn, *v.* plunder, spoil, rob; an *spùinn* duine Dia, *shall a man rob God? Bible*; *n. f.* spoil.

Spuinneadair, spûėnn'-ad-aėr, *n. m.* plunderer, spoiler.

Spuinneadh, spûėnn'-Ă, *pt.* spoiling, plundering.

Spuir, spŭėr, *n. f.* a spur, talon.

Spuirse, spŭrsh'-å, *n. f.* milk-weed, spurge.

Spùll, spûll, *n. f.* nail of a cat; a clutch.

Spullach, spûll'-ach, *a.* nailed, greedy *n. f.* a very greedy, monopolising female.

Spullaire, spûll'-ur-a, *n. m.* greedy man.

Sput, spûtt, *n. f.* a spout; bad liquor *or* toplash; *v.* squirt, spout, pour out; gunna-*spùt*, *a syringe*; a' *spùtadh*, *squirting.*

Sputaire, spût'-ur-a, *n. m.* a bird; syringe.

Srabh, srâv, *n. m.* a straw; a trusadh na *sràbh* is a leigeil nam boitean leis an abhainn, *gathering straws, and allowing the trusses to go with the stream*; *v.* scatter here and there.

Srabhach, srâv'-ach, *a.* scattered, strawy.

Srac, srăchg, *v.* tear, rend violently.

Sracadh, scrăchg'-Ă, *pt. n. m.* tearing; a rent.

Sracaire, srachg'-ur-a, *n. m.* render, tearer.

Sracanta, srăchg'-ant-a, *adj.* turbulent.

Srad, srădd, *n. f.* a spark of fire; quick temper; *v.* emit sparks of fire; sparkle.

Sradadh, srădd'-Ă, *pt.* emitting sparks.

Sradanta, srădd'-ant-å, *adj.* quick-tempered.

Sradrach, srădd'-răch, *n. f.* sparkle; half inebriety.

Sraid, srăējj, *n. f.* a street, a row, rank; *v.* walk the streets, pace, step forward.

Sraideach, srâjj'-ach, *n. f.* a lane; *adj.* full of streets.

Sraideamachd, **Sraidimeachd**, srâjj'-am-achg, *n. f.* walking for pleasure *or* exercise; pacing.

Sraideamaich, srâjj'-am-ēch, *v.* walk for pleasure *or* exercise.

Sraigh, srăē'-y', *or* srrī'-ēy', *n. f.* the cartilage of the nose; cuiridh mi car an *sraigh* do shròine, *I will twist the cartilage of your nose*; *v.* sneeze; tha e a' *sraigheadh*, *he is sneezing*; murdered in many places, **Sreothadh.**

Sraigheartaich, sraī'-art-ēch, *n. f.* sneezing

Srann, srann, *n. f.* a snore, whiz; *v.* snore, whiz; **provincial** for sreann, sryànn.

Srann, srànn, *n. f.* a drink as deep as one's breath will permit him; *v.* drink deep.

Srannadh, srànn'-ă, *n. m.* great offence.

Sraon, srāon, *v.* make a false step. *H. S.*

Sraonadh, srāon'-ă, *n. m.* great offence.

Sraonais, srāon'-ăsh, *n. f.* great snuffiness.

Sraonaiseach, srāon'-ash-ach, *a.* snuffy.

Srath, srhă, *n. m.* a plain beside a river; meadow; flat part of a valley; a valley; luchd-àiteachaidh an t-*srath, the inhabitants of the valley. Bible*; in *Scotch*, strath; *Cornish*, srath; *Welsh*, ysrad; *Latin*, stratum.

Srathach, srhă'-ach, *adj.* full of valleys.

Srathair, srhă'-ĕr, *n. f.* pannier-saddle; bithidh na caidearan, a' tighinn air na *srathraichean, horse-dealers talk of pannier-saddles. Prov*; every one to his shop.

Sream, sryem, rheum, wrinkle.

Sreamaid, sryĕm'-ĕj, *n. f.* a string of slaver, *or* snotter.

Sreang, sréng, *n. f.* a string; charm to prevent harm from an evil eye.

Sreangach, sréng'-ach, *adj.* capillary, in strings.

Sreangaich, sréng'-ĕch, *v.* string; get capillary.

Sreangaichte, sréng'-ĕch-tyå, *pt.* tied; capillary.

Sreann, sryánn, *n. f.* a snore, snort; whiz, buzz, humming noise; *v.* snore, snort.

Sreannartaich, sryànn'-art-ĕch, *n. f.* a continuous buzzing, whizzing; snoring *or* snorting.

Sreann-chorr, sryánn-chôrr', *n.f.* a whirlwind. *Islay.*

Sreap for streup, to climb.

Sreat, Sreatan, srătt'-an, *n.m.* a screech; *sreatan* lughadaireachd, *a screech of blasphemies.*

Sreath, sră², *n. f.* row, rank, stratum; *sreath*-aghaidh, *a van*; *sreath*-chùl, *rear.*

Sreathach, srā²'-ach, *adj.* in ranks *or* rows.

Sreathaich, srā'-ĕch, *v.* place in ranks.

Sreathainn; see Sgreothainn, kiln-straw.

Srein, Sreine, srān'-å, *gen.* of srian, bridle.

Sreinglein, srēng'-lyĕn, *n. f.* strangles; foghach. *North.*

Sreothan, sryŏ'-an, *n. m.* semen, film.

Sreothartaich; see Sraigheartaich, sneezing.

Sreud, srăd, *n. m.* for treud, a drove.

Sreup, srăp, for streup, to climb.

Srian, srĕăn, *n. f.* a bridle, a streak; *v.* bridle.

Srianach, srĕăn'-ach, *a.* bridled, streaked.

Sriante, srĕăn'-tyå, *pt.* bridled, curbed.

Sriut, srĕŭt, *n. m.* torrent of quick sounds.

Sroin, srôĕn, *n f.* a huff; tha *sròin* air, *he is huffed*, or *offended*; *gen.* of sròn.

Sroineis, srôn'-ash, *n f.* snuffling, huffiness.

Sroineiseach, srôen'-ash-ach, *adj.* huffy, snuffy.

Srol, srôll, *n.m.* gauze, crape, veil, banner.

Srolach, srôll'-ach, *a.* dressed with crape.

Sron, srôn, *n. f.* a nose, promontory, *or* peak, supposed to resemble a nose; a huff; tha *sròn* air, *he is huffed, he is offended.*

Sronach, srôn'-ach, *adj.* having a prominent nose; *n. f.* nose-string.

Sronail, srôn'-al, *adj.* nasal.

Sruan, srŭăn, *n. m.* shortbread cake having five corners. *Is.*

Srub, srûb, *v.* suck, inhale drink, as far as your breath will permit you; draw in, imbibe.

Srubadh, srûb'-ă, *pt.* inhaling, imbibing; *n. f.* a large mouthful of liquids.

Srubag, srûb'-ag, *n. f.* a little gulp.

Srubaire, srûb'-ur-å, *n. m.* a sucker, inhaler.

Sruil, srŭ'l, *v.* rinse, half-cleanse; sruthail; *v. n.* gulp, drink; *sruil* ort e, *gulp it up.*

Srulach, srûl'-ach, *a.* coming in streams.

Sruladh, srŭll'-ă, *pt.* half-washing, rinsing, gulping.

Sruladh, srûll'-ă, suction of air; a *srùladh* a tha bho'n dorus, *the suction*, or *stream of air that comes from the door.*

Srullamas, srŭll'-am-as, *n. m.* a person that speaks as if his mouth was filled with liquid.

Sruth, srhŭ, *n. m.* current, stream, tide; tha 'n *sruth* 'nar aghaidh, *the stream is against us, the current is running right a-head*; saobh-*shruth, eddy-tide*; *v.* stream, flow, as water; shed, drip, melt; a' *sruthadh* dheur, *shedding tears*; a' *sruthadh* a nuas, *dropping down*; *sruthaidh* na beantan, *the hills shall melt. B.*; am marbh-*sruth, slack-water*; coileach an t-*sruth, ripple of the current*; le *sruth* is soirbheas, *having fair wind, a favourable tide*; tha'n *sruth* leinn, *the current is favourable*; torrent, a fountain; *sruthannan* na beatha, *the fountains of life*; confhadh an t-*sruth, the rage of the torrent. Oss.*; bhrist faire air monadh an t-*sruth, dawn broke on the hill of streams*; a' dol leis an t-*sruth, going with the stream, going down-hill.*

Sruthach, srŭ'-ach, *adj.* streaming.

Sruthadh, srŭ'-ă, *pt.* flowing, spending, as corn in the shock.

Sruthan, srhu'-an, *n. m.* streamlet, rivulet, rill.

Sruthanach, sru'-an-ach, full of rivulets.

Sruthail, srŭ'l, rinse with water; see Sruil.

Sruthlag, srûll′-ag, *n. f.* the discharge of a mill.

Sta for Stath, st*h*â, advantage, use.

Stabhach, stâv′-ach, *adj.* straddling, wide asunder.

Stabhaic, stav′-èchg, *n. f.* a wry-neck, a sullen, *or* boorish attitude of the head.

Stablair, stâbb′-llaer, *n. m.* a stabler.

Stabull, stâb′-ull, *n. m.* a stable; (*Latin*, stabulum.)

Stac, stachg, *n. m.* a steep rock, conical hill; dullness of hearing.

Stacach, stăchg′-ach, *adj.* dull of hearing; very unready to take fire; peaky, uneven.

Stacachd, stăchg′-achg, *n. f.* deafness; unaptness to take fire.

Stacaiche, stăchg′-èch-à, *n. f.* degree of deafness.

Stachaill, stăch′-èlly, *n. m.* a bar, a barrier.

Stad, stădd′, *n. m.* a stop, period; stopping, detention, impediment, pause; *v.* stop, impede, hinder; tha *stad* na chainnt, *there is an impediment in his speech*; gun *stad, incessantly, unceasingly*; dean *stad, wait, stop, pause*; not so fast.

Stadach, stădd′-ach, *adj.* ceasing, lisping.

Stadachd, stădd′-achg, *n. f.* impediment, detention; tendency *or* proneness to stop.

Stadaich, stădd′-èch, *n. f.* stop, impediment of speech; duine aig an robh *stadaich* na chainnt, *a man who had an impediment of speech. Bible.*

Stadh, staŏ′-gh, *n. m.* stays; the rope that sustains the mast; dhiùlt i tighinn 'sa *stadh, she refused stays*; a' tighinn 'sa *stadh, putting about, as a ship* or *boat*; ar *stadh* is ar tarrainn, cum fallann, *our stays and haulyards, preserve thou*; a swathe of grass, *or* what the scythe cuts at a stroke.

Stadhadh, staŏ′-Ă, *n. m.* a lurch, sudden bend.

Stagarsaich, stàg′-ars èch, *n. f.* staggering, stammering; (*Belgic* staggerer.)

Staid, stăjj, *n. f.* state, condition; is truagh mo *staid, sad is my condition*; an estate, proprietorship.

Staidealachd, stăjj′-all-achg, *n. f.* sedateness.

Staideil, stăjj′-al, *adj.* sedate, portly.

Staidhir, stă′-hèr, *n. f.* a stair, steps.

Staidhreach, stăĕr′-ach, *a.* having a stair, *or* steps.

Staidhrichean, stăĕr′-èch-un, *n. pl.* stairs.

Stail, stâ′l, *n. f.* bandage, strop. *North.*

Stailc, stal′èchg, *n. f.* thump; *a.* lash against.

Stailinn, stâ′l′-ènn, *n. f.* steel; (*Belg.* staal.)

Stailinneach, stâ′l′-ènn-ach, *a.* adamantine.

Staing, sténg, *n. f.* a firm well-built person *or* beast; an insurmountable bar *or* barrier; an objection not easily got rid of. *Is.*; a ditch. *B.*;—pointed rock, peg. *North.*

Staingeach, steng′-ach, *adj.* full of ditches, *or* difficult.

Stair, staor′, *n. f.* a temporary bridge for cattle, *Skye*; (ceasach); stepping-stones. *North.*

Stairirich, properly Stararaich, noise.

Stairn, stâèrn, *n. f.* noise, tramping.

Stairt, stàèrt, *n. f.* considerable distance, trip.

Stairseach, **Stairsneach**, star′-shach, starsh′-nyach, *n. f.* a threshold; starsach.

Stait, stàjty′, *n. m.* a magistrate, great man of a place *or* city; *stàitean* na tìre, neo a bhaile, *the great men of the country*, or *magistrates of the city.*

Staitealachd, stàjty′-all-achg, *n. f.* magisterial conduct *or* gait, stateliness.

Staitail, stàjty″-al, *adj.* magisterial, portly.

Stalc, stal′k, *v.* dash your foot against. *Islay*; thread a hook, tap. *Mainland*; starch. *Lochaber*; gaze, stare. *North*; *n. m.* a dash against, thump.

Stalcadh, stalk′-Ă, *pt.* dashing, thumping, threading *or* hooping; starching, &c.

Stalcanta, stalk′-annt-a, *adj.* stout, firm.

Stalcantachd, stalk′-annt-achg, *n. f.* stoutness.

Stall, stâ′ll, *n. m.* bearing; proper state; cha 'n urrainn mi a thoirt gu *stàll, I cannot bring him* or *it to a bearing*, or *proper state* or *trim.*

Stall, stăll, *v.* dash violently against.

Stalla, stall′-ă, *n. m.* craggy, steep. *N.*

Stalladh, stăll′-Ă, *pt.* dashing, thumping; *n. m.* a smart thump, *or* dash against.

Stallacaire, stall′-achg-ur′-a, *n. m.* a blockhead.

Stallacaireachd, stăll′-achg-ur-achg, *n. f.* stupidity.

Stamac, stam′-ag, *n. f.* stomach; (*Latin*, stomachus.)

Stamh, stáv, *n. m.* a bull's —— dried for the purpose of lashing horses; a kind of tangle. *Skye*; (doire, *Islay.*)

Stamhnaich, stáv′-nnèch, *v.* reduce to order; break a young horse; drub lustily; a' *stamhnachadh, drubbing* or *breaking, as a horse*;—press down, compress. *N.*

Stamb, stámb, *v.* trample, stamp, damn.

Stambadh, stámb′-Ă, trampling, condemning, without a hearing.

Stambte, stámb′-tyà, *pt.* trampled, pressed, cursed, corrupt; duine *stàmbte, a cursed*, or *very wicked fellow.*

Stamp, stămp, *n. m.* a stamp. *Teutonic.*

Stan, stàn, *adj.* below, shìos; *North.*

Stang, stang, *n. m.* a tank, pool.

Stann, stánn, *n. f.* a vat, *or* tun *stann* cléith, *worm-vat*, or *-tun*; a stall, stand, *or* stance, as at a market.

Stannart, stánn'-art, *n. f.* standaid.

Staoig, stäoėg, *n. f.* a clumsy beef-steak; *v.* cut into clumsy steaks, *or* lumps.

Staoin, stãoėn, *n. f.* tin. *B.*; laziness. *Perthshire*; juniper; caoran *staoin, juniper-berries. North.*

Staon, stãon, *v.* bend, curve. *Irish.*

Stapag; see Fuarag; Scotch crowdy.

Staoram, stăor'-um, *n. f.* inclination. *N.*

Staplaich, stăp'-llėch, *n. f.* noise of the sea.

Stapull, stap'-ull, *n. m.* a staple. *Teut.*

Starachd, stăr'-achg, *n. f.* romping, blustering.

Starraraich, star'-ar-ėch, *n f.* great noise.

Starbanach, starv'-an-ach, *n. m.* a stout fellow. *Macdonald.*

Stard, stàrd, *n. f.* a moon-eye.

Stardshuileach, stârd'-hu'l-ach, *a.* moon-eyed.

Starn, stărn, *n. m.* an upstart.

Starr, stârr, *v.* shove violently, dash; *n. m.* sort of grass, *Lewis*; seasg, *Argyle.*

Starrachd, stârr'-achg. *n. f.* roaming. *Sk.*

Starradh, stărr'-Ă, *pt.* pushing violently, dashing;—failing, whim, freak. *H. S.*

Starraich, stârr'-ėch, *n. f.* complete intoxication.

Starrs, starrs, *n. m.* starch.

Starrsach, starrs'-ach, *n. f.* threshold, bar, barrier; na *starrsach* an siod, *as a barrier yonder.*

Starrsaich, stărrs'-ėch, starch, stiffen.

Stath, sttâ*h*, *n. m.* good purpose, *or* end, use, benefit; gnothach air bheag *stàth*, *a thing worth little*; cha'n 'eil *stàth* an sin duit, *that serves no end to you*; cha' n'eil *stàth* bhi tighinn air sin, *to speak of that serves no good purpose*; cha'n'eil *stàth* air so, *this is useless.*

Stathalachd, sttâ*h*'-äll-achg, *n. f.* usefulness.

Stathail, sttâ*h*'-al, *adj.* useful, profitable.

Steabhag, styeff'-ag, *or* styév'-ag, *n. f.* switch.

Steach, styech', *adv.* inside, in, within; 'nuair a thàinig iad a *steach, when they came in.*

Steadhainn, styé'-ėnn, *n. f.* firm, pointed and punctual mode of pronouncing your words.

Steadhainneach, styé'-ėnn-ach, *adj.* making a slight pause between every word in speaking *or* reading; punctual.

Stealdrach, styall'-drrach, *n. f.* a torrent; state of being a good deal intoxicated.

Steall, styâll, *n. f.* a plash, gush; a considerable quantity of any liquid; a torrent, *or* heavy shower of rain; *v.* plash, pour out irregularly.

Steallach, styall'-ach, *a.* plashing, gushing.

Stealladh, styall'-Ă, *pt.* plashing, gushing.

Steallaire, styall'-ur-ă, *n. m.* a cascade, *or* cataract, (eas); a watering-can;—a syringe;—glyster, *or* clyster. *Irish.*

Stearnall, styârn''-all, *n. m.* sea-bird, tern;—a s gn of an inn. *Irish.*

Steic, styèchg, *n. f.* a cow's stake, *or* stall.

Steic-bhraghd, styèch-vrâdd', *n. f.* windpipe. *Irish.*

Steidh, styãė'-y', *n. f.* foundation, basis; is i mo làmh a leag *stéidh* na talmhainn, *it is my hand that has laid the foundations of the earth. B.*; the piling of peats. *Lew.*; *steidh*-theagaisg, *a text*; *v.* found, build upon; pile peats; in *Sutherlandshire*, stéibh.

Steidhealachd, styãey'-all-achg, *n. f.* solidity, steadiness, punctuality, firmness.

Steidheil, styãė'-y-al, *adj.* decisive in character; solid, firm, steady, punctual.

Steidhich, styãė'-yėch, *v.* found; stéidh.

Steidhichte, styãė'-yėch-tyă, *pt.* founded.

Steill, styălly'2, styēlly2, *n. f.* pin *or* peg, on which something is hung. *H. S.*; a long fellow.

Steimhleag, styév'-lyog, *n. f.* hasp of a lock.

Steinle, styén'-lyă, *n. f.* itch; (sgrìobach.) *Irish.*

Steinn, styãėnn, *v.* stain; *v. n.* disappoint; *stèinn* e orm, *he disappointed me, he defeated my purpose.*

Steinneadh, styãėnn'-Ă, *pt.* disappointing, staining; *n. m.* disappointment; a stain.

Steoc, styôchg, *v.* stalk, strut; *n. c.* idler.

Steocair, styôchg'-aėr, *n. m.* stalker; an idler.

Steorn, styôrn, *v.* guide by the stars; *n.* a stare. *Arm.*

Steothag, styŏ'-ag, *n. f.* switch, cane, light staff; *steothaireachd, sauntering with a switch in your hand.*

Steud, styăd, *n. f.* a fine young mare; a charger; race-horse; a stride; *v.* run a race; bu lauithe a' *steudadh* e na ghaoith, *he could run swifter than the wind. Macgregor*; a wave.

Stiall, styĕäll, *n. f.* a long streak *or* stripe of cloth, &c.; *v.* tear in stripes.

Stiallach, styĕäll'-ach, *adj.* striped, streaked.

Stiallaire, styĕäll'-ur-ă, *n. m.* a drawling f—; a long, ugly fellow.

Stic, styēchg, *v.* stick, adhere; (stican, *Sax.*); *n. c.* a bad pet of a person, blackguard; a stake, *or* kiln-rafter.—in *H. S.*, blemish, hurt.

Sticeartach, styèchg'-art-ach, *n. m.* a long person; an apparition that stalks aside houses.

Stidean, styĕjj′-an; see Stìodach, puss.

Stigh, staŏĕ′-y′, ('san tigh,) *adv.* within, in the house; inside; theirig a *stigh, go in*; am bheil e *stigh, is he within?* 'a *stigh* na muigh, *either within* or *without*; cuir a *stigh* e, *put inside, push it in*; *Inter.* away in! in with you! *stigh, stigh, away in! away in with you!*

Stingleag; see Steimhleag.

Stiob, styēbb, *v.* steep, soak; (*Belgic*, stippen.)

Stiobadh, styēbb′-Ă, *pt.* steeping, soaking.

Stiobull, styēbb′-ull, *n. f.* a steeple, spire.

Stiocach, styuchg′-ach, *adj.* lame. *North.*

Stiocall, styúchg′-ăll, *n. m.* buttress. *Islay*

Stiocanta, styéchg′-ant-à, *adj.* adhesive.

Stiodach, styē′d′-ach, *n. f. Inter.* puss! push!

Stiog, styē′g, *n. f.* a stripe in cloth, &c.

Stiogach, styē′g′-ach, *adj.* striped, streaked;—sorry. *N.*; *n. f.* a slim, sleeky female.

Stiom, styēm, *n. f.* a fillet, faltan; ringlet. *Bible.*

Stiorap, stē′r′-ap, *n. f.* a stirrup.

Stiorlach, styéurl′-ach, *n. f.* sorry long female.

Stiorlan, styéúrl′-an, *n. m.* any ugly long thing.

Stiornach, styeùrn′-ach, *n. m.* sturgeon.

Stiubhard, styū′-art, *n. m.* a steward.

Stiubhardachd, styū′-ărt-achg, *n. f.* stewardship.

Stipinn, styēp′-ènn, *n. f.* stipend. (*Latin.*)

Stipinnear, styēp′-ènn-ăĕr, *n. m.* a stipendiary.

Stiuir, styūr′, *n. f.* the helm, rudder; fear na *stiùrach, the helmsman*; iarunn *stiùrach, helm-hinge* or *pivot*; two long feathers in a cock's tail; the long, elastic tail of a lobster; *v.* steer, direct, guide, lead; *stiuir* am bàta, *steer the boat*; *stiuir* dhachaidh e, *direct* or *guide him home.*

Stiuradair, styūr′-add′ăĕr, *n. m.* helmsman, one that steers a vessel.

Stiuradh, styūr′-Ă, *pt.* steering, guiding, directing, managing; *n. m.* direction, guidance, management.

Stob, stȯb, *n. m.* stab; *v.* thrust, prick, set potatoes by making a hole and putting potatoes into it.

Stobach, stȯb′-ach, *adj.* prickly, thorny.

Stobadh, stȯb′Ă, *pt.* planting potatoes, &c.

Stobh, stō, *v.* stew; *stòbhte, stewed.*

Stobh, stȯ, *v.* stow; *v. n.* stick to, as a person; feel affection for.

Stoc, stŏchg, *n. m.* stock, pack of cards, trunk of tree, root, capital, store, cravat; gad bhàsachadh an *stoc, though the stock* (trunk,) *should perish. B.*; *v. n.* object, cast up; tha e a' *stocadh* siod is so rium, *he objects this and that*; cha riog thu leas a bhi *stocadh* sin riumsa, *you need not object that to me,—don't cast up that to me.*

Stocaich, stŏchg′-ĕch, *v.* stock a farm.

Stocaidh, **Stocaich**, stŏchg′-ĕch, *n. f.* stocking-hose; dealg *stocaich, stocking-wire.*

Stocainnich, stŏchg′-ènn-ĕch, *v.* season, as a cask.

Stod, stȯdd′, *n. m.* a huff, pet; sudden fit of peevishness; ghabh e *stod, he took the pet, he was quite huffed at it.*

Stodach, stȯdd″-ach, *a.* huffy, pettish; *n. f.* pet.

Stodaire, stȯdd″-ur-à, *n. m.* a pettish fellow.

Stoipeal, stoyp′-all, *n. m.* bung, stopple.

Stoirm, stŏĕrm, *n. f.* storm; (ais-toirm); *all Languages*; tingling, *or* ringing sensation in the ear.

Stoirmealachd, stŏĕrm′-all-achg, *n. f.* storminess.

Stoirmeil, stŏĕrm′-al, *adj.* stormy, blowy, keen.

Stol, stôll, *n. m.* stool, properly furm; *v.* settle.

Stolda, stôld′-à, *adj.* sedate; solemn in gait.

Stoldachd, stôld′-achg, *n. f.* solemnity of step; sedateness, staidness, tameness.

Stop, stôp, *n. m.* a measure for liquids; pot for liquors; *stòp*-pìnnt, *half-gallon measure*; *stòp*-seipinn, *quart-measure*; *stòp*-bodaich, *half-quart measure*; *stòp*-leabhodaich, *a half-pint measure*; *stòp*-ceathra, *a gill measure.*

Stop, stŏp, *v.* dam up, *or* prevent from running; stop, bung; (*Belgic*, stoppen, stoppe.)

Stopadh, stŏpp′-Ă, *pt.* stopping, bunging.

Stor, stôr, *n. m. poet. cont.* of stòras.

Stor, stōr, *n. m.* a bull—word used to excite a bull, to call him; stòr! stòr! *Perthshire*; in *Islay*, toraidh! tòraidh!

Stor, stōr, *n. m.* steep, high peak. *Skye*; *v.* store.

Storas, stôr′-as, *n. m.* wealth, great riches.

Storasach, stôr′as-ach, *a.* wealthy, rich.

Stoth, stŏ*h*, *n. m.* steam; a *stoth* a thàinig as a' choire, *the steam that came from the cauldron*; stench;—*v.* lop off branches.

Stoth-bhata, sto*h*-vhâtt′-a, *n. f.* steam-boat.

Strabaid, strabb′-ājj, *n. f.* a whore, harlot.

Strabaire, strabb′-ăĕr-à, *n. m.* a whoremonger.

Strabhaig, stra′-ĕg, *n. m.* lay-straw; sgreothainn. *North.*

Strac, strâchg, *n. m.* a drake. *Skye*; a streak *or* plank in boat-building; *v.* aim at; a' *stràcadh* urra, *aiming at her bent on getting her.*

Straic, strâèchg, *n. f.* the brim of a measure, the strike or measure-roller; pride, arising from abundance; gun *stràic, without being proud of wealth*; *v.* roll *or* strike a measure in measuring.

Straiceil, strâèchg′-al, *adj.* purse-proud.

Straighil, strī-yh″-ėl, *v.* thump noisily.

Straighleadh, strī²ll′-ă, *pt.* thumping noisily; *n. m.* a noisy almost harmless blow.

Straighlich, strī′l′-èch, *n. f.* clangor, clashing, blustering, swaggering; noise, *or* bustle.

Streap, strāp, *v.* climb, scale, struggle, *or* scramble; *n. f. pt.* climbing, struggling; scaling, scrambling.

Streapadair, strāp′-ad-aėr, *n. m.* climber, ladder.

Streup, strāp, for streupaid, a row, fray.

Streupaid, strāp′-ăj, *n. f.* row, fray, skirmish.

Streupaideach, strāp′-ăj-ach, *a.* quarrelsome.

Stri, corruption of strìobh, which is used in Knapdale and Sutherlandshire.

Striam, strēăm, *n. m.* a long shred.

Striamalach, strēăm′-al-ach, *n. f.* any thing long and ugly; long ugly person.

Striall, strēăll, *n. f.* a long shred, stripe; *v.* tear in long stripes, as cloth.

Strianach, strēăn -ach, *n. m.* badger, (broc).

Striobh, strēvv, *and* strē, *v.* strive; *n. f.* strife.

Striobhail, strēv′-al, *adj.* emulous.

Strioch, strēch, *v.* draw a line; *n. f.* a line.

Striochd, strēchg, *v.* yield, submit, surrender, strike; cha *strìochdainn* do dhuine, *I would not yield to any one*; b' fheudar dhaibh *strìochdadh, they were compelled to yield*, or *surrender*.

Striochdadh, stre'chg′-ă, *pt.* yielding, submitting, giving up; *n. m.* submission, obedience.

Striochdte, strē′ch′-tyȧ, *pt.* yielded, submissive, compliant.

Strioll, strėúll, *n. f.* a girth, *Irish.*

Striop, strēpp, *n. f.* whoredom; (*Dan.* a female.)

Striopach, strēpp′-ach, *n. f.* a whore.

Striopachas, strēpp′-ach-as, *n. f.* whoredom.

Striopaire, strēpp′-ur-ȧ, *n. m.* whoremonger.

Strodh, strô, *n. m.* (striudheas), prodigality.

Stroic, strôèchg, *v.* tear asunder, lascerate; *n. f.* a long rag, *or* ragged person.

Stroiceadh, strôèchg′-ă, *pt.* tearing asunder.

Struidh, strúė-′y′, *v.* spend, waste, squander.

Struidheas, strúė′-y*h*as, *n. m.* prodigality.

Struidheasach, strúė′-y*h*as-ach, *a.* prodigal.

Struidheasachd, strúė′-y*h*as-achg, *n. f.* extreme extravagance, waste *or* prodigality.

Struidheil, strúė′-y*h*al, *a.* extravagant.

Strup, strŭp, *n. m.* spout of a kettle, (*Dan.*)

Strump, strŭmp, *n. m.* spout of a kettle.

Struth, strhŭ, *n. f.* an ostrich, *Job.* 39. 13.

Stuacach, stŭăchg′-ach, *adj.* stupid, boorish.

Stuacachd, stŭăchg′-achg, *n. m.* stupidity.

Stuacaire, stŭăchg′-ăėr-ȧ, *n. m.* a blockhead.

Stuacaireachd, stŭăchg′-ăėr-achg, *n. f.* stupidity.

Stuadh, stŭă′-gh, *n. f.* a mountain-high wave, pillar, column; *stuadhaibh* deataich, *pillars of smoke. Bible.*

Stuadhach, stŭă′-ach, *a.* having huge waves.

Stuadhadh, stŭă′-ă, *pt.* approaching, approximating; coming near in excellence.

Stuaic, stŭăèchg, *n. f.* a wry-neck and sullen countenance, expressive of discontent, an extreme boorishness *or* stupidity, —little hill. *H. S.*

Stuaidh, stŭăe-y′, *n. f.* a gable of a house; *v.* come near, approximate; cha *stuaidh* thu air, *you will not come near him, this will not approximate it*; cha *stuaidh* so air a lionadh, *this will not near fill it.*

Stuaim, stŭăèm, *n. f.* guardedness; temperance, prudence, modesty; a' reusanachadh ma fhìrinteachd *stuaim*, agus breathanas ri teachd, ghabh Felix eagal mòr, *reasoning about righteousness, temperance, and judgment to come, Felix trembled, Acts* xxiv. 25.; *stuaim* is macantas, *meekness and modesty, Bible*; Geal-làimh na *stuaim, the fair, prudent,* (*cautious*) *hand. Oss.*

Stuama, stŭăm′-a, *adj.* temperate in desire *or* appetite; temperate, moderate; a' teagasg dhuinn gach mì-dhiadhachd agus ana-mianna àicheadh, agus ar beatha a chaitheadh gu *stuama* gu cothromach agus gu Diadhaidh anns an t-saoghal so làthair, *teaching us to deny all ungodliness and worldly lusts, and to spend our lives soberly, righteously, and godly in this present life. Titus* iii. 12; modest.

Stuc, stûchg, *n. m.* a lump; surliness.

Stuc, stûchg, *n. f.* a pinnacle, a conical steep rock; precipice; cliff.

Stucach, stuchg.. stŭk′-ach, *adj.* not apt to burn, not inflammable; surly, morose

Stucach, stûchg- *and* stûk′-ach, *adj.* clifty, prominent; full of bare rocks.

Stugh-cridhe, stŭ-gh-krè′-a, *n. m.* cordial.

Stughaig, stŭ′-ėg, *v.* starch. *N.*; starsaich.

Stuib, stŭėb, *pl.* and *gen.* of s ob.

Stuic, stŭėchg, *pl.* and *gen.* of stoc.

Stuic, stûėchg, *n. f.* wry-neck, as a bull going to fight; scowling side-look of a morose person.

Stuidearra, stŭjj′-urr-a, *adj.* studious.

Stuidearrachd, stŭjj′-urr-achg, *n. f.* study, composure, meditation.

Stuig, stŭėg, *v.* set dogs to; incite, instigate; *n. c.* a bad pet *or* person.

Stuirt, stûėrjt, *n. f.* assumed gravity.

Stuirtealachd, stuėrjty″-all-achg, *n. f.* see Stuirt.

Stuirteil, stuėrjty″-al, *adj.* morose and dignified, but insignificant.

Stur, stûr, *n. m.* dust, motes; lur gun *stùr, diamond unsullied.*

Sturd, Sturdan, stûrd′-an, *n. m.* the herb darnel, the seed of which causes intoxication when mixed with meal; vertigo in sheep, *or* the disease which causes them to reel.

Sturr, stûrr, *n. m.* rugged top of a hill.

Stuth, Stugh, stŭ′-gh′, *n. m.* camlet, stuff, thing, particle; gach *stugh* a th' agam, *every thing I possess*; droch *stugh, bad stuff*; cha bhi *stugh* ort, *nothing will be wrong with you.*

Suacan, sŭăchg′-an, *n. m.* any thing wrought together awkwardly, as clay; — pot. *Macfarlane.*

Suadhadh, sŭă′-ghă, *pt. n. m.* rubbing, friction.

Suaicean, sŭăėchg′-ăėn, *n. m.* bundle of straw. *North.*

Suaicheanta, sŭăėch′-chyant-a, *adj.* curious, novel, new, remarkable, notable.

Suaicheantas, sŭăėch′-chyant-us, *n. m.* novelty, curiosity; cha *suaicheantas* còrr air cladach, *a heron on the shore, is no novelty* or *curiosity*; escutcheon, ensign, standard, armorial, *or* ensign, *or* crest; dha 'm bu *shuaicheantas* guibhas, *whose armorial ensign* or *crest was the fir-crop*; slat-*shuaicheantais, a sceptre.*

Suaidh, sŭăė′-y′, } *v. n.* rub, wipe; mash,
Suadh, sua′-gh, } as potatoes.

Suaidhte, sŭăėy′-tyă, *pt.* rubbed, mashed.

Suail, sŭăėl, *adj.* small. *Macfarlan.*

Suaimh, sŭăėv, *n. m.* luxurious kind of rest.

Suaimhneach, sŭăėv′-nyach, *adj.* enjoying a kind of luxury in ease and quiet, as after great danger *or* fatigue; very tranquil, *or* quiet.

Suaimhneas, sŭăėv′-nyus, *n. m.* luxury of ease and rest; greatest tranquillity *or* quiet; bheir mise *suaimhneas* dhuibh, *I will give you rest. Bible.*

Suaimhneasach, sŭăėv′-nyus-ach, *a.* luxuriating in peace and tranquillity.

Suain, sŭăėn, *n. f.* profound *or* deep sleep; Sweden, Righ na *Suain, the King of Sweden*; a' dol do'n t-*Suain, going to Sweden*; *v.* wreathe. *N.*

Suaineach, sŭăėn′-ach, *adj.* narcotic; sound asleep; in a profound sleep.

Suaineach, sŭăėn′-ach, *adj.* Swedish; *n. m.* a Swede, *or* inhabitant of Sweden.

Suaip, sŭăėp, *n. f.* faint *or* distant resemblance, as persons; tha *suaip* eatorra, *they resemble somewhat each other*; exchange, *or* barter; rinn iad *suaip, they have bartered commodities*; *v.* exchange, *or* barter; *shuaip* iad na h-eich, *they have exchanged* or *bartered the horses.*

Suairce, sŭăėrk-ă, *a.* kind, polite; urbane.

Suairceas, sŭăėrk′-us, *n. m.* kindness, politeness.

Suanach, sŭăn′-ach, *n. f.* hide, skin; a covering *or* mantle. *Mackintyre.*

Suarach, Suarrach, sŭărr′-ach, *adj.* indifferent; tha mi *suarrach* uime, *I am indifferent about it*; insignificant, paltry, inconsiderable; duine na nì *suarrach, a paltry person* or *thing*; bu *shuarrach* dhuit gad a dheanadh tu sin, *it were no great thing, though you should do that, —it were a light or inconsiderable matter though you should do it*; gnothach *suarrach, a paltry* or *shabby thing.*

Suarrachas, suarr′-ach-as, *n. f.* trifling nature *or* quality, paltriness, naught; *suarrachas* a ni so, *the contemptible nature of this thing,—the paltriness of this thing*; na cuir an *suarrachas* an ni so, *do not set at nought,—do not make light of this thing*; neglect, contempt.

Suarraichead, sŭăr′-ėch-ad, *n. f.* degree of indifference, contemptibleness; a' dol an *suarraichead* uime, *getting more indifferent about it.*

Suas, sŭăs, *n. m. adv.* height, eminence, upper part; a *suas, up, upwards*; thoir *suas* ort, *up with you*; chaidh e *suas, he went up*; chaidh e *suas* air beinn, *he went up into a mountain, B.*; cha'n'eil an *suas* air fichead ann, *there is not more than twenty.*

Subailt; see Supail; (*French,* souple.)

Subhach, sŭ′-ach, *adj.* happy, merry.

Subhachas, sŭ′-ach-us, *n. m.* happiness, expression of happiness, mirth, merriment, gladness; is màirg a dheanadh *subhachas* ri dubhachas fir eile, *he is to be pitied that rejoices in another's woe.*

Subhailc, sŭv′-aėlk, *n. f.* virtue; *Bible,* deadh-bheus.

Subhailceach, sŭb′-ăelk-ach, *adj.* virtuous, moral; beusach, deadh-bheusach.

Suchd, sŭchd, *n. m.* sake, account; air *suchd* a mhaitheis, *for goodness sake*; air *suchd* Chrìoda, *for Christ's sake*; air *suchd* nan achd, *for the sake of these objections.*

Sud, mispronunciation of Siod.

Sudh, su'-gh, *n. m.* seam of a plank. *H. S.*

Sug, sûg, *for* sùigh, to suck. *Bible.*

Sug, sûg, *n. m.* merriness, mirth, happiness.

Sug, sŭg, *n. m.* a lamb; *Inter.* mode of calling a lamb. *Argyle.*

Sugach, sûg'-ach, *adj.* merry, cheerful.

Sugair, sûg'-ėr, *v.* make merry, sport.

Sugaire, sûg'-ur-à, *n. m.* Merry-Andrew.

Sugan, sûg'-an, *n. m.* a straw *or* heath-rope.

Sugh, sŭ'-gh, *n. m.* sap, juice, moisture; soup; a receding huge wave; dearest object *or* darling; a *shùgh* mo chridhe, *my dearest! my darling! sùgh* feoile, *soup*, or *juice of beef*; tha'n *sùgh* fuar, *the moisture on the earth is cold*; gnothach gun *sùgh*, *a sapless* or *senseless affair*; *sùgh* nan ubhall, *the sap of the apples.*

Sughadh, sû'-X, *pt.* drinking up, *or* drying up; seasoning, as wood; tha fiodh air *sùghadh*, *the wood is seasoned,—extract the juice*; absorb; *shùigh* e am fallus, *it absorbed the perspiration*; a' *sùghadh* an smior as, *extracting the very marrow from it*; *n. m.* receding wave; extracting, absorption; thug na *sùghaidh* leis e, *the receding waves carried it away.*

Sughail, sú'-ghal, *adj.* juicy, sappy.

Sughan, sù'-an, *n. m.* extract, liquid-flummery.

Sughair, } **Sughmhor**, } sûgh'-ghur, *adj.* sappy, juicy, pithy, succulent.

Sughaireachd, sûgh'-ghur-achg, *n. f.* juiciness, sappiness, succulency, solidity.

Sugh-craobh, sŭgh'-krăov, *n. m.* rasps.

Sugh-lair, sŭ-gh-lâėr', *n. m.* strawberries.

Sugradh, sûg'-krX, *n. m.* play, sport, diversion, joke; cha'n'eil thu ad *shùgradh*, *it is no joke to deal with you*; cha'n e an *sùgradh* cur ris, *it is no joke to master* or *manage him*; agus dh 'éirich iad suas gu *sùgradh*, *and they rose up to play. B.*

Suic, sŭėchg, *n. pl.* ploughshares; snouts.

Suicean, sŭėchg'-äėn, *n. m.* gag for a calf. *North.*

Suidh, sŭė'-y', *v.* sit; sit down; incubate.

Suidhe, súė'-yė, *n. f.* sitting, act or state of sitting; sederunt; dean *suidhe, sit, be seated*; 'na *shuidhe, be sitting* or *seated*; 'na *suidhe, she sitting* or *seated*; beam, saigh. *North.*

Suidheachan, sŭė'-y-hach-an, *n. m.* turf-sofa. *Armst.*; cushion. *Islay*; setting, (in some places.)

Suidheagan, súė'-ghag-an; see Suidhe.

Suidheachadh, súė'-y-hach-X, *pt.* settling, laying foundation, making frame-work; planting *or* colonizing; arranging terms of marriage; letting of houses, farms, &c.; plan, model; air a cheart *suidheachadh*, *upon the same plan, after the came pattern* or *model, as cloth.*

Suidhich, súė'-ėch, *v.* let, set; *shuidhich* e an tigh, neo am baile, *he has let the house* or *farm*; betrothe, settle terms of marriage; *shuidhich* a nighean air, *he betrothed his daughter to him*; win, lay, plant, arrange, settle, appoint; *suidhich* àit' an tachair sinn, *appoint a place where we shall meet*; *shuidhich* iad an stéidh, *they laid the foundation*; *shuidhich* Fionn an t-seilg, *Fingal arranged the hunt*; agus *shuidhich* an Tighearn Dia gàrradh, *and the* Lord God *planted a garden, Bible*; *shuidhich* e beothshlaint urra, *he settled an annuity on her.*

Suidhichte, súė'-ėch-tyà, *pt.* laid, as foundation; settled, appointed, pointed out; tha 'n t-àite *suidhichte, the place is appointed, is determined*; tha mi *suidhichte* air sin a dheanadh, *I am determined to do that*; sedate; duine *suidhichte, sedate person.*

Suidhe-lair, súė-llâėr', *n. m.* frame-work, ground-work.

Suigeart, sŭėg'-artt', *n. m.* blustering kind of expression of joy.

Suigh, sûė-y', evaporate, absorb, dry up, drink up; season *or* dry, as wood; extract; *shùigh* am fiodh, *the wood seasoned*; fiodh *sùighte, seasoned wood*; *shùigh* an t-ombar an dùradan a 'm shùil, *the amber extracted the mote from my eye*; *shùigh* an còs an t-uisge, *the sponge absorbed the water*; *shùigh* am fallus, *the perspiration absorbed*; *sùigh* ort e, *suck it in*; *shùigh* a' phoite, *the pot dried up*; *shùigh* na h-uile deur, *every drop evaporated.*

Suighte, sûey''-tyà, *pt.* absorbed, dried up, evaporated, boiled in, seasoned.

Suil, sû'l, *n. f.* an eye, a spot; expectation, hope; an opening, orifice; superintendance, oversight; glance, sight; bha mo cheud *sùil, my first glance* or *sight was*; thog e a *shùil, he raised his eye*; gun *sùil* r'a theachd, *without any expectation of his coming*; tha *sùil* againn ris, *we expect him*; na biodh *sùil* na dùil agad ris, *have neither expectation or hope of him*; biodh *sùil* agad orra, *watch* or *keep your eye on them*; an cuir tobar a mach as an aon *sùil*, uisge milis is searbh, *will a fountain send forth, at the same opening, sweet water and bitter? Bible*; tha '*shùil* ri teachd, *he expects to come.*

Suileach, sû'l'-ach, *adj.* sharp-sighted; knowing.

Suilbhir, sŭ'l'-vhėr', *adj.* hearty, cheerful.

Suilbhireachd, sŭ'l'-vhėr'-achg, *n. f.* hilarity, cheerfulness.

Suil chrith, sŭ'l'-chrėh, *n. f.* quagmire.

Suileag, sû'l'-ag, *n. f.* spot in cloth; the bell on liquors; small bubble.

Suilleagach, sù'l'-ag-ach, *a.* spotted.

Suil-lighiche, sû'l'-llė-ėch-a, *n. m.* an oculist.

Suim, sûėm, *n. f.* sum; (summa, *Latin*); attention, regard, consideration; cha bhi *sùim* aige do dh' éirig, *he shall not regard a ransom. Bible*; *sùim* nan deich fhathantan, *the sum of the Ten Commandments*; cha'n'eil *sùim*'sam bith aige do d' ghnothach, *he pays no attention to your business*; gabh *sùim, pay attention, attend to.*

Suimealachd, sûėm'-all-achg, *n. f.* attentiveness.

Suimeil, sûėm'-al, *adj.* attentive; momentous, important, considerable.

Suipear, sêp- *or* sŭėp'-ăėr, *n. f.* supper; (*French*, souper); an dèigh na *suipreach, after supper. Bible.*

Suire, sŭėr'-a, *n. f.* sea-nymph. *H. S.*; màidean mhara. *Islay.*

Suireach, sûėr'-ach, *a.* wooing, courting; *n. m.* a courtier, wooer, shuffler.

Suirich, sŭėr'-ėch, *n. f.* courtship, wooing.

Suiriche, sŭėr'-ėch-ȧ, *n. m.* wooer.

Suisd, Suist, sûėshjj, *n. m.* a flail.

Suisdealadh, shûėshjj'-all-ă, *pt.* drubbing, hard work; working night and day.

Suith, sûė- sû'-ėch, (suthaich,) *n. f.* soot.

Suitheach, sûė'-ach, *adj.* sooty; full of soot.

Sulaire, sûl'-ur-ȧ, *n. f.* gannet, amson.

Sulchair, sûl'-chur, *a.* overjoyed.

Sulas, sŭl'-as, *n. m.* complaisance, overjoy, shewing itself by gestures and expression of countenance; air son *sulas* riutsa, *out of sheer complacency to you*; 'se rinn an *sulas, how overjoyed he was.*

Sulasach, sŭl'-as-ach, *adj.* overjoyed, complaisant. *Islay.*

Sult, sŭl'tt, *n. m.* plumpness, fatness.

Sultar, *adj.* } sŭl'tt'-ur, *adj.* plump, fat,
Sultmhor, } in good condition.

Sultaireachd, sŭl'tt'-aėr-achg, *n. f.* plumpness.

Sumag, sŭm'-ag, (pillinn); saddle-cloth.

Sumaich, sŭm'-ėch, *v.* give due number, as cattle at pasture.

Sumaid, Sumainn, sŭm'-ėj'-ėnn, *n. f.* a wave

Sumair, sŭm'-aėr, *n. m.* drone of a pipe. *Gillies.*

Sumanadh; see Sunnanadh.

Sumhail, sû'-ul, *adj* of little bulk; portable; as a person, humble, obedient, obsequious.

Sumhlachadh, sû'll'-ach-ă, *pt.* getting less bulky, creeping in; sitting *or* lying closer and closer; *n. m.* lessening, *or* abridgment of bulk.

Sumhlaich, sû'll'-ėch, *v.* lie *or* pack close together; lessen, abridge, get less bulky.

Sumhlachd, sû'll'-achg, *n. f.* littleness of bulk; obsequiousness, abjectness, littleness; also Sumhlas.

Sunn, pronounced and written Sunnd.

Sunnag, sŭnn'-ag, *n. f.* straw-chair. *N.*

Sunnanadh, sunn'-an-ă, *n. m.* a summons, *part.* serving with summons.

Sunnanaich, sûnn'-an-ėch, *v.* summon.

Sunnd, sûnnd, *n. m.* humour, hilarity; dè 'n *sùnnd* a th'ort, *how do ye do?*

Sunndach, sûnnd'-ach, *adj.* lively, joyous, in good health and spirits.

Supail, sûpp'-al, *adj.* supple, elastic; (*French*, suople); nimble.

Supalachd, sûp'-al-achg, *n. f.* suppleness, elasticity, nimbleness.

Surd, sûrd, *n. m.* successful train *or* mode, eager and willing exertion; business appearance; hilarity; cuir *sùrd* ort, *bestir yourself.*

Surdag, sûrd'-ag, *n. m.* a stride, leap.

Surdail, sûrd'-al, *adj.* prompt, business-like, full of spirits.

Surdalachd, sûrd'-all-achg, *n. f.* alacrity.

Susdal, sûsd'-al, *n. m.* bustle about nothing.

Suthainn, sŭ'-ėnn, *adj.* everlasting, eternal, infinite; gu *suthainn* is gu sìorruith tha, *thou art eternally and for ever. Psalms.*

T

T, t, the sixteenth letter of the Gaelic alphabet, named by the Irish, Teine. It has various sounds, but the most common is *t*, as in town; slender sound, like ch, in choose; or first *t* in Christianity, kris-TYE-an-ė-tė. See Grammar.

T-, t-; it is thus placed before many nouns *sing.* beginning with a vowel, and having the article prefixed, as,—an *t*-each, an *t*-uan, *the horse, the lamb*; 2d, placed in the genitive and nominative, before nouns beginning with sl-, sn-, sr-, which is exemplified under "an" article, page 11.—See also Grammar.

T', t', *for* d' *or* do, thy; as, *t'* athair, *thy father.*

Ta, an Irish tha; *tha* mi, *I am*; in Irish, *ta* mi, *ta* thu, *I am, thou art.*

Tabaid, ttab'-ăj, *n. f.* a row, a fray.

Tabaideach, ttab'-ăj-ach, *a.* quarrelsome.

Tabaideachd, ttăb'-ăj-achg, *n. f.* quarrelsomeness; quarrelsome disposition and habits.

Tabh, tâv, *n. m.* the ocean. *Ossian*; àbh. *Lewis.*

Tabhachd, tâv'-achg, *n. f.* profit, benefit.

advantage; cha'n eil *tàbhachd* sam bith dhomhsa ann, *it is no profit* or *benefit to me*; quantity *or* number; dè'n *tàbhachd* a th' ann, *what quantity is there of it?* ma'n *tàbhachd* sin, *about that quantity*; substantiality, solidity.

Tabhachdach, ttâv'-achg-ach, *adj.* beneficial, advantageous, profitable, efficient, efficacious; buillean *tàbhachdach, effectual* or *efficient blows*; ni *tàbhachdach, a profitable* or *advantageous thing*; solid, substantial.

Tabhair, Irish for thoir, give, grant.

Tabhairn, ttâv'-ern, *n. m.* an inn, a tavern; (*French*, taverne; *Armoric* and *Welsh*, tafern; *Cornish*, tavargn.)

Tabhairt, Irish for Tobhairt.

Tabhairteach, Irish for Tobhartach.

Tabhall, tâv'-all, *n. m.* a sling. *B.*; *Irish.*

Tabhann, taff'-ann, *n. f* barking, yelping.

Tabhannaich, taff'-ann-èch, *n. f.* continuous barking.

Tabhartair, tobhairtear, bestower.

Tabhartas, tobhartas, gift, offering.

Tabhastal, tâv'-ast-al, *n. f.* nonsense. *N.*

Tac, tăchg, *n. f.* space, time; ma'n *tac*-so an uirigh, *about this time last year*; ceithir bliadhna 'na *taic*-so, *this time four years*; improperly written *dachd.*

Tacaid, tăchg'-aj, *n. f.* a tack; stitch *or* pain.

Tacan, tăchg'-an, *n. f.* little time, while.

Tacar, tâchg'-ur, *n. m.* plenty, provisions.

Tachair, tăch'-èr, *v.* meet, light upon, find; *tachraidh* sinn fhathast, *we shall meet yet*; an do *thachair* thu air, *did you light upon it*, or *find it*; *v. n.* happen, come to pass; *thachair* e gu math dhuit, *it has happened well to you*; agus *thacair* gu'n deach e seachad, *and it came to pass that he passed by.*

Tachairt, tăch'-ărjt, *pt.* happening, meeting, act of meeting, *or* coming to pass.

Tachais, tăch-èsh, *v.* scratch the skin.

Tachara, tăch'-ar-a, *n. m.* sprite, trifling person. *Islay*;—orphan. *North.*

Tachas, tăch'-us, *n. m.* itch, itchiness; *pt.* clawing, scratching.

Tachasach, tăch'us-ach, *adj.* itchy.

Tachd, tăchg, *v.* choke, strangle, stop up.

Tachdadh, tăchg'-Ă, *pt.* choking, strangling.

Tachrais, tăch'-rèsh, *v.* wind yarn.

Tachrasach, tăch'-ras-ach, *n. f.* windlass.

Tadh, tâ, *n. m.* a ledge, a layer. *Bible.*

Tag, Tagan, tăg'-an, *n. m.* private, *or* hid purse, as that of a wife.

Tagair, tag'-èr, *v.* claim, crave, plead a cause, prosecute; tha e *tagairt* orm, *he claims of me, he craves me*; *tagair* mo chùis a Dhè, *plead my cause*, O God! *Ps.*

Tagairt, tăg'-ărjt, *pt.* pleading, craving.

Tagarach, tăg'-ar-ach, *adj.* litigious.

Tagartair, tăg'-art-aer, *n. m.* pleader, agent.

Tagartas, tăg'-artt-us, *n. m.* prosecution, law-plea; tha *tagartas* aige an Inbhir-aoradh, *he has a law-plea in Inverary;* claim.

Tagh, taŏ'-gh, *v.* choose, select, elect, make choice; *tagh* a chuid a's fhearr, *select the best, make choice of the best*; *adj.* choice, select, beloved, dear to; is *tagh* leam thu, *I love you, I like you*; ma's *tagh* leat mi, is *tagh* leam thu, is mar an *tagh* na taobh me, *if you love me I love you, otherwise do not come near me*; is *tagh* leam thusa ach is annsa leam esan, *I like you, but he is more dear, dearer to me*; murdered by the Irish, *togh*—and hence the absurdity, is *toigh* leam e, in books, instead of, is *tagh* leam e, *I like it.*

Tagha, ttaŏ'-à, *n. f.* choice, selection; *tagha* gach nì, *choice* or *selection of every thing*; *tagha* a mheàirlich, *a choice thief, a real thief*; rogha is *tagha, pick and choice.*

Taghach, taŏ'-ach. *adj.* fond of; cha'n'eil mi *taghach ma, I am not fond of.*

Taghadh, taŏ'-aŏ gh, *pt.* choosing, electing.

Taghadair, taŏ'-add-aèr, *n. m.* elector, chooser.

Taghairm, tao'-aŏèrm, *n. f.* an echo; militia.

Taghan, taŏ'-an, *n. m.* pole-cat, stinkard.

Taghte, taŏ'-tyà, *pt.* choice, chosen.

Tagradair, tăg'-radd'-ăèr, *n. m.* pleader, agent.

Tagradh, tăg'-rĂ, *pt.* pleading, craving.

Taibh, Taibhean, tăeff'-ăèn, *n. m.* substance.

Taibheanach, tăeff'-ăèn-ach, *adj.* substantial.

Taibhleach, tăev- *or* ttħĭ'-lach, *n. f.* a smart blow, *or* box sideways; smart box,

Taibhis, Taibhse, ttī'-èsh, tăevsh, *n. c.* spectre, apparition, second-sight; spirit, ghost, a vision of the second-sight.

Taibhsear, ttăev'-shyăèr, *n. m.* a visionary, a silly person; one gifted with the second-sight.

Taibhsearachd, tăev'-shyar-achg, *n. f.* bewildered, *or* stupid conduct; second-sight.

Taibid, tăeb'-èjj, *n. f.* taunting speech. *N.*

Taic, tăechg, *n. f.* support, prop, fulcrum; cuir *taic* ri so, *prop this*; cuir *taic* ris a ghéamhlaig, *put a fulcrum to the lever*; contact, collision; thàinig e an *taic* na cartach, *he came in contact with the cart*; nearness, approximation; *taic* ri bliadhna, *near a year*; cum *taic* rium, *support me*; an *taic* a chéile, *in collision with each other*; dependence, preparation; an *taic* an dòmhnuich, *in contact*, or *in preparation for the Sabbath*; na leig do thaic ris a sin, *depend* or *lean not too much to that*; an *taic* a bhalla, *leaning on the wall*; cha ruig mi leas mo *thaic* a leigeil riutsa, *I need not lean much on your patronage* or *support*; laoich ri sleaghan an *taic, heroes leaning on their spears.*

TAICEIL, tăĕchg′-al, *adj.* stout, firm.

TAICEALACHD, tăĕchg′-al-achg, *n. f.* stoutness, solidity, firmness.

TAIFEID, tăĕff′-aj, *n. f.* bow-string. *Macd.*

TAIG, taėg, *n. f.* great attachment. *H. S.*

TAIGEIS, taėg′-ash, *n. f.* Scotch haggis.

TAIGH, taŏe′-y′, proper orthography of tigh.

TAIL, tăel, *n. m.* substance, fee, wages. *Sk.*

TAILCEAS, tă′l′-kus, *n. m.* scorn, disdain.

TAILCEASACH, tă′l′-kus-ach, *a.* disdainful.

TAILEASG, tâ′l′-usg, *n. m.* backgammon.

TAILLEABH, tâ′lly″-uv, *n. m.* apprentice-fee, premium; consequence, result; an do phàidh thu do *thàilleabh, have you paid your apprentice-fee*, or *premium*? air *tàilleabh* a ghnothaich sin, *in consequence of that affair*; gheibh, neo meallaidh mi nis *tàilleabh* mo shaoithreach, *I will now enjoy the result* or *fruits of my labour. Islay.*

TAILLEABHACH, tâlly″-uv-ach, *adj.* consequent, as the result; *n. m.* an apprentice.

TAILLEABHACHD, ta′lly″-uv-achd, *n. f.* apprenticeship, substantiality.

TAILLEAR, tâ′lly′-aėr, *n. m.* a tailor.

TAILLEARACHD, tâlly″-ăėr-achg, *n. f.* sewing.

TAILM, taŏl′-um, *n. m.* tools. *Irish.*

TAILMRICH, taŏl′-um-rėch, *n. f.* noise.

TAILP, tăĕlp, *n. f.* a bundle, parcel. *Irish.*

TAIMH, táėv, *n. m.* death, mortality. *Ir.*

TAIMHLEAC, táėv′-llechg, *n. f.* tombstone. *Irish.*

TAIMHNEULL, ttév′-nnell, *n. f.* slumber. *Ps.*

TAIN, } tàėnn, *n. f.* wealth in flocks;
TAINN, } flocks, cattle. *Islay, Bible*; spoil. *Irish.*

TAINE, táėn″-â, *deg.* thinner, (tana), *n. f.* thinness; na 's *taine, thinner*; is *taine, the thinnest.*

TAINEAD, táėn′-ud, *n. f.* thinness, degree of thinness, degree of tenuity.

TAING, táėng, *n. f.* gratitude, thanks, deep sense of gratitude; gun *tàing* dhuit, *in defiance of you, in spite of you, without thanks to you*; nì mi sin gun *tàing* dhuit, *I will do that in defiance of you*; a′ nochdadh do *thàing, shewing your sense of gratitude.*

TAINGEALACHD, táėng′-all-achg, *n. f.* sentiments of gratitude; taingealas.

TAINGEIL, táėng′-al, *adj.* grateful, thankful, impressed with a sense of gratitude; is *tàingeil* is còir dhuit a bhi, *you ought to be very grateful*; bi *tàingeil* nach ′eil so na′s miosa, *be thankful that things are not worse.*

TAINISTEAR, táėn″-ėsth′-tyaėr, *n. m.* heir-presumptive; next oldest son; one acting for the heir; regent, governor; trustee, tutor.

TAINISTEARACHD, táėn′-ėsh-tyăr′-achg, *n. f.* presumptive heirship, regency, trusteeship.

TAINTEAN, tàėnn′-tyun, *n. pl.* talents, faculties, accomplishments; is mòr na *tàinteann* a bhuilich Dia ort, *great are the talents God has bestowed on you*; bithidh a sgoil na *tàintean* ri d′ bheò dhuit, *your education must prove an accomplishment to you for life.*

TAIP, tă′p, *n. f.* great wealth, without any of the refined manners or education of genteel society; a mass, a lump.

TAIR, tâėr, *n. m.* contempt, reproach; na dean *tàir, do not despise* or *scorn*; a′ *tàir* orm, *despising me, looking down on me*; *v.* get, *Sm.*; come, go, *B.*; mean, *H. Society.*

TAIRBEART, ta′rb′-art, *n. f.* isthmus; name of isthmus of Kintyre, and many other like places in the Highlands; superabundance.

TAIRBEARTACH, ta′rb′-art-ach, *adj.* superabundant, very abundant, almost superfluous; cho *tairbeartach* ′sa tha iad, *they are so superabundant.*

TAIRBEARTAS, tăerb′-art-as, *n. f.* superabundance, overflowing goodness; *tairbeartas* a làmh, *the superabundance of his goodness, Ps.*; murdered toirbeartas.

TAIRBH, taŏėrv, *n. pl.* bulls—of a bull.

TAIRBHE, taŏr′-a, *n. f.* advantage, profit, avail; an t-ainm gun an *tairbhe, the name without the profit* or *benefit*; *tàirbhe* cha dean t′òr-chùl réidh, *thy glossy yellow hair cannot avail.*

TAIRBEALACH, ta′r′-byal ach, *n. m.* defile.

TAIRBHEARTAS, see Tairbeartas, bounty.

TAIREALACHD, tâ′r′-all-achg, *n. f.* contemptuousness, contemptibility, reproachfulness.

TAIREIL, tâ′r′-al, *adj.* contemptuous, disdainful, reproachful, insulting.

TAIRG, ta′rėg, *v.* offer, proffer; propose; bid; *thairg* e airgead dhaibh, *he offered them money*; *tairg* air so, *bid for this—at a sale* or *auction.*

TAIRGIR, tâ′rėg′-ėr, *v.* prophesy, *B.*; obs.

TAIRGIRE, tăerg-ėr-â, *n. m* offerer, bidder.

TAIRGSE, tăerg′-shâ, *n. f.* offer, proposal.

TAIRGSINN, tăerg′-shėnn, *n. f. pt.* offering, bidding, proffering; *n. f.* an offer.

TAIRGSEACH, tăerg′-shyach, *adj.* inviting offering.

Tairis, tăėr'-ėsh, *int.* stand still! see Teirisd and Teiris, *a.* kindly, urbane. *Gillies.*

Tairiseach, tăėr'-ėsh-ach, *adj.* loyal, *Mackenzie.*

Tairisgean, for toirpsgian, peat-spade, fat.

Tairlearach, tâėr'-lyăr-ach, *a.* transmarine. *M'F.*

Tairmeas, tâ'r'-mėss, *n. m.* disdain, contempt.

Tairmeasail, tâ'r'-mėss-al, *adj.* disdainful.

Tairn, taŏėrn, *n. m.* necromancy; iodramanachd.

Tairne, tăėrn'-à, *gen.* of tarrunn, a nail.

Tairneach, tăėrn'-ech, *n. f.* thunder; *a.* extractive.

Tairneanach, tâėrn'-ăėn-ach, *n. f.* thunder.

Tairnnich, nail.

Tairnsinn, taėrsh'-ėnn, *pt.* obtaining. *H.S.*

Tais, tăsh, *adj.* damp, moist, spiritless.

Taisbean, tashb'-aėn, *v.* table, present; *taisbeanan* t-airgead, *table the money*;—reveal, shew; *taisbean* do thrŏcair dhuinn, *reveal thy loving kindness to us*, *Ps.*; *n. m.* a revelation, a vision. *Bible.*

Taisbeanadh, tăshb'-áėn'-Ă, *pt.* revealing; leabhar an *taisbeanaidh*, REVELATIONS.

Taisdeal, tăshj'-al, *n. f.* a journey, voyage. *M'F.*

Taisdealach, tashjj'-al-ach, *n. m.* ghost, a contemptible person; one that scuds *or* vanishes by, *Is.*; a sojourner, traveller, *M'F.*; vagabond, *Gillies.*

Taise, tăsh'-à, *deg.* tais, more soft, spiritless.

Taiseachd, tăsh'-achg, *n. f.* extreme cowardice.

Taisead, tash'-ad, *n. m.* extreme degree of cowardice *or* moistness.

Taiseadach, tăsh'-aŏd-ach, *n. m.* shroud, winding-sheet; ciste is *taiseadach*, *coffin and shroud.*

Taisealachd, tăsh'-al-achg, *n. f.* moistness.

Taisg, tăėshg, *v.* deposit, lay up, hoard; ga' *tasgadh* seachad, *hoarding it up*; *n. m.* store; also tigh-*taisg*, *a store-house*; ni sam tha'n *taisg*, *any thing in store.*

Taisg-airm, tăėshg'-aŏrm, *n. f.* armoury.

Taisgeach, tăėshg'-ach, *n. f.* a store, store-house.

Taisgeadach, tăėshg'-aŏd-ach, *n. f.* wardrobe.

Taisgeal, tăshg'-al, *n. m.* finding any thing that was lost; reward for returning it.

Taisgeal, tăshg'-skell, *n. m.* news.

Taisich, tăsh'-ėch, *v.* moisten; daunt.

Taitinn, tajt'-ėnn, *v.* please, give delight to, satisfy; deamar a *thaitinn* e riut, *how did it please you?*

Taitneach, tajt'-nyach, *adj.* happy, pleasant, agreeable, fascinating, acceptable; is *taitneach* an nì e, *it is a pleasant thing*; *taitneach* do 'n t-sealladh, *pleasant to the sight. B.*; is *taitneach* leam t' fhaicinn, *I am happy to see you.*

Taitneachd, tajt'-nyach, *n. f.* taste, pleasantness, agreeableness.

Taitneadh, tăjt'-nyĂ, *pt.* pleasing.

Taitneas, tajt'-nyas, sensation of taste, *or* quality that gives rise to delight.

Tal, tâ'll, *n. f.* coopers' axe, *or* adze.

Talach, tall'-ach, *n. m.* repining; cha 'n ion duit a bhi *talach*, *you have no reason to repine*, or *grumble*, or *be displeased.*

Taladh, tâ'-la, *pt.* getting attached to; *n. m.* art of getting attached to a person *or* house, particularly as animals.

Talaich, tall'-ėch, *v.* repine, murmur.

Talaidh, tâll'-Ă, *v.* attach to, get fond of.

Talainte, tall'-aėnjt-a, *n. m.* partition. *H. Society.*

Talamh, tal'-uv, *n. m.* earth, land; glas-*talamh*, *unploughed land*; *talamh* dugh, *black land in open weather*, or *absence of snow in winter.*

Talann, tal'-ann, *n. m.* talent. *Bible.*

Talfuinn, tall-fŭėnn', *n. m.* a hoe.

Talla, tall'-a, *n. m.* a hall. *Ossian.*

Talmhaidh, tall'-vė, *adj.* earthy, worldly; nithe *talmhaidh*, *earthly things*,—*worldly*; inntinn *thalmhaidh*. *worldly mind*; weighty, substantial; min *thalmhaidh*, *substantial meal*; pale, sallow. *H. S.*

Talmhaidheachd, tall'-vė-achg, *n. f.* weightiness, substantiality, sallowness, worldliness.

Talmhainn, tall'-vhėnn, *gen.* of talamh.

Talmhantachadh, tal'-ant-ach-Ă, *pt.* growing *or* sticking together, as sods or earth does.

Talmhantaich, tall'-ant-ėch, *v.* grow, as earth; stick together, as sods, &c.

Tamailt, tàm'-alyjt, *n. f* insult, reproach.

Tamailteach, tàm'-alyjt-ach, *adj.* insulting, disparaging, reproachful, taunting; gnàthfhacal *tàmailteach*, *a taunting proverb*, *Bible*; disgraceful.

Tamailtear, tàm'-ăljt-aėr, *n. m.* taunter.

Tamh, tàv, *n. m.* rest, quietness, quiet, refuge; aite *tàimh*, *place of rest* or *refuge*; abode, habitation; c'àite an *tàmh* dhuit, *where is the place of your abode? Sm.*; a' *tamh* san àite so, *dwelling here*; idleness, inactivity; tha i 'na *tàmh*, *she is idle*; tha e 'na *thàmh*, *he is idle*; cha *tàmh* dhuitse, *you don't pass your time in idleness*; leig *tàmh* dhomh, *let me alone*; leig *tàmh* dha sin, *let that alone*; nach leig thu *tàmh* dhomh, *would you not let me alone*; *v.* rest, abide, cease, desist, give over; *tàmh* do d' sgeig, *give over your jeering*, MACDONALD; *Inter.*

tàmh! tàmh! mo leanabh! *sleep! sleep! my child!* 'g obair gun *tàmh, incessantly, unceasingly,* or *indefatigably working.*

Tamhaich, tàv'-èch, *v.* rest, abide.

Tamhaiche, tàv'-èch-å, *n. m.* inhabitant.

Tamhaite, tàv'-âjt-å, *n. m.* habitation.

Tamharach, tàv'-ar-ach, *n. m.* a dolt.

Tamhasg, táv'-ask, *n. m.* spectre, apparition, ghost; b'e do *thamhasg* a bh' ann, *it was your ghost.*

Tamhasgail, táv'-ask-al, *adj.* spectre-like.

Tamull, tám'-ull, *n. m.* while; tacan.

Tana, tán'-a, *adj.* thin, slender, lean, shallow; ni *tana, thin thing*; duine *tana, lean person*; aite *tana,* (as in water,) *a shallow, shoal place*; brochan-*tana, gruel.*

Tanachd, tán'-achg, *n. f.* thinness, &c.

Tanaich, tán'-èch, *v.* get thin *or* shoal.

Tanalach, tán'-al-ach, *n. m.* shoal, *or* shallow water; thin part of a hide; thàinig am bàta o'n doimhneachd gus an *tanalach, the boat came from deep water to shoal water*; *tanalach* na seiche, *the thin of the hide.*

Tannas, tánn'-us; see Tamhasg, ghost.

Taobh, ttãov, *n. m.* side, direction, cause, account; an *taobh* a muigh, *the outside, the exterior*; an *taobh* a stigh, *the inner side, interior*; an *taobh* cùl, *the back part*; *taobh* beoil, *the front*; dè'n *taobh* a chaidh e, *in what direction has he gone?* cò'n *taobh, which side?* ri m' *thaobh, aside me*; thug e a *thaoibh* i, *he seduced her, led her astray*; a *thaoibh* sin, *about that, because of that, on that account*; cha'n eil fhios' am dè 's *taobh* dha, *I do not know what is become of him,—in what direction he has gone*; a *thaobh* sin deth, *on that very account*; *v.* come near, approach; cha do *thaobh* e am baile, *he did not come near the town*; cha *taobh* e sinne, *he will not come near us*; na *taobh* mise, *do not come near me,—keep at arm's-length from me.*

Taobhach, tãov'-ach, *adj.* lateral.

Taobhan, tãov'-an, *n. m.* side-rafter.

Taobhcheum, tãov'-chyãm, *n. f.* digression.

Taobh-leis, tãov-llãsh2', *n. m.* lee-side.

Taobhshruth, tãov'-hrŭh, *n. m.* eddy-tide.

Taod, tãodd', *n. f.* halter, reins.

Taoghail, *for* Tigheil, call when passing.

Taoim, tãoèm, properly taŏem, *n. f.* bilge-water.

Taois, tãŏèsh, *n. f.* dough *or* leaven.

Taoiseadair, tãoèsh'-add'-ăèr, *n. m.* a baker. *Macfarlan.*

Taoisinn, tãoèsh'-ènn, *v.* } knead, leaven,
Taoisnich, tãoesh'-nyèch, } work dough.

Taoitear, túèjt'-aèr, *n. m.* tutor, trustee.

Taom, tãom, *v. n.* bale a boat, pour out; empty, as a dish *or* cart; *taom* am bàta, *bale the boat*; *taom* air e, *pour it on it*; *taom* a' chairt, *empty the cart.*

Taomaire, tãom'-ur-a, *n. m.* a pump.

Taoman, tãom'-an, *n. m.* baling-dish.

Taosg, tãosg, *n. m.* near the full of a dish, cask, pitcher, cart, &c.; in some places used for Taom.

Taosgach, tãosg'-ach, *a.* fickle, uncertain; duine *taosgach, fickle person*; ni *taosgach, an uncertain* or *precarious thing.*

Taosgaid, tãosg'-ăj, *n. f.* fickle female.

Taosgaire, tãosg'-ur-a, *n. m.* fickle man.

Tap, tap, *n. m.* lock of lint on a distaff; *v.* hoop *or* thread a fishing-hook. *Islay.*

Tapachd, tapp'-ach, *n. f.* heroism.

Tapadh, tap'-Ă, *n. m.* heroic feat, achievement; thanks, success; *tapadh* leat, *thank you, Sir,* or *Madam,*—literally, *may you be a hero* or *heroine,* (the thing uppermost in Donald's noddle); air do shlàinte, *here is to your health*; *tapadh* leatsa, *thank you, Sir,* or *Madam, may you be a hero,* &c.

Tapadh-cion, tap'-Ă-kèún, *n. m.* a blunder.

Tapagail, tăp'-ag-al, *n. f.* a blunder.

Tapaidh, tăp'-è, *adj.* heroic, brave, clever, bold, successful in business.

Tapaidheachd, tap'-è-achg; see Tapachd.

Tapan, tap'-Ă, *n. m.* little lock of lint, &c.

Tar, târ, *n. m.* belly; *tar*-geal, *white belly.*

Taran, tar'-an, *n. m.* ghost of unbaptised child. *H. S.*

Tarbh, tărv, *n. m.* a bull; *tairbh, bulls*; *Welsh,* tarw; *Cornish,* tarv; see Tòraidh.

Tarbh-nathrach, tărv'-nár-ach, *n.* dragon-fly.

Tarbhach, tarv'-ach, *a.* supplied with bulls.

Tarbhach, tăr'-ach, *adj.* profitable, beneficial; *tarbhach* do dhuine, *profitable to man. B.*; substantial, productive; bàrr *tarbhach, substantial crop, productive crop*; buille *tarbhach, an effectual blow,* or *pull in rowing.*

Tarbhachd, tăr'-achg, *n. f.* substantiality, productiveness, gainfulness, profit.

Tarbhaichead, tăr'-èch-ad, *n. f.* degree of profit, *or* importance, *or* substantiality.

Tarbhail, târv'-al, *a.* bull-faced, brutish.

Tarbh-taine, târv'-tàèn-å, *n. m.* parish-bull.

Tarbh-reidh, târv'-rrăè-y', *n. m.* farm-bull.

Tarbh-uisge, târv'-ŭshg-ă, *n. m.* water-bull.

Tarcuis, tark'-kŭsh, *n. f.* contempt, dispute.

Tarcuiseach, tark'-kŭsh-ach, *a.* contemptuous.

Tarcuisich, tărk'-kŭsh-èch, *v.* despise, revile.

Targaid, tărg'-aj, *n. f.* target, shield.

TARGAIR, tărg′-ėr, *v.* foretell. *North.*

TARLADH, târ′-lă, *n. m.* great demand, *or* tearing from each other, as a scarce commodity; used in the Bible for tachair, happen.

TARLAID, târ′-llăj, *n. c.* contemptible person.

TARLAIDH, târ′-lì2, *v.* tear, *or* drag away.

TARMACH, tarm′-ach, *n. m.* source of a disease.

TARMACHADH, tărm′-ach-ă, *pt.* gathering, as a tumour; collecting, as matter in a suppuration; originating, congregating, *or* settling.

TARMACHAN, tarm′-ach-an, *n. m.* the bird, ptarmagan.

TARMAICH, tăr′-mėch, *v.* originate, settle.

TARMAS, tăr′-mas, *n. m.* dislike of food. *N.*

TARNACH, tărn′-ach, *n. f.* clap of thunder.

TARR, târr, *n. m.* lowest part of the belly.

TARRACH, tarr′-ach, *n. m.* girth, belly-thong.

TARRAIGHEAL, tarr′-ė-ghyal, *a.* white-bellied; *n. f.* white-bellied cow.

TARRUNN, tărr′-unn, *n. f.* a nail; *tàirnean, nails*; *biortharrunn, coffin-nail, calp, a rivet*; sgolb, *single floorings.*

TARRUINN, tărr′-ėnn, *n. f.* act of drawing *or* extracting; act of drawing near; an extracting plaster; *cuir tarruinn* air, *apply an extracting plaster to it*; a haul, pull; *tarruinn*-chailleach, *dragging in a slovenly manner*; demand; *v. n.* draw, pull, extract, haul; an *tarruinn* thu a mach an Lebhiatan le dubhan, *canst thou draw the Leviathan with a hook*; *tharruinn* e an t-iongar, *it extracted the matter* (from the tumour); *tarruinn* air t'ais, *retract, withdraw*; *tarruinn* fuil, *let blood*; *tarruinn* am fagus, *draw near*; *tarruinn* suas ris, *address him, speak to him.*

TARRSANAN, tărr′-san-ăn, *n. m.* cross-beam.

TARRSUINN, tărr′-sėnn, *adj.* cross, across, traverse, oblique; *adv.* across, traversely, obliquely, from side to side; cuir *tarrsuinn* e, *place it traversely*, or *across*, or *obliquely.*

TARRSUINNEACHD, tărr′-sėnn-achg, *n. f.* obliquely, traverseness, crossness, peevishness.

TARRSANNANACHD, tărr′-sunn-an-achg, *n.f.* bickering, satirizing, lampooning; sort of poetry.

TART, tărt, *n. m.* drought; padhadh, *thirst.*

TARTACH, tărt′-ach, *adj.* droughty, dry.

TARTAR, tărt′-ar, *n. f.* noise of tramping.

TARTARACH, tărt′ar-ach, *adj.* noisy in stamping.

TARTMHOR, tărt′-ur, *adj.* droughty, dry.

TARTMHORACHD, tărt′-ur-achg, *n. f.* dry *or* droughty weather; great drought.

TASAN, tâs′-an, *n. c.* bickering, fretting bickering, scolding, discontented person.

TASANACH, tâs′-an-ach, *adj.* bickering.

TASANACHD, tâs′-an-achg, *n. f.* bickering, fretful disposition *or* habit, fretfulness.

TASDAN, tasd′-an, *n. m.* a shilling.

TASG, tasg, *n. m.* a task, allotted job; tasca, *Welsh*; a store; ann an *taisg, in store.*

TASGAIDH, tasg′ė, *n. f.* treasure, store; tha′ a *thasgaidh*! *yes, my love*! *my darling*!

TASP, tăsp, *n. m.* severe sarcasm.

TASPANNACH, tăsp′-ann-ach, *adj.* very sarcastic, *or* petulant.

TASPAIRE, tăsp′-ur-ȧ, *n. m.* satirist.

TATAIDH, tât′-ē2, *v.* domesticate, as an animal.

TATH, tâ*h*, *v.* join *or* sodder, as hot irons.

TATHADH, tâ′-ă, *pt. n. m.* joining, joint, seam.

TATHAICH, tâ′-ėch, *n. f.* for tighich.

TE, tyă, *n. f.* a female, woman, *or* any object of the feminine gender.

TEAB, tyăb2, *a.* flippant person's mouth.

TEABAD, tyăb′-ad, *n. m.* a stammer. *North.*

TEABAIS, tyăb′-ash, *n. f.* flippancy of speech.

TEABAISEACH, tyăb′-ash-ach, *n. m.* flippant.

TEABANTA, tyăb′-ant-a, *adj.* carping, captious.

TEABANTACHD, tyăb2′-ant-achg, *n. f.* captiousness, flippancy of speech, captious notice.

TEACH, tyech, *n. f.* a house, habitation.

TEACHD, tyechg, (for tigheachd); *n. m.* arrival; air dha *teachd, having arrived*; *pt.* arriving; *teachd* a mach, *increase, product*; *teachd* a steach, *income*; *teachd*-an-tìr, *provision, livelihood.*

TEACHD, tyúchd, tyechg, *v. n.* be fit to contain, hold, find room for; cha *teachd* e an so, *it has not sufficient room here*; an *teachd* e ann, *can it contain it*? an *teachd* e 'san leaba, *has he room in the bed*?

TEACHDAIRE, tyechg′-ur-a, *n. m.* messenger, courier, ambassador, delegate, envoy, missionary.

TEACHDAIREACHD, tyechg′-ur-achg, *n. f.* message, embassy, errand, legation, mission.

TEADALACH, tyăd′-al-ach, *adj.* slow, inactive. *North.*

TEADHAIR, tyaŏ′-ėr, *n. f.* to tether; *v.* tether.

TEADHRAICHEAN, tyaŏr′-ėch-an, *n. pl.* tethers.

TEAGAIR, tyăg′-ėr, *v.* gather milk for butter, by stinting the allowance of a family; economise.

TEAGAISG, tyăg′-ėshg, *v.* instruct by preaching *or* lecturing, teach by precepts.

TEAGAISG'E, tyāg′-ask-tyȧ, *pt.* taught, lectured.

TEAGAMH, tyāg′-áv, *n. m.* doubt, suspense.

TEAGAMHACH, tyāg′-'áv-ach, *adj.* doubtful.

TEAGASG, tyāg′-ask, *n. m.* instruction by lectures; *pt.* teaching by lectures, lecturing; fear *teagaisg, lecturer*; luchd-*teagasg, instructors.*

TEAGLACH, tyāog′-lach, *a.* doubtful, uncertain.

TEAGLACHD, tyāog′-llachg, *n.f.* uncertainty.

TEAGHLACH, tyāoll′-ach, *n. m.* a family, household.

TEAGNADH, tyāg′-nX̆, *n. m.* a tenesmus, as a hen particularly, (applied to persons sometimes); properly teagmhail.

TEALL, tyall, *n.m.* an attack all of a sudden.

TEALLACH, tyall′-ach, *n. m.* a smith's fire-place *or* forge; a hearth *or* fire-place.

TEALLACHAG, tyall′-ach-ag, *n.f.* concubine.

TEALLSANACH, tyall′-san-ach, *n.m.* a sceptic

TEALLSANACHD, tyall′-san-achg, *n. f.* scepticism.

TEAMHAIDH, tyev′-ė, *adj.* pleasant. *North.*

TEAMHALL, tyév′-all, *n. m.* slight swoon *or* stun.

TEAMHARRA, tyév′-urr-a, *adj.* very pertly eloquent; eloquent and flippant, as a young person.

TEAMHRACHD, tyev′-rrachg, *n. f.* flippancy; an impertinent prattle of a young person.

TEAMPULL, tyemp′-ull, *n. m* a temple.

TEANACHD, tyan′-achg, *v.* save. *H. S.*

TEANACHDAS, tyan′-achg-us, *n. m.* deliverance. *H. S.*

TEANACHAIR, tyen′-ach-ur, *n. f.* smith's tongs.

TEANGA, tyéng′-a, *n. f.* a tongue, language, hold of a buckle; Gàidhlig Dhùideach, *the unknown Gaelic tongue.*

TEANGACH, tyéng′-ach, *a.* having many tongues.

TEANGAIR, tyéng′-ăėr, *n. m.* an interpreter, linguist.

TEANGAIREACHD, tyéng′-ăėr-achg, *n. f.* interpreting languages; skill in languages *or* philology, interpreting.

TEANN, tyănn, *adj.* tight, tense, severe, rigid, near, close; tha'n t-sreang *teann, the string is tight*; *teann* air mìosa, *near a month, close upon a month*; duine *teann, a severe* or *rigid person*; *v. n.* draw near, approach, approximate, fall to, commence, begin to move, go, proceed; *teann* as an sin, *away with you*; *theann* iad ri folbh, *they began to move off*; *teann* as an rathad, *leave my way*; *teann* an nios, *come hither*; *teannaibh* r'a chéile, *sit close*; *theann* iad ri treobhadh, *they commenced ploughing.*

TEANNACHADH, tyann′-X̆, *pt.* tightening.

TEANNAICH, tyann′-ėch, *v.* tighten, squeeze.

TEANNACHTE, tyann′-ėch-tyȧ, *pt.* squeezed.

TEANNAIR, tyann′-ur-a, *n.m.* noise in a cave.

TEANNTACHD, tyannt′-achg, *n. f.* strait, difficulty.

TEARB, tyerbb, *v.* separate cattle of any, *or* all kinds.

TEARC, tyerk, *adj.* rare, unusual, scarce.

TEARCEUN, tyerk-èn′, *n. m.* phœnix, rare bird.

TEARMUNN, tyer′-munn, *n. m.* refuge, patron; mo *thearmunn* thu, *thou art my refuge. Psalms.*

TEARN, tyârn, *v* escape, evade; cha b'urra dhuit *teàrnadh, you could not escape*; preserve, protect, defend, rescue, save; Dia 'gar *tearnadh, may God preserve* or *rescue us.*

TEARNADH, tyârn′-X̆, *pt.* preserving, rescuing, escaping; *n.m.* after-birth, (*Lew.*); (*Argyle, slànachadh,*) *preservation, escape, rescue.*

TEARR, tyârr, *n. m.* tar, pitch; *v.* tar.

TEARRACHD, tyarr′-achg, *n. f.* keen sarcasm.

TEARRADH, tyărr′-X̆, *pt.* tarring, daubing.

TEARUINN, tyèr′-ènn, *v.* preserve, rescue.

TEARUINTE, tyèr′-ènn-tyȧ, *pt. adj.* preserved, rescued, secured, safe, guarded, cautious.

TEARUINTEACHD, tyèr′-ėnjt-achg, *n. f.* security *or* protected state, precaution, caution.

TEAS, tyās, *n. m.* heat, warmth, too much of the good things of life, superabundance.

TEASACH, tyās′-ach, *n. m.* cattle running from excessive heat, fever, *Bible*; warm water in milk.

TEASAICH, tyās′-ėch, *v.* heat, warm, become warm.

TEASAICHTE, tyās′-ėch-tya, *pt.* heated, warm.

TEASAIRG, } tyās2′-ruig, *v.* save, interpose
TEASRUIG, } for the purpose of rescuing; relieve, afford relief.

TEASRUIGINN, tyās′-rėg-ėnn, *n. f.* relief, preservation, rescue; *pt.* rescuing, relieving, interfering.

TEIC, tyăėchg, *adj.* due, lawful, legal; cha *teic* na th' ann, *all there are, are too much*; cha *teic* dhuit, *that is more than is due,—more than is lawful*; an *teic* a h'aon, *is not one more than enough*; an *teic* a h-aon deug, *is not eleven more than enough*; bheir mise dhuit gus an abair thu cha *teic, I will give you till you say, it is more than enough.*

TEICH, tyăch, *v.* flee, scamper, be off! desert; o ghuth a bhuaireas *theich* na sluaigh, *at the noise of the tumult, the people fled. Bible*; THEICH E, *he fled, he deserted the army, he took to his heels.*

Teicheadh, tyăch²'-ă, *pt.* fleeing, taking to his heels, scampering; *n. m.* fleeing, desertion.

Teacheach, tyăch-ach, *adj.* fleeing, fleeting. *Macdonald.*

Teid, tyāj, corruption of d'théid, which see.

Teididh, tyāj'-ė, *n. f.* wild-fire; teine. thionnacham. *North.*

Teile, tyāl'-à, *n. f.* lime, *or* linden tree.

Teilg, tyālėg, *n. m.* hook-line; casach. *N.*

Teilleach, tyălly'-ach, *n. m.* blub-cheeked fellow. *North.*

Teine, tyān''-à, *n. m.* fire; *teine*-éibhinn, *bone-fire*; bràight, dreallsach, bràightseal, *teine* thionnachain, *wild-fire, phosphoric light from decayed wood* or *fish*; *teine*-athair, *lightning.*

Teine-de, tyān²'-à-dyā, *n. m.* erysipelas; butterfly. *North*; deallan-dè. *West H.*

Teindire, tyānj'-ur-à, *n. m.* a fire-grate.

Teindreach, tyānjj'-rach, *n. f.* watch-chain, &c.

Teinn, tyānn, *n. f.* predicament, strait, distress; nach e a bha 'na *théinn, what a predicament he was in*! *how he was nonplussed*; an aimsir carraid agus *téinn, in time of fatigue and distress.*

Teinne, tyānn²'-a, tyēnn²'-a, degree more tight, &c.; *n. f.* degree of tightness; tightness, rigidness;—fire.

Teinne, tyānn'-à, *n. f.* link of chain.

Teinnead, tyēnn²'-ad, *n. f.* degree of tightness.

Teinndeachd, tyānnj'-ach, *adj.* fieriness.

Teinndidh, tyānnj'-ė, *adj.* fiery, hot, keen.

Teinndidheachd; see Teinnidheachd.

Teinntean, tyānnj'-an, *n. m.* hearth-stone.

Teinntreach, tyānnj'-rach, *n. f.* flash of lightning.

Teirbheartaich, tyăr'-yart-ėch, *v.* harass. *H. S.*; distribute. *Islay.*

Teirce, tyărk'-a, *adj.* degree of scarceness; na s *teirce, scarcer*; *n. f.* scarceness, scarcity.

Teircead, tyărk'-ad, *n. f.* degree of scarcity.

Teirceachd, tyărk'-achg, *n. f.* fewness, rareness.

Teirig, tyăr²'-ėg, *v. n.* be exhausted, consumed, be spent, run out; *theirig* orm, *all mine is run out, is exhausted*; 'nuair *theirigeas* gual, *teirigidh* obair, *when coals are consumed, smith's work is at an end.*; *theirig* iad, *they are done, they are run out, they are consumed.*

Teirinn, tyăr'-ėnn, *n. m.* alight, descend.

Teiris, **Teirisd**, tyăr²'-ėsh, tyăr'-ėshj, *Int.* stand still! stand! keep quiet! (said to a cow.)

Teirm, tyăėrm², *n. f.* a thumb.

Teismid, tyăsh'-mėj, *n. f.* last will; tiomnadh

Teist, tyăshj, *n. f.* reputation, character, respectability• nach leig a *theist* air chall, *who will not suffer his fame* or *respectability to be bandied with. Psalms.*

Teistealachd, tyăshj'-al-achg, *n. f.* respectability, fame, good name, reputation, esteem.

Teisteanas, tyăshjt'-an-as, *n. m.* testimonials, certificate, reputation, testimony.

Teisteas, tyăshjt'-as, *n. f.* testimony. *B.*

Teisteil, tyăsjt'-al. *adj.* having a respectable character, respectable, reputable.

Teo-chridheach, tyô'-chrė-ach, *adj.* warm hearted, affectionate, kindly.

Teodhadh, tyô'-ă, *pt.* warming, simmering, glowing with love, feeling affection for.

Teoidh, tyōė'-y', *v.* warm, simmer, glow with delight *or* affection; cha do *theòidh* mi riamh ris, *my heart never glowed with delight* or *affection towards him.*

Tioidhte, tyōe'-y'-tyà, *pt.* warmed, simmered.

Teom, tyāom, *adj.* expert, dexterous.

Teomachd, tyāom'-achg, *n. f.* expertness, dexterity, skill, proficiency in any thing.

Teth, tyā², *adj.* hot, impetuous, keen; more properly teith; na 's *teotha, hotter.*

Teth, ty*h*è, *adj.* rancid, insipid, tasteless.

Teuchd, tyèchg, *v.* congeal; reodh. *H. S.*

Teuthachd, tyhè'-achg, *n. f.* rancidness.

Teud, tyădd', *n. f.* musical instrument string.

Teudach, tyădd''-ach, *adj.* stringed.

Teugair, tyăg'-uėr, *v.* gather milk by putting people on short allowance, to make butter.

Teugradh, tyăg'-ră, *pt.* gathering milk economically; *n. m.* milk *or* butter so gathered.

Teugbhoil, tyăg'-v*h*al, *n. f.* agonies of death.

Teum, tyăm, *n. f.* temptation, whim, caprice, *Argyle*;—in Bible, Cowal, a bite, (loiteadh);—*v.* tempt, beguile, draw aside;—in Bible, bite as a serpent does; *theum* nathair mi (loit nathair mi), *a serpent bit me*;—in Argyle, a serpent beguiled, *or* enticed me.

Teumadh, tyăm'-ă, *pt.* tempting, beguiling, biting, snatching.

Teumnach, tyăm'-nach, *adj.* capricious, whimsical; cha 'n 'eil ann ach duine *teumnach, he is a capricious* or *whimsical man*; enticing, inviting, tempting; cha 'n 'eil e na nì *teumnach, it is not an enticing affair.*

Teumnachd, tyăm'-nachg, *n. f.* tempting nature *or* quality; capriciousness.

Teurmnasg, tyărm'-nnăsk, *n. m.* a bandage on the toes and thumbs of a dead person, to prevent his ghost from hurting foes

Thainig, hàn'-ėg, *past v.* thig, came.

Thairis, hăėr'-ėsh, *adv.* over, across, abroad, *or* over the channel *or* seas; chaidh e *thairis, he went abroad,—he left the kingdom*; a' dol *thairis, going abroad* or *cross the sound* or *channel*; copan air cuir *thairis, the cup running over*; beyond, exceeding the bounds, remaining as a surplus; chaidh e *thairis* air sin, *he went beyond that,* or *it is beyond that*; *thairis* air mòran, *beyond many*; thug e *thairis, he over-fatigued himself*; thoir *thairis, give over, be done of it*; chuir iad *thairis* i, *they capsized* (the boat) *her.*

Thairte, hăèrjt'-à, *pre.* and *pro.* beyond her, over her; an abhainn a' cur *thairte, the river overflowing*; see Thairis, &c.

Thall, hăll, *adv.* over, on the other side, beyond, abroad; *adj.* yon, yonder; am baile ad *thall, yonder town*; over against.

Thalla, hall'-a, *v.* come, come along; *thalla* leamsa, *come along with me*; *thallaibh, come you*; *Inter.* thalla! thalla! indeed! indeed! well! well! ay! ay!

Thallad, hăll'-ad, *adv.* yon, yonder.

Th'ann, hănn, (for tha ann), that is, is in that place, exists; co mheud a *th'ann, how many is there?*

Thar, har, over, beyond, across, more than; *thar* fichead, *beyond twenty,—more than twenty*; *thar* a chéile, *at variance*; chuir thu *thar* a chéile iad, *you set them by the ears*; *thar* na còrach, *beyond what is proper.*

Tharad, hăr'-udd, (*pre. pro.*) beyond thee.

Tharaibh, hăr'-uv, (*pre. pro.*) over you.

Tharainn, hăr'-enn, (*pre. pro.*) over us.

Tharam, hăr'-um, (*pre. pro.*) beyond *or* over me; chaidh i *tharam, she capsized on me.*

Tharta, hărt'-à, (*pre. pro.*) beyond them; chaidh am bàta *tharta, the boat capsized on them*; cuir *tharta* e, *put it over them.*

Theab, hāb², *def. v.* theab mi, I had almost; *theab* iad, *they had almost*; *theab* thu mo mharbhadh, *you had almost killed me*;—(used in all the persons.)

Theagamh, hăg'-av, *adv.* perhaps; *theagamh* gu bheil, *perhaps it is so—perhaps so.*

Theid, hāj, *fut. v.* theirig *or* rach, will *or* shall go.

Their, hāèr², *fut. v.* abair; *their* thu, *thou shalt say*; *their* sinn, *we shall say*; *their* iad, *they shall say*; *their* cuid, *some shall say*; *their* leam, *I should think.*

Theirig, hāèr''-èg, *v. n.* go, proceed; *theirig* thusa, *go ye*, or *thou*; *theid* mi, *I shall go*; an *d'theid* thu, *shalt thou go*; chaidh mi, *I went.*

Theirig, *part. v.* teirig, be expended *or* exhausted; *theirig* iad gu léir, *they are all spent, &c.*

Thig, hèg, *v. n.* come; (*fut.* also thig); *thig* thusa leamsa, *come you along with me*; *thig* sinn léibh, *we shall come along with you*; *thàinig* sinn leibh, *we came along with you*; cha d' *thig* sinn leibh, *we shall not come along with you*; cha d' *thàinig* iad, *they did not come*; *v. n.* become, suit, fit, befit; is math a *thig* an còta dhuit, *the coat becomes, fits*, or *suits you well*; deamar a tha e *tighinn* domh, *how does it become me,* or *how does it fit me?* agree with one's taste, be pleased with; deamar *thig* sinn riutsa, *how will that please you?* cha *d'thig* sin gu math ris, *that will not please him well*; recover, escape, get the better of; *thig* e uaith, *he will recover, he will get the better of this*; speak of, reflect upon, speculate about; *thig* iad ort gu farsuinn fial, *they shall speak of you far and wide, every where, and liberally*; bithidh iad a' *tighinn* oirnn, *they shall speak of us,—our conduct will be a matter of reflection.* See Grammar.

Thoir, hòèr, *v. n.* give, deliver, grant, *or* bestow on; *thoir* dhomh, *give me*; *thoir* dhaibh, *give them,* or *to them*; bring, carry, bear; *thoir* so a dh'ionnsuidh, *bring, bear,* or *carry this to him*; *thoir* an ionnsuidh, *bear, carry,* or *bring this to them*; compel, force, constrain; *thoir* air so a dheanadh, *contrain* or *compel,* or *force him to do this*; *thoir* seachad, *deliver, give up*; *thoir* suas, *deliver up, abdicate, resign*; *thoir* ionnsuidh air, *attack, assault him*; *thoir* thu fhèin as, *begone, take to your heels*; *thoir* fios, *inform, invite*; *thoir* as e, *swig it off,—gulp it up*; *thoir* bhuaidh, *bring from,* or *deprive, him of it*; *thoir* an fhaire, *take care, beware*; *thoir* mathanas, *pardon, forgive*; *thoir* leat e, *bring it with you*; *thoir* as a chéile, *disjoin, tear asunder*; *thoir* ionnsuidh air, *attack, assault, make a dash,* or *dart at him*; *thoir* a stigh, *bring in, cultivate, as land*; *thoir* a stigh ort, *get in, away in with you*; *thoir* an suas, e, *cede, surrender,* or *abdicate it*; *thoir* buidheachas, *return thanks*; *thoir* breith, *give the sense, judge*; *thoir* an geall, *give as a bet, pledge, stake, mortgage*; *thoir* géill, *admit, concede, yield, submit*; na d' *thoir* géill da, *don't admit, pay no attention to any thing he says*; *thoir* aigheab, neo oidheirp, *attempt*; *thoir* thairis *give over, be quite exhausted* or *over-fatigued*; *thoir* leum, *jump*; *thoir* dùil eum, *bound*; *thoir* urram, *pay respect, reverence*; *thoir* saighde asad, *make a dash* or *dart at any thing*; *thoir* siorradh neo sgiutadh, *dart, bolt*; *thoir* gu buil, *bring to a successful termination*; *thoir* do leaba ort, *be off to bed.*

Throimh, hroév², (*pre. pro.*) through him; *throibh, through you*; *thrompa, through them, &c.*

Thu, û, (*pers. pron. asp. form*), thou; *thu* féin *or* phéin, *thou* or *thee*, *thyself*;—(*Greek* and *Latin*, tu; *German* and *Swedish*, thu *and* du; *Dan.* du; *Belg.* U; *Sax.* thu *and* tho; *Pers.* too); as, is *tu* an cù, *thou art a dog*; (pronounced us-dû).

Thubhairt, thŭ'-urjt, *past.* abair, said.

Thud, Thut, hûd', hŭt, *Int.* indeed! tut! has it come to this pitch! so much so!

Thug, hŭg, *part.* of thoir, gave; *thug* e domh e, *he gave*, or *has given it me.*

Thuig, hŭég, *past* of *v.* tuig, I understood.

Thuige, hŭég'-â, *adv.* towards, to the wind; thàinig i *thuige, she came to* (as a ship) *as any thing else, it improved*; a' dol *thuige* is uaidh, *going hither and thither*; thainig e *thuige* fhéine, *he came to himself,—recovered his judgment.*

Thuca, hŭchg'-â, *pro. pre.* towards them.

Thug, hŭg, *past. v.* irreg.; thoir; thoir dhaibh, *give them*; *thug* mi dhaibh, *I gave them.*

Thugad, hŭg'-ad, *n. m.pre. pro.* towards thee; *Inter.* out of my way! leave that place! *thugaibh, leave ye that*! also, towards you.

Thun, hŭn, *prep.* to, toward; *thun* an tighe, *towards the house*; *adv.* near, nearly, almost, on the eve; *thun* teirigeachdainn, *nearly expended* or *exhausted*; *thun* éirigh, *on the eve of rising*; *thun* cogaidh, *for war, for the purpose of war*; *thun* mo mhac, *to my sons Os.*

Ti, tyē, *n. m.* an individual; an *tì* is àirde, *the Supreme Being*; oir mar so deir an *tì* àrd agus uasail, *for thus says the high and lofty one. B.*—set design *or* earnest wish, determination; tha e air *tì* mise a mharbhadh, *he is bent on my destruction*; tha e air *tì* cuir as domh, *he is determined to finish my days*; bha *'thì* air mise a sgrios, *his determination was to ruin me, to destroy me.*

Tibhe, tyév'-a, *deg.* tuigh na's tibhe, thicker

Tibhead, tyév'-ad, *n.m.* degree of thickness

Tiamhachd, tyeăv'-achg, *n. f.* dreariness, gloominess; melodious heart-melting sound.

Tiamhaidh, tyĕăv'-ê, *adj.* melancholy, dreary, distressing, dismal; heart-melting, as music; àite *tiamhaidh, a dreary place*; *pt.* port *tiamhaidh, a heart-melting strain* or *tune.*

Tiamhaidheachd; see Tiamhachd.

Tide, tyéj'-â, *n. m.* time; (*Swedish*, tid.)

Tig, for d'thig, dyéj *or* jjég; cha d' *thig* e, *he shall not come.*

Tigh, ttaŏé'-y', *n. m.* a house; 'se 'ainm aoibhneach *tigh* na fëile, *its joyous name is the house of hospitality*, (*Fingal's*); *tigh*-beag, *a necessary, a privy*; *tigh*-marsantachd, *a shop, ware-room*; *tigh*-chon, *dog-kennel*; *tigh*-chalman, *a dove-cot*, or *ducket*; *tigh*-bainne, *dairy*; *tigh*-chaorach, *sheep-cot*; *tigh*-airm, *an armoury. B.*; *tigh*-cìse, *custom-house*; *tigh*-chearc, *hen-house*; an *tigh*-mòr, *mansion-house*; *tigh*-bàinnse, *the house of the wedding*; *tigh*-samhraidh, *a villa*, or *summer-house*; *tigh*-cusbuinn, *custom-house*; *tigh*-dìomhaireachd, *jakes*; *tigh*-eiridinn, *an infirmary*; *tigh*-sgoil, *a school-house*; *tigh*-fasdaidh, *house where one is hired*; *tigh*-leanna, *tigh*-òsd, *an inn, alehouse*; *tigh*-seinnse, *an inn*; (French); *tigh*-strìop, *a bawdy-house*; *tigh*-mòid, *court-house, justice-court*; *tigh*-nigheadaireachd, *wash-house*; *tigh*-sheillean, *a hive*; *tigh*-malairt, *an exchange*; *tigh*-taisg, *tigh*-stòir, *pantry, store-room*; *tigh*-tàimh, *an inn. B.*; *tigh*-teas, *hot-house*; *tigh*-tàinn, *an inn*; *tigh*-réidh, *a banking-house*; *tigh*-righ, *palace*; aig an *tigh, at home*; o'n *tigh, abroad, from home.*

Tigheadas, thī²'-ad-us, *n. m.* a household; air a *thigh* is air a *thigheadas, he having a house and household.*

Tighealt, ttīh'-ăltt, *pt.* calling when passing

Tighearn, tyè'-ărrn, *n. m.* Lord Almighty! a landlord, proprietor; superior title of respect; tha a *thighearn, yea, O Lord*! (tì an fhearainn, *or* tì tharainn.)

Tighearnail, tyè'-arm-al, *adj.* lordly.

Tighearnalachd, tyè'-urn-al-achg, *n. f.* lordliness.

Tighearnas, tyè'-arn-as, *n. m.* proprietorship, lordship, rule, sway, dominion.

Tighich, ttīh'-èch, *n. f.* state of being subject to callers.

Tighil, ttī²h'-èl, *v.* call when passing.

Tighinn, tyè'-ènn, *n. f.* speaking, slandering, back-biting, speculating on the faults of others; *pt.* coming, speaking, agreeing with, &c.

Tilg, tyèl'-ég, *v.* throw, cast off, reproach, cast up to; vomit; *thilg* e, *he threw, vomited*; *thilg* an t-each mi, *the horse threw me off*; *thilg* i searrach, *she cast a foal*; *thilg* e a dheoch, *he vomited his drink*; *thilg* e orm e, *he cast it up to me*; strike with an elf-shot, shoot, fire at; *thilg* e an duine, *he shot the man*; duine *tilgte, a man shot by the fairies,—a man that cares not what he does.*

Tilgeadh, tyelég'-ă, *pt.* casting, throwing, shooting, vomiting, reproaching, a reproach.

Tilgte, tyèlég'-tya, *pt.* thrown, cast; mad.

Till, tyèlly', *v. n.* return, come back; relapse; *thill* ris, *he has got a relapse.*

Tilleadh, tyèlèg'-Ă, *pt.* returning, relapsing; *n.m.* a relapse, return, act of turning.

Tim, tyēm, *n. m.* time; is *tim* teicheadh, *it is time to be off*; *tiomana, times.*

Timchioll, tyem'-chèúl, *n.m.* circuit, compass; ma 'm *thimchioll, about me*, ma *thimchioll* trì, *about three*; ma 'n *timchioll, about them*; *prep. adv.* about, around; *timchioll* fichead, *about twenty*; chaidh e *tiomchioll, he went round*; chaidh e *tiomchioll* orra, *he surrounded them*; a cheud *timchioll* a rinn iad, *the first circuit* or *compass they made.*

Timchiollach, tyèm'-cheal-ach, *adj.* circuitous, circular, encompassing.

Timchiollaich, tyèm'-cheul·èch, *v.* surround, environ, inclose, encompass.

Timchiollaichte, tyēm'-chyall-èch-tyà, *pt.* environed, surrounded, encompassed, encircled, gone round.

Timchioll-ghearr, tyēm-chyall-ghyârr', *v.* circumcise; *timchioll-ghearradh, circumcision, circumcising*; *timchioll-ghearr* clann Israel, *circumcise the children of Israel. Bible.*

Tinn, tyēnn[2], *adj. adv.* unwell, sick; feuch tha t'athair *tinn, behold, thy father is sick*

Tinne, tyēnn[2]'-à, *deg.* of teann; chain. *N.*

Tinneas, tyēnn'-us, *n. m.* sickness, disease; *tinneas*-cloinne, *travail, labour, child-birth, parturition*; *tinneas*-goile, *stomach complaint*; *tinneas*-fairge, *seasickness*; *tinneas*-tuiteamach, *palsy, epilepsy.*

Tinnsgeadail, tyēnn'-skedd-al, *n. m.* bad omen. *North.*

Tiodhlac, tyē'll'-achg, *n. m.* gift, offering.

Tiodhlacadh, tyē'll'-achg-Ă, *pt.* burying, interring; giving; *n. m.* burial, interment.

Tiodhlaic, tye'llk, tyē'll-èchg, *v.* bury, inter.

Tiolam, tyul'-am, *n. m.* snatch, space, a short time; clever opportunity.

Tiolp, tyúlp, *v.* steal by snatching, pilfer; steal one's property, and he almost looking at you; cavil, carp.

Tiolpadair, tyúlp'-ad-aèr, *n. m.* a thief by snatching; pilferer;—a critic. *M'F.*

Tiolpadh, tyulp'-Ă, *pt.* stealing by snatching; pilfering; carping, cavilling.

Tiom, tyē'm, *adj.* easily abashed *or* daunted; tender-hearted, sensitive, timid.

Tioma, tyē'm[2]'-a, *n. f.* delicateness of feeling; a daunt; melting into tears; thàinig *tioma* air, *he was daunted, he melted into tears*; softness of disposition, sensitiveness; thàinig *tioma* air suilean Fhinn, *Fingal melted into tears*; ioma ceud fo *thioma, many a hundred quite unmanned,—quite damped* or *daunted.* Song.

Tiomachd, tyē'm'-achg, *n. f.* delicacy of feeling and sentiment; daunt, damp on the spirits.

Tiomaich, tyēm'-èch, *v.* soften *or* melt into tears, *or* better feelings; Laoch nach *tiomaich, a hero that goes forward dauntlessly. Macdonald*; *thiomaich* a chridhe, *his heart softened.*

Tiomainn, tyēm'-ènn, *v.* resign solemnly, bequeath, bestow; *thiomainn* e spiorad suas, *he solemnly committed his spirit unto God*; swearing by Heaven.

Tiomainte, tyēm'-ènjt-à, *pt.* bequeathed, religiously determined.

Tiomnadair, tyēm[2]'-nad-ăèr, *n.m.* testator

Tiomnadh, tyēm'-nĂ, *n. m.* testament, will; oir tha *tiomnadh* dainnean an déigh bàis dhaoine, *for a testament is binding after men's death. Bible*; an Sean-*Tiomnadh, the Old Testament*; *pt.* committing solemnly, bequeathing.

Tiompan, tyēmp[2]'-an, *n. m.* timbril, cymbal, tabor, *or* drum. *Bible.*

Tiomsaich, tyēm'-sèch, *v.* collect. *H. S.*

Tionail, tyun'-âl, *v.* gather, collect. *B.*

Tional, tyun'-al, *n.m.* collection, collecting

Tionnsgainn, tyunn'-skaènn, *v.* attack *or* fall to of a sudden without any cause. *Islay*;—invent, devise. *Macfarlan*; return; turn. *H. S.*

Tionnsgnadh, tyúnnsk'-nĂ, *pt.* attacking *or* falling to of a sudden; *n. m.* sudden attack *or* commencement; invention.

Tiop, tyèp, *v.* steal by little and little; pilfer.

Tiop, tyēp, *v.* thread a fishing-hook. *Ross-shire.*

Tioram, tyur'-um, *adj.* dry, seasoned, arid, without moisture; flippant in speech;—tiorma, *more dry, arid*, &c.; fair, as weather; uair *thioram, fair weather*; feur *tioram, hay.*

Tiorc, tyurk, *v.* save, deliver. *Irish.*

Tiorma, tyurm'-a, *deg.* of tioram, more *or* most dry, drier, driest.

Tiormachadh, tyurm'-ach-Ă, *pt. n. m.* drying, fair weather; seasoning, as hay, fish, &c.

Tiormachail, tyurm'-ach-al, *adj.* desicative.

Tiormachd, tyurm'-achg, *n. f.* fair weather; continuance of fair weather; flippancy.

Tiormaich, tyurm'-èch, *v.* dry, dry up.

Tiorman, tyurm'-an, *n. m.* meal-ball.

Tiort, tyurt, *n. m.* accident, mishap. *H. S.*

Tiot, tyè'tt, *v.* dispatch quickly. *H. S.*

Tiota, for Tiotamh, moment.

Tiotamh, tyè'tt'-uv, *n. m.* moment, little time.

Tir, tyēr', *n. m.* land, shore; air *tir, ashore, on land*; country, region; o 'n thàinig e an *tir, since he came to the* *country, to this region*; *tìr*-mòr, *continent*; eadar *thìr*-mòr agus eileanan, *both the continent and islands.*

Tir, tyēr', *v.* kiln-dry corn, *Islay*; in *Perthshire*, crōch.

Tireachas, tyēr''-ach-as, *n. f.* patriotism.

Tireadh, tyēr''-ă, *pt.* kiln-drying; *n. m.* the quantity of corn kiln-drying.

Tit, tyējt, *inter.* expressive of wet. *H. S.*

Titheach, tyē*h*'-ach, *adj.* bent *or* determined on, keen for; *tìtheach* air mo mharbhadh, *bent on my destruction.*

Tiugainn, tyū²g'-ènn, *v. def.* come along.

Tiugh, tyū²gh, *adj.* thick, not slender, (thicker, tibhe neo *tiuighe*,) *frequent, in quick succession, as drops of rain*; dull, hazy, dense, gross, clumsy.

Tiughaich, tyŭ'-ěch, *v.* thicken, crowd.

Tiuighe, tyŭ'-è, *adj.* degree thicker, thickest.

Tiuighead, tyŭ²'-ud, *n. f.* degree of thickness.

Tiuigheadas, tyŭ'-ud-us, *n. f.* thickness.

Tlachd, ttlachg, *n. m.* love, attachment; tha *tlachd* aige dhith, *he is attached to her*; pleasure, satisfaction, degree of satisfaction; cha'n fhaigh thu e le *tlachd, you shall not get it with any degree of satisfaction*; beauty, liberality, affection; is beag mo *thlachd* dhith neo dheth, *I have no great affection for her* or *him.*

Tlachdaireachd, *n. f.* } tlachg'-uèr-achg,
Tlachdmhoireachd, } handsomeness, comeliness, pleasantness, blandness.

Tlachdar, tlachg'-ur, *adj.* handsome, lovely, liberal, pleasant, comely; leanaibh *tlachmhor, a goodly child. Bible.*

Tlam, tlàm, *n. m.* handful of wool; awkward handling; *v.* fumble, mix wool.

Tlamadh, tlàm'-ă, *pt.* mixing, fumbling.

Tlath, tlà*h*, *adj.* somewhat moist, humid; tha so *tlàth, this is somewhat moist* or *humid*; balmy, soft, mellow, mild, gentle; uisge *tlàth, balmy* or *genial rain*; smooth, fine to the touch; bu bhuige a' chàint na oladh *thlàth, his speech was softer than smooth oil. Psalms.*

Tlas, tlâs, *n. f.* (tlàthas), balminess, mildness, gentleness; a' tiondadh ascaoine na sìne gu *tlàs, changing the inclemency of the weather to calmness* or *mildness*; smoothness, gentleness.

Tlathaich, tlâ*h*'-ěch, *v.* moisten gently, become balmy *or* gentle, abate gently, as weather; get into gentle perspiration; *tlàthachadh* falluis, *gentle perspiration* or *sweat.*

Tligheachd, tlè'-achg, *n. f.* inclination.

Tliochd, tlyúchg, *n. m.* beginning. *Irish.*

Tlugh, tlŭgh', *n. m.* pair of tongs. *Irish.*

Tlus, ttlŭs, *n. m.* affection, tenderness of manner, gentleness, as weather; balminess, *or* mildness; as clothes next the skin, comfort, comfortable sensation; labhair le *tlus, speak with some degree of affection*; cha'n'eil *tlus* sam bith 'san aodach, *there is no comfort in the clothes*; fheara bu mhòr *tlus* is bàigh, *ye heroes noted for natural affection and clanship*; thig *tlus* is blàs, *balmy weather and genial warmth shall come*; *tlus* nan speur, *the balminess of the air.*

Tlusar, *adj.* } tlŭs'-ur, *adj.* affectionate,
Tlusmhor, } kind; nighean *thlusar, an affectionate daughter*; agreeable to the touch, comfortable; aodach *tlusar, comfortable clothing*; balmy, genial, mild; uair *thlusar, genial* or *mild weather.*

Tlusaireachd, *n. f.* } ttlŭs'-uèr-achg, bal-
Tlusmhoireachd, } miness, genial warmth, *or* comfortable feel *or* sensation.

Tnuth, tunû*h*, trû*h*, *n. f.* envy, malice. *Bible*; grudge, indignation, avarice.

Tnuthar, tunû*h*'-ur, *adj.* malicious.

Tob, tōbb, *n. f.* surprise. *Irish.*

Tobar, tō²b'-ur, *n. m.* well, spring, fountain; *tobraichear* na beatha, *the fountains* (issues) *of life*; *tobar* fioruisg, *a spring-well*; *tobar*-baistidh, *a baptismal font*; *tobar*-tàirne, *a draw-well*; source, origin; an *tobar* bho'm bheil gach buaireadh a sruthadh, *the source whence all temptations flow.*

Tobha, tòv'-à, *n. m.* a rope; *v.* tow.

Tobhair, tò'-aèr, *v.* give, bestow.

Tobhairt, tò'-ărjt, *pt.* giving.

Tobhartach, tò'-art-ach, *adj.* liberal, munificent, charitable; duine *tobhartach, a liberal*, or *charitable man.*

Tobhartas, tò'-art-us, *n. m.* a gift, offering, charity.

Toc, tôchg, *v.* swell up, puff, rise gradually, as a loaf does; swell, as with rage; *thòc* a h-aodann, *her face swelled with rage*; swell with good eating.

Tocadh, tôchg'-ă, *pt.* swelling, puffing.

Toch, toch, *n. f.* the hough *or* ham of a beast; *v.* hough, *or* cut off limbs of cattle; *thoch* iad an crodh, *they houghed the cattle.*

Tochail, toch'-èl, *v.* dig, quarry. *Irish*; *Psalms.*

Tochailt, toch'-aljt, *n. f.* a quarry. *Irish.*

Tochar, toch'-ar, *n. m.* marriage-portion.

Tochd, tôchg, *n. m.* suffocating bad smell.

Tochrais, toch'-rēsh, *v.* reel *or* wind yarn.

Tochras, toch'-ras, *n. m. pt.* winding, reeling.

Todhair, tò'-ĕr, *v.* manure, bleach.

Todhar, tò'-ar, *n. m.* dung dropped by cattle on the field; a field so manured; bleaching; a bleach.

Tog, tōg², *v. n.* build, raise, lift, stir up,

rear, bring up; brew, distil, exact, as tribute; *thog* iad tigh, *they built a house*; a fear a *thog* thu, *the man that reared you*; le glioeas *togar* tigh, *with wisdom a house is built*; *togaidh* fear fiar aimhreit, *a perverse man stirreth up strife*; *thog* tuinn an cinn, *waves reared their heads*; *tog* do throm dhiom, *remove thy burden from me*; do not goad me too much,—do not touch me to the quick; *thog* iad cìs, *they exacted a tribute*; clear up, cheer; cha ... pìob mo chridhe, *bagpipes will not cheer my spirits*; *togaidh* an latha, *the day will clear up*; tog ri, *tog* air, *ascend, report ill of*; *tog* cùis, *appeal*; *thog* e chùis gu Seusar, *he appealed into Cæsar*; *tog* ort thun a mhonaidh, *betake yourself to the mountains*; a' *togail* a bhruthaich, *ascending the acclivity*; *thog* iad air gu'n robh e dèidheil air an òl, *they raised a report that he was addicted to liquor*; a' *thogadh* mo chridhe nuair bhithidh e trom, *that would cheer my heart when drooping*; hoist, weigh; *tog* na siuil, *hoist the sails*; *thog* iad an acair, *they weighed anchor*; *thog* iad a' bhraich, *they brewed* or *distilled the malt*; *tog* do shuil, *raise your eye*.

Togail, tòg'-al, *pt.* raising, rearing, exacting; ascending, hoisting, weighing, &c

Togail, tòg'-al, *n. f.* structure, superstructure, building; a' moladh na *togalach*, *praising the building. Bible*; starvation; air an *togail*, *starving, as a cow*.

Togair, tòg'-èr, *v.* please, wish, incline, desire; ma *thogras* mi fhéin, *just if I please*; a' *togairt* dol dachaidh, *inclining*, or *feeling disposed to go home*.

Togalach, tōg'-al-ach, *gen.* of Togail.

Togalaiche, tōg'-al-èch-à, *n. m.* builder.

Togalaichean, tòg'-al-èch-an, *n. pl.* buildings.

Togarrach, tòg'-arr-ach, *adj.* inviting, enticing; cha'n'eil an latha so *togarrach*, *this day is not inviting*; willing, desirous; tha e *togarrach* a dh' fholbh, *he is desirous to go*.

Toghaidh, tògh''-è, *n. f.* guard, care. *H. Society*.

Toghlainn, tŏll'-ènn, *n. f.* exhalation, fume; tha *toghlainn* ag éiridh, *there is an exhalation rising*; disagreeable heat *or* fume.

Tograch, for Togarrach, willing.

Togte, tòg'-tyà, *pt.* raised, lifted under excitement; tha speuran a chinn *togte*, *he is quite in a frenzy*.

Toibheum, tóev'-vām, *n. f.* blasphemy.

Toibheumach, tóev'-ām-ach, *adj.* blasphemous, offensive, profane.

Toic, tôèchg, *n. f.* a swelling in the body *or* face from good living; wealth, that puffs up.

Toicealachd, tôèchg'-al-achg, *n. f.* purse-pride.

Toicear, tôèchg'-ăĕr, *n. m.* purse-proud man.

Toicearachd, tôèchg'-ăĕr-achg, *n. f.* purse-pride.

Toiceil, tôèchg'-al, *adj.* purse-proud, swelled up with pride of riches; disdain.

Toichiosdal, tôèch'-èsd-al, *n. m.* arrogance.

Toigh, táŏ for tagh; is *toigh* leam, *for* is *tagh* leam, *I like, I am fond of*.

Toil, tŏ'l, *n. f.* inclination, desire, will, wish, pleasure; an tì a ni *toil* Dè, *he that does the will of God*; tha *toil* 'am sin a dheanadh, *I wish to do that*; ma 'se do *thoil* e, *if you please*.

Toileach, tŏ'l'-ach, *adj.* willing, voluntary; tha mi *toileach*, *I am willing*; gach ni is *toileach* le Dia, *every thing God pleases*.

Toileachadh, to'l'-ach-ach-ă, *pt.* pleasing, satisfying, giving pleasure; *n. m.* satisfaction.

Toileachas, tŏ'l'-ach-us, *n. m.* contentment; *toileachas*-inntinn, *mental pleasure* or *satisfaction*.

Toileachd, to'l'-achg, *n. m.* willingness.

Toilealachd, to'l'-al-achg, *n. f.* eagerness, extreme willingness, *or* readiness.

Toilich, to'l'-èch, *v.* satisfy, please, will, wish; ma *thoilicheas* tu, *if you will* or *wish*; *thoilich* mi e, *I satisfied him*.

Toilichte, to'l'-èch-tyà, *pt.* pleased, satisfied; tha mi *toilichte*, *I am content*.

Toil-inntinn, to'l'-ènjt-ènn, *n. f.* gratification, satisfaction, mental enjoyment.

Toill, taŏlly', *v.* deserve, merit; *thoill* thu sin, *you deserved* or *merited that*.

Toillteanach, for Toilltinneach.

Toillteannas, taŏlty''-unn-us, *n. f.* desert, merit; a réir ar *toillteannas*, *according to your desert* or *merit*.

Toilltinn, taŏlly''-tyènn, *pt.* meriting, deserving; dè tha thu a' *toilltinn*, *what do you deserve* or *merit*?

Toilltinneach, taŏlly''-tyènn-ach, *adj.* deserving, meriting; duine *toilltinneach* air bàs, *a person meriting death*.

Toimhseachan, tóèsh'-ach-an, } *n. m.* a riddle;
Toimhseagan, tóèsh'-ag-an, } an enigma.

Toimhsean, tósh'-an, *n. pl.* weights, scales, balances, measures —; faculties. *North*.

Toimhseil, tósh'-shul, *adj.* sensible. *N.*

Toinisg, tóèn''-èshg, *n. f.* common sense.

Toinisgeil, tóèn'-èskg-al, *adj.* sensible.

Toinn, toènn, *v.* twist, wreathe. (*Cas.*); spin, twine; tachrais *or* tochrais. *Bible*.

Toinneamh, tòènn'-uv, *pt.* spinning, twining; *n. m.* arrangement, train; chuir thu as mo *thoinneamh* mi, *you disappointed me,—you deranged my plans.*

Toir, corruption of d'thoir; see Thoir.

Toir, tôer', *n. f.* pursuit, diligent search; teichidh sibh, 'nuair nach bi an *tòir* oirbh, *ye shall flee when there is none in pursuit of you*; tha e air *tòir, he is making a search for*; enough; is *tòir* e fhèin air sin, *he is quite enough for that himself*; band of pursuers; tha'n *tòir* ad dhéigh, *there is a band of pursuers after you.*

Toirbheartas, for Toirbeartas.

Toireasg, for Tuiriasg, saw; sàbh.

Toireann, tŏer'-unn, *n. f.* thunder. *H. S.*

Toirleum, tŏer'-llām. *n. m.* a bound.

Toirm, tŏerm, *n. f.* noise; ruzzling noise, as of people going through a wood; murmuring.

Toirmeasg, tŏem'-usg, *pt. n. m.* forbidding; prohibition *or* hindrance.

Toirlinn, tô2'-lyénn, *v.* alight, come off a horse.

Toirmisg, tŏerm'-èshg, *v.* forbid, prohibit.

Toirmisgte, tŏerm'-èshg-tyâ, *pt.* prohibited.

Toirp, tŏerp, *n. f.* a sod, divot; thick person.

Toirpeanta, tŏerp'-annt-â, *adj.* squat; thick.

Toirpsgian, tŏerp'-skēăn, *n. f.* peat-spade.

Toirt, tŏèrjt, *n. f.* taste in matters; decorum, decency, due regard *or* attention; duine gun *toirt, a person destitute of taste,* or *regardless of decorum*; is beag *toirt* a bhìos air do ghnothach, *your business must be done very awkwardly*; dh' imich e ma'n ordugh le *toirt, he obeyed the summons with due regard to decorum.*

Toirtealachd, tŏèrjt'-al-achg, *n. f.* decency, tastefulness, excellent order *or* arrangement.

Toirteil, tŏèrjt'-al, *adj.* decent, tasteful.

Toiseach, tôsh'-ach, *n. f.* beginning, origin, source; van *or* front, precedence; anns an *toiseach* bha 'm facal, *in the beginning was the word, B.*; *toiseach* a ghnothaich, *the origin of the thing*; *toiseach* an airm, *the van* or *front of the army*; fhuair e an *toiseach* orra, *he got precedence of them*; air *thoiseach, first, foremost*; bow *or* prow of a ship; *toiseach* is deireadh 'na luinge, *the bow and stern of the ship.*

Toiseachadh, tôsh'-ach-ă, *pt. n. m.* commencing, beginning, commencement, origin.

Toiseadrach, tôsh'-add-rach, *n. m.* crowner. *Highland Society.*

Toisg, tŏèshg, *n. m.* an occasion. *R. P.*

Toisgeal; see Taisgeul, reward.

Toisgeal, tŏsh'-gyal, *n. f.* left, sinister; an làmh *thoisgeal*, (làmh chlì), *left hand. H. S.*

Toisich, tôsh'-èch, *v.* begin, commence, fall to; agus *thòisich* iad air cuid do 'n t-sluagh a bhualadh agus a mharbhadh, *and they began to smite and kill some of the people. B.*

Toit, tŏèjt, *n. f.* smoke, fume, steam.

Toiteach, tŏèjt'-ach, *adj.* fumy, vapoury.

Toitean, tŏèjt'-an, *n. m.* collop, steak.

Toitlinn, tŏèjt'-lénn, *n. f.* steam, vapour

Toitlinneach, tŏèjt'-llénn-ach, *n. f.* steam-boat.

Tolg, tolug, *n. f.* a hollow, as in a kettle; *v.* make hollows, as in a kettle *or* cauldron.

Tolgach, tolug'-ach, *adj.* hollowed, freakish.

Toll, tŏ'll, *v.* make holes, bore, perforate; *n. m.* hole, bore, perforation; hollow.

Toll, to'll, *v.* exhale, emit vapours.

Tolladair, tō2ll'-add'-āĕr, *n. m.* borer.

Tolladh, tō2ll'-ă, *pt.* boring, edging in.

Tollainn, to'll'-ènn, *n. f.* exhalation, vapour in damp places in summer; steam, gas.

Tollaire, tō2ll'-ur'-a, *n. f.* one that edges his way; a genteel intruder.

Tolm, tŏ'llum, high hillock; tulm.

Tom, tōm, *n. m.* a bush, thicket, ant-hill; stool. *Islay*; *tòm* ghròiseid, *gooseberry-bush*; tha e air a *thòm, he is at stool*; thug e car ma *thòm* asam, *he jilted me,* or *cheated me, by leaving me*; a volume of a book, (*French,* tome); am bun an *tùim, sheltered only by the thicket*;—knoll.

Tomach, tōm'-ach, *adj.* bushy, tufted.

Tomad, tōm2'-ad, *n. m.* size, bulk. *Armst.*

Tomalt, tōm2'-al'tt, *n. m.* bulk. *Macd.*

Tombaca, tōm2-bâchg'-a, *n. m.* tobacco; (*Persian,* tombako; *Latin,* tabacum.)

Tomh, tó, *v.* point with the finger. *Armst.*; *Bible*; offer, attempt. *Highland Society Dictionary.*

Tomhais, tóv2'-ésh, *v.* measure, survey, weigh, guess, unriddle, resolve an enigma; *tomhais* am fiodh, *measure the wood*; *tomhais* am fearann, *survey the land*; *tomhais* cò choinnic mi, *guess whom I saw?*

Tomhas, tóv2'-us, *n. m.* weight, measure, survey; measurement, dimension; gabh mo *thomhas, take my measure*; de'n *tomhas* th' ann, *what is its measurement?* —*what is its dimensions?* slat-*thomhais, a wand*; thar *tomhais, beyond measure,* or *moderation*; *pt.* measuring, weighing, surveying, guessing.

Tomhlachd, tòv'-lachd, *n. m.* thick milk. *Irish.*

Ton, tòn, *n. f.* breech, *or* fundament.

Tonach, tòn′-ach, *adj. n. f.* large-hipped, *or* a broad-bottomed lady.

Tonaire, tòn′-ur-à, *n. m.* broad-bottomed man.

Tonlagan, tòhl′-ag-an, *n. m.* sliding on the breech; hobbling.

Tonlagain, tòhl′-ag-áen, *v.* hobble, slide on the breech.

Tonn, tōnn[2], *v. n.* splash; 'ga *thonnadh* ma cheann, *splashing it about his head*; pouring out irregularly.

Tonn, tōnn[2], *n. f.* a wave, a splash; a considerable quantity of water *or* liquid; thog *tuinn* an cinn, *waves reared their head*; an *tonn* bhaistidh, *baptism, sacred water*; *tonn* air traigh le féin, *a solitary wave on the shore*; nuallan nan *tonn*, *the raging noise of waves. Ossian.*

Tonnag, tōnn[2]′-ag, *n. f.* a tartan shawl.

Tor, tor, *a.* heavy shower; *n. f.* bush, shrub. *Irish.*

Tora, tor′-a, *n. m.* augre, wimble.

Torach, tor′-ach, *adj.* fruitful, fertile, productive, substantial, rank; sìol *torach, rank*, or *productive corn*; talamh *torach, fertile* or *fruitful land*; efficient, effectual; buillean *torach, efficient* or *energetic pulls, as in rowing.*

Torachd, tŏr′-achg, *n. f.* pursuit, chase; pursuing with hostile intention; strict inquiry; tha e a' *tòrachd, he is making strict inquiry*; a' *tòrachd* chaorach, *searching for sheep*; luchd-*tòrachd, persecutors, pursuers*; air eagal gu'n coinnich an luchd-*tòrachd* sibh, *lest the pursuers meet you. Bible*; fuileachdach 'san *tòrachd, bloody in the chase. Ossian*; craving; tha e *tòrachd* orm, *he craves*, or *insinuates his claim to such.* Song.

Toradh, tŏr′-ă, *n. m.* fruit, produce; thug Càin do *thoradh* an fhearainn, *Cain brought of the fruit* (or produce) *of the land*; consequence, result, effect; *toradh* do ghnìomharan, *the natural effects* or *consequence of your conduct* or *deeds.*

Toranach, tor′-an-ach, *n. m.* grub-worm.

Toraicheas, tor′-èch-us, *n. m.* conception, pregnancy.

Torair, tor′-uėr, *n. m.* grub-worm. *Oss.*

Torc, tork, *n. m.* castrated boar. *Islay*; a boar and a whale. *Ossian*; sovereign, a lord. *Irish*; a' tomhas an *tuirc, measuring the boar,—a great feat in Ossian's time.*

Torchar, tor′-char, *n. m.* a fall, killing.

Torchradh, tor′-chra, *n. m.* transfixing.

Torman, tor′-man, *n. m.* drone of a bagpipe, murmur;—herb, clary. *Irish.*

Torr, tôrr, *n. m.* a mound, *or* large heap; *torr* gainnich, *heap* or *mound of sand*; womb, conical hill. *Oss.*; *v.* heap, hoard; a' *torradh* airgid, *heaping* or *hoarding money*; teem, come alive; air *torradh* le miallan, *teeming with lice*; air *torradh* le gràisg, *teeming with rabble*; *pt.* torradh.

Torrach, torr′-ach, *adj.* pregnant; with child; in the family way.

Torradh, torr′-ă, *n. m.* embankment of a dam; payment for keeping up a mill-dam.

Torradh, tôrr′-ă, *n. m.* burial, interment, funeral; burial solemnities, *or* procession.

Torraich, torr′-èch, *v.* impregnate, teem.

Torraicheas, torr′-èch-us, *n. f.* conception, pregnancy.

Torran, torr′-an, *n. m.* a knoll, hillock.

Tort, tŏrt, *n. m.* a little loaf *or* cake. *Ir.*

Torunn, tŏrr′-unn, *n. f.* loud murmuring noise.

Tosd, ttŏsd, *n. m.* silence; *v.* be silent; *a.* silent; bi ad *thosd, be silent,—hold your peace.*

Tosdach, tosdd′-ach, *adj.* silent, peaceful; talla *tosdach* na dìochuimhne, *the peaceful land of forgetfulness. Ossian.*

Tosg, ttosg, *n. f.* a tusk; *tuisg, tusks*; *v.* cut irregularly.

Tosgach, ttosg′-ach, *adj.* cut in an uneven way.

Tosgaid, tôsg′-ājj, *n. f.* a hogshead; in *Perthshire*, togsaid.

Tosgaire, ttosg′-ur-à, *n. m.* one that cuts irregularly, *or* botches in cutting;—post. *Highland Society.*

Tot, tott′, *v.* roast *or* toast hurriedly on the embers; boil hurriedly.

Tota, tòtt′′-à, *n. m.* a thwart, *or* rower's seat; *tota* bràghad, *bow-thwart*; *tota* deiridh, *stern-thwart.*

Total, ttott′′-al, *n. m.* arrogance. *M'F.*

Toth, tŏ*h*, *n. m.* pudenda. *Shaw*; stench, (stoth.)

Tothag, to*h*′-ag, *n. f.* wonderfully short trowsers.

Tra, for Tràth.

Trabhach, trâv′-ach, *n. f.* rubbish cast a-shore. *Irish.*

Trabhailt, trav′-alljt, *n. f.* mill-hopper.

Trachd, trâchg, *n. m.* a drake.

Tragha, trâ*h*′-a, *gen.* of tràigh.

Traghadh, trâ*h*′-ă, *pt. n. m.* ebbing, ebb.

Traidhtear, haŏejt′-ăėr, *n. m.* rogue.

Traigh, trâè′-y′, *v.* ebb, dry up; *thraigh* e, *it ebbed*; *n. f.* shore, strand, sands, sand-beach; reflux; mar *thràigh* fhuaimear a chuain, *like the raging reflux of the sea*; a dh' ionnsuidh na *tràgha, towards the shore.*

Traigh-gheadh, trâè′-y′-y*h*è-aŏgh, *n. m* stock-gannet, (beautiful bird.)

Traighte, trâè′-y′-tya, *pt.* ebbed, dry.

Traill, trâ′lly′, *n. c.* a drudge, slave.

Traille, trâ''-llyȧ, *n. m.* the fish tusk.

Trailleach, trâėlly''-ach, *n. f.* sea-weeds.

Traillealachd, trâlly''-all.achg, *n. f.* slavishness, utmost degradation, servility.

Trailleil, tràlly''-al, *adj.* slavish, servile; obair *thràilleil, servile work. Bible.*

Trainge, tréng'-ȧ, *n. f.* throng, pressure of business; degree more *or* most throng; (*Scot. Germ.*)

Traisg, trâėshg, *v.* parch with thirst; *thràisg* mo chridhe, *my very heart parched.*

Traisg, traėshg, *v.* fast, abstain from food, observe a fast; *thraisg* e trì làithean, *he abstained from food three days*; c'arson a *thraisg* sibh, *why did you fast? Bible*; in *Irish*, troisg.

Traisgte, traėshg'-tyȧ, *pt.* parched of thirst.

Trait, trajt, *n. f.* cataplasm, fuairlit *M'F.*

Tramailt, trăm'-aljt, *n. f.* a most unaccountable whim *or* freak.

Tramailteach, trăm'-aljt-ach, *adj.* whimsical, capricious, freakish.

Trang, tráng, *adj.* throng, very busy, on good terms; (*German, Swedish, Danish, Scotch.*)

Tra-noin, tra*h*'-nôėn, *n. m.* noon, midday.

Traoghadh, trāo*h*'-Ă, *pt.* subsiding, abating, as a swelling; draining; *n. m.* abatement of a swelling.

Traoigh, trāoė'-y', *v.* subside, abate, drain.

Traoighte, trāoė'-y'-tyȧ, *pt.* subsided, abated, drained.

Traon, trāon, *n. m.* a rail, *or* corn-crake. *Skye*; an treun-ri-treun. *Islay.*

Trap, ttrapp, *n. m.* a trap-stair; snare; (*Danish*); *v.* take places in a class; carp.

Trasd, trasdd', *adv.* across, athwart, obliquely, traverse; awkwardly placed.

Trasdair, trasdd''-aėr, *n. m.* a diameter.

Trasdan, for trosdan, a crutch.

Trasg, trăsg, *n. f.* fasting; a fast; 'na *thrasg, he fasting*; 'na *trasg, she fasting*; dh' éibh iad *traisg, they proclaimed a fast. Bible.*

Trasgadh, trasg'-Ă, *pt.* fasting.

Trasgadh, trâsg'-Ă, *pt.* parching of thirst.

Trath, trâ*h*, *adj. adv.* early, timeously, betimes; early in season; dean *tràth* e, *do it in season*; do it betimes; bi an so *tràth, be here early*; *n. m.* a meal *or* diet; dà *thràth* 'san latha, *two meals a-day*; season, day-time; 'sna *tràthaibh* ceart, *at the proper seasons*; ma *thràth* an fheasgair, *at the time of the evening. B.*

Trathadair, trâh'-ad-aėr, *n. m.* time-keeper.

Trathail, trâ*h*'-al, *adj.* early, in time.

Trathalachd, trâh'-al-achg, *n. f.* seasonableness.

Tre, trā2, *prep.* though (bad, dead.)

Treabh, *Irish for* treobh, plough.

Treabhair, trāv2'-aėr, *n. pl.* houses, *Skye, Lewis*; in *Irish*, a surety, bail, urras.

Treachaill, trėch'-ėlly', *v.* dig a grave (near Inverary). *Provincial.*

Treagha, tré'-ȧ, *prep.* through. *North.*

Treaghaid, tré'-aj, *n. f.* stitch in the side. *North.*

Trealaich, tryall'-ėch, *n. pl.* trifles, trash, a man's ——, in ridicule.

Trealbhaidh, tryall'-vė, *adj.* come to man *or* woman's estate, grown up. *Islay.*

Treall, tryall, *n. f.* short space. *M'F.*

Treun-ri-treun, trén'-rė-trėn', *n. m.* the bird land-rail, *or*, in Scotch, corn-crake.

Treas, trās2, *adj.* the third; an *treas* uair, *thrice, the third time.*

Treasd, trăsd, *n. m.* a long form *or* seat, as in a school; *v.* bespeak, engage. *Islay.*

Treasdach, trăsd'-ach, *a.* thorough-pacing. *H. S.*

Treasg; see Treisg. weavers' paste.

Treastarruinn, trās'-ttăr-ėnn, *n. f.* spirits of wine; thrice-distilled whisky.

Treathghamhnach, trā2'-gháv-nach, *n. f.* a cow that has a calf in two years. *Islay.*

Treathnach, trān'-ach, *n. f.* gimlet. *Ir.*

Treibhdhireach, trèv'-y*h*ēr-ach, *adj* faithful to one's engagement; just, sincere, upright.

Treibhdhireachd, trĕv'-y*h*ēr-achg, *n. f.* faithfulness, sincerity, punctuality, trustiness, uprightness; also tréibhdhireas.

Treig, trāėg, *v.* forsake, leave, abandon, relinquish; na *trèig* mi gu buileach na gu bràth, *forsake thou not me utterly, nor for ever.*

Treigsinn, trāėg'-shėnn, *pt. n. f.* forsaking, abandoning; quitting, relinquishing.

Treigte, trāėg'-tyȧ, *pt.* forsaken, abandoned.

Treine, trāėn'-ȧ, *deg.* of treun, strong, &c.; *n. f.* might, power.

Treis, traŏėsh, *n. f.* a while, spell.

Treise, trāėsh2'-ȧ, *deg.* of laidir and treiseil; more powerful; *n. f.* might, bodily strength, animal power.

Treisead, trāėsh'-ad, *n. f.* degree of strength.

Treiseil, trăėsh'-al, *adj.* powerful in body.

Treisg, trāėshg, *n. f.* weavers' paste; trash.

Treobh, tryȯ, *v.* plough, till.

Treobhadair, tryȯ'-ad-aėr, *n. m.* ploughman.

Treobhadh, tryȯ'-Ă, *pt. n. f.* ploughing.

Treobhaiche, tryȯ'-ėch-a, *n. m.* ploughman.

Treodhaire, tryȯ'-ur-a, *n. m.* smith's nail-mould, *or* shape-iron.

Treoir, tryôer, *n. f.* vigour, energy.

Treorachadh, tryôr′-ach-ad, *pt.* leading, guiding, supporting, directing.

Treoraich, tryôr′-êch, *v.* guide, give strength to accomplish, strengthen.

Treoraichte, tryôr′-êch-tyâ, *pt.* strengthened.

Treubh, trèv, *n. f.* tribe, family, race; do réir air *treubh, according to your tribe. Bible.*

Treubhach, trāv′-ach, *adj.* heroic, gallant.

Treubhanta, trāv′-annt-â, *adj.* heroic, fond of feats *or* atchievements.

Treubhantas, trāv′-annt-as, *n. f.* display of feats *or* atchievements, boasting.

Treubhas, trāv′-as, *n. f.* feat, exploit.

Treubhasach, trāv′-as-ach, *adj.* fond of displaying feats of valour; ostentatious.

Treud, trădd, *n. m.* a drove, flock, herd.

Treudach, trădd′-ach, *adj.* having many flocks *or* herds; gregarious.

Treudaire, trădd′-ur-â, *n. m.* a drover.

Treudaiche, trădd′-êch-a, *n. m.* herdsman.

Treun, trān, *adj.* persevering and successful beyond expectation, as a weak person; mighty, vigorous, *B.*; surprising; is *treun* a fhuaradh thu, *you did surprisingly*; is *treun* leam fhéin a b'urrainn thu, *I am surprised that you were able*; is *treun* a gheibhear thu, *you do surprisingly*; *treun* an neart, *mighty in strength. Psalms*; *n. m.* a hero, *or* brave man; measg *tréin* a shluaigh, *among the brave of his people. Ossian.*

Treunachd, trān′-achg, *n. f.* perseverance and success; surprising conduct.

Treunad, trān′-ad, degree of success, &c.

Treunadas, trān′-add-as, *n. f.* exploits.

Treunair, trān′-ăer, *n. m.* diligent man.

Tri, trē, *adj. n. c.* three; *trì* uairean, *thrice.*

Triall, trĕăll, *v.* stroll, travel, walk; *n. m.* walking, travel, journey; design.

Triallaire, trĕăll′-ur-a, *n. m.* traveller.

Trian, trĕăn, *n. m.* third, third part; gearrar dà *thrian, two-thirds shall be cut. Bible*; particle, ray; *trian* do shoillse, *ray of light. Ossian.*

Triantach, trĕăn′-ach, *adj.* triangular, in thirds.

Triantach, trĕănt′-ach, *n. f.* a triangle.

Triantan, trĕănt′-an, *n. pl.* thirds.

Trianaid, trĕăn′-aj, *n. f.* the Trinity.

Triath, trĕăch, *n. m.* a personage, lord, chief; an *triath* tha borb, *the hero that is fierce. Ossian*; coimeas do'n charraig an *triath, like the headland is the hero*; thog na *triaith* sleagh a bhàis, *the chiefs lifted the spears of death. Ossian*; mo Dhia, 's tu an *triath* ra-mhòr, *thou art, O Lord, a very mighty Lord. Psalms.*

Triathail, trĕăch′-al, *adj.* mighty, lordly.

Tribhileach, trė′-vėl-ach, *n. f.* marsh, trefoil.

Tric, trėchg, *adj.* often, frequent; *adv.* often.

Tricead, tréchg′-ad, *n. f.* degree of frequency.

Tricead, trėchg′-ad, *adj.* thirty. *Armst.*

Trid, trējj, for Frìd, through, throughout.

Tri-deug, trē′-jjā'g, *n. c. adj.* thirteen.

Trid-shoilleir, trēj-hòelly″-aėr, *a.* transparent.

Trid-shoillse, trējj-haŏelly″-shâ, *n. f.* transparency.

Trid-shoillseach, trējj-haŏll′-shyach, *adj.* transparency, limpidness.

Tri-fhoghair, trē-aŏ*h*′-ur, *n. m.* tripthong.

Tri-fichead, trė-fėch′-ud, *n. f.* sixty; aon 's *tri-fichead*, dhà 's *tri-fichead, sixty-one, sixty-two*; a h-aon-deug 's *tri-fichead, seventy-one*; seachd-deug 's *tri-fichead, seventy-seven*; ochd-deug 's *tri-fichead, seventy-eight.*

Tri-ficheadamh, trė-fėch′-ad-uv, *adj.* sixtieth.

Tri-fillte, trė-fėlly″-tyâ, *adj.* threefold.

Trileanta, trėl′-ant-a, *adj.* thirlling *Song.*

Trileachan; see Drilleachan, oyster catcher; sand-piper, *or* sea-poet.

Trilsean, trėlly′-shyaėn; drillsean.

Trilis, tryėl′-ėsh, *n. f.* locks of hair. *Song.*

Trinnsear, truėnn′-shary', *n. m.* plate.

Trioblaid, trėb′-laj, *n. f.* trouble, distress, calamity; is lìonar *trioblaid* agus teinn, thig air an fhìrean chòir, *many straits and calamities fall to the lot of the upright*; le *trioblaid* chruaidh, *with sore distress.*

Trioblaideach, trėb′-lăj-ach, *adj.* distressing, calamitous; ni *trioblaideach, a distressing thing*; sore distressed.

Trioblaich, trēbb′-llėch, *v.* triple; make threefold.

Triobuail, trėb′-ŭăėl, *v.* vibrate, swing.

Triobuilte, trēb′-u'll-tyâ, *a.* triple, threefold.

Triogh, trė′-gh', *n. f.* fit, as of coughing *or* laughing; the chin-cough, hooping-cough.

Trionaid, trēn′-aj, *n. f.* Trinity.

Trionaidach, trēn′-aj-ach, *adj.* Trinitarian; *n. c.* a Trinitarian.

Triopall, trėp′-all, *n. m.* a bunch, (bad).

Trioramhach, trėr′-ráv-ach, *adj.* three-oared; *n. f.* three-oared boat, trireme.

Tri-shiollach, trė′-hėúl-ach, *adj.* having three syllables; *n. m.* word having such.

Tri-shiolladh, trė′-hėull-Ä, *n. m.* tri-syllable.

Tri-shlisneach, trė′-*h*lėsh-nach, *adj.* trilateral.

Triubhas, treŭ′-us, *n. f.* breeches and stockings in one piece; pantaloons.

Triubhsair, treŭs′-aër, *n. f.* trowsers.

Triuchan; see Driuchan.

Triugh, trèaŏgh, *n. f.* hooping-cough, *or* chin-cough.—*North*, triuthach.

Triuir, tryūėr, *n. c.* three; three in number; rug mi dha *triuir* mac, *I bore him three sons. Bible.*

Triuirean, tryūėr′-áėn′, *n. m.* bowl, *or* children's play-bullet; ag iomairt air *triuireanan, playing at bowls,—marbles.*

Trobhd, tròv′-ud, *v.* come hither, come away; come along with me.

Trocair, trôchg′-uėr, *n. f.* mercy, compassion.

Trocaireach, trôchg′-ăĕr-ach, *adj.* merciful.

Trocaireachd, trôchg′-ăėr-achg, *n. f.* mercifulness, compassionate regard, clemency.

Trod, trŏdd, *n. m.* scolding; a scold, reprimand, quarrel among ladies;—starling. *Irish.*

Trodaire, trŏ′dd′-ur-à, *n. m.* scolder.

Trogbhoil, trôg′-v*h*ul, *n. f.* grumbling, murmuring, grunting; eternal scold.

Trogbhoileach, trôg′-v*h*ul-ach, *adj.* apt to murmur, *or* grumble gruntingly.

Troich, troych, *n. c.* a dwarf, ninny.

Troichealachd, troych′-al-achg, *n. f.* dwarfishness, triflingness of person.

Troicheil, troych′-al, *adj.* dwarfish.

Troid, troėjj, *v. n.* scold, reprimand; *throid* mo bhean is gu'n do *throid* i rium, —is *throid* mi rithe o'n a *throid* i rium, *my wife scolded me in earnest,—by my word she scolded me;—and I scolded her, just because she did so. Song.*

Troid, troėjj, *gen.* of trod.

Troidh, traŏė′-yh′, *n. f.* the foot; foot in length; *traidhean,* (trrī-un,) *feet*; (properly, Traidh.)

Troimh, tróė, a curious word for throimh, *through him* or *it.* This word has given great offence throughout the whole Highlands, when used for le d' ìobartan, le d' iompaidh-san, *by your means* or *instrumentality.*

Troisg, Irish for traisg, fast.

Trom, trōm^2, *adj.* heavy, weighty, addicted; *tròm* air an òl, *addicted to liquor*; luxuriant, rank; barr *tròm, rank* or *luxuriant crop*; ponderous, sad, melancholy, profound, *or* deep, as sleep; eallach *trom, a heavy burden, an oppressive burden*; cadal *trom, profound sleep*; an fonn a bristeadh gu *trom, the strain breaking melancholy*; dull, sad; is taitneach ach 's *trom* do ghuth, *pleasant but sad is thy voice. Ossian*; *n. m.* burden, heavy charge; tog do *throm* dhiom, *remove your burden* or *charge from me,—do not be so severe on me*; nach biodh a *throm* oirnn, *that he would not be a burden to us*; embarrassment, impediment, encumbrance; cha bhi sin na *throm* ort, *that will not be an encumbrance to you*; a's *trime,* or *truime, which is heavier.*

Tromachadh, trōm^2′-ach-ă, *pt.* getting heavier, *or* more addicted *or* ponderous; aggravating.

Tromaich, trōm^2′-ėch, *v. n.* get heavier, make more heavy *or* weighty, get more addicted; aggravate.

Tromainntinn, trō^{2}m′-ėnjt-ėnn′, *n. f.* dejection.

Tromainntinneach, trō^{2}m′-ėnjt-ėnn-ach, *adj.* dull, dejected, disconsolate, mournful.

Tromb, trō^{2}mb, *n. f.* Jews' harp.

Trombaid, trō^{2}mb′-aj, *n. f.* a trumpet.

Trombair, trō^{2}mb′-ăėr, *n. m.* trumpeter.

Trombaireachd, trō^{2}mb′-ăėr-achg, *n. f.* harping, carping, canting.

Trombhad, trō^{2}m′-v*h*ad, *n. m.* herb vervain.

Trom-laidhe, trō^{2}m-llăē′-ė, *n. f.* nightmare. *Skye.*

Trom-lighe, trōm-llė′-ė, *n. f.* night-mare. *Islay.*

Trosdan, trosd′-an, *n. m.* a crutch, trap.

Trosg, trŏsk, *n. m.* cod; a lubber.

Trot, trŏt, *n. f.* a sheep's foot; *v.* trot; (*French,* trotter; *German,* trotten; *Italian,* trotare; *Spanish,* trote.)

Trotan, trŏt′-an, *n. m.* trotting.

Troth, trhō, *n. m.* trip, time.

Troth, trō*h*^{2}, *n. m.* a taint.

Truacanta, trūăchg′-ant-a, *adj.* merciful, compassionate.

Truacantachd, trŭăchg′-ant-achg, *n. f.* pity.

Truagh, truao′-gh′, *adj.* sad, miserable, wretched; Och is duin' *truagh* mi, co dh' fhuasglas mi o chorp a' bhàis so? *O wretched man that I am, who shall deliver me from the body of this death?* Rom. vii. and 24.; is *truagh* leam thu, *I pity you*; nach *truagh* mo chàradh, *how piteous is my case*; is *truagh* nach fhaca mi e, *it is a pity I have not seen him*; distressing, sad, melancholy; is *truagh* mar thachair, *sad is this occurrence*; miserly; is *truagh* an tobhartas e, *it is a miserable offering* or *gift*; comharra *truagh* a bhàis, *the dismal symptoms of death. Ossian*; cha *truagh* leam thu, *I do not pity you*; ma's *truagh* leat e, *if you pity him.*

Truaghan, truagh′-an, *n. m.* miserable person.

Truaighe, trūăe′-yhė, *n. f.* pity, woe, mischief; tha an *truaighe* ortsa, *you have* *exceeded all bounds,—you have gone to the mischief*; mo *thruaighe* mi, *woe's me*! mo *thruaighe* thu, *woe unto you*! na cuimhneachadh e *thruaighe* ni's mò, *let him remember his misery no more. Bible*, Acts 31–7.

Truaill, trŭălly', *n. f.* sheath *or* scabbard; tharruinn e a chlaidheamh as a *thruaill, he unsheathed his sword*; *v.* qualify, *or* reduce to a standard, as whisky, &c.; uisge-beatha *truaillte, qualified* or *reduced whisky*; pollute, corrupt, defile; *thruaill* thu am fearann, *you have polluted the land*; cha *truaill* thu thu féin, *thou shalt not pollute yourself. B.*

Truailleachd, trŭăilly''-achg, *n. f.* mean quantity, consideration, *or* disposition.

Truailleachan, trŭăělly''-ach-an, *n. m.* mean person.

Truailleadh, trŭăělly''-ă, *pt.* reducing spirits to a standard; polluting.

Truaillidh, trŭăělly''-ė, *adj.* mean, dastardly, very low *or* shabby; polluting.

Truaillidheachd, trŭăěll'-ė-achg, *n. f.* meanness of disposition, niggardliness.

Truaillte, trŭăělly''-tyȧ, *pt.* reduced, defiled.

Truan, trŭăn, *n. f.* trowel, (*Md.*); spàinn-aoil.

Truas, trŭăs, (for truaghas), pity, compassion; ghabh e *truas* dith, *he pitied her wretchedness*; *truas* mo chor, *the wretchedness of my condition.*

Truasail, trŭăs'-al, *adj.* compassionate.

Trudair, trŭdd'-ur, *n. m.* filthy person, beastly fellow, brutish man.

Trudaireachd, trŭdd'-ur'-achg, *n. f.* filth.

Truid, trŭjj, *n. f.* (also truideag), a starling; tidy, neat female.

Truileach, trŭěl'-ach, *n. f.* a worthless person.

Truille. trŭělly', *n. c.* worthless, dirty person.

Truime, trŭėm'-ȧ, *n. f.* weightiness; *deg.* trom.

Truis, trŭėsh, *v.* gather, tuck, gird, truss; *inter.* gather your tail! be off! said to a dog *or* a person in contempt.

Truis, trûėsh, *n. f.* lasciviousness. *Irish.*

Truisealadh, trŭsh'-al-ă, *n. m.* state of having one's clothes tucked up.

Truiseil, trŭsh'-al, *adj.* lascivious.

Trup, trŭpp, *n. m.* a troop; (*French*, troup; *German*, trùpp, *or* tropp, *Italian*, *Belgian*, *&c.*)

Trupair, trŭpp'-ăėr, *n. m.* trooper; a romp.

Trus, trŭs, *n. m.* a belt, girdle. *Irish.*

Trusadh, trŭs'-ă, *pt.* gathering, trussing; *n. m.* collection, a gathering.

Trusdair, trŭsd'-ar, *n. m.* a debauchee; filthy fellow.

Trusdaireachd, trŭdd'-ăėr-achg, *n. f* filthiness.

Trusgan, trŭsg'-an, *n. m.* suit of clothes dress.

Truthaire, trŭh'-ur-ȧ, *n. m.* bankrupt. *Sk*

Tu, dû *and* tû, *per. pron.* thou; is *tù* an gille, *thou art the right fellow*; is gabh aidh *tu* mi steach fadheòidh a' d' àros glòrmhor féin, *and* THOU *shalt receive me finally into thy glorious habitation.*

Tuagh, tŭă'-gh, *n. f.* hatchet, axe; *tuagh*-airm, *tuagh*-chatha, *a battle axe, a Lochaber-axe*; *tuagh*-chuillse, *tuagh*-fhola, *a fleam*, or *cattle-lancet.*

Tuaicheal; see Tuainealach, dizziness.

Tuaileas, tŭă'l'-us, *n. m.* libel, calumny, defamation, slander.

Tuaileasach, tŭă'l'-us-ach, *adj.* defamatory, calumnious, reproachful, slanderous; *tuaileasachd, calumniousness.*

Tuaimeil, tuaėm'-ėl, *v.* swathe awkwardly; huddle on clothes.

Tuainealaich, tŭăėn'-al-ėch, *n. f.* giddiness, dizziness, amazement, stupidity.

Tuaiream, tuăėr'-um, *n. m.* sense, judgment; cha'n 'eil dith *tuaireim* air, *he does not want sense*; quantity *or* number; dè 'n *tuaiream* a th'ann, *what quantity* or *number may there be of it?* direction, pursuit, aim, shot; dh' fholbh e m'a *tuaiream, he went for her, in pursuit of her*; thilg e m'a *thuaiream* e, *he threw it in her direction*, or *he aimed it at him*; dh'fhàg mi ma'n *tuaiream* so e, *I left it hereabouts*; ma *thuaiream* an aon aite, *much about the same place.*

Tuaireamach, tŭăr''-am-ach, *a.* sensible.

Tuaireap, tŭăėr'-up, *n. f.* a squabble.

Tuairgne, tŭăěrg'-nyȧ, *n. f.* confusion. *B*

Tuairmeachd, tŭăěrm'-achg; see Tuaiream.

Tuairmse, tŭăėrsh'-ȧ; see Tuaiream.

Tuairneag, tŭăėrn'-ag, *n. f.* a cobble, *or* punt of a boat; tidy, neat female.

Tuairnear, tŭăėrn'-ăėr, *n. m.* a turner.

Tuairnearachd, tŭăėrn'-ăėr-achg, *n. f.* turner's trade; working at a lathe.

Tuairsgeul, tŭăėr'-skell, *n. m.* defamation; false report, calumny, slander.

Tuairsgeulach, tŭăėr''-skell-ach, *adj.* defamatory, calumnious, slanderous.

Tuaisd, tŭăėshg, *n. c.* an awkward person; dolt.

Tuaisdeach, tŭăėshg'-ach, *adj.* awkward, stupid.

Tuaisdeachd, tŭăėshg'-achg, *n. f.* stupidity.

Tuaisdear, tŭăėshj'-ăėr, *n. m.* dolt, awkward fellow.

Tuaisdeil, tŭăėshj'-al, *adj.* stupid, awkward.

Tuaith, tŭăėch, *n. f.* lordship, territory.

TUAITHEAL, tŭăĕ'-al, *adj.* northward, sinister.

TUAM, túăm, *n. m.* tomb. *Sm. An. Poems*; grave, cave, moat *or* mound. *Ossian.*

TUAMHSGAOIL, tŭăsg'-ăŏĕl, *v.* roll in clothes, huddle, endeavour to extricate out of a labyrinth, *or* great deal of clothes.

TUAR, tŭăr, *v.* deserve, merit; an ni a *thuar* thu, *what you deserved*; *n. m.* merit, desert;—hue, colour. *Smith*; *pt.* deserving, meriting; dè tha thu a' *tuar* a dheanadh ort, *what do you deserve to be done to you*? tha thu *tuar* do chrochadh, *you deserve to be hanged.*

TUARADH, tŭăr'-Ă, quantity, number; dè'n *tuaradh* a th' ann, *what quantity* or *number is there*? ma'n *tuaradh* sin, *about that quantity.*

TUARASDAL, tŭăr'-asd-al, *n. m.* fee, wages, reward, salary, stipend; desert.

TUASAID, tŭăs'-aj, *n. f.* row, fray, fight.

TUASAIDEACH, tŭăs'-ăj-ach, *adj.* quarrelsome.

TUATH, tŭăh, *n. f. coll.* tenantry, peasantry, country people; the country; air an *tuath, on the country.*

TUATH, tŭăh, *n. f.* the north; bho'n *tuath, from the north, northward*; *adj. adv.* north, northern, northward; gaoth *tuath, north wind*; *tuath* ort, *northward of you.*

TUATHACH, tŭăh'-ach, *n. m.* North Highlander; deasach, *West Highlander.*

TUATHANACH, tŭăhn'-ach, *n. m.* tenant, husbandman, agriculturist.

TUATHANACHAS, tŭăhn'-ach-as, *n. f.* husbandry, agriculture, farming; tenement.

TUBA, tŭba, *n. m.* a tub, vat.

TUBAIST, tŭb'-ăshjt, *n. f.* mischance, mischief, mishap, accident; is trom na *tubaistean* air na sliobastan, *the clumsy are very liable to mischances, to accidents*; *tubaist* ort, *mischief take you*; thaobh *tubaist, by accident*; thig *tubaist* air, *mischief shall befall him. Bible.*

TUBAISTEACH, tŭb'-ashjj-ach, *adj.* unlucky, unfortunate, calamitous, untoward.

TUBAISTEACHD, tŭb'-ashjt-achg, *n. f.* unfortunateness, liability to accidents.

TUBAN, tŭb'-an, *n. m.* a tub. *West*; lock of wool. *North.*

TUBH for Tugh, tŭ'-gh, thatch; *v.* back, as a horse; *tubh* e, *back him in.*

TUBHAILT, tŭ'-aljt, *n. f.* a table-cloth, towel.

TUCH, tûch, *v.* smother, fumigate, grow hoarse; tha mo mhuinneal air a *tùchadh, my throat is becoming hoarse.*

TUCH, tŭch, *inter.* tut! hush!

TUCHAN, tûch'-an, *n. m.* hoarseness, half-smothered fire.

TUCHANACH, tûch'-an-ach, *adj.* hoarse.

TUCHAIRE, tûch'-ur-a, *n. m.* smother.

TUD, tŭd, *inter.* tut! whist!

TUD, tŭd, *n. m.* a little heap, as dough.

TUDAN, tŭd'-an, *n. m.* a little corn-stack; small heap of any thing; manikin.

TUG, corruption of d'thug, ddŭg, (see thug); an d' *thug* e, *has he brought*?

TUGH, tŭgh, *v.* thatch, cover; back.

TUGHA, tŭgh'-a, *n. f.* thatch, covering; tighean *tŭgha, thatched houses* or *cots.*

TUGHADAIR, tŭgh'-ad-aĕr, *n. m.* thatcher.

TUIG, tŭĕg, *v.* understand, comprehend perceive, discern; *thuig* e do chridhe, *h understood thy heart*; cò *thuigeas* uil sheachrain fhéin, *who can his errors understand*; glan o lochd diomhair mi, *cleanse me from secret sins*; an sin *tuigidh* tu eagail an Tighearna, *then thou shalt understand the fear of the Lord.*

TUIGSE, tŭĕgsh'-â, *n. f.* understanding, sense, reason, judgment; a' call a *thuigse, losing his senses,* or *judgment*; skill, knowledge; is beag *tuigse* th agadsa air sin, *you have little skill of that.*

TUIGSEACH, tŭĕgsh'-ach, *adj.* intelligent, prudent, sensible; duine *tuigseach, a prudent* or *intelligent man. Bible*; skilled, expert; *tuigseach* air a leithid sin, *expert in such things.*

TUIGSINN, tŭĕg'-shĕnn, *pt.* understanding, perceiving, discerning.

TUIL, tŭ'l, *n. f.* a flood, torrent, deluge.

TUIL-BHEUM, tŭ'l'-văm, *n. f.* torrent. *M'F.*

TUIL-DHORUS, tŭ'l'-ghor-us, *n. m.* flood-gate; *tuil-dhorsan* Neamh, *the windows of Heaven. Bible.*

TUILICH, tŭ'l'-ĕch, } *n. m.* more, additional
TUILIDH, tŭ'l'-ĕ, } quantity *or* number; thoir dhomh *tuilidh, give me more*; *tuilidh* is a choir, *too much, superabundance, superfluity. Argyle.*

TUILLE, tyŭlly''-á, *n. m.* more, additional quantity *or* number. *Perthshire.*

TUILIDH, tŭ'l'-ĕch, } *adv.* more, any more,
TUILLE, tŭ'lly'-a, } any further; cha till, cha till mi *tuilich, I shall never, never more return*!!! cha bhi mi am ònrachd *tuille, I shall not be any further solitary*; *tuilich* or *tuille* gu bràth, *any more for ever. B.*; *tuilich* cha léir dhuit, *Oscar, Oscar, thou shalt see no more*; cha'n fhaod thu tighinn *tuilich, you must not come any more*; a *thuille* neo *thuilidh* air sin, *moreover*; *tuilidh* na's leoir, *more than is sufficient, more than enough.*

TUILTEAN, tŭ'l'-tyan, *n. pl.* floods, deluges.

TUILTEACH, tŭ'l'-tyach, *n. f.* a torrent; air *tuilteach* gaoithe sgaoil e a sgiathan, *on a torrent of air* (wind) *she spread her wings. Ossian*; *adj.* in torrents, inundating, deluging; frasan *tuilteach, in inundating* or *deluging showers.*

TUIM, tŭĕm, *n. pl.* bushes, ant-hills, (tom.)

Tuimhseach, tŭev′-shach, *a.* beating. *H. Society.*

Tuimhsich, tŭsh′-ėch, *v.* beat, drub. *H. S.*

Tuimpe, tŭėmp′-à, *n. m.* a turnip. *Irish.*

Tuin, tŭėn, *v.* dwell; *n. m.* dwelling. *Ir.*; *Psalms.*

Tuineach, tŭėn′-ach, *n. f.* dwelling, lodging; an i cois na creige do *thuineach, is the shelter of the rock thy lodgings? Oss.*

Tuineachadh, tŭėn′-ach-ă, *pt.* gathering into a place for residence; colonizing, dwelling; *n. f.* dwelling-place.

Tuineachas, tŭėn′-ach-us, *n. m.* colony.

Tuineadh, corruption of Tuineachadh.

Tuinich, tŭėn′-ėch, *v.* settle in a place, plant, *or* colonize; gather, as matter in a suppuration; settle, *or* fix in a place, as a moveable tumour.

Tuinn, tŭėnn, *n. pl.* (tonn), waves.

Tuinne, tuėnn′-à, *gen.* water-mark; an gob na *tuinne, at the water's edge, at the water-mark.*

Tuinneasach, tŭėnn′-as-ach, *a.* mortal. *St.*

Tuir, tŭėr, *v.* sing *or* rehearse an elegy; lament for the dead, deplore; theirigeadh mo dheoir na *tuirinn* gach ànradh, *my tears would fail, were I to deplore every disaster. Sm.*; *tuir* an aithris neoàdhmhor, *deplore the hapless tale—weep out of purgatory.*

Tuirc, ttŭėrk, *n. pl.* boars.

Tuirc, ttŭėrk, *n. f.* Turkey; do'n *Tuirc, to Turkey*; o'n *Tuirc, from Turkey.*

Tuireadh, tŭėr′-ă, *n. m.* an elegy, death-song, a dirge, lamentation for the dead; mourning, wailing; dh' èisd sinn ri *tuireadh* a thruaighe, *we listened to him while wailing his hard fate*; ciod fàth do *thuiridh, what is the cause of your lament?* le *tuireadh* glaoidh, thog e 'cheann, *with the lamentation of death, he raised his head. Smith.*

Tuireann, tŭėr′-unn, *n. m.* anvil, spark. *Ir.*

Tuireasg, tŭĕr′-ask, *n. m.* a saw; an àrdaich an *tuireasg* e féin, *shall the saw raise itself. Bible.*

Tuirl, tŭėrl, *v.* alight, dismount. *Ossian.*

Tuirleum, tŭėr′-lām, *n. m.* a fearful leap.

Tuirleig, tŭrl′-llėg, *n. m.* water-spout.

Tuirlich, tŭėrl′-ėch, *n. f.* rumbling noise.

Tuirlinn for Toirlinn, dismount, alight.

Tuirse, tŭrėsh′-à, *n. f.* sadness. *Perthsh.*

Tuirseach, tŭrėsh′-ach, *adj.* sad; tùrsach.

Tuis, tûsh, *n. f.* incense, frankincense. *B.*

Tuisear, tŭsh′-ur′, *n. m.* censer. *Bible.*

Tuisill, tŭsh-ėlly′, *v.* stumble, stammer.

Tuisleach, tŭsh′-lyach, *adj.* unsteady.

Tuisleadh, tŭsh′-lyă, *pt.* stumbling; *n m.* a stumble, jostle;—delivery. *M'F.*

Tuislich, tŭsh′-llyėch, *v.* stumble, jostle, slip, fall; *thuislich* e, *he stumbled.—N*; *thuismich* e, *he stumbled.*

Tuit, tŭėjt, *v. n.* fall, slip, chance, happen, befall, benight, get dark; be seduced by; *thuit* duinn tachairt, *we met by chance*; *thuit* iad, *they fell*; *thuit* daibh tighinn a stigh, *it happened that they came in*; *thuit* an oidhche oirnn, *we were benighted,—the night came on,—it got dark*; *thuit* i leis, *she was seduced by him*; subside,—set, as the sun; *tuitidh* a ghaoith ach mairidh ar cliù, *the wind shall subside, but our fame shall last*; *thuit* mo ghrian gu sìor, *my sun has set for ever. Ossian*; fail, damp; *thuit* a chridhe, *his heart failed him.*

Tuiteam, tŭėjt′-um, *n. m.* a fall; dusk, dawn; fhuair e *tuiteam, he got a fall*; m'a *thuiteam* na h-oidhche, *about the dawn* or *dusk of the evening*; *pt.* falling, getting dusky; *tuiteamsa, let me fall* or *happen.*

Tuiteamach, tŭėjt′-am-ach, *adj.* falling, accidental, casual; an tinneas *tuiteamach, the falling sickness, epilepsy, apoplexy*; *n. m.* epilepsy. *Bible.*

Tuiteamachd, tuejt′-am-achg, *n. f.* fallability, contingency.

Tuiteamas, tuėjt′-am-as, *n. m.* chance, accident; thachair sinn le *tuiteamas, we met by accident* or *chance*; cha'n'eil *tuiteamas* sam bith gu tachair sinn am feasd, *there is no chance that we shall ever meet*; an event, occurrence; gach droch *thuiteamas, every evil occurrence. Bible*; an dàil gach *tuiteamas, to face any event, in contact with any danger*; cha'n'eil ann ach *tuiteamas, it is only a chance*;—also epilepsy. *Bible.*

Tula, tûll′-a, *adj.* complete, most notorious; ag innseadh no *tula*-bhreug, *telling most notorious lies*; an *tula*-mheairleach, *the notorious thief.*

Tulach, tŭl′-ach, } *n. f.* a knoll; little
Tulaich, tŭl′-ėch, } green eminence; mi am shuidhe air an *tulaich, I sitting on the knoll*; an *tulach* laghach air robh Tuara, *the fine eminence on which Tuara stood*; tomb; chàirich sinn 'san *tulaich* an laoch, *we interred the hero in the tomb,* or *in the green knoll.*

Tulachan, tŭl′-ach-an, *n. m.* a sham-calf, *or* bishop. *Highland Society.*

Tulag, tŭll′-ag, *n. f.* fish pollock. *H. S.*

Tulchainn, tul′-cháėnn, *n. f.* a gable of a house; the breech.

Tulchuis, tu'l′-chŭsh, *n. f.* confidence. *Ir.*

Tulchuiseach, tŭ'l′-chŭsh-ach, *adj.* persevering, plodding, brave; o'n eascaraid *thulchuiseach, from the brave* or *persevering foe. Smith.*

Tulg, tŭlag, *v.* rock, toss, roll; *tulg* a' chreathall, *rock the cradle*; an long a *tulgadh, the ship rolling*; wave, osci'

..ute; an doire a *tulgadh, the grove waving.*

Tulgach, tŭlug'-ach, *adj.* rocking, tossing; uneasy, as a seat; unfixed, *or* uncertain, as an office, *or* employment.

Tulgadh, tŭlug'-ă, *pt.* tossing, rocking, lurching; *n. m.* a lurch, toss,—used by *Armstrong* for Tolg.

Tulm, tŭlum, *n. f.* a knoll, *or* little mound of turf, &c.; eminence.

Tulmach, tŭlum'-ach, *adj.* knolly.

Tum, tŭm, *v.* dip, immerse, duck, immerge, plunge; *thum* iad an còta 'san fhuil, *they dipped the coat in the blood. Bible*; a chas an *tumadh* 'sa chaochan, *his foot immersed in the gurgling streamlet. Ossian.*

Tumadair, tŭm'-ad-ăĕr, *n. m.* baling-dish.

Tumadh, tŭm'-ă, *pt.* dipping, ducking; *n. m.* duck, immersion.

Tumaire, tŭm'-ad-ăĕr, *n. m.* a ducker.

Tum-tam, tŭm-tám', *n. m.* a humdrum; great hesitation, stupid conduct.

Tumte, tŭm'-tyá, *pt.* immerged, dipped.

Tunaich, for Tuinich, settle, dwell.

Tung, tŭng, *n. m.* a family burying-ground inclosed, a tomb, vault. *Argyle.*

Tungaid, tŭng'-aj, *n. f.* a most notorious lie, *or* hellish evasion, a stratagem.

Tungaideach, tŭng'-ăj-ach, *adj.* full of hellish evasions *or* noted lies.

Tunna, tŭnn'-á, *n. m.* a tun weight, dish; (*French*, tonnea, *German*, tonne.)

Tunnadair, tŭnn'-ad-aer, *n. m.* tunner.

Tunnag, tŭnn'-ag, *n. f.* a duck.

Tur, tûr, *n. m.* penetration, mental acuteness, genius, intelligence; cha duine gun *tùr* a dheanadh e, *it is not a man destitute of penetration* or *genius that could accomplish it*; wisdom, understanding; gliocas is *tùr, wisdom and understanding*, (natural acuteness). *Bible*; inntinn is *tùr* nam fear, *the mind and acuteness of the heroes. Ml.*; *v.* invent, devise, contrive, frame; air a *thùradh* le Seumus, *invented by James,—Stewart's songs*; a *thùras* olc, *that devises evil*; a *thùr* oibre ealanta, *to devise* or *plan cunning works. Bible.*; get fair, as weather.

Tur, tùr, *n. m.* a tower, fortification, fort, castle; *Tùr* Bhàbloin, *the Tower of Babel.*

Tur, tûr, *adj.* without condiment, (*or* kitchen, *Scotch*); greim *tur, a dry morsel*; aran *tur, bread without butter and cheese*; buntàta *tur, potatoes, and nothing to eat to them*; *adj.* most completely, *or* entirely; is *tur* a dh' fhairslich e ort, *how completely it has defied you*; tha e mar sin gu *tur, it is so most completely, it is absolutely so, it is wholly so.*

Turach, tûr'-ach, *adj.* towering, turretted.

Turachdach, tŭr'-achg-ach, *adj.* without any thing else than meal, potatoes, &c.

Turadh, tŭr'-ă, *n. m.* absence of rain, fair weather; tha e na *thuradh, it is fair*; rinn e *turadh, it faired, the rain ceased.*

Turail, tûr'-al, *adj.* shrewd, ingenious, acute, inventive, skilful; gach duine toileach, *tùrail, every willing, skilful man.*

Turalachd, tûr'-al-achg, *n. m.* shrewdness.

Turainn, tur'-ăenn, *n. f.* a fit of sickness; fhuair e an droch *thùrainn, he has got a very bad fit of sickness.*

Turainneach, tŭr'-ăenn-achg, *adj.* delicate in health; liable to sickness.

Turainniche, tŭr'-ăenn-ėch-a, *n. m.* invalid.

Turamaich; see Turramanaich.

Turamanaich, tŭr'-am-an-ėch, *n. f.* rocking.

Turcach, tŭrk'-ach, *a.* Turkish; *n. m.* a Turk; turkey hen or cock.

Turcais, tŭrk'-ash, *n. f.* tweezers.

Turlach, tûrr'-llach, *n. m.* a very large fire, having smoke and no flame; big, clumsy person; *n. f.* a monstrous ugly head of hair; *tùrlach* na fèisde, *banquet-fire. Ossian.*

Turloch, tŭr'-lòch, *n. f.* a lake that dries in summer.

Turn, tûrn, *n. m.* job, feat; *turn* odhar, *a mite* or *twelfth of a penny.*

Turr, tûrr, *n. m.* a large heap, tomb; *v.* rock hither and thither.

Turrachadal, tûrr'-a-chad-al, *n. c.* sleeping and rocking, as a person sitting on a chair; slumbering, dozing, lethargy.

Turraig, tŭrr'-ėg, *n. f.* stool in ridicule; air do *thurraig, at stool. Irish.*

Turraim, **Turramain**, tŭrr'-am-ăen, *v.* rock *or* vibrate, as a person lamenting the dead, sitting on a grave.

Turram, *n. m.*, **Turraman**, tŭrr'-am-an, *n. m.* tossing hither and thither, as a person lamenting; vibration, oscillation. *North*, turraban.

Tursa, tûrs'-á, *n. f.* dejection, sadness; waving the head and lamenting; sorrow.

Tursach, tûrs'-ach, *adj.* sad, sorrowful; gu *tùrsach*, trom, *sad and dejected*; Orsa Fionn gu *tùrsach*, said Fingal, mournfully.

Turtur, tûrt'-ur, *n. m.* a turtle. *Bible.*

Turus, tŭr'-us, *n. m.* journey, travel.

Turusachd, tŭr'-us-achg, *n. f.* pilgrimage.

Tus, tûs, *n. m.* beginning, commencement, front, origin; Helen, *tùs* ar cràidh, *Helen, the origin* or *source of our severe affliction*; air *tùs* an airm, *in front* or *van of the army*; air a *thùs* is air a thoiseach, *first and foremost*; tùs-mhuinntir aborigines; 's e *tùs* a ghliocais, eagal De, *the beginning of wisdom, is the fear of God.*

Tut, tûtt', *n. m.* a foist, stink; *v.* foist, stink.

Tutaire, tûtt'-ur-a, *n. m.* foister.

U

U, û, the seventeenth and last letter of the Gaelic alphabet, styled " ùr," the yew-tree; it has seven or eight sounds.—See the Key.

Uabairt, ŭăb'-arjty', *n. f.* expulsion. *N.*

Uabhar, ŭăv'-ur, *n. m.* extreme pride.

Uabheist, uáv'-vāshjj, *n. f.* a monster. *B.*; as properly Uaınbheist, (nasal sound.)

Uachdar, ŭăchg'-ur, *n. m.* surface, top; air *uachdar, on the surface, on the top*; *uachdar* is iochdar, *top and bottom*; cream, upper of a shoe; grugh is *uachdar, curds and cream*;—woof of cloth. *North*; fhuair e làmh an *uachdar, he got the ascendant, the mastery*; a tighinn an *uachdar, coming on the surface, coming above ground,* or *budding, as lint, potatoes, &c.*; an *uachdar* ma seach, *alternately up and down. Ossian.*

Uachdarachd, ŭăchg'-ar-achg, *n. f.* top; o'n *uachdarachd* gus an iochdrachd, *from top to bottom.*

Uachdaran, ŭăchg'-ar-an, *n. m.* a superior, governor, ruler, chief; thàinig *uachdaran* àirid, agus thug e aoradh dha, *a certain Ruler came and worshipped him. Bible.*

Uachdarach, ŭăchg'-rach, *adj.* upper, higher, superficial.

Uachdaranachd, ŭăch'-ar-an-achd, *n. f.* supremacy, dominion, rule; reign, sovereignty; biodh *uachdaranachd* aca, *let them have dominion. Bible.*

Uachdrachd, ŭăchg'-rachg, *n. f.* surface, top; o'n *uachdrachd,* gus an iochdrachd, *from first to last,—from the top to the bottom*; (pronounced often *uarachd.*)

Uaibh, vŭăev, (*pre.* and *pro.* sibh,) from you, at a distance from you; wanted by you; being your duty; tha *uaibh* folbh, *you had better be gone, it is your duty to go*; fada *uaibh, far from you,—at a great distance from you*; cuiribh *uaibh* na Diathan coimheach, *put away the strange gods. Bible.*

Uaibhreach, ŭăev'-ryach, *adj.* arrogant, haughty, self-important, extremely proud; tha Dia a' cur an aghaidh nan *uaibhreach, God resisteth the proud. Bible.*

Uaibh-se, ŭăv'-shà, *emph.* of Uaibh.

Uaibhreachas, ŭăév'-ryach-us, *n. f.* extreme degree of pride *or* vain-glory; great haughtiness; also uaibhreachd.

Uaidh, vŭăey', (*pre. pro.*) from him.

Uaigh, ŭăĕ'-y', *n. f.* a grave, tomb, sepulchre; gus an càrar mi 'san *uaigh, till I am interred.*

Uaigneach, ŭăeg'-nyach, *adj.* solitary, remote, retired; àite *uaigneach, a solitary* or *remote place*; distant, dull; duine *uaigneach, a person distant* or *reserved in manner.*

Uaigneas, ŭăeg'-nyus, *n. m.* lonesomeness, retired manners *or* habits; thug e air *uaigneas* e, *he took him aside, he retired into a secret place with him*; a secret, secrecy, privacy; th' an t-aran a dh' ithear an *uaigneas,* taitneach, *bread eaten in secret, is pleasant*; *uaigneas*-san, *his retired manner* or *disposition.*

Uaignidh, ŭăĕg'-nyė, *adj.* uaigneach.

Uaigneachd, ŭăăg'-nyach, *n. f.* secrecy, solitariness, &c.; retired, morose disposition *or* habits.

Uaill, ŭăėlly', *n. f.* pomp, vanity, vain-glory, inconsistent boasting; na dean *uaill* as an latha màireach, *boast not of to-morrow. Bible.*

Uaillire, ŭălly'-ėr-à, *n. m.* a fop, spark.

Uaill-mhiann, ŭălly'-vhĕăn, *n. f.* ambition.

Uaimhinn, ŭáėv'-ėnn, *n. f.* horror; great horror *or* detestation.

Uaimhinneach, ŭăėv'-ėnn-ach, } *adj.* horrifying.
Uaimhneach, ŭabėv'-nyach, }

Uaimhneachd, ŭăĕv'-nyachg, *n. f.* horrifying nature *or* quality; horridness.

Uaine, ŭăen'-à, *adj.* green, pallid, wan; *n. m.* green, green colour.

Uainead, ŭăĕn'-ad, *n. m.* greenness, pallidness, wanness; degree of greenness.

Uaineachan, ŭăėn'-ach-an, *n. c.* a wan, pallid, miserable-looking person; also uainealach.

Uainich, ŭăėn'-ėch, *v.* get green.

Uainn, vŭăėn, (*pre. pro.*) from us, at a distance from us, wanted by us, missing by us; tha triuir *uainn, we want three, we miss three*; being necessary for us, *or* our duty; tha *uainn* folbh, *it is our duty to go, we had better be gone.*

Uaip, ŭăėp, *v.* bungle, botch.

Uaipe, uăėp'-à, (*pro. pre.*), from her, &c.

Uaipear, ŭăėp'-ăėr, *n. m.* bungler, botcher.

Uair, ŭăėr, *n. f.* an hour, time, weather; time of day *or* night; allotted time, rotation; aon *uair, one hour, one o'clock, once*; dè 'n *uair* a tha e, *what o'clock is it*? ma dhà *uair, about two o'clock*; eadar aon is a dhà, *between one and two*; *uair* 'sam bith, *any time*; na h-uile *uair, at all times*; an *uair* ma dheireadh, *the last time*; a cheud *uair, at first, the first time*; 's e so m' *uair*-sa, *this is my time, this is my turn* or *rotation*; tha *uair* air, *he is subject to fits and starts of good humour* or *generosity*; air *uairibh, sometimes*; an ceart *uair, the very time, presently, immediately, instantly*; gach *uair, at all times*; *uair* eile, *at another time* on a time, at another time, one time; *uair* éiridh iad gu nèamh, *uair* théid iad gu doimhne sìos, *one time they mount to the skies, at another time they sink to the abyss, the deep*; thug mi i'n uaigneas *uair, I brought her apart once*; *uair* a rinn mi sin, *once I did that*; rinn e sin *uair* is *uair, he did that more than once, repeatedly, over and over*; cia lìon *uair* a thig e, *how often shall he come?* 'na *uaireanan, sometimes;* nì mi e air an *uair, I will do instantly, immediately, without losing a moment*; *uair* ma seach, *alternately, in rotation.*

UAIREADAIR, ŭăėr'-add-aer, *n. m.* timepiece, watch; clag-*uaireadair, a clock*; *uaireadair*-gainnich, *sand-glass; uaireadair*-gréine, *sun-dial.*

UAIREIL, ŭăėr'-al, *adj.* hourly.

UAIREIGINN, ŭăėr'-ė-gyėnn, *adv.* sometimes; *uair* na *uaireiginn, sometime or other.*

UAISLE, ŭăėlsh'-ă, *n. m.* genteel extraction, high birth, gentlemanly manners, gentility, liberality; *deg.* of uasal, more *or* most genteel, &c.; (from uis.)

UAISLEACHD, ŭăēshl'-achg, *n. f.* gentility, dignity of port, *or* mind.

UAISLEAD, ŭăēsh'-lyad, degree of gentility.

UAISLEAN, ŭăėsh'-lyun, *n. pl.* gentry.

UAISLICH, ŭăėsh'-lyech, *v.* ennoble, dignify.

UAIT, vhŭăjt, (*pre. pro.*), from thee; *Inter.* away with it! away with it! tha *uait* a bhi folbh, *you had better begone*; tha *uait* a dheanadh, *you better do it*; dè tha *uait? what do you want? bhuait.*

UAITHE, ŭăėch'-ă, (*pro. pre.*), from her, &c.; dè tha *uaithe? what does she want?* thoir *uaithe, tear from her.*

UAITHNE, ŭăĕn'-a, *n. m.* pillar. *B. B.*

UALLACH, ŭăll'-ach, *n. m.* charge; *uallach* an ni sin ormsa, *the charge of that thing to me*; a' guìlan *uallach* tighe Ioseiph, *bearing the charge of the house of Joseph. Bible*; burden, in a moral sense,—hard task; cha'n *uallach* sin air, *that is no hard task for him*; an oppressive weight, responsibility; *uallach* a ghnothaich, *the responsibility of that affair*; is aotrom an t-*uallach* mo gràdh, *my love is a light burden. Oss.*; *adj.* airy, light, indifferent as to weight; thog e gu h-*uallach, he raised it so cleverly*, or *lively*; conceited, light-headed, giddy; duine *uallach, a light-headed person.*

UALLACHAS, ŭăll'-ach-us, *n. m.* conceited ness, vanity, airiness.

UALLACHD, ŭăll'-achg, *n. m.* extreme conceit, *or* vanity, *or* airiness.

ULLAIRE, ŭăll'-ur-ă, *n. m.* coxcomb.

UAM, vŭăm, (*pre. pro.*), from me, wanted by me, at a distance from me; fan *uam, keep at a distance from me, keep from me*; gu ma fada sin *uam, be it far from me*, B.; emphatic *uamsa*, more properly bhuam, bhuamsa.

UAMH,* uá, ŭáv, *n. f.* a cave, den; *n. m.* a chief of savages, terrible fellow—hence uaimhinn, (uamh, chief savage, and binn, sentence to be devoured) cha'n'eil ann ach *uamh* dhuine, *he is only a savage of a fellow.*

UAMHACH, ŭăv'-ach, *adj.* like a cave, in caves.

UAMHAG, ŭă'-ag. *n. f.* tick. *N.*; (seòllann.)

UAMHARR, ŭăv'-urr, *adj.* horrid, horrifying, shocking; atrocious, heinous.

UAMHARRACHD, uăv'-urr-achg, *n. f.* horrifying nature *or* quality; atrocity, heinousness.

UAMBHAS, ŭáv'-vus, *n. m.* horrid deed, atrocity, deed done in a cave, (uamh-bheus): horror, greatest astonishment, enormous quantity; fhuair iad *uamhas* éisg, *they have got an enormous quantity of fish.*

UAMHASACHD, ùáv'-vás-achg, *n. f.* horrification, extreme atrocity; dreadfulness, horribleness, abominableness, loathsomeness.

UAN, ŭán, *n. m.* a lamb; lambs, uain.

UANALACH, ŭán'-al-ach, *n. m.* lambs' wool.

UAN-CAISG, ŭăn-kâshg', *n. m.* Paschal lamb.

UAPA, vŭáp'-a, (*pre. pro.*), from them, distant from them, wanted by them; dè tha *bhuapa? what do they want?* tha *bhuapa* a bhi folbh, *they had better be gone.*

UAS, ŭăs, *n. m.* College-cap used when graduating.

UASAIL, uăs'-al, *adj.* genteel, descended of a respectable family; new, novel, fastidious; duine-*uasal, a gentleman*; bean *uasal, a lady, a gentlewoman*; tha e tuilidh is *uasal* uime, *he is too fastidious about it*; rinn thu do ghnothach gu h-

* Uamh nam fear, the Gentleman's Cave,—a very singular cavern in the Island of St. MacCormaig, in the Sound of Jura, Argyle. It is the fate of every gentleman that enters this cave, that

"Out of his derogate body shall never spring,
A babe to honour him!!!"

What a grand look-out for the Rev. Mr. Malthus!!! Report says, that the celebrated Doctors SAMUEL JOHNSON and MACCULLOCH were storm-staid in this untoward den,—and that this was the reason they vented their spleen on the poor HIGHLANDS and HIGHLANDERS. Government should look about them; St. MacCormaig is in the market.

uasal, a lady, a gentlewoman; tha e tuilidh is *uasal* uime, *he is too fastidious about it*; rinn thu do ghnothach gu h-*uasal, you have made your business like a gentleman*; *n. m.* gentleman. *M'D.*

Uatha, vŭăch'-ă, (*pre. pro.*), from them, off their hands; thoir *uatha, deprive them of, bring from them.*

Ubag, ûb'-ag, *n. f.* an enchantment, incantation, charm, superstitious ceremony.

Ubagach, ŭb'-ag-ach, *adj.* skilled in charms, &c.

Ubagail, ŭb'-ag-ul, *pt.* enchanting.

Ubarraid, ûb'-arr-aj, *n. f.* confusion, fidgetting; lumber, confusion.

Ubarraideach, ûbb'-arr-aj-ach, *a.* turbulent, confused, unsettled, romping, childish

Ubb, Ubh, ûv, ûv, *Inter.* O dear! O dear! my conscience!!!

Ubh, nonsense for Ugh, ŭ'-aŏgh, an egg.

Ubhall, ŭ'-ull, *n. f.* an apple; *ubhal* an sgornain, *the ball of the throttle*; *ubhal* na sùl, *pupil of the eye*; *ubhlan, apples.*

Ubhalach, u'-al-ach, *adj.* apple-bearing.

Ubhladh, ûll'-aŏgh, *n. m.* fine in church courts, ecclesiastical fine; in civil courts, càinn.

Uchd, ŭchg, *n. m.* breast, bosom; *uchd* mo ghaoil, *the breast of my love*; point, or very time; ri *uchd* neo beul bàis, *at the point of death*; (*Perthshire*, tha e aig roinn a' bhàis); clemency, mercy, humanity; fàg gu *uchd* a Moireir e, *refer it to his lordship's clemency* or *humanity*; the face of a hill *or* ascent; a togail an *uchd, ascending the face of a hill,—steep part of a road*; ri *uchd* cruadail, *braving difficulties,—grappling with difficulties*; *uchd*-éideadh, *breast-plate.*

Uchdach, ŭchg'-ach, *n. f.* an ascent *or* side of a hill; a togail na h-*uchdaich, ascending the acclivity*; delivery in speech; 's ann aige tha 'n *uchdach, how grand his delivery*! pith, energy; cha 'n eil *uchdach* aige dha, *he has not energy to encounter such difficulty*; *adj.* prominent, steep.

Uchdardach, ŭchg'-ărdd'-ach, *adj.* high-crested; bold, brave; presumptuous.

Uchdardachd, ŭchg'-ardd'-achg, *n. f.* pomposity, presumptuousness, pomp.

Ughdmhac, ŭchg'-v*h*achg, *n. m.* an adopted son.

Uchdmhacachd, ŭchg'-v*hă*chg-achg, *n f.* adoption; *uchdmhacaich, adopt, take another's son as your own.*

Uchdan, uchg'-an, *n. m.* the instep of a foot *or* shoe; child's bib *or* pinny; a little eminence *or* knoll.

Ud for Ad, that, yon, yonder.

Udal for Udbhoil, distraction for want of a home; tossing about.

Udabac, ûd'-a-bŏchg, *n. m.* porch. ***North.***

Udail, ŭd'-al, *adj.* gloomy; *n. m* churl.

Udalan, ŭd'-all-an, *n. m.* tether-swivel.

Udhar, ŭh'-ur, *n. m.* boil, sore. ***R. M'D.***

Udlaidh, ŭd'-llė, *adj.* dark, gloomy. ***M'F.***

Udrathad. ŭdd'-ră-ad, *n. m.* free egress.

Udbhoil, ŭd'-v*h*al, *n. f.* the state of being tossed from place to place, as a person ejected; state of being absent, a pensioner on the bounty of others, as a person, once in good circumstances; tossing from place to place; cha bhi thu air *udbhoil you shall not be uncared for*; cha 'n fhaic mise air *udbhoil* thu, *I shall not see you a dependant* or *gentle beggar.*

Udbhoileach, ŭd'-val-ach, *adj.* tossed from place to place, as a person.

Ugh, û-gh, *n. m.* an udder, improperly written with *bh*; *ùgh* na boine, *the cow's udder.*

Ugh, ŭgh', *n. f.* an egg; *ugh*-eirig, *pullet's egg*; *ugh*-nid, *a nest-egg*; *uighean, eggs, Bible, Islay*; gealagan *uighe, the white of an egg, Bible*; buidheagan *uighe, the yolk of an egg. Bible.*

Ughdair, } **Ughdarra**, } ŭdd''-urr-a, *n. m.* an author; oir cha 'n e Dia *ùghdarra* na mi-rioghailt ach na sìthe, *for God is not the author of confusion, but of peace. Bible.*

Ughdarrachd, ûdd'-ărr-achg, *n. f.* authorship.

Ughdarras, ûdd''-urr-as, *n. m.* authority, command; a' teagasg mar neach aig' am bheil *ughdarras, teaching as one having authority. Bible.*

Ugsa, ŭg'-sa, *n. f.* the largest kind of coal-fish; in *Scotch*, stenlock.

Uibe, ŭėb'-ă, *n. m.* a batch, *or* a lump of dough; a block of any thing, as marble; lump of a person; ioba more properly, which see.

Uibhir, ŭėv'-ėr[2], *n. f.* an equal quantity or number; tha *uibhir* is *uibhir* aca, *they have share and share alike, they have equal numbers* or *quantity*; *uibhir* eile, *as much again, double that quantity* or *number*; dè'n *uibhir* is th'ann, *how much is there? what quantity* or *number is there? uibhir* is a th'ann, *as much as there are? a sum* or *quantity equivalent to*; *uibhir* na circe, *the equivalent,* or *any thing as valuable as a hen*; na h-*uibhir, a great number* or *quantity*; na h-*uibhir* do dhaoine, *a great number of men*; *uibhir* ri càch, *as much as the rest*; 'se na h-*uibhir* e, *it is so much.*

Uidh, ûĕ, *n. m.* heed, care, journey; intention, hope; gun *uidh* ri sòlas, *without hope of consolation. Sm.*; aig ceann ar n-*uidh, at our journey's end*; ceann-*uidh, destination.*

Uidh, ŭĕ, *n. f.* step, gradation, degree; *uidh* air 'n *uidh*, *by degrees*; gradually; 's ann *uidh* air' n *uidh* a thogar na caisteil, *castles are built by degrees, gradually, by little and little.*

Uidheam, ue″-yum, *n. f.* regimentals, uniform, accoutrements, equipage, materials, apparatus; fodh làn *uidheam*, *dressed in his full accoutrements* or *uniform*; dheanainn sin na biodh an *uidheam* agam, *I would do that, if I had the materials*, or *tools*, or *apparatus*; rigging, instruments.

Uidheamach, ŭĕy″-am-ach, *adj.* well-furnished, *or* provided with materials *or* apparatus.

Uidheamachadh, ŭĕy″-am-ach-Ă, *pt.* preparing, arranging matters; *n. m.* preparation, arrangement.

Uidheamaich, ŭĕy″-am-ėch, *v.* prepare, fit, arrange, furnish with necessary accoutrements, materials, *or* instruments; equip; *uidheamaich* thu fhèin, *equip yourself, dress yourself*; *uidheamaichte, prepared*, &c.

Uig, ûėg, *n. f.* a conical steep rock, nook.

Uilc, ŭĕ'lk, *n. pl.* of Olc; also *gen.*

Uile, ŭ'lă, *adj. adv. n. m.* altogether, all, wholly, quite, every; tha iad mar sin *uile, they are all so*; thàinig iad *uile, they have all come*; tha mi *uile* thoileach, *I am quite willing*; *uile*-léirsinneach, *all-seeing*; na h-*uile, every one, all, the whole.*

Uileachd, ŭ'l′-achg, *n. f.* universality.

Uileann, ŭ'l′-unn, *n. f.* the elbow, corner, angle; *uileann* na beinne, *the angle* or *corner of the mountain*; air *uilinn* nan leac, *on the corner of the flags. Ossian*; 'nuair bha e air *uilinn, when he was embarrassed*; on the eve of failing.

Uilear, ŭ'l′-aėr, *adj.* too much, redundant, superfluous, unnecessary; cha b' *uilear* dhuit a bhi an so, *you would require to be here,—it were not too much for you to be here*; cha b' *uilear* dhuinn cogadh na fàilneachadh, *we were obliged to fight* or *yield. Sm.*; cha b' *uilear* dhuit sin, *you would require that,—that is necessary*; cha b' *uilear* uibhir eile, *as much again is requisite.*

Uilebheist for Ullabheist, monster.

Uile-bheannaichte, ŭ'l′-â-v*h*yánn-ėch tyȧ, *adj.* truly blessed, all holy, completely blessed.

Uile-bhuadhach, ŭ'l′-â-vhŭă-ghach, *adj.* all-victorious, triumphant, victorious.

Uil'-fhiosrach, ŭ'l′-ės-rach, *a.* omniscient.

Uil'-fhiosrachd, ŭ'l′-ės-rachg, *n. m.* omniscience.

Uil'-fhoghainteachd, ŭ'l′-om′-ėnn-tyachg, *n. f.* all-sufficiency; *uil'-fhoghainteach, all-sufficient.*

Uil'-iomlaineachd, ŭ'l′-ėm-lan-achg, *n. f* all-sufficiency, full perfection *or* completeness.

Uil'-iomlan, ŭ'l′-ėm-lán, *adj.* all-perfect.

Uil'-ionadach, ŭ'l′-ĕŭn-ad-ach, *adj.* omnipresent; tha Dia *uil'-ionadach, God is omnipresent.*

Uill, ûlly', *v.* oil, grease, besmear.

Uilleadh, úlly′-Ă, *n. m.* lamp-oil; *pt.* oiling.

Uilleag, uėlly′-ag, *n. f.* a jostle, elbowing.

Uilleagaich, ŭėlly′-ag-ėch, *v.* jostle, elbow.

Uilleann, ŭlly″-unn, *n. m.* honey-suckle. *MS. H.*; *pl.* elbows; see Uileann.

Uillich, ŭlly″-ėch, *v.* oil; *ùillichte, oiled.*

Uillidh, ûlly′-ė, *adj.* oily, greasy.

Uillt, ûėlljt; see àllt, mountain stream.

Uillne, uėly′-nyȧ, *gen.* of Uileann, elbow

Uillnich, ŭlly″-nyėch, *v.* jostle, elbow.

Uilt, ŭlljt, *gen. pl.* of Alt, a joint.

Uime, ŭėm′-ȧ, (*pre. pro.*) about, *or* around him, *or* it; agus chuir iad *uime* aodach purpuir, *and they put on him a purple robe. B.*; of, *or* concerning him, *or* it; cia *uime, about whom*, or *concerning which*; properly ioma. *Islay*; *ioma*-sin, *therefore, for that reason.*

Uimpe, ŭėmp′-ȧ, (*pro. pre.*) about her *or* it.

Uine, ûėn′-ȧ, *n. f.* time, season, space, *or* interval, leisure; *uine* thrì làithean, *the space of three days*; caith t' *uine, pass your time, mispend your time*; ar n-*uine* a' ruith air sgiathaibh, *our time fleeting on wings. Ossian*; 'nuair a bhios *ùine* agam, *when I have leisure.*

Uinich, ûėn′-ėch, *n. f.* bustle, fumbling.

Uinneag, ŭėnn′-ag, *n. f.* window; *uinneagan, windows*; *uinneagan* Nèimh, *the windows of Heaven.*

Uinneagachadh, ŭĕnn′-ag-ach-Ă, *n. m.* dawn; *pt.* dawning.

Uinneagaich, ŭĕnn′-ag-ėch, *v.* dawn, begin to dawn; 'nuair a bha an latha ag *uinneagachadh, when the day began to dawn.*

Uinnean, uĕnn′-un, *n. m.* an onion; corn on the foot.

Uinnlean, uėnn′-llyun, *pl.* of uileann, elbows; properly ùillean.

Uinnsich, uėnnsh′-ėch, *v.* manage. *H. S.*

Uinnse, ŭėnnsh′-ȧ, *n. f.* ash-tree; an ash.

Uinnseann, ŭėnn′-shyunn, *n. m.* wood of the ash-tree.

Uipear for Uaipear, bungler, botcher.

Uipinn, ŭėp′-ėnn, *n. f.* hoard, maoin.

Uir, ûėr', *n. f.* mould, dust, earth, grave; cáirich 'san *ùir, bury, inter*; letter U; fo'n *ùir, in the dust, in the grave*; *ùir*-chòmhnuidh, *tomb. Ossian.*

Uircean, uĕrk′ ăĕn, (oircean), grice.

Uire, ûer″-à, *deg.* of ùr, newer, fresher.

Uiread, ûer″-ud, *n. f.* degree of newness.

Uiread for Urad, as much as.

Uireall, ûer″-all, *n. m.* a ferule, a ring.

Uireallach, ûer″-all-ach, *n. m.* a dagger; dirk.

Uireas, ŭer″-as, *n. f.* want, necessary, family *or* domestic necessary; a maim; a' dol air son *uireasan, going for little family necessaries.*

Uireasach, uer″-as-ach, *adj.* indispensable, very much wanted; ni *uireasach, a thing very much wanted*; defective, maimed, lame; duine *uireasach, a maimed person*; làmh *uireasach, a defective hand, a maimed hand.*

Uireasaich, ŭer′-as-ėch, *n. f.* want, necessary; *uireasaich* 'sam bith a th' ort, *any necessary you want*; dè th' ad *uireasaich, what do you want? what do you lack?* defect, maim, deficiency; dé iad na h-*uireasaichean* a tha dhìth ort, *what are the necessaries you want?*

Uireasuidh, **Uireasbhuidh**, ŭer″-as-ė, *n. f.* want; in *Irish*, uireasbadh, defect, deficiency.

Uirigeoll, } ŭer′-′ėg-all, *n. m.* eloquence,
Uirgheol, } talk, conversation, utterance, speech; cha'n'eil càinnt na *uirigioll* ann am bheul, *there is neither language or speech in my lips. Oss.*

Uirich, **Uirigh**, uer′-ėch, *n. f.* pallet, couch; na laidhe air *uirich, stretched on a pallet.*

Uiridh, ŭer″-ė, *n. f.* last year, (*i. e.* an uair a ruith, the time that has elapsed); an *uiridh, last year*; ma'n am so an *uiridh, about this time last year*; am bliadhna 's an *uiridh, this and last year.*

Uirigh, ŭer′-ėch; see Uirich, couch.

Uirlios, ŭer′-llės, *n. m.* walled garden. *Ir.*

Uirsgeul, ur′-skell, *n. m.* news, intelligence, tale, fable, novel, romance; blarney.

Uirsgeulach, uer′-skell-ach, *a.* fabulous.

Uis, ûsh, *n. f.* courteous reception, hospitality carried to excess almost; unnecessary hurry-burry at one's reception; 's ann rompa bha an *ùis, they met with a most courteous reception.*

Uis, ûsh, *n.f.* use, (feum, properly). *Mainland.*

Uislealachd, ûsh′-all-achg, *n. f.* courtesy, courteousness, highest degree of hospitality;—usefulness, *Mainland*; dignity, *Macdonald*; snugness, comfort, *Irish.*

Uiseil, ûsh′-al, *adj.* courteous, kind, hospitable in the highest degree imaginable; gu *ùiseil, entertained with the utmost hospitality and courtesy*; *ùiseil* aca, *entertained in the politest and most hospitable manner by them,—useful, Mainland*; snug, dignified. *Md.*; *Irish.*

Uiseag, ŭsh′-ag, *n. f.* a lark, skylark.

Uisge, ŭshg′-à, *n. m.* water, rain; billow, a wave; fo'n *uisge, under water, immersed*; th' an t-*uisge* ann, *it is raining*; dh' éirich *uisge, a billow* or *surge arose*; a river, stream; mar *uisge* balbh a ghlinne, *like the smooth stream of the valley*; *uisge*-beatha, *whisky, aquavitæ*; *uisge*-coisrig, *holy* or *consecrated water.*

Uisgeachadh, ŭshg′-ach-Ă, *pt.* raining, watering; ag *uisgeachadh* na talmhainn, *watering the earth, Bible*; *n. m.* irrigation, *or* watering of land.

Uisgealachd, ushg′-al-achg, *n. f.* wateriness.

Uisgeil, ŭshg′-al, *adj.* watering, irrigating.

Uisgichte, ŭshg′-ėch-tyà, *pt.* watered, irrigated.

Uisgidh, ŭshg′-ė, *adj.* watery, waterish.

Uisgidheachd, same as uisgealachd.

Uisinnich, ŭsh′-ėnn-ėch, *v.* use, cleachd.

Uisliginn, ŭsh′-lyė′-gėnn, *n. f.* confusion. *Gillies.*

Uislinn, ŭsh′-llyėnn, *n. f.* sport. *H. S. D.*

Uist, ŭėshjt, *Inter.* hist! silence! hold your peace! not a word!! hush!

Ula, ŭl′-à, *n. m.* a beard. *Smith's Poems*; long grass. *Ossian*; heavy curled hair. *Armstrong.*

Ulag, ŭ'll′-ag, *n. f.* a block, a pulley.

Ulaidh, ŭll′-ė, *n. f.* a hid treasure; darling.

Ulainn, ŭll′-ėnn, *n. m.* charnel-house. *Ir.*

Ulartaich, ŭl′-artt′-ech, *n. f.* howling, wailing.

Ullabheist, ŭll′-a-v*h*āshjt, *n. f.* a monster.

Ullabheisteil, ull′-a-vhăshjt-al, *adj.* monstrous.

Ullachadh, } ŭll′-ach-adh, (from ull-
Ulmhachadh, } amh), *pt.* dressing, making ready; *n. m.* preparation, act of appointing, *or* making a provision.

Ullaich, ûll′-ėch, *v,* prepare, make ready provide; *ûllaichibh* bhur cridhe a chum an Tighearn, *prepare your hearts unto the Lord. Bible*; ullmhaich.

Ullamhachd, ull′-ur-achg, *n. m.* preparedness, readiness, proneness, completion.

Ullamh, ŭll′-uv, *adj.* ambidexterous, prepared, ready, very ready, prone; is *ullamh* le neach, *one is prone* or *ready*; airgiod *ullamh, cash, ready money.*

Ullamh, ŭll′-uv, *n. m.* (uile-lamh, ambidexterous), a Doctor of Medicine, a sage; an t-*ullamh* Iolach is an t-*ullamh* Muileach, *the Islay and the Mull doctors of* *the name of Beaton,** *far-famed for their learning.*

Ullamhaich, ùll'-vhèch, *v.* same as ùllaich.

Ultach, ŭll'-tach, *n. m.* a burden for one's back; *ultach* a dhroma, *as much as he can carry on his back*; *a bundle, faggot,* or *truss, fit to be carried on the back*; (ullamhtach)—in *Perthshire*, a burden between the hands, *or* in the grasp.

Ultach, ŭll'-tach, *n. m.* an Ulster man. *Irish.*

Umad, ŭm'-ad, (*pre. pro.*), about thee, concerning thee, in reference to thee; tilg t'-fhallainn *umad, throw* or *cast your mantle about thee. B.*; a labhairt *umad, speaking about thee,—in reference to thee.*

Umaibh, ŭm'-ėv, (*pre. pro.*), about you, in reference to you, *or* regarding you; concerning you, (ioma *and* sibh); cuiribh *umaibh, cast about you*; labhairt *umaibh, speaking concerning,* or *in reference to you.*

Umaidh, corruption of Umbaidh.

Umaillt, ŭm'-alljt, *n. f.* a degrading submission of one's judgment to curry favour; obsequiousness.

Umailltеach, ûm'-alljt-ach, *adj.* meanly submissive to curry favour; fawning.

Umainn, ŭm'-ènn, (*pre. pro.*), about us, concerning us, &c.; dh' iadh iad *umainn, they surrounded us. Ossian*; ag radh *umainn, saying in reference to us,* or *concerning us.*

Umam, ŭm'-am, (*pre. pro.*), about *or* regarding me; 'n ann *umam*-sa? *is it about me? is it in reference to me?*

Umbadail, ŭm'-ad-al, *adj.* very stupid.

Umbaidh, ûmb'-ė, *n. m.* a blockhead, dolt.

Umh, ŭv, *n. m.* brass *or* copper. *Ir.*; *Bible.*

Umhadair, ŭv'-ăd-âėr, *n. m.* brazier.

Umhail, un²' ul, *n. f.* heed, attention, consideration; na biodh *umhail* agad da, *never mind him, take no heed, pay no regard or attention to him*; gun *umhail* do'n lot na chliabh fèin, *regardless of the wound in his own side*; half-suspicion; chuir mi an *umhail, I half-suspected*; dè'n *umhail* a th'agadsa, *what do you care? what matters it to you?*

Umhail, } ŭ'-ul, *adj.* obedient, submissive,
Umhal, } lowly, humble; cho *umhail* ris a luch fo ladhar a chaoit, *as submissive as the mouse under the paw of the cat*; *umhail* an cridhe, *lowly in spirit*; *umhail* do lagh, *obedient to law. Bible.*

Umhaillt; see ùmaillt.

Umhlachd, ûll'-achg, *n. f.* obeisance, salutation, homage; dean t' *ùmhlachd, make your obeisance, make homage*; obedience, submissiveness; *ùmhlachd* a chreididh, *the obedience of faith. Bible*; rinn e *ùmhlachd* dhà, *he saluted him, he made his obeisance, he bowed to him.*

Umhlaich, ûll' ėch, *v.* submit, obey, make humble *or* submissive to rule.

Umpa, ŭmp'-a, (*pre. pro.*) about them, in reference to them, concerning them; *iompa*, properly labhair e *iompa, he spoke in reference to them.*

Umpaidh, *Irish* for Umbaidh.

Ung, ûng, *v.* anoint, oil; dh' *ùng* thu mo cheann, *thou hast anointed my head. Bible*; *ùngte, anointed, oiled.*

Ungadh, ûng'-Ă, *n. f.* ointment, unction.

Unnlar, ûnn'-lar, *n. m.* floor, layer, course.

Unnsa, ûss'-à, *n. m.* an ounce; *Welsh*, uns.

Untas, ŭnt'-as, *n. m.* windlass. *Irish.*

Up, ŭp, for Ut, push, jostle, shove.

Uprait, corruption of ùbarraid, confusion, &c.

Ur, ûr, *adj.* new, fresh, recent; a ghealach *ùr, the new moon*; sgadan *ùr*, im *ùr, a fresh herring, fresh butter*; novel, curious; ni sam bith *ùr, any thing novel* or *curious*; as-*ùr, a second time, again, anew, afresh*; thòisich iad as-*ùr, they commenced anew*; trusgan *ùr, new suit of clothes*; oiteag *ùr* nan sliabh, *the fresh breeze of the mountains. Oss.*; *ùr* nomha, *quite new*; sgaoil cuirm as *ùr, the feast was spread a second time. Bible, Ossian*; *adv.* afresh, newly, second time; dh'*ùr* thoisich iad, *they have newly begun.*

Ur, ur, for bhur, your; togaibh *'ur* siuil, tàirnibh *'ur* ràimh, *hoist your sails, pull with your oars. Song.* See Ar.

Urabhallach, ŭr'-a-vhăll-ach, *n. f.* the herb devil's-bit. *Irish.*

Urach, ŭr'-ach, *n. m.* bottle, pail. *Irish*; *gen.* of ùir, mould, soil, earth; a' bùrrach

---

* A succession of an order of literati of the name of Beaton, styled Ullamh and Oileamh, existed in Islay and Mull from time immemorial, till the middle of the last century. Doctor Hector Beaton, one of them, got, as a reward, for effecting a cure which baffled the then Faculty of Edinburgh, in the case of one of the Jameses, Kings of Scotland, two farms in Islay. John, the last of the Mull Doctors, has a handsome tombstone in Iona, with a Latin inscription, running thus:—

"Hic jacet Johannis Betonus, Mac
lenorum familiæ, Medicus
qui mortuus est 19 Novembris, 1657,
Æt. 63. Donaldus Betonus fecit 1674,
Ecce cadit jaculo victricis mortis iniquæ
Qui alios solverat ipse mali.
Soli Deo Gloria."

All the proverbs current in the Islands, end thus:—"Mu'n d'thuirt an t-Ullamh Iolach e;—mu'n d'thuirt an t-Ullamh Muileach e," *as the Islay sage used to say;—as the Mull sage used to say*; (an leanabh Iolach, in *Skye.*) *Sm., Is., Armst.*

na h-*ùrach, stirring up the mould* or *earth.*

Urachadh, ûr'-ach-ă, *pt.* renewing, refreshing; *n. m.* refreshment, renewal, recommencement.

Urachd, ûr'-achg, *n.f.* newness, novelty.

Urad, ŭr'-add', *n. m. adv.* equal quantity, *or* number; so much; *urad* is *urad, equal shares, like quantities*; *urad* eile, *as much again*; *urad* a bhidhich, *so much as a meal of meat.*

Uraich, ûr'-èch, *v.* renew, become fresh *or* green; dh' *ùraich* e mo chràdh, *he renewed my torment*; ach ch'an *ùraich* mo gheug, *but my branch shall never become green,* or *bud. Sm.*; *v. a.* refresh, invigorate; dh' *ùraich* an deoch e, *the potions refreshed him, invigorated him.*

Urail, ûr'-al, } *adj.* fresh-looking, as a
Urair, ûr'-ur, } person; flourishing, green, gay; 'san iarmailt *ùrair, in the freshly green firmament*; a choillteach *ùrair, the green woodland.*

Uraireachd, ûr'-ur'-achg, } *n.f.* freshness,
Uralachd, ûr'-al-achg, } youthfulness, as an aged person.

Uranach, ûr'-an-ach, *n. c.* an upstart.

Urball, ŭrb'-all, *n. m.* a tail, a train.

Urchaill, ŭr'-chally', *n. f.* fetters; chain. *Irish*; mould-board of a plough. *N.*;—*W.*, urchair.

Urchair, ŭr'-char', *n.f.* a shot; leig *urchair, fire, shoot at*; a throw, cast, violent push *or* jostle; *urchair* cloiche, a *stone-cast, throw at a stone, hammer,* &c.; beul ri *urchair* gunna air folbh, *about a gun-shot off*; thug e *urchair* dha, *he gave him* or *it a violent push* or *throw*; mould-board of a plough. *West.*

Urchasg, ŭr'-chasg, *n. m.* antidote. *Irish*; physic. *North.*

Urchoid, ŭrch'-oj, *n. f.* harm; calamity. *Bible*; *Psalm-book*;—(obsolete.)

Urla, ûrl'-a, *n. m.* face *or* front. *Ossian*; (obsolete.)

Ur-labhairt, ûr'-lláv-arjt, *n. f.* eloquence. *Macfarlan.*

Urlaim, ûr'-lláèm, *n. f.* readiness. *M'F.*

Urlaimh, ûr'-llév, *adj.* neat, ready. *M'F.*

Urlann, ŭr'-lánn, *n. f.* a sort of staff. *M'F.*

Urlar, ûr'-lăr, *n. m.* floor; air an *ùrlar, on the floor*; a layer, *or* course, vein, as in a mine; cuir *urlar* ma seach 'san dunan, *put a layer,* or *course about in the dung-hill*; properly Unnlar.

Urloinn, ûr'-llaŏènn, *n. f.* beauty. *MSS.*; fore part *or* prow of a ship. *Mackenzie.*

Urnuich, ûrn'-èch, } prayer to God;
Urnuigh, ûrn'-è, *n f.* } dean *ùrnuigh, pray*; uime sin fhuair do sheirbhiseach 'na chridhe an *ùrnuigh* so a dheanadh riut, *therefore thy servant hath found in his heart to pray* (make) *this prayer unto thee.* Sam. vii. 27.; ag *ùrnuigh, praying.*

Urr, *n. m.* a child, infant. *Perthshire.*

Urra, ŭrr'-à, *n. f.* a personage; ann an tigh *urra* mhòir, *in a great personage's house*; author, authority; cò 's *urra* dhuit, *who is your authority?* cha'n'eil sgeul gun *urra* agam, *my version of the story is not without authority* or *author*; owner, proprietor; cò 's *urra* dha so, *who is owner* or *proprietor of this?* cha robh caora riamh gun *urra, a sheep never wanted an owner*; *adj.* able, capable; na b' *urra* mi, *were I able, were I capable*; ma's *urra* mise, *if I can.*

Urra, ŭrr'-a, (*pre. pro.*), on her, owed by her, the matter with her, ailing her; dé th' *urra, what is the matter with her?—what ails her?* dè th' agad *urra, how much does she owe you?* of her, wanted by her; greim *urra, a hold of her*; a dhìth *urra, wanted by her.*

Urrach, ŭrr'-ach, *n. m.* power, ability. *Perthshire.*

Urrachd, ŭrr'-achg, *n. m.* dependance, reliance; cha ruig thu leas *urrachd* a dheanadh as an sin, *you need not put any reliance in that,—place no dependance on that*: an *urrachd* riutsa, *relying on you*; an *urrachd* a chosnaidh, *depending on his daily labour* or *industry*; am *urrachd*-sa, *in dependance on me*; in *Perthshire,* urrach;—cha'n 'eil mi am *urrach, I am not able*; corrupted, murrach.

Urrainn, ŭrr'-ènn, *n.* and *adj.* ability, power, author; cha'n'eil mi am *urrainn, I am not fit, I am not able*; an *urrainn* iad, *are they able?* ni mi na's *urrainn* mi, *I will do all I am capable of doing,—all I can*; an *urrainn* sin a bhi, *is it possible? can that be?*

Urrail, ŭrr'-al, *adj.* self-sufficient.

Urralachd, ŭrr'-all-achg, *n. f.* self-sufficiency.

Urram, ŭrr'-am, *n. f.* respect, reverence, deference; na meadhon bha *urram* do'n rìgh, *in their midst was reverence to the king. Oss.*; air son *urram* do d' t' fhacalsa, *out of deference to your word*; dignity, honour; uaitse tha teachd saibhreas agus *urram, from thee proceed both riches and honour. B.*; precedence, superiority, preference; bheir mi an *urram* dhuit thar na choinnic mi, *I will give you preference above all I ever saw,—you excel all I ever saw*; an *urram* do'n loach, *precedence to the hero*! a toirt *urram, giving honour. Bible.*

Urramach, ŭrr'-am-ach, *adj.* honourable, respectable, reverend, powerful, dignified, worshipful, distinguished; honorary; ball *urràmach, an honorary mem-*

her; principal; sibhse a's urramaiche do'n treud, *you which are the principal of the flock?* respectful, submissive; tha ainm *urramach, his name is reverenced, is distinguished*; rinn è gu h-*urramach, he did it masterly,—he did it in a respectable manner.*

URRAMACHD, ŭrr'-am-achg, *n. f* honourableness, reverence, respectability, homage.

URRAMAICH, ŭrr'-am-èch, *v.* reverence, distinguish, honour, revere, respect.

URRANTA, urr'-annt-à, *adj.* self-sufficient, self-important; confident in strength *or* capacity; bold.

URRANTACHD, ŭrr'-annt-achg, *n. f.* self-sufficiency, self-confidence, audacity, presumption.

URRAS, ŭrr'-as, *n. c.* surety, security, bail, cautioner, warrant; cò thèid an *urras* ort, *who will become security,* or *cautioner,* or *bail for you?* thèid mise an *urras* ortsa, *I can assure, I will warrant you*; ma tha thu an *urras, if you are surety. B.*; cha'n fheàrr an t-*urras* na'n t-earras, *the security* or *bail is not a whit better than the principal*; cha'n'eil *urras* a dhìth orm, *I want no security* or *surety.*

URRASACH, ŭrr'-as-ach, *adj.* secure, sure.

URRASACHD, ŭrr'-as-achg, *n. f.* trust-worthiness; assumption.

URRASAICH, ŭrr'-as-èch, *v.* insure.

URRASAIL, ŭrr'-as-al, *adj.* confident, secure.

URRASAIR, ŭrr'-as-ăèr, *n. m.* insurer.

URSANN, ŭrr'-sènn, *n. f.* door-post, pillar of a gate; door-cheek; *ursannan, door-posts,* or *pillars of a gate.*

URUISG, ûrr'-èshg, *n. f.* a hobgoblin; bòchdan, *Perthshire*; a savage, ugly-looking fellow. *West.*

US, ŭss, *n. m.* impudence, presumption; na biodh a dh' *uss* agad, *presume not, dare not.*

USA, ŭs'-a, *for* asa *or* fasa, (*deg.* furasd.)

USAID, ŭs'-ăj, *n. f.* querulousness; aptness to complain with any, *or* for a very slight reason.

USAIDEACH, ŭs'-aj-ach, *adj.* querulous; too apt to complain; querimonious.

USAIDEACHD, ŭs'-ăj-achg, *n. f.* querulousness; aptness to complain, *or* to weep for little or no reason; querimoniousness.

USGAR, ŭsg'-ur, *n. f.* a jewel, gem; any ornament, necklace, bracelet. *Bible*; *Ir.*

USGARAICHE, ŭsg'-ur-èch-à, *n. m.* a jeweller.

USPAIR, ŭsp'-ăèr, *n. m.* lumpish fellow. *H. Society.*

UT! UT! ŭt, ut, *Inter.* tut! tut! don't!

UT, ŭtt', *v.* push, shove, jostle; dh' *ut* e bhuaidh e, *he pushed him away from him*; *ut* i, *shove her.*

UTAG, ŭtt''-ag, shove, push, jostle.

UTAIG, ûtt''-ăèg, *n. f.* strife, outrage, hubbub, row; lumber, confusion.

UTAIGEACH, ûtt'-ăèg-ach, *adj.* turbulent.

UTAIGEACHD, ût'-áèg-achg, *n. f.* turbulence.

UTAN, ût'-an, knuckle. *Irish*; riuidean.

UTARRAS, ûtt'-arr-as, *n. m.* confused heap *or* mass; romping; lumber, confusion; annoyance, molestation, fidgeting.

UTARRASACH, ûtt''-arr-as-ach, *a.* confused, romping, full of lumber, unsettled.

UTH, û, (*or* ùgh, properly); udder; *ùth, or ùgh* boine, *cow's udder.*

UTHACHD, û*h*'-achg, *n. f.* suicide; thug e *uthachd* dha fhéin, *he committed suicide, he was the cause of his own death, manslaughter*; bheir e *uthachd* dhuit, *he will do away with your life.*

UTHACHDAIL, û*h*'-achg-al, *a.* suicidical.

UTHARD, ŭ'-ard, *adv.* above, as cionn.

UTHNA, ŭ*h*n'-a, *n. f.* the surname Unity.

UTRAS, contraction of ùtarras, confusion.

A CHRIOCH.

ENGLISH-GAELIC DICTIONARY

ENGLISH-GAELIC DICTIONARY

COMPILED BY

John Mackenzie

(This work formed Part II
of MacAlpine's *Pronouncing
Gaelic Dictionary*)

GAIRM PUBLICATIONS
29 Waterloo Street
Glasgow
1979

SBN 901771 19 8

Printed in Great Britain by
ROBERT MACLEHOSE AND CO LTD
Printers to the University of Glasgow

AN

ENGLISH-GAELIC DICTIONARY.

A, *s.* Ceud litir na h-aibidil.
ABACK, *adv.* Air ais.
ABACUS, *s.* Clàr-cunntais; clach-mhullaich.
ABAFT, *adv.* A dh'ionnsaidh an deiridh.
ABAISANCE, *s.* Umhlachd.
ABALIENATE, *v. a.* Thoir thairis do chòir do neach eile.
ABANDON, *v. n.* Fàg, dìobair, tréig.
ABANDONED, *part.* Tréigte.
ABASE, *v. a.* Ìslich, cuir sìos.
ABASED, *part.* Islichte.
ABASEMENT, *s.* Ìsleachadh, irioslachadh, leagail sìos; eas-urram, tàir.
ABASH, *v. a.* Nàraich, athaich.
ABASHMENT, *s.* Breisleachadh, ioghnadh.
ABATE, *v. a.* and *n.* Lughdaich, beagaich.
ABATEMENT, *s.* Lughdachadh, ìsleachadh.
ABBA, *s.* Athair (facal Eabhrach).
ABBACY, *s.* Sealbh, a bhuineas do dh'-aba.
ABBESS, *s.* Ban-aba.
ABBEY, *s.* Abaid, taigh-mhanach.
ABBOT, *s.* Aba.
ABBREVIATE, *v. a.* Giorrach.
ABBREVIATION, *s.* Giorrachadh.
ABBREVIATURE, *s.* Comharradh giorrachaidh.
ABDICATE, *v. a.* Leig dhìot do chòir.
ABDICATION, *s.* Toirt suas, tréigsinn.
ABDITORY, *s.* Ionad falaich.
ABDOMEN, *s.* Iochdar a' chuirp.
ABDOMINAL, *adj.* A bhuineas do'n bhroinn.
ABDOMINOUS, *adj.* Bronnach.
ABDUCE, *v. a.* Cuir o chéile.
ABDUCTION, *s.* Toirt air falbh.
ABECEDARIAN, *s.* Fear-teagaisg na h-aibidil.
ABEARANCE, *s.* Giùlan, iomchar
ABED, *adv.* Air leabaidh.
ABERRANCE, *s.* Seachran o'n t-slighe cheart.
ABERRANT, *adj.* Seachranach.
ABET, *v. a.* Brosnaich, cuidich.
ABETMENT, *s.* Brosnachadh, cuideachadh.
ABETTOR, *s.* Fear-brosnachaidh.
ABEYANCE, *s.* Dlighe laghail àraidh.
ABGREGATE, *v. a.* Tearbadh.
ABHOR, *v. a.* Sgreataich, oilltich.
ABHORRENCE, *s.* Sgreamh, dù-ghràin.
ABHORRENT, *adj.* Fuathach, gràineil.
ABHORRENTLY, *adv.* Gu sgreataidh.
ABHORRING, *s.* Geur-fhuathachadh.
ABIDE, *v. a.* and *n.* Fan, fuirich.
ABIDING, *v.* Fuireach, fantainn, tàmh.
ABJECT, *adj.* Suarach, dìblidh, bochd, truaillidh, tàireil, meallta.
ABJECTION, *s.* Mìotharachd aignidh, no inntinn, suarachas, tràillealachd.
ABILITY, *s.* Comas, cumhachd, &c.
ABILITIES, *s.* Càileachd, comas-inntinn.
ABJUDICATED, *part. adj.* Air a thoirt le breth, o aon neach do neach eile.
ABJUDICATION, *s.* Diùltadh.
ABJUGATE, *v. a.* Fuasgail, saor.
ABJURATION, *s.* Mionnachadh nach deanar ni àraidh; àicheadh. Abjuration oath, *Cùl-mhionnan.*
ABJURE, *v. a.* Cùl-mhionnaich; tréig do bharail.
ABLATION, *s.* Tabhairt air falbh.
ABLATIVE, *adj.* A bheir air falbh.
ABLE, *adj.* Comasach, teòma, sgileil.
ABLE-BODIED, *adj.* Corp-làidir, Treun.

Ablegate, *v. a.* Cuir air theachdaireachd.

Ablepsy, *s.* Doille, cion-fradhairc

Abligate, *v. a.* Ceangail suas.

Ablocation, *s.* Suidheachadh, no leigeil a mach air mhàl.

Abluent, *adj.* Ionnladach, nighteach.

Ablution, *s.* Ionnlad, glanadh; saoradh o chiont.

Abnegate, *v. a.* Àicheadh, diùlt, seachain.

Abnegation, *s.* Àicheadh, diùltadh.

Aboard, *adv.* Air bòrd luinge.

Abode, *s.* Àite còmhnaidh.

Abolish, *v. a.* Thoir thairis; cuir as.

Abolishable, *adj.* A dh' fhaodar a chur as, no a sgrios.

Abolition, *s.* Sgaoileadh, atharrachadh, sgrios.

Abominable, *adj.* Gràineil, fuathor.

Abominableness, *s.* Gràinealachd.

Abominate, *v. a.* Fhuathaich, oilltich.

Abomination, *s.* Gràinealachd, dùghrain.

Aborigines, *s.* Prìomh-mhuinntir.

Abortion, *s.* Torrachas anabaich,

Abortive, *adj.* Anabaich, neo-inbheach.

Above, *prep.* Os-ceann, a bhàrr.

Above, *adv.* Shuas, gu h-àrd.

Above All, *ad.* Os bàrr, gu h-àraidh.

Above-Board, *ad.* Os ceann bùird.

Abound, *v. n.* Fas lìonmhor sìolmhor.

About, *prep.* Mu, mu 'n cuairt, dlù, *About ten thousand*, mu dheich mìle; *They were speaking about you*, bha iad a bruidhinn mu d' dhéibhinn; *About him*, uime, mu'n cuairt da, mu 'thimchioll, mu'dhéibhinn; *aboutthem*, umpa, mu'n cuairt daibh; *about her*, uimpe, mu'n cuairt d'i, mu 'déibhinn, mu 'timchioll; *about whom?* cia uime?

About, *adv.* An cuairt, gu cruinn, gu timchiollach. Ceithirthimchioll, mu'n cuairt; fagus air; air tì, a dol a', gu; timchioll, toirt gu crìch; gu buil, gu teachd; ag iarraidh.

Abrade, *v.a.* Suath dheth, suath air falbh.

Abreast, *adv.* Uchd ri uchd.

Abridge, *v a.* Giorraich, lughdaich.

Abridged, *part.* Giorraichte.

Abroad, *adv.* Mu sgaoil; a muigh, a mach; air aineol, an tìr chéin; an tìr thall. gu, no do, thìr chéin; air gach taobh; an leth muigh.

Abrogate, *v. a.* Cuir lagh air chùl, cuir a leth-taobh.

Abrupt, *adj.* Cas, corrach, creagach; aithghearr, grad, cabhagach, gun uidheamachadh; briste.

Abruption, *s.* Grad-bhriseadh.

Abruptness, *s.* Cabhag, caise, corrachas, bristeachd.

Abscess, *s.* Neasgaid, at, iongrachadh.

Abscind, *v. a.* Gearr dheth, gearr air falbh.

Abscission, *s.* Gearradh dheth, sgudadh.

Abscond, *v. a.* and *n.* Falaich thu féin, teich air fògradh.

Absconder, *s.* Fògarach, fear-cùirn.

Absence, *s.* Neo-làthaireachd; neoaireachail.

Absent, *adj.* Neo-làthaireach, neoaireach, smuain-sheachranach.

Absent, *v. a.* Rach o'n taigh, cùm air falbh.

Absentee, *s.* Neach a ta air falbh o 'dhùthaich.

Absinthiated, *part.* Searbhaichte.

Absinthium, *s.* Lŭs-nam-biast.

Absist, *v. n.* Seas air falbh, leig dhìot.

Absolvatory, *adj.* A mhathas lochd.

Absolve, *v. a.* Saor, math, fuasgail o, crìochnaich, co-lion.

Absolver, *s.* Neach a ghabhas air féin peacadh a mhathadh.

Absolute, *adj.* Iomlan, co-lion: saor, gun chumha; neo-cheannsaichte, neo-cheangailte.

Absoluteness, *s.* Iomlanachd, dligheachas, fuasgailteachd, àrd-chumhachd.

Absolution, *s.* Saoradh, mathanas, fuasgladh.

Absolutory, *adj.* A shaoras, a dh' fhuasglas, a mhathas.

Absonant, *adj.* Mì-chéillidh, baoth.

Absonous, *adj.* Neo-bhinn, searbhghuthach, searbh-ghlŏireach.

Absorb, *v. a.* Sluig, deothail, òl.

Absorbent, *adj.* A shluigeas, a shùghas, a dh-òlas.

Absorbent, *s.* Leigheas sùghaidh, a thiormaicheas leanntaidhean a' chuirp.

Absorpt, *part.* Sluigte, sùghte sìos.

Absorption, *s.* Tiormachadh, sùghadh, slugadh.

Abstain, *v. a.* Seachain, seun, fàg; na gabh, àicheadh dhut féin.

Abstemious, *adj.* Stuama, measarra.

Abstemiousness, *s.* Stuaim, measarrachd.

Absterge, *v. a.* Glan-shuath, suathghlan.

Abstergent, *adj.* A sealbhachadh nàdur glanaidh.

Abstinence, *s.* Measarrachd, stuamachd.

Abstinent, *adj.* Stuama, measarra.

Abstract, *v. a.* As-tharruinn; tarruinn a bhrìgh ás, thoir a shùgh as; dealaich beachdan na h-inntinn o chéile.

Abstract, *adj.* Eadar-dhealaichte, sgairte; dorch, deacair r'a thuigsinn; neo-mheasgaichte.

Abstract, *s.* As-tarruinn suim aith-ghearr, brigh; sùmhlachadh, aith-ghiorrachadh.

Abstraction, *s.* Dealachadh, eadar-dhealachadh, brìgh-tharruinn; neo-aire do nithibh 's an làthair.

Abstruse, *adj.* Doilleir, falachaidh, do-thuigsinn, deacair.

Abstruseness, *s.* Doilleireachd, doimh-neachd, deacaireachd.

Absurd, *adj.* Amaideach, baoth.

Absurdity, *s.* Amaideachd, baogh-altas, faoinealachd.

Absurdly, *adv.* Gu mi-reusonta, mi-chiallach, gòrach.

Abundance, *s.* Pailteas, lìonmhorachd.

Abundant, *adj.* Pailt, saibhir, làn.

Abundantly, *adv.* Gu pailt, gu saibhir.

Abuse, *v.a.* Mi-ghnàthaich, mi-bhuilich; meall, gabh brath; thoir ana-cainnt, maslaich, trod, càin, beum.

Abuse, *s.* Mi-ghnàthachadh, mi-bhuil-eachadh, ana-caitheamh; càineadh, trod, ana-cainnt.

Abuser, *s.* Milltear, struidhear; fear-càinidh, fear ana-cainnt.

Abusive, *adj.* Millteach, strùidheil, ana-caithteach; ana-cainnteach.

Abuttal, *s.* Crìoch no iomall fearainn; sgrìobhadh anns am beil crìochan air an ainmeachadh.

Abutment, *s.* Co-chrìoch, stéidh togalach.

Abyss, *s.* Doimhneachd gun ìochdar; dubh-aigean; ifrinn.

Academic, *s.* Fòghlumach.

Academic, *adj.* A bhuineas do thaigh-fòghlum.

Academy, *s.* Àrd-sgoil.

Acates, *s.* Biadh, teachd-an-tìr.

Accede, *v. n.* Aontaich, strìochd, còrd.

Accelerate, *v. a.* Greas, luathaich.

Acceleration, *s.* Greasad, luath-achadh.

Accent, *s.* Fuaim, fonn, blas cainnte, pong-labhairt.

Accept, *v. a.* Gabh.

Acceptability, *s.* Taitneachd.

Acceptable, *adj.* Taitneach.

Acceptance, *s.* Gabhail le deagh-thoil.

Access, *s.* Rathad, slighe, fosgladh.

Accessary, *s.* Fear-cuideachaidh.

Accessible, *adj*, So-ruigsinn; fosg-arra, fàilteach.

Accession, *s.* Meudachadh, cuideach-adh, leasachadh; tighinn an ceann.

Accessory, *adj.* A mheudaicheas, a chuidicheas.

Accessory, *s.* Aontachair, co-pàirt-iche ann an ciont, co-chiontaiche.

Accident, *s.* Sgiorradh, tubaist, beud.

Accidental, *adj.* Tuiteamach, tubaisteach.

Acclaim, *v. n.* Ard-mhol, dean luath-ghair.

Acclaim, *s.* Luath-ghàir.

Acclamation, *s.* Caithream éibhneis.

Acclamatory, *adj.* Luath-ghaireach, ait, éibhneach.

Acclivity, *s.* Bruthach, uchdach.

Acclivous, *adj.* Bruthachail, uchdach-ail, cas.

Accoil, *v. n.* Dòmhlaich, dùmhlaich.

Accolent, *s.* Fear-àiteachaidh chrìoch.

Accommodable, *adj.* Goireasach.

Accommodate, *v. a.* Thoir coingheall, ceartaich; réitich.

Accommodate, *adj.* Iomchuidh, cubh-aidh.

Accommodation, *s.* Freagarrachd, goireas, ceartachadh, rùm; uidheam, ullachadh; réite, socrachadh, còrdadh.

Accompanier, *s.* Fear-co-thurais.

Accompaniment, *s.* Leasachadh, ni an cois ni no neach.

Accompany, *v. a.* and *n.* Rach an cuideachd, ni no neach.

Accomplice, *s.* Fear-comuinn, pàirt-iche, co-chiontaiche.

Accomplish, *v. a.* Crìochnaich, thoir gu buil thoir gu crìch; co-lion.

Accomplished, *part. adj.* Iomlan, deas, sgiamhach, snasail, eireachdail, àlainn.

Accomplishment. Crìochnachadh, co-lionadh; sgèimhealachd, maise; cosnadh, faotainn, fòghlum.

Accomptant, *s.* Fear-cunntais.

Accord, *v. a.* and *n.* Réitich, aontaich · còrd.

Accord, *s.* Co-chòrdadh.

Accordance, *s.* Còrdadh, co-sheirm.

According, *prep.* A réir, a thaobh.

Accordingly, *adv.* Mar sin, a réir sin.

Accost, *v. a.* Cuir fàilte, fàiltich.

Accostable, *adj.* Faoilidh, furanach.

Account, *s.* Cunntas, àireamh; meas; urram, inbhe, àrd-inbhe, àirde; sgeul, tuairisgeul; rannsachadh, dearbhadh; mìneachadh, soilleireachadh

Account, *v. a.* and *n.* Meas, baralaich, smuainich; àireamh, cunnt; thoir cunntas, aithris, bi freagarrach.

Accountable, *adj.* Freagarrach, a dh'fheumas cunntas a thabhairt.

Accountableness, *s.* Freagarrachd.

Accountant, *s.* Cunntair.

Account-Book, *s.* Leabhar-cunntais.

Accoutre, *v. a.* Uidheamaich, deasaich.

Accoutrements, *s.* Armachd, uidh-eam, airneis.

Accredit, *v. a.* Guidich, dean taobh ri, thoir urram do.

ACCREDITED, *adj.* Earbsach.
ACCRESCENT, *adj.* A chinneas, a dhfhàsas suas.
ACCRETIVE, *adj.* Co-fhàsail, co-chinntinneach.
ACCROACH, *v. a.* Clic, tarruinn chugad le cromaig.
ACCRUE, *v. n.* Thig gu; éirich o, sruth o, tàrmaich.
ACCRUMENT, *s.* Meudachadh, leasachadh, fàs.
ACCUBATION, *s.* Laidhe air uilinn, sìneadh air leabaidh.
ACCUMB, *v. a.* Laidh, no sìn thu féin sìos air t-uilinn.
ACCUMBENT, *adj.* A laidheas air uilinn.
ACCUMULATE, *v. a.* Càrn suas, cruach, cruinnich, cuir r'a chéile, cnuasaich.
ACCUMULATION, *s.* Co-chruinneachadh, cur r'a chéile, càrnadh suas, cnuasachadh, trusadh.
ACCURACY, *s.* Pongalachd, dearbhachd, cinnteachd, sicireachd, soilleireachd, snasmhorachd, freagarrachd.
ACCURATE, *adj.* Pongail, neo-chearbach, cinnteach, ceart, riaghailteach, freagarrach.
ACCURATENESS, *s.* Pongalachd, eagnaidheachd, freagarrachd.
ACCURSE, *v. a.* Mallaich, dìt.
ACCURSED, *part. adj.* Mallaichte; a thoill mallachd.
ACCUSABLE, *adj.* Ri choireachadh, ri chronachadh, a thoill dìteadh.
ACCUSATION, *s.* Casaid, cùis-dhìtidh.
ACCUSATIVE, *adj.* A choiricheas, casaideach.
ACCUSATORY, *adj.* A dhìteas, a chasaideas.
ACCUSE, *v. a.* Dean casaid, dìt, gearain, coirich, tagair.
ACCUSED, *part. adj.* Coirichte.
ACCUSER, *s.* Fear-dìtidh, fear-casaid.
ACCUSTOM, *v. a.* and *n.* Cleachd, gnàthaich.
ACCUSTOMARY, *adj.* Gnàthach.
ACCUSTOMED, *adj.* A réir cleachdaidh, mar bu ghnàthach.
ACE, *s.* Aon; ni meanbh, smùirnean.
ACERB, *adj.* Searbh, geur, goirt.
ACERBATE, *v. a.* Dean searbh, geur, goirt.
ACERBITY, *s.* Blas searbh, geur, goirt.
ACERVATION, *s.* Tòrradh, càrnadh, trusadh.
ACESCENT, *adj.* A' fàs geur.
ACETOSITY, *s.* Searbhas, geurachd, goirteachd, gairgead.
ACETOUS, *adj.* Goirt, searbh, garg.
ACHE, *s.* Pian, goirteas, goimh.
ACHE, *v. n.* Tinn, cràiteach.
ACHIEVE, *v. a.* Crìochnaich gu sona, co-lion gu buadhach.
ACHIEVEMENT, *s.* Euchd, gaisge.
ACHIEVER, *s.* Gaisgeach.
ACHING, *s.* Pian, goirteas, cràdh, acaid.
ACID, *adj.* Geur, goirt, searbh, garg.
ACID, *s.* Ni searbh no geur.
ACIDITY, *s.* Geurachd, searbhachd.
ACIDULATE, *v. a.* Dean searbh, garg.
ACIDULOUS, *adj.* A leth-char goirt.
ACKNOWLEDGE, *v. a.* Aidich t'eòlas air ni no neach, aidich.
ACKNOWLEDGING, *adj.* Aideachail, taingeil.
ACKNOWLEDGMENT, *s.* Aideachadh; buidheachas.
ACME, *s.* Àirde, mullach, spiris.
ACOUSTIC, *adj.* A bhuineas do chlàisdeachd.
ACOUSTICS, *s.* Iocshlaint-chluas.
ACQUAINT, *v. a.* Innis, thoir fios.
ACQUAINTABLE, *adj.* Faoilidh, fosgarra.
ACQUAINTANCE, *s.* Eòlas; fear eòlais. *pl.* luchd-eòlais.
ACQUAINTED, *adj.* Eòlach, fiosrach.
ACQUEST, *s.* Buannachd, tairbh.
ACQUIESCE, *v. n.* Co-aontaich, géill.
ACQUIESCENCE, *s.* Aontachadh, géilleadh.
ACQUIESCENT, *adj.* A cho-aontaicheas.
ACQUIRE, *v. a.* Coisinn, buannaich.
ACQUIRED, *part. adj.* Coisinnte, buannaichte.
ACQUIREMENT, *s.* Cosnadh, ionnsachadh.
ACQUIRER, *s.* Fear-buannachaidh.
ACQUISITION, *s.* Cosnadh, tairbh, buannachd.
ACQUIT, *v. a.* Fuasgail, leig fa-sgaoil.
ACQUITMENT, *s.* Fuasgladh, saoradh.
ACQUITTAL, *s.* Saoradh, glanadh o choire.
ACQUITTANCE, *s.* Sgrìobhadh fuasglaidh.
ACRE, *s.* Acair, acair-fhearainn.
ACRID, *adj.* Teith, searbh, garg, goirt.
ACRIMONIOUS, *adj.* Garg, searbh, teith.
ACRIMONY, *s.* Gargalachd, geuralachd.
ACRITUDE, *s.* Blas geur, searbh, teith.
ACRONYCAL, A laidheas, 's a dh' éireas, leis a' ghréin.
ACROSPIRE, *s.* Gucag, boinne-bàn.
ACROSS, *adv.* Tarsuinn, o thaobh gu taobh.
ACROSS, *prep.* Thar, thairis air.
ACROSTIC, *s.* Ainm-rann.
ACT, *v. a.* and *n.* Gluais, caraich; dèan, gnìomhaich, co-lion: giùlain, iomchair; aobharaich, thoir gu buil; gabh ort, cleasaich, cluich, gabh samhla ort; cuir air ghluasad.
ACT, *s.* Gnìomh, tùrn, reachd; euchd, cleas; achd, dèanadas; earrann àraidh

cluiche; sgrìobhadh achdannan lagail, reachd breithe.
ACTION, *s*. Gnìomh, tùrn, obair; cath, blàr; cùis-lagha.
ACTIONABLE, *adj*. Neo-dhligheach, buailteach do dhìteadh lagha.
ACTIVE, *adj*. Grad, ealamh, deas, fuasgailte; sùrdail, beothail, teòma, gnìomhach tapaidh.
ACTIVITY, *s*. Beothalachd, gnìomhachas.
ACTOR, *s*. Cleasaiche.
ACTRESS, *s*. Bana-chleasaiche.
ACTUAL, *adj*. Cinnteach, dearbhta, fìor.
ACTUARY, *s*. Cléireach cùirte.
ACTUATE, *v. a*. Brosnaich, gluais.
ACUATE, *v. a*. Geuraich, cuir air chois.
ACULEATE, *adj*. Biorach, gathach, dealgach.
ACUMEN, *s*. Rinn, geurachd; géire.
ACUMINATE, *v. n*. Fàs, no éirich suas air modh binneanach.
ACUMINATED, *adj*. Binneanach.
ACUMINATION, *s*. Rinn, binnean.
ACUTE, *adj*. Geur-thùigseach, biorach; guineach; bras, dealasach; carach; smiorail, beothail, mion.
ACUTENESS, *s*. Géire, geurachd.
ADACT, *v. a*. Greas, gluais, iomain.
ADAGE, *s*. Gnà-fhacal, sean-fhacal.
ADAMANT, *s*. Leug, clach-luachor.
ADAMANTINE, *adj*. Cruaidh-leuganta.
ADAM'S-APPLE, *s*. Meall-an-sgòrnain.
ADAPT, *v. a*. Dean freagarrach, ceart aich.
ADAPTABILITY, *s*. Freagarrachd.
ADAPTABLE, *adj*. Freagarrach.
ADAPTATION, *s*. Ceartachadh.
A-DAYS, *adv. i. e*. Now a-days, 'S an àm so; or, 'San linn so.
ADCORPORATE, *v. a*. Ceangail r'a chéile.
ADD, *v. a*. Cuir ris, meudaich, leasaich.
ADDECIMATE, *v. a*. Tog an deachamh.
ADDER, *s*. Aithir, beithir.
ADDER'S-GRASS, *s*. Lŭs-na-nathrach.
ADDER'S-WORT, *s*. Fliogh-na-nathrach.
ADDICT, *v. a*. Thoir suas thu fèin do, cleachdadh; coisrig.
ADDICTED, *adj*. Air a thoirt suas, ro dhéigheil air.
ADDITION, *s*. A cur r'a chéile, a meudachadh, a leasachadh.
ADDITIONAL, *adj*. Barrachd, tuilleadh.
ADDLE, *adj*. Breun, lobh, grod.
ADDLE, *v. a*. Dean fàs, cuir ás.
ADDLE-HEADED, *adj*. Gog-cheannach.
ADDRESS, *v. a*. Guthaich, labhair, sgrìobh.
ADDRESS, *s*. Deas-labhairt; modhalachd; sgrìobhadh seòlaidh air cùl litreach.
ADDUCE, *v. a*. Thoir air aghaidh, tagair.
ADDUCIBLE, *adj*. A ghabhas toirt air aghaidh.
ADDUCTIVE, *adj*. A bheir, suas no sìos.
ADDULCE, *v. a*. Mìslich, dean blasda.
ADEPT *s*. Fear-làn-ealanta.
ADEPT, *adj*. Oileanta, lan-eòlach.
ADEQUATE, *v. a*. Làn-shamhlaich.
ADEQUATE, *adj*. Iomchuidh, co-ionann; freagarrach.
ADEQUATENESS, *s*. Freagarrachd, co-ionannachd.
ADHERE, *v. n*. Dlù-lean, fan dìleas.
ADHERENCE, *s*. Dlù-leanailteachd.
ADHERENT, *adj*. Leanailteach.
ADHERENT, *s*. Fear-leanmhainn.
ADHESION, *s*. Leanmhainneachd.
ADHESIVE, *adj*. Leanailteach.
ADHESIVENESS, *s*. Leanailteachd.
ADHIBIT, *v. a*. Cuir gu feum, gnàthaich
ADJACENT, *adj*. Fagus, dlù.
ADJECT, *v. a* Cuir ris, leasaich, meudaich.
ADJECTION, *s*. Cur ris, meudachadh.
ADJECTIVE, *s*. Buaidh-fhacal.
ADJECTIVELY, *adv*. Mar bhuaidh-fhacal.
ADIEU, *adv*. Soraidh leat.
ADJOIN, *v. a*. Tàth, dlùthaich.
ADJOIN, *v. n*. Dlù, am fagus.
ADJOURN, *v. a*. Cuir dàil gu àm eile.
ADJOURNMENT, *s*. Dàil gu là eile.
ADJUDGE, *v. a*. Thoir còir air ni le breth laghail, thoir binn, thoir breth.
ADJUDICATION, *s*. Toirt còir le breth laghail.
ADJUGATE, *v. a*. Beartaich, cuingich.
ADJUNCT, *adj*. Aonaichte.
ADJUNCTION, *s*. Tàthadh, dlù-cheangal.
ADJUNCTIVE, *adj*. A thàthas r'a chéile.
ADJUNCTIVELY, *adv*. Air mhodh tàthaidh.
ADJUNCTLY, *adv*. An ceangal.
ADJURATION, *s*. Mionnan air son riaghailt a' leantainn.
ADJURE, *v. a*. Gabh mionnan.
ADJURER, *s*. Neach a chuireas mionnan.
ADJUST, *v. a*. Ceartaich, réitich.
ADJUSTMENT, *s*. Ceartachadh, cothromachadh.
ADJUTANCY, *s*. Dreuchd, no inbhe oifigich còmhnaidh; deagh riaghailt.
ADJUTANT, *s*. Oifigeach a ni còmhnadh ri oifigich eile.
ADMENSURATION, *s*. Tomhas.
ADMINISTER, *v. a*. Tabhair, fritheil.
ADMINISTRATION, *s*. Frithealadh, riaghladh, freasdalachadh; luchd-comhairle an rìgh, luchd-riaghlaidh, no stiùraidh na rìoghachd; uachdaranachd; taisbeanadh, tabhairt.
ADMINISTRATIVE, *adj*. Fritheilteach, a bhuilicheas, a riaghlas.
ADMINISTRATOR, *s*. Fear-riaghlaidh,

àrd-fhear comhairle ; fear a ghabh cùram ghnothaichean neach a chaochail.

Administratrix, *s.* Bana-riaghladair.

Admirable, *adj.* Ionmholta, cliùiteach.

Admirably, *adv.* Gu h-iongantach, &c.

Admiral, *s.* Ard-mharaiche, ceannard cabhlaich.

Admiralty, *s.* Luchd-riaghlaidh na cabhlaich cogaidh.

Admiration, *s.* Iongnadh, iongantas, mòr-mheas.

Admire, *v. a.* Gabh gaol no mòr-mheas air ni no neach.

Admirer, *s.* Fear-gaoil, fear-molaidh.

Admissible, *adj.* Ceadachail, a leigear a steach.

Admission, *s.* Leigeadh a steach.

Admittable, *adj.* A dh' fhaodar a leigeadh a steach, no fhulang.

Admittance, *s.* Cead, leigeadh a steach.

Admix, *v. a.* Measgaich, co-mheasgaich.

Admixture, *s.* Co-mheasgadh.

Admonish, *v. a.* Caoin-chronaich.

Admonisher, *s.* Comhairleach.

Admonition, *s.* Caoin-chronachadh.

Ado, *s.* Othail, iomairt, saothair.

Adolescency, *s,* Òg-aois, ùr-fhàs.

Adoors, *adv.* Aig an dorus.

Adopt, *v. a.* Uchd-mhacaich.

Adoption, *s.* Uchd-mhachdachadh.

Adorable, *adj.* Airidh air aoradh.

Adorableness, *s.* Ard-urramachd, ion-mholtachd.

Adoration, *s.* Aoradh, naomh-urram.

Adore, *v. a.* Aor, dean aoradh.

Adorer, *s.* Fear-aoraidh, fear-gaoil.

Adorn, *v. a.* Sgeadaich, sgèimhich, uidheamaich.

Adown, *adv.* Sìos, gu làr.

Adrift, *adv.* Leis an t-srùth ; air iom-adan.

Adroit, *adj.* Deas, ealanta, ealamh.

Adroitness, *s.* Ealantachd, gleusdachd.

Advance, *v. a.* and *n.* Thoir air agh-aidh ; ardaich, meudaich, mòraich ; leasaich, luathaich ; dlùthaich, thig am fagus, thig air t'aghaidh ; cinn, fàs ; tairg, thoir am follais ; dìol roi-làimh ; tog suas, rùisg, taisbean.

Advance, *s.* Dlùthachadh, teannadh, teachd air aghaidh ; féin-thairgse, cuireadh gràidh ; cinntinn, meud-achadh, àrdachadh ; soirbheachahd ; airgead-roi-làimh.

Advancement, *s.* Adhartachd, àrdach-adh, àirde ; teachd air aghaidh, soirbh-eachadh.

Advantage, *s.* Buidhinn, tairbhe, buann-achd, sochair, leas, math, fàth ; co-throm, lamh-an-uachdar.

Advantage, *v. a.* Leasaich, àrdaich.

Advantaged, *adj.* Leasaichte, air dheagh chothrom.

Advantage-ground, *s.* Cothrom-talmhuinn.

Advantageous, *adj.* Buannachail, goir-easach, tarbhach.

Advantageousness, *s.* Feumalachd, buannachd.

Advent, *s.* Teachd ar Slànaighear ; am mìos roi nollaig.

Adventitious, *adj.* Tuiteamach, tub-aisdeach.

Adventual, *adj.* A bhuineas do dh' àm teachd ar Slànaighear.

Adventure, *s.* Tuiteamas, tubaist ; deuch-ainn, feuchainn, ionnsaidh ; cunnart.

Adventure, *v. a.* and *n.* Feuch ri, thoir deuchainn, thoir ionnsaidh ; gabh misneach.

Adventurer, *s.* Fear-deuchainn, fear-iomairt, fear-misnich, fear-fuadain ; fear-dàna.

Adventurous, *adj.* Misneachail, dàna, deuchainneach, gleusda, gaisgeil.

Adverb, *s.* Ceann-bhriathar.

Adverbial, *adj.* Ceann-bhriathrach.

Adversary, *s.* Eas-caraid, nàmhaid.

Adverse, *adj.* Tarsainn, crosda, an aghaidh a chéile, a cur an aghaidh, dìobhalach, àmhgharach, ànrach, call-dach, dochannach, nàimhdeil.

Adverseness, *s.* Crosdachd, tarsainn-eachd, nàimhdeas.

Adversity, *s.* Fàth-bròin, truaighe, an-shocair, doilgheas, cruaidh-chas ; àmhghar, teinn, doilghios.

Advert, *v. a.* and *n.* Thoir fainear, beachdaich, dearc.

Advertence, *s.* Aire, beachd.

Advertent, *adj.* Aireachail, beachdail.

Advertise, *v. a.* Thoir fios follaiseach, rabhaidh.

Advertisement, *s.* Sanas, gairm.

Advertiser, *s.* Fear-naigheachd, fear-sanais.

Advice, *s.* Comhairle seòladh.

Advisable, *adj.* Glic, crionna.

Advise, *v. a.* and *n.* Comhairlich, cuir comhairle ri ; gabh comhairle.

Advisedness, *s.* Comhairleachd, crìon nachd.

Adviser, *s.* Comhairleach.

Adulation, *s.* Sodal, miodal, brosgal.

Adulator, *s.* Sodalaiche, miodalaich.

Adult, *adj.* Air teachd gu h-aois.

Adult, *s.* Neach air teachd gu aois.

Adulterate, *v. a.* and *n.* Dean adh-altras ; mill, truaill, salaich.

Adulteration, *s.* Truailleadh, salach-adh.

Adulterer, *s.* Adhaltraiche.

Adulteress, *s.* Ban-adhaltraiche.

ADULTERINE, *s.* Sliochd adhaltrannach.
ADULTERINE, *adj.* Truaillidh, dìolain.
ADULTEROUS, *adj.* Adhaltrannach.
ADULTERY, *s.* Adhaltras, truailleadh.
ADUMBRANT, *adj.* A bheir fann-choltas.
ADUMBRATION, *s.* Toirt fann-choltas.
ADUNCITY, *s.* Caime, fiaradh, lùbadh.
ADUNQUE, *adj.* Cam, crom, dubhanach.
ADVOCACY, *s.* Dian-thagradh.
ADVOCATE, *s.* Fear-tagraidh.
ADVOCATE, *v. a.* Tagair, seas, dìon.
ADVOCATION, *s.* Tagradh eadar-ghuidhe.
ADVOLATION, *s.* Itealachd, itealaich.
ADVOWEE, *s.* Neach aig am beil beathachadh eaglais r'a thoirt seachad.
ADUST, *adj.* Loisgte cnàmhte.
ADUSTED, *adj.* Loisgte, seargte le teas.
ADZE, *s.* Tàl, croma-sgian.
AEGIS, *s.* Sgiath-chòmhraig.
AERIAL, *adj.* Adharail, iarmailteach.
AERIE, *s.* Nead eòin fhuileachdaich.
AERIFORM, *adj.* Mar an t-adhar.
AEROLOGY, *s.* Eòlas-adhair.
AEROMANCY, *s.* Speuradaireachd.
AEROMETER, *s.* Adhar-mheidh.
AEROMETRY, *s.* Adhar-thomhas.
AERONAUT, *s.* Adhar-sheòladair.
AEROSCOPY, *s.* Speur-choimhead.
AETHIOP'S-MINERAL, *s.* Cungaidh-leighis do phronnasg agus do dh' airgeadbeò.
AETITES, *s.* Clach-iolaire.
AFFABILITY, *s.* Suairceas, ceanaltas.
AFFABLE, *adj.* Suairce, ceanalta.
AFFABLENESS, *s.* Suairceachd.
AFFAIR, *s* Gnothach; cùis, còmhrag.
AFFEAR, *v. n.* Daingnich, suidhich.
AFFECT, *s.* Faireachdainn, mothachadh.
AFFECT, *v. a.* Drùigh air, thoir air faireachdainn; gabh ort, leig ort; gabh déigh air; gluais inntinn.
AFFECTATION, *s.* Cuir am fiachaibh; baoth-choltas.
AFFECTED, *adj.* Luaisgte le droch, no le deagh rùn, sgleòthach, pròiseil.
AFFECTION, *s.* Gràdh, gaol, aigneadh; càil; dealas; galar, eucail, tinneas.
AFFECTIONATE, *adj.* Gràdhach, gaolach, caidreach; teò-chridheach.
AFFECTIONATENESS, *s.* Teò-chridheachd.
AFFECTIOUSLY *adv.* Gu dùrachdach, gu déigheil.
AFFECTIVE, *adj.* Tiomachail, blàthcridheach.
AFFIANCE, *s.* Còrdadh-pòsaidh, earbsa, muinghin, dòchas.
AFFIANCE, *v. a.* Réitich, dean coimhcheangal pòsaidh; cuir dòchas.
AFFIDAVIT, *s.* Mionnan-sgrìobhte.
AFFILE, *v. a.* Dean mìn le eighe.
AFFILIATION, *s.* Uchd-mhacachd.
AFFINED, *adj.* Ceangailte le bann dàimhe, càirdeach.
AFFINITY, *s.* Cleamhnas; dàimh.
AFFIRM, *v. a.* Cuir an céill; dearbh,
AFFIRMABLE, *adj.* Daingneachail.
AFFIRMANCE, *s.* Daingneachadh, suidheachadh; dearbhachd, daingneachadh.
AFFIRMANT, *s.* Fear-dearbhaidh.
AFFIRMATION, *s.* Dearbhadh, daingneachadh.
AFFIRMATIVE, *adj.* Dhearbhte, danarra, dìorrasach.
AFFIRMATIVELY, *adv.* Gu dearbhta.
AFFIRMER, *s* Fear-dearbhaidh.
AFFIX, *v. a.* Co-cheangail, tàth.
AFFIXION, *s.* Co-cheangal, tàthadh.
AFFLICT, *v. a.* Pian, goirtich, sàraich.
AFFLICTEDNESS, *s.* Doilghios, àmhghar.
AFFLICTER, *s.* Fear-sàrachaidh.
AFFLICTINGLY, *adv.* Gu doilghiosach, àmhgharach.
AFFLICTION, *s.* Amhghar, teinn; doilghios, bròn.
AFFLICTIVE, *adj.* Doilghiosach, àmhgharach.
AFFLICTIVELY, *adv.* Gu doilghiosach, cràiteach, &c.
AFFLUENCE, *s.* Tòic, mòr-mhaoin, beartas, saibhreas.
AFFLUENT, *adj.* Saibhir, beartach, pailt.
AFFLUX, *s.* Cruinneachadh, sruthadh; sruth, maoin-ruith.
AFFLUXION, *s.* Sruthadh, cruinneachadh, lìonadh.
AFFORD, *v. a.* Thoir seachad; builich, tabhair, deònaich; bi comasach.
AFFRANCHISE, *v. a.* Saor, dean saor.
AFFRAY, *v. a.* Cuir eagal air, geiltich.
AFFRAY, *s.* Caonnag, sabaid, carraid.
AFFRICTION, *s.* Suathadh r'a chéile.
AFFRIENDED, *adj.* Réitichte.
AFFRIGHT, *v. a.* Cuir eagal.
AFFRIGHT, *s.* Eagal, geilt, giorag.
AFFRIGHTER, *s.* Bòcan, culaidh-eagail.
AFFRIGHTFUL, *adj.* Eagalach, oillteil.
AFFRIGHTMENT, *s.* Geilt-chrith, eagal.
AFFRONT, *v. a.* Nàraich, maslaich.
AFFRONT, *s.* Nàrachadh, masladh, tàir, tarcuis, tàmailt.
AFFRONTING, *adj.* Tarcuiseach, spìdeil
AFFRONTIVE, *adj.* Tarcuiseach, tàmailteach, spìdeil.
AFFUSION, *s.* Dòrtadh, co-mheasgadh.
AFFY, *v. a.* Dean co-cheangal pòsaidh
AFIELD, *adv.* A mach, do'n raon.
AFIRE, *adv.* 'Na theine, gu teinnteach.
AFLAT, *adv.* Air làr, gu sìnteach.
AFLOAT, *adv.* Air uachdar, air snàmh
AFOOT, *adv.* A chois; air chois.
AFORE, *prep.* Air thùs.
AFORE, *adv.* Cheana, roimhe so.

AFORE-GOING, *adj.* Roi-so.
AFOREHAND, *adv.* Roi-làimh.
AFOREMENTIONED, *adj.* Roi-luaighte.
AFORESAID, *adj.* Roi-ainmichte.
AFORETIME, *adv.* 'S an àm a chaidhe.
AFRAID, *adj.* Fo eagal.
AFRESH, *adv.* As ùr, a rithist.
AFRONT, *adv.* Ri aghaidh.
AFT, *adv.* O thoiseach gu deireadh.
AFTER, *prep.* An déigh.
AFTER, *adv.* 'S an àm ri tighinn.
AFTER-AGES, *s.* Linntean ri teachd.
AFTER-ALL, *adv.* Mu dheireadh.
AFTER-BEARING, *s.* Ath-fhàs.
AFTER-CROP, *s.* Ath-bhàrr.
AFTER-DAYS, *s.* Làthaibh ri teachd.
AFTERMOST, *adj.* Deireannach.
AFTERNOON, *s.* Feasgar, an déigh nòine.
AFTER-PAINS, *s.* Ath-phiantan.
AFTER-PROOF, *s.* Ath-dhearbhadh.
AFTER-REPENTANCE, *s.* Ath-aithreachas.
AFTER-STING, *s.* Ath-ghath, ath-ghuin.
AFTER-THOUGHT, *s.* Ath-smuain.
AFTER-TOSSING, *s.* Ath-luasgadh.
AFTERWARD, *adv.* An déigh sin, [often erroneously written "na dhéigh sin."]
AFTERWISE, *adj.* Glic an déigh làimh.
AGAIN, *adv.* A rithist, uair eile.
AGAINST, *prep.* An aghaidh ; fa-chomhair ; thall.
AGAIN-WARD, *adv.* An taobh so a rithst
AGARICK, *s.* Cungaidh-leighis do bhàrr an daraich.
AGAST, AGHAST, *adv.* Grad chlisgeadh.
AGATE, *adv.* Air an rathad, a' falbh.
AGATE, *s.* Agat, clach-luachmhor.
AGATY, *adj.* Aig am beil gnè na h-agait.
AGAZE, *v. a.* Seall le ioghnadh, spleuc.
AGAZED, *adj.* Air bhall-chrith.
AGE, *s.* Ùin ; linn, ginealach ; àm, beatha ; ùin cheud bliadhna ; aois.
AGED, *adj.* Sean, aosda.
AGENCY, *s.* Dèanadachd ; dreuchd firgnothaich air son neach eile.
AGEND, *s.* Seirbhis-eaglais.
AGENT, *s.* Fear-ionaid.
AGENTSHIP, *s.* Gnìomh fir-ionaid.
AGGER, *s.* Balla-daingneachaidh.
AGGERATE, *v. a.* Cuir an àirde, càrn suas.
AGGEROSE, *adj.* Cnocanach, tomanach.
AGGLOMERATE, *v. a* Cruinnich, cearslaich, trus r'a chéile.
AGGLOMERATION, *s.* Meall cruinn, trusadh.
AGGLUTINANT, *adj.* Glaodhach, tàthach.
AGGLUTINATE, *v. a.* Glaodhaich, tàthaich, dlù r'a chéile.
AGGLUTINATION, *s.* Tàthadh, aonadh, dlùthadh.
AGGRANDIZATION, *s.* Meudachadh, àrdachadh, togail suas.
AGGRANDIZE, *v. a.* Àrdaich, tog suas an inbhe, meudaich an urram ; fàs mòr.
AGGRANDIZEMENT, *s.* Meudachadh, àrdachadh, mòrachadh, urramachadh.
AGGRANDIZER, *s.* Fear-àrdachaidh.
AGGRAVATE, *v. a.* An-tromaich.
AGGRAVATION, *s.* An-tromachadh.
AGGREGATE, *adj.* Co-chruinnichte.
AGGREGATE, *s.* An t-iomlan, am meall uile.
AGGREGATE, *v. a.* Cruinnich, trŭs, tòrr.
AGGREGATION, *s.* Co-chruinneachadh ; an t-iomlan.
AGGRESS, *v. n.* Tòisich an aimhreit buail an toiseach.
AGGRESSION, *s.* A' cheud bhuille, a' cheud teine, a' cheud ionnsaidh.
AGGRESSOR, *s.* Fear togail na strìthe, an coireach.
AGGRIEVANCE, *s.* Eucoir, sàrachadh.
AGGRIEVE, *v. a.* Doilghiosaich, léir ; buair ; dochainn, sàraich.
AGHAST, *adj.* Geiltichte, geilt-ghlacte.
AGILE, *adj.* Lùgor, ealamh, clis, grad-charach, fuasgailte, beothail.
AGILENESS, *s.* Lùghorachd.
AGILITY, *s.* Cliseachd, fuasgailteachd.
AGITATE, *v. a.* Gluais, caraich, cuir troi-chéile ; buair ; cnuasaich.
AGITATION, *s.* Carachadh, gluasad, luasgadh, inntinny ; iomairt ; cnuasachadh, buaireas imcheist.
AGITATOR, *s.* Fear-brosnachaidh fear-gluasaid.
AGNAIL, *s.* An galar-iongach.
AGNATE, *adj.* Càirdeach, dìleas.
AGNATIC, *ad* Càirdeach a thaobh athar.
AGNATION, *s.* Sìnnsireachd nam mac, o'n aon athair ; càirdeas, cleamhnas.
AGNUS-CASTUS, *s.* Craobh-na-geamnachd.
AGO, *adv.* O so, o chian.
AGOG, *adv.* Air bhraise, gu h-iollagach.
AGOING, *adj.* A' falbh, air ghluasad.
AGON, *s.* Strì-gill, co-spàirn.
AGONE, *adv.* Seachad, air falbh.
AGONISTES, *s.* Fear-gheall-strìtheach.
AGONIZE, *v. n.* Bi air do gheur chràdh.
AGONIZINGLY, *adv.* Gu ro chràiteach.
AGONY, *s.* Uspagan a' bhàis, piantan bàis, teinn-chràdh, dòrainn ; cruaidhghleac, spàirn.
AGOOD, *adv* Da-rìreadh.
AGRAMMATIST, *s.* Fear neo-fhòghlumite.
AGRARIAN, *adj.* Fearannach.
AGREE, *v. n* Còird, aontaich ; réitich.

AGREEABLE, *adj.* Freagarrach, taitneach, ciatach.

AGREEABLENESS, *s.* Freagarrachd, taitneachd, co-aontachd, samhlachd.

AGREEABLY, *adv.* See Agreeable.

AGREED, *adj.* Còirdte, suidhichte.

AGREEINGLY, *adv.* Do réir sin.

AGREEMENT, *s.* Réite, còrdadh, samhla; co-cheangal.

AGRICULTURAL, *adj.* Tuathanachail, àiteachail.

AGRICULTURE, *s.* Tuathanachas, àiteachd.

AGRICULTURIST, *s.* Tuathanach, treabhaiche.

AGRIMONY, *s.* A' gheurag-bhileach.

AGROUND, *adv.* An sàs, air grunnd.

AGUE, *s.* Am fiabhras-critheach.

AGUED, *adj.* Crith-bhuailte, critheach.

AGUE-TREE, *s.* A chraobh chrithinn.

AH! *interj.* Ah! Aha! mo thruaighe!

AHEAD, *adv.* Air thoiseach.

AHOLD, *adv.* Air fuaradh.

AHOY, *interj.* Ho! hòi!

AHUNGRY, *adj.* Acrach, ciorcach.

AJAR, *adv.* Leth-fhosgailte.

AID, *s.* Cuideachadh, còmhnadh.

AID, *v. a.* Cuidich, cùm suas, cobhair.

AIDANCE, *s.* Cobhair, còmhnadh.

AID-DE-CAMP, *s.* Àrd-theachdair ceannaird feachd.

AIDER, *s.* Fear-cuideachaidh.

AIDLESS, *adv.* Gun chobhair.

AIRET, *s.* A' chorra-ghlas.

AIL, *v. a.* Pian, cràdh; gearain.

AIL, *s.* Tinneas, galar, eucail.

AILMENT, *s.* Dòrainn, tinneas, galar.

AILING, *adj.* Tinn, euslainteach.

AIM, *v. a.* and *n.* Cuimsich, feuch r'a bhualadh, thoir ionnsaidh; comharraich, beachdaich.

AIM, *s.* Cuimse, cuimseachd, ionnsaidh; rùn, dùrachd; barail, seòl.

AIMLESS, *adj.* Neo-chuimseach.

AIR, *s.* Adhar, àileadh, iarmailt; speuran; gaoth; fàile, tòc; fonn, ceòl; aogas, gnè

AIR, *v. a.* Cuir ris an àileadh, sgaoil ris a' ghaoith; teò, blàthaich.

AIR-BORNE, *adj.* Aotrom, air a ghiùlan leis an àileadh.

AIR-BUILT, *adj.* Faoin, gun bhunachar.

AIR-HOLE, *s.* Toll-gaoithe.

AIRINESS, *s.* Fosgailteachd, gaotharachd.

AIRING, *s.* Spaidseireachd, a' gabhail na gaoithe; a' cnocaireachd.

AIRLING, *s.* Creutair òg iollagach.

AIR-GUN, *s.* Gunna-gaoithe.

AIR-PUMP, *s.* Pìob thaosgaidh an àilidh.

AIRY, *adj.* Adharail; àrd 's an adhar; fosgailte, gaothar; aotrom, faoin; fonnor, sunntach.

AISLE, *s.* Cùl-taigh eaglais.

AKE, *v. n.* Mothaich. cràdh; bi goirt, cràdh an cridhe.

AKIN, *adj.* Càirdeach, dìleas coltach

ALABASTER, *s.* Clach-shoilleir.

ALACK, *interj.* Mo thruaighe! mo chreach, mo léireadh; mo dhiobhail!

ALACK-A-DAY, *interj.* Mo chreach an diugh! Mo dhũnaidh!

ALACRIOUSLY, *adj.* Gu sunntach.

ALACRIOUSNESS, *s.* Beothalachd.

ALACRITY, *s.* Sunntachd, smioralachd.

ALAMODE, *adv.* Anns an fhasan.

ALAND, *adv.* Air tìr, air tràigh.

ALARM, *s.* Caismeachd, gaoir-chatha, rabhadh; clisgeadh, fuathas.

ALARM, *v. a.* Buail caismeachd; thoir rabhadh, thoir sanas; buair.

ALARMING, *adj.* Eagalach, cunnartach.

ALARMIST, *s.* Fear-caismeachd.

ALARM-POST, *s.* Crann-tàraidh.

ALAS, *interj.* Och! mo chreach! mo thruaighe! mo dhuilichinn! mo léireadh!

ALAS THE DAY, *interj.* Och mo thruaighe! mis' an diugh!

ALB, *s.* Léine-aifrinn.

ALBEIT, *adv.* Gidheadh, air son sin.

ALBION, *s.* Alba, Albainn.

ALBUGINEOUS, *adj.* Geal, coltach ri gealagan uibhe.

ALBUM, *s.* Leabhar-cuimhneachain.

ALCHYMIST, *s.* Leughadair mhiotailtean.

ALCHYMY, *s.* Eòlas domhainn air gnè mhiotailtean; seòrsa miotailt.

ALCOHOL, *s.* Treas-tarruinn.

ALCORAN, *s.* Bìoball nan Turcach.

ALCOVE, *s.* Leabaidh-àrd suidheachan

ALDER, *s.* Feàrna.

ALDERMAN, *s.* Bùirdeiseach.

ALDERN, *adj.* Deante do dh-fhèarne

ALE, *s.* Leann, lionn.

ALE-BERRY, *s.* Leann teth.

ALE BREWER, *s.* Grùdair.

ALE-HOUSE, *s.* Taigh-leanna.

ALEMBIC, *s.* Poit-thogalach, poit-dubh.

ALERT, *adj.* Furachail, beothail, deas.

ALERTNESS, *s.* Beothalachd.

ALE-VAT, *s.* Dabhach-leanna.

ALE-WIFE, *s.* Bean-taigh-leanna.

ALEXANDERS, *s.* Lũs-nan-gràn-dubh.

ALEXANDRINE, *s.* Seòrsa bàrdachd.

ALEXANDRINE, *adj.* Fad-shreathach.

ALEXITERICAL, *adj.* Nimh-fhògrach.

ALGEBRA, *s.* An cunntas aibidileach.

ALGID, *adj.* Fuar, fionnar reòta.

ALIAS, *adv.* Air dòigh eile.

ALIBI, *adv.* An àit' eile.

ALIBLE, *adj.* Brìghor, susbaineach.

ALIEN, *adj.* Gallda, coimheach.

ALIEN, *s.* Gall, coimheach, coigreach; eilthireach, allamharach.

ALIENABLE, *adj.* So-thoirt thairis.
ALIENATE, *v. a.* Thoir thairis.
ALIENATED, *adj.* Dealaichte, sgaraichte.
ALIENATION, *s.* Dealachadh, dìobradh.
ALIGHT, *v. a.* Teirinn, tùirlinn.
ALIKE, *adv.* Coltach, a réir a chéile.
ALIMENT, *s.* Lòn, biadh, teachd-an-tìr.
ALIMENTAL, *adj.* Biadhar, brìghor.
ALIMENTALLY, *adv.* Gu biadhar.
ALIMENTARY, *adj.* A dh' àraicheas.
ALIMENTATION, *s.* Beathachadh.
ALIMONY, *s.* Lòn mnà aonaraich.
ALIQUANT, *adj.* Còrr-phàirteach.
ALIQUOT, *adj.* Slàn-phàirteach.
ALISH, *adj.* Leannach, mar leann.
ALIVE, *adj.* Beò, beothail, sunntach.
ALKALI, *s.* Salann-na-groide.
ALKALINE, *adj.* Nàdur salann-na-groide.
ALL, *adj.* Uile, iomlan, gu léir, na h-uile ; an t-iomlan.
ALL-ABANDONED, *adj.* Uile-thréigte.
ALL-ABHORRED, *adj.* Uile-fhuathach.
ALL-CHANGING, *adj.* Uile-chaochlaidh-each.
ALL-CHEERING, *adj.* Uile-bheothachail.
ALL-COMPREHENSIVE, *adj.* Uile-thuig-sinneach.
ALL-CONQUERING, *adj.* Uile-bhuadhach.
ALL-CONSUMING, *adj.* Uile-chaithteach.
ALL-DISGRACED, *adj.* Uile-mhaslaichte.
ALL-HALLOWS, *s.* An t-samhainn ùr.
ALL-HEAL, *s.* Slàn-lùs.
ALL-KNOWING, *adj.* Uil'-fhiosrach.
ALL-POWERFUL, *adj.* Uile-chumhachd-ach.
ALL-PRAISED, *adj.* Uile-chliùiteach.
ALL-SAINTS-DAY, *s.* Latha nan uile naomh.
ALL-SEEING, *adj.* Uile-léirsinneach.
ALL-SUFFICIENCY, *s.* Uil'-fhoghain-teachd, uile-dhiongmhaltchd.
ALL-SUFFICIENT, *adj* Uil'-fhoghaint-each, uile-dhiangmhalt.
ALL-SUFFICIENT, *s.* An t-Uil'-fhogh-ainteach, an t-Uile-dhiangmhalt.
ALL-TRIUMPHING, *adj.* Uile-bhuadhach.
ALLAY, *v. a.* Caisg, bac, ciùinich.
ALLAY, *s.* Droch mhiotailt.
ALLAYMENT, *s.* Lagachadh, ìsleachadh.
ALLEGATION, *s.* Dearbhachd.
ALLEGE, *v. a.* Daingnich, cuir an céill.
ALLEGEABLE, *adj.* So-aithriseil.
ALLEGIANCE, *s.* Ùmhlachd, géilleadh, strìochdadh, cìs-rìgh.
ALLEGORICAL, *adj.* Samhlachail.
ALLEGORIZE, *v. n.* Samhlaich.
ALLEGORY, *s.* Samhla, cosamhlachd.
ALLELUIAH, *s.* Cliù do Dhia.
ALLEVIATE, *v. a.* Aotromaich, lùgh-daich ; maothaich, lagaich.
ALLEVIATION, *s.* Aotromachadh, lùgh-dachadh ; lagachadh.
ALLEVIATIVE, *s.* Cofhurtair
ALLEY, *s.* Caol-shràid.
ALLIANCE, *s.* Càirdeas, cleamhnas.
ALLIGATE, *v. a.* Ceangail, snaim.
ALLIGATION, *s.* Snaimeadh, snaim ; seòrsa cùnntais.
ALLIGATURE, *s.* Ceanglachan, lùbag.
ALLISION, *s.* Co-bhualadh.
ALLITERATION, *s.* Sruth-fhacal.
ALLOCATION, *s.* Cur r'a chéile.
ALLODIAL, *adj.* Saor o chìs fearainn
ALLODIUM, *s.* Fearann saor o chìs.
ALLOT, *a.* Roinn le crann.
ALLOTMENT, *s.* Roinn crannachur, cuid.
ALLOTTERY, *s.* Cuibhrionn, crannachur.
ALLOW, *v. a.* Ceadaich, deònaich leig.
ALLOWABLE, *adj.* Ceadaichte, dligheach.
ALLOWANCE, *s.* Cubhrionn, cead
ALLUDE, *v. n.* Ciallaich, snasaich.
ALLURE, *v. a.* Meall, tàlaidh, buair.
ALLURE, *s.* Foill-ghlacadh, ribe.
ALLUREMENT, *s.* Mealladh, tàladh.
ALLURER, *s.* Mealltair, fear-tàlaidh.
ALLURING, *s.* Mealladh, tàladh.
ALLURINGLY, *adv.* Cluaintearach.
ALLURINGNESS, *s.* Mealltaireachd.
ALLUSION, *s.* Sanas, coimeas
ALLUSIVE, *adv.* Sanasach, snasail.
ALLUVION, *s.* Salachar-srutha.
ALLY, *v. a.* Co-cheangail, dean cleamh-nas ri, dlùthaich an càirdeas.
ALLY, *s.* Companach, caraid.
ALMANACK, *s.* Mìosachan.
ALMIGHTINESS, *s.* Uile chumhachd.
ALMIGHTY, *adj.* Uile-chumhachdach.
ALMOND, *s.* Cnò-almoin.
ALMONDS OF THE THROAT, *s.* Fàireagan bhun na teanga.
ALMONER, Fear-roinn dhéircean
ALMONRY, *s.* Taigh-tasgaidh dhéircean
ALMOST, *adv.* Gu inbhe bhig, theab.
ALMS, *s.* Déirc, déircean.
ALMS-HOUSE, *s.* Taigh-bhochd.
ALNAGE, *s.* Slat-thomhais.
ALOES, *s.* Àlos, fiodh cùbhraidh.
ALOFT, *adv.* Gu h-àrd, an àirde, shuas.
ALONE, *adj.* Aonarach ; ònarach.
ALONELY, *adv.* Gu h-aonaranach.
ALONG, *adv.* Air fad ; tre uile, air fhad ; maille ri, còmhla, le ; air aghaidh, air adhart.
ALONGSIDE, *adv.* Ri taobh na luinge.
ALONGST, *adv.* Air fhad, ri fhad.
ALOOF, *adv.* Air falbh, an céin, air fuaradh ; á sealladh, an cleith ; *stand aloof*, seas air falbh.
ALOUD, *adv.* Gu labhar àrd.
ALPHA, *s.* A cheud litir do'n aibidil Ghreugaich ; a' ciallachadh an ceud ni, no nì a's àirde.
ALPHABET, *s.* Aibidil cànain sam bith.
ALREADY, *adv.* Cheana, mar-thà.

ALSO, *adv.* Mar an ceudna.
ALTAR, *s.* Altair, leac-ìobairt, crom-leac.
ALTAR-PIECE, *s.* Dealbh o's ceann altrach.
ALTER, *v. a.* Atharraich, mùth.
ALTERABLE, *adj.* So-atharraichte.
ALTERANT, *adj.* A ni atharrachadh.
ALTERATION, *s.* Atharrachadh.
ALTERATIVE, *adj.* Caochlaidheach.
ALTERATIVE, *s.* Ìocshlaint-ghlanadh.
ALTERCATION, *s.* Connsachadh, trod.
ALTERNATE, *v. a.* Atharraich.
ALTERNATELY, *adv.* Mu'n seach.
ALTERNATION, *s.* Freagradh mu seach.
ALTERNATIVE, *adj.* Atharrachadh, roghainn, an dara h-aon; ann an seòl mùthaidh.
ALTITUDE, *s.* Àirde.
ALTOGETHER, *adv.* Gu léir, gu tŭr, gu buileach, gu h-iomlan; còmhla.
ALUM, *s.* Alm, clach an datha.
ALWAYS, *adv.* Daonnan, an còmhnaidh, a ghnà, riamh; gun atharrachadh.
AM, *v.* Tha mi, ataim, is mi.
AMABILITY, *s.* Aillteachd, bòichead.
AMAIN, *adv.* Gu dian, le neart.
AMALGAMATE, *v. a.* Co-mheasgaich.
AMALGAMATION, *s.* Co-mheasgachadh.
AMANDATION, *s.* Dol air ghnothach.
AMANUENSIS, *s.* Cléireach sgrìobhaidh bhriathran neach eile.
AMARANTH, *s.* Lŭs-a'-ghràidh.
AMARITUDE, *s.* Searbhachd, geurad.
AMASSMENT, *s.* Meall, cruach, cruinnneachadh, trŭsadh.
AMASS, *v. a.* Trŭs, cruinnich, tòrr.
AMATEUR, *s.* Fear-spéis do dh' ealain.
AMATORY, *adj.* Gaol-gheanmhuinneach.
AMAZE, *v. a.* Cuir ioghnadh.
AMAZE, *s.* Ioghnadh, amhluadh, eagal.
AMAZEDLY, *adv.* Mar fo ioghnadh.
AMAZEMENT, *s.* Mòr ioghnadh.
AMAZING, *adj.* Iongantach, uabhasach.
AMAZON, *s.* Bana-ghaisgeach.
AMBAGES, *s.* Cuairt-chaint.
AMBASSADOR, EMBASSADOR, *s.* Tosgaire; teachdaire rìgh gu rìgh eile.
AMBASSADRESS, *s.* Ban-tosgair.
AMBASSAGE, *s.* Tosgaireachd.
AMBER, *s.* Òmar, leann-soilleir.
AMBERGRIS, *s.* Seòrsa do chùngaidh leighis chùraidh air dhreach na luaidhe agus, a leaghas mar chéir.
AMBIDEXTER, *s.* Gleus-fhear, deas-fhear, fear deas-lamhach, fear deas le 'dha làimh; fear leam leat.
AMBIDEXTROUS, *adj.* Co-dheas-lamhach, ealamh air gach làimh; mealltach, foilleil, leam leat.
AMBIGUITY, *s.* Dà-sheadh.
AMBIGUOUS, *adj.* Da-sheadhach.
AMBIGUOUSNESS, *s.* Neo-chinnteachd.
AMBILOGY, *s.* Dubh-cainnt.
AMBIT, *s.* Cuairt.
AMBITION, *s.* Glòir-mhiann.
AMBITIOUS, *adj.* Glòir-mhiannach.
AMBLE, *s.* Fàlaireachd, spaidsearachd.
AMBLER, *s.* Fàlaire, each-marcachd
AMBLINGLY, *adv.* Gu fòill-cheumach.
AMBROSIAL, *adj.* Cùbhraidh, millis.
AMBULATE, *v. a.* Spaidsearaich.
AMBULATION, *s.* Gluasad, falbh.
AMBULATIVE, *adj.* Falbhach.
AMELIORATE, *v. a.* Dean ni's fearr.
AMEN, *adv.* Gum ma h-amhlaidh bhios.
AMENABLE, *adj.* Freagarrach, buailteach.
AMEND, *v. a.* and *n.* Leasaich, ath-leasaich; dean ni's fearr, càirich; fàs ni's fearr, rach am feabhas.
AMENDING, *s.* Leasachadh.
AMENDMENT, *s.* Ath-leasachad.
AMENDS, *s.* Dìoladh, luach, éirig.
AMENITY, *s.* Taitneachd, ciatachd.
AMERCEMENT, *s.* Ubhladh; peanas
AMETHODICAL, *adj.* Neo-dhòigheil.
AMETHYST, *s.* Clach luachmhor.
AMIABLE, *adj.* Ion-ghràdhach, gaolach, taitneach; maiseach, àluinn; càirdeil, caoimhneil.
AMIABLENESS, *s.* So-ghràdhachd, taitneachd, &c.
AMICABLE, *adj.* Caoimhneil, càirdeil.
AMID, AMIDST, *prep.* Am measg.
AMISS, *adv.* Gu h-olc, gu docharach.
AMISS, *s.* Coireachd, coire, olc.
AMISSION, *s.* Call, calldach.
AMITY, *s.* Càirdeas, co-chòrdadh.
AMMUNITION, *s.* Uidheam gunnaireachd, àirneis-chogaidh.
AMNESTY, *s.* Mathanas coitcheann.
AMONGST, *prep.* Am measg, air feadh.
AMONG, *adv.* Am measg, còmhla.
AMORIST, *s.* Suiridheach, leannan.
AMOROUS, *adj.* Gaolach; leannanach brìodalach; gaol-dhùsgach.
AMOUNT, *v. n.* Ruig, thig, cuir an àird' an cùnntas; thig gu suim, àraidh.
AMOUNT, *s.* An t-àireamh iomlan.
AMOUR, *s.* Leannanachd-dhiomhair.
AMPHIBIOUS, *adj.* A thig beò an uisge 's air talamh.
AMPHIBOLOGICAL, *adj.* Dubh-fhaclach.
AMPHIBOLOGY, *s.* Cainnt dhà-sheadhach, cainnt dhorcha.
AMPHIBOLOUS, *adj.* Ioma-chiallachd.
AMPHITHEATRE, *s.* Taigh-cluiche.
AMPLE, *adj.* Mòr, farsuinn, leudach, fiùghantach, foghainteach.
AMPLENESS, *s.* Lànachd, farsuinneachd.
AMPLIATE, *v. a.* Meudaich, farsuinnich.
AMPLIATION, *s.* Meudachadh, farsuinneachadh; lànachadh, leudachadh.
AMPLIFICATE, *v. a.* Meudaich, leudaich.
AMPLIFICATION, *s.* Meudachadh.

AMPLIFY, *v. a.* Meudaich, leudaich.
AMPLITUDE, *s.* Meudachd, lànachd.
AMPUTATE, *v. a.* Gearr air falbh, sgăr.
AMPUTATION, *s.* Gearradh, sgăradh.
AMULET, *s.* Paidirean giosagach, seun.
AMUSE, *v. a.* Toilich, cum o fhadal.
AMUSEMENT, *s.* Caithe-aimsir.
AMUSINGLY. *adv.* Air mhodh taitneach.
AMUSIVE, *adj.* Taitneach, a thogas sproc.
ANABAPTIST, *s.* Anabaisteach.
ANALEPTIC, *adj.* Cofhurtachail.
ANALOGIAL. *adj.* Samhlachail.
ANALOGOUS, *adj.* Co-choltach, co-chòrdadh, co-fhreagarrach.
ANALOGY, *s.* Coltas, samhlachas, co-chòrdadh, fìor choltas r'a chéile.
ANALYSIS, *s.* Mion-rannsachadh.
ANALYST, *s.* Fear-mìneachaidh.
ANALYZE, *v. a.* Bun-rannsaich.
ANARCH, *s.* Fear mi-riaghailt.
ANARCHY, *s.* Mi-riaghailt.
ANARCHICAL, *adj.* Aimhreiteach.
ANASARCA, *s.* Seòrsa meudbhronn.
ANATHEMA, *s.* Ascaoin-eaglais.
ANATHEMATIZE, *v. a.* Sgar o chomunn nan crìosdaidhean.
ANATOMICAL, *adj.* Chorp-ghearradh.
ANATOMIST, *s.* Corp-shnasaire.
ANATOMY, *s.* Corp-shnasadh, corp-ghearradh, corp-rannsachadh; teagasg corp-shnasaidh, eòlas corp-ghearraidh.
ANCESTOR, *s.* Priomh-athair, sinnsear.
ANCESTRY, *s.* Sinnsearachd.
ANCHOR, *s.* Acair luinge.
ANCHOR, *v. a.* and *n.* Tilg acair, laidh air acair, leag acair; stad air acair.
ANCHORAGE, *s.* Acarsaid; càin-acarsaid.
ANCHORED, *adj.* Acraichte, air acair.
ANCHORESS, *s.* Bana-mhanach.
ANCHORET, *s.* Manach diobarach.
ANCIENT, *adj.* Arsaidh, aosda; o shean.
ANCIENT, *s.* Na sean daoine, bratach, fear-brataich.
ANCIENTLY, *adv.* O shean, an céin.
AND, *conj.* Agus, a's 's.
ANDROGENE, *s.* Neach fireann-boireann.
ANECDOTE, *s.* Ùr-sgeul, mion-sgeul.
ANECDOTICAL, *adj.* Ùr-sgeulach.
ANEMOMETER, *s.* Gaoth-mheidh.
ANEW, *adv.* As ùr, a rithist.
ANFRACTUOUS, *adj.* Lùbach, cam.
ANGEL, *s.* Aingeal; bonn òir.
ANGEL, *adj.* Air dhreach aingil.
ANGELICALLY, *adv.* Air mhodh aingil.
ANGELICA, *s.* Lŭs-nam-buadh.
ANGELICAL, *adj.* Coltach ri aingeal.
ANGELIC, *adj.* See Angelical.
ANGER, *s.* Fearg, corraich, mi-thlachd.
ANGER, *v. a.* Brosnaich gu feirg.
ANGLE, *s.* Oisinn gobhal; uileann.
ANGLE, *v. a* Iasgaich le slait.
ANGLED, *adj.* Oisinneach, uinnleach.
ANGLER, *s.* Iasgair-slaite.
ANGLICAN, *adj.* Sasunnach.
ANGLICISM, *s.* Dòigh na Beurla.
ANGLING, *s.* Iasgach le slait.
ANGRY, *adj.* Feargach, corrach, căs.
ANGUISH, *s.* Dòrainn, àmhghar.
ANGULAR, *adj.* Cearnach; gòbhlach.
ANGULARITY, *s.* Cearnachd.
ANGUST, *adj.* Aimhleathan cumhang.
ANHELATION, *s.* Sèitrich, plosgartaich.
ANIMABLE, *adj.* So-bheothachaidh.
ANIMADVERSION, *s.* Cronachadh, rannsachadh.
ANIMADVERT, *v. n.* Thoir achmhasan, cronaich; rannsaich.
ANIMAL, *s.* Ainmhidh, brùid.
ANIMALCULE, *s.* Meanbh-bheathach.
ANIMATE, *v. a.* Beothaich; neartaich.
ANIMATE, *adj.* Beò, beothail, beathail.
ANIMATED, *adj.* Beothaichte, beothail.
ANIMATION, *s.* Beothachadh.
ANIMATIVE, *adj.* Beothachail.
ANIMOSITY, *s.* Gàmhlas, falachd.
ANISE, *s.* Anis, seòrsa luibhe.
ANKER, *s.* Leth-bharaille, buideal.
ANKLE, *s.* Aobrunn, caol na coise.
ANKLED, *adj.* Aobrunnach.
ANNALIST, *s.* Seanachaidh, eachdraiche.
ANNALS, *s.* Eachdraidh bhliadhnach.
ANNEX, *v. a.* Ceangail; snaidhm; cuir ris.
ANNIHILATE, *v. a.* Dìthich, cuir ás.
ANNIHILATION, *s.* Léir-sgrios.
ANNIVERSARY, *s.* Cuirm bhliadhnach.
ANNOTATION, *s.* Mìneachadh.
ANNOTATOR, Fear-mìneachaidh.
ANNOUNCE, *v. a.* Cuir an céill, foillsich.
ANNOY, *v. a.* Cuir dragh, no càmpar air.
ANNOYANCE, *s.* Trioblaid, buaireas.
ANNOYER, *s.* Buaireadair.
ANNUAL, *adj.* Bliadhnail.
ANNUALLY, *adv.* Gach bliadhna.
ANNUITANT, *s.* Fear-suim-bhliadhnail.
ANNUITY, *s.* Suim-bhliadhnail.
ANNUL, *v. a* Cuir ás, dubh a mach.
ANNULAR, *adj.* Faineach.
ANNULET, *s.* Faine ailbheag.
ANNUMERATE, *v. a.* Cuir ris an àireamh.
ANNUMERATION, *s.* Ath-leasachadh.
ANNUNCIATE, *v. a.* Aithris, innis.
ANNUNCIATION, *s.* Latha-feill-Muire.
ANODYNE, *adj.* Furtachail, faothachail.
ANOINT, *v. a.* Ung, suath le ola; coisrig
ANOINTING, *s.* Ungadh, coisrigeadh
ANON, *adv.* An dràst 's a rithist.
ANONYMOUS, *adj.* Neo-ainmichte.
ANOTHER, *adj.* Tuilleadh; neach eile.
ANSATED, *adj.* Cluasach, làmhach.
ANSWER, *v. a.* and *n.* Freagair, thoir freagairt, thoir freagradh; toilich, dean an gnothach; freagair an àite.
ANSWER, *s.* Freagradh, Freagairt.

Answerable, *adj.* Freagarrach.
Ant, *s.* Seangan, sneaghan.
An't. Mu 's e do thoil.
Antagonist, *s.* Nàmhaid, nàmh.
Antecedence, *s.* Tùs-imeachd.
Antecedent, *a.* An toiseach.
Antechamber, *s.* Seòmar-taoibh.
Antedate, *v. a.* Sgrìobh ùine air ais.
Antediluvian, *adj.* Roi 'n Tuil.
Antelope, *s.* Fiadh-ghobhar.
Anthem, *s.* Laoidh-naomha.
Anthology, *s.* Badag-lùs; leabhar rann.
Anthropology, *s.* Corp-eòlas.
Antichrist, *s.* Ana-criosd.
Antichristian, *adj.* Ana-criosdail.
Anticipate, *v. a.* Roi-ghlac.
Anticipation, *s.* Roi-bharail.
Antick, *adj.* Neònach, fiadh-chleasach.
Antidote, *s.* Ùrchasg, ìoc-shlaint.
Antinomy, *s.* Eas-cordadh dà lagha.
Antipathy, *s.* Fuath, gràin, sgreamh.
Antipoison, *s.* Ùr-chasg puinnsein.
Antiquary, **Antiquarian**, *s.* Arsadair, arsair, seann-seanachaidh.
Antiquate, *v. a.* Cuir á cleachdadh.
Antique, *adj.* Aosda; seann-ghnàthach.
Antiquity, *s.* Arsachd, seanachd.
Antiscorbutic, *s.* Claimh-leigheas.
Antitrinitarian, *s.* Fear cur an aghaidh teagasg na Trionaid.
Antitype, *s.* Brìgh-shamhla.
Antler, *s.* Meur cabair féigh.
Antre, *s.* Uamh; gàradh; talamh-toll.
Anvil, *s.* Innean gobha, &c.
Anxiety, *s.* Iomagain, smuairean.
Anxious, *adj.* Iomagaineach.
Any, *adj.* Aon, aon sam bith, cò sam bith.
Anywise, *adv.* Air dhòigh sam bith.
Apace, *adv.* Gu grad, gu luath.
Apart, *adv.* Air leth, gu taobh.
Apartment, *s.* Seòmar air leth.
Apathist, *s.* Duine gun fhaireachdainn.
Apathy, *s.* Cion-mothachaidh.
Ape, *s.* Apa, apag; fear-fanaid.
Ape, *v. a.* Dean atharrais, dean fochaid.
Apeak, *adv.* Ullamh gu sàthadh.
Aperient, *adj.* Math gu fosgladh.
Apert, *adj.* Fuasgailteach, sgarach.
Apertion, *s.* Fosgladh, bearn, bealach.
Aperture, *s.* Fosgladh, sgoltadh.
Apex, *s.* Binnean, barr, mullach, bidean.
Aphorism, *s.* Fìrinn-shuidhichte.
Apiary, *s.* Taigh-sheillein, beachlan.
Apiece, *adv.* Gach aon, an t-aon.
Apish, *adj.* Pròiseil, faoin-bheachdail.
A-pit-pat, *adv.* A' plosgartaich.
Apocalypse, *s.* Taisbeanadh.
Apocrypha. Leabhraichean nach eil fios cò a sgrìobh iad, agus a tha gun ùghdarras 's an eaglais.
Apocryphal, *adj.* Neo-chinnteach.
Apologize, *v. a.* Thoir leisgeul.
Apologue, *s.* Sgeulachd, no ursgeul.
Apology, *s.* Tagradh, leisgeul.
Apophthegm, *s.* Geur-fhacal.
Apoplexy, *s.* An spad-thinneas.
Apostacy, *s* Cùl-shleamhnachadh.
Apostate, *adj.* Mealltach, neo-dhìleas.
Apostatize, *v.n.* Claon o d' chreideamh
Apostleship, *s.* Abstolachd.
Apostolical, *adj.* Abstolach.
Apothecary, *s.* Olla, lusragan.
Appal, *v. a.* Cuir fo eagal.
Apparatus, *s.* Uidheam, acainn.
Apparel, *s.* Earradh, trusgan, aodach.
Apparent, *adj.* Soilleir, a réir coltais.
Apparition, *s.* Sealladh, samhla.
Appeach, *v. a.* Dìt, cronaich, càin.
Appeachment, *s.* Dìteadh, cùis-dhìtidh, casaid, achmhasan.
Appeal, *v. a.* and *n.* Tog do chùis gu cùirt eile; leig gu ràdh; gairm mar fhianais.
Appeal, *s.* Togail cùise o aon chùirt gu cùirt eile 's àirde, tagradh an aghaidh breitheanais; cùis-dhìtidh.
Appear, *v. n.* Thig am fradharc.
Appearance, *s.* Teachd an làthair, sealladh; coltas, cruth; taisbeanadh.
Appease, *v. a.* Réitich, sìthich.
Appeasement, *s.* Sìothchaint, réite.
Appellant, *s.* and *adj.* Fear-dubhlanachaidh, a bhuineas do chùis-thogail.
Appellative, *s.* Co-ainm, tiodal.
Append, *v. a.* Cuir ris.
Appendix, *s.* Ath-sgrìobhadh.
Appertain, *v. n.* Buintain a thaobh còrach no nàduir.
Appertinent, *adj.* Dligheach.
Appetite, *s.* Miann, déigh, togradh, toil; Ana-miann, an-togradh feòlmhor; fadal, fìor-chion; miann; acras.
Appetite, *v. a.* Iarr, biodh toil agad.
Applaud, *v. a.* Àrd-mhol, cuir suas.
Applause, *s.* Ard-mholadh, mòr-chliù.
Applausive, *adj.* Moltach, cliùiteach.
Apple, *s.* Ubhall.
Applicable, *adj.* Freagarrach.
Applier, **Applicant**, *s.* Fear-iarraidh.
Applicate, *v. a.* Co-chuir, cuir ris.
Application, *s.* Co-chur samhlachadh; dian-smuaineachadh, dìchioll.
Applicative, **Applicatory**, *adj.* Dìcheallach, freagarrach.
Apply, *v. a.* and *n.* Co-chuir, càirich air, leag plàsd; cuir air son, builich; dian-smuainich, leag t'inntinn air, cleachd dìcheall; iarr, aslaich.
Appoint, *v. a.* and *n.* Suidhich, ainmich, òrduich; deasaich, uidheamaich.
Appointment, *s.* Suidheachadh, ainmeachadh, òrdachadh; deasachadh.

APPORTION, *v. a.* Dean roinn chothromach.
APPOSITE, *adj.* Iomchuidh, cothromach.
APPOSITIVE, *adj.* Freagarrach.
APPRAISE, *v. a.* Meas, cuir luach air.
APPRECIATE, *v. a.* Meas, tuig a luach.
APPREHEND, *v. a.* Glac, beir, dean greim; tuig, measraich; gabh eagal; thoir fainear.
APPREHENSION, *s.* Smuaineachadh, measrachadh; tuigse, reuson, comas fiosrachaidh; eagal, faiteachas; amharas.
APPREHENSIVE, *adj.* Geur-thuigseach; eagalach, amharasach; mothachail.
APPRENTICE, *s.* Fòghlumaich céirde.
APPRENTICESHIP, *s.* Ùine-ceangail fir céirde.
APPRIZE, *v.* Thoir fios, thoir brath, innis cuir an céill.
APPROACH, *v a.* Thig am fagus; dlùthaich, tarruinn.
APPROACH, *s.* Dlùthachadh, teannadh.
APPROBATION, *s.* Dearbhadh, moladh, taitneas.
APPROPRIATE, *v. a.* Cuir air leth; gabh mar do chuid féin.
APPROPRIATION, *s.* Cur gu feum àraidh.
APPROVABLE, *adj.* Cliù-thoillteanach.
APPROVAL, *s.* See Approbation.
APPROVE, *v. a.* and *n.* Bi toilichte, gabh tlachd; mol; dearbh, fìreanaich.
APPROVEMENT, *s.* Dearbhadh, toil, moladh, taitneachd.
APPROXIMATE, *adj.* Faisg, dlù.
APPROXIMATION, *s.* Dlùthachadh, teachd am fagus; a soìr-dhlùthachadh.
APRIL, *s.* An Giblean.
APRON, *s.* Criosan, aparan.
APROPOS, *adv.* Direach 's an àm; rofhreagarrach.
APT, *adj.* Deas, ealamh, buailteach.
APTITUDE, *s.* Freagarrachd, deasachd; aomadh, buailteachd, claonadh.
APTLY, *adv.* Deas, ealamh, buailteach.
APTNESS, *s.* Freagarrachd, deasachd; buailteachd, aomadh.
AQUA-FORTIS, *s.* Uisge teinntidh, a leaghas gach meatailt ach òr agus *Platina.*
AQUATIC, *adj.* A tighinn beò, no fàs 'san uisge.
AQUEDUCT, *s.* Amar uisge.
AQUEOUS, *adj.* Uisgidh.
AQUILINE, *adj.* Crom-shronach.
ARABIC, *s.* Cainnt nan Arabianach.
ARABLE, *adj.* So-threabhaidh.
ARATION, ARATURE, *s.* Treabhadh, àiteach, àr, rudhar.
ARATORY, *adj.* Treabhach.
ARBITER, *s.* Fear réiteachaidh cùise.
ARBITRARY, *adj.* Aintighearnail, borbsmachdail, iomluath.
ARBITRATE, *v. a.* and *n.* Thoir breith réiteachaidh; suidh am breith.
ARBITRATION, *s.* Breith-réite.
ARBITRATOR, *s.* Àrd-uachdaran.
ARBORESCENT, *adj.* A craobh-fhàs.
ARCADE, *s.* Sràid fo dhion.
ARCHARC, *s.* Roinn-cuairt, bogha.
ARCH, *adj.* Prìomh, àrd.
ARCHANGEL, *s.* Ard-aingeal; an deanntag mharbh.
ARCHANGELIC, *adj.* Ard-aingealach.
ARCHBISHOP, *s.* Ard-easbuig.
ARCHED, *adj.* Crom, air chumadh bogha.
ARCHER, *s.* Boghadair, saighdear.
ARCHERY, *s.* Boghadaireachd.
ARCHETYPE, *s.* Prìomh-shamhla.
ARCHETYPAL, *adj.* Priomh-shamhlachail.
ARCHITECT, *s.* Ard-chlachair.
ARCHITECTURE, *s.* Ard-chlachaireachd.
ARCHIVES, *s.* Tasg-thigh sheann sgrìobhaidhean a's chòraichean.
ARDENT, *adj.* Lasganta; bras, garg, àrd-inntinneach; teas-ghràdhach, càirdeil.
ARDENTLY, *adv.* Dàimheil blàth chridheach.
ARDOUR, *s.* Blàthas, teas; teas-ghràdh.
ARDUOUS, *adj.* Ard, cas; duilich.
ARE, *v.* (3d p. *pl. pr.* tense,) Tha iad.
AREA, *s.* Raon, magh; ionad fosgailte.
ARGUE, *v. a.* and *n.* Reusonaich; connsaich, tagair an aghaidh; dearbh, còmhdaich, dean a mach.
ARGUMENT, *s.* Reuson, argamaid; ceann-aobhair, cùis-thagraidh; brìghsgrìobhaidh, connsachadh, deasbaireachd.
ARGUMENTAL, *adj.* Argumaideach.
ARGUMENTATION, *s.* Reusonachadh, deasbaireachd, connsachadh.
ARGUMENTATIVE, *adj.* Argamaideach, reusonta, deagh-thagarrach; connspaideach, deasbaireach.
ARGUTE, *adj.* Seòlta, carach, geursgreadach.
ARID, *adj.* Tioram, tartmhor, loisgte.
ARIDITY, *s.* Tiormachd, tartmhorachd; cruas-cridhe, fuar-chràbhadh.
ARIGHT, *adj.* Gu ceart, gun chron.
ARISE, *v. n.* Éirich suas, dìrich an àird; mosgail.
ARITHMETICAL, *adj.* Àireamhach.
ARITHMETIC, *s.* Cùnntas, eòlas-àireamh.
ARK, *s.* Àirc; àirc a' cho-cheangail.
ARM, *s.* Gàirdean; loch-mara.
ARM, *v. a.* Armaich, cuir ort t' airm
ARMADA, *s.* Feachd-mara.
ARMAMENT, *s.* Feachd-mara no tìre.

ARMFUL, *s.* Làn na h-achlais, achlasan.
ARMIPOTENT, *adj.* Buadhach, treun an cath.
ARMISTICE, *s.* Sìth ghoirid.
ARMLET, *s.* Meanbh-ghàirdean; bàghan-mara; dìon gàirdean.
ARMORIAL, *adj.* Suaicheantach.
ARMOUR, ARMOR, *s.* Armachd.
ARMOURER, *s.* Fear-dheanamh arm.
ARM-PIT, *s.* Lag-na-h-achlais.
ARMS, *s.* Armachd, beart-chogaidh; suaicheantas, gearradh-arm.
ARMY, *s.* Armailt, feachd.
AROMATIC, AROMATICAL, *adj.* Deagh-bholtrach.
AROMATICS, *s.* Spìsrean.
AROMATIZE, *v. a.* Spìsrich; dean cùbhraidh.
AROSE, *pret.* Dh' éirich.
AROUND, *ad. prep.* Mu'n cuairt.
AROUSE, *v. a.* Dùisg, gluais suas, tog.
ARRAIGN, *v. a.* Deasaich, cùis, cuir an òrdugh, cuir air seòl; thoir an làthair; coirich, dìt, cuir cron ás leth.
ARRAIGNMENT, *s.* Coireachadh, dìteadh.
ARRANGE, *v. a.* Cuir an uidheam, réitich.
ARRANGEMENT, *s.* Réiteachadh.
ARRANT, *adj.* Ro olc, dona.
ARRAS, *s.* Obair-ghréis.
ARRAY, *s.* Riaghailt, uidheam, òrdugh-catha; deasachadh, éideadh.
ARRAY, *v. a.* Cuir an òrdugh, cuir an riaghailt, tarruinn suas; sgeadaich.
ARREAR, *s.* Fiachan gun dìoladh.
ARREST, *s.* Sàradh; glacadh, cur an làimh.
ARREST, *v. a.* Glac, cuir an làimh, cuir an sàs, cuir sàradh, dean greim laghail.
ARRIVAL, *s.* Tighinn, teachd, ruigsinn.
ARRIVE, *v. a.* Ruig tìr; thig.
ARROGANCE, ARROGANCY, *s.* Ladornas, dànadas, uaill, ceannardas, àrdan.
ARROGANT, *adj.* Ladorna, dàna, ceannasach, àrdanach.
ARROGANTLY, *adv.* See Arrogant.
ARROGATE, *v. a.* Gabh ort gu dàna.
ARROW, *s.* Saighead, guin, gath.
ARSENAL, *s.* Arm-lann.
ARSMART, *s.* Lŭs-an-fhogair.
ART, *s.* Eòlas, innleachd; ealain; cèird; seòltachd; alt, dòigh.
ARTERY, *s.* Cuisle, féith.
ARTFUL, *adj.* Innleachdach, seòlta, ealanta; cuilbheartach, carach; eòlach teòma, deas.
ARTFULLY, *adv.* See Artful.
ARTFULNESS, *s.* Ealantachd, seòltachd.
ARTHRITIS, *s.* Tinneas-nan-alt.
ARTICHOKE, *s.* Farusgag.
ARTICLE, *s.* Mion-fhacal; cumha, pong ceann-teagaisg.
ARTICLE, *v. a.* and *n.* Cùmhnantaich, réitich, suidhich; còrd ri, ceangail.
ARTICULAR, *adj.* Altach.
ARTICULATE, *adj.* Pongail, soilleir so-thuigsinn; a bhuineas do dh' altaibh a' chuirp.
ARTICULATE, *v. a.* Abair gu soilleir, pongail; dean cumhachan.
ARTICULATELY, *adv.* See Articulate.
ARTICULATENESS, *s.* Pongalachd.
ARTICULATION, *s.* Ceangal nan alt 's nan cnàmh, alt-cheangal; pong-labhairt.
ARTIFICE, *s.* Car, cuilbheart, dò-bheart, eòlas, teòmachd.
ARTIFICER, *s.* Fear-cèirde.
ARTIFICIAL, *adj.* Innleachdach.
ARTIFICIALITY, *s.* Innleachdas.
ARTIFICIALLY, *adv.* See Artificial.
ARTILLERY, *s.* Gunnachan mòra.
ARTISAN, *s.* Fear-cèirde; fear-ealain.
ARTIST, *s.* Fear-làimh-chèirde; fear teòma, fear-innleachd.
ARTLESS, *adj.* Aineolach, neo-chealgach, fosgailte; cearbach.
AS, *conj.* implying time or action. 'Nuair, an àm; air do; (*answering to* so, *such*, &c.) mar; (in one part of a sentence answering to so, in another), mar, ceart mar, air mheud is; *mar* a thubhairt thu, thachair e; *ceart mar* thubhairt thu, thachair e; *air mheud* 's gu-n robh sin draghail bha so taitneach.
ASBESTINE, *adj.* Neo-loisgeach.
ASCEND, *v. a.* and *n.* Dìrich, streap tog, gabh suas, éirich.
ASCENDANT, *s.* Àirde; uachdranachd, ceannardachd.
ASCENDANT, *adj.* An uachdar, uachdrach, ainneartach; 's an t-sealladh.
ASCENDENCY, *s.* Cumhachd, uachdranachd, smachd.
ASCENSION, *s.* Éiridh, dìreadh.
ASCENSION-DAY, *s.* Latha dol suas ar Slànaighear.
ASCENT, *s.* Éirigh, dol suas, dìreadh rathad-dìridh, slighe dhol suas; bruthach, uchdach, aonach, àirde.
ASCERTAIN, *v. a.* Dean cinnteach, dearbh, socraich, suidhich; faigh fios, cuir á teagamh.
ASCERTAINABLE, *adj.* So dhearbhta, so-fhiosraichte.
ASCERTAINMENT, *s.* Riaghailt shuidhichte.
ASCETIC, *s.* Fear-fàsaich, fear-gnàchrabhach.
ASCITITIOUS, *adj.* Barrachdail.
ASCRIBE, *v. a.* Cuir á leth.
ASCRIPTION, *s.* Cur ás leth.
ASH, *s.* Uinnseann.

Ashame, *v. a.* Nàraich.
Ashamed, *adj.* Nàraichte.
Ashes, *s.* Luath, luaithre.
Ashore, *adv.* Air tìr, air tràigh.
Ashy, *adj.* Air dhreach na luaithre.
Asia, *s.* Aon de cheàrnaibh na cruinne.
Aside, *adv.* Siar, a thaobh, a leth-taobh, ás an t-slighe; leis féin.
Ask, *v. a.* and *n.* Iarr, sir, guidh; ceasnaich, feòraich, faighnaich; fiosraich.
Askance, **Askant**, *adv.* Cam, siar, claon.
Asker, *s.* Fear-iarraidh, fear-achanaich, fear-siridh, fear-rannsachaidh; arc-luachrach uisge.
Askew, *adv.* Gu claon, gu tàireil, gu sanntach; gu cam, a leth-taobh.
Asleep, *adv.* An cadal, an suain.
Aslope, *adv.* Le leathad, fiar, cam.
Asp, **Aspic**, *s.* Nathair nimhe ro mharbhtach.
Asparagus, *s.* Creamh-mac-fiagh.
Aspect, *s.* Snuadh, gnùis, aogas, dreach.
Aspection, *s.* Sealltainn, coimhead, amharc.
Aspen, *s.* Critheann, an critheach.
Asper, *adj.* Garbh, geur, doirbh.
Asperate, *v. a.* Dean garbh, dean doirbh.
Asperation, *s.* Garbhachadh, doirbh-eachadh.
Asperity, *s.* Gairbhe, garbh-fhuaim; gairge, crosdachd, sglàmhrainn, fiat-achd; geurachd.
Asperous, *adj.* See Asper.
Asperse, *v. a.* Cùl-chain, maslaich.
Asperser, *s* Fear-tuaileis.
Aspirate, *v. a.* and *n.* Abair le neart analach.
Aspiration, *s.* Geur-thogradh, beò-iarraidh; ana-mhiann, mòr dhéidh air ni-eigin mòr; labhairt le neart ana-lach.
Aspire, *v. a.* and *n.* Iarr, miannaich, bi'n déidh air; dìrich suas, éirich suas.
Aspirement, *s.* See Aspiration.
Aspiring, *s.* Ard-mhiann; pong, stad.
Ass, *s.* Asal, as.
Assail, *v. a.* Thoir ionnsaidh air, leum air; cas ris, connsaich, aslaich.
Assailable, *adj.* So-bhuailte.
Assailant, *s.* Fear-ionnsaidh, nàmhaid.
Assailant, *adj.* A bheir ionnsaidh, a dh' éireas air, connsachail, strìtheil.
Assailment, *s.* Ionnsaidh.
Assassin, *s.* Mortair, neach a bheir ionnsaidh mharbhaidh.
Assassinate, *v. a.* and *n.* Mort, marbh le foill; thoir ionnsaidh mharbhaidh gu h-uaigneach.
Assassination, *s.* Mortadh, marbhadh le foill.
Assassinator, *s.* Mortair, foille.
Assation, *s.* Ròstadh, ròsladh.
Assault, *s.* Ionnsaidh, aghaidh.
Assault, *v. a.* Thoir ionnsaidh, buail,
Assay, *s.* Deuchainn, feuchainn dearbhadh; tòiseachadh, luach.
Assemblage, *s.* Cruinneachadh, tional.
Assemblance, *s.* Cruinneachadh.
Assemble, *v. a.* and *n.* Chruinnich.
Assembler, *s.* Fear-cruinneachaidh.
Assembling, *s.* Cruinneachadh, tional.
Assembly, *s.* Co-chruinneachadh, àrd-sheanadh.
Assent, *s.* Aontachadh, còrdadh, aont, géill.
Assentment, *s.* Aontachadh.
Assert, *v. a.* Tagair, agair; saor, teasairg.
Assertion, *s.* Tagradh, agairt; facal, ceann-dearbhaidh.
Assertive, *adj.* Tagrach, dian-bhriath-rach, abartach.
Assertor, *s.* Fear-tagraidh, fear-dearbhaidh.
Assess, *v. a.* Leag cìs, no càin, tog cìs meas.
Assessable, *adj.* Cìs-dhiolach.
Assession, *s.* Co-shuidhe chum comh airle no cuideachadh a thabhairt.
Assessionary, *adj.* A bhuineas do luchd-cìse.
Assessment, *s.* Càin; cìs-leagadh.
Assever, **Asseverate**, *v. a.* Dian-bhriathraich, mionnaich.
Asseveration, *s.* Briathar, mionnan.
Assiduity, *s.* Dìchioll, buan-dhùrachd.
Assiduous, *adj.* Dìchiollach, dùrachd, leanmhainneach.
Assign, *v. a.* Òrduich, comharraich, cuir air leth, sònraich; suidhich, socraich, ceartaich; thoir còir seachad.
Assignation, *s.* Coinneamh-leannan-achd; toirt seachad còrach; cur air leth, sònrachadh.
Assignment, *s.* Sònrachadh, cur air leth.
Assimilate, *v. a.* Dean coltach, meirbh, cnàmh.
Assist, *v. a.* and *n.* Cuidich, fòir, dean còmhnadh
Assistance, *s.* Cobhair, còmhnadh.
Assistant, *s.* Fear-còmhnaidh, fear-cuideachaidh, fear-cobhrach.
Assize, *s.* Mòd; luchd-breith, reachd riaghailt.
Ass-like, *adj.* Coltach ri asail.
Associate, *v. a.* and *n.* Dean companas, cùm cuideachdas.
Associate, *s.* Companach.
Association, *s.* Co-aontachadh, co-chomunn, comunn, co-chuideachd; co-chùmhnant, co-réite; co-phàirt, co-cheangaltas.

ASSOIL, *v. a.* Fuasgail, freagair, thoir deagh fhreagairt; cuir mu sgaoil, math; salaich.
ASSORT, *v. a.* Cuir an òrdugh, réitich.
ASSORTMENT, *s.* Cùr an òrdugh, réiteachadh.
ASSUAGE, *v. a.* and *n.* Caisg, lùghdaich, eutromaich; sìthich; traogh, tuit, laidh.
ASSUAGEMENT, *s.* Faothachadh, lasachadh, lùghdachadh, sòcair.
ASSUAGER, *s.* Fear-sìtheachaidh, feareutromachaidh.
ASSUASIVE, *adj.* Ciùineach, a chiùinicheas, a dh' aotromaicheas.
ASSUME, *v. a.* and *n.* Gabh ort, togair; tog, glac; bi ceannasach, uaibhreach.
ASSUMING, *s.* Ladornas, dànadas.
ASSUMING, *adj.* Uaibhreach, ladorna.
ASSUMPTION, *s.* Glacadh, gabhail do t'ionnsuidh féin; barail gun chòmhdachadh; togail suas do nèamh.
ASSURANCE, *s.* Dearbhachd, làn-dearbhachd, cinnteachas; làn-dòchas, beag-narachd, ladornachd, peasanachd; aobhar-dòchais, meamnadh, smioralachd, tréine; dearbhachd an gràdh Dhé.
ASSURE, *v. a.* Dean cinnteach, cuir á teagamh.
ASSURED, *adj.* Cinnteach, dearbhte.
ASSUREDLY, *adv.* Gun teagamh.
ASTERN, *adv.* Gu deireadh na luinge.
ASTHMA, *s.* Luathas-analach.
ASTHMATIC, *v.* Fo 'n luathas-analach.
ASTONISH, *v. a.* Iongantaich, cuir ioghnadh.
ASTONISHMENT, *s.* Ioghnadh.
ASTOUND, *v. a.* Uamhunnaich.
ASTRAY, *adv.* Air seacharan.
ASTRICTION, *s.* Teannachadh, ceangal.
ASTRICTIVE, *adj.* Teanntach.
ASTRIDE, *adv.* Casa-gòbhlach.
ASTRINGE, *v. a.* Teannaich, crup.
ASTRINGENT, *adj.* Ceangaltach.
ASTROLOGER, *s.* Speuradair.
ASTROLOGY, *s.* Speuradaireachd.
ASTRONOMER, *s.* Reulladair.
ASTRONOMICAL, *adj.* Reull-eòlach.
ASTRONOMY, *s.* Reull-eòlas.
ASTRO-THEOLOGY, *s.* Reull-dhiadhachd.
ASUNDER, *adv.* Air leth, o chéile.
ASYLUM, *s.* Ionad-tèarmainn.
ATHEISM, *s.* Aicheadh air bith Dhé.
ATHEIST, *s.* Fear-àicheadh Dhé.
ATHEISTICAL, *adj.* Neo-chreideach.
ATHEIZE, *v. n.* Labhair mar fhearàicheadh Dhé.
ATHLETIC, *adj.* Làidir, calma, fearail.
ATHWART, *adv.* Gu tuaitheal tarsuinn.
ATLAS, *s.* Leabhar dealbha dhùthchannan.
ATMOSPHERE, *s.* An t-àileadh, adhar.
ATOM, ATOMY, *s.* Dadmun, smùirnean, càillean, dùradan, fuilbhean.
ATOMICAL, *adj.* Smùirneanach, deannanach, fuilbheanach, &c.
ATOMISM, *s.* Teagasg nan smùirnean.
ATONE, *v. a.* and *n.* Thoir dìol, érig; dean réite air son chiontach.
ATONEMENT, *s.* Réite, còrdadh; éirig, ìobairt-réite.
ATROCIOUS, *adj.* Aingidh, an-trom, mallaichte, fuilteach, borb.
ATROCIOUSLY, *adv.* Gu h-aingidh, &c.
ATROCITY, *s.* Aingidheachd, buirbe.
ATTACH, *v. a.* Glac; tàlaidh, dlùthaich riut féin.
ATTACHMENT, *s.* Dìsleachd, a leanmhainneachd, dàimh; gràdh, rùn.
ATTACK, *v. a.* Thoir ionnsaidh; cronaich
ATTACK, *s.* Ionnsaidh nàimhdeil.
ATTAIN, *v. a.* and *n.* Faigh, buannaich, coisinn; thig suas; ruig, gabh seilbh thig a dh' ionnsaidh.
ATTAINABLE, *adj.* So-ruigheachd.
ATTAINDER, *s.* Dìteadh lagha, cùirtdhìteadh; truailleachd, coire.
ATTAINMENT, *s.* Buannachd, ionnsachadh; ruigsinn.
ATTAINT, *v. a.* Maslaich; salaich, truaill.
ATTEMPER, ATTEMPERATE, *v. a.* Measgaich; bogaich; dean freagarrach.
ATTEMPT, *v. a.* Thoir ionnsaidh.
ATTEMPT, *s.* Ionnsaidh; oidheirp.
ATTEND, *v. a.* and *n.* Feith, fritheil, fan, fuirich; thoir aire, beachdaich.
ATTENDANCE, *s.* Feitheamh, frithealadh; aire, seirbhis.
ATTENDANT, *adj.* Fritheilteach.
ATTENDANT, *s.* Fear-frithealaidh;
ATTENTION, *s.* Aire, furachras, faicill,
ATTENTIVE, *adj.* Furachail, faicilleach, cùramach.
ATTENUATE, *v. a.* Tanaich; lùghdaich.
ATTENUATION, *s.* Tanachadh, tanachd.
ATTEST, *v. a.* Thoir fianais, tog fianais.
ATTEST, *s.* Fianais, teisteannas.
ATTESTATION, *s.* Teisteas, dearbhadh.
ATTIC, *adj.* Glan-chainnteach, grinnlabhrach.
ATTIRE, *v. a.* Aodaich, còmhdaich, sgeudaich, sgiamhaich, cuir an uidheam.
ATTIRE, *s.* Aodach, eudach, còmhdach, earradh, culaidh, trusgan.
ATTITUDE, *s.* Suidheachadh, seasamh.
ATTORNEY, *s.* Àrd-sgrìobhair lagha.
ATTRACT, *v. a.* Tarruinn, tàlaidh, meall.
ATTRACTION, *s.* Comas tàlaidh no meallaidh, sùghadh.
ATTRACTIVE, *adj.* Tarruinneach, sùghach; tàlaidheach, mealltach.

ATTRACTIVE, *s.* Tàladh, mealladh.
ATTRIBUTE, *v. a.* Cuir ás leth.
ATTRIBUTE, *s.* Feart, buaidh, cliù.
ATTRIBUTION, *s.* Moladh, buaidh-chliù.
ATTRITION, *s.* Caitheamh, rubadh, bleith, min-shuathadh; duilichinn; cràdh inntinn.
ATTUNE, *v. a.* Gleus, cuir am fonn.
AVAIL, *v. a.* Buannaich, coisinn, dean feum.
AVAILABLE, *adj.* Buannachail, tarbhach, feumail; cumhachdach.
AVARICE, *s.* Sannt, spìocaireachd.
AVARICIOUS, *adj.* Sanntach, déidheil, spìocach.
AVAST, *adv.* Cum air do làimh, stad, sguir, gu leòir,
AVAUNT, *interj.* As mo shealladh! air falbh! trŭis!
AUBURN, *adj.* Buidhe-dhonn.
AUCTION, *s.* Reic follaiseach co-thairgseach.
AUCTIONEER, *s.* Fear-reic co-thairgseach.
AUCUPATION, *s.* Eunadaireachd.
AUDACIOUS, *adj.* Dàna, ladorna; beagnàrach, beadaidh.
AUDACIOUSNESS, *s.* Dànachd.
AUDACITY, *s.* Tapachd, misneach.
AUDIBLE, *adj.* Labhrach, àrd-ghuthach.
AUDIENCE, *s.* Éisdeachd; luchd-éisdeachd, co-thional.
AUDITOR, *s.* Fear-éisdeachd.
AUDITORY, *s.* Luchd-éisdeachd; ionad-éisdeachd.
AVE-MARY, *s.* Fàilte-Muire.
AVENGE, *v. a.* Dìol, thoir gu peanas.
AVENGEANCE, *s.* Dìoghaltas, peanas.
AVENGEMENT, *s.* Dìoghaltas, dìoladh.
AVENGER, *s.* Fear-dìolaidh.
AVENUE, *s.* Rathad, slighe, sràid eadar chraobhan.
AVER, *v. a.* Cuir an céill, abair gu barantach.
AVERAGE, *s.* Eadar dhà anabharra.
AVERMENT, *s.* Dearbhadh le fianais;
AVERSE, *adj.* Fuathach, gràinichte.
AVERSION, *s.* Fuath, gràin.
AVERT, *v. a.* Tionndaidh gu taobh.
AUGER, *s.* Tora, sniamhaire, boireal.
AUGHT, *pron.* Ni sam bith, dad.
AUGMENT, *v. a.* Meudaich.
AUGMENT, *s.* Meudachadh, piseach.
AUGMENTATION, *s.* Seòl meudachaidh.
AUGUR, *s.* Fiosaiche, eun-dhruidh.
AUGURATION, *s.* Eun-dhruidheachd.
AUGURY, *s.* Fiosachd le comharraibh.
AUGUST, *s.* Ceud mìos an Fhoghair.
AUGUST, *adj.* Mòr, urramach, naomha.
AVIARY, *s.* Eun-lann.
AVIDITY, *s.* Gionachd, glamaireachd.
AULIC, *adj.* Cùirteil, rìoghail, flathail.
AULN, *s.* Slat-thomhais.

AUNT, *s.* Piuthar athar no màthar.
AVOCATE, *v. a.* Gairm air falbh.
AVOCATION, *s.* Gairm a leth-taobh.
AVOID, *v. a.* and *n.* Seachain; cuitich, cuir cùl.
AVOIDABLE, *adj.* So-sheachante.
AVOKE, *v. a.* Gairm air ais.
AVOLATION, *s.* Itealachadh, fuadach, teicheadh.
AVOUCH, *v. a.* Abair gu daingeann, cuir an céill gu dian; thoir dearbhadh.
AVOUCH, *s.* Aideachadh, fianais, teisteas.
AVOW, *v. a.* Cuir an céill, aidich.
AVOWAL, *s.* Aideachadh fosgailte.
AURELIA, *s.* Spiontag, òg-chnuimh.
AURICLE, *s.* Bilean na cluaise; cluasan a' chridhe.
AURICULA, *s.* Lŭs-na-bann-rìgh.
AURICULAR, *adj.* Teann air a' chluais.
AURIST, *s.* Olla-chluas.
AURORA, *s.* Luibh-chrodh'-an-eich: reull na maidne.
AURORA-BOREALIS, *s.* Na fir-chlis.
AUSCULTATION, *s.* Cluas-aire.
AUSPICE, *s.* Manadh; dìon, caoimhneas.
AUSPICIOUS, *adj.* Sealbhach; sona.
AUSTERE, *adj.* Teann, cruaidh, bodachail; searbh, geur.
AUSTERITY, *s.* Teanntachd, gruamachd: an-iochd.
AUSTRAL, *adj.* A deas, deiseal.
AUTHENTIC, *a.* Fìor, cinnteach.
AUTHENTICATE, *v. a.* Dearbh le ùghdarras.
AUTHENTICITY, *v. a.* Cinnteachd.
AUTHOR, *s.* Ùghdar, fear sgrìobhaidh.
AUTHORITATIVE, *adj.* Ùghdarrach.
AUTHORITY, *s.* Ùghdarras; cumhachd.
AUTHORIZE, *v. a.* Thoir ùghdarras, ceadaich; fìreanaich, dearbh.
AUTOGRAPHY, *s.* Dearbh làmh-sgrìobhaidh.
AUTUMN, *s.* Am foghar.
AUTUMNAL, *adj.* Fogharach.
AVULSION, *s.* Spìonadh, reubadh.
AUXILIAR, AUXILIARY, *s.* Fear-cuideachaidh.
AUXILIATION, *s.* Cuideachadh, còmhnadh, cobhair.
AWAIT, *v. a.* Fuirich, fan, feith.
AWAKE, *v. a.* Dùisg, mosgail.
AWARD, *v. a.* Thoir dìoladh a réir toillteanais.
AWARD, *s.* Breitheanas, binn.
AWARE, *adj.* Faicilleach, furachair.
AWAY, *adv.* Air falbh, trŭs air falbh!
AWE, *s.* Eagal, urram, giorrag.
AWFUL, *adj.* Eagalach, a dhùisgeas urram; urramach; gealtach.
AWFULNESS, *s.* Uabhasachd, eagalachd.
AWHILE, *adv.* Tacan, car tacain.
AWKWARD, *adj.* Cearbach, neo-sgiob-

alta, slaodach, slaopach, neo-làmh-ach, liobasta.
AWKWARDLY, *adv* Gu cearbach.
AWL, *s.* Minidh bhròg.
AWN, *s.* Calg, arbhair no feòir.
AWNING, *s.* Brat-dìona; brat-dubhair.
AWOKE, *the preterite* of to *Awake*, Dhùisg.
AWRY, *adv.* Cam, claon, fiar-shuileach
AXE, *s.* Tuagh; lamh-thuagh.
AXILLA, *s.* Lag na h-achlais, asgail.
AXILLAR, *adj.* Asgaileach.
AXIOM, *s.* Fìrinn shoilleir, fìrinn so-fhaicsinneach; fìrinn shuidhichte.
AXLE, AXLE-TREE, *s.* Aiseal, crann-aisil.
AY, *adv.* Seadh, gu dearbh.
AYE, *adv.* Do ghnà, gu bràth.
AZURNE, *adj.* Speur-ghorm, liath-ghorm.

B

B, Dara litir na h-aibidil.
BAA, *s.* Méilich, méile nan caorach.
BAAL, *s.* Beil, dia bréige, iodhol.
BABBLE, *s.* Gobaireachd, luath-bheul-achd.
BABBLER, *s.* Glagair, beul-gun-fhàith-eam.
BABBLING, *s.* Glagaireachd, glogair-eachd.
BABE, *s.* Naoidhean, naoidheachan, leanaban.
BABOON, *s.* Apa, do'n t-seòrsa is mò.
BACCAATED, *adj.* Neamhnaideach, cuir-neanach.
BACCHANALIAN, *s.* Misgear.
BACHELOR, *s.* Seana-ghille, fear gun bhean, &c. &c.
BACK, *s.* Cùl, cùl-thaobh; druim, croit.
BACK, *adv.* Air ais; an coinneamh a chùil.
BACK, *v. a.* Theirig air muin, marcaich; tog air muin; seas dìon, tagair, neart-aich, cuidich; dìon.
BACKBITE, *v. a.* Cùl-chàin, tog tuaileas.
BACKBITER, *s.* Fear cùl-chàinnt, fear-tuaileis.
BACKED, *part.* Cùltacaichte.
BACKGAMMON, *s.* Tàileasg.
BACKSIDE, *s.* Leth-deiridh, tòn, taobh-cùil.
BACKSLIDER, *s.* Fear-cul-sleamhnach-aidh.
BACKSTAY, *s.* Stadh-cùil.
BACKSWORD, *s.* Claidheamh aon fhaobh-air.
BACKWARD, *adv.* An coinneamh a chùil.
BACKWARD, *adj.* Neo-thoileach, ain-deonach; mall, leasg, tròm.
BACON, *s.* Muic-fheoil chruaidh-shaillt
BAD, *adj.* Olc, dona; aingidh, crosda cronail, ciurrail, tinn, euslan.
BADE, *pret.* of Bid. Dh' iarr.
BADGE, *s.* Suaicheantas; comharradh.
BADGER, *s.* Broc, tùitean, srianach.
BAFFLE, *v. a.* and *n.* Fairtlich air, rach as o, seachainn, mill; faigh làmh an uachdar air, thoir an car á; dean fa-naid no sgeig air.
BAG, *s.* Poca, balg, sac, mala, màileid.
BAGATELLE, *s.* Faoineas, ni gun luach.
BAGGAGE, *s.* Àirneis. treathlaich feachd; imrich; dubh-chaile.
BAGNIO, *s.* Taigh-faircidh, taigh-siùrs-achd.
BAGPIPE, *s.* Pìob Ghàëlach.
BAIL, *s.* Saorsa, no fuasgladh air urras; fear-urrais, urras; crìoch frìthe.
BAIL, *v. a.* Urrasaich, rach an urras air, thoir urras air; fuasgail air urras.
BAILIFF, *s.* Bàillidh, maor, fear-riagh-laidh; peathair; maor-fearainn.
BAILIWICK, *s.* Bàillidheachd.
BAIT, *v. a.* and *n.* Cuir maghar air dubhan; biadh, thoir biadh; sàth ann, thoir ionnsaidh air; sàraich, mar bheathach 's an stuigear coin; stad a chum bìdh.
BAIT, *s.* Maghar; buaireadh, culaidh-bhuairidh, biadh meallaidh.
BAIZE, *s.* Garbh-chlò fosgailte.
BAKE, *v. a.* and *n.* Fuin, taosainn, bruich ann an àmhainn.
BAKEHOUSE, *s.* Taigh-fuine.
BAKEN, *part.* Fuinte, cruadhaichte.
BAKER, *s.* Fuineadair.
BALANCE, *s.* Meidh, toimhsean; dlù-bheachd; co-chothromachadh; barr-achd cudthrom; claban uaireadair.
BALCONY, *s.* For-uinneag, for-aradh.
BALD, *adj.* Maol, sgailceach, lom.
BALDERDASH, *s.* Treamsgal, goileam, earra-ghloir.
BALDNESS, *s.* Maoile, sgailc.
BALDPATE, *s.* Maol-cheann.
BALE, *s.* Bathar truiste, sac, ni sam bith truiste chum iomchar; truaighe.
BALEFUL, *adj.* Truagh, brònach, dògh-ruinneach; millteach, sgriosail.
BALK, *s.* Sail, sparr; balc, bailc, bàn-dhruim eadar dà iomaire; amladh, dìobradh dòchais.
BALK, *v.* Dìobair, tréig.
BALL, *s.* Ball, peileir, co-thional damhsa.
BALLAD, *s.* Duanag, òran, luinneag.
BALLAST, *s.* Fàradh luinge no bàta.
BALLOON, *s.* Inneal dìridh agus seòl-aidh 's na speuraibh.
BALLOT, *s.* Crann, crannchur; tilgeadh chrann.

Balm, *s.* Ìoc-shlaint.
Balmy, *adj.* Ìoc-shlainteach.
Balsam, *s.* Ola-leighis.
Balsamic, *adj.* Furtachail.
Baluster, *s.* Post beag, rongas.
Balustrade, *s.* Sreath phost no rongas.
Bamboo, *s.* Cuilc Ìnnseanach.
Bamboozle, *v. a.* Meall, car.
Ban, *s.* Gairm fhollaiseach.
Banana-tree, *s.* Cuach-Phàdruig.
Band, *s.* Ceangal, bann; cuibhreach, slabhraidh; bann-daingneachaidh; bannal, còisir, cuideachd.
Bandage, *s.* Bann, stiom-cheangail.
Band-box, *s.* Bòsdan sliseig.
Banditti, *s. pl.* Luchd-reubainn.
Bandore, *s.* Inneal-ciùil trì-theudach.
Bandy, *v. a.* and *n.* Tilg a null 'sa nall, iomain air ais 's air, adhart; gabh is thoir, co-iomlaidich; ioma-luaisg.
Bandy-leg, *s.* Cama-chas, cas-cham.
Bandy-legged, *adj.* Cama-chasach.
Bane, *s.* Nimh; aimhleas, sgrios, creach.
Baneful, *adj.* Nimheil, aimhleasach.
Bane-wort, *s.* Lùs-na-h-òidhche.
Bang, *v.* Slacaich, dòrn, garbh-laimhsich.
Bang, *s.* Cnap, dòrn, garbh-bhuille.
Banish, *v. a.* Fuadaich á 'dhùthaich; fògair.
Banishment, *s.* Fògradh, fògairt.
Bank, *s.* Bruach aibhne no uillt; tòrr, tom, dùn; taigh-tasgaidh airgeid.
Banker, *s.* Fear-malairt-airgeid.
Bankrupt, *s.* Fear-briste, ceannaiche briste.
Bankruptcy, *s.* Briseadh, creideis.
Banner, *s.* Bratach, suaicheantas.
Banneret, *s.* Ridire-làraich.
Bannock, *s.* Bonnach, breacag.
Banquet, *s.* Cuilm, cuirm, fleadh.
Banqueting, *s.* Fleadhachas.
Banstickle, *s.* A' bhiorag-lodain.
Banter, *s.* Magadh, fochaid, sgeig.
Bantling, *s.* Isean leinibh, leanaban.
Baptism, *s.* Baisteadh.
Baptismal, *adj.* Baistidh, baisteachail.
Baptist, **Baptizer**, *s.* Fear-baistidh.
Bar, *s.* Crann, crann-tarsuinn, crann-doruis; stad, grabadh, amladh, cnap-starraidh; oitir, sgeir-bhàite; ionad-tagraidh, bhreith; aite roinn na dibhe; geinn.
Bar, *v. a.* Crann, glais, dùin le crann; bac, grab; cum a muigh.
Barb, *s.* Feusag; corran, gath, friobhag.
Barb, *v. a.* Bearr, lomair; riobhagaich, thoir calg, thoir corran; uidheamaich each cogaidh.
Barbarian, *s.* Allmharach, duine borb.
Barbaric, *adj.* Céin-thireach, coimheach.
Barbarism, *s.* Brùidealachd, an-iochdmhorachd, buirbe.
Barbarous, *adj.* Borb, allmhara, fiaghaich; neo-oileanta, brùideil; an-iochdmhor, garg, cruaidh-chridheach.
Barbed, *adj.* Armaichte, beartaichte, fo làn-uidheam-cogaidh; riobhagach, corranach, biorach, gathach, calgach.
Barbel, *s.* Seòrs' éisg, breac-feusagach; a' mhiol gàilleach.
Barber, *s.* Bearradair fuilt no feusaig
Barberry, *s.* Preas nan-gearr-dhearc, gearr-dhearcag.
Bard, *s.* Bàrd, aos-dana, filidh.
Bardic, *adj.* Bardail.
Bare, *adj.* Lom, lomnochd, rùisgte, nochdte, ris, follaiseach; falamh.
Barefaced, *adj.* Bathaiseach; ladorna, leamh, mi-nàrach.
Barefooted, *adj.* Cas-ruisgte.
Bareheaded, *adj.* Ceann-ruisgte.
Barelegged, *adj.* Luirg-ruisgte.
Bargain, *s.* Cùmhnant; luach-peighinn.
Bargain, *v. n.* Cùmhnantaich, còrd.
Barge, *s.* Bàta, bìrlinn.
Barilla, *s.* Luaithre do'n deantear glainne.
Bark, *s.* Cairt, rùsg; bàrca, long bheag.
Bark, *v. a.* and *n.* Rùisg, thoir a chairt dheth.
Barker, *s.* Fear-tathuinn; dreamaire fear-rusgaidh chraobh.
Barky, *adj.* Cairteach, cairtidh.
Barley, *s.* Eòrna.
Barleycorn, *s.* Gràinnean-eòrna, treas earrainn na h-òirlich.
Barm, *s.* Beirm, deasgainn.
Barn, *s.* Sabhal, sobhal, sgiobal.
Barn-yard, *s.* Iolann.
Barnacle, *s.* Bàirneach; an cathan.
Barometer, *s.* Gloine-shìde.
Baron, *s.* Ridire. [Rìgh-tìre.]
Baronage, *s.* Baranachd, ridireachd.
Baroness, *s.* Baintighearn, ban-ridire.
Baronet, *s.* Ridire beag.
Baronical, *adj.* Baranach.
Barony, *s.* Inbhe-barain.
Barrack, *s.* Taigh-feachd.
Barrel, *s.* Baraille, feadan, guna.
Barren, *adj.* Seasg, aimrid, neo-thorach, fàs.
Barrenness, *s.* Aimrideachd, seasgachd.
Barricade, *s.* Balla-bacaidh.
Barricade, *v. a.* Glais suas, duin.
Barricado, *s.* Daingneachd, babhunn, dìdean.
Barrier, *s.* Daingneach, dìon, balla-bacaidh, tùr, dùn; bacadh, amladh

cnapstarraidh; comharradh-crìche, gàradh-crìche.

BARRISTER, *s.* Fear-tagraidh, an cùirt-ibh Shasuinn.

BARROW, *s.* Bara; boglach; tolman; tonn.

BARTER, *s.* Malairt, iomlaid.

BARTER, *v. a.* Iomlaidich, malairtich, suaip, dean malairt, &c.

BARTRAM, *s.* Lŭs-a-bhalla.

BASALTES, *s.* Gnè chloiche.

BASE, *s.* Stéidh, bonn, bunait, iochdar, bunchar.

BASE, *adj.* Suarach, neo-luachmhor, truaillidh, gun fhiù; ìosal, tàireil.

BASENESS, *s.* Suarachas, neo-luach-mhorachd, tàirealachd, truailleachd.

BASHAW, *s.* Thurcach; fear stràiceil.

BASHFUL, *adj.* Gnùis-nàrach, athach; diùid, saidealta.

BASHFULNESS, *s.* Nàire, saidealtas.

BASILICA, *s.* Feith-mheadhon a' ghàir-dean.

BASIN, *s.* Soitheach ionnlaid; long-phort.

BASIS, *s.* Stéidh, bunait; roinn ìochd-rach puist; bunchar, bun.

BASK, *v. a.* and *n.* Grianaich, laidh 's a' bhlàthas.

BASKET, *s.* Bascaid, cliabh, sgùlan, craidhleag.

BASS, *s.* Cas-chlùd.

BASS, *adj.* Dos-fhuaimneach.

BASTARD, *s.* Neach dìolain; ni truaill-idh.

BASTARD, *adj.* Dìolain; truaillidh.

BASTARDIZE. *v. a.* and *n.* Dearbh dìolain; dean dìolanas, faigh urra dhìolain.

BASTE, *v. a.* Gabh air le bata; leagh ìm air.

BASTINADE, BASTINADO, *v. a.* Slachd le bata, gabh air le bata.

BAT, *s.* Ialtag, an dialtag.

BATCH, *s.* Uiread a' dh' aran 'sa dh' fhuinear aig aon àm.

BATE, *s.* Strìth, caonnag, co-strith.

BATE, *v. a.* and *n.* Lughdaich, leag sìos; thoir sìos am prìs, leag am prìs, math.

BATH, *s.* Àit'-ionnlaid, àite-nighe; nighe, ionnlad.

BATHE, *v. a.* and *n.* Ionnlaid, fairig, failc, nigh.

BATHOS, *s.* Sgleò-bhardachd.

BATLET, *s.* Slacan, siomaid, cuaile.

BATON, *s.* Bata, bata-dreuchd àrd-chinn-iùil; comharradh-dìolanais ann an gearradh-arm.

BATTALIA, *s.* Òrdugh-catha.

BATTALION, *s.* Cuideachda shaighdearan bho 500, gu 800 fear.

BATTEN, *s.* Maide, mìr fiodha.

BATTER, *v. a.* and *n.* Buail sìos, pronn, slachd, tilg sìos, leag sìos; claoidh le trom sheirbhis.

BATTER, *s.* Coimeasgadh, glaogh.

BATTERING-RAM, *s.* Reithe-cogaidh, reithe-slachdaidh, ceann-reithe.

BATTERY, *s.* Bualadh sìos, slacadh; innealan slacaidh; balla ghunn-aichean mòra; ionnsaidh nàimhdeil.

BATTLE, *s.* Cath, blàr, còmhrag.

BATTLE-ARRAY, *s.* Òrdugh-catha

BATTLE-AXE, *s.* Tuagh-chatha.

BATTLEDOOR, *s.* Stroidhleagan.

BATTLEMENT, *s.* Barra-bhalla.

BAUBLE, *s.* Déideag, cleas.

BAWL, *v. a.* and *n.* Glaodh, ràn, raoic

BAWREL, *s.* Spearag.

BAY, *adj.* Buidhe-ruadh.

BAY, *s.* Camus, loch-mara, bàgh.

BAY-SALT, *s.* Salann-mara.

BAY-TREE, *s.* Craobh-laibhreis.

BAYONET, *s.* Béigeileid.

BAZAAR, *s.* Àite-margaidh.

BE, *v. n.* Bi; bi ann, bi beò.

BEACH, *s.* Mol, tràigh, cladach.

BEACON, *s.* Taigh-soluis.

BEAD, *s.* Paidirean; grìogag.

BEADLE, *s.* Maor; no maor-eaglais.

BEAGLE, *s.* Cù-luirg.

BEAK, *s.* Gob; sròn; bior-snaois.

BEAKER, *s.* Soitheach-gobach.

BEAM, *s.* Sail; meidh; cròc, garm-ainn; gath-soluis, gath-gréine, deal-radh, boillsgeadh, dearsadh.

BEAM, *v. n.* Dealraich, soillsich, dears soillsich air.

BEAN, *s.* Pònar.

BEAR, *v. a.* and *n.* Giùlain, iomchair, cum suas, fuilig.

BEAR, *s.* Math-ghamhainn, torc.

BEARD, *s.* Feusag; calg, colg.

BEARDLESS, *adj.* Gun fheusag, lom smigeach; smigideach.

BEARER, *s.* Fear-iomchair; fear-giùlain cuirp do'n uaigh.

BEARING, *s.* Suidheachadh, sealltainn, aghaidh; modh, giùlan; cùrsa.

BEAST, *s.* Ainmhidh, beathach; brùid, biast.

BEASTLY, *adj.* Brùideil, biastail.

BEAT, *v. a.* and *n.* Buail, thoir buille; gabh air, faigh buaidh.

BEATIFIC, *adj.* Sona, làn sonais.

BEATIFICATION, *s.* Làn-shona.

BEATING, *s.* Gabhail air, gréidheadh.

BEATITUDE, *s.* Sonas néamhaidh.

BEAU, *s.* Spalpaire, fear, rìmheach; leannan.

BEAVER, *s.* Dobhar-chu, clàr-aghaidh clogaid.

BEAUTEOUS, *adj.* Maiseach, àluinn, bòidheach, sgiamhach, grinn.

Beauteousness, *s.* Maisealachd.
Beautiful, *adj.* Bòidheach, rìmheach.
Beautify, *v. a.* and *n.* Maisich sgiamhaich grinnich.
Beauty, *s.* Maise, àillte, sgèimh.
Beauty-spot, *s.* Ball-seirce.
Becalm, *v. a.* Sàmhaich, foisich, ciùinich.
Because, *conj.* Air son, do-bhrìgh.
Beck, *s.* Sméideadh.
Beckon, *v. n.* Sméid air.
Become, *v. n.* Cinn, fàs freagair.
Becoming, *adj.* Iomchuidh, dligheach, tlachdmhor, ciatach, taitneach, freagarrach.
Bed, *s.* Leabaidh.
Bedash, *v. a.* Eabraich, beubanaich.
Bedding, *s.* Uidheam-leapa.
Bedeck, *v. a.* Sgéimhich, snasaich.
Bedehouse, *s.* Taigh-oiriceis.
Bedew, *v. a.* Dealtraich, driùchdaich.
Bedfellow, *s.* Coimhleapach.
Bedlam, *s.* Taigh-cuthaich.
Bedlamite, *s.* Neach cuthaich.
Bedrid, *adj.* Air an aon-leabaidh, tinn.
Bedstead, *s.* Fiodh-leapa.
Bee, *s.* Beach, seillean.
Beech, *s.* Crann-fàibhile.
Beef, *s.* Mairt-fheoil; mart-biadhta.
Beef-eater, *s.* Gille-taigh-rìgh.
Beer, *s.* Leann-caol.
Beet, *s.* Ainm luis, biotais.
Beetle, *s.* Daolag, fairche, simist.
Beeves *s. pl.* Crodh, daimh, spréidh.
Befal, *v. n.* Tachair thig gu crìch gu teachd.
Befit, *v. a.* Freagair, dean iomchuidh.
Before, *prep.* Roimh; air beulthaobh; an làthair, 'san làthair; mu choinneamh; roimhe, a roghainn air; osceann.
Before, *adv.* Roimhe, roimhe sin; 'san àm a chaidh; gus a nise; cheana.
Beforehand, *adv.* Roi-laimh, air tùs.
Befoul, *v. a.* Salaich, truaill.
Befriend, *v. a.* Dean càirdeas.
Beg, *v. a.* and *n.* Iarr, sir, guidh, thig beò air déircibh, falbh air déirc.
Beget, *v. a.* Gin; tàrmaich.
Beggar, *s.* Déirceach, diol-déirce.
Beggarly, *adj.* Bochd, dìblidh, truagh.
Beggary, *s.* Bochdainn, aimbeairt.
Begin, *v. a.* and *n.* Tòisich, tionnsgain.
Beginner, *s.* Fòghlumaich.
Beginning, *s.* Toiseach, aobhar, prìomhaobhar. tòiseachadh.
Begird, *v. a.* Crioslaich, cuartaich; iadh.
Begone, *interj.* Air falbh thu! á m' fhianais! trùis!
Begot, *pret. v.* Beget. Ghin.
Begotten, *pret. part v.* Beget. Ginte, air a ghineamhuinn.
Beguile, *v. a.* Meall, car breug.
Begun, *pret. part. v.* Begin, Tòisichte.
Behalf, *s.* Deagh-ghean, as leth, air a thaobh, air son.
Behave, *v. a.* Giùlain, gluais, gnàthaich.
Behaviour, *s.* Giùlan gluasad, cleachdadh, gnàthachadh; beus, modh.
Behead, *v. a.* Thoir an ceann dheth.
Behemoth, *s.* An t-Each-uisg.
Behind, *prep.* Air chùl, air deireadh.
Behind-hand, *adv.* An déigh làimhe.
Behold, *v. a.* Faic, seall, amhairc, thoir fainear.
Behold, *interj.* Feuch.
Beholden, *adj.* An comain, fo fhiachaibh.
Behoof, *s.* Ni tha chum buannachd, math.
Behoove, *v. n.* Bi iomchuidh, freagarrach.
Being, *s.* Bith; inbhe, còr, beatha; creutair, tì, urra, neach, cré.
Belabour, *v. a.* Slachd, buail gu minig.
Belch, *v. a.* and *n.* Brùchd a mach, brist gaoth, diobair; taom a mach.
Beldam, *s.* Seanna chailleach chrosda.
Beleaguer, *v. a.* Iomadhruid.
Belfry, *s.* Taigh-cluig.
Belie, *v. a.* Breugaich, thoir a bhreug dha; aithris breugan.
Believe, *v. a.* and *n.* Creid, thoir creideas, biodh creideamh agad.
Believer, *s.* Creideach, Criosdaidh.
Bell, *s.* Clag, glag; àrd onoir cùise.
Belle, *s.* Boireannach, rìmheach.
Belles-lettres, *s.* Snas-chainnt sgrìobhaidh.
Belligerant, *adj.* Bagarach air cogadh.
Bellow, *s.* Beuc, ràn, geum.
Bellowing, *s.* Beucaich, bùirich.
Bellows, *s.* Balg-séididh.
Belly, *s.* Brù, bolg, broinn.
Belman, *s.* Fear-bualaidh cluig.
Belong, *v. n* Buin, bhuneas
Beloved, *part.* Gràdhaichte.
Below, *prep.* Fo, shìos.
Below, *adv.* Gu h-ìosal.
Belt, *s.* Crios, crios-leasraidh.
Bemoan, *v. a.* Dean cumha, caoidh.
Bench, *s.* Being, ionad-suidhe; cathair-bhreitheanais; luchd-ceartais.
Bencher, *s.* Fear-tagraidh an cùirtcheartais; breitheamh.
Bend, *v. a.* Crom, cam, lùb; stiùr, aom; ceannsaich; bi claon, bi fiar.
Bend, *s.* Cromadh, camadh, fiaradh.
Bendable, *adj.* So-lùbaidh.
Beneath, *prep.* Fo, an ìochdar.
Benediction, *s.* Beannachadh.

BENEFACTION, *s.* Tiodhlacadh, deagh-ghniomh.
BENEFACTOR, *s.* Tabhartair; fear fuasg-laidh.
BENEFICE, *s.* Beathachadh eaglais.
BENEFICENCE, *s* Mathas, oircheas.
BENEFICENT, *adj.* Toirbheartach, seirc-eil, fiùghantach, còir
BENEFICIAL, *adj.* Tarbhach, luachmhor, feumail.
BENEFIT, s. Tiodhlac, deagh-ghniomh.
BENEVOLENCE, *s.* Mathas, fiùghantachd, deagh-ghean.
BENEVOLENT, *adj.* Caoimhneil, seirc-eil, mathasach, fiùghantach.
BENIGHT, *v. a.* Dorchaich, duibhrich; cuartaich le dorchadas; cum an ain-eolas.
BENIGN, *adj.* Caoimhneil, fiùghantach, fial, mathasach, tròcaireach.
BENIGNITY, *s.* Tròcaireachd, mathas-achd; caomhalachd.
BENISON, *s.* Beannachd, beannachadh.
BENT, *s.* Camadh, lùbadh, cromadh; claonadh, fiaradh; rùn-suidhichte, toil, togradh; mŭran.
BENUMB, *v. a.* Meilich, einglich.
BEQUEATH, *v. a.* Tiomnaich, fàg mar dhìleab.
BEQUEST, *s.* Dìleab.
BERBERRY, *s.* Goirt-dhearc.
BEREAVE, *v. a.* Buin uaith, creach, rùisg, thoir air falbh.
BERRY, *s.* Dearc, dearcag.
BERYL, *s.* Clach luachmor, beril.
BESEECH, *s.* Iarrtas, achanaich, guidhe.
BESEEM, *v. a.* Bi freagarrach, iom-chuidh.
BESET, *v. a.* Cuartaich, iadh mu thim-chioll; fàth, fheith; buail air.
BESIDE, BESIDES, *prep.* Làmh ri, ri taobh; a bharr, a thuilleadh.
BESIEGE, *v. a.* Séisd, iom-dhruid, teannaich cuartaich.
BESMEAR, *v. a.* Salaich, luidrich, smeur.
BESOM, *s.* Sguab-ùrlair.
BESOTTEDNESS, *s.* Amadanachd.
BESPANGLE, *v. a.* Dealraich, lainnirich.
BESPATTER, *v. a.* Salaich, tilg poll air; càin, mill a chliù.
BESPEAK, *v. a.* Orduich, iarr, roi-làimh, cuir an céill do.
BESPRINKLE, *v. a.* Uisgich, sriodag-aich.
BEST, *adj.* A's fearr, iomlan, math.
BESTIAL, *adj.* Ainmhidheach, brùideil, feòlmhor.
BESTIR, *v. a.* Grad ghluais, éirich, mosgail, caraich.
BESTOW, *v. a.* Thoir seachad, builich.
BESTRIDE, *v. a.* Rach casa-gòbhlach.
BET, *v. a.* Cuir geall.
BETAKE, *v. a.* Theirig, tog ort, imich, falbh.
BETHINK, *v. a.* and *n.* Smuaintich, cuimhnich.
BETIDE, *v. a.* and *n.* Tachair o, érich a mach, tàrladh.
BETIMES, *adv.* 'Na àm, moch, tràthail; an ùin' ghearr, gu luath.
BETOKEN, *v. a.* Ciallaich le, comharr-aich, samhlaich; cuir an céill roi-làimh.
BETONY, *s.* Lŭs-Mhic-Bheathaig.
BETRAY, *v. a.* Brath; dean feall, meall, leig ris rùn-dìomhair caraid; nochd a chum a chall; bi luath-bheulach.
BETRAYER, *s.* Brathadair, mealltair.
BETROTH, *v. a.* Réitich, dean ceangal pòsaidh.
BETTER, *adj.* A chuid a's fearr.
BETWEEN, *prep.* Eadar, sa' mheadhon.
BEVEL, *s.* Oisinn neo-dhìreach.
BEVERAGE, *s.* Deoch rìmheach.
BEVY, *s.* Tòtal-eun; coisir.
BEWAIL, *v. a* and *n.* Dean caoidh, guil, tuireadh, bròn.
BEWARE, *v. n.* Thoir an air, bi air t' fhaicill.
BEWILDER, *v. a.* Seachranaich, iomrall-aich.
BEWITCH, *v. a.* Cuir fo gheasaibh.
BEYOND, *prep.* Roimhe; thall, air an taobh thall; ni's faide na; air nach urrainn e ruigheachd; air thoiseach air; thairis air.
BIAS, *s.* Taobh-chudthrom, aomadh, claonadh, toil, togradh.
BIB, *s.* Bréid-uchd, uchdan leinibh.
BIBBER, *s.* Misgear, pòitear.
BIBLE, *s.* Bìoball an leabhar naomha.
BIBLICAL, *adj.* Bioballach, sgriobturail.
BICE, *s.* Dath buidhe no uaine.
BID, *v. a.* Iarr, thoir cuireadh; òr-duich; thoir tairgse, tairg luach.
BIDDEN, *adj.* Cuirte, air a chuireadh; òrduichte.
BIDDER, *s.* Fear-tairgse.
BIDDING, *s.* Ordugh, earail; tairgse.
BIDE, *v. n.* Còmhnaich, tàmh, gabh còmhnaidh, fuirich; mair, fan.
BIDENTAL, *adj.* Dà-fhiaclach.
BIDING, *s.* Tàmhachd, àros, fardoch, dachaigh, asdail, ionad-còmhnaidh.
BIENNIAL, *adj.* Dà-bhliadhnach.
BIER, *s.* Carbad, giùlan.
BIESTING, *s.* Nòs, ceud-bhainne.
BIFARIOUS, *adj.* Dà-fhillte; dà-sheagh-ach.
BIFEROUS, *adj.* A' giùlan dà bharr 'sa bhliadhna.
BIFORM, *adj*, Dà-chruthach.
BIG, *adj.* Mòr, dòmhail, tomadach; leth-tromach, torrach; làn; àrdanach

BIGAMY, *s.* Pòsadh ri dithis bhan
BIGOT, *s.* Fear dall dhian an creideamh
BIGOTRY, *s.* Dìan eud mi-reusanta an creideamh, dall-eud am beachdaibh àraidh.
BILBERRY, *s.* Braoileag.
BILBOES, *s.* Ceap-chas air bòrd luinge.
BILE, *s.* Sùgh searbh, domblas; leannachadh.
BILIOUS, *adj.* Domblasach.
BILK, *v. a.* Thoir an car as, meall.
BILL, *s.* Gob eòin; sgian-sgathaidh; sgrìobhadh-geallaidh; bann iomlaid; &c.
BILL, *v. n.* Cuir gob ri gob.
BILLET-DOUX, *s.* Litir-leannanachd,
BILLIONS, *s.* Deich ceud mìle do dheich ceud mìle.
BILLOW, *s.* Tonn, sumain, bairlinn.
BIN, *s.* Taigh-taisg.
BINARY, *adj.* Dùbailte, dà-fhillte.
BIND, *v. a.* and *n.* Ceangail, cuibhrich, cuir an cuing; crioslaich, cuir uime; naisg, teannaich; cuir fo mhionnaibh; cum a steach, bac; cuir fo fhiachaibh.
BINDER, *s.* Fear ceangail.
BINDING, *s.* Ceangal, ceanglachan.
BINDWEED, *s.* Iadh-lŭs.
BINNACLE, *s.* Ionad socair na cairt-iùil.
BIOGRAPHER, *s.* Beath'-eachdraich.
BIOGRAPHY, *s.* Beath'-eachdraidh.
BIPAROUS, *adj.* A bheireas dithis còlath.
BIPARTITION, *s.* Roinn dà leth.
BIPED, *s.* Dà-chasach.
BIPENNATED, *adj.* Dà-sgiathach.
BIPETALOUS, *adj.* Dă-bhileach.
BIRCH, *s.* Beithe, slat-chaoil.
BIRD, *s.* Eun, eunlaith.
BIRD'S-CHERRY, *s.* Fiodhag.
BIRTH, *s.* Breith; sinnsireachd, sìol; staid-breith, inbhe; an ni a rugadh.
BIRTHRIGHT, *s.* Còir-bhreith.
BISCUIT, *s.* Briscaid.
BISECT, *v. a.* Gearr 's a' mheadhon.
BISHOP, *s.* Easbuig.
BISHOPRIC, *s.* Easbuigeachd.
BISHOP-WEED, *s.* Lŭs-an-easbuig.
BISSEXTILE, *s.* Bliadhna leum.
BIT, *s.* Mìr, crioman, criomag, bìdeag; cabastair sréine, camagan sréine.
BITCH, *s.* Galla; soigh-chulanach.
BITE, *v. a.* Thoir gréim as.
BITE, *s.* Gréim, làn-beòil; gearradh.
BITING, *s.* Teumadh, beumadh.
BITTACLE, See Binnacle.
BITTER, *adj.* Goirt, searbh, teth, geur; garg, sgaiteach, an-iochdmhor; cràiteach, guineach; mi-thaitneach.
BITTERN, *s.* A chorra-ghràin.
BITTERNESS, *s.* Searbhachd, gamhlas, mi-rùn; crosdachd; doilghios, briseadh-cridhe.
BITUMEN, Bìgh-thalmhuinn.
BIVALVE, BIVALVULAR, *adj.* Dà-dhuilleach, chòmhlach, dà-shligeach, mar fheusgan no coilleag, &c.
BIVOUAC, *v. n.* Dean faire na h-oidhche air eagal nàmhaid.
BLAB, *v. a.* and *n.* Bi luath-bheulach.
BLACK, *adj.* Dubh, dorch, doilleir; gruamach, nuarranta, neulach; gràineil, mallaichte, aingidh; dìomhaireach; muladach, brònach, tùrsach.
BLACKAMOOR, *s.* Duine dubh.
BLACKBIRD, *s.* Lon-dubh.
BLACK-CATTLE, *s.* Crodh, buar, nì, feudail, spréidh, tàn.
BLACKCOCK, *s.* An coilleach-dubh.
BLACKGUARD, *s.* Balach suarach mi-bheusach.
BLACKEN, *v. a.* and *n.* Dubh, dubhaich, dean dubh; dorchaich; cùl-chàin, mill cliù; fàs dorch, bi dubh.
BLACKNESS, *s.* Duibhead, dorchachd.
BLACKSMITH, *s.* Gobha-iarainn.
BLADDER, *s.* Aotroman, balg.
BLADE, *s.* Bileag-fheòir, no fhochainn; lann, iarann claidheimh no sgeine; lasgaire, fear spaideil; cnàimh an t-slinnean.
BLAIN, *s.* Neasgaid, guirean, leus.
BLAMABLE, *adj.* Coireach, ciontach.
BLAMABLENESS, *s.* Ciontachd, coireachd.
BLAME, *v. a.* Coirich, faigh cron do.
BLAME, *s.* Coire; cionta, lochd, cron.
BLAMELESS, *adj.* Neo-choireach, neo-chiontach.
BLANCH, *v. a.* and *n.* Gealaich, dean geal no bàn; rùisg, sgrath; seachain, fàg, leig le; cuir a thaobh, buin gu séimh.
BLAND, *adj.* Caoin, caomh, mìn, tlàth séimh, ciùin, fòill.
BLANDISH, *v. a.* Séimhich, dean caoin, breug, dean cainnt thlà.
BLANDISHMENT, *s.* Cainnt thlà, caoin-mholadh, fòill-labhairt, brosgal.
BLANK, *adj.* Geal, bàn; gun sgrìobhadh.
BLANK, *s.* Aite falamh, mìr pàipeir gun sgrìobhadh; crannchur gun luach, cuspair.
BLANKET, *s.* Plaide, plancaid.
BLASPHEMING, *s.* Toibheumachadh.
BLASPHEMOUSLY, *ad.* Toibheumach.
BLASPHEMY, *s.* Toibheum.
BLAST, *s.* Osag, séideag, oiteag; sgal.
BLAST, *v. a.* Seachd, searg; mill.
BLAZE, *s.* Lasair, solus lasarach, lèus soluis; blàradh.
BLAZE, *v. a.* and *n.* Cuir am farsuinn-

eachd, craobh-sgaoil; dealraich, taisbean thu fein.

Balzon, *v. a.* Dean soilleir comharran ghearradh-arm; sgeadaich gu maiseach; seòl gu follaiseach, taisbean, cuir a mach; àrd-mhol, sgaoil a chliù, dean follaiseach, gairm suas.

Blazon, *s.* Gearradh-arm; soillseachadh, taisbeanadh; moladh, cliù-ghairm.

Bleach, *v. a.* and *n.* Gealaich, dean geal; fàs geal, todhair.

Bleak, *adj.* Lom, fuar, fuaraidh, nochdaidh, gun tuar.

Blear, *adj.* Rèasg-shuileach, prabshuileach, mùsgach, dearg-shuileach, brach-shuileach; doilleir, dorch, neulach.

Bleareyed, *a.* Prab-shuileach.

Bleat, *v. n* Meil, dean mèil.

Bleed, *v. a.* and *n.* Leig fuil, thoir fuil, tarruinn fuil; caill fuil, sil fuil.

Blate, *adj.* Saidealta, nàrach, dùid.

Blemish, *v. a.* Cuir gaoid ann; salaich, truaill.

Blemish, *s.* Ciorram, gaoid, cron, michliù, sgainneal.

Blench, *v. a.* and *n.* Bac, cum air ais; crup, clisg, siap air falbh.

Blench, *s.* Clisgeadh, leum grad.

Blend, *v. a.* Coimeasgaich, cuir toimhe chéile; truaill, salaich, mill.

Bless, *v. a.* Beannaich, dean sona; mol, glòraich, thoir taing.

Blessed, **Blest**, *adj.* Beannaichte, sona; naomha, iomlan sona; air a bheannachadh.

Blessing, *s.* Beannachadh, sonas; naomhachd; sonas nèamhaidh; geanmath Dhé, deagh dhùrachd.

Blight, *s.* Fuar-dhealt, liath-reothadh; crìonadh, seargadh, gealadh.

Blind, *adj.* Dall, gun fhradharc, dorch; dall-inntinneach, aineolach.

Blind, *s.* Sgàile-shùl, dall-bhrat; neach dall.

Blindfold, *v. a.* Dall dorchaich, còmhdaich a shùilean.

Blindfold, *adj.* Sùil-chòmhdaichte.

Blindman's buff, *s.* Dallan-dà.

Blindness, *s.* Doille; aineolas, dorchadas.

Blink, *v. n.* Caog, priob; faic gu doilleir.

Blink, *s.* Sealladh grad, plathadh.

Bliss, *s.* Àrd-shonas; sonas nam flath.

Blissful, *adj.* Làn aoibhneach.

Blister, *s.* Leus, bolgan, éirigh craicinn

Blister, *v. a.* and *n.* Thoir leus air, thoir éirigh craicinn air, tog bolg uisg' air a chraiceann.

Blithe, *adj.* Aoibhinn, ăit, sunntach.

Bloat *v. a.* and *n.* Séid suas, bòc, at.

Bloatedness, *s.* At, bòcadh, séideadh.

Blobber-lip, *s.* Meill, beul tiugh, borr.

Block, *s.* Sgonn, òrda-fiodha; pluc, meall, cnap, ploc; ealag.

Block, *v. a.* Dùin a steach.

Blockade, *s.* Iom-dhruideadh.

Blockhead, *s.* Bumaileir, ùmaidh, baothaire, àmhlar, buamasdair.

Block-tin, *s.* Staoin neo-mheasgte.

Blood, *s.* Fuil; sliochd, sìol, gineal; luchd-dàimh, càirdean.

Blood, *v. a.* Salaich le fuil, còmhdaich le fuil, thoir fuil, mar do chù òg; leig fuil ás.

Blood-hound, *s.* Cù-luirg.

Bloodshed, *s*, Dòrtadh fala.

Bloodshot, *adj.* Fuil-ruitheach.

Bloody, *adj.* Fuileach, fuilteach; fuileachdach.

Bloom, *s.* Blàth; ùr-fhàs, snuadh na h-òige, dreach cinneachaidh.

Bloomy, *adj.* Blàthmhor, ùrar.

Blossom, *s.* Blàth, bàrr-gùg.

Blot, *v. a.* Dubh a mach; salaich, cuir ball dubh air; duaichnich, dorchaich.

Blotch, *s.* Leus, guirean, builgean.

Blow, *s.* Buille, gleadhar, sgealp; bualadh, slachdadh; blàth.

Blow, *v. a.* and *n.* Séid; séid suas, lìon le gaoith, cuir gaoth ann; bi gearranalach, plosg; thig fo bhlàth, cuir blàth a mach; ăt bochd.

Blowze, *s.* Caile phluiceach dhearg.

Blowzy, *adj.* Ruiteach, 's an aghaidh, loisgte leis a' ghréin.

Blubber. *s.* Saill muice-mara; muirteuchd.

Blubber, *v. a.* Bòchd an aghaidh le caoineadh.

Bludgeon, *s.* Bata, slacan, cuaille.

Blue, *adj.* Gorm, liath.

Bluebottle, *s.* Gille-guirmean, cuileag mhòr.

Blueness, *s.* Guirme, guirmead.

Bluff, *adj.* Atmhor, bòcach, gruamach, glagach; maol, neo-gheur.

Blunder, *v. n.* Rach am mearachd, tuislich, tuit an iomrall.

Blunder, *s.* Mearachd, iomrall, tuisleadh.

Blunderbuss, *s.* Gunna-craosach.

Blunt, *adj.* Maol, neo-gheur, gun fhaobhar; neo-thuigseach.

Blunt, *v. a.* Maolaich, thoir air falbh am faobhar; lagaich, cìosnaich.

Bluntness, *s.* Maoilead, cion faobhair; cion tuisge, neo-gheurchuis.

Blur, Ball salach, smal, sal.

Blush, *s.* Rughadh, gnùis-nàire, deirge.

Bluster, *v. a.* and *n.* Beuc, dean toirm mar an sian; bagair, bi gleadhrach.

BLUSTER, *s.* Collaid, gleadhraich ; aimhreit, bòsd, spaglainn.
BLUSTERER, *s.* Glagaire, fear-spaglainn.
BLUSTERING, *s.* Gleadhraich, stairirich.
BLUSTROUS, *adj.* Gleadhrach, spaglainneach.
BOAR, *s.* Torc, cullach, ùmaidh.
BOARD, *s.* Bòrd, clàr, dèile ; cuirm ; bòrd luinge.
BOARD, *v. a.* and *n.* Bòrd, glac soitheach ; cuir air bhòrd ; bi air bhòrd.
BOARDWAGES, *s.* Tuarasdal-bùird.
BOARISH, *adj.* Aineolach brùideil.
BOAST, *v. a.* and *n.* Dean uaill dean spagluinn ; mol thu féin.
BOAST, *s.* Bòsd, uaill, spaglainn.
BOASTER, *s.* Fear-ràiteachais, glagaire, bòsdair.
BOASTFUL, *adj.* Bòsdail, mòr-chuiseach.
BOAT, *s.* Bàta, eithear, sgoth, birlinn, iùrach.
BOATMAN, *s.* Fear-bàta.
BOATSWAIN, *s.* Fear-acuinn luinge.
BOBBIN, *s.* Iteachan.
BOBTAILED, *adj.* Cutach.
BODE, *v. a.* and *n.* Cuir air mhanadh ; innis roi-làimh.
BODEMENT, *s.* Comharradh, tuar, manadh.
BODICE, *s.* Cliabhan-ceangail.
BODILESS, *adj.* Neo-chorporra.
BODILY, *adj.* Corporra
BODKIN, *s.* Putag, dealg,brodaiche.
BODY, *s.* Corp, colunn, ni neo-spioradail ; neach, creutair ; meall, buidheann, meadhon feachd ; cuideachd, communn; spionnadh, treòir, neart.
BODY-CLOTHES, *s.* Aodach-cuim.
BOG, *s.* Féithe, boglach, suil-chrithich.
BOGGLE, *v. n.* Clisg, leum, bi an teagamh.
BOGGLER, *s.* Gealtaire, claghaire.
BOIL, *v. a.* and *n.* Dean teth, bruich ; goil.
BOILER, *s.* Goileadair ; coire.
BOISTEROUS, *adj.* Gailbheach ; fuathasach, stoirmeil ; borb.
BOISTEROUSLY *ad.* Ro gailbheach, stoirmmeil, doireannach.
BOLD, *adj.* Dàna, danara, neo-sgàthach ; gaisgeil, fearail, treubhach ; ladorna, mi-mhodhail.
BOLDEN, *v. a.* Cuir misneach ann.
BOLDNESS, *adj.* Dànachd, neo-sgàthachd ; tapachd ; neo-shaidealtachd ; ladornas, mi-mhodhalachd.
BOLE, *s.* Seòra talmhuinn, tomhas shéa feòrlain.
BOLL, *s.* Cuinnlein déise, lurga déise ; bolla.
BOLSTER, *s.* Adhart, cluasag, ceannadhart.
BOLSTER, *v. a.* Adhartaich, càirich cluasag fo cheann ; cùm taice.
BOLT, *s* Saighead ; crann, dealanach, beithir.
BOLT, *v. a.* and *n.* Glais, dùin ; daingnich le crann, cum ri chéile ; grad leum, briosg.
BOLT-ROPE, *s.* Ball-oire, aoir.
BOLTER, *s.* Criathar ; lìon-glacaidh.
BOLTSPRIT, *s.* Crann-spreòid, cann-uisge.
BOLUS, *s.* Cungaidh-leighis, seòrsa talmhuinn.
BOMB, *s.* Toirm, àrd-fhuaim ; peileir bloighdeach ; urchair-frois.
BOMBARD, *s.* Gunna-mòr toirm-shligneach ; soitheach dibhe.
BOMBARDIER, *s.* Gunnadair toirmshligean.
BOMBARDMENT, *s.* Séisdthoirm-shligean.
BOMBASIN, *s.* Sròl-dubh.
BOMBAST, *s.* Earraghloir, àrd-ghlòir.
BOMBASTIC, *adj.* Earra-ghlòireach.
BOMBULATION, *s.* Fuaim, gleadhraich.
BOMBKETCH, *s.* Long-thoirm-shligneach.
BOMBYX, *s.* Durrag shìoda.
BONASUS, *s.* Damh fiadhaich.
BOND, *s.* Ceangal, bann, còrd ; gealladh.
BOND, *adj.* Ceangailte, tràilleil, daor, fo bhruid.
BONDAGE, *s.* Braighdeanas, daorsa,
BONDMAID, *s.* Ban-tràill, daor, inilt.
BONDMAN, *s.* Tràill, daor-òglach.
BONELACE, *s.* Obair-lìn.
BONELESS, *adj.* Gun chnàimh.
BONFIRE, *s.* Tein aighear, tein-éibhinn.
BONNET, *s.* Boineid, ceann-aodach.
BONNY, *adj.* Bòidheach, maiseach, àlainn, laghach.
BONUM, MAGNUM, *s.* Plumbas mòr.
BONY, *adj.* Cnàmhach, mòr-chnàmhach.
BOOBY, *s.* Buimilear, ùmaidh.
BOOK, *s.* Leabhar, sgrìobhadh.
BOOKBINDER, *s.* Leabhar-cheangladair.
BOOKEEPER, *s.* Fear chumail leabhraichean.
BOOKEEPING, *s.* Eolas rian-chunntais.
BOOK-CASE, *s.* Leabhar-lann.
BOOK-MATE, *s.* Companach sgoill.
BOOKSELLER, *s.* Leabhar-reiceadair.
BOOKWORM, *s.* Reudan, leòmann ; feardian - leughach, fear ro dhéidheil air fòghlum.
BOOM, *s.* Crann-sgoide ; acarsaid, spàrr dìona acarsaid.
BOON, *s.* Tiodhlac, saor-thabhartas.
BOON, *adj.* Cridheil, sunntach, aobhach, ait ; caoimhneil.
BOOR, *s.* Balach, sgonn-òglach cumanta.
BOORISH, *adj.* Mi-mhodhail, neo-oileanta.
BOORISHNESS, *s.* Mi-mhodhalachd.

BOOT, *s.* Bòt, bròg-chalpach.
BOOTH, *s.* Bùth, pàilliun, bothan.
BOOTJACK, *s.* Ceap air son tarruinn bhòtan bharr chas.
BOOTLESS, *adj.* Neo-tharbhach, diomhain, faoin ; neo-bhuadhach.
BOOTY, *s.* Cobhartach, creach, reubainn; cluich cuil-bheartach.
BOOZE, *s.* Prasach mhart.
BORACHINO, *s.* Misgear, searrag leathair.
BOPEEP, *s.* Falach-fead, dìdeagaich.
BORAX, *s.* Salann-tàth.
BORDER, *s.* Oir, bile, crìoch, iomall, bruach, taobh, eirthir, còrsa.
BORDERER, *s.* Fear àiteach nan crìoch.
BORE, *v. a.* and *n.* Toll, gearr toll ; fosgail le tolladh, cladhaich, dean toll.
BORE, *s.* Toll ; tora, boireal, &c.
BOREAS, *s.* A' ghaoth a Tuath.
BORER, *s.* Inneal-tollaidh, tora,boireal.
BORN, *v.* Beirte.
BORNE, *part. pas.* Giùlainte, air a ghiùlan.
BOROUGH, *s.* Baile mòr, baile margaidh, bòrgh.
BORROW, *v. a.* Gabh an coingheall ; iarr iasachd ; gabh iasad.
BORROWER,*s.* Fear-gabhail an coingheall.
BOSCAGE, *s.* Coille, doire, coillteach.
BOSKY. *adj.* Coillteach, preasach, garbh, stobanach.
BOSOM, *s.* Uchd, broilleach, cridhe ; asgail,cliabh.
BOSOM, *v. a.* Achlaisich, dlùthaich, ri d'bhroilleach.
BOSS, *s.* Copan, cnap.
BOSS, *adj.* Copanaichte.
BOTANIC, BOTANICAL, Luidheach.
BOTANIST, Lusragan.
BOTANY, *s.* Luibh-eòlas.
BOTCH, *s.* Leus, guirean, plucan.
BOTCH, *v. a.* Clùd ; càirich gu neoshnasmhor, prab, breòcaich.
BOTCHER, *s.* Prabaire, greòig.
BOTH, *adj.* Le chéile, 'n an dithis, araon.
BOTH, *conj.* Araon, cuideachd, le chéile.
BOTHER, *v. a.* Sàraich, sgìthich, cuir dragh.
BOTTLE, *s.* Searrag, botul.
BOTTOM, *s.* Ìochdar, ni sam bith, srath, gleann.
BOTTOMLESS, *adj.* Gun ìochdar, gun ghrunnd, gun aigeal.
BOTTOMRY *s.* Airgead air fhaotainn an geall air son luinge.
BOUND, *s.* Durrag-bhracha.
BOUGH, *s.* Meur, geug, meangan, fiùran, faillean.
BOUGHT, *part.* Ceannaichte.
BOUNCE, *v. n.* Leum, thoir sùrdag ; bi dàna, ladorna.
BOUNCER, *s.* Fear-spaglainn.
BOUND, BOUNDARY, *s.* Crìoch, comharradh-crìche.
BOUND. *v. a.* and *n.* Crìochnaich, cuir crìoch ri ; bac, pill, dùin a steach ; thoir leum, sùrdag.
BOUND, *adj.* Suidhichte air dol.
BOUNDLESS, *adj.* Neo-chrìochnach.
BOUNDSTONE, *s.* Clach-chliuch.
BOUNTEOUS, BOUNTIFUL, *adj.* Fiùghantach, tabhartach, pàirteach, fialaidh, mathasach
BOUNTY, *s.* Toirbheartas, fialachd, pàirteachd, mathas.
BOURGEON, *v. n.* Meanglanaich, faill-eanaich.
BOURN, *s.* Crioch, iomall, oir, ceann ; allt, sruthan.
BOUSE or BOOSE, *v. a.* Òl gu saìbhir, bi pòit.
BOUSY, *adj.* Misgeach, froganach, soganach.
BOUTADE, *s.* Magaid.
BOW, *s.* Bogha-saighde ; bogha-frois ; bogha-fidhle ; cuing ; bogha dìolaide ; toiseach luinge ; cromadh, lùbadh, sleuchdadh, ùmhlachd.
BOW, *v. a.* and *n.* Crom, lùb, cam, claon ; sleuchd, crom, dean ùmhlachd.
BOWELS, *s.* Mionach, innidh ; taobh staigh ; cridhe, com ; innidh thròcaire, iochd, truas.
BOWER, *s.* Seomar, bùth ; doire sgàilthaigh, bothan-sàmhraidh badan ; féithe chrupaidh ; acair luinge.
BOWERY, *adj.* Sgàileach, bothanach, fionnar, dubharach, doireach, badanach.
BOWL, *s.* Bolla, cuach, ball cruinn.
BOWL, *v. a.* and *n.* Cluich le buill, ruith car ma char.
BOWLEGGED, *adj.* Cam-chasach.
BOWLING-GREEN, *s.* Réidhlean bhall.
BOWMAN, *s.* Saighdear bogha.
BOWSPRIT, *s.* Crann-spreòid.
BOWSTRING, *s.* Taifeid.
BOWYER, *s.* Boghadair ; saor boghachan, saigheid.
BOX, *s.* Bocsa, cobhan, ciste ; dòrn, buille, gleadhar, cnap.
BOX, *v. a.* and *n.* Cuir am bosca ; dean dòrnadh, thoir sgailleag do.
BOXER, *s.* Dòrnaiche, fear-iomairt dhòrn
BOY, *s.* Leanabh gille.
BOYISH,*adj.* Leanabail, faoin, socharach.
BOYISHNESS, *s.* Leanabas, leanabaidheachd, faoineachd.
BRABBLE, *s.* Connsachadh, iorghuill.
BRACE, *v. a.* Crioslaich teannaich, daingnich.
BRACE, *s.* Crios, bann, ceangal, teann-

adan; armachd, uidheam cogaidh; teannachadh, daingneachadh; paidhir, dithis.

Bracelet, *s.* Làmh-fhailean làmh; usgar.

Bracer, *s.* Teannadan, bann-teannachaidh; deoch bheothachaidh.

Brach, *s.* Galla-thòlair, saidh.

Brachial, *adj.* Gàirdeanach.

Brack, *s.* Bealach, bearn, briseadh.

Bracken, *s.* Raineach, roineach.

Bracket, *s.* Ealchainn, sorachan.

Brackish, *adj.* Air bhlas an t-sàile.

Brag, *v. n.* Dean uaill, bi ràiteachail, dean bòsd, dean spaglainn, dùlanaich.

Brag, *s.* Uaill, ràiteachas, bòsd, spaglainn; aobhar-uaill.

Braggadocio, *s.* Spaga-da-glid.

Braggart, **Bragger**, *s.* Fear ùaillmhor, bòsdail, ràiteachail, spaglainneach.

Braid, *v. a,* Figh, dualaich.

Braid, *s.* Dual, ni fighte 'na dhualaibh, dosan-banntraich.

Brails, *s.* Buill-tharruinn sheòl.

Brain, *s.* Eanchainn, eanachaill; ceann, tuigse, tùr.

Brain, *v. a.* Cuir an eanchainn ás.

Brainless, *adj.* Baoth, faoin, neothuigseach, neo-thùrail, gun eanchainn.

Brain-pan, *s.* Copan a' chinn, an claigeann.

Brainsick, *adj.* Tuainealach, amaideach.

Brait, *s.* Daimean greannach neolìobta.

Brake, *s.* Droighionnach; raineach; slacan-lìn; làmh pìob-thaosgaidh; amar-fuine.

Braky, *adj,* Driseach, làn droighnich.

Bramble, *s.* Dris nan smeur dubha.

Bran, *s.* Càth, còrlach, garbhan.

Branch, *s.* Meangan, meanglan, meur, geug, fiùran; earrann, cuid; sliochd, gineal, iarmad.

Branch, *v. a.* Craobh-sgaoil, 'na earrannaibh; sgaoil a mach, meursgaoil; bi bith-bhriathrach; bi cabrach, bi cròcach.

Brancher, *s.* Isean no pùda, speireig.

Branchless, *a.* Neo-gheugach.

Branchy, *adj.* Meanganach, geugach, dosach, cròcach, cabrach.

Brand, *s.* Aithinne, bioran-teine, biordearg, maide connaidh.

Brand, *v. a.* Maslaich, comharraich le iarann dearg.

Brandish, *v. a.* Crath, luaisg, tog suas.

Brandling, *s.* Boiteag-dhrùchda.

Brandy, *s.* Branndaidh.

Brangle, *s.* Co-stri, connsachadh, brionglaid.

Branny, *adj.* Càthach, garbhanach.

Brasier, *s.* Ceard-umha; aghann umha.

Brasil, *s.* Fiodh an datha.

Brass, *s.* Umha; dànachd.

Brassy, *adj.* Umhach, dàna, ladorna.

Brat, *s.* Isean, garrach, droch leanabh.

Bravado, *s.* Fear bòsdail, bagarach, maoidheach.

Brave, *adj.* Misneachail, curanta, dàna, gaisgeil, calma; fearail.

Brave, *v. a.* Dùlanaich, tàirg cath.

Bravely, *adj.* Misneachd.

Bravery, *s.* Misneach, gaisge, treubhantas, fearalas, curantachd.

Bravo, *s.* Fear a mhortas air son duais.

Brawl, *v. a* and *n.* Dean ghleadhrach, dean cànran, dean co-stri, trod, dean stairirich.

Brawler, *s.* Fear-iorghuilleach.

Brawn, *s.* Feòil a' chalpa; cruaidh-fheòil tuirc.

Brawniness, *s.* Spionnadh, neart, lùgh; cruas.

Brawny, *adj.* Féitheach, làidir, cruaidhghreimeach, calpach, gramail.

Bray, *v. a.* and *n.* Pronn, brùth; ràn beuc, sgreuch, bleith.

Bray, *s.* Sitir asail; sgread, sgreuch, ràn, raoichd.

Brayer, *s.* Sitriche, sgreadair; pronnadair, bruthadair.

Braze, *v. a.* Tàth le umha.

Brazen, *adj.* Umhach; ladorna, minàrach.

Brazen-face, *s.* Bathais gun fhalas gun nàire.

Brazenness, *s.* Air dhreach umha; mi-nàire, ladornas.

Breach, *s.* Briseadh, fosgladh, sgàineadh; bealach, bearn; connspaid.

Bread, *s.* Aran; lòn, teachd-an-tìr.

Bread-corn, *s.* Arbhar-arain.

Breadth, *s.* Leud, farsuinneachd.

Break, *v. a.* and *n.* Bris, sgealb, crac; fàs lag, breòite.

Break, *s.* Briseadh, sgealbadh, sgoltadh; bealach, bearn.

Breakers, *s.* Sùmainnean, sgeir-thonn.

Breakfast, *s.* Ceud-longaidh biadhmaidne.

Breast, *s.* Uchd, broilleach, maothan; cìoch, cliabh.

Breastknot, *s.* Dos ribeanan air an uchd.

Breastplate, *s.* Uchd-éideadh.

Breastwork, *s.* Uchd-bhalla.

Breath, *s.* Anail, deò; beatha.

Breathe, *v. a.* and *n.* Analaich, séid; bi beò; leig anail.

Breathing, *s.* Urnaigh dhìomhair, analachadh, séideadh, tarruinn analach

Breathless, *adj.* Plosgartach, séideagach, sgìth, sàraichte; gun deò, gun anail, marbh.
Breech, *s.* Màs, tòn, tulachann, earr, deireadh.
Breeches, *s.* Brìsnean, briogais, triubhais.
Breed, *v. a.* and *n.* Gin, sìolaich, tàrmaich; tog, àraich, ionnsaich, tog suas, àlaich.
Breed, *s.* Seòrsa, gnè, sìol, sliochd; àlach, linn.
Breeding, *s.* Ionnsachadh, fòghlum, oilean, eòlas, togail suas; modh, beus.
Breeze, *s.* Creithleag, cuileag-ghathach, sgairt-ghaoth, tlà-ghaoth.
Breezy, *adj.* Sgairt-ghaothach, tlàghaothach; osagach, oiteagach.
Bret, **Brit**, *s.* Seòrsa liabaig.
Brethren, *s.* Bràithrean.
Breviate, *s.* Gearr-shuim cùise
Brevity, **Briefness**, *s.* Giorrad, aithghiorrad.
Brew, *v. a.* and *n.* Tog, dean togail, bi grùdaireachd.
Brewer, *s.* Grùdaire, fear-togalach.
Brewery, **Brewhouse**, *s.* Taigh-togalach, taigh-grùide.
Bribe, *s.* Duais chlaon-bhreth.
Bribe, *v. a.* Ceannaich le duais.
Bribery, *s.* Duais na h-euceairt.
Brick, *s.* Clach-chreadha.
Brick-dust, *s.* Criadh-dhuslach.
Brick-kiln, *s.* Àth-chreadha.
Bricklayer, *s.* Criadh-chlachair.
Bridal, *adj.* A bhuineas do bhanais, pòsda.
Bride, *s.* Bean-bainnse, bean-òg.
Bridecake, *s.* Bonnach mnà-bainnse.
Bridegroom, *s.* Fear-bainnse.
Bridemaid, *s.* Maighdean-phòsaidh.
Bridewell, *s.* Gainntir, prìosan.
Bridge, *s.* Drochaid.
Bridle, *s.* Srian, taod, ceannsal.
Bridle, *v. a.* and *n.* Srian, stiùr, treòraich, seòl; ceannsaich.
Brief, *adj.* Goirid, gearr, aithghearr.
Brief, *s.* Sgrìobhadh-gearr, suim aithghearr cùise.
Briefness, *s.* Aithghearrachd.
Brier, *s.* Dris, preas-mhucag.
Briery, *adj.* Driseach, deilgneach.
Brig, *s.* Soitheach dà chroinn.
Brigade, *s.* Buidheann mhòr airm.
Brigand, *s.* Spùinnear, creachadair.
Brigandine, *s.* Long chreachaidh, lùireach mhàilleach.
Bright, *adj.* Soilleir, soillseach, deàrsach, dealrach, lainnireach, boillsgeach; glan, geur, tuigseach.
Brighten, *v. a.* and *n.* Soillsich, deàrsaich, soilleirich.
Brightness *s.* Soilleireachd.
Brigose, *adj.* Sabaideach.
Brilliancy, *s.* Lainnearachd.
Brilliant, *adj.* Soillseach, dearsach, baillsgeach, lainnearach.
Brim, *s.* Oir, bile, bruach, iomall; beul.
Brimmer, *s.* Cuach-stràcte, cuach làn.
Brimstone, *s.* Pronnasg, rief.
Brinded, *adj.* Srianach, stiallach.
Brine, *s.* Mearshal, sàl.
Bring, *v. a.* Thoir, tabhair, beir.
Brinish, *adj.* Saillte, air bhlas an t-sàile.
Brink, *s.* Oir, bruach, bile.
Brisk, *adj.* Brisg, beothail, cridheil, sunntach; gleuste, smiorail, tapaidh, clis.
Brisket, *s.* Mìr-uchd, broilleach.
Briskness, *s.* Beothalachd, smioralachd, cliseachd, meamnachd.
Bristle, *s.* Calg muice, friodhan.
Bristle, *v.* Tog friodhan air; cuir calg air.
Bristly, *adj.* Calgach, colgach, friodhanach.
Bristolstone, *s.* Seōrsa, daoimein.
Brista, *s.* Am blàraoghan.
British, *adj.* Breatunnach.
Briton, *s.* Breatunnach, fear a mhuinntir Bhreatuinn.
Brittle, *adj.* Brisg, furasd' a bhriseadh.
Brittleness, *s.* Brisgealachd.
Brize, *s.* Creithleag, speach.
Broach, *v. a.* Cuir bior ann; toll, leig ruith le; labhair, cuir an céill; tionndaidh ris an t-soirbheas.
Broacher, *s.* Bior-ròslaidh; fear-innse.
Broad, *adj.* Leathann; mòr, farsuinn; garbh; drabasta, coma m 'a chainnt, mi-mhodhail.
Broad-cloth, *s.* Clò Sasunnach.
Broadness, *s.* Leud, farsuinneachd.
Broadside, *s.* Làdach ghunnacha-mòra o thaobh luinge.
Broadsword, *s.* Claidheamh-mòr.
Brocade, *s.* Sìoda gréiste.
Brocage, *s.* Buannachd, ceannachd; ceannachd bhaidreagach.
Brocoli, *s.* Seòrsa càil.
Brocket, *s.* Dà-bhliadhnach féigh.
Brogue, *s.* Bròg éille; cainnt thruaillidh.
Broidery, *s.* See Embroidery.
Broil, *v.* Ròsd, bruich air na h-éibhlean.
Broil, *s.* Caonnag, săbaid.
Broken, *part.* Briste.
Broker, *s.* Fear-gnothaich, feardheanamh ghnothaichean air son neach eile; ceannaiche shean-àirneis.
Brokerage, *s.* Duais fir gnothaich.

Bronchial, *adj.* Sgòrnanach.
Bronze, *s.* Umha, dealbh umha.
Bronze, *v. a.* Cruadhaich mar umha.
Brooch, *s.* Bràist.
Brood, *v.* Àlaich, àraich; guir.
Brood, *s.* Sliochd, àl, sìol, gineal, linn.
Brook, *s.* Alltan, sruthan, caochan.
Brook, *v.* Fuilig, giùlain.
Broom, *s.* Bealaidh; sguabach, sguab-ùrlair, sguab-làir.
Broomy, *adj*, Bealaidheach.
Broth, *s.* Eun-bhrìgh, eanaraich.
Brothel, *s.* Taigh-siùrsachd.
Brother, *s.* Bràthair.
Brotherhood, *s.* Bràithreachas.
Brotherly, *adj.* Bràitheil.
Brow, *s.* Mala; clàr-aodainn, bathais; bruach.
Browbeat, *v. a.* Eagalaich, nàraich, cuir fo sproc.
Brown, *adj.* Donn.
Brownish, *adj.* Soilleir-dhonn.
Brownness, *s.* Duinne, doinne.
Brownstudy, *s.* Dubh-smuaintean.
Browse, *s.* Baralach, barrach.
Bruise, *v. a.* Pronn, brùth, mion-phronn.
Bruise, *s.* Bruthadh, ciùrradh, dochann,
Bruit, *v. a.* Innis, aithris, cuir an céill.
Brumal *adj.* Geamhrachail·
Brunette, *s.* Bean dhonn-ghnùiseach.
Brunt, *s.* Garbh-ionnsaidh, teas, strì.
Brush, *s.* Sguab, no sguab-aodaich.
Brush, *v.* Sguab, slìob, suath.
Brushwood, *s.* Frith-choille.
Brusk, *adj.* Borb, mi-mhodhail.
Brutal, *adj.* Garg, brùideil.
Brutality, *s.* Brùidealachd.
Brute, *s.* Ainmhidh, bruid, beathach, creutair gun reusan.
Brutish, *adj.* Brùideil, feòlmhor, allmhara, fiadhaich, borb, garg aineolach, neo-mhothachail.
Bubble, *s.* Gucag, cop, builgean, splangaid, staonag.
Bubble, *v. a.* and *n.* Meall, thoir, an car á; éirich gu gucagach, bi sùileagach.
Bubbler, *s.* Mealltair, cealgair.
Bubbly, *adj.* Spliùgach, splangaideach, ronnach, staonagach.
Buccaniers, *s.* Luchd-spùinnidh air fairge.
Buck, *s.* Boc, damh féigh, uisge sgùraidh, uisge nigheadaireachd; aodach air a nighe; fear spaideil, lasgaire.
Buckbeam, *s.* Seòrsa do thrì-bhilich.
Bucket, *s.* Cuinneag, bucaid.
Buckle, *s.* Bucull, claspa; cas-fhalt, cuairteag, cuach, cuachag.
Buckler, *s.* Sgiath-dhìon, sgiath.
Buckram, *s.* Aodach teann rag lìn.
Buckskin, *s.* Leathair féigh.
Buckthorn, *s.* Sgitheach.
Bucolics, *s.* Oran buachailleachd.
Bud, *s.* Ùr-fhàs, ùr-ròs, gucag.
Budge, *v. n.* Caraich, gluais, glidnich.
Budget, *s.* Balg-solair, poca, màileid.
Buff, *s.* Leathar-sginneir, dath soilleir buidhe.
Buff, Buffet, *v. a.* Buail, dòrn.
Buffalo, *s.* Tarbh-allaidh, damh-fiadhaich.
Buffet, *s.* Còrn-chlar; àmraidh.
Buffoon, *s.* Dù-chleasaich.
Buffoonery, *s.* Dù-chleasachd.
Bug, *s.* Miol fhiodha.
Bugbear, *s.* Bòcan, culaidh-eagail.
Bugle, Buglehorn, *s.* Dùdach, adharcfhoghaid.
Bugloss, *s.* Lŭs-teang'-an-daimh, boglŭs.
Build, *v.* Tog, bi clachaireachd
Builder, *s.* Clachair, fear-togail.
Building, *s.* Togail, taigh, aitreabh.
Built, *s.* Cumadh aitreibh, togail.
Bulb, *s.* Bun cruinn, meacan, meallan.
Bulbous, *adj.* Meacanach, làn ghlùn.
Bulge, *v. n.* Sgàin, sgoilt, bi eu-dìonach, leig a steach uisge; bulgaich, brùchd a mach.
Bulk, *s.* Meudachd, tomad, dòmhlachd; a' chuid a's mò.
Bulkhead, *s.* Clàraidh soithich.
Bulkiness, *s.* Meudachd, dòmhlachd.
Bulky, *adj.* Mòr, dòmhail, tomadach.
Bull, *s.* Tarbh; mearachd facail, droch thuiteamas cainnte.
Bull-baiting, *s.* Gleachd chon a's tharbh.
Bull-dog, *s.* Tarbh-chù, cù feòladair
Bullet, *s.* Peileir, ruagaire.
Bulletin, *s.* Naigheachd cùirt.
Bullion, *s.* Òrd òir, no airgeid.
Bullfinch, *s.* Am buidh-eun-coille.
Bullock, *s.* Tarbh òg, damh.
Bully, *s.* Curaidh ceatharnach dàna.
Bulrush, *s.* Gobhal-luachair.
Bulwark, *s.* Balla-dìdein; obair-ard.
Bumbailiff, *s.* Maor-dubh.
Bumboat, *s.* Bàta-luiristeach.
Bump, *s.* At, meall, cnap, pluc; cròнan nan sgarbh.
Bumper, *s.* Sgailc.
Bumpkin, *s.* Luiriste, gleòsgaire.
Bun, *s.* Aran milis.
Bunch, *s.* Bagaid, gagan, croit.
Bunchy, *adj.* Bagaideach, gaganach.
Bundle, *s.* Pasgan, trusan; ultach.
Bung, *s.* Àrcan buideil.
Bungle, *v.* Greòigich, clùd, dean gu cearbach.
Bungle, *s.* Clùd, bréid, obair sgòdach

Bungler, *s.* Greoig prăbaire.
Bunter, *s.* Sgonn-chaile.
Bunting, *s.* Gealag-bhuachair.
Buoy, *s.* Fleodruinn, bolla, àrca.
Buoy, *v.* Cum an uachdar.
Buoyancy, *s.* Aotromachd, fleodradh.
Buoyant, *adj.* Aotrom, a shnàmhas.
Burden, *s.* Eallach, uallach, éire.
Burden, *v. a.* Uallaich, sacaich, luchdaich.
Burdensome, *adj.* Doilghiosach, cudthromach.
Burdock, *s.* Mac-an-dogha, an Galangreannachair, an seircean-mòr.
Bureau, *s.* Ciste chlàr-sgrìobhaidh.
Burgage, *s.* Gabhaltas baile-margaidh.
Burgess, *s.* Buirdeiseach.
Burgh, *s.* Baile-mòr, bòrgh.
Burgher, *s.* Saoranach, neach aig am bheil seilbh an còraichean baile mhòir.
Burglary, *s.* Briseadh thaighean, spùinneadh na h-oidhche.
Burgomaster, *s.* Baillidh baile mhòir.
Burial, *s.* Adhlacadh, tìodhlacadh.
Burine, *s.* Iaran-grabhalaidh.
Burlesque, *adj.* Sgeigeil, magail.
Burlesque, *s.* Sgeigeireachd, fochaid.
Burly, *adj.* Leathann, dòmhail, dinnte; stàirneach.
Burn, *v. a.* Loisg ; bi losgadh.
Burn, *s.* Losgadh, sgaldadh.
Burnet, *s.* A' bhileach-loisgein.
Burning, *s.* A' losgadh.
Burnish, *v. a.* Lìobh, lainnrich.
Burnisher, *s.* Fear-lìobhaidh, no inneal lìobhaidh.
Burr, *s.* Faillean na cluaise.
Burrow, *v. n,* Cladhaich fo thalamh.
Burst, *v. a.* Sgoilt, sgàin spreadh bhrùchd.
Burst, *s.* Sgàineadh, sgoltadh, spreadhadh.
Burstness, *s.* Màm-sic, beum-sic.
Burstwort, *s.* Lŭs-an-t-sicnich.
Burthen, *s.* See Burden, *s.* and *v.*
Bury, *v. a.* Adhlaic, tìodhlaic.
Bush, *s.* Preas, dos ; bad.
Bushel, *s.* Tomhas àraidh.
Bushy, *adj.* Preasach, dosach, gasach ; badanach, &c.
Business, *s.* Obair, gnothach.
Busk, *s.* Pleaghan-teannachaidh.
Buskin, *s.* Leth-bhòt.
Buss, *s.* Pòg, busag ; bàt-iasgaich.
Bust, *s.* Dealbh duine, bho cheann gu gualainn.
Bustard, *s.* Coileach-Frangach.
Bustle, *s.* Cabhag, iorghuill, othail, drip, collaid, càmparaid.
Bustler, *s.* Fear cabhagach.
Busy, *adj.* Saoithreach, deanadach ; leamh.
Busybody, *s.* Fear-tuaileis
But, *conj.* Ach, gidheadh.
But, *s.* Crìoch, ceann-crìche.
Butcher, *s.* Feòladair.
Butcher, *v. a.* Casgair, marbh, mort.
Butchery, *s.* Feòladaireachd ; mort, taigh-feòladaireachd.
Butler, *s.* Buidealair.
Butment, *s.* Bonn bogha drochaid.
Butt, *s.* Ionad cuimse, àite buill-amais ; buideal mòr, baraille, tocsaid.
Butter, *s.* Ìm.
Butter, *v. a.* Taisich le ìm.
Butterflower, *s.* Buidheag-an t-sàmhraidh.
Butterfly, *s.* Dearbadan-dé, eunandé, dealan-dé, dealbhan-dé, tormagan-dé, calaman-dé.
Buttermilk, *s.* Blàthach.
Butterwort, Badan-measgain.
Buttery, *adj.* Ìmeach, iomacach.
Buttery, *s.* Taigh-tasgaidh, biadh-lann.
Buttock, *s.* Màs, tòn.
Button, *s.* Putan, cnap.
Button, *v. a.* Putanaich.
Buttonhole, *s.* Toll-putain.
Buttress, *s.* Balla-taice.
Buttress, *v. a.* Taicich, goibhlich.
Buxom, *adj.* Aighearach, beothail, meamnach, aotrom, clis.
Buxomness, *s.* Macnasachd, beadarachd, meamnadh.
Buy, *v. a.* Ceannaich.
Buyer, *s.* Fear-ceannachaidh.
Buzz, *v. a.* Aithris os n-iosal, thoir sanas.
Buzz, *s.* Srann, crònan, cagar.
Buzzard, *s.* Clamhan ; sgonn-bhalach, bumailear.
Buzzer, *s.* Fear-cogarsaich, feartuaileis
By, *prep.* Le ; tre, trid, troi ; fag dlù, faisg.
By and by, *adv.* An ùin ghearr.
By-law, *s.* Riagailt comuinn.
By-name, *s.* Frith-ainm, far-ainm, leth-ainm, leas-ainm.
Bystander, *s.* Fear amhairc.
Byword, *s.* Frith-fhacal, sean-fhacal.
Byre, *s.* Bà-theach, bàthach.

C

C, Treas litir na h-aibidil, tha i a seasamh air son : Ceud, cùig fichead.
Cab, *s.* Tomhas Iudhach a chumas trì pinnt.
Cabal, *s.* Coinneamh dhìomhair ; cluaintearachd, claon chomhairle.

CABAL, CABALA, *s.* Am beul-aithris Iudhach.
CABALIST, *s.* Fear fiosrach mu bheul-aithris nan Iudhach.
CABALISTICAL, *adj.* Dìomhair.
CABALLER, *s,* Fear-comhairle dhìomhair, cluaintear.
CABBAGE, *s.* Càl, càl-faobach.
CABBAGE, *v. a.* Goid fuigheall aodaich, an àm a bhi ga ghearradh.
CABIN, *s.* Seòmar luinge; bùth, bothan.
CABINET, *s.* Seòmar-comhairle; tasgaidh; ionad-dìomhair.
CABINET-MAKER, *s.* Saor deanamh àirneis taighe.
CABLE, *s.* Muir-theud, càball.
CACHETICAL, *adj.* Euslan.
CACHEXY, *s.* Euslaint.
CACKLE, *v. n.* Ràc, bi glocail, goir, gàir.
CACODEMON, *s.* Deamhan, an-spiorad.
CADAVEROUS, *adj.* Cairbheach, lobhte, malcte, grod.
CADDIS, *s.* Durrag-chonnlaich.
CADE, *adj.* Tlà, tairis.
CADENCE, *s.* Tuiteam, leagadh, ìsleachadh gutha.
CADET, *s.* Am bràthair is òige; fear a chogas a nasgaidh an dùil ri àrdachadh, fhaighinn san arm.
CADGER, *s.* Ceannaiche trusaidh.
CAG, *s.* Buideal, soire.
CAGE, *s.* Eun-lann, eunadan.
CAJOLE, *v. a.* Breug, meall, ciùinich.
CAJOLER, *s.* Miodalaiche, fear-sodail.
CAITIFF, *s.* Slaightear, droch-bheartach.
CAKE, *s.* Breacag, bonnach, dearnagan.
CALAMINE. *s.* Seòrsa meine.
CALAMITOUS, *adj.* Truagh, dosgainneach.
CALAMITY, *s.* Truaighe, dosgainn. calldachd, àmhghar; doilghios.
CALCAREOUS, *adj.* Cailceach.
CALCINATION, *s.* Losgadh gu luaithre.
CALCINE, *v. a.* Loisg gu luaithre.
CALCULATE, *v. n.* Cunnt, meas; tomhais.
CALCULATION, *s.* Cunntas.
CALCULATOR, *s.* Fear-àireamh.
CALCULOUS, *adj.* Clachach, moraghanach.
CALDRON, *s.* Coire-mòr.
CALEDONIAN, *adj.* Albannach.
CALEFACTORY, *adj.* Teth, a ni teth.
CALEFY, *v. a.* Dean teth, teòdh.
CALENDAR. *s.* Mìosachan.
CALENDER, *v. a.* Liosraich.
CALENDER, *s.* Preas liosrachaidh.
CALENDERER, *s.* Fear-liosraidh.
CALF. *s.* Laogh; calpa na coise.
CALIBER, *s.* Beul gunna.
CALICO, *s.* Aodach canaich.
CALID, *adj.* Teth, loisgeach.
CALIDITY, CALIDNESS, *s.* Dian-theas.
CALIGATION, *s.* Dorchadas, gruamachd.
CALIGINOUS, *adj.* Dorcha, gruamach.
CALIGRAPHY, *s.* Snas-sgrìobhadh.
CALIVER, *s.* Cuilibhear, Gunna-glaic.
CALK, *v. a.* Calc, dìonaich, dùin suas.
CALKER, *s.* Fear-calcaidh, calcadair
CALL, *v. a.* Gairm, goir; glaodh, éigh.
CALL, *s.* Gairm, cuireadh, glaodh.
CALLAT, CALLET, *s.* Caile shuarach.
CALLING, *s.* Gairm, dreuchd; inbhe; aidmheil.
CALLIPERS, *s.* Gobhal-roinne.
CALLOSITY, *s.* Calunn, at gun chràdh.
CALLOUS, *adj.* Cruaidh, teann neomhothachail.
CALLOW, *adj.* Rùisgte, lom.
CALM, *adj.* Sàmhach, ciùin, fèitheach sèimh, tosdach, sìothchail.
CALM, *s.* Fè, ciùine sìth, sàmhchair.
CALMNESS, *s.* Ciùine, sàmhchair.
CALOMEL, *s.* Airgead-beò fiorghlan.
CALORIFIC, *adj.* Teth, a theasaicheas.
CALTROP, *s.* An deanndag arbhair.
CALVE, *v. n.* Beir laogh.
CALUMNIATE, *v.* Cùl-chàin aithris tuaileas.
CALUMNIATION, *s.* Cùl-chàineadh, tuaileas.
CALUMNIATOR, *s.* Fear-cùl-chàinidh.
CALUMNIOUS *adj.* Tuaileasach, sgainnealach.
CALUMNY, *s.* Sgainneal, tuaileas, breug.
CALYCLE, *s.* Ur-bhlàth.
CAMBRIC, *s.* Pearluinn, anart caol,
CAME, *pret.* of Come. Thàinig.
CAMEL, .. Càmhal.
CAMELOTS, *s.* Aodach clòimhe's sìoda.
CAMOMILE, . Lŭs-nan-cam -bhil
CAMP, *s.* Càmpa, feachd-chòmhnaidh.
CAMPAIGN, *s.* Réidhlean, còmhnard; ùine feachd an càmpa.
CAMPAIGNER, *s.* Seann saighdear càmpa.
CAMPESTRAL, *adj.* Machrach, fiadhain.
CAN, *s.* Copan, còrn, cuach.
CANAILLE, *s.* Gràisg, pràbar, fòtus.
CANAL, *s.* Clais uisge.
CANALICULATED, *adj.* Sruthanach.
CANCEL, *v. a.* Dubh a mach.
CANCELLATED, *adj.* Sgrìobhte tarsuinn.
CANCELLATION, *s.* Dubhadh a mach.
CANCER, *s.* Partan, crùbag; aon do na comharran 'sa chuairt-ghréin chnàmhainn.
CANCEROUS, *adj.* Cnàmhainneach.
CANCRINE, *adj.* Partanach, crùbagach.
CANDENT, *adj.* Dian-theth, dearg-theth.

CANDID, *adj.* Saor, neo-chealgach.
CANDIDATE, *s.* Fear-iarraidh.
CANDIDLY, *ad.* Gu h-ionraic.
CANDIFY, *v. a.* Gealaich, dean geal.
CANDLE, *s.* Coinneal.
CANDLEMAS, *s.* Feill-brìde.
CANDLESTICK, *s.* Coinnleir.
CANDOUR, *s.* Glain'-inntinn, suairceas, fosgarrachd.
CANDY, *v. a.* Gréidh le siùcar.
CANE, *s.* Bata, lorg, cuilc.
CANE, *v. a.* Buail le bata, slacuinn.
CANINE, *adj.* Coltach ri cù.
CANISTER, *s.* Bòsdan tèa.
CANKER, *s.* Cnàmhainn, cnuimh; meirg.
CANKER, *v. a.* Truaill, mill, ith air falbh, cnàmh, caith.
CANKEROUS, *adj.* Cnàmhach.
CANNIBAL, *s.* Fear ithe feòla dhaoine.
CANNON, *s.* Gunna mòr.
CANNONIER, *s.* Gunnair.
CANOE, *s.* Curach Innseanach.
CANON, *s.* Riaghailt, lagh, reachd eaglais.
CANONICAL, *adj.* Riaghailteach, laghail, a shuidheachadh le lagh na cléire; spioradail.
CANONIST, *s.* Fear-eòlach air lagh na cléire.
CANONIZATION, *s.* Cur an àireamh nan naomh.
CANOPY, *s.* Sgàil-bhrat, còmhdach-rìoghail, ceann-bhrat.
CANOPY, *v. n.* Còmhdaich le sgàil-bhrat.
CANOROUS, *adj.* Ceòl-bhinn, fonnor
CANT, *s.* Gràisg-chòmhradh; dubh-chainnt.
CANTATA, *s.* Òran-nan-căr.
CANTATION, *s.* Canntaireachd.
CANTEEN, *s.* Canna saighdear.
CANTER, *s.* Cealgair, mealltair.
CANTHARIDES, *s.* Cuileagan Fràngach.
CANTHUS, *s.* Oisinn na sùla.
CANTICLE, *s.* Òran cràbhach; Dàn Sholaimh.
CANTLE, *s.* Mìr, earrann, bloigh.
CANTO, *s.* Earrann do dhuan.
CANTON, *s.* Mìr fearainn, taobh dùthcha.
CANTONIZE, *v. a.* Dean mion-roinn, roinn 'na earrannaibh.
CANVASS, *s.* Aodach cainbe.
CANVASS, *v. a.* Mion-rannsaich, sgrùd, iarr fàbhar.
CANZONET, *s.* Òran beag, duanag,
CAP, *s.* Currac, còmhdach cinn.
CAP, *v. a.* Còmhdaich, cuir currac air.
CAP-A-PIE, O mhullach gu bonn, bho churraic gu bròig.
CAPABILITY, *s.* Cumhachd, comas.
CAPABLE, *adj.* Comasach.
CAPACIOUS, *adj.* Mòr, farsuinn.
CAPACIOUSNESS, *s.* Farsuinneachd.
CAPACITATE, *v. a.* Dean comasach, iomchuidh, ullaich. deasaich.
CAPACITY, *s.* Urrainn, comas, leud, cumhachd.
CAPARISON, *s.* Còmhdach rìmheach eich.
CAPE, *s.* Rudha, ceann-tìre, maol rinn.
CAPER, *s.* Leum, sùrdag; seòrsa peabair.
CAPER, *v. n.* Leum, geàrr sùrdagan.
CAPILLARY, *adj.* Caol mar ròineig.
CAPITAL, *adj.* Prìomh, àrd, mòr, àraidh.
CAPITAL, *s.* Ceann, cuilbh, mullach; prìomh-bhaile, ărd-bhaile, àrd-chathair; earras; litir mhòr; an calpa.
CAPITATION, *s.* Cunntas-cheann cìs-cheann.
CAPITULAR, *s.* Brìgh-sgrìobhaidh.
CAPITULATE, *v. a.* Strìochd air chumha
CAPITULATION, *s.* Cumha-géilleidh, cùmhnantan-strìochdaidh.
CAPON, *s.* Coileach spothte.
CAPRICE, *s.* Sròineas, neònachas, mùiteachd.
CAPRICIOUS, *adj.* Neònach, mùiteach.
CAPSULAR, CAPSULARY, *adj.* Fàs, mar chisteig.
CAPSULATE, CAPSULATED, *adj.* Dùinte, ann am bocsa.
CAPTAIN, *s.* Ard-cheannard, ceann-feadhna, ceann-feachd; caiptin.
CAPTATION, *s.* Suiridhe, moladh, miodal.
CAPTIVE, *s.* Ciomach, braighde.
CAPTIVITY, *s.* Ciomachas, daorsa.
CAPTION, *s.* Glacadh, glacadh laghail.
CAPTIOUS, *adj.* Beumach, connspaideach, corrach, tiolpach, frionasach crosda.
CAPTOR, *s.* Glacadair, fear toirt fo chìs.
CAPTURE, *s.* Glacadh, creachadh; creach, cobhartach.
CAR, *s.* Càrn, carbad, carbad-cogaidh.
CARAT, *s.* Tomhas cheithir gràinnean; tomhas òir.
CARAVAN, *s.* Carbad-mòr; buidheann luchd-turais 's an airde 'n-ear, luchd-siubhail.
CARAVANSARY, *s* Taigh-òsda 's an àirde 'n ear.
CARAWAY, *s.* Lùs-Mhic-Chuimein.
CARBONADE, *v. a.* Dòigh ghearraidh feòla.
CARABINE, *s.* Gunna-glaic.
CARBINER, CARABINER, *s.* Trùpair aotrom.
CARBUNCLE, *s.* Seud dealrach, leug loinnreach, carbuncul; guirean, plucan dearg.

CARCASS, *s.* Cairbh, closach, corp marbh.
CARD, *s.* Cairt, cairt-chluiche, cairt-iùil; càrd, sgrìoban.
CARD, *v. a.* Càrd, cìr; measgaich.
CARD-TABLE, *s.* Clar-chairtean.
CARDIAC, *adj.* Neartachail, ìoc-shlaint-'ach.
CARDINAL, *adj.* Prìomh, àrd, urram-ach.
CARDINAL, *s.* Prìomh-dhiadhair an eaglais na Ròimhe.
CARE, *s.* Iomagain, cùram, aire, faic-eil
CARE, *v. n.* Gabh cùram, gabh suim, bi faicilleach.
CAREEN, *v. a.* Calc, dionaich, càirich.
CAREER, s. Co-liong, reis, cùrsa.
CAREFUL, *adj.* Cùramach, iomagain-each, faicilleach, faireachail, furach-ail.
CAREFULNESS, *s.* Iomagaineachd.
CARELESS, *adj.* Mi-chùramach, dear-madach, coma gun fheart.
CARELESSNESS, *s.* Mi-chùramachd, dear-madachd.
CARESS, *v. a.* Caidrich, gràdhaich, tàlaidh, criodaich.
CARGO, *s.* Luchd luinge.
CARICATURE, *s.* Dealbh-magaidh.
CARIES, CARIOUSITY, *s.* Grodachd.
CARIOUS, *adj.* Grod, lobhte, malcte.
CARLE, *s.* Mùigean, bodach gnù.
CARLINGS, *s.* Lunnan-chas air ùrlar luinge no bàta.
CARMAN, *s.* Cairtear.
CARMINATIVE, *s.* Iocshlaint-lasachaidh.
CARMINE, *s.* Dearg, corcur.
CARNAGE, *s.* Àr, marbhadh, casgradh, léir-sgrios, feòlach.
CARNAL, *adj.* Feòlmhor, corporra, collaidh.
CARNALITY, *s.* Feòlmhorachd.
CARNEOUS, CARNOUS, *adj.* Reamhar, sultmhor.
CARNIVAL, *s.* A' chuirm inid.
CARNIVOROUS, *adj.* Feòil-itheach.
CARNOSITY, *s.* Ain-fheòil,
CAROL, *s.* Coireal, òran-gàirdeachais.
CAROL, *v. a.* Mol, seinn cliù, ceileirich
CAROUSAL, *s.* Fleadh, cuirm, òl.
CAROUSE, *v. a.* Òl, bi air mhisg.
CARP, *s.* Carbhanach uisge.
CARP, *v. n.* Coirich, tiolp, spreig.
CARPENTER, *s.* Saor, saor luinge.
CARPET, *s.* Brat-ùrlair, stràille.
CARPING, *adj.* Coireachail, tiolpach.
CARRIAGE, *s.* Giùlan, beus, carbad.
CARRIER, *s.* Fear giùlain, cairtear, seòrsa calamain.
CARRION, *s.* Blionach, ablach.
CARROT, *s.* Miuran-buidhe.
CARROTY, *s.* Dearg, ruadh.
CARRY, *v. a.* Giùlain iomchair, thoir leat, biodh agad.
CART, *s.* Cairt, càrn.
CART, *v. a.* Giùlain le cairt.
CARTE-BLANCHE, *s.* Paipeir geal.
CARTEL, *s.* Litir chùmhnantan eadar da rìoghachd.
CARTER, *s.* Cairtear.
CARTILAGE, *s.* Maoth-chnaimh.
CARTILAGINOUS, *adj.* Maothanach.
CARTOON, *s.* Dhealbh mòr air paipeir.
CARTOUCH, *s.* Bocsa-peileireach.
CARTRIDGE, *s.* Roidhleag-urchrach.
CARTWRIGHT, *s.* Saor-chairtean.
CARVE, *v. a.* Gearr feoil, fiodh, no clachan, &c.
CARVING, *s.* Gràbhaladh, obair-shnaidhte.
CASCADE, *s,* Eas, cas-shruth.
CASE, *s.* Còmhdach, duille, truaill, cochull; staid, cŏr.
CASEHARDEN, *v. a.* Cruadhaich air an taobh muigh.
CASEKNIFE, *s.* Sgian mhòr.
CASE-SHOT, *s.* Peileirean lanna
CASH, *s.* Airgead ullamh, airgead làimhe.
CASHIER, *s.* Fear-gleidheadh an airg-eid.
CASK, *s.* Buideal, baraille.
CASK, CASQUE, *s.* Clogaid.
CASKET, *s.* Bocsachan.
CASSIA, *s.* Spìosradh; craobh chasia.
CASSOCK, *s.* Casag, cota sagairt.
CAST, *v. a.* Tilg, tilg air falbh; cuir sìos; leag; cuir air cùl; cunnt, air-eamh; leagh, dealbh.
CAST, *s.* Tilgeadh, urchair, buille; le ag-adh, suidheachadh; sgapadh, crath-adh, sgaoileadh; gluasad, claonadh, siaradh; cumadh, dealbh.
CASTAWAY, *s.* Dìobarach, ni air a thilg-eadh, air falbh.
CASTELLAN, *s.* Fear riaghlaidh daing-nich.
CASTELLATED, *adj.* Dùinte, ann an daingneach.
CASTIGATE, *v. a.* Cronaich, smachd-aich.
CASTIGATION, *s.* Cronachadh, peanas.
CASTING-NET, *s.* Lion-sgrìobaidh.
CASTOR, See Beaver.
CASTRAMETATION, *s.* Càmpachadh.
CASTRATE, *v. a.* Spoth; dean ni neo-iomlan.
CASTRATION, *s.* Spoth, gearradh air falbh.
CASUAL, *adj.* Tuiteamach, tubaisteach
CAUSALTY, *s.* Tuiteamas; tubaist.
CASUIST, *s.* Fear fuasglaidh cheistean
CAT, *s.* Cat.

CATACLYSM, *s.* Tuilbheam, dìle.
CATACOMBS, *s. pl.* Uamhannan adhlaic
CATALOGUE, *s.* Clàr-ainm, ainm-chlar.
CATAPHRACT, *s.* Marcach armaichte.
CATAPLASM, *s.* Plàsd, fuar lite.
CATAPULT, *s.* Tailm, no clach-bhogha
CATARACT, *s.* Eas ; galar nan sùl.
CATARRH, *s.* An gàlar smugaideach.
CATARRHAL, *adj.* Smugaideach, ronnach, staonagach.
CATASTROPHE, *s.* Crìoch, droch dheireadh, tubaist.
CATCH, *v. a.* Glac, greimich, beir, ceap.
CATCH, *s.* Glacadh, beirsinn, ceapadh, greim, cothrom ; teum ; luinneag, duanag ; gramaiche.
CATECHISE, *v. a.* Ceasnaich, rannsaich.
CATECHISM, *s.* Leabhar-cheist.
CATECHIST, *s.* Fear-ceasnachaidh, ceistear.
CATECHUMEN, *s.* Ùr-chriosdaidh, leanabh 's a chreideamh.
CATEGORICAL, *adj.* Cinnteach, freagarrach.
CATEGORY, *s.* Òrdugh, dream, treubh, seòrsa, gnè.
CATENARIAN, *adj.* Coltach ri slabhraidh, lùbagach, ailbheagach.
CATENATION, *s.* Tinne, dul, co-cheangal lùbagan.
CATER, *v. n.* Solair, faigh biadh.
CATERCATERER, *s.* Fear-solair.
CATERESS, *s.* Bean-sholair.
CATERPILLAR, *s.* Burras.
CATERWAUL, *v. n.* Dean miagail mar chat.
CATES, *s.* Biadh math, mias bhlasta.
CATGUT, *s.* Teud ; anart ro-gharbh.
CATHARTI, *adj.* Pùrgaideach.
CATHEDRAL, *s.* Ard-eaglais easbuigeach, cathair easbuig.
CATHOLIC, *adj.* Coitcheann ; cumanta.
CATLING, *s.* Sgian-sgaraidh léigh ; teudan.
CATTLE, *s.* Spréidh, crodh, buar, feudail, tàn.
CAVALCADE, *s.* Marc-shluagh.
CAVALIER, *s.* Marcach, ridire ; Rioghalaich.
CAVALIER, *adj.* Gaisgeil, treun, uallach, stràiceil.
CAVALIERNESS, *s.* Mòr-chuis, stràicealachd.
CAVALRY, *s.* Marc-shluagh cogaidh.
CAUDLE, *s.* Deoch bhan-shiùbhla.
CAVE, *s.* Uamh, brugh, toll fo thalamh.
CAVEAT, *s.* Rabhadh, sanas, bacadh.
CAVERN, *s.* Talamh-toll, sloc, uamh.
CAVERNED, CAVERNOUS, *adj.* Uamhach, a' gabhail còmhnaidh an uamhaibh.
CAUGHT, *part. pas.* Glacte.
CAVIL, *v.* Cronaich, coirich, tiolp.
CAVILLATION, *s.* Cronachadh, coireachadh.
CAVILLIER, *s.* Tiolpaire mi-mhoghail féin-bharalach.
CAVITY, *s.* Fàslach, còs, lag, sloc, glac.
CAUL, *s.* Lion-cinn, currac, bréide an crannaig ; currac-an-rìgh.
CAULIFEROUS, *adj.* Cuiseagach, luirgneach.
CAULIFLOWER, *s.* Càl-gruthach.
CAUSAL, *adj.* Aobharach.
CAUSE, *s.* Aobhar, ceann-fàth.
CAUSE, *v. a.* Dean, thoir mu'n cuairt, thoir gu buil.
CAUSELESS, *adj.* Gun aobhar.
CAUSEY, CAUSEWAY, Càbhsair.
CAUSTIC, *s.* A' chlach-loisgeach.
CAUTERY, *s.* Losgadh le iarunn no le cungaidhean léigh.
CAUTION, *s.* Gliocas, cùram, aire, faicill; ràthan, urras, comhairle ; rabhadh, sanas.
CAUTION, *v. a.* Thoir rabhadh, cuir air 'fhaicill.
CAUTIONARY, *adj.* An urras, an geall ; sanasach.
CAUTIOUS, *adj.* Cùramach, faicilleach.
CAUTIOUSNESS, *s.* Faicilleachd.
CAW, *v. n.* Ròc, glaodh mar ròcais.
CEASE, *v. a.* Cuir stad air, cuir crìoch air, caisg ; sguir, leig dhìot ; bàsaich ; dean tàmh.
CEASELESS, *adj.* Buan, gun stad.
CEDAR, *s.* Seudar, craobh sheudair.
CEDE, *v.* Thoir suas, leig dhìot ; géill.
CEIL, *v. a.* Còmhdaich thairis.
CEILING, *s.* Mullach a steach.
CELATURE, *s.* Eòlas gràbhalaidh.
CELEBRATE, *v. a.* Mol, dean iomraiteach ; gléidh, cùm.
CELEBRATION, *s.* Cuimhneachan urramach, cumail féille, moladh, cliù.
CELEBRIOUS, *adj.* Iomraiteach, cliùiteach.
CELEBRITY, *s* Greadhnachas, iomraiteachd.
CELERITY, *s.* Luathas, ealamhachd.
CELESTIAL, *adj.* Nèamhaidh ; diadhaidh, naomha.
CELESTIAL, *s.* Aon do mhuinntir nèimh.
CELIBACY, CELIBATE, *s.* Beatha sagairt manaich no cailliche-duibhe.
CELL, *s.* Cill, còs, fròg, bothan , balgan, pocan.
CELLAR, *s.* Seilear, cùil.
CELTIC, *adj.* Gàëlach.
CELTS, *s.* Gàidheil, luchd-àiteachaidh na Seann Fhrainge.
CEMENT, *s.* Leann-tàth.
CEMENT *v. a.* Tath, cuir r'a chéile.

CEMETERY, *s.* Cladh, ionad-adhlacaidh.
CENOTAPH, *s.* Fàs-chàrn.
CENSE, *v. a.* Ung le tùis, dean deaghbholtrach.
CENSER, *s.* Tùisear, soitheach tùis.
CENSOR, *s.* Fear-cronaichidh.
CENSORIAN, *adj.* Cronachail.
CENSORIOUS, *adj.* Cronachail, achmhasanach, cànranach.
CENSURABLE, *adj.* Toillteannach air achmhasan, ciontach, coireach.
CENSURE, *s.* Coire, achmhasan, cronachadh, ascaoin-eaglais.
CENSURE, *v. a.* Cronaich, coirich; thoir breith, thoir barail.
CENSUS, *s.* Cùnntas, sluagh-chunntas.
CENT, *s.* Giorrachadh air an fhacal laidinn *centum*, ceud.
CENTAGE, *s.* Pàidheadh as a' cheud.
CENTENARY, *s.* Ceud, cùig fichead.
CENTENNIAL, *adj.* Ceud-bliadhnach.
CENTESIMAL, *adj.* Ceudamh.
CENTIFOLIOUS, *adj.* Ceud-dhuilleagach.
CENTRAL, *adj.* Meadhonach.
CENTRE, *s.* Meadhon, buillsgean.
CENTRE, *v. a.* Cuir 's a mheadhon, trus gu meadhon, bi 's a mheadhon.
CENTRIC, *adj.* Suidhichte 's a mheadhon.
CENTRIFUGAL, *adj.* Meadhon-sheachnach.
CENTRIPETAL, *adj.* Meadhon-aomachdail.
CENTUPLE, *adj.* Ceud fillte.
CENTURIATE, *v. n.* Roinn 'n a cheudaibh.
CENTURION, *s.* Ceannard-ceud.
CENTURY, *s.* Ceud bliadhna.
CERATE, *s.* Ìocshlaint chéire.
CERE, *v. a.* Céir, céirich.
CERECLOTH, *s.* Aodach-céire.
CEREMENT, *s.* Leine-lighe chéire.
CEREMONIAL, *s.* Deas-ghnà, dòigh, rian, seòl, riaghailt, modh; riaghailtcràbhaidh.
CEREMONIOUS, *adj.* Deas-ghnàthach, òrdail, dòigheil; làn modhalachd modhail.
CEREMONY, *s.* Deas-gnàth, riaghailtchrabhaidh; modhalachd, dòigh, cleachdadh, modh.
CERRUS, *s.* Searbh-dharach.
CERTAIN, *adj.* Cinnteach, fìrinneach, dearbhta, àraidh.
CERTAINTY, CERTITUDE, *s.* Cinnteachd, dearbhadh.
CERTIFICATE, *s.* Teist, teisteannas.
CERTIFY, *v. a.* Thoir fios, dean cinnteach, dean dearbhta
CERTITUDE, *s.* Cinnteachd, dearbhachd.
CERULEAN, CERULEOUS, *adj.* Gorm, liath-ghorm, speur-ghorm.
CERULIFIC, *adj.* Gorm-dhathach.
CERUMEN, *s.* Céir na cluaise.
CERUSE, *s.* Luaidhe gheal, dath geal.
CESS, *s.* Cìs, càin, màl.
CESSATION, *s.* Stad, socair, sgur, tàmh, clos; fósadh cogaidh, anail-airm
CESSIBLE, *adj* So-thoirt-thairis.
CESSION, *s.* Géilleadh, strìochdadh.
CESTUS, *s.* Crios-gaoil, crios a' ghràidh.
CETACEOUS, *adj.* Orcanach.
CHAFE, *v. a.* and *n.* Suath, blàthaich, teòth; teasaich, feargaich, casaich; bi, frionasach, crosda, feargach.
CHAFE, *s.* Blàthas, teas; fearg, boile, corraich, frionas.
CHAFER, *s.* Daolag-bhuidhe.
CHAFF, *s.* Moll, càth; ni suarach.
CHAFFER, *v. n.* Malairtich, connsaich mu luach.
CHAFFERER, *s.* Fear ceannachd, fear teann am malairt.
CHAFFINCH, *s.* Breac-an-t-sìl.
CHAFFY, *adj.* Càthach, mollach, aotrom, gun bhrìgh.
CHAFINGDISH, *s.* Crubag-ghuail.
CHAGRIN *s.* Frionas, droch-nàdur, mighean, droch-fhonn, farran.
CHAGRIN, *v. a.* Dean frionasach, sàraich.
CHAIN, *s.* Slabhraidh, geimheal, ceangal, cuibhreach, glas-làmh
CHAIN, *v. a.* Ceangail, cuibhrich, geimhlich, cuir air slabhraidh; ceangail r'a chéile.
CHAINSHOT, *s.* Urchair shlabhraidh.
CHAIR, *s.* Cathair, suidheachan.
CHAIRMAN, *s.* Fear cathrach, ceannsuidhe, fear-iomchair.
CHAISE, *s.* Carbad eutrom, carbad dà eich.
CHALDRON, *s.* Salldair, tomhas guail no sìl.
CHALICE, Cupan calpach.
CHALK, *s.* Cailc.
CHALK, *v. a.* Comharraich le cailc.
CHALKY, *adj.* Cailceach.
CHALLENGE, *v. a.* Tairg deas-chòmhrag, dùlanaich.
CHALLENGE, *s.* Gairm-chatha, tairgsecòmhraig, dùlan.
CHALYBEATE, *adj.* Stailinneach, air bhlas iaruinn.
CHAMADE, *s.* Caismeachd, géillidh.
CHAMBER, *s.* Seòmar, ionad-cadail.
CHAMBERLAIN, *s.* Fear-ionaid uachdarain, seumarlan, fear togail màil.
CHAMBERMAID, *s.* Maighdeann sheòmair.
CHAMELEON, *s.* Seòrsa dearc-luachrach.

CHAMIOS, *s.* Seòrsa gaibhre.
CHAMOMILE, *s.* A' buidheag cham-bhil.
CHAMP, *v. a.* and *n.* Cagainn, teum, gearr, criom.
CHAMPAIGN, *s.* Machair, màgh, srath.
CHAMPAIGN, *s.* Seòrsa fìona.
CHAMPION, *s.* Treunlaoch, gaisgeach, curaidh, milidh.
CHANCE, *s.* Tuiteamas, dàn, sealbh.
CHANCEL, *s.* Ionad altair an eaglais.
CHANCRE, *s.* Druis-ghuirean.
CHANDELIER, *s.* Coinnleir meurach.
CHANDLER, *s.* Fear deanamh choinnlean.
CHANGE, *v. a.* Mùth, atharraich; caochail.
CHANGE, *s.* Mùthadh, atharrachadh, caochla, iomlaid.
CHANGEABLE, CHANGEFUL, *adj.* Caochlaideach, luaineach, sgaogach, neo-sheasmhach; so-atharraichte; ioma-chruthach, ioma-dhathach.
CHANGELESS, *adj.* Neo-chaochlaideach.
CHANGELING, *s.* Tàcharan, amadan, ùmaidh; leanabh air fhàgail, no air a ghabhail an àite leinibh eile; àmhlar, sgaogan.
CHANGER, *s.* Fear-atharrachaidh, fear-mùthaidh, fear-malairt airgeid.
CHANNEL, *s.* Amar, clais, leabaidh linne.
CHANT, *v.* Seinn, tog fonn air.
CHANTER, *s.* Fear-canntaireachd; siunnsair.
CHANTICLEER, *s.* Coileach, deagh sheinneadair.
CHAOS, *s.* Mi-riaghailt, aimhreit, troi-chéile.
CHAOTIC, *adj.* Co-measgte, aimhreiteach.
CHAP, *s.* Peasg, fosgladh, sgàineadh; càirean beathaich.
CHAPE, *s.* Teanga, bucail, crampait claidheimh no bata.
CHAPEL, *s.* Eaglais, cill, crùisle.
CHAPELRY, *s.* Cuairt eaglais.
CHAPLAIN, *s.* Ministear teaghlaich, feachd, no luinge.
CHAPLESS, *adj.* Caol-pheirceallach.
CHAPLET, *s.* Blàth-fhleasg, lŭs-chrùn.
CHAPMAN, *s.* Ceannaiche.
CHAPPED, CHAPT, *part. pass.* Peasgte, pronnte.
CHAPTER, *s.* Caibidil; taigh-cléire.
CHAPTREL, *s.* Ceann-mullaich carraigh.
CHAR, *s.* Seòrsa éisg, tarragan, obair-latha.
CHARACTER, *s.* Comharradh, samhla, coltas; litir; iomradh, aithris; cliù, beusan, alla.
CHARACTER, *v. a.* Sgrìob, grabhal; dean iomradh.
CHARACTERISTIC, *adj.* Fìor-shamlachail.
CHARACTERIZE, *v. a.* Thoir cliù, thoir teisteas, aithris buadhan; comharraich; grabhal, sgrìobh.
CHARCOAL, *s.* Gual-fiodha, gual-loisgte.
CHARGE, *v. a.* Earb, thoir comas, earb gnothach, cuir as leth, dìt, faigh cron, buail, thoir ionnsaidh.
CHARGE, *s.* Cùram, gleidheadh; àinte, iompaidh; dreuchd; casaid, coire; cosgas, cìs, urchair.
CHARGEABLE, *adj.* Daor, cosgail, air a chur as leth.
CHARGER, *s.* Mias-mhòr; steud-each.
CHARIOT, *s.* Carbad.
CHARIOTEER, *s.* Carbadair.
CHARITABLE, *adj.* Oircheasach, dèirceach, carthannach; seirceil.
CHARITY, *s.* Caoimhneas, carthannas, gràdh, seirc; déirceachd, tabhartachd
CHARLATAN, *s.* Cleasaiche, léigh-breige mealltair.
CHARLATANICAL, *adj.* Mealltach, aineolach.
CHARLES'S-WAIN, *s.* An griugadan, an crann-reulltach.
CHARLOCK, *s.* An carran-buidhe.
CHARM, *s.* Drùidheachd, buidseachd.
CHARM, *v. a.* Seun, cuir seun air, cuir fo gheasaibh; gairm le drùidheachd.
CHARMER, *s.* Drùidh, geasadair; gràidhean; gràidheag.
CHARMING, *adj.* Taitneach, grinn.
CHARNEL-HOUSE, *s.* Taigh-adhlacaidh.
CHART, *s.* Cairt-iùil.
CHARTER, *s.* Sgrìobhadh, cùmhnant sgrìobhte, bann sgrìobhte; còir sgrìobhte, daingneachd sgrìobhte; dlighe, saorsa.
CHARY, *adj.* Faicilleach, glic, sicir.
CHASE, *v. a.* Sealg, ruaig, fuadaich.
CHASE, *s.* Sealg, faoghaid; tòir, iarraidh; frìth, fad gunna 'san leth a staigh.
CHASM, *s.* Sgàineadh, sgoltadh, bearn.
CHASTE, *adj.* Geamnaidh; glan, fìor-ghlan.
CHASTEN, CHASTISE, *v. a.* Cronaich, smachdaich, peanasaich, claoidh.
CHASTITY, CHASTENESS, *s.* Geamnachd.
CHASTISEMENT, *s.* Smachdachadh, peanas.
CHAT, *v. n.* Dean còmhradh, dean gobaireachd, dean geòlam.
CHAT, *s.* Gobaireachd, frith-chòmhradh.
CHATTEL, *s.* Maoin, àirneis.
CHATTER, *s.* Geòlam, sgeilm.
CHAWDRON, *s.* Mionach beathaich.
CHEAP, *adj.* Saor; air bheag prìs.
CHEAPEN, *v. a.* Lughdaich, leag prìs.
CHEAPNESS, *s.* Saoiread.
CHEAT, *s.* Foill, feall, car; mealltair.

Check, *v. a.* Caisg, bac, grab, cuir fo smachd; cronaich, co-shamhlaich r'a chéile.
Checker, Chequer, *v. a.* Breac, stiallaich, tarruinn stiallan tarsuinn.
Cheek, *s.* Gruaidh, lic.
Cheek-tooth, *s.* Cùlag, fiacaill-chùil.
Cheer, *s.* Cuirm, cuilm, caithream.
Cheer, *v. a.* Misnich, brosnaich.
Cheerer, *s.* Fear-cofhurtachd, fear-sòlais.
Cheerful, *adj.* Ait, suilbhir, aoibhinn
Cheerfulness, *s.* Sùrd, suigeart, sunnt; toil-inntinn, cridhealas.
Cheerless, *adj.* Dubhach, trom.
Cheery, *adj.* Ait, aoibhneach.
Cheese, *s.* Càise.
Cheesemonger. *s.* Ceannaiche-càise.
Cheesevat, *s.* Fiodhan.
Cherish, *adj.* Eiridnich, àraich.
Cherry, *s.* Sirist, craobh-shirìst.
Cherub, *s.* Spiorad nèamhaidh: aìngeal; *Cherubim.*
Cherup, *v. n.* Dean ghuth binn.
Cheslip, *s.* Corra-chòsag.
Chesnut, Chestnut, *s.* Geanm-chnò.
Chess, *s.* Taileasg.
Chess-player, *s.* Fear-feòirne.
Chest, s. Ciste, com, cliabh.
Chevalier,. Ridire, curidh.
Chew, *v. a.* Cagain, cnàmh; cnuasaich.
Chicane, *s.* staraidheachd, innleachd.
Chick, Chicken, *s.* Eireag.
Chickenhearted, *adj.* Gealtach.
Chickenpox, *s.* A' bhreac-òtraich.
Chide, *v. a.* Cronaich, coirich, trod.
Chief, *adj.* Priomh, àrd, araid.
Chieftain, *s.* Ceann-feadhna; ceann-cinnidh.
Chilblain, *s.* Cusp, at-fuachd.
Child, *s.* Leanabh, pàisde.
Childhood, *s.* Leanabachd, leanabas.
Childish, *adj.* Leanabail, leanabaidh.
Childishness, *s.* Leanabachd.
Childless, *adj.* Gun sliochd.
Chiliarch, *s.* Ceannard-mìle.
Chill, *adj.* Fuar, fuaraidh, fionnar.
Chill, *v. a*, Fuaraich, fionnfhuaraich.
Chillness, *s.* Crith-fhuachd.
Chilly, *adj.* Fionnfhuar, fuar, amh.
Chime, *s.* Co-sheirm, co-chòrdadh.
Chimera, *s.* Breisleach, faoin-bheachd.
Chimerical, *adj.* Breisleachail.
Chimney, Luidheir, fàr-leus.
Chin, *s.* Smig, smigead, smeig.
Chincough, *s.* Triuthach.
Chine, *s.* Draonnag, mir-droma, cliathag.
Chink, *s* Sgoltadh, sgàineadh, gàgadh.
Chinky, Gàgach, sgainte.
Chip, *v. a.* Pronn, snaidh; sgàin sgoilt.
Chip, Chiping, *s.* Sliseag, mir, sgealb.
Chirographer, *s.* Fear-sgrìobhaidh.
Chiromancer, *s.* Deàrnadair.
Chiromancy, *s.* Deàrnadaireachd
Chirp, *v. a.* Tog fonn; dean dùrdan.
Chirp, *s.* Bìdeil, ceileirean, bìd.
Chirping, *s.* Ceileireachd.
Chirurgeon, *s.* Làmh-léigh.
Chisel, *s.* Gilb, sgeilb.
Chit, *s.* Paìste, isean; ball brice.
Chitchat, *s.* Pronn-chainnt, gobaireachd, gusgal, briot, geòlam.
Chitterlings, *s.* Mionach, grealach.
Chivalry, *s.* Ridireachd; treubhantas.
Chives, *s.* Meanbh-chalg lŭis.
Choice, . Roghainn, taghadh; brŏd.
Choice, *adj.* Taghte.
Choiceness, *s.* Luachmhorachd, luach.
Choir, *s.* Coisir-chiùil.
Choke, *v. a.* Tachd; mùch.
Choler, *s.* Leanntan, frionas; fearg.
Choleric, *adj.* Feargach, lasanta, cas.
Choose, *v. a.* Tagh, rógḣnaich.
Chop, *v. a.* Sgud, gearr le buille; sluig, pronn.
Chop, *s.* Staoig, sgeanach.
Chopin, *s.* Seipin.
Choppy, *adj.* Làn tholl, gàgach.
Choral, *adj.* Co-sheirmeach.
Chord, *s.* Teud, tafaid.
Chorister, *s.* Fear-seinn.
Chorus, *s.* Co-sheirm; luinneag.
Chosen, *part.* Taghte, roghnaichte.
Chouse, *v. a.* Meall, thoir an car.
Christen, *v. a.* Baist.
Christendom, *s.* A' Chrìosdachd.
Christening, *s.* Baisteadh.
Christian, *s.* Crìosdaidh.
Christian, *adj.* Crìosdail.
Christianity, *s.* Criosdalachd; an creideamh a theagaisg Criosd.
Christianise, *v. a.* Cneasdaich.
Christian-name, *s.* Ainm-baistidh.
Christmas, *s.* Nollaig; àm na nollaig.
Chromatic, *adj.* Dathach.
Chronic, Chronical, *adj.* Tìmeil, leantach.
Chronicle, *s.* Eachdraidh.
Chronicler, *s.* Eachdraiche.
Chronological, *adj.* Eachdraidheach.
Chronology, *s.* Ùin-eachdraidh.
Chronometer, *s.* Uaireadair luinge.
Chuck, *s.* Gloc, gràchdan.
Chuff, *s.* Ùmaidh, burraidh.
Chum, *s.* Companach seòmair.
Chump, *s.* Slacan, fairgean.
Church, *s.* Eaglais, cill; cléir.
Churchman, *s.* Pears-eaglais, ministear.
Churchyard, *s.* Cladh, Reidhlic.
Churl, *s.* Bodach, balach, mùigean.
Churlish, *adj.* Mùgach gnù, iargalta.
Churlishness, *s.* Iargaltas, gruam-

achd, doichioll ; crosdachd, mi-shuairceas.
CHURME, *s.* Toirm, fuaim, borbhan.
CHURN, *s.* Muidhe, crannag.
CHURRWORM, *s.* An t-slat-thomhais.
CHYLE, *s.* Leann-meirbhidh.
CHYMIST, *s.* Feallsanach-brìghe.
CHYMISTRY, Feallsanachd-brìghe.
CICATRICE, *s.* Lorg, làrach.
CICATRIZE, *v. a.* Leighis, slànaich.
CICISBEO, *s.* Gille-baintighearn.
CICURATE, *v. a.* Càllaich, ceannsaich.
CIDER, *s.* Leann-ubhall.
CILICIOUS, *adj.* Gaoisideach, molach.
CIMETER, *s.* Claidheamh-crom.
CINDER, *s.* Gual, guaillean.
CINEREOUS, *adj.* Air dhath na luaithre.
CINGLE, *s.* Crios-tarra, no tarr-iall eich.
CINNAMON, *s.* Caineal.
CINQUEFOIL, *s.* Seamrag chùig-bhileach.
CION, *s.* Faillean, fiùran, ògan.
CIPHER, *s.* An comharradh so (0) ann an cunntas, sgrìobhadh dìomhair.
CIRCLE, *s.* Cuairt, cearcall, buaile, còisir, co-thional.
CIRCLE, *v. a.* Iadh, cuairtich ; cruinnich.
CIRCLET, *s.* Cuairteag camag, buaileag ailbheag.
CIRCUIT, *s.* Cuairt nam mòraireandearga.
CIRCUIT, *v. n.* Cuairtich, rach mu'n cuairt.
CIRCUITOUS, *adj.* Cruinn mu'n cuairt.
CIRCULAR, *adj.* Cuairteach.
CIRCULATE, *v. a.* Cuir timchioll ; cuir mu'n cuairt.
CIRCULATION, *s.* Dol mu'n cuairt.
CIRCUMAMBIENT, *adj.* A' dol mu thimchioll.
CIRCUMAMBULATE, *v. n.* Coisich mu'n cuairt.
CIRCUMCISE, *v. a.* Timchioll-ghearr.
CIRCUMCISION, *s.* Timchioll-ghearradh.
CIRCUMDUCT, *v. a.* Thoir mu'n cuairt, pill, bac, dubh a mach.
CIRCUMFERENCE, *s.* Cuairt-thomhas.
CIRCUMFLEX, *s.* An comharradh so (^) air litir.
CIRCUMFLUENT, *adj.* Cuairt-shruthach.
CIRCUMFORANEOUS, *adj.* Seacharan, o thaigh gu taigh.
CIRCUMFUSE, *v. a.* Dòirt mu'n cuairt.
CIRCUMFUSION, *s.* Ioma-dhòrtadh.
CIRCUMGYRATE, *v. a.* Cuibhlich, paisg gu cruinn.
CIRCUMJACENT, *adj.* Dlù, fagus.
CIRCUMITION, *s.* Cuairteachadh.
CIRCUMLIGATION, *s.* Ceangal mu'ncuairt.
CIRCUMLOCUTION, *s.* Cuairt-chainnt.
CIRCUMMURED, *adj.* Ioma-dhùinte.
CIRCUMNAVIGABLE, *adj.* So-sheòlaidh mu'n cuairt.
CIRCUMNAVIGATE, *v. a.* Seòl mu'n cuairt.
CIRCUMNAVIGATION, *s.* Cuairt-sheòladh
CIRCUMNAVIGATOR, *s.* Seòladair-cuairt na cruinne.
CIRCUMROTATION, *s.* Cuibhleadh, mu'n cuairt.
CIRCUMSCRIBE, *v. a.* Ioma-dhuin.
CIRCUMSCRIPTION, *s.* Ioma-dhunadh.
CIRCUMSPECTION, *s.* Aire, cùram, faicill, furachas, crìonnachd.
CIRCUMSPECTIVE, *adj.* Aireachail.
CIRCUMSTANCE, *s.* Cùis, càs, gnothach, cŏr, staid.
CIRCUMSTANTIAL, *adj.* Mineideach ; pongail.
CIRCUMVALLATE, *v. a.* Daingnich.
CIRCUMVALLATION, *s.* Daingneach.
CIRCUMVECTION, *s.* Cuairt-ghiùlan.
CIRCUMVENT, *v. a.* Meall.
CIRCUMVENTION, *s.* Foill, cealg.
CIRCUMVEST, *v. a.* Aodaich, mu'n cuairt.
CIRCUMVOLVE, *v. a.* Cuir mu'n cuairt.
CIRCUMVOLUTION, *s.* Ioma-roladh.
CIST, *s.* Còmhdach, ciste ; toll, sloc.
CISTERN, . Amar, tobar, linne.
CITADEL, *s.* Dùn, daingneach, caisteal.
CITAL, CITATION, *s.* Achmhasan, cronachadh, bairlinn.
CITE, *v. a.* Gairm, òrduich.
CITESS, *s.* Bean-àitichidh baile-mhòir.
CITIZEN, *s.* Fear-àiteachaidh baile-mhòir.
CITRINE, *adj.* Buidhe-dhonn.
CITY, *s.* Cathair, baile-mòr.
CIVIL, *adj.* Cuideachdail, comunnach ; riaghailteach, rianail, dòigheil ; còir, deagh-bheusach, ciùin, modhail, siobhalta, suairce, a bhuineas do cheartas na tìre ; nach buin do'n eaglais, no do'n arm.
CIVILITY, *s.* Modhalachd, sìobhaltachd, suairceas, grinneas.
CIVILIZE, *v. a.* Ciuinich, teagaisg.
CIVIL-LAW, *s.* Lagh na Rìoghachd.
CIVIL-WAR, *s.* Ar-a-mach.
CLACK, *s.* Clabar muillein.
CLACK, *v. a.* Dean glagan, gliong ; gagaireachd.
CLAD, *part* Aodaichte, sgeadaichte.
CLAIM, *v. a.* Tagair, agair, iarr.
CLAIM, *s.* Agradh, agartas.
CLAIMABLE, *adj.* Agarach, so-agraidh.
CLAIMANT, *s.* Tagaireach, agarach.
CLAMBER, *v. a.* Streap, dìrich suas.
CLAMMY. *adj.* Glaodhach, leantach.
CLAMOROUS, *adj.* Gleadhrach, labhrach.
CLAMOUR, Gàraich, gaoir.
CLAMP, *s.* Cnòt, clabhdan.
CLAN, *s.* Fine, cinneadh.
CLANDESTINE, *adj.* Uaigneach.
CLANG, *s.* Gliong, glang, gliogar.

Clangour, *s.* Gleadhraich, gliongraich.
Clangous, *adj.* Gliongach, glangach.
Clank, *s.* Gleadhar, trost.
Clanship, *s.* Cinneadas.
Clap, *v. a.* Buail r a chéile.
Clap, *s.* Buille, farum, gleadhar, bragh ; bas-ghair, iolach.
Clapper, *s.* Clabar mullein, teangha cluig.
Clapperclaw, *v. a.* Trod, càin.
Clasp, *s.* Cromag, dubhan.
Class, *s.* Buidheann, dreum, cuideachd, seòrsa.
Classical, *adj.* Ionnsaichte, fòghlumte.
Clatter, *v. a.* Bi ri straighlich; dean blabhdaireachd.
Clatter, *s.* Straighlich, gleadhraich.
Clause, *s.* Cuibhrionn; pong.
Clausure, *s.* Dùnadh, druideadh.
Claw, *s.* Spàg, spòg, cròg, ionga; màg dubhan, crudhan, pluit.
Claw, *v. a.* Sgrìob sgròb, reub, tachais.
Clay, *s.* Criadh, eré, criadhach.
Clean, *adj.* Glan ; geamnaidh.
Clean, *v. a.* Glan, nigh, sgùr, ionnlaid.
Cleanliness, **Cleanness**, *s.* Gloinead neo-thruailleachd, fiorghlanachd.
Cleanly, *adj.* Glan, grinn, eireachdail.
Cleanse, *v. a.* Glan, nigh, sgùr, ionnlaid.
Clear, *adj.* Soilleir, soillseach, deàlrach, dearsach, lainnreach, glan; so-thuigsinn; cinnteach ; neo-chiontach ; saor, tuigseach.
Clear, *v. a.* Soilleirich, glan, sgùr, soillsich, dean lainnreach; dean sothuigsinn, rèitich; saor, fìreanaich; sìolaidh.
Clearance, *s.* Barantas-seòlaidh.
Clearer, *s.* Fear-soilleireachaidh.
Clearness, *s.* Soilleireachd.
Clearsighted, *adj.* Glan-fhradharcach.
Cleave, *v.* Sgoilt, spealg, spealt, dlùthlean.
Cleaver, *s.* Sgian-sgoltaidh.
Clef, *s.* Uchdach, stalla.
Cleft, *part.* Sgoilte, roinnte.
Cleft, *s.* Sgoltadh, clais, sgàineadh.
Cleg, *s.* Creithleag-nan-each.
Clemency, *s.* Iochd, bàigh, truas.
Clement, *adj.* Mìn, ciùin, sèimh, bàigheil, caoin, tròcaireach.
Clergy, *s.* Cléir.
Clergyman, *s.* Pears-eaglais.
Clerical, *adj.* Cleireachail.
Clerk, *s.* Cléireach, duine fòghluimte ; sgrìobhaich.
Clerkship, *s.* Cléirsneachd
Clever, *adj.* Tapaidh, deas, eòlach clis.
Cleverness, *s.* Tapachd, cliseachd.
Clew, *s.* Ceirsle ; stiùradh, fear-iùil.
Clew, *v. a.* Paisg siùil.
Click, *v. a.* Bi gliongarsnaich.
Client, *s.* Fear-iarraidh comhairle firlagha.
Cliff, *s.* Creag, sgor, sgùr, stùc.
Cliffy, *adj.* Sgorach, creagach, stùcach.
Climate, **Clime**, *s.* Earrainn-saoghail, àileadh.
Climax, *s.* Dìreadh, éiridh an àirde.
Climb, *v. a.* Dìrich, streap.
Climber, *s.* Fear-streapaidh, lũs streapach.
Climbing, *s.* Streapadh, dìreadh.
Clinch, *v. a.* Daingnich, teannaich, dùin.
Clinch, *s.* Gearr-fhacal.
Clincher, *s.* Greimiche.
Cling, *v. a.* Tiormaich, suas, toinn mu'n cuairt.
Clinic, *s.* Neach an-shocrach tinn.
Clinical, *adj.* Iarganach, eucaileach, euslainteach.
Clink, *v. a.* Thoir gliong.
Clip, *v. a.* Gearr, bearr, lomair, rùisg ; giorraich.
Clipper, *s.* Gearradair, bearradair.
Clipping, *s.* Bearradh, gearradh, lomadh.
Cloak, *s.* Falluinn, cleòc, brat-falaich, sgàile.
Cloak, *v. a.* Còmhdaich, falaich, cleith ceil.
Clock, *s.* Uaireadair, daolag.
Clockwork, *s.* Obair-uaireadair.
Clod, *s.* Clod, ploc, fòd, sgrath ; clodcheann, ùmaidh.
Cloddy, *adj.* Clodach, plocach.
Clodpate, **Clodepole**, *s.* Clod-cheann, ùmaidh.
Clog, *v. a.* Uallaich, luchdaich sacaich bac, tromaich.
Clog, *s.* Eallach, slacan, cudthrom, amaladh, bròg-fhiodha.
Cloister, *s.* Cill-mhanach, taigh chaill eacha-dubha.
Close, *v. a.* Dùin, crìochnaich.
Close, *s.* Dùnadh, mainnir, achadh; crìochnachadh ; ceann, crìoch, deireadh, co-dhùnadh.
Close, *adj.* Dùinte, ceilte, dìomhair, uaigneach ; cumhann ; teann, daingeann, dlù ; dorch, doilleir, neulach.
Closeness, *s.* Dùinteachd, cuingead, teanntachd ; dìomhaireachd uaigneachd.
Closet, *s.* Seòmar-uaigneach, clòsaid.
Closet, *v. a.* Dùin, glais, ceil.
Closure, *s.* Dùnadh, crìochnachadh.

Clot, *s.* Meall, ploc, clod-cheann.
Cloth, *s.* Aodach, clò, tubhailt.
Clothe, *v. a.* Aodaich còmhdaich, sgeadaich.
Clothier, *s.* Ainm uasal air tailear.
Clothing, Clothes, *s.* Aodach, earradh trusgan.
Cloud, *s.* Neul, dubhar, sgò ceò.
Cloud, *v. a.* Neulaich, dorchaich.
Cloudberry, *s.* Oidhreag, foidhreag.
Cloudcapt, *adj.* Neulach, sgothach.
Cloudless, *adj.* Neo-sgòthach.
Cloudy, *adj.* Neulach, neo-soilleir, dubharrach, dorcha, doilleir, gruamach.
Cloven, *part.* Sgoilte.
Clover, *s.* Seamrag, simrag, bileag-chapail, saimir.
Clovered, *adj.* Simeragach, seamragach.
Clough, *s.* Sgòr, stùc, eid-bheann.
Clout, *s.* Luideag, broineag, clùd; tùthag, mìr, brèid, giobal.
Clown, *s.* Luiriste, tuasdar, sgonnbhalach, amadan-àbhachd.
Clownish, *adj.* Tuaisdeach, luiristeach; liobasta, mi-mhodhail.
Cloy, *v. a.* Lìon, sàsaich, cuir gràin air.
Cloyment, *s.* Gràin-bidh, séid.
Club, *s.* Cuaille, lorg, rongas, caman, slacan, A' chairt-chluiche do'n ainm an "dubh-bhileach," no'n "crasg," cuideachd, còisir comunn.
Club, *v. a.* Dìol an lach, cruinn bi cuid fir.
Clublaw, *s.* Làmhachd-làidir.
Cluck, *v. a.* Dean gogail, mar chirc.
Clumps, *s.* Ùmpaidh, slaodair glògair.
Clumisness, *s.* Slaodaireachd, cearbachd.
Clumsy, *adj.* Slaodach, liobasta, trom.
Clung, *part.* Leanta, greimichte.
Clung, *adj.* Tioramaichte, gun saill.
Cluster, *s.* Bagaid, cluigean, dŏs gagan; dornlach.
Clutch, *v. a.* Greimich, glais, glac, teannaich.
Clutch, *s.* Greimeachadh, glacadh, cròg, spòg, mag, dubhan ìne.
Clutter, *s.* Straighlich, stairirich, gleadhraich, garaich.
Clyster, *s.* Cliostar.
Coacervate, *v. a.* Cruinnich, càrn; dùn, tòrr, trŭs.
Coach, *s.* Carbad.
Coact, *v. n.* Co-oibrich, co-shaothraich.
Coaction, *s.* An-toil, aindeoin.
Coactive, *adj.* Ainneartach.
Coadjutant, *adj-* A' co-chuideachadh.
Coadjutor, *s.* Fear-chuidiche.
Coagent, *s.* Co-oibriche.
Coagment, *v. a.* Co-chruinnich. tàth ri chéile.
Coagulate, *v. a.* Binndich, tiughaich righnich.
Coagulation, *s.* Binndeachadh.
Coal, *s.* Al-ghual, gual.
Coal, *v. a.* Gual, loisg gu gual; comharraich le gual.
Coalery. *s.* Toll-guail, sloc-guail.
Coal-fish, *s.* Ucsa, ucas.
Coalesce, *v. n.* Aonaich, tathaich.
Coalescence, *s.* Aonadh, tàthadh.
Coalition, *s.* Glaodhadh, r'a chéile.
Coaly, *adj.* Gualach, air dhreach guail.
Coaptation, *s.* Co-fhreagradh.
Coarse, *adj.* Garbh neo-fhìnealta; mi-mhodhail, garg.
Coarseness, *s.* Gairbhe, drabasdachd.
Coast, *s.* Oirthir, eirthir còrsa, slios.
Coast, *v. a.* Seòl cois an fhearann.
Coat, *s.* Còta; éideadh, aodach.
Coax, *v. a.* Breug, tàlaidh, meall.
Cobble, *v. a.* Cairich, bréidich.
Cobbler, *s.* Greusache sheanna-bhrog; gròig.
Cobirons, *s.* Iaruinn cnap-cheannach.
Cobweb, *s.* Lìon an damhain-allaidh.
Cochineal, *s.* Càrnaid.
Cock, *s.* Coileach; molan-feòir.
Cock, *v. a.* Tog suas; sgrog, cuir air lagh.
Cockade, *s.* Suaicheantas, fàbhar, coc-àrd.
Cockatrice, *s.* Righ-nathair.
Cocker, *v. a.* Criodaich tàlaidh.
Cockerel, *s.* Coilleach eireig
Cocket, *s.* Teisteanas taigh-cuspuinn.
Cockle, *s.* Coilleag, srùban; cogull.
Cockloft, *s.* Lobhta mullaich, spiris.
Cockney, *s.* Lunnainneach.
Cockpit, *s.* *s.* Blàr-catha choileach.
Cocksure, *adj.* Làn-chinnteach.
Cod, *s.* Bodach-ruadh, trosg; cochull, plaosg, mogull.
Codicil, *s.* Leasachadh tiomnaidh.
Codle, *v. a.* Slaop, leth-bhruich.
Coefficacy, *s.* Co-oibreachadh.
Coemption, *s.* Co-cheannachd.
Coequal, *adj.* Co-ionann.
Coerce, *v. a.* Bac, ceannsaich, cùm fo smachd.
Coercible, *adj.* So-cheannsaichte.
Coercion, *s.* Casg, smachd.
Coercive, *adj.* Ceannsalach, smachdail.
Co-essential, *adj.* Aon-bhitheach.
Co-eternal, *adj.* Co-shuthainn.
Coeval, *s.* Co-aimsireach.
Coeval, Coevous, *adj.* Co-aosda, co-aimsireil.
Coexist, *v. n.* Bi co-bhitheach.
Coexistence, *s.* Co-bhith.
Coexistent, *adj.* Co-bhitheach.
Coffer, *s.* Ciste, còbaraid, ulaidh.

COFFIN, *s.* Ciste-mhairbh, ciste-laidhe.
COG, *v. a.* Dean miodal, bi carach.
COG, *s.* Cogus ratha muillein.
COGENCY, *s.* Cumhachd, neart.
COGENT, *adj.* Làidir, spionndail.
COGITATION, *s.* Smuain, beachdachadh.
COGNATE, *adj.* Càirdeach, dàimheil.
COGNATION, *s.* Càirdeas, dàimh.
COIF, *s.* Bréid, beannag.
COIL, *v. a.* Trus, cruinnich.
COIL, *s.* Cuairteag, còrd-chearcall.
COIN, *s.* Cùinneadh, airgead.
COINCIDE, *v. n.* Coinnich, co-aontaich.
COINCIDENCE, *s.* Cò-dhalachadh; co-fhreagradh.
COINCIDENT, *adj.* Co-chòrdadh.
COINER, *s.* Fear-cùnnidh.
COITION, *s.* Mairiste, cliathadh; modh siolaichidh.
COLATION, COLATURE, *s.* Sìoladh.
COLD, *adj.* Fuar, fionnar, fuaraidh.
COLD, *s.* Fuachd, fuarachd, fionnfhuar; cnatan.
COLDNESS, *s.* Fuarachd, fuairead, fionn-fhuaireachd.
COLE, *s.* Guaillean, eibhil-mharbh.
COLEWORT, *s.* Càl-bloinigein.
COLIC, *s.* Greim-mionaich.
COLLAPSE, *v. n.* Crùp, trŭs.
COLLAR, *s.* Bràid, coileir.
COLLAR-BONE, *s.* Cnaimh an uga.
COLLAR, *v. a.* Beir air amhaich, glac air sgòrnan.
COLLATE, *v. a.* Coimeas, feuch r'a chéile.
COLLATERAL, *adj.* Co-shìnte, taobh ri taobh.
COLLATION, *s.* Buileachadh, greim-blasda; coimeas.
COLLATOR, *s.* Fear sgrùdaidh.
COLLEAGUE, *s.* Companach, coimpire.
COLLECT, *v. a.* Cò-chruinnich, tion-ail.
COLLECT, *s.* Urnaigh ghoirid.
COLLECTION, *s.* Co-chruinneachadh.
COLLECTIVE, *adj.* Co-chruinnichte.
COLLECTOR, *s.* Fear-trusaidh, cis-mhaor.
COLLEGE, *s.* Oil-taigh, àrd-sgoil.
COLLEGIAN, *s.* Fòghlumach ard-sgoile.
COLLIER, *s.* Gualadair.
CAULIFLOWER, *s.* Cal-dìtheanach.
COLLIGATION, *s.* Co-cheangal, co-nasg-adh.
COLLISION, *s.* Co-bhualadh, gleadhar.
COLLOCATE, *v. a.* Suidhich, cairich, sochraich.
COLLOCATION, *s.* Suidheachadh, soc-rachadh.
COLLOP, *s.* Toitean, staoig.
COLLOQUIAL, *adj.* Conaltrach.
COLLOQUY, *s* Co-labhairt.
COLLUSION, *s.* Co-chealg, cuilbheart.
COLLUSIVE, *adj.* Cuilbheartach.
COLLY, *v. a.* Dubh le gual.
COLON, *s.* Pung; an caolan mu'n cuairt.
COLONEL, *s.* Cornaileir, còirneal.
COLONIST, *s.* Fear-àiteachaidh tìr chéin.
COLONIZE, *v. a.* Tìrich, àitich.
COLONY, *s.* Luchd-imriche.
COLORATE, *adj.* Dathte.
COLOUR, *s.* Dath; neul, tuar, fiamh, dreach; coltas, riochd; bratach, suaicheantas.
COLOUR, *v. a.* Dath; cuir dath air.
COLOURIST, *s.* Dathadair.
COLT, *s.* Searrach, bìoraiche.
COLUMBARY, *s.* Taigh chalaman.
COLUMBINE, *s.* Lŭs-a'-chalamain.
COLUMN, *s.* Colbh, carragh; sreath.
COLUMNAR, *adj.* Colbhach, carraghail.
COMATE. Companach.
COMB, *s.* Cìr; cìrean; cìr-mheala, copan.
COMBAT, *s.* Cò-chòmhrag, co-chair-eachd.
COMBATANT, *s.* Fear-còmhraig; gaisg-each.
COMBINATE, *adj.* Naisgte, ceangailte.
COMBINATION, *s.* Co-aontachd, co-cheangal.
COMBINE, *v. a.* Co-cheangail, co-aont-aich, co-thàth.
COMBUSTIBLE, *adj.* So-loisgeach, tior-am.
COMBUSTION, *s.* Fal-losgadh, ùparait.
COME, *v. n.* Thig; trobhad.
COMEDIAN, *s.* Cleasaiche,
COMEDY, *s.* Cluich, àbhachd.
COMELINESS, *s.* Eireachdas, ciatachd.
COMELY, *adj.* Eireachdail, ciatach.
COMET, *s.* Reull chearbach.
COMFIT, *s.* Greim milis, mìlsean.
COMFORT, *s.* Co-fhurtachd, sòlas.
COMFORTABLE, *adj.* Socrach, sòlasach.
COMFORTLESS, *adj.* Neo-shuaimh-neach.
COMIC, COMICAL, *adj.* Abhachdach, cridheil, sùgach, ait, cleasanta, neòn-ach.
COMING, *s.* Teachd, tighinn.
COMMA, *s.* Gearr-phung.
COMMAND, *v. a.* Orduich, àint, iarr, ceannsaich.
COMMAND; *s.* Uachdranachd, ard-chumh-achd, ùghdarras, smachd, ceannas, tighearnas; riaghladh, òrduchadh, àinte.
COMMANDER, *s.* Uachdaran, ceannard.
COMMANDMENT, *s.* Òrdugh, iarrtas, àinte. (*Irish idiom* àithne.)
COMMEMORATE, *v. a.* Cuimhnich.
COMMEMORATION, *s.* Cuimhneachan.

COMMENCE, *v. a.* Tòisich, siùd.
COMMENCEMENT, *s.* Tionnsgnadh, tùs, tòiseachadh.
COMMEND, *v. a.* Mol, cliùthaich.
COMMENDABLE, *adj.* Cliù-thoillteannach.
COMMENDATION, *s.* Cliù, moladh; teachdaireachd gaoil.
COMMENDATORY, *adj.* Cliùiteach.
COMMENSURATE, *adj.* Co-thoimhseach.
COMMENT, *v. a.* Mìnich, leudaich.
COMMENT, *s.* Brìgh-mhìneachadh.
COMMENTARY, *s.* Mìneachadh.
COMMENTATOR, *s.* Fear-mìneachaidh.
COMMERCE, *s.* Malart; co-chomunn.
COMMERCE, *v. n.* Malairtich, cum comunn.
COMMERCIAL, *adj.* Malairteach.
COMMINATION, *s.* Bagradh, maoidheadh.
COMMINGLE, *v. a.* Co-mheasgaich.
COMMINUTE, *v. a.* Pronn, mìnich.
COMMINUTION, *s.* Mion-phronnadh.
COMMISERABLE, *adj.* Truagh.
COMMISERATION, *s.* Co-mhothachadh, bàigh.
COMMISERATIVE, *adj.* Iochdmhor.
COMMISSARY, *s.* Comasdair.
COMMISSION, *s.* Earbsa, barantas; ùghdarras; còir.
COMMISSION, *v. a.* Earb, ùghdarraich.
COMMISSIONER, *s.* Fear-ùdarrais.
COMMIT, *v. a.* Earb, cuir an comus leig fo chumhachd; thoir seachad, tiomain; cuir am prìosan, cuir an làimh; cuir an gnìomh, ciontaich.
COMMITTEE, *s.* Cuideachd-riaghlaidh.
COMMIX, *v. a.* Co-mheasg, measgaich.
COMMIXION, *s.* Co-mheasgadh.
COMMODE, *s.* Cionnabharr.
COMMODIOUS, *adj.* Goireasach.
COMMODIOUSNESS, *s.* Goireas.
COMMODITY, *s.* Tairbh, bathar.
COMMODORE, *s.* Ceannard-cabhlaich.
COMMON, *adj.* Coitcheann, suarach.
COMMON, *s.* Ionaltradh coitcheann.
COMMONER, *s.* Diun'-an-uasal.
COMMONALTY, *s.* Mall-shluadh.
COMMONITION, *s.* Comhairle, rabhadh.
COMMONNESS, *s.* Coitcheanntas.
COMMONS, *s.* Tuath-chomhairle.
COMMONWEALTH, *s.* An shuagh.
COMMOTION, *s.* Buaireas, luasgan aimhreìt ùparait, troi-chéile.
COMMUNE, *v. n.* Co-labhair.
COMMUNICANT, *s.* Comanaiche.
COMMUNICATE, *v. a.* and *n.* Compàirtich, builich, thoir seachad; aithris, innis, cuir an céill, taisbein, co-labhair, co-roinn; bi an compairt.
COMMUNICATION, *s.* Compàirteachadh, conaltradh, cur an céill; slighe-fhosgailte; co-chaidreamh; co-chainnt.
COMMUNICATIVE, *adj.* Compàirteach, còmhraidhteach.
COMMUNION, *s.* Còmpanas, comonnachadh, comunn.
COMMUNITY, *s.* Sluagh na Rìoghachd compàirt.
COMMUTABLE, *adj.* Iomlaideach.
COMMUTATION, *s.* Iomlaid, éirig.
COMMUTE, *v. a.* Mùth; dìol éirig.
COMPACT, *s.* Co-cheangal, cùmhnanta.
COMPACT, *adj.* Teann, daingeann.
COMPACTNESS, *s.* Daingneachd.
COMPANION, *s.* Companach.
COMPANY, *s.* Cuideachd, comunn.
COMPANY, *v. a.* Comunnaich.
COMPARABLE, *adj.* Co-ionann.
COMPARATIVE, *adj.* A réir coimeis.
COMPARE, *v. a.* Coimeas.
COMPARE, *s.* Samhla.
COMPARISON, *s.* Coimheart.
COMPART, *v. a.* Compàirtich.
COMPARTMENT, *s.* Roinn, earrann.
COMPARTITION, *s.* Compàirteachadh.
COMPASS, *v. a.* Cuairtich, iomadhruid.
COMPASS, *s.* Cuairt, cearcall; farsuinneachd, tomhas, meud, leud; crìochan; uchdach; cùmbaist, gobhal-roinn; cairt-iùil cumadair.
COMPASSION, *s.* Truas, iochd.
COMPASSIONATE, *adj.* Truacanta.
COMPATIBILITY, *s.* Co-chòrdalachd.
COMPATIBLE, *adj.* Co-chòrdail.
COMPATRIOT, *s.* Fear-dùthcha.
COMPEER, *s.* Companach, còimpir.
COMPEL, *v. a.* Co-éignich.
COMPELLATION, *s.* Fàilte, furan.
COMPENDIOUS, *adj.* Geàrr-bhrìgheach.
COMPENSATE, *v. a.* Dìol, pàidh, ìoc.
COMPENSATION, *s.* Làn-dìoladh.
COMPETENCY, *s.* Pailteas, fòghnadh.
COMPETENT, *adj.* Iomchuidh, comasach.
COMPETITION, *s.* Co-dheuchainn, co-stri.
COMPETITOR, *s.* Fear co-shreip.
COMPILATION, *s.* Co-chruinneachadh.
COMPILE, *v. a* Co-chruinnich, tionail.
COMPILER, *s.* Fear-trusaidh.
COMPLACENCY, *s.* Tlachd, suairceas.
COMPLACENT, *adj.* Modhail, suairce.
COMPLAIN, *v. n.* Gearain, talaich; dean casaid.
COMPLAINANT, *s.* Fear-agairt dìolaidh.
COMPLAINER, *s.* Fear-gearain, fear-cumha.
COMPLAINT, *s.* Gearan, casaid; galar.
COMPLAISANCE, *s.* Modhalachd.
COMPLAISANT, *adj.* Sìobhalta, modhail, suilbhir, suairce, faoilidh.
COMPLANATE, COMPLANE, *v. a.* Dean còmhnard, dean réidh.
COMPLEMENT, *s.* Co-lìonadh.
COMPLETE, *adj.* Iomlan, colionta.

COMPLETE, *v. a.* Dean iomlan.
COMPLETEMENT, *s.* Coilionadh.
COMPLETENESS, *s.* Iomlanachd.
COMPLETION, *s.* Co-lionadh.
COMPLEX, *adj.* Ciogailteach, deacair.
COMPLEXION, *s.* Fuar, neul, dreach, snuadh, coltas, fiamh.
COMPLEXLY, *ad.* Doilleireach.
COMPLIANCE, *s.* Striochdadh, géilleadh.
COMPLAINT, *adj.* Aontach, suairce.
COMPLICATE, *adj.* Cho-mheasgach.
COMPLICATE, *v. a.* Co-fhilltich, co-dhual, co-amlaich.
COMPLICATION, *s.* Co-amladh, co-dhualadh.
COMPLIER, *s.* Fear-co-aontachaidh.
COMPLIMENT, *s.* Moladh, miodal.
COMPLIMENTAL, *adj.* Miodalach.
COMPLINE, *s.* Aoradh feasgair.
COMPLOT, *s.* Co-bhann, co-chealg.
COMPLOT, *v. a.* Gabh claon-chombairle.
COMPLY, *v. n.* Co-aontaich, géill.
COMPONENT, *adj.* A' deanamh suas.
COMPORT, *v. a.* Giùlain, fuilig.
COMPORT, COMPORTMENT, *s.* Giùlan, gnàths, beus.
COMPORTABLE, *adj.* Freagarrach.
COMPOSE, *v. a.* Co-dhean, dean suas, co-chuir, co-dhlùthaich; càirich, socraich, leag, suidhich, ceartaich; sgrìobh; sìthich, ciùinich, dean samhach.
COMPOSED, *part.* Suidhichte, socraichte.
COMPOSER, *s.* Ŭghdar, sgrìobhair.
COMPOSITION, *s.* Sgrìobhadh; co-thlamadh; co-shuidheachadh; suidheachadh, socrachadh, riaghailt.
COMPOSITOR, *s.* Fear-suidhichidh.
COMPOST, COMPOSTURE, *s.* Mathachadh, leasachadh, aolaich.
COMPOSURE, *s.* Suidheachadh, sàmhchalr, riaghailt; sìthealachd.
COMPOTATION, *s.* Co--phòitearachd.
COMPOUND, *v. a.* and *n.* Coimeasg, cuir cuideachd, measg, co-dhean; dean facal dùbailte; dean co-chòrdadh; còrd ri luchd fiachan; thig gu cumhachan.
COMPOUND, *adj.* Coimeasgte, dùbailte.
COMPOUND, *s.* Coimeasgadh.
COMPREHEND, *v. a.* Measraich, tuig.
COMPREHENSIBLE, *adj.* So-mheasraichte.
COMPREHENSION, *s.* Tuigse, eòlas.
COMPREHENSIVE, *adj.* Tuigseach. ciallach.
COMPRESS, *v. a.* Dlùthaich, teannaich.
COMPRESSIBLE, *adj.* So-dhinnte.
COMPRESSION, *s.* Teannachadh.
COMPRESSURE, *s.* Bruthadh, dinneadh.
COMPRIZE, *v. a.* Cum, gabh, gléidh.
COMPROBATION, *s.* Co-dhearbhadh.
COMPROMISE, *s.* Cùmhnanta-réitich.
COMPROMISE, *v. a.* and *n.* Co-chòrd.
COMPTROL, *v. a.* Ceannsaich, smachdaich.
COMPTROLLER, *s.* Fear-riaghlaidh.
COMPULSATORY, *adj.* Éigineach.
COMPULSION, *s.* Co-éigneachadh.
COMPULSIVE, COMPULSORY, *adj.* Ainneartach.
COMPUNCTION, Agartas-cogais.
COMPURGATION, *s.* Co-dhaingneachadh.
COMPUTABLE, *adj.* So-àireamh.
COMPUTATION, *s.* Àireamh, suim.
COMPUTE, *v. a.* Meas, cunnt.
COMRADE, *s.* Companach.
CON, *v. a.* Aithnich; breithnich, smuainich, ionnsaich air do mheaghair.
CONCATENATE, *v. a.* Co-thàth.
CONCATENATION, *s.* Co-thàthadh.
CONCAVE, *adj.* Còsach, co-chòsach.
CONCAVITY, *s.* Còs, co-chòs.
CONCEAL, *v. a.* Ceil, cleith falaich.
CONCEALABLE, *adj.* So-fhalach.
CONCEALMENT, *s.* Ionad-falaich, cleith.
CONCEDE, *v. a.* and *n.* Co-cheadaich, leig seachad, aontaich, géill, strìochd, fuilig, deònaich, aidich, leig thairis, luasaich.
CONCEIT, *s.* Beachd, smuain, barail; tuigse; fein-bheachd, féin-spéis féinmheas, mac-meanmnainn.
CONCEIT, *v. a.* Smuainich, beachdaich.
CONCEITED, *adj.* Féin-bheachdail.
CONCEIVABLE, *adj.* So-shaoilsinn.
CONCEIVE, *v. a.* Cnuasaich, tionnsgainn, breithnich, saoil; fàs torrach.
CONCEIVER, *s.* Beachdair.
CONCENTRATE, *v. a.* Co-chruinnich.
CONCENTRATION, *s.* Co-chruinneachadh.
CONCENTRE, *v. a.* Thoir gu meadhon.
CONCENTRIC, *adj.* Aon-mheadhonach
CONCEPTION, *s.* Gineamhuinn, meas rachadh.
CONCERN, *v. a.* Gabh gnothach.
CONCERN, *s.* Gnothach, cùis; cùram.
CONCERNING, *prep.* Mu thimchioll, mu dhéibhinn, a thaobh.
CONCERNMENT, *s.* Gnothach; cùram.
CONCERT, *v. a.* and *n.* Co-shuidhich, co-rùnaich, gabh comhairle gu dìomhair; co-shocraich, co-chomhairlich.
CONCERT, *s.* Co-chomhairle, co-shuidheachadh, co-shocrachadh, co-rùn; co-sheirm, còisir-chiùil.
CONCESSION, *s.* Strìochdadh, ceadachadh, géilleadh, toirt thairis.
CONCH, *s.* Slige, faochag.

CONCILIATE, *v. a.* Réitich buannaich.
CONCILIATION, *s.* Réiteachadh.
CONCILIATOR, *s.* Fear-réiteachaidh.
CONCINITY, *s.* Freagarrachd.
CONCISE, *adj.* Goirid, gearr.
CONCISENESS, *s.* Aithghiorrad.
CONCISION, *s.* Co-ghearradh, sgudadh.
CONCITATION, *s.* Co-éiridh.
CONCLAMATION, *s.* Co-ghàir.
CONCLUDE, *v.* Co-dhùin, dùin, crioch-naich.
CONCLUSION, *s.* Co-dhùnadh.
CONCLUSIVE, *adj.* Crìochnach.
CONCOCT, *v. a.* Cnàmh, meirbh.
CONCOCTION, *s.* Meirbheadh.
CONCOCTIVE, *adj.* Cnàmhach.
CONCOMITANT, *adj.* Co-aontaichte.
CONCOMITANT, *s.* Companach.
CONCORD, *s.* Co-fhreagairt, co-shéirm, co-fhonn, co-chòrdadh.
CONCORDANCE, *s.* Co-chòrdachd.
CONCORDANT, *adj.* Co-chòrdail.
CONCORDATE, *s.* Co-bhann, co-ghairm.
CONCORPORATE, *v. a.* Co-chruinnich.
CONCOURSE, *s.* Co-chruinneachadh
CONCRETE, *v. a.* Co-chrùinnich.
CONCRETE, *adj.* Co-chruinnichte.
CONCRETION, *s.* Meall chruinnichte.
CONCUBINE, *s.* Coileapach.
CONCUPISCENCE, *s.* Ana-mhiann.
CONCUPISCENT, *adj.* Collaidh.
CONCUR, *v. n.* Aontaich.
CONCURRENCE, *s.* Co-aontachd, co-chuideachadh, toil.
CONCURRENT, *adj.* Co-aontach.
CONCUSSION, *s.* Criothnachadh.
CONDEMN, *v. a.* Dìt, cronaich.
CONDEMNATION, *s.* Dìteadh, binn.
CONDENSATE, *adj.* Tiughaichte.
CONDENSATION, *s.* Tiughachadh.
CONDENSE, *v. a.* Co-dhlùthaich.
CONDENSITY, *s.* Dinnteachd.
CONDESCEND, *v. n.* Ìslich, irioslaich, strìochd, deònaich, ceadaich.
CONDESCENSION, Irioslachd.
CONDIGN, *adj.* Toillteannach, iom-chuidh.
CONDIMENT, *s.* Amhlon, annlann.
CONDITE, *v. a.* Saillteich, saill.
CONDITION, *s.* Cor, staid; cumha, cùmhnanta, inbhe.
CONDITIONAL, *adj.* Air chumha.
CONDITIONARY, *adj.* Cùmhnantaichte.
CONDOLE, *v. n.* Co-ghuil.
CONDOLENCE, *s.* Co-ghal.
CONDONATION, *s.* Mathadh.
CONDUCE, *v. a.* Co-chèimnich, treò-raich, stiùr, seòl an t-slighe; co-chuid-ich.
CONDUCIBLE, *adj.* Comhnachail.
CONDUCIVE, *adj.* Cuideachail.
CONDUCT, *s.* Rian, dòigh, riaghladh; stiùradh, treòrachadh; buidheann dhìona; giùlan, beus, caithe'-beatha.
CONDUCT, *v. a.* Treòraich, stiùr, seòl.
CONDUCTOR, *s.* Fear-iùil, fear-treòr-achaidh; ceannard.
CONDUIT, *s.* Pìob-uisge, guitear.
CONE, *s.* Bidean, stalla.
CONFABULATE, *v. n.* Co-labhair.
CONFABULATION, *s.* Conaltradh.
CONFECTION, *s.* Mìlsean.
CONFECTIONER *s.* Mìlseanaich.
CONFEDERACY, *s.* Cùmhnant.
CONFEDERATE, *v. a.* Co-aontaich, co-cheangail.
CONFEDERATE, *s.* Companach.
CONFEDERATION, *s.* Co-chaidreamh.
CONFER, *v. a.* Thabhair, builich, bàirig; co-labhair.
CONFERENCE, *s.* Còmhradh.
CONFESS, *v. a* Aidich; faoisidich; éisd faoisid; taisbean, cuir an céill; co-aontaich, ceadaich.
CONFESSION, *s.* Aidmheil; faoisid.
CONFESSOR, *s.* Fear-aidmheil a' chreid-imh; sagart-faoisid; fear-aideach-aidh.
CONFEST, *adj.* Aidichte, soilleir.
CONFIDANT, CONFIDENT, *s.* Fear-rùin-eachd, caraid dealaidh.
CONFIDE, *v. a.* Earb, cuir earbsa.
CONFIDENCE, *s.* Earbsa, muinghinn, bun; dòchas, misneach; dànadas, ladornas.
CONFIDENT, *adj.* Cinnteach, dearbhte, earbsach, dearbh-chinnteach, neo-theagmhach; danarra, teann, dalma; muinghinneach, dòchasach; dàna, ladorna.
CONFIDENTIAL, *adj.* Càirdeil, dìleas.
CONFIGURATION, *s.* Co-fhreagradh.
CONFIGURE, *v. a.* Dean co-dhreachte.
CONFINE, *s.* Crìoch, iomall, oir.
CONFINE, *v. a* Cum a steach.
CONFINEMENT, *s.* Prìosanachadh.
CONFIRM, *v. a.* Daingnich, socraich.
CONFIRMABLE, *adj.* So-dhearbhte.
CONFIRMATION, *s.* Co-dhearbhadh; dol fo làimh an easbuig.
CONFISCATE, *v. a.* Ar-phuntaich.
CONFISCATION, *s.* Ar-phuntachadh.
CONFIX, *v. a.* Daingnich, suidhich.
CONFLAGRANT, *adj.* Co-lasach.
CONFLAGRATION, *s.* Co-lasadh.
CONFLATION, *s.* Co-ghàir; co-leaghadh.
CONFLICT, *v. n.* Cathaich, dean strì.
CONFLICT, *s.* Strì, spàirn, còmhrag, sabaid, dòrainn, cràdh.
CONFLUENCE, *s.* Co-choinneachadh shruth; co-thional.
CONFLUENT, *adj.* A' co-shruthadh.
CONFLUX, *s.* Ionbhar; co-thional.
CONFORM, *v.* Co-aontaich, géill.

CONFORMABLE, *adj.* Co-chòrdail, coltach.
CONFORMATION, *s.* Co-chruth, cumadh, dealbh.
CONFORMIST, *s.* Fear co-aontachaidh.
CONFORMITY, *s.* Co-fhreagarrachd, coltas, samhlachas.
CONFOUND, *v. a.* Aimhreitich, cuir thar a chéile; coimeasg, cuir an imcheist; tuairgnich, nàraich; mill, sgrios.
CONFOUNDED, *ad* Gràineil, fuathach.
CONFOUNDER, *s.* Buaireadair, blaomair, fear tuairgnidh.
CONFRATERNITY, *s.* Co-bhràthaireachas.
CONFRONT, *v. a.* Seas mu choinneamh; cuir aghaidh ri aghaidh.
CONFRONTED, *part.* Air an toirt aghaidh ri aghaidh.
CONFUSE, *v. a.* Aimhreitich, breislich, cuir thar a chéile; mi-riaghailtich, dorchaich; tuairgnich.
CONFUSION, *s.* Breisleach, tuairgneadh; aimhreit, buaireas, aimlisg; aimheal.
CONFUTABLE, *adj.* So-àicheadh.
CONFUTATION, *s.* Breugnachadh.
CONFUTE, *v. a.* Breugnaich.
CONGEAL, *v. a.* Reòdh, ragaich.
CONGEALABLE, *adj.* Reòdhtachail.
CONGEALMENT, *s.* Reodhadh, eighneadh.
CONGEE, CONGE, *s.* Umhlachd, cromadh, lùbadh.
CONGENIAL, *adj.* Co-ghnéitheach.
CONGEON, *s.* Duairc, arachd.
CONGER, *s.* Easgann mhara.
CONGEST, *v. a.* Càrn, cruach, tòrr.
CONGESTION, *s.* Leannachadh, trusadh.
CONGLACIATE, *v. a.* Tionndaidh gu eigh.
CONGLOBATE, *v. a.* Dean meall cruinn.
CONGLOBATE, *adj.* Co-chruinn.
CONGLOMERATE, *v. a.* Ceirslich.
CONGLOMERATE, *adj.* Ceirslichte.
CONGLOMERATION, *s.* Co-thrŭsadh.
CONGLUTINATION, *s.* Aonadh.
CONGOU, *s.* Seòrsa do thì fìnealta.
CONGRATULANT, *adj.* Co-ghàirdeachail.
CONGRATULATE, *v. a.* Dean co-ghàirdeachas.
CONGRATULATION, *s.* Co-ghàirdeachas.
CONGRATULATORY, *adj.* Co-ghàirdeachail.
CONGREGATE, *v. a.* Co-thionail.
CONGREGATION, *s.* Co-thional.
CONGRESS, *s.* Coinneamh, còdhàil.
CONGRESSIVE, *adj.* A' coinneachadh.
CONGRUENCE, CONGRUITY, *s.* Freagarrachd, co-fhreagarrachd, còrdachd.
CONGRUENT, *adj.* Co-fhreagarrach.
CONGRUOUS, *adj.* Co-fhreagarrach.
CONIC, CONICAL, *adj.* Bideanach.
CONJECTOR, CONJECTURER, *s.* Fear-baralach.
CONJECTURAL, *adj.* Baralach.
CONJECTURE, *s.* Barail, tuaiream.
CONJECTURE, *v. a.* Baralaich.
CONJOIN, *v. a.* and *n.* Co-dhlùthaich, aonaich, co-aontaich, co-cheangail, co-thàth; co-naisg.
CONJOINT, *adj.* Co-cheangailte, co-dhlùithte, co-naisgte.
CONJUGAL, *adj.* Pòsachail, pòsta.
CONJUGATE, *v. a.* Co-cheangail, co-naisg co-dhlùthaich.
CONJUGATION, *s.* Co-cheangal.
CONJUNCTION, *s.* Aonadh, co-cheangal, coinneachadh; facal aonaidh, càraid.
CONJUNCTIVE, *adj.* Co-cheangailte.
CONJUNCTURE, *s.* Co-chuideachd, coinneachadh, tachairt, còdhail; càs, cùis, éigin, àm sònraichte, iomacheist; co-cheangal, co-nasgadh; co-chòrdalachd.
CONJURATION, *s.* Mìonnachadh, grìosad; drùidheachd; co-chealg.
CONJURE, *v. a.* Grìos, mionnaich; co-cheangail fo mhionnaibh; cuir fo gheasaibh; gnàthaich drùidheachd.
CONJURER, *s.* Drùidh, fiosaiche.
CONJUREMENT, *s.* Grìosad, aslachadh.
CONNASCENCE, *s.* Co-bhreith; aonadh.
CONNATE, *adj.* Co-bhreithte.
CONNATURAL, *adj.* Co-ghnèach.
CONNECT, *v. a.* Co-naisg.
CONNECTED, *part.* Aonaichte.
CONNEX, *v. a.* Co-naisg, snaidhm.
CONNEXION, *s.* Aonadh, dàimh.
CONNIVANCE, *s.* Leigeadh seachad.
CONNIVE, *v. n.* Caog, smèid; reach seachad.
CONNOISSEUR, *s.* Fear fiosrach.
CONNUBIAL, *adj.* Pòsachail, posta.
CONQUASSATE, *v. a.* Coluaisg.
CONQUER, *v. a.* Buadhaich, ceannsaich; cìosnaich.
CONQUERABLE, *adj.* So-cheannsachadh.
CONQUEROR, *s.* Buadhaiche.
CONQUEST, *s.* Buaidh-làrach.
CONSANGUINITY, *s.* Càirdeas, dàimh.
CONSCIENCE, *s.* Cogais, ceartas, còir.
CONSCIENTIOUS, *adj.* Cogaiseach.
CONSCIONABLE, *adj.* Ceart, reusonta.
CONSCIOUS, *adj.* Féin-fhiosrach.
CONSCIOUSLY, *ad.* Féin-fhiosrachail.
CONSCIOUSNESS, *s.* Féin-fhiosrachd.
CONSCRIPT, *v.* Sgrìobte sìos.
CONSECRATE, *v. a.* Coisrig, seun.
CONSECRATE, *adj.* Coisrigte, seunte
CONSECRATION, *s.* Coisrigeadh, seunadh.
CONSECUTION, *s.* Leanmhainn.
CONSECUTIVE, *adj.* Leanmhainneach.
CONSEMINATE, *v. a.* Co-chuir sìol am measg a chéile.
CONSENT, *v. n.* Aontaich, géill còrd.
CONSENT, *s.* Aonta.

Consentaneous, *adj.* Freagarrach.
Consentient, *adj.* A dhaon bharail.
Consequence, *s.* Toradh, buaidh, brìgh.
Consequent, *adj.* Leanmhainneach.
Consequential, *adj.* Cudthromach, mòr-bheachdail.
Consequently, *adv.* Uime sin.
Conservation, *s.* Gleidheadh, dìon.
Conservatory, *adj.* Ionad-tasgaidh.
Conserve, *v. a.* Taisg, gléidh, dìon; dean milis.
Conserve, *s.* Biadh blasta.
Consider, *v. a.* and *n.* Smuainich, beachd-smuainich, thoir fainear, sgrùd, rannsaich, cnuasaich; dìol, duaisich; cuimhnich.
Considerable, *adj.* Fiùghail, luach-mhor, cudhromach.
Considerably, *ad.* Fiùghalachd.
Considerate, *adj.* Ciallach, glic.
Consideration, *s.* Smuaineachadh, beachd-smuaineachadh, toirt fainear, rannsachadh, sgrùdadh; crìonnachd, gliocas; geur-bheachd; meas, urram; luach, dìoladh; aobhar, fàth.
Consign, *v. a.* Thoir seachad.
Consignment, *s.* Toirt seachad.
Consimility, *s.* Aon-choltachd.
Consist, *v. n.* Mair, buanaich.
Consistence, **Consistency**, *s.* Staid, cŏr, bith; cumadh, dreach; seasmhachd, buanachd, maireannachd; co-chòrdadh.
Consistent, *adj.* Co-chòrdach, do réir.
Consistory, *s.* Ionad-ceartais 's an eaglais.
Consociate, *s.* Companach.
Consociate, *v. a.* Dlùthaich; aonaich.
Consociation, *s.* Co-chomunn.
Consolable, *adj.* So-fhurtachail.
Consolation, *s.* Sòlas, furtachd.
Consolatory, *adj.* Sòlasach, furtachail.
Console, *v. a.* Sòlasaich, furtaich.
Consoler, *s.* Co-fhurtair.
Consolidate, *v. a.* Cruadhaich.
Consolidation, *s.* Cruadhachadh.
Consonance, *s.* Co-sheirm, co-aont.
Consonant, *adj.* Co-fhreagarrach.
Consonant, *s.* Co-fhòghar.
Consonous, *adj.* Leadarra, binn.
Consort, *s.* Céile, coisir; aonachd.
Consort, *v.* Aonaich, measgaich; pòs; rach an cuideachd.
Conspicuity, *s.* Soilleireachd.
Conspicuous, *adj.* Faicsinneach, soilleir, ainmeil, cliùiteach, inbheach.
Conspiracy, *s.* Feall, foill ceannairc.
Conspirator, **Conspirer**, *s.* Fealltair, fear-foille, cluaintear.
Conspire, *v. a.* Suidhich, droch-bheart, dean co-fheall.
Conspurcate, *v. a.* Truaill.
Constable, *s.* Maor-sìthe.
Constableship, *s.* Maorsainneachd-sìth.
Constancy, *s.* Seasachd, neo-chaochlaidheachd, maireannachd, bunailteachd; dìlseachd.
Constant, *adj.* Seasach, daingeann, maireannach; bunailteach; dìleas.
Constellation, *s.* An grigleachan.
Consternation, *s.* Fuathas, uabhas.
Constipate, *v. a.* Tiughaich, dinn, dlùthaich, teannaich; lìon suas, duin, iom-dhruid; ceangail.
Constipation, *s.* Dlùthachadh.
Constituent, *adj.* Dùileach, prìomh.
Constituent, *s.* Fear-òrduchaidh.
Constitute, *v. a.* Suidhich, tog, stéidhich; socraich.
Constitution, *s.* Suidheachadh, togail; stéidheadh, socrachadh, càileachd; aoradh; *the constitution of man*, aoradh mhic an duine.
Constitutional, *adj.* Càileachdail, freumhail; aorachail, laghail, reachdail.
Constrain, *v. a.* Co-éignich.
Constraint, *s.* Eigin, aindeoin.
Constriction, *s.* Teannachadh.
Constringe, *v. a.* Teannaich.
Constringent, *adj.* Teannachail.
Construct, *v. a.* Tog, dèan, dealbh, cùm, suidhich.
Construction, *s.* Togail, deanamh, dealbh, cumadh, suidheachadh.
Construe, *v. a* Réitich; mìnich.
Constuprate, *v. a.* Eignich, truaill.
Consubstantial, *adj.* De'n aon bhrìgh.
Consul, *s.* Ard-chomhairleach.
Consult, *v. a.* Faigh comhairle.
Consultation, *s.* Comhairle.
Consumable, *adj.* So-chaithte.
Consume, *v. a.* Searg, caith, sgrios.
Consumer, *s.* Milltear, struidhear.
Consummate, *v. a.* Foirfich, crìochnaich, co-lion.
Consummation, *s.* Foirfeachadh.
Consumption, s. Caitheamh, éiteach.
Consumptive, *adj.* Caithteach.
Contact, *s.* Co-bhualadh.
Contagion, *s.* Gabhaltachd, plàigh.
Contagious, *adj.* Gabhaltach.
Contain, *v. a.* Cùm; bac, ceannsaich.
Contaminate, *adj.* Truaillidh.
Contamination, *s.* Truailleadh.
Contemper, **Contemperate**, *v. a.* Ciùinich, maothaich.
Contemplate, *v. a.* Beachd-smuainich.
Contemplation, *s.* Dlùth-aire.
Contemplative, *adj.* Smuainteachail.

CONTEMPLATOR, *s.* Fear-beachdachaidh, fear smuainteachail.
CONTEMPORARY, *adj.* Co-aimsireil.
CONTEMPORARY, *s.* Co-aoiseach.
CONTEMPT, *s.* Tàir, tarcuis, dimeas.
CONTEMPTIBLE, *adj.* Tàireil, suarach.
CONTEMPTUOUS, *adj.* Tarcuiseach.
CONTEND, *v. a.* Cathaich, dean strì.
CONTENDER, *s.* Fear-co-strì.
CONTENT, *adj.* Buidheach, toilichte.
CONTENT, *v. a.* Toilich, riaraich.
CONTENTATION, *s.* Toileachas, socair.
CONTENTED, *part.* Riaraichte, toilichte.
CONTENTION, *s.* Strì, connspaid.
CONTENTIOUS, *adj.* Connspaideach.
CONTENTLESS, *adj.* Neo-thoilichte.
CONTENTMENT, *s.* Toileachas-inntinn.
CONTENTS, *s.* Clar-innse.
CONTEST, *v. a.* Tagair; dean strì.
CONTEST, *s.* Strì, cath, arabhaig.
CONTESTABLE, *adj.* Tagluinneach.
CONTEXT, *s.* Co-theagasg.
CONTEXTURE, *s.* Co-fhilleadh, dealbh.
CONTIGUITY, *s.* Fagusachd.
CONTIGUOUS, *adj.* Dlù do 'chéile.
CONTINENCE, or CONTINENCY, *s.* Féin-smachd; stuamachd; measarrachd.
CONTINENT, *adj.* Geamnaidh, beusach.
CONTINENT, *s.* Tìr-mòr, a mhòr-thìr.
CONTINENTAL, *adj.* Mòr-thìreach.
CONTINGENT, *adj.* Tuiteamach.
CONTINGENT, *s.* Tuiteamas; cuid, còir.
CONTINUAL, *adj.* Sior, daonnan.
CONTINUALLY, *ad.* Do ghnà, gun sgur.
CONTINUANCE, *s.* Mairsinneachd.
CONTINUATION, *s.* Buanachadh.
CONTINUE, *v. a.* Buanaich, mair.
CONTINUITY, *s.* Dlù-leanmhuinneachd.
CONTORT, *v. a.* Toinn, sniomn, fiar.
CONTORTION, *s.* Toinneamh, fiaradh.
CONTRA (Facal laidinn), An aghaidh.
CONTRABAND, *adj.* Mi-laghail, toirmsgte, neo-cheadaichte.
CONTRACT, *v. a.* and *n.* Giorraich, lughdaich, teannaich, beagaich; réitich, dean ceangal pòsaidh; crup, preas; cumhnantaich.
CONTRACT, *s.* Cùmhnant, réiteach.
CONTRACTIBLE, *adj.* So-ghiorrachadh.
CONTRACTION, *s.* Giorrachadh.
CONTRACTOR, *s.* Fear-cùmhnantachaidh.
CONTRADICT, *v. a.* Cuir an aghaidh.
CONTRADICTION, *s.* Co-àicheadh.
CONTRADICTORY, *adj.* Neo-chòrdail.
CONTRADISTINCTION, *s.* Eadar-dhealachadh.
CONTRARIETY, *s.* Neo-fhreagarrachd.
CONTRARIWISE, *adv.* Direach an aghaidh.
CONTRARY, *adj.* An aghaidh.
CONTRAST, *s.* Eadar-dhealachadh.
CONTRAST, *v. a.* Cuir an aghaidh.
CONTRAVENE, *v. a.* Thig an aghaidh.
CONTRAVENTION, *s.* Cur an aghaidh.
CONTRIBUTARY, *adj.* Co-chìseachd.
CONTRIBUTE, *v. a.* Cuidich, cuir leis.
CONTRIBUTION, *s.* Cuideachadh, tabhartas, tional, co-roinn; cìs-airm.
CONTRITE, *adj.* Brùite, aithreachail.
CONTRIVANCE, *s.* Dealbh, dealbhadh; innleachd, suidheachadh.
CONTRIVE, *v. a.* Dealbh, faigh innleachd.
CONTRIVER, *s.* Fear-innleachd.
CONTROL, *s.* Smachd, ùghdarras.
CONTROL, *v. a.* Ceannsaich.
CONTROLLABLE, *adj.* So-cheannsaichte.
CONTROLLER, *s.* Fear-riaghlaidh.
CONTROVERSIAL, *adj.* Connsachail.
CONTROVERSY, *s.* Connspaid, strì.
CONTROVERT, *v. a.* Cuir an aghaidh.
CONTROVERTIBLE, *adj.* So-thagradh.
CONTROVERTIST, *s.* Fear-connspaid.
CONTUMACIOUS, *adj.* Ceann-laidir.
CONTUMACIOUSNESS, CONTUMACY, *s.* Eas-ùmhlachd, crosdachd.
CONTUMELIOUS, *adj.* Talcuiseach.
CONTUMELY, *s.* Tàir, talcuis.
CONTUSE, *v. a.* Brùth, pronn.
CONTUSION, *s.* Bruthadh, pronnadh.
CONVALESCENCE, *s.* Ath-shlàinte.
CONVALESCENT, *adj.* Ath-shlàinteach.
CONVENE, *v. a.* Tionail, gairm cuideachd, trus.
CONVENIENCE, *s.* Goireas, deisealachd.
CONVENIENT, *adj.* Goireasach.
CONVENT, *s.* Manachainn.
CONVENTICLE, *s.* Coinneamh dhìomhair a chum aoraidh.
CONVENTION, *s.* Co-chruinneachadh.
CONVENTIONAL, *adj.* Cùmhnantaichte.
CONVENTIONARY, *adj.* A réir cùmhnaint.
CONVERGE, *v. n.* Co-aom.
CONVERGENT, *s.* Co-aomach.
CONVERSABLE, *adj.* Fosgarach, conaltrach, còmhraiteach.
CONVERSANT, *adj.* Fiosrach, mioneòlach.
CONVERSATION, *s.* Còmhradh.
CONVERSE, *v. n.* Labhair, dean seanachas.
CONVERSION, *s.* Iompachadh.
CONVERT, *v. a.* Iompaich; bi air t'iompachadh.
CONVERT, *s.* Iompachan.
CONVERTIBLE, *adj.* So-thionndadh.
CONVEX, *adj.* Cruinn, dronnach.
CONVEXITY, *s.* Dronnachd.
CONVEY, *v. a.* Giùlain, iomchair.
CONVEYANCE, *s.* Seòl-iomchair; còir sgrìobhte, riaghladh diamhair.
CONVEYANCER, *s.* Sgrìobhadair chòraichean.
CONVEYER, *s.* Fear-giùlain, fear-iomachair.

CONVICT, *v. a.* Còmhdaich, dìt.
CONVICT, *s.* Ciontach.
CONVICTION, *s.* Dearbhadh, dìteadh.
CONVICTIVE, *adj.* A dhearbhas.
CONVINCE, *v. a.* Dearbh.
CONVINCIBLE, *adj.* So-dhearbhaidh.
CONVIVIAL, *adj.* Fleadhach.
CONUNDRUM, *s.* Toimhseachan.
CONVOCATE, *v. a.* Co-chruinnich.
CONVOCATION, *s.* Co-chruinneachadh.
CONVOLVE, *v. a.* Co-fhill, co-thoinn.
CONVOLUTION, *s.* Co-fhilleadh.
CONVOY, *v. a.* Dìon air turas.
CONVULSE, *v. a.* Grad-chlisg.
CONVULSION, *s.* An tinneas ospagach.
CONVULSIVE, *adj.* Grad-chlisgeach, buaireasach, creathneachail.
CONY, *s.* Coinean.
COO, *v. n* Dean dùrdail mar chalaman.
COOK, *s.* Còcaire, fear-deasachaidh.
COOK, *v. a.* Deasaich, bruich.
COOKERY, *s.* Còcaireachd, deasachadh.
COOL, *adj.* Fionnar; fuar, amhaidh.
COOL, *v. a.* Fuaraich, fionnaraich.
COOLNESS, *s.* Fionnarachd.
COOM, *s.* Sùidhe; blonag-rotha.
COOMB, *s.* Tomhas cheithir cheithreamh.
COOP, *s.* Baraille; eunlan.
COOP, *v. a.* Dùin suas.
COOPER, *s.* Cùbair.
CO-OPERATE, *v. n.* Co-oibrich.
CO-OPERATION, *s.* Co-oibreachadh.
CO-ORDINATE, *adj.* Co-inbheach,
COOT, *s.* An dù-lach.
COP, *s.* Ceann, mullach, bàrr.
COPARCENARY, COPARCENY, *s.* Co-oighreachas, co-phairteachas.
COPARTNER, *s.* Fear-comhpairt.
COPARTNERSHIP, *s.* Combanas.
COPE, *s.* Currac-sagairt; sreath-mhullaich, no clach-mhullaich.
COPE, *v. a.* Connsaich.
COPIER, COPYIST, *s.* Fear ath-sgrìobhaidh.
COPING, *s.* Sreath-mhullaich-balla.
COPIOUS, *adj.* Làn, pailt, lìonmhor.
COPIOUSNESS, *s.* Pailteas.
COPPER, *s.* Copar.
COPPER-PLATE, *s.* Clò-chlàr copair.
COPPERAS, *s.* Copar dubhaidh.
COPPERSMITH, *s.* Ceàrd-copair.
COPPICE, COPS, *s.* Preas-choille.
COPULATE, *v. a.* Càraidich.
COPULATION, *s.* Càraideachadh, maraist.
COPY, *s.* Leth-bhreac, mac-samhail.
COPY, *v. a.* Ath-sgrìobh.
COQUETRY, *s.* Guaineas, gogaideachd.
COQUETTE, *s.* Gogaid, guanag.
CORAL, *s.* Croimheal.
CORALLINE, *adj.* Croimhealach.
CORANT, *s.* Damhsa-clis.
CORBAN, *s.* Aite-gleidhidh dhéirc.
CORD, *s.* Còrd, sreang, ball, ròp.
CORDAGE, *s.* Buill, acuinn-luinge.
CORDIAL, *s.* Deoch-eiridinn.
CORDIAL, *adj.* Eiridneach, càirdeal.
CORDIALITY, *s.* Blàth-ghradh, catharanas.
CORDOVAN, CORDWAIN, *s.* Leathar eich.
CORE, *s.* Cridhe, buisgean.
CORIANDER, *s.* Lus-a'choire.
CORK, *s.* Àrc, àrcan.
CORKY, *adj.* Àrcach, àrcanach.
CORMORANT, *s.* Sgarbh.
CORN, *s.* Gràn, sìol; arbhar.
CORNCHANDLER, *s.* Grainsear.
CORN-MARIGOLD, *s.* A' bhuidheag-shamhraidh.
CORNELIAN, *s.* Clach luachmhor.
CORNEOUS, *adj.* Adharcach.
CORNER, *s.* Oisinn, cearn; cùil.
CORNET, *s.* Dùdach; fear brataich eachraidh.
CORNETER, *s.* Dùdaire.
CORNICE, *s.* Bàrr-mhaise, barr-bhile
CORNICLE, *s.* Adharcag, sgrogag.
CORNIGEROUS, *adj.* Cròcach.
CORNUCOPIA, *s.* Adharc-shaibhreis.
COROLLARY, *s.* Co-dhùnadh.
CORONATION, *s.* Crunadh.
CORONER, *s.* Breitheamh mòid.
CORONET, *s.* Ridir-chrùn.
CORPORAL, *s.* Corpaileir.
CORPORALITY, *s.* Corporrachd.
CORPORATE, *adj.* Aonaichte.
CORPORATION, *s.* Comunn.
CORPOREAL, CORPORAL, *adj.* Corporra.
CORPS, *s.* Buidheann airm.
CORPSE, *s.* Corp marbh.
CORPULENCE, *s.* Sultmhorachd.
CORPULENT, *adj.* Dòmhail.
CORPUSCLE, *s.* Dùradan smùirnean.
CORPUSCULAR, *adj.* Smùirneanach.
CORRADE, *v. a.* Suath, sgrìob r'a chéile.
CORRADIATION, *s.* Co-dhealradh.
CORRECT, *v. a.* Smachdaich, cronaich; ceartaich.
CORRECT, *adj.* Ceart, poncail.
CORRECTION, *s.* Smachdachadh, cronachadh, ceartachadh.
CORRECTIVE, *adj.* Ceartachail.
CORRECTNESS, *s.* Ceartachd, eagarachd, pongalachd, snasmhorachd.
CORRELATE, *s.* Co-charaid.
CORRELATIVE, *adj.* Co-dhàimheach.
CORRESPOND, *v. n.* Co-fhreagair, co-sgrìobh litrichean.
CORRESPONDENCE, *s.* Co-fhreagradh; co-sgrìobhadh litrichean; caidreamh, càirdeas, co-chomunn.
CORRESPONDENT, *adj.* Co-fhreagarrach.
CORRESPONDENT, *s.* Co-sgrìobhair.
CORRIGIBLE, *adj.* So-chronachadh.
CORROBORANT, *dj.* Co-neartachail.
CORROBORATE, *v. a.* Co-neartaich.

CORROBORATION, *s.* Co-dhearbhadh.
CORRODE, *v. a.* Cnàmh, caith, meirgnich.
CORRODENT, *adj.* Cnàimhteach.
CORROSIBLE, *adj.* So-chnàimhteach.
CORROSION, *s.* Cnàmh, meirgneadh.
CORROSIVE, *adj.* Cnàimhteach.
CORROSIVENESS, *s.* Cnàimhteachd.
CORRUGANT, *adj.* Preasach.
CORRUGATION, *s.* Preasadh, casadh.
CORRUPT, *v.* Grod, lobh, dean breun; truaill, salaich, mill, lochdaich, dochunn; breòth, breun.
CORRUPT, *adj.* Truaillidh, salach, olc.
CORRUPTER, *s.* Truailleadair.
CORRUPTIBLE, *adj.* So-thruaillidh.
CORRUPTION, *s.* Truailleachd.
CORRUPTIVE, *adj.* Lobhtach, breothach.
CORRUPTNESS, *s.* Truailleadh.
CÒRSAIR, *s.* Long-spùinnidh.
CORSE, *s.* Corp, cairbh, closach.
CORSLET, or CORSLET, *s.* Uchd-éideadh.
CORTICAL, *adj.* Cairtidh, sgrothach.
CORUSCANT, *adj.* Deàlrach, lainnreach.
CORUSCATION, *s.* Deàlradh, deàrsadh.
CORYMBIATED, *adj.* Bagaideach.
COSMETIC, *s.* Cungaidh mhaise.
COSMOGONY, *s.* Cé-chruthachadh.
COSMOGRAPHER, *s.* Cé-sgrìobhair.
COSMOGRAPHY, *s.* Cé-sgrìobhadh.
COSMOPOLITE, *s.* Faodalaich.
COSSET, *s.* Uan-pheat, peat uain.
COST, *s.* Luach, fiach, cosgais.
COSTAL, *adj.* Aisinneach.
COSTARD, *s.* Ceann, cnuac; ubhall.
CÒSTIVE, *adj.* Ceangailte, teann; dùinte.
COSTLINESS, *s.* Cosgas, stròdhalachd.
COSTLY, *adj.* Cosgail, daor, strùidheil.
COSTUME, *s.* Aodach-suaicheanta.
COT, COTTAGE, *s.* Bothan.
COTEMPORARY, *adj.* Co-aimsireil.
COTERIE, *s.* Bannal, cuideachd, coisir.
COTQUEAN, *s.* Fear cailleachail.
COTTAGER, *s.* Coitear, croitear.
COTTILION, *s.* Damhsa Fràngach.
COTTON, *s.* Canach, aodach canaich.
COUCH, *v.* Càirich, cuir a laidhe; cuir air lagh; crùb, crom, dean laidhe.
COUCH, *s.* Leabaidh; uraigh-làir.
COUCHANT, *adj.* Sìnte, 'na laidhe.
COUCH-GRASS, *s.* Feur-a'-phuint.
COVE, *s.* Bàgh, lùb, camus; uamh, dìon.
COVENANT, *s.* Co-cheangal, cùmhnant.
COVENANT, *v. a.* Cùmhnantaich, daingnich, co-cheangail.
COVENANTER, *s.* Cùmhnantach.
COVER, *v. a* Còmhdaich; falach, ceil.
COVER, *s.* Còmhdach; falach, brat, sgàil.
COVERING, *s.* Còmhdach, aodach.
COVERLET, COVERLID, *s.* Brat-uachdair.
COVERT, *s.* Dìdean, ionad-falaich, dìon, fasgadh; doire, badan-dlù.
COVERT, *adj.* Falaichte, dìomhair
COVERTNESS, *s.* Dìomhaireachd.
COVET, *v. a.* Sanntaich, miannaich.
COVETABLE, *adj.* Ion-mhiannaichte.
COVETOUS, *adj.* Sanntach.
COVEY, *s.* Mathair-ghuir le 'h-àlach.
COUGH, *s.* Casad, casadaich.
COULTER, *s.* Coltar, sgoiltear.
COUNCIL, *s.* Co-chomhairle; chomhairle, seòladh, earail, luchd-tagraidh.
COUNSEL, *v. a.* Comhairlich, earalaich.
COUNSELLOR, *s.* Comhairleach-lagha.
COUNT, *v. a.* Aireamh, cunntas.
COUNTENANCE, *s.* Gnùis, aghaidh, aodann, fiamh, dreach, snuadh; dìon tearmunn, dìdeann.
COUNTENANCE, *v. a.* Dìon, seas.
COUNTER, *s.* Clàr-malairt.
COUNTER, *adv.* Càlg-dhìreach, an aghaidh, dìreach an aghaidh.
COUNTERACT, *v. a.* Grab, bac-amail.
COUNTERBALANCE, *v. a.* Co-chothromaich.
COUNTERCHANGE, *s.* Co-mhalairt.
COUNTER-EVIDENCE, *s.* Ath-fhianais.
COUNTERFEIT, *adj.* Mealltach.
COUNTERFEIT, *s.* Feall-chùinneadh.
COUNTERMAND, *v. a.* Ath-òrduich.
COUNTERMARCH, *v. n.* Ais-imich.
COUNTERMOTION, *s.* Ath-ghluasad.
COUNTERPANE, *s.* Brat-uachdair leapa.
COUNTERPART, *s.* Leth-bhreach.
COUNTERPLOT, *s.* As-innleachd.
COUNTERPOISE, *v. a.* Co-chothromaich.
COUNTERTIDE, *s.* Saobh-shruth.
COUNTESS, *s.* Ban-iarla.
COUNTLESS, *adj.* Do-àireamh.
COUNTRY, *s.* Dùthaich, tìr.
COUNTRYMAN, *s.* Fear-dùthcha.
COUNTY, *s.* Siorramachd.
COUPLE, *s.* Càraid, dithis.
COUPLE, *v.* Càraidich.
COUPLET, *s.* Ceathramh, càraid rann.
COURAGE, *s.* Misneach, cruadal.
COURAGEOUS, *adj.* Misneachail.
COURAGEOUSNESS, *s.* Misneachd.
COURIER, *s.* Teachdair, gille-ruith.
COURSE, *s.* Slighe, coliong; ionad-iomchar, giùlan, caithe-beatha, seòl, gnàthas, gnà; riaghailt.
COURSE, *v. a.* Ruag, lorgaich, lean.
COURT, *s.* Cùirt, lùchairt, lios; taighmòid; mòd; miodal, sodal.
COURT, *v. a.* Dean suiridhe.
COURTEOUS, *adj.* Cùirteil, aoidheil, suairce, caoimhneil.
COURTEOUSNESS, *s.* Cùirtealachd, aoidhealachd, suairceas, caoimhnealachd.
COURTESAN, *s.* Strìopach, siùrsaich.
COURTESY, *s.* Modhalachd, modh.
COURTIER, *s.* Cùirtear; suiridheach.
COURTLINESS, *s.* Cùirtealachd; cuirleis.
COURTLY, *adj.* Cùirteil, cuirteiseach.

COURTSHIP, *s.* Suiridhe, leannanachd.
COUSIN, *s.* Co-ogha.
COW, *s.* Bò, mart; *v.* eagalaich.
COWARD, *s.* Cladhaire, gealtaire.
COWARDICE, *s.* Cladhaireachd, geilt.
COWARDLY, *adj.* Gealtach, eagalach.
COWER, *v. n.* Crùb, dean crùban.
COWHERD, *s.* Buachaille.
COWL, *s.* Currac-manaich, cuinneag-uisg.
COWLED, *adj.* Curraiceach, boineideach.
COWSLIP, *s.* Bròg-na-cuthaig.
COXCOMB, *s.* Cìrean; sgeamhanach.
COXCOMICAL, *adj.* Proiseil.
COY, *adj.* Nàrach, màlda, beusach; sàmhach, saidealt.
COYNESS, *s.* Saidealtas, màldachd.
COZEN, *v. a.* Meall, thoir an car á.
COZENAGE, *s.* Ceilg, foill.
COZENER, *s.* Cealgair, mealltair.
CRAB, *s.* Partan, duine dreamach.
CRABBED, *adj.* Dreamach, dranndanach, frionasach, cas.
CRABBEDLY, *ad.* Dreamasach, dranndanachd, frionasachd, caiseachd.
CRACK, *s.* Sgàineadh, brag, bristeadh.
CRACK, *v. a.* Sgoilt, sgàin; spreadh.
CRACK-BRAINED, *adj.* Mi-chéillidh.
CRACKER, *s.* Fear-spaglainn.
CRACKLE, *v. n.* Dean cnacail, cnac.
CRADLE, *s.* Creathall, lunn bàta.
CRAFT, *s.* Ceàird, ìnnleachd, seòltachd, teòmachd; loingeas beaga.
CRAFTINESS, *s.* Cluaintearachd, foill.
CRAFTSMAN, *s.* Fear-cèirde.
CRAFTY, *adj.* Carach, fealltach.
CRAG, *s.* Creag, sgòrr sgeir.
CRAGGED, CRAGGY, *adj.* Creagach.
CRAM, *v. a.* Dinn, glaimsich.
CRAMBO, *s.* Rann-chòmhradh, rannachd, duanaireachd.
CRAMP, *s.* Iodha; glamaire-teannachaidh, inneal-dlùthaidh.
CRAMP, *v. a.* Bac, grab, ceangail.
CRANE, *s.* Còrra-sgriach, corra-ghlas, corra-riabhach; inneal-togail; pìob-tharruinn.
CRANIUM, *s.* Claigeann, cnuac.
CRANK, *s.* Crangaid; fiar-char, fiaradh.
CRANK, *adj.* Corrach, guanach.
CRANKLE, *v. a.* Lùb, cam, fiar.
CRANNIED, *adj.* Tolltach, sgàinteach.
CRANNY, *s.* Gàg, sgàineadh, cùil, peisg.
CRAPE, *s.* Sròl-duth dù-shròl.
CRAPULENCE, *s.* Amh-dheoch, no tinneas-poit.
CRASH, *s.* Stairn, stairirich.
CRATCH, *s.* Prasach, mainnir.
CRAVAT, *s.* Suaineach-muineil.
CRAVE, *v. a.* Iarr, tagair; guidh.
CRAVEN, *s.* Fùidsidh, gealtaire.
CRAVING, *s.* Miann, miannachadh.
CRAW, *s.* Sgroban, goile, giaban.
CRAWFISH, CRAYFISH, *s.* Giomach-uisge.
CRAWL, *v. a.* Crùb, snàig.
CRAZE, *v. a.* Bris, cuir air mi-chéill.
CRAZINESS, *s.* Breòiteachd; mi-chéill.
CRAZY, *adj.* Lag, breòite; méaranta,
CREAK, *v. n,* Sgread, dìosgain.
CREAM, *s.* Uachdar, bàrr.
CREAM-FACED, *adj.* Bàn-neulach.
CREAMY, *adj.* Uachdarach, barragach.
CREASE, *s.* Filleadh, preasag.
CREATE, *v. a.* Cruthaich, dean dealbh.
CREATION, *s.* An Cruthachadh, a' chruitheachd.
CREATIVE, *adj.* Cruthachail.
CREATOR, *s.* Cruthadair; Cruithear.
CREATURE, *s.* Creutair, cré, dùil, bith.
CREDENCE, *s.* Creideas, meas.
CREDENDA, *s.* Pongan-creidimh.
CREDENT, *adj.* Creideach.
CREDENTIALS, *s.* Litrichean, teisteis.
CREDIBILITY, CREDIBLENESS, *s.* Creideas, teistealachd.
CREDIBLE, *adj.* Creideasach.
CREDIT, *s.* Creideas; cliù, meas.
CREDIT, *v. a.* Creid; thoir dàil.
CREDITABLE, *adj.* Teisteil; measail.
CREDITOR, *s.* Fear-féich.
CREDULITY, *s.* Baoghaltachd.
CREDULOUS, *adj.* Baoghhalta.
CREED, *s.* Creud, aidmheil, creideamh.
CREEK, *s.* Bàgh, geodha, camus, cùil.
CREEP, *v. a.* Snaig, crùb, dean magaran, fabh air do mhàgan.
CREEPER, *s.* An ìath-shlat.
CRESCENT, *s.* Leth-chearcall.
CRESS, *s.* Biolair an fhuarain.
CRESSET, *s.* Crann-tàra, gath-solais.
CREST, *s.* Ite-mullaich, bad-mullaich.
CRESTED, *adj.* Dosach, cìreanach.
CREST-FALLEN, *adj.* Fo thùrsa, fo sproc, fo leann-dubh.
CRETACEOUS, *adj.* Cailceach.
CREVICE, *s.* Sgoltadh, sgàineadh, còs.
CREW, *s.* Sgioba bàta no luinge, gràisg, pàbar.
CRIB, *s.* Prasach; bothan, crùban.
CRIB, *v. a.* Goid, dùin suas, fàngaich.
CRIBLE, *s.* Criathar.
CRIBRATION, *s.* Criathradh.
CRICK, *s.* Giosgan; tinneas-miunneil.
CRICKET, *s.* Greollan, cuileag-theallaich.
CRIER, *s.* Fear-éigheachd.
CRIME, *s.* Ceannairce, eucoir, coire, cron, cionta, lochd.
CRIMINAL, CRIMINIOUS, *adj.* Coireach, ciontach, eucorach.
CRIMINAL, *s.* Ceannairceach, fear do-bheirt, ciontach.
CRIMELESS. *adj.* Neo chiontach.

CRIMINATION, *s.* Coireachadh, dìteadh.
CRIMINATORY, *adj.* Coireachail.
CRIMP, *v. a.* Cas, preas, dualaich.
CRIMSON, *adj.* Craobh-dhearg.
CRINGE, *s.* Crùbadh, strìochdadh tràill-eil, bochd-ùmhladh.
CRINGE, *v. a.* Crùb, strìochd.
CRINKLE, *s.* Preasag, preasadh, crupadh.
CRIPPLE, *s.* Bacach, crùbach, cripleach.
CRISIS, *s.* Cunnart, faothachadh.
CRISP, CRISPY, *adj.* Cas, bachlagach, cuachach, brisg, pronn,
CRISPATION, *s.* Toinneamh, dualadh, cuachadh, preasadh.
CRISPNESS, CRISPITUDE, *s.* Caise, caisead, preasachd, cuachagachd, brisgead.
CRITERION, *s.* Comharradh, dearbhadh.
CRITIC, *s.* Breitheamh, tiolpaire.
CRITICAL, *adj.* Eagnaidh, poncail, teannbhreitheach, tiolpach ; cunnartach.
CRITICISE, *v. a.* Geur-bhreithnich.
CRITICISM, CRITIQUE, *s.* Geur-bhreithneachadh, geur-rannsachadh, mionsgrùdadh.
CROAK, *v. n.* Ròc, dean ròcail.
CROCK, *s.* Soitheach-creadha, crogan.
CROCODILE, *s.* An lonach-sligeach.
CROCKERY, *s.* Gach seorsa soithichean creadha.
CRONY, *s.* Caraid fear cagair.
CROOK, *s.* Cromag ; camag cròcan, dubhan, lùb.
CROOK, *v. a.* Crom, cam, lùb ; aom.
CROOKED, *adj.* Cam, crom, fiar, cròcanach, lùbach ; crosta.
CROOKEDNESS, *s.* Caime, cruime, fiarachd, lùbachd, aingeachd, crosdachd.
CROP, *s.* Sgròban eoin ; mullach ; bàrr, arbhar.
CROP, *v. a.* Bearr, gearr, buain, lomair.
CROPFULL, *adj.* Làn sgriòbain, sàthaichte.
CROSIER, *s.* Cromag-an-aithreachais ; bachull-easbuig.
CROSLET, *s.* Croiseag ; suacan.
CROSS, *s.* Crăsg, crois, crann-ceusaidh.
CROSS, *adj.* Tarsuinn ; fiar, cam, trasda ; deacair, doirbh, àmhgharach ; aingidh, crosta ; frionasach ; mishealbhach, tuaitheal.
CROSS, *v. a.* Cuir tarsainn ; seun ; coisrig rach thairis.
CROSS-EXAMINE, *v. a.* Ath-cheasnaich.
CROSSBOW, *s.* Bogha saigheid.
CROSS-GRAINED, *adj.* Gearr-ghraineach, craindidh, crosta.
CROSSNESS, *s.* Crasgachd ; reasgachd.
CROTCH, *s.* Gobhal, cromag, dubhan, bacan.
CROTCHET, *s.* An comharradh [so].
CROUCH, *v. n.* Lùb, crom, crùb ri làr ; dean miodal.
CROUP, *s.* Breaman, rumpull ; dronn.
CROW, *s.* Feannag ; geimhleag ; gairmcoilich
CROWD, *s.* Dòmblachd, gràisg.
CROWD, *v. a.* Dòmhlaich, mùch ; teannaich, dinn.
CROWN, *s.* Coron, crùn ; fleasg ; mullach a' chinn, bàrr ; bonn chùig tasdan.
CROWN, *v. a.* Crùn ; sgeadaich, maisich ; crìochnaich.
CRUCIAL, *adj.* Crasgach, tarsainn, trasta, fiar.
CRUCIBLE, *s.* Suacan, poit-leaghaidh.
CRUCIFIX, *s.* Crois-sheunaidh.
CRUCIFIXION, *s.* Ceusadh.
CRUCIFORM, *adj.* Crasgach, tarsainn.
CRUCIFY, *v. a.* Ceus, croch ri cram.
CRUDE, CRUDY, *adj.* Amh, anabaich.
CRUDENESS, CRUDITY, *s.* Neo-mheirbhteachd, an-abaichead.
CRUEL, *adj.* An-iochdmhor, cruaidhchridheach, borb, garg, fuilteach, neothruacanta, aingidh, mi-thlŭsail.
CRUELTY, *s.* An-iochdmhorachd.
CRUET, *s.* Searrag bheag, olla.
CRUISE, *v. n.* Dean tòireachd mara.
CRUISER, *s.* Long-thòireachd.
CRUM, *s.* Mìr, pronnag, criomag, bideag, sprùileag.
CRUMBS, *plur.* Spruileach, fuigheal.
CRUMBLE, *v. a.* Pronn, criom ; bris.
CRUMMY, *adj.* Pronnagach.
CRUPPER, *s.* Cuirpean, bod-chrann, beairt-dheiridh eich.
CRURAL, *adj.* Luirgneach, cosach.
CRUSADE, CROISADE, *s.* Cogadh-nacroise.
CRUSH, *v. a.* Brùth, faisg, pronn, teannaich ; ceannsaich, sàraich.
CRUSH, *s.* Bruthadh, pronnadh, mùchadh, dìnneadh, teannachadh.
CRUST, *s.* Slige, sgrath, rùsg, cochull.
CRUSTACEOUS, *adj.* Alt-shligeach.
CRUSTY, *adj.* Sligeach ; dranndanach.
CRUTCH, *s.* Lorg, treŏsdan, crasg, cuaille, bata-laimhe.
CRY, *v. a.* Glaodh, éigh, gairm ; guil.
CRY, *s.* Eigh, iolach, beuc, ràn ; gul.
CRYPTICAL, *adj.* Còsach, uaigheach.
CRYSTAL, *s.* Criostal, glaine-shòilleir.
CUB, *s.* Cuilean, isean.
CUBATION, *s.* Suidhe, laidhe sìos.
CUBE, *s,* Ceithir-chearnag.
CUBIC, CUBICAL, *adj.* Ceithir-chearnach, ceithir-oisinneach.
CUBIT, *s.* Làmh-choille.
CUBITAL, *adj.* Làmh-choilleach.
CUCKOLD, *s.* Fear ban-adhaltraiche
CUCKOLD, *v. a.* Dean adhaltras.
CUCKOLDY, *adj.* Truagh, dìblidh.

CUCKOO, *s.* Cuach, cuthag.
CUCUMBER, *s.* Cular.
CUD, *s.* Cìr. ["A chnàmhas a chìr." Bible.]
CUDDLE, *v. n.* Laidh sìos, laidh ri làr.
CUDDY, *s.* Baothaire, balaoch.
CUDGEL, *s.* Bata, cuaille, rongas.
CUDGEL, *v. a.* Buail le bata, slac.
CUDWEED, *s.* An cnàmh-lus.
CUE, *s.* Dronn, feaman, rumpull, roinns, earball, deireadh; sanas.
CUFF, *s.* Dòrn, cnap, bun-dùirn.
CUIRASS, *s.* Uchd-éideadh, uchd-bheart.
CUIRASSIER, *s.* Saighdear armaichte.
CUISH, *s.* Leas-bheart, leás-dhion.
CULDEES, *s.* Cùildich, coilltich.
CULLENDER, *s.* Liolachan.
CULLY, *s.* Suiridheach socharach.
CULM, *s.* Seòrsa do ghual mìn.
CULPABLE, *adj.* Ciontach, coireach.
CULPRIT, *s.* Ciontach, coireach.
CULTIVATE, *v. a.* Leasaich, àitich, treabh, thoir a steach.
CULTIVATION, *s.* Àiteach, treabhadh, leasachadh; ionnsachadh.
CULTURE, *s.* Treabhadh, leasachadh.
CULVER, *s.* An smùdan.
CULVERIN, *s.* Gunna fada, cuilbheir.
CUMBER, *v. a.* Tromaich, cuir maille.
CUMBERSOME, *adj.* Trom, draghail.
CUMBRANCE, *s.* Uallach, dragh.
CUMBROUS, *adj.* Trom, Sgì, sàrachail.
CUMIN, *s.* Lus-Mhic-Chuimein.
CUMULATE, *v. a.* Tòrr, càrn, cruach.
CUMULATION, *s.* Càrnadh, tòrradh.
CUNEAL, CUNEIFORM, *adj.* Geinneach.
CUNNING, *adj.* Seòlta, sgileil; carach, cluainteach, sligheach, cealgach.
CUNNING, CUNNINGNESS, *s.* Seòltachd, gliocas; cuilbheartachd, cluaintearachd, cealgaireachd, caraireachd.
CUP, *s.* Cupan, copan, còrn, cuach.
CUPBEARER, *s.* Gille-cupain.
CUPBOARD, *s.* Còrn-chlar.
CUPIDITY, *s.* Ana-mhiann, sannt.
CUPOLA, *s.* Cruinn-mhullach.
CUR, *s.* Madadh, cù, duine dreamach.
CURABLE, *adj.* So-leigheas.
CURACY, *s.* Frith-mhinistearachd.
CURATE, *s.* Frith-mhinistear.
CURB, *s.* Camagan sréine, cabstar; bacadh, grabadh, éis.
CURB, *v. a.* Ceannsaich, bac.
CURD, *s.* Gruth, slamban.
CURD, CURDLE, *v. a.* Binndich.
CURE, *s.* Leigheas, cungaidh-leighis.
CURE, *v. a.* Leighis, slànaich; sàill.
CURELESS, *adj.* Do-leigheas.
CURFEW, *s.* Clag-smàlaidh.
CURIOSITY, *s.* Neònachas, ioghnadh.
CURIOUS, *adj.* Iongantach, neònach.
CURL, *adj.* Cutach, gearr.
CURL, *s.* Dual, bachlag, cam-lub.
CURL, *v. a.* Bachlaich, cas, dualaich.
CURLED, *adj.* Bachlach, dualach.
CURLEW, *s.* Guilbneach.
CURMUDGEON, *s.* Spìocaire.
CURRANT, *s.* Dearcag-fhrangach.
CURRENCY, *s.* Sgaoileadh, ruith; ruithchainnt, deas-bhriatharachd; airgead-bainne.
CURRENT, *adj.* Iom-ruitheach; measail, coitcheann; gnàthaichte.
CURRENT, *s.* Buinne, cas-shruth.
CURRICLE, *s.* Carbad dà-rotha.
CURRIER, *s.* Fear-gréidhidh leathair.
CURRISH, *adj.* Sabaideach, mosach.
CURRYCOMB, *s.* Cìr-eich, càrd-eich.
CURSE, *v. a.* Mallaich, mionnaich.
CURSE, *s.* Mallachd, droch guidhe.
CURSED, *adj.* Mallaichte, aingidh.
CURSORINESS, *s.* Prabadh-thairis.
CURSORY, *adj.* Luath, neo-chùramach.
CURTAIL, *v. a.* Giòrraich.
CURTAIN, *s.* Cùirtein, brat-sgàile.
CURVATION, *s.* Cromadh, camadh.
CURVATURE, *s.* Cruime, caime, lùb.
CURVE, *v. a.* Crom, cam, fiar, lùb.
CURVET, *v. a.* Leum, gearr, sùrdag.
CURVET, *s.* Leum, cruinn-leum, sùrdag.
CURVILINEAR, *adj.* Cam-sgrìobach.
CUSHION, *s.* Săsag, pillean.
CUSP, *s.* Adharc na gealaich' ùir.
CUSPATED, CUSPIDATED, *adj.* Rinneach.
CUSPIDATE, *v. a.* Geuraich, bioraich.
CUSTARD, *s.* Ubhagan, uibheagan.
CUSTODY, *s.* An làimh; cùram.
CUSTOM, *s.* Àbhaist; gnàthachadh, modh, gnàths; cuspunn.
CUSTOMARY, CUSTOMABLE, *adj.* Àbhaisteach, gnàthach, gnàthachail.
CUSTOMER, *s.* Gnà-cheannaiche.
CUSTOMHOUSE, *s.* Taigh–cuspuinn.
CUT, *v. a.* Gearr; sgath, sgud, bèarr.
CUT, *s.* Gearradh, sgathadh; leòn; mìr, dealbh, cumadh.
CUTANEOUS, *adj.* Craicneach.
CUTICLE, *s.* Craicionn-uachdrach.
CUTLASS, *s.* Claidheamh-cutach.
CUTLER, *s.* Gobha-lann.
CUTLERY, *s.* Lannan staillinn.
CUT-THROAT, *s.* Mortair.
CUTTING, *s.* Mìr, sliseag; gearradh.
CUTTLE, *s.* Fear-tuaileis, draosdaire.
CYCLE, *s.* Cuairt, ré mìos.
CYGNET, *s.* Eala òg, isean eala.
CYLINDER, *s.* Rothlair, rothair.
CYLINDRICAL, *adj.* Cruinn-fhada.
CYMAR, *s.* Falluinn, sgàilean.
CYMBAL, *s.* Tiompan.
CYNIC, CYNICAL, *adj.* Dranndanach, sgaiteach.
CYNOSURE, *s.* Reull nah-àirde tuath.
CYPRESS, *s.* Craobh-bhròin.

Cyst, *s.* Balgan-iongrach.
Czar, *s.* Ainm iompaire Ruisia.
Czarina, *s.* Ainm ban-iompaire Ruisia.

D

D, *s.* Ceathramh litir na h-aibidil.
Dab, *v. a.* Frith-bhuail, dean ballach le uisge.
Dab, *s.* Seòrsa liabaig, meall, pluc, buille, fear ceàirde.
Dabble, *v. a.* Luidir, taisich, crath thairis le uisge.
Dabbler, *s.* Greoigean, fear gun sgil.
Dace, *s.* Seòrs do dh'iasg abhna.
Daffodil, Daffodilly, *s.* Lŭs-a-chrom-chinn.
Dagger, *s.* Cuinnsear; sgian mhor.
Daggle, *v. a.* Eabair, luidir, fliuch.
Daggletail, *adj.* Salach, luidirte.
Daily, *adv.* Gach là, gu lathail.
Dainty, *adj.* Blasda, taitneach, milis, sòghmhor; grinn, finealta, muirneach, moiteil, modhail; mìn, ciatach.
Dairy, *s.* Taigh-bainne; bothan-àiridh.
Daisied, *adj.* Nòineanach; neòineanach.
Dairymaid, *s.* Banarach, banachaig.
Daisy, *s.* Nòinean, neòinean.
Dale, *s.* Dail, gleann, glac.
Dalliance, *s.* Beadradh, sùgradh, dàil.
Dallop, *s.* Fàilean, tòrr, dùn.
Dam, *s.* Màthair-chuaine, tuil-dhoras.
Damage, *s.* Dolaidh, beud, dochann, cron; luach calla.
Damage, *v. a.* Dochainn, mill.
Damageable, *s.* So-mhilleadh; cronail, ciùrrail.
Damask, *s.* Anart-geug-ghréiste.
Dame, *s.* Baintighearna, bean-taighe.
Damn, *v. a.* Dìt gu peanas sìorruidh, mallaich; dìt.
Damnable, *adj.* Mallaichte, sgriosach.
Damnation, *s.* Dìteadh sìorruidh.
Damned, *adj.* Damainte, mallaichte.
Damnify, *v. a.* Dochainn, mill.
Damp, *adj.* Tais, àitidh, fliuch, bog.
Damp, *v. a.* Taisich, fliuch, bogaich.
Damsel, *s* Cailin; maighdean, gruagach, ainir, finne, ribhinn.
Dance, *v. n.* Dàmhsadh.
Dancing, *s.* Dàmhsa.
Dandelion, *s.* Am beàrnan-brìde.
Dandle, *v. a.* Siùd, crath, caidrich cniadaich, tàthlaidh breug.
Dandruff, *s.* Carr, sgailc-mhullaich.
Danewort, *s.* Fliogh-a'-bhalla.
Danger, *s.* Cunnart, baoghal, gàbhadh.
Dangerless, *adj.* Neo-chunnartach.
Dangerous, *adj.* Cunnartach.
Dangle, *v. n.* Crath mar chluigean, bi co-bhogadan.
Dangler, *s.* Gille-bhan, sliomair.
Dank, *adj.* Àitidh, tungaidh, bog.
Dapper, *adj.* Beag, lurach, guamach.
Dapperling, *s.* Luspardan, duairc.
Dapple, *adj.* Balla-bhreac.
Dare, *v. a.* Dùlanaich, thoir dùlan.
Daring, *adj.* Dàna, dalma, ladorna, neo-sgàthach.
Dark, *adj.* Dorch, doilleir; dubh.
Darken, *v. a.* Dorchaich, doilleirich.
Darkness, *s.* Dorchadas, duibhre.
Darksome, *adj.* Doilleir, dubharach.
Darling, *s.* Annsachd, luaidh, mùirninn.
Darling, *adj.* Gaolach, gràdhach.
Darn, or **Dearn**, *v. a.* Cnòdaich, càirich.
Darnel, *s.* Dìthein, bùidheag.
Dart, *s.* Gath, guin, gàinne.
Dash, *v. a.* and *n.* Buail air, tilg le neart, spealg, brist, pronn, spealt, spairt, taom, coimeasg, truaill; nàraich.
Dash, *s.* Buille, tilgeil; dubh-sgriach.
Dastard, *s.* Cladhaire, gealtaire.
Dastardly, *adj.* Cladhaireach, gealtach, fiamhach, eagalach.
Data, *s.* Fìrinnean suidhichte.
Date, *s.* Àm, an latha de'n mhìos.
Date, *v. a.* Comharraich àm.
Dateless, *adj.* Gun àm ainmichte.
Dative, *adj.* Tabhartach.
Daub, *v. a.* Smeur, buaichd, slìob.
Dauber, *s.* Sgleogaire.
Daughter, *s.* Nighean, inghean.
Daunt, *v. a.* Geiltich, mi-mhisnich.
Dauntless, *adj.* Neo-sgàthach.
Daw, *s.* An t-eun do'n ainm, a' chadhag.
Dawn, *s.* Camhanaich, briseadh na fàire, glasadh an latha.
Day, *s.* Latha. [Poetically, "Là, and lò."]
Day-book, *s.* Leabhar-lathail.
Day-break, *s.* Briseadh na fàire.
Day-light, *s.* Solus an latha.
Day-star, *s.* Reull na maidne.
Dazzle, *v. a.* Deàrs, deàrsaich, soillsich, boillsgich.
Deacon, *s.* Foirfeach.
Deaconry, *s.* Dreuchd foirfich.
Dead, *adj.* Marbh, trom. [*The dead*, Na mairbh.]
Deaden, *v. a.* Marbh, lagaich, fannaich.
Deadly, *adj.* Marbhtach, bàsmhor.
Deadness, *s.* Marbhantachd, laigsinn.
Deaf, *adj.* Bodhar, gun chlaisteachd.
Deafen, *v. a.* Bodhair, dean bodhar.

DEAFNESS, *s.* Buidhre, boidhre.
DEAL, *s.* Cuibhrionn; déile, clàr.
DEAL, *v. a.* Roinn, riaraich.
DEALBATE, *v. a.* Gealaich, cuir ri todhar.
DEALBATION, *s.* Gealachadh, todhar.
DEALER, *s.* Fear-malairt, ceannaiche, fear roinn chairtean.
DEALING, *s.* Gnothach, déilig.
DEAMBULATION, *s.* Sràid-imeachd.
DEAN, *s.* Deadhan, fear ionaid easbuig.
DEANERY, *s.* Dreuchd deadhain.
DEAR, *adj.* Gaolach, gràdhach, prìseil, daor.
DEARTH, *s.* Gainne, dìth, gort, airc teircead.
DEARTICULATE, *v. a.* Thoir ás a' chéile.
DEATH, *s.* Bàs, eug, aog.
DEATHLESS, *adj.* Neo-bhàsmhor.
DEATHLIKE, *adj.* Aog-neulach.
DEATHWATCH, *s.* Am Biog-ghairm.
DEBAR, *v. a.* Bac, cum air ais, toirmisg.
DEBARK, *v. a.* Cuir air tìr, rach air tìr.
DEBASE, *v. a.* Truaill, ìslich; maslaich.
DEBASEMENT, *s.* Truailleadh, isleachadh, maslachadh.
DEBATE, *s.* Connsachadh, tagradh.
DEBATE, *v. a.* Connsaich, tagair.
DEBAUCH, *v. a.* Truaill, salaich.
DEBAUCH, *s.* Misg, neo-mheasarrachd.
DEBAUCHEE, *s.* Geòcaire, misgear.
DEBAUCHERY, *s.* Mi-gheamnachd, geòcaireachd, pòitearachd.
DEBENTURE, *s.* Bann-sgrìobhaidh.
DEBILE, *adj.* Fann, lag, marbhanta.
DEBILITATE, *v. a.* Fannaich, lagaich.
DEBILITY, *s.* Laige, anmhuinneachd.
DEBONAIR, *adj.* Fìnealta, grinn, suairce.
DEBT, *s.* Fiachan, feich, comain.
DEBTOR, *s.* Fear-fhiach.
DECADE, *s.* Deich.
DECAGON, *s.* Deich-shlisneach.
DECAMP, *v. n.* Rach imrich, atharraich campa, triall, imich, gluais air falbh.
DECANT, *v. a.* Taom ás, gu fòill.
DECANTER, *s.* Searrag ghlaine.
DECAPITATE, *v. a.* Dì-cheannich.
DECAPITATION, *s.* Dì-cheannadh.
DECAY, *v. a.* Caith, crìon, searg, seac.
DECAY, *s.* Crìonadh, seargadh, seacadh, caitheamh as.
DECEASE, *s.* Bas, caochla, eug.
DECEASE, *v. n.* Bàsaich, caochail.
DECEIT, *s.* Ìogan, cealg, gò, foill.
DECEITFUL, *adj.* Cealgach, foilleil.
DECEIVE, *v. a.* Meall, car, breug.
DECEIVER, *s.* Mealltair, cealgair.
DECEMBER, *s.* Mìos meadhonach a' gheamhraidh.
DECENCY, *s.* Eireachdas, beusachd, loinn; modh, stuamachd.
DECENNIAL, *adj.* Deich bliadhnail.
DECENT, *adj.* Eireachdail, ciatach, loinneil, grinn, còir, beusach, ceanalta, modhail, stuama, freagarrach.
DECEPTIBLE, *adj.* So-mhealladh.
DECEPTION, *s.* Mealladh, foill, cealg.
DECEPTIVE, *adj.* Meallta, foilleil, cealgach, carach.
DECIDE, *v. a.* Thoir breith, co-dhùin.
DECIDENCE, *s.* Malcadh, tuiteam dheth; seargadh, seacadh.
DECIDER, *s.* Breitheamh, fear-réite.
DECIDUOUS, *adj.* Seargach.
DECIMAL, *adj.* Deich-roinneach.
DECIMATION, *s.* Deachamh.
DECIPHER, *v. a.* Leugh sgrìobhadh dorch, comharraich, cuir comharradh air; mìnich, dean soilleir.
DECISION, *s.* Co-dhùnadh; crìoch.
DECISIVE, *adj.* Co-dhùnach, dearbhach.
DECISIVELY, *ad.* Dearbhte, cinnteach.
DECK, *v. a.* Còmhdaich, sgiamhaich.
DECK, *s.* Clar-uachdair, bòrd-luinge.
DECLAIM, *v. a.* Tagair, dean àrd-ghlòir, labhair gu snas-bhriathrach.
DECLARATION, *s.* Cur an céill, daingneacadh cùise.
DECLARATIVE, *adj* Foillseachail.
DECLARE, *v a.* Nochd, taisbean, innis, aithris, cuir an céill; aidich.
DECLENSION, *s.* Ìsleachadh, cromadh, téarnadh; dol sìos; lùbadh, claonadh, aomadh.
DECLINABLE, *adj.* So-aomaidh.
DECLINATION, *s.* Isleachadh, lagachadh, seargadh; tearnadh; cromadh, lùbadh, camadh, fiaradh; seacharan, claonadh; mùthadh.
DECLINATOR, *s.* Inneal faotainn a' chòmhnaird.
DECLINE, *v. a.* and *n.* Crom, aom, lùb, cam; seachainn, diùlt, ob, leig seachad; crom, seac; claon, rach a thaobh; crìon, searg caith ás.
DECLINE, *s.* Téarnadh, cromadh, dol sìos, caitheamh, crìonadh, seacadh, seargadh.
DECLIVITY, *s.* Téarnadh, bruthach, leathad, cromadh, fiaradh.
DECOCT, *v. a.* Bruich, goil; meirbh.
DECOCTION, *s.* Goil, bruicheadh.
DECOLLATE, *v. a.* Cuir an ceann dheth.
DECOMPOSE, *v. a.* Eadar-dhealaich.
DECOMPOUND, *v. a.* Ath-mheasgaich, cuir air leth.
DECORATE, *v. a.* Sgeadaich, maisich.
DECORATION, *s.* Sgeadachadh.
DECOROUS, *adj.* Ciatach, cubhaidh.
DECORTICATE, *v. a.* Rùisg, plaoisg.
DECORUM, *s.* Deagh-bheus, stuaim, eireachdas.
DECOY, *v. a.* Meall, tàlaidh, breug.
DECOY, *s.* Culaidh-thàlaidh, buaireadh.
DECOY-DUCK, *s.* Tunag threòrachaidh.

Decrease, *v. a.* Lùghdaich, beagaich.
Decree, *v. n.* Roi-òrduich, suidhich, àithn, socraich, sònraich.
Decree, *s.* Reachd-cheangal; breith cùise, roi-òrdugh.
Decrepit, *adj.* Breòite, fann.
Decrepitude, *s.* Breòiteachd.
Decrescent, *adj.* A' crìonadh.
Decretal, *adj.* Reachdach.
Decretal, *s.* Leabhar-lagha.
Decretory, *adj.* Reachdach, laghail.
Decry, *v. n.* Cronaich, coirich, càin.
Decumbant, *adj.* Liùgach.
Decuple, *adj.* Deich-fillte.
Decursion, *s.* Ruith le bruthach.
Dedentition, *s.* Tilgeadh nam fiacal.
Dedicate, *v. a.* Coisrig, naomhaich; seun cuir fo thèarmann.
Deduce, *v. a.* Tarruinn uaith; cuir sìos an òrdugh; thoir as; beagaich, lughdaich.
Deducement, *s.* Co-dhùnadh.
Deduct, *v. a.* Lughdaich, beagaich, thoir sìos.
Deduction, *s.* Co-dhùnadh; co-ghearradh, lughdachadh, beagachadh.
Deed, *s.* Gnìomh, dèanadas; euchd; reachd-dhaingneachaidh.
Deem, *v. a.* Meas, co-dhùin; saoil.
Deep, *adj.* Domhain; trom, eagnaidh, tùrail.
Deep, *s.* An doimhne; an cuan; aigeal.
Deeply, *ad.* Gu trom, brònach.
Deer, *s.* Fiagh. [Erroneously written "Fiadh."]
Deface, *v. a.* Dubh a mach, mill.
Defacement, *s.* Sgrìobadh ás, sgrios.
Defalcation, *s.* Lughdachadh.
Defamation, *s.* Tuaileas, mì-chliù.
Defamatory, *adj.* Tuaileasach.
Defame, *v. a.* Tuaileasaich, cul-chàin.
Defatigate, *v. a.* Sgìthch, claoidh.
Default, *s.* Dearmad, dì-chuimhn; coire, lochd, cionta, fàillinn.
Defaulter, *s.* Fear dearmaid corach.
Defeasance, *s.* Briseadh cùmhnainte.
Defeasible, *adj.* Nach seas lagh.
Defeat, *s.* Ruaig, teicheadh, call-catha.
Defeat, *v. a.* Ruaig, buadhaich.
Defeature, *s.* Atharrachadh gnùise.
Defecate, *v. a.* Glan, sìolaidh; sgùr.
Defecation, *s.* Fior-ghlanadh.
Defect, *s.* Easbhuidh, fàillinn, uireasbhuidh, dìth; coire, gaoid.
Defection, *s.* Easbhuidh, fàillneachadh; ceannairc.
Defective, *adj.* Neo-iomlan, neo-choimhlionta; ciorramach.
Defence, *s.* Dìon, dìdean, tèarmann, daingneachd; leithsgeul, fireanachadh.
Defenceless, *adj.* Neo-armaichte, gun tèarmann, nochdte, lom; lag, fann
Defend, *v. a.* Dìon, teasraig, tèaruinn.
Defendant, *s.* Fear-dìona.
Defender, *s.* Fear-tagraidh.
Defensible, *adj.* Tèarmannach.
Defer, *v. a.* and *n.* Cuir air dàil, dàilich leig gu comhairle neach eile; fuirich, dean maille.
Deference, *s.* Meas, urram, ùmhlachd; strìochdadh, géilleadh.
Defiance, *s.* Dùlan; dùlanachadh.
Deficiency, *s.* Neo-iomlaineachd, easbhuidh, dìth; fàillinn.
Deficient, *adj.* Neo-iomlan.
Defile, *v. a.* Salaich, truaill.
Defile, *s.* Cunglach, caol ghleann.
Defilement, *s.* Truailleadh, sal
Defiler, *s.* Truailleadair.
Definable, *s.* So-mhìnachaidh.
Define, *v. a.* Mìnich, soilleirich
Definite, *adj.* Comharraichte.
Definiteness, *s.* Soilleireachd.
Definition, *s.* Mìneachadh.
Definitive, *adj.* Dearbhte, soilleir.
Deflagrable, *adj.* Loisgeach.
Deflagrability, *s.* So-loisgeach.
Deflect, *v. n.* Crom, lùb, aom, claon.
Deflection, *s.* Lùbadh, claonadh.
Deflexure, *s.* Cromadh, lùbadh.
Defloration, *s.* Òigh-thruailleadh.
Deflower, *v. a.* Éignich, truaill òigh.
Defluous, *adj.* Silteach, sruthach.
Defluxion, *s.* Téarnadh leanntan.
Deforcement, *s.* Cumail á seilbh.
Deform, *v. a.* Duaichnich, mi-chùm.
Deformity, *s.* Mi-dhreach, mi-dhealbh, neo-chumaireachd, ea-cuandachd.
Defraud, *v. a.* Meall, car.
Defrauder, *s.* Mealltair, cealgair.
Defray, *v. a.* Dìol, ìoc, pàidh.
Deft, *adj.* Sgiamhach, lurach, ealamh.
Defunct, *adj.* Marbh, tŭr-ás.
Defunction, *s.* Bàsachadh, eug, aog.
Defy, *v. a.* Dùlanaich; dean tàir.
Degeneracy, *s.* Claonadh, on chòir, cul-sleamhnachadh.
Degenerate, *v. n.* Tuit air falbh, rach am measad.
Degenerate, *adj.* An-dualach, suarach, truagh.
Degeneration, *s.* Dol am measad, an-dualchas, cùl-sleamhnachadh.
Deglutition, *s.* Slugadh.
Degradation, *s.* Isleachadh; truaillachd.
Degrade, *v. a.* Ìslich, beagaich.
Degree, *s.* Inbhe, àirde, staid, cor; ceum, glùn, ginealaich.
By Degrees, *adv.* Uidh air uidh.
Dehort, *v. a.* Comhairlich.
Dehortation, *s.* Comhairleachadh.

Deicide, *s.* Bàs ar Slànaighear.
Deject, *v. a.* Mi-mhisnich; tilg sìos.
Dejection, *s.* Smuairean, mulad.
Dejecture, *s.* Òtrach, salachar, inneir.
Deification, *s.* Dia-dheanamh.
Deify, *v. a.* Diadhaich, àrd-mhol.
Deign, *v. a.* Deònaich, ceadaich.
Deist, *s.* Ana-creideach.
Deistical, *adj.* Ana-creideach.
Deity, *s.* Dia, diadhachd.
Delactation, *s.* Cur o'n chìch.
Delapsed, *adj.* A' tuiteam sìos.
Delate, *v. a.* Giùlain, iomchair; casaidich, dean casaid air.
Delation, *s.* Giùlan, iomchar; dìteadh.
Delay, *v. a.* Cuir dàil, cuir maille; bac, fuirich, cum an amharus.
Delay, *s.* Dàil, càird maille, màirneal, seamsan, stad.
Delectable, *adj.* Taitneach, sòlasach.
Delectation, *s.* Tlachd, sòlas.
Delegate, *v. a.* Cuir air falbh; earb.
Delegate, *s.* Fear-ionaid, teachdair.
Delete, *v. a.* Dubh a mach,
Deleterious, *adj.* Marbhtach.
Deleterious, *s.* Martach, sgriosail.
Deliberate, *v. a.* Meòraich.
Deliberate, *adj.* Smuainteach; socrach, cùramach.
Deliberation, *s.* Faicilleachd, cùram.
Deliberative, *adj.* Faicilleach, meòrachail, smuainteachail.
Delicacy, *s.* Mìlseachd; mìneachd, màldachd; fìnealtachd, suairceas, grinneas, ceanaltachd; mùirn; séimhealachd; meurantachd.
Delicate, *adj.* Blasda, milis, taitneach; mìlseanach, sòghail; fìnealta, grinn, mìn, ceanalta, meuranta, lag.
Delicateness, *s.* Mùirn, mìneachd.
Delicious, *adj.* Milis, blasda, taitneach.
Deligation, *s.* Ceangal suas, trusadh.
Delight, *s.* Aighear, aiteas; tlachd
Delight, *v. a.* and *n.* Toilich, taitinn, dean subhach, dean aoibhneach; gabh tlachd, faigh tlachd.
Delightful, *adj.* Sòlasach, ciatach.
Delineate, *v. a.* Dealbh, dreachd, tarruinn, nochd an dathaibh.
Delineation, *s.* Dealbh, dreachd, tarruinn, cumadh.
Delinquency, *s.* Coire, cron, lochd.
Delinquent, *s.* Coireach, ciontach.
Deliquate, *v. a.* Leagh.
Delirious, *adj.* Breisleachail, gòrach.
Delirium, *s.* Breisleach, mearaichinn.
Deliver, *s.* Cuir fa-sgaoil, saor; teasraig; tiomain, thoir seachad, liubhair.
Deliverance, *s.* Liùthradh, saorsa.
Deliverer, *s.* Fear-saoraidh.
Delivery, *s.* Liubhairt, tèarnadh.

Dell, *s.* Coire, glacag, lagan.
Delude, *v. a.* Meall, car.
Delve, *v. a.* Ruamhair, àitich.
Delve, *s.* Dìg, sloc, toll.
Delver, *s.* Fear ruamhair.
Deluge, *s.* Tuil, dìle, lighe.
Deluge, *v. a.* Tuilich, bàth.
Delusion, *s.* Mealladh, cealg, feall.
Delusive, Delusory, *adj.* Meallta̤ch, cealgach, carach, fealltach.
Demagogue, *s.* Ceannard-gràisge.
Demand, *v. a.* Iarr, tagair; sir; feoraich, tagradh, tagartas.
Demand, *s.* Iarruidh, iarrtas, sireadh.
Demandant, *s.* Fear-tagraidh.
Demander. Tagradair, fear-tagraidh.
Demean, *v. a.* Giùlain, ìslich.
Demeanour, *s.* Giùlan, beus, iomchar.
Demerit, *s.* Droch thoillteannas.
Demi, *s.* Leth.
Demigration, *s.* Imirich.
Demise, *s.* Bàs, caochla, eug.
Demise, *v. a.* Tiomain, fàg, dìleab.
Demission, *s.* Ìsleachadh, suarachas.
Demit, *v. a.* Cuir fo sproc.
Democracy, *s.* Co-fhlaitheachd.
Democratical, *adj.* A bhuineas do cho-fhlaitheachd.
Demolish, *v. a.* Sgrios.
Demolisher, *s.* Sgriosadair.
Demolition, *s.* Leagadh gu làr.
Demon, *s.* Deamhan, diabhol.
Demoniac, *adj.* Deamhanaidh.
Demonology, *s.* Deamhan-eòlas.
Demonstrable, *adj.* So-dhearbhadh.
Demonstrate, *v. a.* Co-dhearbh.
Demonstration, *s.* Co-dhearbhadh.
Demonstrative, *adj.* Dearbh-chinnteach, lan-shoilleir.
Demoralization, *s.* Milleadh dheaghbheusan, truailleadh.
Demulcent, *adj.* Maoth, bog.
Demur, *v. a.* and *n.* Cuir teagamh ann; dàilich, màirnealaich; dean maille; bi an ioma-chomhairle.
Demur, *s.* Teagamh, ioma-chomhairle.
Demure, *adj.* Stuama, socrach.
Demurrage, *s.* Dìoladh maille luinge.
Den, *s.* Garaidh, faic, uamh; còs.
Dendrology, *s.* Craobh-eòlas.
Deniable, *s.* So-àicheadh.
Denial, *s.* Àicheadh; diùltadh.
Denier, *s.* Fear-àicheidh.
Denigrate, *v. a.* Dubh, duaichnich.
Denizen, *s.* Saoranach, bùirdeiseach.
Denominate, *v. a.* Ainmich, gairm.
Denomination, *s* Ainm.
Denominative, *adj.* Ainmeannach.
Denotation, *s.* Comharrachadh
Denote, *v. a.* Comharraich, taisbean.
Denounce, *v. a* Bagair; casaidich, innis air, cuir an céill.

DENSE, *adj.* Tiugh, dlu, teann.
DENSITY, *s.* Tiuighead, dlùths.
DENTAL, *adj.* Fiaclach.
DENTICULATED, *adj.* Mion-fhiaclach.
DENTIFRICE, *s.* Fùdar-fhiacal.
DENTIST, *s.* Léigh-fhiacal.
DENTITION, *s.* Fiaclachadh.
DENUDATE, DENUDE, *v. a.* Rùisg, lomair, faobhaich, feann.
DENUNCIATION, *s.* Cronachadh follaiseach, cuir an céill.
DENY, *v. a.* Àicheadh, diùlt, ob.
DEOBSTRUCT, *v. a.* Glan, réitich.
DEODAND, *s.* Naomh-thiodhlac.
DEPART, *v. n.* Fàg, imich, triall, coisich, siubhail; bàsaich, caochail.
DEPARTMENT, *s.* Gnothach, dreuchd.
DEPARTURE, *s.* Falbh, fàgail, triall; siubhal, caochla, bàs, éug.
DEPEND, *v. n.* Bi am freasdal, earb, cuir muiniginn, cuir ùidh.
DEPENDANCE, *s.* Eiseamalachd.
DEPENDANT, *adj.* Eisimeileach.
DEPENDANT, DEPENDENT, DEPENDER, *s.* Ìochdaran, fear-eiseamail.
DEPENDENT, *adj.* An crochadh.
DEPHLEGM, *v. a.* Glan o mhùsgan.
DEPICT, *v. a.* Dealbh, dreach, cùm, tarruinn dealbh mìnich, soilleirich, cuir sìos an òrdugh.
DEPILOUS, *adj.* Maol, lom; gun fhalt.
DEPLETION, *s.* Falmhachadh.
DEPLORABLE, *adj.* Brònach, muladach.
DEPLORE, *v. a.* Caoidh, caoin, dean tuìreadh, dean cumha, dean bròn.
DEPLUMATION, *s.* Spìonadh itean.
DEPLUME, *v. a.* Spìon dẹth iteach.
DEPONE, *v. a.* Mionnaìch.
DEPONENT, *s.* Fianais air a mhionnan
DEPOPULATE, *v. a.* Fàsaich.
DEPOPULATION, *s.* Fàsachadh.
DEPORT, *v. a.* Giùlain, iomchair, gluais.
DEPORT, DEPORTMENT, *s.* Giùlan, cleachdadh, caitheamh-beatha.
DEPORTATION, *s.* Fògradh.
DEPOSE, *v. a.* and *n.* Leig dhiòt; cuir a bhàrr na cathrach, ìslich, tàmailtich, cuir á inbhe; cuir a thaobh, leig seachad; fianaisich, thoir fianais.
DEPOSIT, *v. a.* Taisg, cuir an làmhan; thoir an geall; cuir air riadh; cuir a thaobh.
DEPOSITION, *s.* Mionnan, fianais air mhionnaibh; dì-chathrachadh, easonarachadh; cur á dreuchd eaglais.
DEPOSITORY, *s.* Taigh-tasgaidh.
DEPRAVATION, *s.* Truailleadh.
DEPRAVE, *v. a.* Truaill, mill, salaich.
DEPRAVEDNESS, *s.* Truailleachd, aingeachd.
DEPRAVER, *s.* Fear-truaillidh, fearmillidh, milltear.
DEPRAVEMENT, DEPRAVITY, *s.* Truailleachd, aingeachd.
DEPRECATE, *v. a.* Aslaich; guidh.
DEPRECATION, *s.* Aslachadh, guidhe.
DEPRECIATE, *v. a.* Cuir an dimeas.
DEPREDATE, *v. a.* Spùinn, goid, creach,
DEPREDATION, *s.* Spùinneadh, creach.
DEPREDATOR, *s.* Spùinneadair.
DEPREHEND, *v. a.* Cuir an làimh.
DEPRESS, *v. a.* Brùth sìos, tilg sìos; leag; ìslich, ùmhlaich, cuir fo sproc
DEPRESSION, *s.* Dinneadh, cudthrom, cumail fodha; tuiteam sìos, leagadh, tèarnadh; ìsleachadh, mi-mhisneachadh, trom-inntinn, sproc.
DEPRESSOR, *s.* Fear cumail fodha.
DEPRIVATION, *s.* Toirt air falbh, dìobradh; call, creachadh, calldach.
DEPRIVE, *v. a.* Buin uaithe, thoir uaithe.
DEPTH, *s.* Doimhneachd; tulchuis.
DEPULSION, *s.* Fuadach air falbh.
DEPURATE, *adj.* Fìr-ghlan, gun druaip.
DEPURATION, *s.* Glanadh, sìoladh.
DEPUTATION, *s.* Teachdaireachd.
DEPUTE, *v. a.* Sònraich, sŏcraich.
DEPUTY, *s.* Fear-ionaid, fear gnothaich.
DERANGEMENT, *s.* Eas-òrdugh.
DERELICTION, *s.* Dìobradh, tréigsinn.
DERIDE, *v. a.* Sgeig, fochaidich, mag.
DERISION, *s.* Sgeig, magadh, fochaid, fanaid; cùis-mhagaidh.
DERISIVE, *adj.* Sgeigeil, magail.
DERIVABLE, *adj.* Air am beil còir shinnsearach; ag éiridh o.
DERIVATION, *s.* Tarruinn; facal fhreumhachd, sruth-chlaonadh.
DERIVATIVE, *adj.* A teachd o ni eile.
DERIVE, *v. a.* Tarruinn, dean facalfhreumhachd, sruth a dh'ionnsaidh.
DERNIER, *adj.* Deireannach.
DEROGATE, *v. a.* Lùghdaich, lagaich.
DEROGATION, *s.* Cur an suarachas.
DEROGATORY, DEROGATIVE, *adj.* Tarchuiseach, easonarach, mi-chliùiteach.
DERVIS, DERVISE, *s.* Sagart Turcach.
DESCANT, *s.* Òran, ròlaist.
DESCANT, *v. a.* Dean canntaireachd.
DESCEND, *v. a.* Teirinn; tùirlinn.
DESCENDANT, *s.* Gineal, sliochd, sìol, linn, iarmad, pòr, clann.
DESCENDENT, *adj.* A' tèarnadh, do shliochd, do shìol.
DESCENSION, *s.* Téarnadh, tuirlinn, teachd le bruthach.
DESCENT, *s.* Tearnadh, dol sìos; aomadh, leathad, leth-bhruthach; ìsleachadh, teachd a nuas.
DESCRIBE, *v. a.* Thoir tuairisgeul.
DESCRIPTION, *s.* Dreach, tuairisgeul.
DESCRY, *v. a.* Faigh a mach, dearc, faic fad' ás, beachdaich fad ás.
DESECRATION, *s.* Mi-naomhachadh.

DESERT, *s.* Fàsach, dìthreabh; mathas.
DESERT, *v. a.* Tréig, fàg, diobair.
DESERTER, *s.* Fear-teichidh.
DESERTION, *s.* Tréigsinn, teicheadh.
DESERTLESS, *adj.* Neo-thoillteannach.
DESERVE, *v. n.* A bhi fiùghail, airidh.
DESICCATE, *v. a.* Tiormaich, traodh.
DESIDERATUM, *s.* Ionndran.
DESIGN, *v. a.* Rùnaich, cuir romhad, sònraich, comharraich; tionnsgainn.
DESIGN, *s.* Rùn, tionnsgnadh, miann, beachd, smuain; samhlachas.
DESIGNATION, *s.* Sònrachadh.
DESIGNER, *s.* Dreachdadair, fear-dealbhaidh, fear-tionnsgnaidh.
DESIGNING, *adj.* Innleachdach, carach, seòlta, cealgach, sligheach.
DESIRABLE, *adj.* Ion-mhiannaichte.
DESIRE, *s.* Toil, iarraidh, miann, togradh, déidh, càil, dùrachd.
DESIRE, *v. a.* Miannaich, sanntaich, iarr, tagair, togair sir.
DESIROUS, *adj.* Miannach, togarrach.
DESIST, *v. n.* Stad, sguir, foisich.
DESISTANCE, *s.* Stad, sgur, fosadh.
DESISTIVE, *adj.* Crìochneach.
DESK, *s.* Bòrd-sgrìobhaidh.
DESOLATE, *adj.* Neo-àitichte; fàsail.
DESOLATE, *v. a.* Fàsaich. dìth-làraich.
DESOLATION, *s.* Fàsachadh, fàsalachd.
DESPAIR, *s.* An-dòchas, an-earbsa.
DESPAIR, *v.* Cuir an eu-dòchas; thoir thairis dùil, bi an eu-dòchas.
DESPATCH, *s.* Teachdaireachd, cabhag, luaths, ealamhachd, deifir.
DESPERATE, *adj.* Eu-dòchasach, anearbsach; gun athadh; ainmheasach, ainniseach, caillte, truagh.
DESPERATION, *s.* Eu-dòchas.
DESPICABLE, *adj.* Tàireil, suarach.
DESPISABLE, *adj.* Suarach, dìblidh.
DESPISE, *v. a.* Dean tàir, dean tarcuis.
DESPITE, *s.* Gamhlas, fearg, diomb, mì-run, spìd, droch-mhéinn, fuath, tailceas, táir; dùlan, aindeoin.
DESPITEFUL, *adj.* Gamhlasach.
DESPOIL, *v. a.* Spùinn, creach, slad.
DESPOLIATION, *s.* Spùinneadh, creach.
DESPOND, *v. n.* Caill dòchas.
DESPONDENCY, *s.* An-dòchas, mi-mhisneach, an-earbsa; trium-inntinn.
DESPONDENT, *adj.* Du-dòchasach, muladach, trom-inntinneach.
DESPONSATE, *v. a.* Réitich.
DESPOT, *s.* Aintighearna.
DESPOTIC, *adj.* Aintighearnail.
DESPOTISM, *adj.* Aintighearnas, ceannasachd, smachdalachd.
DESSERT, *s.* Biadh os ceann gach bìdh.
DESTINATE, *v. a.* Sònraich, crioch.
DESTINATION, *s.* Sònrachadh.
DESTINE, *v. a.* Òrduich, sònraich.
DESTINY, *s.* Dàn; crannchur sìorruidh.
DESTITUTE, *adj.* Falamh; ainniseach, bochd, daoibhir.
DESTITUTION, *s.* Ainnis, airc, dìth.
DESTROY, *v a.* Sgrios, marbh.
DESTROYER, *s.* Milltear, sgriosadair.
DESTRUCTIBLE, *adj.* So-sgriosadh.
DESTRUCTION, *s.* Léir-sgrios, milleadh, fàsachadh, marbhadh, toirt gu neo-ni, dol a dhìth, di-mhilleadh.
DESTRUCTIVE, *adj.* Sgriosail, millteach.
DESUETUDE, *s.* Ana-cleachdadh.
DESULTORY, *adj.* Bristeach, luaineach, neo-bhunailteach, neo-shuidhichte.
DESUME, *v. a.* Thoir o ni sam bith.
DETACH, *v. a.* Dealaich, cuir air leth.
DETACHMENT, *s.* Cuideachd airm.
DETAIL, *v. a.* Innis gu poncail.
DETAIL, *s.* Mion-chunntas.
DETAIN, *v. a.* Cùm air ais, cùm an làimh, gléidh, bac, grab.
DETECT, *v. a.* Faigh a mach, leig ris.
DETECTION, *s.* Faotainn a mach.
DETENTION, *s.* Gleidheadh; cumail an làimh, amladh, grabadh, bacadh.
DETER, *v. a.* Mi-mhisnich, bac le eagal.
DETERGE, *v. a.* Siab, glan, nigh.
DETERGENT, *adj.* Siabach, glanail.
DETERIORATION, *s.* Dol am miosad.
DETERMINABLE, *adj.* So-dheanamh a mach, so chuir a thaobh.
DETERMINATE, *adj.* Suidhichte, sònraichte, cinnteach, crìochnaichte.
DETERMINATION, *s.* Rùn suidhichte.
DETERMINE, *v. a.* Sònraich, suidhich.
DETERSION, *s.* Glanadh, siabadh.
DETEST, *v. a.* Fuathaich, gràinich.
DETESTABLE, *adj.* Fuathach, gràineil.
DETESTATION, *s.* Fuath, gràin, sgreamh.
DETHRONE, *v. a.* Dìth-chathairich.
DETONATION, *s.* Tàirn-thoirm.
DETRACT, *v. a.* Di-mhol, cùl-chàin.
DETRACTION, *s.* Cùl-chaineadh, tuaill-eas, di-moladh, sgainneal.
DETRACTORY, *adj.* Tarcuiseach.
DETRIMENT, *s.* Dìobhail, call, dolaidh.
DETRIMENTAL, *adj.* Diobhalach.
DETRUDE, *v. a.* Pùc sìos, ìslich.
DETRUNCATE, *v. a.* Gearr, bearr, sgud.
DETRUSION, *s.* Pùcadh sìos.
DEVASTATE, *v. a.* Fàsaich, creach, mill, sgrios ás.
DEVASTATION, *s.* Fàsachadh, sgrios.
DEUCE, *s.* Dithis; an diabhol,
DEVELOP, *v. a.* Foillsich, taisbein.
DEVEST, *v. a.* Faobhaich, rùisg, saor uaithe, thoir air falbh.
DEVIATE, *v. n.* Rach am mearachd.
DEVIATION, *s.* Seachran, faontradh, iomrall, mearachd, claonadh air falbh; peacadh, cionta.
DEVICE, *s.* Innleachd, tionnsgal, tionnsg

nadh, cleas, car, dealbh ; rùn, comhairle, smuain ; gearradh-arm ; seòltachd, ealantas.
DEVIL, *s*. Diabhol, deamhan, donas.
DEVILISH, *adj*. Diabhlaidh, deamhnaidh, donasach.
DEVIOUS, *adj*. Iomrallach, seachranach.
DEVISE, *v. a*. Suidhich innleachd ; beachdaich, tionnsgain.
DEVISED, *part*. Socraichte, suidhichte.
DEVOID, *adj*. Falamh, fàs, as eugmhais.
DEVOIR, *s*. Dleasanas, aire, seirbhis.
DEVOLVE, *v. a*. Cuir car mu char.
DEVOTE, *v. a*. Coisrig ; thoir seachad.
DEVOTEE, *s*. Saobh-chreideach.
DEVOTION, *s*. Diadachd ; cràbhadh, aoradh ; ùrnuigh ; teas-ghràdh, dùrachd, toirt suas a' chridhe.
DEVOUR, *v. a*. Ith suas, glàm, glut, beubanaich, riasail ; sgrios, mill, cuir ás, ith gu glamach.
DEVOUT, *adj*. Diadhaidh, cràbhach.
DEW, *s*. Dealt, drùchd, no driùchd.
DEWDROP, *s*. Cuirnean, braon.
DEWLAP, *s*. Caisean-uchd, sprogaill.
DEWY, *s*. Dealtach, drùchdach, braonach, cuirneanach.
DEXTERITY, *s*. Deisealachd, tapachd, ealamhachd ; teòmachd, seòltachd.
DEXTEROUS, *adj*. Deiseil, teòma, seòlta.
DEXTRAL, DEXTER, *adj*. Deas, deiseil.
DIABETES, *s*. An ruith-fhuail.
DIABOLICAL, *adj*. Diabhlaidh.
DIACODIUM, *s*. Sùgh a' chadolain.
DIACOUSTICS, *s*. Fuaim-iùil.
DIADEM, *s*. Crùn, coron, fleasg.
DIAGONAL, *adj*. Trasta, tarsuinn, fiar, bho oisinn gu oisinn. *s*. Trastan.
DIAGRAM, *s*. Dealbh.
DIAL, *s*. Uaireadair-gréine.
DIALECT, *s*. Cànan, cainnt.
DIALECTI, *s*. Reusonach.
DIALING, *s*. Tarruinn uaireadair gréine.
DIALOGIST, *s*. Fear co-labhairt.
DIALOGUE, *s*. Co-labhairt, còmhradh.
DIAMETER, *s*. Cuairt-thomhas.
DIAMETRICAL, *adj*. Croislineach.
DIAMOND, *s*. Daoimein, daoimean.
DIAPASON, *s*. Co-shéirm-nan-uil-fhuaim.
DIAPER, *s*. Anart-gréiste.
DIAPHORETIC, *adj*. Fallasach.
DIAPHRAGM, *s*. An sgairt.
DIARRHŒA, *s*. A' ghearrach.
DIARY, *s*. Leabhar-latha.
DIBBLE, *s*. Pleadhag.
DICE, *s*. Dìsnean.
DICER, *s*. Cearraiche dhìsnean.
DICTATE, *v*. Deachd, seòl, òrduich.
DICTATE, *s*. Riaghailt, deachdadh.
DICTATION, *s*. Deachdadh, òrduchadh.
DICTATOR, *s*. Ard-uachdaran Ròimheach.
DICTATORIAL, *adj*. Ceannsalach.
DICTATORSHIP, *s*. Ceannsalachd.
DICTION, *s*. Labhradh, deachdadh.
DICTIONARY, *s*. Facalair.
DIDACTIC, DIDACTICAL, *adj*. Seòlach.
DIE, DYE, *s*. Dath; dìsne; seula-cùinnidh.
DIE, *v. n*. Bàsaich, eug, caochail.
DIER, DYER, *s*. Dathadair.
DIET, *s*. Lòn, biadh ; coinneamh fhlath.
DIET, *v. a*. Beathaich ; biadh, àraich.
DIFFER, *v. a*. and *n*. Eadar-dhealaich, cuir eadar-dhealachadh ; bi air t'eadar-dhealachadh ; connsaich, cuir a mach air ; dealaich am barail.
DIFFERENCE, *s*. Eadar-dhealachadh, mùthadh ; atharrachadh, caochla ; connsachadh, connspaid, cur a mach.
DIFFERENT, *adj*. Air leth ; de ghnè eile.
DIFFICULT, *adj*. Deacair, duilich, doirbh, cruaidh, draghail ; docair.
DIFFICULTY, *s*. Duilgheadas, deacaireachd, docaireachd, dorratas; cruaidhchàs, teinn, imcheist, airc.
DIFFIDENCE, *s*. An-amharas, mi-earbsa.
DIFFIDENT, *adj*. An-amharasach.
DIFFLUENT, *adj*. Silteach, fuasgailt.
DIFFORMITY, *s*. Neo-chumaireachd.
DIFFUSE, *v. a*. Dòirt a mach, taom.
DIFFUSE, *adj*. Sgapte, sgaoilte.
DIFFUSED, DIFFUSEDLY, *adj*. Sgaoilte.
DIFFUSEDNESS, *s*. Sgaoilteachd.
DIFFUSION, *s*. Sgaoileadh.
DIG, *v. a*. Cladhaich, tochail, treachail, bùraich, ruamhair.
DIGEST, *v. a*. Eagaraich, cuir an òrdugh ; meirbh, cnàmh ; cnuasaich.
DIGESTIBLE, *adj*. Meirbheach.
DIGESTION, *s*. Meirbheadh.
DIGGER, *s*. Fear-cladhaich.
DIGIT, *s*. Tri cheathram na h-òirlich.
DIGNIFIED, *part*. Urramaichte.
DIGNIFY, *v. a*. Àrdaich, urramaich.
DIGNITARY, *s*. Àrd-shagart.
DIGNITY, *s*. Àirde, urram, inbhe,
DIGRESS, *v. n*. Claon, rach fiar.
DIGRESSION, *s*. Seacharan, seanachais.
DIKE, *s*. Clais, dìg, cam-rath ; gàradh.
DILACERATE, *v. a*. Riasail, stròic, reub.
DILAPIDATE, *v. a*. Dìth-làraich, fàsaich.
DILAPIDATION, *s*. Tuiteam sìos.
DILATE, *v. a*. Sgaoil a mach, leudaich ; aithris gu mion.
DILATORY, *adj*. Mall, màirnealach.
DILEMMA, *s*. Argamaid-ribidh.
DILIGENCE, *s*. Dìchioll, dùrachd.
DILIGENT, *adj*. Dìchiollach, dèanadach.
DILUTE, *v. a*. Tanaich, lagaich.
DILUTION, *s*. Tanachadh.
DILUVIAN, *adj*. Tuilteach, dìleach.
DIM, *adj*. Doilleir, dorcha, gruamach.
DIM, *v. a*. Doilleirich, dorchaich, neulaich, duibhrich, gruaimich.
DIMENSION, *s*. Tomhas, meud, tomad.

DIMINISH, *v. a.* Lughdaich, beagaich.
DIMINUTION, *s.* Lughdachadh.
DIMINUTIVE, *adj.* Beag, meanbh, leibideach, crion, bìdeach.
DIMITY. Seòrsa do dh'aodach canaich.
DIMNESS, *s.* Doilleireachd, dubharachd.
DIMPLE, *s.* Lagan, copan.
DIMPLY, *adj.* Laganach, copanach.
DIN, *s.* Toirm, fuaim, stairirich.
DINE, *v.* Gabh dinneir.
DINGLE, *s.* Gleann, glac, lag.
DINGY, *adj.* Lachdunn,
DINNER, *s.* Diothad, dinneir.
DINT, *s.* Buille, gleadhar, stràc, coilleag; lorg; neart, spionnadh.
DINUMERATION, *s.* Cunntas aon an déigh aon, cunntas a lion aon a's aon.
DIOCESAN, *s.* Easbuig.
DIOCESE, *s.* Sgìreachd easbuig.
DIP, *v. a.* Tùm, bog; taisich.
DIPHTHONG, *s.* Dà-fhòghair.
DIPLOMA, *s.* Còir sgrìobhte.
DIRE, DIREFUL, *adj.* Eagalach, uabhasach, oillteil.
DIRECT, *adj.* Dìreach, soilleir, sothuigsinn, neo-fhiar.
DIRECT, *v. a.* Cuir dìreach, seòl, stiùr; cuimsich, treòraich.
DIRECTION, *s.* Seòladh, treòrachadh.
DIRECTLY, *ad.* Air ball, dìreach.
DIRECTOR, *s.* Fear-seòlaidh.
DIRECTORY, *s.* Leabhar-seòlaidh.
DIRENESS, *s.* Uamharrachd.
DIREPTION, *s.* Spùinneadh, slad.
DIRGE, *s.* Tuireadh, cumha, corranach.
DIRK, *s.* Biodag, cuinnsear.
DIRT, *s.* Salachar; inneir, aolach; mosaiche, poll, clàbar.
DIRTINESS, *s.* Salacharachd, mosaiche.
DIRTY, *adj.* Salach, mosach, neo-ghlan.
DIRTY, *v. a.* Salaich, truaill; maslaich.
DIRUPTION, *s.* Sgàineadh, sgoltadh.
DISABILITY, *s.* Neo-chomas, laige.
DISABLE, *v. a.* Dean neo-chomasach.
DISABUSE, *v. a.* Cuir ceart.
DISADVANTAGE, *s.* Calldachd, call.
DISADVANTAGEOUS, *adj.* Ana-cothromach, dìobhalach, caillteach.
DISAFFECT, *v. a.* Dean mi-thoilichte.
DISAFFECTED, *adj.* Mi-thoilichte.
DISAFFECTION, *s.* Mi-dhìlseachdh.
DISAGREE, *v. n.* Mi-chòrd, eas-aontaich.
DISAGREEABLE, *adj.* Neo-thaitneach.
DISAGREEMENT, *s.* Eas-aonachd, eucoltas, neo-chòrdadh.
DISALLOW, *v. a.* Toirmisg, bac; diùlt.
DISALLOWABLE, *adj.* Neo-cheadaichte.
DISANIMATE, *v. a.* Marbh; mi-mhisnich, meataich.
DISAPPEAR, *v. n.* Rach á sealladh, teich.
DISAPPOINT, *v. a.* Meall, dìobair.
DISAPPOINTMENT, *s.* Mealladh.
DISAPPROBATION, DISAPPROVAL, *s.* Cronachadh, coireachadh, achmhasan, dìteadh, mi-thaitneadh.
DISAPPROVE, *v. a.* Coirich, cronaich, dìt, dì-moil.
DISARM, *v. a.* Dìth-armaich.
DISARRAY, *s.* Aimhreit, aimhreidh, easòrdugh, mi-riaghailt; rùsgadh.
DISASTER, *s.* Truaighe, tubaist, sgiorradh, bochduinn, calldachd.
DISASTROUS, *adj.* Mi-shealbhach, sgiorrail, tubaisteach; truagh, caillteach.
DISAVOUCH, DISAVOW, *v. a.* Aicheidh, na aithnich.
DISAVOWAL, DISAVOWMENT, *s.* Àicheadh, diùltadh.
DISBAND, *v. a.* Leig fa-sgaoil, leig air falbh, sgaoil, sgap.
DISBARK, *v. a.* Cuir air tìr á luing.
DISBELIEF, *s.* As-creideamh.
DISBELIEVE, *v. a.* Na creid.
DISBELIEVER, *s.* As-creideach.
DISBURDEN, *v. a.* Neo-luchdaich, eutromaich, cuir dheth eallach.
DISBURSE, *v. a.* Cosg, cuir a mach airgead, dean cosgais.
DISBURSEMENT, *s.* Cur-a-mach.
DISCARD, *v. a.* Cuir air falbh.
DISCERN, *v. a.* Faic, thoir fainear; beachdaich, dearc.
DISCERNIBLE, *adj.* So-fhaicinn, soilleir.
DISCERNING, *part.* Beachdail, tuigseach.
DISCERNMENT, *s.* Deagh-bhreithneachadh, tuigse, eòlas, géire, tùr.
DISCERP, *v. a.* Srac, stròic, thoir ás a chéile 'na mhìrean.
DISCHARGE, *v. a.* Eutromaich, neoluchdaich; tilg a mach, leig as; caith urchair; dìol, ìoc, pàidh, thoir seachad; saor; cuir air falbh; co-lìon.
DISCHARGE, *s.* Fuasgladh, sgaoileadh, leigeadh ás, no air falbh; urchair; taomadh, sruth; cur á dreuchd; saoradh, saorsa; pàidheadh, dìoladh; litir shaoraidh; co-lionadh.
DISCIPLE, *s.* Deisciobul, sgoilear, fear leanmhuinn.
DISCIPLESHIP, *s.* Deisciobulachd.
DISCIPLINE, *s.* Oideas, oilean, teagasg, ionnsachadh, fòghlum, riaghladh, riaghailt; ùmhlachd, smachd.
DISCIPLINE, *v. a.* Oileanaich, ionnsaich, teagaisg, fòghluim; stiùr, seòl, riaghail; smachdaich, ceannsaich.
DISCLAIM, *v. a.* Àicheidh, cuir cùl ri.
DISCLOSE, *v. a.* Foillsich, cuir os-àird, leig ris; innis, nochd.
DISCLOSURE, *s.* Leigeadh ris, seòladh, taisbeanadh, nochdadh, foillseachadh.
DISCOLOUR, *v. a.* Mill dath.
DISCOMFIT, *v. a.* Ceannsaich, ruag.
DISCOMFITURE, *s.* Teicheadh, ruaig.

DISCOMFORT, *s.* An-shocair, mulad.
DISCOMMEND, *v. a.* Di-moil.
DISCOMMODE, *v. a.* Cuir dragh air.
DISCOMMODIOUS, *adj.* Draghail.
DISCOMPOSE, *v. a.* Aimhreitich.
DISCOMPOSURE, *s.* Aimhreit, tuairgneadh, buaireas; troi' chéile.
DISCONCERT, *v. a.* Cuir troi' chéile, feargaich, dorranaich; cuir fa-sgaoil.
DISCONFORMITY, *s.* Neo-fhreagarrachd.
DISCONGRUITY, *s.* Mi-chòrdadh.
DISCONSOLATE, *adj.* Tùrsach, brònach, dubhach, neo-éibhneach.
DISCONTENT, DISCONTENTED, *adj.* Mi-thoilichte; neo-thoilichte, mi-shuaimhneach.
DISCONTENT, *s.* Mi-thoileachadh.
DISCONTENTEDNESS, DISCONTENTMENT, *s.* Neo-thoileachas-inntinn, neo-thoilealachd.
DISCONTINUANCE, DISCONTINUATION, *s.* Neo-mhairsinneachd, bristeachd; stad, sgur, leigeadh seachad.
DISCONTINUE, *v. a.* Sguir, leig seachad, leig dhìot, teirig.
DISCORD, *s.* Aimhreit, mi-chòrdadh.
DISCORDANCE, *s.* Neo-fhreagarrachd.
DISCORDANT, *adj.* Neo-fhreagarrach, aimhreiteach; neo-chòrdail; eu-coltach, neo-sheasmhach.
DISCOVER, *v. a.* Faigh a mach, foillsich, nochd; leig fhaicinn, seall, leig ris, dean aithnichte.
DISCOVERY, *s.* Faotainn a mach; foillseachadh, nochdadh, taisbeanadh.
DISCOUNT, *s.* Leigeadh sìos; riadh airgeid làimhe.
DISCOUNT, *v. a.* Ath-dhìol.
DISCOUNTENANCE, *v. a.* Mi-mhisnich, amhairc air le anntlachd.
DISCOUNTENANCE, *s.* Fuaralachd.
DISCOURAGE, *v. a.* Mi-mhisnich.
DISCOURAGEMENT, *s.* Mi-mhisneachadh
DISCOURSE, *s.* Còmhradh, co-labhairt, conaltradh; cainnt, searmoin.
DISCOURTEOUS, *adj.* Neo-aoidheil, mi-mhodhail, neo-shuairce, neo-shìobhalta, dalma, borb, ladorna.
DISCOUS, *adj.* Leathann, farsuinn.
DISCREDIT, *s.* Masladh, tàir, mì-chliu.
DISCREDIT, *v. a.* Na creid.
DISCREET, *adj.* Glic, faicilleach, cùramach; modhail, sìobhalt.
DISCREPANCE, *s.* Eadar-dhealachadh.
DISCRETION, *s.* Gliocas, ciall, crìonntachd; saor-inntinneachd, toil.
DISCRETIONARY, *adj.* A réir toile.
DISCRIMINATE, *v. a.* Eadar-dhealaich.
DISCRIMINATION, *s.* Eadar-dhealachadh, mùthadh, aithneachadh, comharradh air leth, suaicheantas.
DISCUMBENCY, *s* Còrr-shuidhe.
DISCURSIVE, *adj.* Luaineach, falbhach, siùbhlach; reusonach, luasganach.
DISCUSS, *v. a.* Feuch, rannsaich, sgrùd.
DISCUSSION, *s.* Feuchainn, deuchainn, rannsachadh, sgrùdadh, cnuasachadh, argamaid, reusonachadh.
DISDAIN, *v. a.* Cuir suarach, tarcuisich, na b' fhiach leat.
DISDAIN, *s.* Tàir, tarcuis, dìmeas, spìd.
DISDAINFUL, *adj.* Tarcuiseach.
DISEASE, *s.* Tinneas, euslaint, galar.
DISEASED, *adj.* Tinn, galarach.
DISEMBARK, *v. a.* Cuir air tìr.
DISEMBITTER, *v. a.* Milsich.
DISEMBOGUE, *v. a.* Sruth, dòirt, taom; brùchd, steall.
DISENCHANT, *v. a.* Saor o gheasaibh.
DISENCUMBER, *v. a.* Dìth-luchdaich, thoir dheth uallach.
DISENGAGE, *v. a.* Fuasgail, dealaich, cuir fa-sgaoil, réitich, bi fuasgailte.
DISENGAGED, *part.* Neo-cheangailte.
DISENTANGLE, *v. a.* Fuasgail, réitich.
DISENTHRAL, *v. a.* Saor o thràilleachd.
DISENTHRONE, *v. a.* Dìth-chathraich.
DISFAVOUR, *s.* Mi-fhàbhar.
DISFIGURATION, *s.* Mi-dhealbh.
DISFIGURE, *v. a.* Duaichnich.
DISFRANCHISE, *v. a.* Cuir á còir.
DISGORGE, *v. a.* Dìobhair, sgeith, tilg.
DISGRACE, *s.* Eas-urram, cion-fàbhair; masladh, tàmailt, nàire, aobhar-nàire.
DISGRACE, *v. a.* Maslaich, tàmailtich, eas-urramaich; nàraich; cuir á fàbhar.
DISGRACEFUL, *adj.* Maslach, nàr.
DISGUISE, *v. a.* Cleith, falaich, atharraich cruth, cuir an aimh-riochd.
DISGUISE, *s.* Còmhdach meallta.
DISGUST, *s.* Gràin, sgreamh, fuath, déisinn, anntlachd, daoch.
DISGUST, *v. a.* Gràinich, cuir sgreamh air, cuir déisinn air, sgreataich; fuathaich, cuir mìothlachd air.
DISGUSTING, DISGUSTFUL, *adj.* Déisinneach, gràineil, fuathach, sgreamhail.
DISH, *s.* Soitheach, mias.
DISH, *v. a.* Cuir am mèis.
DISHABILLE, *s.* Neo-uidheam.
DISHEARTEN, *v. a.* Mi-mhisnich.
DISHERIT, *v. a.* Cuir á oighreachd.
DISHEVEL, *v. a.* Cléig falt.
DISHONEST, *adj.* Eas-ionraic, bradach; cealgach, fealltach, mi-onarach.
DISHONESTY, *s.* Eas-ionracas.
DISHONOUR, *s.* Eas-urram, eas-onoir, masladh, tàmailt; mi-chliu.
DISHONOUR, *v. a.* Eas-urramaich, maslaich, nàraich; truaill.
DISHONOURABLE, *adj.* Mi-chliùiteach, maslach, nàr, tàmailteach.
DISINCLINATION, *s.* Mi-thoil.

DISINCLINE, *v. a.* Dean neo-thoileach, dean neo-aontachail.
DISINCLINED, *adj.* Neo-aontachail.
DISINGENUITY, *s.* Mealltaireachd.
DISINGENUOUS, *adj.* Carach, lùbach, fealltach, sligheach, dùbailte.
DISINHERIT, *v. a.* Buin uaithe a chòir-bhreith.
DISINTER, *v. a.* Tog á uaigh.
DISINTERESTED, *adj.* Neo-fhéineil, glan, fialaidh ; coma.
DISJOIN, *v. a.* Dealaich, eadar-dhealaich.
DISJOINT, *v. a.* Cuir ás an alt ; bris.
DISJOINTED, *adj.* As an alt, dealaichte.
DISJUNCT, *adj.* Dealaichte.
DISJUNCTION, *s.* Dealachadh.
DISK, *s.* Aodann, aghaidh ; peileastair.
DISLIKE, *s.* Fuath, sgreamh, gràin.
DISLIKE, *v. a.* Fuathaich, sgreamhaich.
DISLIKEN, *v. a.* Dean eugsamhail.
DISLOCATE, *v. a.* Cuir á àite.
DISLOCATION, *s.* Carachadh, cur á àite ; dol as an alt, cur á alt.
DISLODGE, *v. a.* Cuir á àite.
DISLOYAL, *adj.* Mì-rioghail, neo-dhìleas.
DISLOYALTY, *s.* Mi-rioghalachd.
DISMAL, *adj.* Oillteil, uamharra, eagalach, dubhach, brònach, neo-shuilbhear.
DISMANTLE, *v. a.* Rùisg, cuir dheth a chòmhdach ; tilg sìos, leag gu làr.
DISMAY, *v. a.* Oilltich, clisg, cuir eagal.
DISMAY, *s.* Oillt, eagal, uamhunn.
DISMEMBER, *v. a.* Spìon ás a chéile, thoir ball o bhall.
DISMISS, *v. a.* Cuir air falbh, sgaoil ; thoir cead ; cuir á dreuchd.
DISMISSION, *s.* Cuir air falbh, cur air theachdaireachd ; ceadachadh falbh.
DISMOUNT, *v. a.* Teirinn ; cuir no tilg sìos ; tuirlinn.
DISOBEDIENCE, *s.* Eas-umhlachd.
DISOBEY, *v. a.* Na toir ùmhlachd.
DISOBLIGE, *v. a.* Thoir oilbheum, cuir mìothlachd.
DISOBLIGING, *adj.* Mi-choingheallach.
DISORDER, *s.* Mi-riaghailt, aimhreit, buaireas, troi' chéile ; tinneas, galar.
DISORDER, *v. a.* Mi-riaghailtich, aimhreitich, cuir thar a chéile.
DISORDERLY, *adj.* Mi-riaghailteach.
DISORGANIZE, *v. a.* Eas-orduich.
DISOWN, *v. a.* Àicheidh, na gabh ri.
DISPARAGEMENT, *s.* Masladh, tàir, tarcuis, mì-chliu, sgainneal.
DISPARITY, *s.* Neo-ionannachd.
DISPASSIONATE, *adj.* Stòlda, ciùin, socrach, neo-bhuaireasach.
DISPEL, *v. a.* Sgap, sgaoil, fuadaich, fògair, iom-ruag, iom-sgaoil.
DISPENSARY, *s.* Taigh ìocshlaintean.
DISPENSATION, *s.* Compàirteachadh, riarachadh ; buileachadh, dòigh bhuileachaidh ; cead peacachaidh.
DISPENSE, *v. a.* Roinn, riaraich ; dean suas cungaidh leighis ; thig as-eugais.
DISPEOPLE, *v. a.* Fàsaich, dìth-làraich.
DISPERGE, *v. n.* Crath, sgiot.
DISPERSE, *v. a.* Sgap, sgaoil, iom-sgaoil.
DISPERSER, *s.* Sgapadair.
DISPERSION, *s.* Sgaoileadh, sgapadh.
DISPIRIT, *v. a* Mi-mhisnich, tiomaich, lagaich spiorad ; claoidh, cìosnaich.
DISPLACE, *v. a.* Cuir á 'àite.
DISPLANT, *v. a.* Cuir imrich, fuadaich.
DISPLANTATION, *s.* Imrich lŭis ; fuadach, cur imrich, fàsachadh.
DISPLAY, *v. a.* Sgaoil a mach, foillsich, taisbean ; fosgail, leig ris.
DISPLEASE, *v. a.* Mi-thoilich, thoir oilbheum, feargaich.
DISPLEASURE, *s.* Mi-thaitneachd, neo-thoileachas-inntinn ; diomb, fearg.
DISPLOSION, *s.* Spreadhadh, brùchdadh.
DISPORT, *s.* Cluiche, mireag, fala-dhà.
DISPOSAL, *s.* Buileachadh, riarachadh ; comas buileachaidh ; riaghladh, stiùradh, seòladh ; toirt seachad.
DISPOSE, *v. a.* Suidhich, cuir an òrdugh, builich, ceartaich, òrduich ; giùlain, iomchair ; dean ri, builich.
DISPOSITION, *s.* Riaghailt, dòigh, seòl, suidheachadh, rian ; nàdur, aomadh, gnè, càil ; aigne, dùrachd.
DISPOSSESS, *v. a.* Cuir á seilbh.
DISPOSSESSION, *s.* Cur á seilbh.
DISPOSURE, *s.* Comas buileachaidh.
DISPRAISE, *s.* Di-moladh.
DISPRAISE, *v. a.* Di-moil, cronaich.
DISPREAD, *v. a.* Sgap, sgaoil.
DISPROOF, *s.* Àicheadh, dearbhadh 'n a bhréig, breugnachadh.
DISPROPORTION, *s.* Neo-ionannachd.
DISPROPORTIONABLE, DISPROPORTIONATE, *adj.* Mi-fhreagarrach.
DISPROVE, *v. a.* Dearbh 'na bhréig.
DISPUTABLE, *adj.* Tagarach.
DISPUTANT, *s.* Deasbair, connspaidiche.
DISPUTATION, *s.* Connsachadh, reusonachadh, deasbaireachd.
DISPUTATIOUS, DISPUTATIVE, *adj.* Connsachail, connspaideach.
DISPUTE, *v.* Connsaich, cothaich, tagair ; reusanaich, bi deasbaireachd.
DISPUTE, *s.* Connsachadh, deasbaireachd.
DISPUTELESS, *adj.* Neo-àicheach.
DISQUALIFICATION, *s.* Neo-fhreagarrachd, neo-iomchuidheachd.
DISQUALIFY, *v. a.* Dean neo-iomchuidh.
DISQUIET, DISQUIETUDE, *s.* Iomaguin, neo-fhoisneachd.
DISQUIET, *v. a.* Trioblaidich, cuir càmpar air cuir dragh air.

Disquietful, *adj.* Mi-shuaimhneach.
Disquisition, *s.* Rannsachadh, sgrùdadh, deuchainn, deasbaireachd.
Disregard, *s.* Dìmeas, tarcuis.
Disregard, *v. a.* Dean dìmeas air.
Disregardful, *adj.* Tarcuiseach.
Disrelish, *s.* Anablas, gràin, sgreamh.
Disrelish, *v. a.* Sgreamhaich, sgreataich, gràinich, fuathaich, gabh gràin.
Disreputable, *adj.* Neo-mheasail.
Disreputation, **Disrepute**, *s.* Mi-chliù, droch ainm.
Disrespect, *s.* Eas-urram, tarcuis.
Disrobe, *v. a.* Faobhaich.
Disruption, *s.* Bristeadh, sgàineadh.
Dissatisfaction, *s.* Mi-thoileachadh.
Dissatisfy, *v. a.* Mi-thoilich.
Dissect, *v. a.* Cuir as a chéile ; sgrùd.
Dissection, *s.* Corp-shnasadh.
Dissemblance, *s.* Neo-choltas.
Dissemble, *v. a.* Cuir an aimhriochd, falaich, ceil, meall.
Dissembler, *s.* Cealgair, mealltair.
Disseminate, *v. a.* Craobh-sgaoil.
Dissemination, *s.* Craobh-sgaoileadh.
Disseminator, *s.* Fear craobh-sgaoilidh.
Dissension, *s.* Aimhreit, ceannairc.
Dissent, *v. n.* Bi air chaochla baralach, mi-chòrd ; eas-aontaich ; sgar.
Dissent, *s.* Eas-aontachadh, dealachadh, caochla barail.
Dissenter, *s.* Fear-dealachaidh o'n eaglais shuidhichte.
Dissentious, *adj.* Eas-aontach.
Dissertation, *s.* Òraid, searmoin.
Disservice, *s.* Ciurradh, dochann, cron.
Disserviceable, *adj.* Caillteach.
Dissever, *v. a.* Géarr, sgar.
Dissimilar, *adj.* Eu-coltach.
Dissimilarity, **Dissimilitude**, *s.* Eu-coltas, eu-cosmhalachd.
Dissimulation, *s.* Cealgaireachd, gnùis-mhealladh, cluain, cuilbheart.
Dissipate, *v. a.* Sgaoil, sgap, caith.
Dissipation, *s.* Ana-caitheamh.
Dissociate, *v. a.* Eadar-dhealaich, sgar.
Dissoluble, *adj.* So-leaghadh.
Dissolve, *v. a* Leagh ; sgaoil, cuir o chéile, fuasgail, cuir fa-sgaoil ; eadar-dhealaich, sgar o chéile.
Dissolvent, *adj.* Leaghach, a leaghas.
Dissolvable, *adj.* So-leaghach.
Dissolute, *adj.* Neo-shuidhichte, neo-gheimnidh, fuasgailte, macnasach, baoiseach, drùiseil, strothail, ana-measarra.
Dissoluteness, *s.* Fuasgailteachd, stròthalachd, neo-gheamnuidheachd, ana-measarrachd.
Dissolution, *s.* Leaghadh ; fuasgladh, dol as a chéile ; caochladh, bàs.
Dissonance, *s.* Ràcaireachd.
Dissonant, *adj.* Searbh, neo-fhonnmhor.
Dissuade, *v. a.* Ath-chomhairlich.
Dissuasive, *adj.* A' comhairleachadh an aghaidh, earalach.
Dissyllable, *s.* Facal dà lididh.
Distaff, *s.* Cuigeal.
Distance, *s.* Astar, céin, uidhe ; ùine.
Distance, *v. a.* Fàg fad' air dheireadh.
Distant, *adj.* Fad' air falbh, fad' ás ; céin, fad' uaithe ; neo-dhaimheil.
Distaste, *s.* Droch-bhlas, searbhachd, gràin, anntlachd, fuath, déisinn.
Distasteful, *adj.* Neo-bhlasta, searbh.
Distemper, *s.* Tinneas, galar, eucail.
Distemper, *v. a.* Cuir galar ann, dean tinn, dean eucaileach ; buair.
Distend, *v. a.* Leudaich, farsuinnich.
Distention, *s.* Leudachadh, farsuinneachadh, sgaoileadh a mach.
Distich, *s.* Càraid rann, ceathramh òrain.
Distil, *v. a.* Tarruinn ; leagh, sruth.
Distillation, *s.* Tarruinn, sruthadh.
Distiller, *s.* Grùdaire, fear-togalach.
Distinct, *adj.* Soilleir, poncail.
Distinction, *s.* Eadar-dhealachadh.
Distinctive, *adj.* Tuigseach, soilleir.
Distinguish, *v. a.* Eadar-dhealaich.
Distinguishable, *adj.* So-aithneachadh.
Distinguished, *adj.* Comharraichte.
Distort, *v. a.* Toinn, snìomh, fiar.
Distortion, *s.* Sreamadh, casadh, toinneamh, fiaradh, snìomh.
Distract, *v. a.* Roinn, cuir as a chéile ; cuir an imcheist ; cuir air bhreitheal, buair.
Distracted, *adj.* Buairte, claoidhte, sàraichte ; air a chuthach, air bhoile.
Distraction, *s.* Eas-aonachd, mi-chòrdadh, mi-riaghailt, iom-sgaradh, aimhreit, eas-òrdugh ; buaireadh, bruaillean, imcheist, breathal ; cuthach.
Distrain, *v. a.* Glac, cuir an gréim.
Distress, *s.* An-shocair, àmhghar, tinneas ; teanntachd, cruaidh-chàs, teinn, airc ; claoidh, sàrachadh ; glacadh laghail.
Distress, *v. a.* Sàraich, claoidh.
Distressed, *adj.* Truagh, àmhgharach, an-shocrach.
Distribute, *v. a.* Roinn, compàirtich;
Distribution, *s.* Roinn, compàirteachadh, riarachas, comh-roinn.
Distributive, *adj.* Compàirteach.
District, *s.* Cèarn, mòr-roinn dùthcha.
Distrust, *v. a.* Mi-chreid, an-earb.
Distrustful, *adj.* Mi-chreideasach, an-earbsach.
Disturb, *v. a.* Buair, cuir dragh ; cuir troi' chéile.

Disturbance, *s.* Buaireas, tuairgneadh, aimhreit.
Disturber, *s.* Buaireadair.
Disunion, *s.* Dealachadh, eadar-sgaradh, eas-aonachd, mi-chòrdadh.
Disunite, *v.* Eadar-sgar, dealaich.
Disunity, *s.* Eas-aonachd, eadar-sgarachdainn, tearbadh.
Disuse, **Disusage**. *s.* Mi-chleachdadh.
Disuse, *v. a.* Cuir á cleachdadh.
Ditch, *s.* Clais, dìg, feuth.
Ditcher, *s.* Dìgear.
Dithyrambic, *s.* Duanag òil.
Dittany, *s.* Lŭs-a'-phìobairc.
Ditto, *adv.* An ni ceudna.
Ditty, *s.* Òran, luinneag, duanag.
Divan, *s.* Àrd-chomhairl an Turcaich.
Divarication, *s.* Caochla baralach.
Dive, *v.* Rach fo'n uisge ; rannsaich a steach, rach á sealladh.
Diver, *s.* An gobha-uisg ; shnàmhaich fo'n uisg ; fear-rannsachaidh.
Diverge, *v. n.* Ioma-sgaoil.
Divergent, *adj.* A' dol gach rathad.
Divers, *adj.* Iomadh, iomadach.
Diverse, *adj.* Eug-samhail, air leth.
Diversification, *s.* Mùthadh, atharrachadh, caochla ; eug-samhlachd.
Diversify, *v. a.* Mùgh, atharraich, dean eug-samhail.
Diversion, *s.* Criodhalas, aighear, fearas-chuideachd ; claonadh.
Diversity, *s.* Eu-coltas, iomadachd.
Divert, *v. a.* Tionndaidh air falbh ; cum o fhadal, breug, cum cluich ri.
Divertisement, *s.* Aighear, cluiche.
Divertive, *adj.* Àbhachdach, sùgach.
Divest, *v. a.* Rùisg, faobhaich.
Divide, *v.* Roinn, eadar-sgar, dealaich, cuir dealachadh eadar, cùm o chéile ; pàirtich ; eas-aontaich, mi-chòrd.
Dividend, *s.* Earrann, roinn, cuid.
Divider, *s.* Roinneadair.
Dividual, *adj.* Roinnte, pàirtichte.
Divination, *s.* Fàisneachd, fiosachd.
Divine, *adj.* Diadhaidh, nèamhaidh.
Divine, *s.* Diadhair, sagart, pears'-eaglais ; ministear.
Divine, *v. a.* Baralaich.
Diviner, *s.* Fàisniche, fiosaiche.
Divinity, *s.* Diadhachd ; Dia ; diadhaireachd ; ni neo-thalmhaidh.
Divisible, *adj.* So-roinn, pàirteachail.
Division, *s.* Roinn, pàirteachadh; eadardhealachadh ; pàirt, cuid, earrann.
Divisor, *s.* Àireamh leis an roinnear, fear-roinne roinneadair.
Divorce, **Divorcement**, *s.* Dealachadh phòsaidh ; litir-dhealachaidh.
Divorce, *v. a.* Dealaich càraid phòsta ; cuir air falbh.
Diuretic, **Diuretical**, *adj.* Fual-bhrosnachail.
Diurnal, *adj.* Lathail, gach latha.
Diurnal, *s.* Leabhar-latha.
Divulge, *v. a.* Foillsich, taisbean, innis gu follaiseach, dean follaiseach.
Dizziness, *s.* Tuainealaich, clò-ghalar.
Dizzy, *adj.* Tuainealach ; aotrom.
Do, *v.* Dean, gnàthaich ; cuir an gnìomh ; crìochnaich ; atharraich, mùth ; biodh gnothach agad ri.
Docible, **Docile**, *adj.* So-ionnsachadh, soirbh, soitheamh, callta.
Docility, **Docibleness**, *s.* Soirbheachd.
Dock, *s.* Copag ; long-phort.
Docket, *s.* Sgrìobhadh-seòlaidh air bathar, gearr-sgrìobhadh.
Dockyard, *s.* Long-lann.
Doctor, *s.* Olla ; ollamh ; lighich ; léigh.
Doctorship, *s.* Ollamhachd.
Doctrinal, *adj.* Oileanach.
Doctrine, *s.* Teagasg, ionnsachadh.
Document, *s.* Àithne, riaghailt, dearbhadh-sgrìobhte.
Dodecagon, *s.* Dealbh dà thaobh dheug-shlisneach.
Dodge, *v. n.* Meall, bi ri mi-chleasan.
Doe, *s.* Earb, eilid, maoisleach.
Doer, *s.* Deanadair, fear-gnothaich.
Doff, *v. a.* Cuir dhìot, cùir dàil.
Dog, *s.* Cù, madadh, balgaire.
Dog, *v. a.* Lorgaich, lean, srònaich.
Dogbrier, *s.* Con-dris.
Dogdays, *s.* An t-iuchar.
Doge, *s.* Uachdaran Bhénis.
Dogged, *adj.* Gnù, breun, coimheach, doirbh, iargalta.
Doggerel, *s.* Treallain, reòlaist, bàrdachd shuarach.
Dogish, *adj.* Brùideil, dreamach, crost.
Dogma, *s.* Barail shuidhichte, teagasg gnàthaichte.
Dogmatic, **Dogmatical**, *adj.* Ùghdarrach, fein-bharalach, dearrasach.
Dogmatism, *s.* Danarrachd, dearras.
Dogmatist, *s.* Fear teann 'na 'bharail.
Dogstar, *s.* Reull an iuchair.
Doings, *s.* Dèanadais, gnìomharran.
Dole, *s.* Compàirteachadh, co-roinn.
Dole, *v. a.* Builich, compàirtich, riaraich, roinn.
Doleful, *adj.* Brònach, dubhach, tùrsach, gearanach, doilghiosach ; déisinneach, aonaranach, cianail, tiamhaidh, trom.
Doll, *s.* Liùdhag, leanabh-liùdhag.
Dollar, *s.* Bonn airgeid.
Dolorific, *adj.* Doilghiosach, trioblaideach, àmhgharach, muladach.
Dolorous, *adj.* Muladach, brònach, tiamhaidh, piantail, doilghiosach, amhgharach.

DOLOUR, *s.* Bròn, doilghios, tùrsa, cràdh, dòghruinn, pian.
DOLPHIN, *s.* An leumadair.
DOLT, *s.* Burraidh, ùmaidh, gurraiceach, tàmhanach.
DOLTISH, *adj.* Pleòisgeach, gurraiceil, trom-cheannach, ùmanta.
DOMAIN, *s.* Uachdranachd, fearann-saor; baile 'n tighearna.
DOME, *s.* Aitreabh, taigh, àros, teach; crom-thogail, astail.
DOMESTIC, *adj.* Teachail, a bhuineas do'n taigh; dìomhair, uaigneach; soirbh, callaichte.
DOMESTIC, *s.* Fear-muinntir, seirbhiseach a chòmhnaidh 's an teaghlach.
DOMESTICATE, *v. a.* Cùm aig an taigh, càllaich.
DOMICILE, *s.* Dachaigh, aros, fàrdoch, taigh, astail, còmhnaidh.
DOMINATE, *v. a.* Riaghail, ceannsaich, cùm fo smachd.
DOMINATION, *s.* Cumhachd, uachdranachd; aintighearnas, ceannsalachd, cruaidh-smachd.
DOMINEER, *v.* Riaghail, sàraich; bi ain-tighearnail.
DOMINICAL, *adj.* Sàbaideach; a bhuineas do'n phaidir.
DOMINION, *s.* Uachdranachd, àrd-cheannas; cumhachd, ùghdarras; iompaireachd, rìoghachd; lamh-an-uachdar.
DON, *s.* Duin'-uasal Spàinteach.
DONATION, *s.* Tabhartas, tiodhlac, deagh-ghean.
DONATIVE, *s.* Tabhartas, déirc.
DONE, *part. pass.* of the verb *to do.* Deante.
DONOR, *s.* Tabhartaiche, tabhartach.
DOOM, *v. a.* Thoir a mach binn, dìt, thoir breith air; òrduich, àithn, sònraich, rùnaich.
DOOM, *s.* Breitheanas, binn; dìteadh; òrduchadh, crannchur, dàn; milleadh, sgrios; breithneachadh.
DOOMSDAY, *s.* Latha-luain.
DOOMSDAY-BOOK, *s.* An leabhar-dubh.
DOOR, *s.* Dorus, comhla.
DOORPOST, *s.* Ursainn.
DOQUET, *s.* Barantas.
DORMANT, *adj.* Cadaltach; dìomhair, os n-ìosal, falaichte.
DORMITORY, *s.* Seòmar-cadail.
DORMOUSE, *s.* An dall-luch.
DORN, *s.* Dronnag, seòrs' éisg.
DOSE, *s.* Tomhas cungaidh leigis; balgam searbh; làn-broinne.
DOT, *s.* Pong, punc, dùradan.
DOT, *v. a.* Comharraich, cuir buill air, puncaich, dean puncan.
DOTAGE, *s.* Breitheal, breisleach, leanabas, shean aois.
DOTARD, DOTER, *s.* Leannanach ro gaolach, seann duine leanabail.
DOTE, *v. n.* Bi 'na d' bhreitheal; bi an trom-ghaol; beachdaich air le gràdh.
DOTTEREL, *s.* An t-amadan-mòintich.
DOUBLE, *adj.* Dùbailte, dà-fhillte; a dhà uibhir; fealltach, carach, cealgach.
DOUBLE, *v. a.* Dùblaich, dùbail, cuir dà-fhillte; dean uibhir eile; bi dùbailte, fàs uibhir eile; bi carach.
DOUBLE, *s.* Dùbladh, dùblachadh, uibhir eile; car, cleas; leth-bhreac.
DOUBLE-DEALER, *s.* Cluaintear, cealgair.
DOUBLET, *s.* Peiteag, siostacota; dithis.
DOUBLE-TONGUED, *adj.* Cealgach.
DOUBT, *v. a.* Cuir an teagamh, cuir an amharus, cuir an umhail, na h-earbás; bi'n ioma-chomhairle, bi 'n iomacheist.
DOUBT, *s.* Teagamh, ioma-chomhairle, ioma-cheist; neo-chinnteachd; anamharus, an-earbsa.
DOUBTFUL, *adj.* Teagmhach, mi-chinnteach, neo-shoilleir; amharasach, anearbsach, sgàthach.
DOUBTFULNESS, *s.* Teagamh, mi-chinnteachd; doilleireachd; tuiteamas.
DOUBTLESS, *adj.* Cinnteach, gun teagamh, gun amharus.
DOUBTLESS, *adv.* Gu cinnteach, gun teagamh, gun cheist, gun amharus.
DOVE, *s.* Calaman, calman.
DOVECOT, DOVEHOUSE, *s.* Calm-lann, tùcaid, taigh-chalaman.
DOVETAIL, *s.* Amladh, fiaclachadh.
DOUGH, *s.* Taois.
DOUGHTY, *adj.* Gaisgeil, euchdail, flathail, calma, smiorail, curanta.
DOUGHY, *adj.* Taoiseach, plamacaidh.
DOUSE, *v. n.* Tùm, thoir leagadh do.
DOWAGER, *s.* Banntrach uasal.
DOWDY, *s.* Té shlaopach neo-chruinneil, sgumrag, sgliughaisg.
DOWDY, *adj.* Sgumragach, slaopach, sgleòideach, sgluisgeach.
DOWER, DOWRY, *s.* Tochradh; cuibhrionn banntraich.
DOWERLESS, *adj.* Gun tochradh.
DOWLAS, *s.* Tùlainn, anart asgairt.
DOWN, *s.* Réidhleach, clòimh-itean, mìn-chlòimh, mìn-fhalt.
DOWN, *prep.* Sìos, le bruthach.
DOWNCAST, *adj.* Airtneulach, trom, smuaireanach, dubhach.
DOWNFAL, *s.* Tuiteam, leagadh, ìsleachadh; sgrios.
DOWNHILL, *s.* Leathad, leacann.
DOWNLYING, *part.* Dlù, do'n t-sop.
DOWNRIGHT, *adj.* Soilleir, fosgailte, saor, dìreach; calg-dhìreach, tréidhireach, neo-chealgach; follaiseach, as an aodann.

Downright, *adv.* Gu buileach, gun stad ; gu soilleir, gu neo-chealgach.

Downward, Downwards, *adv.* A nuas sìos, le bruthach

Downward, *adj.* A' dol le bruthach, a' téarnadh, a' cromadh ; smuaireanach, muladach.

Downy, *adj.* Clòimheach, taìris ; bog, mìn, maoth, ploiteach.

Doxy, *s.* Strìopach ; aigeannach.

Doze, *v. n.* Clò-chaidil.

Dozen, *s.* Dusan, a dhà-dheug.

Dozy, *adj.* Cadalach ; lunndach.

Drab, *s.* Garbh-chlò ; siùrsach, strìopach, strapaid ; mosag, caile bhreun.

Drachm, *s.* Seann chùinneadh Greugach ; an t-ochdamh cuid do dh' unnsa.

Dread, *adj.* Eagalach, uabhasach.

Draff, *s.* Treasg, dràbhag cnàmhag.

Draft, *s.* Bann Airgeid.

Drag, *v. a.* Slaoid, tarruinn, spìon.

Drag, *s.* Lion-tarruinn, tarruinn ; greimiche ; càrn-slaoid.

Draggle, *v. a.* Luidir, salaich, slaod tre 'n pholl.

Dragnet, *s.* Lion-sgrìobaidh.

Dragon, *s.* Dràgon, nathair-sgiathach.

Dragonfly, *s.* Tarbh-nathrach.

Dragoon, *s.* Saighdear eachraidh.

Drain, *v. a.* Traogh, tarruinn, tiormaich, siothlaidh.

Drain, *s.* Guitear, clais.

Drake, *s.* Dràc, ràc.

Dram, *s.* Drăma, dràm.

Drama. *s.* Dàn-chluiche.

Dramatic, *adj.* Cluìcheach, a bhuineas do dhàn-chluiche.

Dramatist, *s.* Ùghdar cluiche.

Draper, *s.* Ceannaiche aodaich.

Drapery, *s.* Obair-aodaich ; aodaichean.

Draught, *s.* Tarruinn ; srùbadh, deoch ; uiread 's a dh' òlas neach air aon tarruinn.

Draughts. Tàileasg.

Draw, *v. a.* Tarruinn, dragh, slaod ; spìon, spiod, spiol ; deoghail ; sìn, dean fada ; tàlaidh, meall ; crup ; dealbh.

Drawbridge, *s.* Drochaid-thogalach.

Drawer, *s.* Fear-tarruinn ; cisteagthairnneach.

Drawing-room, *s.* Seòmar coinneachaidh.

Drawl, *v. n.* Màirnealaich, labhair gu slaodach.

Drawl, *s.* Draoluinn, ràsan.

Drawn, *part.* Tàirnnte.

Draw-well, *s.* Tobar tharruinn.

Dray, *s.* Cairt-leanna.

Dread, *s.* Eagal, oillt, geilt, gealtachd, fiamh ; cùis-eagail.

Dread, *adj.* Eagalach, oillteil.

Dread, *v. n.* Oilltich, criothnaich.

Dreadful, *adj.* Eagalach, uabhasach.

Dreadless, *adj.* Neo-eagalach, neosgàthach, gun fhiamh.

Dream, *s.* Aisling, bruadar ; breisleach.

Dream, *v.* Bruadair, faic aisling, aislingich ; smuainich gu faoin.

Dreamer, *s.* Bruadaraiche, aislingiche.

Dreamless, *adj.* Saor o bhruadaraibh.

Drear, Dreary, *adj.* Muladach, brònach, tiamhaidh ; aonaranach, dorcha, déisinneach.

Dreariness, *s.* Uamharrachd, dubhachas, uaigneachd.

Dredge, *s.* Prac, lion-eisearan.

Dredge, *v. a.* Cuir fathadh.

Dreggy, *adj.* Druaipeil, dràbhagach.

Dregs, *s.* Druaip, dràbhag, salchar ; grùid, grunnd ; fuaigheall, sguabadh.

Drench, *v. a.* Fliuch, bogaich ; taisich ; sgùr, purgaidich ; nigh, glan.

Drench, *s.* Purgaideach.

Dress, *v. a.* Sgeadaich, còmhdaich, breaghaich, sgiamhaich, uidheamaich, ceartaich, deasaich ; gréidh.

Dress, *s.* Aodach, earradh, sgeadach, uidheam ; rìomhadh.

Dresser, *s.* Fear-sgeadachaidh ; còrnchlàr.

Dressing-room, *s.* Seòmar-sgeadachaidh.

Dribble, *v. n.* Srid, sil, braon, fras ; tuit 'n a d' bhoinnean.

Drier, *s.* Tiorman.

Drift, *s.* Cathadh ; cùrsa, brìgh, ciall.

Drift, *v. a.* Iomain, cuir le gaoith ; cuir 'na chuithe.

Drill, *v. a.* Toll ; teagaisg arm.

Drill, *s.* Caochan ; tora, sniamhaire, gimileid ; teagasg-airm.

Drink, *v.* Òl, srùb, sùgh, gabh deoch.

Drink, *s.* Deoch.

Drinkable, *adj.* A ghabhas òl.

Drinker, *s.* Misgear, pòitear.

Drip, *v. n.* Sil, sruth, snith.

Drip, *s.* Sileadh, braon, snithe.

Dripping-pan, *s.* Aghann-shilidh.

Drive, *v.* Greas, buail air aghart ; iomain, fuadaich, saodaich, ruag ; cuir an éigin.

Drivel, *v. a.* Bi sileadh ronn.

Drivel, *s.* Ronn, sgleog, splangaid staonag, smugaid.

Driveller, *s.* Ronnaire, sgleogaire, spliugaire ; amhlar.

Driven, Droven, *part.* Fògairte, fuadaichte, iomanaichte.

Driver, *s.* Ceannaire, fear-greasaidh ; iomanaiche.

Drizzle, *v.* Braon, sil ; snith.

Drizzly, *adj* Braonach, ciùrach.

Drock, *s.* Sgonnan.

Droll, *s.* Cleasaiche, àmhailt.

DROLL, *adj.* Neònach, cleasach.
DROLLERY, *s.* Cleasachd, àbhachd, fearas-chuideachd.
DROMEDARY, *s.* Dromadair, droman.
DRONE, *s.* Seillein dìomhain ; leisgean, lunndair, rongair ; torman, dos.
DRONISH, *adj.* Lunndach, cadalach, diomhanach, rongach, slaodach.
DROOP, *v. n.* Searg, crìon, crom, meath ; fàs lag, caith air falbh ; aom.
DROOPING, *part.* A' siothladh ás.
DROP, *s.* Boinne, braon, driog.
DROP, *v. a.* Sil, fras, braon, driog ; leig seachad, leig dhìot ; fras ; tuit, bàsaich.
DROPPING, *s.* Sileadh, snithe.
DROPLET, *s.* Braon, cuirnean, driog.
DROPSICAL, *adj.* Meud-bhronnach.
DROPSY, *s.* Meud-bhronn.
DROSS, *s.* Sal, smùrach, dus, spruilleach.
DROSSY, *adj.* Salach, meirgeach.
DROVE, *s.* Treud, greigh, dròbh.
DROVER, *s.* Dròbhair.
DROUGHT, DROUTH, *s.* Tiormachd, tart, turadh ; pathadh.
DROUGHTY, *adj.* Tioram, tartmhor ; pàiteach, teth.
DROWN, *v.* Bàth ; tuilich ; bi air do bhàthadh.
DROWSINESS, *s.* Trumadas, cadaltachd, tromsanaich ; lunndaireachd.
DROWSY, *adj.* Cadalach, tromsanach, trom-cheannach.
DRUB, *v. a.* Spuac, cnapaich, slacuinn.
DRUB, *s.* Spuac, cnap, buille, dòrn.
DRUDGE, *v. n.* Dean sìor-obair, oibrich gun tamh ; dean dubh-obair, dean obair thràilleil.
DRUDGE, *s.* Dubh-chosannach, tràill.
DRUDGERY, *s.* Dubh-chosnadh, tràillealachd, obair dhìblidh, saothair.
DRUG, *s.* Cungaidh leighis ; ni gun diù.
DRUGGET, *s.* Drògaid.
DRUGGIST, *s.* Fear-reic chùngai-leighis.
DRUID, *s.* Drùidh, draoidh.
DRUIDICAL, *adj.* Drùidheil.
DRUIDISM, *s.* Drùidheachd.
DRUM, *s.* Druma.
DRUMMER, *s.* Drumair.
DRUMSTICK, *s.* Bioran-druma.
DRUNK, *adj.* Air mhisg, misgeach.
DRUNKARD, *s.* Misgear, pòitear.
DRUNKENNESS, *s.* Misg, pòitearachd.
DRY, *adj.* Tioram ; pàiteach, iotmhor.
DRY, *v.* Tiormaich, siab ; seac.
DRYNESS, *s.* Tiormachd ; seacadh.
DRY-NURSE, *s.* Banaltrum-thioram.
DUB, *v. a.* Dean ridire, cuir an inbhe ridire ; urramaich, àrdaich an inbhe.
DUB, *s.* Buille, cnap, dòrn.
DUBIOUS, *adj.* Neo-chinnteach, teagmhach, neo-shoilleir.
DUBITABLE, *adj.* Teagmhach.
DUCAL, *adj.* Diùcail.
DUCAT, *s.* Bonn naoidh a's shé sgillean.
DUCK, *s.* Tunnag ; lach ; cromadh-cinn, facal tàlaidh.
DUCK, *v.* Cuir fo'n uisge, tùm ; rach fo'n uisge ; crùb.
DUCKING, *s.* Tumadh, bogadh.
DUCKING-STOOL, *s.* An stòl-dubh.
DUCKLEGGED, *adj.* Clàr-chasach, spàgach, plùitach, spògach.
DUCKLING, *s.* Òg-lachan.
DUCT, *s.* Seòladh ; slighe, pìob-ghiùlain.
DUCTILE, *adj.* Sùbailte, so-lùbadh, sotharruinn, so-ghéillidh, maoth.
DUCTILITY, *s.* Sùbailteachd, ciùineachd.
DUDGEON, *s.* Cuinnsear, biodag ; gruaim, dod, droch-mhéinn.
DUE, *adj.* Fiachnaichte, dligheach, iomchuidh, cubhaidh ; dìreach, neomhearachdach.
DUE, *adv.* Gu dìreach.
DUE, *s.* Còir, dlighe ; fiacan, càin, màl.
DUEL, *s.* Còmhrag-dithis.
DUELLIST, *s.* Céile-chòmhraig.
DUENNA, *s.* Seann bhan-oide-foghluim.
DUET, *s.* Ceòl-dithis.
DUG, *s.* Sine.
DUKE, *s.* Diùc.
DUKEDOM, *s.* Seilbh diùc.
DULCET, *adj.* Milis, taitneach ; binn, fonnmhor ; ciatach ; tiamhaidh.
DULCIFY, DULCORATE, *v. a.* Mìlsich, dean-milis.
DULCIMER, *s.* Seòrs' inneil ciùil.
DULL, *adj.* Trom-inntinneach, smuaireanach ; boaghalta, neo-gheur, tromcheannach, pleòisgeach, maol-aigneach ; maol, tiugh ; plubach, luidseach, clod-cheannach ; neo-chridheil.
DULL, *v. a.* Cuir 'na bhreislich, cuir tuairgneadh air ; maol ; dean trominntinneach, mi-mhisnich ; fàs trominntinneach.
DULLARD, *s.* Burraidh, ùmaidh.
DULNESS, *s.* Neo-thuisge, gloidhcealachd, pleòisgeachd, mi-ghéire ; truime, dùsal ; tromsanaich, cadaltachd ; maillead, màirnealachd, màidheanachd ; dorchacdh ; maoile.
DULY, *adv.* Gu h-iomchuidh, gu freagarrach, gu riaghailteach.
DUMB, *adj.* Balbh ; tosdach, sàmhach.
DUMBNESS, *s.* Balbhachd ; tosdachd.
DUMPS, *s.* Airtneal, leann-dubh, tromsanaich ; tuirtealachd.
DUMPISH, *adj.* Trom-inntinneach, dubhach, smuaireanach.
DUN, *adj.* Ciar, lachdunn, odhar ; duaichnidh, dorcha.
DUN, *v. a.* Tagair, tathainn, bodhair.
DUN, *s.* Fear-tagraidh fhiach ; dùn.
DUNCE, *s.* Ùmaidh, burraidh.

DUNG. *s.* Inneir, buachar mathachadh, todhar, aolach.
DUNG, *v. a.* Mathaich, leasaich, inneirich, aolaich ; tothair.
DUNGEON, *s.* Prìosan, toll-dubh.
DUNGHILL, *s.* Òtrach, dùnan, sitig, dun-aolaich ; breunan.
DUNGY, *adj.* Salach, breun, làn òtraich.
DUPE, *s.* Maoilean, fear socharach.
DUPE, *v. a.* Thoir an car á, meall, gabh brath na sochair air.
DUPLICATE, *s.* Dùblachadh.
DUPLICATION, *s.* Dùblachadh ; filleadh.
DUPLICITY, *s.* Dùbailteachd.
DURABLE, *adj.* Maireannach, buan.
DURABILITY, *s.* Maireannachd, buanas.
DURANCE, *s.* Prìosanachadh, prìosan.
DURATION, *s.* Maireannachd, buanas, fad ùine, no aimsire.
DURING, *prep.* Ré.
DURST, *pret.* of *to dare.* Dàna.
DUSK, *adj.* Ciar, doilleir, dubharach.
DUSK, *s.* Doilleireachd, eadar-sholus ; feasgar, beul na h-oidhche ; duibhre.
DUSKISH, DUSKY, *adj.* A leth-char dorcha, no ciar.
DUST, *s.* Dus, duslach, ùir, smùr, stùr ; ùir a' bhàis ; an uaigh.
DUST, *v. a.* Sguab, cuir an stùr dheth ; crath stùr air.
DUSTY, *adj.* Smùirneach, làn duslaich.
DUTCHESS, *s.* Ban-diùc.
DUTCHY, *s.* Dùthaich fo riadhladh diùc
DUTEOUS, DUTIFUL, *adj.* Dleasanach.
DUTY, *s.* Dleasanas, dlighe ; càin, cìs.
DWARF. *s.* Duairc, troich, luspardan, luch-armann, fathanach.
DWARFISH, *adj.* Duairccach, crìon, troicheanta, fachanta, beag.
DWELL, *v. n.* Fuirich ; còmhnaich, tuinich, gabh tàmh ; lean air.
DWELLER, *s.* Fear-àiteachaidh, fear-còmhnaidh, tàmhaidh.
DWELLING, *s.* Taigh-còmhnaidh, dachaigh, fàrdach ; astail, ionad-còmhnaidh.
DWINDLE, *v. n.* Beagaich, lughdaich, crìon, searg, caith air falbh.
DYING, *part.* Bàsachadh ; dath.
DYNASTY, *s.* Uachdaranachd.
DYCRASY, *s.* Droch coimeasgadh fala.
DYSENTERY, *s.* An sgaoilteach, a'ghearrach, an sgàird, an tinneas-gearraidh.
DYSURY, *s.* Éigin-fhuail, galar-fuail.

E

E, *s.* Cùigeamh litir na h-aibidil.

EACH, *pron.* Gach, gach aon.
EAGER, *adj.* Dian, dealasach, togarrach, miannach, bras ; dùrachdach.
EAGERNESS, *s.* Déine, miannachd, dùrachd, togairt ; braise, caise.
EAGLE, *s.* Iolaire, fìr-eun ; a' bhratach Ròmanach.
EAGLE-EYED, *adj.* Bior-shuileach.
EAGLESPEED, *s.* Luathas na h-iolaire
EAGLET, *s.* Isean iolaire.
EAR, *s.* Cluas, cluas-chiùil ; dias.
EARL, *s.* Iarla.
EARLDOM, *s.* Iarlachd, oighreachd iarla.
EARLESS, *adj.* Bodhar, maol.
EARLY, *adj.* Moch, tràth, tràthail, mochthrathach, madainneach.
EARL-MARSHAL, *s.* Ard-mharasgal.
EARN, *v. a.* Coisinn, buannaich.
EARNEST, *adj.* Dùrachdach, dealasach, dian, dìchiollach ; suidhichte, leagte, togarrach ; cudthromach, àraidh.
EARNEST, *s.* Earlas ; da-rìreadh.
EARNING, *s.* Cosnadh, tuarasdal.
EAR-RING, *s.* Cluas-fhail.
EARTH, *s.* Talamh, ùir, cruinne.
EARTHLY, *adj.* Talmhaidh.
EARTH-WORM, *s.* Cnuimh-thalmhuinn, neach truagh, dìblidh, spiocaire.
EARTH-NUT, *s.* Braonan.
EARTHQUAKE, *s.* Crith-thalmhuinn.
EARWIG, *s.* Fiolan, fiolar.
EASE, *s.* Fois, tàmh, socair, suaimhneas ; lasachadh, faothachadh.
EASE, *v. a.* Faothaich, lasaich, aotromaich, lùghdaich, thoir fois.
EASEFUL, *adj.* Sàmhach, socrach.
EASEMENT, *s.* Cobhair, còmhnadh, furtachd, fuasgladh, faothachadh.
EASINESS, *s.* Furastachd ; soirbheachd ; fois, tàmh, socair, suaimhneas.
EAST, *s.* Ear, an airde 'n ear.
EASTER, *s.* Càisg, a' chàisg.
EASTERLY, *adj.* and *ad.* An ear, o'n ear.
EASTWARD, *ad.* O'n àird an ear, gus an àird an ear.
EASY, *adj.* Furasta ; soirbh, socrach, sàmhach, aig fois, foisneach , soghéilleadh ; saor, fosgailte.
EAT, *v.* Ith ; caith ; cnàmh.
EATABLE, *adj.* A dh' fhaodar itheadh.
EAVES, *s.* Anainn, barra-bhalla.
EAVESDROPPER, *s.* Fear-farcluaise.
EBB, *s.* Tràghadh ; crìonadh, seargadh.
EBB, *v. n.* Tràigh, traogh ; crìon.
EBON, EBONY, *s.* Fiodh cruaidh dubh.
EBRIETY, *s.* Misg, misgearachd.
EBULLITION, *s.* Goil.
ECCENTRIC, *adj.* A' dol o'n mheadhon ; mi-riaghailteach, neònach, seachranach, iomrallach.
ECCENTRICITY, *s.* Aomadh o'n mheadhon, neònachas.

Ecclesiastic, *s.* Sagart, pears-eaglais.
Ecclesiastic, *adj.* Eaglaiseil.
Echo, *s.* Mac-talla; ath-ghairm.
Eclaircissement, *s.* Soilleireachadh.
Eclat, *s.* Greadhnachas, glòir, urram.
Eclectic, *s.* Roghainneachadh.
Eclipse, *s.* Ball-dubh; dubhar.
Ecliptic, *s.* Grian-chrios.
Eclogue, *s.* Òran buachailleachd.
Economical, *adj.* Gléidhteach, caontach, cùramach, grùndail.
Economist, *s.* Fear caontach, fear crionna, fear-gléidhteach.
Economise, *v. a.* Gléidh, cuir gu deagh bhuil, steòrnaich.
Economy, *s.* Banas-taighe, steòrnadh, dòighealachd, deagh-riaghladh teaghlaich; caontachd, gléidhteachd; dòigh, rian, seòl.
Ecstacy, *s.* Mor-ghàirdeachas, àrd-éibhneas, subhachas.
Ecstatic, *adj.* Làn aoibhneis, ro aoibhneach, subhach, sòlasach.
Edacious, *adj.* Gionach, geòcach, lonach, glutach, glamach.
Edacity, *s.* Glàmhaireachd, geòcaireachd, craosaireachd.
Edder, *s.* Barran.
Eddy, *s.* Saobh-shruth, sruth-cuairteig.
Edentated, *adj.* Cabach, gun fhiaclan.
Edge, *s.* Faobhar; roinn; oir, bile.
Edging, *s.* Oir, fàitheam; stìm.
Edgeless, *adj.* Maol, neo-gheur.
Edgetool, *s.* Faobhar-gearraidh.
Edgewise, *adv.* Air a roinn; air oir.
Edict, *s.* Reachd, òrdugh folluiseach.
Edification, *s.* Togail suas, oileanachadh; teagasg, ionnsachadh, fòghlum.
Edifice, *s.* Aitreabh, togail, taigh, àros.
Edify, *v. a.* Teagaisg, ionnsaich.
Edit, *v. a.* Deasaich air son clò-bhualaidh.
Edition, *s.* Clò-bhualadh, cur a mach.
Editor, *s.* Fear-deasachaidh leabhair air son clò-bhualaidh.
Educate, *v. a.* Fòghluim, ionnsaich, teagaisg, tog suas.
Education, *s.* Fòghlum, muineadh, ionnsachadh, teagasg, togail suas.
Eduction, *s.* Foillseachadh.
Edulcoration, *s.* Millseachadh.
Eek, *v. a.* Cuir ri, meudaich.
Eel, *s.* Easgann.
Effable, *adj.* So chur an céill, sonochdadh, so-innseadh.
Efface, *v. a.* Dubh a mach, mill, duaichnich, cuir mi-dhreach air
Effect, *s.* Eifeachd, buaidh, buil, toradh, crìoch, gnìomh; co-dhùnadh, deireadh.
Effect, *v. a.* Co-lion, thoir gu crìch; dèan, cuir an gnìomh.
Effective, *adj.* Foghainteach, buadhach, comasach.
Effectively, *ad.* Gu cumhachdach, le eifeachd, gu buadhach.
Effectless, *adj.* Neo-eifeachdach.
Effectual, *adj.* Eifeachdach.
Effectuate, *v. a.* Coimhlion.
Effeminacy, *s.* Meatachd, buige, neosmioralachd; sòghalachd, macnus.
Effeminate, *adj.* Meata, bog, meathchridheach; macnusach, soghmhor.
Effervescence, *s.* Goil, oibreachadh le teas.
Efficacious, *adj.* Éifeachdach, buadhach, comasach, foghainteach.
Efficacy, *s.* Comas, cumhachd, neart, buaidh, éifeachd.
Efficience, *s.* Gnìomhachd, tairbhe, cumhachd.
Efficient, *adj.* Éifeachdach, tarbhach, comasach, diongmhalta, treun, foghainteach, buadhach.
Effigy, *s.* Ìomhaigh, dealbh, cruth.
Efflorescence, *s.* Blàth, teachd fo bhlàth, bristeadh a mach.
Efflorescent, *adj.* A' teachd fo bhlàth.
Effluence, *s.* Sruthadh.
Effluent, *adj.* A' sruthadh, a' teachd o.
Effluvia, *s.* Tòchd.
Effluxion, *s.* Sruthadh, sileadh.
Effort, *s.* Ionnsaidh, deuchainn.
Effraible, *adj.* Eagalach, uabhasach.
Effrontery, *s.* Bathaiseachd, ladornas, dalmachd, mi-nàire.
Effulgence, *s.* Dearrsadh, boillsgeadh, lannaireachd, soillseachd.
Effulgent, *adj.* Dearrsach, boillsgeach, dealrach, soillseach.
Effuse, *v. a.* Doirt, taom.
Effusion, *s.* Dòrtadh, taomadh, taosgadh, cur thairis; ana-caitheamh; toirbheartachd, buileachadh.
Egg, *s.* Ubh.
Eglantine, *s.* Preas nan ròs.
Egotism, *s.* Féin-iomradh, féin-mholadh.
Egotist, *s.* Fear-fein-mholaidh.
Egotistical, *adj.* Féin-mholtach.
Egotize, *v. n.* Bi labhairt umad féin.
Egregious, *adj.* Comharraichte, sònraichte, ainmeil; ana-cuimseach.
Egregiously, *ad.* Gu h-ana-cuimseach.
Egress, Egression, *s.* Dol a mach, triall, imeachd, siubhal.
Eight, *s.* Ochd.
Eighth, *adj.* Ochdamh.
Eighteen, *adj.* Ochd-deug.
Eighthly, *adv.* Anns an ochdamh àite.
Eightscore, *adj.* Ochd fichead.
Eighty, *adj.* Ceithir fichead.
Either, *pron.* An dara h-aon, an dàrna fear, aon air bith dhiù.

EJACULATE, *v. a.* Cuir a mach, tilg.
EJACULATION, *s.* Guidhe, achanaich.
EJACULATORY, *adj.* Tilgeadh a mach le cabhaig, mar ùrnaigh ghoirid; cabhagach, calamh.
EJECT, *v. a.* Tilg a mach, cuir a mach; fògair, diobair, cuir air falbh.
EJECTION, *s.* Cur a mach, fògradh, fuadach; cur ás.
EJECTMENT, *s.* Bàirligeadh, bàirlinn; fògradh, cur air falbh.
EJULATION, *s.* Cumha, no tuireadh.
EKE, or EEK, *v. a.* Meudaich, leasaich, cuir ri; lìon, dean suas.
EKE, *ad.* Mar an ceudna.
ELABORATE, *adj.* Saoithreachail.
ELABORATELY, *ad.* Le mòr-shaothair.
ELANCE, *v. n.* Saighdeadh a mach.
ELAPSE, *v. n.* Rach seachad, rach thart, ruith air falbh.
ELASTIC, *adj.* Sùbailte, caoiniallach, lùbach, a' leum air ais.
ELASTICITY, *s.* Sùbailteachd, lùbachd.
ELATE, *adj.* Uaibhreach, àrdanach, air a thogail suas, stràiceil.
ELATE, *v. a.* Tog suas, dean uaibhreach, dean stràiceil.
ELATION, *s.* Uaibhreachd, mòralachd, àilleas, uaill, àrdan, stràic.
ELBOW, *s.* Uileann; lùb, oisinn.
ELBOW-CHAIR, *s.* Cathair-ghàirdean.
ELD, *s.* Aois, seann aois, breòiteachd.
ELDER, *adj.* Ni's sine, ni's aosmhoire.
ELDER, ALDER, *s.* Craobh fhearna.
ELDERLY, *adj.* Sean, aosmhor.
ELDERS, *s.* Seann daoine, seanairean, athraichean; foirfich.
ELDERSHIP, *s.* Seanaireachd, urram na h-aoise; dreuchd foirfich.
ELDEST, *adj.* A's sine, a's aosda.
ELECAMPANE, *s.* Aillean.
ELECT, *v. a.* Roghnaich, tagh; roi'-thagh, roi'-òrduich.
ELECT, ELECTED, *part.* Taghte, roghnaichte; roi'-òrduichte, air a roi'-thaghadh.
ELECTION, *s.* Taghadh, roghnachadh, sònrachadh; roghainn; roi'-thaghadh, roi'-shònrachadh; taghadh fir àirdchomhairle.
ELECTIVE, *adj.* Roghainneach, roghnach, taghach.
ELECTOR, *s.* Taghadair; prionns' aig am beil facal ann an taghadh iompaire na Gearmailte.
ELECTORAL, *adj.* Aig am beil urram fir taghaidh.
ELECTORATE, *s.* Oighreachd taghadair.
ELECTRICAL, *adj.* A' tarruinn le gné an dealanaich.
ELECTRICITY, *s.* Gné an dealanaich.
ELEEMOSYNARY, *adj.* Déirceach.
ELEGANCE, *s.* Grinneas, eireachdas, maise, ciatachd, maisealachd, bòidhchead, dreach, àille.
ELEGANT, *adj.* Eireachdail, maiseach, grinn, fìnealta, ciatach, àillidh.
ELEGIAC, *adj.* Marbhrannach, cianail.
ELEGY, *s.* Marbhrann, cumha, tuireadh; dàn tiamhaidh.
ELEMENT, *s.* Ceud-aobhar; dùilthionnsgnaidh; dùil; na ceithir dùilean, 's iad sin, talamh, gaoth, teine 's uisge.
ELEMENTAL, ELEMENTARY, *adj.* Dùileach, dùileachail, prìomh, neomheasgte.
ELEPHANT, *s.* Elephant, an ceithirchasach a's mò th' air thalamh.
ELEPHANTINE, *adj.* A bhuineas do dh' elephant.
ELEVATE, ELEVATED, *part.* Ardaichte.
ELEVATE, *v. a.* Tog suas, àrdaich, tog an inbhe, urramaich, séid suas, dean uaibhreach.
ELEVATION, *s.* Àirde, togail suas; àrdachadh, urramachadh, cur an onoir.
ELEVEN, *adj.* A h-aon-deug.
ELF, *s.* Sìthiche, duine-sìth, tàcharan, màileachan; droch spiorad, diabhol; gàrlaoch, sìochaire, luspardan.
ELICIT, *v. a.* Thoir a mach, tarruinn a mach.
ELIGIBLE, *adj.* Airidh air roghainn.
ELIMINATE, *v. n.* Cuir a mach air dorus.
ELIMINATION, *s.* Fogradh, tilgeadh air falbh.
ELINGUID, *adj.* Balbh, gun chainnt.
ELISION, *s.* Gearradh, sgathadh dheth; eadar-sgaradh, dealachadh.
ELIXIR, *s.* Cungaidh-leighis, ìoc-shlaint.
ELK, *s.* Lon, làn-damh.
ELL, *s.* An t-slat-thomhais Albannach; slat chùig cairteil.
ELLIPSIS, *s.* Cumadh uibhe, bèarn an cainnt.
ELLIPTICAL, *adj.* Air chumadh uibhe; bèarnach an cainnt.
ELM, *s.* Leamhan.
ELOCUTION, *s.* Ur-labhairt, deas-chainnt, briathrachas, uirghioll, labhairt.
ELOGE, ELOGY, EULOGY, *s.* Moladh.
ELONGATE, *v. a.* Fadaich, tarruinn a mach, sìn a mach; rach an céin.
ELONGATION, *s.* Sìneadh a mach, fadachadh; triall, imeachd.
ELOPE, *v. a.* Ruith air falbh, teich, rach am fuadach.
ELOPEMENT, *s.* Teicheadh, ruith air falbh, fuadach, dol am fuadach.
ELOQUENCE, *s.* Ùr-labhairt, deaschainnt, snas-labhairt, fileantachd.
ELOQUENT, *adj.* Ùr-labhairteach, deaschainnteach, fileanta.

Else, *pron.* Eile, aon eile.
Elsewhere, *adv.* An ait' eile, an àit' eigin eile, an ionad eile.
Elvish, *adj.* Baobhanta, siachaireil.
Elucidate, *v. a.* Mìnich, dean so-thuigsinn, soilleirich.
Elucidation, *s.* Mìneachadh, soilleireachadh.
Elucidator, *s.* Fear-soilleireachaidh.
Elude, *v. a.* Seachain, faigh ás le car; meall, teich fo-lùib.
Elusion, *s.* Seachnadh, cleas.
Elusive, **Elusory**, *adj.* Mealltach, carach, cleasach, cuilbheartach.
Elute, *v. a.* Ionnlaid, nigh.
Elysian, *adj.* Mar phàrras, ro-thaitneach, ro aobhneach.
Elysium, *s.* Pàrras nan cinneach.
Emaciate, *v.* Searg, meath.
Emaciation, *s.* Reangadh, caitheamh ás, seargadh, meathadh le gort.
Emaculate, *v. a.* Glan o bhuill shalach.
Emanant, *adj.* A' sruthadh, a' sileadh o.
Emanate, *v. a.* Sruth, ruith, brùchd.
Emanation, *s.* Sruth, sileadh, ruith.
Emancipate, *v. a.* Fuasgail, saor, thoir saorsa bho chuing.
Emancipation, *s.* Fuasgladh, toirt o chuing.
Emasculate, *v. a.* Spoth; lagaich, meataich.
Embalm, *v. a.* Spìosraich, lion le spìosradh, cuir spìosraidh air.
Embar, *v. a.* Dùin a steach.
Embargo, *s.* Bacadh, grabadh-seòlaidh.
Embark, *v.* Cuir air bòrd, cuir air luing; rach air bòrd; gabh gnothach o's làimh.
Embarrass, *v. a.* Aimhreitich; cuir an ioma-cheist.
Embarrassment, *s.* Ioma-cheist,teinn.
Embassage, **Embassy**, *s.* Tosgaireachd.
Embattle, *v. a.* Cuir an òrdugh blàir.
Embay, *v. a.* Fliuch, nigh, dùin an geotha, druid an camus.
Embellish, *v. a.* Sgeadaich, maisich, sgiamhaich, breaghaich.
Embellishment, *s.* Sgèimh, sgeadachadh, breaghachd, rìomhadh.
Embers, *s.* Grìosach, beò-ghrìosach.
Embezzle, *v. a.* Goid ni a chaidh earbsadh riut; ceil cuid neach eile.
Embezzlement, *s.* Goid, cumail cuid neach eile, mi-ghnàthachadh airgeid.
Emblaze, **Emblazon**, *v. a.* Òraich, dean lainnireach; tarruinn gearradh arm; sgiamhaich le suaicheantas.
Emblem, *s.* Sàmhla, riochd, coltas, cruth-dhealbh, mac-samhail.
Emblematic, **Emblematical**, *adj.* Samhlach.
Emboss, *v. a.* Gràbhal, breac, cnapaich carbh; dualaich, dùin a stigh.
Embossment, *s.* Eiridh, breac-dhualachadh, gràbhaladh, obair-ghréis.
Embowel, *v. a.* Thoir am mionach ás; cuir am broinn.
Embrace, *v. a.* Iath 'nad' ghlacaibh, cniadaich, caidrich, pòg; fàiltich.
Embrace, *s.* Iathadh an glacaibh, pòg, fàilteachadh, cniadachadh, caidreamh.
Embrasure, *s.* Barra-bhalla.
Embrocate, *v. a.* Suath le acainn leighis.
Embrocation, *s.* Suathadh le acainn leighis.
Embroider, *v. a.* Gréis, cuir obair ghréis air.
Embroiderer, *s.* Gréiseadair.
Embroidery, *s.* Obair-ghréis.
Embroil, *v. a.* Aimhreitich, cuir thar a chéile, dean mi-riaghailt; cuir an ioma-cheist, buair.
Embryo, *s.* Ceud-fhàs, torrachas anabaich.
Emendation, *s.* Leasachadh, càradh, ceartachadh, atharrachadh.
Emerald, *s.* Smàrag, clach uasal uaine.
Emerge, *v. a.* Éirich an àirde, thig an uachdar, thig ás; thig am fradharc.
Emergency, *s.* Éiridh an uachdar; teachd am fradharc; tubaist, càs, tachartas.
Emergent, *adj.* Ag éiridh, a' teachd am follais; tuiteamach, tubaisteach, cruadalach.
Emersion, *s.* Éiridh, teachd am fradharc.
Emery, *s.* Seorsa mèinn iarainn.
Emetic, *s.* Purgaid thilgidh.
Emication, *s.* Lainnir, dealradh.
Emigrant, *s.* Céin-thìreach, eilthireach, fear-imrich.
Emigrate, *v. n.* Rach imrich gu tìr eile, fàg an dùthaich.
Eminence, *s.* Airde, mullach; mòrinbhe, meas, urram; mòrachd, àrdonoir.
Eminent, *adj.* Àrd, mòr, urramach; measail, ainmeil; sònraichte, comharraichte.
Emissary, *s.* Fear-brathaidh, teachdaire dìomhair; fear cur a mach.
Emission, *s.* Leigeadh a mach, leigeadh fa-sgaoil.
Emit, *v. a.* Leig a mach, cuir uat.
Emmet, *s.* Seangan, sneaghan.
Emollient, *adj.* Tlàth, caomh, maoth, tairis, tlùsail.
Emollient, *s.* Ìocshlaint-thlusail.
Emolument, *s.* Buannachd, tairbhe.
Emotion, *s.* Gluasad-inntinn.

EMPALE, *v. a.* Daingnich, ioma-dhruid, ceus, troimh-lot.
EMPANNEL, *v. a.* Gairm luchd deuchainn gu cùirt.
EMPASSION, *v. a.* Cuir fo bhuaireas.
EMPEROR, *s.* Iompaire.
EMPHASIS, *s.* Neart a' ghutha.
EMPHATIC, EMPHATICAL, *adj.* Làidir, neartmhor, brìoghmhor.
EMPIRE, *s.* Ard-uachdaranachd, mòr-chumhachd ; mòr-rìoghachd.
EMPIRIC, *s.* Léigh gun eòlas.
EMPIRIC, EMPIRICAL, *adj.* Deuchainneach, teagmhach, a' toirt dheuchainnean.
EMPLASTIC, *adj.* Ronnach, glaodhach, plàsdach, righinn.
EMPLOY, *v. a.* Thoir obair, gnàthaich, cleachd.
EMPLOY, EMPLOYMENT, *s.* Gnothach, obair ; dreuchd, cèaird.
EMPLOYER, *s.* Fear toirt oibreach.
EMPORIUM, *s.* Baile-margaidh.
EMPOVERISH, *v. a.* Dean bochd, dean ainniseach.
EMPOWER, *v. a.* Thoir comas, thoir ùghdarras ; dean comasach.
EMPRESS. *s.* Ban-iompaire.
EMPRISE, *s.* Gabhail os-làimh chunnartach dheacair.
EMPTINESS, *s.* Falamhachd, àite falamh'; aineolas.
EMPTY, *adj.* Falamh ; fàs.
EMPTY, *v.* Falmhaich, tráigh ; fasaich, fàs falamh
EMPURPLE, *v. a.* Dean dath dearg.
EMPUZZLE, *v. a.* Cuir an ioma-cheist, cuir am breislich.
EMPYREAL, *adj.* Nèamhaidh, fiorghlan.
EMPYREAN, *s.* Nèamh nan Nèamh, na flaitheas a's àirde.
EMPYREUM, EMPYREUMA, *s.* Bràthlosgadh.
EMULATE, *v. a.* Dean co-fharpais, dean co-strì, dean strì.
EMULATION, *s.* Co-fharpais, strì, spàirn, co-dheuchainn ; farmad, eud, co-stri.
EMULATIVE, *adj.* Co-fharpaiseach.
EMULATOR, *s.* Fear-co-fharpais, fear-strìghe.
EMULGE, *v. a.* Bligh ás, falmhaich.
EMULOUS, *adj.* Co-spairneach, buaidhdhéigheil.
ENABLE, *v. a.* Dean comasach, thoir comas.
ENACT, *v. a.* Òrduich, sònraich.
ENACTED, *part.* Òrduichte, socraichte.
ENAMEL, *v. a.* Dealtraich ; bi dealtradh.
ENAMOUR, *v. a.* Gràdhaich, cuir an gaol.
ENCAGE, *v. a.* Cuir an cuing, cròidh.
ENCAMP, *v.* Campaich.
ENCAMPMENT, *s.* Campachadh.
ENCHAFE, *v. a.* Feargaich, fraochaich, brosnaich.
ENCHAIN, *v. a.* Ceangail air slabhraidh.
ENCHANT, *v. a.* Cuir fo gheasaibh ; dean ro-shòlasach.
ENCHANTER, *s.* Geasadair, drùidh.
ENCHANTMENT, *s.* Drùidheachd ; àrd-shòlas, aoibhneas.
ENCHANTRESS, *s.* Bana-bhuidsich, ban-fhiosaiche ; té mhealladh gràidh, té ro mhaiseach.
ENCHASE, *v. a.* Leag ann an òr, maisich.
ENCIRCLE, *v. a.* Cuartaich, ioma-dhruid.
ENCLOSE, *v. a.* Dùin, cuartaich, ioma-dhruid.
ENCLOSURE, *s.* Dùnadh, iathadh, ioma-dhruideadh ; àite dùinte.
ENCOMIUM, *s.* Moladh, cliù.
ENCOMPASS, *v. a.* Cuartaich, iadh.
ENCORE, *adv.* A rithist, uair eile.
ENCOUNTER, *s.* Còmhrag ; cath ; dian-chòmhradh ; tachairt, coinneamh.
ENCOUNTER, *v. a.* Coinnich, thoir coinneamh, thoir ionnsaidh, thoir aghaidh air ; tachair an cath.
ENCOURAGE, *v. a.* Misnich, brosnaich, beothaich, thoir misneach, cuir misneach ann.
ENCOURAGEMENT, *s.* Misneach, brosnachadh ; còmhnadh.
ENCROACH, *v. n.* Thig, no rach, thar crìch, gun fhios no gun chòir.
ENCROACHMENT, *s.* Gabhail gun chòir
ENCUMBER, *v. a.* Luchdaich, grab, cuir trom air, bac, cuir éis air.
ENCUMBRANCE, *s.* Cudthrom, uallach, eallach, éire, grabadh.
ENCYCLOPEDIA, *s.* Cuairt-fhòghluim, uile-fhòghlum, eòlas gach nì.
END, *s.* Deireadh, crìoch, finid ; ceann, dùnadh, co-dhùnadh, foircheann, bàs.
ENDAMAGE, *v. a.* Ciùrr, dochainn.
ENDANGER, *v. a.* Cunnartaich, cuir an cunnart, cuir am baoghal.
ENDEAR, *v. a.* Tàlaidh, tarruinn spéis, dean gràdhach.
ENDEARMENT, *s.* Gràdhmhorachd, beadradh, gràdh, gaol, fàth-gaoil.
ENDEAVOUR, *s.* Ionnsaidh, deuchainn, dìchioll, spàirn, strì.
ENDEAVOUR, *v.* Thoir ionnsaidh, thoir deuchainn, dean dìchioll, feuch ri.
ENDICT, ENDICTE, *v. a.* Coirich, cuir as leth.
ENDICTMENT, *s.* Dearbhadh air dìteadh laghail.
ENDLESS, *adj.* Neo-chrìochnach, gun cheann, maireannach, sìorruidh, bith-bhuan ; a ghnà.
ENDORSE, *v. a.* Cùl-sgrìobh.
ENDORSEMENT, *s.* Cùl-sgrìobhadh.

Endow, *v. a.* Thoir tochradh, thoir cuibhrionn.

Endowment, *s.* Saibhreas, beartas; tiodhlac airgeid; càil, tuigse, eòlas.

Endue, *v. a.* Builich, bàirig, tiodhlaic.

Endurance, *s.* Maireannachd, buantas; foighidinn, fulang, giùlan le.

Endure, *v.* Fuilig, giùlain le; mair, fuirich.

Enemy, *s.* Nàmh, nàmhaid, eascaraid, fear-fuatha, an diabhol.

Energetic, *adj.* Làidir, neartmhor; gnìomhach, deanadach, éifeachdach, tàbhachdach.

Energy, *s.* Neart, spionnadh, tàbhachd; feart, lùgh.

Enervate, **Enerve**, *v. a.* Lagaich, meataich.

Enfeeble, *v. a.* Lagaich, anmhannaich.

Enfeoff, *v. a.* Cuir an seilbh, gabh seilbh.

Enfetter, *v. a.* Cuibhrich, geimhlich.

Enfilade, *s.* Aisir dhìreach réith.

Enforce, *v.* Neartaich, thoir spionnadh, spàrr, fòirn; earalaich; dearbh.

Enforcement, *s.* Co-éigneachadh, aindeoin, éigin.

Enfranchise, *v. a.* Dean 'na shaoranach.

Enfranchisement, *s.* Saorsa bailemargaidh, saoradh.

Engage, *v.* Gabh os làimh, geall, ceangail, freagair air son; meall, tàlaidh, gabh muinntearas.

Engagement, *s.* Gabhail os làimh, gealladh, cùmhnant; cath, còmhrag, blàr, cò-strì.

Engender, *v. a.* Gin; beir; bi gintinn.

Engine, *s.* Inneal, uidheam, beairt.

Engineer, *s.* Fear cuimseachadh ghunnacha-mora ris na nàimhdean an àm catha; fear deanamh inneal.

Engird, *v. a.* Ioma-dhruid, crioslaich.

English, *adj.* Sasunnach.

Englut, *v. a.* Sluig suas, glut.

Engorge, *v.* Sluig, glàm.

Engrapple, *v. n.* Teann-ghlac, greimich, dean co-strì.

Engrasp, *v. a.* Teann-ghlac, greimich.

Engrave, *v. a.* Gràbhal; gearr, snaidh.

Engraver, *s.* Gràbhalaiche.

Engraving, *s.* Gràbhaladh, gearradh.

Engross, *v. a.* Tiughaich, dean domhail, dean tomadach, meudaich, dean reamhar; glac chugad an t-iomlan; dean ath-sgrìobhadh garbh.

Enhance, *v. a.* Àrdaich, tog an luach; cuir barrachd meas air; meudaich, antromaich.

Enigma, *s.* Tòimhseachan, cruaidhcheist.

Enigmatical, *adj.* Cruaidh-cheisteach, dorcha; doirbh r'a thuigsinn.

Enjoin, *v. a.* Òrduich, earalaich.

Enjoinment, *s.* Òrduchadh, seòladh.

Enjoy, *v. a.* Meal, sealbhaich; gabh tlachd ann; bi sona.

Enjoyment, *s.* Toil-inntinn, mealtainn, sonas, suaimhneas

Enkindle, *v. a.* Fadaidh, las, beothaich; dùisg, brosnaich.

Enlarge, *v.* Meudaich, leudaich, cuir am farsuinneachd; bi bith-bhriathrach.

Enlargement, *s.* Meudachd, meudachadh, farsuinneachd; fuasgladh; saoradh; leudachadh.

Enlighten, *v. a.* Soillsich, soilleirich, thoir fradharc; teagaisg, ionnsaich.

Enlist, *v. a.* Rach ri àireamh.

Enliven, *v. a.* Beothaich, misnich.

Enmity, *s.* Naimhdeas, mì-run, gamhlas, fuath, falachd.

Ennoble, *v. a.* Uaislich, àrdaich, dean urramach; dean ainmeil, dean cliùiteach.

Ennoblement, *s.* Uaisleachadh, àrdachadh, togail an urram.

Ennui, *s.* Cianalas, airtneul, fadal.

Enodation, *s.* Snaim-fhuasgladh.

Enormity, *s.* Uabhasachd, anabarrachd; gràinealachd, déisinn.

Enormous, *adj.* Aingidh, déisinneach; uabhasach, fuathasach.

Enough, *adv.* Gu leòir.

Enow, *adj.* the *plr.* of Enough, Ni's leòr.

Enrage, *v. a.* Feargaich, fraochaich, cuir corraich air.

Enrank, *v. a.* Cuir an òrdugh.

Enrapture, *v. a.* Dean ro-aoibhneach, dean ro ait.

Enrich, *v. a.* Beartaich, dean beartach, saibhrich; mathaich, leasaich.

Enring, *v. a.* Iath mu'n cuairt.

Enrobe, *v. a.* Sgeadaich, éid, còmhdaich.

Enrol, *v. a.* Sgrìobh sìos ainm ann an leabhar-ainmean; paisg.

Enrolment, *s.* Ainm-chlàr.

Ensanguine, *v. a.* Dath le fuil.

Enshrine, *v. a.* Taisg gu cùramach, cuir an naomh-thasgadh.

Ensign, *s.* Bratach, meirghe, suaicheantas; fear-brataich.

Enslave, *v. a.* Dean 'na thràill, thoir gu tràilleachd.

Enslavement, *s.* Tràillealachd.

Ensteep, *v.* Tùm fo'n uisge.

Ensue, *v. a.* Lean, thig an lorg, bi leanmhainn.

Ensurance, *s.* Urras an aghaidh cunnairt.

Ensure, *v. a.* Dean cinnteach, cuir á cunnart.

Entablature, Entablement, *s.* Barra-bhailc.
Entail, *v. a.* Cuir fo chòir dhligheach.
Entail, *s.* Suidheachadh, riaghailt, seilbh oighreachd.
Entame, *v. a.* Càllaich, dean soirbh.
Entangle, *v. a.* Rib, cuir an sàs; aimhreitich, cuir an ioma-cheist.
Enter, *v. a.* Inntrinn, rach a steach; tòisich gnothach.
Enterprise, *s.* Ionnsaidh chunnartach.
Entertain, *v. a.* Thoir cuirm, dean biatachd; cum còmhradh ri; rùnaich.
Entertainment, *s.* Cuirm, fleagh, aoidheachd, biadhtachd; co-labhairt; fearas-chuideachd.
Enthrone, *v. a.* Cuir rìgh air a chathair; àrdaich.
Enthusiasm, *s.* Blàthas-inntinn.
Enthusiast, *s.* Fear dealasach; fear-baoth-chreidimh.
Enthusiastic, *adj.* Dealasach, dian, blàth-aigneach, àrd-inntinneach; baoth-chreideach.
Entice, *v. a.* Meall, tàlaidh, buair, thoir a thaobh.
Enticement, *s.* Mealladh, tàladh gu olc, buaireadh, culaidh-mheallaidh.
Enticer, *s.* Fear-tàlaidh, mealltair.
Entire, *adj.* Iomlan, coimhlionta, slàn, uile, làn; neo-mheasgte; neo-thruaillte.
Entirely, *ad.* Gu léir.
Entitle, *v. a.* Thoir còir; urramaich, thoir tiodal; sgrìobh tiodal.
Entity, *s.* Beò-bhith, beò-dhùil.
Entomb, *v. a.* Adhlaic, tìodhlaic.
Entrails, *s.* Mionach, grealach, caolain.
Entrance, *s.* Leigeadh a steach, comas dol a steach; dol a steach, slighe dhol a steach; tòiseachadh; gabhail seilbh.
Entrance, *v. a.* Rach am platha, cuir am paisean; giulain an inntinn o nithibh faicsinneach.
Entrap, *v. a.* Rib, glac, cuir an sàs; gabh cothrom air.
Entreat, *v. a.* Guidh, aslaich, grìos, iarr gu dùrachdach.
Entreaty, *s.* Guidhe, achanaich, iarrtas, aslachadh.
Entry, *s.* Dorus; dol a steach; gabhail seilbh, inntrinn; sgrìobhadh, no cur sìos ann an leabhar.
Enubilous, *adj.* Speur-ghlan, soilleir, sàr-ghlan.
Enucleate, *v. a.* Sgaoil, réitich.
Envelop, *v. a.* Paisg, còmhdaich; falaich, cuartaich.
Envelope, *s.* Pasgadh, còmhdach.
Envenom, *v. a.* Puinnseanaich; truaill; feargaich, cuir air boile.
Enviable, *adj.* Airidh air farmad.
Envious, *adj.* Farmadach.
Environ, *v. a.* Cuartaich, ioma-dhruid.
Environs, *s.* Iomall, coimhearsnachd.
Enumerate, *v. a.* Cunnt, àireamh.
Enumeration, *s.* Cunntas, àireamh.
Enunciate, *v. a.* Cuir an céill, innis, aithris, gairm, foillsich.
Enunciation, *s.* Aithris, nochdadh, cur an céill.
Enunciative, *adj.* Aithriseach.
Envoy, *s.* Teachdaire rìgh gu rìgh eile.
Envy, *v. a.* Gabh farmad ri sonas neach eile.
Envy, *s.* Farmad; tnù, mì-run, fuath, doilghios air son sonas neach eile.
Epaulette, *s.* Babag-ghuailne oifigich.
Ephemera, *s.* Fiabhras nach mair ach aon latha; cnuimh nach bi beò ach aon latha.
Ephemeral, *adj.* Neo-mhaireannach.
Ephemeris, *s.* Leabhar-latha.
Ephemerist, *s.* Speuradair.
Epic, *s.* Dàn-mòr, duan-eachdraidh.
Epicure, *s.* Geòcaire, craosaire, glutaire.
Epicurean, *adj.* Geòcach, sòghmhor, craosach, glutach.
Epicurism, *s.* Sògh, geòcaireachd, sàimh, ròic; teagasg Epicuruis.
Epidemic, Epidemical, *adj.* Gabhaltach, sgaoilteach, plàigheach.
Epidermis, *s.* Craiceann a muigh a' chuirp.
Epiglottis, *s.* Claban an sgòrnain.
Epigram, *s.* Gearr-dhuanag.
Epigrammatist, *s.* Fear-facail, duanaire, bàrd-rann.
Epilepsy, *s.* An tinneas tuiteamach.
Epileptic, *adj.* Tuiteamach.
Epilogue, *s.* Oraid, crìoch cluiche.
Epiphany, *s.* Féill an Taisbeanaidh.
Episcopacy, *s.* Easbuigeachd.
Episcopal, *adj.* Easbuigeach.
Episcopalian, *s.* Fear do chreidimh an easbuig.
Episode, *s.* Sgeul am meadhon dàin.
Epistle, *s.* Litir, teachdaireachd-dhiomhair.
Epistolary, *adj.* A bhuineas do litrichibh.
Epitaph, *s.* Sgrìobhadh air leac-lighe.
Epithalamium, *s.* Beannachadh-bàird, òran pòsaidh, dàn bainnse.
Epithet, *s.* Facal-buaidh, foir-ainm.
Epitome, *s.* Giorradan, brìgh sgeòil.
Epitomise, *v. a.* Giorraich, coimhghearr.
Epoch, Epocha, *s.* Àm o'n cunntar aimsir, àm ainmeil sam bith.

EPULARY, *adj.* Fleadhach ; cuirmeach.
EPULATION, *s.* Cuirm, fleadh, féisd, aighear, subhachas.
EUPOLOTIC, *s.* Iocshlaint leighis.
EQUABILITY, *s.* Co-ionannachd.
EQUABLE, *adj.* Ionann, co-chothromach, dìreach.
EQUAL, *adj.* Ionann, co-ionann, coimeas ; comasach ; réidh, còmhnard ; dìreach, ceart, neo-chlaon-bhreitheach.
EQUAL, *s.* Coimpire, leth-bhreac, seise.
EQUAL, EQUALIZE, *v. a.* Coimeas, dean ionann, dean coltach.
EQUALITY, *s.* Ionannachd, co-ionannachd, coimeas, còmhnardachd.
EQUANIMITY, *s.* Socair-inntinn, fois.
EQUATION, *s.* Co-fhreagarrachd.
EQUATOR, *s.* Cearcall meadhon na talmhuinn.
EQUERRY, *s.* Fear coimhid each an rìgh.
EQUIDISTANT, *adj.* Aig an aon fhad.
EQUILATERAL, *adj.* Co-shlisneach.
EQUILIBRIUM, *s.* Co-chothrom.
EQUINOCTIAL, *s.* Cearcall na co-fhad-thràth.
EQUINOCTIAL, *adj.* A bhuineas do'n cho-fhad-thràth.
EQUINOXES, *s.* Co-fhad-thràth.
EQUIP, *v. a.* Deasaich, cuir an uidheam, ullamhaich, sgeadaich.
EQUIPAGE, *s.* Carbad rìmheach 'na làn uidheam ; coisridh, frithealadh ; acainn, àirneis, fasair.
EQUIPMENT, *s.* Deasachadh, uidheamachadh ; acainn, airneis.
EQUIPOISE, *s.* Co-chudthrom.
EQUIPONDERANT, *adj.* Co-chudthromach, co-chothromach.
EQUIPONDERATE, *v. n.* Co-chudthromaich.
EQUITABLE, *adj.* Ceart, cothromach.
EQUITY, *s.* Ceartas, cothrom ; ceartbhreitheanas.
EQUIVALENT, *adj.* Co-ionann, co-luachmhor, co-chudthromach.
EQUIVALENT, *s.* Ni co-luachmhor.
EQUIVOCAL, *adj.* Teagmhach, dà-sheadhach, neo-chinnteach.
EQUIVOCATE, *v. a.* Dean teagmhach, dean dà-sheadhach, dean cleith-inntinn.
EQUIVOCATION, *s.* Dubh-chainnt.
EQUIVOCATOR, *s.* Fear dubh-chainnt.
ERA, *s.* Linn, àm, aimsir.
ERADIATION, *s.* Dèarsadh, deàlradh.
ERADICATE, *v. a.* Spion á bun.
ERADICATION, *s.* Spionadh á bun, sgrios.
ERASE, *v. a.* Mill, sgrios ; dubh a mach.
ERASEMENT, *s.* Dubhadh ás, sgrios.
ERE, *adv.* Roimhe, roi', mu'n, mas.
ERECT, *v. a.* Tog, tog dìreach ; àrdaich, tog suas.
ERECT, *adj.* Dìreach, neo-chrom ; misneachail, sgairteil.
ERECTION, *s.* Éiridh, togail, seasamh
ERECTNESS, *s.* Dìrichead.
EREMITE, *s.* Maol-ciaran, aonrach.
EREMITICAL, *adj.* Aonaranach, cianail, dubhach cràbhach.
ERENOW, *adv.* Roimhe so.
EREWHILE, *adv.* A chianamh.
ERINGO, *s.* Critheann-cladaich, seòrsa luibhe.
ERMELINE, ERMINE, *s.* Seórsa neas.
EROSION, *s.* Cnàmhuinn.
ERR, *v. n.* Rach air iomrall no air faontradh, rach air seachran, rach am mearachd.
ERRABLE, *adj.* Mearachdach.
ERRAND, *s.* Gnothach, teachdaireachd.
ERRANT, *adj.* Iomrallach, seachranach.
ERRATA, *s.* Mearachdan clò-bhualaidh.
ERRATIC, *adj.* Iomrallach, seachranach.
ERRING, *adj.* Mearachdach, seachranach.
ERRONEOUS, *adj.* Mearachdach, neo-shuidhichte, iomrallach, faondrach ; neo-fhior, neo-cheart, breugach.
ERROR, *s.* Mearachd ; iomrall, seachran, peacadh.
ERST, *adv.* Air thùs, roimhe so.
ERUBESCENCE, *s.* Deirge, ruthadh.
ERUCTATION, *s.* Brùchd.
ERUDITION, *s.* Ionnsachadh, fòghlum.
ERUGINOUS, *adj.* Méirgeach.
ERUPTION, *s.* Brùchdadh, bristeadh a mach ; broth.
ERUPTIVE, *adj.* A' bristeadh a mach ; brothach, guireanach.
ERYSIPELAS, *s.* Ruaidhe.
ESCALADE, *s.* Streapadh balla.
ESCALOP, *s.* Eisear shlaopte.
ESCAPE, *v. a.* Teich, tàr as ; seachain.
ESCAPE, *s.* Teicheadh, seachnadh, dol ás o chunnart.
ESCHEW, *v. a.* Seachain, na gabh gnothach ri, teich uaithe.
ESCORT, *s.* Coimheadachd ; dìon, freiceadan.
ESCULENT, *s.* Teachd-an-tìr.
ESCUTCHEON, *s.* Sgiath-teaghlaich, suaicheantas brataich.
ESPECIAL, *adj.* Àraidh, sònraichte.
ESPLANADE, *s.* Cùl balla daingnich ; àilean.
ESPOUSALS, *s.* Ceangal pòsaidh, còrdadh.
ESPOUSE, *v. a.* Dean ceangal pòsaidh ; pòs ; dìon, teasairg.
ESPY, *v. a.* Faic, beachdaich, comharraich ; gabh sealladh.
ESQUIRE, *s.* Tiotal duin'uasail is ìsle na ridire.

Essay, *v. a.* Feuch, thoir ionnsaidh, thoir deuchainn.
Essay, *s.* Deuchainn, feuchainn, òraid.
Essayist, *s.* Fear sgrìobhaidh òraidean.
Essence, *s.* Gnè, brìgh, sùgh, bladh.
Essential, *adj.* Feumail, nach gabh seachnadh, ro-àraidh, prìomh.
Establish, *v. a.* Suidhich, stéidh, socraich, daingnich, leag, riaghailtich.
Established, *part.* Suidhichte.
Establishment, *s.* Suidheachadh, socrachadh, stéidheachadh; daingneachadh, tuarasdal, teachd a steach.
Estate, *s.* Oighreachd, seilbh, fearann, cor, inbhe.
Esteem, *v. a.* Meas, cuir luach air; coimeas; urramaich, meas luachmhor.
Esteem, *s.* Meas, urram, onoir, miadh.
Estimable, *adj.* Luachmhor, prìseil, miadhail; measail, urramach.
Estimableness, *s.* Luachmhorachd, miadhalachd.
Estimate, *v. a.* Meas, cuir luach air.
Estimate, *s.* Cunntas, àireamh, meas; prìseachadh.
Estimation, *s.* Meas, luachmhorachd, urram, onoir; barail, breth.
Estival, *adj.* Samhrachail; ni a bhuineas do'n t-sàmhradh.
Estrange, *v. a.* Cum air falbh, tarruinn air falbh, dean fuathach, dean 'na choigreach.
Estrangement, *s.* Fad ás, gluasad air falbh.
Estuary, *s.* Abar, caolas, bàgh, camus.
Etching, *s.* Dealbh-sgrìobhaidh.
Eternal, *adj.* Bìth-bhuan, suthainn, sìorruidh, maireannach; neo-chrìochnach; gun toiseach.
Eternity, *s.* Siorruidheachd, bithbhuantachd.
Ether, *s.* Àile fìor-ghlan, adhar fìnealta.
Ethereal, *adj.* Adharach, adharail; nèamhaidh, spioradail.
Ethic, **Ethical**, *adj.* Modhannach, modhail beusach.
Ethics, *s. pl.* Modhannan, riaghailt nam modhannan, lagh nam beus.
Ethnic, *adj.* Pàganach.
Etiquette, *s.* Modh, deas-ghnàth.
Etymological, *adj.* A bhuineas do dh' fhacal-fhreumhachd.
Etymology, *s.* Facal-fhreumhachd.
Etymon, *s.* Freumh-fhacal.
Eulogical, *adj.* Moltach.
Eulogise, *v. a.* Mol, cliùthaich.
Eulogy, *s.* Moladh, cliù.
Eunuch, *s.* Caillteanach, òlach.
Euphony, *s.* Binn-fhuaim, binnead.
Eurus, *s.* A' ghaoth an ear.
Evacuate, *v. a.* Falmhaich dean falamh, fàsaich; fàg, falbh as; leig fuil.
Evacuation, *s.* Falmhachadh; glanadh, purgaideachadh; fàgail, falbh.
Evade, *v. a.* Seachain, faigh as, tàr as.
Evanescence, *s.* Diombuanachd, caochlaidheachd, faileas.
Evangelical, *adj.* Soisgeulach.
Evangelist, *s.* Soisgeulaiche.
Evangelize, *v. a.* Searmonaich an soisgeul.
Evaporate, *v. a.* Cuir 'na smùid, cuir 'na cheò.
Evaporation, *s.* Dol 'na smùid; tiormachadh.
Evasion, *s.* Leithsgeul, seachnadh; car, seamaguad, cur seachad, no gu taobh.
Eucharist, *s.* Comanachadh, suipeir an Tighearna.
Eucharistical, *adj.* A bhuineas do'n chomanachadh.
Eve, **Even**, *s.* Feasgar, anamoch, àrd-fheasgar, eadar-sholus, beul na h-oidhche; trasg roi' latha féille.
Even, *adj.* Réidh, còmhnard, co-ionann, neo-chaochlaidheach, co-shìnte, dìreach, neo-chlaon; ciùin, sèimh; do dh' àireamh a ghabhas roinn.
Even, *adv.* Eadhon.
Evenhanded, *adj.* Ceart, dìreach, neo-chlaon-bhreitheach, cothromach.
Evening, *s.* Feasgar, beul na h-oidhche.
Evenness, *s.* Còmhnardachd, réidheachd, ionannachd, riaghailteachd; sèimheachd, ciùine.
Even-song, *s.* Aoradh feasgair.
Event, *s.* Cùis, ni, tachartas, tuiteamas; crìoch, buil, toradh.
Eventful, *adj.* Cudthromach, tùiteamach, a bheir iomadh nì mu'n cuairt.
Even-tide, *s.* Trà-feasgair.
Ever, *adv.* Aig àm sam bith, idir, riamh; daonnan, gu bràth, an còmhnaidh, a chaoidh, gu sìorruidh.
Evergreen, *s.* Luibh no craobh shioruaine.
Evergreen, *adj.* Sìor-uaine.
Everlasting, *adj.* Sìorruidh, bithbhuan, maireannach.
Everlasting, *s.* Sìorruidheachd.
Everliving, *adj.* Neo-bhàsmhor.
Evermore, *adv.* Gu bràth, o so suas.
Every, *adj.* Gach, na h-uile, gach aon.
Evict, *v. a.* Cuir á seilbh, thoir uaith le ceartas.
Eviction, *s.* Cur á seilbh.
Evidence, *s.* Dearbhachd, dearbhadh; còmhdach, teisteas; fianais.
Evident, *adj.* Soilleir, dearbhte, cinnteach, follaiseach.
Evil, *adj.* Olc, dona, droch; aingidh.
Evil, **Evilness**, *s.* Olc, aingidheachd:

do-bheirt dochann, cron, urchaid; truaighe, call.

Evilminded, *adj.* Droch-inntinneach.

Evilspeaking, *s.* Cùl-chaineadh, sgainneal, tuaileis.

Evince, *v. a.* Dearbh, dean-soilleir, còmhdaich, co-dhearbh.

Evincible, *adj.* So-dhearbhadh.

Evitable, *adj.* So-sheachnadh.

Evocation, *s.* Éigheach, glaodhaich.

Evolation, *s.* Itealaich, falbh air iteig.

Evolve, *v. a.* Fuasgail.

Evolution, *s.* Teachd á filleadh.

Evulsion, *s.* Spìonadh á bun.

Ewe, *s.* Othaisg, caora.

Ewer, *s.* Soitheach-ionnlaid.

Exacerbation, *s.* Feargachadh.

Exact, *adj.* Ceart, dòigheil, pungail, riaghailteach; freagarrach.

Exact, *v. a.* Iarr mar chòir, tagair; àithn, earalaich.

Exaction, *s.* Iarraidh gu smachdail; daor-chàin, trom-chìs.

Exactness, *s.* Pungalachd, dòigheal-achd, riaghailteachd, ceartas.

Exaggerate, *v. a.* Meudaich, cuir am meud, cuir ri.

Exaggeration, *s.* Meudachadh.

Exagitation, *s.* Luasgadh, tulgadh.

Exalt, *v. a.* Àrdaich, tog an àird, tog gu h-urram; tog suas.

Exaltation, *s.* Àrdachadh, togail an àirde; éiridh gu h-urram; àirde, urram, inbhe.

Examination, *s.* Ceasnachadh, ranns-achadh, min-sgrùdadh.

Examine, *v. a.* Ceasnaich, cuir ceist-ean, fidir; rannsaich, sgrùd.

Examiner, *s.* Fear-sgrùdaidh.

Example, *s.* Samhla; eiseamplair, ball-sampuill.

Exasperate, *v. a.* Farranaich, fearg-aich, buair, brosnaich.

Exasperation, *s.* Brosnachadh, buair-eadh, farranachadh.

Excavate, *v. a.* Cladhaich, tochail, bùraich.

Exceed, *v.* Theirig thairis air, thoir barrachd; rach tuilleadh 's fada, rach thar tomhas.

Exceeding, *adj.* Anabarrach, ro-mhòr.

Excel, *v.* Thoir barrachd, thoir barr, faigh buaidh, coisinn buaidh; bi os ceann, bi ni's cliùthaichte, bi ni's ainmeile.

Excellence, Excellency, *s.* Gastachd, feothas, mathas; àirde, àrdachd, mòr-achd; òirdheirceas.

Excellent, *adj.* Òirdheirc, gasta, luachmhor, barrail, math.

Except, *v.* Fàg a mach, cuir air cùl, diùlt, ob, cuir an leth a muigh.

Except, Excepting, *prep.* Ach, saor o; mur, mur eil.

Exception, *s.* Cur an taobh a mach, fàgail a mach, diùltadh, obadh; coire, cunnuil, cron.

Exceptionable, *adj.* Buailteach do choire.

Exceptious, *adj.* Crosda, dreamasach, dreamlainneach.

Excerptor, *s.* Taghadair.

Excerpt, *adj.* Taghte, raoghnaichte.

Excerption, *s.* Taghadaireachd, raogh-nachadh.

Excess, *s.* Anabharr, tuilleadh 'sa chòir; ana-measarrachd.

Excessive, *adj.* Anabarrach, fuathas-ach; ana-measarra.

Excet, *v. a.* Gearr air fabh, gearr ás.

Exchange, *v. a.* Malartaich, iomlaidich.

Exchange, *s.* Iomlaid, malairt, suaip, co-cheannachd; mùthadh luach airg-eid rìoghachdan; Ionad-malairt.

Exchequer, *s.* Cùirt ionmhais a' chrùin.

Excisable, *adj.* Buailteach do bhi air a ghlacadh, no, buailteach do chìs rìgh.

Excise, *s.* Cìs-Rìgh.

Exciseman, *s.* Gàidsear, cìs-mhaor.

Excision, *s.* Gearradh ás, sgrios.

Excitation, *s.* Gluasad, carachadh, brosnachadh, dùsgadh, buaireadh.

Excite, *v. a.* Dùisg, brosnaich, gluais, misnich.

Excitement, *s.* Culaidh-bhrosnachaidh.

Exclaim, *v. n.* Glaodh, éigh, gairm.

Exclamation, *s.* Glaodh, iolach; comh-arradh iongantais, mar e so [!]

Exclamatory, *adj.* Gairmeach, ard-ghuthach, labhrach.

Exclude, *v. a.* Dùin a mach, bac, toir-misg; cùm air ais.

Exclusion, *s.* Dùnadh a mach; diùlt-adh, bacadh, toirmeasg; tilgeadh air falbh.

Exclusive, *adj.* A' bacadh, a' dùnadh a mach, a' diùltadh, a' toirmeasg.

Excogitate, *v.* Breithnich, tionnsgain, cnuasaich, beachdaich; smuaintich.

Excogitation, *s.* Beachd-smuainteach-adh, tionnsgnadh.

Excommunicate, *v. a.* Cuir á comunn nan criosdaidhean.

Excommunication, *s.* Ascaoin-eaglais, cur á comunn nan criosdaidhean.

Excoriate, *v. a.* Feann, rùisg, thoir an craiceann deth, faobhaich.

Excoriation, *s.* Rùsgadh, call craicinn; creach, spùinneadh.

Excrement, *s.* Cac, aolach, inneir.

Excrescence, *s.* Meall, flùth foinne, plucan.

Excruciate, *v. a.* Cràidh, pian, claoidh.

Excruciation, *s.* Cràdh, pian, dòruinn.
Excubation, *s.* Faire rè na h-òidhche.
Exculpate, *v. a.* Saor, gabh a leith-sgeul, fìreanaich.
Excursion, *s.* Cuairt, siubhal, sgrìob, turas, astar, falbh.
Excursive, *adj.* Turasach, falbhach, siùbhlach.
Excusable, *adj.* Leisgeulach, so-mhathadh.
Excuse, *v. a.* Gabh leisgeul, math.
Excuse, *s.* Leisgeul.
Excuseless, *adj.* Gun leisgeul.
Execrable, *adj.* Fuathach, daochail, gràineil, oillteil; mallaichte.
Execrate, *v. a.* Mallaich, guidh olc.
Execration, *s.* Mallachd, droch ghuidhe.
Exect, *v. a.* Gearr air fabh, gearr ás.
Execute, *v.* Dean, cuir an gnìomh, co-lion; marbh.
Execution, *s.* Cur an gnìomh, co-lionadh ; cur gu bàs, crochadh.
Executioner, *s.* Crochadair.
Executive, *adj.* Gnìomhach, gnìomh-chomasach, cumhachdach.
Executor, *s.* Fear-cùraim tiomnaidh.
Executrix, *s.* Bean-cùraim tiomnaidh.
Exemplar, *s.* Eiseamplair.
Exemplary, *adj.* Eiseamplaireach, cliù-thoillteannach, deagh-bheusach.
Exemplify, *v. a.* Mìnich le cosamhlachd.
Exempt, *v. a.* Saor, leig seachad.
Exemption, *s.* Saorsa, ceadachadh dol saor.
Exercise, *s.* Saothair, cleachdadh corporra, sràid-imeachd, gluasad, falbh; iomairt, gnàthachadh, gnìomh; oileanachadh; seirbhis an Tighearna.
Exercise, *v.* Oibrich, gnàthaich, cleachd, dean, cùm ri saothair, cuir an gnìomh, cleachd saothair chorporra.
Exert, *v. a.* Feuch ri, dean spàirn, dean dìchioll, cuir chuige, saothraich, oibrich, thoir ionnsaidh.
Exertion, *s.* Ionnsaidh, deuchainn, dìchioll, spàirn.
Exfoliate, *v. a.* Sgrath, sgar.
Exhalation, *s.* Éiridh 'na smùid no 'na cheò; ceò, grian-dheatach, ceathach.
Exhaust, *v. a.* Tràigh, tiormaich, falmhaich, taosg.
Exhaustless, *adj.* Neo-thraoghach.
Exhaustible, *adj.* So-traoghadh.
Exhaustion, *s.* Tràghadh, traoghadh.
Exhibit, *v. a.* Nochd, taisbean, feuch, foillsich, leig ris.
Exhibition, *s.* Nochdadh, foillseachadh, taisbeanadh, leigeadh ris.
Exhilarate, *v. a.* Cuir aoibhneas air dean cridheil, dean sunntach.
Exhilaration, *s.* Cridhealas, sunnt.
Exhort, *v. a.* 'Earalaich, comhairlich.
Exhortation, *s.* Comhairleachadh.
Exhumation, *s.* Toirt ás an uaigh.
Exigence, Exigency, *s.* Feum, easbhuidh, dìth, uireasbhuidh; cruaidhchas, teanntachd, éigin.
Exigent, *adj.* Éigineach, cruaidh, cruadalach.
Exigent, *s.* Eigin, teanntachd, cruaidhchas.
Exile, *s.* Fògradh, fuadach; fear-fuadain, fògarach, dìobarach.
Exile, *v. a.* Fògair, cuir ás an tìr.
Exist, *v. n.* Bi, bi beò, bi làthair.
Existence, Existency, *s.* Bith, beatha.
Existent, *adj.* A ta beò, a làthair.
Exit, *s.* Falbh, triall, siubhal, caochladh.
Exodus, *s.* Turas á àite no tìr, dara Leabhar Mhaois.
Exonerate, *v. a.* Neo-luchdaich, saor, fìreanaich.
Exoneration, *s.* Eutromachadh, fìreanachadh.
Exoptation, *s.* Dian-iarrtas, dianthogradh.
Exorable, *adj.* So-chomhairleachadh.
Exorbitance, *s.* Ana-cuimse, uamharrachd, anabarrachd.
Exorbitant, *adj.* Ana-cuimseach, anabarrach, fuathasach, thar tomhas.
Exorcise, *v. a.* Fògair deamhan, fuadaich droch spiorad, cuir spiorad fo gheasaibh.
Exorcist, *s.* Fear chur spioradan fo gheasaibh, druidh, geasadair.
Exordium, *s.* Roi'-ràdh, tùs-labhairt.
Exotic, *adj.* Coimheach, a bhuineas do dhùthaich eile.
Expand, *v. a.* Sgaoil, fosgail a mach; meudaich, at.
Expanse, *s.* Còmhnard mòr, fosgladh farsuinn, sìneadh; an iarmailt.
Expansion, *s.* Sgaoileadh, fosgladh, sìneadh a mach; farsuinneachd.
Expansive, *adj.* Sgaoilteach, so-shìneadh a mach.
Expatiate, *v. n.* Sìn a mach; leudaich.
Expatriate, *part.* Fògairte, fuadaichte.
Expect, *v. a.* Bitheadh dùil agad; amhairc air son.
Expectancy, *s.* Dùil, dòchas; earbsa.
Expectant, *adj.* Dòchasach, an dùil.
Expectation, *s.* Dùil, dòchas.
Expectorate, *v. a.* Cuir a mach o'n chridhe.
Expectoration, *s.* Cur a mach le casad.

EXPEDIENCE, EXPEDIENCY, *s.* Freagarrachd, iomchuidheachd, feumalachd.
EXPEDIENT, *adj.* Freagarrach, iomchuidh, cothromach.
EXPEDITE, *v. a.* Luathaich, cabhagaich.
EXPEDITION, *s.* Luathas, cabhag, graide; ionnsaidh, turas-cogaidh.
EXPEDITIOUS, *adj.* Ullamh, ealamh, luath, grad, cabhagach.
EXPEL, *v. a.* Tilg a mach, cuir air falbh; fògair, fuadaich; cum uat.
EXPEND, *v. a.* Caith, cosg.
EXPENSE, *s.* Cosgas, cur a mach airgeid.
EXPENSELESS, *adj.* Neo-chosgail.
EXPENSIVE, *adj.* Cosgail, caithteach, struidheil; daor, luachmhor.
EXPENSIVENESS, *s.* Cosgalachd, struidhealachd; luachmhorachd.
EXPERIENCE, *s.* Cleachdadh, deuchainn; féin-fhiosrachadh, gnàth, eòlas, aithne, cleachdadh.
EXPERIENCE, *v. a.* Aithnich, fairich, mothaich, faigh fios faireachdainn; gnàthaich.
EXPERIENCED, *part.* Gnàthaichte ri, cleachdte, gnàth-eòlach.
EXPERIMENT, *s.* Deuchainn dhearbhaidh.
EXPERIMENTAL, *adj.* Deuchainneach.
EXPERT, *adj.* Ealanta, teòma, seòlta; deas, ealamh.
EXPERTNESS, *s.* Seòltachd, teòmachd.
EXPIABLE, *adj.* So-dhìoladh, so-ìocadh.
EXPIATE, *v. a.* Ioc, thoir éirig, thoir dìoladh air son coire.
EXPIATION, *s.* Dìoladh, ìocadh, athdhìoladh.
EXPIATORY, *adj.* Réiteachail, a ni dìoladh.
EXPIRATION, *s.* Tarruinn na h-analach, séideadh analach; crìoch, ceann; call an deò, bàsachadh.
EXPIRE, *v.* Séid, analaich; bàsaich, thoir suas an deò; crìochnaich, thig gu crìch.
EXPLAIN, *v. a.* Dean so-thuigsinn, soilleirich, foillsich.
EXPLANATION, *s.* Mìneachadh, soilleireachadh, soillseachadh.
EXPLANATORY, *adj.* Mìneachail.
EXPLICABLE, *adj.* So-mhìneachadh.
EXPLICATE, *v. a.* Fosgail, soilleirich.
EXPLICATION, *s.* Fosgladh, soilleireachadh, mìneachadh, fuasgladh, réiteachadh; eadar-theangachadh.
EXPLICIT, *adj.* Soilleir, so-thuigsinn, pungail.
EXPLODE, *v. a.* Spreadh, tilg á mach le spreadhadh; tilg a mach le tàir, cuir an neo-shuim.
EXPLOIT, *s.* Euchd, treubhantas, mòrghnìomh.
EXPLORE, *v. a.* Feuch, rannsaich, sgrùd, sir.
EXPLOSION, *s.* Spreadhadh, bragh.
EXPORT, *v. a.* Cuir do thìr eile.
EXPORTATION, *s.* Cur bathar thar muir.
EXPOSE, *v. a.* Nochd, foillsich, leig ris, rùisg, taisbean; dean ball-magaidh dheth; cuir an cunnart.
EXPOSITION, *s.* Mìneachadh, soilleireachadh; suidheachadh, leigeil ris; eadar-theangachadh.
EXPOSITOR, *s.* Fear-mìneachaidh, eadartheangair.
EXPOSTULATE, *v. n.* Reusonaich; connsaich, cothaich.
EXPOSTULATION, *s.* Reusonachadh, deasbaireachd; connsachadh, cothachadh; casaid.
EXPOSURE, *s.* Foillseachadh, leigeil ris, taisbeanadh; gàbhadh, cunnart; suidheachadh.
EXPOUND, *v. a.* Mìnich, foislich dean soilleir, leig ris.
EXPOUNDER, *s.* Fear-mìneachaidh.
EXPRESS, *v. a.* Cuir an céill, innis, aithris; nochd, foillsich, taisbean; fàisg, brùth á mach.
EXPRESS, *adj.* Soilleir, pungail, follaiseach; a dh' aon ghnothach; a dh' aon obair.
EXPRESS, *s.* Teachdaire-cabhaig, teachdaireachd-chabhaig.
EXPRESSIBLE, *adj.* So-innseadh.
EXPRESSION, *s.* Dòigh labhairt, aithris, cainnt; fàsgadh.
EXPRESSIVE, *adj.* Làn seadh, brìoghor, seadhach, làidir.
EXPROBATE, *v. a.* Cronaich, maslaich.
EXPROBATION, *s.* Cronachadh.
EXPUGN, *v. a.* Buadhaich, cìosnaich, ceannsaich.
EXPUGNATION, *s.* Buadhachadh, ceannsachadh.
EXPULSION, *s.* Fògradh, fuadach, cur a mach.
EXPULSIVE, *adj.* A dh' fhògras, a dh' fhuadaicheas.
EXPUNGE, *v. a.* Dubh a mach, sgrìob ás
EXPURGATION, *s.* Glanadh, sgùradh, ionnlad.
EXPURGE, *v. a.* Glan, ionnlaid.
EXQUISITE, *adj.* Gasta, taghte, òirdheirc, grinn, co-lionta; ro mhothachail.
EXQUISITENESS, *s.* Òirdheirceas, grinneas, sgiultachd.
EXTANT, *adj.* Maireann, foliaiseach, a làthair; beò.
EXTEMPORANEOUS, EXTEMPORARY, *adj.* Bharr làimhe, gun ullachadh.

Extempore, *adv.* Gun ullachadh roi' làimh.
Extemporise, *v. n.* Labhair gun ullachadh.
Extend, *v. a.* Sìn, sgaoil; leudaich, meudaich, farsuinnich; bàirig, compàirtich; ruig air.
Extension, *s.* Sìneadh, ruigheachd, sgaoileadh, farsuinneachd, leud, meud.
Extensive, *adj.* Farsuinn, leathann, mòr.
Extensiveness, *s.* Farsuinneachd, meud, leud.
Extent, *s.* Farsuinneachd, meud, leud, fad, dòmhladas.
Extenuate, *v. a.* Lughdaich, caolaich, beagaich, tanaich; gabh leisgeul, aotromaich coire.
Extenuation, *s.* Lughdachadh, beagachadh, gabhail leisgeil; aotromachadh; tanachadh, caolachadh.
Exterior, *adj.* Air an taobh muigh.
Exterminate, *v. a.* Spìon á 'fhreumhaibh, dìthich, sgrios; thoir as a bhun, fògair.
Extermination, *s.* Sgrios, milleadh.
Extern, External, *adj.* A muigh, air an taobh muigh.
Externally, Exteriorly, *adv.* A muigh, air an taobh muigh.
Extersion, *s.* Suathadh, air falbh.
Extimulate, *v. a.* Spor, brosnaich.
Extimulation, *s.* Sporadh, brodadh, brosnachadh.
Extinct, *adj.* Crìochnaichte, nach eil a làthair; marbh.
Extinction, *s.* Cur ás, smàladh; dol ás, mùchadh; milleadh, sgrios, fògradh.
Extinguish, *v. a.* Cuir ás, mùch, smàl ás; mill, sgrios, caisg.
Extinguisher, *s.* Smàladair.
Extirpate, *v. a.* Spìon á bun, sgrios, dìthich.
Extirpation, *s.* Toirt á 'fhreumhan, spìonadh á bun, sgrios.
Extol, *v. a.* Ard-mhol, cliùthaich.
Extort, *v. a.* Dean fòirneart, thoir air falbh le ainneart.
Extortion, *s.* Fòirneart, foireigneadh.
Extortioner, *s.* Fear foireignidh.
Extract, *v. a.* Tarruinn á, thoir á.
Extract, *s.* As-tarruinn, brìgh, sùgh.
Extraction, *s.* Tàrmachadh, sloinneadh, taruinn a mach.
Extrajudicial. *adj.* Neo-laghail.
Extraneous, *adj.* Coimheach.
Extraordinary, *adj.* Neo-ghnàthach; neo-chumanta, sònraichte, àraid, anabarrach iongantach.
Extravagance, Extravagancy, *s.* Ana-measarrachd, ana-caitheamh, struidhealachd; mi-riaghailt, dol ás an t-slighe; buaireas.
Extravagant, *adj.* Strùidheil, anacaithteach; mi-riaghailteach, anacuimseach.
Extreme, *adj.* Anabarrach, ro-mhòr iomallach, a's faide muigh; deireannach.
Extreme, *s.* Iomall, deireadh, ceann thall, crìoch.
Extremity, *s* Ceann a's faide mach, crìoch, iomall, oir; gnè an aghaidh gnè eile; cruaidh-chas, teinn, éigin.
Extricate, *v. a.* Saor, fuasgail.
Extrication, *s.* Saoradh, fuasgladh, toirt á amladh.
Extrinsic, Extrinsical, *adj.* Air an leth a muigh, a bhuineas do ni eile.
Extrinsically, *adv.* O 'n leth a muigh.
Extrusion, *s.* Tilgeadh a mach.
Exuberance, *s.* Cùs, mòr-phailteas.
Exuberant, *adj.* Pailt, làn, lìonmhor, tarbhach, a' cur thairis.
Exudation, *s.* Fallus.
Exudate, Exude, *v. n.* Cuir fallus dhiot.
Exulcerate, *v. a.* Leannaich, eargnaich; bi 'g iongrachadh.
Exult, *v. n.* Dean uaill, dean aoibhneas, dean gàirdeachas; dean meoghail, bi ri aighear.
Exultance, Exultation, *s.* Uaill, gàirdeachas, aoibhneas, subhachas, aighear, meoghail.
Exundate, *v. a.* Cuir thairis.
Exundation, *s.* Ro-phailteas, làn.
Exuperable, *adj.* So-cheannsachadh.
Exuscitate, *v. a.* Èirich, dùisg, tog suas.
Exustion, *s.* Losgadh, cnàmh, caitheamh as le teìne.
Eyas, *s.* Isean seabhaic.
Eye, *s.* Sùil; crò snàthaid.
Eye, *v. a.* Beachdaich, faic, seall, cum sùil air, dearc, amhairc.
Eyeball, *s.* Ubhall na sùl, clach na sùl.
Eyebright, *s.* Lùs-nan-leac.
Eyebrow, *s.* Mala.
Eyelash, *s.* Fabhradh.
Eyeless, *adj.* Gun sùilean.
Eyelet, *s.* Toll-fradhairc.
Eyelid, *s.* Rosg, rasg.
Eyesalve, *s.* Sàbh-shùl.

Eyesight, *s.* Sealladh, fradharc, léirsinn, léirsinn-shùl.

Eyesore, *s.* Culaidh ghràin, culaidh-mhì-thlachd, cuis-dhéisinn.

Eyetooth, *s.* Fiacaill-chrìche.

Eyewitness, *s.* Fianais-shùl.

Eyre, *s.* Mòd ceartais.

Eyry, *s.* Nead iolaire, fìthich, seabhaic, no nead eun-feòil-itheach sam bith eile.

F

F, *s.* Sèathamh litir na h-aibidil.

Fable, *s.* Spleagh, uirsgeul, sgeulachd.

Fable, *v.* Innis breugan, innis sgeulachd, labhair faoin-sgeul spleaghach.

Fabled, *part.* Iomraiteach an uirsgeulan, ainmeil ann an sgeul.

Fabric, *s.* Togail, aitreabh, taigh.

Fabricate, *v. a.* Tog, dealbh, cothog.

Fabulist, *s.* Spleaghaire, sgeulaiche.

Fabulous, *adj.* Spleaghach, uirsgeulach, faoin-sgeulach, breugach.

Face, *s.* Aghaidh, gnùis, aodann tuar, aogas ; uachdar, beul-thaobh ; dreach.

Face, *v. a.* Cuir aghaidh ri, thoir aghaidh air, tachair, coinnich ; seas mu choinneamh ; tionndaidh t' aghaidh mu'n cuairt.

Facetious, *adj.* Cridheil, sunntach, àbhachdach, sùgach, sùigeartach, ait.

Facile, *adj.* Furasda, soirbh, sodheanamh, ciùin, fòil.

Facilitate, *v. a.* Dean furasta, dean soirbh, dean réidh, réitich.

Facility, *s.* Furastachd, ullamhachd, teòmachd ; sùbailteachd, géilleachdainn, socharachd.

Facing, *s.* Lìnig, aghaidh, còmhdach.

Facinorous, *adj.* Aingidh, olc, dona.

Fact, *s.* Gniomh, gnothach, beart, tùrn ; fìrinn.

Faction, *s.* Luchd-tuairgnidh ; aimhreit, tuairgneadh, eas-aonachd.

Factious, *adj.* Aimhreiteach, buaireasach, easaontach, ceannairceach.

Factor, *s.* Seamarlan, bàilidh.

Factory, *s.* Taigh-dhèantaichean, ionad luchd gnothaich ; taigh-cèairde.

Factotum, *s.* Gille-gach-gnothaich.

Faculty, *s.* Comas, cumhachd; càil, buaidh-inntinn ; seòltachd, dòigh ; comunn luchd-teagaisg àrd-sgoile.

Facundity, *s.* Fileantachd.

Fade, *v.* Caith, seachd ; teich á sealladh ; caill dath ; searg, crìon, meath.

Fading, *s.* Crìonadh, seargadh, seacadh, caitheamh ás.

Fæces, *s.* Òtrach, anabas, aolach, dràbhag, druaip.

Fag, *v. n.* Fàs, sgith, fannaich.

Fag, Fag-end, *s.* Ceànn-aodaich, fuigheall, deireadh.

Fagot, *s.* Cual chonnaidh, fiodh fadaidh, &c.

Fail, *v.* Tréig, dìobair, fàg ; fàillinnich, bi an easbhuidh ; teirig, rach ás, sguir ; fannaich, fàs lag; thig gearr air.

Failing, *s.* Fàillinn, fàillneachadh ; seargadh, seacadh ; uireasbhuidh, tuisleadh, coire.

Failure, *s.* Easbhuidh, uireasbhuidh ; tuisleadh, coire, fàillinn.

Fain, *adj.* Sòlasach, sunntach, deònach, toileach, an geall.

Fain, *adv.* Gu toileach, gu deònach, le làn toil.

Faint, *v.* Fannaich, rach am paisean, fàs lag, fàs fann, caill do spiorad, bi fo dhiobhail-misnich.

Faint, *adj.* Lag, fann. anfhann ; neo-shoilleir ; breòite, gun chlì, gealltach, meat, tais, fo dhiobhail-misnich ; neo-smiorail, neo-sgairteil.

Faint-hearted, *adj.* Lag-chridheach, gealtach, tais, meat, cladharra,

Fainting, *s.* Fannachadh, paisean, neul, laigse.

Faintish, *adj.* Fann, a' fàs fann.

Faintness, *s.* Laigse, laigsinn, anfhannachd ; neo-smioralachd, marbhantachd ; lag-chridheachd, cladhaireachd.

Fair, *adj.* Maiseach, sgiamhach, bòidheach, àillidh ; geal, fionn ; taitneach, maiseach, ciatach, glan, soilleir ; ceart, cothromach, dìreach ; sìobhalta, suairce.

Fair, *s.* Maise-mnà, àile ; féill.

Fairing, *s.* Faidhrean.

Fairness, *s.* Maise, maisealachd, bòidhchead, àilleachd ; ceartas, onoir, ionracas, tréidhireachd ; soilleireachd.

Fairy, *s.* Sìthiche ; bean-shìth.

Fairy, *adj.* A bhuineas do shìthichean.

Faith, *s.* Creideamh ; muinghinn, dòchas, earbsa ; creideas, barail ;

dìlseachd ; onoir, fìrinn ; gealltanas, gealladh.

FAITHFUL, *adj.* Creideach ; dìleas ; ionraic, trèidhireach, onorach ; fìreanach, fìreanta.

FAITHFULNESS, *s.* Trèidhireachd, ionracas ; dìlseachd, seasmhachd.

FAITHLESS, *adj.* Mi-chreideach ; midhìleas, mealltach, cealgach.

FAITHLESSNESS, *s.* Mi-dhìlseachd.

FALCHION, *s.* Claidheamh crom.

FALCON, *s.* Seabhac seilge.

FALCONER, *s.* Seabhacair, fear-ionnsachaidh sheabhac.

FALCONRY, *s.* Seabhacaireachd.

FALL, *v. n.* Tuit ; teirinn ; traogh, sìolaidh.

FALL, *s.* Tuiteam, leagadh, léir-sgrios ; tuiteam sìos, ìsleachadh ; téarnadh càs, bruthach ; eas, steall.

FALLABILITY, *s.* Buailteachd do mhearachd.

FALLACIOUS, *adj.* Mearachdach, mealltach, carach, cealgach.

FALLACY, *s.* Mealltachd, feallsachd, cealgachd.

FALLIBLE, *adj.* Tuiteamach, buailteach do mhearachd, fàillinneach.

FALLING, *s.* Tuiteam, peacadh.

FALLING-SICKNESS, *s.* An tinneastuiteamach.

FALLOW, *adj.* Dearg-shoilleir, buidheshoilleir ; Talamh bàn, neothreabhte.

FALLOW, *s.* Treabhadh-sàmhraidh, eilgheadh.

FALSE, *adj.* Breugach, fallsa, neofhìor ; mearachdach ; meallta, midhìleas.

FALSEHEARTED, *adj.* Meallta, foilleil, cealgach.

FALSEHOOD, FALSITY, *s.* Breug ; mealltaireachd, cealg.

FALSIFY, *v.* Dean breugach, breugnaich, dearbh 'na bréig ; àicheadh an fhìrinn.

FALTER, *v. n.* Bi liotach, dean gagail chainnte, bi manntach ; fàs sgìth.

FALTERING, *s.* Teabadaich, laigse, teachd gearr.

FAME, *s.* Cliù, alla, ainm ; iomradh.

FAMED, *adj.* Ainmeil, allail, cliùiteach, iomraiteach ; measail.

FAMELESS, *adj.* Neo-iomraiteach.

FAMILIAR, *adj.* Aoidheil, saor, ceanalta, furanach, faoilidh ; càirdeil ; eòlach, coitcheann, tric.

FAMILIAR, *s.* Fear eòlais, còmpanach ; leannan-sìth.

FAMILIARITY, *s.* Eòlas, còmpanas ; saorsa còmhraidh.

FAMILIARIZE, *v. a.* Dean eòlach, gnàthaich, cleachd.

FAMILY, *s.* Teaghlach ; sliochd, àl, clann, gineal ; cinneadh, fine, dream.

FAMINE, *s.* Gort, airc, gainne.

FAMISH, *v.* Cuir gu bàs le gort.

FAMOUS, *adj.* Ainmeil, cliùiteach, measail, iomraiteach, sònraichte.

FAN, *s.* Gaotharan, sgàileagan ; guit, fasgnag, dallanach.

FAN, *v. a.* Fuaraich, gluais, an t-àileadh ; fasgain.

FANATIC, *s.* Neach air boile le baoth chreideamh.

FANATIC, FANATICAL, *adj.* Boathchreideach, saobh-chreideach.

FANATICISM, *s.* Baoth-chreideamh, saobh-chreideamh.

FANCIFUL, *adj.* Mac-meanmnach, neònach, iongantach, saobhsmuainteach.

FANCIFULNESS, *s.* Neònachas, iongantas, macmeamnainn.

FANCY, *s.* Mac-meamna, saobhsmuain ; barail, miann, déidh, tlachd.

FANCY, *v.* Smuainich, saoil, baralaich, beachdaich ; miannaich, gabh déidh ; bi 'n dùil.

FANE, *s.* Teampull, eaglais, coilleachgaoithe.

FANFARON, *s.* Curaidh, gaisgeach.

FANG, *s.* Tosg, ionga, dubhan, pliùt.

FANGED, *adj.* Tosgach, iongach, dubhanach, spògach, pliùtach.

FANGLE, *s.* Faoin, ionnsaidh, faoin innleachd.

FANTASTIC, FANTASTICAL, *adj.* Macmeamnach, iongantach, neo-sheasmhach, faoin, neònach, gòrach, gogaideach, guanach.

FAR, *adv.* Fada, fád' ás, fad' air falbh, an céin ; gu mòr.

FAR, *adj.* Fada, fad' ás.

FARCE, *s.* Ealaidh, baoth chluich.

FARCICAL, *adj.* Àbhachdach, a bhuineas do chluich baoth.

FARCY, *s.* Claimh-each.

FARDEL, *s.* Trusgan ; cual, ultach.

FARE, *v. n.* Ith, gabh lòn ; siubhail, imich, gabh turas ; tàrladh dhut, bi an cor.

FARE, *s.* Luach giùlain, duais, dìoladh faraidh ; biadh, lòn, teachd-an-tìr.

FAREWELL, *ad.* Soraidh leat, slàn leat, beannachd leat.

FARFETCHED, *adj.* Air a tharriunn fad ás, air teachd o chéin.

Farinaceous, *adj*. A bhuineas do mhin, air bhlas mine.

Farm, *s*. Baile fearainn, gabhail fhearainn, tuathanas.

Farmer, *s*. Tuathanach, gabhaltaiche.

Farmost, *adj*. A's faid ás.

Farrago, *s*. Brudhaiste, bròthas, brochan, cumasg.

Farrier, *s*. Marc-lighich, léigh-each, gobha-chruidhean.

Farrow, *s*. Cuain, àlach muice.

Farrow, *v. a.* Beir uirceanan.

Fart, *s*. Braim, breim, bram.

Farther, *adv*. Ni's fhaide as, a thumeadh, a bhàrr.

Farther, *adj*. Ni's faide, ni's iomallaiche; air taobh thall.

Farther, *v. a.* Cuir air adhart, cuidich.

Fartherance, *s*. Cuideachadh, còmhnadh.

Farthest, *adj*. A's faid' ás, a's iomallaiche.

Farthing, *s*. Feòirlinn, fàirdein.

Farthingale, *s*. Cearcall-còta.

Fascinate, *v. a.* Cuir fo gheasaibh.

Fascination, *s*. Buidseachd.

Fashion, *s*. Modh, seol; fasan; cleachdadh, gnàths, cumadh, cruth, dealbh, dèanamh, dreach, samhla, coltas; dòigh, nòs; uaisle.

Fashion, *v. a.* Cùm, dealbh, dreach.

Fashionable. *adj*. Fasanta, gnàthaichte, nòsail, cleachdail.

Fast, *s*. Trasg, Trasgadh.

Fast, *adj*. Daingeann, teann, neoghluasadach, diongmhalta; luath.

Fasten, *v*. Daingnich, teannaich, ceangail; greimich, gabh greim.

Fastening, *s*. Ceangal, daingneachadh.

Fastidious, *adj*. Àilleasach, moiteil, tarcuiseach, àileanta, arralach.

Fasting, *s*. Trasgadh, trasg.

Fat, *adj*. Reamhar, sultmhor, feòlmhor.

Fat, *s*. Reamhrachd, saill, sult, blonag.

Fatal, *adj*. Marbhtach, bàsmhor, sgriosail, millteach; an dàn.

Fatalist, *s*. Fear creidsinn 's an dàn.

Fatality, *s*. Roi'-òrduchadh, dàn.

Fate, *s*. Dàn; dàil, manadh; bàs; sgrios.

Fated, *adj*. Roi'-òrduichte, an dàn.

Father, *s*. Athair.

Father, *v. a.* Gabh ri mar athair, uchdmhacaich; aidick mar do ghniomh no do sgrìobhadh; cuir as leth, cuir air.

Father-in-law, *s*. Athair-céile.

Fatherless, *adj*. Gun athair.

Fatherly, *adj*. Athaireil.

Fathom, *s*. Aitheamh.

Fathom, *v. a.* Tomhais aitheamh, ruig air, faigh a mach; tomhais doimhneachd.

Fathomless, *adj*. Gun ghrunnd, gun iochdar, gun aigein.

Fatigable, *adj*. So-sgìtheachadh.

Fatigue, *v. a.* Sgìthich, sàraich.

Fatigue, *s*. Sgìos, saothair, sàrachadh, allaban.

Fatling, *s*. Beathach reamhar, ainmhidh air a bhiadhadh air son a mhàrbhadh.

Fatness, *s*. Reamrachd, reamhad, sultmhorachd; geir, saill.

Fatten, *v*. Reamhraich, biadh; fàs reamhar.

Fatuity, *s*. Baothaireachd.

Fatuous, *adj*. Baoth, gòrach, faoin, amaideach; lag, faileasach.

Fault, *s*. Coire, cron, lochd, gaoid, cionta.

Faultless, *adj*. Neo-lochdach, neochiontach, neo-choireach; iomlan, gun mheang.

Faulty, *adj*. Ciontach, coireach, mearachdach; olc, dona.

Favour, *v. a.* Cuidich, bi fàbharach, nochd càirdeas, dean còmhnadh le, còmhnaich.

Favour, *s*. Fàbhar, deagh-ghean, bàigh, maidhean, taobh, càirdeas; suaicheantas.

Favourable, *adj*. Fàbharach, bàigheil.

Favoured, *part*. A fhuair cothrom no fàbhor, dheth am beil spéis.

Favourite, *s*. Annsachd, ceist, luaidh.

Fawn, *s*. Laogh féigh, fiagh òg; meann earba.

Fawn, *v. n.* Dean miodal, dean sodal, dean cùirteas; strìochd, lùb.

Fealty, *s*. Ùmhlachd, dlighe iochdarain d'a uachdaran.

Fear, *s*. Eagal, geilt, sgàth, fiamh.

Fear, *v*. Gabh eagal, gabh fiamh; bi fo eagal, geiltich; bi am fiamh, bi fo chùram, bi fo iomaguin.

Fearful, *adj*. Gealtach, meat, lagchridheach, eagalach, fiamhail; oillteill, uamhunnach, uabhasach.

Fearfulness, *s*. Gealtachd, meatachd, geilt, eagal, fiamh, sgàth, oillt, uabhas.

FEARLESS, *adj.* Neo-ghealtach, gun athadh, neo-fhiamhach.
FEASIBLE, *adj.* So-dheanamh, coltach.
FEAST, *s.* Cuirm, fleadh, cuilm.
FEAST, *v. a.* Dean cuirm, thoir fleadh; gabh cuirm, gabh fleadh.
FEAT, *s.* Gnìomh, éuchd, treubhantas; cleas, car neònach.
FEAT, *adj.* Ealamh, sgiobalta, deas, teòma; grinn, snasmhor.
FEATHER, *s.* Ite, iteag.
FEATHER, *v. a.* Sgeadaich le itean.
FEATHER-BED, *s.* Leabaidh chloimhiteach, leabaidh itean.
FEATHERED, *adj.* Iteagach, iteach.
FEATURE, *s.* Tuar, aogas, cruth, dreach; cumadh, cruitheachd, dealbh.
FEBRILE, *adj.* Fiabhrasach.
FEBRUARY, *s.* Ceud mhìos an earraich.
FECULENCE, *s.* Drabhas, gruid druaip.
FECULENT, *adj.* Drabhasach, druaipeil.
FECUND, *adj.* Torrach, sìolmhor.
FECUNDITY, *s.* Sìolmhorachd.
FED, *prep.* and *part.* of *to feed.* Àraichte.
FEDERAL, *adj.* A bhuineas do chùmhnant.
FEE, *v. a.* Tuarasdalaich, gabh.
FEE, *s.* Duais, dìoladh, tuarasdal.
FEEBLE, *adj.* Lag, fann, anfhann.
FEEBLENESS, *s.* Laigse, anfhannachd.
FEED, *v.* Biadh, àraich, beathaich, cùm suas.
FEED, *s.* Biadh, lòn, ionaltradh.
FEEDER, *s.* Fear-biadhaidh; fear-ithe.
FEEL, *v. a.* Fairich, mothaich, laimhsich; feuch, rannsaich.
FEELING, *s.* Faireachduinn, faireachadh, mothachadh, càileachd.
FEIGN, *v.* Gabh ort, leig ort; aithris gu breugach.
FEINT, *s.* Coltas breugach, gabhail air.
FELICITATE, *v. a.* Dean sona, fàiltich.
FELICITOUS, *adj.* Sona, sòlasach.
FELICITY, *s.* Sonas, sòlas.
FELINE, *adj.* Mar chat.
FELL, *adj.* Borb, fiadhaich, allaidh garg, allamhara.
FELL, *s.* Seiche, bian, craiceann.
FELL, *v.a.* Leag gu làr, buail sìos, spad, smàil; gèarr sìos, mar chraoibh.
FELLMONGER, *s.* Ceannaiche-bhoiceann.
FELLOW, *s.* Companach, coimpire; lethbhreac; gille; dubh-bhalach.
FELLOW, *v. a.* Càraidich, paidhrich.
FELLOWSHIP, *s.* Companas, compantas, comunn, co-bhann, caidreamh.
FELO-DE-SE, *s.* Féin-mhortair.
FELON, *s.* Slaoightear.
FELONIOUS, *adj.* Aingidh, fealltach, olc, ciontach.
FELONY, *s.* Coire bàis.
FELT, *s.* Aodach gaoisideach; bian.
FELUCCA, *s.* Bàta sè-ràmhach.
FEMALE, *s.* Bean, boireannach, bainionnach, té.
FEMALE, *adj.* Boireann, bainionn.
FEMINALITY, *s.* Nàdur nam ban.
FEMININE, *adj.* Boireann, bainionnach; caomh, bog, maoth, mìn, màlda.
FEMORAL, *adj.* Sléisneach, màsach.
FEN, *s.* Boglach, càthar, mòinteach.
FENCE, *s.* Dìon, callaid, dìg, daingneach, bàbhunn.
FENCE, *v.* Dùin, iomadhruid, cuairtich.
FENCELESS, *adj.* Gun challaid, fosgailte.
FENCER, *s.* Basbair, cliaranach.
FENCIBLE, *adj.* So-dhion.
FENCING, *s.* Basbaireachd, cliaranachd.
FEND, *v.* Dìon, cum dhìot; connsaich; tagair.
FENDER, *s.* Dìonadair.
FENNEL, *s.* Lus-an-t-saoidh.
FENNY, *adj.* Mòinteachail, bog.
FEOFF, *v. a.* Cuir an seilbh fuinn.
FEOFFMENT, *s.* Cur an seilbh.
FERINE, *adj.* Fiadhaich, garg.
FERINENESS, FERITY, *s.* Gairge, buirbe, allamharrachd, fiadhaichead.
FERMENT, *v. a.* Cuir fo bhuaireas, tog an àirde; bi fo bhuaireas, oibrich.
FERMENT, *s.* Buaireas, mi-riaghailt, oibreachadh, troi'-chéile.
FERMENTATION, *s.* Buaireas, oibreachadh.
FERN, *s.* Raineach, rŏineach.
FERNY, *adj.* Raineachail, làn rŏinich.
FEROCIOUS, *adj.* Fiadhaich, garg, allamharra, an-iochdmhor.
FEROCITY, *s.* Fiadhaichead, gairge, buirbe, an-iochd.
FERRET, *s.* Feòcullan, coinneas; stìom.
FERRET, *v. a.* Cuir á toll.
FERRIAGE, *s.* Faradh, airgead-aisig.
FERRUGINOUS, *adj.* Do ghné iaruinn.
FERRY, *v.* Aisig; rach thar aiseag.
FERRY, *s.* Aiseag.
FERRYMAN, *s.* Fear-aiseig, portair.
FERTILE, *adj.* Torach, sìolmhor, biadhchar, pailt, lìonmhor.
FERTILITY, *s.* Sìolmhoireachd, tarbhachd, toraicheas.
FERTILIZE, *v. a.* Dean torach, dean sìolmhor, leasaich, mathaich.
FERULA, *s.* Slat-sgiùrsaidh, sgiùrs.

Fervency, *s.* Dealas, teas-inntinn, dian-thogradh, dĕine, beò-dhùrachd.
Fervent, *adj.* Teth, air ghoil; dian, bras, cas, dealasach; dùrachdach, blàth.
Fervid, *adj.* Teth, air ghoil, loisgeach; bras, dian, dealasach, deòthasach.
Fervidness, *s.* Dĕine, braise, dealas, deòthas.
Fervour, *s.* Teas, blàthas; teas inntinn, dealas, dĕine, beò-dhùrachd.
Festal, *adj.* Cuirmeach, fleadhach.
Fester, *v. n.* Eargnaich, at, iongraich.
Festival, *s.* Fĕill, cuirm-bhliadhnail.
Festive, *adj.* Fleadhach, cuirmeach, fĕisdeach, aoibhneach.
Festivity, *s.* Aoibhneas, aighear, subhachas, gàirdeachas.
Fetch, *v. a.* Thoir leat, thoir an so.
Fetch, *s.* Innleachd, seòl, car, cleas.
Fetid, *adj.* Breun, lobhte, grod.
Fetlock, *s.* Luidhean, fiarag.
Fetor, *s.* Droch bholadh, droch thòchd.
Fetter, *s.* Cuibhreach, geimheal.
Fetter, *v. a.* Geimhlich, cuibhrich.
Fetus, **Fœtus**, *s.* Ceud-fhàs.
Feu, *s.* Gabhail, gabhaltas.
Feud, *s.* Aimhreit, strì, eas-aonachd, connsachadh, falachd, cogadh.
Feudal, *adj.* A bhuineas do shuidheachadh fearainn.
Feudatory, *s.* Gabhaltaiche.
Fever, *s.* Fiabhras, cuartach, teasach.
Feverish, **Feverous**, **Fevery**, *adj.* Fiabhrasach, teth, loisgeach; mùiteach, neo-shuidhichte.
Few, *adj.* Tearc, ainneamh, gann.
Fewness, *s.* Teircead, gainnead.
Fiat, *s.* Breitheanas, binn.
Fib, *s.* Breug, frìth-bhreug.
Fib, *v. n.* Innis breugan.
Fibber, *s.* Breugaire.
Fibre, *s.* Freumh chaol, teudag,
Fibula, *s.* Cnàimh-caol na lurga.
Fickle, *adj.* Caochlaideach, mùiteach, luasganach, luaineach, neo-shuidhichte, neo bhunailteach.
Fickleness, *s.* Caochlaideachd, mùiteachd, luasganachd, neo-bhunailteachd, neo-sheasmhachd.
Fiction, *s.* Naigheachd breugach; uirsgeul, sgeulachd.
Fictitious, **Fictitiously**, *adj.* Feallsach, mealltach, faoin, breugach.
Fiddle, *s.* Fiodhall.
Fiddle, *v. a.* Dean fidhleireachd; bi diomhanach.
Fiddlefaddle, *s.* Babhdaire, beagseadh, faoineis.
Fiddler, *s.* Fìdhleir.
Fiddle-string, *s.* Teud fìdhle.
Fidelity, *s.* Trĕidhireas, fìrinn; dìlseachd, seasmhachd.
Fidget, *v. n.* Dean iomairt, bi luasganach.
Fie, *interj.* Ud! ud! mo nàire!
Fief, *s.* Gabhail fhearainn; fo-uachdaran.
Field, *s.* Machair, raon, achadh, faiche, màgh; blàr, farsuinneachd.
Fieldfare, *s.* An liathtruisg.
Field-piece, *s.* Gunn'-àraich.
Fiend, *s.* Diabhol, deamhan.
Fierce, *adj.* Fiadhaich, droch-mheinneach, feargach, garg, borb, buaireasach; laidir, treun.
Fierceness, *s.* Fiadhaichead, buirbe, gairge, buaireas, guinideachd, fuilteachd; ainteas, teinntidheachd; braise, buaireas.
Fiery, *adj.* Teinnteach, lasarra, loisgeach; dian, bras, cabhagach; feargach, frionasach, garg, droch-mheinneach; dealrach, soillseach.
Fife, *s.* Fìdeag-Ghallda.
Fifer, *s.* Fear-fìdeig.
Fifteen, *adj.* Cùig-deug.
Fifth, *adj.* Cùigeadh.
Fifthly, *adv.* 'S a chuigeadh àite.
Fifty, *adj.* Caogad, leth-cheud.
Fig, *s.* Fìgis, crann-fìge.
Fight, *s.* Cath, còmhrag; caonnag, tuasaid, sabaid.
Fighter, *s.* Curaidh, gaisgeach, fearcòmhraig, fear sabaideach.
Figurable, *adj.* A ghabhas cumadh, a ghabhas dealbh.
Figurative, *adj.* Samhlachail.
Figure, *s.* Dealbh, cumadh, dreach, cruth; pearsa, aogas, coltas, samhla.
Figure, *v. a.* Cum, dreach, dealbh; dean eug-samhail; samhlaich; smuainich.
Figwort, *s.* Am farach-dubh.
Filament, *s.* Sreang chaol, toinntean.
Filbert, *s.* Cnò, faoisgeag.
Filch, *v. a.* Goid, slad, dean mĕirle.
File, *s.* Eighe, lìomhan; ainm-chlar.
Filial, *adj.* Macail, dleasanach.
Filiation, *s.* Dàimh mic ri athair.
Filings, *s.* Smùrach ĕighe.
Fill, *v. a.* Lìon, luchdaich; sàsaich, dean buidheach; fàs làn.
Fill, *s.* Làn, sàth, leoir, teann-shàth.
Fillet, *s.* Stìom, crios; tiugh na slĕisde.

FILLET, *v. a.* Ceangail le stìom, cuir crios air, cuir cuairteag uime.
FILLIP, *v. a.* Thoir cliùdan.
FILLIP, *s.* Spadag, cliùdan.
FILLY, *s.* Loth, lothag.
FILM, *s.* Sgrath, sgannan, sgàilean.
FILMY, *adj.* Sgrathach, sgàileanach.
FILTER, *v. a.* Sìolaidh.
FILTER, *s.* Sìolachan.
FILTH, *s.* Salchar, anabas, druaip.
FILTHY, *adj.* Salach, musach, drabhasach; neo-ghlan, truaillidh.
FILTRATE, *v. a.* Sìolaidh.
FILTRATION, *s.* Sìoladh, glanadh.
FIN, *s.* Iteach éisg, ite, sgiath.
FINABLE, *adj.* Airidh air ùbhladh.
FINAL, *adj.* Deireannach.
FINANCE, *s.* Teachd a steach, màl, cìs, càin.
FINANCIER, *s.* Fear trusaidh cìs rìgh.
FIND, *v. a.* Faigh; tachair air; faigh a mach, amais, fairich, aithnich; co-dhùin; cum suas, beathaich.
FINE, *adj.* Grinn, fìnealta, caol; glan, fìor ghlan, soilleir; geur, tana.
FINE, *s.* Ùbhladh, peanas.
FINE, *v. a.* Glan, ath-ghlan; dean fìnealta; leag ùbhladh.
FINENESS, *s.* Grinnead, fìnealtachd, grinneas, bòidhchead, maise; mìnead, caoilead.
FINERY, *s.* Breaghachd, rìmheadh.
FINESSE, *s.* Càr, cleas, cealg.
FINGER, *s.* Meur, corrag.
FINGER, *v. a.* Meuraich, laimhsich.
FINICAL, *adj.* Moiteil, cùirteil, grinn, gogaideach, leòmach, aralach.
FINING-POT, *s.* Suacan-leaghaidh.
FINISH, *s.* A' Chrìoch, am foircheann.
FINISH, *v. a.* Crìochnaich; co-lion.
FINISHER, *s.* Fear-crìochnachaidh.
FINITE, *adj.* Crìochnach, crìochnaichte.
FINITELESS, *adj.* Neo-chrìochnach.
FINNY, *adj.* Iteach.
FIR, *s.* Giubhas, no ghiuthas.
FIRE, *s.* Teine, teas, ainteas.
FIRE, *v.* Cuir ri theine, loisg; fadaidh, beothaich, bruidich; tilg.
FIRE-ARMS, *s.* Airm-theine.
FIREBRAND, *s.* Aithinne; brathadair.
FIRE-CROSS, *s.* Crois-tàra, crann-tàra.
FIRELOCK, *s.* Gunna, musgaid.
FIREMAN, *s.* Fear-casgaidh teine.
FIREPAN, *s.* Aoghan-theine.
FIRING, *s.* Connadh, gual, mòine.
FIRKIN, *s.* Buideal naoi galoin.
FIRM, *adj.* Daingeann, làidir, teann; seasmhach, diongmhalta, bunailteach, neo-ghluasadach.
FIRMAMENT, *s.* Speur, iarmailt, adhar.
FIRMAMENTAL, *adj.* Iarmailteach, adharach, speurach, neamhaidh.
FIRMNESS, *s.* Daingneachd, greimealas; maireannachd, seasmhachd, cinnteas, diongmhaltas, bunailteachd.
FIRST, *adj.* Ceud, ceudamh; an tùs, an toiseach; prìomh.
FIRST, *adv.* An tùs, air toiseach, roimh; ann sa' cheud àite.
FIRST-FRUITS, *s.* Ceud-thoradh.
FIRSTLING, *s.* Ceud-ghin; no ceud-fhàs.
FISCAL, *s.* Ionmhas, tighinn a stigh rìoghachd.
FISH, *s.* Iasg; *gen.* éisg.
FISH, *v.* Iasgaich; bi 'g iasgach.
FISHER, FISHERMAN, *s.* Iasgair.
FISHERY, *s.* Iasgach.
FISH-HOOK, *s.* Dubhan iasgaich.
FISHING, *s.* Iasgaireachd.
FISHMEAL, *s.* Tràth bìdh de dh' iasg.
FISHMONGER, *s.* Còpair.
FISHY, *adj.* Mar iasg.
FISSILE, *adj.* Sgoilteach, so-sgoltadh.
FISSURE, *s.* Sgoltadh, sgàineadh, gàg.
FIST, *s.* Dòrn.
FIT, *adj.* Iomchuidh, freagarrach.
FIT, *v.* Dean freagarrach, dean iomchuidh; cuir an uidheam, cuir an òrdugh, ceartaich.
FITCH, *s.* Peasair-luch.
FITCHAT, FITCHEW, *s.* Feòcullan.
FITFUL, *adj.* Làn ghreisean, plathach.
FITNESS, *s.* Freagarrachd, deisealachd.
FIVE, *adj.* Cùig, còig.
FIVEFOLD, *adj.* Cùig-fillte.
FIVES, *s.* An galair-greidh.
FIX, *v.* Suidhich, socraich, daingnich, dean teann, spàrr; beachdaich; gabh gu fois.
FIXATION, FIXEDNESS, *s.* Suidheachadh, maireachduinn, seasmhachd; daingneach, dùiread; bunailteachd, diongmhaltachd.
FIXTURE, *s.* Ni tàirngte, no ceangailte.
FIZGIG, *s.* Seòrsa mòr-ghath.
FLABBY, *adj.* Bog, maoth; plamcaidh, neo-ghramail.
FLACCID, *adj.* Lag, tais, anfhann, maoth, so-lubaidh.
FLACCIDITY, *s.* Anfhainne, laigse.
FLAG, *v. a.* Fannaich, lagaich; caill treòir, fàs lag.
FLAG, *s.* Seileasdair; bratach; leac.
FLAGELET, *s.* Gall-fheadan.
FLAGELLATION, *s.* Sgiùrsadh.
FLAGGY, *adj.* Lag, anfhann, fuasgailte.

Flagitious, *adj.* Aingidh, droch-mhuint, olc, ciontach.
Flagitiousness, *s.* Aingidheachd.
Flagon, *s.* Cuinneag dhibhe.
Flagrancy, *s.* Teas, ainteas.
Flagrant, *adj.* Teth, deòthasach, dùrachdach, dealasach; follaiseach, soilleir, anabarra, fuathasach, amasgaidh.
Flagship, *s.* Long an aird-cheannaird.
Flail, *s.* Sùiste, uideal.
Flake, *s.* Lòineag, tlàm, toban; breath.
Flaky, *adj.* Lòineagach, tlàmach, fuasgailte; 'na bhreathan.
Flame, *s.* Lasair; teas-inntinn, déine.
Flambeau, *s.* Dòrn-leus céire.
Flamen, *s.* Sagart pàganach.
Flammability, *s.* Lasantachd.
Flammation, *s.* Lasadh, losgadh.
Flammiferous, *adj.* Lasrach, loisg-each.
Flamy, *adj.* Lasrach, lasanta.
Flank, *s.* Slios, loch-bhléin, taobh.
Flannel, *s.* Cùrainn-chneas.
Flap, *s.* Libeag, bad air chrathadh, clib, clìbeag, cliban.
Flap, *v.* Buail air falbh; crath.
Flap-eared, *adj.* Spad-chluasach.
Flare, *v. a.* Dealraich, dèarrs, boillsg.
Flash, *s.* Boillsgeadh, dreòs, dèars-adh, lasadh; caoir, plathadh.
Flash, *v.* Deàlraich, dèarrs, boillsg.
Flash, *a.* Spaideil, rimheach.
Flask, *s.* Adharc-fhùdair, searrag-pòcaid.
Flat, *adj.* Còmhnard, réidh, mìn; ìosal, sìnte, leagte gu làr; cianail, neo-chridheil, neo-smiorail; 'as an aghaidh.
Flat, *s.* Còmhnard, réidhlean, lòn, fàn, fearann iosal, lom.
Flatness, *s.* Còmhnardachd, réidh-eachd; marbhantachd, neo-bhrisg-ead, neo-smioralachd; neo-fhonn-mhorachd, dùrantachd.
Flatten, *v.* Dean còmhnard, dean réidh; leag sios, leudaich, dean leath-ann; mi-mhisnich, cuir fo sproc.
Flatter, *v. a.* Dean miodal, dean sodal, mol gu breugach.
Flatterer, *s.* Miodalaich, sodalaich.
Flattery, *s.* Miodal, sodal, miolasg, gabhann, brosgul.
Flattish, *adj.* Còmhnard, staoin.
Flatulency, *s.* Gaothmhorachd; falamhachd, faoineachd, diomhanas.
Flatulent, **Flatuous**, *adj.* Gaoth-mhor, atmhor, falamh, faoin, gaoth-ach.
Flaunt, *s.* Basdal, lòiseam.
Flavour, *s.* Blàs, bòladh cùbhraidh.
Flavorous, *adj.* Blasda; cùbhraidh.
Flaw, *s.* Gaoid, sgàineadh, sgoltadh; ciorram, coire, meang.
Flax, *s.* Lìon, cuiseag-anairt.
Flax-dresser, *s.* Seiclear-lìn.
Flaxen, *adj.* De lìon, lìn; fada réidh.
Flay, *v. a.* Feann, faobhaich.
Flea, *s.* Deargann.
Fleam, *s.* Cuisleag cruidh, tuadh-fhala.
Fledge, *adj.* Iteagach, sgiathach.
Flee, *v. n.* Teich, ruith, tàr ás.
Fleece, *s.* Rùsg, lomradh.
Fleece, *v. a.* Rùisg, lomair; creach.
Fleeced, *part.* Ruiste, creachte.
Fleecy, *adj.* Clòimheach, rùsgach.
Fleer, *v. n.* Mag, sgeig, fochaidich.
Fleer, *s.* Fochaid, magadh, sgeig, fanaid; gàire fanaid, dréin fhochaid.
Fleet, *s.* Cabhlach, loingeas.
Fleet, *adj.* Luath, siùbhlach, clis.
Fleet, *v. n.* Siubhail grad.
Fleeting, *adj.* Siùbhlach, diombuan.
Fleetness, *s.* Luathas, siùbhlachd.
Flesh, *s.* Feòil.
Fleshly, *adv.* Gu corporra, feòlmhor.
Fleshy, *adj.* Feòlmhor, reamhar, sultmhor, làn.
Fletcher, *s.* Leistear, fear dheanamh shaighead.
Flew, *pret.* of *to fly*. Dh'itealaich.
Flewed, *adj.* Spreilleach, craosach.
Flexibility, *s.* Sùbailteachd.
Flexible, **Flexile**, *adj.* Sùbailte, so-lùbadh; so-chomhairleach.
Flexion, *s.* Cromadh, lùbadh, cam-adh.
Flexuous, *adj.* Lùbach, cam, crom.
Flexure, *s.* Fiaradh, camadh, crom-adh, claonadh.
Flight, *s.* Teicheadh, ruaig; iteal-aich, falbh air sgiathan; teas-inntinn, àrd-smuain; ealtainn.
Flighty, *adj.* Fiadhaich, luaineach, neo-shuidhichte, neo-bhunailteach, macmeanmnach.
Flimsy, *adj.* Lag, faoin, neo-ghramail, anfhann, neo-sgoinneil, cearbach.
Flinch, *v. n.* Sèap, fannaich, crup.
Flincher, *s.* Cladhaire, gealtaire.
Fling, *v.* Tilg, thoir urchair; sgap, sgaoil, crath; fas neo-cheannsaichte.
Fling, *s.* Tilgeadh, urchair; fochaid, innisg, anaisg, beum-tàire.
Flint, *s.* Ailbhinn, spor, airtein.
Flinty, *adj.* Ailbhinneach, clachach.
Flippancy, *s.* Beulchaireachd, leóg-aireachd.

Flippant, *adj.* Luath-bheulach bruidhneach; gobach, peasanach, beagnarach, beadaidh.

Flirt, *v.* Tilg, thoir urchair ghrad; dean gobaireachd.

Flirt, *s.* Grad-char, lù-chleas, bladhm; gòdag, gogaid, goileag, leòdag.

Flirtation, *s.* Gogaideachd, beadradh.

Flit, *v.* Cuir imrich; rach imrich.

Flitch, *s.* Cliathach shaillte muice.

Flitter, *s.* Giobal, broineag, lùireach.

Float, *v.* Snàmh, bi air fleodradh.

Flock, *s.* Greigh; treud, ealt, ealta.

Flock, *v. n.* Trus, tionail, cruinnich.

Flood, *s.* Tuil, dìle; lìonadh.

Flood, *v. a.* Còmhdaich le uisge.

Floodgate. *s.* Tuil-dhorus.

Floodmark, *s.* Àirde làin mhara; dubh-chladach.

Flook, or **Fliuke**, *s.* Soc acrach; lèabag, leobag, liabag.

Floor, *s.* Ùrlar, làr.

Floor, *v. a.* Cuir ùrlar ann.

Flooring, *s.* Ùrlar, fiodh-ùrlair.

Floral, *adj.* Lusach, flùranach.

Florid, *adj.* Lusach, flùranach; ùrail, ruiteagach; sgiamhach.

Floridness, *s.* Ruiteachas, deirge.

Florist, *s.* Lusragan.

Flounce, *v.* Sgiot, spairt; siubhail le sraon ann an uisg.

Flounce, *s.* Froinis; plub, sgiotadh.

Flounder, *s.* Leòbag, lèabag, liabag.

Flounder, *v. n.* Dean spàirn.

Flour, *s.* Min-chruineachd, mhìn.

Flourish, *v.* Cuir fo bhlàth; crath gu fraoidhneasach; fas suas, soirbhich; bi àrd-ghlòireach, dean spagluinn, dean uaill.

Flourish, *s.* Mòrachd, maise, glòir, uaill, bòsd; blàth, ùr-fhàs, duilleachadh; fuaim thrompaidean.

Flout, *v.* Sgeig, mag, fochaidich; dean fochaid, dean fanaid.

Flout, *s.* Magadh, tàir, fanaid.

Flow, *v.* Ruith, sil; éirich, ăt; bi pailt, bi sgaoilteach.

Flow, *s.* Lìonadh, éiridh, sruth, tuil; pailteas, lànachd; ard-ghlòir, deas-chainnt.

Flower, *s.* Blàth, ùr-fhàs; a chuid a's fèarr, brod.

Flower-de-luce, *s.* Seileasdair.

Floweret, **Flowret**, *s.* Flùran, plùran.

Flowery, *adj.* Flùranach, gucagach.

Fluctuant, *adj.* Luaineach, neo-shuidhichte, luasganach, neo-bhunailteach.

Fluctuate, *v. n.* Bi air udail, luaisg, tulg; bi neo-sheasmhach, bi 's an ioma-chomhairle.

Fluctuation, *s.* Udal, luasgadh, tulgadh; ioma-chomhairle, ima-cheist; crathadh, luasgadh, tilgeadh a nùll 's a nall.

Flue, *s.* Piob-deataich, sòrn.

Fluency, *adj.* Ùr-labhairt, réidheachd, sruthadh, deas-chainnt.

Fluent, *adj.* Sruthach, silteach, leaghach; a' gluasad, ruitheach; deas-labhrach, réidh am bruidhinn.

Fluid, *adj.* Uisgidh, sruthach, leaghach.

Fluid, *s.* Uisge, staid uisge.

Fluidity, *s.* Uisgealachd, tanachd.

Flummery, *s.* Làgan; brosgul.

Flurry, *s.* Cabhag, othail; osag.

Flush, *v. a.* Cuir rughadh ann, dean ruiteach; fàs dearg.

Flush, *s.* Bladhmadh, dian-ghluasad.

Fluster, *v. a.* Cuir sogan air; cuir 'na chabhaig.

Flute, *s.* Duiseal, feadan.

Flutter, *v.* Dean itealaich.

Flutter, *s.* Udal, tulgadh, luasgan, crathadh; cabhag, troimhe chéile; eacharais.

Flux, *s.* Sruthadh, ruith, siubhal, dol seachad, dol air falbh; a' ghèarrach, lionadh, trusadh.

Flux, *adj.* Neo-sheasmhach, siùbhlach.

Fluxion, *s.* Sruthadh, sileadh, siubhal; sruth.

Fly, *v.* Seachain, teich, tréig, leig dhìot, fàg, dìobair, cuir cùl ri; falbh air iteig.

Fly, *s.* Cuileag; roth; carbad faraidh.

Flyingfish, *s.* Iasg-sgiathach.

Foal, *s.* Searrach.

Foam, *s.* Cop, cobhar.

Foam, *v. n.* Cuir cop dhiot; bi feargach.

Foamy, *adj.* Cobharach, copach.

Fob, *s.* Pòcait bheag.

Focus, *s.* Buillsgean.

Fodder, *s.* Fodar, conlach, innlinn.

Foe, *s.* Nàmhaid, nàmh; eas-caraid.

Foetus, **Fetus**, *s.* Ceud-fhàs.

Fog, *s.* Ceò, ceathach; ath-bharr feòir.

Foggy, *adj.* Neulach, ceòthach.

Foible, *s.* Fàillinn, beag-chionta.

Foil, *v. a.* Ruaig, gabh air, faigh làmh an uachdar, fairtlich, claoidh.

Foil, *s.* Ruaig, fairtleachadh, claoidh; dealtradh, òradh; claidheamh-maol.

Foin, *s.* Sàthadh, buille-thuige.

Fold, *s.* Mainnir, fang, buaile, crò; treud, buar; filleadh, pleat.
Fold, *v.a.* Fangaich, cuir am mainnir; fill, paisg, cuir dà fhilt.
Foliage, *s.* Duilleach, duilleagan.
Foliate, *adj.* Duilleagach.
Foliate, *v. a.* Dean 'na dhuilleagan.
Foliation, *s.* Blàth chuairteag.
Folio, *s.* Leabhar nan duilleag a's mò.
Folk, *s.* Muinntir, sluagh, pobull.
Follow, *v.* Lean, ruag; thig an lorg; géill; thig 'na dhéigh.
Follower, *s.* Fear-leanmhuinn.
Folly, *s.* Amaideachd, gòraich.
Foment, *v. a.* Blàthaich, teòth; nigh; bruidich, brosnaich, misnich.
Fomentation, *s.* Bruideachadh.
Fon, *s.* Amadan, amhlar.
Fond, *adj.* Amaideach, beadarrach, deòthasach; déidheil.
Fond, **Fondle**, *v.* Tataidh; gràdhaich, cniadaich.
Fondling, *s.* Annsachd, luaidh.
Fondness, *s.* Déidh; gràdh, gaol.
Font, *s.* Tobar-baistidh.
Food, *s.* Biadh, lòn, teachd-an-tìr.
Fool, *s.* Amadan, burraidh, baothaire.
Fool, *v.* Dean amadan deth, meall, thoir a chreidsinn air, thoir an car á; cluich, caith aimsir.
Foolery, *s.* Amaideachd; gòraich.
Foolhardy, *adj.* Dàna, mi-chiallach.
Foolish, *adj.* Gòrach, amaideach.
Foolishness, *s.* Amaideachd, gòraich.
Foot, *s.* Cas, troidh; bun, bonn.
Foot, *v.* Imich, coisich; damhs.
Football, *s.* Ball-coise, ball-iomain.
Footboy, *s.* Gille-ruith, gille-coise.
Footing, *s.* Àite-seasaimh, bunait, suidheachadh, stéidh, seilbh; staid, còr.
Footman, *s.* Gille duin'-uasail.
Footpad, *s.* Spùinneadair rathaidmhòir,
Footpath, *s.* Rathad-coise.
Footstep, *s.* Lorg coise; cas-cheum.
Fop, *s.* Spailpean, lasgaire, gaoithean.
Foppery, *s.* Amaideachd, spailpeis.
Foppish, *adj.* Amaideach, gòrach; spailleiceil, spailpeil, farumach.
Foppishness, *s.* Spailleic, spailpeis.
For, *prep.* Air son, a chionn, do bhrìgh, a thaobh; air sgàth; fa chomhair; air taobh; a dh' ionnsaidh.
Forage, *v.* Spùill, creach; solair.
Forage, *s.* Biadh, lòn, innlinn.
Forasmuch, *conj.* A chionn, do-bhrìgh a thaobh; air sgàth.
Forbear, *v.* Seachain, ob; giùlain le, caomhain, fuilig, leig le; sguir; dean maille; caisg.
Forbearance, *s.* Seachnadh, obadh leigeadh seachad, sgur, stad; fadfhulangas, deagh-mhèin; caomhalachd, bàigh.
Forbid, *v.* Toirmisg; caisg, cùm air ais.
Forbidden, *part.* Toirmisgte.
Forbidding, *part. adj.* Sgreataidh.
Force, *s.* Neart, spionnadh; ainneart; éifeachd, tàbhachd, feart, brìgh; armailt, feachd.
Force, *v.* Co-éignich, thoir a dh' aindeoin; gnàthaich ainneart; spàrr, teannaich.
Forceps, *s.* Turcais, clobha-léigh.
Forcible, *adj.* Laidir, neartmhor; éifeachdach, tàbhachdach, brìoghmhor; aindeonach, éigneach.
Ford, *s.* Àth, faoghail.
Ford, *v. a.* Coisich tre abhainn.
Fordable, *adj.* Tana, eu-domhain.
Fore, *adj.* Air tùs, air toiseach, roimhe.
Forebode, *v.n.* Innis roi'-làimh, roi'-innis, cuir air mhanadh, fàisnich, roi'-aithnich.
Forecast, *v.* Dealbh, tionnsgain; uidheamaich; suidhich ìnnleachd.
Forecast, *s.* Uidheamachadh, deasachadh, seòladh. ìnnleachd, dealbh, tionnsgal.
Forecastle, *s.* Toiseach luinge.
Forecited, *part.* Roi'-ainmichte.
Foreclose, *v. a.* Dùin, druid a stigh.
Foredo, *v. a.* Creach, claoidh.
Foredoom, *v. a.* Roi'-òrduich roi'-shuidhich.
Forefather, **Foregoer**, *s.* Priomhathair, seanair, sinnsear.
Forefront, *s.* Clàr-aghaidh.
Forego, *v. a.* Dealaich, cuir dhìot, cuitich, tréig, fàg, dìobair.
Foreground, *s.* Réidhlean; beulthaobh.
Forehand, *adj.* Roi'-làimh.
Forehead, *s.* Clar-aodainn, bathais.
Foreign, *adj.* Gallda, coimheach.
Foreigner, *s.* Gall, coimheach, allmharach, coigreach, eilthireach, deòra.
Forejudge, *v. a.* Roi'-bhreithnich.
Foreknow, *v. a.* Roi'-aithnich.
Foreknowledge, *s.* Roi'-fhiosrachadh.
Foreland, *s.* Rudha, roinn, àird, sròn.
Forelock, *s.* Dosan, ciabhag.
Foreman, *s.* Fear-amhairc-thairis.

Foremast, *s.* Crann toisich.
Forementioned, *adj.* Roi'-luaighte.
Foremost, *adj.* Prìomh, air thoiseach.
Forenamed, *adj.* Roi'-ainmichte.
Forenoon, *s.* Roi' mheadhon latha.
Forensic, *adj.* A bhuineas do mhòd lagha.
Foreordain, *v. a.* Roi'-òrduich.
Forepart, *s.* Toiseach, aghaidh.
Forerunner, *s.* Roi'-ruithear.
Foresay, *v. a.* Roi'-innis.
Foresail, *s.* Seol-toisich.
Foresee, *v. a.* Faic roi' làimh.
Foresight, *s.* Roi'-shealladh.
Forest, *s.* Frìdh, coille, fàsach.
Forestall, *v. a.* Ceannaich roi' làimh.
Forestaller, *s.* Fear-millidh margaidh.
Forester, *s.* Peathair, forsair.
Foretaste, *s.* Roi'-bhlasad.
Foretell, *v.* Roi'-innis, fàisnich.
Forethink. *v. a.* Roi'-smaoinich.
Forethought, *s.* Roi'-smuain.
Foretoken, *s.* Comharradh, sanas.
Foretop, *s.* Dŏs-mullaich, cìrean.
Foreward, *s.* Toiseach, aghaidh.
Forewarn, *v. a.* Cuir air earalas.
Forfeit, *s.* Ùbhladh.
Forfeiture, *s.* Arbhartachadh.
Forge, *s.* Ceardach, teallach.
Forge, *v. a.* Cùm, dealbh, dean goibhneachd; dealbh gu feallsa.
Forgery, *s*, Dealbhadh mealltach.
Forget, *v. a.* Dì-chuimhnich, dearmaid.
Forgetful, *adj.* Dì-chuimhneach.
Forgetfulness, *s.* Dì-chuimhne.
Forgive, *v. a.* Math, thoir mathanas.
Forgiveness, *s.* Mathanas.
Forgotten, *part.* Dì-chuimhnichte.
Fork, *s.* Gobhal, gobhlag.
Fork, *v. n.* Fàs gobhlach, cuir a mach dias.
Forked, **Forky**, *adj.* Gòbhlach.
Forktailed, *adj.* Earra-ghobhlach.
Forlorn, *adj.* Aonaranach, truagh.
Form, *s.* Cumadh, dreach, dealbh, cruth, aogas, riochd, dòigh; fasan, cleachdadh, modh, nŏs, seŏl, àitesuidhe; buidhean.
Form, *v. a.* Cruthaich, dealbh, cùm.
Formal, *adj.* Riaghailteach, dòigheil.
Formality, *s.* Deas-ghnàth, modh, dòigh; òrdugh, puncalachd.
Formation, *s.* Cumadh, dealbh.
Former, *adj.* Roi'; roi'-ainmichte; a chaidh seachad.
Formidable, *adj.* Eagalach, uabhasach, fuathasach, cunnartach, deacair.
Formless, *adj.* Gun dealbh, gun chruth.
Formula, *s.* Riaghailt shuidhichte.
Fornicate, *v. n.* Dean strìopachas.
Fornication, *s.* Strìopachas.
Fornicator, *s.* Fear-strìopachais.
Fornicatress, *s.* Strìopach, siùrsach.
Forsake, *v. a.* Trèig, cuir cùl ri.
Forsaken, *part.* Trèigte.
Forsooth, *adv.* Gu dearbh.
Forswear, *v.* Cuir cùl ri fo mhionnaibh; thoir mionnan-eithich.
Fort, *s.* Daingneach, dùn, dìdean.
Forth, *adv.* O so suas; air aghart.
Forthcoming, *part.* Ullamh gu teachd a làthair.
Forthwith, *adv.* Gun dàil, gun mhaille.
Fortieth, *adj.* Dà fhicheadamh.
Fortifiable, *adj.* So-dhìonadh.
Fortification, *s.* Eòlas-daingneachd; daighneach, dìdean, dìon.
Fortify, *v. a.* Dìon, daingnich; neartaich, dean làidir; misnich.
Fortilage, **Fortin**, **Fortlet**, *s.* Daingneach beag.
Fortitude, *s.* Misneach, cruadal.
Fortnight, *s.* Ceithir-latha-deug
Fortress, *s.* Daingneach, dìdean.
Fortuitous, *adj.* Tuiteamach.
Fortuitousness, *s.* Tuiteamas.
Fortunate, *adj.* Sona, seamhsail.
Fortune, *s.* Sealbh, àgh; crannchur; oighreachd, saibhreas; tochradh.
Fortunehunter, *s.* Fear-tòir air tochradh.
Fortuneteller, *s.* Fiosaiche, dearnadair.
Forty, *adj.* Dà fhichead.
Forum, *s.* Taigh-coinneamh.
Forward, *adj.* Dian, dùrachdach, iarrtach; dealasach teth, cas, bras; obann, ceann-laidir, beadaidh; luath, tràthail; grad, ealamh, cabhagach.
Forward, *v. a.* Greas, cuir air aghart.
Forwardness, *s.* Togarrachd, dèine, braise, dùrachd; tràthalachd, ladornas.
Foss, *s.* Dìg, clais.
Fossil, *adj.* Tochailteach.
Fossil, *s.* Tochailt.
Foster, *v. a.* Altrum, àraich, beathaich, àlaich, tog suas.
Fosterage, *s.* Altrum, togail, àrach.
Fosterbrother, *s.* Co-dhalta.
Fosterchild, **Fosterling**, *s.* Dalta.
Fought, *pret.* and *part.* of *to fight.* Bhuail, buailte.

FOUL, *adj.* Salach, mosach, neo-ghlan, truaillidh; grâineil, déisinneach; duaichnidh; drabhasach.

FOUL, *v. a.* Salaich, duaichnich.

FOULNESS, *s.* Salchar, mosaiche; truailleachd, grâinealachd; déisinn, gràinde.

FOUND, *pret.* and *part.* of *to find.*

FOUND, *v. a.* Stéidhich, suidhich; tog suas; socraich; tilg, leagh.

FOUNDATION, *s.* Stéidh, bunait.

FOUNDER, *s.* Fear-suidheachaidh airgeid; leaghadair.

FOUNDER, *v.* Dean crùbach; theirig fodha.

FOUNDERY, FOUNDRY, *s.* Taigh-leaghaidh.

FOUNDLING, *s.* Faodailiche, faodalach.

FOUNT, FOUNTAIN, *s.* Tobar, fuaran; màthair-uisge, mathair-aobhair, toiseach, tùs, bun.

FOUNTFUL, *adj.* Fuaranach.

FOUR, *adj.* Ceithir.

FOURFOLD, *adj.* Ceithir-fillte.

FOURFOOTED, *adj.* Ceithir-chasach.

FOURSCORE, *adj.* Ceithir-fichead.

FOURTEEN, *adj.* Ceithir-deug.

FOURTEENTH, *adj.* Ceathramh-deug.

FOURTH, *adj.* Ceathramh.

FOURTHLY, *adv.* 'S a' cheathramh àite.

FOWL, *s.* Eun, ian.

FOWLER, *s.* Eunadair.

FOWLING, *s.* Eunach.

FOWLING-PIECE, *s.* Gunn'-eunaich.

EOX, *s.* Sionnach, madadh-ruadh.

FOXCASE, *s.* Bian sionnaich.

FOXGLOVE, *s.* Lùs-nam-ban-sìth.

FOXHOUND, *s.* Gadhar-sionnaich.

FOXHUNTER, *s.* Brocair.

FRACTION, *s.* Bristeadh, mìr, bloigh.

FRACTIONAL, *adj.* Bristeach.

FRACTIOUS, *adj.* Crosda, càs.

FRACTURE, *s.* Bristeadh.

FRACTURE, *v. a.* Bris, bloighdich.

FRAGILE, *adj.* Brisg, bristeach, lag.

FRAGILITY, *s.* Brisgead, breòiteachd.

FRAGMENT, *s.* Fuigheal, spruilleach.

FRAGRANCE, FRAGRANCY, *s.* Cùbhraidheachd, deagh bhòladh.

FRAGRANT, *adj.* Cùbhraidh.

FRAIL, *adj.* Lag, breòite, gun treòir; anfhann, so-lùbadh.

FRAILTY, *s.* Anmhuinneachd; laigsinn.

FRAME, *v. a.* Dealbh, cruthaich, cùm.

FRAME, *s.* Cumadair, cumadh, dealbh, dreach, cruth.

FRANCHISE, *s.* Saorsa; còir.

FRANCHISE, *v. a.* Saor, thoir còir.

FRANGIBLE, *adj.* Brisg, pronn.

FRANION, *s.* Leanan; companach.

FRANK, *adj.* Faoilidh, saor, furanach.

FRANK, *s.* Litir-shaor; bonn Fràngach deich sgillinn; fail-muice.

FRANK, *v. a.* Saor litir; cuir am fail.

FRANKINCENSE, *s.* Saor-thùis.

FRANKNESS, *s.* Fosgailteachd, saorsa.

FRANTIC, *adj.* Air boile, air chuthach, mearanach; feargach, buaireasach.

FRATERNAL, *adj.* Brâithreil.

FRATERNITY, *s.* Brâithreachas.

FRATRICIDE, *s.* Mort-bràthar.

FRAUD, *s.* Mealltaireachd, foill.

FRAUDULENCE, FRAUDULENCY, *s.* Mealltaireachd, cealgaireachd.

FRAUDULENT, FRAUDFUL, *adj.* Carach, cealgach, foilleil, fealltach.

FRAUGHT, *part.* Luchdaichte, làn

FRAY, *s.* Cath, còmhrag, caonnag.

FREAK, *v. a.* Breac, ballaich, stiallaich.

FREAKISH, *adj.* Luaineach, neònach.

FRECKLE, *s.* Breacadh-seunain.

FRECKLED, *adj.* Breac-bhàllach.

FREE, *adj.* Saor, neo-cheangailte.

FREE, *v. a.* Saor, fuasgail, leig fasgaoil.

FREEBOOTER, *s.* Fear-reubainn.

FREEDOM, *s.* Saorsa, saorsainn, cead.

FREEHOLD, *s.* Fearann-saor, oighreachd.

FREEHOLDER, *s.* Fear fearainn-shaoir.

FREEMAN, *s.* Duine saor; fear-chòraichean, tràill a fhuair a shaorsa.

FREENESS, *s.* Saorsainn; fosgailteachd.

FREESTONE, *s.* Gaireal, saoireal.

FREETHINKER, *s.* As-creideach.

FREEZE, *v. a.* Reòdh, meilich.

FREIGHT, *v. a.* Luchdaich, far.

FREIGHT, *s.* Luchd; faradh.

FRENCH, *s.* Fràngaich; fràingis.

FRENCH, *adj.* Fràngach.

FRENETIC, *adj.* Air boile, mearanach.

FRENZY, *s.* Boile, bàinidh, mearan.

FREQUENCY, *s.* Coitcheanntas.

FREQUENT, *adj.* Tric, minig.

FREQUENT, *v. a.* Taghail, tathaich.

FREQUENTER, *s.* Fear-tathaich.

FREQUENTLY, *adv.* Gu tric, gu minig.

FRESCO, *s.* Fionnaireachd, duibhre.

FRESH, *adj.* Fionnar; ùr, ùrail.

FRESHEN, *v. a.* Ùraich, fàs ùr.

FRESHNESS, *s.* Ùralachd, ùrachd.

FRET, *s.* Buaireas, iomairt, frionas.

FRET, *v.* Luaisg, càraich; suath, caith às; feargnaich; gabh fearg.

FRETFUL, *adj.* Frionasach, càs.

FRETFULNESS, *s.* Frionas, càise.

FRETTY, *adj.* Cnapach, plucanach.
FRIABLE, *adj.* Brisg, so-phronnadh.
FRIAR, *s.* Brathair-bochd.
FRIARY, *s.* Crùisle.
FRIBBLE, *s.* Spalpaire.
FRICTION, *s.* Suathadh, rubadh.
FRIDAY, *s.* Di-h-aoine.
FRIEND, *s.* Caraid, daimheach.
FRIENDLESS, *adj.* Gun charaid.
FRIENDLINESS, *s.* Daimhealach.
FRIENDLY, *adj.* Càirdeil, daimheil.
FRIENDSHIP, *s.* Càirdeas, dàimh.
FRIEZE, FRIZE, *s.* Clò molach.
FRIGATE, *s.* Long bheag chogaidh.
FRIGHT, FRIGHTEN, *v. a.* Cuir eagal air, oilltich, clisg, geiltich, sgeunaich.
FRIGHT, *s.* Eagal, geilt, oillt, clisgeadh.
FRIGHTFUL, *adj.* Eagalach, oillteil.
FRIGID, *adj.* Fuar, fuaralach, neo-chaoimhneil, tioram; neo-bheothail.
FRIGIDITY, *s.* Fuaralachd; marbhantachd.
FRIGORIFIC, *adj.* A' deanamh fuar.
FRILL, *v. n.* Crithnich, crith.
FRILL, *s.* Grinneas-uchd.
FRINGE, *s.* Fraoidhneas, oir.
FRINGY, *adj.* Fraoidhneasach.
FRIPPERY, *s.* Bàrlagan, ribagan.
FRISK, *v. n.* Leum, gèarr, sùrdag; damhs.
FRISKINESS, *s.* Mire, mireagachd.
FRISKFUL, *adj.* Mireagach, mear.
FRITH, *s.* Caolas mara, seòrsa lìn.
FRITTER, *s.* Mìrean, crioman.
FRITTER, *v. a.* Bris; pronn, bruan.
FRIVOLITY, *s.* Faoineas, faoineachd.
FRIVOLOUS, FRIVOLOUSNESS, *adj.* Faoin, suarach, dìblidh.
FRIZZLE, *v. a.* Cuairsg, căs, sniamh.
FRIZZLE, *s.* Camag, caisreag.
FRO, *adv.* Air ais, suas.
FROCK, *s.* Gùn beag; còta-gearr.
FROG, *s.* Losgann, leumnachan, gille-cràigean.
FROLIC, *s.* Mire, sùgradh, beadradh.
FROLIC, FROLICSOME, *adj.* Mireagach, sùgach, cleasanta.
FROM, *prep.* O, bho, uaithe; as.
FROND, *s.* Geug-dhuilleagach.
FRONT, *s.* Aghaidh, aodann; toiseach.
FRONT, *v.* Thoir aghaidh, coinnich; seas mu chcinneamh.
FRONTIER, *s.* Crìoch, oir, iomall.
FRONTISPIECE, *s.* Clàr-aghaidh.
FRONTLESS, *adj.* Beag-narach, ladorna.
FROST, *s.* Reodhadh, reothadh.
FROSTBITTEN, *adj.* Seargte le reothadh.
FROSTY, *adj.* Reòta, fuaralach; liath.
FROTH, *s.* Cop, cobhar, sgùm.
FROTHY, *adj.* Copach, cobharach, faoin.
FROUZY, *adj.* Laidir, breun, doilleir.
FROWARD, *adj.* Daobhaidh, crosda, danarra, do-cheannsachadh.
FROWARDNESS, *s.* Dearras, danarrachd.
FROWN, *v. a.* Amhairc le gruaim.
FROWN, *s.* Gruaim, sgraing, mùig.
FROZEN, *part. pass.* of *to freeze.* Reòte; fuaralach.
FRUCTIFEROUS, *adj.* Measach.
FRUCTIFY, *v. a.* Dean torach; giùlain meas, bi sìolmhor.
FRUCTUOUS, *adj.* Sìolmhor, measach.
FRUGAL, *adj.* Caomhantach, glèidhteach.
FRUGALITY, *s.* Caomhnadh, crìontachd.
FRUIT, *s.* Meas; toradh; sliochd.
FRUITAGE, *s.* Measach.
FRUITBEARING, *part.* A' giùlan meas.
FRUITERY, *s.* Lobhta-mheas.
FRUITFUL, *adj.* Torach, sìolmhor.
FRUITFULNESS, *s.* Sìolmhorachd, pailteas.
FRUITION, *s.* Mealtainn, sealbhachadh.
FRUITLESS, *adj.* Neo-thorach; neo-tharbhach, faoin; aimrid, seasg.
FRUMENTACIOUS, *adj.* Do ghràn.
FRUMENTY, *s.* Brochan-cruithneachd.
FRUMP, *v. a.* Mag, cuir 'na thosd.
FRUSH, *v. a.* Bris, bruan, pronn, brùth.
FRUSTRANEOUS, *adj.* Neo-tharbhach, faoin.
FRUSTRATE, *v. a.* Meall, mill dùil; bac, dìobair, cuir a thaobh.
FRY, *s.* Sìol-èisg, gramasgar, gràisg.
FRY, *v. a.* Ròist ann an aghainn.
FRYINGPAN, *s.* Aghann; friochdan.
FUB, *v. a.* Cuir dhiot le brèig.
FUDDLE, *v.* Cuir air mhisg; bi air mhisg.
FUEL, *s.* Connadh.
FUGACIOUS, *adj.* Luaineach, siùbhlach.
FUGACIOUSNESS, FUGACITY, *s.* Luaineachd, siùbhlachd, luathas, diombuanachd, neo-chinnteachd, neo-sheasmhachd.
FUGITIVE, *adj.* Siùbhlach, faileasach.
FUGITIVE, *s.* Fògarach dìobarach.
FULCRUM, *s.* Gobhal cùl-taic.
FULFIL, *v. a.* Coimhlion.
FULFILMENT, *s.* Coimhlionadh.
FULGENCY *s.* Dèarsadh, dealradh.

Fulgent, Fulgid, *adj.* Dèarsach, dealrach, boillsgeach.
Fuliginous, *adj.* Smalach, ceothach.
Full, *adj.* Làn, lìonta ; sàsaichte.
Full, *s.* Làn, làine, iomlaine.
Full, *adv.* Gu h-uile, gu h-iomlan.
Full, *v. a.* Luaidh, fùc.
Full-blown, *adj.* Fo làn-bhlàth.
Full-grown, *adj.* Aig làn-fhàs.
Fuller, *s.* Fùcadair.
Fuller's-earth, *s.* Criadh-an-fhùcadair.
Full-eyed, *adj.* Meall-shuileach.
Fulminant, *adj.* Tàirnich.
Fulminate, *v.* Dean tàirnich.
Fulmination, *s.* Tàirneanach, toirm ; ascaoin-eaglais.
Fulness, *s.* Lànachd, làine, pailteas.
Fulsome, *adj.* Gràineil, breun, salach.
Fumado, *s.* Iasg tioram cruaidh.
Fumage, *s.* Cìs-teallaich.
Fumble, *v.* Dean gu cearbach ; laimhsich gu cèarr ; prab.
Fumbler, *s.* Prabaire, fear-cearbach.
Fume, *s.* Deathach ; ceò, smùd, ceathach ; toth, corraich.
Fumet, *s.* Buachar féigh.
Fumid, *adj.* Ceòthach, smùdanach.
Fumigate, *v. n.* Cuir smùid, toit.
Fumigation, *s.* Deatach, smùd.
Fumous, Fumy, *adj.* Smoky, deatachail, smùideach, toiteach.
Fun, *s.* Fearas-chuideachd, fala-dhà.
Function, *s.* Dreuchd, cèaird.
Fund, *s.* Stoc, stòras, maoin.
Fundament, *s.* Tòn, leth-deiridh.
Fundamental, *adj.* Bunaiteach, sònraichte.
Funeral, *s.* Tìodhlacadh, adhlacadh.
Funeral, Funereal, *adj.* A bhuineas do thìodhlacadh ; brònach, dubhach, muladach.
Fungous, *adj.* Spongach.
Fungus, *s.* Ballag-bhuachair.
Funk, *s.* Droch bholadh.
Funnel, *s.* Lìonadair ; pìob-tharruinn.
Funny, *adj.* Cridheil, sùgach.
Fur, *s.* Bian ; craiceann-fionnaidh.
Furacious, *adj.* Bradach.
Furacity, *s.* Braid, meirle.
Furbelow, *s.* Froinis, fraoidhneas.
Furbish, *v. a.* Lìomh, loinnrich.
Furious, *adj.* Air a chuthach, air bàinidh ; mearanach, feargach ; garg, borb, lasanta.
Furl, *v. a.* Paisg, trus, fill.
Furlong, *s.* An t-ochdamh cuid do mhìle, dà cheud a's dà fhichead slat.
Furlough, *s.* Fòrlach saighdear.
Furnace, *s.* Fùirneis, àmhuinn.
Furnish, *v. a.* Uidheamaich ; thoir seachad ; sgiamhaich, maisich, breaghaich.
Furniture, *s.* Àirneis, uidheam.
Furrier, *s.* Fear-reic bhian.
Furrow, *s.* Clais ; preas.
Furry, *adj.* Molach, ròmach.
Further, *v. a.* Cuidich, cuir air aghart.
Furthermore, *adv.* Os bàrr, a bharr.
Furthermost, Furthest, *s.* Is fhaid' air falbh, is iomalaiche.
Fury, *s.* Cuthach, bàinidh, boile ; fearg, corraich, buaireas ; boil' inntinn, déine ; baobh chuthaich, banifrinneach.
Furze, *s.* Conusg.
Furzy, *adj.* Conusgach.
Fuse, *v.* Leagh ; gabh leaghadh, bi leaghadh.
Fusee, Fusil, *s.* Gunna-glaice.
Fusible, *adj.* Leaghach, so-leaghadh.
Fusibility, *s.* Nàdur leaghach.
Fusileer, *s.* Saighdear gunna-glaice.
Fusion, *s.* Leaghadh.
Fuss, *s.* Ùparaid, fuaim, cabhag.
Fustian, *s.* Aodach air a dheanamh do chanach agus do lion ; àrd-ghlòir.
Fustiness, *s.* Bréine, liatas.
Fusty, *adj.* Breun, malcaidh, liath.
Futile, *adj.* Faoin, dìomhain, gun luach ; bruidhneach, lonach.
Futility, *s.* Lon, beilean ; faoineas, dìomhanas ; gòraich.
Future, *adj.* Ri teachd, a thig.
Future, Futurity, *s.* Àm ri teachd ; ni ri teachd no ri tachairt.
Fuzz-ball, *s.* Balgan-péiteach.
Fy, O Fie ! *interj.* Mo nàire !

G

G, *s.* Seachdamh litir na h-aibidil.
Gabardine, *s.* Earrasaid.
Gab, Gabble, *v. n.* Bi gobaireachd
Gabble, *s.* Briot, glocaireachd.
Gabbler, *s.* Glogair, gobaire.
Gabel, *s.* Cìs, càin.
Gable, *s.* Stuadh, tulchann.
Gad, *s.* Geinn stàilinn.
Gad, *v. n.* Ruith air chéilidh.
Gadder, *s.* Fear-ceilidh.
Gadding, *s.* Céilidh.

GADFLY, *s.* Gleithir, creithleag.
GAELIC, *s.* Gàëlig, gàëlic.
GAG, *v. a.* Glomharaich, cuir sparrag.
GAG, *s.* Glomhar, sparrag, cabstair.
GAGE, *s.* Geall, earlas ; tomhas.
GAGE, *v. a.* Cuir geall.
GAIETY, *s.* Aiteas, cridhealas, aoibhneas, aigeantas ; sunnt, mire ; breaghas.
GAILY, *adv.* Gu h-ait, gu cridheil, gu h-aoibhneach, gu sunntach ; gu breagha.
GAIN, *s.* Buannachd, buidhinn.
GAIN, *v.* Buannaich, coisinn ; faigh.
GAINER, *s.* Fear-buannachd.
GAINFUL, *adj.* Buannachdail, tarbhach.
GAINSAY, *v. a.* Cuir an aghaidh, thoir a bhreug do ; àicheadh.
GAINSTAND, *v. a.* Cuir an aghaidh.
GAIRISH, *adj.* Basdalach, lòiseamach.
GAIT, *s.* Slighe ; gluasad, siubhal.
GALAXY, *s.* Co-sholus-reull.
GALE, *s.* Gaoth sgairteil ; gaoth threun.
GALL, *s.* Domhlas ; gamhlas.
GALL, *v. a.* Cràidh, ciùrr, rùisg ; claoidh ; feargaich.
GALLANT, *adj.* Basdalach, rìmheach, uallach, spaideil ; curanta, flathail.
GALLANT, *s.* Lasgaire, suiridheach.
GALLANTRY, *s.* Basdal, spairiseachd, rìmheachas ; treubhantas ; suiridhe.
GALLERY, *s.* Aisir eadar dà sheòmar ; ăradh, lobhta.
GALLEY, *s.* Birlinn, iùbhrach.
GALLEY-SLAVE, *s.* Traill-iomraidh.
GALLIARD, *s.* Lasgaire rìmheach.
GALLIGASKINS, *s.* Mogain, osain mhòra.
GALLIPOT, *s.* Poit-chreadha.
GALLON, *s.* Galan, ceithir-chărt.
GALLOP, *s.* Cruinn-leum, teann-ruith.
GALLOP, *v. n.* Marcaich le cruinnleum.
GALLOWAY, *s.* Each nach eil thar ceithir làmhan deug air àirde.
GALLOWS, *s.* Croich.
GAMBADOES, *s.* Triubhais-mharcachd.
GAMBLE, *v. n.* Cluich air son airgeid.
GAMBLER, *s.* Fear-cluiche ; mealltair.
GAMBOL, *v. a.* Damhs, leum, dean mireag, dean ruideis, dean lŭ-chleas.
GAMBOL, *s.* Mireag, leumnaich ; lŭchleas, cleas abhachdach.
GAMBREL, *s.* Cas-deiridh eich.
GAME, *s.* Cluiche ; fearas-chuideachd, magadh, culaidh-bhùird ; sealg, eòin agus beathaichean seilge.
GAME, *v. n.* Cluich air son airgeid.
GAMECOCK, *s.* Coileach-catha.
GAMEKEEPER, *s.* Peathair-seilge.
GAMESOME, *adj.* Sùgach, mireagach.
GAMESTER, *s.* Ceărrach.
GAMING, *s.* Ceărrachd.
GAMMON, *s.* Ceithreamh deiridh muic'.
GANDER, *s.* Gànradh.
GANG, *s.* Buidheann, còisridh, bannal.
GANGLION, *s.* Màm.
GANGRENE, *s.* Buirbein, an-fheòil.
GANGRENE, *v. a.* Lobh, grod, cnàmh.
GANGRENOUS, *adj.* Cnàimhteach, grod.
GANTLET, *s.* Buill'-o-gach-fear.
GAOL, *s.* Gainntir, prìosan.
GAOLER, *s.* Fear gleidhidh prìosain.
GAP, *s.* Bealach, bearn ; fosgladh.
GAPE, *v. n.* Dean mèananaich, spleuchd.
GAPER, *s.* Steòcaire ; miannaiche.
GARB, *s.* Éideadh, earradh, aogas.
GARBAGE, GARBISH, *s.* Gairetheann, mionach, grealach.
GARBLE, *v. a.* Eadar-dhealaich, tagh.
GARDEN, *s.* Lios, gàradh.
GARDENER, *s.* Gàradair, gàirnealair.
GARDENING, *s.* Gàirnealaireachd.
GARGARISM, GARGLE, *s.* Deoch-glanaidh beòil a's slugain.
GARGLE, *v. a.* Nigh, glan, sruthail.
GARLAND, *s.* Blàth-fhleasg, lŭs-chrùn.
GARLAND, *v. a.* Maisich le blàthfhleasg.
GARLIC, *s.* Creamh, gaïrgean.
GARMENT, *s.* Aodach, earradh.
GARNER, *s.* Ionad-tasgaidh sìl.
GARNET, *s.* Clach luachmhor, gàirneid.
GARNISH, *v. a.* Maisich, sgiamhaich.
GARNISH, GARNITURE, *s.* Sgeadachadh.
GARRET, *s.* Seòmar-mullaich.
GARRETTEER, *s.* Fear-seòmair-mullaich.
GARRISON, *s.* Saighdearan baile dìona ; dùn, tùr, daingneach.
GARRISON, *v. a.* Cuir saighdearan air baile dìon ; dìdinn, daingnich.
GARRULITY, *s.* Gobaireachd, geòileam.
GARRULOUS, *adj.* Gobach, luathbheulach.
GARTER, *s.* Gartan, glùinean.
GARTH, *s.* Dòmhlad, tiuighead.
GASCONADE, *s.* Spagluinn, spleadhas.
GASH, *s.* Gearradh, beum, lot domhain.
GASP, *v. n.* Plosg, tarruinn ospag.
GASP, *s.* Àinich, plosg, ospag.
GASTRIC, *adj.* Meirbheach.
GASTROTOMY, *s.* Gearradh-bronn.
GATE, *s.* Geata, dorus, cachaileith.
GATHER, *v.* Cruinnich, tionail, trus.

Gatherer, *s.* Fear-cruinneachaidh.
Gathering, *s.* Co-chruinneachadh.
Gathers, *s.* Fillidhean, pleatan.
Gaude, Gaudery, *s.* Basdalachd, breaghachd, rìmheachd.
Gaudy, *adj.* Lòiseamach, basdalach, rìmheach, breagh.
Gauge, *v. a.* Tomhais soitheach.
Gauge, *s.* Riaghailt thomhais shoithichean.
Gauger, *s.* Fear tomhais shoithichean.
Gaunt, *adj.* Tana, lom; gun fheòil.
Gauntlet, *s.* Làmh-dhion, dòrn-bheart.
Gauze, *s.* Sròl.
Gauntree, *s.* Làir-mhaide.
Gawk, *s.* Cuthag; baothaire.
Gawky, *adj.* Sgleòbaideach, sgleòideach.
Gay, *adj.* Cridheil, sunntach, sùgach, beò; rìmheach, grinn.
Gayety, *s.* Cridhealas, aiteas, basdal.
Gaze, *v. n.* Beachdaich, dùr-amhairc.
Gazer, *s.* Spleuchdaire.
Gazette, *s.* Litir-naigheachd.
Gazetteer, *s.* Fear-naigheachd.
Gazing-stock, *s.* Culaidh-bhùirst.
Gear, Geer, *s.* Àirneis, cuid, eudail, maoin; goireas, uidheam; beairt.
Geese, *s. plural* of Goose. Geòidh.
Gelantine, Gelatinous, *adj.* Tiugh; righinn.
Geld, *v. a.* Spòth; buin uaithe.
Gelder, *s.* Spòthadair.
Gelding, *s.* Gearran.
Gelid, *adj.* Fuar, reòdhte.
Gelidity, *s.* Fuachd mòr, reòtachd.
Gem, *s.* Seud, neamhnaid; ùr-fhàs.
Gemination, *s.* Dùblachadh.
Gemini, *s.* Na leth-aoin, aon do chomharran na cuairt-ghréine.
Geminous, *adj.* Dà-fhillt.
Gemmary, *adj.* Seudach, leugach.
Gender, *s.* Gné, gin, seòrsa.
Gender, *v.* Gin, tàrmaich; àraich.
Genealogical, *adj.* Sloinnteachail.
Genealogist, *s.* Sloinntear.
Genealogy, *s.* Sloinntearachd.
General, *adj.* Coitcheann, cumanta; gnàthaichte, farsuinn an seadh.
General, *s.* Seanailear; ceann-feachd.
Generalissimo, *s.* Àrd-sheanailear.
Generality, *s.* Coitcheanntas, cumantas; a' chuid a's mò.
Generate, *v. a.* Gin, sìolaich, tàrmaich, thoir a mach.
Generation, *s.* Gineamhuinn; sliochd, àlach, àl, glùn-ginealaich; linn.
Generative, *adj.* Sìolmhor.
Generical, *adj.* Gnèitheach.
Generosity, *s.* Fiùghantachd, fialachd, toirbheartachd, uaisle suairceas.
Generous, *adj.* Fiùghantach, faoilidh, flathail, fial, tabhartach, suairce; uasal, làidir, beothail.
Genesis, *s.* Leabhar nan ginealach
Genet, *s.* Each spàinnteach.
Geneva, *s.* Sùgh an aitil.
Genial, *adj.* Gnèitheach; tlùsail, caoimhneil; nàdurra, dàimheil, cridheil.
Genitals, *s.* Buill-dìomhair.
Genitive, *adj.* Gineamhuinneach.
Genius, *s.* Duine mhòr-cheud-fathan; cumhachd inntinn; nàdur, aomadh inntinn.
Genteel, *adj.* Modhail; spéiseil; suairce; eireachdail; grinn.
Genteelness, *s.* Modhalachd, suairceas, eireachdas, grinneas.
Gentian, *s.* Lùs-a'-chrùbain.
Gentile, *s.* Cinneach, geintealach.
Gentilism, *s.* Pàganach.
Gentility, *s.* Speisealachd, uaisle.
Gentle, *adj.* Uasal, inbheach; modhail, beusach; ciùin, sèimh, caomh, màlda; sìtheil, soitheamh.
Gentleman, *s.* Duin'-uasal.
Gentlemanlike, *adj.* Mar dhuin'-uasal, flathail.
Gentleness, *s.* Uaisle; ciùine.
Gentlewoman, *s.* Bean-uasal.
Gentry, *s.* Uaislean, daoin-'uaisle.
Genuflexion, *s.* Glùn-lùbadh.
Genuine, *adj.* Fìor, neo-thruaillte.
Genus, *s.* Dream, seòrsa, gnè.
Geographer, *s.* Cruinn'-eòlaiche.
Geography, *s.* Cruinne-eòlas.
Geology, *s.* Eòlas air gnè na cruinne.
Geomancer, *s.* Fiosaiche, druidh.
Geomancy, *s.* Fiosachd, druidheachd.
Geometer, *s.* Fear-eolais tomhais.
Geometral, Geometric, Geometrical, *adj.* A bhuineas do thomhas.
Geometry, *s.* Eòlas-meudachd.
Georgic, *s.* Dàn-tuathanachais.
Geranium, *s.* Lùs-gnà-ghorm.
German, *s.* Bràthair, daimheach.
Germe, Germin, *s.* Fiùran, faillean.
Germinate, *v. n.* Thoir air fàs, thig fo bhlàth.
Germination, *s.* Ùr-fhàs, blàth.
Gestation, *s.* Tòrrachas, leth-tromachd.
Gesticulate, *v. n.* Dean àmhailtean.
Gesticulation, *s.* Lù-chleasachd, àmhailtean.
Gesture, *s.* Car, carachadh, gluasad.
Get, *v.* Faigh; coisinn, solair; gin.
Getting, *s,* Faighinn; cosnadh.

Gewgaw, *s.* Rud faoin, ni suarach.
Ghastful, *adj.* Gruamach, oillteil.
Ghastly, *adv.* Gu h-aogaidh, oillteil.
Ghost, *s.* Tannasg, spiorad; tàsg.
Ghostly, *adj.* Spioradail.
Giant, *s.* Fomhair, famhair, athach.
Giantess, *s.* Ban-athach.
Giantlike, Giantly, *adj.* Athanta.
Gibber, *v. n.* Labhair gun seadh.
Gibberish, *s.* Goileam, cainnt chèard.
Gibbet, *s.* Croich.
Gibbosity, Gibbousness, *s.* Bolgachd, plucachd.
Gibbous, *adj.* Crotach, plucach, meallach.
Gibcat, *s.* Cat-luathainn.
Gibe, *s.* Fochaid, magadh; sgeig.
Giblets, *s.* Bàrr sgiathan geòidh.
Giddily, *adv.* Gu guanach; gun chùram.
Giddiness, *s.* Tuainealaich, guanachd, gogaideachd; gòraiche.
Giddy, *s.* Guanach, tuainealach; sgaogach, gaoitheanach, gòrach, faoin.
Giddy-brained, *adj.* Sgaog-cheannach, it-cheannach.
Gier-eagle, *s.* An Iolair'-fhionn.
Gift, *s.* Tìodhlac, tabhartas, gibht.
Gifted, *adj.* Tìodhlaicte, comasach.
Gig, *s.* Carbad beag; bàta-caol.
Gigantic, *adj.* Athach, tomadach.
Giggle, *v. n.* Dean frith-ghàire.
Gild, *v. a.* Òr, òraich.
Gilder, *s.* Fear-òraidh.
Gilding, *s.* Òradh.
Gill, *s.* Stòp-cairteil, giùran; sprogaill; lŭs-na-staoine, eighean-làir.
Gilly-flower, *s.* [Corruption from July flower.] Lŭs-leth-an-t-sàmhraidh.
Gilt, *s.* Òr-dhealt.
Gim, Gimmy, *s.* Snasmhor, grinn.
Gimlet, *s.* Gimileid.
Gin, *s.* Ribe, lìon; sùgh an aitil.
Ginger, *s.* Dinnsear.
Gingerbread, *s.* Aran-milis.
Gingerly, *adv.* Gu caomhail.
Gingival, *adj.* Càireanach.
Gingle, *v.* Dean glìongraich; gliong.
Ginglymus, *s.* Alt-cheangal.
Gipsy, *s.* Cèard-fiosachd, ban-fhiosaiche, baobh-shiùbhlach.
Gird, *v.* Crioslaich, cuairtich.
Girder, *s.* Sail-ùrlair.
Girdle, *s.* Crios-leasraidh.
Girl, *s.* Caileag, cailin, nìonag.
Girlish, *adj.* Mar chaileag, mar phàiste.
Girt, Girth, *s.* Giort-tarra, beartbhronn dìolta; dòmhlad, gairbhead, cuairt.
Girth, *v. a.* Crioslaich, giortaich.
Give, *v. a.* Tabhair, thoir, bàirig, builich, thoir seachad.
Giver, *s.* Fear-buileachaidh.
Giving, *s.* Buileachadh, tabhairt.
Gizzard, *s.* Sgròban, giaban.
Glaciation, *s.* Reodhadh, dĕigh.
Glacious, *adj.* Dĕigheach, eighreadail, reòdhte.
Glacis, *s.* Bruach daingnich.
Glad, *adj.* Ait, aoibhinn, toilichte.
Glad, Gladden, *v. a.* Dean aoibhneach, dean éibhinn, dean ăit, sòlasaich.
Glade, *s.* Réidhlean, blàr, ridhe, ìòm.
Gladiator, *s.* Cliaranach, basbair.
Gladness, *s.* Aoibhneas, toil-inntinn.
Gladsome, *adj.* Aoibhneach, ăit.
Glare, *s.* Gealagan uibhe.
Glance, *s.* Pladhadh, grad-shealladh.
Glance, *v. n.* Grad amhairc, gabh pladhadh dheth, ruith fiar, thoir siaradh.
Gland, *s.* Fàireag.
Glanders, *s.* Gràineasadh.
Glandulous, Glandular, *adj.* Faireagach.
Glare, *v.* Boillsg, dealraich, soillsich, dèarsaich; seall gu fiadhaich; dèars, bi loinnreach.
Glare, *s.* Boillsgeadh, dealradh, soillse, lannair; sealladh fiadhaich.
Glaring, *adj.* Follaiseach, ro shoillear.
Glass, *s.* Glaine; sgàthan.
Glassy, *adj.* Glaineach, réidh, mìn, soilleir.
Glave, *s.* Claidheamh mòr.
Glaze, *v. a.* Còmhdaich le glaine.
Glazier, *s.* Glaineadair.
Gleam, *s.* Boillsgeadh, pladhadh, dril.
Gleam, *v. n.* Boillsg, dèars, soillsich.
Gleamy, *adj.* Boillsgeach, dèarsach.
Glean, *v. a.* Trŭs; dioghlum.
Gleaner, *s.* Fear dioghluim.
Gleaning, *s.* Dioghlum, tional.
Glebe, *s.* Fonn ministear, fòd.
Glede, *s.* Clamhan gòbhlach,
Glee, *s.* Mire, sunnt, aiteas, cridhealas; luinneag, òran sùgraidh.
Gleeful, *adj.* Cridheil, sunntach.
Gleet, *s.* Sileadh, iongar.
Glefty, *adj.* Silteach, iongarach.
Glen, *s.* Gleann.
Glewy, *adj.* Glaodhach, righinn.
Glib, *adj.* Sleamhainn, mìn, réidh.
Glibness, *s.* Sleamhnad, mìnead.
Glide, *v. n.* Gluais eutrom, falbh ciùin.

GLIMMER, *v. n.* Dean fann-sholus.
GLIMMER, GLIMMERING, *s.* Fann-sholus, frith-sholus.
GLIMPSE, *s.* Pladhadh, boillsgeadh, sealladh grad, aiteal.
GLISTEN, *v. n.* Soillsich, boillsg, dealraich.
GLISTER, *v. n.* Soillsich, dèarrs, boillsg.
GLITTER, *v. n.* Deàrs, boillsg, bi lainnearach, bi breagha.
GLITTER, GLITTERING, *s.* Dèarsadh, boillsgeadh, lainnir.
GLOBATED, GLOBED, *adj.* Cruinn.
GLOBE, *s.* Ball cruinn; cruinne; dealbh na cruinne.
GLOBOSE, GLOBULAR, GLOBULOUS, *adj.* Cruinn, cuarsgach.
GLOBOSITY, *s.* Cruinn-chumadh.
GLOMERATE, *v. a.* Cuairsg, cruinnich.
GLOMERATION, *s.* Cuairsgeadh.
GLOOM, *s.* Gruaim, duibhre, dubhar; mi-ghean, mùig, smalan, truim-inntinn.
GLOOMINESS, *s.* Duibhre, doilleireachd; mùgaich, gruamachd, mi-ghean.
GLOOMY, *adj.* Doilleir, neulach, dubhnarach; gulmach, gruamach, mùgach, trom-inntinneach.
GLORIFICATION, *s.* Glòrachadh.
GLORIFY, *v. a.* Glòraich, cliùthaich; thoir aoradh, thoir urram, thoir glòir; thoir gu glòir, naomhaich.
GLORIOUS, *adj.* Glòrmhor, òirdheirc, allail, naomha.
GLORY, *s.* Glòir, cliù; sonas nèimh; urram, àrd-mholadh.
GLORY, *v. a.* Dean uaill, dean bòsd.
GLOSS, *s.* Mìneachadh, lìomh, dealradh.
GLOSS, *v.* Mìnich, cuir cleòc air, thoir leithsgeul bòidheach; lìomh, sgeadaich.
GLOSSARY, *s.* Sanasan, leabhar-mìneachaidh shean-fhacal.
GLOSSINESS, *s.* Lìomharrachd.
GLOSSY, *adj.* Lìomharra, mìn.
GLOVE, *s.* Làmhainn, meatag.
GLOVER, *s.* Làmhainnear.
GLOUT, *v.* Amhairc gruamach.
GLOW, *v.* Dèarrs, soillsich le teas; dian-loisg; bi teth, bi blàth; bi feargach, lăs.
GLOW, *s.* Caoir dhearg, teas, soillse; lainnir, ainteas, dian-chorraich.
GLOW-WORM, *s.* Cuileag-shnìomhain.
GLOZE, *v. n.* Dean miodal, dean miolasg.
GLOZE, *s.* Miodal, sodal, miolasg.
GLUE, *s.* Glaodh; slaman tàth.
GLUE, *v. a.* Glaodh; co-thàth.
GLUM, *adj.* Dorcha, gruamach.
GLUT, *v. a.* Sàsaich; glàm, glut.
GLUT, *s.* Glàmadh, slugadh, làn, sàth.
GLUTINOSITY, GLUTINOUSNESS, *s.* Glaoghach, rìghneach, leantach.
GLUTINOUS, *adj.* Glaodhach, righinn.
GLUTTON, *s.* Glaimsear, geòcaire, craosaire, glàimhear.
GLUTTONOUS, *adj.* Craosach, geòcach.
GLUTTONY, *s.* Geòcaireachd, craos.
GNARLED, *adj.* Meallach, plucach.
GNASH, *v.* Buail r'a chéile, dean gìosgan; cas dréin.
GNASHING, *s.* Dìosgan, gìosgan.
GNAT, *s.* Meanbh-chuileag.
GNAW, *v. a.* Caith, ith, cnàmh, creim, cagainn, teum.
GNOMON, *s.* Clag-làmh, no mheur.
GO, *v. n.* Falbh, imich, theirig, rach, siubhail, coisich, gluais; tàr ás.
GOAD, *s.* Bior-greasaidh.
GOAD, *v. a.* Greas le bior greasaidh, spŏr; bruidich, stuig, cuir thuige.
GOAL, *s.* Ceann-crìche, crìoch, deireadh, ceann-thall; ceann tòiseachaidh réise.
GOAT, *s.* Gobhar, gabhar.
GOATHERD, *s.* Buachaille ghobhar.
GOATISH, *adj.* Macnusach, drùiseil.
GOBB, *v. a.* Sluig, ith gu lonach.
GOBBET, *v. a.* Sluig gun chagnadh.
GOBLET, *s.* Aghann, copan, cuach.
GOBLIN, *s.* Fuath, bòcan, ùruisg màilleachan, glaistig, baobh.
GOD, *s.* Dia; dia, iodhol.
GODCHILD, *s.* Dalta.
GODDESS, *s.* Ban-dia.
GODFATHER, *s.* Oide, goistidh.
GODHEAD, *s.* Diadhachd.
GODLESS, *adj.* Aindiadhaidh
GODLESSNESS, *s.* Aindiadhachd.
GOD-LIKE, *adj.* Mar dhia.
GODLINESS, *s.* Diadhachd.
GODLY, *adj.* Diadhaidh, cràbhach.
GODMOTHER, *s.* Muime.
GOGGLE, *v. n.* Spleuchd, seall fiar.
GOGGLE-EYED, *adj.* Fiar-shuileach.
GOING, *s.* Falbh, imeachd.
GOLD, *s.* Òr.
GOLDEN, *adj.* Òrdha, òir, òrach, do dh' òr; òr-bhuidhe, àr-bhuidhe.
GOLDFINCH, *s.* Lasair-choille.
GOLDHAMMER, *s.* Buidhein-coille.
GOLDSMITH, *s.* Òr-cheard.
GONDOLA, *s.* Seòrsa bàta, eithear beag.
GONE, *part. pret.* from *to go.* Air triall, air falbh, thairis, marbh millte.
GONORRHŒA, *s.* An clap silteach.

Good, *adj.* Math, deagh; fallain.
Good, *s.* Math; leas, tairbhe.
Goodwill, *s.* Deagh-thoil.
Goodliness, *s.* Maise, eireachdas.
Goodly, *adj.* Maiseach, sgiamhach, bòidheach, ciatach, eireachdail; sultmhor, dòmhail, tomadach.
Goodness, *s.* Mathas, deagh-bheus.
Goods, *s.* Cuid, maoin, bathar.
Goody, *s.* Mo bheanag.
Goose, *s.* Gèadh; iarunn-tàillear.
Gooseberry, *s.* Gròiseid.
Goosequill, *s.* Gèadhach.
Gorbellied, *adj.* Bronnach.
Gore, *s.* Fuil, flann-fhuil; gaorr.
Gore, *v. a.* Gaorr, troi' lot, sàth.
Gorge, *s.* Sgòrnan, slugan; biadh.
Gorge, *v. a.* Gloc, lìon, sàsaich; sluig; ith, ionaltair.
Gorgeous, *adj.* Rìmheach, lòiseamach, greadhnach.
Gorget, *s.* Gòrsaid.
Gorgon, *s.* Culaidh-dhéisinn.
Gormandize, *v. n.* Glut, ith gu lonach.
Gormandizer, *s.* Glaimsear, geòcaire.
Gorse, *s.* Conusg, droighneach.
Gory, *adj.* Air eabradh le fuil.
Goshawk, *s.* Seabhac-mhòr.
Gosling, *s.* Isean geòidh.
Gospel, *s.* Soisgeul; [*etymo.* so-sgeul.]
Gossamer, *s.* Lŭs-chlòimh.
Gossip, *s.* Goistidh; sgimilear; briot.
Gossip, *v. n.* Bi bruidhneach, bi gobaireachd; bi sŏganach.
Got, **Gotten**, *part. pass.* of *to get.* Fhuaras, fhuaradh.
Govern, *v.* Riaghail, rìoghaich; stiùr, seòl, steòrn; ceannsaich, smachdaich, cùm an òrdugh.
Governable, *adj.* So-cheannsachadh.
Governess, *s.* Ban-oid-ionnsachaich.
Government, *s.* Uachdranachd, riaghladh, flaitheachd; ceannsachd, ceannsalachd.
Governor, *s.* Riaghladair; oidionnsachaidh.
Gouge, *s.* Gilb chruinn.
Gourd, *s.* Luibh-sgàile.
Gout, *s.* Tinneas-nan-alt.
Gouty, *adj.* Gu h-olc le tinneas-nanalt; a bhuineas do thinneas-nan-alt.
Gown, *s.* Gùn, earrasaid.
Gownsman, *s.* Fear-gùin.
Grace, *s.* Fàbhar, deagh-ghean tròcair, mathanas; gràs, subhailc, diadhachd; maise, eireachdas; loinn, àilleachd; altachadh.
Grace, *v. a.* Sgeadaich, maisich.
Grace-cup, *s.* A' cheud deoch slàinte.
Graceful, *adj.* Àluinn, maiseach, ciatach, grinn.
Gracefulness, *s.* Eireachdas, maise.
Graceless, *adj.* Gun ghràs, aingidh.
Gracious, *adj.* Tròcaireach, gràsmhor, mathasach; fàbharach, caomh, bàigheil.
Graciousness, *s.* Gràsmhorachd, caomhalachd, tròcair, bàigh.
Gradation, *s.* Ceum, éiridh, dìreadh riaghailteach, ceum air cheum.
Gradatory, *adj.* A' dol o cheum gu ceum.
Grade, *s.* Inbhe, ceum.
Gradual, *adj.* A' chuid 'sa chuid.
Graduate, *v. a.* Thoir tiodal ionnsachaidh do; gabh ceum ionnsachaidh; àrdaich dean ni's fèarr; gluais o cheum gu ceum.
Graduate, *s.* Sgoilear, tiodail.
Graduality, **Graduation**, *s.* Dol air aghart, ceumnachadh; buileachadh tiodal ionnsachaidh.
Graft, **Graff**, *s.* Faillean, fiùran.
Graft, **Graff**, *v. a.* Tàth, alp; cothàth; bi suidheachadh fhaillean.
Grain, *s.* Sìlean, gràinne, sìol, gràn; calg; nàdur, gnè.
Grained, *adj.* Calgach, garbh, molach.
Grains, *s.* Treasg, drabh.
Grainy, *adj.* Grànach; gràinneanach.
Gramineal, **Gramineous**, *adj.* Feurach, lŭsanach.
Graminivorous, *adj.* Feur-itheach.
Grammar, *s.* Eòlas ceart-chainnt.
Grammarian, *s.* Fear ceart-chainnteach, snas-bhriathraiche.
Grammatical, *adj.* Ceart-chainnteach, snas-bhriathrach.
Grampus, *s.* Cana, puthag.
Granary, *s.* Sìol-lann, sgiobal.
Granate, **Granite**, *s.* Graineal.
Grand, *adj.* Urramach, ainmeil; mòr, greadhnach, breagha; prìomh; àrd, uasal.
Grandchild, *s.* Ogha.
Grandee, *s.* Duine cumhachdach.
Grandeur, *s.* Mòrachd, greadhnachas; meamnachd, mòr-chuis.
Grandfather, *s.* Seanair.
Grandiloquence, *s.* Àrd-ghlòir.
Grandinious, *adj.* Sneachdaidh.
Grandmother, *s.* Seanamhair.
Grandness, *s.* Mòrachd, meudachd
Grandsire, *s.* Priomh-athair.
Grandson, *s.* Ogha.
Grange, *s.* Grainnseach.
Granivorus, *adj.* Gràn-itl each.
Grannam, **Grandam**, *s.* Seanamhair.

Grant, *v. a.* Ceadaich, aidich, deonaich; builich, tiodhlaic, bàirig.
Grant, *s.* Buileachadh, tabhairt, tiodhlacadh; tiodhlac, tabhartas; ceadachach, aideachadh.
Grantor, *s.* Fear tiodhlacaidh.
Granulary, *adj.* Gràinneach.
Granulation, *s.* Pronnadh.
Granulous, *adj.* Gràinneanach.
Grape, *s.* Fìon-dhearc.
Graphical, *adj.* Dealbhach.
Grapnel, *s.* Greimiche.
Grapple, *v.* Greimich, glac, beir air, gleachd, teannaich.
Grasp, *v.* Greimich, glac, teannaich; dean greim; theirig an sàs.
Grasp, *s.* Greimeachadh, glacadh, greim; seilbh, cumail.
Grass, *s.* Feur.
Grasshopper, *s.* Fionnan-feòir, leumnach uaine, dreòlan-teasbhuidh.
Grassy, *adj.* Feurach.
Grate, *s.* Cliath-theine.
Grate, *v.* Suath, sgrìob, meil; thoir sgreuch air, dean fuaim sgreuchach.
Grateful, *adj.* Taingeil, buidheach; taitneach, tlachdmhor, ciatach.
Grater, *s.* Sgrìobadair; sgrìoban.
Gratification, *s.* Toileachadh, sòlasachadh, sàsachadh; toil-inntinn, sòlas.
Gratify, *v. a.* Toilich, taitinn; sàsaich, duaisich, dìol.
Grating, *s.* Cliath-iaruinn.
Grating, *part. adj.* Sgreuchach, sgreadach.
Gratis, *adv.* A nasgaidh.
Gratitude, Gratefulness, *s.* Taingealachd, buidheachas.
Gratuitous, *adj.* Saor-thiodhlaicte.
Gratuity, *s.* Saor-thiodhlac.
Gratulation, *s.* Fàilte, fàilteachadh; co-ghàirdeachas, co-bhuidheachas.
Gratulatory, *adj.* Sòlasach, coghàirdeachail.
Grave, *s.* Uaigh.
Grave, *v.* Gèarr, gràbhal; tarruinn, sgrìobh.
Grave, *adj.* Stòlda, suidhichte, sàmhach, cudthromach; trom, tormanach.
Graveclothes, *s.* Aodach mairbh.
Gravel, *s.* Grinneal; galar-fuail.
Gravel, *v. a.* Còmhdaich le grinneal; amail, grab, bac.
Gravelly, *adj.* Grinnealach.
Graver, *s.* Fear-gràbhalaidh; inneal gràbhalaidh, gilb-ghràbhalaidh.
Gravidity, *s.* Leth-tromachas.
Graving, *s.* Gràbhaladh, obair gràbhalaiche.
Gravitate, *v. n.* Tuit, theirig le bruthach.
Gravitation, *s.* Tuiteam, tèarnadh.
Gravity, Graveness, *s.* Cudthrom, truimead; antromachadh, stòldachd, suidheachadh-inntinn.
Gravy, *s.* Sùgh feòla.
Gray, *adj.* Glas, liath; ciar
Grayish, *adj.* Liath-ghlas.
Graze, *v.* Feuraich, cuir air feur; ionaltair, ith feur, suath, bean.
Grazier, *s.* Àireach, fear sprèidhe
Grazing, *s.* Ionaltradh.
Grease, *s.* Crèis, geir, saill.
Grease, *v. a.* Buaic, smeur.
Greasiness, *s.* Reamhrachd.
Greasy, *adj.* Crèiseach, geireach.
Great, *adj.* Mòr, dòmhail; lìonmhor, fada; àrd; uaibhreach, àrdanach; làn, torrach.
Greatness, *s.* Mòrachd, meudachd; mòralachd, àrd-inbhe, urram, cumhachd; uaill, uaibhreachas, àrdan.
Greaves, *s.* Cas-bheairt.
Greece, *s.* A' Ghrèig.
Greediness, *s.* Sannt, gionach, lon.
Greedy, *adj.* Sanntach, gionach, cìocrach, lonach, glutach, glàmhach.
Green, *adj.* Uaine, gorm; glas; ùrail, ùr; àitidh, fliuch, tais; anabaich.
Green, *s.* Dath uaine no gorm; rèidhlean, àilean, lèan, raon.
Green-cloth, *s.* Am bòrd-uaine.
Greenness, *s.* Uainead, guirme; anabaicheachd, anabaichead; ùraireachd.
Greensickness, *s.* An galar-uaine.
Greet, *v. n.* Fàiltich, furanaich; dean co-ghàirdeachas; cuir beannachd.
Greeting, *s.* Fàilte, furan, beannachd.
Gregarious, *adj.* Greigheach.
Grenade, Grenado, *s.* Peileir spealgach.
Grenadier, *s.* Saighdear àrd.
Greyhound, *s.* Mìol-chù, gaothar.
Grice, *s.* Orcan, uircean.
Gridiron, *s.* Branndair.
Grief, *s.* Bròn, doilghios, mulad, bristeadh-cridhe.
Grievance, *s.* Dochunn, cruaidhchas.
Grieve, *v.* Cràidh, dochainn; dean tùrsach; caoidh; bi fo bhròn.
Grievous, *adj.* Doilghiosach, cràidhteach, searbh; trom, anabarrach.
Griffin, Griffon, *s.* Leòghan-sgiathach.
Grig, *s.* Easgann bheag; creutair guanach, mireagach.

Grim, *adj.* Gruamach, mùgach, duaichnidh, gnù, neo-aoidheil.
Grimace, *s.* Gruaim, mùig.
Grimness, *s.* Gruamachd.
Grin, *v. n.* Cuir dréin ort.
Grin, *s.* Dréin, braoisg.
Grind, *v.* Meil, bleith, pronn; suath, geuraich; dean bleith, bi bleith.
Grinder, *s.* Muillear, meiltear; muileann, cùl-fhiacail.
Grindstone, *s.* Clach-gheurachaidh.
Gripe, *v.* Greimich, glac; cum daingean; teannaich, fàisg; cràidh.
Gripe, *s.* Greim; fàsgadh, teannachadh; éigin, cruaidh-chas; greim mionaich.
Grisly, *adj.* Déisinneach, oillteil.
Grist, *s.* Gràn caoin.
Gristle, *s.* Maothan, brisgein.
Gristly, *adj.* Maothanach.
Grit, *s.* Garbhan, còrlach.
Grizzled, **Grizzly**, *adj.* Gris-fhionn.
Groan, *v. n.* Osnaich, gearain, cnead.
Groan, *s.* Acain, osna, gearan, cnead.
Groat, *s.* Ceithir sgillinn, gròt.
Grocer, *s.* Ceannaiche sùcair, tì, a's spiosraidh, &c.
Grog, *s.* Spiorad a's uisge co-mheasgte.
Groin, *s.* Loch-bhléin.
Groom, *s.* Gill'-each.
Groove, *s.* Uamh, sloc; clais.
Grope, *v. n.* Smeuraich.
Gross, *adj.* Garbh, tiugh, dòmhail, reamhar, sultmhor; déisinneach, neo-cheanalta, neo-thaitneach; neo-ghlan, neo-fhìnealta; iomlan, uile.
Gross, *s.* A' chuid mhòr, a' chuid a s mò; an t-iomlan; dà dhusan-deug.
Grossness, *s.* Gairbhead, tiuighead, dòmhlachd; reamhrachd; ùmpadalachd.
Grot, **Grotto**, *s.* Sgàil-thaigh.
Grotesque, *adj.* Mi-dhealbhach, eucuanda mi-nadurach.
Grove, *s.* Doire, coille, badan.
Grovel, *v. n.* Snàig, màg; bi suarach, bi ìosal.
Ground, *s.* Talamh; làr, fonn; fearann, tìr; dùthaich; aobhar, bun, bunchar, toiseach.
Ground, *v. a.* Suidhich 's an talamh; socraich air làr; stéidhich, taic; bonn-shuidhich.
Ground-ivy, *s.* Athair-lùs, staoin.
Groundless, *adj.* Gun aobhar.
Groundsel, **Grunsel**, *s.* Grunnasg.
Groundwork, *s.* Bunabhas, stéidh.
Groupe, *s.* Grunnan, dòrlach.
Grouse, *s.* Eòin fhraoich.
Grow, *v. n.* Thoir fàs air; fàs, cinn, meudaich; at, éirich suas.
Growl, *v. n.* Dean grùnsgul, dean borbhanaich; talaich.
Growling, *s.* Grùnsgul, talach, borbhan.
Grown, *part.* Cinnichte, air fàs.
Growth, *s.* Fàs, cinneas; toradh; meudachadh, teachd air aghart.
Grub, *v. a.* Bùraich, cladhaich.
Grub, *s.* Cnuimh mhìllteach.
Grubble, *v. n.* Smeuraich.
Grudge, *v.* Maoidh air, talaich; gabh farmad ri; bi neo-thoileach; bi farmadach, bi gamhlasach.
Grudge, *s.* Mì-run, gamhlas, tnu; falachd; farmad, diomb.
Gruel, *s.* Brochan, easach.
Gruff, **Grum**, *adj.* Gruamach, mugach, doirbh, neo-aoidheil.
Grumble, *v. n.* Talaich, dean duarmanaich, gearain, dean grùnsgul.
Grumbler, *s.* Fear-talaich.
Grumbling, *s.* Gearan, duarmanaich.
Grunt, **Gruntle**, *v. n.* Dean gnosail, sgiamh mar mhuic.
Grunt, *s.* Gnosail, osna, cnead, acain.
Gruntling, *s.* Uircean, orcan.
Guarantee, *s.* Urras; dearbhachd.
Guard, *v. a.* Dìon, dìdinn, gléidh.
Guard, *s.* Freiceadan; faire, earalas.
Guardian, *s.* Fear-gleidhidh, fear-dìona.
Guardian, *adj.* Dìonach, gléidhteach.
Guardianship, *s.* Dreuchd fir-diona.
Guardless, *adj.* Gun dìon.
Guardship, *s.* Long-dhìona.
Gudgeon, *s.* Clibist; bronnag.
Guess, *v.* Thoir tuaiream, tomhais; thoir barail, baralaich.
Guess, *s.* Barail, tuaiream, meas.
Guest, *s.* Aoidh, coigreach.
Guidance, *s.* Seòladh, steòrnadh, stiùradh, treòrachadh, riaghladh.
Guide, *v. a.* Seòl, steòrn, treòraich.
Guide, *s.* Fear-treòrachaidh, fear-seòlaidh; fear-steòrnaidh; fear-riaghlaidh, stiùradair.
Guideless, *adj.* Seachranach, gun treòir.
Guild, *s.* Comunn, buidheann.
Guile, *s.* Cealg, foill, cluain.
Guileful, *adj.* Cealgach, foilleil.
Guileless, *adj.* Neo-chealgach, neo-fhoilleil, tréidhireach, gun ghò.
Guillemot, *s.* Eun-a'-chrùbain.
Guillotine, *s.* Inneal dìth-cheannaidh.
Guilt, *s.* Cionta, cron, easaontas.
Guiltiness, *s.* Cionta, aingeachd.

GUILTLESS, *adj.* Neo-chiontach.
GUILTY, *adj.* Ciontach; aingidh.
GUINEA, *s.* Bonn òir sgillinn thar fhichead Shasunnach.
GUISE, *s.* Seòl, modh, dòigh; aogas, éideadh.
GULES, *adj.* Dearg an gearradh-arm.
GULF, *s.* Camus, geodha, bàgh; dubh-aigean; coire cuairteig, slugan.
GULL, *v. a.* Meall, thoir car á.
GULL, *s.* Car, cleas, mi-chleas, cuil-bheart; baothaire; faoileag.
GULLET, *s.* Sgòrnan, slùgan, eitigh-each.
GULLY, *s.* Clais dhomhain uisge.
GULP, *v. a.* Gloc, glut, sluig.
GUM, *s.* Bìth; càirean.
GUM, *v. a.* Buaic le bìth, dlùthaich le bìth.
GUMMINESS, *s.* Rìghnead, rìghneachas.
GUMMY, *adj.* Bìtheanta, righinn.
GUN, *s.* Gunna.
GUNNER, *s.* Gunnair.
GUNNERY, *s.* Gunnaireachd.
GUNPOWDER, *s.* Fùdar-gunna.
GUNSHOT, *s.* Urchair gunna.
GUNSMITH, *s.* Gobha-ghunnachan.
GUNSTONE, *s.* Peileir gunna mhòir.
GUNWALE, GUNNEL, *s.* Beul-mòr bàta no luinge.
GURGLE, *v. n.* Dean glugan.
GURNET, GURNARD, *s.* Cnùdan, cnò-dan, crùdan.
GUSH, *v. n.* Spùt, sruth, brùchd, taoisg.
GUSH, *s.* Brùchd, spùt, taosg.
GUSSET, *s.* Guiseid, eang.
GUST, *s.* Blas; sàth-mhiann, déidh, taitneachd; osag, oiteag, cuairt-ghaoth.
GUSTATION, *s.* Blasad, blasachd.
GUSTFUL, *adj.* Blasda, taitneach.
GUSTO, *s.* Blas, miann, aomadh-inntinn.
GUSTY, *adj.* Stoirmeil, gaothar.
GUT, *s.* Caolan; geòcaireachd.
GUT, *v. a.* Thoir am mionach á; spùill, spùinn, creach.
GUTTER, *s.* Guiteir.
GUTTLER, *s.* Glutaire, geòcaire.
GUTTURAL, *adj.* Tùchanach, a' labh-airt troi 'n sgòrnan.
GUZZLE, *v. a.* Sluig, òl gu bras.
GUZZLER, *s.* Geòcaire, pòitear.
GYMNASIUM, *s.* Sgoil-lù-chleas.
GYMNASTIC, *adj.* Lù-chleasach.
GYNECOCRACY, *s.* Rìaghladh mnà.
GYRATION, *s.* Cur mu chuairt.
GYRE, *s.* Cuairt, cearcall.
GYVES, *s.* Geimhlean, glas-chas, ceap.

H

H, *s.* Ochdamh litir na h-aibidil.
Ha! *interj.* Ha!
HABERDASHER, *s.* Ceannaich'-aod-aichean.
HABERDASHERY, *s.* Aodaichean.
HABERDINE, *s.* Trosg saillt' tioram.
HABERGEON, *s.* Uchd-éideadh.
HABILIMENT, *s.* Éideadh, earradh.
HABIT, *s.* Còr, staid; uidheam, earr-adh, éideadh; cleachdadh, gnàth-achadh.
HABITABLE, *adj.* Freagarrach air son còmhnaidh.
HABITANT, *s.* Tàmhaiche.
HABITATION, *s.* Ionad-còmhnaidh.
HABITUAL, *adj.* Cleachdach, gnàth-ach, gnàthaichte.
HABITUATE, *v. a.* Cleachd, gnàthaich.
HABITUDE, *s.* Càirdeas, còrdadh; gnàthachadh, cleachdadh.
HACK, *v. a.* Spealg, géarr, eagaich.
HACK, *s.* Each réidh.
HACKLE, *v. a.* Seicil, cìr.
HACKNEY, *s.* Each réidh; tàrlaid.
HADDOCK, *s.* Adag.
HAFT, *s.* Cas, samhach.
HAG, *s.* Baobh, ban-draoidh, buid-seach; cailleach ghrannda mi-aoidh-eil.
HAGGARD, HAGGARDLY, *adj.* Fiadh-aich, borb, garg; duaichnidh, grann-da, oillteil.
HAGGESS, *s.* Taigeis.
HAGGISH, *adj.* Basbhaidh, duaichnidh.
HAGGLE, *v.* Gearr, pronn, eagaich.
HAGGLER, *s.* Fear gearraidh; fear righinn an co-cheannachd.
HAIL, *s.* Mheallan, geal-shìon.
HAIL! *interj.* Fáilte! slàinte!
HAILSTONE, *s.* Clach-mheallain.
HAIR, *s.* Falt, ròine, fuiltean: fionn-adh, gaoisid, calg.
HAIRBRAINED, *adj.* Sgaogach.
HAIRINESS, *s.* Romaiche.
HAIRY, *adj.* Ròmach, molach, roin-each, fionnach.
HALBERD, *s.* Pic-chatha.
HALCYON, *adj.* Sèimh, ciùin.
HALE, *adj.* Slàn, cridheil, sùgach.
HALE, *v. a.* Slaoid, dragh.
HALF, *s.* Leth.
HALFBLOOD, *adj.* Riataich.
HALFPENNY, *s.* Bonna-sè.
HALIMASS, *s.* Latha nan uile naomh.
HALING, *s.* Draghadh, slaodadh.

HALL, *s.* Talla-mòid; lùchairt.
HALLELUJAH, *s.* Moladh do Dhia.
HALLOO, *v. a.* Stuig, leig, brosnaich, glaodh; beuc, dean gàir.
HALLOW, *v. a.* Naomhaich, coisrig.
HALLUCINATION, *s.* Mearachd.
HALO, *s.* Roth na gréine, no na gealaiche.
HALSER, HAWSER, *s.* Muir-theud; taod, còrd; ball bàta.
HALT, *v. n.* Bi crùbach, bi bacach; stad, seas; bi 'n imcheist; bi teabadaich.
HALT, *adj.* Crùbach, bacach.
HALT, *s.* Crùbaiche; stad, seasamh.
HALTER, *s.* Taod, tobha na croiche.
HALVE, *v. a.* Roinn 'na dhà leth.
HAM, *s.* Spàg, sliasaid, ceithreamhdeiridh; sliasaid shaillte chrochte.
HAMLET, *s.* Baile beag, clachan.
HAMMER, *s.* Òrd.
HAMMER, *v.* Buail le òrd.
HAMMOCK, *s.* Leaba chrochta.
HAMPER, *s.* Cliabh, sgùlan.
HAMPER, *v. a.* Cuibhrich, cuir amladh air; cuir an sàs, cuir an ribe.
HAMSTRING, *s.* Féithe na h-iosgaid.
HAND, *s.* Làmh; tomhas cheithir òirleach; dòigh, seòl.
HAND, *v. a.* Thoir as do làimh, sìn, thoir, tabhair, thoir seachad.
HANDBREADTH, *s.* Leud boise.
HANDCUFF, *s.* Glas-làmh.
HANDICRAFT, *s.* Cèaird.
HANDFUL, *s.* Làn dùirn, dòrlach.
HANDINESS, *s.* Làmhchaireachd.
HANDKERCHIEF, *s.* Éideadh muineil.
HANDLE, *v. a.* Laimhsich.
HANDLE, *s.* Làmh, cǎs, cluas.
HANDMAID, *s.* Banoglach.
HANDSAW, *s.* Sàbh làimhe.
HANDSEL, HANSEL, *s.* Sainnseal.
HANDSOME, *adj.* Maiseach, àillidh, eireachdail, bòidheach; mòr, gasda.
HANDWRITING, *s.* Lamh-sgrìobhaidh.
HANDY, *adj.* Làmhchair, deas, ealamh.
HANG, *v.* Croch; bi'n imcheist.
HANGER, *s.* Cuinnsear.
HANGING, *adj.* An crochadh, a crochadh.
HANGMAN, *s.* Crochadair.
HANK, *s.* Iarna.
HANKER, *v. n.* Bi'n geall air.
HAP, *s.* Tubais; tuiteamas, tachairt.
HAPHAZARD, *s.* Tuiteamas, tubaist.
HAPLESS, *adj.* Mi-shealbhar, mishona, neo-sheamhsar.
HAPLY, *adv.* Theagamh.
HAPPEN, *v. n.* Tachair, tuit a mach.
HAPPINESS, *s.* Sonas, àgh, sealbh.
HAPPY, *adj.* Sona, sòlasach, àghmhor, sealbhach, rathail; deas, ealamh.
HARANGUE, *s.* Òraid, seanachas.
HARASS, *v. a.* Claoidh, sàraich, léir.
HARBINGER, *s.* Roi-ruithear, teachdair.
HARBOUR, HARBOURAGE, *s.* Cala, acarsaid, dìon, dìdean.
HARBOUR, *v.* Gabh ri, thoir fasgadh do; gabh còmhnaidh, gabh dìon.
HARD, *adj.* Cruaidh, teann, daingeann; duilich r'a thuigsinn; deacair, doirbh; dòghruinneach, cràidhteach; an-iochdmhor, cruadalach, garg; gann.
HARD, *adv.* Am fagus, dlù, teann; gu dìchiollach, gu dian, gu dùrachdach.
HARDEN, *v. a.* Cruadhaich, teannaich, lean ri; dean ladorna; fàs cruaidh, fàs teann.
HARDFAVOURED, *adj.* Duaichnidh.
HARDIHOOD, *s.* Cruadal, danarrachd.
HARDINESS, *s.* Cruadal; dànachd.
HARDNESS, *s.* Cruas; an-iochd, buirbe.
HARDS, *s.* Ascart.
HARDSHIP, *s.* Cruaidh-chas, teanntachd, fòirneart, teinn; éigin.
HARDWARE, *s.* Bathar cruaidh.
HARDY, *adj.* Dàna, ladorna, danarra; gaisgeil; cruadalach, fulangach.
HARE, *s.* Maigheach, gearr.
HAREBELL, *s.* Currac-na-cuthaige.
HAREBRAINED, *adj.* Gaoitheanach.
HARRIER, *s.* Tòlair mhaigheach.
HARK, *interj.* Éisd! cluinn! tost!
HARLEQUIN, *s.* Àmhuilteach.
HARLOT, *s.* Strìopach, siùrsach.
HARLOTRY, *s.* Strìopachas.
HARM, *s.* Cron, aimhleas, lochd, coire, ciorram, dolaidh, call, beud, dochair.
HARM, *v. a.* Ciùrr, dochainn, lochdaich.
HARMFUL, *adj.* Cronail, lochdach.
HARMLESS, *adj.* Neo-chiontach, neochronail, neo-lochdach; sàbhailte.
HARMONIC, HARMONICAL, *adj.* Cofhuaimneach, co-cheòlach; binn.
HARMONIOUS, *adj.* Co-chòrdach.
HARMONIST, *s.* Fear-ciùil.
HARMONIZE, *v. a.* Dean co-fhuaimneach; co-fhreagair.
HARMONY, *s* Co-sheirm, co-chòrdadh, co-fhreagairt; co-cheòl; càirdeas.
HARNESS, *s.* Fasair; armachd.
HARP, *s.* Clàrsach, cruit-chiùil.
HARP, *v. a.* Cluich air clàrsaich.
HARPER, *s.* Clàrsair, cruitear.
HARPOON, *s.* Mòr-ghath muice-mara.

Harpooner, *s.* Fear tilgidh mŏr-ghath na muice-mara.
Harpsichord, *s.* Cruit-chiŭil.
Harpy, *s.* Gionair, glàmair.
Harridan, *s.* Sean strìopach sheargte.
Harrow, *s.* Cliath-chliata.
Harrow, *v. a.* Cliath; buair.
Harsh, *adj.* Searbh, garg, borb, reasgach, frithearra; neo-bhinn; coimheach, cruaidh, teann.
Harshness, *s.* Searbhachd, gairge, gairgead; neo-fhonnmhorachd; reasgachd; buirbe.
Hart, *s.* Damh fĕigh.
Hartshorn, *s.* Sugh chabar fĕigh.
Harvest, *s.* Foghar, toradh.
Harvesting, *part. v.* Fogharadh.
Harvest-home, *s.* Deireadh buana.
Hash, *v. a.* Pronn, gèarr, bloighdich.
Hash, *s.* Feòil phronn.
Hassock, *s.* Cluasag ghlŭin.
Haste, *s.* Cabhag, greasad; fearg.
Haste, Hasten, *v. a.* Greas, luathaich, brosnaich, cuir cabhag air; deifirich, dean cabhag.
Hastings, *s.* Luath-pheasair.
Hastiness, *s.* Greasachd, deifir, cabhag, luaths; frionas, crosdachd, conasachd.
Hasty, *adj.* Luath, cabhagach; deifireach, grad, ealamh; bras, crosda, dian, lasanta, obann, clis.
Hasty-pudding, *s.* Mèilean, stăpag.
Hat, *s.* Bioraid, ăd.
Hatch, *v.* Guir, thoir a mach eòin; thoir gu crìch; àlaich, tàrmaich.
Hatch, *s.* Gur, linn, àlach; dorus bŭird luinge.
Hatchet, *s.* Làmh-thuadh.
Hate, *v. a.* Fuathaich, gràinich, oilltich, sgreamhaich.
Hate, Hatred, *s.* Fuath, gràin, oillt, sgreamh, gairisinn, gamhlas, mìrun, naimhdeas.
Hateful, *adj.* Fuathach, gràineil, gairisneach, sgreamhail, sgreataidh, dĕisinneach.
Hatter, *s.* Fear-dèanamh ădan.
Have, *v. a.* Biodh agad; giŭlain, caith; seilbhich, meal; iarr, agair.
Haven, *s.* Cala, acarsaid, seŏlait.
Having, *s.* Sealbh, maoin.
Haugh, *s.* Lèanan.
Haughtiness, *s.* Àrdan, uaibhreachas, uaill, uabhar.
Haughty, *adj.* Àrdanach, uaibhreach, mòr-chuiseach, àileasach, àrd-inntinneach; stràiceil, meamnach.
Haul, *v. a.* Tarruinn, slaoid.
Haum, *s.* Fodar, connlach.
Haunch, *s.* Sliasaid, màs, cruachann.
Haunt, *v. a.* Taghail, taghaich.
Havock, *s.* Àr, milleadh, sgrios.
Haw, *s.* Sgeachac; găgail.
Haw, *v. n.* Briudhinn gu găgach.
Hawk, *s.* Seabhac, speireag.
Hawk, *v. n.* Éigh bathar gu 'reic; sealg le seabhaic; ròc, casadaich.
Hawker, *s.* Seabhacair; fear-éigheach bathair, ceannaiche-màlaid.
Hawthorn, *s.* Sgitheach, droigheann.
Hay, *s.* Feur-saidhe.
Haymaker, *s.* Fear caoineachaidh feòir.
Hayrick, Haystack, *s.* Curracacfheòir, tŭdan, mŏlan.
Hazard, *s.* Cunnart; tuiteamas.
Hazard, *v. a.* Cuir an cunnart; feuch ri, feuch cuid tuiteamais.
Hazardous, *adj.* Cunnartach.
Haze, *s.* Ceŏ, ceathach, smŭd.
Hazel, *s.* Calltunn.
Hazel, Hazelly, *adj.* Air dhath calltuinn.
He, *pron.* Ĕ, se, esan; firionnta.
Head, *s.* Ceann; ceannard; toiseach; tuigse; mullach; neach; barr, uachdar; àirde, cead, comas, saorthoil.
Head, *v. a.* Treòraich, stiŭr, riaghail; dìth-cheann; cuir ceann air.
Headach, *s.* Ceann-ghalair, cràdh cinn.
Head-bands, *s.* Beannag.
Head-dress, *s.* Anard-cinn.
Headland, *s.* Ceann-tìre, maol, rutha.
Headless, *adj.* Gun cheann, gun cheannard; neo-thŭrail, aineolach.
Headlong, *adj.* Cas, corrach, grad; bras, obann, cabhagach.
Headlong, *adv.* An coinneamh a chinn; gu bras, gu h-obann; gu neo-smaointeachail.
Headpiece, *s.* Clogaid, tuigse.
Headstall, *s.* Claigeann aghastair.
Headstrong, *adj.* Ceann-laidir.
Heady, *adj.* Dian, bras, cas; cabhagach, ceann-laidir; a' dol 'sa' cheann.
Heal, *v.* Leighis, slànaich, dean gu math; fàs gu math, fàs slàn.
Healing, *part.* Leigheasach.
Health, *s.* Slàinte, fallaineachd.
Healthful, Healthsome, *adj.* Slàn, fallain; slàinteil.
Healthy, *adj.* Slàn, fallain; slàinteil.
Heap, *s.* Tòrr, dŭn, cărn, cruach.
Heap, *v. a.* Cărn, cruach, cruinnich.
Hear, *v.* Cluinn, éisd.
Hearer, *s.* Fear-éisdeachd.

HEARING, *s.* Clàisneachd; éisdeachd.
HEARKEN, *v. n.* Éisd, cluinn.
HEARSAY, *s.* Iomradh, fathunn.
HEARSE, *s.* Carbad-mhàrbh.
HEART, *s.* Cridhe; meadhon.
HEARTACH, *s.* Briseadh-cridhe.
HEARTBURNING, *s.* Losgadh-bràghad.
HEART-EASE, *s.* Socair inntinn.
HEARTFELT, *adj.* A' ruigheachd a chridhe.
HEARTSTRINGS, *s.* Féithean a' chridhe.
HEARTEN, *v. a.* Misnich, beothaich.
HEARTH, *s.* Teinntean, cagailt.
HEARTHMONEY, *s.* Cìs-teallaich.
HEARTINESS, *s.* Tréidhireas; cridhealas, sunnt, beathalachd.
HEARTLESS, *s.* Lag-chridheach.
HEARTY, *adj.* Dùrachdach, dìleas; slàn, slàinteil; cridheil, treòrach, sunntach.
HEAT, *s.* Teas; blàths, bruthainn; buaireas, ainteas; braise.
HEAT, *v. a.* Teasaich, teò; cuir air boile, cuir air ghoil; blàthaich.
HEATER, *s.* Uidheam teasachaidh, iarunn teinntidh.
HEATH, *s.* Fraoch.
HEATHCOCK, *s.* Coileach-fraoich.
HEATHEN, *s.* Cinneach, geintealach.
HEATHEN, HEATHENISH, *adj.* Pàganach; fiadhaich, allamharra.
HEATHENISM, *s.* Pàganachd.
HEATHY, *adj.* Fraochach, làn fraoich.
HEAVE, *s.* Togail, ospag, plosg.
HEAVE, *v.* Tog suas, luaisg; bòrc, bòc; plosg, tarruinn osna; ăt, éirich suas.
HEAVEN, *s.* Nèamh, speur, adhar, iarmailt; flatshonas, flaitheas.
HEAVENLY, *adj.* Nèamhaidh, flathail, naomha, diadhaidh.
HEAVINESS, *s.* Cudthrom, truime, truimead; airtneal, cianalas, sproc, mulad, trom-inntinn.
HEAVY, *adj.* Trom, cudthromach; airtnealach, cianail, trom-inntinneach, neo-shunntach; leisg, lunndach, cadalach, trom-cheannach, pleoisgeach; neulach, dorcha.
HEBDOMAND, *s.* Ùine sheachd latha.
HEBDOMADAL, HEBDOMADARY, *adj.* Seachduineil.
HEBREW, *s.* Eabhrach; Eabhra.
HEBREW, *adj.* Eabhrach.
HECATOMB, *s.* Ìobairt-cheud.
HECTIC, HECTICAL, *adj.* Gnàthach, fiabhrasach.
HECTOR, *s.* Bagaire, bòsdair.
HEDGE, *s.* Fàl-gléidhte, callaid.
HEDGE, *v.* Dùin le fàl, druid suas le droighionn, cuairtich le callaid.
HEDGEBORN, *adj.* An-uasal.
HEDGEHOG, *s.* Cràineag.
HEDGER, *s.* Fear-togail fàil-gléite.
HEED, *v. a.* Thoir fainear, thoir aire.
HEED, *s.* Cùram, aire, faicill.
HEEDFUL, *adj.* Cùramach, faicilleach, furachair; aireachail, aireach.
HEEDLESS, *adj.* Neo-chùramach.
HEEDLESSNESS, *s.* Dearmadachd.
HEEL, *s.* Sàil; cas beathaich.
HEEL, *v.* Cuir spuir air coileach; aom, claon, laidh air aon taobh.
HEFT, *s.* Làmh, cas, sămhach.
HEGIRA, *s.* Ceann cunntais aimsir nan Arabach.
HEIFER, *s* Agh, atharla.
HEIGH-HO! *interj.* Oich O!
HEIGHT, *s.* Àirde, àirdead; mullach, binnein; inbhe; iomlanachd.
HEIGHTEN, *v. a.* Àrdaich, tog suas, meudaich; leasaich; an-tromaich.
HEINOUS, *adj.* Uabhasach, amasgaidh, anabarrach, an-trom.
HEINOUSNESS, *s.* Uabhasachd, uabharrachd, amasgaidheachd.
HEIR, *s.* Oighre.
HEIR, *v. a.* Seilbhich mar oighre.
HEIRESS, *s.* Ban-oighre.
HEIRLESS, *adj.* Gun oighre.
HEIRLOOM, *s.* Ball-sinnsireachd.
HEIRSHIP, *s.* Staid oighre.
HELIOSCOPE, *s.* Gloine gréine.
HELL, *s.* Ifrinn, irinn, iutharn.
HELLENIC, *adj.* Greugach.
HELLISH, *adj.* Ifrinneach.
HELM, *s.* Clogaid; falmadair.
HELMED, *adj.* Clogaideach.
HELMET, *s.* Clogaid.
HELMSMAN, *s.* Stiùradair.
HELP, *v.* Cuidich, cobhair, foir, comhnaich, furtaich; cuir air aghart; thoir cobhair, thoir cuideachadh.
HELP, *s.* Cuideachadh, cobhair, còmhnadh, taic; fuasgladh, furtachd.
HELPFUL, *adj.* Cuideachail, cobharach, comhnachail.
HELPLESS, *adj.* Bochd, truagh, gun chòmhnadh, gun chobhair.
HELPMATE, *s.* Co-chuidiche.
HELTER-SKELTER, *adv.* Uathrais-air-thàrais; muin air mhuin.
HELVE, *s.* Sămhach tuaidhe.
HEM, *s.* Fàitheam; cnead, casad.
HEM, *v. a.* Cuir fàitheam air, cuir oir ri; iomadhruid, cuairtich; cnead, dean casad.
HEMISPHERE, *s.* Leth-chruinne.
HEMISTICH, *s.* Leth-rann.

HEMLOCK, *s.* Iteotha, minmhear.
HEMORRHAGE, *s.* A' ghèarrach-fhala.
HEMORRHOIDS, *s.* Neasgaidean fola.
HEMP, *s.* Còrcach.
HEMPEN, *adj.* Cainbe, còrcaich.
HEN, *s.* Cearc.
HENCOOP, *s.* Crò-chearc.
HENPECKED, *adj.* Fo smachd mnatha.
HENROOST, *s.* Spardan, spiris, iris.
HENCE! *interj.* or *adv.* As a' so! uaithe so; air falbh, fad' ás; o'n aobhar so, o'n bhun so.
HENCEFORTH, HENCEFORWARD, *adv.* Uaithe so a mach.
HEPTAGON, *s.* Seachd-shlisneach.
HEPTAGONAL, *adj.* Seachd-shlisneach.
HEPTARCHY, *s.* Riaghladh sheachd-nar.
HER, *pron.* I, ise.
HERALD, *s.* Àrd-mhaor-rìgh; teachd-aire.
HERALDRY, *s.* Dreuchd àrd mhaoir rìgh; eòlas ghearradh-arm.
HERB, *s.* Lŭs, luibh.
HERBACEOUS, *adj.* Lŭsach.
HERBAGE, *s.* Feur, feurach.
HERBAL, *s.* Clar-ainm luibhean.
HERBALIST, *s.* Lŭsragan.
HERBY, *adj.* Lŭsach, luibheach.
HERCULEAN, *adj.* Mòr, làidir.
HERD, *s.* Greigh, buar, treud.
HERD, *v.* Buachaillich; comunnaich.
HERDSMAN, *s.* Buachaille,
HERE, *adv.* An so, 's an àite so.
HEREABOUTS, *adv.* Mu thimchioll so, uime so, mu'n cuairt da so.
HEREAFTER, *adv.* 'San àm ri teachd; 'san ath-shaoghal, 'san ath-bheatha.
HEREAFTER, *s.* Ath-shaoghal.
HEREBY, *adv.* Le so, leis a' so.
HEREDITABLE, *adj.* A' teachd mar oighreachd.
HEREDITARY, *adj.* Dùthchasach, a' teachd le còir oighre.
HEREIN, HEREINTO, *adv.* An so.
HEREOF, *adv.* Uaithe so.
HEREON, HEREUPON, *adv.* Air a' so.
HEREOUT, *adv.* As a' so.
HERESY, *s.* Saobh-chreideamh.
HERETIC, *s.* Saobh-chreideach.
HERETICAL, *adj.* Saobh-chreidmheach.
HERETO, HEREUNTO, *adv.* Gu so.
HERETOFORE, *adv.* Roi' so.
HEREUPON, *adv.* Air a' so.
HEREWITH, *adv.* Leis a' so, le so.
HERIOT, *s.* Càrbhaist.
HERITAGE, *s.* Oighreachd.
HERMAPHRODITE, *s.* Neach firionn-boireann.
HERMIT, *s.* Ònaran.
HERMITAGE, *s.* Bothan onarain.
HERNIA, *s.* Màm-sice.
HERO, *s.* Curaidh, gaisgeach, laoch.
HEROIC, HEROICAL, *adj.* Gaisgeil, treun, foghainteach, buadhach, euchdach.
HEROESS, HEROINE, *s.* Ban-laoch, bana-ghaisgeach, bann-seud.
HEROISM, *s.* Euchd, gaisge, treuntas.
HERN, HERON, *s.* Corra-ghriodhach.
HERONRY, *s.* Aite nead nan còrr.
HERRING, *s.* Sgadan.
HERSELF, *pron.* Ise, i-féin.
HESITATE, *v. a.* Stad, bi 'n imcheist, sòr, ŏb, seun.
HESITATION, *s.* Teagamh, amharus.
HETERODOX, *adj.* Saobh-chreid-mheach.
HETEROGENEOUS, *adj.* Iol-ghnèitheach.
HEW, *v.* Gèarr, sgud, snaidh, sgath; cùm, dreach.
HEXAGON, *s.* Sé-shlisneag.
HEXAMETER, *s.* Bàrdachd shè-chas.
HEXANGULAR, *adj.* Sé-oisinneach.
HEY! *interj.* Il! Ìl!
HEYDAY, *s.* Mire, braise.
HIATUS, *s.* Bèarn, fosgladh.
HIBERNAL, *adj.* Geamhrachail.
HICCIUS-DOCCIUS, *s.* Cleasaiche.
HICCOUGH, *s.* Aileag.
HID, HIDDEN, *part.* Falaichte.
HIDE, *v. n.* Ceil, falaich.
HIDE, *s.* Seiche, seic, boicionn.
HIDE-AND-SEEK, *s.* Falach-fead.
HIDEOUS, *adj.* Uamharra, oillteil, eag-alach, déisinneach; gairisneach, sgreataidh, gràineil, grannda.
HIE, *v. n.* Falbh, greas, deifrich, dean cabhag.
HIERARCHY, *s.* Riaghladh-eaglais.
HIEROGLYPHIC, *s.* Dealbh-sgrìobhadh.
HIEROGLYPHICAL, *adj.* Samhlachail.
HIGH, *adj.* Àrd; mòr; uasal, urram-ach; spagluinneach, bòsdail; àrd-anach, uaibhreach, mòr-chuiseach.
HIGHLAND, *s.* Àrd-thir, braidhe.
HIGHLAND, *adj.* Gàëlach.
HIGHLANDER, *s.* Gàël.
HIGHMINDED, *adj.* Àrd-inntinneach.
HIGHNESS, *s.* Àirde; mòrachd.
HIGH-WATER, *s.* Muir-làn.
HIGHWAY, *s.* Rathad-mòr.
HIGHWAYMAN, *s.* Fear reubainn.
HILARITY, *s.* Cridhealas.
HILL, *s.* Beinn, monadh, sliabh.
HILLOCK, *s.* Cnoc, sìthean, tòrr.
HILLY, *adj.* Monadail, beanntach.
HILT, *s.* Dòrn-bheirt claidheimh.
HIMSELF, *pron.* E-féin.
HIND, *s.* Eilid, agh féigh; sgalag.

HINDER, *v. a.* Bac, grab ; cùm air ais.
HINDRANCE, *s.* Grabadh, bacadh.
HINDERMOST, HINDMOST, *adj.* Deireannach, air deireadh.
HINGE, *s.* Cùl-cheangal, bann.
HINT, *v. a.* Thoir sanas, thoir rabhadh.
HINT, *s.* Sanas, rabhadh.
HIP, *s.* Alt na sléisne, muc-fhàileag; trom-inntinn.
HIPPOPOTAMUS, *s.* An t-each-uisge.
HIPSHOT, *adj.* As an leis.
HIRE, *v. a.* Tuarasdalaich, gabh air thuarasdal; thoir air son tuarasdail, suidhich.
HIRE, *s.* Tuarasdal, duais, pàidheadh.
HIRELING, *s.* Tuarasdalaiche.
HIRSUTE, *adj.* Ròmach, molach.
HIS, *poss. pron. mas.* A.
HISS, *v.* Dìt, éigh sìos.
HIST ! *interj.* Uist ! eist !
HISTORIAN, *s.* Seanachaidh.
HISTORICAL, *adj.* Eachdrachail.
HISTORIOGRAPHER, *s.* Eachdraiche.
HISTORIOGRAPHY, *s.* Eachdaireachd.
HISTORIOLOGY, *s.* Eòlas eachdraidhe.
HISTORY, *s.* Eachdraidh.
HISTRIONIC, *adj.* Cluicheach.
HIT, *v.* Buail, cuimsich, amais.
HIT, *s.* Buille ; tuiteamas, tapas.
HITCH, *v. n.* Bi'n amladh ; gluais.
HITCHEL, *s.* Seicil, cìr-lin.
HITHE, *s.* Geodha, camus.
HITHE, *s.* Lamraig, seòlait.
HITHER, *adv.* An so, an taobh so.
HITHERTO, *adv.* Gus a nise, fathast.
HITHERWARD, *adv.* Chum an àite so.
HIVE, *s.* Beach-lann, sgeap.
HO ! *interj.* O ! ho !
HOAR-FROST, *s.* Liath-reodhadh.
HOARD, *s.* Tasgaidh, ulaidh.
HOARD, *v. a.* Càrn, taisg ; trus.
HOARINESS, *s.* Léithead.
HOARSE, *adj.* Tùchanach, garbh.
HOARSENESS, *s.* Tùchadh, rùsgadh cléibh.
HOARY, HOAR, *adj.* Liath, glas.
HOAX, *s.* Mealladh.
HOBBLE, *s.* Ceum crùbaiche.
HOBBY, *s.* Seòrsa seabhaic ; each-maide, làir-mhaide.
HOBGOBLIN, *s.* Màileachan, bòcan.
HOBNAIL, *s.* Tarunn crudha.
HOCK, *s.* Fìon Gearmailteach.
HOCUS-POCUS, *s.* Cleasaiche, mealltair.
HOD, *s.* Amar-aoil.
HODGEPODGE, *s.* Brochan-breac.
HOE, *s.* Fàl-fuinn, sgrìoban.
HOE, *v. a.* Cladhaich le fàl-fuinn.
HOG, *s.* Cullach, torc spothte.
HOGSHEAD, *s.* Togsaid.
HOGCOTE, HOGSTY, *s.* Fail mhuc.
HOGGISH, *adj.* Gionach, mosach.
HOG-HERD, *s.* Mucair.
HOGWASH, *s.* Biadh mhuc.
HOIDEN, *s.* Caile gun oilean.
HOIST, *v. a.* Tog suas.
HOLD, *v.* Cùm greim ; gléidh.
HOLD, *s.* Greim, greimeachadh ; cumail, gleidheach ; ceàrn luinge ; daingneach.
HOLDER, *s.* Fear-séilbhe.
HOLDFAST, *s.* Gramaiche.
HOLE, *s.* Toll ; sloc.
HOLIDAY, HOLYDAY, *s.* Latha-féile.
HOLINESS, *s.* Naomhachd, diadhachd.
HOLLAND, *s.* Olaind.
HOLLOW, *adj.* Còsach, fàs, falamh ; cealgach, foilleil.
HOLLOW, *s.* Còs, cobhan, sloc, lag.
HOLLOWNESS, *s.* Còsaichead, falamhachd ; mealltaireachd, neo-sheasmhachd.
HOLLY, *s.* Cuileann.
HOLLYHOCK, *s.* An ròs-mall.
HOLOCAIST, *s.* Iobairt-loist.
HOLOGRAPH, *s.* Dearbh-sgrìobhadh.
HOLY, *adj.* Naomha ; coisrigte.
HOMAGE, *s.* Dligheachas, dleasannas, seirbhis ; ùmhlachd, strìochdadh.
HOME, *s.* Dachaigh, teach.
HOME, *adv.* Dhachaigh, gu 'thìr dùthchais ; gu 'chogais ; gu ceann.
HOMEBRED, *adj.* Nàdurra, dualach, dùthchasach ; neo-fhìnealta, socharach.
HOMELINESS, *s.* Neo-ghrinneas.
HOMELY, *adj.* Neo-ghrinn.
HOMER, *s.* Tomhas thrì pinnt.
HOMESPUN, *adj.* Neo-eireachdail.
HOMEWARD, *adv.* Dhachaigh.
HOMICIDE, *s.* Mort ; mortair.
HOMILY, *s.* Searmoin.
HOMOGENEOUS, *adj.* Co-ghnéitheach.
HOMOLOGOUS, *adj.* Co-ionann.
HONE, *s.* Clach-gheurachaidh.
HONEST, *adj.* Ionraic, onarach.
HONESTY, *s.* Ionracas, onair.
HONEY, *s.* Mil, meal.
HONEYCOMB, *s.* Cìr-mheala.
HONEYMOON, *s.* Mìos nam pòg.
HONEYSUCKLE, *s.* Lùs-a'-chraois.
HONIED, *adj.* Mileach, milis, blasda.
HONORARY, *adj.* Urramach.
HONOUR, *s.* Onair, urram ; meas.
HONOUR, *v. a.* Onaraich, cuir urram air ; àrdaich, tog gu urram ; glòraich, urramaich.
HONOURABLE, *adj.* Òirdheirc, urramach, onarach ; àrd, fiùghantach ; ceart, dìreach.

HOOD, *s*. Cionnabharr.
HOODWINK, *v. a.* Dall; meall, falaich.
HOOF, *s*. Crodhan, ionga, ladhar.
HOOFED, *adj*. Crodhanach, ladhrach.
HOOK, *s*. Dubhan, cromag; corran.
HOOK, *v. a.* Glac le dubhan, clic.
HOOKED, *adj*. Dubhanach, cromagach.
HOOP, *s*. Cearcall, cuairteag.
HOOP, *v*. Cuir cearcall air; cuairtich, iomadhruid; glaodh, éigh, dean ulfhartaich.
HOOPING-COUGH, *s*. An triuthach.
HOOT, *v. n.* Sgànraich, fuadaich; goir mar chomhachaig; glaodh, dean iolach.
HOP, *v*. Leum, dean beiceis, falbh air leth chois; bi bacach, bi crùbach.
HOP, *s*. Lùs-an-leanna; frith-leum.
HOPE, *s*. Dòchas, dùil.
HOPE, *v. n.* Biodh dùil, agad ri.
HOPEFUL, *adj*. Dòchasach, earbsach.
HOPELESS, *adj*. Eu-dòchasach.
HOPPER, *s*. Treabhailt; fear-beiceis.
HOPPLE, *v. n.* Deighnich, spearaich.
HORAL, HORARY, *adj*. Uaireil.
HORDE, *s*. Ceathairne.
HORIZON, *s*. Cuairt nan speur.
HORIZONTAL, *adj*. Còmhnard, réidh.
HORN, *s*. Adharc, eabar; còrn.
HORNBOOK, *s*. Leabhar na h-aibidil.
HORNED, *adj*. Adharcach, cròcach.
HORNET, *s*. Connsbeach.
HORNOWL, *s*. Comhachag adharcach.
HORNPIPE, *s*. Damhsa grad-charach.
HORNY, *adj*. Adharcail; cruaidh.
HOROGRAPHY, *s*. Eòlas uairean.
HOROLOGE, *s*. Uaireadair.
HOROSCOPE, *s*. Suidheachadh nan reull aig àm breith.
HORRIBLE, *adj*. Oillteil, uabhasach.
HORRID, *adj*. Oillteil, eagalach; déisinneach, sgreataidh; garbh, doirbh; gruamach, dorcha.
HORRIFIC, *adj*. Oillteil, uamharr, uabhasach, eagalach.
HORROR, *s*. Eagal, uamhunn, oilltchrith, ball-chrith; uamhaltachd.
HORSE, *s*. Each; marc-shluagh.
HORSEBACK, *s*. Marcachd.
HORSEBEAN, *s*. Ponar-nan-each.
HORSEGUARDS, *s*. Freiceadan each.
HORSEHAIR, *s*. Gaoisid-each.
HORSEMAN, *s*. Marcaiche.
HORSEMANSHIP, *s*. Marcachd.
HORSEWAY, *s*. Each shlighe.
HORTATION, *s*. Comhairleachadh.
HORTATIVE, *adj*. Earalach.
HORTICULTURE, *s*. Gàradaireachd.
HOSANNA, *s*. Moladh do Dhia.
HOSE, *s*. Osan, osain, mogain.
HOSIER, *s*. Fear-reic osan.
HOSPITABLE, *adj*. Fialaidh, faoilidh, fial, fiùghantach, aoidheil, furanach, fàilteach.
HOSPITAL, *s*. Tigh eiridinn.
HOSPITALITY, *s*. Aoidheachd.
HOST, *s*. Fear-taighe, fear-taigh-òsda; arm, feachd, armailt.
HOSTAGE, *s*. Fear-gill, braighde-gill.
HOSTESS, *s*. Bean-taighe, bean-taigh-òsda.
HOSTILE, *adj*. Naimhdeil, eascairdeach.
HOSTILITY, *s*. Naimhdeas, eascairdeas.
HOSTLER, *s*. Gill-each.
HOT, *adj*. Teth, teinntidh, loisgeach; bras, dian, garg, lasanta; deònach.
HOTBED, *s*. Leabaidh-theth.
HOTEL, *s*. Àrd-thaigh-òsda.
HOTHOUSE, *s*. Taigh-teth.
HOTNESS, *s*. Teas, gairgead, ainteas, braise, boile.
HOTSPUR, *s*. Fear dian, fear feargach.
HOVEL, *s*. Sgàth-thaigh, bruchlag, bothan.
HOVER, *v. n.* Itealaich; croch os ceann; iadh timchioll air; bi 'n ioma-cheist, bi 'n ioma-chomhairle.
HOUGH, *s*. Iosgaid, bac-na-h-iosgaid.
HOUGH, *v. a.* Gèarr iosgaid.
HOUND, *s*. Tòllair, gaothar, cùseilge.
HOUR, *s*. Uair, fad thri-fichead mionaid.
HOURGLASS, *s*. Glaine-ghainmhich.
HOURLY, *adv*. Gach uair.
HOUSE, *s*. Taigh, fàrdoch, teach.
HOUSE, *v*. Cuir a stigh, thoir fasgadh; gabh fasgadh, gabh dìon, dean còmhnaidh.
HOUSEBREAKER, *s*. Spùinneadair thaighean.
HOUSEBREAKING, *s*. Bristeadh agus spùinneadh thaighean.
HOUSEHOLD, *s*. Teaghlach.
HOUSEKEEPING, *s*. Banas-taighe.
HOUSELESS, *adj*. Gun àite-còmhnaidh.
HOUSEMAID, *s*. Maighdean-sheòmair.
HOUSEWIFE, *s*. Bean-taighe.
HOUSEWIFERY, *s*. Riaghladh teaghlaich.
HOW, *adv*. Cia mar, cia cho mòr; ciod an dòigh, cionnas; c'ar son, ciod an t-aobhar.
HOWBEIT, *adv*. Gidheadh.
HOWEVER, *adv*. Ciod air bith an dòigh; cò-dhiù; gidheadh.
HOWL, *v. n.* Dean ulfhartaich, dean

donnalaich; dean gul éigheach, dean burral.
HOWL, *s.* Donnal, burral, ràn, raoichd, gul éigheach, sgal.
HOY, *s.* Seòrsa bàta.
HUBBUB, *s.* Glaodh, iolach, gàir; othail, mi-riaghailt, aimhreit.
HUCKSTER, *s.* Frith-cheannaiche.
HUDDLE, *v.* Cuir umad gun dòigh; cuir thar a chéile, tilg air muin a chéile; dòmhlaich, thig muin air mhuin.
HUE, *s.* Dath, dreach, neul, tuar; iolach, glaodhaich, ruaig.
HUFF, *s.* Dod, sròineas, stuirt.
HUFF, *v.* Séid, bòc, ăt le àrdan.
HUFFISH, *adj.* Uaibhreach, àrdanach.
HUG, *v. a.* Glac gu caidreach, fàiltich, cniadaich; glac teann; féin chaidrich.
HUGE, *s.* Mòr, anabarrach, gailbheach, tomadach.
HUGENESS, *s.* Meudachd, anabarrachd, tomadachd.
HUGGER-MUGGER, *s.* Cuigeann, tasgaidh diamhair, ionad-falaich.
HULK, *s.* Tàrlaid luinge, slige luinge; dreall, sgonn.
HULL, *s.* Cochull, rùsg, plaosg; slige luinge.
HULLY, *adj.* Cochullach, plaosgach.
HUM, *v. n.* Dean torman, dean dùrdail, dean cronan; mol.
HUM, *s.* Srann, dranndan, gàir sheillein, crònan, torman.
HUMAN, *adj.* Daonna, talmhaidh.
HUMANE, *adj.* Bàigheil, caomh, seirceil, truacanta, tròcaireach, caoimhneil.
HUMANITY, *s.* Daonnachd, nàdur a chinne-dhaonna; bàighealachd, truacantachd, cneasdachd.
HUMANKIND, *s.* Cinne-daonna.
HUMBLE, *adj.* Ùmhal, iriosal, sèimh.
HUMBLE, *v. a.* Irislich, irioslaich, ùmhlaich; ciosnaich, thoir fo smachd; thoir gu strìochdadh.
HUMDRUM, *s.* Umaidh.
HUMECTATION, *s.* Fliuchadh, bogachadh.
HUMID, *adj.* Àitidh, fliuch, bog.
HUMIDITY, *s.* Fliche, àitidheachd.
HUMILIATION, *s.* Irioslachadh.
HUMILITY, *s.* Irioslachd, ùmhlachd.
HUMMING-BIRD, *s.* An t-eun dranndanach, am beag-eun.
HUMORIST, *s.* Fear neònach, fear mac-meanmnach, fear gun srian; fear àbhachdach, àmhailteach.
HUMOROUS, *adj.* Neònach; aighearach, sùgach, àbhachdach, neo-riaghailteach.
HUMORSOME, *adj.* Frithearra, conusach; neònach, luasganach.
HUMOUR, *s.* Càil, nàdur, aomadh-inntinn; àbhachd, fearas-chuideachd, cridhealas; leann-tàth.
HUMOUR, *v. a.* Toilich; géill, strìochd.
HUMP, *s.* Păit, meall, croit.
HUMPBACK, *s.* Druim crotach.
HUMPBACKED, *adj.* Crotach.
HUNCH, *s.* Meall, cnap, păit.
HUNDRED, *adj.* Ceud, ciad.
HUNDREDTH, *adj.* An ceudamh.
HUNG, *part.* Crochte.
HUNGER, *s.* Acras; ciocras.
HUNGRY, *adj.* Acrach, air acras.
HUNKS, *s.* Daormunn, spìocaire.
HUNT, *v.* Sealg, dean fiaghach, dean sealgaireachd; ruag, dlù-lean; rannsaich; stiùr lothainn chon.
HUNT, *s.* Faoghaid; ruaig, sealg.
HUNTER, *s.* Sealgair; giomhanach.
HUNTING, *s.* Sealgaireachd, fiaghach.
HUNTRESS, *s.* Ban-sealgair.
HUNTSMAN, *s.* Sealgair.
HURDLE, *s.* Càrn-slaodaidh, cliath.
HURL, *v. a.* Tilg sios, cuibhil.
HURL, *s.* Iorghuill, tuasaid, săbaid.
HURLY, HURLYBURLY, *s.* Buaireas, ùparaid, othail, iomairt.
HURRICANE, *s.* Doinionn, gaillionn, stoirm, ioma-ghaoth, an-uair.
HURRY, *v.* Greas, luathaich, deifrich; dean cabhag.
HURRY, *s.* Cabhag, buaireas, othail.
HURT, *v. a.* Ciùrr, dochainn, goirtich, cràidh, leòn, lot, dean dochair air.
HURT, *s.* Dochann, ciurradh, leòn; coire, cron, dochair.
HURTFUL, *adj.* Cronail, dochannach.
HURTFULNESS, *s.* Cronalachd.
HURTLEBERRY, *s.* Dearcag-choille.
HUSBAND, *s.* Fear-pòsta, céile.
HUSBAND, *v. a.* Caomhain.
HUSBANDMAN, *s.* Treabhaiche.
HUSBANDRY, *s.* Treabhadh, tuathanachas; caomhnadh.
HUSH, *v.* Caisg, cuir sàmhach; mùch; bi sàmhach, bi tosdach.
HUSHMONEY, *s.* Brìob air son a bhi sàmhach.
HUSK, *s.* Cochull, rùsg, plaosg, mogull, mogunn.
HUSKY, *adj.* Cochullach, rùsgach, plaosgach; garbh, reasgach.
HUSSAR, *s.* Seòra trùpair.
HUSSY, *s.* Dubh-chaile, botrumaid.
HUSTINGS, *s. pl.* Mòd, coinneamh.
HUSTLE, *v. a.* Coimeasg.

Hut, *s.* Bothan, bruchlag.
Hutch, *s.* Ciste-shìl.
Huzza ! *interj.* Co-ghàir, iolach.
Hyacinth, *s.* Seòrsa neòinein; dath.
Hydra, *s.* Ua-bheist ioma-cheannach.
Hydraulics, *s. pl.* Eòlas air tarruinn uisge tre phìoban.
Hydrocele, *s.* Meud-bhronn.
Hydrocephalus, *s.* Uisge 'sa cheann.
Hydrographer, *s.* Fear-tarruinn dealbh na mara.
Hydrography, *s.* Muir-eòlas.
Hydromancy, *s.* Fàisneachd le uisge.
Hydrometer, **Hygrometer**, *s.* Meidh-uisge.
Hydrophobia, *s.* Cuthach nan con.
Hydrostatics, *s. pl.* Eòlas tomhais uisge.
Hyemal, *adj.* A bhuineas do'n gheamhradh.
Hydrus, *s.* Nathair uisge.
Hyena, *s.* Ainmhidh-fiadhaich.
Hymen, *s.* Dia a' phòsaidh; maighdeanas.
Hymeneal, *adj.* Pòsachail.
Hymn, *s.* Laoidh, dàn spioradail.
Hymn, *v. a.* Mol le laoidhibh.
Hymnic, *adj.* Laoidheach.
Hyp, *v. a.* Cuir fo sproc.
Hyperbole, *s.* Aibheiseachadh, spleadhachas, spleadh.
Hyperbolical, *adj.* Spleadhach.
Hyperbolize, *v. a.* Dean spleadhachas.
Hyperborean, *adj.* Tuath; fuar.
Hypercritic, *s.* Gann-thiolpair.
Hypercritical, *adj.* Gann-thìolpach.
Hypermeter, *s.* Ni thar tomhas.
Hyphen, *s.* Comharradh ceangail fhacal mar e so (-).
Hypnotic, *s.* Ìoc-shlaint chadail.
Hypochondriac, *s.* Leann-dubh.
Hypocist, *s.* Ioc-shlainte cheanghail.
Hypocrisy, *s.* Cealgaireachd.
Hypocrite, *s.* Cealgair, mealltair.
Hypocritical, *adj.* Cealgach.
Hypothesis, *s.* Barail gun dearbhadh.
Hypothetical, *adj.* Baralach.
Hyrst, **Herst**, *s.* Doire, badan-coille.
Hyssop, *s.* Hisop, seòrsa luibh.
Hysterical, *adj.* Ospagach, air am beil tinneas nan neul, no tinneas builg.
Hysterics, *s.* An tinneas paiseanach.

I

I, *s.* Naothamh litir na h-aibidil.
I, *pron.* Mì; *emph.* mise.
Iambic, *s.* Cam-dhàn.
Iambic, *adj.* Cam-dhànach.
Ice, *s.* Eigh, deigh, éithre.
Icehouse, *s.* Taigh-eighe.
Ichor, *s.* Ruith-iongrach.
Ichorous, *adj.* Silteachail.
Icthyology, *s.* Eòlas nan iasg.
Icthyophagy, *s.* Iasg-itheannaich.
Icicle, *s.* Caisean-reòdhta.
Icon, *s.* Ìomhaigh.
Iconolater, *s.* Dealbh-aoradair.
Icy, *adj.* Eigheach, reòdhta.
Idea, *s.* Smuain, barail, dealbh-inntinn.
Ideal, *adj.* A réir barail, dealbh-inntinneach.
Identical, **Indentic**, *adj.* Ceudna, ionann, ceart-cheudna.
Identification, *s.* Dearbhadh ionannachd.
Identify, *v. a.* Dearbh ionannachd.
Identity, *s.* Ionannachd.
Idiom, *s.* Gnàths-cainnte.
Idiomatic, *adj.* Gnàths-chainnteach.
Idiotism, *s.* Amadanachd.
Idle, *adj.* Leisg, monaiseach; dìomhain, dìomhanach; gun ghnothach; neo-éifeachdach; faoin, suarach, baoth.
Idleness, *s.* Dìomhanachd, dìomhanas; faoineas, neo-nitheachd; neo-éifeachd.
Idler, *s.* Leisgean, lunndaire, dìomhanaiche, bataire, droll.
Idol, *s.* Iomhaigh, iodhol.
Idolater, *s.* Fear-iodhol-aoraidh.
Idolatrous, *adj.* Iodhol-aorach.
Idolatry, *s.* Iodhol-aoradh.
Idolish, *adj.* Iodholach.
Idolize, *v.* Gabh mar iodhol.
If, *conj.* Ma, na, mur, *ma* 's urra mi, *na* 'n abrainn, *na* 'm biodh e air teachd; *mur* tig e.
Igneous, *adj.* Teinntidh, lasarra, lasanta, loisgeach.
Ignis-fatuus, *s.* Spiorad-lodain, teinesionnachain, srada-bianain.
Ignite, *v. a.* Cuir teine ri, fadaidh; las, gabh teine.
Ignition, *s.* Lasadh, losgadh.
Ignoble, *adj.* An-uasal, neo-inbheach; mìothar, suarach, iosal.
Ignominious, *adj.* Nàr, maslach, dìblidh, tarcuiseach.
Ignominy, *s.* Nàire, mì-chliù.

Ignoramus, *s.* Burraidh, sgonn.
Ignorance, *s.* Aineolas, an-fhios.
Ignorant, *adj.* Aineolach.
Ile, *s.* Dias, aisir.
Iliac, *adj.* Caolanach.
Ill, *adj.* Olc, dona; tinn, euslan.
Ill, *s.* Olc, aingidheachd, cron.
Illapse, *s.* Sleamhnachadh; ionnsaidh, tachartas, tuiteamas.
Illaudable, *adj.* Neo-airidh.
Illegal, *adj.* Neo-dhligheach, milaghail, neo-cheadaichte.
Illegality, *s.* Mi-laghalachd.
Illegibility, *s.* Do-leughtachd.
Illegible, *adj.* Do-leughadh, neoshoilleir, dorcha.
Illegitimate, *adj.* Dìolain.
Illegitimacy, *s.* Dìolanas.
Illiberal, *adj.* Neo-uasal, neo-fhialaidh; spìocach, crìon, gortach.
Illiberality, *s.* Cruas, spìocaiche.
Illimitable, *adj.* Neo-chrìochnachail.
Illimited, *adj.* Neo-chrìochnaichte.
Illiteracy, *s.* Neo-fhòghlumachd.
Illiterate, *adj.* Neo-fhòghluimte.
Illiterateness, *s.* Neo-fhoghluimteachd.
Illnature, *s.* Droch-nàdur.
Illness, *s.* Tinneas, galar, euslaint.
Illogical, *adj.* Mi-reusonta.
Ill-starred, *adj.* Neo-shealbhach.
Illude, *v. a.* Meall, thoir an car á.
Illume, Illumine, Illuminate, *v. a.* Soillsich, soilleirich, dealradh.
Illumination, *s.* Soillseachadh, soilleireachadh, dealradh, dearsadh.
Illuminative, *adj.* Soillseach.
Illusion, *s.* Mealladh, mearachd.
Illusive, *adj.* Mealltach, faoin.
Illusory, *adj.* Cealgach, carach.
Illustrate, *v. a.* Soillsich, mìnich.
Illustration, *s.* Mìneachadh.
Illustrative, *adj.* Mìneachail.
Illustrator, *s.* Fear-mìneachaidh.
Illustrious, *adj.* Uasal, ainmeil.
Image, *s.* Iomhaigh, samhla.
Imagery, *s.* Ìomhaighean; faoinsmuaintean; samhlaidhean.
Imaginable, *adj.* A dh' fhaodar a smuaineachadh.
Imaginary, *adj.* Faoin-bharaileach.
Imagination, *s.* Mac-meanmainn; smuain-inntinn; breithneachadh; faoin-bheachd; innleachd.
Imaginative, *adj.* Mac-meanmnach.
Imagine, *v. a.* Smaoinich, beachdaich; dealbh, tionnsgain.
Imbecile, *adj.* Lag-chuiseach, fann.
Imbecility, *s.* Lag chuiseachd,
Imbibe, *v. a.* Òl, sùigh, deoghail.
Imbitter, *v. a.* Searbhaich, dean searbh; dean mi-shona, léir; buair.
Imbody, *v.* Corpaich; co-chorpaich; co-aonaich.
Imbolden, *v. a.* Misnich, brosnaich.
Imbosom, *v. a.* Uchdaich, tàlaidh; caidrich, gràdhaich.
Imbound, *v. a.* Iomadhruid, cuairtich.
Imbow, *v. a.* Cuir bogha air.
Imbower, *v. a.* Sgàilich, còmhdaich.
Imbricated, *adj.* Eagach, slocach.
Imbrication, *s.* Eagachadh, sloc.
Imbrown, *v. a.* Donnaich, dean donn.
Imbrue, *v. a.* Fliuch, bog, tùm.
Imbrute, *v. a.* Ìslich, dean brùideil.
Imbue, *v. a.* Snuadhaich, dath.
Imitability, *s.* So-shamhlachd.
Imitable, *adj.* So-shamhlachdail.
Imitate, *v. a.* Co-shamhlaich, aithris, lean eiseamplair, dean coltach ri.
Imitation, *s.* Lean-shamhlachadh.
Imitative, *adj.* Aithriseach.
Imitator, *s.* Fear-aithris.
Immaculate, *adj.* Glan, fìor-ghlan.
Immane, *adj.* Anabarrach, fuathasach; borb, garg.
Immanity, *s.* Buirbe, brùidealachd.
Immarcessible, *adj.* Neo-sheargach.
Immartial, *adj.* Neo-ghaisgeanta.
Immaterial, *adj.* Neo-chorporra, spioradail; neo-nitheach.
Immateriality, *s.* Neo-chorporrachd, spioradalachd, neo-nitheachd.
Immature, *adj.* An-abaich.
Immaturity, *s.* An-abaichead.
Immeability, *s.* Neo-ghluaisneachd.
Immeasurable, *adj.* Do-thomhas.
Immechanical, *adj.* Neo-ealanta.
Immediate, *adj.* Dlù, aig làimh; grad, ealamh, clis.
Immediately, *adv.* Gu grad, gu luath, gun dàil, gun stàd, air ball.
Immedicable, *adj.* Do-leigheas.
Immelodious, *adj.* Neo-bhinn.
Immemorial, *adj.* Cian, o chian.
Immense, *adj.* Fuathasach mòr.
Immensity, *s.* Anabarrachd.
Immensurable, *adj.* Do-thomhas
Immerge, Immerse, *v. a.* Cuir fodha, tùm, bogaich ann an uisg'.
Immersion, *s.* Tumadh, cur fodha, bogadh; dol fodha.
Immethodical, *adj.* Mi-riaghailteach, mi-dhòigheil, neo-sheòlta.
Immethodically, *adv.* Gun riaghailt.
Immigration, *s.* Teachd a nall.
Imminence, *s.* Cunnart, gàbhadh.
Imminent, *adj.* Cunnartach, gàbhaidh.

IMMIX, IMMINGLE, *v. a.* Co-measgaich, co-mheasg.
IMMIXABLE, *adj.* Do-mheasgadh.
IMMOBILITY, *s.* Neo-ghluasadachd.
IMMODERATE, *adj.* Ana-meas-arra.
IMMODERATION, *s.* Ana-measarrachd.
IMMODEST, *adj.* Mi-nàrach, beag-narach; mi-stuama, neo-ghlan.
IMMODESTY, *s.* Ladornas; mi-stuaim.
IMMOLATE, *v. a.* Thoir ìobairt, ìobair.
IMMOLATION, *s.* Ìobradh.
IMMORAL, *adj.* Mi-bheusach, eas ionraic, eucorach, droch-bheartach.
IMMORALITY, *s.* Mi-bheus, eas-ionracas, eucoir, droch-bheart.
IMMORTAL, *adj.* Neo-bhàsmhor.
IMMORTALITY, *s.* Neo-bhàsmhorachd.
IMMORTALIZE, *v. a.* Dean neo-bhàsmhor.
IMMOVEABLE, *adj.* Neo-ghluasadach.
IMMUNITY, *s.* Saorsa; fuasgladh, cead.
IMMURE, *v. a.* Druid, cuir an sàs.
IMMUTABILITY, *s.* Neo-chaochlaideachd.
IMMUTABLE, *adj.* Neo-chaochlaideach.
IMP, *s.* Mac, màileachan.
IMP, *v. a.* Cuir ri, meudaich.
IMPACT, *v. a.* Teannaich, spàrr, dinn.
IMPAIR, *v. a.* Lughdaich, dìobhailich, mill; fàs ni's miosa.
IMPALPABLE, *adj.* Do-fhaireachdainn, mìn, meanbh.
IMPARITY, *s.* Neo-ionannachd.
IMPART, *v. a.* Tabhair, tìodhlaic, compàirtich; soilleirich; co-roinn.
IMPARTIAL, *adj.* Ceart-bhreitheach, neo-chlaon, dìreach, cothromach, còir.
IMPARTIALITY, *s.* Neo-leth-bhreitheachd, neo-chlaonachd, cothrom.
IMPASSABLE, *adj.* Do-shiubhal.
IMPASSION, *v. a.* Feargaich, brosnaich.
IMPASSIONED, *adj.* Brosnaichte.
IMPATIENCE, *s.* Mi-fhaighidinn, neo-chruadal; boile, ainteas, caise, braise.
IMPATIENT, *adj.* Neo-fhoighidneach; neo-shocrach, cas, dian.
IMPAWN, *v. a.* Thoir an geall.
IMPEACH, *v. a.* Càsaidich, dìt gu follaiseach, cuir as leth; bac, grab.
IMPEACHMENT, *s.* Casaid, dìteadh, cùis-dhìtidh; coire, masladh.
IMPEARL, *v. a.* Neamhnaidich.
IMPECCABILITY, *s.* Neo-chiontas.
IMPECCABLE, *adj.* Neo-chiontach.
IMPEDE, *v. a.* Bac, cuir maille air.
IMPEDIMENT, *s.* Bacadh, cnap-starraidh.
IMPEL, *v. a.* Greas, cuir air aghaidh.
IMPEND, *v. n.* Croch os-ceann, bi aig làimh.
IMPENETRABLE, *adj.* Do-tholladh, do-dhrùigheadh; dùinte; do ghluasad.
IMPENITENCE, *s.* Neo-aithreachas.
IMPENITENT, *adj.* Neo-aithreachail.
IMPENNOUS, *adj.* Neo sgiathach.
IMPERATIVE, *adj.* Ceannsalach.
IMPERCEPTIBLE, *adj.* Neo-fhaicsinneach, neo-lèirsinneach, do-mhothachadh.
IMPERFECT, *adj.* Neo-fhoirfe, neo-iomlan, neo choimhlionta.
IMPERFECTION, *s.* Neo-iomlanachd.
IMPERFORATE, *adj.* Neo-tholldach.
IMPERIAL, *adj.* Rìoghail, àrd-urramach, àrd-uachdaranach.
IMPERIOUS, *adj.* Aintighearnail, cruaidh-smachdail, fòirneartach; ceannsachail, smachdail; uachdaranach; uaimhreach.
IMPERIOUSNESS, *s.* Ceannasachd, smachdalachd; aintighearnas.
IMPERISHABLE, *adj.* Neo-bhàsmhor.
IMPERSONAL, *adj.* Neo-phearsanta.
IMPERSPICUOUS, *adj.* Neo-shoilleir.
IMPERSUASIBLE, *adj.* Do-chomhairleachadh.
IMPERTINENCE, *s.* Beadaidheachd; mi-mhodh, leamhadas, dànadas, gòraich.
IMPERTINENT, *adj.* Amaideach; leamh, beadaidh, mi-mhodhail, ladorna, dàna, beag-narach.
IMPERVIOUS, *adj.* Air nach drùighear
IMPETRABLE, *adj.* So-fhaotainn.
IMPETRATE, *v. a.* Faigh le achanaich.
IMPETUOSITY, *s.* Braise, caise, dèine.
IMPETUOUS, *adj.* Ainteasach, fiadhaich, feargach; càs, bras, dian.
IMPETUS, *s.* Dèine, sitheadh, deann, neart.
IMPIERCEABLE, *adj.* Do-tholladh.
IMPIETY, *s.* Ain-diadhachd, mi-naomhachd, aingeachd; droch-bheart.
IMPINGE, *v. a.* Buail, tuit air muin.
IMPIOUS, *adj.* Ain-diadhaidh.
IMPLACABLE, *adj.* Gamhlasach, dochasgadh.
IMPLANT, *v. a.* Suidhich, socraich.
IMPLAUSIBLE, *adj.* Neo-choltach.
IMPLEMENT, *s.* Inneal, ball-deise.
IMPLICATE, *v. a.* Rib, bac, caisg.
IMPLICATION, *s.* Ribeadh, bacadh, seadh, ciall.
IMPLICATIVE, *adj.* Fillteach, seadhachail.
IMPLICIT, *adj.* Fillte, ribte, iomfhillte; seadhaichte; earbsach, an crochadh air, ùmhal.

Implore, *v. a.* Aslaich, guidh, grìos.
Imply, *v. a.* Fill, ciallaich.
Impoison, *v. a.* Puinnseanaich.
Impolite, *adj.* Mi-mhodhail.
Impolitic, *adj.* Neo-sheòlta.
Imponderous, *adj.* Aotrom.
Imporous, *adj.* Neo-chòsach, dlù.
Import, *v. a.* Thoir o chéin, faigh o chéin; seadhaich, ciallaich.
Import, *s.* Cudthrom, brìgh, bladh, seadh, toirt.
Importance, *s.* Cudthrom, mòr-thoirt, seadh, stà.
Important, *adj.* Cudthromach, toirteil, brìoghmhor, feumail.
Importation, *s.* Toirt dhachaigh.
Importunate, *adj.* Iarrtachail.
Importune, *v. a.* Sàraich le iarrtas.
Importunity, *s.* Leamhachas.
Impose, *v. a.* Leag air; àithn, cuir mar fhiachaibh air; meall, thoir an car.
Imposition, *s.* Leagail, leagail air; éigin, ainneart; mealladh, foill.
Impossibility, *s.* Neo-chomasachd.
Impossible, *adj.* Eu-comasach.
Impost, *s.* Cìs, càin, cuspunn.
Imposthumate, *v. n.* Iongraich, ăt.
Imposthume, *s.* Iongrachadh.
Impostor, *s.* Mealltair, slaightear.
Imposture, *s.* Mealladh, foill, ceilg.
Impotence, **Impotency**, *s.* Laigse, anfhannachd, lag-chuiseachd, neo-chomas.
Impotent, *adj.* Lag, anfhann, neo-chomasach, fann, lag-chuiseach.
Impound, *v. a.* Dùin ann am punnd.
Impracticable, *adj.* Do-dheanamh.
Imprecate, *v. a.* Guidh olc.
Imprecation, *s.* Droch ghuidhe.
Impregnable, *adj.* Do-ghlacadh.
Impregnate, *v. a.* Dean torrach.
Impregnation, *s.* Torrachas.
Imprejudicate, *adj.* Neo-chlaon-bhreathach.
Impreparation, *s.* Neo-uigheam.
Impress, *v. a.* Clò-bhuail; comharraich; glac, ceap.
Impressible, *adj.* So-chomharrachadh.
Impression, *s.* Comharradh, athailt; dealbh, cruth, riochd; clò-bhualadh.
Impressive, *adj.* Drùighteach.
Impressure, *s.* Comharradh, lòrg.
Imprimis, *adv.* Anns a' cheud àite.
Imprint, *v. a.* Comharraich; drùigh.
Imprison, *v. a.* Cuir am prìosan.
Imprisonment, *s.* Prìosanachadh.
Improbability, *s.* Mi-choltas.
Improbable, *adj.* Mi-choltach.
Improbate, *v. a.* Toirmisg, di-mol.
Improbation, *s.* Toirmeasg.
Improbity, *s.* Eas-ionracas, foill.
Improper, *adj.* Neo-iomchuidh.
Impropriety, *s.* Neo-fhreagharrachd.
Improvable, *adj.* So-leasachadh.
Improve, *v.* Leasaich; rach am feabhas.
Improvement, *s.* Leasachadh; feabhas, teachd air aghaidh; ionnsachadh.
Improvidence, *s.* Neo-fhreasdalachd.
Improvident, *adj.* Neo-fhreasdalach.
Imprudence, *s.* Gòraich, amaideachd.
Imprudent, *adj.* Gòrach, amaideach.
Impudence, *s.* Dànadas, ladornas.
Impudent, *adj.* Dàna, ladorna.
Impugn, *v. a.* Coirich, faigh cron.
Impugnation, *s.* Coireachadh.
Impuissance, *s.* Anmhuinneachd.
Impulse, *s.* Faireachadh, togradh.
Impulsive, *adj.* Brosnachail.
Impunity, *s.* Saor o dhioghaltas.
Impure, *adj.* Neo-ghlan, truaillidh.
Impurity, *s.* Neo-ghloine; sal.
Impurple, *v. a.* Dean dearg.
Imputable, *adj.* So-chur as leth.
Imputation, *s.* Cur as leth; casaid.
Impute, *v. a.* Cuir cron as leth.
In, *prep.* Ann, an, am, anns, 's.
In, *prefix.* Do, neo, eu, as, an.
Inability, *s.* Neo-chomas, laigse.
Inaccessible, *adj.* Do-ruigsinn.
Inaccuracy, *s.* Neo-phoncalachd.
Inaccurate, *adj.* Mearachdach.
Inaction, *s.* Tàmh, fois, clos.
Inactive, *adj.* Neo-ghnìomhach.
Inactivity, *s.* Neo-ghnìomhachas.
Inadequate, *adj.* Neo-fhreagarrach.
Inadequacy, *s.* Neo-fhreagarrachd.
Inadvertence, *s.* Neo-churam.
Inadvertent, *adj.* Neo-chùramach.
Inalienable, *adj.* Do-dhealachadh.
Inane, *adj.* Fàs, faoin, falamh.
Inanimate, *adj.* Marbhanta.
Inanity, *s.* Faoineachd, fàsachd.
Inapplicable, *adj.* Neo-fhreagarrach.
Inaptitude, *s.* Neo-iomchuidheachd.
Inarticulate, *adj.* Manntach.
Inattention, *s.* Neo-aire.
Inattentive, *adj.* Neo-aireil.
Inaudible, *adj.* Do-chluinntinn.
Inaugurate, *v. a.* Coisrig.
Inauguration, *s.* Coisrigeadh.
Inauration, *s.* Òradh, òrachadh.
Inauspicious, *adj.* Mi-shealbhach.
Inborn, *adj.* Nàdurra.
Incalculable, *adj.* Do-àireamh.
Incantation, *s.* Ubag, ubhaidh, geas.
Incantatory, *adj.* Ubagach.
Incapability, *s.* Neo-chomasachd.

INCAPABLE, *adj.* Neo-urrainneach.
INCAPACIOUS, *adj.* Cumhang.
INCAPACITATE, *v. a.* Dean mi-chomasach.
INCAPACITY, *s.* Neo-chomas.
INCARCERATE, *v. a.* Prìosanaich.
INCARCERATION, *s.* Prìosanachadh.
INCARN, *v.* Fàs 'na fheòil.
INCARNATE, *v. a.* Gabh cruth feòla.
INCARNATE, *adj.* 'S an fheòil.
INCARNATINE, *v. a.* Càrnaidich.
INCARNATION, *s.* Corp-ghabhail.
INCASE, *v. a.* Còmhdaich, dùin.
INCAUTIOUS, *adj.* Mi-fhaicilleach.
INCAUTIOUSNESS, *s.* Mi-fhaicilleachd.
INCENDIARY, *s.* Loisgeadair; brathadair, ceann-aimhreit, buaireadair.
INCENDIARY, *adj.* Buaireasach.
INCENSE, *s.* Tùis.
INCENSE, *v. a.* Buair, feargaich.
INCENSORY, *s.* Tùisear.
INCENTIVE, *s.* Brosnachadh, buaireadh; cùis-aimhreit; mathair-aobhair.
INCENTIVE, *adj.* Brosnachail.
INCESSANT, *adj.* Daonnan, sìor.
INCEST, *s.* Col, con-dàimh.
INCESTUOUS, *adj.* Colach, con-dàimheach.
INCH, *s.* Òirleach.
INCHIPIN, *s.* Am poca-buidhe.
INCHMEAL, *s.* Mìr-oirleich.
INCHOATE, *v. a.* Tòisich.
INCHOATION, *s.* Tòiseachadh.
INCHOATIVE, *adj.* Ceud-cheumach.
INCIDE, *v. a.* Gearr, roinn.
INCIDENCE, INCIDENT, *s.* Tuiteamas, tachartas.
INCIDENT, INCIDENTAL, *adj.* Tuiteamach, tachartach, buailteach.
INCINERATE, *v. a.* Dù-loisg.
INCINERATION, *s.* Dù-losgadh.
INCIPIENT, *adj.* Tòiseachail, ceud.
INCIRCUMSPECTION, *s.* Neo-aire.
INCISED, *adj.* Gèarrte.
INCISION, INCISURE, *s.* Gearradh; tolladh.
INCISIVE, *adj.* Gearrtach, geur.
INCISOR, *s.* A' ghearr-fhiacail.
INCITATION, INCITEMENT, *s.* Brosnachadh, misneachadh, beothachadh.
INCITE, *v. a.* Brosnaich, gluais, beothaich, tog, misnich.
INCIVILITY, *s.* Mi-mhodhalachd.
INCLEMENCY, *s.* An-iochd.
INCLEMENT, *adj.* An-iochdmhor.
INCLINABLE, *adj.* Deònach, togarrach, dèidheil, toileach, miannach.
INCLINATION, *s.* Aomadh; toil, togradh; dèidh, miann, iarrtas, deòin; gaol, tòirt, ùidh; cromadh, camadh, claonadh.
INCLINE, *v.* Aom, crom, claon, lùb sleuchd; togair, miannaich.
INCLOSE, *v. a.* Duin, ioma-dhruid.
INCLUDE, *v. a.* Iath; cùm.
INCLUSION, *s.* Cumail, cuairteachadh.
INCLUSIVE, *adj.* A' gabhail a stigh.
INCOAGULABLE, *adj.* Do-bhinnteachadh.
INCOG, INCOGNITO, *adv.* Gu falaichte, gu dìomhair.
INCOHERENCE, *s.* Neo-leanailteachd, fuasgailteachd; neo-aontachas, eascordadh.
INCOHERENT, *adj.* Fuasgailte, sgaoilte, neo-cheangailte; neo-fhreagarrach, neo-aontachail, baoth.
INCOMBUSTIBLE, *adj.* Neo-loisgeach.
INCOME, *s.* Teachd a steach.
INCOMMENSURABLE, *adj.* Do-thomhas.
INCOMMISCIBLE, *adj.* Do-mheasgadh.
INCOMMODE, *v. a.* Cuir dragh air.
INCOMMODIOUS, *adj.* Neo-ghoireasach, draghail, neo-fhreagarrach.
INCOMMUNICABLE, *adj.* Do-phàirteachadh, do-labhairt, do-innseadh.
INCOMMUNICATED, *adj.* Neo-phàirtichte.
INCOMMUNICATING, *adj.* Neo-chompanta.
INCOMMUTABLE, *adj.* Do-mhalartach.
INCOMPACT, *adj.* Fuasgailte, sgaoilte.
INCOMPARABLE, *adj.* Gun choimeas.
INCOMPASSIONATE, *adj.* An-tròcaireach, neo-thlùsail, cruaidh-chridheach.
INCOMPATIBILITY, *s.* Neo-fhreagarrachd.
INCOMPATIBLE, *adj.* Neo fhreagarrach.
INCOMPETENCY, *s.* Neo-chomasachd.
INCOMPETENT, *adj.* Neo-chomasach.
INCOMPLETE, *adj.* Neo-choimhlionta.
INCOMPLIANCE, *s.* Diùltadh, raige.
INCOMPOSED, *adj.* Neo-shuidhichte.
INCOMPREHENSIBILITY, INCOMPREHENSIBLENESS, *s.* Do-thuigsinneachd.
INCOMPREHENSIBLE, *adj.* Do-thuigsinn.
INCOMPRESSIBLE, *adj.* Do-theannachadh.
INCONCURRING, *adj.* Neo-aontachail.
INCONCEALABLE, *adj.* Do-chlèith.
INCONCEIVABLE, INCONCEPTIBLE, *adj.* Do-smuaineachadh, do-bharalachadh, do-thuigsinn.
INCONCLUSIVE, *adj.* Neo-chinnteach.

INCONCLUSIVENESS, *s.* Neo-chinnteachd.
INCONCOCT, *adj.* An-abaich.
INCONCOCTION, *s.* An-abaicheachd.
INCONCURRING, *adj.* Neo-chòrdaidh.
INCONCUSSIBLE, *adj.* Do-ghluasad.
INCONDITE, *adj.* Neo-riaghailteach.
INCONDITIONAL, INCONDITIONATE, *adj.* Neo-chùmhnantach.
INCONFORMITY, *s.* Neo-aontachd.
INCONGRUENCE, INCONGRUITY, *s.* Neo-fhreagarrachd, ea-coltas.
INCONGRUOUS, INCONGRUENT, *adj.* Neo-fhreagarrach.
INCONNEXION, *s.* An-dàimh.
INCONSCIONABLE, *adj.* Neo-chogaiseach.
INCONSIDERABLE, *adj.* Suarach.
INCONSIDERABLENESS, *s.* Suarachas.
INCONSIDERATE, *adj.* Neo-chùramach, dearmadach, neo-aireil.
INCONSIDERATENESS, *s.* Neo-airealachd, neo-chùramachd.
INCONSISTENCY, *s.* Mi-chòrdadh.
INCONSISTENT, *adj.* Neo-fhreagarrach.
INCONSOLABLE, *adj.* Dù-bhrònach.
INCONSONANCY, *s.* Neo-aontachd.
INCONSTANCY, *s.* Neo-bhunailteachd.
INCONSTANT, *adj.* Neo-bhunailteach.
INCONTESTABLE, *adj.* Do-àicheadh.
INCONTIGUOUS, *adj.* Neo-dhlù.
INCONTINENCE, *s.* Mi-stuamachd.
INCONTINENT, *adj.* Mi-stuama.
INCONTROVERTIBLE, *adj.* Dearbhte.
INCONVENIENCE, *s.* Neo-iomchuidheachd, neo-fhreagarrachd, neo-ghoireasachd, dragh, duilichinn, anacothrom.
INCONVENIENT, *adj.* Mi-ghoireasach.
INCONVERTIBLE, *adj.* Do-mhùthadh.
INCONVINCIBLE, *adj.* Rag-mhuinealach.
INCORPORAL, INCORPOREAL, INCORPORATE, *adj.* Neo-chorporra.
INCORPORALITY, *s.* Neo-chorporrachd.
INCORPORATE, *v.* Measgaich, co-cheangail, co-chomunnaich ; cuir cruth air, corpaich ; aonaich.
INCORPORATION, *s.* Coimeasgadh ; co-chomunn ; aonachadh.
INCORPOREITY, *s.* Neo-chorporrachd.
INCORRECT, *adj.* Mearachdach.
INCORRECTLY, *adv.* Gu mearachdach.
INCORRECTNESS, *s.* Docharachd.
INCORRIGIBLE, *adj.* Do-cheannsachadh, aingidh.
INCORRIGIBLENESS, *s.* Do-cheannsachd, aingidheachd.
INCORRUPT, *adj.* Neo-thruaillte.
INCORRUPTIBILITY, *s.* Neo-sheargte.
INCORRUPTIBLE, *adj.* Neo-thruaillidh.
INCORRUPTION, *s.* Neo-thruailleachd.
INCORRUPTNESS, *s.* Ionracas, tréidhireas.
INCRASSATE, *v. a.* Dean tiugh.
INCRASSATION, *s.* Tiughachadh.
INCRASSATIVE, *adj.* Tiughachail.
INCREASE, *v.* Meudaich, cuir am meud, lìonmhoraich ; fàs lìonmhor, cinn, rach am meud, fàs mòr.
INCREASE, *s.* Fàs, cinntinn, meudachadh ; teachd a mach, tuilleadh ; toradh, cinneas ; sìol, sliochd, gineal.
INCREDIBILITY, *s.* Neo-chreidsinneachd.
INCREDIBLE, *adj.* Do-chreidsinn.
INCREDULITY, *s.* As-creidimh.
INCREDULOUS, *adj.* As-creideach.
INCREMABLE, *adj.* Do-losgadh.
INCREMENT, *s.* Fàs, meudachadh ; leasachadh ; toradh, piseach.
INCRIMINATE, *v. a.* Casaidich, dìt.
INCRUST, *v. a.* Cuir rùsg air.
INCRUSTATION, *s.* Rùsg, sgròth.
INCUBATE, *v. n.* Guir, laidh air uibhean.
INCUBATION, *s.* Gur.
INCUBUS, *s.* An trom-lighe.
INCULCATE, *v. a.* Dian-chomhairlich.
INCULCATION, *s.* Dian-chomhairleachadh.
INCUMBENCY, *s.* Laidhe, leagail taic ; beatha, ùine-beatha.
INCUMBENT, *adj.* A' leagail taic air, a' laidhe ; dligheach, mar fhiachaibh.
INCUMBENT, *s.* Sealbhadair beathachaidh, pears'-eaglais.
INCUMBER, *v. a.* Cuir eallach air.
INCUR, *v. a.* Bi buailteach do ; toill.
INCURABLE, *adj.* Do-leigheas.
INCURIOUS, *adj.* Coma, suarach, mu.
INCURSION, *s.* Ionnsaidh, ruathar.
INCURVATE, *v. a.* Lùb, crom, cam.
INCURVATION, *s.* Lùbadh, cromadh.
INCURVITY, *s.* Lùbadh, cruime, caime.
INDAGATE, *v. a.* Rannsaich.
INDAGATION, *s.* Lorgachadh, rannsachadh, fidreachadh, leantainn.
INDIGATOR, *s.* Fear-rannsachaidh.
INDART, *v. a.* Sàth a steach.
INDEBTED, *adj.* Am fiachaibh ; fo chomain, an comain.
INDECENCY, INDECORUM, *s.* Mi-chiatachd, mi-bheus, neo-eireachdas.
INDECENT, *adj.* Neo-eireachdail, neo-chumhaidh.
INDECIDUOUS, *adj.* Neo-thuiteamach.
INDECISION, *s.* Neo-chinnteachd.
INDECISIVE, *adj.* Neo-chinnteach.

INDECLINABLE, *adj.* Neo-atharrachail.
INDECOROUS, *adj.* Neo-bheusach, mi-mhodail, neo-eireachdail, mi-chiatach.
INDEED, *adv.* Gu fìrinneach, gu dearbh, gu deimhinn.
INDEFATIGABLE, *adj.* Do-sgìtheachadh.
INDEFEASIBLE, *adj.* Do-chur an aghaidh.
INDEFECTIBLE, *adj.* Neo-fhàilneach.
INDEFENSIBLE, *adj.* Do-dhìonadh.
INDEFINABLE, *adj.* Do-ainmeachadh.
INDEFINITE, *adj.* Neo-chrìochnach, neo-shònraichte.
INDELIBERATE, *adj.* Cabhagach, cas.
INDELIBLE, *adj.* Do-mhilleadh.
INDELICACY, *s.* Mi-mhodh, mi-shuairceas, neo-cheanaltas.
INDELICATE, *adj.* Mi-mhodhail.
INDEMNIFICATION, *s.* Ath-dhìoladh; urras.
INDEMNIFY, *v. a.* Dìon o challdach.
INDEMNITY, *s.* Làn-mhathanas.
INDEMONSTRABLE, *adj.* Do-dhearbhadh.
INDENT, *v.* Eagaich, fiaclaich, gròb; cùmhnantaich.
INDENT, INDENTATION, *s.* Eagachadh, fiaclachadh, gròbadh.
INDENTURE, *s.* Cèird-chùmhnant.
INDEPENDENCE, INDEPENDENCY, *s.* Saorsa; neo-eiseamaileachd.
INDEPENDENT, *adj.* Saor; neo-eiseamaileach.
INDESCRIBABLE, *adj.* Do aithris.
INDESTRUCTIBLE, *adj.* Do-mhilleadh.
INDETERMINABLE, *adj.* Do-shònrachadh.
INDETERMINATE, *adj.* Neo-shònraichte, neo-mheasraichte.
INDETERMINED, *adj.* Neo-shuidhichte.
INDEVOTED, *adj.* Neo-dhìleas.
INDEVOTION, *s.* Mi-dhiadhachd.
INDEVOUT, *adj.* Neo-chràbhach.
INDEX, *s.* Clàr-innseadh leabhair; làmh-uaireadair; comharradh-corraig mar e so ☞.
INDEXTERITY, *s.* Neo-ealantachd.
INDIAN, *s.* and *adj.* Innseanach.
INDICATE, *v. a.* Taisbean, foillsich, innis, comharraich a mach.
INDICATION, *s.* Comharradh, innseadh, foillseachadh; rabhadh, sanas, fios.
INDICATIVE, *adj.* Taisbeanach, foillseachail, innseachail.
INDICTION, *s.* Cuir an cèill, gairm, rabhadh follaiseach.
INDICTMENT, *s.* Dìteadh-sgrìobhte.
INDIFFERENCE, *s.* Coimhiseachd; neo-shuim, neo-chùram, neo-aire.
INDIFFERENT, *adj.* Coimhis; neo-aireil, coma, dearmadach; neo-chlaon-bhreitheach; meadhonach, an eatarras.
INDIGENCE, *s.* Bochdainn, ainniseachd, truaighe, gainne.
INDIGENOUS, *adj.* Dùthchasach.
INDIGENT, *adj.* Bochd, gann, truagh; falamh, fàs.
INDIGESTED, *adj.* Mi-riaghailteach; fuasgailte, sgaoilte; neo-mheirbhte.
INDIGESTION, *s.* Cion-meirbhidh.
INDIGITATE, *v. a.* Nochd, feuch.
INDIGITATION, *s.* Nochdadh, feuchainn.
INDIGNANT, *adj.* Feargach, diombach.
INDIGNATION, *s.* Fearg, corraich.
INDIGNITY, *s.* Dimeas, tàmailt, tàir, tarcuis, masladh.
INDIGO, *s.* Guirmean.
INDIRECT, *adj.* Neo-dhìreach, fiar, cam; mealltach, foilleil.
INDIRECTNESS, *s.* Fiaradh, caime.
INDISCERNIBLE, *adj.* Do-fhaicsinneach.
INDISCERPTIBLE, *adj.* Do-sgarachdainn.
INDISCOVERABLE, *adj.* Do-rannsachadh.
INDISCREET, *adj.* Neo-chrìonna.
INDISCRETION, *s.* Neo-chrìonnachd.
INDISCRIMINATE, *adj.* Feadh a chéile.
INDISCUSSED, *adj.* Neo-rannsaichte.
INDISPENSABLE, *adj.* Neo-seachnach.
INDISPOSE, *v. a.* Neo-uidheamaich.
INDISPOSITION, *s.* Euslaint; fuath.
INDISPUTABLE, *adj.* Cinnteach.
INDISPUTABLENESS, *s.* Cinnteachas.
INDISSOLUBLE, *adj.* Do-leaghadh; neo-sgaranta; buan, maireannach.
INDISTINCT, *adj.* Neo-shoilleir.
INDISTINCTNESS, *s.* Neo-shoilleireachd, neo-chinnteachas, doilleireachd.
INDISTURBANCE, *s.* Ciùineachd.
INDIVIDUAL, *adj.* Leis féin.
INDIVIDUAL, *s.* Aon, ùrra, neach.
INDIVIDUALITY, *s.* Pearsantachd, bith air leth.
INDIVIDUALLY, *adv.* Air leth, fa-leth.
INDIVISIBLE, *adj.* Do-sgarachadh.
INDIVISIBILITY, *s.* Do-roinnteachd.
INDOCIBLE, INDOCILE, *adj.* Do-ionnsachadh, dùr, fiadhaich.
INDOCILITY, *s.* Do-theagaisgeachd.
INDOLENCE, *s.* Leisg, dìomhanas.
INDOLENT, *adj.* Leisg, dearmadach.
INDRAUGHT, *s.* Camus, bàgh, cala, leigeadh a steach.

INDRENCH, *v. a.* Tùm, fliuch, bogaich, fluch, bàth.

INDUBITABLE, *adj.* Neo-theagmhach.

INDUBITATE, *adj.* Soilleir.

INDUCE, *v. a.* Thoir air; thoir air aghaidh.

INDUCEMENT, *s.* Aobhar brosnachaidh, cuireadh, misneach, comhairle.

INDUCT, *v. a.* Cuir an seilbh, thoir a steach.

INDUCTION, *s.* Dol a stigh, sealbhachadh; deanamh a mach.

INDUCTIVE, *adj.* Earalach, treòrachail; seadhach.

INDUE, *v. a.* Còmhdaich.

INDULGE, *v. a.* Leig le, toilich; beadraich, breug; thoir cead do.

INDULGENCE, *s.* Caoimhneas, caomhalachd, maoth-chaidreamh; bàigh, deagh-gean; saor-thìodhlac; toileachadh; cead-peacaidh.

INDULGENT, *adj.* Caoimhneil, caidreach, fial; caomh, bàigheil; faoinghràdhach; truacanta.

INDULT, INDULTO, *s.* Ùghdarras.

INDURATE, *v.* Cruadhaich, fàs cruaidh.

INDURATION, *s.* Cruadhachadh; cruas; cruas cridhe.

INDUSTRIOUS, *adj.* Gnìomhach, dìchiollach, dèanadach, aghartach.

INDUSTRY, *s.* Dìchioll, saothair, deanadachd, gnìomhachas.

INDWELLER, *s.* Fear-còmhnaidh.

INEBRIATE, *v.* Misgich, bi air mhisg.

INEBRIATION, *s.* Misg, daorach.

INEFFABILITY, *s.* Do labhartachd.

INEFFABLE, *adj.* Do-innseadh.

INEFFECTIVE, *adj.* Neo-bhuadhach, fann, neo-dhrùiteach.

INEFFECTUAL, *adj.* Neo-tharbhach, fann.

INEFFICACIOUS, *adj.* Neo-éifeachdach.

INEFFICACY, *s.* Neo-chomasachd.

INELEGANCE, *s.* Mi-mhaise, mi-loinn.

INELEGANT, *adj.* Neo-mhaiseach, miloinneil, mi-dhreachmhor, mi-eireachdail.

INELOQUENT, *adj.* Neo-fhileanta.

INEPT, *adj.* Neo-fhreagarrach, baoth.

INEPTITUDE, *s.* Neo-fhreagarrachd.

INEQUALITY, *s.* Neo-choimeasachd, neo-ionannachd; eadar-dhealachadh.

INEQUITABLE, *adj.* Mi-cheart.

INERRABLE, *adj.* Neo-mhearachdail.

INERT, *adj.* Trom, marbhanta, leisg.

INERTNESS, *s.* Marbhantachd.

INESCATION, *s.* Tàladh, buaireadh.

INESTIMABLE, *adj.* Os ceann luach.

INEVIDENT, *adj.* Mi-shoilleir, dorcha.

INEVITABLE, *adj.* Do-sheachnadh.

INEXCUSABLE, *adj.* Neo-leithsgeulach.

INEXHALABLE, *adj.* Nach éirich 'na cheò.

INEXHAUSTIBLE, *adj.* Do-thraoghadh.

INEXISTENCE, *s.* Neo-bhith.

INEXISTENT, *adj.* Neo-bhitheach.

INEXORABLE, *adj.* Do-lùbadh.

INEXPEDIENCE, *s.* Neo-iomchuidheachd.

INEXPEDIENT, *adj.* Neo-iomchuidh.

INEXPERIENCE, *s.* Cion-eòlais.

INEXPERIENCED, *adj.* Neo-chleachdte.

INEXPERT, *adj.* Neo-ealanta.

INEXPIABLE, *adj.* Do-réiteachadh.

INEXPLICABLE, *adj.* Do-mhineachadh.

INEXPLORABLE, *adj.* Do rannsachadh.

INEXPRESSIBLE, *adj.* Do-innseadh.

INEXTINCT, *adj.* Neo-mhùchte.

INEXTINGUISHABLE, *adj.* Do-mhùchadh.

INEXTIRPABLE, *adj.* Do-spìonadh.

INEXTRICABLE, *adj.* Do-fhuasgladh.

INFALLIBILITY, *s.* Do-mhearachdas.

INFALLIBLE, *adj.* Neo-mhearachdach.

INFAMOUS, *adj.* Maslach, olc.

INFAMY, *s.* Masladh, mi-chliù, sgainneal.

INFANCY, *s.* Leanabachd; tùs.

INFANT, *s.* Naoidh, (*etymo.* nuadh-thì,) naoidheachan, naoidhean, leanabh, leanaban, pàisde.

INFANTICIDE, *s.* Naoidh-mhortair.

INFANTILE, INFANTINE, *adj.* Leanabaidh, leanabail, leanabanta.

INFANTRY, *s.* Saighdearan coise.

INFATUATE, *v. a.* Dall, buair, cuir fo gheasaibh.

INFATUATED, *adj.* Buairte, as a chiall.

INFATUATION, *s.* Dalladh, buaireadh.

INFEASIBLE, *adj.* Do-dheanamh.

INFECT, *v. a.* Cuir galar no tinneas air; truaill, lìon le truailleachd.

INFECTION, *s.* Galar-ghabhail.

INFECTIOUS, *adj.* Gabhaltach.

INFECUND, *adj.* Neo-thorach, seasg.

INFECUNDITY, *s.* Neo-thorachas.

INFELICITY, *s.* Mi-shonas, mi-àgh.

INFER, *v. a.* Co-dhùin, thoir fainear.

INFERENCE, *s.* Co-dhùnadh, seadh.

INFERRIBLE, *adj.* So-thuigsinn o, a thuigear le.

INFERIOR, *adj.* Ìochdrach; suarach, ni's suaraiche, ni's neo-inbhiche.

INFERIOR, *s.* Ìochdaran.

INFERIORITY, *s.* Ìochdranachd, neo-inbheachd, neo-luachachd.

INFERNAL, *adj.* Ifrinneach, dona.

INFERTILE, *adj.* Mi-thorach, aimrid

INFERTILITY, *s.* Mi-thorachas.

INFEST, *v. a.* Taghaich, claoidh, cuir dragh air.

INFESTIVE, *adj.* Neo-shunntach.

INFIDEL, *s.* Ana-creideach.

INFIDELITY, *s.* As-creideamh; anacriosdachd; mealltaireachd.

INFINITE, *adj.* Neo-chrìochnach, neomheasraichte.

INFINITELY, *adv.* Gun tomhas, gun chrìoch, mòran ni's, gu mòr ni's.

INFINITENESS, INFINITUDE, INFINITY, *s.* Neo-chrìochnachd, anabarrachd.

INFIRM, *adj.* Euslan, anfhann, breòite; neo-dhaingeann.

INFIRMARY, *s.* Taigh-eiridinn.

INFIRMITY, *s.* Laigse, anfhannachd, anmhainneachd; breòiteachd, fàillinn, euslaint, tinneas.

INFIRMNESS, *s.* Laigse, eucail.

INFIX, *v. a.* Sàth a steach; daingnaich.

INFLAME, *v. a.* Loisg, lăs, cuir r'a theine; feargaich, buair; brosnaich; ăt, gabh fearg, iongraich.

INFLAMMABLE, *adj.* So-lasadh, lasaireach, lasanta.

INFLAMMATION, *s.* Cur r'a theine, lasadh, losgadh; brosnachadh; iongrachadh, ainteas.

INFLAMMATORY, *adj.* Lasarra, loisgeach, buaireasach, feargach.

INFLATE, *v. a.* Séid, suas, cuir gaoth ann; dean ardanach, dean moiteil.

INFLATION, *s.* Séideadh, ăt; moit, féinbheachd, féin-spèis.

INFLECT, *v. a.* Lùb, fiar, crom.

INFLECTIVE, *adj.* A lùbas, a chromas.

INFLEXIBILITY, INFLEXIBLENESS, *s.* Neo-lùbtachd, raige, raigead; ragmhuinealas, reasgachd.

INFLEXIBLE, *adj.* Do-lùbadh, dochromadh, rag; dùr, reasgach, ceannlaidir; do-atharrachadh, do-chaochladh.

INFLICT, *v. a.* Leag peanas air, peanasach, pian, sàraich, goirtich, cràidh.

INFLICTION, *s.* Leagadh peanais, peanasachadh, sàrachadh, peanas.

INFLICTIVE, *adj.* Peanasail.

INFLUENCE, *s.* Cumhachd, ceannardachd, uachdranachd.

INFLUENCE, *v. a.* Stiùr, lùb, aom, treòraich, earalaich, comhairlich.

INFLUENT, *adj.* A' lìonadh, a' sruthadh a steach.

INFLUENTIAL, *adj.* Cumhachdach, buadhach, uachdranail.

INFLUX, *s.* Tighinn a steach, sruthlìonaidh.

INFOLD, *v. a.* Fill, paisg.

INFOLIATE, *v. a.* Còmhdaich le duilleach.

INFORM, *v. a.* Teagaisg, thoir eòlas, casaidich, innis; thoir brăth.

INFORMAL, *adj.* Mi-riaghailteach.

INFORMALITY, *s.* Mi-riaghailt.

INFORMANT, *s.* Fear-brătha.

INFORMATION, *s.* Naigheachd, sgeul; rabhadh, brăth; ionnsachadh, oilean, fiosrachadh.

INFORMER, *s.* Fear-innsidh.

INFORMIDABLE, *adj.* Neo-eagalach.

INFORMITY, *s.* Neo-chumaireachd.

INFORTUNATE, *adj.* Mi-shealbhach.

INFRACT, *v. a.* Bris, bris cùmhnant.

INFRACTION, *s.* Briseadh.

INFRAMUNDANE, *adj.* Fo'n t-saoghal.

INFRANGIBLE, *adj.* Do-bhristeadh.

INFREQUENCY, *s.* Ainminigeas.

INFREQUENT, *adj.* Ainmig, ainneamh.

INFRIGIDATE, *v. a.* Fuaraich, ragaich.

INFRIGIDATION, *s.* Fuachd-ragachadh.

INFRINGE, *v. a.* Mill, sgrios, bac.

INFRINGEMENT, *s.* Bristeadh.

INFRUGIFEROUS, *adj.* Neo-thorach.

INFUMATE, *v. a.* Tiormaich sa' cheò.

INFURIATE, *adj.* Air boile, cuthaich.

INFURIATE, *v. a.* Cuir air boile.

INFUSE, *v. a.* Dòirt ann, dòirt a steach; bogaich, cuir am bogadh.

INFUSIBLE, *adj.* A ghabhas cur ann.

INFUSION, *s.* Dòrtadh a steach; teagasg, deachdadh; bogachadh; sùgh, deoch.

INFUSIVE, *adj.* Dòirteach; leaghtach.

INGEMINATION, *s.* Ath-aithris.

INGENERATE, INGENERATED, *adj.* Neoghinte.

INGENIOUS, *adj.* Innleachdach, tùrail, geur-chuiseach, seòlta, teòma, ealanta, innealta.

INGENUITY, *s.* Innleachd, tùralachd, teòmachd, seòltachd, ealantachd, innealtachd.

INGENUOUS, *adj.* Fosgarra, fìrinneach, ceart, còir, fialaidh.

INGLORIOUS, *adj.* Neo-allail, suarach; dìblidh, gun déidh air cliù.

INGOT, *s.* Geinn òir no airgeid.

INGRAFF, INGRAFT, *v. a.* Alp; suidhich faillean o aona chraoibh ann an craoibh eile.

INGRAFTMENT, *s.* Alpadh.

INGRATE, *s.* Neonach, mi-thaingeil.

INGRATIATE, *v. a.* Mol thu féin do; faigh caoimhneas o neach.

INGRATITUDE, *s.* Mi-thaingealachd.

INGREDIENT, *s.* Earrann-measgachaidh.

INGRESS, *s.* Dol a steach, slighe.

Ingulph, *v. a.* Tilg sios ann an slugan.

Ingurgitate, *v.* Sluig, sìos, dean geòcaireachd.

Ingurgitation, *s.* Geòcaireachd.

Inhabit, *v.* Àitich, sealbhaich; còmhnaich, tàmh, fuirich.

Inhabitable, *adj.* So-àiteachadh.

Inhabitant, *s.* Fear-àiteachaidh.

Inhale, *v. a.* Tarruinn t' anail, gabh a steach leis an anail.

Inharmonious, *adj.* Neo-bhinn.

Inherent, *adj.* Ann-féin, nàdurra, dualach, neo-ghinte, leanabhaineach.

Inherit, *v. a.* Gabh mar oighreachd, faigh mar oighreachd.

Inheritable, *adj.* Oighreachail.

Inheritance, *s.* Oighreachd, sealbh dlighe, maoin dhligheach.

Inheritor, *s.* Oighre, sealbhadair.

Inheritress, **Inheritrix**, *s.* Ban-oighre, bann-sealbhadair.

Inhibit, *v. a.* Bac, cum air ais, grab, cuir stad air; toirmisg, diùlt.

Inhibition, *s.* Bacadh, grabadh, stad, amladh; toirmeasg, casg.

Inhospitable, *adj.* Neo-fhialaidh, iargalta, coimheach doichiollach.

Inhospitality, *s.* Neo-fhialachd, iargaltachd, coimhiche, doichiollachd, mosaiche, spìocaiche, crìonachd, cruas, mùgaireachd, doirbheachd.

Inhuman, *adj.* Neo-dhaonairceach, mi-dhaonna, borb, an-iochdmhor, cruaidh-chridheach.

Inhumanity, *s.* Mi-dhaonnachd, an-iochdmhorachd, buirbe.

Inhumate, **Inhume**, *v. a.* Adhlaic, tòrr, tiodhlaic.

Inhumation, *s.* Adhlacadh, tòrradh.

Inject, *v. a.* Tilg a stigh, tilg suas.

Injection, *s.* Tilgeadh a steach; a' chungaidh a thilgear a steach.

Inimical, *adj.* Neo-chàirdeil, mi-rùnach.

Inimitable, *adj.* Do-leanmhainn, do-shamhlach; gun choimeas.

Iniquitous, *adj.* Eucorach, peacach, aingidh, ciontach, olc.

Iniquity, *s.* Eucoir, peacadh, aingeachd, ana-ceartas, cionta, olc.

Initial, *adj.* Toiseachail, air thoiseach.

Initiate, *v.* Fòghluim, teagaisg; tionnsgain, tòisich.

Initiation, *s.* Ceud thòiseachadh.

Initiatory, *adj.* Tòiseachail.

Injudicial, *adj.* Mi-riaghailteach.

Injudicious, *adj.* Neo thuigseach, neo-chrìonna, neo thùrail.

Injunction, *s.* Àinte, earail, dian-iarrtas, òrdugh.

Injure, *v. a.* Docharaich, lochdaich, ciùrr, dochannaich, dean coire do.

Injurious, *adj.* Cronail, eucorach, ana-ceart; coireach, ciontach; aimhleasach, docharach; tarcuiseach, tàmailteach.

Injury, *s.* Lochd, leth-trom, ciurradh, ana-cothrom, dochair; dochunn, dìobhail, call, calldach; tàir, tarcuis, càineadh.

Injustice, *s.* Ana-ceartas, eucoir, ana-cothrom; easaontas, olc.

Ink, *s.* Dubh, dubh-sgrìobhaidh.

Inkle, *s.* Stìom, stiall, caol-chrios.

Inkling, *s.* Sanas, faireachadh, rabhadh.

Inky, *adj.* Dubh, dorcha.

Inland, *adj.* Braigheach.

Inland, *s.* Bràighe-dùthcha.

Inlapidate, *v. a.* Fàs mar chlòich.

Inlay, *v. a.* Ioma-dhreachaich.

Inlet, *s.* Dorus, fosgladh, rathad, bealach, caolas, aisir.

Inly, *adj.* Meadhonach, dìomhair.

Inmate, *s.* Co-thàmhaiche.

Inmost, **Innermost**, *adj.* A's fhaide steach.

Inn, *s.* Taigh-òsda, taigh-òil, taigh-leanna.

Innate, *adj.* Neo-ghinte, nàdurra, gnèitheach, dualach.

Innavigable, *adj.* Do-sheòladh.

Inner, *adj.* A's fhaide steach.

Innholder, **Innkeeper**, *s.* Òsdair.

Innocence, *s.* Neo-chiontachd, neo-chiontas; neo-lochdachd, neo-chronalachd; fìreantachd, ionracas, neo-chiont; tréidhireas.

Innocent, *adj.* Neo-chiontach, neo-choireach, glan; neo-lochdach.

Innocuous, *adj.* Neo-chronail, neo-lochdach.

Innovate, *v. a.* Ùr-ghnàthaich, dean ùr-chaochla; atharraich.

Innovation, *s.* Ùr-ghnàthachadh.

Innovator, *s.* Ùr-ghnàthadair.

Innoxious, *adj.* Neo-lochdach, neo-choireach, neo-chiùrrail.

Innuendo, *s.* Fiar-rabhadh.

Innumerable, *adj.* Do-àireamh.

Inoculate, *v.* Suidhich; cuir a' bhreac air.

Inoculation, *s.* Suidheachadh, alpadh; cur na brice.

Inodorous, *adj.* Gun fhàileadh.

Inoffensive, *adj.* Neo-lochdach, soitheamh, ciùin, suairce, neo-bhuaireasach.

Inoffensiveness, *s.* Suairceas.
Inofficious, *adj.* Mi-mhodhail.
Inopportune, *adj.* An-aimsireil.
Inordinacy, *s.* Ana-cuimse.
Inordinate, *adj.* Ana-cuimseach, mi-riaghailteach, aimhreiteach.
Inordinateness, *s.* Aimhreit.
Inorganical, *adj.* Neo-ghleusta.
Inosculate, *v. n.* Buin r'a chéile, co-cheangail, tàthaich,
Inosculation, *s.* Aonadh, dlùthachadh, tàthadh, co-bhuntainn, pòg.
Inquest, *s.* Sgrùdadh, ceasnachadh, rannsachadh laghail; iarraidh, sireadh.
Inquietude, *s.* Mi-shuaimhneas, neo-fhoisneachd, an-shocair.
Inquinate, *v. a.* Truaill, salaich, mill.
Inquination, *s.* Truailleadh, salachadh.
Inquire, *v.* Feòraich, farraid, iarr, faighnich; rannsaich, sir, dean sgrùdadh.
Inquirer, *s.* Fear-rannsachaidh, fear-ceasnachaidh, fear-sgrùdaidh.
Inquiry, *s.* Ceasnachadh, feòraich, rannsachadh, sireadh, sgrùdadh.
Inquisition, *s.* Rannsachadh laghail, mion-cheasnachadh, sireadh; cùirt a chaidh a shocrachadh air son saobh-chreideamh fhaotainn a mach.
Inquisitive, *adj.* Rannsachail, faighneachdail, fidreachail.
Inquisitiveness, *s.* Faighneachdas, geur-rannsachadh, fidreachadh.
Inquisitor, *s.* Fear-ceasnachaidh, fear-rannsachaidh, fear-sgrùdaich.
Inroad, *s.* Ionnsaidh, ruathar, ruaig.
Insalubrious, *adj.* Neo-fhallain.
Insalubrity, *s.* Neo-fhallaineachd.
Insane, *adj.* Cuthaich, mearanach.
Insaneness, **Insanity**, *s.* Cuthach, mearan-céille, boile.
Insatiable, **Insatiate**, *adj.* Do-shàsachadh, do-riarachadh, do-thoileachadh, gionach, geòcach, glùtach, lònach, craosach, cìocrach.
Insatiableness, *s.* Lòin-chraois.
Insaturable, *adj.* Do-lìonadh.
Inscribe, *v. a.* Sgrìobh air.
Inscription, *s.* Sgrìobhadh, tiodal, gràbhaladh, cuimhne.
Inscrutable, *adj.* Do-rannsachadh.
Insculpture, *s.* Gràbhaladh, snaidheadh.
Insect, *s.* Cuileag, cnuimh, biastag.
Insectator, *s.* Fear-tòrach.
Insecure, *adj.* Neo-thèarainte.
Insecurity, *s.* Neo-thèarainteachd.
Insensate, *adj.* Neo-thuigseach.
Insensibility, *s.* Neo-mhothachadh.
Insensible, *adj.* Neo-mhothachail, neo-thuigseach; neo-chaidreach.
Inseparable, *adj.* Do-dhealachadh, do-sgaradh, do-fhuasgladh.
Insert, *v. a.* Suidhich, gabh a steach.
Insertion, *s.* Suidheachadh, cur ann.
Inside, *s.* An taobh a staigh.
Insidious, *adj.* Meallta, cealgach, foilleil, carach, cuilbheartach, sligheach.
Insidiousness, *s.* Mealltachd, ceilg, foillealachd, cuilbheartachd.
Insight, *s.* Fiosrachadh, geur-bheachd.
Insignia, *s.* Suaicheantas.
Insignificance, *s.* Faoineas.
Insignificant, *adj.* Faoin, suarach, tàireil, neo-luachmhor.
Insincere, *adj.* Neo-fhìrinneach, neo-dhùrachdach, neo-thréidhireach, cealgach, claon, foilleil, carach.
Insincerity, *s.* Neo-fhìrinneachd, neo-thréidhireas, ceilg, foillealachd.
Insinuant, *adj.* Miodalach, brionnalach, seòlta.
Insinuate, *v.* Cuir a steach le faicill; dean miodal, dean brosgal; faigh a staigh air; thoir leth-shanas, leth-chiallaich.
Insinuation, *s.* Cur a staigh, sàthadh; miodal, sodal, brosgal, brionnal.
Insinuative, *adj.* Seòltach, miodalach, sodalach, brosgalach.
Insipid, *adj.* Neo-bhlasda, neo-shunntach, neo-sheadhach, marbhanta, tioram, trom, amhaidh.
Insipidity, *s.* Neo-bhlasdachd; marbhantachd, tiormachd, truime, amhaidheachd.
Insipience, *s.* Neo-ghliocas, gòraiche, baothaltachd, baothaireachd.
Insist, *v. n.* Seas air, socraich air, lean air, buanaich air, seas ri, cùm air.
Insition, *s.* Suidheachadh mheanglan an craobhan.
Insnare, *v. a.* Rib, glac, cuir an sàs.
Insobriety, *s.* Ana-measarrachd, misg.
Insociable, *adj.* Neo-chòmhraideach, neo-chonaltrach, neo-chòmpanta.
Insolate, *v. a.* Cuir ri gréin.
Insolation, *s.* Grianachadh.
Insolent, *adj.* Uaibhreach, stràiceil, beadaidh, tarcuiseach.
Insolence, *s.* Uaibhreachas, tàir, àrdan, stràic, beadaidheachd.
Insolvable, *adj.* Do-fhuasgladh, do-mhìneachadh, do-réiteachadh; do-dhìoladh, do-ìocadh.

INSOLUBLE, *adj.* Do-leaghadh.
INSOLVENCY, *s.* Bristeadh creideis.
INSOLVENT, *adj.* Briste.
INSOMUCH, *adv.* A' mheud agus gu.
INSPECT, *v. a.* Rannsaich, beachdaich.
INSPECTION, *s.* Amharc, geur-amharc, mion-rannsachadh, sgrùdadh, dearcadh; cùram, sùl amharc.
INSPECTOR, *s.* Fear-rannsachaidh, fear-sgrùdaidh; fear-coimhid, fear-cùraim.
INSPIRABLE, *adj.* A ghabhas tarruinn a steach.
INSPIRATION, *s.* Analachadh, sùghadh analach; deachdadh an Spioraid, teagasg nèamhaidh.
INSPIRE, *v.* Analaich air; cuir 's an inntinn; tarruinn a steach, sùigh, tarruinn t' anail.
INSPIRIT, *v. a.* Beothaich, dùisg suas, brosnaich, misnich.
INSPISSATE, *v. a.* Tiughaich, dean tiugh.
INSPISSATED, *adj.* Tiughaichte.
INSPISSATION, *s.* Tiughachadh.
INSTABILITY, *s.* Neo-bhunailteachd.
INSTALL, *v. a.* Cuir an dreuchd.
INSTALLATION, *s.* Cur an seilbh dreuchd, suidheachadh an dreuchd, dreuchd-shuidheachadh.
INSTALMENT, *s.* Dreuchd-ionad; earrann-dhìoladh.
INSTANT, *adj.* Dian, éigneach, dian-iarrtasachd, dùrachdach, cabhagach, bras, ealamh.
INSTANT, *s.* Tìota, àm, tamall, uair.
INSTANTANEOUS, *adj.* An gradaig.
INSTANTLY, INSTANTANEOUSLY, *adv.* Gu grad, gu h-obann, gu h-ealamh, gu clis.
INSTATE, *v. a.* Suidhich, cuir an inbhe.
INSTAURATION, *s.* Ath-aiseadh.
INSTEAD, *adv.* An àite, air son.
INSTEEP, *v. a.* Bogaich, tùm an uisg.
INSTEP, *s.* Uachdar na traidhe.
INSTIGATE, *v. a.* Brosnaich, buair.
INSTIGATION, *s.* Brosnachadh, buaireadh.
INSTIGATOR, *s.* Buaireadair.
INSTIL, *v. a.* Sil, sil a stigh; teagaisg.
INSTILLATION, *s.* Sileadh-a-stigh; teagasg, mion-theagasg.
INSTINCT, *adj.* Beò, beothail, beathail.
INSTINCT, *s.* Aomadh nàdurra, nàdur, ciall, gnè.
INSTINCTIVE, *adj.* Gnèitheil, nàdurrach.
INSTITUTE, *v. a.* Suidhich, socraich.
INSTITUTE, *s.* Reachd, lagh, rian, òrdugh, seòl suidhichte; àinte, fìrinn shuidhichte.
INSTITUTION, *s.* Suidheachadh, òrduchadh; lagh, reachd; oilean, foghlum.
INSTITUTOR, *s.* Fear-suidheachaidh, fear-òrduchaidh; fear-teagaisg.
INSTRUCT, *v. a.* Teagaisg, oileanaich, seòl, comhairlich, ionnsaich.
INSTRUCTION, *s.* Teagasg, oilean, seòladh, eòlas, comhairle; àinte, ionnsachadh.
INSTRUCTIVE, *adj.* Teagasgach.
INSTRUCTOR, *s.* Oid-ionnsachaidh, fear-teagaisg, fear-fòghluim.
INSTRUMENT, *s.* Inneal, ball, beart, arm; inneal-ciùil; bann-sgrìobhte; meadhon, ball-acuinn.
INSTRUMENTAL, *adj.* 'Na mheadhon air.
INSUAVITY, *s.* Neo-thaitneachd.
INSUBJECTION, *s.* Eas-ùmhlachd.
INSUBORDINATION, *s.* Mi-riaghailt.
INSUBSTANTIAL, *adj.* Neo-bhrìoghor.
INSUFFERABLE, *adj.* Do-fhulang, do-ghiùlan, do-iomchar; déisinneach.
INSUFFICIENCY, *s.* Neo-choimhlionta-chd, neo-dhiongmhaltachd, eas-bhuidheachd, neo-fhoghainteachd.
INSUFFICIENT, *adj.* Neo-choimhlionta, neo-dhiongmhalta, neo-fhoghainteach.
INSULAR, *adj.* Eileanach, 'na aonar, leis féin.
INSULATED, *adj.* Dealaichte, air leth.
INSULT, *s.* Tàmailt, masladh, tàir, tarcuis, dimeas, beum, toibheum.
INSULT, *v. a.* Tàmailtich, thoir tàmailt, maslaich, cuir gu nàire.
INSULTER, *s.* Fear-tarcuis.
INSUPERABILITY, *s.* Do-cheannsachd, do-chlaoidhteachd; do-dheantachd.
INSUPERABLE, *adj.* Do-cheannsachadh; do-chlaoidheadh, do-shàrachadh; do-dhèanamh, do-fhairtleach.
INSUPPORTABLE, *adj.* Do-ghiùlan.
INSUPPORTABLENESS, *s.* Do-ghiùlantachd.
INSUPPRESSIBLE, *adj.* Do-fhalach.
INSURANCE, *s.* Urras, airgead urrais.
INSURE, *v. a.* Faigh no thoir urras air.
INSURGENT, *s.* Ceannaircach.
INSURMOUNTABLE, *adj.* Thar comas.
INSURRECTION, *s.* Ar-a-mach.
INTACTIBLE, *adj.* Do-fhaireachadh.
INTANGIBLE, *adj.* Do-bheantainn.
INTEGER, *s.* Slàn-àireamh, an-t-iomlan.
INTEGRAL, *adj.* Slàn, iomlan, coimhlionta, neo-bhriste.

Integral, *s.* An t-iomlan.
Integrity, *s.* Tréidhireas, ionracas; gloine, neo-chiontas.
Integument, *s.* Còmhdach, cochull.
Intellect, *s.* Tuigse, toinisg. ciall.
Intellective, *adj.* Tuigseach, ciallach; inntinneil, mothachail.
Intellectual, *adj.* Inntinneil, inntinneach; tuigseach, ciallach.
Intelligence, *s.* Fios, fiosrachadh, eòlas, tuigse; spiorad.
Intelligent, *adj.* Tuigseach, eòlach, fiosrach, fòghluimte, ionnsaichte.
Intelligible, *adj.* So-thuigsinn.
Intemerate, *adj.* Neo-thruaillte.
Intemperament, *s.* Droch càileachd.
Intemperance, *s.* Ana-measarrachd.
Intemperate, *adj.* Ana-measarra, mi-stuama; glùtail; lasanta, feargach.
Intemperature, *s.* Mi-riaghailt san iormalt, anabharra.
Intenable, *s.* Do-chumail.
Intend, *v. a.* Cuir romhad, sònraich, rùnaich, togair; thoir fainear.
Intendent, *s.* Fear-freasdail.
Inteneration, *s.* Maothachadh, taiseachadh, tlàthachadh.
Intense, *adj.* Teann, cruaidh, teannaichte; dlù-aireach; dian.
Intenseness, *s.* Teinne, teanntachd; déinead, déine; ro-aire, dlù-aire.
Intention, *s.* Rùn, miann, sannt, cur romhad, aire, beachd.
Intentional, *adj.* Rùnaichte, le deòin.
Intentive, *adj.* Dlù-aireach, dùrachdach.
Intentness, *s.* Ro-aire, geur-aire.
Inter, *v. a.* Adhlaic, tìodhlaic.
Intercalary, *adj.* Barrachdail.
Intercalation, *s.* Eadar-chur.
Intercede, *v. a.* Dean eadar-ghuidhe.
Intercept, *v. a.* Glac 's an t-slighe, beir air; cuir bacadh air.
Intercession, *s.* Eadar-ghuidhe.
Intercessor, *s.* Eadar-mheadhonair.
Interchain, *v. a.* Co-cheangail.
Interchange, *v. a.* Malairtich.
Interchange, *s.* Iomlaid, malairt.
Interchangeable, *adj.* Co-iomlaideach, co-mhalairteach.
Intercipient, *adj.* Eadar-ghlacach.
Intercision, *s.* Bacadh, amladh.
Interclude, *v. n.* Dùin a mach.
Interclusion, *s.* Dùnadh a mach.
Intercolumniation, *s.* Eadar dhà charragh.
Intercostal, *adj.* Eadar dhà aisne.
Intercourse, *s.* Co-chomunn.
Interdict, *v. a.* Toirmisg, seun, bac.
Interdiction, *s.* Bacadh, toirmeasg, grabadh, iomasgaradh.
Interdictory, *adj.* Toirmeasgach.
Interest, *v.* Cuir fo chùram, cuir fo smuain; gabh gnothach ri, gabh cùram do; gluais, drùidh air; tog déidh.
Interest, *s.* Leas, math, buannachd, tairbhe, feum; cumhachd, ùghdarras; comh-roinn, comh-pàirt, lethphàirt; ocar, riadh.
Interfere, *v. n.* Dean meachranachd.
Interference, *s.* Eadraiginn.
Interfulgent, *adj.* Eadar-dhealrach.
Interfused, *adj.* Eadar-thaomte.
Interjacent, *adj.* Eadar-laidheach.
Interject, *v.* Dean eadraiginn.
Interjection, *s.* Guth-fhacal.
Interim, *s.* An t-àm, 's an àm.
Interjoin, *v. a.* Eadar-dhlùthaich.
Interior, *adj.* An leth stigh.
Interknowledge, *s.* Co-eòlas.
Interlace, *v. a.* Eadar-fhigh.
Interlapse, *s.* Eadar-ùine.
Interlard, *v. a.* Measgaich le.
Interleave, *v. a.* Eadar-dhuilleagaich.
Interline, *v. a.* Eadar-shreathaich.
Interlineation, *s.* Eadar-shreathadh, eadar-sgrìobhadh.
Interlocation, *s.* Eadar-shuidheachadh.
Interlink, *v. a.* Eadar-theinich.
Interlocution, *s.* Eadar-labhairt.
Interlocutor, *s.* Eadar-labhairtair
Interlocutory, *adj.* Conaltrach.
Interlope, *v. n.* Eadar-leum.
Interloper, *s.* Sgimilear.
Interlucent, *adj.* Eadar-shoillseach.
Interlude, *s.* Eadar-chluiche.
Interlunar, *adj.* Eadar dhà sholus.
Intermarriage, *s.* Co-chleamhnas.
Intermeddle, *v. n.* Dean meachranachd.
Intermedial, **Intermediate**, *adj.* Eadar-mheadhonach.
Intermedium, *s.* Eadar-uidhe.
Interment, *s.* Tìodhlacadh, adhlacadh.
Intermention, *v. a.* Eadar-ainmich.
Intermigration, *s.* Iomlaid àite.
Interminable, **Interminate**, *adj.* Neo-chrìochnach, neo-iomallach, gun chrìoch.
Intermination, *adj.* Bagradh.
Intermingle, *v. a.* Coimeasgaich.
Intermission, *s.* Stad, clos, tàmh; eadar-ùine; lasachadh, faothachadh.

Intermissive, Intermittent, *adj.* Neo-bhitheanta, neo-ghnàthach.

Intermit, *v.* Sguir, stad, leig tàmh dha; faothaich, lasaich, clos rè ùine.

Intermix, *v.* Coimeasg.

Intermixture, *s.* Coimeasgadh.

Intermundane, *adj.* Eadar-dhà shaoghal.

Intermural, *adj.* Eadar-dhà-bhalla.

Intermutual, *adj.* Eadar-mhalairteach, eadar-iomlaideach.

Internal, *adj.* 'S an leth a' steach.

Internuncio, *s.* Eadar-theachdair.

Interpellation, *s.* Bairlin, gairm.

Interpoint, *v. a.* Eadar-phoncaich.

Interpolate, *v. a.* Eadar-sgrìobh, spàrr an àite nach buin do.

Interpolation, *s.* Eadar-sgrìobhadh, eadar-sparradh.

Interpolator, *s.* Fear-breugachaidh seagha le mi-sgrìobhadh.

Interposal, Interposition, *s.* Eadraiginn, teachd 's an rathad.

Interpose, *v.* Eadar-chuir, eadarshuidhich; cuir grabadh air, amail; tairg cuideachadh; dean eadraiginn.

Interposition, *s.* Eadraiginn.

Interpret, *v. a.* Mìnich, soilleirich; eadar-theangaich.

Interpretable, *adj.* So-mhìneachadh, so-shoilleireachadh.

Interpretation, *s.* Mìneachadh, soilleireachadh, eadar-theangachadh, brìgh, seadh.

Interpreter, *s.* Fear-mìneachaidh.

Interreign, Interregnum, *s.* Eadarriaghladh.

Interrogate, *v.* Ceasnaich, rannsaich, fidrich, cuir ceistean.

Interrogation, *s.* Ceasnachadh, rannsachadh, cur cheistean; ceist, faighneachd, comharradh-ceiste (?).

Interrogative, *adj.* Faighneachdach, ceisteach, ceasnachail.

Interrogative, *s.* Ceist-fhacal.

Interrogatory, *s.* Ceist, ceasnachadh, faighneachd.

Interrogatory, *adj.* Ceasnachail.

Interrupt, *v. a.* Cuir stad air, bac.

Interrupted, *adj.* Bristeach, briste.

Interruption, *s.* Stad, briseadh, briseadh a steach, stad-chur; eadarchur, grabadh, bacadh; cnap-starraidh; stad, clos.

Intersect, *v. a.* Co-ghearr, gearr tarsainn; eadar-chuir, eadar-shuidhich.

Intersection, *s.* Eadar-ghearradh.

Intersperse, *v. a.* Eadar-sgap.

Interstice, *s.* Eadar-fhosgladh.

Interstitial, *adj.* Eadar-fhosglach.

Intertexture, *s.* Eadar-fhighe.

Intertwine, *v. a.* Eadar-thoinn.

Interval, *s.* Eadar-uidhe, eadarionad; eadar-ùine, eadar-àm; faothachadh.

Intervene, *v. n.* Thig eadar.

Intervenient, *adj.* A thig eadar.

Intervention, *s.* Eadar-thighinn.

Intervert, *v. a.* Cuir gu buil eile.

Interview, *s.* Co-shealladh.

Intervolve, *v. a.* Eadar-fhill.

Interweave, *v. a.* Eadar-fhigh.

Intestate, *adj.* Gun tiomnadh.

Intestinal, *adj.* Caolanach.

Intestine, *adj.* 'S an leth a staigh; corporra.

Intestine, *s.* A' ghrealach.

Inthral, *v. a.* Cìosnaich cuir fo dhaorsa.

Inthralment, *s.* Braighdeanas.

Intimacy, *s.* Comunn, co-chomunn, dlù eòlas, companas, caidreamh.

Intimate, *adj.* Mion-eòlach, caidreach; dlù, fagus, teann air.

Intimate, *s.* Caraid, còmpanach.

Intimate, *v. a.* Innis, thoir sanas.

Intimation, *s.* Fios, rabhadh, sanas.

Intimidate, *v. a.* Gealtaich, eagalaich.

Into, *prep.* A staigh, a steach, gu; a stigh ann; a dh' ionnsaidh.

Intolerable, *adj.* Do-ghiùlan, dona.

Intolerant, *adj.* Neo-fhulangach.

Intonation, *s.* Torrunn, tairnthoirm.

Intoxicate, *v. a.* Cuir air an daoraich, misgich.

Intoxicated, *adj.* Air mhisg.

Intoxication, *s.* Misg, daorach.

Intractable, *adj.* Do-cheannsachadh, ceann-laidir, dùr.

Intransmutable, *adj.* Do-mhùthadh, do-atharrachadh.

Intrap, *v. a.* Cuir an sàs, glac, rib.

Intrench, *v.* Cladhaich, tochail, treachail; dìon le clais; bris a steach air.

Intrenchment, *s.* Clais-dhaingneachd, dìdean threachailte.

Intrepid, *adj.* Gaisgeil, curanta.

Intrepidity, *s.* Curantachd.

Intricacy, *s.* Aimhreit, deacaireachd.

Intricate, *adj.* Aimhreidh, deacair, ioma-cheisteach, ioma-lùbach.

Intrigue, *s.* Rùn-aimhleis, comhairle dhìomhair, cùis-leannanachd; innleachd meallaidh, feall, cuilbheart.

Intrigue, *v. n.* Meall, cleasaich, dean leannanachd dhìomhair.

Intrinsic, Intrinsical, *adj.* Nàdurra, gnèitheil, ann féin, dlùdhaimheil.

Introduce, *v. a.* Thoir 's an làthair, thoir am fianais, thoir am follais, thoir a staigh; thoir air aghart.

Introduction, *s.* Treòrachadh, toirt an làthair, toirt am fianais; roiràdh.

Introductive, *adj.* Treòrachail.

Intromission, *s.* Meachranachd, buintinn ri cuid neach eile; cur a steach.

Intromit, *v.* Cuir a stigh, leig a staigh; buin ri cuid neach eile.

Introspection, *s.* Sealltainn a staigh.

Introvenient, *adj.* A thig a steach.

Intrude, *v. n.* Fòirn, spàrr a staigh; thig gun chuireadh; bris a steach.

Intruder, *s.* Sgimilear, fear-fòirnidh.

Intrusion, *s.* Sgimeilearachd, fòirneadh.

Intrusive, *adj.* Leamh, beag-narach.

Intrust, *v. a.* Earb ri, cuir earbs' ann.

Intuition, *s.* Beachd-eòlas, grad-eòlas.

Intuitive, *adj.* So-thuigsinn; geur-thuigseach, grad-thuigseach.

Intwine, *v. a.* Toinn, fill, figh, snìomh.

Inumbrate, *v. a.* Sgàil, cuir sgàil air.

Inunction, *s.* Ungadh, ol'-ùngadh.

Inundate, *v.* Còmhdaich le uisge.

Inundation, *s.* Tuil-chòmhdach.

Inurbanity, *s.* Neo-shuairceas.

Inure, *v. a.* Ri, cuir an cleachdadh, cleachd.

Inurement, *s.* Cleachdadh.

Inurn, *v. a.* Adhlaic, tìodhlaic, tòrr.

Inustion, *s.* Losgadh, lasadh.

Inutile, *adj.* Neo-fheumail, suarach.

Inutility, *s.* Neo-fheumalachd.

Inutterable, *adj.* Do-labhairt.

Invade, *v. a.* Thoir ionnsaidh air, bris a steach; leum air, cas ri, buail air.

Invader, *s.* Nàmhaid, fear brisidh a steach, fear-fòirnidh.

Invalescence, *s.* Slainte, lùgh, neart.

Invalid, *adj.* Lag, anfhann, neothreòrach, fann.

Invalid, *s.* Neach tinn, euslainteach, neach gun chlì.

Invalidate, *v. a.* Lagaich, dìobhalaich, anfhannaich.

Invalidity, *s.* Laigse, anfhannachd.

Invaluable, *adj.* Os ceann luach.

Invariable, *adj.* Neo-chaochlaideach.

Invariableness, *s.* Neo-chaochlaideachd, maireannachd, gnàthachas.

Invaried, *adj.* Neo-atharraichte.

Invasion, *s.* Briseadh a staigh, ionnsaidh naimhdeil.

Invasive, *adj.* Ainneartach.

Invective, *s.* Achmhasan, geur-achmhasan, cronachadh, beum.

Invective, *adj.* Beumnach, aoireil.

Inveigh, *v. a.* Càin, faigh cron.

Inveigle, *v. a.* Meall, thoir a thaobh, mi-chomhairlich, rib.

Inveigler, *s.* Mealltair, mi-chomhairleach.

Invent, *v. a.* Faigh ìnnleachd ùr, faigh a mach, tionnsgail; fealltaich.

Invention, *s.* Ùr-innleachd, ùr-ghleus, breug-dhealbhadh.

Inventive, *adj.* Innleachdach, ealanta, tùrail, tionnsgalach.

Inventor, *s.* Fear a dhealbhas innleachd ùr; fear deanamh bhreug.

Inventory, *s.* Maoin-chunntas.

Inverse, *adj.* Tarsainn, air chaochla dòigh.

Inversion, *s.* Rian-atharrachadh.

Invert, *v. a.* Cuir bun-os-ceann.

Invest, *v. a.* Éid, sgeadaich, còmhdaich; cuir an seilbh, cuir an dreuchd; cuairtich, ioma-dhruid, séisd; cuir umad.

Investigable, *adj.* So-rannsachadh.

Investigate, *v. a.* Rannsaich.

Investigation, *s.* Rannsachadh.

Investiture, *s.* Còir-sheilbhe.

Investment, *s.* Éideadh, earradh, aodach, culaidh, trusgan.

Inveteracy, *s.* Danarrachd, buantasuilc; cian mhairsinn an olc.

Inveterate, *adj.* Sean, buan; danarra, dìorrasach, dùr, dian, cruadhaichte.

Inveteration, *s.* Buanachadh, cruadhachadh.

Invidious, *adj.* Fuath-thogalach, farmadach, mì-runach, gamhlasach, naimhdeil.

Invidiousness, *s.* Fuath-thogalachd.

Invigorate, *v. a.* Neartaich, beothaich, lùghaich, brosnaich.

Invigoration, *s.* Neartachadh.

Invincible, *adj.* Do-cheannsachadh.

Inviolable, *adj.* Do-thruaillidh.

Inviolate, *adj.* Neo-chiùrrte, neothruaillte, neo-bhriste.

Invisibility, *s.* Do-fhaicsinneachd.

Invisible, *adj.* Do-fhaicsinneach.

Invitation, *s.* Cuireadh, iarraidh.

Invite, *v.* Iarr, gairm, thoir cuireadh; tàlaidh.
Inviter, *s.* Fear-cuiridh, fear-gairme.
Invitingly, *adj.* Gu tàlaidheach.
Invocate, *v. a.* Guidh, grias.
Invocation, *s.* Ùrnuigh, achanich.
Invoice, *s.* Maoin-chlàr.
Involve, *v. a.* Cuairtich iadh mu; seadhaich; co-aonaich, co-cheangail; rib; cuir troi-chéile, aimhreitich, cuir an ceann a chéile.
Involuntary, *adj.* Neo-thoileach.
Involution, *s.* Filleadh, cuairteachadh; cochull, cuairt-chòmhdach.
Invulnerable, *adj.* Do-leònadh.
Inward, Inwardly, *adv.* A steach; gu diamhair.
Inwrap, *v. a.* Fill, cuairtich, iomchòmhdaich; dorchaich, doilleirich.
Inwreathe, *v. a.* Stìom-chuairtich, coronaich.
Irascibleness, *s.* Lasantachd, feargachd, crosdachd.
Irascible, *adj.* Lasanta, feargach, crosda.
Ire, *s.* Fearg, corraich, fraoch, boile.
Ireful, *adj.* Feargach, lasanta, crosda.
Iris, *s.* Bogha-frois, bhogha-braoin; cearcall na sùl; seileastair.
Irksome, *adj.* Sgìth, buaireasach.
Iron, *s.* Iarunn; cuibhreach.
Iron, *adj.* Iaruinn, iarnach; cruaidh.
Iron, *v. a.* Iarnaich; dean mìn.
Ironical, *adj.* Magail, dà-sheadhach.
Ironmonger, *s.* Ceannaiche-cruadhach.
Irony, *s.* Sgeigearachd, fochaid.
Irradiance, Irradiancy, *s.* Dealradh, dearsadh, soillse.
Irradiate, *v.* Dealraich, loinnrich; soillsich, soilleirich; sgiamhaich.
Irradiation, *s.* Dèarsadh, dealradh; soilleireachadh, soillseachadh.
Irrational, *adj.* Eu-céillidh.
Irrationality, *s.* Eu-céillidheachd.
Irreclaimable, *adj.* Do-leasachadh.
Irreconcileable, *adj.* Do-réiteachadh.
Irreconciled, *adj.* Neo-réitichte.
Irrecoverable, *adj.* Caillte, dofhaotainn air ais; do-leasachadh.
Irreducible, *adi.* Do-briseadh.
Irrefragable, *adj.* Do-àicheadh.
Irrefutable, *adj.* Do-dhiùltadh.
Irregular, *adj.* Mi-riaghailteach.
Irregularity, *s.* Mi-riaghailt, easòrdugh; mi-dhòigh; mi-bheus.
Irrelative, *adj.* Aonarach, leis féin.
Irrelevant, *adj.* Neo-fhreagarrach.
Irrelievable, *adj.* Do-fhuasgladh.
Irreligion, *s.* Aindiadhachd.
Irreligious, *adj.* Aindiadhaidh.
Irremediable, *adj.* Do-shlànachadh.
Irremissible, *adj.* Do-mhathadh.
Irremoveable, *adj.* Do-ghluasad.
Irrenowned, *adj.* Neo-chliùiteach.
Irreparable, *adj.* Do-leasachadh.
Irrepentance, *s.* Neo-aithreachas.
Irreprehensible, *adj.* Neo-choireach.
Irrepresentable, *adj.* Do-shamhlachadh.
Irrepressible, *adj.* Do-cheannsachadh.
Irreproachable, *adj.* Neo-choireach, neo-chiontach.
Irreproveable, *adj.* Neo-chinteach.
Irresistible, *adj.* Do-chur 'na aghaidh.
Irresolute, *adj.* Neo-bhunailteach.
Irresolution, *s.* Neo-sheasmhachd.
Irretentive, *adj.* Ao-dhìonach.
Irretrievable, *adj.* Do-leasachadh.
Irreverence, *s.* Neo-urram.
Irreverent, *adj.* Mi-mhodhail.
Irreversible, *adj.* Do-atharrachadh.
Irrevocable, *adj.* Do-aisig.
Irrigate, *v. a.* Uisgich, fliuch, bog.
Irrigation, *s.* Uisgeachadh, bogadh.
Irrision, *s.* Gàireachdaich, fochaid.
Irritable, *adj.* Dranndanach, crosda.
Irritate, *v. a.* Brosnaich, feargaich.
Irritation, *s.* Brosnachadh, frionas.
Irruption, *s.* Briseadh a steach, ionnsaidh, ruathar.
Irruptive, *adj.* Brùchdach, ionnsaidheach, ruatharach.
Is, *v.* Is; *it is*, is e, no, thà e, is mì, is tu, &c. no, tha mì, tha thu, &c.
Ischury, *s.* Casg-uisge; galar-fuail.
Isinglass, *s.* Glaodh-éisg.
Island, Isle, *s.* Eilean, innis, I.
Islander, *s.* Eileanach.
Isolated, *adj.* Air leth, aonarach.
Issue, *s.* Ruith, dòrtadh, sruthadh; buil, crìoch, toradh; silteach; gineal, sliochd, clann, sìol.
Issue, *v.* Thig a mach, bris a mach thig o, sruth o; cuir a mach.
Issueless, *adj.* Gun sliochd, aimrid.
Isthmus, *s.* Doirlinn, tairbeart.
Itch, *s.* Cloimh, sgrìobach, tachas; dian-iarrtas, miann, fìleadh.
Itchy, *adj.* Claimheach, clamhach.
Item, *s.* Ni ùr; leth-shanas.
Iterable, *adj.* So-aithris.
Iterant, *adj.* Aithriseach.
Iteration, *s.* Ath-aithris.
Iterative, *adj.* Ath-aithriseach.
Itinerant, *adj.* Siùbhlach, turasach.

Itinerary, *s.* Leabhar-siubhail.
Itself, *pron.* E-féin, no i-féin.
Ivory, *s.* Deud elephaint.
Ivy, *s.* Iadh-shlat, eidheann.

J

J, *s.* Deicheamh litir na h-aibidil.
Jabber, *v. n.* Bi geolamach.
Jabberer, *s.* Geolamaiche.
Jacent, *adj.* Sìnteach, 'na shìneadh.
Jacinth, *s.* Clach-luachmhor.
Jack, *s.* Iain; greimiche-bhòt; geadas; lùireach-mhàilleach; sorchan tuirisg; bratach luinge.
Jackalent, *s.* Blaghastair balaich.
Jackal, *s.* Fear-solair an leògh-ainn.
Jackanapes, *s.* Peasan, bùban.
Jackass, *s.* Asail-fhireann.
Jackdaw, *s.* Cathag-fhireann.
Jacket, *s.* Peiteag mhuilichinneach.
Jacobin, *s.* Manach glas.
Jacobine, *s.* Calman cìreanach.
Jacobite, *s.* Fear-leanmhainn teaghlach nan Stiùbhartach.
Jactitation, *s.* Iom-luasgadh.
Jaculation, *s.* Tilgeadh, caithe.
Jade, *s.* Sean-each; caile.
Jade, *v. a.* Sgìthich, claoidh; maslaich, sàraich; géill, sìolaidh.
Jadish, *adj.* Gun chlì, neo-sheasmhach.
Jag, *v. a.* Eagaich, fiaclaich.
Jag, *s.* Eag, bearn, căb.
Jaggy, *adj.* Eagach, fiaclach, bèarnach, căbach.
Jail, *s.* Prìosan, carcair, gainntir.
Jailer, *s.* Fear gleidhidh prìosain.
Jalap, *s.* Seòrsa purgaid.
Jam, *s.* Mìlsean-measa.
Jam, *v. a.* Teannaich, stailc, dinn.
Jamb, *s.* Ursann, taobh-thaic.
Jangle, *v. n.* Dean gobaireachd, dean gleadhraich.
Jangler, *s.* Fear-bruidhneach.
Janitor, *s.* Dorsair.
Jantiness, *s.* Iollagachd.
Janty, Jaunty, *adj.* Iollagach, sgeilmeil.
January, *s.* Ceud mhìos na bliadhna.
Japan, *s.* Obair lìomhaidh.
Jar, *v. n.* Gliong, buail, co-bhuail; cuir an aghaidh, dean aimhreit.
Jar, *s.* Gliongadh; mi-chòrdadh soitheach creadha.
Jargon, *s.* Brolaich, goileam.
Jasper, *s.* Seòrsa cloiche, iaspar.
Jaundice, *s.* A' bhuidheach.
Jaundiced, *adj.* Fo 'n bhuidhich.
Jaunt, *v. n.* Thoir sgrìob, rach air turas.
Jaunt, *s.* Cuairt, sgrìob, turas.
Javelin, *s.* Gath, leth-shleagh.
Jaw, *s.* Giall, peirceall, carbad.
Jawed, *adj.* Giallach, peirceallach.
Jay, *s.* Pigheid, sgreuchan-coille.
Jealous, *adj.* Eudmhor.
Jealousy, *s.* Eud, eudmhorachd.
Jeer, *v.* Mag, sgeig, fochaidich; dean magadh, dean fochaid.
Jehovah, *s.* Iehobhah; ainm Dhé 's a' chainnt Eabhraich.
Jejune, *adj.* Falamh, neo-tharbhach, faoin; neo-bhlasda.
Jejuneness, *s.* Falamhachd, fàsachd; tiormachd, neo-bhlasdachd.
Jelly, *s.* Slaman-milis.
Jennet, *s.* Each spàinteach.
Jeopardy, *s.* Cunnart, gàbhadh.
Jerk, *v. a.* Buail, grad bhuail, suas.
Jerk, *s.* Grad bhuille, grad-thulgadh.
Jerkin, *s.* Peiteag; cota-gearr.
Jessamine, *s.* Lŭs curaĭdh.
Jest, *s.* Àbhcaid, fala-dhà.
Jester, *s.* Cleasaiche, amhlair.
Jesuit, *s.* Feall-chreideach.
Jesuitical, *adj.* Fealltach.
Jet, *s.* Clach-dhubh; steall, spùtan.
Jet, *v. n.* Grad shruth, steall.
Jettee, *s.* Laimhrig.
Jew, *s.* Iùdhach.
Jewel, *s.* Seud, leug, usgar, àilleagan.
Jeweller, *s.* Seudair.
Jewess, *s.* Ban-Iùdhach.
Jew's Harp, *s.* Tromp.
Jiffy, *s.* Tiota, priobadh nan sùl.
Jig, *s.* Port-cruinn; damhsa-cruinn.
Jilt, *s.* Ban-mhealltair.
Jingle, *s.* Gliong, gliongan.
Job, *s.* Gnothach, car-oibre.
Job, *v.* Sàth, gon; reic a's ceannaich.
Jobber, *s.* Fear-mhion-ghnothach.
Jockey, *s.* Dròbhair each; mealltair.
Jockey, *v. a.* Thoir an car á, meall.
Jocose, Jocular, *adj.* Àbhcaideach, beadarrach, mear, macnusach, aighearach, mireagach.
Jocoseness, Jocosity, Jocularity, *s.* Abhcaideachd, beadarrachd, cleasantachd, macnusachd, aighearachd, mireagachd.
Jocund, *adj.* Mear, aighearach, cridheil.

Jocundity, *s.* Aighearachd, cridhealas.
Jog, Joggle, *v.* Put, purr, crath; dean bogadaich, crath-ghluais; mall-imich.
Jogger, *s.* Slaodaire, leisgean.
Join, *v.* Ceangail, dlùthaich, caignich, cuir r'a chéile; aonaich.
Joiner, *s.* Saor.
Joint, *s.* Alt; teumadh.
Joint, *adj.* Coitcheann; co-shealbhach, co-oibreachail, co-phàirteach.
Joint, *v. a.* Altaich; aonaich, cuir r'a chéile; gearr 'na altaibh.
Jointed, *adj.* Altach, lùdnanach.
Jointer, *s.* Locair-dhlùthaidh.
Jointly, *adv.* Cuideachd, le chéile.
Jointure, *s.* Tighinn a steach bliadhnach-banntraich.
Joist, *s.* Sail, spàrr.
Joke, *s.* Àbhcaid, fala-dhà.
Joking, *s.* Fala-dhà, àbhcaid.
Jole, *s.* Ceann-aghaidh; ceann éisg.
Jollity, *s.* Subhachas, cridhealas, aighear; fleadhachas; maise, àilleachd.
Jolly, *adj.* Aotrom, aigeannach, cridheil, subhach, aoibhneach; beothail, mear, fleadhach, ăit; reamhar, sultmhor, fallain; maiseach, dreachmhor.
Jolt, *v.* Crath, crith, luaisg.
Jolt, *s.* Crathadh, crith, luasgadh.
Jonquille, *s.* Lŭs-a'-chrom-chinn.
Jorden, *s.* Poit-leapa, poit-fhuail.
Jostle, *v. a.* Put, utagaich, tulg.
Jot, Jota, *s.* Ponc, dad, tiodal.
Jovial, *adj.* Fonnmhor, aighearach, ăit, suilbhearra, subhach.
Jovialness, Joviality, *s.* Fonnmhorachd, ăiteas, suilbhearrachd.
Journal, *s.* Cunntas-lathail, leabhar-latha, paipeir-naigheachd.
Journalist, *s.* Fear cunntais-lathail.
Journey, *s.* Turas, cuairt, astar.
Journeyman, *s.* Fear-cèirde air thuarasdal.
Joust, *s.* Còmhrag, falagha.
Joy, *s.* Aoibhneas, gàirdeachas, ăiteas, aighear; subhachas, sòlas.
Joy, *v.* Dean ăit, guidh math le; dean aoibhneach, sòlasaich; bi ăit, dean gàirdeachas, bi aoibhneach.
Joyful, *adj.* Aoibhneach, ăit, subhach.
Joyful, *adj.* Làn-éibhneis, subhach.
Joyfulness, *s.* Aoibhneas, sonas, subhachas, ăiteas.
Joyfully, *adv.* Gu h-éibhinn, ăit.
Joyless, *adj.* Neo-aoibhneach, neo-shòlasach, dubhach, trom.
Jubilant, *adj.* Buaidh-ghaireach.
Jubilee, *s.* Gàirdeachas, fleadhachas, àrd-fhéill; bliadhna shaorsa.
Jocundity, *s.* Taitneachd, taitneas.
Judaical, *adj.* Iùdhach.
Judaism, *s.* Creideamh nan Iùdhach.
Judge, *s.* Breitheamh.
Judge, *v. a.* Thoir breth, thoir a mach binn; meas, thoir barail air; breithnich, feuch, rannsaich cùis.
Judgment, *s.* Breitheanas; breth, barail, tuisge, breithneachadh, ciall, geur-bheachd; binn, dìteadh; làtha a' bhreitheanais.
Judicatory, *s.* Mòd laghail.
Judicatory, *adj.* Breth-thabhairteach.
Judicature, *s.* Riaghladh-ceartais.
Judicial, Judiciary, *adj.* Laghail, a réir ceartais; peanasach, dìoghaltach.
Judicious, *adj.* Tuigseach, crìonna, glic, ciallach, seòlta, geur-chùiseach.
Judiciously, *adv.* Gu tuigseach.
Jug, *s.* Soitheach-dibhe, noigean creadha.
Juggle, *v. a.* Dean cleasachd; meall.
Juggle, *s.* Cleasachd, foill.
Juggler, *s.* Cleasaiche; mealltair.
Jugular, *adj.* Sgòrnanach.
Juice, *s.* Sùgh, brìgh, blagh.
Juiceless, *adj.* Neo-bhrioghmhor, blian.
Juiciness, *s.* Brìoghmhorachd.
Juicy, *adj.* Sùghmhòr, brìoghmhor.
Julap, *s.* Uisg millis.
July, *s.* An seachd-mhìos, mìos deireannach an-t-sàmhraidh.
Jumble, *v. a.* Cuir troi' chéile, co-measgaich, crath an ceann a' chéile.
Jumble, *s.* Coimeasgadh, dreamsgal.
Jump, *v. a.* Leum, gearr sùrdag.
Jump, *s.* Leum, sùrdag.
Juncate, *s.* Ceapaire-càise.
Juncous, *adj.* Riasgach.
Junction, *s.* Ceangal, co-aonadh.
June, *s.* An òg mhìos, mìos meadhoin an t-Sàmhraidh.
Junior, *adj.* A's òige, ìochdrach.
Juniper, *s.* Aitean, aiteal.
Junk, *s.* Long Ìnnseanach; seanna càball.
Junket, *v. n.* Gabh cuirm fhalaich.
Junta, Junto, *s.* Comhairle, comhairle-riaghlaidh, flath-chomhairle.
Juratory, *adj.* Mionnachail.
Juridical, *adj.* Lagh-ghnàthach.
Jurisconsult, *s.* Comhairleach lagha.

JURISDICTION, *s.* Uachdranachd laghail.
JURISPRUDENCE, *s.* Eòlas lagha.
JURIST, *s.* Fear-lagha, fear-breithe.
JUROR, JURYMAN, *s.* Fear-sgoltadh breith.
JURY, *s.* Luchd-sgoltadh breith.
JURYMAST, *s.* Crann-éigin.
JUST, *adj.* Ceart, dìreach, fìrinneach, ionraic, tréidhireach; dligheach; cothromach, iomlan.
JUSTICE, *s.* Ceartas, còir, cothrom.
JUSTICESHIP, *s.* Dreuchd fir-ceartais.
JUSTICIARY, *s.* Fear-ceartais.
JUSTIFIABLE, *adj.* So-thagradh.
JUSTIFIABLENESS, *s.* So-thagraidheachd.
JUSTIFICATION, *s.* Fìreanachadh.
JUSTIFICATOR, *s.* Fear-saoraidh.
JUSTIFY, *v. a.* Fìreanaich, saor; dìon.
JUSTLE, *v.* Put, purr, utagaich.
JUSTLY, *s.* Gu h-ionraic gu ceart.
JUSTNESS, *s.* Ceartas, ceartachd.
JUT, *v. n.* Seas a mach, tulg a mach.
JUTTY, *v. a.* Sìn a mach, cuir am fad.
JUVENILE, *adj.* Leanabaidh, òg, ògail.
JUVENILITY, *s.* Ògalachd.
JUXTAPOSITION, *s.* Fagusachd.

K

K, *s* An t-aon litir deug do'n aibidil.
KAIL, *s.* Càl.
KALENDAR, *s.* Mìosachan, féillire.
KALI, *s.* Feamainn.
KAM, *adj.* Fiar, crom, cam, claon.
KAW, *v. n.* Ròc, dean ròcail.
KAW, *s.* Ròc fithich no feanaig.
KAYLE, *s.* Cluich-nan-naodh-toll.
KECK, *v. a.* Dìobhair, sgreamhaich.
KECKLE, *v. a.* Suain càball.
KECKSY, *s.* An gunn'-uisge, iteodha.
KEDGER, *s.* Acair bheag, gramaiche.
KEEL, *s.* Druim-iochdair luinge, no bàta.
KEELFAT, *s.* Dabhach-fhuarachaidh.
KEELHALE, *v. a.* Leth-bhàth.
KEEN, *adj.* Geur, faobharach; sgaiteach, coimheach, nimheil; dian, togarrach, dùrachdach; beur.
KEENNESS, *s.* Géire; fuachd; beurachd, dùrachd, eudmhorachd; deine.
KEEP, *v. a.* Cùm, gléidh; coimhid dìon, teasraig; bac, cuir stad air cùm air ais; cùm suas, beathaich; ceil, cùm ort; mair; buanaich, rach air t' aghaidh.
KEEP, *s.* Daingneach.
KEEPER, *s.* Fear-gleidhidh, fear-coimhid.
KEEPING, *s.* Cùram, cùram-gleidhidh, aire; coimhid, dìon, gleidheadh.
KEEPSAKE, *s.* Cuimhneachan.
KEG, *s.* Buideal beag, gingean, gòthan
KELL, *s.* An sgairt, brat a' mhionaich.
KELP, *s.* Celp, luath feamnach.
KELSON, KEELSON, *s.* Druim-uachdair luinge no bàta.
KEN, *v. a.* Aithnich, an céin.
KEN, *s.* Sealladh, fad fradhairc; aithne.
KENNEL, *s.* Taigh-chon; saobhaidh guitear, clais-shalachair.
KEPT, *pret.* and *part. pass.* of *to keep.* Gléidhte, cùmta.
KERCHIEF, *s.* Breid an càradh crannaig, beannag.
KERN, *s.* Bràdh, saighdear, coise.
KERN, *v.* Cruadhaich; meallanaich.
KERNEL, *s.* Eitein, biadh cnuthan.
KERNELLY, *adj.* Eiteineach; fàireagach.
KERSEY, *s.* Garbh-Chlò.
KESTREL, *s.* Coilleach, seabhaic.
KETCH, *s.* Sgùda, long throm.
KETTLE, *s.* Coire, goileire.
KETTLEDRUM, *s.* Gall-druma.
KEY, *s.* Iuchair; mìneachadh; fonn, séis; laimhrig, seòlait.
KEYAGE, *s.* Cìs-laimhrig.
KEYHOLE, *s.* Toll-iuchrach.
KEYSTONE, *s.* Clach-ghlasaidh.
KIBE, *s.* Cùsp, peisg, gàg.
KICK, *v. a.* Breab, buail le d' chois.
KICK, *s.* Breab, buile coise.
KICKSHAW, *s.* Annas, faoineas.
KID, *s.* Meann, cualag fhraoich.
KIDNAP, *v. a.* Goid clann no daoine.
KIDNAPPER, *s.* Mèirleach cloinne.
KIDNEY-BEAN, *s.* Am pònar-àirneach.
KIDNEYS, *s.* Àirnean.
KILDERKIN, *s.* Leth-bharaille.
KILL, *v. a.* Marbh, cuir gu bàs.
KILLER, *s.* Marbhaiche, fear-casgairt.
KILLOW, *s.* Dubh-smùir; sùthaidh.
KILN, *s.* Àth, àtha.
KIMBO, *adj.* Fiar, cuagach, cam.
KIN, *s.* Cinneadh, fine, dàimh, càirdeas.
KIND, *adj.* Còir, caoimhneil, mathasach; bàigheil, carthannach, fialaidh.
KIND, *s.* Gnè, gineal; modh, seòl.
KINDLE, *v.* Lăs; beothaich, cuir chuige; brosnaich, cuir air boile; gabh teine, gabh.

Kindler, *s.* Brathadair, fear-lasaidh; fear-brosnachaidh, buaireadair.

Kindliness, *s.* Deagh-ghean, carthannas, tlùs, còiread.

Kindly, *adj.* Bàigheil, caoimhneil.

Kindness, *s.* Caomhalachd, seirc.

Kindred, *s.* Càirdeas, dàimh; cleamhnas; càirdean, cinneadh, luchd-dàimh.

Kindred, *adj.* Aon-ghnèitheach co-ghnèitheach; dàimheil, càirdeach.

Kine, *s.* Crodh, spréidh, feudail, buar.

King, *s.* Rìgh.

Kingcraft, *s.* Eòlas-riaghlaidh.

Kingdom, *s.* Rìoghachd, dùthaich.

Kingfisher, *s.* An gobha-uisge, an cruiteun.

Kingly, *adj.* Rìoghail, flathail, mòrdha.

Kingsevil, *s.* Tinneas an rìgh, an easba-bhràghaid.

Kingship, *s.* Rìoghalachd.

Kinsfolk, *s.* Luchd-dàimh, càirdean.

Kinsman, *s.* Fear-dàimh, caraide.

Kinswoman, *s.* Bean-dàimhe, banacharaid.

Kipper, *s.* Bradan tiormaichte.

Kirk, *s.* Eaglais, eaglais na h-Albann.

Kirtle, *s.* Fallainn, aodach-uachdair.

Kiss, *v. a.* Pòg, thoir pòg.

Kiss, *s.* Pòg.

Kit, *s.* Miosair dhùinte; fiodhall bheag.

Kitchen, *s.* Taigh-còcaireachd; seomar-deasaichidh; annlann.

Kitchen-garden, *s.* Gàradh-càil.

Kitchen-maid, *s.* Banna-chòcair.

Kite, *s.* Clamhan, clamhan-gòbhlach; ball-cluich' àraidh.

Kitten, *s* Piseag; *v. n.* Beir piseagan.

Knack, *s.* Làmhchaireachd, ealantachd.

Knag, *s.* Snuaim, cnag; meur a' choin.

Knaggy, *adj.* Snaimeach, plucanach.

Knap, *s.* Meall, flùth, maol, àird.

Knap, *v.* Sgath dheth, sgud, criom; sgailc, buail.

Knapsack, *s.* Abarsgaic, crapsaic.

Knare, Knur, Knurle, *s.* Cruaidh-shnaim; gath.

Knave, *s.* Slaightear, mealltair.

Knavery, *s.* Slaightearachd, fealltachd.

Knavish, *adj.* Cluainteach, mealltach, foilleil, fealltach.

Knavishness, *s.* Cluaintearachd.

Knead, *v. a.* Taoisinn, aoibrich, fuin.

Kneading-trough, *s.* Losaid, amar-fuine, clàr-fuine.

Knee, *s.* Glùn, lùgh.

Kneedeep, *adj.* Gu ruig na glùinean.

Kneepan, *s.* Falaman a' ghlùin.

Kneel, *v. n.* Strìochd, lùb do ghlùn.

Knell, *s.* Beum-cluig, clag-bàis.

Knew, *pret.* of to *know.* Dh' aithnich.

Knife, *s.* Sgian, corc; cuinnsear.

Knight, *s.* Ridire (*etymol.* Rìgh-tìre.)

Knight, *v. a.* Ridirich, dean 'na ridire.

Knighthood, *s.* Ridireachd.

Knightly, *adj.* Ridireach.

Knit, *v. a.* Figh; ceangail, dlùthaich.

Knitter, *s.* Figheadair.

Knob, *s.* Cnap, cnag, snaim.

Knobbed, Knobby, *adj.* Cnapach, gathach, cairgeach, snaimeach.

Knock, *s.* Buille, sgailc, cnap.

Knock, *v.* Buail; cnap, sgailc; spad, buail sìos; buail aig dorus.

Knocker, *s.* Băs-ri-crann; glagan-doruis.

Knoll, *v.* Beum mar chlag, séirm.

Knoll, *s.* Tolm, tolman, tom, toman, dùn.

Knot, *s.* Snaim; ceangal, bann, co-bhann; comunn, buidheann; bagaid.

Knot, *v.* Snaim; aimhreitich; aonaich, dlùthaich.

Knotgrass, *s.* A ghlùineach-dhearg.

Knotted, Knotty, *adj.* Snaimeach.

Know, *v.* Aithnich, fiosraich; ionnsaich; comharraich; tuig; bi eòlach.

Knowing, *adj.* Eòlach, ealanta, seòlta, fiosrach, gleusta; glic, oileanta.

Knowingly, *adv.* Gu h-eòlach.

Knowledge, *s.* Eòlas; aithne, tuigse, fios, fiosrachd; fòghlum, ionnsachadh, soilleireachd, fiosrachadh, tùr.

Knuckle. *s.* Rùdan, alt.

Knuckle, *v. n.* Strìochd, géill.

Knuckled, *adj.* Rùdanach, altach.

Knuckles, *s.* Uilt nam meur.

Knuff, *s.* Slaodaire.

Koran, *s.* Bìoball *Mhahomet.*

L

L, *s.* An dara litir deug de'n aibidil.

La ! *interj.* Feuch ! seall ! faic !

Label, *s.* Comharradh sgrìobhte.

Labial, *adj.* Bil-fhuaimneach.

Laborant, *s.* Feallsanach-brìghe.

Laboratory, *s.* Bùth dhrogaichean.

Laborious, *adj.* Saoithreachail, gnìomhach, dìchiollach; doirbh, deacair, sgìth.

Labour, *s.* Saothair; saothair-chloinne; obair.

Labour, *v.* Saothraich, oibrich, dean dìchioll, gabh saothair ri; dean spàirn; bi 'n teanntachd, bi 'n teinn; bi 'n saothair-chloinne.

Labourer, *s.* Fear-oibre, oibriche.

Labyrinth, *s.* Cuairt aimhreidh, iomachuairt.

Laburnum, *s.* Bealaidh Frangach.

Lace, *s.* Sreang, stìom, stiall, iall; balt air fhighe.

Lace, *v. a.* Ceangail, sreangaich, iallaich; rìomhaich, grinnich.

Lacerate, *v. a.* Reub, srac, sgoilt.

Laceration, *s.* Reubadh, sracadh.

Lacerative, *adj.* Sracach, reubach.

Lachrymal, *adj.* Deurach, deurachail.

Lachrymary, *adj.* Deurach.

Lachrymation, *s.* Gul, caoidh, sileadh dheur.

Lack, *v.* Bi am feum; bi dh' easbhuidh, bi 'n uireasbhuidh.

Lack, *s.* Uireasbhuidh, easbhuidh, dìth, gainne, ainnis, aimbeart.

Lackaday! *interj.* O! mis' an diugh!

Lackbrain, *s.* Baoghaire, ùmaidh.

Lacker, *s.* Sùgh lìomhaidh.

Lacker, *v. a.* Cuir sùgh-lìomhaidh air.

Lackey, *s.* Gille coise.

Lackey, *v. a.* Fritheil, feith.

Lacklustre, *adj.* Neo-dhealrach.

Laconic, *adj.* Gearr, aithghearr, gearr-chainnteach, gearr-bhriathrach.

Laconism, *s.* Gearr-chainnteachd.

Lactage, *s.* Toradh bainne.

Lactary, *s.* Taigh-baine; *adj.* Bainneach.

Lactation, *s.* Deoghal, cìoch-thabhairt.

Lacteal, *s.* Cuisle-goile.

Lacteous, **Lateal**, *adj.* Bainneach.

Lactescent, **Latific**, *adj.* Bainneach.

Lad, *s.* Òganach, òigear, balachan; gille.

Ladder, *s.* Fàradh, dreimire.

Lade, *v. a.* Luchdaich, lìon; tilg a mach, taom, falmhaich; tarruinn uisge.

Lading, *s.* Luchd, làn.

Ladle, *s.* Liagh, ladar, lodar.

Lady-bird, **Lady-cow**, *s.* An daolag dhearg bhreac.

Lady-day, *s.* Latha Muire naoimh.

Lady-like, *s.* Bainndidh, màlda, miùinte, suairce, sgiamhach.

Ladyship, *s.* Baintighearnas.

Lag, *adj.* Deireannach, athaiseach; màirnealach, leisg, trom, mall; air deireadh.

Lag, *v. n.* Dean màirneal, tuit air deireadh, mall-ghluais, fiurich air deireadh.

Laic, **Laical**, *adj.* Pobullach, nach buin do 'n chléir.

Laid, *pret. part.* of *to lay.* Càirichte, socraichte, suidhichte.

Lain, *pret. part.* of *to lie.* Air laidhe.

Lair, *s.* Saobhaidh, brocluinn.

Laird, *s.* Tighearna, uachdaran.

Laity, *s.* Am pobull; an sluagh air leth o'n chléir, am mall-shluagh.

Lake, *s.* Loch-uisge; dath dù-dhearg.

Lamb, *s.* Uan, uainean.

Lambent, *adj.* Cluicheach, mireagach.

Lambkin, *s.* Uanan, uanachan.

Lame, *adj.* Bacach, crùbach.

Lame, *v. a.* Dean bacach, dean crùbach.

Lameness, *s.* Bacaiche, crùbaiche.

Lament, *v.* Caoidh, guil, dean bròn; dean tuireadh, bi brònach, bi dubhach.

Lament, *s.* Cumha, caoidh, tuireadh.

Lamentable, *adj.* Tùrsach, brònach, airsnealach, muladach, dubhach.

Lamentation, *s.* Tuireadh, cumha.

Lamina, *s.* Sgrath thana, rùsg tana.

Laminated, *adj.* Sgrathach, leacach.

Lammas, *s.* Lùnasdal, liùnasd-fhéill.

Lamp, *s.* Lòchran, crùisgean.

Lamp-black, *s.* Dubhadh sùthaidh.

Lampoon, *s.* Aoir, aoireadh.

Lampoon, *v. a.* Aoir, càin, màb.

Lampooner, *s.* Aoireadair, éisg.

Lamprey, *s.* Seòrsa easgainn.

Lanarious, *adj.* Clòimheach.

Lance, *s.* Sleagh, lann, gath, pìc.

Lance, *v. a.* Gon, bruidich; leig fuil.

Lancer, *s.* Saighdear sleagha.

Lancet, *s.* Sgian-fhala, cuisleag.

Lancitate, *v. a.* Srac, sgoilt, sgàin.

Lancitation, *s.* Sracadh, reubadh.

Land, *s.* Tìr, dùthaich, fearann; talamh, talamh tioram; oighreachd.

Land, *v.* Cuir air tìr, rach air tìr.

Landed, *adj.* Fearannach.

Land forces, *s.* Feachd-tìre.

Landholder, *s.* Fear-fearainn.

Landing, *s.* Ceann staighreach; laimhrig.

Landlady, *s.* Ban-uachdaran; bean-an-taighe.
Landlocked, *adj.* Tìr-dhruidte.
Landlord, *s.* Uachdaran; fear-an-taighe.
Landmark, *s.* Comharradh-crìche.
Landscape, *s.* Dealbh tìre, aghaidh, dùthcha.
Landwaiter, *s.* Maor-cuspuinn.
Landward, *adv.* Gu tìr.
Lane, *s.* Caol-sràid, frith-rathad.
Language, *s.* Cainnt, cànan.
Languid, *adj.* Lag, fann, anfhann; marbhanta, trom, neo-shunntach.
Languidness, *s.* Marbhantachd, laige.
Languish, *v. n.* Fannaich, fàs lag, searg ás, caith ás, crìon.
Languishment, *s.* Lagachadh, fannachadh, crìonadh, seargadh ás, sìoladh seachad; tlàth-shealladh.
Languor, *s.* Laigse, sgìos, anfhannachd.
Lank, *adj.* Seang, neo-chullach, bochd.
Lankness, *s.* Seangachd, neo-lànachd.
Lansquenet, *s.* Saighdear-coise; cluiche àraidh chairtean.
Lantern, *s.* Trillsean; lanntair.
Lap, *s.* Uchd; glùn.
Lap, *v.* Fill nu'n cuairt.
Lapdog, *s.* Measan, crann-chù.
Lapidary, *s.* Leug-ghearradair.
Lapper, *s.* Filleadair, fear-pasgaidh.
Lappet, *s.* Beannag-chinn, filleag.
Lapse, *s.* Aomadh, tuiteam, slaodadh, réidh-shruth; tapag, mearachd.
Lapse, *v. a.* Sleamhnaich, tuit; fàilnich, rach am mearachd; tuislich; cùl-shleamhnaich, tuit o'n chreideamh.
Lapwing, *s.* An t-adharcan-luachrach.
Larboard, *s.* Taobh clì luinge.
Larceny, *s.* Braide, mion-mhèirle.
Larch, *s.* Guibhas-learaig.
Lard, *s.* Muc-bhlonag, saill.
Lard, *v. a.* Lìon le saill; reamhraich.
Larder, *s.* Taigh-bìdh.
Lardon, *s.* Staoig muic-fheola.
Large, *adj.* Mòr, tomadach; farsuinn.
Largeness, *s.* Meudachd, leud; farsuinneachd.
Largess, *s.* Tìodhlac, saor-thabhartas.
Lark, *s.* Uiseag, riabhag.
Larum, *s.* Clag caismeachd, maoim.
Larynx, *s.* Bràigh an sgòrnain.
Lascivious, *adj.* Macnusach, drùiseil.
Lasciviousness, *s.* Drùisealachd.
Lash, *s.* Iall-sgiùrsair; buille.
Lash, *v. a.* Sgiùrs, buail le slait; aoir, ceangail.
[La]ss, *s.* Nighean, cailin, òg-bhean, ainnir, finne, gruagach, cruinneag, òigh, maighdean.
Lassitude, *s.* Sgìos, airtneul, laigse.
Last, *adj.* Deireannach, air deireadh.
Last, *adv.* Mu dheireadh; Anns an àite mu dheireadh.
Last, *v. a.* Mair, buanaich, seas, fan.
Last, *s.* Ceap bhròg.
Lastage, *s.* Cuspunn faraidh.
Lasting, *adj.* Maireannach, buan.
Latch, *s.* Dealan-doruis, claimhean.
Latchet, *s.* Barr-iall, iall-bròige.
Late, *adj.* Anmoch, fadalach, màirnealach; deireannach; nach maireann.
Late, *adv.* Mu dheireadh, gu h-anmoch.
Lately, Latterly, *adv.* O cheann ghoirid.
Lateness, *s.* Anmoichead.
Latent, *adj.* Falaichte, dìomhair.
Lateral, *adj.* Leth-taobhach.
Lath, *s.* Lathus, spealt.
Lathe, *s.* Beairt-thuairnearachd.
Lather, *v.* Dean cop, tog cobhar.
Lather, *s.* Cop, cobhar-shiabuinn.
Latin, *s.* Laideann, laidionn.
Latinize, *v. a.* Tionndaidh gu laideann.
Latish, *adj.* Leth-anmoch.
Latitude, *s.* Leud, farsuinneachd, meudachd, sgaoilteachd, fuasgailteachd.
Latitudinarian, *s.* Saobh-chreideach, baoth-chreideach.
Latration, *s.* Comhartaich, tathunn.
Latria, *s.* An t-àrd-aoradh.
Latten, *s.* Umha, iaran-geal.
Latter, *adj.* Deireannach.
Lattice, *s.* Cliath-uinneag.
Laud, *s.* Cliù, moladh, àrd-mholadh.
Laud, *v. a.* Cliùthaich, àrd-mhol.
Laudable, *adj.* Ion-mholta, cliùiteach.
Laudanum, *s.* Deoch-chadail.
Laudation, *s.* Àrd-chliù.
Laudatory, *adj.* Moltach, cliùteach.
Laugh, *v.* Dean gàire; dean fochaid.
Laughable, *adj.* Neònach, a thogas gàire.
Laughing-stock, *s.* Cullaidh-mhagaidh.
Laughter, *s.* Gàireachdaich, fearaschuideachd, ăit-iolach.
Launch, *v.* Cuir air snàmh; leudaich; gabh farsuinneachd; grad thòisich air; gabh gu fairge.
Laundress, *s.* Bean-nighe.
Laundry, *s.* Taigh-nighe.
Laureate, *s.* Am Bàrd rìoghail.
Laurel, *s.* Craobh laibhreis.

LAVE, *v.* Nigh, ionnlaid, fairic, failc.
LAVENDER, *s.* Lüs-na-tùise.
LAVER, *s.* Saitheach-nighe; saigheach-ionnlaid.
LAVISH, *adj.* Struidheil, stròdhail, barr-sgaoilteach; neo-stéidhichte.
LAVISH, *v. a.* Struidh, barr-sgaoil, sgap, dean ana-caitheamh.
LAVOLT, or LAVOLTA, *s.* Damhsa-mear.
LAW, *s.* Lagh, reachd, riaghailt; stàtunn, òrdugh; bunait, stéidh.
LAWFUL, *adj.* Laghail, ceadaichte.
LAWFULNESS, *s.* Laghalachd, ceartas.
LAWGIVER, *s.* Lagh-thabhairtair.
LAWLESS, *adj.* Neo-laghail, mi-laghail, an-dligheach, ana-ceart.
LAWN, *s.* Réidhlean, achadh, faiche eadar-dà-choill; anart grinn.
LAWSUIT, *s.* Cùis-lagha.
LAWYER, *s.* Fear-lagha.
LAX, *adj.* Fuasgailte, saor; fuasgailteach, neo-cheangailte, neo-theann; neo-dhiongmhalta, neo-eagnaidh; lasach, neo-dhaingeann; fuasgailte 'sa' chorp.
LAX, *s.* A' ghearrach, seòrs' éisg.
LAXATION, *s.* Lasachadh, fuasgladh.
LAXATIVE, *adj.* Fuasgailteach, purgaideach; sgaoilteach.
LAXITY, LAXNESS, *s.* Sgaoilteachd, neo-theanntachd, fuasgailteachd; fosgailteachd.
LAY, *pret.* of *to lie.* Laidh.
LAY, *v.* Càirich, cuir; suidich; leag sìos, buail sìos; sgaoil air; ciùinich, sìthich, cuir gu fois; cuir geall; taisg.
LAY, *s.* Òran, duanag, luinneag, fonn.
LAY, *adj.* Nach buin do'n chléir.
LAYER, *s.* Sreath, breath; failleau, mean-glan; cearc-ghuir.
LAYMAN, *s.* Fear nach buin do'n chléir.
LAZAR, *s.* Fear fo eucail ghràineil, lobhar.
LAZARHOUSE, LAZARETTO, *s.* Taigh leighis nam mùireach, taigh nan lobhar.
LAZINESS, *s.* Leisg, lunndaireachd, màirnealachd, dìomhanas.
LAZY, *adj.* Leisg, lunndach, dìomhain; màirnealach, mall.
LEA, LEE, *s.* Achadh, cluan, raon, faiche, glas-talamh, fiadhair.
LEAD, *s.* Luaidhe.
LEAD, *v.* Treòraich, stiùr.
LEADEN, *adj.* Luaidheach; trom, neo-ghluasadach, marbhanta; dùr.
LEADER, *s.* Fear-treòrachaidh; ceannfeadhna; fear-ceann-sreatha.
LEADING, *part.* Prìomh, àrd, ceud.
LEADING, *s.* Treòrachadh, stiùradh.
LEAF, *s.* Duilleag, duille.
LEAFLESS, *adj.* Gun duilleach, lom.
LEAFY, *adj.* Duilleagach, fo bhlàth.
LEAGUE, *s.* Co-cheangal, comh-phàirt, fad thrì mìle.
LEAGUE, *v. n.* Dean co-cheangal, aonaich.
LEAK, *v. a.* Leig uisg' a mach, no steach; bi ao-dionach, sil, snith.
LEAKAGE, *s.* Dioll calldach ao-dìona.
LEAKY, *adj.* Ao-dionach; bruidhneach, fosgailte, luath-bheulach.
LEAN, *v. n.* Leag do thaic ri, leig do chudthrom air; aom; crom thu féin.
LEAN, *adj.* Bochd, tana, caol, gun fheòil; neo-shultmhor, tioram, neo-bhrìoghail.
LEAN, *s.* Blìonach, feòil gun saill.
LEANNESS, *s.* Caoile, tainead; tiormad.
LEAP, *v.* Leum; thoir leum.
LEAP, *s.* Leum, cruinn-leum; briosgadh.
LEAPYEAR, *s.* Bliadhna-léim.
LEARN, *v. n.* Fòghlum, ionnsaich.
LEARNED, *adj.* Fòghlumte, ionnsaichte; eòlach, fiosrach; leabhrach.
LEARNER, *s.* Fòghlumaiche, sgoilear.
LEARNING, *s.* Fòghlum, ionnsachadh.
LEASE, *s.* Gabhail, suidheachadh.
LEASE, *v. n.* Dìoghluim, tionail suas.
LEASH, *s.* Iall, bann, ceanglàchan.
LEASING, *s.* Breugan, mealltaireachd.
LEAST, *adj.* A's lugha, a's bige, a's crìne.
AT LEAST, *adv.* Air a' chuid a's lugha, co-dhiù.
LEATHER, *s.* Leathar, seiche cairtidh.
LEATHERN, *adj.* Leathair, mar leathar.
LEAVE, *s.* Cead; comas.
LEAVE, *v.* Fàg, tréig, cùlaich.
LEAVEN, *s.* Taois; *v. a.* Taoisinn.
LEAVES, *s.* the *plur.* of *leaf.* Duilleach, duilleagan.
LEAVINGS, *s.* Fuighleach, fuigheall.
LECHER, *s.* Fear-siùrsachd.
LECHEROUS, *adj.* Drùiseil, collaidh.
LECHERY, *s.* Drùisealachd.
LECTION, *s.* Leughadh.
LECTURE, *s.* Seanachas mìneachaidh; achmhasan, cronachadh, trod.
LECTURE, *v. n.* Mìnich, cronaich teagaisg am follais.
LECTURER, *s.* Fear-teagaisg.
LED, *pret. part.* of *to lead.* Treòraichte.

LEDGE, *s.* Stìm-oire, oir.
LEDGER, *s.* Leabhar cunntais.
LEE, *s.* Làib; taobh an fhasgadh.
LEECH, *s.* Deal, seil-uisge.
LEEK, *s.* Creamh-gàraidh.
LEER, *s.* Caog-shealladh, fiar-shealladh.
LEER, *v. n.* Amhairc siar, dean caog-shùil.
LEES, *s.* Laìb, dràib, druaip.
LEET, *s.* Mòd ceartais uachdarain.
LEEWARD, *adj.* Air fasgadh.
LEFT, *pret. part.* of *to leave.* Fàgte, tréigte, cùlaichte.
LEFT-HANDED, *adj.* Clìth-lamhach, cearr-lamhach, ciotach.
LEG, *s.* Lurga, căs, calpa.
LEGACY, *s.* Dìleab.
LEGAL, *adj.* Laghail, ceadaichte, dligheach.
LEGALITY, LEGALNESS, *s.* Dligheachas, dligheachd.
LEGALIZE, *v. a.* Dean laghail, dean ceadaichte.
LEGATE, *s.* Teachdaire Pàp na Ròimhe.
LEGATEE, *s.* Fear dìlib, dìleabach.
LEGATION, *s.* Teachdaireachd.
LEGATOR, *s.* Fear-tiomnaidh.
LEGEND, *s.* Seanachas, faoinsgeul, sgeulachd; seann sgrìobhadh.
LEGENDARY, *adj.* Seann-sgeulach.
LEGERDEMAIN, *s.* Lù-chleasachd, claon-char.
LEGGED, *adj.* Căsach, spògach.
LEGIBILITY, *s.* Soilleireachd.
LEGIBLE, *adj.* So-leughadh, soilleir.
LEGION, *s.* Feachd Ròmhanach mu chùig mìle fear.
LEGISLATE, *v. a.* Dean lagh, thoir reachd.
LEGISLATION, *s.* Lagh-thabhartas.
LEGISLATIVE, *adj.* Lagh-thabhairteach.
LEGISLATOR, *s.* Lagh-thabhartair.
LEGISLATURE, *s.* Lagh-chumhachd.
LEGITIMACY, *s.* Dligheachd-breithe, fior-ghlaine.
LEGITIMATE, *adj.* Neo-dhìolain, dligheach.
LEGITIMATION, *s.* Dlighe-thabhairt.
LEGUME, LEGUMEN, *s.* Sìol cochullach, frŏs, fras, peasair, pònair.
LEGUMINOUS, *adj.* Cochullach mar pheasair no mar phònair.
LEISURABLE, *adj.* Athaiseach, socrach.
LEISURE, *s.* Athais, socair, fois.
LEISURELY, *adj.* Athaiseach, mall.
LEMAN, *s.* Leannan.
LEMON, *s.* Seòrsa meas, liomaid.
LEND, *v. a.* Thoir an iasad, thoir an coingheall.
LENDER, *s.* Conghalaich, iasadaiche.
LENGTH, *s.* Fad, feadh, sìneadh, astar.
LENGTHEN, *v.* Cuir am fad, dean ni's faide, sìn, sìn a mach.
LENGTHWISE, *adv.* Air fhad.
LENIENT, *adj.* Ciùin, caoin, maoth, tlàth, tairis, fuasgailteach.
LENIENT, *s.* Ìocshlaint-thaiseachaidh.
LENIFY, *v. n.* Ciùinich, taisich, maothaich.
LENITIVE, *adj.* Ciùineachail, maothachail.
LENITIVE, *s.* Leigheas-maothachaidh.
LENITY, *s.* Bàigh, iochd, tròcair, ciùine, caomhalachd, caoimhneas.
LENS, *s.* Seòrsa do ghlain-amhairc.
LENT, *s.* An carghus, àm trasgaidh.
LENTIL, *s.* Peasair-nan-luch.
LENTITUDE, *s.* Slaodaireachd, leisg.
LENTOR, *s.* Rìghneachd; màirnealachd.
LENTOUS, *adj.* Righinn, rag, slamach.
LEOPARD, *s.* An liopard.
LEPER, *s.* Lobhar, mùireach.
LEPEROUS, LEPROUS, *s.* Lobharach, luibhreach, mùireach.
LEPOREAN, LEPORINE, *adj.* Maigheachail.
LEPROSY, *s.* A' mhuir, an luibhre.
LESS, LESSER, *adv.* Ni's lugha, ni's bige.
LESSEE, *s.* Fear-gabhalach, tuathanach.
LESSEN, *v.* Lughdaich, cuir an lughad; ìslich; fàs ni's lugha.
LESSON, *s.* Earann-leughaidh, leasan, ionnsachadh, teagasg; trod, achmhasan.
LESSOR, *s.* Fear-suidheachaidh fearainn, &c.
LEST, *conj.* Mu, mu 'n, air eagal gu.
LET, *v. a.* Leig, ceadaich; suidhich, thoir air ghabhail.
LET, *s.* Bacadh, stad, grabadh, maille.
LETHAL, *adj.* Bàsmhor, fuilteach, millteach.
LETHARGIC, *adj.* Marbhanta, cadalach, airsnealach, trom.
LETHARGY, *s.* An suain-ghalar.
LETHE, *s.* Deoch dhì-chuimhne.
LETHIFEROUS, *adj.* Bàsmhor, marbhtach.
LETTER, *s.* Litir, fear-ceadachaidh.
LETTERS, *s.* Fòghlum, ionnsachadh.
LEVEE, *s.* Ceathairne duine mhòir.
LEVEL, *adj.* Còmhnard, réidh.
LEVEL, *v.* Dean còmhnard, dean réidh - leag sìos, leag gu làr; dean coinbheach; gabh cùimse; thoir ionnsaidh.

Level, *s.* Còmhnard, réidh-ionad; co-àirde, co-chuimse, co-inbheachd.
Leveller, *s.* Fear-islichidh.
Levelness, *s.* Còmhnardachd.
Lever, *s.* Geimhleag, inneal-togail.
Leveret, *s.* Cuilein maighich.
Leviable, *adj.* So-thogail mar chìs.
Leviathan, *s.* An cinionnan-crò.
Levigate, *v. a.* Lìomh; mìn-mheil, mìn-phronn; suath.
Levigation, *s.* Lìomhadh, meileadh, suathadh.
Levite, *s.* Lebhitheach, neach do threubh Lebhi, sagart.
Levitical, *s.* Lebhitheach, sagartach.
Levity, *s.* Aotruime, aotromachd; gòraiche, gogaideachd; dìomhanas, amaideachd; neo-stòldachd.
Levy, *v. a.* Tog daoine, dean suas feachd.
Levy, *s.* Togail; feachd, armailt, cruinneachadh, buidheann.
Lewd, *adj.* Olc, aingidh, mi-bheusach; ana-miannach, drùiseil, draosda, collaidh.
Lewdness, *s.* Mì-nàire, mi-stuamachd; aingidheachd; anamiann, draosdachd.
Lexicographer, *s.* Fear-dèanamh facalair, facalairiche.
Lexicography, *s.* Facladaireachd.
Lexicon, *s.* Facalair, leabhar-fhacal.
Liable, *adj.* Buailteach, buailteach do.
Liar, *s.* Breugadair, breugaire.
Libation, *s.* Ìobairt-fhiona.
Libel, *s.* Aoir, aoireadh; casaid-sgrìobhte, cùis-chasaid, cùis-dhìtidh.
Libel, *v. a.* Aoir; càin; maslaich.
Libeller, *s.* Aoireadair, fear-càinidh.
Libellous, *adj.* Tàir-chainnteach, maslachail, tuaileasach.
Liberal, *adj.* Fiùghantach, uasal, flathail, fial, fialaidh; tabhairteach, toirbheartach, pailt-lamhach, faoilidh.
Liberality, *s.* Fialaidheachd, tabhairteachd, toirbheartachd, aoidheachd, aoidhealachd.
Liberate, *v. a.* Cuir fa sgaoil, saor.
Liberation, *s.* Cur fa sgaoil, fuasgladh.
Liberator, *s.* Fear-fuasglaidh.
Libertine, *s.* Duine gun smachd, fear-aìmhreit; ana-creideach, fear neo-mheasarra; saoranach.
Libertine, *adj.* Ana-creideach.
Libertinism, *s.* Ain-diadhachd.
Liberty, *s.* Saorsa; cead, sochair, dlighe.
Libidinous, *adj.* Connanach, anamiannach, neo-gheamnaidh, collaidh, drùiseil.
Librarian, *s.* Fear-gleidhidh leabhraichean, fear-leabhar-lann.
Library, *s.* Leabhar-lann, seòmar leabhraichean.
Libration, *s.* Co-chothromachadh.
Lice, *s.* the *plural* of *louse.* Mialan.
Licence, *s.* Ro-shaorsa; cead reic comas.
License, *v. a.* Ceadaich, thoir cead reic laghail seachad.
Licentiate, *s.* Fear-barantais.
Licentious, *adj.* Mi-bheusach.
Licentiousness, *s.* Mi-bheus.
Lichen, *s.* Crotal, griaman.
Licit, *adj.* Laghail, dligheach.
Lick, *v. a.* Ìmlich.
Lick, *s.* Buille, cnap, dòrn.
Lickerish, *adj.* Sòghmhor, geòcach.
Licorice, *s.* Maide-milis, cara-meala.
Lictor, *s.* Maor Ròimheach.
Lid, *s.* Brod; fabhradh, rŏsg.
Lie, *s.* Breug, spleagh.
Lie, *v. n.* Innis breug, dean breug; laidh; caidil.
Liege, *s.* Tighearna, uachdaran.
Liege, *adj.* Uachdranach.
Lieu, *s.* Àite, ionad, riochd.
Lieve, *adv.* Gu toileach, gu deònach.
Lieutenancy, *s.* Fo-uachdranachd.
Lieutenant, *s.* Fo-uachdaran.
Life, *s.* Beatha, deò; caithe-beatha; beothalachd, meanmnachd.
Lifeguard, *s.* Freiceadan diona rìgh.
Lifeless, *adj.* Marbh, gun deò; marbhanta; neo-bheothail, neo-shunntach, tròm.
Lifetime, *s.* Aimsir, ùine, làithean.
Lift, *v. a.* Tog; àrdaich, cuir suas.
Lift, *s.* Togail; eallach.
Lifter, *s.* Fear-togalach; gadaiche, mèirleach.
Ligament, *s.* Ceanglachan, ceangal.
Ligature, *s.* Bann-cheangail.
Light, *s.* Solus; soillse; eòlas, soilleireachd, fòghlum; lòchrann.
Light, *adj.* Aotrom, eutrom; lùghor; suarach, beag; neo-shuidhichte, gòrach, guanach, gogaideach; soilleir, soillseach.
Light, *v.* Las, soillsich, beothaich; thoir solus do; tuit air, amais air; teirinn, thig a nuas.
Lighten, *v.* Dealraich, dèars, boillsg, soillsich, soilleirich; aotromaich.
Lighter, *s.* Bàta-luchda.
Lightfingered, *adj.* Bradach.
Lighterman, *s.* Sgiobair bàta-luchda.

LIGHTHEADED, *adj.* Gŏg-cheannach; sgaogach, aotrom, air mhearan-céille.
LIGHTHEARTED, *adj.* Sunntach, aighearach, suigeartach, cridheil.
LIGHTHOUSE, *s.* Taigh-soluis.
LIGHTNESS, *s.* Aotromachd, aotruime; luaineachas, guaineas.
LIGHTNITG, *s.* Dealanach, tein'-adhair.
LIGHTSOME, *adj.* Soilleir, soillseach, dealrach; sunntach, aighearach, cridheil.
LIGNEOUS, *adj.* Fiodhach, mar fhiodh.
LIKE, *adj.* Coltach; ionann.
LIKE, *s.* Mac-samhail, samhail, samhla.
LIKE, *adv.* Ionann agus, amhail, mar; coltach.
LIKELIHOOD, *s.* Coltas, cosmhalachd.
LIKELY, *adj.* Coltach; dreachmhor.
LIKEN, *v. a.* Samhlaich, coimeas.
LIKENESS, *s.* Samhla, coltas, cosamhlachd; dealbh; mac-samhail.
LIKEWISE, *adv.* Mar an ceudna, fòs.
LILY, *s.* Lili, lilidh.
LILYLIVERED, *adj.* Cladhaireach, gealtach.
LIMATURE, *s.* Duslach-eadha.
LIMB, *s.* Ball, ball-cuirp.
LIMBER, *adj.* So-lùbadh, maoth.
LIMBERNESS, *s.* So-lùbaidheachd, maothachd.
LIMBO, *s.* Gainntir; ifrinn.
LIME, *s.* Aol; *v. a.* Aol, aolaich.
LIMEKILN, *s.* Àth-aoil.
LIMIT, *s.* Crioch, iomall, ceann-crìche.
LIMIT, *v. a.* Cuir crìoch ri, cuir crìoch mu, suidhich crìochan.
LIMITARY, *adj.* Iomallach.
LIMITATION, *s.* Crìoch-chur, bacadh ùine shuidhichte, iomal.
LIMN, *v. a.* Tarruinn dealbh.
LIMNER, *s.* Fear-tarruinn dhealbh.
LIMP, *v. n.* Bi bacach, bi crùbach.
LIMP, *s.* Crùbaiche, bacaiche.
LIMPET, *s.* Bàirneach.
LIMPID, *adj.* Troi-shoilleir, glan.
LIMPIDNESS, *s.* Troi-shoilleireachd.
LIMY, *adj.* Aolach.
LINCHPIN, *s.* Tarunn-aisil.
LINDEN, *s.* Teile, crann-teile.
LINE, *s.* Sgrìob, fad, sìneadh; sreang; driamlach; sreath-sgrìobhaidh; crios-meadhoin an t-saoghail; sliochd, sìol, gineal; deicheamh-earrann na h-oirlich.
LINE, *v. a.* Lìnig, cluthaich.
LINEAGE, *s.* Linn, sliochd, iarmad, clann, cinneadh, fine, sìol, teaghlach, gineal.
LINEAL, *adj.* Sìnte, sreathach, tarruinnte; dìreach, dligheach, dùthchasach.
LINEAMENT, *s.* Cruth, dreach, dualachas, comharradh-gnùise.
LINEATION, *s.* Stiall, sgrìob, sgriach.
LINEN, *s.* Anart, lion-aodach.
LINEN, *adj.* Anartach, mar anart.
LINEN-DRAPER, *s.* Ceannaich'-anairt.
LING, *s.* Fraoch; langa.
LINGER, *v. n.* Bi fad' am pèin, bi fo chràdh-thinneas; bi an iom-chomhairle; cuir dàil ann, dean dàil, bi fada ri, gabh ùine.
LINGERER, *s.* Slaodaire, màirnealaich, leisgean, lunndaire.
LINGO, *s.* Cànan, cainnt.
LINGUACIOUS, *adj.* Bruidhneach, cainnteach, gobach, geŏpach.
LINGUIST, *s.* Cànanaich, teangair.
LINIMENT, *s.* Cungaidh-leighis, sàbh.
LINING, *s.* Lìnig, lìnigeadh.
LINK, *s.* Tinne, dùl; leus, dòrnais.
LINK, *v.* Co-cheangail, tàth, figh 's a chéile; co-dhlùthaich, aon; cuir am bannaibh; bi'n dlùthachd.
LINNET, *s.* Am breacan-beithe.
LINSEED, *s.* Frŏs-lìn, fras-lìn.
LINSEY-WOOLSEY, *s.* Drògaid.
LINSTOCK, *s.* Bior-fadaidh-cluaise.
LINT, *s.* Lìon; caiteas.
LINTEL, *s.* Ard-dorus, for-dhorus.
LION, *s.* Leòghann; erroneously written, "Leomhann" and "leobhan."
LIONESS, *s.* Ban-leòghann.
LIP, *s.* Bile, lip, oir.
LIPOTHYMY, *s.* Paisean, breisleach, neul.
LIPPED, *adj.* Bileach, busach; oireach.
LIPPITUDE, *s.* Prabaiche, brach-shuileachd.
LIQUABLE, *adj.* So-leaghadh.
LIQUATION, *s.* Leaghadh.
LIQUATE, *v. n.* Leagh, fàs tana.
LIQUEFACTION, *s.* Leaghadh.
LIQUEFIABLE, *adj.* So-leaghadh.
LIQUEFY, *v. a.* Leagh, fàs tana.
LIQUESCENT, *adj.* Leaghtach.
LIQUID, *adj.* Tana; bog, soilleir; mìn.
LIQUID, *s.* Uisge, ni tana sam bith.
LIQUIDATE, *v. a.* Glan air falbh, lùghdaich, fiachan.
LIQUIDITY, *s.* Tainead, leaghtachd, uisgealachd.
LIQUOR, *s.* Deoch làidir.
LISP, *v. n.* Dean liotaiche; bi liotach, bi manntach.
LIST, *s.* Clàr-ainm, ainm-chlàr togradh, miann, toil; stiall, stìom.

List, *v.* Tog, cuir an àireamh; gabh mar shaighdear; éisd, thoir an aire do; dean far-chluais.
Listed, *adj.* Stiallach, grianach.
Listen, *v. n.* Eisd; dean far-chluais.
Listless, *adj.* Coma; neó-chùramach, neo-mhothachail, gun aire.
Listlessness, *s.* Cion-umhaill, coéiseachd, neo-mhothachalachd, neo-chùram.
Lit, *pret.* of *to light.* Las, bheothaich, shoillsich.
Litany, *s.* An Leadan, fiurm ùrnaigh.
Literal, *adj.* Litireil, litireach.
Literary, *adj.* Ionnsaichte, fòghluimte, grinn fhòghluimte.
Literati, *s.* Luchd-fòghluim.
Literature, *s.* Ionnsachadh, fòghlum.
Lithography, *s.* Leac-sgrìobhadh.
Lithotomist, *s.* Léigh fuail-chloich.
Litigant, *s.* Lagh-thagradair.
Litigant, *adj.* Lagh-thagartach.
Litigate, *v. a.* Agair lagh air.
Litigation, *s.* Tagairt-lagha.
Litigious, *adj.* Connspaideach.
Litigiousness, *s.* Tagluinneachd.
Litter, *s.* Crò-leabaidh; connlach; cuain, lir; treamsgal.
Litter, *v. a.* Beir, beir àl; sgap mu'n cuairt.
Little, *adj.* Beag, bìdeach; crìon, meanbh, suarach.
Little, *s.* Beagan, rud-beag.
Littleness, *s.* Bige, lughad, crìonad; mìotharachd, suarachas.
Littoral, *adj.* Cladachail.
Liturgy, *s.* Ùrnaigh choitcheann.
Live, *v. n.* Bi beò; thig beò; mair beò.
Live, *adj.* Beò; beothail, beathail.
Livelihood, *s.* Teachd-an-tìr, lòn.
Liveliness, *s.* Beothalachd, sunntachd.
Livelong, *adj.* Fadalach, buan, sgìth.
Lively, *adj.* Sunntach, beothail; meanmnach, aighearach, mear.
Liver, *s.* Atha, sgòchraich, grùthan.
Liver-colour, *adj.* Dù-dhearg.
Livery, *s.* Éideadh-suaicheantais seirbheisich.
Liveryman, *s.* Gille-suaicheantais.
Livid, *adj.* Dù-ghorm.
Lividity, *s.* Dù-ghuirme.
Living, *part. adj.* Beò, beothail.
Living, *s.* Teachd-an-tìr, beathachadh.
Lixivial, *adj.* Saillt, salannach.
Lixiviate, *adj.* Saillteach, salannach.
Lixivium, *s.* Uisge làn salainn.
Lizard, *s.* Arc-luachrach.
Lo! *interj.* Faic! feuch! seall! amhairc!
Load, *s.* Luchd, eallach, éire, cudthrom; trom, truime, uallach.
Load, *v. a.* Luchdaich, eallaich, lìon, cuimrigich, cuir fo éire; cuir urchair an gunna; tromaich.
Loadstone, *s.* Clach-iùil.
Loaf, *s.* Builionn, muilion.
Loam, *s.* Trom-thalamh.
Loamy, *adj.* Laomaidh.
Loan, *s.* Iasad, iasachd, coinghealI.
Loath, *adj.* Aindeonach, neo-thoileach.
Loathe, *v. a.* Fuathaich, sgreataich roimh; gabh gràin.
Loathful, *adj.* Fuathmhor, deisinneach.
Loathing, *s.* Gràin, fuath, sgreat.
Loathsome, *adj.* Gràineil, sgreataidh.
Loathsomeness, *s.* Sgreamhalachd.
Lob, *s.* Slaodaire, liobasdair, buimilear.
Lobby, *s.* Foir-sheòmar.
Lobe, *s.* Duilleag an sgamhain, earrann.
Lobster, *s.* Giomach.
Local, *adj.* Dùthchail, ionadail.
Locality, *s.* Àite, còmhnaidh.
Location, *s.* Suidheachadh ann.
Lock, *s.* Glas; gleus gunna; bachlag, dual, ciabhag.
Lock, *v.* Glais; druid, dùin; bi dùinte, bi glaiste.
Locker, *s.* Àite-gleidhidh, àite-glaiste.
Locket, *s.* Glasag-mhuineil.
Lockram, *s.* Anart-asgairt.
Locomotion, *s.* Gluasad, siubhal.
Locomotive, *adj.* Gluasadach, siùbhlach.
Locust, *s.* Locust.
Lodge, *v.* Cuir an ionad còmhnaidh; suidhich, socraich, càirich; gabh còmhnaidh.
Lodge, *s.* Taigh-geata, taigh-fasgaidh.
Lodgement, *s.* Cruinneachadh, dòmhlachadh; seilbh-ghlacaidh, toirt a mach daingnich.
Lodger, *s.* Fear-fàrdaich, aoidh.
Lodging, *s.* Fàrdoch, còmhnaidh dìon, fasgadh.
Loft, *s.* Ùrlar, ùrlar-déile, lobhta.
Loftiness, *s.* Àirde, àrd-smuainteachd; mòr-chuis, àrdan, féinbheachd.
Lofty, *adj.* Àrd, mòr, uasal; allail, òirdheirc; mòr-chuiseach, àrdanach, féin-bheachdail, uaibhreach.

Log, *s.* Sgonn, òrda fiodha; tomhas Eabhruidheach.
Loggerhead, *s.* Gurraiceach, amhlair, baothaire, ùmaidh.
Logic, *s.* Ealain reusonachaidh.
Logical, *adj.* Dian-chiallach.
Logician, *s.* Fear dian-reusonachaidh.
Logwood, *s.* Fiodh an datha.
Loin, *s.* Leasraidh, am blian.
Loiter, *v. a.* Dean màirneal, bi dìomhanach, bi ri steòcaireachd.
Loiterer, *s.* Steòcaire, leisgean, lunndaire, slaodaire.
Loll, *v.* Dean leth-laidhe ri, leag do thaic air.
Lone, *adj.* Aonarach; leis féin.
Loneliness, Loneness, *s.* Aonaranachd; dìomhaireachd, uaigneachd.
Lonely, Lonesome, *adj.* Aonarach, aonaranach; dìomhair, uaigneach.
Long, *adj.* Fada, buan, maireannach.
Long, *v. n.* Miannaich, bi miannach, biodh a mhiann ort, gabh fadal.
Long-boat, *s.* Bàta-mòr luinge.
Longevity, *s.* Fad-shaoghalachd.
Longimanous, *adj.* Fad-làmhach.
Longing, *s.* Miann, togradh, geall, déidh, dian-thogradh.
Longitude, *s.* Fad; iar-astar; earastar.
Longitudinal, *adj.* Air fhad.
Longsome, *adj.* Fadalach; sgìtheil.
Longsuffering, *adj.* Fad-fhulangach.
Longsuffering, *s.* Fad-fhulangas.
Longways, *adj.* Air fhad.
Longwinded, *adj.* Fad-anaileach; sgìth.
Looby, *s.* Burraidh, blaghastair.
Loof, Luff, *v. a.* Teann ri soirbheas, thoir a dh' ionnsaidh na gaoithe; fan ri gaoith; cùm ri fuaradh.
Look, *v.* Sir, iarr, rannsaich; dearc, seall air, amhairc, beachdaich; feuch, mion-rannsaich.
Look! *interj.* Seall! faic! feuch!
Look, *s.* Snuadh, dreach, aogas, sealladh, tuar, fiamh, neul; faicinn, amharc.
Looking-glass, *s.* Sgàthan.
Loom, *s.* Beart, beart-fhigheadair.
Loon, *s.* Slaoightear, crochaire.
Loop, *s.* Lùb, eag-shùl, eag-amhairc.
Loophole, *s.* Toll, fosgladh; dorusteichidh, cuilbheart, car.
Loopholed, *adj.* Sùileach, tolltach, lùbach.
Loose, *v.* Fuasgail, lasaich; cuir mu sgaoil, leig fa sgaoil; thoir cead; cuir saor; leig ás.
Loosen, *v.* Lasaich, fuasgail; thoir ás a chéile; bi sgaoilteach.
Looseness, *s.* Fuasgailteachd, neodhaingneachd; macnus; mi-riaghailteachd, buaireasachd; fuasgladh cuirp, a' ghearrach.
Lop, *v. a.* Gèarr, bèarr, sgud, sgath.
Loppings, *s.* Barrach, sgathach.
Loquacious, *adj.* Bruidhneach, abartach, beul-fhuasgailte, gòbach.
Loquacity, *s.* Abarachd, gòbaireachd.
Lord, *s.* Tighearna, uachdaran, triath, morair.
Lord, *v. n.* Dean morair dheth; bi aintighearnail, bi stràiceil; dean cruaidh riaghladh.
Lording, Lordling, *s.* Tighearna beag.
Lordliness, *s.* Flathaileachd, mòrachd, urram, àrd-inbhe; stràic, stràicealachd, mòr-chuis.
Lordship, *s.* Tighearnas, moraireachd.
Lore, *s.* Fòghlum, oilean, teagasg.
Lorimer, Loriner, *s.* Fear deanamh shrian, srianadair.
Lorn, *adj.* Tréigte, caillte, aonaranach.
Lose, *v.* Caill; leig á fradharc.
Loseable, *adj.* So-chall.
Loser, *s.* Fear-calldaich, am fear a chaill.
Loss, *s.* Call; teagamh.
Lost, *pret.* of *to lose.* Caillte.
Lot, *s.* Crannchur; roinn, earrann.
Lotion, *s.* Cungaidh-nighe.
Lottery, *s.* Crannchur, tuiteamas.
Loud, *adj.* Ard-fhuaimneach, tartarach, labhar; farumach.
Loudness, *s.* Labhrachd, toirm, farum.
Lounge, *v. n.* Bi dìomhain, bi lunndach.
Lounger, *s.* Lunndaire, fear-dìomhain.
Louse, *s.* Miol, mial.
Lousewort, *s.* An lùs-riabhach.
Lousiness, *s.* Mialachas, mosaiche.
Lousy, *adj.* Mialach, làn mhial.
Lout, *s.* Burraidh, sgonn balaich.
Loutish, *adj.* Ludaireach, balachail.
Lovage, *s.* Lùs-an-liùgaire.
Love, *v. a.* Gràdhaich, thoir gaol, thoir gràdh; gabh tlachd.
Love, *s.* Gaol, gràdh, déidh; miann, suiridhe; càirdeas, deagh-rùn; gràidhean, gràidheag; mo ghràdh, mo ghaol, mo rùn.
Loveknot, *s.* Bad-leannanachd.
Loveletter, *s.* Litir-leannanachd.
Loveliness, *s.* Ionmhuinneachd.
Lovelorn, *adj.* Tréigte, cùlaichte.

LOVELY, *adj.* Caomh, àillidh, maiseil.
LOVER, *s.* Fear-gaoil, leannan.
LOVESICK, *adj.* Tinn le gaol, an gaol.
LOVESONG, *s.* Òran-gaoil.
LOVESUIT, *s.* Suiridhe.
LOVETALE, *s.* Sgeula-gaoil.
LOVING, *part. adj.* Gràdhach, caoimhneil, caomh; gràdh-bhriathrach.
LOVINGKINDNESS, *s.* Caoimhneas-gràidh.
LOVINGNESS, *s.* Caomhalachd, gràdhalachd, caoimhneas.
LOW, *adj.* Ìosal; domhain; neo-fhuaimneach, neo-labhar; muladach, trom-inntinneach, tùrsach; mosach, mìothar; neo-allail, bochd.
LOW, *v. n.* Dean géimnich, dean langanaich.
LOWER, *v.* Ìslich, thoir sìos, ceannsaich; lùghdaich luach; sìolaidh sìos.
LOWER, *s.* Gruaim, mùig.
LOWERMOST, *adj.* Iochdrach, a's ìsle.
LOWLAND, *s.* Fonn còmhnard, machair.
LOWLINESS, *s.* Irioslachd, macantas, suairceas; mìotharachd, tàirealachd.
LOWLY, *adj.* Iriosal, macanta, stuama, ciùin, soitheamh; an-uasal, mìothar, suarach; neo-allail, ìosal.
LOWNESS, *s.* Ìsleachd, suarachas, neo-inbheachd; ùmhlachd; trom-inntinn, mulad.
LOWSPIRITED, *adj.* Trom-inntinneach, dubhach, muladach.
LOYAL, *adj.* Rìoghail, dìleas; tairis, fìrinneach, tréidhireach.
LOYALIST, *s.* Fear-dìleas do'n rìgh.
LOYALTY, *s.* Dìlseachd, tréidhireas.
LUBBER, LUBBARD, *s.* Rag-bhalach, steòcaire, slaodaire, gurraiceach, boganach, claghaire.
LUBBERLY, *adj.* Slaodach, bog, gealtach, claghaireach.
LUBRIC, LUBRICOUS, *adj.* Sleamhain, neo-sheasmhach.
LUBRICATE, *v. a.* Lìomh, dean sleamhainn, fàg sleamhainn.
LUBRICITY, *s.* Sleamhnachd, slìomachd, macnus, macnusachd.
LUCE, *s.* Geadas, gead-iasg.
LUCENT, *adj.* Lìomhaidh, lainnearach.
LUCERNE, *s.* Seòrsa feòir.
LUCID, *adj.* Lainnearach, deàrsach, dealrach; soilleir, glan, troi-shoilleir, trìd-shoilleir.
LUCIDITY, *s.* Lainnearachd, dearsachd.
LUCIFER, *s.* An diabhol; reull na maidne.
LUCIFEROUS, LUCIFIC, *adj.* Soillseach, soilleir, soills-thabhartach.
LUCK, *s.* Tuiteamas, tachartas, dàn, tapadh, càs; crannchur.
LUCKLESS, *adj.* Mi-shealbhach, mi-shona.
LUCKY, *adj.* Sealbhach, sona.
LUCRATIVE, *adj.* Buannachdail, airgeadach, tarbhach.
LUCRE, *s.* Buannachd, cosnadh.
LUCTATION, *s.* Strì, spàirn, deuchainn.
LUCUBRATE, *v. n.* Dean faire, oibrich 's an oidhche, no, le solus coinnle.
LUCUBRATION, *s.* Saothair oidhche, sgrìobhadh le solus coinnle.
LUDICROUS, *adj.* Àbhachdach.
LUDIFICATION, *s.* Magadh, fanaid.
LUFF, *v. n.* Cùm ris a' ghaoith.
LUG, *v. a.* Slaoid, spìon leat.
LUG, *s.* An lugas, am biathain-tràghad.
LUGGAGE, *s.* Goireas-turais; trealaich.
LUKEWARM, *adj.* Meagh-bhlàth.
LUKEWARMNESS, *s.* Meagh-bhlàths.
LULL, *v. a.* Cuir gu cadal, cuir sàmhach.
LULLABY, *s.* Òran fulasgaidh, crònan.
LUMBAGO, *s.* An leum-droma.
LUMBER, *s.* Trealaich, sean-àirneis.
LUMBER, *v.* Dòmhlaich, gluais trom.
LUMINARY, *s.* Solus; fear-eòlais, fear soillseachaidh; fear-naidheachd.
LUMINOUS, *adj.* Soillseach, dealrach; soilleir, glan; dearsach, boillsgeach.
LUMP, *s.* Meall, sgonn, an t-iomlan.
LUMPING, LUMPISH, *adj.* Trom, marbhanta, leasg, tomadach.
LUMPISHLY, *adv.* Gu tròm, gu marbhanta.
LUMPY, *adj.* Meallanach, cnapanach.
LUNACY, *s.* Cuthach-na-gealaich, mearan-céille.
LUNAR, LUNARY, *adj.* Gealachail.
LUNATED, *adj.* Leth-chruinn.
LUNATIC, *s.* Fear-cuthaich, fear-mearain, fear-aotromais.
LUNATION, *s.* Cuairt na gealaich.
LUNCH, LUNCHEON, *s.* Biadh meadhoin latha.
LUNETTE, *s.* Leth-ghealach, solus-ùr.
LUNGS, *s.* Sgamhan.
LUNGWORT, *s.* Crotal-coille.
LURCH, *s.* Teinn, teanndachd, drip.
LURCH, *v.* Thoir an car á, dean frithghoid, siolc; dean ceilg.
LURCHER, *s.* Cù-seilg, gaothar.
LURE, *s.* Culaidh bhuairidh, mealladh.
LURE, *v. a.* Buair, tàlaidh, meall.
LURID, *adj.* Duaichnidh, gruamach.
LURK, *v. n.* Dean feall-fhalach.
LURKER, *s.* Gadaich-chùl-phreas.

Luscious, *adj.* Sòghmhor, ro-bhlasda.
Lush, *adj.* Trom-dhathach.
Lust, *s.* Miann-feòlmhor; ann-tog-radh, ana-miann.
Lustful, *adj.* Ana-miannach, coll-aidh.
Lustiness, *s.* Spionnadh, sultmhor-achd, dòmhalachd.
Lustral, *adj.* Ionnladach, a ghlanas.
Lustration, *s.* Glanadh le uisge.
Lustre, *s.* Dealradh, dearsadh, lainn-ear, soillse; mòr-chliù, ainmealachd; ùine chùig bliadhna.
Lustring, *s.* Sìoda boillsgeil.
Lusty, *adj.* Làidir, calma, neartmhor, sultmhor, foghainteach, reamhar, garbh.
Lute, *s.* Inneal-ciùil àraidh, crèadh-ghlaodh.
Lute, *v. a.* Cuir crèadh-ghlaodh air.
Lux, **Luxate**, *v. a.* Cuir ás an ǎlt.
Luxuriance, **Luxuriancy**, *s.* Mòr-chinneas, ro-phailteas, reamhrachd.
Luxuriant, *adj.* Ro-phailt, fàsmhor.
Luxurious, *adj.* Sòghail, geòcach; ròiceal, ana-miannach.
Luxuriousness, *s.* Sòghalachd.
Luxury, *s.* Sòghalachd; sògh, ana-barra, ana-miann, neo-ghloine.
Lycanthropy, *s.* An troma-tàisean.
Lying, *s.* Deanamh bhreug; laidhe.
Lymph, *s.* Uisge, sùgh glan.
Lymphatic, *adj.* Uisgeach, uisgeil.
Lympheduct, *s.* Soitheach-uisge.
Lyre, *s.* Clàrsach, cruit.
Lyric, **Lyrical**, *adj.* Fonnmhor, ceòlmhor, cruit-bhinn.
Lyrist, *s.* Cruitear, clàrsair.

M

M, *s.* An treas litir deug do'n aibidil.
Macaroni, *s.* Sgèamhanach, lasgaire.
Macaronic, *s.* Measgachadh.
Macaroon, *s.* Aran-millis.
Macaw, *s.* A' pharaid.
Mace, *s.* Suaicheantas inbhe; bata maol; seòrsa spìosraidh.
Macebearer, *s.* Fear-iomchair slat-shuaicheantais.
Macerate, *v. a.* Cnàmh, caith air falbh; claoidh, sàraich, pian; brùth; bogaich, taisich an uisge.
Maceration, *s.* Cnàmh, caitheadh ás; sàrachadh, bruthadh; bogach-adh, taiseachadh.
Machinal, *adj.* Innleachdach.
Machinate, *v. a.* Dean innleachd.
Machination, *s.* Dealbhadh, tionn-sgaladh, droch-innleachd.
Machine, *s.* Beairt-innleachd.
Machinery, *s.* Obair ealanta, obair innleachdach, obair ghluasadach.
Machinist, *s.* Fear-dheanamh bheairt-innleachd.
Mackerel, *s.* Ronnach, reannach.
Macrology, *s.* Fad-sheanachas.
Macrocosm, *s.* An cruinne-cé, a' chruitheachd, an domhan, an saoghal.
Mactation, *s.* Ìobradh; càsgairt.
Macula, **Maculation**, *s.* Ballach-adh, sallachadh.
Maculate, **Macle**, *v. a.* Ballaich, salaich.
Maculation, *s.* Ballachadh, salachadh.
Mad, *adj.* Air a chuthach, mearanach.
Mad, **Madden**, *v.* Cuir air chuthach.
Madam, *s.* Baintighearna.
Madbrained, *adj.* Mearanach, bras.
Madcap, *s.* Fear-fiadhaich, fear-mearain, fear-cuthaich.
Madder, *s.* An ruadh dhath, màdar.
Made, *pret.* of *to make.* Rinn; dèante.
Madhouse, *s.* Taigh-cuthaich.
Madefy, *v. a.* Taisich, bogaich.
Madness, *s.* Cuthach, mearan.
Madrigal, *s.* Òran dùthcha.
Magazine, *s.* Taigh-tasgaidh.
Maggot, *s.* Spiantag, cnuimheag, baoth-smuain, magaid.
Maggoty, *adj.* Cnuimheach, spian-tagach; baoth-smuainteach.
Magi, *s.* Speuradairean na h-airde an ear.
Magic, *s.* Drùidheachd, geasan.
Magic, **Magical**, *adj.* Drùidheil, geasagach.
Magician, *s.* Drùidh, fiosaiche.
Magisterial, *adj.* Tighearnail; ceannasach, làdasach, stràiceil.
Magistracy, *s.* Uachdranachd.
Magistrate, *s.* Bàillidh, uachdaran, fear-riaghlaidh, breitheamh.
Magnanimity, *s.* Mòr-inntinneachd.
Magnanimous, *adj.* Mòr-inntinneach.
Magnesia, *s.* Gnè do dh' fhùdar pùrgaide.
Magnet, *s.* Clach-iùil.
Magnetic, **Magnetical**, *adj.* Tarr-uinneach, mar a' chlach iùil.
Magnetism, *s.* Cumhachd tarruinn da ionnsaidh féin, mar th' aig a' chloich iùil.

Magnificence, *s.* Mòrdhalachd.
Magnificent, *adj.* Òirdheirc, mòr-chuiseach; glonnmhor; àrd.
Magnifier, *s.* Fear-meudachaidh, fear-àrdachaidh; gloine-mheudach-aidh.
Magnify, *v. a.* Meudaich; àrdaich, tog, urramaich.
Magnitude, *s.* Meudachd, meud.
Magpie, *s.* Pioghaid.
Maid, Maiden, *s.* Maighdeann, òigh, cailin, caileag, gruagach, nighean, ainnir, finne, cruinneag; ban-oglach.
Maiden, *adj.* Òigheach, maighdeann-ach; glan, ùr, fìor-ghlan, neo-thruaillidh.
Maidenhair, *s.* An dubh-chăsach.
Maidenhead, Maidhood, Maiden-hood, *s.* Maighdeannas.
Mail, *s.* Lùireach-mhàilleach, deise-chruadhach; màla, balg-litrichean.
Maim, *v. a.* Leòn, ciurr, dochainn.
Maim, *s.* Dochunn, ciurradh; bac-aiche, crùbaiche; cron, coire; gaoid.
Main, *adj.* Prìomh, ceud, àraidh; mòr, àrd, fuathasach; cudthromach, sònraichte.
Main, *s.* A' mhòr chuid; tomad; an lear, an cuan, an fhairge mhòr.
Mainland, *s.* Tìr-mòr, a' mhòr-thìr.
Mainmast, *s.* Crann-mòr, an crann-meadhoin.
Mainprize, *s.* Tabhairt air urras.
Mainsail, *s.* An seòl-mòr, an seòl-meadhoin.
Mainsheet, *s.* Sgòd an t-siùil mhòir.
Maintain, *v.* Gléidh, cùm; daingnich, dean seasmhach; dìon, seas, buan-aich, coisinn; cùm suas, beathaich, thoir teachd-an-tìr do; tagair, còmh-daich.
Maintainable, *adj.* So-dhìon, so-ghleidheadh, so-thagradh, so-sheas-amh, so-chòmhdachadh.
Maintenance, *s.* Dìon, taic, fasgadh, tèarmann; tsachd-an-tìr, beathach-adh; seasmachd, maireannachd, daingneachd.
Maintop, *s.* Bàrr a' chroinn mhòir.
Mainyard, *s.* Slat shiùil a chroinn mhòir.
Maize, *s.* Cruithneachd Innseanach.
Majestic, Majestical, *adj.* Mòrdha, urramach, flathail; àrd.
Majesty, *s.* Mòrachd, mòrdhalachd, greadhnachas, òirdheirceas; àrd-chumhachd; rìoghalachd.
Major, *adj.* A's mò, a's urramaiche.
Major, *s.* Ard-oifigeach, màidsear.
Majoration, *s.* Meudachadh.
Majority, *s.* A' mhòr chuid; làn-aois, mòid.
Make, *v.* Dèan, dean suas; dealbh; thoir air, co-éignich gu; dèan air, coisinn air; ruig.
Make, *s.* Dèanamh, cumadh, cruth.
Makebate, *s.* Ball-aimhleis, ceann-buaireis.
Maker, *s.* An Cruthadair; fear-dèan-amh, dealbhadair, cumadair.
Makepeace, *s.* Fear-eadraiginn.
Making, *s.* Deanamh, deàlbh.
Maladministration, *s.* Mi-riagh-ladh, mi-steòrnadh, mi-bhuileach-adh.
Malady, *s.* Galar, euslaint, tinneas, eucail.
Malapert, *adj.* Beadaidh, dàna, bath-aiseach, dalma, leamh, lonach.
Malapertness, *s.* Beadaidheachd, ladornas, dalmachd.
Malcontent, *adj.* Mi-thoilichte, neo-riaraichte.
Male, *s.* Fireann, firionn, firionnach
Malecontent, *s.* Fear-mi-thoilichte, fear gearanach, fear tuaireapach, fear-talaich.
Maledicted, *adj.* Mallaichte.
Malediction, *s.* Mallachd.
Malefaction, *s.* Coire, droch-bheart, lochd, oilbheum, ciont.
Malefactor, *s.* Fear-droch-bheirt, eucorach, ciontach.
Malefic, *adj.* Buaireasach, cronail.
Malevolence, *s.* Mi-rùn, gamhlas, fuath, nimhealachd, miosgainn.
Malevolent, *adj.* Mì-runach, gamh-lasach, nimheil, miosgainneach.
Malice, *s.* Mì-run, gamhlas, droch-mhèinn, nàimhdeas, tnù.
Malicious, *adj.* Gamhlasach, mì-runach, droch-mhèinneach, naimh-deil.
Maliciousness, *s.* Falachd, droch-mhèinneachd, nimhealachd.
Malign, *adj.* Gabhaltach, guineach, nimheil, millteach.
Malign, *v. a.* Fuathaich; dochainn, ciurr, dean cron do.
Malignancy, Malignity, *s.* Droch-mhèinn; millteachd, sgriosalachd.
Malignant, *adj.* Millteach, sgriosail.
Malkin, *s.* Bhreun-chaile, dubh-chaile.
Mall, *s.* Simid, òrd; sràid.
Mall, *v. a.* Slaicinn, buaill.
Mallard, *s.* Dràc fiadhaich.
Malleability, *s.* Fulang ùird.
Malleable, *adj.* So-oibreachadh.
Malleate, *v. a.* Oibrich air innean.

MALLET, *s.* Fairche, slacan, simid.
MALLOWS, *s.* Lŭs-nam-meall-mòra.
MALT, *s.* Braich.
MALT, *v. n.* Brach, gabh brachadh.
MALTSTER, *s.* Brachadair.
MALTREAT, *v. a.* Droch ghréidh.
MALVERSATION, *s.* Mealltaireachd.
MAM, MAMMA, *s.* Màthair.
MAMMON, *s.* Beartas, saibhreas.
MAN, *s.* Duine, fear.
MAN, *v. a.* Cuir sgioba air, &c.
MANACLES, *s.* Glas làmh, cuibhreach.
MANAGE, *v.* Stiùr, riaghail, òrduich; ceannsaich; steòrn.
MANAGE, MANAGEMENT, MANAGERY, *s.* Riaghladh, stiùradh; seòltachd, sicireachd, innleachd; iomairt, cleachdadh.
MANAGEABLE, *adj.* So-iomairt, so-riaghladh, so-stiùradh, so-cheannsachadh.
MANAGER, *s.* Fear-riaghlaidh, fear-stiùraidh; fear-steòrnaidh.
MANATION, *s.* Sruthadh, brùchdadh.
MANCHET, *s.* Aran-milis, aran-cridhe.
MANCIPATE, *v. a.* Cuir fo dhaorsa.
MANDAMUS, *s.* Òrdugh rìoghail.
MANDATARY, *s.* Pears'-eaglais pàpanach.
MANDATE, *s.* Àinte, òrdugh, earail.
MANDATORY, *adj.* Àinteil, earalach.
MANDIBLE, *s.* Peirceall, gial.
MANDIBULAR, *adj.* Peirceallach.
MANDRAKE, *s.* A chara-mhill.
MANDUCATE, *v. a.* Cagainn, ith.
MANDUCATION, *s.* Cagnadh, itheadh.
MANE, *s.* Muing, gath-muinge.
MANEGE, *s.* Sgoil-mharcachd.
MANES, *s.* Tàsg, spiorad, tannasg.
MANFUL, *adj.* Fearail, duineil.
MANFULNESS, *s.* Fearalas, duinealas.
MANGE, *s.* Cloimh, galar spréidhe.
MANGER, *s.* Prasach, frasach.
MANGLE, *v. a.* Reub, srac, mill, thòir á sa chéile; dean ablach dheth; mìnich anart.
MANGLE, *s.* Muillean mìneachaidh.
MANGY, *adj.* Cloimheach, clamhrach.
MANHOOD, *s.* Làn-aois; fearalas.
MANIA, *s.* Boile-cuthaich.
MANIAC, *s.* Neach cuthaich.
MANIACAL, *adj.* Air boile cuthaich.
MANIFEST, *adj.* Follaiseach, soilleir.
MANIFEST, *s.* Chunntas luchd luinge.
MANIFEST, *v. a.* Taisbean, soilleirich, foillsich, nochd, feuch, leig ris.
MANIFESTATION, *s.* Foillseachadh.
MANIFESTNESS, *s.* Soilleireachd.
MANIFESTO, *s.* Gairm-fhollaiseach.
MANIFOLD, *adj.* Iom-fhillteach.
MANIKIN, *s.* Duairc, luspardan.
MANIPLE, *s.* Lan-dùirn; prasgan.
MANKIND, *s.* An cinneadh-daonna.
MANLIKE, MANLY, *adj.* Duineil, fearail, gaisgeil.
MANLINESS, *s.* Duinealas, fearalachd.
MANNA, *s.* Mana, aran nèamhaidh, &c.
MANNER, *s.* Modh, seòl, alt, rian; gnà, gnàths, cleachdadh, nòs; gnè, seòrsa; tuar, snuadh, sealladh, aogas.
MANNERLY, *adj.* Beusach, modhail.
MANNERS, *s.* Deas-ghnà, oilean.
MANŒUVRE, *s.* Sicireachd.
MANOR, *s.* Fearann tighearna.
MANSE, *s.* Taigh ministear.
MANSION, *s.* Taigh tighearna.
MANSLAUGHTER, *s.* Mort, casgairt.
MANTLE, *s.* Falluinn, aodach-uachdair.
MANTUA, *s.* Gùn baintighearna.
MANTUA-MAKER, *s.* Ban-tàillear.
MANUAL, *adj.* Làmhach.
MANUDUCTION, *s.* Làmh-threòrachadh, làmh-stiùradh.
MANUFACTORY, *s.* Bùth cèirde.
MANUFACTURE, *s.* Làmh-obair.
MANUFACTURE, *v. a.* Oibrich, dèan.
MANUFACTURER, *s.* Fear-lâimh-oibre.
MANUMISSION, *s.* Saoradh tràille.
MANUMIT, *v. a.* Saor o dhaorsa.
MANURABLE, *adj.* So mhathachadh.
MANURE, *v. a.* Leasaich, mathaich.
MANURE, *s.* Màthachadh, inneir.
MANUSCRIPT, *s.* Leabhar-sgrìobhte.
MANY, *adj.* Iomadh, lìonmhor.
MANY-COLOURED, *adj.* Ioma-dhathach.
MANY-CORNERED, *adj.* Ioma-bheannach.
MANY-HEADED, *adj.* Ioma-cheannach.
MANY-LANGUAGED, *adj.* Ioma-chainnteach.
MANY-TIMES, *adv.* Iomadh uair, tric.
MAP, *s.* Dealbh dùthcha, no baile, &c.
MAR, *v. a.* Léir, mill, dochainn, truaill.
MARASMUS, *s.* An tinneas caitheamh.
MARAUDER, *s.* Saighdear-spùinnidh.
MARBLE, *s.* Marmor, marbhal.
MARBLE, *v. a.* Breacaich, srianaich.
MARCH, *s.* Am màrt, mìos a' mhàirt; feachd-shiubhal; ceum stòlda; portsiubhail; crìoch, iomall, oir.
MARCH, *v.* Màrsail, imich le feachdcheum; triall, gluais; ceumnaich, gluais gu stàtail; gluais an òrdugh.
MARCHIONESS, *s.* Bana-mharcus.
MARCHPANE, *s.* Seòrs' aran-milis.
MARCID, *adj.* Caol, seargte, glaisneulach.
MARE, *s.* Làir.
MARESCHAL, *s.* Ard-mharascal.

Margarite, Margarites, *s.* Neamhnaid, déideag.

Margent, Margin, *s.* Oir, bile, iomall, crìoch, beul, leth-oir.

Marginal, *adj.* Iomallach, bileach, leth-oireach.

Margrave, *s.* Duin-uasal Gearmailteach.

Marigold, *s.* A' bhile-bhuidhe.

Marine, *adj.* Mara, muireach.

Mariner, *s.* Maraiche, seòladair.

Maritime, *adj.* Fairgeach.

Mark, *s.* Marg; bonn airgeid thrìtasdain deug as gròt; comharradh; làrach, athailt, lorg; dearbhadh, còmhdach; ball-amais, cuspair.

Mark, *v.* Comharraich; beachdaich, thoir fainear; seall, amhairc.

Market, *s.* Féill, margadh, faighir; reic, a's ceannachd.

Marketable, *adj.* A ghabhas reic.

Marksman, *s.* Fear-cuspaireachd.

Marl, *s.* Lagus, criadh-mhathachaidh.

Marlline, *s.* Sreang sgeinnidh.

Marquis, *s.* Oighre diùc, marcus.

Marriage, *s.* Pòsadh.

Marriageable, *adj.* Aig aois-pòsaidh.

Married, *adj.* Pòsta.

Marrow, *s.* Smior, smear.

Marrow-fat, *s.* A' pheasair mhòr.

Marrowless, *adj.* Neo-smiorach.

Marry, *v.* Pòs; thoir am pòsadh.

Marsh, Marish, *s.* Lòn; boglach, breun-loch, féith.

Marsh-mallow, *s.* Lŭs-nam-meall mòra, an cnap-lŭs.

Marsh-marigold, *s.* Lŭs-buidhebealltainn, lŭs Muire.

Marshal, *s.* Marasgal.

Marshal, *v. a.* Tarruinn suas, cuir an òrdugh; roi'-imich, treòraich.

Marshalship, *s.* Marasgalachd.

Marshy, *adj.* Bog, fliuch, féitheach.

Mart, *s.* Àite margaidh.

Marten, *s.* Taghán; gobhlan-gaoithe.

Martial, *adj.* Cathach, gaisgeanta, curanta, crodha, treun.

Martialist, *s.* Curaidh, gaisgeach.

Martingal, *s.* Srian-cheannsachaidh.

Martinmas, *s.* An fhéill-màrtainn.

Martyr, *s.* Martarach, fear-fianais.

Martyrdom, *s.* Bàs air son creidimh.

Martyrology, *s.* Eachdraidh mhartarach.

Marvel, *s.* Iongantas, iongnadh.

Marvel, *v. n.* Gabh iongnadh.

Marvellous, *adj.* Iongantach, neònach.

Marvellousness, *s.* Neònachas.

Masculine, *adj.* Firionn; duineil.

Mash, *s.* Measgan, coimeasgadh, magul lìn.

Mash, *v. a.* Pronn, brùth, masg.

Mask, *s.* Cidhis; leithsgeul, car.

Masker, *s.* Fear-cidhis.

Mason, *s.* Clachair.

Masonic, *adj.* Clachaireach.

Masonry, *s.* Clachaireachd.

Masquerade, *s.* Cluiche-chidhis.

Masquerader, *s.* Fear-cidhis.

Mass, *s.* Meall, dùn, torr; tomad; a' mhòr-chuid; aifrionn.

Massacre, *s.* Casgradh, mort.

Massacre, *v. a.* Casgair, marbh, mort.

Massiness, Massiveness, *s.* Cudthrom, tomad, truimead.

Massive, Massy, *adj.* Cudthromach, trom, tomadach.

Mast, *s.* Crann; cnò.

Master, *s.* Maighistear, fear-taighe; fear-riaghlaidh, fear-stiùraidh, uachdaran, tighearna; sgiobair; fear-teagaisg.

Master, *v. a.* Dean maighistearachd, riaghail; ceannsaich; bi ealanta, bi gleusda.

Masterliness, *s.* Àrd-ealantachd.

Masterly, *adj.* Ealanta, grinn.

Masterpiece, *s.* Àrd-ghnìomh, euchd.

Mastership, Mastery, *s.* Maighistearachd, uachdranachd, ceannsal; urram, buaidh; ealain, eòlas.

Mastication, *s.* Cagnadh.

Masticatory, *s.* Leigheas-cagnaidh.

Mastich, *s.* Bìgh, seòrsa glaoidh.

Mastiff, *s.* Cù mòr, balgaire.

Mastless, *adj.* Gun chrann.

Mastlin, Meslin, *s.* Prac.

Mat, *s.* Brat luachrach.

Match, *s.* Lasadan, brathadair.

Match, *s.* Mac-samhail, fear-dùlain; leth-bhreac; pòsadh; comh-strì.

Match, *v.* Co-fhreagair; pòs, thoir am pòsadh, bi pòsta.

Matchable, *adj.* Co-ionannach.

Matchless, *adj.* Gun choimeas.

Mate, *s.* Céile; còmpanach.

Material, *adj.* Corporra; feumail, sònraichte.

Materialist, *s.* Fear-àicheadh spiorad.

Materiality, *s.* Corporrachd.

Materials, *s.* Deisealasan.

Maternal, *adj.* Màithreil.

Maternity, *s.* Màthaireachd.

Mathematician, *s.* Fear-eòlais thomhas a's àireamh.

Mathematics, *s.* Eòlas tomhas a's àireamh.

MATIN, *adj*. Madainneach, moch.
MATINS, *s*. Aoradh maidne, madainnean, maidnean. *Md.*
MATRICE, or MATRIX, *s*. Bolg, machlag; laghadair, inneal cumaidh.
MATRICIDE, *s*. Mòrt màthar.
MATRICULATE, *v. a*. Cuir sìos ainm an co-chomunn oil-taighean Shasuinn.
MATRICULATION, *s*. Ainm-ghabhail.
MATRIMONIAL, *adj*. Pòsachail.
MATRIMONY, *s*. An dàimh-phòsaidh.
MATRON, *s*. Bean; seanna bhean; bean-taighe.
MATRONLY, *adj*. Sean; màithreil.
MATTER, *s*. Ni corporra, ni talmhaidh; brìgh, ni, rud, stuth; cùis, gnothach, aobhar, mathair-uilc, cùisghearain, cùis-thalaich; iongar.
MATTOCK, *s*. Piocaid, matag.
MATTRESS, *s*. Leabaidh-ìochdrach.
MATURATION, *s*. Abachadh.
MATURATIVE, *adj*. Abachail.
MATURE, *adj*. Abaich; deas, ullamh.
MATURITY, *s*. Abaichead, coimhliontachd.
MAUDLIN, *adj*. Leth-mhisgeach, frŏganach, sŏganach; *s*. Lŭs-âraidh.
MAUGRE, *adv*. A dh' aindeoin.
MAUL, *s*. Fairche, slacan mòr.
MAUL, *v. a*. Buail, gréidh, spuac, brùth, pronn, slacraich, dochainn, ciurr.
MAUND, Sgùlan-laimhe, seòrs' ùird.
MAUNDER, *v. n*. Dean monmhar, dean bòrbhan.
MAUSOLEUM, *s*. Taigh adhlacaidh.
MAW, *s*. Goile; sgròban eòin.
MAWKISH, *adj*. Sgreamhail, sgreataidh, déisinneach.
MAWKISHNESS, *s*. Sgreamhalachd.
MAW-WORM, *s*. Cnuimh goile.
MAXIM, *s*. Fìrinn-shuidhichte, gnàfhacal, sean-fhacal.
MAY, *v. auxil*. Faod, faodaidh, feudaidh.
MAY, *s*. Am màigh, an céitean.
MAY-DAY, *s*. Latha bealltainn.
MAYOR, *s*. Àrd bhaillidh baile-mhòir.
MAYORALTY, *s*. Ceannardachd bailemhòir,
MAYORESS, *s*. Banna-bhaillidh.
MAZZARD, *s*. Cnàimh a' pheirceill.
MAZE, *s*. Cuairt-shloc; tuaineal, imacheist, ioma-chomhairle.
MAZY, *adj*. Cuairteach, troi' chéile.
ME, *pron*. Mi, mise.
MEAD, *s*. Madh, leann-meala.
MEAD, MEADOW, *s*. Lòn, àilean, cluan, miadan, miadair, faiche.
MEADOW-SWEET, *s*. Cneas-Cuchulainn, lŭs-cuchulainn.
MEAGER, *adj*. Caol, bochd, tana, lom, gun fheòil; acrach, gortach, gann.
MEAGERNESS, *s*. Caoile, tainead, luime.
MEAL, *s*. Trà bìdh; min.
MEALMAN, *s*. Ceannaiche mine.
MEALY, *adj*. Tioram, mar mhin.
MEALY-MOUTHED, *adj*. Tlàth-bheulach, sodalach, brosgalach, mìnbhriathrach, cealgach.
MEAN, *adj*. Ìosal, suarach, mìodhoir, tàireil; dìblidh, dìmeasach.
MEAN, *s*. Meadhonachd, cuibheasachd; tomhas, riaghailt.
MEAN, *v. a*. Rùnaich, cuir romhad, togair; ciallaich; biodh a mhiann ort.
MEANDER, *s*. Cuairt-char, fiaradh.
MEANDER, *v. n*. Lùb, fiar, crom.
MEANING, *s*. Rùn-suidhichte; ciall, seadh, brìgh bladh; tuigse.
MEANNESS, *s*. Ìsleachd, bochdainn, suarachas; tàirealachd; spìocaireachd, mosaiche.
MEANT, *part. pass*. of *to mean*. Ciallaichte, rùnaichte.
MEASLES, *s*. A' ghriuthach a' ghriùthrach, a' ghriobhach.
MEASURABLE, *adj*. A ghabhas tomhas.
MEASURE, *s*. Tomhas, cuimse, riaghailt, inneal-tomhais; gu leòir, ni's leòir; cuibhrionn, cuid, roinn, earrann; measarrachd.
MEASURE, *v. a*. Tomhais.
MEASURELESS, *adj*. Do-thomhas.
MEASUREMENT, *s*. Tomhas.
MEASURER, *s*. Fear-tomhais.
MEAT, *s*. Feòil; biadh, teachd an-tìr.
MECHANIC, *s*. Fear-cèirde.
MECHANIC, MECHANICAL, *adj*. Cèirdeil, innleachdach, saoithreachail, ionnsaichte an cèird; oibreachail.
MECHANICS, *s*. Ealain-chèirde.
MECHANICIAN, MECHANIST, *s*. Fearcèirde, fear-eulain.
MECHANISM, *s*. Ealain-ghluasadachd.
MEDAL, *s*. Seanna-chùinneadh, bonncuimhne.
MEDDLE, *v*. Buin ri, bean ri; dean eadraiginn, cuir làmh ann: biodh làmh agad ann.
MEDDLER, *s*. Beadagan, meachranaiche.
MEDIATE, *v*. Sìthich, réitich, dean réidh; dean eadraiginn; bi eadardithis.
MEDIATION, *s*. Eadraiginn, réite, réiteachadh, sìtheachadh, eadar-ghuidhe.
MEDIATOR, *s*. Eadar-mheadhonair.

Mediatory, *adj.* Eadar-mheadhonach.
Mediatorship, *s.* Eadar mheadhonaireachd.
Mediatrix, *s.* Bean-shìtheachaidh.
Medicable, *adj.* So-leigheas.
Medical, Medicinal, *s.* Léigh.
Medicament, *s.* Cungaidh-leighis.
Medicate, *v. a.* Measgaich le iocshlaint.
Medicinal, *adj.* Ioc-shlainteach.
Medicine, *s.* Eòlas-leighis, iocshlaint.
Mediety, *s.* Meadhon, meadhonachd.
Mediocre, *adj.* Meadhonach, an eatorras, cùibheasach.
Mediocrity, *s.* Eatorras, cùibheas.
Meditate, *v.* Tionnsgain, deilbh; smuainich, cnuasaich, beachdsmaointich.
Meditation, *s.* Smaointean, breithneachadh, beachd-smaointean.
Meditative, *adj.* Smaointeachail.
Mediterranean, Mediterraneous, *adj.* Meadhon-thìreach, eadarthìreach.
Medium, *s.* Inneal; eadar-mheadhon.
Medley, *s.* Coimeasgadh, treamsgal.
Medullar, Medullary, *adj.* Smiorach, beo-smiorach.
Meed, *s.* Duais; tiodhlac, tabhartas.
Meek, *adj.* Macanta, ciùin, màlda, soitheamh, mìn, sèimh, iriosal.
Meekness, *s.* Macantas, irioslachd.
Meer, *s.* Loch; crìoch.
Meet, *adj.* Iomchuidh, freagarrach.
Meet, *v. n.* Còmhlaich, coinnich, tachair; cùm còdhail; cruinnich.
Meeting, *s.* Cruinneachadh, cothional, còdhail, coinneachadh.
Meetly, *adv.* Gu h-iomchuidh.
Meetness, *s.* Iomchuidheachd.
Megrim, *s.* Galar-cinn, ceann-ghalar.
Melancholic, Melancholy, *adj.* Dubhach, fo leanndubh, trom; brònach; muladach, tiamhaidh.
Melancholy, *s.* Leann-dubh, mulad; truime-inntinn, dù-bhròn; dubhachas, cianalas, tùrsa.
Meliorate, *v. a.* Leasaich, càirich.
Melioration, Meliority, *s.* Leasachadh, càradh, feabhas.
Mellifluous, *adj.* Mileach, mealach, mil-shruthach.
Mellow, *adj.* Tlàth-fhuaimneach; làn-abaich; air mhisg.
Mellowness, *s.* Làn-abachd; tlàthghuthachd, buigead.
Melodious, *adj.* Leudarra, fonnmhor, binn, ceileireach, ceòl-bhinn.
Melody, *s.* Ceòl-bhinneas, binneas.
Melon, *s.* Meal-bhucan.
Melt, *v.* Leagh, taisich, bogaich, caith ás.
Melter, *s.* Leaghadair.
Member, *s.* Ball, ball-cuirp.
Membrane, *s.* Féith-lianan, cochull.
Membraneous, *adj.* Féith-liananach.
Memento, *s.* Cuimhneachan, sanas.
Memoir, *s.* Mion-eachdraidh.
Memorable, *adj.* Ainmeil, cliùiteach.
Memorandum, *s.* Cuimhneachan.
Memorial, *s.* Cuimhneachan-duaise.
Memorialist, *s.* Fear-cuir-an-cuimhne, fear-cuimhneachaidh.
Memory, *s.* Cuimhne, meadhair.
Men, *plural* of *man.* Daoine, fir.
Menace, *v. a.* Bagair, maoidh.
Menace, *s.* Bagradh, maoidheadh.
Menage, Menagerie, *s.* Co-chruinneachadh fhiadh-bheathaichean.
Mend, *v. a.* Càirich, dean suas; leasaich; cuidich; rach am feabhas, cinn ni's fearr.
Mendacity, *s.* Breugaireachd.
Mender, *s.* Fear-càradh.
Mendicant, *s.* Déirceach, deòra,
Menial, *s.* Seirbheiseach.
Menology, *s.* Mìosachan.
Menstrual, *adj.* Mìosach.
Menstruum, *s.* Uisge-tarruinn.
Mensurate, *v. a.* Tomhais.
Mensuration, *s.* Tomhas.
Mental, *adj.* Inntinneach, inntinneil.
Mention, *s.* Ainmeachadh, iomradh.
Mention, *v. a.* Ainmich, aithris.
Mephitical, *adj.* Lobte, grod, breunbholtrach.
Mercantile, *adj.* Malairteach, margail.
Mercenary, *adj.* Gionach, sanntach.
Mercenary, *s.* Seirbhiseach-duaise.
Mercer, *s.* Ceannaiche sìoda.
Mercery, *s.* Ceannachd shìoda.
Merchandise, *s.* Ceannachd; bathar.
Merchant, *s.* Ceannaiche.
Merchantman, *s.* Long cheannachd.
Merciful, *adj.* Tròcaireach, iochdmhor, bàigheil.
Merciless, *adj.* An-tròcaireach, an-iochdmhor, cruaidh-chridheach.
Mercurial, *adj.* Beò-airgeadach.
Mercury, *s.* Airgiod-beò; sunnt.
Mercy, *s.* Tròcair, iochd, mathanas.
Mercy-seat, *s.* Cathair-na-tròcair.
Mere, *adj.* Fìor, a mhàin.
Merely, *adv.* A mhàin, dìreach.
Meretricious, *adj.* Macnusach, fallsail.
Meridian, *s.* Meadhon-latha, trà-

nòine, àird' an latha; cridhe na h-airde-deas.

MERIDIONAL, *adj.* Deiseal, mu dheas.

MERIT, *s.* Fiùghantas, fiùghalach, òirdheirceas.

MERITORIOUS, *adj.* Airidh, cliùiteach.

MERLE, *s.* An lon-dubh.

MERLIN, *s.* Seòrsa seabhaic.

MERMAID, *s.* Maighdeann-mhara.

MERRIMENT, *s.* Aighear, subhachas, meoghail, mire, sùgradh, àiteas, sùigeart, fonn.

MERRY, *adj.* Aoibhinn, àit; mear, mireagach, aighearach, subhach, geanail, suigeartach.

MERRY-ANDREW, *s.* Baoth-chleasaiche.

MERRYTHOUGHT, *s.* An cnàimh-pòsaidh, cnaimh-uchd eòin.

MESENTERY, *s.* Lìon a mhionaich.

MESH, *s.* Mogull-lìn.

MESS, *s.* Mias; comh-ith; biadh cuideachd.

MESS, *v. n.* Ith; rach an comh-ith.

MESSAGE, *s.* Teachdaireachd.

MESSENGER, *s.* Teachdaire, gille-ruith; maor, earraid.

MESSIAH, *s.* Mesiah, an Slànaighear.

MESSMATE, *s.* Fear-comh-ith.

MESSUAGE, *s.* Taigh-còmhnaidh.

MET, *pret.* and *part.* of *to meet.* Choinnich, chòmhlaich; coinnichte, còmhlaichte.

METAL, *s.* Meatailt, miotailt.

METALLIC, *adj.* Meatailteach.

METALLINE, *adj.* Làn meatailt.

METALLURGY, *s.* Obair-mheatailtean.

METAMORPHOSIS, *s.* Cruth-chaochla, cruth-atharachadh.

METAPHOR, *s.* Briathar-samhla, samhla.

METAPHORICAL, *adj.* Samhlachail.

METAPHRASE, *s.* Eadar-theangachadh.

METAPHYSICAL, *adj.* Domhain, dìomhair, àrd-fhiosrach.

METAPHYSICS, *s.* Eòlas nithibh inntinneach.

METATHESIS, *s.* Atharrachadh.

METE, *v. a.* Tomhais, cothromaich.

METEOR, *s.* Driug, dreag.

METEOROGIAL, *adj.* Driugach.

METEOROLOGIST, *s.* Speuradair.

METEOROLOGY, *s.* Speuradaireachd.

METER, *s.* Fear-tomhais.

METEWAND, METEYARD, *s.* Slat-thonhais.

METHEGLIN, *s.* Leann-meala.

METHINKS, *v. imp.* Air leam.

METHOD, *s.* Dòigh, seòl, rian, modh.

METHODICAL, *adj.* Dòigheil, òrdail, seòlta, rianail.

METHODICALLY, *adv.* Gu dòigheil.

METHODIST, *s.* Fear dealachaidh o eaglais Shasuinn.

METHODIZE, *v. a.* Cuir air dòigh.

METHOUGHT, *pret.* of *methinks.* Shaoil mi, shaoil leam.

METONYMY, *s.* Samhla, modh-samhla.

METOPOSCOPY, *s.* Gnùis-fhiosachd.

METRE, *s.* Rannachd, dàn.

METRICAL, *adj.* Rannach, rann-rèidh.

METROPOLIS, *s.* Àrd-bhaile-mòr.

METROPOLITAN, *s.* Àrd-easbuig.

METTLE, *s.* Smioralachd; stuth.

METTLED, METTLESOME, *adj.* Smiorail, misneachail, duineil, fearail, cruadalach.

MEW, *s.* Eun-lann; fang; faoileag.

MEW, *v.* Druid suas, dean prìosanaich; tilg na h-itean; dean miamhail, mar chat.

MEWL, *v. n.* Ràn, mar naoidhean.

MICE, *plural* of *mouse.* Luchan.

MICHAELMAS, *s.* An Fhéill-Mìcheil.

MICKERY, *s.* Siolcaireachd, frith-ghoid.

MICROCOSM, *s.* An saoghal beag; corp an duine.

MICROSCOPE, *s.* Glaine mheudachaidh.

MID, MIDST, *adj.* Eadar-mheadhonach.

MID-DAY, *s.* Meadhon-latha.

MIDDLE, *adj.* Meadhon.

MIDDLE, *s.* Meadhon, buillsgean.

MIDDLEMOST, MIDMOST, *adj.* 'Sa' mheadhon, sa' bhuillsgean, sa' chridhe.

MIDDLING, *adj.* Meadhonach, an eatorras, cùibheasach.

MIDGE, *s.* Meanbh-chuileag.

MID-HEAVEN, *s.* Meadhon nan speur.

MID-LEG, *s.* Leth a' chalpa.

MIDNIGHT, *s.* Meadhon oidhche.

MIDRIFF, *s.* An sgairt.

MIDSHIPMAN, *s.* Òg-oifigeach luinge.

MIDSTREAM, *s.* Coilleach-an-t-srutha.

MIDSUMMER, *s.* An Fhéill-Eoin.

MIDWAY, *s.* Leth an rathaid.

MIDWAY, *adv.* 'Sa mheadhon.

MIDWIFE, *s.* Bean-ghlùine.

MIDWIFERY, *s.* Banas-glùine.

MIDWINTER, *s.* An Fhéill-Shlinnein.

MIEN, *s.* Snuadh, dreach, aogas, tuar, gnùis, coltas, cruth.

MIGHT, *pret.* of *may.* Dh' fhaodadh.

MIGHT, *s.* Cumhachd, neart, spionnadh.

MIGHTINESS, *s.* Mòr-chumhachd.

MIGHTY, *adj.* Cumhachdach, neartmhor, treun euchdach; smachdail, uachdranach, ùghdarrach; làidir, foghainteach

MIGRATE, *v. n.* Rach imrich, falbh.
MIGRATION, *s.* Imrich, dol imrich.
MILCH, *adj.* Bainneach, bainnear.
MILD, *adj.* Bàigheil; mìn, ciùin, sèimh; neo-gheur, milis, blasda.
MILDEW, *s.* Crith-reothadh, cith-reodhadh, liath-reodhadh, fuar-dhealt, mill-cheò; liathtas.
MILDNESS, *s.* Bàighealachd; ciùine.
MILE, *s.* Mìle, 1760 slat.
MILESTONE, *s.* Clach-mhìle.
MILFOIL, *s.* Earr-thalmhuinn.
MILIARY, *adj.* Caol, meanbh.
MILITANT, *adj.* Cogach, cathach.
MILITARY, *adj.* Cathachail, cogail.
MILITATE, *v. n.* Cuir an aghaidh.
MILITIA, *adj.* Feachd-dùthcha.
MILK, *s.* Bainne; sùgh-luibhean.
MILK, *v. a.* Bleodhainn, bligh, leig.
MILKEN, *adj.* Bainneach, bliochdach.
MILKINESS, *s.* Bainneachas.
MILKMAID, *s.* Banarach, banachaig.
MILKPAIL, *s.* Currasan, cuman.
MILKSOP, *s.* Boganach; gealtaire, claghaire; fear-cailleachail.
MILKTEETH, *s.* Ceud fhiaclan searr-aich.
MILKWHITE, *adj.* Geal mar bhainne.
MILKY, *adj.* Bainneach; maoth, ciùin.
MILKY-WAY, *s.* Geal-shruth nan speur.
MILL, *s.* Muileann, meiligir.
MILL, *v. a.* Bleith, meil, pronn.
MILL-DAM, *s.* Linne-muilinn.
MILLENARY, *s.* Mìle-bliadhna.
MILLENIUM, *s.* Ùine mìle bliadhna tha cuid a' saoilsinn, anns an riagh-ail Criosd fathast air thalamh maille ris na naoimh, an deigh na h-ais-éirigh.
MILLEPEDE, *s.* Corra-chòsag.
MILLER, *s.* Muillear.
MILLESIMAL, *adj.* Mìlteabh, mìleadh.
MILLINER, *s.* Bhean ghrinneis.
MILLINERY, *s.* Grinneas bhan.
MILLION, *s.* Deich ceud mìle.
MILLIONTH, *adj.* An deicheamh ceud-mìle.
MILLSTONE, *s.* Clach-mhuilinn.
MILT, *s.* Mealag éisg; an dubh-liath.
MILTER, *s.* Iasg mealagach.
MIMIC, *s.* Fear-atharais.
MIMIC, MIMICAL, *adj.* Atharraiseach, fochaideach, fanaideach.
MIMICRY, *s.* Atharrais, sgeigireachd.
MINCE, *v. a.* Mìn-ghearr; falbh le meanbh-cheum, imich gu mùirn-each.
MIND, *s.* Inntinn, tuigse; tùr; toil, déidh, togradh; smuaintean; beachd.
MIND, *v. a.* Thoir an aire, thoir fain-ear, beachdaich; cuir an cuimhne.
MINDED, *adj.* Togarrach, deònach.
MINDFUL, *adj.* Faicilleach, cùramach.
MINDLESS, *adj.* Neo-aireil, neo-chùr-amach, neo-fhaicilleach.
MINE, *pron. posses.* Mo, leamsa.
MINE, *s.* Shloc-mèinne, àite mèinne; sloc séisdidh.
MINE, *v. a.* Cladhaich fodha; mill gun fhios, mill gu diomhair.
MINER, *s.* Fear-cladhaich mèinne.
MINERAL, *s.* Mèinn.
MINERAL, *adj.* Mèinneach.
MINERALIST, *s.* Mèinneadair.
MINERALOGIST, *s.* Fear mèinn-eòlach.
MINERALOGY, *s.* Mèinn-eòlas.
MINGLE, *v. a.* Measgaich, coimeasg, cuir an ceann a chéile; truaill; cuir troi' chéile.
MINGLE, *s.* Measgadh, coimeasgadh.
MINIATURE, *s.* Meanbh-dhealbh.
MINIKIN, *adj.* Beag, crìon, meanbh.
MINIM, MINUM, *s.* Duairce; punc-chiùil àraid.
MINIMUM, *s.* A' chuid a's lugha.
MINIMUS, *s.* An creutair a's lugha.
MINION, *s.* Peasan, beadagan-millte.
MINION, *adj.* Mùirneach, greannar.
MINISTER, *s.* Ministear [*often erro-neously written* "ministir"]; fear-riaghlaidh, fèar-comhairle; teachd-aire.
MINISTER, *v.* Fritheil; tabhair, buil-ich, bairig, thoir seachad.
MINISTERIAL, *adj.* Ministearach, frìtheilteach.
MINISTRATION, *s.* Ministrealachd.
MINISTRY, *s.* Dreuchd, seirbheis; min-istrealachd; meadhonachd, luchd-riaghlaidh, luchd-comhairle.
MINNOW, *s.* Am bior-deamhnaidh.
MINOR, *s.* Neach fo làn-aois.
MINORATE, *v. a.* Lughdaich, beagaich.
MINORATION, *s.* Lughdachadh.
MINORITY, *s.* Òg-aois; a' chuid a's lugha.
MINSTER, *s.* Cill-mhanach.
MINSTREL, *s.* Cruitear, clàrsair.
MINSTRELSY, *s.* Cruitearachd, ceòl, coisir-chiùil.
MINT, *s.* Mionnt, meannt; taigh-cùinnidh.
MINUTE, *adj.* Meanbh, beag, mion.
MINUTE, *s.* Mionaid, trì ficheadamh earrann na h-uarach; gearr-chunnt-as, sgrìobhadh.
MINUTE, *v. a.* Sgrìobh gearr-chunntas.
MINUTE-BOOK, *s.* Leabhar chuimhne.
MINUTENESS, *s.* Meanbhachd, bige.

Minutely, *adv.* Gu meanbh, gu mion, gu mionaideach.
Minutiæ, *s.* Meanbh-phoncan.
Minx, *s.* Gaorsach, caile bheag-narach, aigeannach.
Miracle, *s.* Mìorbhuil.
Miraculous, *adj.* Mìorbhuileach.
Miraculously, *adv.* Gu mìorbhuileach, gu h-iongantach.
Mirador, *s.* Aradh, lobta.
Mire, *s.* Poll, làthach, eabar, clàbar.
Mire, *v. a.* Salaich, eabraich.
Mirror, *s.* Sgàthan.
Mirth, *s.* Mire, sùgradh, aighear.
Mirthful, *adj.* Aighearach, cridheil, sùgach; aoibhneach.
Miry, *adj.* Clàbarach, eabarach.
Misadventure, *s.* Mi-shealbh, donas.
Misadvise, *v. a.* Mi-chomhairlich.
Misadvised, *adj.* Mi-chomhairlichte.
Misaimed, *adj.* Mi-chuimsichte.
Misanthrope, *s.* Fear-fuathachaidh dhaoine, fuathadair dhaoine.
Misanthropy, *s.* Fuath do dhaoine.
Misapplication, *s.* Mi-bhuileachadh.
Misapply, *v. a.* Mi-bhuilich.
Misapprehend, *v. n.* Mi-bhreithnich.
Misapprehension, *s.* Mi-bhreithneachadh, mi-thuigsinn.
Misbecome, *v. n.* Bi mi-chiatach.
Misbegotten, *adj.* Dìolain.
Misbehave, *v. n.* Cleachd mi-bheus.
Misbehaviour, *s.* Droch-giùlan.
Misbelief, *s.* Saobh-chreideamh.
Misbeliever, *s.* Saobh-chreideach.
Miscalculation, *s.* Mear-chunntadh.
Miscalculate, *v. a.* Dean mearchunntadh, dean mi-chunntadh.
Miscarriage, *s.* Aisead-anabaich.
Miscarry, *v. n.* Beir anabaich; rach am mearachd, mi-ghiùlain.
Miscellaneous, *adj.* Measgaichte.
Miscellany, *s.* Co-measgadh.
Mischance, *s.* Tubaist, droch-dhàn.
Mischief, *s.* Aimhleas, cron, lochd.
Mischievous, *adj.* Aimhleasach, cronail, do-bheairteach.
Miscible, *adj.* So-mheasgadh.
Mis-citation, *s.* Mi-aithris.
Misclaim, *s.* Tagradh gun chòir.
Misconception, *s.* Barail mhearachdach, mi-bharail.
Misconduct, *s.* Mi-riaghladh; droch ghiulan, mi-bheus.
Misconjecture, *s.* Beachd mearachdach, mi-bheachd.
Misconstruction, *s.* Mi-mhìneachadh, mi-sheadh.
Misconstrue, *v. a.* Mi-mhìnich.
Miscreance, *s.* As-creideamh.
Miscreant, *s.* As-creideach, saobhchreideach, ann-spiorad, baobh.
Misdeed, *s.* Dò-bheart, droch-bheart.
Misdeem, *v. a.* Thoir mi-bhreth air.
Misdemeanour, *s.* Mi-ghniomh, coire.
Misdoubt, *v. a.* Cuir an teagamh.
Misemploy, *v. a.* Mi-bhuilich.
Misemployment, *s.* Mi-bhuileachadh.
Miser, *s.* Spìocaire, fìneag.
Miserable, *adj.* Truagh, neo-shona, ainnis; gortach, gann, cruaidh.
Miserableness, *s.* Truaighe, gainne.
Misery, *s.* Truaighe, bochdainn, dòruinn; mi-shealbh.
Misfashion, *v. a.* Mi-dhealbhaich, mi-chùm, cuir an droch riochd.
Misfortune, *s.* Mi shealbh, tubaist.
Misgive, *v. a.* Cuir am mi-earbsa.
Misgiving, *s.* Teagamh; mi-earbsa.
Misgovern, *v. a.* Mi-riaghal.
Misguide, *v. a.* Mi-threòraich.
Misguidance, *s.* Mi-threòrachadh.
Mishap, *s.* Mi-thapadh, droch thuiteamas, sgiorradh, tubaist.
Misinfer, *v. a.* Mi-mheasraich.
Misinform, *v. a.* Thoir fios meallta.
Misinterpret, *v. a.* Mi-bhreithnich.
Misjudge, *v. a.* Thoir mi-bhreth.
Mislay, *v. a.* Mi-shuidhich.
Mislead, *v. a.* Mi-threòraich.
Mislike, *v. a.* Bi mi-thoilichte le.
Mislike, *s.* Mi-thoileachadh, gràin.
Misly, *adj.* Ciurach, braonach.
Mismanage, *v. a.* Mi-bhuilich.
Mismanagement, *s.* Mi-bhuileachadh.
Misname, *v. a.* Thoir frith-ainm.
Misnomer, *s.* Mi-ainmeachadh.
Misobserve, *v. a.* Mi-bheachdaich.
Misogamist, *s.* Fuathadair pòsaidh.
Misogyny, *s.* Fuath bhan.
Misorder, *v. a.* Mi-òrduich, mi-stiùr.
Mispend, *v. a.* Mi-chaith, mi-bhuilich.
Mispersuasion, *s.* Droch-iompaidh.
Misplace, *v. a.* Mi-shuidhich.
Mispoint, *v. a.* Mi-phoncaich.
Misprint, *s.* Mearachd clò-bhualaidh.
Misprison, *s.* Tàire dearmad, dìchuimhne, ceiltinn; mearachd.
Misproportion, *s.* Mi-chuimse.
Misrecite, *v. a.* Mi-abair.
Misreckon, *v. a.* Mi-chunnt.
Misrelate, *v. a.* Mi-innis.
Misreport, *v. a.* Mi-aithris.
Misrepresent, *v. a.* Thoir mi-theist.
Misrule, *s.* Mi-riaghailt, buaireas.
Miss, *s.* Òigh, maighdeann uasal.
Miss, *v.* Mearachdaich, rach iomrall; mi-amais; thig gearr, caill; ionndrainn; leig seachad.
Missal, *s.* Leabhar-aifrionn.

Missile, *adj.* Tilgte leis an làimh.
Mission, *s.* Teachdaireachd.
Missionary, *s.* Teachdaire, searmonaiche, ministear-siubhail.
Missive, *s.* Litir-chumhachan.
Mist, *s.* Ceò, eitheach, ceathach, braon.
Mistake, *v.* Rach iomrall, mi-thuig.
Mistake, *s.* Mearachd, iomrall.
Mistime, *v. a.* Mi-thràthaich.
Mistiness, *s.* Ceòthachd, neulachd.
Mistletoe, *s.* An t-uil-ìoc.
Mistress, *s.* Banna-mhaighstear; bann-seilbheadair, bean-theagaisg, coimhleapach.
Mistrust, *s.* An-earbsa, teagamh.
Mistrustful, *adj.* Mi-earbsach.
Mistrustfully, *adv.* Gu h-an-earbsach, gu neo-dhòchasach.
Misty, *adj.* Ceòthach, ceòthar, citheach; dorcha, doilleir, neulach.
Misunderstand, *v. a.* Mi-thuig.
Misunderstanding, *s.* Mi-thuigse, mearachd, mi-bhreithneachadh, aimhreit, mi-chòrdadh.
Misusage, **Misuse**, *s.* Droch bhuileachadh, mi-bhuileachadh, droch-càramh; ni-ghnàthachadh.
Mite, *s.* Fìneag; dadmunn; tùrn, an dara cuid deug do sgillinn.
Mithridate, *s.* Deoch-nimh-chasg.
Mitigate, *v. a.* Lughdaich, aotromaich; lasaich, sàmhaich, ciùinich; bogaich, maothaich.
Mitigation, *s.* Lughdachadh, aotromachadh; lasachadh, sèimheachadh; bogachadh, maothachadh.
Mitre, *s.* Crùn-easbuig; coron.
Mitred, *adj.* Crùnte mar easbuig.
Mittens, *s.* Meatagan, làmhainean.
Mittimus, *s.* Òrdugh prìosanachaidh.
Mix, *v. a.* Measgaich.
Mixture, *s.* Measgachadh, measgadh.
Mizenmast, *s.* An crann-deiridh.
Moan, *v.* Caoidh, guil, gearain, caoin, dean cumha, dean tuireadh.
Moan, *s.* Caoidh, gearan, acan, iargain, caoineadh, tuireadh.
Moat, *s.* Dìg, ruith uisge mar dhìdean.
Mob, *s.* Prasgan-buairidh, gràisg.
Mob, *v. a.* Tionail gràisg.
Mobby, *v.* Leann-buntàta.
Mobility, *s* Gluasadachd; gràisg.
Moble, *v. a.* Sgeadaich gu cearbach.
Mock, *v. a.* Mag, dean fanaid.
Mock, *adj.* Meallta, feallsa, breugach.
Mockable, *adj.* Ion-fhochaideach.
Mockery, *s.* Sgeigeireachd, fanaid.
Mode, *s.* Modh, dòigh, gnè; seòl, cumadh; rian, gnàths.
Model, *s.* Cumadh; riaghailt, tomhas.
Model, *v. a.* Dealbh, cùm.
Moderate, *adj.* Ciùin, stuama, sèimh; measarra, cuimseach; meadhonach, cùibheasach.
Moderate, *v. a.* Ciùinich, ceannsaich, dean measarra; riaghail.
Moderately, *adv.* Gu fòil.
Moderation, *s.* Ciùineachd, stuaim.
Moderator, *s.* Fear-riaghlaidh.
Modern, *adj.* Ùr, neo-shean.
Modernise, *v. a.* Dean ùr, ùraich.
Modest, *adj.* Nàrach, màlda, stuama; banail, beusach, bìth.
Modesty, *s.* Beusachd, màldachd, stuamachd, measarrachd.
Modicum, *s.* Cuibhrionn bheag.
Modification, *s.* Atharrachadh.
Modify, *v. a.* Atharraich, cùm; ciùinich, taisich; lagaich.
Modish, *adj.* Fasanta, nòsach.
Modishness, *s.* Fasantachd, nòsachd.
Modulate, *v. a.* Cuir fonn-ciùil air.
Modulation, *s.* Binneas; gleus.
Modulator, *s.* Fear-gleusaidh.
Modus, *s.* Dìoladh deachaimh.
Moiety, *s.* Leth, leth-earrann.
Moil, *v.* Eabraich, salaich, làbanaich; sgìthich, sàraich; oibrich 's an làthaich, luidrich.
Moist, *adj.* Àitidh, bog, tais.
Moisten, *v. a.* Taisich, bogaich.
Moistness, *s.* Àitidheachd, buige.
Moisture, *s.* Taiseachd, fliche, buige.
Mole, *s.* Ball-dòrain, miun; famh, ùir-reodhadh.
Molecatcher, *s.* Famhoir.
Molehill, *s.* Famh-thòrr.
Molest, *v. a.* Cuir dragh air, buair.
Molestation, *s.* Aimheal, dragh.
Molewarp, **Mouldwarp**, *s.* Famh.
Mollient, *adj.* Maoth, taiseachail.
Mollification, *s.* Maothachadh.
Mollify, *v. a.* Bogaich, taisich, maothaich; ceannsaich, ciùinich; lasaich.
Molosses, **Molasses**, *s.* Druaip an t-siùcair.
Molten, *part. pass.* from to *melt.* Leaghte.
Molting, **Moulting**, *part. a.* A' cur nan itean, a' tilgeadh a' bhreun fhionnaidh, a' tilgeadh nan cabar, &c.
Moly, *s.* Creamh fhiadhaich.
Mome, *s.* Burraidh, amhlar; post.
Moment, *s.* Toirt, brìgh, toradh, luach, tiota.
Momentary, *adj.* Grad-ùineach, goirid.
Momentous, *adj.* Cudthromach, toirteil, feumail.
Monachal, *adj.* Manachail.

MONACHISM, *s.* Beatha-manaich.
MONADE, *s.* Ni neo-fhaicsinneach.
MONARCH, *s.* Àrd-righ.
MONARCHIAL, *adj.* Àrd rioghail.
MONARCHICAL, *adj.* Aon-fhlathach.
MONARCHY, *s.* Aon-fhlathachd.
MONASTERY, *s.* Manachainn.
MONASTIC, *adj.* Manachail.
MONDAY, *s.* Di-luain.
MONEY, *s.* Airgead-làimhe.
MONEYED, *adj.* Airgeadach, beartach.
MONEYLESS, *adj.* Gun airgead, bochd.
MONGER, *s.* Fear reic a's ceannaich.
MONGREL, *adj.* Eadar-dà-ghnè.
MONGREL, *s.* Beathach-eadar-dà-ghnè.
MONISH, *v. a.* Comhairlich.
MONISHER, *s.* Fear-comhairle.
MONITION, *s.* Earail.
MONITIVE, *adj.* Comhairleach.
MONITOR, *s.* Comhairleach.
MONITORY, *adj.* Comhairleach.
MONITORY, *s.* Comhairle.
MONK, *s.* Manach; (*etymo.* Math-neach, math *and* neach.)
MONKEY, *s.* Ap, apa, amadan gòrach.
MONKISH, *adj.* Manachail, aonarach.
MONOCULAR, MONOCULOUS, *adj.* Leth-shùileach, aon-sùileach.
MONODY, *s.* Òran-mòr.
MONOGAMY, *s.* Aon-phòsadh.
MONOLOGUE, *s.* Féin-labhairt.
MONOMACHY, *s.* Còmhrag-dithis.
MONOPETALOUS, *adj.* Aon-duilleagach.
MONOPOLIST, *s.* Léir-cheannaiche.
MONOPOLIZE, *v. a.* Léir-cheannaich.
MONOPOLY, *s.* Léir-chomas-reic.
MONOSYLLABLE, *s.* Facal aon lididh.
MONOSTICH, *s.* Ochd-rann.
MONOTONY, *s.* Aon-ghuthachd.
MONOTONOUS, *adj.* Aon-ghuthach.
MONSTER, *s.* Uile-bheist; ni mi-nàdurrach, ni gràineil; cuis-uabhais.
MONSTROUS, *adj.* Mi-nàdurra; fuath-asach, uabhasach, oillteil, sgreat-aidh, gairsinneach.
MONERO, *s.* Curac-mharcachd.
MONTH, *s.* Mìos, mì.
MONTHLY, *adj.* Mìosach, mìosail.
MONUMENT, *s.* Barpa, càrn-cuimhne; carragh, leac.
MONUMENTAL, *adj.* Barpail, càrnach.
MOOD, *s.* Suidheachadh; seòl, gleus, dòigh, corraich, fraoch, friodh.
MOODY, *adj.* Feargach, corrach; gruamach, greannach, frionasach, cas, bras, tiamhaidh; trom, mulad-ach, brònach, dubhach.
MOON, *s.* Gealach, rè, mìos.
MOON-BEAM, *s.* Gath-gealaich.
MOON-CALF, *s.* Uile-bheist, burraidh.
MOON-EYED, *adj.* Ròsp-shuileach.
MOONLIGHT, *s.* Solus-gealaich.
MOONSTRUCK, *adj.* Mearanach.
MOOR, *s.* Sliabh mhonadh; càthair, mòinteach; duine-dubh.
MOOR, *v.* Tilg acair; bi acraichte.
MOORHEN, *s.* Cearc-fhraoich.
MOORING, *s.* Cala, acarsaid.
MOORISH, MOORY, *adj.* Sliabhach; mòinteachail, mònadail; mar dhaoine-dubha.
MOORLAND, *s.* Sliabh, cathair.
MOOSE, *s.* An lòn Americanach.
MOOT, *v. a.* Tagair, connspaidich.
MOOT-*CASE* or *POINT*, *s.* Cùis-thag-raidh theugamhach.
MOOTED, *adj.* Spìont á bun.
MOP, *s.* Moibeal, maban, sguab-làir.
MOPE, *v. n.* Bi trom, bi neo-shunnt-ach, bi tùrsach, bi turra-chadalach.
MOPE, MOPUS, *s.* Rongaire; aisliniche.
MOPPET, MOPSEY, *s.* Fear-brèige; duine-maide; liùbhag.
MORAL, *adj.* Modhannail, beusach, beus-theagasgail.
MORAL, *s.* Modh, modhalachd, beus; dheagh bheus.
MORALIST, *s.* Fear-teagaisg dheagh bheus, fear-beusach.
MORALITY, *s.* Deagh beusachd, modh-alachd, subhailcean.
MORALIZE, *v.* Dean deagh-bheusach; teagaisg deagh-bheusan.
MORALIZER, *s.* Fear-dheanamh dheagh bheus, fear-teagaisg bheus.
MORALS, *s.* Deagh-bheusan, modh-annan, subhailcean.
MORASS, *s.* Boglach, mòinteach.
MORBID, *adj.* Euslainteach, galarach.
MORBIDNESS, *s.* Euslainteachd.
MORBIFIC, *adj.* Galarach, mi-fhallain.
MORBOSE, *adj.* Euslan, galarach.
MORDACIOUS, *adj.* Beumach; sgobach.
MORE, *adv.* Ni's mò, ni bu mhò; tuill-eadh, barrachd, fòs.
MORE, *s.* Tuilleadh, barrachd.
MOREOVER, *adv.* Os bàrr, a' bharr a thuilleadh, air so.
MORION, *s.* Clogaid, ceann-bheairt.
MORN, MORNING, *s.* Madainn.
MOROSE, *adj.* Gruamach, mùgach.
MOROSENESS, *s.* Gruamaiche, mùg-aiche, doirbhe, dùire.
MORPHEW, *s.* Leus-mùire, luibhre.
MORRIS-DANCE, *s.* Dàmhs-nan-clag.
MORROW, *s.* Am màireach.
MORSE, *s.* An t-each-mara.
MORSEL, *s.* Greim, criomag, crioman, mìr, bideag, rud beag.
MORT, *s.* Iolach séilge.

MORTAL, *adj.* Bàsmhor; bàs-dhualach, marbhtach, sgriosail; daonna, talmhaidh.
MORTAL, *s.* Duine, bith-bàsmhor creutair-talmhaidh.
MORTALITY, *s.* Bàsmhorachd; marbhtachd; nàdur-daonna.
MORTAR, *s.* Aol-tàthaidh; soitheach pronnaidh; gunna-thoirm-shligean.
MORTGAGE, *v. a.* Thoir fearan seachad an geall airgeid.
MORTGAGEE, *s.* Fear-gabhail fearain an geall argeid.
MORTGAGER, *s.* Fear-tabhairt fearain an geall airgeid.
MORTIFICATION, *s.* Grodadh, breothadh; claoidh, doilghios.
MORTIFY, *v.* Claoidh, marbh, thoir bàs; ceannsaich, smachdaich; ìslich, cuir doilghios air; breoth, grod.
MORTISE, *s.* Toll-alpaidh.
MORTMAIN, *s.* Seilbh-beatha.
MORTUARY, *s.* Dìleab do 'n eaglais.
MOSAIC, MOSAICAL, *adj.* A bhuineas do lagh agus do fhrithealadh Mhaois; bhreac-dhualadh air clachan, &c.
MOSCHETO, *s.* Creathlag Innseanach.
MOSQUE, *s.* An eaglais Thurcach.
MOSS, *s.* Mòinteach, mòine; còinneach, coinnteach, liath-sgrath.
MOSSY, *adj.* Mòinteachail, còinneachail, coinnteachail., liathsgrathach.
MOST, *adj.* A's mò, a' chuid a's mò.
MOST, *s.* A chuid a's mò, a' chuid mhòr, a' mhòr chuid.
MOSTLY, *adv.* Mar a's trice, cha mhòr nach, 's beach nach.
MOTE, *s.* Dùradan, smùirnean.
MOTH, *s.* Leòman, raodan, cnuimh.
MOTH-EATEN, *part.* Raodanaite.
MOTHER, *s.* Màthair; deasgann.
MOTHERLESS, *adj.* Gun mhàthair.
MOTHERLY, *adj.* Màithreil; caomh.
MOTHERY, *adj.* Deasgainneach.
MOTHY, *adj.* Leòmanach, raodanach.
MOTION, *s.* Gluasad, car; deò, beatha; siubhal, ceum; tairgse, iarrtas, comhairle.
MOTIONLESS, *adj.* Neo-ghluasadach.
MOTIVE, *s.* Cuspair-gluasaid, aobharbrosnachaidh.
MOTLEY, *adj.* Iom-dhathach, iomghnèitheach, measgaichte.
MOTTO, *s.* Facal-suaicheantais.
MOVE, *v.* Gluais, atharraich, caraich; cuir air ghluasad; cuir iompaidh air, aom gu; feargaich, brosnaich; buair, luaisg; imich, siubhail, triall, bi beò, bi gluasadach.
MOVEABLE, *adj.* So-ghluasad.
MOVEABLES, *s.* Earnais, treathlaich.
MOVELESS, *adj.* Do-ghluasad.
MOVEMENT, *s.* Gluasad, carachadh.
MOVING, *part. adj.* Drùighteach, brònach.
MOULD, *s.* Liathtas; ùir, talamh; molltair, cumadair; dealbh, cruth, cumachd.
MOULD, *v. a.* Dealbh, riochdaich, cùm; lobh, fàs liath.
MOULDER, *v.* Crìon, tionndaidh gu luaithre; fàs 'na d' luaithre.
MOULDERING, *part. adj.* A' tionndadh gu ùir, a' tionndadh gu smùir.
MOULDINESS, *s.* Liathtas.
MOULDING, *s.* Stiom-oire.
MOULDY, *adj.* Air liathadh, liath.
MOULT, *v. a.* Tilg na h-itean.
MOUND, *s.* Tòrr, tom tolm, bruachdhìona, fàl-sgéithe.
MOUNT, *s.* Sliabh, beinn, cnoc.
MOUNT, *v.* Dìrich, streap; cuir air muin eich; sgeadaich, grinnich; éirich suas; leum air muin eich; rach air freiceadan.
MOUNTAIN, *s.* Sliabh, beinn, monadh, cruach, meall, màm, tòrr, àrd, aonach, fireach.
MOUNTAINEER, *s.* Braidheach, Gäël, fear-sléibhe, fear-monaidh.
MOUNTAINOUS, *adj.* Sléibhteach, beanntach, monadail, garbh.
MOUNTEBANK, *s.* Lighiche-bréige, baoth-cleasaiche.
MOUNTING, *s.* Spàngan-sgeadachaidh.
MOURN, *v.* Caoidh, caoin, guil; bi fo bhròn, dean caoidh, bi tùrsach.
MOURNER, *s.* Fear-bròin, fear-caoidh.
MOURNFUL, *adj.* Brònach, tùrsach, muladach, dubhach, tiamhaidh.
MOURNING, *s.* Bròn, mulad, caoidh, tuireadh, tùrsa, caoineadh, cumha; éideadh-bròin.
MOUSE, *s.* Luch.
MOUSER, *s.* Sealgair-luch.
MOUSE-TRAP, *s.* Cặt-cnaige.
MOUSE-EAR, *s.* Lŭs-nam-mial.
MOUTH, *s.* Beul, craos; clab.
MOUTH, *v.* Labhair àrd, glaodh, gabh làn beòil; glac 'n ad chraos.
MOUTHFUL, *s.* Lan-beòil; balgum.
MOUTHLESS, *adj.* Gun bheul.
MOW, *v.* Gearr, buain le fàladair; speal, sgud, gearr sìos.
MOW, *s.* Mìr, cruach, tŭdan.
MOW-BURN, *s.* Brachadh-dearg.
MOWER, *s.* Spealadair.
MOXA, or MOXO, *s.* Coinnteach Innseannach.
MUCH, *adv.* Mòran, iomadh, ioma.

Much, *s.* Mòran; cùs ro, glé.
Mucid, *adj.* Sleamhainn, sliobach, ceòthach, àitidh, air liathadh.
Mucidness, *s.* Sleamhnachd, liathtachd, àiteachd.
Mucilage, *s.* Slamban, sleamhnachd.
Mucilaginous, *adj.* Slambanach, slambach; barragach; sleamhainn.
Muck, *s.* Inneir, mathachadh; aolach, salchar, buachar.
Muck, *v. a.* Mathaich, innearaich.
Muckhill, *s.* Otrach, dùnan, sitig.
Muckiness, *s.* Otrach, salachar, anabas, mosaiche.
Muck-worm, *s.* A' chnuimheagbhuachair, a' chnuimh-aolaich.
Mucky, *adj.* Otrachail, salach.
Mucous, **Muculent**, *adj.* Ronnach, sglongach, smugach, slamach.
Mucronated, *adj.* Barra-chaol.
Mucus, *s.* Ronn, sglong, sglongaid.
Mud, *s.* Eabar, làthach, poll, clàbar.
Muddiness, *s.* Sal, druaipealachd.
Muddle, *v. a.* Cuir troi' chéile, salaich, truaill; cuir air leth-dhaoraich, dean frŏganach, dean sŏganach.
Muddy, *adj.* Salach, drabastach; eabarach; gruamach, dorcha.
Mudsuccer, *s.* Calum-dubh.
Muff, *s.* Mùtan, làmh-bhian.
Muffle, *v.* Ceil, cuir sgàil air, còmhdaich; paisg, trŭs.
Muffler, *s.* Gnùis-bhrat.
Mufti, *s.* Àrd-shagart Turcach.
Mug, *s.* Soitheach òil, cuach, noigean.
Muggish, **Muggy**, *adj.* Tais, fliuch, àitidh; doilleir, mùgach.
Mughouse, *s.* Taigh leanna, taigh-òil.
Mugwort, *s.* An liath-lŭs, gròban.
Mulatto, *s.* Neach-lachdunn.
Mulberry, *s.* Smeur, maol-dhearc.
Mulct, *s.* Ùbhladh, peanas.
Mule, *s.* Muileid, muilead.
Muller, *s.* Brâ-bhleith dhathan.
Mullet, *s.* An cearbanach.
Mulligrubs, *s.* An greim-moinaich.
Mullock, *s.* Anabas, mosaiche.
Multangular, *adj.* Ioma-chèarnach.
Multifarious, *adj.* Ioma-ghnèitheach, ioma-chùiseach.
Multifidous, *adj.* Iom' earrainneach.
Multiform, *adj.* Ioma-chruthach.
Multiformity, *s.* Ioma chruthachd.
Multilateral, *adj.* Ioma-shliosach.
Multilineal, *adj.* Ioma-shreathach.
Multiloquous, *adj.* Ioma-bhriathrach, iom'-fhaclach.
Multinominal, *adj.* Iom'-ainmeach.
Multiparous, *adj.* Ioma-ghinteach.
Multipede, *s.* Ioma-chasach.
Multiple, *adj.* Ioma-fillteach.
Multipliable, *adj.* So-mheudachadh.
Multiplicand, *s.* Àireamh a mheudaichear le àireamh eile.
Multiplication, *s.* Meudachadh.
Multiplicator, *s.* Am meudachair.
Multiplicity, *s.* Iomadachd.
Multiplier, *s.* Fear-meudachaidh.
Multiply, *v. a.* Siolaich, lìonmhoraich; meudaich.
Multipotent, *adj.* Ioma-chumhachdach, ioma-bhuadhach.
Multisonous, *adj.* Ioma-ghuthach.
Multitude, *s.* Mòr-shluagh; cruinneachadh, dòmhlachadh.
Multitudinous, *adj.* Iom'-fhillteach.
Multocular, *adj.* Ioma-shùileach.
Multure, *s.* Meilteir, cìs, molltair.
Mum! *interj.* Tosd! éisd!
Mum, *s.* Leann cruithneachd.
Mumble, *v.* Dean prondal bruidhne, labhair gu glugach, leth labhair.
Mumbler, *s.* Glugaire, fear manndach, fear-liodach.
Mumm, *v. a.* Dean cluich-chidhis.
Mummer, *s.* Fear-cidhis, chleasaiche.
Mummery, *s.* Balbh-chleasachd.
Mummy, *s.* Corp-spiosraichte.
Mump, *v. a.* Cagainn; abair gu manntach; iarr déirc.
Mumper, *s.* Fear-iarraidh dhéirc.
Mumps, *s* Gruaim, tosd-fhearg, stŭrd; stŭirt; an tinneas-plocach.
Mundane, *adj.* Saoghalta, talmhaidh.
Mundanity, *s.* Saoghalachd.
Mundation, *s.* Glanadh, sgŭradh.
Mundify, *v. a.* Glan, dean glan.
Munerary, *adj.* Tìodhlacail.
Mungrel, *adj.* Dialoin.
Municipal, *adj.* Comunnach; a bhuineas do bhaile mòr.
Munificence, *s.* Toirbheartas.
Munificent, *adj.* Toirbheartach.
Muniment, *s.* Daingneach, dìdean; dìon, tèarmann; daingneachdsgrìobhaidh, còraichean, ranntanan bann-sgrìobhte.
Munition, *s.* Daingneach, dìon.
Mural, *adj.* A bhuineas do bhalla.
Murder, *s.* Mort, murt.
Murder, *v. a.* Mort, dean mort.
Murderer, *s.* Mortair, fear-casraidh.
Murderous, *adj.* Mortach, fuilteach.
Muriatic, *adj.* Saillte.
Murk, *s.* Moignean mheas, dorchadas.
Murky, *adj.* Dorcha, doilleir, dubh.
Murmur, *s.* Borbhan, torman, dùrdan, crònan; monmhor, gearan, talach, cànran.
Murmur, *v. a.* Dean borbhan, dean

crònan, dean torman, dean mon-mhor.
MURMURER, *s.* Gearanaiche, fear-tal-aich, fear-cànrain.
MURRAIN, *s.* Tinneas-dubh na spréidhe.
MURREY, *adj.* Dù-dhearg, dû-ruadh.
MUSCLE, *s.* Féith, feith-lùthaidh.
MUSCOSENESS, MUSCOSITY, *s.* Coinn-teach, coinneach.
MUSCULAR, *adj.* Fèitheach, neart-mhor, stairbeanta, laidir.
MUSE, *v.* Beachd-smuainich, cnuas-aich, trom-smuainich.
MUSE, *s.* Buaidh na bàrdachd; *The muses.* A' cheòlraidh.
MUSEUM, *s.* Taigh-iongantais.
MUSHROOM, *s.* Ballag-bhuachair.
MUSIC, *s.* Ceòl, binneas, fonn.
MUSICAL, *adj.* Ceòlmhor, bìnn.
MUSICIAN, *s.* Fear-ciùil.
MUSING, *s.* Beachd-smuainteachadh.
MUSK, *s.* Seòrsa, deagh boltraich.
MUSKET, *s.* Musg, gunna-saighdear.
MUSKETEER, MUSQUETEER, *s.* Saigh-dear-musgaide.
MUSKETOON, *s.* Gearr-ghunna.
MUSKY, *adj.* Cùbhraidh, boltrachail.
MUSLIN, *s.* Anart-grinn, péarluinn.
MUSROL, *s.* Iall-sròine sréine.
MUSSEL, *s.* Feusgan, clab-dubh.
MUSSULMAN, *s.* Mahomatanach.
MUST, *verb imperf.* Feumaidh, feumar, 's éigin, b' éigin, 's fheudar, b' fheudar, &c.
MUSTACHES, MUSTACHOES, *s.* Caisean-feusaig, feusag bil'-uachdair.
MUSTARD, *s.* Sgeallan.
MUSTER, *v. n.* Cruinnich, co-chruinn-ich, truis, tionail.
MUSTER, *s.* Sealladh airm, feachd-shealladh; cruinneachadh, feach-thional buidheann.
MUSTER-MASTER, *s.* Fear-cruinneach-aidh shaighdearan.
MUSTER-ROLL, *s.* Ainm-chlàr feachd.
MUSTINESS, *s.* Liathtas, àiteachd.
MUSTY, *adj.* Àitidh, mùsgach, dong-aidh, liath; trom, lunndach.
MUTABILITY, *s.* Caochlaidheachd.
MUTABLE, *adj.* Caochlaidheach.
MUTATION, *s.* Atharrachadh.
MUTE, *adj.* Balbh, tosdach, bìth.
MUTE, *s.* Balbhan, balbh.
MUTELY, *adv.* Gu tosdach.
MUTENESS, *s.* Tosdachd, balbhachd.
MUTILATE, *v. a.* Ciurramaich, gearr dheth, sguidh deth.
MUTILATION, *s.* Ciurramachadh.
MUTINE, MUTINEER, *s.* Fear-ceann-airc, fear-àr-a mach.
MUTINOUS, *adj.* Ceannairceach.
MUTINY, *v. n.* Dean àr-a-mach.
MUTINY, *s.* Ar-a-mach, ceannairc.
MUTTER, *v.* Dean dranndan, dean dùrdan, dean gearain, talaich.
MUTTON, *s.* Muilt-fheoil; caora.
MUTTON-FIST, *s.* Garbh-dhòrn-dearg.
MUTUAL, *adj.* A réir a' chéile, aon-tachail, mu seach, a bhuineas do dhithis.
MUTUALITY, *s.* Co-iasad, coingheall.
MUZZLE, *s.* Beul; bus-iall, glas-ghuib.
MUZZLE, *v.* Bus-iallaich, cuir glas-ghuib, glomharaich.
MY, *pron. poss.* Mo, m'.
MYOGRAPHY, *s.* Féith-eòlas.
MYOLOGY, *s.* Féith-theagasg.
MYOTOMY, *s.* Féith-shnasadh.
MYRIAD, *s.* Àireamh, dheich mìle.
MYRMIDON, *s.* Ceatharnach-mi-mhoil.
MYRRH, *s.* Mir, spiosraidh chùraidh.
MYRTLE, *s.* Miortal, lùs cùbhraidh.
MYSELF, *pron.* Mi-féin, mise féin.
MYSTAGOGUE, *s.* Fear leigeadh ris dìomhaireachd.
MYSTERIOUS, *adj.* Domhain, dìomhair.
MYSTERIOUSLY, *adv.* Gu diamhair.
MYSTERIOUSNESS, *s.* Dìomhaireachd.
MYSTERIZE, *v. a.* Diamhairich, dorch-naich, doileirich.
MYSTERY, *s.* Dìomhaireachd.
MYSTIC, MYSTICAL, *adj.* Dìomhair, dorcha, do-thuigsinn.
MYTHOLOGICAL, *adj.* Faoin-sgeulach.
MYTHOLOGIST, *s.* Faoin-sgeulaiche.
MYTHOLOGY, *s.* Faoin sgeulachd; eachdraidh nan dia bréige.

N

N, *s.* Ceathramh litir deug na-h-aibidil.
NAB, *v. a.* Grad-ghlac, foill-ghlac.
NADIR, *s.* Am ball 's isle do'n chruinne.
NAG, *s.* Each beag; each òg.
NAIL, *s.* Ionga; tarung; tomhas dhà òirleich a's cairteal.
NAILER, *s.* Gobha thàirngnean.
NAKED, *adj.* Lonmochd; rùisgte, nochdaidh, gun arm; soilleir, fosg-ailte, lom.
NAKEDNESS, *s.* Nochdachd, luime.
NAME, *s.* Ainm; iomradh; cliù, alla.
NAME, *v. a.* Ainmich; goir air ainm.

NAMELESS, *adj.* Neo-ainmeil, gun ainm.
NAMELY, *adv.* Gu sònràichte.
NAMESAKE, *s.* Fear-cinnidh, co-ainm.
NANKEEN, *s.* Seòrsa do dh' aodach canaich.
NAP, *s.* Dùsal, pràmh; cnap.
NAPE, *s.* Alt chùl a' mhuineil.
NAPKIN, *s.* Neapuig, nèapaigin.
NAPLESS, *adj.* Gun chaitean, lom.
NAPPY, *adj.* Cobharach, ròmach.
NARABLE, *adj.* So-aithris.
NARCISSUS, *s.* Lŭs-a'-chroma-chinn.
NARCOTIC, *adj.* Cadalach, tuainealach, breisleachail.
NARRATE, *v. a.* Innis, aithris.
NARRATION, NARATIRE, *s.* Aithris, sgeul, iomradh, tuaireasgeul.
NARRATIVE, *adj.* Aithriseach, innseach.
NARRATOR, *s.* Fear-aithris, fear-innsidh, fear-eachdraidh, seanachaidh.
NARROW, *adj.* Cumhann, aimhleathan, caol, sanntach; spìocach, mosach.
NARROWLY, *adv.* Gu cumhann.
NARROWMINDED, *adj.* Sanntach, spìocach, beag-aigneach.
NARROWNESS, *s.* Cuingead, bochdainn, spìocaireachd.
NASAL, *adj.* Srònach, glòmach.
NASTILY, *adv.* Gu salach, gu truaillidh, gu drabasta.
NASTINESS, *s.* Trustaireachd; drabastachd, draosdachd, salachar.
NASTY, *adj.* Salach, mosach, truaillidh.
NATAL, *adj.* Dùthchasach.
NATION, *s.* Fine, cinneadh, cinneach, sluagh, muinntir, dùthaich, rìoghachd.
NATIONAL, *adj.* Dùthchasach, dùthchail cinneadail.
NATIVE, *adj.* Nàdurrach, gnèitheil; dùthchasach, dualach.
NATIVE, *s.* Dùthchasaiche; *plr. Natives.* Gnà-mhuinntir.
NATIVITY, *s.* Breith; tìr-bhreith.
NATURAL, *adj.* Nàdurrach, nàdurra; gnèitheil; dàimheil, caoimhneil; tlàth, dìolain.
NATURAL, *s.* Amadan, staid nàduir.
NATURALIST, *s.* Fear-eòlaich nàdurra.
NATURALIZATION, *s.* Gabhail a steach coigrich do dhùthaich.
NATURALIZE, *v. a.* Dean nàdurrach.
NATURALLY, *adv.* Gu nàdurrach.
NATURALNESS, *s.* Nàdurrachd.
NATURE, *s.* Nàdur, gnè, seòrsa; càil; mèinn; an domhan, an cruthachadh; dàimh, nàdurrachd.
NAUGHT, *adj.* Olc, aingidh, truaillidh, dona, droch.
NAUGHT, *s.* Neo-ni.
NAUGHTINESS, *s.* Droch-mhèinn, olcas.
NAUGHTY, *adj.* Olc, aingidh, dona, truaillidh, crosda, droch.
NAUSEA, *s.* Togradh gu dìobhairt.
NAUSEATE, *v.* Sgreataich; cuir sgreat air, gabh sgreat roimh.
NAUSEOUS, *adj.* Sgreataidh, sgreamhail, déisinneach, grâineil.
NAUSEOUSNESS, *s.* Sgreamhalachd, deisinneachd, sgreatachd, gràin.
NAUTICAL, *adj.* Fairgeach, cuanach.
NAVAL, *adj.* Longach, cabhlachail.
NAVE, *s.* Cìoch, cuibhle; meadhon eaglais.
NAVEL, *s.* Imleag; meadhon.
NAVIGABLE, *adj.* So-sheòladh, domhainn.
NAVIGABLENESS, *s.* Doimhneachd-uisge.
NAVIGATE, *v. a.* Seòl, thairis an luing.
NAVIGATION, *s.* Maraireachd, sgoilmhara.
NAVIGATOR, *s.* Maraiche, sgoilearmara.
NAVY, *s.* Cabhlach, luingeas-chogaidh.
NAY, *adv.* Ni-h-eadh, cha n-è.
NEAF, *s.* Dòrn.
NEAL, *v. a.* Dean tais no cruaidh le blàthas teine; adhairt.
NEAP-TIDE, *s.* Conn-tràigh.
NEAR, NEARLY, *adv.* Fagus, faisg, aig làimh, dlù; an dàimh, an cleamhnas.
NEAR, *adj.* Faisg, dlù, fagus, teann; dàimheil, dlù o; gann, spìocach.
NEARNESS, *s.* Fagusachd, dlùthachd, faisgeachd; dàimh, dìlseachd; gainne, spìocaireachd, gortachd.
NEAT, *adj.* Snasmhor, grinn, cuimir.
NEATLY, *adv.* Gu snasmhor.
NEATNESS, *s.* Snasmhorachd, grinneas, sgiultachd.
NEB, *s.* Gob eoin, beul.
NEBULOUS, *adj.* Neulach, ceòthach.
NECESSARIES, *s.* Feumalachd, goireas.
NECESSARY, *adj.* Feumail, goireasach; dualach, neo-sheachanta.
NECESSARY, *s.* Taigh-fuagairt.
NECESSITATE, *v. a.* Éignich.
NECESSITATION, *s.* Éigneachadh.
NECESSITOUS, *adj.* Aimbeartach.
NECESSITUDE, *s.* Aimbeart, gainne.
NECESSITY, *s.* Airc, éigin, aimbeart, do-sheachnaidheachd; dàn.
NECK, *s.* Muineal, amhach.
NECKCLOTH, *s.* Éideadh muineil.
NECKED, *adj.* Muinealach, sgòrnanach.
NECKLACE, *s.* Usgar-bràgaid, seudmuineil; paidearan.

Necromancer, *s.* Taracadair, fiosaiche, fàidh draoidh.
Necromancy, *s.* Taracandachd, drùidheachd, fiosachd.
Necromantic, *adj.* Fiosachdail.
Nectar, *s.* Deoch mhilis nan dia bréige.
Nectareous, Nectarine, *adj.* Milis, mar dheoch nan dée bréige.
Nectarine, *s.* Seòrsa plùmbais.
Nectary, *s.* Cuach-mhile nam flùran.
Need, Neediness, *s.* Dìth, feum, easbhuidh, airc.
Need, *v.* Feum; bi a dhìth, bi feumach.
Needful, *adj.* Feumach, bochd, truagh, ainniseach.
Needle, *s.* Snàthad; bior-gréisidh dealg na cairt-iùil.
Needlemaker, *s.* Gobha-shnàthad.
Needlework, *s.* Obair-ghréis.
Needless, *adj.* Gun fheum, dìomhain.
Needs, *adv.* Feumaidh, 's éigin.
Needy, *adj.* Bochd, ainniseach, feumach, dòghlum.
Nefarious, *adj.* Ro-aingidh, mallaichte, uamhar, grâineil, fuathasach.
Negation, *s.* Diùltadh, àicheadh.
Negative, *adj.* Diùltach, àicheanach.
Negative, *s.* Am facal, àicheadh, cha, ni.
Negatively, *adv.* Gu h-aicheadhach.
Neglect, *v. a.* Dean, dearmad; cuir suarach, dean tàir, cuir an neoshùim.
Neglect, *s.* Dearmad; dìmeas, tâir, neo-shùim, mi-chùram.
Neglectful, *adj.* Dearmadach, neochùramach; dìmeasach, neo-shuimeil.
Negligence, *s.* Dearmadachd.
Negligent, *adj.* Dearmadach, neoaireil, mi-chùramach.
Negotiate, *v. n.* Dean gnothach, thoir gu buil, thoir gu h-ìre.
Negotiation, *s.* Co-ghnothach, cùmhnant, socrachadh.
Negro, *s.* Duine-dubh.
Neigh, *s.* Guth eich, sitir.
Neigh, *v. n.* Dean sitir, dean sitrich.
Neighbour, *s.* Nàbaidh, coimhearsnach.
Neighbour, *adj.* Coimhearsnachail, nàbaidheach, dlù.
Neighbourhood, *s.* Nàbaidheachd, coimhearsnachd; luchd-coimhearsnachd.
Neighbourly, *adj.* Coingheallach, càirdeil.
Neither, *conj.* Cha, cha mhò, cha-n e, ni mò, ni h-è, &c.
Nemoral, *adj.* Badanach, doireach.
Neoteric, *adj.* Ùr, nodha, nuadh.
Nephenthe, *s.* Iocshlaint leigheis nan uile phian, &c.
Nephew, *s.* Mac peathar na bràthar.
Nephretic, *adj.* Àirneach; leigheasach air a' ghalar-fhuail.
Nerve, *s.* Féith-mhothachaidh.
Nerve, *v. a.* Neartaich, lùghaich, spionntaich.
Nerveless, *adj.* Gun lùgh, gun bhrì, gun seadh, gun bhladh.
Nervous, Nervy, *adj.* Mion-mhothachail, féitheach; neartmhor, lùghmhor.
Nervousness, *s.* Féith-laigseachd.
Nescience, *s.* Ain-fhios, aineolas.
Nest, *s.* Nead; còs, còmhnaidh.
Nest-egg, *s.* Ubh-nid.
Nestle, *v. n.* Neadaich, crùb sìos, gabh fasgadh, laidh clùth; cuir an nead, cuir an còs; eiridnich.
Nestling, *s.* Isean, eun òg 's an nead.
Net, *s.* Lìon, eangach, ribe.
Nether, *adj.* Ìochdrach; ifrinneach.
Nethermost, *adj.* A's ìochdraiche.
Netting, *s.* Obair-lìn, lìon-obair.
Nettle, *s.* Feanntag, deanntag.
Nettle, *v. a.* Brosnaich, feargaich.
Never, *adv.* Gu bràth, gu suthainn, gu dilinn, a chaoidh; riamh, am feasd: "*cha*-n fhaic mi *gu bràth* e, *cha*-n fhaca mi *riamh* e."
Nevertheless, *adj.* Gidheadh.
Neurotomy, *s.* Gearradh-fhéithean.
Neuter, Neutral, *adj.* Neo-phàirteach, nach buin do thaobh seach taobh.
Neutrality, *s.* Neo-phàirteachd.
New, *adj.* Ùr, nuadh; annasach.
Newfangled, *adj.* Mùirneach mu annasaibh, no fasanan ùra.
Newish, *adj.* Breac-ùr, a leth char ùr.
Newly, *adv.* Gu h-ùr gu h ùrail.
Newness, *s.* Ùrachd, nuadhachd.
News, *s.* Naidheachd, ùr-sgeul.
Newsmonger, *s.* Fear-naidheachd.
Newspaper, *s.* Litir-naidheachd.
Newt, *s.* Arc-luachrach bheag.
Next, *adj.* A's faisge, a's dlù, an ath.
Next, *adv.* Anns an ath àite; a rithist, an déigh sin.
Nib, *s.* Gob eoin, rinn snàthaid.
Nibbed, *adj.* Gobach, srònach.
Nibble, *v.* Spiol, creim, teum, tiolp.
Nice, *adj.* Poncail, faicilleach, eagnaidh; eagallach, fiamhach, amharusach; grinn, innealta; duilich, deac-

air; aralach, blasda; àluinn, taitneach.

Niceness, *s.* Eagnaidheachd, poncalachd, aralachd.

Nicety, *s.* Poncalachd; grinneas, innealtachd; cùram, faiceilleachd; mùirn, mùirnealachd.

Niche, *s.* Oisinn, cùil, frògh.

Nick, *s.* An ceart àm; eag.

Nick, *v. a.* Amais, buail dìreach; eagaich; thoir an car, meall.

Nickname, *s.* Frith-ainm, far-ainm, leth-ainm, aithnisg.

Nickname, *v.* Thoir frith-ainm.

Niece, *s.* Nighean bràthar no peathar.

Niggard, *s.* Spìocaire, fìneag.

Niggard, Niggardly, *adj.* Spìocach, mosach, cruaidh, gann, gortach, sanntach, lom.

Niggardish, *adj.* A leth-char spìocach, rud eigin cruaidh.

Niggardliness, *s.* Spìocaireachd.

Nigh, Nighly, *adv.* Fagus do, goirid o, làimh ri, dlù, an taice.

Night, *s.* Oidhche, dorchadas.

Nightcap, *s.* Currac-oidhche.

Nightdew, *s.* Braon-oidhche.

Nightdress, *s.* Eideadh-oidhche.

Nightfire, *s.* Teine-fionn, teine-sionnachain, teine-bianain.

Nightingale, *s.* An spìdeag.

Nightly, *adv.* Gach oidhche.

Nightman, *s.* Fear-cartaidh.

Nightmare, *s.* An trom-lighe.

Nightshade, *s.* Lŭs-na-h-oidhche.

Nightwarbling, *s.* Ceilleireachd-oidhche, canntaireach-oidhche.

Nightwatch, *s.* Faire na h-oidhche.

Nigrescent, *adj.* A' fàs dorcha, dorganta, dubh.

Nimble, *adj.* Luath, lùghmhor, clis.

Nimblefooted, *adj.* Lùgh-chasach.

Nimbleness, *s.* Luaths, clise.

Nine, *adj.* Naodh, naoidh, naoi.

Ninefold, *s.* Naoidh-fillte.

Nineteen, *adj.* Naoidh-deug.

Ninety, *adj.* Ceithir fichead 's a deich, naoidheanna. *Ir.*

Ninny, Ninnyhammer, *s.* Leth-chiallach, baothbhallan, amadan.

Ninth, *adj.* An naodhamh.

Ninthly, *adv.* Anns an naodhamh àite.

Nip, *v. a.* Spiol, pioc, teum, thoir greim á.

Nip, *s.* Bid, bideag, gòmag; osag, on-fhadh; beum.

Nippers, *s.* Turcais; greimiche.

Nipple, *s.* Sine; ceann na cìche.

Nit, *s.* Sneagha, sneamh.

Nitid, *adj.* Soilleir, boillsgeach, dèarsach, soillseach.

Nitre, *s.* Mear-shalunn.

Nitrous, *adj.* Mear-shailt.

Nitty, *adj.* Sneaghach.

Nival, *adj.* Sneachdach, làn sneachda.

Niveous, *adj.* Sneachdaidh, sneachda-gheal; geal mar shneachda.

Nizy, *s.* Gurraiceach, tamhasg.

No, *adv.* Ni, cha, cha n-e; cha n-ann, cha n-eil, ni h-eadh, &c.

No, *adj.* Air bith, neach sam bith, aon, sam bith.

Nobility, *s.* Àrd-uaisleachd, àrd-uaislean; maithean, mòr-uaislean; àrd-urram, mòrachd.

Noble, *adj.* Uasal, flathail; mòr, àrd, allail, urramach; fiùghantach, fial.

Noble, *s.* Ard-uasal, morair, flath.

Nobleman, *s.* Ard-dhuin-uasal morair, maith; *plur.* Maithean.

Nobleness, *s.* Ard-uaisleachd, flath-alachd, fiallach.

Noblesse, *s.* Mòr-uaislean.

Nobly, *adv.* Gu mòrdha, gu h-allail.

Nobody, *s.* Aon, a h-aon, aon air bith, neach, neach sam bith: *(preceded by a negative in the sentence.)*

Nocent, Nocive, *adj.* Ciontach, coireach; cronail, aimhleasach, dochannach, ciùrrail.

Noctambulist, *s.* Coisiche-cadail, fear a bhios a' coiseachd 'na chadal.

Noctuary, *s.* Cunntas-oidhche.

Nocturn, *s.* Cràbhadh-oidhche.

Nocturnal, *adj.* Oidhcheach.

Nod, *v.* Aom, claon; crith, crithich; lùb, crom, dean cromadh cinn; dean turra-chadal.

Noddle, *s.* Claigeann gun chiall.

Noddy, Noodle, *s.* Buamasdair, burraidh, bàirisg, ùmaidh.

Node, *s.* Meall, cnap, snaim.

Nodous, *adj.* Cnapanach, meallanach.

Noggin, *s.* Noigean, gogan.

Noise, *s.* Fuaim, farum, tartar, toirm, torman; glaodh, gleadhar, sgread, iolach, gàir; buaireas.

Noiseless, *adj.* Neo-fhuaimneach.

Noisiness, *s.* Fuaimneachd, farum-achd, gleadhrachd, tartarachd, bruidhneachd.

Noisome, *adj.* Cronail, ciurrail, aimh-leasach; neo-fhallain; sgreataidh, sgreamhail, déisinneach.

Noisy, *adj.* Fuaimneach, farumach, tartarach, gleadhrach, buaireasach.

Nolition, *s.* Aindeonachd, aindeoin.

Nombles, *s.* Grealach féigh.

Nomenclator, *s.* Fear toirt ainmean.

NOMENCLATURE, *s.* Facalair-ainm.
NOMINAL, *adj.* Ainmeach, fo ainm.
NOMINATE, *v. a.* Gairm air 'ainm.
NOMINATION, *s.* Còir ainmeachaidh.
NOMINATIVE, *s.* *(in grammar.)* Ainm-fhacal.
NOMINEE, *s.* Neach-ainmichte.
NONAGE, *s.* Òg-aois, aois-leanabais.
NON-APPEARANCE, *s.* Neo-theachd-an-lathair.
NON-COMPLIANCE, *s.* Diùltadh.
NON-CONFORMIST, *s.* Fear-aicheadh a' chreidimh shuidhichte.
NONCONFORMITY, *s.* Neo-aontachd.
NONDESCRIPT, *adj.* Neo-shloinnte.
NONE, *adj.* Aon, neach, ni, neach sam bith, ni sam bith ; a' bheag.
NONENTITY, *s.* Neo-bhith.
NONESUCH, *s.* Ainm ubhail àraidh.
NONEXISTENCE, *s.* Neo-bhitheachd.
NONJUROR, *s.* Fear-diùltaidh mhionnan do 'n righ dhligheach.
NONPAREIL, *s.* Barrachd, òirdheirceas, meanbh-litir clò-bhualaidh.
NONPLUS, *s.* Iomacheist.
NONPLUS, *v. a.* Cuir an iomacheist.
NONRESIDENT, *s.* Fear á dhùthaich féin, fear o'n bhaile.
NONRESIDENT, *adj.* Neo-chòmhnaidheach, neo-thàmhach.
NONRESISTANCE, *s.* Làn-ghéill.
NONRESISTANT, *adj.* Làn-ghéilleach.
NONSENSE, *s.* Neo-sheadh, bòilich.
NONSENSICAL, *adj.* Neo-sheadhach.
NONSPARING, *adj.* Neo-thròcaireach.
NONSUIT, *v. a.* Cuir stad air cùis lagha.
NOOK, *s.* Cùil, oisinn, cèarn.
NOON, *s.* Ard-mheadhon-latha.
NOONDAY, NOONTIDE, *s.* Nòin, meadhon-latha, àird' an làtha.
NOOSE, *s.* Lùb-ruithe, snaim-ruithe.
NOOSE, *v. a.* Snaim, rib, cuir an sàs.
NOR, *conj.* No, ni mò, ni's mò, n'as mò, cha mhò.
NORMAL, *adj.* Riaghailteach.
NORTH, *s.* An àirde-tuath ; tuath.
NORTHERLY, NORTHERN, NORTHWARD, *adj.* Tuathach, tuath, á tuath.
NORTHEAST, *s.* An àird' an ear-thuath.
NORTHSTAR, *s.* Reull na h-àirde tuath.
NORTHWARD, *adv.* Mu thuath.
NORTHWEST, *s.* An àird' an iar-thuath.
NORTHWIND, *s.* A' ghaoth á tuath.
NORWEGIAN, *s.* and *adj.* Lochlunnach.
NOSE, *s.* Sròn ; fàile, sicireachd.
NOSE, *v.* Srònaisich, gabh fàile.
NOSEGAY, *s.* Giobag bhlàth-luibhean.
NOSSLE, *s.* Rinn-a-mach, iomal.
NOSOLOGY, *s.* Eòlas, ghalaran.
NOSTRIL, *s.* Cuinnean, pollair.
NOSTRUM, *s.* Leigheas dìomhair.
NOT, *adv.* Cha, ni, cha-n é, ni h-eadh.
NOTABLE, *adj.* Ainmeil, sònraichte.
NOTABLENESS, *s.* Ainmealachd.
NOTARY, *s.* Nòtair, fear-lagha.
NOTATION, *s.* Pùngachadh, cur sìos.
NOTCH, *s.* Eag, gàg, peasg.
NOTE, *s.* Comharradh ; fios, aire ; inbhe, cliù, iomradh ; mì-chliù, tàir ; pong-chiùil ; cuimhneachan ; litir bheag ; bann, bann-sgrìobhte ; mìneachadh.
NOTE, *v. a.* Comharraich, cuir sios, thoir fainear, beachdaich.
NOTED, *part.* Ainmeil, sònraichte.
NOTEDNESS, *s.* Ainmealachd.
NOTELESS. *adj.* Neo-ainmeil.
NOTHING, *s.* Neo-ni, dad, sìon.
NOTHINGNESS, *s.* Neo-nitheachd.
NOTICE, *s.* Aire, beachd ; fios, sanas.
NOTICE, *v. a.* Beachdaich, thoir fainear, thoir an aire.
NOTIFICATION, *s.* Cur-an-céill.
NOTIFY, *v. a.* Cuir an céill, foillsich.
NOTION, *s.* Breithneachadh, smuain.
NOTIONAL, *adj.* Inntinneach, beachdach.
NOTORIETY, *s.* Fiosrachadh follaiseach.
NOTORIOUS, *adj.* Comharraichte ainmeil, suaicheanta.
NOTORIOUSNESS, *s.* Allail.
NOTT, *v. a.* Gearr, bearr, lomair.
NOTWITHSTANDING, *conj.* Gidheadh.
NOTUS, *s.* A' ghaoth á deas.
NOUGHT, *s.* Neo-ni.
NOUN, *s.* Ainm, ainm-ni.
NOURISH, *v. a.* Àraich, tog, eiridnich
NOURISHABLE, *adj.* So-àraich, so-thogail, so-bheathachadh.
NOURISHMENT, *s.* Beathachadh, àrach.
NOVATION, *s.* Nuadhachadh, mùthadh, atharrachadh.
NOVEL, *adj.* Nuadh, annasach, ùr.
NOVELIST, *s.* Ùr-sgeulaiche.
NOVELTY, *s.* Ùrachd, annas.
NOVEMBER, *s.* Ceud-mhìos a' gheamhraidh.
NOVERCAL, *adj.* Muimeach.
NOVICE, *s.* Neach neo-theòma, neach aineolach, ùr-chreideach.
NOVITIATE, *s.* Ùr-thoiseach.
NOVITY, *s.* Urachd, annas.
NOW, *adv.* A nise, an dràsta, an ceartuair, 's an àm so, 'sa' cheart àm, air an uair.
NOWADAYS, *adv.* Anns na làithibh so.
NOWHERE, *adv.* An àite sam bith : *with a preceding negative.*

NOWISE, *ad.* Idir, air dòigh sam bith: *requiring a negative to precede.*
NOXIOUS, *adj.* Ciurrail, cronail, dochannach; neo-fhallain.
NOXIOUSNESS, *s.* Dochannachd, neo-fhallaineachd.
NOZLE, *s.* Smeachan, bus, gnos.
NUBBLE, *v. a.* Spuaic, dean brùite.
NUBIFEROUS, *adj.* Neulach.
NUBILATE, *v. a.* Neulaich, dorchaich.
NUBILE, *adj.* Infhir, aig aois pòsaidh.
NUCIFEROUS, *adj.* Cnòdhach, cnùdhach.
NUCLEUS, *s.* Eitean, mathair-iongarach.
NUDATION, *s.* Lomadh, rùsgadh.
NUDE, *adj.* Lom, rùisgte, lomnochd.
NUDITY, *s.* Lom, nochdachd, luime.
NUGACITY, NUGALITY, *s.* Gusgul, briot, pronna-ghlòir.
NUGATORY, *adj.* Faoin, diamhain, baoth, gun fhiù.
NUISANCE, *s.* Trustaireachd, salachar.
NULL, *s.* Ni gun fheun, gun stàth.
NULL, *adj.* Neo-stàthach, gun fheum.
NULLITY, *s.* Neo-thairbh; neo-bhìth.
NUMB, *adj.* Fuar-rag, rag le fuachd.
NUMB, *v. a.* Meilich, ragaich le fuachd.
NUMBER, *v. a.* Àir, cunnt, dean suas.
NUMBER, *s.* Mòran, iomadh; iomadaidh àireamh, cunntas, uimhir, uibhir; fonn, rannachd.
NUMBERER, *s.* Fear-àireamh.
NUMBERLESS, *adj.* Gun-àireamh.
NUMBNESS, *s.* Marbh-fhuachd.
NUMERABLE, *adj.* So-àireamh.
NUMERAL, *adj.* Àireamhach.
NUMERARY, *adj.* A bhuineas do dh' àireamh.
NUMERATION, *s.* Àireamhachadh.
NUMERATOR, *s.* Fear-àireamh.
NUMERICAL, *adj.* Àireamhail.
NUMERIST, *s.* Uaimhiriche.
NUMEROUS, *adj.* Lìonmhor, iomadaidh, iomadach.
NUMMARY, *adj.* Airgeadach.
NUMSKULL, *s.* Ploc-cheann, amadan.
NUN, *s.* Cailleach-dhubh, piuthar-bhochd; tè aonaranach.
NUNCHION, *s.* Biadh-eadar-dha-thràth.
NUNCIO, *s.* Teachdaire o'n Phàpa.
NUNCUPATIVE, NUNCUPATORY, *adj.* A chuireas an céill gu follaiseach, le càinnt beoil.
NUNNERY, *s.* Cill chailleacha-dubha.
NUPTIAL, *adj.* A bhuineas do phòsadh.
NUPTIALS, *s.* Pòsadh, banais.
NURSE, *s.* Banaltrum, bean-eiridnidh.
NURSE, *v. a.* Altrum, àraich, eiridnich.
NURSERY, *s.* Gàradh-altrum; seòmar-altrum, seòmar cloinne.
NURSING, *s.* Banaltrumachd.
NURSLING, *s.* Dalta, bann-dalta.
NURTURE, *s.* Àrach, teachd-an-tìr, lòn, oilean; fòghlum.
NURTURE, *v. a.* Àraich, tog suas, teagaisg, fòghlum, ionnsaich.
NUSTLE, *v. a.* Caidrìch; cniadaich.
NUT, *s.* Cnò, cìoch cuibhle.
NUTATION, *s.* Clisgeadh, oilt-chrith.
NUTGALL, *s.* Am buicean-daraich.
NUTMEG, *s.* A' chnò-mheannt.
NUTRICATION, *s.* Seòl-beathachaidh.
NUTRICIOUS, NUTRITIVE, *adj.* Beathachail, àrachail.
NUTRICTION, *s.* Buaidh-àraich.
NUTRIMENT, *s.* Beathachadh, lòn.
NUTRIMENTAL, *adj.* Beathachail, biadhar, àrachail.
NUTRITURE, *s.* Biadhadh, beathachadh, àrach.
NUT-TREE, *s.* Craobh-chnò.
NUZZLE, *v. a.* Falaich do cheann mar ni leanabh.
NYMPH, *s.* Ban-dia nan coilltean, ainnir, rìbhinn, maighdean.

O

O, *s.* Cùigeamh litir deug na h-aibidil.
O! *interjection.* O! a!
OAF, *s.* Amadan, ùmaidh, ònaid.
OAFISH, *adj.* Baoth, amadanach.
OAFISHNESS, *s.* Baoghaltachd.
OAK, *s.* Darag, darach.
OAKAPPLE, *s.* Cnò-dharaich.
OAKEN, *adj.* Daraich, do dharach.
OAKLING, *s.* Òg-dharach.
OAKUM, *s.* Calcas.
OAR, *s.* Ràmh, suaibe.
OAR, *v.* Iomair, dean iomaradh.
OATCAKE, *s.* Bonnach-coirce.
OATEN, *adj.* Corcach, coirceach, coirce.
OATH, *s.* Mòid, boid, mionnan.
OATH-BREAKING. *s.* Eitheach.
OATMALT, *s.* Braich-choirce.
OATMEAL, *s.* Min-choirce.
OATS, *s.* Corc, coirc, coirce.
OBAMBULATION, *s.* Coiseachd mu'n cuairt, cuairt-iomachd.
OBCONICAL, *adj.* Bonna-chaol.
OBCORDATE, *adj.* Air cumadh cridhe.
OBDUCE, *v. a.* Còmhdaich, thairis.
OBDUCTION, *s.* Còmhdachadh.

Obduracy, *s.* Cruas-cridhe, neo-aithreachas, rag-mhuinealas.
Obdurate, *adj.* Cruaidh-chridheach, rag-mhuinealach, neo-aithreachail.
Obduration, Obdurateness, *s.* Rag-mhuinealas, cruas-cridhe.
Obdurately, *adv.* Gu neo-gheilleach, gu neo-umhailte.
Obedience, *s.* Ùmhlachd, géill.
Obedient, *adj.* Ùmhal, so riaghladh.
Obediential, *adj.* Ùmhlachdail.
Obeisance, *s.* Fàilte, ùmhlachd, beic.
Obelisk, *s.* Carragh-chrasgach, an comharradh so (†) air marbhan leabhair.
Oberation, *s.* Siubhal-seacharain.
Obese, *adj.* Reamhar, meath, cullach.
Obey, *v. a.* Strìochd, géill, freagair.
Obit, *s.* Falair, alair.
Obituary, *s.* Clàr-innsidh nam marbh.
Object, *s.* Cuspair, ni, cùis, crìoch.
Object, *v. a.* Cuir an aghaidh, diùlt.
Objection, *s.* Cunnuil; cur an aghaidh, tagradh; fàth-gearain, coire, talach.
Objective, *adj.* Cuspaireach, cùiseach.
Objector, *s.* Fear-diùltaidh.
Objuration, *s.* Bòid-cheangail.
Objurgate, *v. a.* Cronaich, trod.
Objurgation, *s.* Achmhasan, trod.
Objurgatory, *adj.* Achmhasanach.
Oblation, *s.* Tabhartas, ìobairt.
Obligation, *s.* Ceangal, còir, dleasanas; cùmhnant; comain.
Obligatory, *adj.* Ceangaltach, cùmhnantach, comaineach.
Oblige, *v. a.* Cuir mar fhiachaibh air, thoir air; cuir fo chomain, cuir comain air.
Obligee, *s.* Neach fo-chomain.
Obliging, *adj.* Coingheallach, suairce.
Oblique, *adj.* Neo-dhìreach, siar.
Obliqueness, Obliquity, *s.* Fiaradh, siaradh, camadh, cromadh; claonadh, cluaintearachd.
Obliterate, *v. a.* Dubh a mach, mill.
Obliteration, *s.* Dubhadh ás, milleadh.
Oblivion, *s.* Di-chuimhne; mathanas.
Oblivious, *adj.* Dì-chuimhneach.
Oblong, *adj.* Cruinn-fhada.
Obloquy, *s.* Coire, cùl-chainnt, masladh.
Obmulescence, *s.* Balbhachd.
Obnoxious, *adj.* Buailteach do.
Obnubliate, *v. a.* Dorchaich, neulaich, dubharaich.
Obole, *s.* Deich gràinean.
Obreption, *s.* Feath-laidhe, eun-laidhe.
Obscene, *adj.* Draosda, drabasda, neo-ghlan truaillidh, salach; dẽisinneach, sgreataidh.
Obscenity, *s.* Draosdachd, drabasdachd, neo-ghlaine.
Obscuration, *s.* Doilleireachd, duirche.
Obscure, *adj.* Dorcha, doilleir, dubharach; uaigneach, falaichte; deacair, dìomhair; neo-ainmeil.
Obscure, *v. a.* Dorchaich, doilleirich, neulaich; ceil, falaich; sgàilich, dean deacair.
Obscureness, Obscurity, *s.* Duirche, doilleireachd; uaigneas; deacaireachd, doirbheachd.
Obsecration, *s.* Achanaich.
Obsequies, *s.* Bròn-tiodhlaicidh.
Obsequious, *adj.* Ùmhal, strìochdail.
Obsequiousness, *s.* Strìochdalachd.
Observable, *adj.* So-fhaicinn, comharraite; soillir.
Observably, *adv.* Gu comharraite.
Observance, *s.* Modh, urram, ùmhlachadh; aoradh, gnà-aoradh; aire, faicill, cùram; riaghailt; spéis, meas.
Observant, *adj.* Aireil, faicilleach, cùramach; spéis-thabhartach.
Observation, *s.* Beachd, beachdachadh, dearcadh, aire, toirt-fainear; sealladh, amharc; fiosrachadh; deasghnàthachadh, frithealadh.
Observator, Observer, *s.* Fear-amhairc, fear-aire, fear-coimheid, fear-beachdachaidh.
Observatory, *s.* Taigh-amhairc reull.
Observe, *v.* Beachdaich, seall, amhairc; thoir fainear, fiosraich; frithEil, faic; bi air t' fhaicill.
Obsession, *s.* Séisd, séisdeadh.
Obsolete, *adj.* A cleachdadh.
Obstacle, *s.* Grabadh, bacadh, cnapstarra; ball-toirmisg.
Obstinacy, *s.* Rag-mhuinealas.
Obstinate, *adj.* Ceann-laidir, rag.
Obstinately, *adv.* Gu reasgach.
Obstinateness, *s.* Rag-mhuinealachd,
Obstipation, *s.* Dunadh suas.
Obstreperous, *adj.* Gleadhrach.
Obstriction, *s.* Daingneachadh, bann.
Obstruct, *v. a.* Bac, dùin suas.
Obstruction, *s.* Ceap-starra, bacadh; ball-toirmisg.
Obstructive, *adj.* Grabach, amlach.
Obstruent, *adj.* Grabanta, éiseil.
Obstupefaction, *s.* Tuaineulachd.
Obtain, *v. a.* Buannaich, coisinn, faigh; mair, buanaich; bi seasmhach.
Obtainable, *adj.* So-fhaotainn.
Obtainment, *s.* Buannachadh, coisnadh, faotainn.

Obtemperate, *v. a.* Strìochd, géill.
Obtend, *v. a.* Cuir an aghaidh, cum a mach.
Obtenebration, *s.* Dorchadas, duibbre, doillearachd.
Obtention, *s.* Cur an aghaidh.
Obtest, *v.* Aslaich, guidh, grìos.
Obtestation, *s.* Aslachadh, griosad.
Obtrectation, *s.* Cùl-chàineadh.
Obtrude, *v. a.* Rach gun chuireadh.
Obtruder, *s.* Sgimilear.
Obtrusion, *s.* Sgimilearachd.
Obtrusive, *adj.* Sgimilearach.
Obtund, *v. a.* Maolaich; lagaich.
Obtuse, *adj.* Maol, neo-gheur; clod-cheannach, marbhanta, troma-cheannach.
Obtusely, *adv.* Gu roinn, maol.
Obtuseness, *s.* Maoile, neo-gheire.
Obtusion, *s.* Maoladh.
Obverse, *adj.* Air a bheul-fodha.
Obvert, *v. a.* Tionndaidh chuige.
Obviate, *v. a.* Thig 'san rathad, bac, grab, coinnich.
Obvious, *adj.* Soilleir, furasda; réidh.
Obviousness, *s.* Soilleireachd.
Occasion, *s.* Tuiteamas, tachartas, cothrom, fàth, àm; aobhar; feum.
Occasion, *v. a.* Aobharaich, tàrmaich; thoir mu'n cuairt.
Occasional, *adj.* Tachartach, air uairibh, tuiteamach.
Occasionally, *adv.* An dràsd, 's a rithist, air uairibh.
Occident, *s.* An iar, an airde 'n iar.
Occidental, **Occiduous**, *adj.* Iar, siar, iarach.
Occiput, *s.* Cùl a' chinn.
Occlude, *v. a.* Dùin suas.
Occult, *adj.* Dìomhair, falaichte.
Occultation, *s.* Reull-fhalach.
Occultness, *s.* Dìomhaireachd.
Occupancy, *s.* Séilbh-ghabhail.
Occupant, *s.* Fear-sealbhachaidh.
Occupate, *v. a.* Gabh séilbh.
Occupation, *s.* Sealbh-ghlacadh; obair, dreuchd, ceaird, gnothach.
Occupier, *s.* Fear-séilbhe, sealbhadair.
Occupy, *v.* Gabh sealbh, séilbhich, gléidh; saoithrich, gnàthaich, caith; lean; cuir gu buil.
Occur, *v. n.* Thig 's a chuimhne; thig 's an rathad; tachair.
Occurrence, *s.* Tachartas, tuiteamas
Occursion, *s.* Co-bhuille, co-bhualadh.
Ocean, *s.* Cuan, lear, fairge, muir, aibheis.
Ocellated, *adj.* Sùileach, coltach ri sùil.
Ochre, *s.* Ruadh-chailc, cailc-dhatha.
Ochreous, *adj.* Ruadh-chailceach.
Octagon, *s.* Ochd-shlisneag.
Octagonal, *adj.* Ochd-chearnach.
Octangular, *adj.* Ochd-oisinneach.
Octavo, *adj.* Ochd-dhuilleagach.
Octennial, *adj.* Ochd-bhliadhnach.
October, *s.* Mios deireannach an fhoghair.
Octonocular, *adj.* Ochd-shùileach.
Octopetalous, *adj.* Ochd-bhileach.
Octuple, *adj.* Ochd-fhillteach.
Ocular, *adj.* Fo'shealladh sùl
Oculist, *s.* Léigh-shùl, sùil-léigh.
Odd, *adj.* Còrr, gàbhaidh, neònach, ioghantach; sònraichte.
Oddity, *s.* Neònachas, neach iongantach, annas.
Oddness, *s.* Còrr, neo-ghnàthachd.
Odds, *s.* Barrachdas; lamh an uachdar; tuasaid, sabaid, carraid.
Ode, *s.* Duanag, luinneag, rann.
Odious, *adj.* Fuathmhor, gràineil.
Odiousness, *s.* Fuathmhorachd.
Odium, *s.* Fuath, gamhlas, coire.
Odoriferous, *adj.* Cùbhraidh.
Odorous, *adj.* Boltrachail, cùbhraidh.
Odour, *s.* Cùbhraidheachd, bòladh.
Oecumenical, *adj.* Coitcheann.
Oeiliad, *s.* Priobadh, caogadh.
O'er, *adv.* contracted from *over*. Thall.
Of, *prep.* De dhe, a; o; mu, mu dhéibhinn; á, as; am measg.
Off, *adv.* Dheth; as; air cùl.
Off, *interj.* Air falbh! teich as mo shealladh! as m' fhianais!
Off, *prep.* De, dhe; o.
Offal, *s.* Spruilleach, fuighleach, dràib, blionach.
Offence, *s.* Cionta, coire, droch-bheart; oilbheum, tàmailt; ionnsaidh, ruathar.
Offenceful, *adj.* Cronail, ciùrrail; oilbheumach, tàmailteach.
Offenceless, *adj.* Neo-oilbheumach.
Offend, *v.* Feargaich, brosnaich; thoir ionnsaidh, buail; dean coire.
Offender, *s.* Ciontach, coireach.
Offensive, *adj.* Oilbheumach; dochannach, cronail; ionnsaidheach; mi-thaitneach, fuathmhor.
Offensiveness, *s.* Cron, dochair; gràinealachd, fuathmhorachd.
Offer, *v.* Tairg; ìobair; nochd, tòisich; thig 's an làthair, bi am fagus; thoir ionnsaidh.
Offer, *s.* Tairgse.
Offering, *s.* Tabhartas, ìobairt.
Offertory, *s.* Tabhartas; ionad-tasgaidh iobairtean.

Office, *s.* Seirbhis, feum; gnothach, obair; seòmar-gnothaich.
Officer, *s.* Oifigeach.
Official, *adj.* Dreuchdail.
Officiate, *v.* Coimhlion; fritheil.
Officious, *adj.* Còir, caoimhneil, coingheallach; bleideil.
Officiousness, *s.* Bleidealachd.
Offing, *s.* Stiùradh o thìr.
Offscouring, *s.* Anabas, salchar.
Offset, *s.* Meangan, fiùran, ùr-fhàs.
Offspring, *s.* Iarmad, sliochd, sìol, àl, gineal, clann.
Offuscate, *v. a.* Neulaich, gruamaich, doilleirich.
Oft, Often, Oftentimes, Oftimes, *adv.* Gu tric, gu minig.
Often, *adj.* Tric, minig, iomadh uair.
Ogee, Ogive, *s.* Seòrsa do bhreacdhualadh air clachan aitribh.
Ogle, *v. n.* Claon-amhairc, caog.
Ogling, *s.* Claon-amharc, caogadh.
Oh! *interj.* O! och! mo thruaighe!
Oil, *s.* Ola, ùilleadh, eòlan.
Oil, *v. a.* Olaich, ùill, ùillich.
Oiliness, *s.* Olachd, ùillidheachd.
Oily, *adj.* Olach, ùilleach.
Ointment, *s.* Ola-ungaidh, ola-leighis, acuinn sàbh.
Old, Olden, *adj.* Sean, aosmhor aosda; àrsaidh.
Oldfashioned, *adj.* Sean-ghnàthach.
Oldish, *adj.* A leth-char sean.
Oldness, *s.* Seanachd, aosdachd.
Oleaginous, Oleose, Oleous, *adj.* Eòlanach, ùilleach.
Olfactory, *adj.* Fàileach, fàileanta.
Oligarchy, *s.* Iar-fhlaitheachd.
Olivaster, *adj.* Lachdunn, riabhach.
Olive, *s.* Crann-ola, dearcan-ola, meas a' chroinn ola.
Ombre, *s.* Cluich triùir air cairtean.
Omega, *s.* Deireadh, crìoch, an litir dheireannach do'n aibidil Ghreugaich.
Omelet, *s.* Sgreabhag, bonnachuibhe.
Omen, *s.* Manadh, roi'-chomharradh.
Omer, *s.* Tomhas Eabhreach thrì pinnt.
Ominate, *v.* Fàisnich, roi-innis.
Ominous, *adj.* Droch-thargrach.
Omission, Omittance, *s.* Dearmad, dì-chuimhn, neo-chùram, neo-aire.
Omit, *v. a.* Dearmaid, dì-chuimhnich; fàg ás, fàg a mach.
Omniferous, *adj.* Uile-thabhartach.
Omnific, *adj.* Uile-dhèanadach.
Omniform, *adj.* Uile-chruthach.
Omnigenous, *adj.* Uile-ghnèitheach.
Omnipotence, Omnipotency, *s.* Uile-chumhachd, uile-chomas.
Omnipotent, *adj.* Uile-chumhachdach, uile-chomasachd.
Omnipresence, *s.* Uile-làthaireachd.
Omnipresent, *adj.* Uile-làthaireach.
Omniscience, *s.* Uil'-fhiosrachd.
Omniscient, *adj.* Uil'-fhiosrach.
Omnivorous, *adj.* Uile-shluigeach.
Omnology, *s.* Co-choltas, samhlachas.
On, *prep.* and *adv.* Air.
On! *interj.* Air aghart! air t'aghart!
Once, *adv.* Aon uair; uair, uair-eigin.
One, *adj.* Aon, a h-aon.
One, *s.* Neach, urra, aon fear, té.
One-eyed, *adj.* Leth-shuileach, cam.
Oneirocritic, *s.* Fear-breathnachaidh bhruadar.
Onerary, *adj.* Luchdail, lòdail.
Onerate, *v. a.* Luchdaich, sacaich.
Oneration, *s.* Luchdachadh.
Onerous, *adj.* Trom, sàrachail.
Onion, *s.* Uinnean.
Only, *adv.* A mhàin.
Onset, *s.* Ionnsaidh, ruathar.
Ontology, *s.* Eòlas-bhithean.
Onward, *adv.* Air aghart, air aghaidh.
Onyx, *s.* Clach-onics, seud shoilleir.
Ooze, *s.* Dràib, làthach; sileadh.
Ooze, *v. n.* Snith, sil, drùidh.
Oozy, *adj.* Dràibeach, silteach.
Opacity, *s.* Duirche, doilleireachd.
Opacous, Opaque, *adj.* Dorcha.
Opal, *s.* Seud àraidh, clach-uasal.
Open, *v.* Fosgail; mìnich; tòisich.
Open, *adj.* Fosgailte; soilleir, follaiseach; fosgarra, réidh, saor.
Openeyed, *adj.* Furachail, leirsinneach.
Openhanded, *adj.* Toirbheartach; fiallaidh, fiùghantach.
Openhearted, *adj.* Saor-chridheach.
Openheartedness, *s.* Fiùghalachd.
Opening, *s.* Fosgladh; bealach.
Openly, *adv.* Gu fosgailt.
Openmouthed, *adj.* Beul-fhosgailte, beul-fharsuinn, geòcach; gleadhrach.
Openness, *s.* Fosgailteachd, soilleireachd, soillseachd; follaiseachd.
Opera, *s.* Ceòl-chluich, cluich-ciùil.
Operate, *v. n.* Gnìomhaich, oibrich.
Operation, *s.* Gnìomhachd, obair.
Operative, *adj.* Gnìomhach.
Operator, *s.* Gnìomharraiche.
Operose, *adj.* Sàrachail, draghail.
Opertanious, *adj.* Diamhaireach.
Ophthalmic, *adj.* Fradharcail.
Ophthalmy, *s.* Galar-nan-sùl.

OPIATE, *s.* Cungaidh-chadail.
OPINIATIVE, *adj.* Rag-bharalach.
OPINION, *s.* Barail, beachd.
OPIUM, *s.* Cungaidh-chadail.
OPPONENT, *adj.* Eascairdeach.
OPPONENT, *s.* Nàmhaid, eascaraid.
OPPORTUNE, *adj.* Tràthail, àmail.
OPPORTUNITY, *s.* Fàth, cothrom.
OPPOSE, *v.* Cuir an aghaidh, bac, grab; dùbhlanaich; taisbean, nochd; coinnich.
OPPOSELESS, *adj.* Do-dhùbhlanach.
OPPOSITE, *adj.* Fa chomhair.
OPPOSITION, *s.* Aghaidh-ri-aghaidh, co-strì, neo-aonachd.
OPPRESS, *v. a.* Sàraich, claoidh.
OPPRESSION, *s.* Sàrachadh, fòirneart, cruaidh-chas, àmhghar, deuchainn, truaighe.
OPPRESSIVE, *adj.* An-iochdmhor, cruaidh; fòirneartach; trom.
OPPRESSOR, *s.* Fear-sàrachaidh, fear-fòirneirt, fear-foireignidh.
OPPROBRIOUS, *adj.* Sgainnéalach.
OPPROBRIOUSNESS, *s.* Sgainnealachd.
OPPROBRIUM, *s.* Masladh, mì-chliù.
OPPUGN, *v. a.* Cuir an aghaidh.
OPPUGNANCY, *s.* Cothachadh.
OPTATIVE, *adj.* Iarrtach, iarrtanach.
OPTIC, *adj.* Léirsinneach, fradharcach.
OPTIC, *s.* Sùil; inneal-fradhairc.
OPTICIAN, *s.* Fear-eòlais-fradhairc.
OPTICS, *s.* Eòlas-fradhairc.
OPTIMACY, *s.* Mòr-uaislean.
OPTION, *s.* Roghainn, comas taghaidh.
OPULENCE, OPULENCY, *s.* Saibhreas, beartas, pailteas, maoin, toic.
OPULENT, *adj.* Saibhir, beartach.
OR, *conj. either.* No, air neo.
ORACLE, *s.* Facal, taisbean; guth-àite; fear ro-ghlic.
ORACULAR, ORACULOUS, *adj.* Taisbeanach, briathrach, smachdail; dorcha, &c.
ORAL, *adj.* Beul-aithriseach.
ORANGE, *s.* Òr-ubhall, òr-mheas.
ORATION, *s.* Òraid, deas-chainnt, duan.
ORATOR, *s.* Fear deas-chainnteach.
ORATORICAL, *adj.* Deas-chainnteach, ùr-labhrach, binn-ghlòireach.
ORATORIO, *s.* Naomh-cheòl.
ORATORY, *s.* Deas-chainnt, ùr-labhradh, òraideachd.
ORB, *s.* Cruinne, cuairt, cearcall, rath, roth, reull; sùil, rosg.
ORBATE, *adj.* Gun chuid, gun chàirdean, gun sliochd.
ORBATION, *s.* Call-sliochda, bochdainn.
ORBED, *adj.* Cruinn, cuairteach.
ORBICULAR, *adj.* Leth chruinn.
ORBIT, *s.* Reull-chuairt, reull-shlighe.
ORCHARD, *adj.* Ubhall-ghart, lios-mheas, gàradh-abhaill.
ORCHESTRA, ORCHESTRE, *s.* Ionad-luchd-ciùil; lobhta-ciùil.
ORDAIN, *v. a.* Sònraich, socraich, suidhich, cuir air leth, òrduich.
ORDEAL, *s.* Cruaidh-dheuchainn.
ORDER, *s.* Òrdugh, suidheachadh, dòigh; riaghailt, àinte; ceannsal.
ORDER, *v. a.* Òrduich, ceartaich, riaghail; cuir an òrdugh, suidhich, socraich; àint.
ORDERLESS, *adj.* Mi-riaghailteach.
ORDERLY, *adj.* Riaghailteach, dòigheil.
ORDINABLE, *adj.* So-shònrachadh.
ORDINAL, *adj.* Riaghailteach.
ORDINAL, *s.* Leabhar riaghailtean.
ORDINANCE, *s.* Reachd, riaghailt, lagh.
ORDINARY, *adj.* Riaghailteach, dòigheil, suidhichte; gnàthaichte; cumanta, ìosal, suarach; neo-àluinn.
ORDINARY, *s.* Cléir-bhreitheamh; seòl-suidhichte; gnà-dhreuchd.
ORDINATE, *v. a.* Sònraich, suidhich.
ORDINATION, *s.* Suidheachadh.
ORDINATIVE, *adj.* Ùghdarrach.
ORDNANCE, *s.* Gunnachan mòra.
ORDURE, *s.* Gaorr, inneir, buachar.
ORE, *s.* Mèinn miotailte.
ORGAL, *s.* Druaip fìona.
ORGAN, *s.* Ball; òraghan.
ORGANIC, ORGANICAL, *adj.* Innealach.
ORGANISM, *s.* Ball-shuidheachadh.
ORGANIST, *s.* Òraghanaiche.
ORGANIZATION, *s.* Cruth-shuidheachadh, dealbhadh.
ORGANIZE, *v. a.* Cruth-shuidhich.
ORGASM, *s.* Fraoch-feirge, déine.
ORGIES, *s.* Misg, ruidhtearachd.
ORIENT, *adj.* Camhanach, soills-bhristeach, loinnireach, deàrsach, ear.
ORIENT, *s.* An ear, an aird' an ear.
ORIENTAL, *adj.* Earach, searach, soir.
ORIFICE, *s.* Beul, fosgladh, toll.
ORIGIN, *s.* Tùs, toiseach, bun, ceud-aobhar, màthair-aobhar; sinnsearrachd.
ORIGINAL, *adj.* Prìomh, tùsail.
ORIGINALITY, *s.* Tùsalachd,
ORIGINARY, *adj.* Tàrmachail, tùsail.
ORIGINATE, *v. a.* Tàrmaich, tòisich; gin, thoir gu bith.
ORISON, ORAISON, *s.* Ùrnaigh.
ORNAMENT, *s.* Ball-maise, ball.
ORNAMENT, *v. a.* Ball-mhaisich, maisich, sgeudaich.
ORNAMENTAL, *adj.* Ball-mhaiseach.
ORNATE, *adj.* Grinn, breagha.

ORNITHOLOGY, *s.* Eun-eòlas.
ORPHAN, *s.* Dìlleachdan.
ORPIMENT, *s.* Seòrsa mèinn.
ORPINE, *s.* Lŭs-nan-laogh.
ORTHODOX, *adj.* Ceart-chreideach.
ORTHODOXY, *s.* Fallaineachd-teagaisg.
ORTHOEPY, *s.* Ponc-labhairt.
ORTHOGRAPHER, *s.* Ceart-sgrìobhair.
ORTHOGRAPHICAL, *adj.* Ceart-sgrìobte.
ORTHOGRAPHY, *s.* Ceart-sgrìobhadh.
ORTHOLOGY, *s.* Ceart-chunntas.
ORTS, *s.* Fuigheall, farstus, sprùilleach.
OSCILLATION, *s.* Luasgan, udal.
OSCILLATORY, *adj.* Luasganach.
OSCITANCY, OSCITATION, *s.* Meunanaich.
OSCITANT, *adj.* Meunanach, tromcheannach.
OSIER, *s.* Craobh sheilich.
OSPRAY, *s.* An iolair-uisge.
OSSICLE, *s.* Meanbh-chnaimh.
OSSIFICATION, *s.* Cnâimheachadh.
OSSIFRAGE, *s.* Seors' iolaire.
OSSIFY, *v. a.* Dean 'na chnàimh.
OST, OUST, *s.* Dabhach-thìridh.
OSTENSIBLE, *adj.* So-nochdadh.
OSTENSIVE, *adj.* Taisbeanach.
OSTENT, *s.* Coltas, tuar, dreach, aogas.
OSTENTATION, *s.* Faoin-ghlòir, uaill.
OSTENTATIOUS, *adj.* Faoin-ghlòireach.
OSTENTATIOUSNESS, *s.* Faoin-uaill.
OSTLER, *s.* Gille-stàbaill.
OSTRICH, *s.* Sruth, sruth-chàmhal.
OTHER, *pron.* Eile.
OTHERWISE, *adv.* Air mhodh eile, no.
OTTER, *s.* Dòran, biast-dubh.
OUGHT, or AUGHT, *s.* Ni, ni-eigin dad, rud, ni sam bith.
OUGHT, *v. imp.* Is còir, is cubhaidh.
OUNCE, *s.* Ùnnsa.
OUR, *pron. poss.* Ar.
OURSELVES, *pron. recip.* Sinn-féin.
OUSEL, *s.* Lon, fiagh mòr.
OUST, *v. a.* Falmhaich; tilg a mach.
OUT, *adv.* A muigh, a mach; o'n taigh; ann am mearachd; an ioma-chomh airle; ás, air falbh.
OUT! *interj.* Gabh a mach! a mach!
OUTBRAVE, *v. a.* Cuir fo gheilt.
OUTBREAK, *s.* Briseadh a mach.
OUTCAST, *s.* Dìobarach, fògarrach.
OUTCRAFT, *v. a.* Cuir a mach le seòltachd.
OUTCRY, *s.* Gaoir, gàir, iolach.
OUTDARE, *v. a.* Cuir a mach le dànadas.
OUTDO, *v. a.* Buadhaich, fairtlich air.
OUTER, *adj.* A muigh, a mach.
OUTERMOST, *adj.* A's fhaide 'mach.
OUTFACE, *v. a.* Nàraich, cuir a mach.
OUTGROW, *v. a.* Fàs thairis, fàs.
OUTGUARD, *s.* Freiceadan-iomaill.
OUTKNAVE, *v. a.* Meall am mealltair.
OUTLANDISH, *adj.* Alabharra.
OUTLAST, *v. a.* Mair ni 's faide na.
OUTLAW, *s.* Fear-cùirn, fògarrach, ceathairneach-coille, coilltear.
OUTLAW, *v. a.* Cuir air choilltearachd.
OUTLAWRY, *s.* Binn-fhògraidh.
OUTLINE, *s.* Dealbh; crìoch, iomall.
OUTLIVE, *v. a.* Fan beò ni's fhaide na.
OUTLOOK, *s.* Faicill, faire, aire.
OUTMOST, *adj.* Iomallach.
OUTRAGE, *s.* Sàbaid, eucoir, ainneart.
OUTRAGE, *v.* Càin, màb, maslaich, dean aimhleas, dean caonnag.
OUTRAGEOUS, *adj.* Cuthachail, fiadhaich; sàbaideach, aimhleasach, ainneartach; ana-measarra, mallaichte; ro-aingidh.
OUTRAGEOUSNESS, *s.* Cuthach, fearg.
OUTRIGHT, *adv.* Gu buileach, gu h-iomlan, gu tŭr; gu h-ealamh, gun dàil.
OUTRUN, *v. a.* Ruith seachad air.
OUTSCORN, *v. a.* Dean dìmeas air.
OUTSELL, *v. a.* Reic ni's daoire.
OUTSHINE, *v. a.* Deàrs a mach.
OUTSHOOT, *v. a.* Tilg seachad air.
OUTSIDE, *s.* An taobh a muigh.
OUTSKIRT, *s.* Oir-iomall, iomall.
OUTSPREAD, *v. a.* Sgaoil a mach.
OUTSTRIP, *v. a.* Fàg air deireadh.
OUTVIE, *v. a.* Faigh barrachd.
OUTWARD, *adj.* Air an taobh muigh; faicsinneach; corporra; céin.
OUTWARD, *adv.* Gu tìr chéin.
OUTWARDLY, *adv.* Do réir coltais o'n taobh a mach.
OUTWARDS, *adv.* A chum an taobh a mach, an leth a muigh.
OUTWIT, *v. a.* Meall, thoir an car á.
OUTWORK, *s.* Balla muigh-daingnich.
OVAL, *adj.* Air chumadh uibhe.
OVARIOUS, *adj.* Ubhach, uibheach.
OVARY, *s.* Machlag, uibheagan.
OVATION, *s.* Mion-chaithream.
OVEN, *s.* Àmhuinn.
OVER, *prep.* and *adv.* Os-ceann; thar; thairis; tarsainn, air a tharsainn; null; thall, a' nall; seachad, seach; a rithist; tuilleadh agus, a bharrachd, a bharr air, os-barr.
OVERACT, *v. a.* Dean tuilleadh 's a' chòir, rach thar a' chòir.
OVERANXIOUS, *adj.* Ro-chùramach.
OVERARCH, *v. a.* Drochaitich.
OVERAWE, *v. a.* Sgàthaich, eagalaich.
OVERBALANCE, *v. a.* Taobh-thromaich.
OVERBALANCE, *s.* Taob chuidthrom.

OVERBEAR, *v. a.* Cùm fo smachd.
OVERBID, *v. a.* Tairg barrachd.
OVERBOARD, *adv.* A mach thar stoc.
OVERBOIL, *v. a.* Mill le bruich.
OVERBURDEN, *v. a.* An-luchdaich.
OVERBUY, *v. a.* Ceannaich ro dhaor.
OVERCAST, *v. a.* Dorchaich, neulaich.
OVERCHARGE, *v. a.* Iarr tuilleadh 'sa' chòir; dean tuilleadh 's làn.
OVERCLOUD, *v. a.* Neulaich; dubharaich, gruamaich.
OVERCOME, *v. a.* Buadhaich, ceannsaich, faigh buaidh.
OVERDO, *v. a.* Dean tuilleadh 's a' chòir.
OVERDRIVE, *v. a.* Iomain ro luath.
OVEREAGER, *adj.* Ro-dhian, ro-bhras.
OVERFLOW, *v.* Cuir thairis, sruth thairis, lion thairis.
OVERFLOWING, *s.* Ro-làn; cur thairis.
OVERFORWARDNESS, *s.* Ro-dhéine.
OVERGROW, *v. a.* Fàs ro-mhòr.
OVERGROWTH, *s.* Ro-fhàs, ro-chinneas.
OVERHALE, *v. a.* Ath-sgrùd.
OVERHEAD, *adv.* Gu h-àrd; os ceann.
OVERHEAR, *v.* Dean farchluais.
OVERJOY, *v. a.* Dean ùr-ghàirdeachas.
OVERJOY, *s.* Ùr-ghàirdeachas.
OVERLAY, *v. a.* Mùch; còmhdaich thairis.
OVERLOAD, *v. a.* An-luchdaich.
OVERLOOK, *v. a.* Amhairc sios air; dean dìmeas air; seall thairis air.
OVERMATCH, *v. a.* Fairtlich air.
OVERMUCH, *adj.* Tuille 's a chòir.
OVERPAY, *v. a.* Dìol tuille 's a chòir.
OVERPLUS, *s.* Barrachd, an còrr.
OVERPOWER, *v. a.* Faigh làmh-an-uachdar, ceannsaich.
OVERPRIZE, *v. a.* Meas thar a luach.
OVERREACH, *v. a.* Faigh os ceann, meall, thoir an car.
OVERRULE, *v. a.* Cùm fo smachd; cuir fo smachd, diùlt.
OVERRUN, *v. a.* Sàraich, mill, claoidh, spùinn; rach thairis air; ioma-sgaoil, sgaoil thairis; cuir thairis, ruith thairis.
OVERSEE, *v. a.* Amhairc thairis.
OVERSEER, *s.* Fear-coimhid.
OVERSET, *v. a.* Tilg bun os ceann.
OVERSHADE, *v. a.* Dùibhrich, neulaich, sgàilich.
OVERSHADOW, *v. a.* Cuir sgàil air.
OVERSIGHT, *s.* Coimhead, mearachd.
OVERSOON, *adv.* Mò 's luath.
OVERSPENT, *adj.* Sàraichte, claoidhte.
OVERSPREAD, *v. a.* Sgaoil thairis.
OVERSTOCK, *v. a.* Dòmhlaich, an-lìon.
OVERSTRAIN, *v.* Thoir dian-ionnsaidh.
OVERT, *adj.* Fosgailte, soilleir.
OVERTAKE, *v. a.* Beir, glac', thig suas.
OVERTHROW, *v. a.* Tilg bun os ceann; ceannsaich; mill, sgrios, cuir ás da.
OVERTHWART, *adj.* Mu choinneamh, mu chomhair, tarsainn, trasd.
OVERTIRE, *v. a.* Dù-sgìthich, sàraich.
OVERTOP, *v. a.* Éirich os ceann.
OVERTURE, *s.* Fosgladh; foillseachadh, soillseachadh.
OVERTURN, *v. a.* Tilg sios, mill, sgrios.
OVERVALUE, *v. a.* Meas thar a luach.
OVERWEEN, *v. n.* Bi féin-bheachdail.
OVERWHELM, *v. a.* Mùch, brùth.
OVERWORK, *v. a.* Sgìthich le obair.
OVERWORN, *part.* Air caitheamh ás.
OVERWROUGHT, *part.* Claoidhte le obair, sàraichte.
OVIFORM, *adj.* Cruinn mar ubh.
OVIPAROUS, *adj.* Ubh-bheirteach.
OWE, *v. a.* Bi fo fiachaibh do.
OWL, OWLET, *s.* A chomhachag, a' chailleach-oidhche.
OWN, *pron.* Féin; mo chuid féin.
OWN, *v. a.* Gabh ri, gabh le; aidich.
OWNER, *s.* Sealbhadair, fear-seilbhe.
OWNERSHIP, *s.* Sealbh, maoin, còir.
OX, *s.* Damh; *plr.* OXEN. Daimh.
OXEYE, *s.* Am bréinean-brothach.
OXGANG, *s.* Damh-imir, tomhas fearainn fhichead acair.
OXLIP, *s.* Bròg-na-cuthaig.
OXTONGUE, *s.* Am bog-lùs.
OXYCRATE, *s.* Fion-guer agus uisge.
OXYMEAL, *s.* Fion-geur agus mil.
O YES! *interj.* Eisdibh! thugaibh! aire! thugaibh fainear!
OYSTER, *s.* Eisir, eisear.

P

P, *s.* Sèathamh litir deug na h aibidil.
PABULAR, PABULOUS, *adj.* Biadhar, innlinneach, feurach, ionaltrach.
PACATED, *adj.* Siochail, sìtheil.
PACE, *s.* Ceum, gàmag; imeachd, gluasad; tomhas chùig troidhean.
PACE, *v.* Ceimnich, gluais; tomhais le gàmagan.
PACER, *s.* Ceumaiche, falaire.
PACIFIC, *adj.* Sìothchail, ciùin, sèimh.
PACIFICATION, *s.* Sìtheachadh.
PACIFICATOR, *s.* Fear deanamh sìthe.
PACIFICATORY, *adj.* Sìth-dhèanadach.

Pacifier, *s.* Fear-ciùineachaidh.
Pacify, *v. a.* Sìthich, ciùinich.
Pack, *s.* Eallach, uallach, cuallach, trusachan; sac, luchd; lothainn chon; droch comunn, gràisg.
Pack, *v.* Trus, ceangail suas, paisg.
Packer, *s.* Fear-trusaidh, fear-ceangail, fear-pacaidh.
Packet, *s.* Ceanglachan, sac, sacan; long-aisig, bàt-aisig.
Packhorse, *s.* Each saic.
Packsaddle, *s.* Srathair.
Packthread, *s.* Sgeinnidh.
Pact, Paction, *s.* Cùmhnant.
Pad, *v. n.* Coisich gu fòill; dean reubainn rathaid mhòir.
Padar, *s.* Garbhan, garbh-mhin.
Paddle, *v. a.* Iomair; luidrich.
Paddle, *s.* Ràmh beag; pleadhan.
Paddock, *s.* Mial-mhàg, cràigean.
Padlock, *s.* Glas-chrochaidh.
Pæan, *s.* Dàn-buaidh-chaithream.
Pagan, *s.* Pàganach, ana-criosdaidh.
Paganism, *s.* Pàganachd.
Page, *s.* Taobh-duilleig; gille-freasdail, gille-bùirde.
Pageant, *s.* Greadhnachas.
Pageant, *adj.* Greadhnach, faicheil.
Pageantry, *s.* Greadhnachd, faichealachd, mòralachd.
Pagnial, *adj.* Duilleagach.
Paid, *pret.* and *part. pass.* of *to pay.* Pàighte, diolte.
Pail, *s.* Cuinneag, cuman, miodar.
Pain, *s.* Cràdh, pian; péin, goimh, guin, dòrainn.
Pain, *v. a.* Cràidh, pian, claoidh.
Painful, *adj.* Cràiteach, piantach.
Painfulness, *s.* Àmhghar, cràdh.
Painim, *s.* As-creideach.
Painless, *adj.* Neo-chraiteach.
Painstaker, *s.* Fear-saoithreachail.
Painstaking, *adj.* Saoithreachail.
Paint, *v. a.* Dreach-dhath, dealbh.
Paint, *s.* Dreach-dhath, lì.
Painter, *s.* Fear-dreach-dhathaidh.
Painting, *s.* Dreach-dhathadh; dealbh.
Pair, *s.* Càraid; lànan; dithis.
Pair, *v. a.* Càraidich, aonaich.
Palace, *s.* Lùchairt, mùr-rìoghail.
Palatable, *adj.* Blasda, milis.
Palate, *s.* Bràighe-beòil.
Palatine, *adj.* Rìoghail.
Pale, *adj.* Bàn, glaisneulach.
Pale, *v. a.* Dean bàn; ioma-dhruid.
Pale, *s.* Cliath-mhaide, buaile; lann, post; dùthaich, cearn.
Palefaced, *adj.* Glas-ghnùiseach.
Palender, *s.* Long-chòrsaireachd.
Paleness, *s.* Glaisneulachd, bànachd.

Paleous, *s.* Mogunnach, cathach, rùsgach, salach.
Palfrey, *s.* Each-marcachd baintighearna.
Paliament, *s.* Falluinn, trusgan.
Paling, *s.* Cliath-dhìdinn, ataigin.
Palisade, Palisado, *s.* Callaid, banniom-dhruididh.
Palisade, *v. a.* Druid le callaid, cuir callaid mu thimchioll.
Palish, *adj.* Glasdaidh, bànaidh.
Pall, *s.* Brat-mairbh; falluinn àirdeasbuig.
Pall, *v.* Fàs mi-bhlasda, dean mibhlasda; lagaich; sàsaich, fàs lag.
Pallet, *s.* Sëid, leabaidh-làir.
Palliate, *v. a.* Falluinnich, còmhdaich; gabh leisgeul, thoir leisgeul, lughdaich coire no cionta; lasaich.
Palliation, *s.* Leisgeulachadh, lughdachadh coire no cionta; faothachadh, fuasgladh, lasachadh.
Palliative, *adj.* Leisgeulach, lughdachail; lasachail, fuasglach.
Pallid, *adj.* Bàn, glasdaidh.
Pallmall, *s.* Seòrsa cluiche.
Palm, *s.* Craobh-phailm; buaidh; bois, bàs, dèarna; tomhas trì òirlich.
Palm, *v. a.* Falaich 's a bhois; meall; slìob, cnìadaich.
Palmipede, *adj.* Dlù-spàgach.
Palmister, *s.* Dearnadair.
Palmistry, *s.* Dearnadaireachd.
Palmy, *adj.* Pailmeach; buadhach.
Palpability, *s.* So-bheanailteachd.
Palpable, *adj.* So-bheanailteach.
Palpation, *s.* Mothachadh.
Palpitate, *v. n.* Plosg, buail.
Palpitation, *s.* Plosgartaich.
Palsical, Palsied, *adj.* Pairiliseach.
Palsy, *s.* Pairilis, crith-thinneas.
Paltriness, *s.* Fagharsachd.
Paltry, *adj.* Fagharsach, suarrach.
Pam, *s.* Am mùnsaidh, am balach.
Pamper, *v. a.* Sàthaich, sàsaich.
Pamphlet, *s.* Duilleachan. *Kk.*
Pan, *s.* Aghann; falman a' ghlùin.
Panacea, *s.* Uil'-ic, uil-ioc.
Panada, Panado, *s.* Aran air a bhruich ann an uisge.
Pancake, *s.* Loireag, foileag.
Pancreas, *s.* Am brisgean-milis.
Pandemic, *adj.* Dùthchasach.
Pander, *s.* Fear-strìopachais.
Pane, *s.* Ceàrnag ghloine; mìr.
Panegyric, *s.* Moladh, dàn-molaidh.
Panegyrist, *s.* Bàrd-molaidh.
Panel, *s.* Ceàrnag; ainm-chlàr luchdbreith.
Pang, *s.* Guin, goimh, cràdh, pian.

PANG, *v. a.* Gon, cràidh, pian.
PANIC, *s.* Clisgeadh, maoim.
PANIC, *adj.* Clisgeach, grad-eagalach.
PANNEL, *s.* Srathair, sumag, plàt.
PANNIER, *s.* Curran, cliabh.
PANOPLY, *s.* Làn-armachd; lan-fhăs-air, làn-uidheam.
PANT, *v. n.* Plosg; miannaich, bi 'n ro gheall air.
PANT, *s.* Plosgadh, àinich.
PANTALOON, *s.* Triubhas; cleasaiche.
PANTHEON, *s.* Teampull nan uile dhia bréige.
PANTHER, *s.* Fiadh-bheathach ballach.
PANTILE, PENTILE, *s.* Crom-shlige-chrè.
PANTLER, *s.* Fear-gleidhidh arain.
PANTOMIME, *s.* Baoth-chleasaiche.
PANTRY, *s.* Seomar-bìdh.
PAP, *s.* Ceann-cìche; biadh-leinibh.
PAPA, *s.* Athair, facal cloinne.
PAPACY, *s.* Pàpanachd.
PAPAL, *adj.* Pàpanach.
PAPER, *s.* Pàipeir, pàpair.
PAPER, *v. a.* Paisg am pàipeir, pàip-eirich.
PAPER-MAKER, *s.* Fear deanamh phàipeirean.
PAPERMILL, *s.* Muileann-pàipeir.
PAPER-STAINER, *s.* Dathadair phàip-eirean.
PAPILLARY, PAPILLOUS, *adj.* Cìoch-ach.
PAPIST, *s.* Pàpanach.
PAPISTICAL, *adj.* Pàpanach.
PAPPOUS, *adj.* Clòimheach.
PAPPY, *adj.* Bog, sùghmhor.
PAR, *s* Co-ionannachd.
PARABLE, *s.* Co-shamhla.
PARABOLICAL, *adj.* Co-shamhlachail.
PARACLETE, *s.* An Comhfhurtair.
PARADE, *s.* Feachd-riaghailt; uaill.
PARADISE, *s.* Pàrras, nèamh.
PARADOX, *s.* Dubh-fhacal, frith-bhar-ail.
PARADOXICAL, *adj.* Baoth-bharail-each.
PARAGON, *s.* Eiseamplair coimhlionta, ni no neach ro-òirdheirc; còmpanach.
PARAGRAPH, *s.* Earrann air leth.
PARALLEL, *adj.* Co-shìnte; co-ionann.
PARALLEL, *s.* Sgrìob-dhìreach; ion-annachd; samhailt, leth-bhreac.
PARALLEL, *v. a.* Co-shìn; coimeas, samhlaich.
PARALLELISM, *s.* Co-shìnteachd, co-samhla.
PARALYSIS, *s.* Pairilis.
PARALYTIC, *adj.* Pairiliseach, crith-anach.
PARALYZE, *v. a.* Pairilisich, cuir fo lag-chrith.
PARAMOUNT, *s.* Am prìomh, an t-àrd.
PARAMOUR, *s.* Leannan, ban-suiridh-each.
PARAPET, *s.* Obair àrd, uchd-bhalla.
PARAPHERNALIA, *s.* Maoin mnà.
PARAPHRASE, *s.* Eadar-mhìneachadh.
PARAPHRAST, *s.* Fear-mìneachaidh.
PARASITE, *s.* Fear-sodail, ri uaislean.
PARASITICAL, *adj.* Sodalach, miodal-ach, sgimeileireach.
PARASOL, *s.* Grian-sgàilean.
PARBOIL, *v. a.* Leth-bhruich, slaop.
PARCEL, *s.* Trusachan, aslachan.
PARCEL, *v. a.* Roinn na earrannan.
PARCH, *v.* Tiormaich le teas, déasg.
PARCHEDNESS, *s.* Déasgachd, sgreadh-adh, tiormachd.
PARCHMENT, *s.* Craiceannsgrìobhaidh.
PARD, PARDALE, *s.* Liobard.
PARDON, *v. a.* Math, thoir mathanas.
PARDON, *s.* Mathanas, loghadh.
PARDONABLE, *adj.* So-mhathadh.
PARDONABLENESS, *s.* So-mhathachd.
PARE, *v. a.* Sgrathaich, gèarr, bearr.
PARENT, *s.* Pàrant, athair no màth-air.
PARENTAGE, *s.* Breith, sìnnsearachd.
PARENTAL, *adj.* Athaireil, no màith-reil.
PARENTHESIS, *s.* Mìneachadh am meadhon sgrìobhaidh, air a chomh-arrachadh mar (so).
PARENTICIDE, *s.* Mort athar, no màthar.
PARER, *s.* Inneal-bearraidh.
PARERGY, *s.* Ni neo-chudthromach.
PARHELION, *s.* Grian-bréige.
PARIETAL, *adj.* Taobh-bhabhunnach.
PARING, *s.* Rusg, sliseag, sgrath.
PARISH, *s.* Sgìreachd, sgìre.
PARISHIONER, *s.* Fear-sgìreachd.
PARISYLLABICAL, *adj.* Coilideach.
PARITY, *s.* Co-ionannachd.
PARK, *s.* Pàirce, frìth, lann.
PARLEY, PARLE, *s.* Còmhradh.
PARLEY, *v. n.* Dean gnothach le còmh-radh beoil.
PARLIAMENT, *s.* Pàrlamaid, àrd-chomhairle rìgh.
PARLIAMENTARY, *adj.* Pàrlamaideach.
PARLOUR, *s.* Seòmar-suidhe.
PARLOUS, *adj.* Geur, beòthail, peas-anach.
PAROCHIAL, *adj.* Sgìreachdail.
PARODY, *s.* Atharrais dàin.
PAROLE, *s.* Gealltannas, beòil.
PAROXYSM, *s.* Ath-philleadh, tinnis, &c.
PARRICIDAL, *adj.* Athair-mhortach.

PARRICIDE, *s.* Mortair athar.
PARROT, *s.* Parraid.
PARRY, *v. n.* Seachainn, cuir seachad, dean grad-charachd.
PARSIMONIOUS, *adj.* Gléidhteach, spìocach, cruaidh, gann.
PARSIMONY, *s.* Spìocaireachd.
PARSLEY, *s.* Fionnas-gàraidh.
PARSNIP, PARSNEP, *s.* An curran-geal.
PARSON, *s.* Pears-eaglais, ministear.
PARSONAGE, *s.* Beathachadh-eaglais.
PART, *s.* Cuid, earrann, roinn, cuibhrionn; gnothach, obair.
PART, *v. a.* Roinn; sgar; eadardhealaich; dealaich; gabh cead o; thoir seachad.
PARTAKE, *v.* Compàirtich, roinn ri.
PARTAKER, *s.* Compàirtiche.
PARTIAL, *adj.* Claon-bhretheach, lethbhretheach; bà'gheil ri, aon taobh.
PARTIALITY, *s.* Claon-bhretheachd.
PARTIALIZE, *v. a.* Dean claon-bhretheach.
PARTICIPABLE, *adj.* So-phàirteachadh.
PARTICIPANT, *adj.* Co-roinnteach.
PARTICIPATE, *v.* Compàirtich.
PARTICIPATION, *s.* Co-roinn, compàirt.
PARTICLE, *s.* Dad, mion-fhacal.
PARTICULAR, *adj.* Àraidh, sònraichte; poncail; còrr.
PARTICULAR, *s.* Ni-àraidh, neachsònraichte, ponc.
PARTICULARITY, *s.* Àraidheachd.
PARTICULARIZE, *v. a.* Sònraich.
PARTING, *s.* Dealachadh, siubhal.
PARTISAN, *s.* Fear-leanmhainn; sleagh.
PARTITION, *v. a.* Roinn; eadar-sgar.
PARTITION, *s.* Roinn, cailbhe.
PARTLET, *s.* Cearc, stìm.
PARTLY, *adv.* Ann an cuid.
PARTNER, *s.* Còmpanach, fear-pàirt.
PARTNERSHIP, *s.* Còmpanas, co-roinn.
PARTOOK, *pret.* of *to partake.* Chompairtich.
PARTRIDGE, *s.* Cearc-thomain.
PARTS, *s.* Buadhan nàdurrach, buadhan-inntinn, ceudfathan; earrannandùthcha; pàirtean. *R.D.*
PARTURITION, *s.* Breith, aisead.
PARTY, *s.* Dream, cuideachd, buidheann; bannal; neach-air-leth; freiceadan.
PARTY-COLOURED, *adj.* Ioma-dhathach.
PARTY-MAN, *s.* Fear-aon taoibh.
PARVITUDE, PARVITY, *s.* Mionaideachd; eagarachd, pungalachd.
PASCHAL, *adj.* Càisgeach, càisgeil.
PASS, *v.* Rach thairis, gabh seachad, rach thar; rach troimh; buadhaich; dearmaid, dì-chuimhnich; leig le, òrduich; leig seachad, math; thoir binn a mach.
PASS, *s.* Glac, bealach, slighe, rathad; cead siubhail; cor, inbhe.
PASSABLE, *adj.* So-imeachd; an eatarais, cuibheasach.
PASSADE, PASSADO, *s.* Uspag.
PASSAGE, *s.* Turas, aisir; slighe; trannsa; earrann, ceann.
PASSENGER, *s.* Fear-turais, fear-aisig.
PASSIBLE, *adj.* So-athailteachadh.
PASSING, *part. adj.* Anabarrach.
PASSING-BELL, *s.* Clag-bàis.
PASSION, *s.* Boile; fearg, corraich, buaireas; déigh, miann, gràdh; fulangas Chriosd.
PASSION-WEEK, *s.* Seachdain-na ceusda.
PASSIONATE, *adj.* Cas, crosda, feargach, lasanta, grad.
PASSIONATENESS, *s.* Lasantachd, caise.
PASSIVE, *adj.* Fulangach, ciùin.
PASSIVENESS, PASSIVITY, *s.* Fulangachd, foighidneachd, ciùineachd.
PASSOVER, *s.* A chàisg; an t-uan càisge.
PASSPORT, *s.* Litir-cead-siubhail.
PAST, *part.* Seachad, a thréig.
PAST, *s.* An ùine a chaidh, an t-âm a dh' fhalbh, an linn a thréig.
PASTE, *s.* Glaodh flùir.
PASTEBOARD, *s.* Paipeir-glaodhte.
PASTERN, *s.* Rùdan eich, glùn eich.
PASTIME, *s.* Fearas-chuideachd.
PASTOR, *s.* Aodhair, pears'-eaglais.
PASTORAL, *adj.* Aodharachail.
PASTORAL, *s.* Òran-dùthcha.
PASTORSHIP, *s.* Aodharachd.
PASTRY, *s.* Biadh fuinte, pitheannan.
PASTURABLE, *adj.* So-ionaltradh.
PASTURAGE, *s.* Feurach, ionaltradh.
PASTURE, *s.* Ionaltradh, feurachas.
PASTURE, *v.* Ionaltair, feuraich.
PASTY, *s.* Pithean.
PAT, *adj.* Iomchuidh, freagarrach.
PAT, *s.* Coilleag; boiseag.
PAT, *v. a.* Slìob, buail aotrom.
PATCH, *s.* Breaban, bréid, tùthag.
PATCH, *v. a.* Clùd, càirich, tùthagaich, bréideich, cnòdaich.
PATCHER, *s.* Clùdaire, cnòdaire.
PATE, *s.* Claigeann, ceann.
PATENT, *adj.* Fosgailte, follaiseach.
PATENT, *s.* Sgrìobhadh còrach o'n rìgh.
PATENTEE, *s.* Fear-còrach.
PATERNAL, *adj.* Athaireil.
PATERNITY, *s.* Athaireachd.
PATERNOSTER, *s.* A' phaidir.

Path, Pathway, *s.* Ceum, slighe, rathad, aisridh, cas-cheum.
Pathetic, Pathetical, *adj.* Drùighteach, tiamhaidh, cianail.
Pathless, *adj.* Gun rathad, gun slighe.
Pathology, *s.* Eòlas-ghalar.
Pathos, *s.* Déine, dian-labhairt, drùighteachd.
Pathway, *s.* Frith-rathad.
Patience, *s.* Foighidinn, fulangas.
Patient, *adj.* Foighidneach, fulangach, foisneach.
Patient, *s.* Neach tinn, euslan.
Patly, *adv.* Gu freagarrach, iomchuidh.
Patriarch, *s.* Prìomh-athair.
Patriarchal, *adj.* Prìomh athaireil.
Patrician, *adj.* Uasal, àrd, flathail.
Patrician, *s.* Àrd-uasal, àrd-fhlath.
Patrimonial, *adj.* Dligheach, sinnsearrach, dualach.
Patrimony, *s.* Oighreachd-sinnsearachd, dualachas.
Patriot, *s.* Fear-gràidh d'a dhùthaich, tìr-ghràdhaiche.
Patriotism, *s.* Gràdh dùthcha.
Patrol, *s.* Freiceadan sràide.
Patron, *s.* Fear comaraidh, fear-taic.
Patronage, *s.* Comaradh, dìon, taic.
Patroness, *s.* Ban-chomaraidh.
Patronise, *v. a.* Dìon, cùm suas, seas, thoir comaradh.
Patronymick, *s.* Ainm sìnnsearachd.
Patten, *s.* Bròg fhiodha agus iaruinn.
Patter, *v. a.* Dean stairirich.
Pattern, *s.* Ball-sampuill ; cumadh.
Paucity, *s.* Ainneamhachd, gainne.
Paunch, *s.* Brù, mionach, maodal.
Pauper, *s.* Dìol-déirce, bochd.
Pauperism, *s.* Déirceachd.
Pause, *s.* Stad, anail, grabadh, tosd.
Pause, *v. n.* Fuirich, smuainich, thoir fainear; stad, clos; bi aig fois.
Pave, *v. a.* Ùrlaraich, leag ùrlar.
Pavement, *s.* Ùrlar-cloiche, càbhsair.
Paver, Paviour, *s.* Càbhsairiche.
Pavilion, *s.* Pàilliun, bùth.
Paw, *s.* Spòg, spàg, màg, cràg, cròg.
Paw, *v. a.* Crògairich, bùraich, sgrìob, cladhaich an talamh mar tharbh; buail leis a chois toisich ; dean miodal.
Pawn, *v. a.* Thoir an geall.
Pawnbroker, *s.* Malairtear-gìll.
Pay, *v. a.* Dìol, pàidh, ìoc.
Pay, *s.* Tuarasdal, luach-saothreach.
Payable, *adj.* Ri dhìoladh.
Payment, *s.* Dìoladh, pàidheadh.
Pea, *s.* Peasair, gràinne peasarach.
Peace, *s.* Sìth; sìothchaint; fois, tamh, réite, socair-inntinn.
Peace! *interj.* Tosd ! clos !
Peace-offering, *s.* Sìth-thabhartas.
Peaceable, *adj.* Soitheamh, sìothchail ; foistinneach ; sàmhach.
Peaceableness, *s.* Sìthealachd.
Peaceful, *adj.* Sìochail, ciùin.
Peacefulness, *s.* Siochainnt.
Peacemaker, *s.* Fear-sìtheachaidh.
Peachick, *s.* Isean na peucaig.
Peacock, *s.* Coileach-peucag.
Peahen, *s.* Peucag, eucag, feucag.
Peak, *s.* Stùc, scòrr, binnein, bàrr.
Peal, *s.* Stàiririch, toirm, torrunn.
Pear, *s.* Peur, meas ioma-ghnè.
Pearl, *s.* Neamhnad ; leus-sùl.
Pearly, *adj.* Neamhnadach.
Peasant, *s.* Fear dubh-chosnaidh.
Peasantry, *s.* Tuath cheatharn.
Peasecod, *s.* Balg peasrach.
Peat, *s.* Mòine ; fàd mhòine.
Pebble, Pebblestone, *s.* Éideag.
Pebbly, *adj.* Éideagach.
Peccability, *s.* Buailteachd do'n pheacadh.
Peccadillo, *s.* Meanbh-chorc.
Peccancy, *s.* Droch-mhèinn.
Peccant, *adj.* Ciontach, peacach; droch-mhèinneach, aingidh.
Peccavi, *pret. v.* Pheacaich mi.
Peck, *s.* Peic, ceithreamh.
Peck, *v. a.* Pioc, gobhaich; spiol.
Pectoral, *adj.* Uchdail, broileachail.
Pectoral, *s.* Uchd-éideadh.
Peculation, *s.* Mèirle, goid.
Peculate, *v. n.* Dean gadaidheachd.
Peculiar, *s.* Àraidh, sònraichte.
Peculiarity, *s.* Buaidh air-leth.
Pecuniary, *adj.* Airgeadach.
Pedagogue, *s.* Beadagan sgoileir.
Pedal, *adj.* Casach, luirgneach.
Pedant, *s.* Beadagan fòghluim.
Pedantic, *adj.* Uailleil á beaganfòghluim.
Pedantry, Pedanticness, *s.* Moit ionnsachaidh.
Pedestal, *s.* Bun-carraigh.
Pedestrial, Pedestrious, *adj.* Air chois, a' coiseachd.
Pedestrian, *s.* Coisiche.
Pedicle, *s.* Cuiseag, lurga duilleig.
Pedicular, Pediculous, *adj.* Mialach.
Pedigree, *s.* Sìnnsearrachd.
Pedler, *s.* Ceannaiche-màileid.
Pedlery, *s.* Frith-cheannachd.
Pedling, *s.* Frith-cheannach.
Pedobaptism, *s.* Naoidh-bhaisteadh.
Pedobaptist, *s.* Naoidh-bhaistiche.

Pendoncle. *s.* An lurga ta ceangal a' mheas ris a' chraoibh.
Peel, *v. a.* Rùisg, plaoisg, creach.
Peel, *s.* Rùsg, plaosg; greidilein.
Peep, *v. n.* Thoir caog-shealladh, amhairc troi' tholl, gabh sealladh bradach, dean dìdeagaich.
Peep, *s.* Grad shealladh; caogadh, sealladh bradach, dìdeag.
Peer, *s.* Flath, morair, còmpanach.
Peerage, Peerdom, *s.* Flathachd, moraireachd.
Peeress, *s.* Bana-mhorair.
Peerless, *adj.* Gun choimeas.
Peerlessness, *s.* Neo-choimeasachd.
Peevish, *adj.* Dreamach, dranndanach, frionasach, cas, corrach, feargach, crosda.
Peevishness, *s.* Dranndanachd, caise.
Peg, *s.* Cnag, stéill, ealachag.
Pelf, *s.* Maoin, saibhreas, beartas.
Pelican, *s.* Pelican, eun mòr fàsaich.
Pellet, *s.* Peileir, ruagaire.
Pellicle, *s.* Sgrath, sgannan.
Pellitory, *s.* Lŭs-a'-bhalla.
Pellmell, *adv.* Troi' chéile.
Pellucid, *adj.* Trìd-shoilleir, soilleir.
Pelt, *s.* Peleid, craiceann, bian, seiche; buille, cnap, sgailc.
Pelt, *v. a.* Tilg air, buail, caith air.
Pelting, *part.* Tilgeadh chlach, &c.
Peltmonger, *s.* Ceannaiche-chraiceann, boiceannaich.
Pen, *s.* Peann, crò, buaile, fang.
Penal, *adj.* Peanasach, dìoghaltach.
Penality, *s.* Buailteachd do pheanas.
Penalty, *s.* Peanas, pian, ùbhladh.
Penance, *s.* Aithridh. *Md.*
Pence, *s. pl.* of *penny.* Sgillinn.
Pencil, *s.* Peann-luaidhe.
Pendant, *s.* Fàinne-cluaise; grinneas crochte; bratach-bheag.
Pendency, *s.* Dàil, teagamh.
Pendent, *adj.* An crochadh; thairis air.
Pending, *adj.* An crochadh, a' teagamhach.
Pendulous, *adj.* An crochadh, crochte.
Pendulum, *s.* Cudthrom-siùdain.
Penetrable, *adj.* So-dhrùigheadh.
Penetrant, *adj.* Drùighteach, geur.
Penetrate, *v.* Drùigh; toll; faigh troimhe, breathnaich.
Penetration, *s.* Tolladh, deargadh, drùigheadh; breithneachadh; geurthuigse.
Penetrative, *adj.* Geur, drùighteach; geur-chuiseach.
Peninsula, *s.* Tairbeart, rŏs.
Penitence, *s.* Aithreachas.
Penitent, *adj.* Aithreachail.
Penitent, *s.* Iompachan. *S.*
Penitential, *adj.* Aithreachail.
Penitentiary, *s.* Ionad-aithreachais.
Penknife, *s.* Sgian-pheann.
Penman, *s.* Ùghdar, sgrìobhair.
Penmanship, *s.* Sgrìobhaireachd.
Pennant, *s.* Ball-tàirnne; bratach.
Pennated, *adj.* Sgiathach.
Penniless, *adj.* Gun pheighinn, ainnis.
Pennon, *s.* Bratach.
Penny, *s.* Peighinn, sgillinn.
Pennyworth, *s.* Luacha-peighinn.
Pension, *s.* Saor-dhuais bhliadhnach.
Pensionary, *adj.* Saor-dhuaiseach.
Pensioner, *s.* Fear-saor-dhuais.
Pensive, *adj.* Trom smaointeachail.
Pensiveness, *s.* Tron smaointinneachd.
Pent, *part. pass.* of *to pen.* Punnte.
Pentacapsular, *adj.* Cùig-chlaiseach.
Pentachord, *s.* Cruit-nan-cùig-teud.
Pentædrous, *adj.* Cùig-shliseach.
Pentagon, *s.* Cùig-chearnag.
Pentangular, *adj.* Cùig-chearnach.
Pentapetalous, *adj.* Cùig-dhuilleach.
Pentateuch, *s.* Cùig leabhraichean Mhaois.
Pentecost, *s.* A' chaingeis.
Pentecostal, *adj.* Caingeiseach.
Penthouse, *s.* Taigh-sgàile.
Pentile, *s.* Chlach-mhullaich-chré.
Penurious, *adj.* Spìocach, crìon.
Penuriousness, *s.* Spìocaiche, crìne.
Penury, *s.* Bochduinn, ainniseachd.
People, *s.* Pobull, sluagh, aiteam.
People, *v. a.* Lìon le sluagh.
Pepper, *s.* Spìosraidh, peabar.
Pepper, *v. a.* Peabraich; slac, spuaic.
Peppercorn, *s.* Smùirnein, dùradan.
Peppermint, *s.* Mionnt, meant.
Peradventure, *adv.* Theagamh.
Perambulate, *v. a.* Cuairt-imich.
Perambulation, *s.* Cuairt-imeachd.
Perceivable, *adj.* So-fhaicsinn.
Perceive, *v. a.* Beachdaich, tuig.
Perceptibility, *s.* So-léirsinneachd.
Perceptible, *adj.* So-léirsinneach.
Perception, *s.* Amharc, beachd; eòlas, fiosrachadh; mothachadh.
Perceptive, *adj.* Léirsinneach, beachdach.
Perch, *s.* Creagag, muc-locha, tomhas chùig slat gu leth; spiris, spàrr.
Perch, *v.* Cuir air spiris; rach air spardan; suidh mar eun.
Perchance, *adv.* A theagamh.
Percipient, *adj.* Geur-bheachdach
Percolate, *v. a.* Sìolaidh.
Percolation, *s.* Sìoladh.

Percolator, *s.* Sìolachan.
Percuss, *v. a.* Buail, thoir buille.
Percussion, *s.* Bualadh, buille, farum.
Perdition, *s.* Sgrios; bàs-sìorruidh.
Perdu, *adv.* Am falach; am fagus.
Perdulous, *adj.* Caillte.
Peregrinate, *v. n.* Dean céin-thuras.
Peregrination, *s.* Céin-thuras.
Peregrinator, *s.* Taisdealach.
Peregrine, *adj.* Céinthireach.
Peremptory, *adj.* Smachdail, teann.
Perennial, *adj.* A mhaireas ré bliadhna; sìor-maireannach.
Perenity, *s.* Buan-mhaireannachd.
Perfect, *adj.* Iomlan, foirfe, coimhlionta; làn-eòlach; neo-choireach, fìor-ghlan; cinnteach, dearbhte.
Perfect, *v. a.* Dean iomlan, dean foirfe, dean coimhlionta; làn-chrìochnaich.
Perfection, *s.* Iomlanachd, foirfeachd, coimhliontachd, diongmhaltachd.
Perfectness, *s.* Iomlanachd, foirfeachd; làn-mhathas.
Perfidious, *adj.* Cuilbheartach, meallta, foilleil, sligheach.
Perfidiousness, *s.* Cuilbheartachd.
Perforate, *v. a.* Toll, toll troimh.
Perforation, *s.* Tolladh.
Perforator, *s.* Sniomhaire, tora.
Perforce, *adv.* A dh' aindeoin, air éigin.
Perform, *v. a.* Coimhlion.
Performance, *s.* Coimhlionadh.
Performer, *s.* Fear-coimhlionaidh, fear-cluiche.
Perfume, *s.* Boltrach, cùbhraidhach.
Perfume, *v. a.* Dean cùbhraidh.
Perfumer, *s.* Boltraiche, ceannaiche bholtraichean.
Perfunctory, *adj.* Dearmadach, neochùramach; neo-choimhlionta.
Perhaps, *adv.* Math a dh' fheudte.
Pericardium, *s.* Cochull a' chridhe.
Pericranium, *s.* Cochull na h-eanchain.
Peril, *s.* Cunnart, baoghal, gàbhadh.
Perilous, *adj.* Cunnartach, gàbhaidh.
Perimeter, *s.* Cuairt-thomhas.
Period, *s.* Cuairt; ùine, àm, ré; crìoch, ceann, deireadh; pong.
Periodical, *adj.* Riaghailteach, aig àmaibh suidhichte.
Periphery, *s.* Cuairt-thiughadh.
Periphrasis, *s.* Cuairt-labhairt.
Periphrastic, *adj.* Cuairt-labhrach.
Perish, *v.* Rach a dhìth, faigh bàs, bàsaich; rach am mugha.
Perishable, *adj.* Bàsmhor, claoidhteach, dìtheachail.
Perjure, *v. a.* Thoir mionnan-eithich.
Perjurer, *s.* Fear-eithich.
Perjury, *s.* Eitheach.
Periwig, *s.* Gruag-thilgte, pìorbhuic.
Periwinkle, *s.* Gille-fionn, faochag.
Perk, *v. n.* Bi guanach, bi gogcheannach.
Permanence, Permansion, *s.* Buanas, maireannachd, seasmhachd.
Permanent, *adj.* Buan, maireannach.
Permiscible, *adj.* So-choimeasgadh.
Permissible, *adj.* Ceadaichte.
Permission, *s.* Cead, saorsa, comas.
Permissive, *adj.* Ceadachail.
Permit, *v. a.* Ceadaich; fuilig, luthasaich, thoir suas.
Permit, *s.* Baranta-cuspuinn.
Permutation, *s.* Malairt, mùthadh.
Pernicious, *adj.* Millteach, sgriosail.
Perniciously, *adv.* Gu sgriosail.
Peroration, *s.* Co-dhùnadh òraid.
Perpend, *v. a.* Gabh dlù-bheachd.
Perpendicular, *adj.* 'Na sheasamh dìreach.
Perpendicular, *s.* Direachan.
Perpension, *s.* Smuaineachadh.
Perpetrate, *v. a.* Ciontaich.
Perpetration, *s.* Ciontachadh.
Perpetual, *adj.* Sìor-mhaireannach.
Perpetuate, *v. a.* Cùm an gnàchleachdadh.
Perpetuity, *s.* Sìor-mhaireannachd.
Perplex, *v. a.* Cuir an ioma-chomhairle.
Perplexed, *adj.* Ioma-cheisteach, deacair, duilich.
Perplexity, *s.* Ioma-chomhairle.
Perquisite, *s.* Frith-bhuannachd.
Perry, *s.* Peur-leann.
Persecute, *v. a.* Geur-lean, iomaruag.
Persecution, *s.* Geur-leanmhainn.
Persecutor, *s.* Fear-geur-leanmhainn.
Perseverance, *s.* Buan-leanaltas.
Perseverant, *adj.* Buan-leanailteach.
Persevere, *v. n.* Buanaich, lean.
Persist, *v. n.* Lean ri, bi seasmhach.
Persistance, *s.* Seasmhachd.
Persistive, *adj.* Buanachail.
Person, *s.* Neach, urra; pearsa.
Personable, *adj.* Cumair; tlachmhor.
Personage, *s.* Urra, neach fiùghail.
Personal, *adj.* Aon-urrach, pearsanta.
Personality, *s.* Aon-urralachd, féinachd; athais, innisg.
Personally, *adv.* Gu h-aon-urrach.
Personate, *v. a.* Gabh cosltas, neach eile.
Personation, *s.* Dol an riochd neach eile.

PERSONIFICATION, *s.* Riochd-samhlachadh.
PERSONIFY, *v. a.* Riochd-shamhlaich.
PERSPECTIVE, *s.* Glain-amhairc; fradharc; sealladh.
PERSPECTIVE, *adj.* Fradharcach.
PERSPICACIOUS, *adj.* Geur-fhradharcach.
PERSPICACITY, *s.* Geur-shùileachd.
PERSPICUITY, *s.* Soilleireachd.
PERSPICUOUS, *adj.* Soilleir, so-thuigsinn.
PERSPIRABLE, *adj.* Fallusach.
PERSPIRATION, *s.* Fallus, cur falluis.
PERSPIRE, *v. n.* Cuir fallus dhiot.
PERSUADE, *v. a.* Comhairlich; earalaich, cuir iompaidh; dean deònach.
PERSUASIBLE, *adj.* So-chomhairleach.
PERSUASION, *s.* Comhairle, earalachadh; barail, creideamh.
PERSUASIVE, PERSUASORY, *adj.* Comhairleach, earaileach, iompaidheach.
PERT, *adj.* Clis, beothail, ealamh, beadaidh, ladorna, goileamach.
PERTAIN, *v. a.* Buin do.
PERTINACIOUS, *adj.* Danarra, rag.
PERTINACITY, *s.* Danarrachd, raige, rag-mhuinealachd, déine.
PERTINENCE, *s.* Iomchuidheachd.
PERTINENT, *adj.* Iomchuidh, cubhaidh.
PERTLY, *adv.* Gu clis, gu beadaidh.
PERTNESS, *s.* Beadaidheachd.
PERTURBATE, *v. a.* Buair, aimhreitich.
PERTURBATION, *s.* Iomagain; buaireas.
PERTUSION, *s.* Tolladh; toll.
PERUKE, *s.* Gruag, Fara-ghruag.
PERUSAL, *s.* Leughadh; rannsachadh.
PERUSE, *v. a.* Leugh; rannsaich.
PERVADE, *v. a.* Trid-shiubhail.
PERVASION, *s.* Trid-shiubhal, dol troi'.
PERVERSE, *adj.* Fiar, claon; dian 's an eucoir, rag-mhuinealach, aingidh; mallaichte, crosta.
PERVERSENESS, *s.* Rag-mhuinealachd, aingealtas, dalmachd.
PERVERSION, *s.* Fiaradh, claonadh.
PERVERT, *v. a.* Fiar, claon; truaill.
PERVERTIBLE, *adj.* So-chlaonadh.
PERVICACIOUS, *adj.* Reasgach, dàna.
PERVICACITY, *s.* Danarrachd.
PERVIOUS, *adj.* Neo-dhìonach.
PEST, *s.* Plàigh; dragh, buaireas.
PESTER, *v. a.* Cuir dragh, buair.
PESTHOUSE, *s.* Taigh-leighis na plàighe.
PESTIFEROUS, *adj.* Plàigheach, marbhtach, gabhaltach.
PESTILENCE, *s.* Plàigh, sgrios-ghalar.
PESTILENT, *adj.* Plàigheach, gabhaltach.
PESTLE, *s.* Plocan-pronnaidh.
PET, *s.* Dod, frionas; uan-pheata.
PETAL, *s.* Duilleag, bileag.
PETALOUS, *adj.* Duilleagach, bileagach.
PETITION, *s.* Achanaich, iarrtas, guidhe, aslachadh.
PETITION, *v. a.* Guidh, aslaich, iarr.
PETITIONARY, *adj.* Aslachail.
PETITIONER, *s.* Fear-aslachaidh.
PETRIFACTION, *s.* Tionndadh gu cloich.
PETRIFY, *v. a.* Tionndaidh gu cloich.
PETTICOAT, *s.* Còta-bàn.
PEITTFOGGER, *s.* Fear-lagha gun fhiù, ball-donais; luimeire.
PETTIFOGGING, *adj.* Suarach.
PETTINESS, *s.* Bige, crìne.
PETTISH, *adj.* Dodach, frionasach.
PETTY, *adj.* Beag, suarrach, crìon.
PETULANCE, *s.* Beadaidheachd.
PETULANT, *adj.* Beadaidh, leamh, peasanach, bleideil; goileamach, beag-narach, mi-mhodhail.
PEW, *s.* Suidheachan-eaglais.
PEWET, *s.* A' chrann-lach.
PEWTER, *s.* Staoin, feòdar.
PEWTERER, *s.* Cèard-staoine.
PHALANX, *s.* Dlù-fheachd.
PHANTASM, *s.* Faoin-bharail.
PHANTOM, *s.* Sgleò-shealladh, faileas.
PHARISAICAL, *adj.* Cràbhach o'n leth a mach; cealgach.
PHARMACY, *s.* Eòlas leigheasan.
PHAROS, *s.* Taigh-soluis, taigh-faire.
PHASIS, *s.* Aghaidh, cruth, dealbh.
PHEASANT, *s* An easag.
PHENIX, PHŒNIX, *s.* An tearc-eun.
PHENOMENON, *s.* Sealladh iongantach.
PHIAL, *s.* Searrag bheag.
PHILANTHROPY, *s.* Gradh-daonna; caomhalachd; seirc.
PHILIPPIC, *s.* Màbaireachd, càineadh.
PHILOLOGER, PHILOLOGIST, *s.* Cànanaich; cainntear.
PHILOLOGY, *s.* Eòlas-chànan.
PHILOMEL, *s.* An spìdeag.
PHILOSOPHER, *s.* Feallsanach, teallsanach, càileadair.
PHILOSOPHER'S-STONE, *s.* Clach-nambuadh.
PHILOSOPHICAL, *adj.* Teallsanta, ionnsaichte, eagnaidh, fiosrach.
PHILOSOPHY, *s.* Feallsanachd, teallsanachd, eagnaidheachd, reusonachadh, àrd-fhoghlum.
PHILTER, *s.* Eòlas-gràidh. *Mt.*
PHIZ, *s.* Aogas, aghaidh, aodann.
PHLEBOTOMIST, *s.* Fear tarruinn fala.
PHLEBOTOMIZE, *v. a.* Tarruinn fuil.
PHLEBOTOMY, *s.* Fuil-tharruinn.
PHLEGM, *s.* Ronn; leanntan-cuirp.

PHLEGMATIC, *adj.* Ronnach; trom.
PHLEME, *s.* Tuadh-fhala.
PHOSPHORUS, *s.* Reull na maidne, &c.
PHRASE, *s.* Dòigh-labhairt; facal.
PHRASEOLOGY, *s.* Modh-labhairt.
PHTHISIC, *s.* Tinneas-caithe, éiteach.
PHTHISICAL, *adj.* Caithteach, éiteachail, searganach.
PHYLACTERY, *s.* Crios air an robh sgrìobhaidhean sònraicht' aig na h-Iudhaich.
PHYSIC, *s.* Eòlas leighis; cungaidhean-leighis; teallsanachd-nàduir.
PHYSICAL, *adj.* Nàdurra, càileadarach, leigheasach.
PHYSICIAN, *s.* Léigh, lighiche.
PHYSIOGNOMIST, *s.* Gnùis-fhiosaiche.
PHYSIOGNOMY, *s.* Gnùis-fhiosachd; aogas, aogasg.
PHYSIOLOGIST, *s.* Teallsanach ghnèithean a's chàilean.
PHYSIOLOGY, *s.* Teallsanachd ghnèithean a's chàilean.
PHYLOLOGY, *s.* Lùs-eòlas.
PIA-MATER, *s.* Cochull na h-eanchainn.
PICK, *v.* Tagh, gabh roghadh a's taghadh; tog, tionail; cuir air leth, glan; fosgail glas; tiolp; spiol, criom.
PICKAXE, *s.* Piocaid.
PICKED, PIKED, *adj.* Guineach, geur.
PICKEER, *v.* Spùinn, spùill.
PICKLE, *s.* Picill; staid, còr, càradh.
PICKLE, *v. a.* Saill, dean saillte.
PICKLOCK, *s.* Glas-phiocaidh.
PICKPOCKET, *s.* Frith-mhèirleach.
PICKTOOTH, *s.* Bior-fhiacall.
PICTURE, *s.* Dealbh, dreach, coltas.
PICTURESQUE, *adj.* Bòidheach, àillidh.
PIDDLE, *v. a.* Pioc, bi faoineasach.
PIE, *s.* Pithean; pioghaid.
PIECE, *s.* Mìr, roinn, earrann; caob, bloigh; gunna; bonn.
PIECE, *v.* Cuir mìr ri; ceangail, tàth, tuthagaich.
PIECEMEAL, *adj.* Aon-fhillte, air leth.
PIECEMEAL, *adv.* Mìr air mhìr.
PIED, *adj.* Breac, ballach, balla-bhreac.
PIER, *s.* Seòlait, laimhrig; carragh.
PIERCE, *v.* Toll, sàth; drùigh, gluais; lot, gon, guin.
PIERCER, *s.* Brodaiche, bior-tollaidh.
PIETY, *s.* Cràbhadh; diadhachd.
PIG, *s.* Uircean, oircein; gàta.
PIGEON, *s.* Calman, calaman, colm.
PIGGIN, *s.* Pigean, soitheachan.
PIGMENT, *s.* Dath, lìth.
PIGMY, *s.* Duairce, troich, luspardan.
PIGNUT, *s.* Cnò-thalmhuinn.
PIKE, *s.* Geadas, crann-shleagh.
PIKESTAFF, *s.* Crann-sleagha.
PILASTER, *s.* Carragh ceithir-chearnach.
PILCHARD, PILCHER, *s.* Sgadan-sligeach.
PILCHER, *s.* Faluinn air a lìnigeadh le bian.
PILE, *s.* Post; cruach, dùn; aitreabh.
PILE, *v.* Tòrr, cruach, càrn; lìon.
PILEWORT, *s.* An searraiche.
PILFER, *v.* Tiolp, dean braide.
PILFERER, *s.* Frith-mheirleach.
PILGRIM, *s.* Eilthireach, fear-cuairt.
PILGRIMAGE, *s.* Eilthireachd.
PILL, *s.* Cungaidh leighis.
PILLAGE, *s.* Creach, spùinn, togail.
PILLAGE, *v. a.* Spùinn, spùill, creach.
PILLAR, *s.* Carragh, colbh; fear-cultaic.
PILLION, *s.* Sumag, peallag, pilleag.
PILLORY, *s.* Ballan-stiallach, brangas.
PILLOW, *s.* Adhartan, cluasag.
PILLOW-BEER, *s.* Còmhdach-cluasaig.
PILOSITY, *s.* Ròmaiche, molaiche.
PILOT, *s.* Fear-iùil luinge.
PILOT, *v. a.* Treòraich; stiùr.
PILOTAGE, *s.* Duais-threòraichidh.
PILOUS, *adj.* Ròmach, molach.
PIMENTO, *s.* Peabar-dubh.
PIMP, *s.* Maor-shiùrsaichean.
PIMPERNEL, *s.* Seamrag-Muire.
PIMPING, *adj.* Leibideach, crìon.
PIMPLE, *s.* Biucean, plucan, guirean.
PIN, *s.* Dealg, prìne; cnag, dùl.
PINCERS, *s.* Turcais, teannchar.
PINCH, *v.* Fàisg, gòmagaich; teannaich; brùth; goirtich, ciùrr; éignich, sàraich, pioc, claoidh; caomhainn, bi gann.
PINCH, *s.* Gòmag; teanntachd.
PINCHBECK, *s.* Seòrsa meatailte.
PINCUSHION, *s.* Prìneachan.
PINE, *s.* Craobh ghiubhais.
PINE, *v.* Caoidh, searg, caith ás.
PINFOLD, *s.* Punnd, fang.
PINION, *s.* Cleite, ite-sgéithe; glaslàmh, ceangal-nan-dà-chaol.
PINION, *v. a.* Ceangail na sgiathan; cuibhrich, ceangail na lamhan.
PINK, *s.* Luibh àraidh; seòrs' éisg; roghadh, taghadh; dath bàn-dhearg.
PINK, *v.* Bior, toll; sàth; caog.
PINMONEY, *s.* Airgead pòcaid bhan.
PINNACE, *s.* Geòla, sgoth luinge.
PINNACLE, *s.* Binnein, turraid.
PINNER, *s.* Ceanna-bharr.
PINT, *s.* Pinnt, leth-chart.
PIONEER, *s.* Saighdear-tochlaidh.
PIOUS, *adj.* Diadhaidh, cràbhaidh.
PIP, *s.* Pìochan, galar-chearc.
PIPE, *s.* Pìob, feadan; guth, anail.

PIPE, *v.* Dean pìobaireachd.
PIPER, *s.* Pìobaire.
PIPING, *adj.* Lag, faoin, goileach.
PIPKIN, *s.* Soitheachan creadha.
PIQUANT, *adj.* Beur, geur, goirt, teth.
PIQUE, *s.* Falachd, mì-run, gamhlas.
PIQUE, *v. a.* Feargaich; farranaich.
PIRACY, *s.* Muir-spùinneadh.
PIRATE, *s.* Spùinneadair-mara.
PIRATICAL, *adj.* Spùinneach.
PISCARY, *s.* Cead-iasgaich.
PISCATION, *s.* Iasgaireachd.
PISCATORY, *adj.* Iasgach.
PISCIVOROUS, *adj.* Iasg-itheach.
PISH! *interj.* Fŭith! fŭidh! fŭich!
PISMIRE, *s.* Seangan, sneaghan.
PISS, *s.* Mùn; fual; *v. n.* Mùin.
PISTOL, *s.* Daga, dag; seòra cùinidh.
PISTON, *s.* Slat-stealladair.
PIT, *s.* Toll, sloc; aigein; uaigh.
PITAPAT, *s.* Plosgadh-cridhe; luasanalach; plosgartaich.
PITCH, *s.* Bìgh, àirde, tomhas.
PITCH, *v.* Suidhich; òrduich; tilg, tilg an coinneamh a chinn; tuit an comhair do chinn; tagh.
PITCHER, *s.* Pigidh-uisge.
PITCHFORK, *s.* Gobhlag aolaich.
PITCHY, *adj.* Bìgheach; doilleir, dubh.
PITCOAL, *s.* Ala-ghual.
PITEOUS, *adj.* Muladach, brònach, tùrsach, truagh; truacanta.
PITFALL, *s.* Tallamh-toll, toll-fofhraoch, sloc-thuislidh.
PITH, *s.* Glaodhan; spionnadh.
PITHINESS, *s.* Spionnadh, treòir.
PITHLESS, *adj.* Neo-spionntail, fann.
PITHY, *adj.* Glaodhanach; spionntail, laidir, smiorail.
PITIABLE, *adj.* Truagh, bochd.
PITIFUL, *adj.* Truacanta, tròcaireach; teò-chridheach, truagh; muladach, brònach; leibideach.
PITILESS, *adj.* Neo-thruacanta, aniochdmhor, cruaidh-chridheach, mithròcaireach; gun truas.
PITTANCE, *s.* Cuibhrionn, rud beag truagh.
PITY, *s.* Truacantas, truas.
PITY, *v.* Gabh truas.
PIVOT, *s.* Udalan; cuairt-udalan.
PIX, *s.* Naomh-chiste.
PLACABLE, *adj.* So-chìosnachadh, soirbh, ciùin.
PLACARD, PLACART, *s.* Fuagradh; sanas-follaiseach.
PLACE, *s.* Àite, ionad; còmhnaidh; toiseach; dreuchd.
PLACE, *v. a.* Suidhich, socraich.
PLACID, *adj.* Ciùin, socrach, soirbh.
PLACIDNESS, *s.* Ciùineachd, soirbheachd.
PLAGIARISM, *s.* Mèirle-sgrìobhaidh.
PLAGIARY, PLAGIARIST, *s.* Mèirleach-sgrìobhaidh.
PLAGUE, *s.* Plàigh; claoidh; dragh, buaireadh.
PLAGUE, *v. a.* Pian, buair, leamhaich.
PLAGUY, *adj.* Plàigheach; draghail
PLAICE, *s.* Leubag-mhòr.
PLAID, *s.* Breacan; suaineach.
PLAIN, *adj.* Réidh, còmhnard, min, lom; fosgailte; saor, soilleir, soirbh.
PLAIN, *s.* Còmhnard, réidhlean, réidhleach, faiche, blàr, lòm.
PLAINDEALING, *s.* Tréidhireachd.
PLAINNESS, *s.* Còmhnardachd, réidheachd, mìneachd; fosgailteachd, tréidhireachd; neo-sgeamhalachd.
PLAINT, *s.* Gearan, caoidh, acan, bròn.
PLAINTIVE, *adj.* Tiamhaidh.
PLAINTIFF, *s.* Fear-agairt.
PLAIT, *s.* Filleadh, filleag, dual, pleat.
PLAN, *s.* Innleachd; dealbh, cumadh.
PLAN, *v. a.* Dealbh, deilbh, suidhich.
PLANCHED, *adj.* Déileach.
PLANCHER, *s.* Déile, bòrd.
PLANE, *s.* Locair; còmhnard.
PLANE, *v. a.* Locair, locraich.
PLANET, *s.* Reull, reull-shiùbhlach.
PLANETARY, *adj.* Reulltach.
PLANK, *s.* Bòrd, clàr, déile.
PLANK, *v. a.* Bòrdaich, clàraich.
PLANNER, *s.* Fear-tionnsgain.
PLANT, *s.* Luibh, meacan; fiùran.
PLANT, *v.* Suidhich; cuir sìolaich; socraich, daingnich.
PLANTAIN, *s.* Cuach-Phàdruig.
PLANTATION, *s.* Suidheachadh; ùr-àiteachadh; toirt a staigh.
PLANTER, *s.* Fear-suidheach, fear-àiteachaidh.
PLANTING, *s.* Suidheachadh.
PLASH, *s.* Lochan, pollag; fiùran meanglan.
PLASH, *v. a.* Luidrig; figh air a' chéile.
PLASHY, *adj.* Lodanach, uisgidh, fuarraidh.
PLASM, *s.* Molldair, ladhadair, cumadair.
PLASTER, *s.* Sglàib; plàsda-leighis.
PLASTER, *v. a.* Sglàibrich; glaodh, cuir plàsd' air.
PLASTERER, *s.* Sglàibeadair.
PLASTIC, *adj.* Cruth-thabhairteach.
PLAT, *s.* Mìr fearainn, goirtean.
PLATE, *s.* Lann; éideadh-màilleach; obair-airgeid; truinnsear.
PLATE, *v. a.* Lannaich; airgeadaich.

Platform, *s.* Còmhnard; dealbh, clàr-aghaidh.
Platoon, *s.* Gunnairean.
Platter, *s.* Mias-mhòr; dualadair.
Plaudit, *s.* Caithream aoibhneis, luath-ghair, iolach.
Plausibility, *s.* Ceart choltas.
Plausible, *adj.* Coltach, beulchar.
Play, *v.* Cluich; dean fearas-chuid-eachd; dean mire, dean àbhachd, dean sùgradh; meall, mag, dean fochaid; oibrich, gluais.
Play, *s.* Cluiche, mire, sùgradh, aighear; cleas; macnus; comas-gluasaid.
Player, *s.* Fear-cluiche, cleasaiche.
Playfellow, *s.* Còmpanach-cluiche.
Playful, *adj.* Cleasanta, beadrach, mireagach, sùgrach, mear.
Playhouse, *s.* Taigh-cluiche.
Playsome, *adj.* Mireagach, sùgach.
Plaything, *s.* Ball-cluiche.
Plea, *s.* Cùis-thagraidh; leisgeul.
Plead, *v. a.* Dìon, tagair; agair reusonaich.
Pleader, *s.* Fear-tagraidh.
Pleading, *s.* Tagradh, agairt.
Pleasant, *adj.* Taitneach, ciatach: tlachdmhor, sunntach, faoilidh, cridheil.
Pleasantness, *s.* Taitneachd, tlachd, ciatachd, tlachdmhorachd; sunnt, cridhealas.
Pleasantry, *s.* Cridhealas, aighear.
Please, *v.* Toilich, riaraich, taitinn.
Pleasurable, *adj.* Taitneach, ciatach.
Pleasure, *s.* Taitneas, tlachd, toil-eachadh, toil-inntinn, ciataidh.
Plebeian, *s.* Duine cumanta, balach.
Plebeian, *adj.* Cumanta, suarach.
Pledge, *s.* Geall; deoch-slàinte.
Pledge, *v. a.* Cuir an geall, òl air, slàinte.
Pleiades, *s.* An griglean.
Plenary, *adj.* Làn, foirfe; iomlan.
Plenipotence, *s.* Làn-chumhachd.
Plenipotent, *adj.* Làn-chumhachd-ach.
Plenipotentiary, *s.* Àrd-theachdair.
Plenitude, *s.* Lànachd; pailteas.
Plenteous, *adj.* Pailt, tarbhach.
Plentiful, *adj.* Lìonmhor; tòrach.
Plenty, *s.* Pailteas; lànachd, saibh-reas.
Plethora, Plethory, *s.* Làntachd, cuirp, dòmhlachd cuirp.
Plethoric, *adj.* Làn, dòmhail.
Pleurisy, *s.* An treaghaid.
Pleuritic, *adj.* Treaghaideach.
Pliable, *adj.* Sùbailte, maoth.
Pliableness, *s.* Sùbailteachd.
Pliant, *adj.* So-lùbadh.
Pliers, *s.* Greimiche, turcais.
Plight, *s.* Cor, càradh, inbhe, cùis.
Plight, *v. a.* Thoir geall, thoir urras.
Plinth, *s.* Bunait carraigh, stéidh.
Plod, *v. n.* Saoithrich, oibrich, imich gu trom; dian-chnuasaich.
Plodder, *s.* Fear-trom-shaoithreach.
Plot, *s.* Croit, goirtean; innleachd; feall-chomhairle; cuilbheart, foill.
Plot, *v.* Tionnsgainn; suidhich; dean foill; dean as-innleachd.
Plover, *s.* Feadag.
Plough, *s.* Crann, crann-àraidh.
Plough, *v. a.* Treabh, àr; reub.
Ploughman, *s.* Treabhaiche.
Ploughsharf, *s.* Soc croinn.
Pluck, *v. a.* Spìon, buain.
Pluck, *s.* Tarruinn, spìonadh; cridhe; sgamhan agus grùthan beathaich.
Plug, *s.* Plucan, cnag, geinn.
Plug, *v. a.* Plucaich, geinnich, dùin.
Plum, *s.* Plumbas; 100,000*l.*
Plumage, *s.* Iteach.
Plumb, *v. a.* Feuch doimhneachd, feuch dìrichead.
Plumb, *adv.* Dìreach 'na sheasamh.
Plumber, *s.* Ceard-luaidhe.
Plume, *s.* Ite, fàbhar, dŏs-mullaich, seŏcan.
Plume, *v.* Tog itean; cuir dŏs air, dosaich; séid suas, ăt.
Plumingerous, *adj.* Iteagach.
Plummet, *s.* Sreang-thomhais doimh-neachd; cudthrom luaidhe.
Plump, *adj.* Sultmhor, dòmhail, reamhar, reachmhor, taiceil, tiugh.
Plump, *v. n.* Plub, plum.
Plumpness, *s.* Sultmhorachd, somalt-achd, domhladachd.
Plumpudding, *s.* Marag phlumbais.
Plumy, *adj.* Còmhdaichte le itean.
Plunder, *s.* Cobhartach, creach.
Plunder, *v. a.* Spùinn; tog creach.
Plunderer, *s.* Spùinneadair.
Plunge, *v.* Tùm, cuir fodha; tilg sàth.
Plunge, *s.* Tumadh, bogadh; àmh-ghar, airc, teinn.
Plural, *adj.* Iomarra.
Pluralist, *s.* Fear dà dhreuchd.
Plurality, *s.* Iomadachd.
Plush, *s.* Seòrsa clò.
Pluvial, Pluvious, *adj.* Frasach, braonach, robach, fliuch.
Ply, *v.* Saoithrich, oibrich ri, iomair, dian-ghnàthaich, grìos, aslaich, guidh; lùb.
Ply, *s.* Aomadh, car, laidhe; filleadh.

Pneumatic, *adj.* Gaothach.
Pneumatics, *s.* Eòlas gaoithe, &c.
Pheumatology, *s.* Eòlas bhith-spioradail.
Pneumonics, *s.* Leigheas sgamhain.
Poach, *v.* Slaop; dean goid frìthe.
Poacher, *s.* Mèirleach sìthne.
Poachy, *adj.* Àitid, bog.
Pock, *s.* Bòc, guirean brice; pocan.
Pocket, *s.* Pòcaid, pòca, pùidse.
Pocket, *v. a.* Cuir 's a' phòcaid.
Pocket-book, *s.* Leabhar-pòcaid.
Poculent, *adj.* A dh' fhaodair òl.
Pod, *s.* Cochull, plaosg, sgrath, rùsg.
Poem, *s.* Dàn, duan, laoidh.
Poesy, *s.* Bàrdachd, rannachd.
Poet, *s.* Bàrd, filidh, aos-dàna.
Poetaster, *s.* Sgonna-bhàrd.
Poetess, Poetress, *s.* Bana-bhàrd.
Poetic, Poetical, *adj.* Bàrdail.
Poetry, *s.* Bàrdachd, ranntachd.
Poignancy, *s.* Gairge, gèire, seirbhe.
Poignant, *adj.* Garg, geur, searbh.
Point, *s.* Roinn, bior; barr-iall; rudha, sròn; neart, seadh, brìgh, tiota; cor; ponc, comharradh; ball; cuspair, an dearbh nì.
Point, *v. a.* Geuraich, thoir roinn air, bioraich; seòl, comharraich; cuimsich; poncaich; feuch, nochd.
Pointed, *adj.* and *part.* Geur, biorach; poncail, eagnaidh.
Pointer, *s.* Cù-eunaich.
Pointless, *adj.* Maol; gun roinn.
Poise, *s.* Co-chothrom.
Poise, *v. a.* Co-chothromaich.
Poison, *s.* Nimh, puinnsean.
Poison, *v. a.* Nimhich; truaill, mill.
Poisonous, *adj.* Nimheach, nimheil.
Poitrel, *s.* Uchd-bheairt eich, &c.
Poke, *s.* Poca, balg, màileid.
Poke, *v. a.* Smeuraich, rùraich.
Poker, *s.* Bioran-griosaich.
Pole, *s.* Crann, maide, cabar, cuaille; cùig slat gu leth.
Polecat, *s.* Feòcullan, taghan.
Polemic, *adj.* Connspaideach.
Polemic, *s.* Connspaidiche.
Polestar, *s.* An reull-iùil thuath.
Police, *s.* Riaghladh baile, &c.
Policy, *s.* Innleachd-riaghlaidh; seòltachd, steòrnadh, crìontachd, gliocas.
Polish, *v.* Lìomh, liomhaich, sgéimhich; oileanaich.
Polish, *s.* Lìomhadh, loinnireachd.
Polisher, *s.* Fear-lìomhaidh.
Polite, *adj.* Modhail, oileanach.
Politeness, *s.* Modhalachd.
Politic, Political, *adj.* Eòlach, eagnaidh, seòlta, domhain, carach; cuilbheartach; a bhuineas do dh'-eòlas-riaghlaidh.
Politician, *s.* Fear eòlach mu innleachdan riaghlaidh.
Politics, *s.* Inleachdan riaghlaidh.
Politure, *s.* Liomharachd.
Polity, *s.* Modh riaghlaidh.
Poll, *s.* Ceann; ainm-chlàr.
Poll, *v. a.* Sgud, bèarr, sgath dheth; spùinn, creach, lom; gabh ainmean; gèarr falt.
Pollard, *s.* Craobh bhearrte; damh gun chròic; garbhan, pronn.
Polenger, *s.* Preas-choille.
Pollute, *v. a.* Truaill, salaich, measgaich le salchar.
Polluted, *part.* and *adj.* Truaillte.
Pollution, *s.* Truailleadh, salchadh.
Poltroon, *s.* Gealtaire, cladhaire.
Polyanthus, *s.* Sòbhrach-gheamhraidh.
Polygamy, *s.* Ioma-phòsadh.
Polyglot, *adj.* Ioma-chainnteach.
Polygon, *s.* Ioma-chèarnag.
Polypous, *adj.* Ioma-chasach.
Polypus, *s.* Ăt-cuinnein.
Polysyllable, *s.* Ioma-shiola.
Polytheism, *s.* Creideamh nan-ioma dia.
Pomade, *s.* Ola-cinn, ola-fuilt.
Pomatum, *s.* Ungadh fuilt.
Pomegranate, *s.* Gràn-ubhall.
Pommel, *s.* Ubhal claidheimh.
Pommel, *v. a.* Slad, slacainn, pronn.
Pomp, *s.* Greadhnachas, uaìll.
Pomposity, *s.* Mòr-chuis.
Pompous, *adj.* Mòr-chuiseach, uailleil.
Pompousness, *s.* Mòralachd.
Pond, *s.* Linne, uisge-tàimh.
Ponder, *v.* Smuainich, beachdsmuainich, fìdrich, cnuasaich.
Ponderosity, *s.* Cudthromachd; cùramachd.
Ponderous, *adj.* Cudthromach, cùramach, laidir.
Ponent, *adj.* Iar, iarach.
Poniard, *s.* Cuinnsear.
Pontage, *s.* Cìs-drochaid.
Pontiff, *s.* Àrd-shagart, am pàpa.
Pontifical, *adj.* Àrd-shagartach.
Pontifical, *s.* Leabhar nan deasghnàth.
Pontificate, *s.* Pàpanachd.
Ponton, *s.* Drochaid-fhleodraidh.
Pony, *s.* Each beag.
Poop, *s.* Deireadh luinge, uisge-tàimh.
Poor, *adj.* Bochd, aimbeartach, dòlum, ainnis; ìosal, suarrach, leibideach; truagh, cruaidh; caol, seang.
Poorly, *adj.* Euslainteach, tinn.

Pop, *s.* Sgailc, bragh, braghadh.
Pope, *s.* Am pàpa.
Popedom, *s.* Pàpachd.
Popery, Papistry, *s.* Pàpanachd.
Popgun, Potgun, *s.* Gunna-sgailc.
Popinjay, *s.* An snagan-daraich.
Popish, *adj.* Pàpanach.
Poplar, *s.* Chritheann, critheach.
Poppy, *s.* An crom-lùs.
Populace, *s.* An sluagh, an cumanta.
Popular, *adj.* Taitneach do 'n t-sluagh; cumanta; so-thuigsinn.
Popularity, *s.* Sluagh-thaitneachd.
Populate, *v. n.* Fàs-lìonmhor, sìolaich; lian le sluagh.
Population, *s.* Sluagh tìre.
Populous, *adj.* Sluaghmhor.
Porcelain, *s.* Criadh fhìnealta.
Porch, *s.* Sgàil-thaigh, foir-dhorus.
Pore, *s.* Pòr, tollan-falluis.
Pore, *v. n.* Geur-amhairc; geur-sgrùd, geur-bheachdaich.
Poreblind, *adj.* Dalladh-eunain.
Pork, *s.* Muic-fheòil ùr.
Porker, Porkling, *s.* Uircean.
Porosity, *s.* Tolltachd, còsachd.
Porous, Pory, *adj.* Tolltach, pòrach.
Porpoise, Porpus, *s.* Péileag, cana.
Porridge, Potage, *s.* Lite.
Porringer, *s.* Soitheach beag creadha.
Port, *s.* Port; cala, acarsaid, dorus, geata; iomchar, giùlan; fion-dearg.
Portable, *adj.* So-ghiùlan.
Portal, *s.* Dorus-àrd, geata mòr.
Portcullis, *s.* Drochaid-thogalach.
Portend, *v. a.* Fàisnich, fiosaich.
Portent, *s.* Droch comharradh.
Portentous, *adj.* Droch thargrach.
Porter, *s.* Dorsair; gille-teachdaireachd; dù-leann, dubh-lionn.
Porterage, *s.* Duais iomchair.
Portglaive, Portglave, *s.* Fear-iomchair claidheimh, gille-claidheimh.
Porthole, *s.* Toll gunna mhòir.
Portico, *s.* Sràid chòmhdaichte.
Portion, *s.* Earrann, roinn, cuid.
Portion, *v. a.* Roinn; thoir dlighe no tochradh do.
Portliness, *s.* Stàtalachd, foghainteachd, riochdalachd.
Portly, *adj.* Stàtail, foghainteach.
Portmanteau, *s.* Màileid-turais.
Portrait, *s.* Dealbh duine, sàmhla.
Portray, *v. a.* Tarruinn dealbh.
Portress, *s.* Bann-dorsair.
Pose, *v. a.* Cuir 'na thosd, cuir an ioma-cheist; ceasnaich.
Position, *s.* Suidheachadh.
Positional, *adj.* Ionadach.
Positive, *adj.* Fìor, fìrinneach; dearbh-chinnteach, dearbhte; dìreach, sònraichte, soilleir; féin-bharalach; suidhichte, stéidhichte, socraichte, ùghdarrach.
Positiveness, *s.* Cinnteachd, dearbhtachd; féin-bharalachd.
Posse, *s.* Buidheann, feachd.
Possess, *v. a.* Sealbhaich, gabh seilbh.
Possession, *s.* Sealbhachadh, seilbh.
Possessive, Possessory, *adj.* Seilbheach, seilbheachail.
Possessor, *s.* Sealbhadair.
Posset, *s.* Bainne air a bhinndeachadh le fìon, &c.
Possibility, *s.* Comas, comasachd.
Possible, *adj.* Comasach.
Post, *s.* Gille-litrichean; post; turas-cabhagach; ionad-freiceadain; dreuchd; àite; gnothach.
Post, *v. n.* Dean turas cabhagach.
Postage, *s.* Duais giùlain litreach.
Postboy, *s.* Fear carbaid-rathaid.
Postchaise, *s.* Carbad-duaise.
Posterior, *adj.* Deireannach.
Posteriors, *s.* Leth-deiridh, màsan.
Posterity, *s.* Na linntean ri teachd.
Postern, *s.* Dorus beag, frith-gheata.
Posthaste, *s.* Cabhag, grad-shiubhal.
Posthumous, *adj.* An déigh bàis.
Postillion, *s.* Gille-carbaid.
Postman, *s.* Gille-litrichean.
Postmaster, *s.* Maighstir-phost.
Post-office, *s.* Taigh-litrichean.
Postpone, *v. a.* Cuir dàil ann.
Postscript, *s.* Fath-sgrìobhadh.
Postulate, *s.* Beachd no fìrinn gun dearbhadh.
Postulation, *s.* Togail gun dearbhadh; beachd gun dearbhadh.
Posture, *s.* Suidheachadh, laidhe, dòigh suidhe no seasamh no laidhe; staid, seòl.
Posy, *s.* Blàth-dhos, blàth-bhad.
Pot, *s.* Poit, prais, praiseach.
Pot, *v. a.* Cuir am poit.
Potash, *s.* Luath luibhean.
Potation, *s.* Pòit, pòitearachd.
Potato, *s.* Buntàta.
Potbellied, *adj.* Bronnach.
Potch, *v. a.* Dean goid, dean meirle.
Potcompanion, *s.* Còmpanach òil.
Potency, *s.* Ùghdarras, uachdranachd.
Potent, *adj.* Cumhachdach, treun.
Potentate, *s.* Righ, àrd-uachdaran.
Potential, *adj.* Comasach; buadhach, neartmhor.
Potentiality, *s.* Comasachd.
Potentness, *s.* Neartmhorachd.
Pother, *s.* Gleadhraich, buaireas.

Potion, *s.* Deoch.
Potsherd, *s.* Spreadhan, pigean, sligechreadha. *Bi.*
Potter, *s.* Criadhadair.
Pottery, *s.* Criadhadaireachd.
Pottle, *s.* Tomhas cheithir pinnt.
Pouch, *s.* Pocaid, pòca, brù mhòr.
Poult, *s.* Isean-eòin, pùda.
Poulterer, *s.* Fear-reic eun.
Poultice, *s.* Fuar-lite, fuarag.
Poultry, *s.* Cearcan, eòin-taighe.
Pounce, *s.* Spòg, cràg; inean eòin.
Pound, *s.* Pund; pund-Sasunnach; punnd spréidhe.
Pound, *v. a.* Pronn, brùth, bleith; cuir am punnd.
Poundage, *s.* Airgead-puinnd.
Pour, *v. a.* Dòirt, taom, bruchd.
Pout, *s.* Bodach-ruadh, pollach.
Pout, *v. n.* Cuir gnoig ort, cuir spliug ort, cuir spreill ort.
Poverty, *s.* Bochdainn, ainnis.
Powder, *s.* Fùdar, dùs, smùr, sad.
Powder, *v. a.* Mìn-phronn, dean 'na smùr; crath smùr air; fùdaraich, crath salann air.
Powder-horn, *s.* Adharc-fhùdair.
Powdery, *adj.* Mìn, pronn.
Power, *s.* Cumhachd, comas.
Powerful, *adj.* Cumhachdach.
Powerfulness, *s.* Neartmhorachd.
Powerless, *adj.* Lag-chuiseach, fann.
Pox, *s.* Breac; a' bhreac-Fhràngach.
Practicable, *adj.* So-dheaneamh.
Practical, *adj.* Cleachdail, cleachdte.
Practice, *s.* Cleachdadh, àbhais; gnàth, innleachd, dòigh.
Practic, *adj.* Cleachdach; teòma.
Practise, *v.* Cleachd, gnàthaich.
Practitioner, *s.* Fear-cleachdaidh.
Pragmatical, *adj.* Beadaidh, leamh.
Praise, *s.* Cliù, moladh.
Praise, *v. a.* Mol, cliùthaich.
Praiseworthiness, *s.* Ion-mholtachd.
Praiseworthy, *adj.* Ion-mholta.
Prame, *s.* Bàta-leathann, coite.
Prance, *v. n.* Leum, geàrr sùrdag, sùrdagaich; céimnich gu h-uallach.
Prancing, *adj.* Leumnach, sùrdagach, beiceiseach, meamnach.
Prank, *s.* Cleas, cleasachd, meamna, àbhcaid, mire; droch-cleas.
Prate, *v. n.* Dean goileam, dean lonais, dean beulais.
Prate, *s.* Faoin-chainnt, lonais.
Prater, *s.* Glagaire, gobaire.
Prating, *s.* Glagaireachd, goileam.
Pratingly, *ad.* Gu goileamach.
Pratler, *s.* Goileamaiche.
Pratique, *s.* Teisteanas-slàinte.
Prattle, *s.* Faoin-chainnt, gobaireachd, briotas, briot.
Prattle, *v. n.* Dean gobaireachd.
Pravity, *s.* Truaillidheachd.
Prawn, *s.* Am muasgan-caol.
Pray, *v.* Dean ùrnaigh, guidh.
Prayer, *s.* Ùrnaigh, guidhe, iarrtas.
Prayerbook, *s.* Leabhar-ùrnaigh.
Preach, *v.* Searmonaich.
Preacher, *s.* Searmonaiche.
Preaching, *s.* Searmonachadh.
Preamble, *s.* Roimh-ràdh.
Precarious, *adj.* Neo-chinnteach.
Precariousness, *s.* Neo-chinnteachd.
Precariously, *adv.* Gu teagamhach, gu baoghalach.
Precaution, *s.* Faicill, roi'-chùram.
Precaution, *v. a.* Roi' earalaich.
Precede, *v. a.* Roi'-imich, rach roimhe.
Precedence, *s.* Roi'-imeachd, toiseach, tùs; inbhe, roi'-àite.
Precedent, *adj.* Roimhe, tùsach.
Precedent, *s.* Eiseamplair.
Precedently, *adv.* Roi'-làimh.
Precentor, *s.* Fear-togail-fuinn.
Precept, *s.* Àinte, reachd, riaghailt.
Preceptive, *adj.* Reachdach, àinteil.
Preceptor, *s.* Oid'-ionnsachaidh.
Precession, *s.* Roi'-shiubhal.
Precinct, *s.* Comharradh-crìche.
Precious, *adj.* Luachmhor, prìseil.
Preciousness, *s.* Luachmhorachd.
Precipice, *s.* Sgòrr, càs-chreag.
Precipitance, *s.* Caise, braise, cabhag, deifir, braisead, déine.
Precipitant, *adj.* Càs, bras, dian.
Precipitate, *v.* Tilg sìos, tilg an comhair a' chinn, cabhagaich, deifirich; tuit sìos, sìolaidh gu grunnd.
Precipitate, *adj.* Chabhagach, deifireach, neo-fhaicilleach.
Precipitately, *adv.* An comhair a' chinn.
Precipitation, *s.* Caise, braise; tuiteam sìos; sioladh gu grunnd.
Precipitous, *adj.* Cas, corrach, sgorrach, creagach; bras.
Precipitousness, *s.* Caise, braise.
Precise, *adj.* Poncail, eagarrach, fuirmeil.
Precision, **Preciseness**, *s.* Poncalachd, eagarrachd.
Preclude, *v. a.* Dùin a mach, grab, bac, cuir bacadh air.
Preclusive, *adj.* Toirmeasgach.
Precocious, *adj.* Roi'-abaich.
Precociousness, *s.* Roi'-abaichead.
Precocity, *s.* Roi'-abaichead.
Precognition, *s.* Roi'-fhiosrachadh.
Preconceit, *s.* Roi'-bheachd.

Preconceive, *v. a.* Roi'-bheachdaich.
Preconception, *s.* Roi'-bheachd.
Preconcert, *v.* Roi'-shuidhich.
Precontract, *s.* Roi'-chùmhnant.
Precontract, *v.* Roi'-chùmhnantaich.
Precurse, *s.* Roi'-ruith.
Precursor, *s.* Roi'-ruith-ear.
Precursory, *adj.* Roi'-ruitheach.
Predaceous, *adj.* Creachach.
Predatory, *adj.* Reubainneach.
Predecessor, *s.* Roi'-shealbhadair.
Preedestinarian, Predestinator, *s.* Creideach an roi'-òrduchadh Dhé.
Predestinate, *v. a.* Roi'-òrduich.
Predestination, *s.* Roi'-òrduchadh Dhé, roi'-thaghadh Dhé.
Predestine, *v. a.* Roi'-òrduich.
Predetermination, *s.* Roi'-òrduchadh, roi'-shònrachadh.
Predetermine, *v. a.* Roi'-òrduich, roi'-shònraich, roi'-rùinich.
Predicament, *s.* Còr, ìre, gne.
Predicate, *s.* Tuairisgeul, aithris.
Predicate, *v.* Abair, innis, aithris, cuir an céill.
Predication, *s.* Innse; iomradh.
Predict, *v. a.* Roi'-innis, roi'-aithris.
Predictive, *adj.* Roi'-innseach.
Prediction, *s.* Fàisneachd.
Predictor, *s.* Fiosaiche, fàidh.
Predigestion, *s.* Roi'-mheirbheadh.
Predilection, *s.* Roi'-thlachd.
Predispose, *v. a.* Roi'-uidheamaich.
Predisposition, *s.* Roi'-uidheamachadh, roi'-ullachadh.
Predominance, Predominancy, *s.* Barrachd, uachdranachd, lamh-an-uachdar, buaidh, ceannas.
Predominant, *adj.* Uachdranach, ceannasach, buadhach.
Predominate, *v. n.* Buadhaich.
Pre-elect, *v. a.* Roi'-thagh.
Pre-eminence, *s.* Àrd-bhuaidh.
Pre-eminent, *adj.* Àrd-bhuadhach.
Pre-engage, *v. a.* Roi'-cheangail.
Pre-engagement, *s.* Roi'-cheangal, roi'-ghealladh, roi'-chumhnant.
Pre-establishment, *s.* Roi'-shuidheachadh, roi'-shocrachadh.
Pre exist, *v. n.* Bi ann roi'-làimh.
Pre-existence, *s.* Roi'-bhith.
Pre-existent, *adj.* Roi'-bhitheach.
Preface, *s.* Roi'-ràdh.
Preface, *v. n.* Roi'-abair.
Prefatory, *adj.* Roi'-ràdhach.
Prefect, *s.* Ceannard, fear-dìona.
Prefer, *v. a.* Roghnaich, àrdaich.
Preferable, *adj.* Ni's fèarr.
Preference, *s.* Roghainn.
Preferment, *s.* Ardachadh.
Prefiguration, *s.* Roi'-shamhlachadh.
Prefix, *v. a.* Roi'-shuidhich.
Prefix, *s.* Roi'-fhacal.
Pregnable, *adj.* So-ghlacadh.
Pregnancy, *s.* Leth-tromachd.
Pregnant, *adj.* Torrach, leth-tromach, làn, trom; tarbhach, sìolmhor.
Pregustation, *s.* Roi'-bhlasad.
Prejudge, *v. a.* Roi'-bhreithnich.
Prejudgment, *s.* Roi'-bhreth, claon-bhreth.
Prejudication, *s.* Roi'-bhreithneachadh, claon-bhreithneachadh.
Prejudice, *s.* Claon-bhàigh; cron.
Prejudice, *v.* Cuir an droch bheachd, cuir an claon-bharail; dochainn le claon bhreth; ciùrr, lochdaich.
Prejudicial, *adj.* Claon-bhretheach; cronail, aimhleasach.
Prelacy, *s.* Easbuigeachd.
Prelate, *s.* Easbuig.
Prelatical, *adj.* Easbuigeach.
Prelection, *s.* Searmonachadh.
Preliminary, *adj.* Tòiseachail.
Preliminary, *s.* Ceud-thùs, toiseach.
Prelude, *s.* Deuchainn-ghleusta; toiseach, roi' ghnothach, roi'-chùis.
Prelude, *v. a.* Roi'-thaisbean.
Prelusive, *adj.* Roi'-làimheach.
Premature, *adj.* Roi' mhithich, roi 'n àm, roi'-abaich.
Prematurely, *adv.* Gu h-ann-tràthail, roi'n mhithich.
Premeditate, *v. a.* Roi'-thionnsgain, roi'-bheachdaich, roi'-chnuasaich.
Premeditation, *s.* Roi'-thionnsgnadh, roi'-bheachdachadh, roi'-chnuasachadh.
Premerit, *v. a.* Roi'-thoill.
Premier, *adj.* Prìomh, a's àirde.
Premier, *s.* Àrd-chomhairliche.
Premise, *v. a.* Roi'-mhìnich.
Premises, *s.* Roi'-fhìrinnean; taighean, aitreabh, fearann.
Premium, *s.* Duais-barrachd.
Premonish, *v. a.* Roi'-earalaich.
Premonition, *s.* Roi'-fhiosrachadh.
Premonstrate, *v. a.* Roi'-thaisbean.
Prenominate, *v. a.* Roi'-ainmich.
Prenomination, *s.* Roi'-ainmeachadh.
Preoccupation, *s.* Roi'-ghabhail; claon-bhàigh.
Preoccupy, *v. a.* Roi'-shealbhaich.
Preominate, *v. a.* Roi'-innis.
Preopinion, *s.* Roi'-bharail.
Preordain, *v. a.* Roi'-òrduich.
Preordination, *s.* Roi'-òrduchadh.
Preparation, *s.* Uidheamachadh.
Preparative, *s.* Gleusadh.
Preparatory, *adj.* Ullachail.

Prepare, *v. a.* Ullaich, uidheamaich, deasaich, dean rèidh.
Preparedness, *s.* Ullamhachd.
Prepense, *adj.* Roi'-smuaintichte, roi'-bheachdaichte, suidhichte, socraichte, rùnaichte.
Preponderance, *s.* Barrachd cudthrom, barrachd cothrom.
Prepose, *v. a.* Roi'-chuir.
Preposition, *s.* Roi'-bhriathar.
Prepossess, *v. a.* Roi'-shealbhaich.
Prepossession, *s.* Roi'-sheilbh.
Prepossessor, *s.* Roi'-shealbhadair.
Preposterous, *adj.* Docharach.
Preposterously, *adv.* Gu docharachd, gu h eu-céillidh.
Prerequire, *v. a.* Roi'-iarr.
Prerequisite, *adj.* Roi'-fheumail.
Preresolve, *v. a.* Roi'-shuidhich.
Prerogative, *s.* Còir-dhlighe.
Prerogatived, *adj.* Còir-dhligheach.
Presage, Presagement, Manadh, fàisneachd, sanus.
Presage, *v. a.* Roi'-innis, roi'-thaisbean, targair, dean fiosachd.
Presbyter, *s* Fear-cléire, cléireach, pears'-eaglais ; sagart.
Presbyterial, *adj.* Cléireachail.
Presbyterian, *s.* Fear-dion cléire, no phears-eaglais.
Presbytery, *s.* Cléir.
Prescience, *s.* Roi'-fhios.
Prescient, *adj.* Roi'-fhiosrach.
Prescribe, *v.* Thoir seòladh.
Prescript, Prescription, *s.* Seòladh, òrdugh, riaghailt, riaghailt-léigh.
Presence, *s.* Làthaireachd, làthair; dreach, tuar, aogas, dealbh, cruth; tapachd, teòmachd.
Presentation, Presention, *s.* Roi'-fhaireachadh, roi'-fhiosrachd, roi'-bheachd.
Present, *adj.* A làthair, dlù, làthaireach, aig làimh ; 's an àm, 's a' cheart àm; an cuimhne; fo bheachd.
Present, *s.* Tìodhlac, tabhartas.
Present, *v. a.* Thoir an làthair, cuir 's an làthair, nochd, taisbean ; tairg, tabhair; thoir seachad, thoir do, builich, air, thoir còir do.
Presentable, *adj.* So-bhuileachadh, so-thaisbeanadh, so-nochdadh.
Presentation, *s.* Tairgsinn, buileachadh, tabhairt, taisbeanadh, nochdadh, cur 's an làthair.
Presentee, *s.* Neach a fhuair còir air beathachadh eaglais.
Presently, *adv.* 'S a cheart àm, an ceart uair, air an uair, gu grad, gu clis, gu luath.
Presentiment, *s.* Roi'-bheachd.
Presentment, *s.* Tabhairt.
Presentness, *s.* Cliseachd.
Preservable, *adj.* So-ghleidheadh.
Preservation, *s.* Saoradh, tèarnadh, gleidheadh, tasgaidh, dìon.
Preservative, *s.* Cungaidh-leighis.
Preserve, *v. a.* Saor, teasraig, dìon, gléidh ; gréidh, dean suas le cungaidh.
Preserve, *s.* Meas gréidhte.
Preserver, *s.* Fear teasraiginn.
Preside, *v. n.* Riaghail, riaghailtich.
Presidency, *s.* Riaghlaireachd.
President, *s.* Fear-riaghlaidh.
Presignification, *s.* Roi'-sheadh.
Presignify, *v. a.* Roi'-sheadhaich.
Press, *v.* Fàisg, brùth ; claoidh, sàraich ; éignich, co-éignich ; sparr, cuir iompadh ; fòirn.
Press, *s.* Bruthadair, fàsgadair ; clò-chlàr ; dòmhlachd, mùchadh ; déine, braise ; còrnchlar.
Pressgang, *s.* Luchd-ghlacaidh.
Pression, *s.* Bruthadh, fàsgadh.
Pressman, *s.* Fear clò-bhualaidh.
Pressmoney, *s.* Airgead-glacaidh.
Pressure, *s.* Bruthadh, fàsgadh, teannachadh ; éigin, ainneart.
Prest, *adj.* Grad, clis, luath.
Presumable, *adj.* So-shaoilsinn.
Presume, *v. a.* Roi'-chreid, roi'-bheachdaich, gabh mar fhìrinn; abair gun dearbhadh ; gabh ort, gabh mar dhànadas ; thoir ionnsaidh ladorna, thoir dàn-ionnsaidh.
Presumption, *s.* Roi'-bheachd ; faoindhànadas ; coltas cudthromach ; dànadas, ladornas ; dall-earbsa.
Presumptive, *adj.* Roi'-smuainichte ; a réir coltais, coltach ; dàna, ladorna.
Presumptuous, *adj.* Àrdanach, dalma; aindiadhaidh, neo-urramach.
Presumptuousness, *s.* Uaimhreachas, ladornas, dalmachd.
Presupposal, *s.* Roi'-bharail.
Presuppose, *v. a.* Roi'-bharalaich.
Pretence, *s.* Leithsgeul, sgàth, faoinsgeul ; cur an ìre, gabhail air féin.
Pretend, *v.* Leig ort, gabh ort; dean mealladh, gabh feall-choltas ; agair, tagair.
Pretender, *s.* Fear-agairt còrach, air ni nach bun da.
Pretensions, *s.* Agartas, còire ; faoin-choltas.
Preterit, *adj.* A chaid seachad.
Preternatural, *adj.* Mi-nàdurra.
Pretext, *s.* Còmhdach, falach, lei sgeul.

Pretor, *s.* Breitheamh Ròmhanach, ard-bhailidh baile-mhòir.

Prettiness, *s.* Grinneas, briaghachd, bòidhchead, bòidhche.

Pretty, *adj.* Grinn, briagha, bòidheach, lurach, laoghach.

Pretty, *adv.* An eatorras; a leth char.

Prevail, *v. a.* Buadhaich, coisinn.

Prevailing, *adj.* Buadhach.

Prevalent, *adj.* Buadhach, cumanta.

Prevalently, *adv.* Gu buadhach.

Prevaricate, *v. n.* Dean breug, bi leam-leat.

Prevarication, *s.* Breugnachadh.

Prevaricator, *s.* Fear-breugnachaidh.

Prevent, *v.* Bac, grab, caisg.

Prevention, *s.* Bacadh, grabadh; roi'-ghabhail.

Preventive, *adj.* Bacail; dìon, dìdeanach, teasraigeach.

Preventive, *s.* Cùngaidh-phillidh.

Previous, *adj.* Air thoiseach, roimh.

Previously, *ad.* Roi'-làimh.

Previousness, *s.* Tùs, tùsachd.

Prey, *s.* Creach, cobhartach.

Prey, *v. n.* Thig beò air reubainn; spùinn, creach; ith suas.

Price, *s.* Luach, prìs; duais.

Price, *v. a.* Meas, cuir luach air.

Prick, *v.* Bior, stob, lot; dean biorach; spor, stuig, brosnaich; gon; dean goirt, dean searbh; sgeadaich thu féin; dean comharradh ciùil.

Prick, *s.* Stob, bior; dealg; gonadh, agartas coguis; cuspair, ball-amais, comharradh-ciùil; bioradh, brodadh; lòrg maigheich.

Pricket, *s.* Dà-bhliadhnach féigh.

Prickle, *s.* Bior, dealg, calg, colg.

Prickly, *adj.* Biorach, guineach.

Pride, *s.* Àrdan, uabhar, uaill, stràic, pròis, moit, uaibhreachas, mòr-chuis.

Pride, *v. a.* Àrdaich thu féin; bi uaibhreach; dean uaill á.

Prier, *s.* Fear dian-sgrùdaidh.

Priest, *s.* Sagart, pear-eaglais.

Priestcraft, *s.* Cléir-sheòltachd.

Priestess, *s.* Bann-sagart.

Priesthood, *s.* Sagartachd.

Priestliness, *s.* Sagartalachd.

Priestly, *adj.* Sagartail.

Priestridden, *adj.* Fo chuing shagart.

Prig, *s.* Méirleach, beadagan.

Prim, *adj.* Fuirmeil, leòmach, eagarach, frionasach, sgeilmeil.

Primacy, *s.* Àrd-shagartachd.

Primary, *adj.* Ceud, prìomh.

Primate, *s.* Àrd-shagart.

Primateship, *s.* Àrd-shagartachd, àrd-easbuigeachd, ceannardachd eaglais.

Primatical, *adj.* Àrd-shagartach, àrd-easbuigeach.

Prime, Primal, *adj.* Moch, prìomh, deagh, sònraichte, gasda; ceud, tùsach; òirdheirc, urramach.

Prime, *s.* An òg-mhadainn, a' chamhanaich, briseadh na fàire, mochthrath; taghadh, roghadh; blàthòige, tréine neirt; ùr-fhàs, earrachd; foirfeachd, àrd-choimhliontachd, lànachd; tùs, toiseach.

Prime, *v. n.* Cuir a steach fùdarcluaise.

Primely, *adv.* Gu sònraichte math.

Primeness, *s.* Tùs; urram.

Primer, *s.* Leabhar-cloinne.

Primeval, *adj.* Sean-aimsireil, àrsaidh, sean-ghnàthach, ceud-aimsireil.

Primitive, *adj.* Prìomh, tùsach, air thoiseach, o thoiseach.

Primitive, *s.* Bun-fhacal.

Primitiveness, *s.* Prìomhachd.

Primity, *s.* Prìomhachd, tùsachd.

Primogenial, *adj.* Ceud-ghinte.

Primogenitor, *s.* Ceud-sinnsear.

Primogeniture, *s.* Sinnsearrachd.

Primrose, *s.* Sòbhrach, seòbhrach.

Prince, *s.* Prionnsa, flath.

Princedom, *s.* Prionnsachd.

Princelike, *adj.* Prionnsail.

Princeliness, *s.* Prionnsalachd.

Princely, *adj.* Mòr, flathail.

Princess, *s.* Banna-phrionnsa.

Principal, *adj.* Ceud, prìomh, àraidh, sònraichte.

Principal, *s.* Ceannard, ceann.

Principality, *s.* Ceannardachd.

Principally, *adv.* Gu sònraite; thar chàch.

Principle, *s.* Dùil; màthair-aobhair, aobhar; bun, freumh, gineadair; fìrinn-shuidhichte, stéidh; fàth, ceud-fàth; ceart, ceartas, còir.

Print, *v. a.* Comharraich; clòbhuail.

Print, *s.* Comhárradh, athailt, lorg; inneal comharrachaidh, laghadair; dealbh, clò-bhualadh.

Printer, *s.* Clò-bhuailtear.

Printing, *s.* Clò-bhualadh.

Printless, *adj.* Gun lòrg.

Prior, *adj.* Air tùs.

Prior, *s.* Àrd-mhanach, aba.

Prioress, *s.* Ban-aba.

Priority, *s.* Toiseach, toiseachd.

Priorship, *s.* Abachd.

Priory, *s.* Comunn mhanach, abaid.
Prism, *s.* Gloine-sgaraidh ghathan soluis.
Prison, *s.* Gainntir, prìosan.
Prisoned, *part.* Prìosanaichte.
Prisoner, *s.* Prìosanach, ciomach.
Prisonment, *s.* Prìosanachd.
Pristine, *adj.* Priomh, sean, àrsaidh.
Prithee, *(abbreviation for I pray thee.)* Guidheam ort.
Privacy, *s.* Uaigneachd, aonarachd, dìomhaireachd, falach, cleith.
Private, *adj.* Uaigneach, dìomhair, falaichte, neo-fhollaiseach, neo-choitcheann; saighdear-cumanta.
Privateer, *s.* Long-spùinnidh.
Privateness, *s.* Diomhaireach.
Privately, *adv.* Gu diomhair.
Privation, *s.* Toirt air falbh, dìobhail, call, uireasbhuidh, dìth.
Privative, *adj.* A' toirt air falbh, dosgainneach.
Privilege, *s* Sochair, dlighe, còir.
Privilege, *v. a.* Builich sochair air, thoir sochair do, saor o chìs.
Privity, *s.* Rabhadh dìomhair.
Privy, *adj.* Uaigneach ; fiosrach air.
Privy, *s.* Taigh-fuagairt, taigh-beag.
Prize, *s.* Duais, geall ; creach.
Prize, *v. a.* Meas, cuir mòr mheas air, cuir luach air.
Pro, *prep.* Air son, as leth.
Probability, *s.* Coltachd, coltas.
Probable, *adj.* Cosltach, coltachail.
Probat, **Probate**, *s.* Dearbhadh, còmhdach, deanamh a mach.
Probation, *s.* Dearbhadh, feuchainn.
Probationary, *adj.* Deuchainneach.
Probationer, *s.* Deuchainniche.
Probe, *s.* Bior-tomhais lotan.
Probe, *v. a.* Sir, iarr, rannsaich.
Probity, *s.* Fìrinn, trèidhireas.
Problem, *s.* Ceist.
Problematical, *adj.* Ceisteach.
Proboscis, *s.* Gnos, soc fada.
Procedure, *s.* Dòigh, stiùradh.
Proceed, *s.* Toradh, teachd a mach.
Proceed, *v. n.* Imich, gluais, rach air t' aghaidh; rach a mach; sruth, tarmaich, éirich o; thig air aghaidh; cuir air aghaidh.
Proceeding, *s.* Dol, imeachd, siubhal, teachd air aghaidh.
Procerity, *s.* Àirde.
Process, *s.* Dol air aghaidh, siubhal, gluasad ; sruth, sruthadh ; seòl, dòigh, innleachd ; cùis-lagha.
Procession, *s.* Mòr-chuideachd, mòrbhuidheann siubhail.
Proclaim, *v. a.* Glaodh, foillsich, éigh.
Proclamation, *s.* Glaodhaich.
Proclivity, *s.* Aomadh, claonadh, togradh, déidh, miann, ealamhachd.
Procrastinate, *v.* Dean maille, cuir dàil, bi màirnealach.
Procrastination, *s.* Dàil, màirneal.
Procreant, *adj.* Torrach, sìolmhor.
Procreate, *v. a.* Gin, sìolaich, dèan.
Procreation, *s.* Gineamhuinn.
Procreative, *adj.* Gineamhuinneach.
Procreator, *s.* Gineadair.
Proctor, *s.* Fear-gnothaich.
Proctorship, *s.* Dreuchd fir gnothaich.
Procurable, *adj.* So-fhaotainn.
Procurator, *s.* Procadair.
Procure, *v. a.* Faigh, coisinn.
Procurer, *s.* Fear-solair.
Procuress, *s.* Bean-sholar strìopach.
Prodigal, *adj.* Struidheil, caithteach.
Prodigal, *s.* Struidhear.
Prodigality, *s.* Stròdhalachd.
Prodigious, *adj.* Uabhasach, anabarrach, còrr, eagalach.
Prodigy, *s.* Mìorbhuill, iongantas, neònachas, uabhas.
Produce, *v. a.* Thoir 'san làthair, nochd, taisbean ; thoir mar fhianais.
Produce, *s.* Toradh, cinneas.
Producible, *adj.* So-nochdadh.
Produce, *s.* Toradh, suim, tomad, fàs, cinntinn, àireamh, obair.
Production, *s.* Dèanamh, obair, toirt a mach, toirt am fianais ; toradh.
Productive, *adj.* Tarbhach, torach, sìolmhor, lìonmhor, pailt, gineadach.
Proem, *s.* Roi'-ràdh.
Profanation, *s.* Mi-naomhachadh.
Profane, *adj.* Mi-naomha.
Profane, *v. a.* Mi-naomhaich.
Profaneness, *s.* Mi-naomhachd.
Profaner, *s.* Fear mi naomhachaidh.
Profess, *v.* Aidich, cuir an céill, nochd, taisbean, dean aideachadh.
Profession, *s.* Cèaird, obair, dreuchd, ealain ; aideachadh.
Professional, *adj.* Ealainneach.
Professor, *s.* Fear-aidmheil.
Professorship, *s.* Dreuchd fhir-aidmheil.
Proffer, *v. a.* Tairg, thoir tairgse, thoir ionnsaidh.
Proffer, *s.* Tairgse ; deuchainn, oidheirp, ionnsaidh.
Proficience, **Proficiency**, *s.* Teachd air aghart, aghartachd.
Proficient, *s.* Fear-ionnsaichte.
Profile, *s.* Leth-aghaidh.

Profit, *s.* Buannachd, tairbhe, feum.
Profit, *v.* Buannaich, tarbhaich, dean math do, buidhinn; coisinn.
Profitable, *adj.* Buannachdach, buannachdail; tarbhach, feumail.
Profitableness, *s.* Buannachd.
Profitless, *adj.* Neo-tharbhach.
Profligacy, *s.* Mi-stuamachd.
Profligate, *adj.* Mi-stuama.
Profligate, *s.* Struidhear.
Profound, *adj.* Domhain; tul-chuiseach, tùrail; iriosal, ùmhal; ro-ionnsaichte, foghlumte.
Profundity, *s.* Doimhneachd.
Profuse, *adj.* Pailt, sgaoilteach.
Profuseness, *s.* Pailteachd; ana-measarrachd, ana-caitheamh.
Profusion, *s.* Pailteas; sgapadh, ana-caitheamh, struidheas.
Progeneration, *s.* Sìolachadh.
Progenitor, *s.* Gineadair, athair.
Progeny, *s.* Sìol, gineal, sliochd, clann, iarmad, teaghlach, àl.
Prognostic, *s.* Fiosachd, targradh.
Prognosticate, *v. a.* Roi'-innis, targair, dean fìosachd, dean fàisneachd.
Prognostication, *s.* Fiosachd, fàisneachd, targandachd, roi'-innse.
Prognosticator, *s.* Fiosaiche.
Progress, Progression, *s.* Cùrsa, siubhal, imeachd; dol air aghart, teachd air aghart; triall, turas, astar.
Progressional, Progressive, *adj.* Siùbhlach, a dol air aghart, aghartach.
Prohibit, *v. a.* Bac, toirmisg, diùlt.
Prohibition, *s.* Bacadh, toirmeasg.
Prohibitory, *adj.* A' toirmeasgach.
Project, *v.* Tilg; tionnsgainn, cnuasaich; croch thar; sìn a mach.
Project, *s.* Tionnsgnadh, dealbh, cnuasachd, innleachd, seòl.
Projectile, *adj.* Gluasadach.
Projection, *s.* Tilgeadh, caitheamh air aghart, crochadh thar; dealbh, tionnsgnadh.
Projector, *s.* Fear tionnsgnaidh.
Projecture, *s.* Crochadh thar, stùc, sròn.
Prolific, *adj.* Clannmhor, sìolmhor, torrach; lìonmhor.
Prolification, *s.* Sìolmhorachd.
Prolix, *adj.* Draolainneach, seamsanach, màirnealach, fadalach.
Prolixity, *s.* Draolainneachd, fadalachd, athaiseachd, maidheanachd.
Prologue, *s.* Duan roi' chluich.
Prolong, *v. a.* Sìn a mach, cuir dàil, cuir seachad.
Prolongation, *s.* Sìneadh a mach; dàil, cur seachad.
Promenade, *s.* Sràid, sràid-imeachd.
Prominence, *s.* Sròn, gob, roinn.
Prominent, *adj.* Soilleir, follaiseach, a' seasamh a mach.
Promiscuous, *adj.* Coimeasgte.
Promise, *v.* Geall, thoir gealladh.
Promiser, *s.* Fear geallaidh.
Promissory, *adj.* Gealltannach.
Promontory, *s.* Roinn, rudha, sroin àird, maol, ceann-tìre.
Promote, *v. a.* Tog gu inbhe, àrdaich.
Promoter, *s.* Fear àrdachaidh.
Promotion, *s.* Àrdachadh.
Prompt, *adj.* Deas, ealamh, ullamh, èasgaidh, iasgaidh, clis, tapaidh.
Prompt, *v. a.* Cuidich, thoir còmhnadh do; deachdaich, innis; brosnaich, cuir thuige, stuig; cuir an cuimhne.
Prompter, *s.* Fear-sanais, fear-cuimhne; fear-earalachaidh, comhairliche.
Promptitude, Promptness, *s.* Graide, tapachd.
Promulgate, Promulge, *v. a.* Craobh-sgaoil, foillsich.
Promulgation, *s.* Craobh-sgaoileadh, foillseachadh.
Promulgator, *s.* Fear foillseachaidh, fear-nochdaidh.
Prone, *adj.* Crom, a' cromadh; air a bhroinn, an coinneamh a' chinn; claon, ag aomadh corrach, càs.
Proneness, *s.* Cromadh, lùbadh sìos; laidhe air bolg; leathad; aomadh, claonadh, lùbadh, miann, toil, togradh.
Pronoun, *s.* Riochd-fhacal.
Pronounce, *v. a.* Abair, labhair, cuir a mach gu poncail, aithris.
Pronunciation, *s.* Dòigh-labhairt.
Proof, *s.* Dearbhadh, fianais, daingneachadh, còmhdach; deuchainn, feuchainn; dearbhadh clò-bhualaidh.
Proof, *adj.* Daingeann, làidir, a sheasas an aghaidh, dìonach.
Proofless, *adj.* Neo-dhearbte.
Prop, *v. a.* Cum suas, goibhlich.
Prop, *s.* Taic, cul-taic, colbh, gobhal, cumail suas.
Propagate, *v.* Sìolaich, tàrmaich; craobh-sgaoil, leudaich, meudaich; cuir air aghart; gin; bi sìolmhor.
Propagation, *s.* Sìolachadh, craobh-sgaoileadh, leudachadh.
Propagator, *s.* Fear-sgaoilidh, fear craobh sgaoilidh, fear leudachaidh.
Propel, *v. a.* Cuir air aghart, spàrr.

Propend, *v. n.* Aom, claon, fiar
Propensity, *s.* Aomadh, claonadh, lùbadh, toil, déidh.
Proper, *adj.* Àraidh, àraid, sònraichte; iomchuidh, cubhaidh, freagarrach; ceart, cothromach; fìor, neo-shamhlachail; eireachdail.
Properly, *adv.* Gu cubhaidh.
Property, *s.* Buaidh, càil, nàdur, gnè; seilbh, maoin, cuid, còir; earras, eudail.
Prophecy, *s.* Fàisneachd, targradh.
Prophesy, *v.* Fàisnich, targair.
Prophet, *s.* Fàidh, fiosaiche.
Prophetess, *s.* Ban-fhàidh.
Prophetic, *adj.* Fàisneachail.
Propinquity, *s.* Fagusachd; dàimh.
Propitiate, *v. a.* Réitich, ciùinich.
Propitiation, *s.* Réiteachadh; ìobairt-réitich, dìoladh, éirig.
Propitiatory, *adj.* Réiteachail.
Propitious, *adj.* Fàbharrach, gràsmhor, tròcaireach, caoimhneil.
Propitiously, *adv.* Fàbharach.
Proplasm, *s.* Laghadair.
Proponent, *s.* Fear-tairgse.
Proportion, *s.* Co-ionannachd; cofhreagarrachd; coimeas; cumadh, dealbh, meudachd.
Proportion, *v. n.* Cuimsich, coimeas; dean co-fhreagarrach, cùm.
Proportionable, *adj.* Co-fhreagarrach, dealbhach, cumadail.
Proportional, *adj.* Co-ionann.
Proportionate, *adj.* Co-fhreagarrach.
Proposal, *s.* Tionnsgnadh, comhairl'-inntinn; tairgse.
Propose, *v. a.* Tairg, thoir tairgse.
Proposer, *s.* Fear-tairgse.
Proposition, *s.* Ciall-ràdh; tairgse.
Propound, *v. a.* Tairg, nochd, taisbein.
Proprietor, *s.* Sealbhadair.
Propriety, *s.* Iomchuidheachd, freagarrachd, ceartas; seilbh-chòir.
Prorogue, *v. a.* Sìn a mach; cuir dàil, cuir seachad.
Prosaic, *adj.* Rŏsgach.
Proscribe, *v. a.* Dìt gu bàs, thoir binn.
Proscription, *s.* Dìteadh gu bàs.
Prose, *s.* An-duan, rŏsg. *Md.*
Prosecute, *v. a.* Lean, dlù-lean; giùlain air aghart; tagair.
Prosecution, *s.* Leantainn, cur air aghart; agairt, tagradh.
Proselyte, *s.* Ùr-chreideach.
Prosodian, **Prosodist**, *s.* Duanaire.
Prosody, *s.* Ranntachd.
Prospect, *s.* Sealladh, fradharc; àitefradhairc ionad-seallaidh; dùil, beachd.
Prospective, *adj.* A' sealltainn roimhe, a' beachdachadh fad' ás; glic, sicir, fad-sheallach.
Prosper, *v.* Soirbhich, dean sona, cuidich le; buadhaich; cinn, fàs, thig air t' aghart.
Prosperity, *s.* Soirbheachadh, sonas, sealbh, răth, piseach.
Prosperous, *adj.* Sealbhach, sona, àdhmhor, rathail.
Prostitute, *v. a.* Truaill, mill, mibhuilich.
Prostitute, *s.* Strìopach, siùrsach.
Prostitution, *s.* Truailleadh, mibhuileachadh; strìopachas.
Prostrate, *adj.* Sìnte, 'na laidhe air a bhlian; strìochdte; sleuchdte.
Prostrate, *v. a.* Tilg sìos, sleuchd.
Prostration, *s.* Sleuchdadh tuiteam sìos, cromadh sìos; lagachadh.
Protect, *v. a.* Dìon, teasraig, sàbhail.
Protection, *s.* Dìon, tèarmunn.
Protective, *adj.* Tèarmunnach.
Protector, *s.* Fear-tèarmmainn.
Protend, *v. a.* Cùm a mach, sìn a mach.
Protest, *v.* Tog fianais an aghaidh, gairm fianais, cuir fianais air.
Protest, *s.* Cur an aghaidh, fianaisthogte.
Protestant, *adj.* Ath-leasaichte.
Protestant, *s.* Protastanach.
Protestation, *s.* Briathar, bòid.
Prothonotary, *s.* Àrd-nòtair.
Prototype, *s.* Roi'-shamhla.
Protract, *v. a.* Sìn a mach, cuir dàil.
Protraction, *s.* Dàil, fadal.
Protractive, *adj.* Seamsanach.
Protrude, *v.* Pùc, spàrr; dinn.
Protrusion, *s.* Pùcadh, sparradh.
Protuberance, *s.* Pluc, meall, ăt.
Protuberant, *adj.* Plucach, meallach.
Proud, *adj.* Bòsdail, beachdail; uaibhreach, àrdanach, mòr-chuiseach; mòr, àrd, stàtail; basdalach, spleaghach, uallach, leòmach; ain-fheoilleach, ătmhor.
Provable, *adj.* So-dhearbhadh.
Prove, *v.* Dearbh, còmhdaich; feuch, cuir gu deuchainn; fàs, tionndaidh a mach.
Proveditor, **Provedore**, *s.* Fearsolair bìdh do luchd-feachda.
Provender, *s.* Innlinn, biadh spréidhe, fodar, feur; feur-saoidh.
Proverb, *s.* Gnà-fhacal, sean-fhacal.

PROVERBIAL, *adj.* Gnà-fhaclach.
PROVIDE, *v. a.* Ullaich, solair, solaraich; tionail; cùmhnantaich.
PROVIDENCE, *s.* Freasdal; crìonnachd, faicill, faicilleachd; caomhantachd.
PROVIDENT, *adj.* Solarach, cùramach, faicilleach, freasdalach.
PROVIDENTIAL, *adj.* Freasdalach.
PROVIDER, *s.* Solaraiche.
PROVIDING, *s.* Cnuasachadh.
PROVINCE, *s.* Mòr-roinn; dùthaich, tìr; siorrachd; gnothach, dreuchd.
PROVINCIAL, *adj.* Dùthchail, neochoitcheann.
PROVISION, *s.* Deasachadh, ullachadh, uidheam, solar, cnuasachadh; biadh, lòn; cùmhnant, bann.
PROVISIONAL, *adj.* Air chois car ùine; a réir cùmhnanta.
PROVISO, *s.* Bann, cùmhnant.
PROVOCATION, *s.* Brosnachadh, buaireadh, chùis-chorraich, farran.
PROVOKE, *v. a.* Buair, brosnaich, feargaich, farranaich, cuir corraich.
PROVOKER, *s.* Fear-brosnachaidh.
PROVOKING, *adj.* Farranach, buaireasach, brosnachail.
PROVOST, *s.* Prothaist.
PROW, *s.* Toiseach luinge.
PROWESS, *s.* Gaisge, treuntas.
PROWL, *v.* Èalaidh air son cobhartaich.
PROWLER, *s.* Èaladair; sèapaire.
PROXIMATE, PROXIME, *adj.* Fagus, dlù, faisg, am fagus.
PROXIMITY, *s.* Fasgusachd, dhùthachd, nàbaidheachd, coimhearsnachd.
PROXY, *s.* Fear-ionaid fir eile.
PRUDE, *s.* Uailleag, leòmag.
PRUDENCE, *s.* Gliocas, crionnachd.
PRUDENT, *adj.* Glic, crìonna, sicir.
PRUDENTIAL, *adj.* Faicilleach, cùram.
PRUDERY, *s.* Moitealachd.
PRUDISH, *adj.* Moiteil, pròiseil.
PRUNE, *v.* Sgath, bèarr, meang.
PRUNE, *s.* Plumbas seargte.
PRUNELLO, *s.* Seòrsa aodaich sìoda.
PRUNER, *s.* Sgathadair, bearradair.
PRUNING-KNIFE, *s.* Sgian-bhearraidh, sgian-sgathaidh.
PRURIENCE, PRURIENCY, *s.* Tachas; mòr-dhéidh, fìleadh.
PRURIENT, *adj.* Tachasach.
PSALM, *s.* Sàlm, laoidh naomha.
PSALMIST, *s.* Sàlmaire.
PSALMODY, *s.* Sàlmadaireachd.
PSALTER, *s.* Sàlmadair.
PSALTERY, *s.* Salltair.
PSEUDO, *adj.* Feallsa, baoth, faoin.
PSHAW! *interj.* Fŭigh! fŭigh ort!
PUBERTY, PUBESCENCE, *s.* Aois-leannanachd, inbhidheachd.
PUBESCENT, *adj.* Inbheach.
PUBLIC, *adj.* Follaiseach, fosgailte, aithnichte, sgaoilte; coitcheann.
PUBLIC, *s.* Sluagh, am mòr-shluagh.
PUBLICAN, *s.* Cìs-mhaor; òsdair.
PUBLICATION, *s.* Foillseachadh, sgaoileadh, craobh-sgaoileadh, cur-a-mach.
PUBLICLY, *adv.* Gu follaiseach.
PUBLICNESS, *s.* Follaiseachd.
PUBLISH, *v. a.* Foillsich, dean aithnichte; gairm, glaodh, cuir a mach.
PUBLISHER, *s.* Fear chuir a mach leabhraichean.
PUCELAGE, *s.* Maighdeannas.
PUCK, *s.* Tuath; siochair.
PUCKER, *v. a.* Liorcaich, cas, preas.
PUDDING, *s.* Marag.
PUDDLE, *s.* Poll, eabar, làthach, làib.
PUDDLE, *v. a.* Làbanaich, salaich.
PUDDLY, *adj.* Làibeach, ruaimleach.
PUDENCY, PUDICITY, *s.* Màldachd, nàrachd, beusachd.
PUERILE, *adj.* Leanabaidh, leanabail.
PUERILITY, *s.* Leanabachd, leanabantas.
PUFF, *s.* Osag, oiteag, séideag, feochan, tŏth, moladh-bréige.
PUFF, *v. a.* Séid suas, bòchd, ăt; bi 'g àinich.
PUFFIN, *s.* Seòrsa eòin, am buthaid; seòrsa éisg, am bolgan-beiceach.
PUFFY, *adj.* Gaothar, osagach, oiteagach, ătmhor; falamh, bolgach
PUG, *s.* Cù beag, ap, apag.
PUGH! *interj.* Ab! ab!
PUGILISM, *s.* Dòrnaireachd.
PUGILIST, *s.* Dòrnair.
PUISNE, *adj.* Òg, beag, crìon, meanbh, ìochdarach, suarrach.
PUISSANCE, *s.* Cumhachd, neart.
PUISSANT, *adj.* Cumhachdach, treun.
PUKE, PUKER, *s.* Deoch dìobhairt.
PUKE, *v. a.* Sgéith, tilg, dìobhair.
PULCHRITUDE, *s.* Bòidhche, maise.
PULE, *v. n.* Dean bìogail; guil, caoin
PULL, *v. a.* Tarruinn, slaoid, spìon.
PULL, *s.* Tarruinn, spioladh, slaod.
PULLET, *s.* Eireag.
PULLEY, *s.* Ulag, fulag.
PULMONARY, PULMONIC, *adj.* Sgamhanach, a bhuineas do'n sgamhan.
PULP, *s.* Laoghan, glaodhan; taois.
PULPIT, *s.* Cùbaid, crannag.
PULPOUS, *adj.* Bogar laoghanach, sùghmhor, brìoghmhor; feòlmhor.

Pulpousness, *s.* Bogarachd, sùghmhorachd, laoghanachd.
Pulpy, *adj.* Bog, bogar, sùghmhor.
Pulsation, *s.* Bualadh cuisle.
Pulse, *s.* Cuisle, gluasad na fala; peasair; pònair; no pòr mogulach sam bith.
Pulverization, *s.* Mìn-phronnadh.
Pulverize, *v. a.* Mìn-phronn.
Pulvil, *s.* Fàileadh cùbhraidh.
Pumice, *s.* Sligeart, mìn-chlach.
Pump, *s.* Taòsgair; bròg-dhamhsa.
Pump, *v. n.* Taòisg, taom; tarruinn.
Pun, *s.* Gearr-fhacal, beum.
Pun, *v. n.* Beum, gearr.
Punch, *s.* Tolladair, farraiche; deoch làidir; dù-cleasaiche; amadan; fear beag, staigean; bun, cnapanach.
Punch, *v. a.* Toll, brŭdaich.
Puncheon, *s.* Togsaid gu leth.
Punctilio, *s.* Modh, modhalachd.
Punctilious, *adj.* Modhail, moiteil.
Punctual, *adj.* Poncail, cinnteach.
Punctuality, *s.* Poncalachd.
Punctuation, *s.* Poncadh, pungadh.
Puncture, *s.* Toll stuib, peasgadh, toll-stainge.
Pungency, *s.* Géiread, gairgead.
Pungent, *adj.* Geur, goirt, garg; guineach, biorach, dealgach; teumnach, beumnach.
Puniness, *s.* Crìne, suarraichead.
Punish, *v. a.* Peanasaich, pian, cràidh, smachdaich.
Punishable, *adj.* So-pheanasachadh, so-phianadh; buailteach do pheanas, airidh air peanas.
Punishment, *s.* Dìoghaltas.
Punition, *s.* Peannas.
Punk, *s.* Siùrsach, strìopach.
Punster, *s.* Beumadair.
Puny, *adj.* Òg; crìon, beag; suarrach, leibideach; fann, lag, truagh.
Pup, *v. n.* Beir cuileanan.
Pupil, *s.* Clach na sùl; sgoilear.
Pupilage, *adj.* Leanabantachd, òige.
Puppet, *s.* Fear-bréige.
Puppy, *s.* Cuilean; balach bòsdail gun iùl gun mhodh.
Purblind, *adj.* Gearr-sheallach.
Purblindness, *s.* Dalladh-eun.
Purchasable, *adj.* So-cheannach.
Purchase, *v. a.* Ceannaich.
Purchase, *s.* Ceannach; cùnradh.
Purchaser, *s.* Fear ceannaich.
Pure, *adj.* Fìor-ghlan; soilleir; neo-thruaillichte, slàn, fallain; geanmnaidh, màlda, macanta; neo-choireach.
Purely, *adv.* Gu fìorghan, gu'n druaip gun choire; gun ghò.
Pureness, *s.* Fìor-ghloine; soilleireachd; teistealachd, geanmnaidheachd; neo-chiontas.
Purgation, *s.* Glanadh, sgùradh.
Purgative, *adj.* Purgaideach, sgùrach, glanadach.
Purgative, *s.* Pùrgaid.
Purgatory, *s.* Purgadair, ionadglanaidh nan aithrichean naomha, àite glanaidh anmannan o thruaillleachd a' pheacaidh, mu'n téid iad a steach do néimh.
Purge, *v.* Glan, sgùr, purgaidich; nigh, ionnlaid; cairt; soilleirich.
Purge, *s.* Sgùradh-cuim.
Purification, *s.* Glanadh, sìoladh, &c.
Purifier, *s.* Fear-glanaidh.
Purify, *v. a.* Tŭr-ghlan; sìolaidh.
Puritan, *s.* Fear-rò-chràbhaidh; neach chràbhach o'n taobh muigh.
Puritanical, *adj.* Ro chràbhach; cealgach, mealltach.
Purity, *s.* Glaine, gloine, gloinead, fìor-ghloine; neo-chiontas; geanmnaidheachd, macantas, teistealachd.
Purl, *s.* Leann luibheanach.
Purl, *v. n.* Dean torman, dean crònan.
Purlieu, *s.* Iomall, buaile.
Purling, *part. adj.* Tormanach.
Purlion, *v. a.* Goid, siolpadh.
Purpartry, *s.* Ciùbhroinn.
Purple, *adj.* Crò-dhearg, flannach.
Purplish, *adj.* Gòrm-dhearg.
Purport, *s.* Ciall, brìgh, rùn, seadh.
Purport, *v. n.* Bi los, cuir romhad.
Purpose, *v. a.* Rùnaich, miannaich, cuir romhad, sònraich, bi 'm brath.
Purpose, *s.* Gnothach; cùis; rùn, miann, togradh, smuain; deòin.
Purposely, *adv.* A dh' aon obair, a dh' aon ghnothach; le deòin.
Purr, *v. n.* Dean crònan, dean dùrdan.
Purse, *s.* Sporan; ionmhas.
Purser, *s.* Gille-sporain.
Pursuable, *adj.* So-leantainn.
Pursuance, *s.* Leantainn.
Pursuant, *adj.* A réir, do réir.
Pursue, *v.* Lean, tòraich; mair.
Pursuer, *s.* Fear-tòire, fear-agairt.
Pursuit, *s.* Ruaig, ruagadh, tòir; leantainn, geur-leanmhainn, &c.
Pursuivant, *s.* Maor; teachdaire.
Pursy, *adj.* Bronnach, pocanach.
Purtenance, *s.* Grealach, mionach.
Purvey, *v.* Solair, cnuasaich, cruinnich, teachd-an-tìr.
Purveyance, *s.* Solar bìdh.
Purveyor, *s.* Fear solaraidh, bìdh.

PURULENCE, PURULENCY, *s.* Iongar.
PURULENT, *adj.* Làn iongrach.
PUS, *s.* Iongar, salchar-lot.
PUSH, *v. a.* Pùc, purr, starr, sàth, stailc; put, putàgaich, utagaich.
PUSH, *s.* Pùcadh, purradh, utag, putadh, starradh, sàthadh, stailceadh; urchair; càs, deuchainn, teanntachd.
PUSHING, *adj.* Aghartach, teòma, beothail; dìchiollach, oidhirpeach.
PUSILLANIMITY, *s.* Cladhaireachd.
PUSILLANIMOUS, *adj.* Gealtach.
PUSS, *s.* Stìoda, stìdidh, ainm cait.
PUSTULE, *s.* Guirean, bucaid; ăt, bristeadh a mach, plucan.
PUSTULOUS, *adj.* Guireanach, bucaideach, plucanach, builgeineach.
PUT, *v.* Cuir; socraich; suidhich, &c.
PUT, *s.* Dubh-bhalach.
PUTATIVE, *adj.* Smuainichte.
PUTID, *adj.* Crìon, ìosal, dìblidh, suarrach, faoin, fagharsach.
PUTREFACTION, *s.* Bréine, breuntas.
PUTREFY, *v.* Grod, lobh, malc, breun.
PUTRID, *adj.* Loibheach, grod, malcte.
PUTRIDNESS, *s.* Breuntas, loibhteachd.
PUTTING-STONE, *s.* Clach-neart.
PUTTOC, *s.* Am beilbhean-ruadh.
PUTTY, *s.* Taois cailc.
PUZZLE, *v. a.* Cuir an ioma-cheist.
PUZZLE, *s.* Ima-cheist, toimhseachan.
PYGMEAN, *adj.* Beag, duairceach.
PYGMY, PIGMY, *s.* Duairce, arrachd, troich, gircean, luch-armunn.
PYRAMID, *s.* Biorramaid, bior-charragh, bior-stùc, carragh barra-chaol.
PYRAMIDAL, PYRAMIDICAL, *adj.* Barrachaol, biorach, binneineach.
PYRE, *s.* Cairbh-theine.
PYRETICS, *s.* Ùr-chasg-fhiabhras.
PYRITES, *s.* Chlach-theine.
PYROMANCY, *s.* Teine-fhiosachd.
PYROTECHNICS, *s.* Obair-theine.
PYROTECHMY, *s.* Eòlas obair-theine.
PYRRHONISM, *s.* Teagamhachd.
PYTALISM, *s.* Ronn, shilleadh.
PYX, *s.* Bocsa nan abhlan coisrighte.

Q

Q, *s.* Seachdamh litir deug na h-Aibidil.
QUACK, *v. n.* Ràc mar thunnaig; dean gagail, gabh ort.
QUACK, *s.* Sgoitich, feall-léigh.
QUACKERY, *s.* Sgoiteachd.
QUADRAGESIMAL, *adj.* Carghusach.
QUADRANGLE, *s.* Ceithir-chearnag.
QUADRANGULAR, *adj.* Ceithir-chearnach, ceithir-oisinneach.
QUADRANT, *s.* Ceithreamh, seòrsa inneal tomhais, carst-cearcaill.
QUADRANTAL, *adj.* Ceithir-chrunn.
QUADRATE, *s.* Ceithir shlisneag.
QUADRATE, *adj.* Ceithir shliosach.
QUADRATURE, *s.* Ceithir-chearnadh.
QUADRENNIAL, *adj.* Ceithir-bhliadhnach; ceithir-bhliadhnachail.
QUADRIFID, *adj.* Ceitheir-earrannach.
QUADRILATERAL, *adj.* Ceithir-shlisneach, ceithir-shliseach.
QUADRILLE, *s.* Seòrsa damhsa; gnè do cluiche air chairtean.
QUADRIPARTITE, *adj.* Ceithreannaichte.
QUADRUPED, *s.* Ceithir-chasach.
QUADRUPLE, *adj.* Ceithir fillte.
QUAFF, *v. a.* Òl, sguab ás e.
QUAGGY, *adj.* Bog, ruaimleach, féitheach.
QUAGMIRE, *s.* Suil-chritheach, boglach.
QUAIL, *s.* Gearra-goirt.
QUAINT, *adj.* Cuimir; snasmhor, greannar, fìnealta, freagarrach.
QUAINTNESS, *s.* Fìnealtachd; cuimireachd; freagarrachd.
QUAKE, *v. n.* Crith, criothnaich.
QUAKE, *s.* Crith, criothnachadh.
QUALIFICATION, *s.* Deasachadh, uidheamachadh; taiseachadh; lughdachadh; feart, buaidh, càil, gné.
QUALIFY, *v. a.* Deasaich, ullai h; dean freagarrach, taisich.
QUALITY, *s.* Inbhe, uaillse, àirde; gnè, buaidh, càil, feart; uaillsean.
QUALM, *s.* Òrrais, sleogadh.
QUALMISH, *adj.* Òrraiseach, sleogach.
QUANDARY, *s.* Teagamh.
QUANTITY, *s.* Meud, uibhir, tomad; cudthrom; na h-urrad.
QUANTUM, *s.* An t-iomlan.
QUARANTINE, *s.* Ùine dhà fhichead là is éigin do luingeas a thig o chéin fuireach, mu m faod iad tighinn gu chala.
QUARREL, *s.* Còmh-strì, connsachadh, droch còrdadh, iorghuill, tuasaid, sabaid, aimhreite, cur a mach; trod.
QUARREL, *v. n.* Troid, connsaich.
QUARRELSOME, *adj.* Sabaideach, tuasaideach, brionglaideach, carraideach, connspaideach, crosda, aimhreiteach, trodach.
QUARRELSOMENESS, *s.* Tuasaideachd, brionglaideachd, strangalachd.

QUARRY, *s.* Gairbheal; seòrsa saighde.
QUARRY, *v. n.* Tochail, cladhaich; bùraich; thig beò air, &c.
QUART, *s.* Càrt, ceathramh.
QUARTANAGUE, *s.* Am fiabhrais-crith-anach.
QUARTER, *s.* ceathramh; àite, cearn, ionad, tìr, dùthaich, earrann baile no dùthcha, àirde; ràidhe, cairteal; cairtealan, bàigh, tròcair, iochd.
QUARTER, *v. a.* Roinn 'na cheithir earrannan, gabh còmhnaidh, cùir suas, fan, fuirich
QUARTERAGE, *s.* Cuid ràithe, luathas-achadh ràithe.
QUARTER-DECK, *s.* Càr-uachdair deiridh luinge.
QUARTERLY, *adj.* and *adv.* Ràitheil, gach ràithe; uair 'san ràithe.
QUARTERMASTER, *s.* Maighistear chairtealan feachda.
QUARTERN, *s.* Cairteal, ceithreamh.
QUARTERS, *s.* Cairtealan.
QUARTERSESSION, *s.* Mòd-ràithe.
QUARTERSTAFF, *s.* Ursann-chatha.
QUARTO, *adj.* Ceathramh.
QUASH, *v. a.* Mùch, caisg, cum sìos, cum sàmhach; cuir air chùl, ceann-saich.
QUASHING, *s.* Mùchadh, casgadh.
QUATERNARY, QUATERNION, QUATERNITY, *s.* Ceithrear.
QUATRAIN, *s.* Rann cheithir-sreath anns am beil am facal is deireann-aiche anns gach sreath a' freagairt ma seach.
QUAVER, *v. n.* Crith, crath; bog, ceil-eirich.
QUAY, *s.* Laimhrig, clacharan.
QUEAN, *s.* Dubh-chaile, strìopach.
QUEASY, *adj.* Tinn, sleogach.
QUEEN, *s.* Bann-righ, bànrinn.
QUEER, *adj.* Neònach, iongantach.
QUEERNESS, *s.* Neònachas.
QUELL, *v.* Mùch, cum fodha; smachd-aich, caisg, cìosnaich; ceannsaich.
QUENCH, *v.* Cuir ás, mùch, bàth.
QUENCHABLE, *adj.* So-mhùchadh.
QUENCHLESS, *adj.* Do-mhùchadh.
QUERIST, *s.* Ceasnaiche, sgrùdaire.
QUERN, *s.* Bràdh, muilleann-làimhe.
QUERPO, *s.* Seacaid, deacaid.
QUERULOUS, *adj.* Gearanach, casaid-each, dranndanach, sraonaiseach.
QUERULOUSNESS, *s.* Dranndanachd.
QUERY, *s.* Ceisd, ceist foighneachd.
QUEST, *s.* Sireadh, rannsachadh, foigh-neachd, sgrùdadh, tòir, iarrtas, iarr-aidh, deidh.
QUESTION, *s.* Ceist, teagamh; amh-arus, connspaid, deasbaireachd foighneachd.
QUESTION, *v.* Feòraich, foighneachd, ceasnaich, sgrùd, farraid, cuir an teagamh.
QUESTIONABLE, *adj.* Teagamhach.
QUESTIONARY, *adj.* Ceasnachail, rann-sachail, sgrùdach.
QUESTIONLESS, *adj.* Gun teagamh, gun amharus, cinnteach.
QUESTUARY, *adj.* Gionach, sanntach.
QUIB, *s.* Geur-fhacal, car-fhacal.
QUIBBLE, *v. n.* Thoir beum.
QUIBBLER, *s.* Car-fhaclaiche.
QUICK, *adj.* Grad, ealamh; beò, beoth-ail, smiorail, tapaidh, ullamh, deas, luath, clis, èasgaidh; cabhagach.
QUICK, *s.* Beò; beò-fheòil.
QUICKBEAM, *s.* An Gall-uinnsean.
QUICKEN, *v.* Beothaich, ath bheoth-aich, brosnaich, greas, deifirich; geuraich.
QUICKENER, *s.* Brosnachair; beoth-achair; greasadair.
QUICK-LIME, *s.* Aol-teth, aol-beò.
QUICKLY, *adv.* Gu luath, gu grad, gu clis.
QUICKNESS, *s.* Luathas, graide, beoth-alachd, deifir, cabhag, tapadh, tap-achd, smioralas; géire.
QUICKSAND, *s.* Beò-ghaineamh.
QUICKSET, *s.* Planntan sgithich.
QUICKSIGHTED, *adj.* Bior-shuileach, grad-sheallach, grad-shuileach.
QUICKSILVER, *s.* Airgead beò.
QUIDDITY, *s.* Car-cheist, car fhacal.
QUIESCENCE, QUIESCENCY, *s.* Sàmh-chair, suaimhneas, fois, tàmh, sèimhe, socair, bailbhe.
QUIESCENT, *adj.* Sàmhach, féitheil, socrach, balbh, tosdach, ciùin.
QUIET, *adj.* Sàmhach, tosdach, ciùin; màlta, macanta, suairce, socrach; suaimhneach; soitheamh; aig fois.
QUIET, *s.* Fois, sàmhchair, sèimhe, ciùineas, tàmh, sìth, suaimhneas; tosdachd, tosd.
QUIET, *v. a.* Caisg, cuir sàmhach, ciùinich, sìochaich, foisnich, socraich.
QUIETISM, *s.* Sìth-inntinn.
QUIETLY, *adv.* Gu ciùin; aig fois.
QUIETNESS, *s.* Sàmhchair, ciùineachd, ciùineas, sìth; sèimhe, fois, fèith.
QUIETUDE, *s.* Sìth, fois, socair, tàmh.
QUILL, *s.* Cléite, ite, sgeithe.
QUILT, *s.* Cùibhrig, brat-leapa.
QUINCE, *s.* Cuinnse, craobh-chuinnse.
QUINCUNX, *s.* Craobh-shuidheachadh ioma-shreathach.
QUINQUANGULAR, *adj.* Cuig-chearnach.

Quinquefoliated, *adj.* Cùig-bhileach.
Quinquennial, *adj.* Cùig-bliadhnach.
Quinsey, *s.* Àt bràghaid.
Quint, *s.* Cùignear, cùig.
Quintal, *s.* Ceud punnt.
Quintessence, *s.* Làn-bhrìgh, bladh, feart; an cùigeamh bith.
Quintuple, *adj.* Cùig-fillte, a chùig uiread, air aithris, cùig uairean.
Quip, *s.* Fochaid, sgeig, beum.
Quire, *s.* Ceithir clair fichead pàipeir.
Quire, *v. n.* Co-sheinn, co-sheirm.
Quirister, *s.* Fear co-sheirm.
Quirk, *s.* Car, cuilbheart; slighe; cleas; beum.
Quit, *v. a.* Fàg; tréig, cuidhtich, cuir cùl ri; dealaich; pàigh, dìol.
Quit, *adj.* Saor, ionann, cuidhte.
Quitchgrass, *s.* Feur-nan-con.
Quite, *adv.* Gu tŭr, gu léir.
Quittance, *s.* Cuidhteas; saorsa.
Quiver, *s.* Dòrnlach, balg-shaighead.
Quiver, *v. n.* Crith, ball-chrith.
Quodlibet, *s.* Car, car-fhacal.
Quoif, Quoiffure, *s.* Ceannabharr.
Quoit, *s.* Peileastair.
Quorum, *s.* Àireamh-àraidh.
Quotation, *s.* Còmhdachadh, earrann o sgrìobhadh neach eile.
Quote, *v. a.* Ainmich ùghdar, thoir mar ùghdar, thoir mar ùghdarras.
Quoth, *v. imperf.* Arsa, ars'.
Quotidian, *adj.* Lathail, gach latha.
Quotient, *s.* A' cho liugha uair.

R

R, *s.* Ochdamh litir deug na-h-Aibidil.
Rabbet, *s.* Tàth, gleus, gròbadh.
Rabbi, Rabbin, *s.* Olla Iùdhach.
Rabbit, *s.* Coinean.
Rabble, *s.* Gràisg, pràbar.
Rabid, *adj.* Cuthaich, borb, garg.
Race, *s.* Réis, ruith, steud, co-ruith; coimhliong; blàr-réis; gineal, ginealach; sliochd, siol, clann, fine, cinneadh, teaghlach.
Racer, *s.* Falaire, steud-each.
Racemiferous, *adj.* Bagaideach.
Raciness, *s.* Searbhas, goirteas.
Rack, *s.* Inneal pianaidh, cuidhlesgaraidh; prasach.
Rack, *v. a.* Sàraich, claoidh, pian.
Racket, *s.* Callaid; gleadhraich, straoidhlich, săbaid.
Rackrent, *s.* Màl-mòr; màl-sàrachaidh; àrd-mhàl.
Racoon, *s.* Broc Americanach.
Racy, *adj.* Làidir, deagh-bholtrach.
Radiance, *s.* Lannair, soillse, boillsgealachd, loinnreachas; dealradh, dearsadh; glòir.
Radiant, *adj.* Lannaireach, soillseach, boillsgeil, boillsgeach, dealrach, dearrsach; glan, soilleir.
Radiate, *v. n.* Dealraich, soillsich.
Radiation, *s.* Dealrachd, lannaireachd, boillsgealachd.
Radical, *adj.* Nàdurra; gnéitheil.
Radicate, *v. a.* Freumhaich.
Radish, *s.* Meacan, curran-dearg.
Radius, *s.* Roth; lànag, spòg.
Raffle, *v. n.* Dìsnich, tilg dìsnean.
Raffle, *s.* Crannchur-gill.
Raft, *s.* Ràth, slaod-uisge, ràmhach.
Rafter, *s.* Taobhan, tarsunan.
Rag, *s.* Giobal, luideag, clùd, cearb, broineag, giobag.
Ragamuffin, *s.* Sgonn-bhalach.
Rage, *s.* Boile, bàinidh, fearg, cuthach, fraoch, corraich, buaireadh.
Ragged, *adj.* Luideagach, luideach, clùdach; broineagach; giobalach, giobagach.
Raging, *adj.* Buaireasach, feargach, fraochail, air a' chuthach, air boile.
Ragout, *s.* Feòil air a deasachadh, a réir seòl nam Fràngach.
Ragwort, *s.* Am buaghallan.
Rail, *s.* Cliath, iadh-lann.
Rail, *v.* Druid, cuir fàl suas; càin.
Railing, *s.* Iadh-lann; callaid.
Raillery, *s.* Sgallais, sglàmhradh.
Raiment, *s.* Aodach, earradh.
Rain, *v. a.* Sil; fras; dòirt; dean uisge.
Rain, *s.* Frasachd, fearr-shion, uisge.
Rainbow, *s.* Bogha-frois.
Rain-goose, *s.* An learg.
Rainy, *adj.* Frasach, fliuch, silteach.
Raise, *v. a.* Tog suas; àrdaich; dùisg.
Raisin, *s.* Fion-dhearc chaoinichte.
Rake, *s.* Ràsdal, ràcan; trusdar.
Rake, *v.* Ràsdalaich, ràc, cruinnich, trŭs, tionail r'a chéile; sgrùd.
Rakehell, *s.* Drùisear, trustar.
Rakish, *adj.* Ana-measarra.
Rally, *v.* Ath-bhrosnaich, athchruinnich feachd.
Ram, *s.* Reithe.
Ram, *v.* Spàrr, starr, stailc.
Ramble, *s.* Iomrall, spaidsearachd.
Ramble. *v. a.* Iomrallaich.

Rambler, *s.* Fear-fàrsain.
Rambling, *adj.* Seacharanach, luaineach, fàrsanach.
Ramification, *s.* Craobh-sgaoileadh; sgaoileadh, meurachadh, iomasgaoileadh.
Ramify, *v. a.* Meuraich, sgaoil.
Rammer, *s.* Farraiche; slat gunna.
Ramous, *adj.* Meanglanach, meurach.
Ramp, *s.* Leum, sùrdag.
Ramp, *v. n.* Leum, sùrdagaich.
Rampant, *adj.* Ruith-leumnach, ruideiseach, sùrdagach, àrd-leumnach; macnusach, a seasamh air na casan deiridh.
Rampart, **Ramptre**, *s.* Bàbhunn, balla-dionaidh, baideal.
Ran, *pret.* of *to run.* Ruith.
Rancid, *adj.* Trom-fhàileach, breun.
Rancorous, *adj.* Mi-rùnach, gamhlasach, fuathach, tnùthar.
Rancour, *s.* Mi-rùn, gamhlas.
Random, *s.* Tubaist, tuaram.
Random, *adj.* Tubaisteach, tuaireamach; air thuaram.
Rang, *pret.* of *to ring.* Sheirm, bheum.
Range, *s.* Òrdugh, sreud, sreath, breath; cuairt, creadhal-theine.
Range, *v. a.* Cuir an òrdugh, marasglaich; cuir am breathan, riaghailtich; cuairtich; siubhail, rach sìos a's suas.
Ranger, *s.* Fear-rannsaichidh; fidriche; peathair; forsair, maor coille.
Rank, *adj.* Làidir, àrd, garbh mar fheur; breun, faileach.
Rank, *v.* Rangaich, sreathaich, cuir an òrdugh, cuir taobh ri taobh, inbhich; àitich, gabh àite no inbhe.
Rank, *s* Sreath, sreud; inbhe; staid.
Rankle, *v. n.* Feargaich, ŭt.
Ranny, *s.* An dallag.
Ransack, *v. a.* Rannsaich, creach.
Ransom, *s.* Éirig, dìol, pàigheadh, fuasgladh; saorsa.
Ransom, *v. a.* Fuasgail, saor.
Rant, *v. n.* Dean stairirich.
Rant, *s.* Gleadhraich, beucail.
Ranter, *s.* Ministear-bòilich; ranntair.
Rantipole, *adj.* Mi-gheamnaidh.
Ranunculus, *s.* Lŭs-an-ròcais.
Rap, *v. n.* Buail, grad-bhuail.
Rap, *s.* Buille, sgailleag, pailleart.
Rapacious, *adj.* Fòirneartach, gionach, lonach, craosach.
Rapacity, *s.* Creachadaireachd, sannt.
Rape, *s.* Cùis-éigin, truailleadh.
Rapid, *a.* Cas, bras, dian, grad, luath, ealamh, ullamh, clis.
Rapidity, *s.* Braise, déine, graide.
Rapine, *s.* Creachadh.
Rapier, *s.* Chlaidheamh-bruididh.
Rapture, *s.* Éibhneas, mòr-aoibhneas; àrd-thoileachadh.
Raptured, *adj.* Éibhinn.
Rapturous, *adj.* Aoibhneach.
Rare, *adj.* Ainmig, tearc, gann; annasach; ainneamh, sàr-mhath,
Raree-show, *s.* Faoin-shealladh; neònachas, iongantas-féille. *R. D.*
Rarefaction, *s.* Tanachadh; meudachadh, sgaoileadh.
Rarify, *v. a.* Tanaich; leudaich.
Rarely, *adv.* Gu h-ainmig, gu tearc, gu h-ainneamh, gu gann.
Rareness, **Rarity**, *s.* Ainmigead, teirce, annas, ganntachd.
Rascal, *s.* Sloightear, crochaire.
Rascallion, *s.* Dù-bhalach.
Rascality, *s.* Pràbar, gràisg.
Rascally, *adj.* Dìblidh, suarrach.
Rase, *v. a.* Spion á bun; mill.
Rash, *adj.* Dàna, ceann-laidir, bras, cas, grad, obann, dian; cabhagach.
Rash, *s.* Briseadh a mach, brŏth.
Rasher, *s.* Sliseag mhuic-fheola.
Rashness, *s.* Dànadas, braisead.
Rasp, *s.* Suidheag, sùghag; eighe.
Rasp, *v. a.* Eigheich.
Raspberry, *s.* Sugh-craobh.
Rasure, *s.* Sgrìobadh-ás.
Rat, *s.* Radan, rodan.
Ratable, *adj.* Luachail, prìseil.
Ratafia, *s.* Seòrsa dibhe làidir.
Rate, *s.* Prìs, luach, fiach.
Rate, *v. a.* Meas; prìsich; troìd.
Rather, *adv.* Docha, fearr; an àite, an àite sin, ni's ro thoiliche.
Ratification, *s.* Daingneachadh.
Ratify, *v. a.* Daingnich, socraich.
Ratiocinate, *v. a.* Reusonaich.
Ratiocination, *s.* Reusonachadh.
Rational, *adj.* Reusonta, tuigseach.
Rationality, *s.* Reusonachd.
Ratsbane, *s.* Puinnsein nan radan.
Rattle, *v. n.* Dean gleadhraich.
Rattle, *s.* Faoin-chainnt, glag; clach-bhalg; gleadhraich, staireараich stàirn, braoidhlich.
Rattling, *adj.* Gleadhrach.
Rattlesnake, *s.* An nathair-ghlagain.
Rattoon, *s.* Sionnach-Innseanach.
Raucity, *s.* Tùchanachd.
Ravage, *v. a.* Sgrios, dean fàs, fàsaich, creach, spùill, léir-sgrios.
Ravage, *s.* Sgrios, fàsachadh, creachadh, spùilleadh, léir-sgrios.
Rave, *v. n.* Bi air boile, bi 'm breislich.
Ravel, *v. a.* Rib; cuir air aimhreith;

buair; cuir an ioma-cheist; fuasgail, thoir ás a' chéile

Ravelin, *s*. Obair-dhìon air chumadh na leth-ghealaich.

Raven, *s*. Fitheach, coirbidh.

Ravenous, *adj*. Cìocrach, slugach, glamhach, geocach, craosach.

Ravenousness, *s*. Miann-creich.

Ravish, *v. a*. Thoir air éigin, thoir cùis a dh' aindeoin; truaill, mill; toilich, dean aoibhinn.

Ravisher, *s*. Fear-éigneachaidh, fear fòirneirt; fear-truaillidh.

Ravishment, *s*. Éigneachadh, éigin, truailleadh; làn-éibhneas.

Raw, *adj*. Amh, amhaidh; glas, ùr; fuar; neo-abaich; neo-mhèirbhte; neo-theòma.

Rawboned, *adj*. Cnàmhach.

Rawness, *s*. Amhachd; aineolas.

Ray, *s*. Gath-soluis; leus.

Raze, *s*. Carraig-dhinnsear.

Raze, *v. a*. Tilg sìos, leag; lom-sgrios, fàsaich; dubh a mach.

Razor, *s*. Ealtainn, bearr-sgian.

Razure, *s*. Dubhadh a mach.

Reach, *v*. Ruig; sìn; faigh.

Reach, *s*. Cumhachd; comas urrainn, ruigsinn, ruigheachd; comas ruigsinn, ruigheachd; sìneadh.

Reaction, *s*. Ath-ghluasad.

Read, *v*. Leugh, tuig; rannsaich.

Read, *pret*. and *part*. Leughte.

Readeption, *s*. Ath-fhaotainn.

Reader, *s*. Leughair, leughadair.

Readily, *adv*. Gu réith, gu toileach.

Readiness, *s*. Ullamhachd, deise.

Reading, *s*. Leughadh, leubhadh.

Readmission, *s*. Ath-leigeil a steach.

Readmit, *v. a*. Ath-ghabh a staigh.

Ready, *adj*. Ullamh, réith deas, deasaichte; ealamh, toileach; furas.

Reaffirm, *v. a*. Ath-chòmhdaich.

Reaffirmance, *s*. Ath-chòmhdachadh.

Real, *adj*. Fìor; cinnteach.

Reality, *s*. Fìrinn, cinnteachd.

Realize, *v. a*. Thoir gu buil.

Really, *adv*. Gu fìor; a rìreadh.

Realm, *s*. Rìoghachd, dùthaich.

Ream, *s*. Buinnseal paipeir.

Reanimate, *v. a*. Ath-bheothaich.

Reannex, *v. a*. Ath-cheangail.

Reap, *v. a*. Buain; buannaich.

Reaper, *s*. Buanaiche.

Rear, *s*. Deireadh feachd; deireadh.

Rear, *v. a*. Tog, àraich; éirich.

Rearmouse, Raremouse, *s*. Ialtag.

Reascend, *v*. Ath-dhìrich.

Reason, *s*. Reuson, toinisg, tuigse; ciall; aobhar, fàth, ceannfàth.

Reason, *v. a*. Reusonaich, deasbairich.

Reasonable, *adj*. Reusonta, ciallach; measarra, meadhonach, cuimseach; ceart, cothromach.

Reasoning, *s*. Deasbaireachd, reusonachadh; argamaid.

Reassemble, *v. a*. Ath-chruinnich.

Reassert, *v. a*. Ath-dhearbh.

Reassume, *v. a*. Ath-ghabh.

Reassure, *v. a*. Thoir ath-chinnte.

Reave, *v. a*. Thoirt leat le ainneart.

Rebaptize, *v. a*. Ath-bhaist.

Rebate, *v. a*. Math; lughdaich.

Rebel, *s*. Fear ar-a-mach.

Rebel, *v. a*. Dean ar-a-mach.

Rebellion, *s*. Ar-a-mach.

Rebellious, *adj*. Ceannairceach.

Reboation, *s*. Ath-gheum.

Rebound, *v*. Leum air ais.

Rebuff, *s*. Ath-bhualadh; diùltadh.

Rebuff, *v. a*. Buail air ais; diùlt.

Rebuild, *v. a*. Ath-thog.

Rebuke, *v. a*. Thoir achmhasan.

Rebuke, *s*. Achmhasan, cronachadh.

Rebus, *s*. Dealbh-fhacal, seòrsa toimhseachain.

Recall, *v. a*. Gairm air ais.

Recall, *s*. Ath-ghairm ais-ghairm.

Recant, *v. a*. Seun, àicheadh.

Recantation, *s*. Seunadh, àicheadh.

Recapitulate, *v. a*. Ath-innis.

Recapitulation, *s*. Ath-innseadh.

Recaption, *s*. Ath-ghlacadh.

Recede, *v. n*. Rach air t' ais.

Receipt, *s*. Gabhail ri; bann-cuidhteachaidh, cuidhteas.

Receivable, *adj*. So-fhaotainn.

Receive, *v. a*. Gabh, gabh ri, faigh.

Receiver, *s*. Fear-gabhail.

Recent, *adj*. Ùr, o cheann ghoirid.

Recentness, *s*. Nuadhachd.

Receptacle, *s*. Ionad-tasgaidh.

Reception, *s*. Furmailt, fàilte; dibeatha, gabhail, gabhail ri.

Receptive, *adj*. So-ghabhail.

Recess, *s*. Uaigneas, dìomhaireachd, sàmhchair; fàgail, sgur, tàmh, clos, fosadh, fòis.

Recession, *s*. Pilltinn, dol air ais.

Rechange, *v. a*. Ath-mhùth.

Eecipe, *s*. Comhairle sgrìobhte léigh.

Recipient, *s*. Gabhadair.

Reciprocal, *adj*. Malairteach, air gach taobh, o gach taobh, a réir a' chéile; m'a seach.

Reciprocate, *v. a*. Malairtich, dean mu 'n seach, dean a réir a' chéile.

Reciprocation, *s*. Co-mhùthadh.

Recital, Recitation, *s*. Aithris; innseadh, sgeulachd.

RECITATIVE, RECITATIVO, *s.* Fonn, sèis, canntaireachd.
RECITE, *v. a.* Ath-aithris; ath-innis.
RECKLESS, *adj.* Neo-chùramach, coma.
RECKON, *v.* Cunnt; meas, saoil.
RECKONING, *s.* Cunntadh, meas, lach.
RECLAIM, *v. a.* Leasaich, ath-leasaich, iompaich, ais-ghairm; ceannsaich, smachdaich.
RECLINE, *v. n.* Sìn, leth-laidh, laidh air do leth-taobh; claon sìos; crom sìos, leig taice.
RECLOSE, *v. a.* Ath-dhùin.
RECLUSE, *adj.* Aonaranach, uaigneach.
RECOAGULATION, *s.* Ath-bhinndeachadh.
RECOGNIZANCE, *s.* Gealladh, bann.
RECOGNIZE, *v. a.* Aidich; aithnich.
RECOGNITION, *s.* Aideachadh, cuimhneachadh; aithneachadh.
RECOIL, *v. n.* Leum no clisg air t' ais.
RECOINAGE, *s.* Ath-chùinneadh.
RECOLLECT, *v. a.* Cuimhnich; athchruinnich, ath-thionail.
RECOLLECTION, *s.* Cuimhne.
RECOMMENCE, *v. a.* Ath-thòisich.
RECOMMEND, *v. a.* Mol; cliùthaich.
RECOMMENDATION, *s.* Moladh, cliù.
RECOMMENDATORY, *adj.* Moladach.
RECOMPENSE, *v. a.* Ath-dhìol, dean suas.
RECOMPENSE, *s.* Ath-dhìoladh.
RECONCILE, *v. a.* Dean rèith, rèitich.
RECONCILABLE, *adj.* So-rèiteachadh.
RECONCILEMENT, *s.* Rèite, sìth.
RECONCILIATION, *s.* Ath-rèite.
RECONDITE, *adj.* Dìomhair, dorcha, domhain, do-thuigsinn.
RECONDICTORY, *s.* Taigh-tasgaidh.
RECONDUCT, *v. a.* Ath-threòraich.
RECONNOITRE, *v. a.* Beachdaich.
RECONQUER, *v. a.* Ath-cheannsaich.
RECONSECRATE, *v. a.* Ath-choisrig.
RECONVENE, *v. n.* Ath-chruinnich.
RECORD, *v. a.* Sgrìobh, cùm air chuimhne.
RECORD, *s.* Leabhar-cuimhne.
RECORDER, *s.* Seanachaidh; meamhraiche; eachdraiche.
RECOUNT, *v. a.* Innis, cuir an cèill.
RECOURSE, *s.* Ath-philleadh.
RECOVER, *v.* Faigh air ais; thig uaithe; fàs gu math.
RECOVERABLE, *adj.* So-leigheas.
RECOVERY, *s.* Faotainn air ais; dol am feabhas, leigheas, fàs gu math.
RECREANT, *adj.* Gealtach, neo-dhuineil.
RECREATE, *v. a.* Ath-bheothaich, athùraich; toilich, sòlasaich, aotromaich.
RECREATION, *s.* Caitheamh-aimsir; culaidh-shùgraidh, lasachadh.
RECREATIVE, *adj.* Ùrachail; lasacail.
RECREMENT, *s.* Dràbhag; salachar.
RECREMENTAL, RECREMENTITIOUS, *adj.* Dràbhagach, deasgannach.
RECRIMINATE, *v. a.* Ath-choirich.
RECRIMINATION, *s.* Ath-choireachadh.
RECRUIT, *v. a.* Ath-neartaich, athleasaich; tog saighdearan.
RECRUIT, *s.* Saighdear ùr.
RECTANGLE, *s.* Ceart-chearnag.
RECTANGULAR, *adj.* Ceart-chearnach.
RECTIFIABLE, *adj.* So-cheartachadh.
RECTIFICATION, *s.* Ceartachadh.
RECTIFIER, *s.* Fear ceartachaidh.
RECTIFY, *v. a.* Ceartaich, leasaich, cuir gu dòigh; ath-tharruinn.
RECTILINEAR, *adj.* Dìreach.
RECTITUDE, *s.* Dìrichead; ionracas.
RECTOR, *s.* Ministear sgìreachd shasunnach; ceannard, riaghladair.
RECTORY, *s.* Aitreamh, agus gliobh-ministear sgìreachd easbuigeach, &c.
RECUBATION, RECUMBENCY, *s.* Lethlaidhe; sìneadh, aomadh.
RECUMBENT, *adj.* 'Na leth-laidhe.
RECUR, *v.* Thig an aire, thig an cuimhne.
RECURRENCE, RECURSION, *s.* Pilltinn, ath-philltinn, ath-thachairt.
RECURRENT, *adj.* Ath-phìlltinneach.
RECURVATION, *s.* Cùl-aomadh, cromadh an comhair a chùil.
RECUSANT, *s.* Fear a dhiùltas caidreamh a' mhòr-chomuinn.
RECUSE, *v. a.* Diùlt, àicheamh.
RED, *adj.* Dearg, ruadh, flannach.
REDBREAST, *s.* Am brù-dhearg.
REDDEN, *v.* Deargaich; dean dearg; fàs dearg, cinn dearg.
REDDISHNESS, *s.* Deirgeachd, ruadhan.
REDE, *s.* Comhairle, sanus.
REDEEM, *v. a.* Saor; ath-cheannaich.
REDEEMABLE, *adj.* So-shaoradh.
REDEEMER, *s.* Fear-saoraidh, Slànaighear an-t-saoghail.
REDELIVER, *v. a.* Ath-shaor, liubhair; thoir air ais.
REDEMPTION, *s.* Èirig; saorsa, saorsainn, sàbhaladh, ath-fhuasgladh.
REDEMPTORY, *adj.* Èirigeil.
REDLEAD, *s.* Basg-luaidhe, basg-ùir.
REDNESS, *s.* Deirge, ruaidhe.
REDOLENCE, REDOLENCY, *s.* Cùbhraidheachd, boltrachas.
REDOLENT, *adj.* Cùbhraidh, deaghbholtrachail.
REDOUBLE, *v. a.* Dùblaich.
REDOUBT, *s.* Dùn beag, dùn catha.

Redoubtable, *adj.* Eagalach, fuathasach, uabhasach.
Redound, *v. n.* Pill air, thig air ais air; tuit air.
Redress, *v. a.* Cuir ceart, ceartaich, leasaich; furtaich; dìol; dean suas.
Redress, *s.* Leasachadh, dìoladh, dìol. fuasgladh, furtachd; deanamh suas.
Reduce, *v. a.* Lughdaich, dean ni's lugha; cuir an lughad; ìslich, irioslaich; ceannsaich, smachdaich.
Reducement, *s.* Lughdachadh, ceannsachadh, smachdachadh.
Reducible, *adj.* So-lughdachadh.
Reduction, *s.* Lughdachadh, cur an lughad, beagachadh; sàrachadh.
Redundance, Redundancy, *s.* Anabharra, lìon mhorachd, làine.
Redundant, *adj.* Làn-phailt.
Reduplicate, *v. a.* Ath-dhùblaich.
Reduplication, *s.* Ath-dhùblachadh.
Reduplicative, *adj.* Dùbailte.
Ree, *v. a.* Criathair, ridilich.
Reed, *s.* Cuilc; ribheid; slinn.
Reedify, *v. a.* Ath-thog.
Reedy, *adj.* Cuilceach.
Reek, *s.* Deathach, smùid, toit.
Reek, *v. n.* Cuir smùid dhiot.
Reeky, *adj.* Smùideach, toiteach.
Reel, *s.* Ceangaldair, crois-thachrais.
Reel, *v. n.* Tachrais, siùganaich.
Re-election, *s.* Ath-thaghadh.
Reembark, *v. a.* Ath-chuir air bòrd.
Reenforce, *v. a.* Ath-neartaich.
Reenforcement, *s.* Ath-neartachadh.
Reenjoy, *v. a.* Ath-shealbhaich.
Reenter, *v. a.* Ath-inntrinn.
Re-establish, *v. a.* Ath-shocraich.
Reeve, Reve, *s.* Stiùbhard.
Re-examine, *v. a.* Ath-cheasnaich.
Refectory, *s.* Pronn-lios; proinn-lis.
Refer, *v.* Leig gu breth.
Reference, *s.* Leigeil gu breth.
Refine, *v. a.* Tŭr-ghlan.
Refined, *adj.* Tŭr-ghlan, fiorghlan.
Refinement, *s.* Fior-ghlanadh; snas, glaine; grinneas, finealtachd.
Refiner, *s.* Leaghadair.
Refit, *v. a.* Ath-chàirich, tog a rithist.
Reflect, *v. a.* Tilg air ais; smaointich, ath-smaointich.
Reflection, *s.* Smaoin; ath-smaointeachadh; beachd; seadh, sùim; cronachadh coire; ais-thilgeadh; ath-shoillse.
Reflective, *adj.* Smaointeachail, smuaireanach; a thilgeas faileas; sgàthanach.
Reflector, *s.* Fear-smaointeachaidh.
Reflex, *adj.* Ath-bhuailte.
Reflexible, *adj.* So-thilgeadh air ais, so-lùbadh, so-aomadh.
Reflourish, *v. n.* Ath-chinn, ath-fhàs.
Reflow, *v. n.* Ath lìon; ath-shruth.
Refluent, *adj.* A' tràghadh.
Reflux, *s.* Tràghadh, traŏghadh.
Reform, *v.* Leasaich, ath-leasaich; ath-dhealbh, ath-chruth; ceartaich.
Reform, *s.* Leasachadh; feabhas; ceartachadh.
Reformation, *s.* Ath-leasachadh, leasachadh; atharrachadh, ceartachadh.
Reformer, *s.* Fear-leasachaidh.
Refract, *v. a.* Tionndaidh, cuir gu taobh; claon gathan soluis.
Refraction, *s.* Tionnda; claonadh.
Refractive, *adj.* So-thionndadh.
Refragable, *adj.* So-chur an aghaidh.
Refrain, *v.* Cum air ais, smachdaich, ceannsaich; cum ort, na dean; caomhain.
Refrangible, *adj.* So-chlaonadh, (mar ghath soluis ;) so-sgaradh.
Refresh, *v. a.* Ùraich, neartaich, beothaich, ath-bheothaich.
Refreshment, *s.* Ùrachadh; fois, tàmh, lasachadh; lòn, biadh.
Refrigerant, *adj.* Fionnar, fallain.
Refrigerate, *v. a.* Fionnaraich.
Refrigeration, *s.* Fionnarachadh.
Refrigerative, *adj.* Fionnar.
Refuge, *s.* Tearmann, dìon, dìdean, fasgath; sgàth, sgàile.
Refugee, *s.* Fògarrach.
Refulgence, *s.* Lainnireachd.
Refulgent, *adj.* Lainnireach.
Refund, *v. a.* Dòirt air ais; dìol, ath-dhìol, dean suas, aisig.
Refusal, *s.* Diùltadh, àicheadh; ŏbadh, seunadh.
Refuse, *v.* Diùlt, àicheidh; ŏb, seun.
Refuse, *s.* Fuigheall, fuighleach, sprùileach, deireadh, diù, fartas, fòtus, deasgann, drabh.
Refuser, *s.* Fear-diùltaidh.
Refutal, *s.* Cur a mach; tosdadh.
Refutation, *s.* Cur a mach, tosdadh; dìteadh, breugnachadh.
Refute, *v. a.* Cuir a mach, cuir sàmhach, cuir an aghaidh; dìt, breugnaich.
Regain, *v. a.* Ath-choisinn.
Regal, *adj.* Rìoghail.
Regale, *v. a.* Ath-bheothaich; thoir cuirm, dean fleaghachas.
Regalement, *s.* Cuirm, ròic, fleagh.
Regalia, *s.* Suaicheantais rìoghail.
Regality, *s.* Rìoghalachd.
Regard, *v. a.* Gabh suim, gabh beachd, thoir suim, thoir fainear,

thoir an aire; gabh seadh, gabh cùram, gabh meas, thoir urram.
Regard, *s.* Suim, beachd, seadh, aire, cùram, meas, urram.
Regardful, *adj.* Furachair, faicilleach, cùramach, suimeil, aireachail.
Regardless, *adj.* Neo-chùramach, neo-fhaicilleach, dearmadach.
Regardlessness, *s.* Mi-chùramachd.
Regency, *s.* Tàinistearachd.
Regenerate, *v. a.* Ath-ghin, ath-bhreith, ath-nuadhaich.
Regenerate, *adj.* Ath-ghinte, ath-bhreithte, ath-nuadhaichte.
Regeneration, *s.* Ath-ghineamhuinn, ath-bhreith, ath-nuadhachadh.
Regent, *s.* Tàinistear; riaghlair.
Regermation, *s.* Ath-bhriseadh.
Regicide, *s.* Rìgh-mhort.
Regimen, *s.* Lòn-riaghladh.
Regiment, *s.* Feachd-mìle, *rĕiseamaid.*
Regimental, *adj.* Feachda.
Region, *s.* Tìr, dùthaich, fearann, fonn, cearn, àirde; talamh, roinn, ceithreamh.
Register, *s.* Clàr-cuimhne.
Register, *v. a.* Sgrìobh, cuir sìos.
Regorge, *v. a.* Tilg; sgeith; ath-shluig.
Regrant, *v. a.* Ath-bhuilich.
Regrade. *v. n.* Rach air t' ais, fàs ni's mion.
Regrate, *v. n.* Ceannaich roì-làimh.
Regress, *s.* Pilltinn, dol air ais.
Regression, *s.* Pilleadh, teachd air ais.
Regret, *s.* Duilichinn, farran.
Regret, *v. a.* Bi duilich, bi farranach.
Regular, *adj.* Riaghailteach.
Regularity, *s.* Riaghailt.
Regulate, *v. a.* Riaghlaich; seòl.
Regulation, *s.* Riaghailt; reachd.
Regulator, *s.* Conn-riaghlaidh; treòraiche, fear-seòlaidh; conn. *Md.*
Regurgitate, *v.* Dòirt air ais.
Regurgitation, *s.* Dòrtadh air ais.
Rehear, *v. a.* Ath-chluinn.
Rehearsal, *s.* Ath-innseadh.
Rehearse, *v. a.* Ath-aithris.
Reign, *v. n.* Rìoghaich, riaghlaich.
Reign, *s.* Rìoghachadh, riaghlachadh.
Reimburse, *v. a.* Ath-dhìol.
Reimbursement, *s.* Ath-dhìoladh.
Rein, *s.* Iall-cheannaireachd; srian.
Rein, *v. a.* Ceannsaich, smachdaich.
Reinforce, *v. a.* Ath-neartaich.
Reinforcement, *s.* Ath-neartachadh.
Reins, *s.* Na h-airnean, caol an droma.
Reinsert, *v. a.* Ath-chuir sìos.
Reinspire, *v. a.* Ath-bheothaich.
Reinstate, *v.* Cuir an ath-sheilbh.
Reinvest, *v. a.* Cuir an seilbh a rithist; cuir ath-shéisd ri baile.
Reiterate, *v. a.* Aithris a rithisd, 'sa rithisd.
Reiteration, *s.* Ath-aithris.
Reject, *v. a.* Diùlt, tilg air falbh.
Rejection, *s.* Diùltadh; dìmeas.
Rejoice, *v.* Dean gàirdeachas, dean aoibhneas, dean luath-ghàir, dean mire, bi ăit, bi sùgach.
Rejoin, *v.* Cuir ri chéile rithisd; ath-choinnich; ath-fhreagair.
Rejoinder, *s.* Ath-fhreagairt.
Rejudge, *v. a.* Ath-sgrùd, ath-cheasnaich, ath-rannsaich.
Rekindle, *v. a.* Ath-bheothaich.
Relapse, *v. n.* Tuislich, no tuit air ais, gabh ath-thinneas.
Relapse, *s.* Tuiteam air ais, fàs ni's miosa, ath-philleadh tinneis.
Relate, *v.* Innis, aithris, cuir an céill; buin do, buin ri.
Related, *part.* and *adj.* Inniste, air innseadh, aithriste, air aithris; càirdeach, dìleas.
Relation, *s.* Innseadh, aithris, cur an céill; sgeul, naidheachd; caraid.
Relative, *s.* Caraid, ban-charaid, fear-cinnidh, dàimheach.
Relative, *adj.* Dàimheil; dìleas, a thaobh.
Relax, *v.* Lasaich; fuasgail; dearmadaich, cuir air dì-chuimhne; dean socair.
Belaxation, *s.* Lasachadh, fuasgladh, socair, athais, fois; dearmadachd.
Relay, *s.* Mùthadh each.
Release, *v. a.* Fuasgail, cuir fa sgaoil.
Relegate, *v. a.* Fuadaich, fògair.
Relegation, *s.* Fuadach, fògradh.
Relent, *v. a.* Maothaich; taisich, bogaich, ciùinich, gabh truas.
Relentless, *adj.* Neo-thruacanta.
Reliance, *s.* Earbsa, muinghinn.
Relic, *s.* Fuigheall, fuighleach, fàgail, iarmad; cuimhneachan.
Relict, *s.* Banntrach.
Relief, *s.* Lasachadh, còmhnadh, furtachd, faothachadh, cobhair, fuasgladh, cuideachadh; sòlas.
Relievable, *adj.* So-lasachadh, so-chòmhnadh, so-chuideachadh.
Relieve, *v. a.* Lasaich, cobhair, cuidich; thoir còmhnadh; mùth, atharraich.
Relievo, *s.* Dealbh grabhailte, &c.
Religion, *s.* Diadhachd, cràbhadh, creideamh, aidmheil.
Religionist, *s.* Baoth-chreideach.

RELIGIOUS, *adj.* Diadhaidh, cràbhach, cneasta, naomha, creideach.
RELINQUISH, *v. a.* Tréig, cuir cùl.
RELISH, *s.* Blăs taitneach; déidh, miann, sòlas, toil, tlachd.
RELISH, *v.* Fàilich; dean blăsta, blăstaich, gabh tlachd do ni; bi blăsta.
RELUCENT, *adj.* Deàrsach, soilleir.
RELUCTANCE, *s.* Aindeonachd.
RELUCTANT, *adj.* Aindeonach.
RELUME, RELUMSE, *v. a.* Ath-las.
RELY, *v. a.* Earb, cuir dòchas, cuir muinghinn, dean bun.
REMAIN, *v. n.* Fuirich, fan.
REMAINDER, *s.* Fuigheall, fuighleach.
REMAINS, *s.* Duslach; corp marbh.
REMAND, *v. a.* Cuir air ais, gairm air ais, cuir fios air ais.
REMARK, *s.* Beachd, rădh.
REMARK, *v. a.* Beachdaich, thoir fainear; comharraich a mach.
REMARKABLE, *adj.* Comharraichte, sònraichte; suaicheanta.
REMEDY, *s.* Leigheas, ìoc-shlaint, cungaidh leigheis; comas, còmhnadh.
REMEDY, *v. a.* Leighis, slànaich.
REMEMBER, *v. a.* Cuimhnich.
REMEMBRANCE, *s.* Cuimhneachan.
REMEMBRANCER, *s.* Meŏraiche.
REMIGRATION, *s.* Ath-imrich, pilleadh.
REMIND, *v. a.* Cuimhnich.
REMINISCENCE, *s.* Cuimhneachadh.
REMISS, *adj.* Tais, mi-thapaidh; neochùramach, dearmadach, leisg, neoaireachail, neo-shuimeil, mall, màirnealach.
REMISSIBLE, *adj.* So-mhathadh.
REMISSION, *s.* Mathanas; saorsa.
REMISSNESS, *s.* Màirneal, neo-aire, dearmad, neo-chùram, neo-shuim.
REMIT, *v.* Lasaich; math, lùghdaich, thoir suas; dàilich, cuir dàil; cuir air ais.
REMITTANCE, *s.* Sùim airgeid, a chuireas neach gu neach eile; pàigheadh.
REMNANT, *s.* Fuigheall, fuighleach, iarmad; an còrr.
REMONSTRANCE, *s.* Cur an aghaidh.
REMONSTRATE, *v. a.* Connsaich, reusonaich, thoir reuson, cuir an aghaidh, earalaich.
REMORSE, *s.* Agartas-cogais; truacantachd, iochdmhorachd.
REMORSEFUL, *adj.* Truacanta, maoth.
REMORSELESS, *adj.* An-iochdmhor.
REMOTE, *adj.* Iomallach, cian, an céin, air astar, fad' ás, fad' air falbh.
REMOTENESS, *s.* Céin, iomallachd.
REMOTION, *s.* Carachadh, gluasad.
REMOVABLE, *adj.* So-ghluasad.
REMOVAL, *s.* Gluasad, imrich.
REMOVE, *v.* Cuir ás àite, cuir air falbh, cuir air imrich; falbh, gluais rach air imrich.
REMOVE, *s.* Falbh; imeachd, gluasad, carachadh, mùthadh.
REMOUNT, *v. a.* Ath-dhìrich.
REMUNERABLE, *adj.* So-dhìoladh.
REMUNERATE, *v. a.* Ath-dhìol, pàigh.
REMUNERATION, *s.* Dìol, ath-dhìoladh.
RENARD, *s.* Ruairidh, ainm a' mhadaidh-ruaidh; cealgaire.
RENASCENT, *adj.* Ath-ghineach.
RENAVIGATE, *v. a.* Ath-sheòl.
RENCOUNTER, *s.* Còmhrag, co-strì.
RENCOUNTER, *v.* Coinnich, buail; rach an dàil, thoir ionnsaidh, dean còmhrag, thoir coinneamh; còmhlaich, tachair air.
REND, *v. a.* Srac, reub; beubanaich.
RENDER, *v. a.* Ìoc, dìol, ath-dhìol; builich, thoir, tabhair; bàirig eadartheangaich', mìnich; thoir thairis, liobhair; tiomain.
RENDEZVOUS, *s.* Ionad-còmhlachaidh.
RENDITION, *s.* Liobhairt, toirt suas.
RENEGADE, RENEGADO, *s.* Naomhthréigeach; fear ceannairceach.
BENEW, *v. a.* Ath-nuadhaich.
RENEWAL, *s.* Ath-nuadhachadh.
RENNET, *s.* Binid; deasgainn.
RENOVATE, *v. a.* Nuadhaich, ùraich.
RENOVATION, *s.* Nuadhachadh.
RENOUNCE, *v. a.* Diùlt, ŏb, tréig.
RENOWN, *s.* Cliù, alla, iomradh.
RENOWNED, *adj.* Cliùiteach, allail, iomraiteach, ainmeil.
RENT, *s.* Sracadh, reub; bèarn; gearradh; màl, tighinn a steach; cìs.
RENT, *v.* Gabh no thoir air son màil; srac, reub, stroic, sgoilt.
RENT, *part.* Sracte, reubte.
RENTAL, *s.* Màl oighreachd.
RENTER, *s.* Màladair; tuathanach.
RENUMERATE, *v. a.* Ath-dhiol, athchunnt.
RENUNCIATION, *s.* Cùlachadh.
REORDAIN, *v. a.* Ath-òrduich.
REORDINATION, *s.* Ath-òrduchadh.
REPAID, *part.* Pàighte, ath-dhìolte.
REPAIR, *v.* Càirich, leasaich, imich, falbh, siubhail; tog ort.
REPAIR, *s.* Càramh; leasachadh.
REPAIRABLE, REPARABLE, *adj.* So-leasachadh, so-chàradh.
REPARATION, *s.* Càramh, dìoladh.
REPARTEE, *s.* Freagairt-geur, beum.
REPASS, *v. n.* Ath-shiubhail.
REPAST, *s.* Biadh, lòn, teachd-an-tìr
REPAY, *v. a.* Ath-dhìol, pàigh, ìoc.

Repeal, *v. a.* Cuir sìos, cuir air chùl, thoir gu neo-ni.
Repeal, *s.* Cur air chùl, cur sìos.
Repeat, *v. a.* Aithris; abair a rìthist; abair air do theangaidh.
Repeatedly, *adv.* Gu minig, gu tric.
Repeater, *s.* Fear-aithris; uaireadear.
Repel, *v. a.* Tilg air ais, diùlt.
Repent, *v. n.* Gabh aithreachas.
Repentance, *s.* Aithreachas.
Repentant, *adj.* Aithreachail.
Repercuss, *v. a.* Buail air.
Repercussion, *s.* Cur air ais.
Repertory, *s.* Ionad-tasgaidh.
Repetition, *s.* Ath-aithris; ath-chantain; ath-dhèanamh; ath-iarrtas.
Repine, *v. n.* Dean talach, dean frionas, dean gearan.
Repiner, *s.* Fear talaich.
Replace, *v. a.* Cuir 'na àite a rithist.
Replant, *v. a.* Ath-shuidhich.
Replenish, *v. a.* Lion; airneisich.
Replete, *adj.* Làn, iomlan.
Repletion, *s.* Làine, sàth, lìontachd.
Replication, *s.* Freagairt.
Reply, *v. n.* Freagair, thoir freagairt.
Reply, *s.* Freagrairt.
Repolish, *v. a.* Ath-lìobhaich.
Report, *v. a.* Innis, aithris; abair.
Report, *s.* Fathunn, biùthas; iomradh, sgeul; fuaim, bragh, làmhach.
Reporter, *s.* Fear-naidheachd.
Reposal, *s.* Foisneachadh.
Repose, *v.* Foisnich, gabh tàmh.
Repose, *s.* Fois, tàmh; cadal.
Reposite, *v. a.* Taisg; cuir seachad.
Reposition, *s.* Tasgaidh, cur suas.
Repository, *s.* Ionad-tasgaidh.
Repossess, *v. a.* Ath-shealbhaich.
Repossession, *s.* Ath-shealbhachadh.
Reprehend, *v. a.* Cronaich, coirich.
Reprehender, *s.* Fear-cronachaidh.
Reprehensible, *adj.* Ion-choireachadh, airidh air achmhasan.
Reprehension, *s.* Achmhasan.
Reprehensive, *adj.* Achmhasanach.
Reprehensory, *adj.* Achmhasanach.
Represent, *v. a.* Feuch; nochd; foillsich, taisbean, cuir an céill; dealbh; riochdaich.
Representation, *s.* Nochdadh, foillseachadh, taisbeanadh, coltas; riochd, dealbh, ìomhaigh, aogas.
Representative, *s.* Fear-ionaid.
Representment, *s.* Iomhaigh; sàmhla.
Repress, *v. a.* Caisg; sàraich; ceannsaich, cìosnaich, smachdaich; mùch; cùm fodha.
Repress, **Repression**, *s.* Càsg, sàrachadh. ceannsachadh, cìosnachadh, mùchadh, cumail fodha.
Repressive, *adj.* Smachdail.
Reprieve, *v. a.* Cuir dàil am peanas.
Reprieve, *s.* Mathadh, dàil peanais.
Reprimand, *v. a.* Achmhasanaich.
Reprimand, *s.* Achmhasan, trod.
Reprint, *v. a.* Ath-chlò-bhuail.
Reprisal, *s.* Éirig; ath ghabhail.
Reproach, *v. a.* Cronaich; maslaich; cuir ás leth, tilg suas.
Reproach, *s.* Cronachadh, maslachadh; mì-chliù, masladh, sgainneal, tàmailt, aithis; tailceas, innisg, ilisg.
Reproachable, *adj.* Maslachail.
Reproachful, *adj.* Maslach, nàr, gràineil, tàmailteach; tailceasach, beumach, toibheumach.
Reprobate, *s.* Daoidhear.
Reprobate, *adj.* Olc, aingidh, baoth.
Reprobate, *v. a.* Mi-cheadaich; diùlt; cuir cùl; dìt.
Reprobation, *s.* Dìteadh; di-meas.
Reproduce, *v. a.* Ath-thoir a mach.
Reproduction, *s.* Ath-thoirt a mach.
Reproof, *s.* Sglamhradh, trod.
Reprovable, *adj.* Airidh air trod.
Reprove, *v. a.* Sglàmhraich; coirich.
Reprune, *v. a.* Ath-sgath, ath-bhearr.
Reptile, *s.* Biast-shnàigeach; trùdar.
Reptile, *adj.* Snàgach, snàigeach.
Republic, *s.* Co-fhliatheachd.
Republican, *adj.* Co-fhlaitheachdach.
Republican, *s.* Fear-co-fhlaitheachd.
Repudiate, *v. a.* Dealaich.
Repudiation, *s.* Dealachadh.
Repugnant, *adj.* Mi-thoileach.
Repulse, *v. a.* Cùm air ais
Repulse, *s.* Ais-bhualadh, pilleadh.
Repulsive, **Repulsory**, *adj.* Ais-bhuailteach, doirbh, oillteil.
Repurchase, *v. a.* Ath-cheannaich.
Reputable, *adj.* Cliùiteach.
Reputation, *s.* Cliù, meas, alla.
Repute, *v. a.* Meas; creid; saoil.
Repute, *s.* Cliù, meas, iomradh.
Request, *s.* Iarrtas, achanaich.
Request, *v. a.* Iarr, sir, guidh.
Requiem, *s.* Laoidh-guidhe, air son nam marbh, marbh-rann, tuireadh.
Require, *v. a.* Iarr; sir; feum.
Requisite, *adj.* Feumail, iomchuidh.
Requisite, *s.* Ni feumail.
Requital, *s.* Dìol, pàigheadh, éirig.
Requite, *v. a.* Ath-dhìol, ath-phàigh.
Rereward, *s.* Feachd-deiridh.
Resale, *s.* Ath-reic.
Resalute, *v. a.* Ath-fhàiltich.
Rescind, *v. a.* Gearr, cuir sìos lagh.
Rescission, *s.* Sgathadh, gearradh.

Rescribe, *v. a.* Ath-sgrìobh.
Rescript, *s.* Reachd rìgh.
Rescue, *s.* Saoradh, fuasgladh.
Rescue, *v. a.* Saor, sgaoil; tèarainn.
Research, *s.* Rannsachadh, ceasnachadh, sgrùdadh, ath-shireadh.
Research, *v. a.* Rannsaich, ceasnaich.
Resemblance, *s.* Samhla, coltas.
Resemble, *v. a.* Bi coltach, coimeas.
Resent, *v. a.* Gabh gu dona, gabh gu h-olc, gabh mar thàmailt; dìoghail.
Resentful, *adj.* Feargach.
Resentment, *s.* Fearg, dìoghaltas.
Reservation, *s.* Cùl-earalas, falach.
Reserve, *v. a.* Taisg, caomhain.
Reserve, *s.* Tasgadh, gleighteanas, cùl-earalas; stuaim, nàire, macantas.
Reserved, *adj.* Màlda, stuama, macanta; dùinte; fada thall, mùgach; neo-shaor; caomhainte, taisgte.
Reservedness, *s.* Fiatachd, mùig.
Reservoir, *s.* Màthair-uisge.
Resettlement, *s.* Ath-shocrachadh.
Reside, *v. n.* Fuirich, gabh còmhnaidh, cuir suas; traogh, sìolaidh.
Residence, **Resiance**, *s.* Ionad-còmhnaidh, fàrdoch, tàimheach.
Resident, **Resisant**, *adj.* A' fuireach.
Resident, *s.* Teachdaire rìgh.
Residue, *s.* Fuigheall, iarmad.
Resign, *v. a.* Thoir suas; géill.
Resignation, *s.* Toirt-seachad; ùmhlachd, strìochdadh, géilleadh.
Resignment, *s.* Toirt suas.
Resilience, *s.* Leum air ais.
Resin, **Rosin**, *s.* Ròiseid, bìth.
Resinous, *adj.* Ròiseideach, bìtheach.
Resist, *v. a.* Cuir an aghaidh.
Resistance, *s.* Strì, cur an aghaidh.
Resistible, *adj.* So-bhacadh.
Resistless, *adj.* Do-bhacadh, dian.
Resoluble, *adj.* So-leaghadh.
Resolute, *adj.* Suidhichte, sònraichte, dàn, danarra, misneachail, gramail, bunailteach, seasmhach.
Resolution, *s.* Rùin-seasmhach, inntinn, misneach; sònrachadh; bunailteachd, bunaiteachd; fuasgladh, mìneachadh.
Resolvable, *adj.* So-sgrùdadh.
Resolve, *v.* Sònraich; cuir romhad; fuasgail, sgrùd; leagh.
Resolve, *s.* Rùn-suidhichte.
Resolved, *adj.* Sònraichte, suidhichte.
Resolvedly, *adv.* Gu suidhichte.
Resolvent, *adj.* Leaghach.
Resonant, *adj.* Ath-fhuaimneach.
Resorb, *v.* Ath-shluig.
Resort, *v. n.* Taghaich; rach.
Resort, *s.* Tional, co-thional, cruinneachadh; coinneamh, cò-dhail.
Resound, *v. a.* Ath-fhuaimnich.
Resource, *s.* Cùl-earalas, tèarmann; seòl, dòigh, rathad.
Respect, *v. a.* Urramaich, thoir meas.
Respect, *s.* Urram, meas, spéis.
Respectable, *adj.* Measail.
Respectful, *adj.* Modhail, beusach.
Respective, *adj.* Sònraichte; àraid.
Respectively, *adv.* Fa leth.
Respersion, *s.* Spultadh, spairteadh.
Respiration, *s.* Analachadh, fois.
Respire, *v. n.* Analaich, leag t' anail.
Respite, *s.* Fois, anail, tàmh; fosadh.
Respite, *v. a.* Thoir fois; cuir dàil.
Resplendence, *s.* Dealrachd dealradh, loinnireachd, dearrsadh, soillse.
Resplendent, *adj.* Dealrach, lonnrach, dearrsach, boillsgeil.
Respond, *v. a.* Ath-fhreagair.
Respondent, *s.* Fear freagairt.
Response, *s.* Freagairt.
Responsible, *adj.* Freagarrach.
Responsion, *s.* Freagradh.
Responsive, **Responsory**, *adj.* Freagairteach; ath-fhuaimneach.
Rest, *s.* Fois, tàmh, cadal, sìth, sàmhchair, socair, suaimhneas, ciùineas, clos; fosadh, sgur; fèith; taic, prop, stad; a' chuid eile; càch.
Rest, *v. n.* Gabh fois; caidil, leig t' anail, sguir, dean tàmh, gabh gu clos; fuirich, fan; earb ri, earb á.
Restauration, *s.* Nuadhachadh.
Restful, *adj.* Sàmhach, ciùin.
Restiff, **Restive**, **Resty**, *adj.* Ceannlaidir, reasgach, stadach, rag.
Restifness, *s.* Reasgachd.
Restitution, *s.* Toirt air ais, dìoladh.
Restless, *adj.* Mì-fhoisneach, mìfhoighidneach; mi-shuaimhneach; luaineach, neo-shuidhichte, iomairteach, aimhreiteach, buaireasach.
Restlessness, *s.* Mi-fhoisneachd, neofhoisneachd, mi-fhoighidinn, mishuaimhneas, dìth foise.
Restorable, *adj.* So-aiseag.
Restoration, *s.* Ath-aiseag.
Restorative, *adj.* Leigheasail.
Restorative, *s.* Leigheas-beothachaidh, iocshlaint-neanrtachaidh.
Restore, *v. a.* Thoir air ais; athdhìol; leighis, ath-bheothaich.
Restrain, *v. a.* Bac; caisg; cùm air ais, toirmisg, ceannsaich, cùm fodha, smachdaich, cùm fo cheannsal.
Restraint, *s.* Bacadh, maille, toirmeasg, grabadh, ceannsachd.

Restrict, *v. a.* Bac, ceannsaich, grab, cùm, a steach; ceangail.
Restriction, *s.* Bacadh; grabadh, cuibhreachadh, ceangal.
Restrictive, *adj.* Ceanglach.
Restringent, *adj.* Ceanglach.
Resust, *v.* Tachair, thig gu buil.
Result, *s.* Buil, crìoch; deireadh.
Resume, *v. a.* Ath-thionnsgain.
Resumption, *s.* Ath-thionnsgnadh.
Resurrection, *s.* Ais-éirigh.
Resurvey, *v. a.* Ath-bheachdaich.
Resuscitate, *v. a.* Ath-dhùisg.
Resuscitation, *s.* Ath-dhùsgadh.
Retail, *v. a.* Reic 'na bheaganan.
Retailer, *s.* Frith-cheannaiche.
Retain, *v. a.* Cùm, gléidh, coimhid.
Retake, *v. a.* Ath-ghlac, ath-ghabh.
Retaliate, *v. a.* Ath-dhìol, dìol air ais; thoir buille air son buille.
Retaliation, *s.* Ath-dhìoladh.
Retard, *v.* Bac, grab, cùm air ais, cuir maill' air, cuir éis air.
Retardation, *s.* Bacadh, grabadh.
Retch, *v. n.* Sgèith, sgeath, tilg.
Retention, *s.* Cumail; cuimhneachadh; cuimhne; dùnadh.
Retentive, *adj.* Dìonach; cuimhneachail, cumailteach.
Reticular, Retiform, *adj.* Lìonanach; mar lìon; sùileagach, sgannanach.
Retinue, *s.* Coigleachd.
Retire, *v.* Rach gu taobh; falbh.
Retired, *adj.* Uaigneach; aonaranach.
Retirement, *s.* Uaigneas.
Retort, *v. a.* Ais-thilg, tilg air ais.
Retort, *s.* Geur-fhreagairt; seòrsa do shoitheach glainne.
Retouch, *v. a.* Ath-bhean ri; leasaich.
Retrace, *v. a.* Ath-lòrgaich.
Retract, *v. a.* Tarruinn air ais.
Retractation, *s.* Ath-bhaireal.
Retraction, *s.* Ais-tarruinn.
Retreat, *s.* Ionad dìomhair; tèarmann, dìdean, àite teichidh, fasgadh; teicheadh-airm, ruaig.
Retreat, *v. n.* Teich; gabh dion.
Retrench, *v. a.* Gearr dheth, sgăth.
Retrenchment, *s.* Lughdachadh, &c.
Retribute, *v. a.* Ath-dhìol, phàigh.
Retribution, *s.* Ath-dhìoladh.
Retributive, *adj.* Dioghalt.
Retrieve, *v. a.* Faigh air ais, aisig, ath-bhuidhinn; ath-ghairm.
Retrievable, *adj.* A dh' fhaodair fhaighinn air ais.
Retrocession, *s.* Dol air ais.
Retrospect, *s.* Sealltainn air ais.
Retrospection, *s.* Sealladh air ais.
Return, *v.* Thig air ais, pìll; dìol, pàigh, ìoc; thoir air ais, cuir air ais.
Return, *s.* Pilleadh; teachd air ais; dìoladh, pàigheadh, freagairt; tairbhe; buannachd.
Reunion, *s.* Ath-aonadh.
Reveal, *v. a.* Nochd, foillsich, taisbean, leig ris; innis, aithris.
Revel, *s.* Cuirm; ruidhtearachd.
Revel, *v. n.* Dean pòit, dean ròic; dean ruidhtearachd.
Revelation, *s.* Taisbeanadh.
Reveller, *s.* Craosaire, pòitear.
Revelrout, *s.* Gràisg-phrasgan.
Revelry, *s.* Ruidhtearachd, pòitearachd, baoisleachd.
Revenge, *v. a.* Gabh dìoghaltas, thoir aichbheil, thoir dìoladh.
Revenge, *s.* Dìoghaltas, dìoladh.
Revengeful, *adj.* Dìoghaltach.
Revenger, *s.* Fear-dìoghaltais.
Revenue, *s.* Teachd a staigh, màl; cìs.
Reverberate, *v. a.* Dean ath-ghairm.
Reverberation, *s.* Ath-ghairm.
Reverberatory, *adj.* Ath-fhuaimneach; ath-phillteach.
Revere, *v. a.* Thoir àrd urram, thoir àrd meas, urramaich.
Reverence, *s.* Urram; ùmhlachd.
Reverence, *v. a.* Urramaich.
Reverend, *adj.* Urramach, measail.
Reverent, *adj.* Iriosal, ùmhal, ùmhlachdail, strìochdail.
Reverently, *adv.* Le urram.
Reversal, *s.* Atharrachadh breitheanais, ath-bhreth.
Reverse, *v. a.* Cuir bun os ceann; atharraich, mùth, caochail.
Reverse, *s.* Atharrachadh, caochla.
Reversible, *adj.* Atharrachail.
Reversion, *s.* Ath-shealbhachadh; còir-sealbhachaidh.
Revert, *v.* Mùth, atharraich; pill.
Revertible, *adj.* So-thiondadh.
Revery, Reverie, *s.* Smaoin, tromsmaoin; beachd-smaoin.
Revest, *v. a.* Ath-sgeudaich.
Review, *v. a.* Ath-bheachdaich; rannsaich; sgrùd.
Review, *s.* Ath-bheachdachadh; rannsachadh; sgrùdadh, beachdachadh.
Reviewer, *s.* Fear-Rannsachaidh.
Revile, *v. a.* Càin, maslaich.
Reviler, *s.* Fear-càinidh, fear-tarcuis.
Revisal, Revision, *s.* Ath-leughadh; ath-sgrùdadh, mion-sgrùdadh.
Revise, *v. a.* Ath-leugh; ath-sgrùd.
Revise, *s.* Ath-leughadh; ath-sgrùdadh, ath-cheartachadh.
Reviser, *s.* Sgrùdaire, fear sgrùdaidh.

Revisit, *v. a.* Ath-thaghaich.
Revival, *s.* Ath-bheothachadh.
Revive, *v.* Ath-bheothaich; ùraich; thig beò a rithisd; thig thuige; dùisg, brosnaich; glac misneach.
Revocable, *adj.* So-atharrachadh.
Revocate, *v. a.* Gairm air ais.
Revocation, *s.* Ais-ghairm.
Revoke, *v. a.* Tarruinn air ais.
Revolt, *v. n.* Dean ar-a-mach; éirich
Revolt, *s.* Ar-a-mach; éirigh.
Revolve, *v.* Uim-chuairtich; cnuasaich, beachd-smuainich.
Revolution, *s.* Cuairt; uim-chuartachadh, atharrachadh; ceannairc; teachd Righ Uilleam a's Màiri.
Revulsion, *s.* Lionadh air ais.
Revulsive, *adj.* Ath-thàirneach.
Reward, *v. a.* Ath-dhìol, dìol, pàigh.
Reward, *s.* Dìol, dìoladh, pàigheadh, duais, luach-saoithreach.
Rhapsodist, *s.* Àrd-ghlòraiche.
Rhapsody, *s.* Àrd-ghlòir.
Rhetoric, *s.* Ùr-labhradh.
Rhetorical, *adj.* Ùr-labhrach.
Rhetorician, *s.* Ùr-labhartaiche.
Rheum, *s.* Ronnan, tias, mùsgan.
Rheumatic, *adj.* Lòinidheach.
Rheumatism, *s.* Lòinidh; alt-ghalar.
Rheuminess, *s.* Mùsganachd.
Rheumy, *adj.* Mùsgach, ronnach.
Rhinoceros, *s.* An Sròn-adharcach.
Rhomb, *s.* Ceithir-shlisneach, &c.
Rhomboid, *s.* Am bradan-leathunn.
Rhubarb, *s.* Luibh-na-pùrgaid.
Rhyme, *s.* Rann; dàn; duan.
Rhyme, *v. n.* Rannaich, dean rann.
Rhymer, *s.* Rannair, duanair.
Rhythmical, *adj.* Duanach, binn.
Rib, *s.* Aisinn; reang, tarsannan.
Ribald, *s.* Baobh, trusdar drabasda.
Ribaldry, *s.* Dràosdachd.
Riband, **Ribbon**, *s.* Stìom, ribean.
Ribwort, *s.* Slàn-lùs.
Rice, *s.* Gràn Innseanach.
Rich, *adj.* Beairteach, saibhir, toiceil; cosgail, luachmhor, prìseil, pailt, torrach; tarbhach, reamhar.
Riches, *s.* Beairteas, saibhreas, maoin, stòras, earras, pailteas, toic.
Richly, *adv.* Gu saibhir pailt.
Richness, *s.* Reamhrachd, saibhreachd, torraichead, beairtichead.
Rick, *s.* Cruach, rucan; cuidhleag, mulan, tudan.
Rickets, *s.* An teannadh.
Rickety, *adj.* Teannadach.
Rid, *v. a.* Cuir fa-sgaoil, saor, fuasgail; cuir air falbh; dìobair, fuadaich.
Riddance, *s.* Fuasgladh; saoradh.
Riddle, *s.* Toimhseachan; ruideal; criathar-garbh.
Riddle, *v.* Ruidealaich, ruidil.
Ride, *v.* Marcaich; smachdaich.
Rider, *s.* Marcaiche, marc-neach.
Ridgil, **Ridgling**, *s.* Rùda.
Ridge, *s.* Druim, croit, mullach; fireach, creachann, aonach; màgh, gead, imire.
Ridgy, *adj.* Druimeanach.
Ridicule, *s.* Fanaid, sgeig; ceòl-gàire; fearas-chuideachd.
Ridicule, *v. a.* Dean sgeig.
Ridiculous, *adj.* Ceòl-ghaireach, aighearach, neònach.
Riding, *s.* Marcachd, earrann, dùthcha.
Ridinghood, *s.* Deìse-mharcachd.
Rife, *adj.* Pailt, lìonmhor.
Rifle, *v. a.* Spùinn, creach, slad.
Rift, *s.* Sgoltadh, gàg; brùc.
Rift, *v.* Sgoilt, sgag, sgàin; brùc.
Rig, *v. a.* Uidheamaich; sgeadaich.
Rigadoon, *s.* Damhsa Fràngach.
Rigation, *s.* Fliuchadh, uisgeachadh.
Rigging, *s.* Buill agus acainn luinge.
Riggish, *adj.* Drùiseil, neo-gheimnidh.
Right, *adj.* Ceart; cubhaidh; freagarrach; dìreach; tréidhireach, còir.
Right, *s.* Ceartas; còir, dlighe.
Right, *v. a.* Thoir ceartas, cuir ceart.
Righteous, *adj.* Fìreanach, tréidhireach, còir, math, ionraic, cothromach; subhailceach.
Righteousness, *s.* Fìreantachd tréidhireas, ionracas.
Rightful, *adj.* Dligheach, ceart.
Rightly, *adv.* Gu ceart.
Rigid, *adj.* Rag; forganta, geurtheann, doirbh; dùr, cruaidh, fuar, leacanta.
Rigidity, *s.* Raige; dùiread, cruas.
Rigour, *s.* Cruas, fuachd; déine.
Rigorous, *adj.* Cruaidh, cruadalach, gàbhaidh; min-phongail.
Rill, **Rillet**, *s.* Caochan, sruthan, alltan, srùlag.
Rim, *s.* Oir, iomall, bile.
Rime, *s.* Liath-reothadh, crith-reothadh, cith-reothadh.
Rimple, *v. a.* Preas, luirc, càs.
Rimy, *adj.* Ceòthar; liath le reothadh.
Rind, *s.* Cairt, rùsg, cochull.
Rind, *v. a.* Rùisg, plaoisg, cairt.
Rindle, *s.* Guitear, claiseag.
Ring, *s.* Fàinne; ailbheag, cearcall, cuairteag, beum cluig.
Ring, *v. a.* Beum, seirm, buail.
Ringdove, *s.* An smùdan.
Ringer, *s.* Fear-cluig.
Ringleader, *s.* Ceann-gràisge.

Ringlet, *s.* Dualag. bachlag, ciabhag, fainneag, cuachag, cleachdag.
Ringtail, *s.* Bréid-air-tòin.
Ringworm, *s.* Buaileag-thimcheill.
Rinse, *v. a.* Srùthall, nigh, ruinnsich.
Rinser, *s.* Sruthlair, nigheadair.
Riot, *s.* Tuaireap, aimhreite.
Riot, *v. n.* Tog tuaireap.
Rioter, *s.* Fear-tuaireap.
Riotous, *adj.* Tuaireapach.
Rip, *v. a.* Srac, reub, srac suas, srac ás a' chéile, sgoilt; nochd, innis, foillsich, taisbean, leig ris.
Ripe, *adj.* Abaich; foirfidh; inbheach.
Ripe, Ripen, *v. n.* Abaich.
Ripeness, *s.* Abaichead; foirfeachd.
Ripple, *v. n.* Faochanaich, crith.
Rippling, *s.* Tonn-luasgadh.
Rise, *v. n.* Éirich; dìrich; bris a mach, dean ceannairc, dean àr-a-mach, dean tuaireap.
Rise, *s.* Éiridh, dìreadh; tùs.
Risen, *part.* Air éiridh.
Risible, *adj.* Gàireachail.
Risk, *s.* Cunnart, gàbhadh.
Risk, *v. a.* Cuir an cunnart.
Rite, *s.* Deas-ghnàth.
Ritual, *adj.* Deas-ghnàthach.
Ritual, *s.* Leabhar dheas-ghnàth.
Rival, *s.* Co-dheuchainniche, cò-shaoithriche; co-shuirdhiche.
Rival, *adj.* Co-strìgheach.
Rivalry, *s.* Comh-dheuchainn, co-dheuchainneachd, comh-eud.
Rive, *v.* Reub, srac, sgàin, sgoilt.
Rivel, *v. a.* Căs, preas, liurc.
Riven, *part.* Reubte, sracte, sgàinte.
River, *s.* Abhuinn, (*etymo.* Àbh-bhuinne, àbh *and* buinne, water and stream,) erroneously written "amhainn." The true Scottish *gen.* of this noun is abhna *and* abhunn; "aibhne" is the Irish *genitive.*
River-dragon, *s.* An croghall-mòr.
River-horse, *s.* An t-each-uisge.
Rivet, *s.* Sparrag, teannachan.
Rivet, *v. a.* Sparr, teannaich.
Rivulet, *s.* Sruthan, caochan, srùlag.
Rixdollar, *s.* Bonn cheithir tastain a's shè sgillinn.
Roach, *s.* Seòrs' éisg.
Road, *s.* Rathad, ròd slighe, aisridh, acarsaid; bàdh, bàdhan, poll, òban, calla.
Roam, *v.* Seabhaid; rach air seachran, rach gu taobh, bi 'san athamanaich, rach air fàrsan.
Roan, *adj.* Grìs-fhionn, riabhach.
Roar, *v. n.* Beuc, geum, éigh, glaodh, sgairtich, ràn; roic; dean burral.
Roar, *s.* Beuc, geum, roic, éigh, glaodh, ràn, sgairt, burral, ulfhart.
Roast, *s.* Ròsta; *v. a.* Ròist.
Rob, *v. a.* Spùill, creach, slad.
Robber, *s.* Creachadair, spùilleadair, fear-reubainn, fear-slaide.
Robbery, *s.* Reubainn, creach.
Robe, *v. a.* Sgeadaich, còmhdaich.
Robe, *s.* Falluinn, trusgan.
Robin-red-breast, *s.* Am brù-dhearg.
Robust, *adj.* Garbh, làidir, calma, neartmhor, comasach, lùghor, féitheach, gramail, garg.
Robustness, *s.* Neart, spionnadh.
Rocambole, *s.* Creamh-nan-creag.
Rochealum, *s.* An t-àlm-fiorghlan.
Rochet, *s.* Léine-aifrionn; seòrs' éisg.
Rock, *s.* Carraig, creag, sgòrr-bheann; cuigeal; tèarmunn, dìdean.
Rock, *v.* Luaisg, tulg, siudanaich; fuluaisg, cuir a chadal; bi air udal.
Rocket, *s.* Seòrs' obair-theine.
Rocky, *adj.* Creagach, carraigeach, garbh; clachach, cruaidh.
Rod, *s.* Slat; sgiùrsair.
Rode, *pret.* of *to ride.* Mharcaich.
Roe, *s.* Earba, ruadhag; iùchair éisg.
Roebuck, *s.* Boc-earba.
Rogation, *s.* Seadhan, aslachadh.
Rogation-week, *s.* Seachduin bhogadh-nan-gad, an seachdamh latha roi'n chàingis.
Rogue, *s.* Sloightear, cealgair.
Roguery, *s.* Sloightearachd.
Roguish, *adj.* Sloighteil, carach.
Roist, *v. n.* Dean gleadhraich.
Roll, *v.* Fill; cuir căr air chăr; tonn-luaisg, cuairsg, cuairtich, cuir mu chuairt, rach mu chuairt.
Roll, *s.* Rola, ruileag.
Roller, *s.* Cuairsgean.
Roman, *adj.* Ròmanach.
Romance, *s.* Ròlaist, spleaghraich.
Romancer, *s.* Reòlaistiche, spleaghaire.
Romanist, *s.* Pàpanach.
Romantic, *adj.* Ròlaisteach, spleaghach, spleighreach.
Rome, *s.* An Ròimh.
Romish, *adj.* Ròimheach, pàpanach.
Romp, *s.* Dubh-caile; garbh-chluich.
Romp, *v. n.* Dean garbh-chleasachd.
Romping, *s.* Garbh-chleasachd.
Rondeau, *s.* Iorram, ùilean.
Ronion, *s.* Umarlaid, bronnag.
Rood, *s.* Ròd, an ceathramh cuid do dh' acair fearainn; crois a' Phàpa.
Roof, *s.* Mullach taighe, fraigh, tudhadh; uachdar a' chàirein.
Roof, *v. a.* Cuir mullach air taigh.
Rook, *s.* Ròcas; cealgair.

Rook, *v. n.* Thoir an car á; meall, creach, spuinn, spuill, slad.
Rookery, *s.* Ionad-ròcas.
Room, *s.* Seòmar, rùm; àite; ionad.
Roomy, *adj.* Farsainn, leathann.
Roost, *s.* Spàrr, spiris, iris, fàradh.
Roost, *v. n.* Rach air spiris.
Root, *s.* Freumh; stoc, bun; meacan, tùs, mathair-aobhair, aobhar.
Root, *v.* Freumhaich, gabh freumh; suidhich, daingnich; sgrios; spìon ás a' bhun; mill.
Rooted, *adj.* Freumhaichte.
Rootedly, *adv.* Gu domhainn, gu daingeann, gu teann.
Rope, *s.* Tobha, ròp, ball.
Rope, *v. n.* Righnich, fàs tiugh.
Ropedancer, *s.* Dhamhsair ròp.
Ropemaker, *s.* Fear deanamh ròp.
Ropiness, *s.* Rìghneachd.
Ropy, *adj.* Righinn, bìthanach.
Roquelaure, Roquelo, *s.* Cleòca fireanaich; faluinn-uachdair.
Rosary, *s.* A' chonair, paidirean.
Roscid, *adj.* Driùchdach, drùchdach.
Rose, *s.* An ròs, an dris-bhil.
Rose, *pret.* of *to rise.* Dh' éirich.
Rosed, *adj.* Dearg, ruiteach.
Roseate, *adj.* Ròsach, ruiteach.
Rosemary, *s.* Ròs-Muire.
Roset, *s.* Gnè do dhath dearg.
Rosin, *s.* Reòiseid.
Rostrum, *s.* Gob; claigeann toisich luinge, crannag, sgalan.
Rosy, *adj.* Ruiteach, mar ròs.
Rot, *v.* Gròd, lobh, breò, malc.
Rot, *s.* An tòchd; malcadh-tioram, grodadh, lobhadh.
Rotary, Rotatory, *adj.* Cuairteach, rothach, cuairsgeach.
Rotation, *s.* Dol-mu'n-cuairt.
Rote, *v. a.* Ionnsaich air do theangaidh.
Rote, *s.* Sriut, facail air teangaidh.
Rotten, *adj.* Grod, lobhte, malcte, breun, breoite, cnàmhte.
Rotund, *adj.* Cruinn.
Rotunda, *s.* Togail chruinn.
Rotundity, *s.* Cruinnead; cruinne.
Rouge, *s.* Dearg, dath dearg.
Rough, *adj.* Garbh; molach, ròmach, ròinneach; gruamach, gnò; dòbhaidh, gailbheach, garbh, gàbhaidh, doinionnach, stuadh-ghreannach; garg, searbh, geur, goirt; dealgach; creagach, clachach.
Roughcast, *s.* Dealbh gun liobhach.
Rough-draught, *s.* Ceud-tharruinn.
Roughen, *v.* Dean garbh, fàs garbh; fàs gruamach, sgaiteach no coimheach; fàs gailbheach.
Roughly, *adv.* Gu garbh.
Roughness, *s.* Gairbhead, molaichead, romaiche, gairge, coimheachas; seirbhe; gailbheichead, fiadhaichead.
Round, *adj.* Cruinn, cearclach; slàn, neo-bhriste, glan, cuimir, riochdail; pongail, luath; sgairteil; mòr.
Round, *s.* Cuairt, cearcall; car.
Round, *adv.* Mu' n cuairt; air gach taobh; timchioll, mu thimchioll.
Roundelay, *s.* Luinneag, coilleag.
Roundhouse, *s.* Prìosan, gainntir.
Roundish, *adj.* A leth-char cruinn.
Roundnesss, *s.* Cruinnead mìnead.
Rouse, *v.* Dùisg; caraich; brosnaich; mosgail, brosgail; brod.
Rousing, *adj.* Brosnachail, mosglach.
Rout, *s.* Pràbar, cumasg; ruaig.
Rout, *v.* Ruag, sgiùrs, sgap.
Route, *s.* Rathad, slighe.
Rove, *v.* Bi air fàrsan, rach air iomrall, siubhail gu luaineach.
Rover, *s.* Fear-fàrsain, almharrach; fear luaineach; creachadair mara.
Roving, *adj.* Fàrsanach, seachranach; iomralltach, neo-shuidhichte.
Row, *s.* Sréad, sreath, breath, sàbaid.
Row, *v. a.* Iomair, dean iomaradh, [*often erroneously written and expressed* "iomram;" the *imperative mood sing.* "let me row."]
Rowel, *s.* Spuir, silteach eich.
Rower, *s.* Iomaraiche, ràmhaiche.
Royal, *adj.* Rìoghail.
Royalist, *s.* Fear rìoghail.
Royalty, *s.* Rìoghalachd.
Roynish, *adj.* Crìon; suarrach.
Rub, *v.* Suath; tachais; sgrìob; teannaich; glan, sgùr.
Rub, *s.* Suathadh; bacadh, maille; cruadal.
Rubber, *s.* Sgrìobadair; inneal suathaidh; seòrs' èighe.
Rubbish, *s.* Salachar, trusdaireachd.
Rubify, *v. a.* Dearg, deargaich.
Rubric, *s.* An sgrìobhadh dearg.
Ruby, *s.* Ruiteachan, rùban; deargsheud; guirean no plucan dearg.
Ructation, *s.* Brùc, brùcail.
Rudder, *s.* Stiùir.
Ruddiness, *s.* Deirge, ruthadh.
Ruddle, *s.* Céir dhearg, clach-dhearg.
Ruddy, *adj.* Ruiteach, dearg.
Rude, *adj.* Borb; balachail, doirbh, mi-mhodhail; brùideil, aineolach, neo-fhoghluimte, neo-shnasmhor; neo-ghrinn, neo-ealanta; neo-sgileil, neo-theòma.
Rudeness, *s.* Buirbe; mi-mhodh; brùidealachd; aineolas; déine.

Rudiment, *s.* Tionnsgnadh, ceud thoiseach, ceud-fhoghlum.
Rudimental, *adj.* Tionnsgnach.
Rue, *v. a.* Crean, gabh aithreachas.
Rue, *s.* An rùdh, an ruadh-lùs.
Rueful, *adj.* Muladach, brònach, dubhach, trom creanachail.
Ruefulness, *s.* Mulad, doilghios.
Ruff, *s.* Gibeag-muineil; seòrs' éisg.
Ruffian, *s.* Fear-brùideil.
Ruffian, *adj.* Bruideil, olc.
Ruffle, *v. a.* Cuir á òrdugh; buair; tog greann mar ni gaoth air uisge.
Ruffle, *s.* Frilleag, gibeag; sàbaid.
Rug, *s.* Brat-teallaich.
Rugged, *adj.* Garbh, creagach, sturrach; bacach, bacanach, stacach; droch-mhuinte, doirbh, borb, brùideil; mi-mhodhail; gailbheach.
Ruggedness, *s.* Gairbhe; buirbe.
Rugose, *adj.* Caisreagach, phreasach.
Ruin, *s.* Léir-sgrios; lom-sgrios; dol sìos; mi-shealbh; làrach.
Ruin, *v. a.* Léir-sgrios; dìth-mhill, dean truagh, tilg sìos, leag; creach.
Ruinate, *v. a.* Thoir gu bochdainn.
Ruination, *s.* Léir-chreach
Ruinous, *adj.* Sgriosal, millteach.
Rule, *s.* Riaghailt; àithne; òrdugh; riaghladh; smachd, ceannas; nòs, gnàth, àbhaist; lagh, reachd.
Rule, *v. a.* Riaghail; stiùr; smachdaich; cuir gu dòigh.
Ruler, *s.* Uachdaran, riaghladair.
Rum, *s.* Deoch làidir o shiùcar.
Rumble, *v. n.* Dean rùcail.
Ruminant, *adj.* A chnàmhas cìr.
Ruminate, *v.* Cnàmh cìr; cnuasaich.
Rumination, *s.* Cnàmhadh cìre, athchagnadh, cnuasachadh.
Rummage, *v.* Rannsaich; sgrùd, sir.
Rummer, *s.* Glaine; còrn, cuach.
Rumour, *s.* Fathunn, iomradh, sgeul.
Rumour, *v. a.* Sgaoil, innis, aithris.
Rump, *s.* An dronn, an rumpull, am feaman, bun an earbaill, mìr-cagnaidh nam bàrd.
Rumple, *s.* Preasag; càs, lorc.
Rumple, *v. a.* Preas, cas, liurc.
Run, *v.* Ruith, greas, steud; teich; sruth; leagh; troi'-lot, bior, sàth.
Run, *s.* Ruith, steud; gluasad, slighe.
Runagate, *s.* Dìobarach, claghaire.
Rundlet, **Runlet**, *s.* Buideal.
Rung, *s.* Rong, rongas.
Runnel, *s.* Sruthan, srùlag, caochan.
Runner, *s.* Steudair, gille-ruithe, teachdaire; clach-mhuilinn.
Runnet, *s.* Binid; deasgainn.
Running, *adj.* Steudach; siùbhlach.
Runnion, *s.* Sgonn-bhalach, ùmaidh.
Runt, *s.* Mart beag; arrach.
Rupee, *s.* Bonn Innseannach is fiach da thastan a's trì sgillinn.
Ruption, *s.* Briseadh, sgaoileadh.
Rupture, *s.* Mam-sic; sgàineadh, aimhreit, eas-còrdadh.
Rupture, *v. a.* Bris, sgàin, sgaoil.
Rural, *adj.* Dùchail, tìreil.
Rush, *s.* Luachair, buigneach; ni suarrach sam bith; dian-ruith.
Rush, *v. n.* Brùc, ruith, pùc, buail air aghart; stiall; thoir ionnsaidh làidir, thoir garbh-ionnsaidh.
Rush-light, *s.* Coinneal-buaic-sitheig.
Rusk, *s.* Briosgaid chruaidh.
Rushy, *adj.* Luachrach; luachaireach.
Russet, *adj.* Donn, dù-ruadh.
Russet, *s.* Drògaid, éideadh dùthcha.
Russeting, *s.* Ubhal-an-eich.
Rust, *s.* Meirg, ruadh-smal.
Rust, *v.* Meirg; meirgeich.
Rustic, *adj.* Dùthchail; neo-shnasmhor, aineolach; sìmplidh.
Rustic, *s.* Galla-bodach, fear-dùcha.
Rustical, *adj.* Borb; aineolach.
Rusticate, *v.* Tuinich san dùthaich; fuadaich do 'n dùthaich.
Rusticity, *s.* Sìmplidheachd, neosheòltachd, neo-chealgachd.
Rustle, *v. n.* Dean starbhanaich.
Rustling, *s.* Starbhanaich.
Rusty, *adj.* Meirgeach, làn.
Rut, *s.* Clais-càs-cùirn, dàmhair no daradh nam fiagh, cullachd nan torccoille, &c. &c.
Ruth, *s.* Truas, truacantas, bàigh.
Ruthful, *adj.* Muladach, brònach, truagh; caomh, bàigheil, truacanta.
Ruthless, *adj.* Cruaidh, borb, cruadalach, neo-thruacanta.
Ruttish, *adj.* Coinnanach; drùiseil; macnusach; teth, air dàradh.
Rye, *s.* Seagal, siogal.
Ryegrass, *s.* Feur-cuir.

S

S, *s.* Naothamh litir deug na h-Aibidil.
Sabaoth, *s.* Feachd, armailt, sluagh.
Sabbath, *s.* Sàbaid; dòmhnach.
Sabbatical, *adj.* Sàbaideach.
Sable, *s.* Dù-radan, dù-rodan.
Sable, *adj.* Dubh, dorcha, ciar.

SABRE, *s.* Claidheamh crom.
SABULOUS, *adj.* Grinnealach.
SACCHARINE, *adj.* Siùcarach, milis.
SACERDOTAL, *adj.* Sagartach.
SACHEL, *s.* Pocan; sacan, balgan.
SACK, *s.* Sac, poca; balg, soire, creach, reubainn; seòrsa fìona.
SACK, *v. a.* Sacaich, cuir an sac; creach; sgrios baile.
SACKBUT, *s.* Seòrsa pìob chiùil.
SACKCLOTH, *s.* Saic-aodach.
SACKPOSSET, *s.* Bainne agus fion.
SACRAMENT, *s.* Sàcramaid; bòid.
SACRAMENTAL, *adj.* Sàcramaideach.
SACRED, *adj.* Naomha, seunta, coisrigte, diadhaidh.
SACREDNESS, *s.* Naomhachd.
SACRIFIC, *adj.* Ìobairteach.
SACRIFICE, *s.* Ìobairt, tabhartas.
SACRIFICE, *v. a.* Ìobair, thoir suas, ìoc, marbh; thoir thairis.
SACRIFICIAL, *adj.* Ìobairteach.
SACRILEGE, *s.* Ceall-shlad, ceall-ghoid, goid nithe naomha, aircheall.
SACRILEGIOUS, *adj.* Ceall-shladach; a' truailleadh nithean naomha.
SACRINGBELL, *s.* An clagan-coisrigidh.
SACRISTAN, *s.* Cleireach sagairt; maoreaglais; fear-gleidhidh nan nithe coisrichte.
SACRISTY, *s.* Ionad tasgaidh nithe naomha no coisrichte.
SAD, *adj.* Brònach, dubhach, muladach, tùrsach, trom, dòlasach, doilghiosach, neo-éibhinn; dorcha; nàr, maslach; olc, aingidh.
SADDEN, *v. a.* Dean brònach, dean dubhach, dean muladach, dean tùrsach no trom; dean doilghiosach, cuir fo sproc; fàs muladach.
SADDLE, *s.* Dìollaid, pillean.
SADDLE, *v. a.* Dìollaidich.
SADDLER, *s.* Dìolladair.
SADNESS, *s.* Bròn, dubhachas, mulad, truime, sproc, doilghios.
SAFE, *adj.* Tèaruinte, slàn, sàbhailte.
SAFEGUARD, *s.* Dìon, dìdean, tèarmunn, tèaruinteachd. coimheadachd.
SAFETY, *s.* Tèaruinteachd.
SAFFRON, *s.* An cròch.
SAFFRON, *adj.* Buidhe; cròchach.
SAG, *v.* Luchdaich, tromaich; sacaich.
SAGACIOUS, *adj.* Geur-chùiseach, glic, tuigseach, toinisgeil, fad-sheallach, sicir, crìonna.
SAGACITY, *s.* Géir-chùis, tuigse, toinisg, gliocas, crìonnachd.
SAGE, *s.* Slàn-lùs; duine glic.
SAGE, *adj.* Glic, foghluimte; sicir.
SAGO, *s.* Seòrsa gràin Innseanach.
SAID, *pret.* and *part.* of *say.* Thubhairt; mar a thùbhradh.
SAIL, *s.* Seòl; brat-siùil.
SAIL, *v.* Seòl, bi seòladh.
SAILFISH, *s.* An cairbean.
SAILOR, *s.* Seòladair, maraiche.
SAILYARD, *s.* Slat-shiùil.
SAINFOIN, *s.* An saoidh-dhearg.
SAINT, *s.* Naomh.
SAINT, *v.* Naomhaich, àireamh am measg nan naomh.
SAINTED, *adj.* Naomha, cràbhach.
SAINTLY, SAINTLIKE, *adj.* Naomha, diadhaidh beannaichte, cneasta.
SAKE, *s.* Son, sgàth, &c.
SAKER, *s.* Seòrsa de ghunna mòr.
SALACIOUS, *adj.* Macnusach, drùiseil, neo-gheimnidh, baoiseach.
SALACITY, *s.* Macnus, drùis.
SALAD, *s.* Biadh-lùs, luibhean.
SALAMANDER, *s.* A' chorra-chagailt.
SALARY, *s.* Tuarasdal bliadhna.
SALE, *s.* Reic, màrgadh.
SALEABLE, *adj.* So-reic, margail.
SALESMAN, *s.* Fear-reic, ceannaiche.
SALIENT, *adj.* Leumnach, sùrdagach; stìnleagach; plosgartach.
SALINE, SALINOUS, *adj.* Saillte.
SALIVA, *s.* Smugaid, seile, ronn.
SALIVATE, *v. a.* Ronnaich.
SALIVATION, *s.* Sileadh ronn.
SALLOW, *s.* Geal-sheileach.
SALLOW, *adj.* Bànaidh, glasdaidh.
SALLY, *s.* Brùc, ionnsaidh.
SALLY, *v. n.* Brùc, bris a mach, thoir ionnsaidh.
SALMAGUNDI, *s.* Ioma-chumasg, [mios air a dheanamh suas le feòil phronn, sgadan, ola, fion-geur, peabar a's uinneinean.]
SALMON, *s.* Bradan.
SALMONTROUT, *s.* Bànag, geala-bhreac.
SALOON, *s.* Àrd-thalla.
SALT, *s.* Salann; *adj.* Saillte.
SALTCELLAR, *s.* Saillear.
SALTER, *s.* Ceannaiche-salainn.
SALTERN, *s.* Obair-shalainn.
SALTISH, *adj.* A leth-char saillte.
SALTNESS, *s.* Saillteachd.
SALTPETRE, *s.* Mear-shalann.
SALUBRITY, *s.* Slàinte, fallaineachd.
SALUTARY, *adj.* Slàinteil, slàn.
SALUTATION, *s.* Fàilte; furan.
SALUTE, *v. a.* Cuir fàilte, cuir furan, dean beatha, fàiltich, furanaich, pòg.
SALUTE, *s.* Fàilte, furan, pòg.
SALUTIFEROUS, *adj.* Slàinteachail.
SALVABLE, *adj.* Ion-shàbhaladh.
SALVATION, *s.* Saoradh, saorsainn, sàbhaladh; slàinte; slànachadh.

Salve, *s.* Sàbh-leigheis, ìoc, ùngadh.
Salver, *s.* Mias, aisead.
Salvo, *s.* Leithsgeul, cuir-seachad.
Same, *adj.* Ionann, ceudna; ceart.
Sameness, *s.* Co-ionannachd.
Samlet, *s.* Glas-bhreac, bradan òg.
Samphire, *s.* Lùs-nan-cnàmh.
Sample, *s.* Samhla, eiseamplair.
Sampler, *s.* Foir-theagaisg fuaigheil.
Sanable, *adj.* So-leigheas.
Sanative, *adj.* Leigheasach.
Sanctification, *s.* Naomhachadh.
Sanctifier, *s.* Fear naomhachaidh.
Sanctify, *v. a.* Naomhaich; coisrig.
Sanctimonious, *adj.* Cràbhach.
Sanctimony, *s.* Naomhachd.
Sanction, *s.* Aontachadh; ùghdarras; rùn; toil; comas, cead; reachd; òrdugh.
Sanctitude, **Sanctity**, *s.* Naomhachd; diadhachd, glaine, mathas.
Sanctuary, *s.* Ionad-naomha; tèarmunn, dìdean, comaraich.
Sand, *s.* Gainmheach, grinneal.
Sandal, *s.* Bonn-bhròg; cuaran.
Sandblind, *adj.* Gearr-sheallach.
Sandstone, *s.* Clach ghainmheich.
Sandy, *adj.* Gaineamhainneach.
Sane, *adj.* Glic, ciallach; fallain.
Sang, *pret.* of *to sing.* Shéinn.
Sanguinary, *adj.* Fuilteach, fuileach, fuileachdach, garg, borb, marbhtach.
Sanguine, *adj.* Flann-dearg; teth, blàth, dian, deòthasach, earbsach, dian-dhòchasach, toileil.
Sanguineous, *adj.* Fuilteach, fuileach.
Sanhedrim, *s.* Ard-chomhairle nan Ìudhach.
Sanicle, *s.* Seorsa luibh, (*the Yorkshire sanicle.* Am bodan dubh.)
Sanious, *adj.* Iongarach.
Sanity, *s.* Gliocas, toinisg, ciall, tuigse, slàinte, càil-inntinn.
Sank, *pret* of *to sink.* Air siothladh, air dol fodha, air dol gu grunnd.
Sap, *s.* Brìgh, sùgh, snothach.
Sap, *v.* Fo-chladhaich, mill.
Sapid, *adj.* Sùghmhor, blasda, milis.
Sapidity, *s.* Blasdachd, mìlseachd.
Sapience, *s.* Gliocas, tuigse, tùr.
Sapient, *adj.* Glic, tuigseach, tùrail.
Sapless, *adj.* Gun sùgh, gun bhrìgh.
Sapling, *s.* Faillean, fiùran, ògan.
Saponaceous, **Saponary**, *adj.* Siabunnach, mar shiabunn.
Sapor, *s.* Blas.
Sapphire, *adj.* Sàpir, lèig ghorm.
Sappiness, *s.* Sùgharachd; ùraireachd.
Sappy, *adj.* Sùghar, brìghmhor.
Saraband, *s.* Damhsa Spàinteach.
Sarcasm, *s.* Gearradh, beum; tearrachd, geur-mhagadh.
Sarcastic, **Sarcastical**, *adj.* Beumnach, geur, tearrachdail, sgeigeil.
Sarcenet, *s.* Sìoda, fìnealta.
Sarcle, *v. a.* Dean gart-ghlanadh.
Sarcophagous, *adj.* Feòil-itheach.
Sarchophagus, *s.* Tuamh, tunga.
Sardine, **Sardonyx**, *s.* Seòrsa do chloich luachmhoir.
Sarsaparilla, *s.* Seòrsa do luibh iocshlainteach a tha tighinn ás na h-Innseachan shuas.
Sash, *s.* Crios; bann; stiom sròl; uinneag-thogalach.
Sassafras, *s.* Luibh ioc-shlainteach a tha tighinn á America.
Satan, *s.* Sàtan, an diabhol, an-t-aibhistear, an t-àbharsair, an riabhach-mòr, an donus, an dòlas, am buaireadair, am fear is miosa.
Satanic, **Satanical**, *adj.* Diabhlaidh, deamhnaidh, aingidh, ifrinneach.
Satchel, *s.* Pocan-màileid.
Sate, **Satiate**, *v. a.* Sàth, lìon gu sàth, sàthaich; làn-toilich.
Satellite, *s.* Cuairt-reull.
Satiate, *adj.* Sàthach, sàsaichte, lìonta, làn, toilichte, buidheach.
Satiety, *s.* Teannadh, teann-shàth, sàth, leòir.
Satin, *s.* Sròl, seòrsa sìoda.
Satire, *s.* Aoir, tearrachd.
Satiric, **Satirical**, *adj.* Aoireil, beumach, sgaiteach, tearrachdail.
Satirist, *s.* Eisg, beithir-bheuma, aoireadair, tearracadair.
Satirize, *v. a.* Dean aoireadh; càin.
Satisfaction, *s.* Taitneas, sàsachadh; lan-toileachadh; dìoladh, éirig.
Satisfactory, *adj.* Taitneach.
Satisfied, *adj.* Toilichte; sàsaichte; sàthach; buidheach.
Satisfy, *v.* Toilich, sàsaich; dìol; dean cinnteach; thoir toileachas inntinn, taitinn ri, thig ri, dean buidheach, riaraich.
Saturable, *adj.* So-shàsachadh.
Saturant, *adj.* Sàsachail, lìontach.
Saturate, *v. a.* Sàsaich, lìon.
Saturday, *s.* Di-sathuirne.
Saturity, *s.* Sàth, làn, leòir.
Saturn, *s.* Sathuirn; aon do na reulltan seacharanach; luidhe.
Saturnian, *adj.* Sona; òrdha.
Saturnine, *adj.* Dorcha, gruamach; dubhach, bròнach, tròm.
Satyr, *s.* Seòrsa apa; dia-coille.
Sauce, *s.* Leannra; sùgh.
Saucebox, *s.* Peasan, fear lonach.

SAUCEPAN, *s.* Sgeileid, aghann.
SAUCER, *s.* Chopan iochdrach.
SAUCINESS, *s.* Beadaidheachd, peasanachd, gobaireachd, mi-mhod.
SAUCY, *adj.* Gobach, lonach, mimhodhail, làsdach, stràiceil, beadaidh; peasanach.
SAUNTER, *v. n.* Spaidseirich.
SAUSAGE, *s.* Ìsbean, marag gheal.
SAVAGE, *adj.* Allmharra, fiadhaich, borb, allaidh; brùideil; ain-iochdmhor; neo-thruacanta, cruaidhchridheach.
SAVAGE, *s.* Borbanach, duine fiadhaich.
SAVAGENESS, *s.* Buirbe, fiadhaichead, an-iochdmhorachd, brùidealachd, allmharrachd, neo-thruacantachd.
SAVANNA, *s.* Magh fada réidh.
SAVE, *v. a.* Saor, teasairg, sàbhail, tèaruinn, dìon, gléidh, coimhid; caomhain.
SAVE, *adv.* Ach; saor o.
SAVED, *part.* Saorte, sàbhailte, tèaruinte, gléidhte; caomhainte.
SAVIN, *s.* Seòrsa luibh; samhan.
SAVING, *adj.* Caontach, grunndail, gléidhteach, spìocach, crìon.
SAVING, *adv.* Ach, saor o.
SAVINGNESS, *s.* Caontachd; grunndalachd, spìocaireachd.
SAVIOUR, *s.* Slànaighear.
SAVORY, *adj.* Garbhag ghàraidh.
SAVOUR, *s.* Fàile, boltrach, blas.
SAVOUR, *v.* Cuir fàileadh, amhairc coltach ri; seall mar.
SAVOURINESS, *s.* Boltrachd, mìlse.
SAVOURY, *adj.* Boltrachail, cùbhraidh, fàileach, milis; blasta.
SAVOY, *s.* Seòrsa càil.
SAW, *pret.* of *see.* Chunna, chunnaic, bheachdaich, dhearc.
SAW, *s.* Sàbh, tuireasg; sean-fhacal.
SAW, *v. a.* Sàbh, dean sàbhadh.
SAWDUST, *s.* Min-sàibh, sadach shàbhaidh, garbhan tuirisg.
SAWFISH, *s.* Am fiaclachan.
SAWPIT, *s.* Sloc sàbhaidh.
SAWYER, *s.* Sàbhadair.
SAXIFRAGE, *s.* Lŭs-nan-cluas.
SAY, *v. a.* Abair, innis, labhair, aithris.
SAYING, *s.* Ràdh, facal, briathar.
SCAB, *s.* Creim, sgreab, sgab, càrr; cloimh, broth, tachas, sgrìobach, guirean.
SCABBARD, Truaill, duille.
SCABBY, *adj.* Creimeach, sgreabach, sgabach, carrach, cloimheach, clomhach, clamhrach, brothach; truagh, dìblidh, mosach.
SCABROUS, *adj.* Garbh, neo-mhìn, molach, robach, neo-bhinn.
SCAFFOLD, *s.* Sgàlan; lobhta.
SCAFFOLDING, *s.* Lobhtachan, sgàlain.
SCALADE, SCALADO, *s.* Fàrachadh, toirt a mach baile le streap.
SCALD, *v. a.* Sgailt, loisg, plod.
SCALD, *s.* Càrr, sgreab; losgadh, sgalltadh, plodadh.
SCALE, *s.* Slige chothrom, lann éisg; fàradh, dreimire; sgreab, sgrath, sgròilleag; aon do chomharran na gréin-chrios; an aibidil chiùil.
SCALE, *v. a.* Streap, streap le fàradh, cothromaich; lannaich, sgrath, sgròillich.
SCALED, *adj.* Lannach, sligeach.
SCALINESS, *s.* Lannachd.
SCALL, *s.* Luibhre, càrr, mùir.
SCALLION, *s.* Creamh gàraidh.
SCALLOP, *s.* Slige-chreachainn; eagachadh, fiaclachadh.
SCALP, *s.* Còmhdach a' chlaiginn.
SCALPEL, *s.* Sgian ghearraidh léigh.
SCALY, *adj.* Lannach; sligeach.
SCAMBLE, *v.* Sgròbaich; bi tuasaideach, beubanaich, reub, stròic.
SCAMBLE, *s.* Tuasaid; streapaid.
SCAMMONY, *s.* Seòrsa pùrgaid.
SCAMPER, *v. n.* Thoir do bhuinn ás.
SCAN, *v. a.* Tomhais; ceasnaich, sgrùd.
SCANDAL, *s.* Sgainneal, tuaileas, toibheum, droch-alla, oilbheum, cùlchaineadh, dìmeas.
SCANDALIZE, *v. a.* Sgainnealaich, maslaich, tuaileasaich, dean tàir, nàraich.
SCANDALOUS, *adj.* Maslach, tàmailteach, sgainnealach, nàr.
SCANDALOUSLY, *adv.* Gu maslach.
SCANNING, *s.* Tomhas-rann.
SCANT, *adj.* Gann, tearc; gortach.
SCANTINESS, *s.* Gainnead, crìne.
SCANTLET, *s.* Beagan, criomag; roinn.
SCANTY, *adj.* Gann; cumhann, crìon; gearr, beag, bochd, spìocach.
SCAPE, *v. a.* Teich, tar ás, seachuinn.
SCAPULA, *s.* Cnaimh an t-slinnein.
SCAPULAR, *adj.* Slinneineach.
SCAR, *s.* Aile, athailt; leòn, sgòrr.
SCAR, *v. a.* Comharraich, leòn.
SCARAB, *s.* Daol, daolag dhubh.
SCARCE, *adj.* Gann; tearc; tĕirc; ainmig; ana-minig; ainneamh.
SCARCE, SCARCELY, *adv.* Air éiginach gann, is gann.
SCARCENESS, SCARCITY, *s.* Gainnead, gainne, teirce, tearcad, ainmigead; daorsa.
SCARE, *v. a.* Fuadaich, fògair saodaich, cuir eagal air.

SCARECROW, *s.* Bodach-ròcais; buachaill'-bréige, fear-bréige, bòchdan.
SCARF, *s.* Tonnag, guailleachan.
SCARFSKIN, *s.* Craiceann; sgannan.
SCARIFICATION, *s.* Sgròilleachadh.
SCARIFY, *v. a.* Sgŏr; sgrìob, sgoch.
SCARLET, *s.* and *adj.* Sgàrlaid.
SCATCHES, *s.* Casan-corrach.
SCATE, *s.* Sgait, sòrnan; bròg-spéidhilidh, speidhleachan.
SCATE, *v. n.* Speidhil.
SCATHE, *v. a.* Sgath, mill, caith.
SCATTER, *v.* Sgap, sgaoil, sgainnir; bi sgaoilte, bi sgapte.
SCATTERING, *s.* Sgapadh, sgaoileadh.
SCAVENGER, *s.* Clàbadair.
SCELERAT, *s.* Daoidhear, daoidh.
SCENE, *s.* Coltas; taisbeanadh, roinncluiche; sgàil-bhrat, no brat-crochaidh taigh-cluiche.
SCENERY, *s.* Riochd-àite; dealbhcholtas.
SCENT, *s.* Fàileadh, bòladh, lòrg.
SCENT, *v. n.* Cuir a mach fàileadh.
SCENTED, *adj.* Boltrach.
SCEPTIC, *s.* Fear as-creideach.
SCEPTICAL, *adj.* Neo-chreideach.
SCEPTICISM, *s.* Mi-chreideamh, teagamh.
SCEPTRE, *s.* Colbh, slat-rìoghail.
SCHEDULE, *s.* Sgrìobhadh, ròla paipeir.
SCHEME, *s.* Dòigh, modh, innleachd.
SCHEMER, *s.* Fear-innleach.
SCHISM, *s.* Eas-aontachd eaglais.
SCHISMATIC, *s.* Fear tréigsinn eaglais.
SCHISMATICAL, *adj.* Eas-aontach.
SCHOLAR, *s.* Sgoilear, foghlumach.
SCHOLARSHIP, *s.* Sgoilearachd, ionnsachadh, foghlum, oilean.
SCHOLASTIC, SCHOLASTICAL, *adj.* Sgoilearach, ionnsaichte, foghlumte.
SCHOLIAST, *s.* Fear-mìneachaidh.
SCHOLIUM, *s.* Mìneachadh.
SCHOOL, *s.* Sgoil; taigh-fòghluim.
SCHOOLFELLOW, *s.* Co-sgoilear.
SCHOOLMASTER, *s.* Maighstear-sgoile.
SCHOOLMISTRESS, *s.* Ban-mhaighstear sgoile, ban-oid'-fhoghluim.
SCIATIC, *s.* Lòini, lòinidh.
SCIATICAL, *adj.* Gu h-olc leis an loini.
SCIENCE, *s.* Ealain; ceird-èolas.
SCIENTIFIC, *adj.* Ealanta; ionnsaichte.
SCIMITAR, *s.* Claidheamh-crom.
SCINTILLATE, *v. n.* Sradagaich.
SCINTILLATING, *adj.* Sradagach.
SCINTILLATION, *s.* Sradadh, caoireadh.
SCION, *s.* Faillean, maothan, fiùran.
SCIRRHOSITY, *s.* Cruadhachadh fàireig.
SCIRRHOUS, *adj.* Cruaidh mar fhàireig.
SCIRRHUS, *s.* At fàireig, beum-sice.
SCISSIBLE, SCISSILE, *adj.* So-sgoltadh, so-ghearradh, so-sgaradh.
SCISSORS, *s.* Siosar; deimheas bheag.
SCISSURE, *s.* Sgoltadh, sgàineadh, gàgadh, sgadadh, peasgadh, sgreadhadh.
SCLEROTIC, *adj.* Cruaidh, greannach.
SCOAT, *v. n.* Cuir stad air cuibhle.
SCOFF, *v. n.* Mag, dean fanaid.
SCOFFINGLY, *ad.* Gu fanaideach.
SCOFFER, *v.* Sgeigear; fear fochaid.
SCOLD, *v. a.* Troid; cronaich.
SCOLDING, *adj.* Sglàmhrach, eallsgail.
SCOLLOP, *s.* An creachann.
SCONCE, *s.* Sgàth-dhùn; dìon; ùbhladh; ceann; coinnlear-meurach.
SCOOP, *s.* Liagh, ladar, taoman.
SCOOP, *v. a.* Sluaisdich, cladhaich.
SCOPE, *s.* Rùn, ciall, miann; rùm, àite, comas; fuasgladh.
SCOPULOUS, *adj.* Creagach, garbh.
SCORBUTIC, *adj.* Carrach, tachasach.
SCORCH, *v.* Loisg, dàth; gread.
SCORE, *s.* Sgrioch; sgrìob; sreath; sgàth; fiachan, cunntas; fichead.
SCORIOUS, *adj.* Salach; stùrach.
SCORN, *v.* Dean dìmeas, dean tàir.
SCORN, *s.* Dìmeas, tarcuis, fanaid.
SCORNER, *s.* Fear-fanaid, sgeigeir.
SCORNFUL, *adj.* Dìmeasach, fanaideach, sgeigeil, tàireil, tarcuiseach.
SCORPION, *s.* Nathair-nimhe, (Esec. ii. 6;) aon do chomharran a' ghréinchrios.
SCOT, *s.* Albannach.
SCOTCH, *v. a.* Gearr, peasg, sgoch.
SCOTCH, *s.* Gearradh, peasg, sgoch.
SCOTCH, SCOTTISH, *adj.* Albannach.
SCOT-FREE, *adj.* Saor; gun phàigheadh.
SCOTOMY, *s.* Tuainealaich.
SCOTTICISM, *s.* A' Bheurla Albannach.
SCOUNDREL, *s.* Slaoightire.
SCOUR, *v. a.* Glan, soilleirich; nigh; sgànraich; teich, ruith.
SCOURER, *s.* Glanadair.
SCOURGE, *s.* Sgiùrsair, sgiùrsadh.
SCOURGE, *v. a.* Sgiùrs, peanasaich.
SCOUT, *s.* Fear-coimheid, beachdair.
SCOUT, *v. n.* Beachdaich air gluasad nàmhaid.
SCOVEL, *s.* Moibeall, meaban.
SCOWL, *v. a.* Bi fo ghruaim, cuir mùig ort.
SCRAG, *s.* Blianach, feòil bhochd.
SCRAGGY, *adj.* Blian, bochd; creagach.
SCRAMBLE, *v. n.* Smearaich, streap.
SCRAMBLE, *s.* Streapais, streap.
SCRAP, *s.* Crioman, crimeag, pronnan, mìr, pioc; fuigheall; bruanag.
SCRAPE, *s.* Cruaidh-chas, teanntachd; dragh; sgrìob.

Scrape, *v.* Sgrìob; sgròb; cnuasaich, teanail, trùs; bi sgrìobadh.
Scraper, *s.* Sgrìobachan, sgrìobadair; droch-fhìdhleir; spìocaire.
Scratch, *v. a.* Sgrìob, sgròb; tachais.
Scratch, *s.* Sgrìob, sgròb; sgrioch.
Scratches, *s.* Galar-each.
Scraw, *s.* Sgrath, rùsg.
Scrawl, *s.* Sgròbaireachd.
Screak, *v. n.* Sgread, sgreuch, sgiamh.
Scream, *v. n.* Sgread, sgreuch, sgriach, sgairt, glaodh ràn, sian.
Screech, *v. n.* Sgreuch, sgread.
Screechowl, *s.* A' chailleach-oidhche.
Screen, *v. a.* Dìon, sgàilich, falaich.
Screen, *s.* Dìon, sgàilean, fasgadh.
Screw, *s.* Bidhis, no bitheas, *from* biast, *a beast or worm.*
Scribble, *v. a.* Dean sgròbail sgrìobhaidh.
Scribble, *s.* Sgròbail, droch sgrìobhadh.
Scribbler, *s.* Ùghdar suarach, droch sgrìobhaiche.
Scribe, *s.* Sgrìobhaiche.
Scrine, *s.* Tasgaidh sgrìobhaidhean.
Scrip, *s.* Màla, màileid, pocan, balg, sporan; duilleag-sgrìobhaidh.
Scriptory, *adj.* Sgrìobte, sgrìobhach.
Scriptural, *adj.* Sgriobturail.
Scripture, *s.* Sgriobtur.
Scrivener, *s.* Sgrìobhadair.
Scrofula, *s.* Easba-bràgaid, tinneas-an-rìgh, silteach.
Scrofulous, *adj.* Guireanach, silteach, leanntach.
Scroll, *s.* Ròla, ròl.
Scrotum, *s.* Magairle, clach-bhalg.
Scrub, *s.* Spìocaire, sgrubaire, sgruimbean; seann sguabach.
Scrub, *v. a.* Glan, nigh, suath.
Scrubbed, **Scrubby**, *adj.* Suarrach, spìocach, crìon, gun fhiù.
Scruple, *s.* Amharus, teagamh, ioma-cheist, ioma-chomhairle; tomhas léigh, fichead gràinn' air chothrom.
Scruple, *v. n.* Cuir amharus, sòr, bi 'n teagamh, bi 'n ioma-chomhairle.
Scrupulosity, *s.* Amharus, teagamh, amharusachd, teagamhachd.
Scrupulous, *adj.* Teagamhach.
Scrupulousness, *s.* Teagamhachd faicilleachd.
Scrutable, *adj.* So-sgrùdadh, so-rannsachadh.
Scrutinize, *v. a.* Sgrùd, rànnsaich, ceasnaich, mion-cheasnaich.
Scrutiny, *s.* Sgrùdadh, rannsachadh.
Scrutoire, *s.* Clàr-sgrìobhaidh.
Scud, *v. n.* Ruith roi 'n ghaoith, teich.
Scuffle, *s.* Brionglaid, tuasaid, collaid, caonnag, sabaid, aimhreit.
Sculk, *v. n.* Dean cùiltearachd.
Sculker, *s.* Cùiltear, fògaraiche.
Scull, *s.* Claigeann; pleadhan.
Sculler, *s.* Eithear-pleadhain.
Scullery, *s.* Taigh-sguideileireachd.
Sculling, *s.* Pleadhanachd.
Scullion, *s.* Sguidleir; dubh-chaile
Sculptor, *s.* Grabhaltaiche.
Sculpture, *s.* Gràbhaladh.
Scum, *v. a.* Sgùm, thoir cobhar dheth.
Scum, *s.* Barrag, uachdar, cobhar.
Scurf, *s.* Sgrath; creim, càrr, sgreab.
Scurfy, *adj.* Sgrathach, creimeach, carrach, sgreabach.
Scurrility, *s.* Sglàmhrainn.
Scurrilous, *adj.* Sglàmhrainneach, sgainnealach, ana-cainnteach.
Scurrilousness, *s.* Sglamhrainneachd.
Scurvy, *s.* An tachas-tioram.
Scurvy, *adj.* Sgabach, carrach, suarrach, diblidh.
Scurvygrass, *s.* Lùs-nam-mial.
Scut, *s.* Feaman maigheich.
Scutcheon, *s.* Suaicheantas.
Scuttle, *s.* Sgùile; dian-choiseachd.
Scythe, *s.* Speal, fàladair.
Sea, *s.* Muir, cuan, fairge, garbhthonn, sùmainn, sùmaid.
Seabeach, *s.* Tràigh, cladach, mol.
Seabeaten, *s.* Tonn-bhuailte.
Seaboy, *s.* Giullan maraiche.
Seabreach, *s.* Briseadh mara.
Seabreeze, *s.* Lear-ghaoth.
Seacalf, *s.* Ròn; codrum.
Seacoast, *s.* Taobh na mara.
Seafarer, *s.* Maraichte, seòladair.
Seafight, *s.* Cath mara.
Seafowl, *s.* Eun-mara.
Seagirt, *adj.* Lear-chuartaichte.
Seagreen, *adj.* Liath-ghorm.
Seagull, *s.* Farspag, farspach.
Seal, *s.* Ròn; seula; comharradh.
Seal, *v. a.* Seulaich; seul; daingnich, naisg; dùin.
Sealing-wax, *s.* Ceur-sheulachaidh.
Seam, *s.* Sgăr; fuaigheal; tàthadh, aonadh; geir, muc-bhlonag.
Seam, *v. a.* Tàth; fuaigh, fàitheim.
Seamaid, *s.* Maighdean-mhara
Seaman, *s.* Seòladair, maraiche.
Seamew, *s.* Faoilinn, faolag.
Seamless, *adj.* Gun tàth; gun fhàitheam; gun sgar.
Seamoss, *s.* Coireall, lìnean.
Seamstress, *s.* Ban-fhuaghlaiche.
Seapiece, *s.* Dealbh mara.
Seapink, *s.* Neoinean cladaich.
Seaport, *s.* Long-phort, cala.

Sear, *v. a.* Loisg; crannaich.
Searce, *s.* Criathar; siolachan.
Searce, *v. a.* Criathair; dràbh.
Searcer, *s.* Criathradair.
Search, *v. a.* Rannsaich; sgrùd.
Search, *s.* Sireadh, rannsachadh; sgrùdadh; iarraidh; tòir.
Searching, *s.* Sireadh, rannsachadh.
Searcloth, *s.* Brèid-cèire.
Seasickness, *s.* Tinneas na mara.
Season, *s.* Àm, aimsir, tràth; cothrom, àm iomchuidh, mithich.
Season, *v. a.* Grèidh, leasaich, dean blasta; dean ri, cleachd ri.
Seasonable, *adj.* Àmail; tràthail, iomchuidh, freagarrach.
Seat, *s.* Suidheachan, cathair, àite-suidhe; àros, àite-còmhnaidh.
Seat, *v. a.* Suidh; dean suidhe, socraich, daingnich.
Secede, *v. n.* Teich, rach a thaobh.
Seceder, *s.* Fear-trèigsinn.
Secern, *v. a.* Sgar; criathair.
Secession, *s.* Trèigsinn, fàgail.
Seclude, *v. a.* Dùin a mach, dealaich, cuir air leth.
Seclusion, *s.* Uaigneas, aonaranachd, dùnadh a mach.
Second, *s.* Tiota; fear-còmhnaidh.
Second, *adj.* Dara; faisge, faigse.
Second, *v. a.* Cuidich; cobhair.
Secondary, *adj.* Ìochdrach, dara, ni's ìsle.
Secondary, *s.* Fear-ionaid.
Secondhand, *adj.* Ath-ghnàthach.
Secondly, *adv.* Anns an dara h-àite.
Secresy, *s.* Uaighneas, cleith.
Secret, *adj.* Dìomhair, uaigneach; falaichte; falachaidh, ceilte.
Secret, *s.* Rùn-dìomhair, cogar, cagar.
Secretary, *s.* Rùn-chlèireach.
Secrete, *v. a.* Falaich, ceil, cleith; dealaich, sgar; sìolaidh; fàisg.
Secretion, *s.* Fàsgadh, sìola; dealachadh.
Secretness, *s.* Dìomhaireachd.
Sect, *s.* Dream, luchd-co-bharail.
Sectary, *s.* Fear dealachaidh o'n Eaglais choitcheann.
Sectator, *s.* Fear-leanmhainn.
Section, *s.* Roinn; earrann, cuibhrionn, gearradh.
Sector, *s.* Roinneadair.
Secular, *adj.* Saoghalta, talmhaidh.
Secularity, *s.* Saoghaltachd.
Secundine, *s.* Ath-bhreith.
Secure, *adj.* Tèaruinte; seasgair, neo-chunnartach, gun chùram, cinnteach, muinghinneach, misneachail.
Secure, *v. a.* Tèaruinn; dean cinnteach, gabh aig; dìon, dean diongalta; glac.
Security, *s.* Dìon, dìonadh, fasgadh; tèaruinteachd, cinnte, urras; seasgaireachd, mi-chùram, cion-aire, neo-shùim.
Sedan, *s.* Cathair-iomchair.
Sedate, *adj.* Ciùin, sàmhach, bìth, socrach, soimeach, màlda, suidhichte, stèidheil, stòlda.
Sedateness, *s.* Ciùineachd, socair.
Sedentary, *adj.* Suidheach.
Sedge, *s.* Seileasdair.
Sedgy, *s.* Seileasdaireach.
Sediment, *s.* Grunnd, grùid, dràbhag, deasgann, druaip.
Sedition, *s.* Ceannairc, àr-a-mach, èirigh, buaireas.
Seditious, *adj.* Ceannairceach, buaireasach, buaireante.
Seditiously, *adv.* Gu ceannairceach.
Seduce, *v. a.* Thoir a thaobh; buair; meall; truaill.
Seducement, *s.* Buaireadh, mealladh.
Seducible, *adj.* So-mhealladh.
Seduction, *s.* Mealladh, buaireadh, truailleadh, mealltaireachd.
Sedulity, *s.* Dìchioll, dìchiollachd, dùrachd, tulchuiseachd.
Sedulous, *adj.* Dìchiollach, dùrachdach, aghartach, saoithreachail.
Sedulously, *adv.* Gu dìchiollach.
See, *s.* Cathair-easbuig.
See, *v. a.* Faic, seall, amhairc; dearc; feuch.
See! *interj.* Faic! seall! feuch! amhairc!
Seed, *s.* Siol, iarmad, fras; fros, pòr; gineal, clann, sliochd.
Seed, *v. n.* Sìolaich; cuir fras dhìot.
Seedling, *s.* Faillean, fiùran, ògan.
Seedsman, *s.* Fear cuir.
Seedtime, *s.* Àm cuir an t-sìl.
Seedy, *adj.* Sìolach, pòrach.
Seeing, *s.* Fradharc; lèirsinn; faicinn.
Seeing, *adv.* A chionn, do brìgh.
Seek, *v. a.* Iarr, rannsaich; sir, feòraich, fiosraich, lean, bi air tòir.
Seel, *v. n.* Aom gu taobh.
Seel, *s.* Luasgadh luinge, tulgadh tuinn.
Seem, *v. a.* Bi mar; gabh ort, leig ort.
Seeming, *s.* Aogas, coltas; beachd.
Seemliness, *s.* Eireachdas, bòidhchead, maise.
Seemly, *adj.* Eireachdail, ceanalta, bòidheach, eugasach, maiseach, grinn, ciatach; freagarrach, iomchuidh, cubhaidh.
Seen, *adj.* Eòlach, fiosrach.

Seer, *s.* Fear seallaidh, tàisear, fear da-shealladh; fiosaiche, fàidh.
Seesaw, *s.* Udalanachd.
Seethe, *v.* Bruich, carra-bhruich; goil, bi air ghoil.
Segment, *s.* Gearradh-cuairteig.
Segregate, *v. a.* Dealaich; sgăr, cuir a thaobh.
Segregation, *s.* Dealachadh, sgăr-adh, sgărachdainn.
Seine, *s.* Seòrsa lìn-iasgaich.
Seize, *v. a.* Glac, greimich, dean greim air, cuir làmh air, gabh.
Seizin, *s.* Gabhail seilbh.
Seizure, *s.* Glacadh; greim; fasdadh.
Seldom, *adv.* Gu h-ainmig, gu tearc; ainmig, tearc, teirc.
Select, *v. a.* Tagh, rŏghnaich.
Select, *adj.* Taghte, rŏghnaichte.
Selection, *s.* Taghadh, rŏghnachadh.
Self, *pron.* Féin, e-féin, fhéin.
Self-conceit, *s.* Féin-spéis.
Self-conceited, *adj.* Fein-spéiseil;
Self-denial, *s.* Féin-àicheadh.
Self-evident, *adj.* Làn-shoilleir.
Self-existence, *s.* Féin-bhith.
Self-interest, *s.* Féin-bhuannachd.
Selfish, *adj.* Féineil, féin-chùiseach.
Selfishness, *s.* Féin-eileachd.
Self-same, *adj.* Ceart, ionann.
Self-will, *s.* Féin-thoil; reasgachd.
Sell, *v. a.* Reic.
Sellander, *s.* Sgăb-glùin-eich.
Seller, *s.* Reiceadair, fear-reic.
Selves, *s. plur.* of *self.* Sinne, sinn-féin.
Selvage, *s.* Oir aodaich, balt.
Semblance, *s.* Samhla, coltas, aogas, dreach, riochd; suaip.
Semi, *s.* Leth.
Semiannular, *adj.* Leth-chruinn.
Semibribe, *s.* A' Phong-thomhais.
Semicircle, *s.* Leth-chearcall.
Semicircular, *adj.* Leth-chearclach.
Semicolon, *s.* Pong stada mar so (;).
Semilunar, *adj.* Air chumadh na gealaich ùire.
Seminal, *adj.* Siolach, pòrach.
Seminary, *s.* Sgoil; lios froise.
Semination, *s.* Sìolchur, cur.
Semiquaver, *s.* Pong-dha-chritheach.
Semitone, *s.* Leth-phung.
Semivowel, *s.* Leth-fhoghair.
Sempiternal, *adj.* Sìorruidh.
Sempiternity, *s.* Siorruidheachd.
Senary, *adj.* Sèathnar, seiseir.
Senate, *s.* Àrd-chomhairle.
Senator, *s.* Comhairleach.
Send, *v. a.* Cuir, cuir fios, cuir air ghnothach; cuir a mach, sgaoil.
Seneschal, *adj.* Àrd-stiùbhard.
Senile, *adj.* Sean; seantaidh, aosda.
Senior, *s.* Am fear is sine.
Senior, *adj.* Is sine, n'is sine.
Seniority, *s.* Aois, sinead.
Senna, *s.* Seòrsa pùrgaid.
Senocular, *adj.* Sè-shuileach.
Sensation, *s.* Mothachadh; càil, beachd, faineachadh; faireachdainn.
Sense, *s.* Mothachadh; càil, beachd; brìgh; barail, seadh; ciall; tuigse, toinisg, geur-mhothachadh.
Senseless, *adj.* Neo-mhothachail, gun mhothachadh; gun chàil; neo-thuigseach; baoghalta, amaideach, gun tuigse, gun toinisg; gun chiall.
Sensibility, *s.* Mothachadh, moth-achalachd; càil.
Sensible, *adj.* Mothachail; so-fhair-eachdainn; tùrail; tuigseach.
Sensitive, *adj.* Mothachail.
Sensual, *adj.* Feòlmhor, collaidh; sòghmhor, nàdurra; mi-gheimnidh, macnusach.
Sensorium, **Sensory**, *s.* Ionad a' mhothachaidh, ball-a' mhothachaidh.
Sensualist, *s.* Fear mi-gheimnidh; fear macnusach; drùisear, trusdar.
Sensuality, *s.* Feòlmhorachd, coll-aidheachd, macnus, macnusachd, mi-gheimnidheachd.
Sensualize, *v. a.* Dean feòlmhor, dean macnusach; truaill.
Sentence, *s.* Binn, breth.
Sentence, *v. a.* Thoir breth, dìt, thoir binn, thoir a mach binn.
Sententious, *adj.* Brìghmhor; drùighteach, goirid, gearr.
Sententiousness, *s.* Giorrad cainnte, brìghmhorachd, brìgh.
Sentient, *adj.* Mothachail.
Sentiment, *s.* Smuain, barail, beachd, rùn, miann, dùrachd.
Sentinel, **Sentry**, *s.* Fear-faire fear-freiceadain, freiceadan.
Sentry-box, *s.* Bothan-faire.
Separable, *adj.* So-dhealachadh.
Separate, *v. a.* Dealaich, sgăr, tearb, roinn, cuir ás a' chéile; cuir air leth, rach a thaobh, rach air leth.
Separate, *adj.* Dealaichte, roinnte, ás a chéile, o chéile, air leth; leis-féin.
Separation, *s.* Dealachadh, sgăradh, tearbadh; sgaoileadh.
Seposition, *s.* Cur air leth.
Sepoy, *s.* Saighdear-Innseanach.
Sept, *s.* Cinneach, gineal, fine.
Septangular, *adj.* Seachd oisinneach.
September, *s.* Mìos meadhonach an fhoghair, an seachd mìos.

Septenary, *adj*. Seachdnar.
Septennial, *adj*. Seachd-bliadhnach.
Septentrion, *s*. An àirde tuath.
Septentrional, *adj*. Tuathach.
Septilateral, *adj*. Seachd-shlisneach.
Septuagint, *s*. Bìoball Greugais nan trì-fichead 's a deich fear-mìneachaidh.
Septuple, *adj*. Seachd-fillte.
Sepulchral, *adj*. Tuamach.
Sepulchre, *s*. Tuam, uaigh.
Sepulchre, *v. a*. Adhlaic, tìodhlaic.
Sepulture, *s*. Adhlacadh, tiodhlacadh.
Sequacity, *s*. Rìghneachd.
Sequel, *s*. An ni a leanas, crìoch, deireadh, ceann-thall.
Sequence, *s*. Leanmhainn.
Sequent, *adj*. Leanmhainneach.
Sequester, *v. a*. Cuir gu taobh, cuir air leth, cuir sàradh.
Sequestered, *adj*. Air leth, diomhair, uaigneach.
Sequestration, *s*. Dealachadh; tabhairt air falbh buannachd seilbhe.
Sequestrator, *s*. Fear-sàraidh.
Seraglio, *s*. Taigh-bhan Mhahomat.
Seraph, *s*. Àrd-aingeal.
Seraphic, *adj*. Ainglidh, fiorghlan.
Seraphim, *s*. Aingeal.
Sere, *adj*. Tioram, seacte, seargte.
Serenade, *s*. Ceòl-leannanachd.
Serene, *adj*. Soineannta; fèitheil, ciùin, foisneach; soilleir, sàmhach, maiseach, farasda.
Serenely, *adv*. Gu soireanta, ciùin.
Sereneness, **Serenity**, *s*. Soireanntachd, ciùineas, fèith, sàmhchair, fois, sèimheachd.
Serenitude, *s*. Soireanntas, ciùine.
Serge, *s*. Cùrainn.
Sergeant, *s*. Ceannard air dà shaighdear dheug; àrd-fhear-lagha.
Series, *s*. Sreath, srèad, òrdugh.
Serious, *adj*. Suidhichte, dùrachdach; stòlda, smuaireanach, foisneach; diadhaidh; cudthromach, trom.
Seriousness, *s*. Stòldachd; farasdachd; aire dhùrachdach.
Sermon, *s*. Searmoin, teagasg.
Sermonize, *v. n*. Searmonaich.
Serosity, *s*. Uisgealachd.
Serous, *adj*. Uisgidh, uisgeil, tana.
Serpent, *s*. Nathair, beithir.
Serpentine, *adj*. Lùbach, carach.
Serrate, **Serrated**, *adj*. Gròbach, fiaclach, cabach; eagach.
Serum, *s*. Meug fala.
Servant, *s*. Seirbheiseach, gille, òglach, sgalag, ban-oglach, beanmhuinntir, searbhanta.
Serve, *v*. Dean seirbheis; thoir ùmhlachd; cuidich, foghain; toilich riaraich.
Service, *s*. Seirbheis; muinntearas, dreuchd, obair; dleasnas, còmhnadh, feum, stà, deagh thùrn; aoradh; cùrsa, riarachadh, saighdearachd.
Serviceable, *adj*. Feumail; iomchuidh; stàthmhor; èasgaidh, dìchiollach.
Servile, *adj*. Tràilleil; dìblidh, suarrach; truaillidh, eisimeileach.
Servility, **Servileness**, *s*. Dìblidheach, tràillealachd; suarrachas.
Servitor, *s*. Seirbhiseach.
Servitude, *s*. Daorsa, tràillealachd seirbheis; muinntearas.
Sess, *s*. Cìs, càin.
Session, *s*. Àm suidhe mòid, suidhe mòid.
Set, *v*. Suidhich, socraich, àitich, planntaich; sònraich, òrduich; cuir ceart cnàimh.
Set, *part*. Suidhichte, socraichte, sònraichte; riaghailteach; àitichte, gnàthach.
Set, *s*. Srèud, dòrlach do ni sam bith; càraid, leth-bhreacan; bannal, buidheann, cuideachd; planntan.
Seton, *s*. Silteach.
Settee, *s*. Làmhsaid; beinc.
Setter, *s*. Fear-suidheachaidh, cùeunaich, cù-luirg.
Setting, *s*. Suidheachadh; dol fodha.
Settle, *s*. Cathair, suidheagan.
Settle, *v*. Socraich, suidhich; àitich; tuinich; sìolaidh; traogh, ciùinich, caisg.
Settlement, *s*. Socrachadh, suidheachadh; còrdadh, sònrachadh, bann; àiteachas; tuineachas.
Seven, *adj*. Seachd. seachdnar, mòrsheisear.
Sevenfold, *adj*. Seachd-fillte.
Seventeen, *adj*. Seachd-deug.
Seventeenth, *adj*. Seachdamh-deug.
Seventh, *adj*. Seachdamh.
Seventhly, *adv*. Anns an t-seachdamh àite.
Seventy, *adj*. Tri-fichead 's a deich.
Sever, *v*. Sgăr, thoir ás a' chéile, dealaich; tearb, cuir air leth.
Several, *adj*. Iomadh, iomadaidh.
Several, *s*. Iomadh, leth-fa-leth.
Severance, *s*. Dealachadh, sgaradh.
Severe, *adj*. Geur, cruaidh, teann, doirbh; gruamach; an-iochdmhor, borb, neo-thruacanta, garg, geurtheann; gàbhaidh, gaillionnach.

SEVERITY, *s.* Cruadhas, cruas, gèire; teinne, teinnead; doirbhe, ain-iochd, buirbe; neo-thruacantas; docair, gairge, gàbhadh; truime.

SEW, *v. a.* Fuaigh, lean.

SEWER, *s.* Fuaghalaiche; gille cuirme; guitear, clais uisge.

SEX, *s.* Gineal, cineal, gnè.

SEXAGENARY, *adj.* Tri fichead bliadhna dh' aois.

SEXAGONAL, *adj.* Sè-shlisneach.

SEXTANT, *s.* An sèathamh cuid do chearcall.

SEXTON, *s.* Fear-cluig; maor-eaglais.

SEXTUPLE, *adj.* Sè-fillte; a shè uiread.

SHABBINESS, *s.* Suarraichead, crìne, leibideachd, spìocaireachd.

SHABBY, *adj.* Suarrach, crìon, leibideach.

SHACKLE, *v. a.* Geimhlich, cùingich.

SHACKLES, *s.* Ceanglaichean.

SHADE, *s.* Sgàil, dubhar, duibhre, doirche, duirche; dìon, fasgadh; sgàil, sgàilean; taibhse, tannasg.

SHADE, *v. a.* Sgàil, duibhrich, dorchaich; dìon, cuir sgàil air.

SHADINESS, *s.* Duibhre, duirche.

SHADOW, *s.* Faileas; dubhar, dùbhradh; dìon, fasgadh, fàbhar, tèarmann; comharradh, lorg; samhla.

SHADOW, *v. a.* Duibhrich, dorchaich, dubharaich, sgàilich; cuir faileas.

SHADOWY, *adj.* Faileasach, sgàileach; dubharach, dorcha, samhlachail.

SHADY, *adj.* Dubharach, sgàileach.

SHAFT, *s.* Saighead; cas, samhach.

SHAG, *s.* Fionnadh, calg; seòrsa eudaich, seòrsa eoin.

SHAGGY, *adj.* Molach, ròmach, roinneach, rŏbach, rònach, caiteanach, peallagach, giobach.

SHAGREEN, *s.* Craicionn-mùrlaich.

SHAKE, *v.* Crath; cuir air chrith; luaisg; crith, criothnaich; tri-bhuail.

SHAKE, *s.* Crathadh; bogadh, luasgadh; crith, tri-bhualadh.

SHAKER, *s.* Crathadair; bogadair.

SHALL, *v. defective;* it has no tenses but *shall* future, and *should* imperfect. Ni.

SHALLOON, *s.* Clò-greòsgach.

SHALLOP, SHALLOOP, *s.* Sgoth, curach.

SHALLOW, *adj.* Tana, eu-domhain; fàs, faoin; lag.

SHALLOW, *s.* Tanalach; àthan, oitir.

SHALLOWNESS, *s.* Tainead; eu-doimhne, tanalachd; baoghaltachd.

SHAM, *v. a.* Meall, thoir an car á.

SHAM, *s.* Mealladh; leithsgeul; cur dheth; cur seachad; cleas, car.

SHAM, *adj.* Fallsail, mealltach.

SHAMBLES, *s.* Margadh feòla.

SHAMBLING, *adj.* Luidseach.

SHAME, *s.* Nàire, masladh; mì-chliù, tàir, tàmailt, eas-onair.

SHAME, *v.* Nàraich, cuir gu nàire, maslaich, gabh nàire.

SHAMEFACED, *adj.* Gnùis-nàrach.

SHAMEFUL, *adj.* Nàr, nàrach, maslach, tàmailteach, tàireil, sgainnealach.

SHAMELESS, *adj.* Beag-nàrach, mi-nàrach dàna; beadaidh, ladorna.

SHAMOIS, or CHAMOIS, *s.* Fiadh-ghobhar, gobhar-allaidh.

SHAMROCK, *s.* Seamrag, seamair. *M.d.*

SHANK, *s.* Lurga; cas, samhach.

SHANKY, *adj.* Luirgneach.

SHAPE, *v. a.* Cùm, dealbh, cruth.

SHAPE, *s.* Cumadh, cumachd, dealbh.

SHAPELESS. *adj.* Neo-chuimir, neo-chumadail, mi-dhealbhach, neo-eireachdail, gun chumadh, á cumadh.

SHAPELINESS, *s.* Cumadalachd, cuimireachd, deagh chumadh, eireachdas.

SHAPELY, *adj.* Cuimir, cumadail cùmte dealbhach, eireachdail, dreachmhor.

SHARD. *s.* Bloigh, bloighd, sgealb spreaghan, pigean, plaosg, lŭs àraidh; seòrsa éisg.

SHARE, *v. a.* Roinn, pàirtich, riaraich; gabh pàirt, faigh cuibhrionn.

SHARE, *s.* Roinn, earrann, cuid, cuibhrionn; crannchur; comaidh; soc.

SHARER, *s.* Fear-roinn, fear-comaidh.

SHARK, *s.* Iasg fuilteach craosach; fear cuilbheartach gionach.

SHARP, *adj.* Geur; smiorail, sgairteil, tapaidh, ealamh, dealasach, deas; faobharach, biorach, guineach, lotar; beur; geur, goirt, garg; sgreadanach, cruaidh.

SHARPEN, *v.* Geuraich, roinnich; bioraich, faobharaich, thoir roinn; thoir faobhar.

SHARPER, *s.* Beuraiche, cealgair, mealltair, caraiche; gadaiche, meirleach.

SHARPNESS, *s.* Beurachd, gèire, gèiread; guineachas; faobhar.

SHARP-SET, *adj.* Acrach, ciocrach.

SHARPSIGHTED, *adj.* Geur-shuileach, bior-shuileach, biorach.

SHARPWITTED, *adj.* Geur, beumach.

SHATTER, *v. a.* Bris, bruan, bloidich, dean 'na mhìreannan.

SHAVE, *v. a.* Bearr, lom, lomair.

SHAVEGRASS, *s.* A bhiorag.

SHAVER, *s.* Bearradair.

SHAVING, Bearradh; sliseag.

SHAWL, *s.* Neapuig-mhòr.

SHE, *adj.* Boireann, boireannach.

SHE, *pron.* I, ise, si.

SHEAF, *s.* Sguab; dòrlach.
SHEAR, *v. a.* Buain; bearr, lom, lomair.
SHEARER, *s.* Buanaiche.
SHEARING, *s.* Buain.
SHEARS, *s.* Siosar, deamhais.
SHEATH, *s.* Truaill, duille.
SHEATHE, SEATH, *v. a.* Truaill, cuir an truaill, cuir an duile.
SHED, *v. a.* Dòirt, taom, sil; cuir.
SHED, *s.* Bùth, sgàil; bothan,
SHEEN, *adj.* Loinnreach; glan, soilleir.
SHEEN, *s.* Boilsgeadh, deàrsadh.
SHEEP, *s. sing.* and *pl.* Caora, othaisg, òisg; caoirich, meanbh-chrobh.
SHEEPCOT, SHEEPFOLD, *s.* Crò-chaorach, bothan-chaorach, fang, mainnir.
SHEEPHOOK, *s.* Cromag cìobair, bachall buachailleachd.
SHEEPISH, *adj.* Baoghalta; nàrach.
SHEEPISHNESS, *s.* Baoghaltachd, faiteachas, gnuls-nàire, diùideachd.
SHEEPSHEARING, *s.* Lomairt; àm rùsgadh nan caorach.
SHEEP'S-EYE, *s.* Gràdh-shealladh.
SHEEPWALK, *s.* Ionaltradh chaorach.
SHEER, *adj.* Glan, fior-ghlan.
SHEER OFF, *v. n.* Goid air falbh; teich, ás an rathad, seup.
SHEET, *s.* Clàr paipeir; braithlin, brailìn, lian-bhrat, lìon-aodach, lìon-anard; pill; seòl, bréid, sgòd-siùil.
SHEET, *v. a.* Còmhdaich, paisg.
SHEETANCHOR, *s.* Acair-bhàis.
SHEKEL, *s.* Bonn airgeid Iùdhach.
SHELF, *s.* Sgeilp; còrn-chlar, sgeir.
SHELL, *s.* Slige, sgrath, plaosg.
SHELL, *v. a.* Plaoisg, sgrath, fosgail.
SHELLFISH, *s.* Maorach, faoch.
SHELLY, *adj.* Sligeach; faochagach.
SHELTER, *s.* Fasgadh, dìon, tèarmann, dìdean, sgàil.
SHELTER, *v.* Dìon, tèarmainn.
SHELVING, *adj.* Claon, aomta, corrach.
SHELVY, *adj.* Ao-domhainn; sgeireach, creagach.
SHEPHERD, *s.* Aodhair, cìbeir.
SHEPHERDESS, *s.* Bana-chìbeir.
SHEPHERDY, *s.* Cìbeireachd.
SHERBET, *s.* Seòrsa dibhe.
SHERD, *s.* Slige-chreadha, pigean.
SHERIFF, *s.* Siorra, siorram.
SHERIFFALTY, *s.* Siorraidheachd.
SHERRY, *s.* Fion Spàinteach.
SHEW, *v. a.* Feach, nochd, foillsich, dearbh; cuir an céill, mìnich, leig, ris, taisbean, dean aithnichte.
SHIELD, *s.* Sgiath, targaid; dìon, dìdean, tèarmann.
SHIELD, *v. a,* Dìon, gléidh, tèaruinn, coimhead, còmhdaich.
SHIFT, *v.* Caraich, glidich, mùth, rach á h-àite; tionndaidh, solair, rach ás.
SHIFT, *s.* Seòl, modh, dòigh; innleachd; cleas; laoim, car, cuilbheart; léine boireannaich; mùthadh, atharrachadh.
SHIFTER. *s.* Cealgair, caraiche.
SHIFTING, *s.* Carachadh, imrich.
SHIFTING, *adj.* Cealgach, carach.
SHIFTLESS, *adj.* Neo-innleachdach; neo-sholarach, &c.
SHILLING, *s.* Tastan, sgillinn-Shasunnach.
SHIN, *s.* Faobhar na lurgann.
SHINE, *v. n.* Dealraich, dèarrs, soillsich, loinnir; bi sònraichte, bi suaicheant; bi urramach.
SHINE, *s.* Aimsir ghrianach; dealradh.
SHINESS, *s.* Fiatachd, coimheachas.
SHINGLES, *s.* Seòrsa do theine dé.
SHINY, *adj.* Deàlrach, dèarrsach.
SHIP, *s.* Long, soitheach, bàrc.
SHIP, *v. a.* Cuir air bòrd luinge.
SHIPBOARD, *s.* Bòrd-luinge.
SHIPMAN, *s.* Maraiche, seòladair.
SHIPPING, *s.* Cabhlach, luingeas.
SHIPWRECK, *s.* Long-bhriseadh.
SHIPWRIGHT, *s.* Saor luingeis.
SHIRE, *s.* Siorrachd, siorramachd.
SHIRT, *s.* Léine, cneas-lìn.
SHITTIM, *s.* Seòrsa fiodha Arabach.
SHITTLECOCK, *s.* Coileach-sraide; callchircean, circe-ball.
SHIVE, *s.* Sliseag; sgealb, bloigh; mìr arain, sliseag arain.
SHIVER, *v.* Crith; bruan; bris; spealg.
SHIVER, *s.* Sgealb, spealg, bruan.
SHIVERING, *s.* Ball-chrith 'crithfhuachd, crith; briseadh, sgealbadh, sgoltadh, spealgadh.
SHAOL, *s.* Oitir; tanalach; cailcean, sgeir; sgaoth, sgann.
SHOALY, *adj.* Tana, ao-dhomhainn, oitireach, sgeireachd, cailceanach.
SHOCK, *s.* Crith, criothnachadh; oilbheum; oillt; gràin, déisinn; ionnsaidh; ruathar; adag, rucan, mulan, cù molach,
SHOCK, *v.* Adagaich; rucanaich; crith, crath, criothnaich; thoir oilbheum, cuir déisinn, cuir gràin air, cuir gairisinn air, thoir ionnsaidh.
SHOCKING, *adj.* Oillteil, eagalach, gràineil; gairisineach déisinneach.
SHOE, *s.* Bròg, crudha.
SHOE, *v. a.* Brògaich, crùdhaich.
SHOEBOY, *s.* Gille-bhròg.
SHOEMAKER, *s.* Greusaiche, (*etymo.* gréidh-seiche, the old Gaelic word for a tanner,) corrupted "griasaiche."
SHOOT, *v.* Tilg; cuir a mach, fàs.

SHOOT, *s.* Meangan, meanglan, faillean, maothan, ùr-fhas, fiùran, ògan.
SHOOTER, *s.* Fear tilgidh.
SHOP, *s.* Bùth; bathair, bùth-oibre.
SHOPBOARD, *s.* Bòrd-oibreach.
SHOPKEEPER, *s.* Fear-bùth.
SHORE, *s.* Tràigh, cladach, tìr, taobh mara, guitear, clais uisge; taic, prop.
SHORELESS, *adj.* Gun tràigh.
SHORN, *part.* and *part.* of *to shear.* Lomairte, lomte, bearrte, buainte.
SHORT, *adj.* Goirid; gearr; beag; crìon; cutach; gann; ath-ghearr; crosda, dreamach, càs.
SHORTEN, *v. a.* Giorraich.
SHORTLIVED, *adj.* Gearr-shaoghalach.
SHORTNESS, *s.* Giorrad, giorradas.
SHORT-SIGHTED, *adj.* Gearr-sheallach.
SHOT, *pret.* and *p. part.* of *to shoot.* Thilg; tilgte.
SHOT, *s.* Urchair, braidhe, spraidhe, làmhach, peileirean; lach.
SHOTFREE, *s.* Lach-shaor, saor.
SHOUGH, *s.* Cù molach.
SHOULDER, *s.* Gualainn, slinnean.
SHOULDERBELT, *s.* Crios-guaille.
SHOULDERBLADE, *s.* Cnàimh-slinnein.
SHOUT, *s.* Caithream, glaodh, iolach.
SHOUT, *v. n.* Glaodh, tog iolach.
SHOVE, *v. a.* Pùc, fùc, pùt, dinn.
SHOVE, *s.* Pùcadh, pùtadh, ùpag.
SHOVER, *s.* Sluasaid.
SHOW, *s.* Iongantas-féille, *R. D.;* seall-adh-iongantais; ball-amhairc; greadhnachas, mòr-chuis; spaglainn.
SHOW, *v. a.* Feuch, nochd, leig ris, foillsich, taisbean.
SHOWBREAD, SHEWBREAD, *s.* Aran-taisbeanta, aran-coisrigte.
SHOWER, *s.* Fras, fros; sileadh.
SHOWER, *v. a.* Fras, dòirt, sil, taom, sgap, sgaoil; bi frasach.
SHOWERY, *adj.* Frasach, silteach.
SHOWY, *adj.* Briagha, grinn; greadhnach, rìmheach, basdalach, faicheil.
SHRED, *s.* Mìr, bìdeag, cearb.
SHREW, *s.* Té ladorna; bana-cheard.
SHREWD, *adj.* Sicir, glic, ciallach; dùbailte, cealgach, seòlta, geur; olc.
SHRIEK, *v.* Sgread, sgreuch, sgairt, glaodh, ràn, sian, thoir sgăl.
SHRIFT, *s.* Aideachadh.
SHRILL, *adj.* Sgreadach, cruaidh, sgalanta, sgalach, binn, geur.
SHRIMP, *s.* Carran; duairce.
SHRINE, *s.* Naomh-chiste.
SHRINK, *v. n.* Crup; geiltich, ath.
SHRINK, *s.* Crupadh, crìonadh, seargadh, seacadh, preasadh.
SHRIEFT, *s.* Faoisid peacaidh.
SHRIVE, *v. a.* Éisd ri faoisid.
SHRIVEL, *v. a.* Crup, preas, preasagaich, searg, liurc; sgreag.
SHRIVELLED, *adj.* Preasach.
SHROUD, *s.* Marbh-phaisg, ais-leine, linnseach, aodach-mairbh; còmhdach.
SHROUD, *v.* Còmhdaich, dìon, thoir fasgadh; gabh fasgadh.
SHROVETIDE, *s.* Di-mairt-inid.
SHRUB, *s.* Preas; deoch mhillis.
SHRUBBY, *adj.* Preasach.
SHRUG, *v. a.* Crup, crùb, clòimhdich.
SHRUG, *s.* Clòimhteachadh; giùig.
SHUDDER, *v. n.* Criothnaich, oilltich.
SHUDDER, *s.* Ball-chrith, oillt, allsga.
SHUFFLE, *v.* Cuir thar a chéile, cuir troi' chéile; coimeasg.
SHUFFLE, *s.* Coimeasgadh; cleas, cuilbheart, seamaguad.
SHUN, *v. a.* Seachain.
SHUT, *v. a.* Dùin, druid.
SHUT, *adj.* Dùinte, druidte.
SHUTTER, *s.* Comhla uinneige.
SHUTTLE, *s.* Spàl, spàla. *D. B.*
SHY, *adj.* Fiata, coimheach, taghanta, fiadhaich; moiteil; faicilleach; amharusach.
SHYNESS, *s.* Fiatachd, mòitealachd.
SIBILATION, *s.* Feadail, fead.
SICAMORE, SYCAMORE, *s.* Crann-sice.
SICK, *adj.* Tinn, euslainteach.
SICKEN, *v.* Fàs tinn; gabh tinneas; dean tinn, cuir galar air.
SICKLE, *s.* Corran, corran-buana.
SICKLY, *adj.* Tinn, euslainteach.
SICKNESS, *s.* Tinneas, euslainte, eucail.
SIDE, *s.* Taobh, slios; oir, cliathach.
SIDE, *v.* Aom; cùm taobh ri, cuidich, cuir le; gabh taobh.
SIDELONG, *adj.* Leth-taobhach.
SIDESADDLE, *s.* Dìollaid-boireannaich.
SIDEWAYS, SIDEWISE, *adv.* An comhair a thaoibh, a leth-taobh.
SIEGE, *s.* Séisd, iom-dhruideadh.
SIEVE, *s.* Criathar.
SIFT, *v. a.* Criathair, criathraich.
SIFTER, *s.* Criathradair, criathraiche.
SIGH, *s.* Osunn, osann, acain, osna.
SIGH, *v. a.* Osnaich, dean osann.
SIGHING, *s.* Osnaich; acain.
SIGHT, *s.* Sealladh; fradharc, léirsinn.
SIGHTLESS, *adj.* Gun fradharc, dall.
SIGHTLY, *adj.* Taitneach, maiseach.
SIGN, *s.* Comharradh, mìorbhuil, iongantas; àile, lòrg; bratach, meirghe; samhla; smèid; dealbh, sop-reic, comharradh-ceannaich.
SIGN, *v. a.* Cuir do làmh ri, cuir t' ainm ri; comharraich; ciallaich.
SIGNAL, *s.* Sanus, fios, comharradh.

SIGNAL, *adj.* Sònraichte, ion-chomharraichte, mòr, àraidh.
SIGNALIZE, *v. a.* Dean ainmeil.
SIGNATURE, *s.* Ainm-sgrìobhte, comharradh, suaicheantas; fo-sgrìobhadh, littir-chomharrachaidh.
SIGNET, *s.* Seula; saoil; seula rìgh.
SIGNIFICANCY, *s.* Ciall; seadh, sùim, meas, urram, brìgh, bladh; cothrom, cudthrom.
SIGNIFICANT, *adj.* Ciallachail, ciallaidheach, cudthromach.
SIGNIFICATION, *s.* Ciall, brìgh; seadh.
SIGNIFICATIVE, *adj.* Seadhach.
SIGNIFY, *v.* Feuch, innis, dean aithnichte, cuir an céill, thoir sanus, thoir fios; ciallaich.
SIGNPOST, *s.* Colbh-seòlaidh.
SILENCE, *s.* Sàmhchair, ciùineas, sèimhe, fèith, tàmh, fois.
SILENCE, *interj.* Tŏst! bi sàmhach!
SILENCE, *v. a.* Cuir sàmhach, cuir 'na thosd.
SILENT, *adj.* Sàmhach, tosdach, balbh, ciùin, bìth.
SILICIOUS, *adj.* Ròinneach, ròmach; clachach, sgorach, sporach.
SILK, *s.* Sìoda; *adj.* Sìoda.
SILKEN, *adj.* Sìoda, sìodail; mìn.
SILKMERCER, *s.* Marsanta-sìoda.
SILK-WEAVER, *s.* Breabadair-sìoda.
SILKWORM, *s.* Cnuimh-shìoda.
SILKY, *adj.* Sìodach, sìodail; mìn.
SILL, *s.* Clach an doruis.
SILLINESS, *s.* Faoineachd; baoghaltachd; amaideachd, gòraich.
SILLY, *adj.* Faoin, baoghalta, fachanta, neo-thùrail, amaideach, gòrach, simplidh; socharach.
SILVAN, SYLVAN, *adj.* Coillteach, coilltidh, coillteachail.
SILVER, *s.* Airgead.
SILVER, *adj.* Airgiodach; airgeid.
SILVERSMITH, *s.* Ceàrd airgeid.
SIMAR, *s.* Earrasaid.
SIMILAR, *adj.* Coltach, co-ionann.
SIMILARITY, *s.* Co-ionannachd, coltas.
SIMILE, *s.* Samhla, coimeas.
SIMILITUDE, *s.* Cosmhalachd.
SIMMER, *v. n.* Bruich, earrabhruich.
SIMONY, *s.* Ceall-shlad, goid no reic nithe naomha, no ni a bhuineas do dh' eaglais.
SIMPER, *s.* Fàite, fèith-ghàire.
SIMPER, *v. n.* Dean snodh-ghàire.
SIMPLE, *adj.* Glan, neo-thruaillte; aon-fhillte; sìmplidh, neo-chiontach, neo-chronail; còir, onarach; iriosal; amaideach, baoghalta, socharach, aineolach, neo-theòma.
SIMPLE, *s.* Ni aon-ghneitheach; ni leis féin, lŭs, luibh.
SIMPLER, SIMPLEST, *s.* Lighiche-lŭs.
SIMPLETON, *s.* Baothalan, baothaire.
SIMPLICITY, *s.* Sìmplidheachd, aon-fhillteachd, ionracas; socharachd; baoghaltachd.
SIMPLIFY, *v. a.* Dean so-thuigsinn.
SIMPLY, *adv.* Gu h-amaideach.
SIMULATION, *s.* Cealgaireachd.
SIMULTANEOUS, *adj.* Còlath, maraon, a dh' aon bheum, cuideachd.
SIN, *s.* Peacadh; cionta, lochd.
SIN, *v. n.* Peacaich; ciontaich.
SINCE, *adv.* A chionn; o chionn, o'n.
SINCE, *prep.* O, bho; o 'n àm sin.
SINCERE, *adj.* Tréidhireach, [*commonly written* tréibhdhireach*], ionraic, onorach, fìrinneach, neo-chealgach.
SINCERITY, *s.* Tréidhireas ionracas.
SINECURE, *s.* Oifigeach, diamhainn.
SINEW, *s.* Féith; féith-lùghaidh.
SINFUL, *adj.* Peacach, mi-naomh, olc.
SING, *v.* Séinn, gabh òran; mol.
SINGE, *v. a.* Dàth, doth.
SINGER, *s.* Fear-séinn, òranaiche.
SINGLE, *adj.* Aon-fhillte; neo-phòsta, àraidh; aonaranach; glan, iomlan, foirfe.
SINGLENESS, *s.* Aon-fhillteachd; foirfeachd, ionracas.
SINGULAR, *adj.* Sònraichte; àraid, àraidh, air leth, neònach, iongantach; còrr, aineamh.
SINGULARITY, *s.* Sònraichead, àraidheachd, neònachas.
SINGULARIZE, *v. a.* Dean sònraichte.
SINISTER, *adj.* Cèarr, clì; olc, eas-ionraic; neo-cheart, neo-chothromach; mi-shealbhar, mi-shona.
SINK, *v.* Cuir fodha; bàth, tom, tùm, ceil, sàraich, ìslich; rach fodha; rach air chùl, rach gu neo-ni; traogh.
SINK, *s.* Clais; guitear; sloc.
SINLESS, *adj.* Neo-lochdach, neo-chiontach, neo-thruaillidh.
SINNER, *s.* Peacach, peacair.
SIN-OFFERING, *s.* Ìobairt pheacaidh.
SINUATE, *v. a.* Lùb, crom, fiar.
SINUOUS, *adj.* Lùbach, carach.
SINUS, *s.* Camas, geotha, bàdh.

---

* Various words of this kind are to be met with in old Gaelic books, as "*saoidhbhreas*," wealth; "*aoidhbhneas*," joy, &c. The quiescent consonants *dh* and *bh*, in all such words, have long since been rejected by Dr Smith and others—this word alone excepted; thus rendering it, without any good reason, the most repulsive combination of letters now in the language.

Sip, *v.* Òl, srùbagaich.
Sip, *s.* Balgam, srùbhag.
Siphon, *s.* Pìob-uisge.
Sir, *s.* A shàir, a mhaighstir.
Sire, *s.* Athair; a rìgh!
Siren, **Syren**, *s.* Bain-dia; bean tàlaidh gu sgrios.
Siren, *adj.* Meallta, a' tàladh.
Sirius, *s.* Reull a' choin.
Sirocco, *s.* Gaoth an eara-dheas.
Sirrah, *s.* Ainm dìmeas; a dhuine so.
Sister, *s.* Piuthar.
Sisterhood, *s.* Peathrachas.
Sisterly, *adj.* Piutharail.
Sit, *v.* Suidh, dean suidhe.
Site, *s.* Suidheachadh, àite, làrach.
Sitter, *s.* Suidhear; eun-guir.
Sitting, *s.* Suidhe; gur.
Situate, **Situated**, *adj.* Suidhichte.
Situation, *s.* Àite; inbhe, cŏr; staid, suidheachadh.
Six, *adj.* Sè; sianar.
Sixfold, *adj.* Sè fillte; a shè uiread.
Sixpence, *s.* Sè-sgillinn.
Sixscore, *s.* Sè fichead.
Sixteen, *adj.* Sè deug.
Sixteenth, *adj.* Seathamh deug.
Sixth, *adj.* Sèathadh, sèathamh.
Sixth, *s.* An sèathamh cuid.
Sixtieth, *adj.* Trì ficheadamh.
Sixty, *adj.* Trì fichead.
Size, *s.* Meud, meudachd, tomad.
Size, *v. a.* Tomhais; sònraich.
Sizy, *adj.* Righinn, glaodhar.
Skate, *s.* Sgait; brŏg-spéilidh.
Skean, *s.* Cuinnsear, sgian.
Skein, *s.* Sgeinn, sgéinnidh.
Skeleton, *s.* Craimhneach.
Skeptic, *s.* Fear teagamhach.
Skeptical, *adj.* Teagamhach.
Sketch, *s.* Ceud tharruinn.
Sketch, *v. a.* Dealbh, tarruinn.
Skewer, *s.* Bior-feŏla; dealg.
Skiff, *s.* Sgoth, curach, eather.
Skilful, *adj.* Sgileil, eolach, teŏma.
Skilfulness, *s.* Sgil, teŏmachd.
Skill, *s.* Sgil, eŏlas, teŏmachd.
Skilled, *adj.* Sgileil, seŏlta, eŏlach.
Skillet, *s.* Coireachan, sgeileid.
Skim, *v. a.* Sgiob, siab; sgùm, thoir uachdar dheth, tog barrag dheth.
Skimmer, *s.* Sgùman, sgumadair.
Skim Milk, *s.* Bainne-lom.
Skin, *s.* Craiceann, bian, seiche; rùsg.
Skin, *v.* Fionn, feann, faobhaich, thoir an craiceann do, rùisg; còmhdaich le craiceann.
Skinker, *s.* Gille-copain.
Skinner, *s.* Craiceanniche.
Skinny, *adj.* Tana, caol, cruaidh.
Skip, *v.* Leum; sùrdagaich; rach thairis, rach seach.
Skip, *s.* Leum, sùrdag, frith-leum.
Skipper, *s.* Sgiobair.
Skirmish, *s.* Arabhaig.
Skirt, *s.* Sgŏd; oir cearb; sgioball; iomall, fraidhe, taobh.
Skit, *s.* Aoir; slios-bhualadh.
Skittish, *adj.* Fiadhta, gealtach, sgeunach; luaineach, aotrom, guanach, mear.
Skreen, *s.* Creathar-garbh; fasgath.
Skull, *s.* Claigeann.
Skulk, *v. n.* Falaich bi cuiltearachd.
Sky, *s.* Speur, iarmailt, adhar, *often erroneously written* "Athar."*
Skylark, *s.* Riabhag, uiseag.
Skylight, *s.* Adhar-leus.
Skyrocket, *s.* Seŏrsa obair-theine.
Slab, *s.* Leac, cùl-déile.
Slabber, *v. n.* Sil ronn; smugaich, ronnaich, fliuch, salaich.
Slabby, *s.* Ronnach smugaideach.
Slack, *adj.* Lăs, lăsach, fuasgailte, neo-dhaingeann, neo-dhiongmhalta; tais, mall, màirnealach, athaiseach; neo-chùramach; fann, lag.
Slack, **Slacken**, *v.* Lasaich, dean lasach, fuasgail, failnich, fannaich; dean maille.
Slack, *s.* Gual mìn, gual pronn.
Slackness, *adj.* Lasaiche, lasaichead, fuasgailteachd; màirnealachd, athaiseachd, mi-chùram.
Slag, *s.* Luaithre no sal iaruinn.
Slake, *v. a.* Mùch, caisg, bàth.
Slain, *part. pass* of *to Slay*. Mharbhadh, chaidh ás.
Slain, *s.* Slinn breabadair.
Slander, *s.* Tuaileas, sgainneal.
Slander, *v. a.* Cul-chàin, maslach.
Slanderer, *s.* Fear-tuaileis.
Slanderous, *s.* Tuaileasach.
Slant, *v.* Claon, fiar, aom.
Slant, **Slanting**, *adj.* Claon, fiar, aomte, aomadh, neo-dhìreach.
Slap, *s.* Sgailc, boiseag, pailleart, sgealp, déiseag.
Slap, *v. a.* Sgailc, déiseagaich.
Slapdash, *adv.* Muin air mhuin.

---

* This error is very apt to mislead those unacquainted with Gaelic grammar, who might suppose it to imply *father*, of which it is the genitive. For example, in the Gaelic translation of Ephes. ii. 2, we read "cumhachd an *athair*," the power of the *air*, by many, at first sight, understood, notwithstanding the letter *i*, as, "the power of the *father*." Written "cumhachd an *adhair*," the distinction must be at once apparent

Slash, *v. a.* Gearr, sgath; beum.
Slash, *s.* Gearradh, leòn, beum.
Slate, *s.* Sglèat, leac.
Slate, *v. a.* Sgleat, sglèataich.
Slater, *s.* Sglèatair.
Slattern, s. Straille, dràic sgliùrach, trusdar caile, sgumrag,
Slaughter, *s.* Ar, marbhadh, casgradh, spadadh.
Slaughter, *v. a.* Casgair, marbh.
Slaughterhouse, *s.* Taigh-spadaidh, taigh-casgraidh, broth-thaigh.
Slaughterman, *s.* Fear-spadaidh.
Slave, *s.* Tràill, brŭid, braighde, ciomach, tàrlaid.
Slaver, *v. n.* Sil ronnan.
Slaver, *s.* Ronnan, staonag.
Slavery, *s.* Braighdeannas, daorsa, tràillealachd.
Slavish, *adj.* Tràilleil.
Slavishness, *s.* Tràillealachd.
Slay, *v. a.* Marbh casgair.
Slayer, *s.* Mortair; marbhaiche.
Sled, **Sledge**, *s.* Càrn-slaoid; òrd-mòr gobha.
Sleek, **Sleeky**, *adj.* Mìn, slìogach, slìom, sliobach, sleamhainn.
Sleekness, *s.* Mìnead, slìobachd.
Sleep, *s.* Pràmh, suain; cadal.
Sleepiness, *s.* Cadalachd; truime.
Sleepless, *adj.* Gun chadal.
Sleepy, *adj.* Cadalach, cadaltach.
Sleet, *s.* Clàmhainn, glìob.
Sleet, *v. n.* Cuir clàmhainn.
Sleety, *adj.* Clàmhainneach.
Sleeve, *s.* Muilicheann.
Sleight, *s.* Cleas, seòl, căr.
Slender, *adj.* Tana, caol, seang, bochd, meuranta; beag, crìon, gann.
Slenderness, *s.* Caoile, caoilead, tainead; dìth tomaid; gainne.
Slice, *s.* Sliseag; mìr tana.
Slice, *v. a.* Sliseagaich, snaidh.
Slide, *v. n.* Sleamhnaich, speidhil.
Slide, *s.* Sleamhnachadh, spéileadh.
Slight, *s.* Dearmad, dìmeas, tàir.
Slight, *adj.* Tana; neo-ghramail; faoin, beag, suarrach, eutrom.
Slight, *v. a.* Dearmaid, dearmadaich, cuir air dìmeas, no air bheag sùim.
Slightness, *s.* Caoilead, tainead, anfhannachd; eutreòir; fadharsachd.
Slim, *adj.* Seang, caol, maoth.
Slime, *s.* Làthach; clàbar.
Sliminess, *s.* Bìtheantachd; rìghneachd, sleamhneachd.
Slimy, *adj.* Bìtheanta, righinn, sleamhainn, tiugh.
Sling, *s.* Crann-tabhaill, bann.
Sling, *v. a.* Tilg le crann-tabhaill, &c.
Slink, *v. n.* Sèap, siap, snăg air falbh, goid air falbh.
Slip, *s.* Tuisleadh; mearachd; cai; crioman, stiall; cuiseag, maothan.
Slip, *v.* Sleamhnaich, spéil, tuislich; snàg; dean mearachd.
Slipknot, *s.* Lùb-ruithe.
Slipper, *s.* Bròg-sheòmair.
Slipperiness, *s.* Sleamhnachd;
Slippery, **Slippy**, *adj.* Sleamhainn mùghtach.
Slit. *v. a.* Sgoilt, sgoch, gearr.
Slit, *s.* Sgoltadh, sgoch, gearradh.
Sliver, *v. a.* Sgoilt, sgath.
Sliver, *s.* Spealtag, spithag,
Slobber, *v.* Dean fliuch le smugaidean, splàngraich.
Sloe, *s.* Áirneag; draighneag.
Sloop, *s.* Saitheach aon chroinn.
Slop, *v. a.* Òl gu gionach; spliut, spairt, sguab ás.
Slope, *s.* Leathad, claon-bhruthach; fiaradh, claonadh.
Slope, *adj.* Claon, aom, fiar cam.
Sloppy, *adj.* Eabarach, fliuch.
Slot, *s.* Lorg féigh; beul-maothain.
Sloth, *s.* Leisg, dìomhanas.
Sloth, *s.* A'Chorra-leisg.
Slothful, *adj.* Leisg, slaodach.
Slouch, *s.* Cromadh, slaodaire, cuacaire, sealladh dìblidh.
Slough, *s.* Rumach, làthach; càthar; cochull, mogunn.
Sloughy, *adj.* Feuthach, clàbarach.
Sloven, *s.* Straille dràic; tàsan, liobasdair; slaodaire.
Slovenly, *adj.* Dràichdeil, slaodach, liobasda, salach, rapach.
Slow, *adj.* Mall, màirnealach, athaiseach, tàsanach, slaodach; leisg.
Slowness, *s.* Maille; màirnealachd, athaiseachd, slaodachd.
Slowworm, *s.* An dall-chnuimh.
Slubber, *v. a.* Dean air dòigh sam bith, pat thairis.
Slubberdegullion, *s.* Trŭsdar.
Sludge, *s.* Poll, eabar, làthach.
Slug, *s.* Leisgean, slaod; rong; seilcheag; peileir-greannach.
Sluggard, *s.* Leisgean, lunndaire.
Sluggish, *adj.* Leisg, lunndach, cadalach; trom, marbhanta, mall.
Sluice. *s.* Tuil-dhorus.
Slumber, *v. n.* Caidil, gabh pràmh.
Slumber, *s.* Clò-chadal dùsal, pràmh.
Slumberous, *adj.* Cadalach, trom.
Slur, *v. a.* Salaich, mill, truaill; meall.
Slur, *s.* Tàir, athais, dìmeas.
Slut, *s.* Botramaid, bréineag.
Sluttish, *adj.* Salach, breun, mosach.

Sluttishness, *s.* Mosaiche.
Sly, *adj.* Carach, sligheach, mealltach.
Smack, *s.* Blăs, deagh-bhlas; sgleog pòige; long aon chrannach.
Small, *adj.* Beag, crìon, cutach; caol; meanbh; mìn, pronn.
Small-coal, *s.* Gual-caoranach.
Smallness, *s.* Bigead, crine, lughad, caoile, caoilead; laigead, di-neart.
Smallpox, *s.* A' Ghall-bholgach; a' bhreac; a' bhăn-ghucach; a' bhean-mhath. *N. H.*
Smalt, *s.* Guirmean, dath gorm.
Smart, *adj.* Sgairteil, tapaidh, beothail; sgealparra, smiorail, geur.
Smart, *s.* Pian, guin, goimh, cràdh.
Smart, *v. n.* Pian, goirtich, crean.
Smartness, *s.* Sgairtealachd, tapadh, beothalachd, smioralas, géire.
Smatch, *s.* Blăs; fàileadh.
Smattering, *s.* Leth-eòlas.
Smear, *v. a.* Smiùr, buaichd.
Smell, *v.* Snòtaich, srònaisich; biodh fàileadh dhìot.
Smell, *s.* Fàileadh, bòladh.
Smelt, *s.* Am mòrgadair.
Smelt, *v. a.* Leagh.
Smelter, *s.* Leaghadair.
Smerk, *v. n.* Amhairc gu tlà, ghràdhach, &c.
Smerk, Smirk, *adj.* Cridheil; sunntach.
Smiket, *s.* Còta-bàn boireannaich.
Smile, *v. n.* Dean fàite; dean snodha ghàire; bi mìog-shuileach.
Smile, *s.* Fàite, fèith-ghàire, fiamhghàire, snodha-gàire; miog-shealladh.
Smite, Smitten, *part. pass.* of *to smite.* Buailte, marbh, millte.
Smite, *v. a.* Buail, marbh, mill.
Smith, *s.* Gobha, gobhainn.
Smithery, Smithy, *s.* Cèardach.
Smock, *s.* Léine boirionnaich.
Smockfaced, *adj.* Smigeideach, lom.
Smoke, *s.* Smùid, ceò, deatach.
Smoke, *v.* Tilg smùid, no toit; gabh pìob thombaca, faigh air fhàileadh; lòrgaich a mach.
Smoke-dry, *v. a.* Tiormaich san tŏit.
Smoky, *adj.* Toiteach, ceòthach.
Smooth, *adj.* Mìn. sleamhainn réidh, còmhnard; tlà, ciùin; sèimh; lom.
Smooth, *v. a.* Mìnich; dean réidh; dean còmhnard, slìob, lìomh; sleamhnaich, ciùinich.
Smoothness, *s.* Mìnead; lìomhachas; sleamhnad, ciùinead.
Smote, *pret.* of *to smite.* Bhuail, mharbh, mhill.
Smother, *v. a.* Mùch, tachd, caisg.
Smother, *s.* Toitearlach, casg.
Smug, *adj.* Deas, sgeinmeil, sgeilmeil, spailpeanta; cuimir, sgiult.
Smuggle, *v. a.* Dean cùiltearachd.
Smuggler, *s.* Ciùltear.
Smuggling, *s.* Cùiltearachd.
Smugness, *s.* Sgeinmealachd.
Smut, *s.* Salachar, draosdachd.
Smutty, *adj.* Salach; draosda.
Snack, *s.* Roinn, cuid, cuibhrionn.
Snaffle, *s.* Srian-sròine.
Snail, *s.* Seilicheag, seilcheag.
Snake, *s.* Rìghinn, nathrair-shuairc.
Snakeroot, *s.* Seòrsa luibh.
Snaky, *adj.* Nathaireil; lùbach.
Snap, *v.* Cnac, bris, teum, beum, gearr, tiolam; glac gu grad.
Snap, *s.* Cnac, teum, beum, tiolam.
Snapper, *s.* Tiolpadair, beumaire.
Snappish, *adj.* Tiolamach; beumach; dranndanach, dreamach, crosda.
Snap-sack, *s.* Àbarsgaig saighdear.
Snare, *s.* Ribe, painntir, lion, eangach, ceap-tuislidh, goisid.
Snare, *v. a.* Rib, glac, painntirich.
Snarl, *v. n.* Dean dranndan, dean grunsgul; labhair gu căs.
Snarler, *s.* Dranndanaich; diorrasan.
Snatch, *v.* Glac, beir air; tiolp, teum, thoir tiolam, thoir sitheadh.
Snatch, *s.* Greis; tiolp, làn-beòil.
Sneak, *v. n.* Fèathlaidh, snàig, crùb.
Sneaking, *adj.* Snàgach, dìblidh.
Sneer, *v. a.* Seall gu tarcuiseach, dean gàire, dean fanaid, măg.
Sneer, *s.* Sealladh-măgaidh, sealladh, fanaideach, facal tàireil; beum.
Sneeze, *v. n.* Dean sreothart.
Sneeze, *s.* Sreothart, sreothartaich.
Sneezewort, *s.* Am meacanragaim,
Snicer, *v. n.* Dean faoin-ghaire.
Snick and Snee, *s.* Biodagraich.
Snipe, *s.* An meannan-adhair.
Snivel, *v. n.* Dean smùchanaich.
Snore, *s.* Srann-chadal.
Snort, *s.* Srannartaich, séidrich.
Snout, *s.* Soc; gnos, sòrn, sròn.
Snow, *s.* Sneachda.
Snowdrop, *s.* A' ghealag-làir.
Snowy, *adj.* Sneachdach; sneachdaidh.
Snub, *s.* Cruaidh-shnaimh, gath.
Snuff, *s.* Smàl coinnle; snaoisean.
Snuff, *v.* Sròineisch; snòtaich, gabh snòitean; smàl.
Snuffbox, *s.* Bocsa-snaoisein.
Snuffers, *s.* Smàladair.
Snuffle, *v. n.* Labhair gu glòmach.
Snug, *adj.* Clùmhar, còsach.
Snuggle, *v. n.* Laidh gu clùmhar.
So, *adv.* Mar sin, mar so, mar sud, air an dòigh so, air an dòigh sin, air

an dòigh ud, air an t-seòl so, air an t-seòl sin, air an t-seòl ud.

Soak, *v.* Bog, sùgh; fliuch; sùig, òl.

Soap, *s.* Siabunn.

Soar, *v. n.* Itealaich gu h-àrd; éirich.

Sob, *s.* Osann, osna, ospag, plosg.

Sob, *v. n.* Dean osann, dean osnaich.

Sober, *adj.* Measarra, stuama, geimnidh, ciùin; riaghailteach.

Sober, *v. a.* Dean measarra; dean ciùim, thoir gu céill.

Soberness, Sobriety, *s.* Measarrachd; stuamachd, geimnidheachd, ciùineas.

Sociable, *adj.* Caidreach, caideara, cuideachdail, càirdeil; còmpanta, conaltrach.

Sociableness, *s.* Caireamhachd; caidearach; còmpantachd.

Social, *adj.* Caidreamhach, comunnach, daonnach.

Society, *s.* comunn, cuideachd; aonachd; cinneadh-daonna; còisir.

Socinian, *s.* Fear cumail a mach nach co-ionann Criosd ri Dia, fearleanmhainn Socinuis.

Sock, *s.* Fochann, bréid-bròige.

Socket, *s.* Ceal; lag na sùl.

Sod, *s.* Fàl, fàilean, tobhta.

Sodality, *s.* Còmpanas, comunn.

Sodden, *part.* Leth-bhruich.

Sofa, *s.* Langsaid, làmhsaid.

Soft, *adj.* Bog, bogar; tais; maoth, tlà; mìn, ciùin, sèimh; farasda, fòil, caomh, baoghalta.

Soft, *interj.* Socair! air do shocair!

Soften, *v.* Bogaich, taislich, maothaich, ciùinich.

Softly, *adv.* Gu fòil, gu ciùin.

Softness, *s.* Buige, taise; caoimhneas, ciùineas, maothalachd; taisealachd.

Soil, *v. a.* Salaich, dubh, truaill; mathaich, innearaich.

Soil, *s.* Ùir, talamh; fearann, tìr; inneir, aolach, salchar; sal.

Sojourn, *v.n.* Còmhnaich, gabh còmhnaidh; tuinich, fan, fuirich.

Sojourn, *s.* Còmhnaidh, cuairt.

Sojourner, *s.* Fear-cuairt, aoidh.

Sojourning, *s.* and *part.* Cuairt; eilthire, turas.

Solace, *s.* Sòlas; co-ghàirdeachas.

Solace, *v. a.* Thoir sòlas, furtaich.

Solan-goose, *s.* Sùlair, guga.

Solar, Solary, *adj.* Gréine; grianach.

Sold, *pret. part.* of to *sell.* Reicte.

Soldier, *s.* Saighdear, milidh.

Soldiership, *s.* Saighdearachd.

Soldiery, *s.* Saighdearan.

Sole, *s.* Bonn coise na bròige; lèabag.

Sole, *v. a.* Cuir bonn air.

Sole, *adj.* A mhain, aon-fhillte.

Solecism, *s.* Baoth-labhradh.

Solely, *adv.* A mhàin; gu sònraichte.

Solemn, *adj.* Sòlaimte, greadhnach; foirmeil; tiamhaidh, trom.

Solemnity, *s.* Sòlaimteachd; deasghnàth bliadhnail; greadhnachas.

Solemnize, *v. a.* Urramaich; coimhid gu deas-ghnàthach.

Solicit, *v. a.* Aslaich, guidh, grìos.

Solicitation, *s.* Aslachadh, guidhe, grìosadh; sireadh; mosgladh, dùsgadh, brosnachadh.

Solicitor, *s.* Fear-tagairt.

Solicitous, *adj.* Iomaguineach, cùramach; déidheil.

Solicitress, *s.* Ban-achanaiche.

Solicitude, *s.* Iomaguin, ro-chùram.

Solid, *adj.* Teann, daingeann, tiugh, trom, tarbhach; neò-fhàs, làidir; fior; glic, suidhichte.

Solid, *s.* Tiugh, a'chuid theann do'n chorp; ni sam bith aig am beil fad, leud, agus tiuighead.

Solidity, *s.* Tairbhe, tiuighead, taicealachd; gramalas; ciall, toinisg.

Solidness, *s.* Tiuighead; ciall.

Soliloquist, *s.* Féin-labhairtiche.

Soliloquize, *v. a.* Labhair riut-féin.

Soliloquy, *s.* Féin-labhairt.

Solitary, *adj.* Aonaranach; uaigneach, fàs; tiamhaidh; ùdlaidh.

Solitude, *s.* Uaigneas; fàsach.

Solo, *s.* Port aon inneil.

Solstice, *s.* Grian-stad.

Soluble, *adj.* So-leaghadh, fuasglach.

Solution, *s.* Dealachadh; leaghadh; ni leaghte; fuasgladh, mìneachadh.

Solutive, *adj.* Purgaideach.

Somatology, *s.* Corp-theagasg.

Solve, *v. a.* Fuasgail, mìnich.

Solvency, *s.* Comasachd air ìocadh.

Solvent, *adj.* Comasach air ìocadh.

Some, *adj.* Cuid, roinn, feadhainn.

Sombre, Sombrous, *adj.* Dorcha, neulach, gruamach, dubh.

Somebody, *s.* Neach-eigin, cuid-eigin.

Somehow, *adv.* Air chor-eigin.

Somerset, Summerset, *s.* Căr-a'-mhuiltean, căr-a'-mhuiltean air an stob.

Something, *s.* Rud-eigin, ni-eigin.

Something, *adv.* A leth-char.

Sometime, *adv.* Uair-eigin.

Sometimes, *adv.* Air uairibh.

Somewhat, *s.* Beagan, rud-eigin.

Somewhat, *adv.* A leth-char.

Somewhere, *adv.* An àit'-eigin.

Somniferous, Somnific, *adj.* Cadalach, cadaltach, dùsalach.

Somnolency, *s.* Cadaldachd.

Son, *s.* Mac, *from* "meac," an extraction. *Dim* "meacan," hence macan.
Son-in-law, *s.* Cliamhuinn.
Song, *s.* Àmhran, òran; dàn.
Songster, *s.* Òranaiche.
Songstress, *s.* Ban-òranaiche.
Soniferous, Sonorific, Sonoriferous, *adj.* Fuaimneach.
Sonnet, *s.* Luinneag, duanag.
Sonorous, *adj.* Ard-ghuthach.
Soon, *adv.* A chlisge, gu luath, an ùin ghearr, gu tràthail, luath, grad.
Soot, *s.* Sùithe; *etymo.* Sùgh-thigh.
Sooted, *adj.* Sùidhte, làn sùithe.
Sooth, *s.* Fìrinn; dearbh-fhìrinn.
Soothe, *v. a.* Breug, tàlaidh; ciùinich.
Soothsay, *v. a.* Fàisnich.
Soothsayer, *s.* Fiosaiche, fàidh.
Soothsaying, *s.* Fiosachd, fàisneachd.
Sooty, *adj.* Sùitheach, dorcha.
Sop, *s.* Ròmag, stapag.
Sop, *v. a.* Tùm ann an spiorad.
Soph, *s.* Stuidear òg Sasunnach.
Sophism, *s.* Cealg-ràdh.
Sophist, Sophister, *s.* Breug-reusonaiche, feallsanach carach.
Sophistical, *adj.* Fallsa, cealgach.
Sophisticate, *v. a.* Truaill, mill.
Sophistication, *s.* Truailleadh.
Sophistry, *s.* Reusonachd mheallta.
Soporiferous, Soporific, *adj.* Cadalach, cadaltach, pràmhail.
Sorcerer, *s.* Fiosaiche, drùidh.
Sorceress, *s.* Ban-drùidh, baobh.
Sorcery, *s.* Drùidheachd, fiosachd.
Sord, *s.* Àilean, lianan.
Sordes, *s.* Mosaiche; anabas, draib.
Sordid, *adj.* Salach, mosach, crìon, mìodhur, biastail, spìocach.
Sore, *s.* Creuchd, lot, cneadh.
Sore, *adj.* Goirt, cràiteach, piantail.
Sorel, *s.* Tri-bhliadhnach buic.
Sorrel, *s.* Sealbhag; biadh-eunain.
Sorrow, *s.* Mulad, bròn.
Sorrowful, *adj.* Muladach, brònach.
Sorry, *adj.* Duilich, muladach, brònach; suarrach, dìblidh, truagh.
Sort, *s.* Seòrsa, gnè; modh, dòigh.
Sort, *v.* Cuir gu dòigh, cuir an òrdugh; seòrsaich; roinn; riaghailtich.
Sortance, *s.* Freagarrachd.
Sortment, *s.* Cur an òrdugh.
Sot, *s.* Burraidh, ùmaidh, misgear.
Sottish, *adj.* Misgeach, ùmadail.
Soul, *s.* Anam; deò, spiorad.
Sound, *adj.* Slàn, fallain; glic.
Sound, *s.* Caolas; tanalach mara.
Sound, *v.* Dean fuaim, dean toirm; gleang; tomhais doimhneachd; sgrùd, rannsaich; séinn, mol, séirm.
Sounding, *adj.* Fuaimneach.
Soundness, *s.* Fallaineachd, slàinte fìrinn, tréidhireas.
Soup, *s.* Eanaraich, eun-bhrigh.
Sour, *adj.* Goirt, geur, garg, searbh; doirbh, crosda, dùr, gruamach.
Source, *s.* Tobar; ceud-aobhar, mathair-aobhair, bun, freumh.
Sourish, *adj.* A leth char goirt.
Sous, *s.* Bonn-Fràngach.
Souse, *adv.* Le splad; le sic.
South, *s.* An àirde deas, deas.
South, *adj.* Deas, deasach.
South-east, *s.* An eara-dheas.
Southerly, *adj.* Deas, á deas, mu dheas; deiseal.
Southwest, *s.* An iar-dheas.
Sovereign, *s.* Rìgh; òr-fhichead-tastan.
Sovereign, *adj.* Rioghail; còrr.
Sovereignty, *s.* Uachdaranachd.
Sow, *s.* Muc, crain, orc.
Sow, *v.* Cuir, sìol-chuir; sgaoil.
Sowens, *s.* Làgan, càbhraich.
Space, *s.* Uidhe, rùm; farsuinneachd; ùin; àm, tìm; astar, greis.
Spacious, *adj.* Farsuinn, mòr.
Spaciousness, *s.* Farsuinneachd.
Spaddle, *s.* Pleadhan, pleadhag.
Spade, *s.* Spaid; caibe, coibe.
Spall, *s.* A' ghualainn.
Span, *s.* Réis, naoi-òirlich.
Span, *v. a.* Tomhais le réis.
Spangle, *s.* Spangan *M.d.*
Spangle, *v. a.* Loinnrich, boillsg.
Spaniel, *s.* Cù-eunaich; sgimileir.
Spanish, *adj.* Spàinteach.
Spanner, *s.* Gleus-gunna.
Spar, *s.* Tarsannan, crann, glas.
Spar, *v.* Duin, glais; dòrn, cath.
Sparable, *s.* Mion-tharung.
Spare, *v.* Caomhain, sàbhail, bi bàigheil ri; seachainn, bi caonntach.
Spare, *adj.* Gann, truagh; caonntach.
Sparerib, *s.* Aisinn air bheag feòla.
Sparing, *adj.* Gann, spìocach.
Spark, *s.* Srad, sradag; dril; lasgaire, gasganach, òganach spairiseach.
Sparkle, *s.* Tuireann; lannair, dealradh, sradagraich.
Sparkle, *v.* Lannair, dealraich; sradagaich; deàrrs, boillsg, soillsich.
Sparkling, *adj.* Loinnreach, dealrach; sradagach; drilseach, soillseach.
Sparrow, *s.* Gealbhonn, glas-eun.
Sparrow-grass, *s.* Creamh-mac-féigh.
Sparrowhawk, *s.* An speireag.
Spasm, Spasmodical, *s.* Féith-chrupadh, orc, ìonga, ìne.
Spasmodic, *adj.* Féith-chrupach, orcach, iodhach, ìneach.

Spat, *s.* Maoirneag.
Spatter, *v.* Spult, salaich; tilg smugaid, cùl-chàin.
Spatterdashes, *s.* Casa-gearra.
Spatula, *s.* Spaideal, maide-poite.
Spaw, *s.* Tobar-mheine.
Spawl, *s.* Smugaid, splangaid.
Spawn, *v.* Cladh; sìolaich.
Spawn, *s.* Iuchraichean éisg; sìol.
Spawner, *s.* Iasg-iochrach.
Spawning, *s.* Cladh, mealagachadh.
Spay, *v. a.* Spoth ainmhidhean boireann.
Speak, *v.* Labhair, bruidhinn, abair, can, bruidhnich; innis, luaidh, aithris.
Speakable, *adj.* So-labhairt, còmhraideach, conaltrach.
Speaker, *s.* Fear-labhairt.
Speaking, *s.* Bruidheann, labhairt.
Spear, *s.* Sleagh, craosach, mòrghath,
Spearmint, *s.* Mionntainn.
Spearwort, *s.* Glais-leun.
Special, *adj.* Àraidh, sònraichte; òirdheirc, prìomh; neo-choitcheann.
Species, *s.* Gné, seòrsa, dream.
Specific, *adj.* Àraid, àraidh, sònraichte.
Specific, *s.* Ùrchasg; iocshlaint.
Specify, *v. a.* Comharraich, ainmich.
Specimen, *s.* Samhla; sampull.
Specious, *adj.* Greadhnach; dealbhach, aogasach, coltach.
Speck, *s.* Smal, sal, ball.
Speck, *v. a.* Salaich, ballaich.
Speckle, *s.* Spotag, ball beag.
Speckle, *v. a.* Ballaich, breacaich.
Speckled, *adj.* Ballach, balla-bhreac.
Spectable, *s.* Sealladh, ball-amhairc.
Spectacles, *s.* Speuclair.
Spectator, *s.* Fear-amhairc.
Spectre, *s.* Tannasg, bòcan.
Speculate, *v.* Smaointich, beachdaich, cnuasaich; cunnartaich.
Speculation, *s.* Beachdachadh, smaointeachadh, rannsachadh, deuchainn, dealbhadh.
Speculative, *adj.* Beachdail, smuainteachail, tionnsgnach.
Speculator, *s.* Dealbhadair, tionnsgnaiche; fear-beachdachaidh.
Speculum, *s.* Sgàthair.
Speech, *s.* Cainnt, cànan, bruidheann; labhairt, seanachas, òraid, uirghioll.
Speechless, *adj.* Balbh, gun chainnt.
Speed, *v.* Greas, luathaich, deifirich.
Speed, *s.* Luaths, deifir, cabhag; *good speed*, deagh shoirbheachadh.
Speedy, *adj.* Luath, cabhagach.
Spell, *s.* Òradh, giseag, seun; greis.
Spell, *v. n.* Litirich.
Spelter, *s.* Seòrsa miotailt.
Spend, *v.* Caith, builich, caisg; claoidh.
Spendthrift, *s.* Struidhear.
Sperm, *s.* Sìol-siolachaidh.
Spermaceti, *s.* Blonag muice mara.
Spermatic, *adj.* Sìolach.
Spew, *v.* Tilg, sgeith, dìobhuir.
Sphacelus, *s.* Cnàmhuin.
Sphere, *s.* Cuairt cruinne, cruinnecé; ball cruinn; inbhe, àite.
Spheric, **Spherical**, *adj.* Cruinn, cuairteach, guairneach, guairsgeach.
Sphericalness, **Sphericty**, *s.* Cruinnead, cuairteachd, guairsgeachd.
Spherics, *s.* Cruinn-eòlas.
Spherule, *s.* Cruinne beag.
Spice, *s.* Spìosraidh.
Spicery, *s.* Spìosraidh, peabar.
Spick and Span, *adv.* Ùr nogha.
Spicy, *adj.* Spìosrach; cùbhraidh.
Spider, *s.* Damhan-allaidh.
Spigot, *s.* Spiocaid, leigeadair.
Spike, *s.* Dias arbhair, bior iaruinn.
Spike, *v. a.* Tàirng, spàrr bior iaruinn.
Spikenard, *s.* Boltrachan, spiocnard,
Spill, *v.* Dòirt; taom, caill, mill.
Spilth, *s.* Ni taomte sam bith.
Spin, *v.* Snìomh, toinn, cuir dàil.
Spinage, *or* **Spinach**, *s.* Bloinigean.
Spindle, *s.* Dealgan, fearsaid.
Spindle-shanked, *adj.* Caol-chasach.
Spine, *s.* Cnàimh na droma.
Spinet, *s.* Seòrsa-inneal-ciùil.
Spiniferous, *adj.* Deilgneach.
Spink, *s.* An lasair-choille.
Spinster, *s.* Bana-chalanaich, bansniomhaich, boireannach neo-phòsta.
Spiny, *adj.* Deilgneach, driseach.
Spiracle, *s.* Toll gaoithe, toll caol.
Spiral, *adj.* Snìomhanach.
Spire, *s.* Stìopull; binein.
Spirit, *s.* Spiorad; tannasg, anam; misneach, smior, smioralas, smearalas, beothalas; nàdur, gné, càil; deò, beatha; uisge-beatha, deoch làidir.
Spirit, *v. a.* Misnich, brosnaich; meall; tàlaidh, goid air falbh.
Spirited, *adj.* Misneachail, smiorail, duineil, beò, sgairteil.
Spiritedness, *s.* Misneach, smioralas.
Spiritless, *adj.* Neo-mhisneachail, neo-smiorail, neo-dhuineil, neo-bheò, neo-sgairteil; gealtach, tròm, marbh, neo-shunntach.
Spiritual, *adj.* Spioradail, neo-chorporre, nèamhaidh; naomha, diadhaidh, inntinneach.
Spirituality, *s.* Spioradalachd, neochorporrachd, cràbhadh.
Spiritualize, *v. a.* Naomhaich, glan.
Spirituous. *adj.* Làidir mar dheoch.
Spirt, *v.* Sgiùrd, spùt, steall.

Spiry, *adj.* Barra-chaol; spiriseach.
Spit, *s.* Bior, feòla, bior-ròsta.
Spit, *v.* Cuir air bior; tilg smugaid.
Spitchcock, *s.* Easgann ròiste.
Spite, *s.* Gamhlas, mì-run falachd, miosgainn, fuath.
Spite, *v. a.* Farranaich, feargaich.
Spiteful, *adj.* Gamhlasach.
Spitefulness, *s.* Gamhlasachd.
Spittle, *s.* Smugaid, seile.
Splash, *v. a.* Spairt, spliut.
Splahsy, *adj.* Salach, làthachail.
Splay, *v. a.* Cuir ás an ălt.
Splayfoot, *adj.* Spliathach, pliutach.
Spleen, *s.* An dubh-liath, fearg; farmad, gamhlas; beum-corraich; airsneul.
Spleenful, *adj.* Farmadach, gamhlasach, feargach, crosda.
Splendent, *adj.* Loinnreach, dearsach, dealrach, boillsgeil, soillseach.
Splendid, *adj.* Dealrach, loinnreach; ro ghrinn; greadhnach, basdalach.
Splendour, *s.* Dealradh, dearrsadh, lainnir, boillsgeadh; greadnachas.
Splenetic, *adj.* Frionasach, crosta.
Splenetive, *adj.* Teinntidh, dian.
Splice, *v. a.* Tâth, teum.
Splint, *s.* Bloigh, *pl.* bloighdean.
Splinter, *s.* Sgealban, spealg.
Split, *v. a.* Sgoilt, sgealb; bris, bruan; crac; srac, sgàin.
Splutter, *s.* Tuasaid, sabaid, caonnag, aimhreite, connsachadh, ùprait.
Spoil, *v.* Spùinn, spùill, creach, mill, truaill, cuir a dholaidh.
Spoil, *s.* Cobhartach, creach.
Spoiler, *s.* Spùilleadair, fear reubainn, milltear; fear truaillidh.
Spoke, *s.* Tarsanan ratha.
Spokesman, *s.* Fear-labhairt.
Spoliation, *s.* Spùilleadh, milleadh.
Sponsal, *adj.* Maraisteach, pòsaidh.
Sponsor, *s.* Goistidh, urras.
Spontaneous, *adj.* Saor, deònach.
Spontaneously, *adv.* A dheòin.
Spontaneousness, *s.* Deònachd.
Spool, *s.* Iteachan; tachras.
Spoon, *s.* Spàin.
Spoonful, *s.* Làn spàine.
Sport, *s.* Cluich spòrs; fala-dhà, fearas-chuideachd; àbhachd, sealg.
Sport, *v.* Cluich, dean mire, dean sùgradh, dean spòrs, dean meoghail.
Sportful, *adj.* Cridheil, sunntach, aighearach, mireagach, sùgach.
Sportfulness, *s.* Cridhealas, mire.
Sportive, *adj.* Mear, cridheil, aighearach, sùgach, suigeartach.
Sportsman, *s.* Giomanach, sealgair.
Spot, *s.* Smal, ball, ionaid; tàmailt.
Spot, *v. a.* Salaich; ballaich, truaill.
Spotless, *adj.* Gun smal, gun bhall, gun ghaoid, gu ghò, gun choire.
Spotted, *adj.* Ballach, balla-bhreac, salach, truaillidh.
Spousal, *s.* Pòsadh, maraiste.
Spouse, *s.* Céile, céile-pòsta.
Spout, *s.* Steall, pìoban; srùlag.
Spout, *v. a.* Spùt, steall, doirt.
Spoutfish, *s.* Muirsgian.
Sprain, *s.* Snìomh, siachadh.
Sprat, *s.* Gearra-sgadan, sàrdail.
Sprawl, *v. n.* Smògaich, snàig.
Spray, *s.* Cathadh mara; barr-géige.
Spread, *v.* Sgaoil; sgap; còmhdaich; sìn a mach, foillsich.
Spreut, *part.* Sgapte, sgaoilte.
Sprig, *s.* Faillean, maothan, fiùran.
Spright, *s.* Tannasg.
Sprightliness, *s.* Beothalas.
Sprightly, *adj.* Beò, meamnach, mear, smiorail, cridheil, sunntach, suilbhear; aotrom.
Spring, *v.* Fas, cinn; sruth a mach; spùt; leum, thoir leum.
Spring, *s.* Earrach; leum, cruinnleum, sùrdag; fuaran, sùbailteachd.
Springe, *s.* Ribe, gòisid.
Springhalt, *s.* Ceum-crùbaich.
Springle, *s.* Dul, lub-ruithe.
Springtide, *s.* Reothairt; aislear.
Sprinkle, *v.* Crath, sgap; sgaoil.
Sprinkling, *s.* Crathadh, sgapadh, sgaoileadh, maoth-fhliuchadh.
Sprit, *s.* Ogan, maoth-fhailean.
Sprite, *s.* Spiorad, tannasg, màileachan.
Spritsail, *s.* Seòl-spreòid.
Sprout, *v. n.* Cuir a mach faillean.
Sprout, *s.* Faillean, fiùran, maothan, buinneag, ùr-fhàs, gineag.
Spruce, *adj.* Sgeilmeil, sgiolta; snasmhor; spailpeanta; deas.
Spruce, *s.* Seòrsa giubhais.
Spruceness, *s.* Sgilmeileachd.
Spud, *s.* Duirceall.
Sprunt, *s.* Maide garbh cutach.
Spume, *s.* Cobhar, cop.
Spumous, **Spumy**, *adj.* Cobharach.
Spung, *s.* Spong, fàisgean.
Spungy, *adj.* Spongach, còsagach.
Spunk, *s.* Brathadair, lasadan.
Spun, *pret.* and *p. part.* of to *spin.* Shniomh; sniomhte.
Spur, *s.* Spor; spuir; brosnachadh.
Spur, *v. a.* Spor, greas, stuig, brod.
Spurious, *adj.* Mealltach, truaillidh.
Spurling, *s.* Spéirleag.
Spurn, *v.* Breab; cuir dimeas air diùlt le tàire dean tarcuis air.
Spurn, *s.* Breab, dimeas, tarcuis.

Spurt, *s.* Briosgadh.
Sputter, *v.* Dean bladaireachd.
Spy, *s.* Beachdair, fear-brathaidh.
Spy, *v.* Beachdaich, faigh a mach; brath, rannsaich; dearc leis an t-sùil.
Spyboat, *s.* Bàta brathaidh.
Spyglass, *s.* Glain'-amhairc.
Squab, *adj.* Neo-chlòimhichte, goirid, cutach, bunach, dòmhail; tiugh; reamhar, pocanach.
Squab, *s.* Săsag, suidheachan.
Squabbish, Squabby, *adj.* Feolmhor, dòmhail, trom, somalta.
Squabble, *v. n.* Connsaich, dean strì.
Squabble, *s.* Tuasaid, sabaid, connsachadh, brionglaid, buaireas.
Squabbler, *s.* Buaireadair.
Squadron, *s.* Earrann cabhlaich no feachd.
Squalid, *adj.* Salach; mosach, déisneach, sgreamhail.
Squall, Squal, *v. n.* Sgread, sgiamh.
Squall, *s.* Sgal gaoithe, sgread, sgiamh, sgrèach.
Squally, *adj.* Oiteagach, gaòthar.
Squamos, Squamous, *adj.* Lannach.
Squander, *v. a.* Caith, strùigh, sgap, cosg, mill.
Squanderer, *s.* Strùighear.
Square, *adj.* Ceithir-chèarnach; cothromach; ceart, ionraic.
Square, *s.* Ceithir-chearnag.
Square, *v.* Dean ceithir chèarnach; socraich, dean cothromach; riaghailtich; cuir an òrdugh.
Squash, *s.* Splad, splaitseadh.
Squat, *v. n.* Crùb, liùg, laidh sìos.
Squat, *s.* Crùban, gurraban.
Squat, *adj.* Saigeanta, cutach, bunach.
Squeak, *v. n.* Sgiamh; sgread, sian.
Squeak, *s.* Sgiamh chabhagach.
Squeamish, *adj.* Òrraiseach, grath-arra, àilleasach, faralach.
Squeeze, *v. a.* Teannaich, mùch; brùth, fàisg; sàraich, claoidh.
Squelch, *s.* Splad, plaidse.
Squib, *s.* Paipeir sradagach.
Squint, *adj.* Claon, fiar-shuileach.
Squint, *v.* Seall claon no fiar.
Squinteyed, *adj.* Fiar-shuileach.
Squire, *s.* Ridire beag.
Squire, *v. a.* Comhaidich, treòraich.
Squirrel, *s.* An fheòrag.
Squirt, *v. a.* Sgiort, steall, taosg.
Squirt, *s.* Stealladair, gunn-uisge.
Stab, *v. a.* Troi-lot, sàth.
Stab, *s.* Sàthadh, lot, leòn.
Stability, *s.* Bunailteachd, buansheasamh, maireannachd; cinnteachd.

Stable, *adj.* Daingeann, buan, bunaiteach, seasmhach, maireannach, diongmhalta.
Stable, *s.* Stàbull, marc-lann, eachlann.
Stack, *s.* Cruach, mulan, ruc, tudan.
Stack, *v. a.* Cruach, cruinnich, càrn.
Stadle, *s.* Lorg, trostan; òg-chrann.
Staff, *s.* Bata, lorg; bachall; cuaille; samhach, cas; suaicheantas; cùltaic.
Stag, *s.* Damh cabrach féigh.
Stage, *s.* Ionad-cluiche, ceann-uidhe.
Stage-coach, *s.* Càrbad-réidh.
Staggard, *s.* Damh féigh ceithirbhliadhnach.
Stagger, *v.* Breathlaich, tuainealaich, tuislich, bi gu tuiteam; bi 'n ioma-cheist; oilltich, cuir am breathal, cuir air boile.
Staggers, *s.* Galair each.
Stagnant, *adj.* Neo-ghluasadach.
Stagnate, *v. n.* Stad mar ni uisge.
Stagnation, *s.* Lodachadh, stad.
Staid, *adj.* Stòlda, suidhichte, glic.
Stain, *s.* Ball, sal, spot, coire, truailleadh; lochd, gaoid; dath, lì; tàmailt, nàire, mi-chliù.
Stain, *v. a.* Salaich, ballaich; truaill; nàraich; maslaich.
Stair, *s.* Staidhir, staidhre.
Staircase, *s.* Ionad-staidhreach.
Stake, *s.* Post, maolanach; carragh, colbh; geall; cipein, bacan.
Stake, *v. a.* Gramaich, daighnich, gabh aige; cuir geall.
Stalacilites, *s.* Caisean-snidhe.
Stale, *adj.* Sean; goirt; searbh.
Stale, *v. n.* Mùin, dean uisge.
Staleness, *s.* Seanndachd, goirteas.
Stalk, *v. n.* Ceumnaich; spaisdeirich, imich gu stàtail; eulaidh.
Stalk, *s.* Ceum uallach; cas cuiseige, cuinnlein, cuiseag, gas, galan.
Stalkinghorse, *s.* Each-séilge.
Stalky, *adj.* Cuiseagach, cuinnleineach, gasach, galanach.
Stall, *s.* Prasach, buaigheal, bualaidh, ionad-biathaidh mhart no each.
Stall, *v. a.* Biath, cuir am bà-thaigh.
Stallion, *s.* Òigeach, àigeach, greigheach, greigheire. *Ir.*
Stamina, *s.* Brìgh, stuth; smior, bun.
Stammer, *v. n.* Bi manndach no liodach, dean gagaireachd.
Stammerer, *s.* Fear manndach, liodach, gagaire, glugaire.
Stamp, *v.* Stailc; pronn, brùth; comharraich.
Stamp, *s.* Àile; dealbh, comharradh

uidheam comharrachaidh, seòrsa, sliochd.

Stanch, *v.* Cuir stad air fuil, &c.

Stanch, *adj.* Dian; diongmhalta, daingeann, làidir, bunaiteach, fìrinneach, fior, dìleas.

Stanchion, *s.* Cùl-taic, gobhal, gàd.

Stand, *s.* Seasamh, àite-seasaimh; stad, teagamh; ioma-cheist; bùth.

Stand, *v.* Seas, seasamh; dean seasamh, fuirich, fan, stad; mair; fuilig, giùlain; buanaich.

Standard, *s.* Suaicheantas, bratach, meirghe; craobh; riaghailt-shuidhichte, modh-seasmhach.

Standel, *s.* Seanna chraobh.

Standing, *s.* Seasamh; buanachadh; mairsinn; cor; inbhe.

Standing, *part. adj.* Suidhichte, socraichte, seasmhach, buan.

Standish, *s.* Seas-dubh. *I. R.*

Stang, *s.* Cùig slat gu leth.

Stannary, *s.* Méinn staoine.

Stanza, *s.* Rann, ceithreamh.

Staple, *s.* Margadh shuidhichte; stìnleag, stapall.

Staple, *adj.* Socraichte, margail.

Star, *s.* Rionnag, reull.

Starboard, *s.* Taobh deas luinge.

Starch, *s.* Stalcair, stalc.

Starch, *v. a.* Stalcaich, stalc.

Starched, *adj.* Stalcanta.

Stare, *v. n.* Spleuc, geur-bheachdaich.

Stare, *s.* Spleuc, geur-amharc.

Stargazer, *s.* Reuladair, speuradair.

Stark, *adj.* Fìor, iomlan; rag, làidir; teann, dearrasach.

Starkly, *adv.* Gu rag, gu làidir.

Starlight, *s.* Reull-sholus.

Starlike, *adj.* Rionnagach, reannagach, drilinneach.

Starling, *s.* Druid, druid-dubh.

Starred, *adj.* Rionnagach, reulltach.

Starry, *adj.* Rionnagach, reulltach.

Starshoot, *s.* Sgeith-rionnaige.

Start, *v.* Clisg, grad-leum, criothnaich, grad-éirich, falbh, siubhail; cuir clisgadh air; cuir ás an alt; cuir ás àite; cuir san rathad.

Start, *s.* Clisgeadh; briosgadh, grad-leum; teannadh air falbh; toiseach.

Starting, *s.* Clisgeadh, briosgadh, leum.

Startle, *v.* Clisg, cuir clisgeadh air; oilltich, cuir eagal air, cuir maoim air; crùp, crùb

Startish, **Startlish**, *adj.* Gealtach, eagalach, maoimeach.

Starve, *v.* Cuir gu bàs le gort no fuachd; meilich.

Starvling, *s.* Fear-caoile, creutair truagh, gortach.

Statary, *adj.* Ceangailte, suidhichte.

State, *s.* Staid, inbhe, cŏr, gné; rìoghachd, dùthaich; mòr-chuis, greadhnachas, mòralachd, luchd-riaghlaidh, stàta.

State, *v. a.* Cuir an céill, aithris gu puncail, thoir cunntas.

Stateliness, *s.* Stàidealachd, greadhnachas, mòralachd, uaill.

Stately, *adj.* Stàideil, greadhnach, flathail, rìmheach, uallach, allail.

Statement, *s.* Cunntas.

Statesman, *s.* Fear-stàta, comhairleach-rìoghachd.

Statics, *s.* Eòlas-cothromachaidh.

Station, *s.* Seasamh; àite, ionad; dreuchd, post, oifig, inbhe.

Station, *v. a.* Socraich; suidhich.

Stationary, *adj.* Socraichte, aitichte.

Stationery, *s.* Bathar phàipeirean.

Stationer, *s.* Reiceadair phàipeirean.

Statuary, *s.* Gràbhalaiche.

Statue, *s.* Ìomhaigh; riochd.

Stature, *s.* Àirde, àirdead.

Statute, *s.* Lagh, reachd, òrdugh.

Stave, *v.* Cuir 'na chlàraibh.

Stave, *s.* Clàr; *plur.* Staves. Clàir.

Stay, *v.* Fuirich, fan, feith, stad, seas; buanaich; còmhnaich, tuinich; cùm, bac, caisg, gabh roimh; cùm suas; cum taic ri.

Stay, *s.* Fanachd, fatainn, fuireach, feitheamh, buanachd, stad; dàil; bacadh; taic, cùl-taic; dìon, tèarmann; stadh; cliabh.

Stayed, *adj.* Suidhichte, socraichte, stòlte, socrach; bacte, grabte; ciùin, ciùinichte.

Stays, *s.* Stadhannan; cliabh mnatha.

Stead, *s.* Ionad, riochd; stà, feum.

Steadfast, *adj.* Bunaiteach, suidhichte, daingeann, seasmhach, buan.

Steadfastness, *s.* Bunailteas.

Steadiness, *s.* Bunailt; seasmhachd.

Steady, *adj.* Bunailteach, gramail; daingeann; socrach, suidhichte.

Steady, *v. a.* Socraich, daingnich, cum suas.

Steak, *s.* Staoig, toitean; fillean.

Steal, *v.* Goid; dean mèirle.

Stealth, *s.* Goid, mèirle, braide.

Steam, *s.* Toit, smùid.

Steed, *s.* Steud; steud-each; falaire.

Steel, *s.* Stàilinn, cruaidh.

Steel, *v. a.* Cruadhaich, stàilinnich.

Steel, *adj.* Stàilinneach, cruaidh.

Steely, *adj.* Cruaidh mar stàilinn

Steelyard, *s.* Biorsamaid.

STEEP, *adj.* Corrach, cǎs.
STEEP, *s.* Bruach, uchdach, bruthach.
STEEP, *v. a.* Bogaich, tùm, taisich.
STEEPLE, *s.* Stìopall, binean.
STEEPNESS, *s.* Caisead, corraichead.
STEEPY, *adj.* Corrach, cǎs, creagach.
STEER, *s.* Damh òg; tarbh òg.
STEER, *v.* Stiùr, seòl; treòraich.
STEERAGE, *s.* Stiùradh, seòladh, riaghladh, steòrnadh, seòmar-mòr luinge.
STEERSMAN, *s.* Stiùradair.
STELLAR, STELLARY, *adj.* Rionnagach.
STELLATION, *s.* Drillinn.
STELLION, *s.* Arc-luachrach bhallach.
STEM, *s.* Lorg, cas, cuiseag; bun, stoc; sliochd, clann, gineal, teaghlach; toiseach luinge.
STEM, *v. a.* Gabh roimh, cum roimh, bac, caisg, cuir stad air.
STENCH, *s.* Droch thòchd, bréine.
STENOGRAPHY, *s.* Gearr-sgrìobhadh.
STENTORIAN, *adj.* Àrd-labhrach.
STENTOROPHONIC, *adj.* Àrd-ghlòireach.
STEP, *v. n.* Thoir ceum, imich, ceumnaich, coisich, gluais, rach, falbh.
STEP, *s.* Ceum; gluasad, imeachd.
STEPDAME, STEPMOTHER, *s.* Muime.
STEPDAUGHTER, *s.* Dalta nighin.
STEPFATHER, *s.* Oide, fear màthar.
STERCORACEOUS, *adj.* Inneireach.
STERCORATION, *s.* Mathachadh.
STERILITY, *s.* Fàsalachd; seasgad.
STERLING, *adj.* Fìor, firinneach.
STERLING, *s.* Airgead Sasunnach.
STERN, *adj.* Gruamach, duairceach, gnù, gnò, cruaidh; neo-thruacanta.
STERN, *s.* Deireadh luinge.
STERNNESS, *s.* Gruaim, gruamaiche; cruathas, duairceas; an-iochd.
STERNON, STERNUM, *s.* Cnàimh a' bhroilich, cnaimhe-uchda.
STEW, *v. a.* Stòbh; earr-bhruich.
STEW, *s.* Stòbh; taigh-teth.
STEWARD, *s.* Stiùbhard.
STEWARDSHIP, *s.* Stiùbhardachd.
STICK, *s.* Bioran, maide, bata, lorg.
STICK, *v.* Sàth; lot; lean, coimhlean; dlùthaich ri; lean ri; stad; cùm ri.
STICKLE, *v. n.* Connsaich; seas ri.
STICKLER, *s.* Fear-cuidichidh, fear a chumas taobh ri neach; fear a chumas a mach gu dian.
STICKY, *adj.* Righinn, leanailteach.
STIFF, *adj.* Rag, do-lùbadh; reasgach, dùr; teann, cruaidh, deacair.
STIFFEN, *v.* Dean rag, ragaich.
STIFFNECKED, *adj.* Rag-mhuinealach.
STIFFNESS, *s.* Reasgachd, raige.
STIFLE, *v.* Mùch, tachd; cùm fodha, caisg, falaich, ceil; cuir ás.
STIGMA, *s.* Comharradh-maslaidh; lorg, tàmailt, sgainneal, mi-chliù.
STIGMATIZE, *v. a.* Comharraich le tàire; cuir fo thàmailt.
STILE, *s.* Staidhir, ceum bealaich; meur uaireadair gréine.
STILETTO, *s.* Cuinnsear.
STILL, *adj.* Sàmhach, ciùin, sèimh.
STILL, *s.* Poit-dubh, poit-thogalach; sàmhchair, tosd.
STILL, *v. a.* Ciùinich, cuir sàmhach, caisg, sìthich.
STILLNESS, *s.* Ciùineas, tost, fèith.
STILTS, *s.* Trosdain; casan-cǒrrach.
STIMULATE, *v. a.* Spor, brod, stuig, brosnaich, cuir thuige, buair.
STIMULUS, *s.* Sporadh, brodadh, brosnachadh, buaireadh.
STING, *s.* Gath; guin, goimh.
STING, *v. a.* Gath, cuir gath, gathaich, guin, leòn, lot, cràidh.
STINGINESS, *s.* Spìocaireachd.
STINGO, *s.* Seann lionn.
STINGY, *adj.* Cruaidh; sanntach.
STINK, *s.* Bòladh breun; tòchd; tùt.
STINKARD, *s.* Spìocaire; bréinean.
STINT, *v. a.* Socraich; cùm a staigh.
STINT, *s.* Crìoch, ceann, bacadh; earrann, cuibhrionn, cuid.
STIPEND, *s.* Stìopain; tuarasdal, pàidheadh suidhichte.
STIPENDIARY, *s.* Fear-tuarasdail.
STIPULATE, *v. a.* Cùmhnantaich, socraich, sònraich, suidhich.
STIPULATION, *s.* Cùmhnant.
STIPULATIVE, *adj.* Cùmhnantach.
STIPULATOR, *s.* Cùmhnantaiche.
STIR, *v.* Gluais, caraich, glidich; brosnaich; beothaich; stùig, cuir thuige; tog.
STIR, *s.* Buaireas, othail, ùinich, aimhreit, strìth, iomairt.
STIRRER, *s.* Buaireadair, brosnaiche, fear moch-éiridh.
STIRRUP, *s.* Cǎs-dul, stiorap.
STITCH, *v. a.* Fuaigh; tàth.
STITCH, *s.* Greim snàthaid, greim fuaigheil; guin, goimh, treathaid.
STITHY, *s.* Innein.
STIVE, *v. a.* Dòmhlaich, dean teth.
STOCK, *s.* Stoc; post, bun; baothaire; gurraiceach, ùmaidh; sìol, sliochd, clann, gineal, pòr, teaghlach; stòr, stòras, maoin; pac.
STOCK, *v. a.* Lìon, stocaich; cruach, càrn, cruinnich.
STOCKDOVE, *s.* Smùdan.
STOCKFISH, *s.* Trosg tioram.

Stocking, *s.* Stocain, osan.
Stocklock, *s.* Glas-chip.
Stocks, *s.* Ceap-peanais.
Stoic, *s.* Teallsanach a ta leanmhainn Sèno.
Stole, *s.* Còta fada; rìoghail; brat.
Stolidity, *s.* Baothaireachd.
Stomach, *s.* Goile, stamac, maodal; sannt bìdh, acras, àrdan, misneach, toil, togradh, déigh.
Stomach, *v.* Gabh gu dona, gabh corraich; gabh fearg.
Stomacher, *s.* Uchd-chrios.
Stomachic, *s.* Leigheas goile.
Stone, *s.* Clach, ăl.
Stone, *adj.* Cloiche, do chloich.
Stone, *v. a.* Clach, tilg clachan.
Stonecast, *s.* Urchair cloiche.
Stonefruit, *s.* Clach-mheas, gach meas anns am beil clach.
Stonehorse, *s.* Òigeach, àigeach.
Stonepit, *s.* Clach-thochailt.
Stony, *adj.* Clachach, làn chlach, sgàirneach; cruaidh; an-iochdmhor.
Stool, *s.* Stòl, sorchan, suidheagan; ionad-suidhe; tom, fuasgladh cuirp.
Stoop, *v. n.* Crom, lùb, aom, géill, strìochd, crùb, ìslich.
Stoop, *s.* Cromadh, lùbadh, aomadh, tuiteam; crùbadh.
Stop, *v. a.* Stad, cuir stad, bac, toirmisg, cùm, grab, caisg, cuir dheth, cuir dàil; sguir, leig dhiot, fan, fuirich.
Stop, *s.* Stad, grabadh, toirmeasg; fanachd, fuireach; dàil.
Stoppage, *s.* Aobhar stad, bacadh; stad, sgur, dàil, maille, grabadh.
Stopple, Stopper, *s.* Àrcan.
Store, *s.* Maoin, stòras, beairteas, pailteas, stoc, ionmhas; faodail, feudail; tasg-thaigh.
Store, *v.* Uidheamaich, lìon, stòr, stocaich, taisg, càrn suas, cuir seachad.
Storehouse, *s.* Taigh-stòir.
Stork, *s.* A chorra-bhàn.
Storm, *s.* Anradh, doireann, gaillionn, doinionn, stoirm, toirm, an-uair; ionnsaidh air baile-dìona.
Storm, *v.* Thoir ionnsaidh làidir, tog gaillionn no doinionn; bi fo chorraich; cuir séisd. *D. B.*
Stormy, *adj.* Ànradhach, gaillionnach, doinionnach, gaothar; crosta.
Story, *s.* Naidheachd, sgeul, sgeulachd; uirsgeul, eachdraidh; breug, ùrlar, lobhta.
Stot, *s.* Damh.
Stout, *adj.* Làidir, treun, foghainteach, calma, comasach, toirteil, gramail, garbh, tiugh; tùrail; dàna, danarra, misneachail.
Stoutness, *s.* Treise, spionnadh, tréine, gramalas, dànadas; reasgachd, misneach.
Stove, *s.* Taigh-teth; àmhuinn, seòrsa fùirneis.
Stow, *v. a.* Taisg, càrn suas.
Stowage, *s.* Àite-tasgaidh.
Strabism, *s.* Caogadh.
Straddle, *v. n.* Imich gu gobhlach.
Straggle, *v. n.* Rach air iomrall, rach air seacharan, rach air faontradh.
Straggler, *s.* Fear-fuadain.
Straight, *adj.* Dìreach; deas.
Straight, Straightways, *adv.* Gu grad, gu h-ealamh, air ball, gu luath, gun stad, gun dàil.
Straighten, *v. a.* Dìrich.
Strain, *v.* Fàisg; sìolaidh; teannaich, dlùthaich; siach, sniomh, cumhannaich, dean spàirn.
Strain, *s.* Fonn; siachadh, snìomh, spàirn, nàdur.
Strainer, *s.* Sìolachan.
Strait, *adj.* Teann, cumhann, aimhleathan; dlù; cruaidh, duilich, docair, deacair.
Strait, *s.* Caolas, cneas mara, cunglach, àirleag; càs, teinn, teanntachd; bochdainn, sàrachadh, uireasbhuidh.
Straiten, *v. a.* Teannaich, dean aimhleathan; sàraich, claoidh.
Straitness, *s.* Cuingead, cuinge, cruadhas, teanntachd.
Strand, *s.* Tràigh, cladach; bruach.
Strand, *v.* Cuir air, rach air; cuir no rach air cladach.
Strange, *adj.* Iongantach, neònach, miorbhuileach; coimheach, coigreach, allmharra, gallda; fiadhaich, aineamh, annasach; anabarrach.
Strange, *interj.* Iongantach!
Stranger, *s.* Coigreach, allmharrach.
Strangle, *v. a.* Tachd, mùch, croch.
Strangles, *s.* An galar-greidh.
Stranguary, *s.* An galar-fuail.
Strap, *s.* Crios. iall, stiom, giort.
Strappado, *s.* Sgiùrsadh.
Strapping, *adj.* Mòr, calma, deas, foghainteach, tlachdmhor.
Strata, *s.* Leapaichean, sreathan.
Stratagem, *s.* Cuilbheart, cogaidh.
Stratum, *s.* Leabaidh, breath, sreath.
Straw, *s.* Connlach; fodar.
Strawberry, *s.* Sùbh-làir.
Stray, *v. n.* Rach air seacharan, rach air iomrall; rach am mearachd.
Stray, *s.* Ainmhidh seacharain.

Streak, *s.* Stiall, stìom, srian.
Streak, *v. a.* Stiall, stiallaich.
Streaky, *adj.* Stiallach, srianach.
Stream, *s.* Sruth; buinne.
Stream, *v.* Sruth, ruith, dòirt.
Streamer, *s.* Bratach, sròl, meirghe.
Streamlet, *s.* Caochan, sruthan.
Streamy, *adj.* Sruthanach.
Street, *s.* Sràid.
Strength, *s.* Neart, spionnadh, tréine, treise; marsainn, lùgh, treòir; cumhachd; gramalas; dìon; tèarmann; dùn, daighneach; armailt.
Strengthen, *v.* Neartaich; beothaich; daingnich; socraich.
Strengthener, *s.* Neartachair.
Strenuous, *adj.* Dàna; gaisgeil, misneachail; dùrachdach; curanta, dian, dealasach.
Streperous, *adj.* Àrd-fuaimneach.
Stress, *s.* Cudthrom; cothrom; strìth; spàirn; eallach; éigin.
Stretch, *v. a.* Sìn, sgaoil; ragaich; sìn a mach; leudaich.
Stretch, *s.* Sìneadh; ionnsaidh.
Stretcher, *s.* Ragadair; sìneadair; lunn-chas, luchd-iomaraidh.
Strew, *v. n.* Sgaoil, sgap, crath.
Striæ, *s.* Claisean slige-chreachainn no slige-coileige.
Striate, Striated, *adj.* Claiseach.
Stricken, *part.* Buailte.
Strickle, *s.* Stràcadair. *Sk.*
Strict, *adj.* Teann, cruaidh, geur; doirbh; leacanta; poncail, dìreach.
Stricture, *s.* Crupadh, teannachadh; buille; beantainn.
Stride, *v. n.* Thoir sìnteag, thoir sùrdag, rach gobhlach, thoir ceum fada.
Stride, *s.* Sìnteag, sùrdag, fad-cheum.
Strife, *s.* Strìth, còmh-strith, connsachadh, caonnag, buaireas, ùtag, săbaid, tuasaid, aimhreite.
Strike, *v.* Buail, dòrnaich; géill.
Striker, *s.* Fear-bualaidh.
Striking, *part. adj.* Drùighteach, iongantach, neònach.
String, *s.* Sreang, sreangan, toinntean, còrd; teud-chiùil.
String, *v. a.* Sreangaich, teudaich.
Stringed, *adj.* Teudaichte.
Stringent, *adj.* Ceangaltach.
Stringy, *adj.* Sreangach, teudach.
Strip, *v. a.* Rùisg, lom, nochd, faobhaich, sgath; cairt, sgrath, plaoisg.
Strip, *s.* Stiall, stiom.
Stripe, *v. a.* Stiall, stiallaich; buail; sgiùrs, sgiuts.
Stripling, *s.* Òganach, balachan.
Strive, *v. n.* Dean spàirn, dean strìth.
Striving, *s.* Co-strìth, gleachd.
Stroke, *s.* Buille, gleadhar, stràc.
Stroke, *v. a.* Mìnich, slìog, slìob.
Stroking, *s.* Slìobadh, suathadh.
Stroll, *v. n.* Sràid-imich, seabhaid.
Stroller, *s.* Sabhdaire, spaisdear.
Strong, *adj.* Làidir, neartmhor, treun, lùghmhor, calma, foghainteach, gramail; fallain, slàinteil; dian, deòthasach; diongmhalta; daingeann; teann.
Strow, *v. a.* Sgaoil; sgap; crath.
Structure, *s.* Togail; aitreabh.
Struggle, *v. n.* Gleachd; dean spàirn, dean strìth; streap, dean iomairt; saoithrich.
Struggle, *s.* Gleachd, spàirn, strìth.
Strumpet, *s.* Siùrsach, strìopach.
Strut, *v. n.* Imich gu stràiceil; bòc
Strut, *s.* Ceum uallach.
Stub, *s.* Bun, òrda, durc.
Stub, *v. a.* Spion as á bhun.
Stubbed, *adj.* Bunach, stumpach, gearr, goirid, geinneach, cutach.
Stubble, *s.* Asbhuain, stailcneach.
Stubborn, *adj.* Rag, rag-mhuinealach, reasgach, eas-ùmhal.
Stubbornness, *s.* Ragaireachd, reasgachd, danarrachd, eas-ùmhlachd.
Stubby, *adj.* Cutach, stobanach, bunach, bunanta, goirid.
Stuckle, *s.* Stùcan, adag, sgrùdhan.
Stud, *s.* Tarag, tacaid; greigh.
Student, *s.* Sgoilear, stuidear.
Studied, *adj.* Ionnsaichte.
Studious, *adj.* Déidheil air foghlum; smuainteachail; meòrach.
Study, *s.* Smuainteachadh; cnuasachd, seòmar, meòraich, meòrachadh.
Study, *v.* Smuainich, smaointich; cnuasaich, meòraich, beachdaich, thoir fainear, breithnich, ionnsaich.
Stuff, *s.* Stuth; cùngaidh; seòrsa clò.
Stuff, *v.* Lìon, lìon gu sàth; spàrr, dinn; bòc; ăt, ith séid.
Stuffing, *s.* Lìonadh, dinneadh, sparradh, mìlsean am feòil.
Stultiloquence, *s.* Glòireamas; baois.
Stum, *s.* Fion ùr; braileis.
Stumble, *v.* Tuislich, sleamhnaich.
Stumble, *s.* Tuisleadh, sleamhnachadh, cliobadh, mearachd, sgiorradh.
Stumbler, *s.* Fear-tuislidh.
Stumbling, *s.* Tuisleadh, sleamhnachadh, spéidhleadh, clibeadh.
Stumblingblock, *s.* Ceap-tuislidh.
Stump, *s.* Bun; stoc, ceapan.
Stumpy, *adj.* Bunach, cutach.
Stun, *v. a.* Cuir tuaineal, cuir tàineal
Stunt, *v. a.* Cum o fhàs.

Stupefaction, *s.* Neo-mhothachadh.
Stupendous, *adj.* Fuathasach, uabhasach, iongantach, anabarrach.
Stupid, *adj.* Dùr; baoghalta.
Stupidity, *s.* Baoghaltachd.
Stupify, *v. a.* Cuir tuaineal.
Stupor, *s.* Tuaineal; tàineal.
Sturdiness, *s.* Neart, spionnadh, gramalas, duinealas, bunantachd.
Sturdy, *adj.* Làidir, neartmhor, bunanta, gramail, calma, garbh.
Sturgeon, *s.* An stirean.
Sturk, *s.* Gamhainn.
Stutter, *v. n.* Bi manndach, bi liodach, bi gagach bi glugach.
Stutterer, *s.* Fear manndach, fear liodach, gagaire, glugaire.
Sty, *s.* Fail mhuc.
Stygian, *adj.* Ifrinneach.
Style, *s.* Modh-labhairt; dòigh-labhairt; modh-sgrìobhaidh; dòigh-sgrìobhaidh; tiodal, ainm; seòl, modh, dòigh.
Style, *v. a.* Ainmich, goir.
Styptic, *adj.* Casgach air fuil.
Styptic, *s.* Leigheas casg-fala.
Suasible, *adj.* So-earalachadh.
Suavity, *s.* Mìlse; taitneachd.
Subacid, *adj.* A leth-char goirt; rudeigin searbh.
Subacrid, *adj.* A leth-char geur.
Subaltern, *s.* Ìochdaran.
Subdue, *v. a.* Ceannsaich, ciùinich, sàraich, cuir fodha, cìosnaich.
Subduer, *s.* Fear-ceannsachaidh.
Subject, *v. a.* Cuir fo smachd, smachdaich, ceannsaich, sàraich, cuir fo cheannsal; dean buailteach do.
Subject, *adj.* Ùmhal; fo smachd, ceannsaichte, fo chìs; buailteach.
Subject, *s.* Ìochdaran; ceann-eagair, ceann-teagaisg, stéidh-theagaisg.
Subjection, *s.* Ceannsachadh, ceannsal, ceannasachd, smachd.
Subjoin, *v. a.* Cuir ri; fàth-sgrìobh.
Subjugate, *v. a.* Ceannsaich, cìosnaich, cuir fo cheannas.
Subjugation, *s.* Cèannsachadh.
Subjunction, *s.* Leasachadh.
Sublimation, *s.* Togail le neart teine.
Sublime, *v. a.* Tog le neart teine.
Sublime, *adj.* Àrd; òirdheirc; mòr; uaibhreach, greadhnach; urramach.
Sublimity, *s.* Àirde; òirdheirceas.
Sublunar, **Sublunary**, *adj.* Talmhaidh, saoghalta; tìmeil.
Submarine, *adj.* Fo 'n mhuir.
Submerge, *v. a.* Cuir fo 'n uisge.
Submersion, *s.* Cur fo 'n uisge.
Submission, *s.* Ùmhlachd, géill.
Submissive, *adj.* Ùmhal, iriosal.
Submissively, *adv.* Gu h-ùmhal.
Submissiveness, *s.* Ùmhlachd.
Submit, *v.* Géill, strìochd, lùb.
Subordinacy, *adj.* Ìochdranachd.
Subordinate, *adj.* Ìochdarach.
Subordination, *s.* Ìochdaranachd.
Suborn, *v. a.* Solair os n-iosal; brìob.
Subornation, *s.* Foill-cheannach.
Suborner, *s.* Fear-foille.
Subpœna, *s.* Rabhadh laghail
Subscribe, *v. n.* Fo-sgrìobh
Subscriber, *s.* Fo-sgrìobhair.
Subscription, *s.* Fo-sgrìobhadh; còmhnadh, cuideachadh, aontachadh.
Subsequence, *s.* Leantainn.
Subsequent, *adj.* A leanas.
Subserve, *v. a.* Fritheil; cuidich.
Subservience, *s.* Frithealadh.
Subservient, *adj.* Fritheilteach, cuideachail, còmhnachail; feumail.
Subside, *v. n.* Traogh, tràigh, tuit sìos; ciùinich, ìslich, sìolaidh.
Subsidency, *s.* Traoghadh, tràghadh, sìoladh, tuiteam sìos.
Subsidiary, *adj.* Cuideachail.
Subsidy, *s.* Cuideachadh, còmhnadh.
Subsign, *v. a.* Cuir ainm ri.
Subsist, *v. n.* Buanaich, thig beò, thig suas, bi beò, beathaich.
Subsistence, *s.* Bith; beatha; buanachadh, tighinn beò, beathachadh, teachd-an-tir, lòn.
Subsistent, *adj.* Beò, maireann.
Substance, *s.* Bìth; corp; brìgh, bladh, stuth, tairbhe; maoin, saibhreas, beairteas.
Substantial, *adj.* Fìor; beò; corporra; làidìr; gramail; socrach, tàbhachadh tarbhach; beairteach reachdmhor, biadhchar, brighor.
Substantiality, *s.* Corporrachd.
Substantiate, *v. a.* Fìrinnich.
Substantive, *s.* Ainm.
Substitute, *v. a.* Cuir an àite.
Substitute, *s.* Fear-ionaid.
Subsultive, *adj.* Leumnach, clisgeach.
Subtend, *v. n.* Sìn mu choinneamh.
Subtense, *s.* Sreang bogha.
Subterfuge, *s.* Leithsgeul, cleas.
Subterranean, **Subterraneous**, *adj.* Fo-thìreach, iochdrach, fo 'n talamh.
Subtile, *adj.* Tana, caol; seang; finealta, sligheach; geur, carach, cealgach, cuilbheartach, eòlach, seòlta, innleachdach.
Subtileness, *s.* Taine, caoile, finealtachd; géire, cuilbheartachd.
Subtiliate, *v. a.* Tanaich, dean tana.
Subtiliation, *s.* Tanachadh.

Subtilty, *s.* Taine, tainead, fìnealtachd; car, cuilbheart, innleachd.
Subtle, *adj.* Carach, cuilbheartach, seòlta, eòlach, slìgheach.
Subtract, *v. a.* Thoir uaithe.
Subtraction, *s.* Toirt uaithe.
Suburb, *s.* Iomall baile.
Subversion, *s.* Tilgeadh sìos, sgrios.
Subversive, *adj.* Millteach, sgriosail.
Subvert, *v.* Tilg bun os ceann.
Succedaneous, *adj.* An àite ni eile.
Succedaneum, *s.* Ni an àite ni eile.
Succeed, *v.* Lean, thig an déigh, thig an lòrg, thig an àite; soirbhich.
Success, *s.* Soirbheachadh, àgh; buaidh; sealbh, rath, sonas, sèamhas.
Successful, *adj.* Soirbheasach, àghmhor, buadhach, sealbhach.
Succession, *s.* Leantainn, leanachd; lorg slighe; còir-sheilbh.
Successive, *adj.* Leantainneach; a leanas; an òrdugh, an riaghailt.
Successor, *s.* Fear-ionaid, fear a thig an àite fir eile.
Succinct, *adj.* Cuimir, truiste; deas, gearr, aith-ghearr, cutach.
Succory, *s.* Lŭs-an-t-siùcair.
Succour, *v. a.* Cuidich, cobhair, furtaich, thoir furtachd.
Succour, *s.* Còmhnadh, cuideachadh, cobhair, furtachd.
Succulent, *adj.* Brìoghmhor, sùghmhor, sultmhor.
Succumb, *v. n.* Géill, strìochd, lùb.
Succussion, *s.* Crathadh, bogadanaich,
Such, *pron.* A leithid; mar.
Suck, *v.* Sùigh, deoghail; srùb.
Suck, *s.* Sùgadh, sùghadh, deoghal. srùbadh, bainne-cìche.
Sucker, *s.* Deoghladair; sùghair, srùbair; faillean, fiùran, maothan.
Sucket, *s.* Mìlsean.
Suckle, *v. a.* Thoir cìoch, àraich.
Suckling, *s.* Cìochran, naoidhean.
Suction, *s.* Sùghadh; deoghal.
Sudden, *adj.* Grad, obann, cas, ealamh, cabhagach, disgir.
Suddenly, *adv.* Gu h-obann.
Sudorific, *adj.* Fallusach.
Suds, *s.* Cobhar shiabuinn.
Sue, *v.* Cuir thuige, lean, tagair, agair, guidh, aslaich, sir, iarr.
Suet, *s.* Geir, ìgh, blonag.
Suety, *adj.* Reamhar, blonagach.
Suffer, *v. a.* Fuilig, giùlain, iomchair; leig le; ceadaich.
Sufferable, *adj.* So-fhulang.
Sufferance, *s.* Fulang, foighidinn, giùlan; cead, comas.
Sufferer, *s.* Fulangaiche.
Suffering, *s.* Fulangas, foighidinn, pian, cràdh.
Suffice, *v.* Foghain; sàsaich.
Sufficiency, *s.* Diongmhaltas; foghainteachd; éifeachd; pailteas; foghnadh; leòir, na 's leòir, sàsachadh.
Sufficient, *adj.* Diongmhalta, foghainteach, comasach, iomchuidh, freagarrach, leòir, na 's leòir.
Suffocate, *v. a.* Tachd, mùch.
Suffocation, *s.* Tachdadh, mùchadh.
Suffocative, *adj.* Tachdach, mùchach.
Suffragan, *s.* Easbuig-cuideachaidh.
Suffragant, *s.* Comh-oibriche.
Suffrage, *s.* Tagh-ghuth; aontachadh, còmhnadh.
Suffuse, *v. a.* Còmhdaich, sgaoil air.
Suffusion, *s.* Còmhdachadh.
Sugar, *s.* Siùcar.
Sugary, *adj.* Siùcarach, milis.
Suggest, *v. a.* Thoir sanus; cuir an ceann, cuir an cuimhne, cuir an aire; cagair.
Suggestion, *s.* Sanus, rabhadh, cagar.
Suicide, *s.* Féin-mhortair; féin-mhort.
Suit, *s.* Iarrtas, iarraidh; sireadh; cùis, cùis-lagha, cùis-tagraidh; culaidh, deise, trusgan; suiridhe.
Suit, *v.* Freagarraich, freagair; uidheamaich; deasaich; éid; còird.
Suitable, *adj.* Freagarrach, iomchuidh, cumhaidh.
Suitableness, *s.* Freagarrachd.
Suiter, **Suitor**, *s.* Suirdhiche; leannan; fear-aslachaidh.
Suitress, *s.* Ban-aslachaidh.
Sulkiness, *s.* Gruaim, moit, mùig.
Sulky, *adj.* Gruamach, iargalta, mùgach, coimheach, neo-aoidheil.
Sullen, *adj.* Doirbh, doichiollach; gnò, gnù; dùr, reasgach, cianail.
Sullenness, *s.* Doirbheas, doireanntachd, gruamaichead; mùgalachd dùiread, reasgachd.
Sully, *v. a.* Salaich, truaill; mill
Sulphur, *s.* Pronnasg, rif, riof.
Sulphureous, *adj.* Pronnasgach.
Sulphury, *adj.* Pronnasgach.
Sultan, *s.* Rìgh nan Turcach.
Sultana, *s.* Ban-righ nan Turcach.
Sultry, *adj.* Bruthainneach, blàth.
Sum, *s.* Àireamh, sùim, brìgh.
Sum, *v. a.* Àireamh, sùim, cunnt.
Sumless, *adj.* Do-àireamh.
Summary, *adj.* Aithghearr, gearr.
Summary, *s.* Giorrachadh.
Summer, *s.* Sàmhradh; sail-ùrlair.
Summerhouse, *s.* Tigh-sàmhraidh.
Summerset, *s.* Căr-a'-mhuiltein.
Summit, *s.* Mullach, binnein, barr.

Summon, *v. a.* Gairm, òrduich.
Summoner, *s.* Maor, gairme.
Summons, *s.* Gairm gu mòd, bàirlinn.
Sumpter, *s.* Each-saic.
Sumptuary, *adj.* A riaghladh cosgais.
Sumptuous, *adj.* Cosgail; sòghail.
Sumptuousness, *s.* Cosgalachd.
Sun, *s.* Grian, lò-chrann. *Ob.*
Sunbeam, *s.* Gath-gréine, deò-grein.
Sunburnt, *adj.* Grian-loiste.
Sunday, *s.* Di-dòmhnaich.
Sunder, *v. a.* Dealaich, sgar.
Sundew, *s.* Lŭs-na-fearna-guirme.
Sundial, *s.* Uaireadair-gréine.
Sundry, *s.* Iomadaidh.
Sundries, *s. pl.* Ioma nithe.
Sunflower, *s.* Neòinean-gréine.
Sunk, *part.* of *sink.* Air dol fodha.
Sunless, *adj.* Gun ghrian, gun teas.
Sunny, *adj.* Grianach; deisearach.
Sunrise, *s.* Èiridh na gréine.
Sunset, *s.* Laidhe na gréine.
Sunshine, *s.* Dèarsadh na gréine.
Sunshiny, *adj.* Grianach dèarsach.
Sup, *v.* Òl; gabh suipeir.
Sup, *s.* Balgum, làn-beòil.
Superable, *adj.* Sò-cheannsachadh.
Superabound, *v. n.* Bi lìonmhor.
Superabundance, *s.* Tuille 's a chòir.
Superabundant, *adj.* Anabarra pailt.
Superadd, *v. a.* Cuir ri.
Superaddition, *s.* Cuir ris.
Superannuate, *v. a.* Meas mò 's sean.
Superb, *adj.* Rìmheach, greadhnach.
Supercargo, *s.* Fear-cùram luchda.
Supercilious, *adj.* Àrdanach, uallach.
Superciliousness, *s.* Àrdan, uaill.
Supereminence, *s.* Barrachd.
Supereminent, *adj.* Barrachdach.
Supererogation, *s.* Bàrra-ghniomh.
Superexcellent, *adj.* Barraichte.
Superfice, *s.* Uachdar.
Superficial, *adj.* Uachdrach; suarrach, faoin; neo-dhiongmhalta, neoghramail; neo-ionnsaichte; aodhomhain; air bheag eòlais.
Superficialness, *s.* Suarraichead; eu-doimhneachd, beag-eòlas.
Superficies, *s.* An taobh a muigh, an t-uachdar, am barr.
Superfine, *adj.* Barr-fhìnealta.
Superfluity, *s.* Anabharra.
Superfluous, *adj.* Neo-fheumail.
Superflux, *s.* Anacuimse.
Superhuman, *adj.* Thar nàdur-daonna.
Superincumbent, *adj.* Air muin.
Superintend, *v. a.* Amhairc thairis.
Superintendency, *s.* Riaghladh.
Superintendent, *s.* Riaghladair.
Superior, *adj.* Is àirde, is fearr.
Superiority, *s.* Barrachd; ceannas, &c.
Superlative, *adj.* Is airde, còrr.
Superlatively, *adv.* Gu barrachdail.
Supernal, *adj.* Nèamhaidh.
Supernatural, *adj.* Thar nàduir.
Supernumerary, *adj.* Còrr.
Superscribe, *v. a.* Sgrìobh air taobh muigh no air cùl litreach.
Superscription, *s.* Cùl-sgrìobhadh.
Supersede, *v.* Cuir air chùl.
Superstition, *s.* Saobh-chràbhadh.
Superstitious, *adj.* Saobh-chràbhach.
Superstruct, *v. a.* Tog, tog air.
Superstruction, *s.* Togail.
Superstructure, *s.* Air-thogail.
Supervise, *v. a.* Seall thairis.
Supervisor, *s.* Fear-rannsachaidh.
Supine, *adj.* Air druime-direach, leisg, màirnealach, coma.
Supineness, *s.* Leisg, tromasanachd.
Supper, *s.* Suipeir.
Supperless, *adj.* Gun suipeir.
Supplant, *v. a.* Cuir á àite le foill.
Supple, *adj.* Sùbailte, so-lùbadh, maoth; carach, miodalach, brosgalach, sodalach, goileamach.
Supplement, *s.* Leasachadh.
Supplemental, Supplementary, *adj.* Leasachail, ath-leasachail.
Suppleness, *s.* Sùbailteachd.
Suppliant, *adj.* Aslachail.
Suppliant, Supplicant, *s.* Fear-aslachaidh, achanaiche.
Supplicate, *v. a.* Aslaich, guidh.
Supplication, *s.* Aslachadh, guidhe, grìosadh, ùrnaigh, achanaich.
Supply, *v. a.* Dean suas; cum ri, seas air son, dean àite.
Supply, *s.* Còmhnadh, cobhair furtachd, deanamh suas, co-leasachadh.
Support, *v. a.* Cùm suas, cùm taic ri, dean cùl-taic, cùm taobh ri, dean còmhnadh le, cuidich, cobhair; beathaich, dìon.
Support, *s.* Taic, cùl-taic; sorchan, còmhnadh, cobhair, cuideachadh.
Supportable, *adj.* So-ghiùlan, so-iomchar, so-fhulang.
Supporter, *s.* Fear cumail suas, dionadair; cul-taic.
Supposable, *adj.* So-shaoilsinn.
Suppose, *v. a.* Saoil, smaointich, baralaich, beachdach.
Supposition, *s.* Saoilsinn, barail, smuain, beachd.
Supposititious, *adj.* Fallsa; breugach.
Supposititiousness, *s.* Fallsachd.
Suppress, *v. a.* Ceannsaich, lùb, cùm fodha, sàraich. falaich, ceil, mùch, cùm sàmhach; cùm a stigh.

SUPPRESSION, *s*. Ceannsachadh, cumail fodha, lùbadh, falach, ceiltinn, mùchadh, cleìth.
SUPPRESSOR, *s*. Ceileadair, mùchadair.
SUPPURATE, *v. a*. Iongraich.
SUPPURAITON, *s*. Iongrachadh.
SUPPURATIVE, *adj*. Iongarach.
SUPRAMUNDANE, *adj*. Os ceann-an-t-saoghail, uachdrach.
SUPRAVULGAR, *adj*. Os ceann a chumanta, barraichte, barrail.
SUPREMACY, *s*. Ard-cheannas, ceannasachd, àrd-uachdranachd,
SUPREME, *adj*. Ard, is àirde.
SURAL, *adj*, Calpach; luirgneach.
SURANCE, *s*. Barantas; urras.
SURCEASE, *v*. Sguir, stad, cuir stad air, cuir crìoch air.
SURCEASE, *s*. Sgur; stad, fosadh.
SURCHARGE, *v, a*. An-luchdaich.
SURCHARGE, *s*. An-luchd, an-truime.
SURCINGLE, *s*. Crios-tàrra, giort.
SURCOAT, *s*. Còt'-uachdair.
SURD, *adj*. Bodhar.
SURDITY, *s*. Buidhre.
SURE, *adj*. Cinnteach, neo-thuisleach, neo-mhearachdach, fìor, fiosrach; daingeann; tèaruinte.
SURE, SURELY, *adv*. Air chinnte, gun teagamh; gu dearbh, gu dimhin, gu fior, gu fìrinneach.
SURFACE, *s*. Uachdar, aghaidh, taobh a muigh, luth a muigh.
SURFEIT, *v*. Sàsaich, lìon, gu sàth; ith gu sàth.
SURFEIT, *s*. Sàsachadh; sàth; tarbhas, teann-shàth, séid, gràin le ithe.
SURGE, *s*. Sùmainn, bòc-thonn.
SURGE, *v. n*. At; éirich, bòc.
SURGEON, *s*. Dearg-léigh, làmh-léigh.
SURGERY, *s*. Dreuchd làmh-léigh.
SURGY, *adj*. Sùmainneach, stuadhach.
SURLINESS, *s*. Iargaltachd.
SURLY, *adj*. Iargalta, doirbh, gruamach, nuarranta, mi-mhodhail; neo-shìobhalta, gnò, gnù, gnùtha.
SURMISE, *s*. Barail, umhaill, saoilsinn.
SURMOUNT, *v. a*. Rach os ceann, rach thairis, buadhaich, thoir buaidh, faigh lamh-an-uachdar.
SURMOUNTABLE, *adj*. So-cheannsachadh.
SURNAME, *s*. Sloinneadh.
SURNAME, *v. a*. Sloinn.
SURPASS, *v. a*. Thoir bàrr, fairtlich, buadhaich; bi os ceann.
SURPASSING, *adj*. Òirdheirc; barrail.
SURPLICE, *s*. Leine-aifrionn.
SURPLUS, *s*. Còrr, barrachd, barrachdas, còrrlach, fuigheall, fuighleach.
SURPRISE, *s*. Ioghnadh, iongantas; fuathas; clisgeadh, uabhas; teachd gun fhios; glacadh gun fhios.
SURPRISE, *v. a*. Thig gun fhios, cuir ioghnadh, clisg, glac gun fhios; thig gun fhaireachadh.
SURPRISING, *part. adj*. Iongantach, neònach, mìorbhuileach.
SURRENDER, *v*. Strìochd, géill; thoir suas; thoir air ais.
SURRENDER, *s*. Strìochdadh, géilleachdainn; toirt thairis, toirt suas.
SURREPTITIOUS, *adj*. Meallta, bradach.
SURROGATION, *s*. Cur an àite neach.
SURROUND, *v. a*. Cuartaich, iomadhruid, iadh mu thimchioll.
SURTOUT, *s*. Còt'-uachdair, faluinn.
SURVEY, *v. a*. Gabh beachd, amhairc, gabh sealladh; tomhais fearann.
SURVEY, *s*. Sealladh, beachd, seall-tuinn thairis; tomhas.
SURVEYOR, *s*. Fear tomhais; fear riaghlaidh, fear-beachdachaidh.
SURVIVE, *v*. Mair beò, bi làthair, mair an déigh, bi beò an déigh.
SURVIVER, SURVIVOR, *s*. An t-aon a bhios a làthair an déigh bàs neach eile.
SUSCEPTIBILITY, *s*. Faireachdainn.
SUSCEPTIBLE, SUSCEPTIVE, *adj*. Mothachail, beothail; a' faireachadh.
SUSCEPTION, *s*. Gabhail.
SUSCIPIENT, *s*. Fear-gabhail.
SUSCITATE, *v. a*. Dùisg, brosnaich.
SUSPECT, *v*. Cuir an amharas, cuir umhaill; bi amharasach, cùm an teagamh; baralaich; saoil ciontach, smaoinich ciontach.
SUSPECTED, *adj*. Fo amharas.
SUSPEND, *v. a*. Croch, cuir an crochadh, dàilich, cuir dàil; cuir á dreuchd car ùine, cùm an ioma-cheist.
SUSPENSE, *s*. Eu-cinnte, teagamh.
SUSPENSION, *s*. Crochadh; bacadh, cur dheth, dàileachadh, grabadh; cumail air ais.
SUSPICION, *s*. Amharus, an-amharus, umhaill; teagamh.
SUSPICIOUS, *adj*. Amharusach; eu-cinnteach; fo amharus.
SUSPIRATION, *s*. Osunn, osnaich.
SUSPIRE, *v. n*. Tarruinn anail; tarruinn osunn, osnaich.
SUSTAIN, *v. a*. Cùm suas, giùlain; cùm taic ri; cuidich; fuilig, cùm beò.
SUSTENANCE, *s*. Biadh, lòn, beathachadh, teachd-an-tìr.
SUSTRATE, *v. n*. Dean cagarsnaich.
SUSTRATION, *s*. Cagar, torman.
SUTLER, *s*. Ceannaiche.
SUTURE, *s*. Tàthadh, ceangal-chnàmh.
SWAB, *s*. Moibean, sguab-làir.

Swab, *v. a.* Glan le moibean.
Swaddle, *v. a.* Paisg, sgaoil.
Swaddle, *s.* Aodach suainidh.
Swag, *v. n.* Croch gu tròm; bi tromsanaich.
Swagger, *v. n.* Dean spaglainn; dean buamasdaireachd, bi spaillichdeil, dean bòsd, dean ràiteachas.
Swaggerer, *s.* Buamasdair, bladhastair, fear spagluinneach, fear spaillichdeil; fear bòsdail.
Swaggy, *adj.* Trom, liobasta, lòdail.
Swain, *s.* Òganach, òigear, fleasgach; tuathanach, buachaille.
Swallow, *s.* Gòbhlachan-gaoithe.
Swallow, *v. a.* Sluig.
Swamp, *s.* Boglach, féith, càthar.
Swampy, *adj.* Bog, càtharach.
Swan, *s.* Eala (*often erroneously written* "ealadh").
Sward, *s.* Fàilean; fòd, sgrath, feur, rùsg; craiceann muice.
Swarm, *s.* Sgaoth, sgann.
Swarm, *v. n.* Cruinnich mar sgaoth.
Swarthy, *adj.* Ciar, odhar, lachdun.
Swash, *s.* Pluinnse, plubartaich.
Swash, *v. a.* Dean plubartaich; dean gleadhraich, dean fuaim.
Swathe, *v. a.* Paisg, spaoil.
Sway, *v.* Riaghail, òrduich; seòl, stiùr; aom; bi cumhachdach.
Sway, *s.* Iomairt, truime; cumhachd; seòladh, riaghladh; smachd.
Sweal, Swale, *v. n.* Caith ás.
Swear, *v.* Mionnaich, thoir mionnan; cuir gu mionnan, gabh mionnan.
Swearer, *s.* Mionntair.
Swearing, *s.* Mionnachadh.
Sweat, *s.* Fallus.
Sweat, *v.* Cuir fallus dhìot, cuir am fallus; saoithrich.
Sweaty, *adj.* Fallusach; goirt.
Sweep, *v.* Sguab, glan; sguids.
Sweep, *s.* Sguabadh; deannadh.
Sweepings, *s.* Trusdaireachd, fòtus.
Sweepnet, *s.* Lìon-sgrìobaidh.
Sweepstakes, *s.* Fear-chosna'-gach-gill.
Sweet, *adj.* Milis, blasda, ùr; cùbhraidh; caoimhneil, caoin, caomh, beulchar, tlà; taitneach, sòlasach, sèimh, ciùin; binn, ceòlmhor; ciatach, laoghach, bòidheach, lùrach, grinn, greannar, màlda.
Sweet, *s.* Mìlse, mìlseachd.
Sweetbread, *s.* Aran-milis.
Sweetbrier, *s.* Feara-dhris.
Sweeten, *v.* Mìlsich; dean milis.
Sweetheart, *s.* Leannan.
Sweetish, *adj.* A leth-char milis.
Sweetmeat, *s.* Mìlsean, biadh-milis.
Sweetness, *s.* Mìlseachd.
Swell, *v.* Ăt, séid, bòc; séid suas, bolg a mach; meudaich, fàs dòmhail.
Swell, *s.* Ăt, séid, dòmhladas; tonn, sumainn, sùmaid.
Swelling, *s.* Ăt, iongrachadh, éiridh, cnap, meall; séideadh, bòcadh.
Swelter, *v.* Tiormach, crion, sgreag.
Sweltry, *adj.* Bruthainneach.
Swerve, *v. n.* Claon, fiar, aom; lùb, rach a thaobh.
Swift, *adj.* Luath, siùbhlach, luainneach, lùghar, lùghmhor, grad, ealamh; clis; deas, èasgaidh.
Swift, *s.* Gobhlan-gainmhich.
Swiftness, *s.* Luathas, luas.
Swig, *v.* Òl gu lonach; gabh balgam mòr.
Swill, *v.* Òl gu lonach; bogaich, fliuch; cuir air mhisg.
Swill, *s.* Sŏs, biadh mhuc.
Swim, *v.* Snàmh; gluais gu fòil.
Swim, *s.* Balg-snàmha.
Swimmer, *s.* Snàmhaiche.
Swimming, *s.* Snàmh; tuaineal.
Swindle, *v. a.* Meall, thoir an car á.
Swindler, *s.* Mealltair, cealgair.
Swindling, *s.* Mealltaireachd.
Swine, *s.* Muc; mucan.
Swineherd *s.* Mucair.
Swing, *v.* Seòg, seòganaich, luaisg, tulg, udail, siùdain, siùd.
Swing, *s.* Greallag; siùdan, tulgadh, seògan, luasgan, luasgadh; cead-féin.
Swinge, *v. a.* Sgiùrs, buail, gabh air.
Swinging, *adj.* Mòr; garbh.
Swingle, *v. n.* Luaisg, seòg, siùd.
Swinish, *adj.* Mucanta; salach.
Switch, *s.* Slat-chaoil, slatag.
Switch, *v. a.* Buail le slait, sgiùrs.
Swivel, *s.* Udalan, seòrsa gunna.
Swobber, *s.* Sguabadair.
Swoon, *v. n.* Rach an neul, rach am plathadh, rach am preathal.
Sword, *s.* Claidheamh, slacan. *Md.*
Swordfish, *s.* An brod-iasg.
Swordman, *s.* Fear-claidheimh.
Swordplayer, *s.* Basbair.
Sycophant, *s.* Sodalaiche.
Sycophantic, *adj.* Sodalach.
Syllabic, Syllabical, *adj.* Lideachail, dùrdach, smideachail.
Syllable, *s.* Lideadh, dùrd, smid.
Syllabus, *s.* Ceann-eagair.
Syllogism, *s.* Argamaid chuairteach.
Sylph, *s.* Sìthiche; màileachan.
Syllogistical, *adj.* Co-argainneach.
Sylvan, *adj.* Coillteach; dubharach.
Sylvan, *s.* Dia-coille.
Symbol, *s.* Samhla, coltas, crùth.
Symbolical, *adj.* Samhlachail.

SYMBOLIZE, *v.* Samhlaich, riochdaich.
SYMMETRICAL, SYMMETRAL, *adj.* Co-fhreagarrach, dealbhach, cumadail.
SYMMETRY, *s.* Co-fhreagarrachd; cumadh, cumadalachd, cumaireachd.
SYMPATHETIC, *adj.* Co-mhothachail; truacanta, co-fhulangach, bàigheil.
SYMPATHIZE, *v. a.* Co-mhothaich, co-fhuilig, comh-fhairich.
SYMPATHY, *s.* Co-mhothachadh, co-fhulangas, truacantas, bàigh.
SYMPHONIOUS, *adj.* Co-shéirmeach.
SYMPHONY, *s.* Co-shéirm.
SYMPTOM, *s.* Comharradh, coltas.
SYMPTOMIC, *adj.* A' tachairt air uairibh.
SYNAGOGUE, *s.* Sinagog. *B.*
SYNCOPE, *s.* Neul; giorrachadh facail.
SYNOD, *s.* Seanadh.
SYNODICAL, *adj.* A bhuineas do sheanadh, seanadhail.
SYNONYMOUS, *adj.* Co-chiallach.
SYNONYMY, *s.* Co-fhacal.
SYNOPSIS, *s.* Giorrachadh.
SYNTAX, *s.* Cur ri chéile fhacal.
SYNTHESIS, *s.* Co-thàthadh.
SYRINGE, *s.* Steallaire, gun-uisge.
SYSTEM, *s.* Riaghailt; dòigh, seòl.
SYSTEMATICAL, *adj.* Riaghailteach.
SYSTOLE, *s.* Crìonadh cridhe; giorrachadh air lideadh fada.

T

T, *s.* Ficheadamh litir na h-Aibidil.
TABBY, *s.* Seorsa sìoda.
TABBY, *adj.* Slatach; stiallach.
TABEFY, *v. n.* Caith, searg, meath.
TABERNACLE, *s.* Pàilliun, bùth.
TABERNACLE, *v. n.* Pàilliunaich.
TABID, *adj.* Éiteachail, gaoideil.
TABLATURE, *s.* Grinneas-balla.
TABLE, *s.* Bòrd; clàr; clàr-innseadh.
TABLECLOTH, *s.* Anart-bùird.
TABLEMAN, *s.* Fear-feòirne.
TABLET, *s.* Bòrdan, clàran.
TABOUR, *s.* Druma-bheag.
TABOURINE, *s.* Druma-meòir.
TABULAR, *adj.* Cèarnach, leacach.
TABULATED, *adj.* Còmhnard, leacach.
TACHE, *s.* Cromag, lùb, dùl.
TACIT, *adj.* Sàmhach, tòsdach, balbh.
TACITURNITY, *s.* Sàmhchair, tòst.
TACK, *v.* Tàth, fuaigh; tionndaidh.
TACK, *s.* Tacaid; aonta; siubhal luinge an aghaidh na gaoithe.
TACKLE, *s.* Acuinn, cungaidh, uidheam; buill; saighead.
TACKLING, *s.* Acuinn-luinge, uidheam.
TACTIC, *adj.* A bhuineas do dh' òrdugh catha.
TACTICS, *s.* Feachd-oilean, cath-ghleus, rian-arm. *Oss.*
TADPOLE, *s.* Ceann-phollag, ceann-simid. *Arg.*
TAFFETA, TAFFETY,* *s.* Seòrsa sìoda.
TAG, *s.* Othaisg; aigilean.
TAG, *v. a.* Tàth, ceangail, fuaigh.
TAIL, *s.* Earball, earr, feaman, breaman, runnsan, rùmpull, ruinns, dronn.
TAILOR, *s.* Tàillear.
TAINT, *v.* Salaich, truaill, mill; bi salach no truaillidh.
TAINT, *s.* Ball, sal, salchar; gaoid; galar; coire, truailleadh.
TAINTURE, *s.* Ball-dubh, salachadh.
TAKE, *v.* Gabh, glac, beir air, cuir làmh air; cuir an làimh.
TAKING, *s.* Glacadh, gabhail, trioblaid.
TALBOT, *s.* Gaothar-ballach.
TALE, *s.* Sgeulachd, sgeul, ùr-sgeul; faoin-sgeul; spleadh.
TALEBEARER, *s.* Fear-tuaileis; breugaire, fear-geòlaim, gobaire.
TALENT, *s.* Tàlann, suim àraidh airgeid; càil, ceud-fàth, comas, feart.
TALISMAN, *s.* Dealbh druidheachd.
TALK, *v. n.* Labhair, bruidhnich.
TAL *s.* Labhairt, bruidheann, cainnt, brosgal, seanachas; conaltradh; iomradh, falthunn; gobais, goileam.
TALKATIVE, *adj.* Bruidhneach, gobach, goileamach, còmhraiteach, beulach, beulchar; brosgalach.
TALKATIVENESS, *s.* Goileam, lonais, gobaireachd, gobais, gusgul.
TALKER, *s.* Geoileamaiche, gobaire.
TALKING, *s.* Còmhradh, cainnt, labhairt, bruidheann, conaltradh.
TALL, *adj.* Àrd, mòr, fada.
TALLNESS, *s.* Àirde.
TALLAGE, *s.* Càin, cìs.
TALLOW, *s.* Geir, igh, blonag.
TALLY, *v.* Dean freagarrach.
TALLY, *s.* Cunntas-eag.

---

* The ancient silk bow-string, denominated *taifeid*, was made of this kind of silk. The fanciful philologists, who would have us to believe that every Gaelic word is of itself pure, furnishes far-fetched definitions of this term. Others take it for an *arrow*, a mistake still more gross. See the "History of Rob Roy," in "Cuirtear nan Gleann," where the contributor, in the poetical part of it, speaks of "*taifeid gheur!*"

Talmud, Thalmud, *s.* Leabhar beul-aithris nan Iùdhach.
Talon, *s.* Ionga, pliut, spuir, spor.
Tamarind, *s.* Meas Innseanach.
Tambarine, *s.* Druma bheag; criathar mion.
Tame, *adj.* Callda, callaidh; ciùin; soirbh; soitheamh; socrach; sòirbh; ceannsaichte.
Tame, *v. a.* Callaich, ciùinich; ceannsaich, dean soirbh, dean soimeach.
Tameness, *s.* Callaidheachd, ciùine; socair; sèimheachd, soirbhe.
Tammy, Taminy, *s.* Stŭth-cŭrainn.
Tamper, *v. a.* Bean ri, bean do, meachranaich, cleachd innleachdan.
Tan, *v.* Cairt; cairtich.
Tang, *s.* Blas làidir, fuaim, guth.
Tangible, *adj.* So-laimhseachadh.
Tangle, *v. a.* Rib, cuir an sàs, cuir air aimhreidh, amhlaich.
Tangle, *s.* Slat-mhara, barr-staimh.
Tank, *s.* Amar-uisge.
Tankard, *s.* Curraighean.
Tanner, *s.* Fear deasachaidh leathair.
Tanpit, *s.* Sloc-cartaidh.
Tansy, *s.* Lŭs-na-Fràing.
Tantalize, *v. a.* Thoir a mach miann.
Tantamount, *adj.* Co-ionann.
Tantivity, *adv.* Le cabhaig.
Tap, *v. a.* Maoth-bhuail, bean; cnag; bris air, fosgail, leig, tarruinn á.
Tap, *s.* Maoth-bhuille; goc, pìobantaosgaidh, pìob-tharruinn.
Tape, *s.* Stìom, crios caol, stiall.
Taper, *adj.* Barra-chaol.
Taper, *v. n.* Dean caol, a' chuid 's a' chuid; fàs barra-chaol.
Taper, *s.* Dreòs, coinneal-chéire.
Tapestry, *s.* Obair-ghréis.
Tapster, *s.* Buidealair.
Tar, *s.* Bìth, teàrr; seòladair.
Tarantula, *s.* Damhan-allaidh.
Tardiness, *s.* Athaiseachd.
Tardy, *adj.* Athaiseach, mall, màirnealach, slaodach, socrach, leisg.
Tare, *s.* Cogull, dìthean.
Target, *s.* Targaid, sgiath.
Tariff, *s.* Cairteal co-cheannachd.
Tarnish, *v.* Salaich, mill; fàs dubh.
Tarpawling, *s.* Cainb-thearra.
Tarry, *v.* Fuirich, stad, dean maille.
Tart, *adj.* Garg, searbh, geur, goirt.
Tart, *s.* Pithean-meas.
Tartan, *s.* Breacan; cadath, catas.
Tartar, *s.* Tart-thìreach, Tartair; sgrisleach, cruaidh-sgrath.
Tartary, *s.* An Tart-thìr.
Tartness, *s.* Gairgead, seirbhe.
Task, *s.* Obair r'a dèanamh; gnìomh.
Tassel, *s.* Cluigein, babaid, babag; froinich; lŭs-na-màighdeinn.
Tases, *s.* Leis-bheart.
Taste, *v.* Blais, gabh blas; feuch.
Taste, *s.* Blas; feuchainn, aithne.
Tastefulness, *s.* Blasdachd.
Tasteless, *adj.* Neo-bhlasta.
Tastelessness, *s.* Neo-bhlastachd.
Taster, *s.* Fear-blasaid; còrn.
Tatter, *v. a.* Reub, srac, stròic.
Tatter, *s.* Luideag, stròic, cearb.
Tatterdemalion, *s.* Luinnsear, ruibealtaich, fear-luideagach.
Tattle, *v. n.* Dean goileam, labhair gu gobach; dean briot.
Tattle, *s.* Goileam, briot, gobair.
Tattler, *s.* Goileamaiche, gobaire.
Tattoo, *s.* Drumadh dhachaigh.
Taunt, *v. a.* Beum, sgeig, mag, dean fochaid air; maslaich.
Taunt, *s.* Beum, geur-fhacal, beurrfhacal; magadh, sgeig, fanaid.
Taunter, *s.* Beumadair.
Tautological, *adj.* Cuairt-bhriathrach, aithriseach.
Tautology, *s.* Cuairt-bhriathran.
Tavern, *s.* Taigh-òsda.
Taw, *v.* Gealaich leathar, alm.
Taw, *s.* Cluiche air bhulagan.
Tawdry, *adj.* Fàoin-bhreagh.
Tawny, *adj.* Odhar, lachdunn, ciar.
Tax, *s.* Cìs-Rìgh, càin.
Tax, *v. a.* Cìs, càin, leag cìs, cuir càin; cronaich, coirich, cuir as leth.
Taxable, *adj.* Buailteach do chìs.
Taxation, *s.* Cìs-leagadh.
Tea, *s.* Tea, tì, teatha. *Irish.*
Teach, *v.* Teagaisg, ionnsaich, oileanaich, foghluim, innis.
Teachable, *adj.* So-theagasg.
Teacher, *s.* Oid-ionnsaich, fear-teagaisg, maighistear-sgoile.
Teague, *s.* Éireannach.
Teal, *s.* Crann-lach.
Team, *s.* Feun; greigh, graidh.
Tear, *s.* Deur, boinne; sracadh, reubadh, stroiceadh.
Tear, *v.* Srac, stròic, reub; spìon, thoir ás a' chéile; bi air boile.
Tearful, *adj.* Deurach, caointeach.
Tease, *v. a.* Cìr, spiol; tlàm; buair, faranaich, cuir dragh air.
Teasel, *s.* Lŭs-an fhŭcadair.
Teat, *s.* Sine, deala.
Technical, *adj.* Ealanta.
Techy, Tetchy, *adj.* Frionasach, dreamach, dodach, crosda, dìorrasach, gèarr, cas, cabhagach.
Ted, *v. a.* Sgaoil feur-saoidh.
Te Déum, *s.* Laoidh naomha.

Tedious, *adj.* Mall, màirnealach, maidheanach, seamsanach; buan.
Teem, *v.* Beir, thoir a mach; bi torrach, bi làn, cuir thairis.
Teemful, *adj.* Torrach, sìolmhor.
Teemless, *adj.* Neo-thorrach.
Teens, *s.* Deugan; eadar dà bliadhna dheug a's fichead bliadhna.
Teeth, *plural* of *tooth.* Fiaclan.
Tegument, *s.* Rùsg, sgrath, cochull.
Teint, *s.* Dath, lì, neul.
Telegraph, *s.* Céin-chagair.
Telescope, *s.* Gloine-amhairc.
Tell, *v.* Innis, aithris, nochd, cuir an céill, foillsich; abair, cunnt, àireamh; thoir fios, cuir fios.
Teller, *s.* Fear-innsidh, cunntair.
Telltale, *s.* Gobaire; fear-aithris; fear-tuaileis.
Temerarious, *adj.* Bras, dàna, cas.
Temerity, *s.* Braise, dànadas.
Temper, *v. a.* Ciùinich; measarraich; measgaich, coimeasg; thoir gu staid fhreagarrach.
Temper, *s.* Nàdur, gné, càil-aignidh; gean; measarrachd, stuaim; ciall; faobhar; fadhairt. *Md.*
Temperament, *s.* Càil, càileachd, staid, nàdur.
Temperance, *s.* Measarrachd, stuamachd, foighidinn, ciùineas.
Temperate, *adj.* Measarra, stuama, foighidneach, ciùin; macanta.
Temperature, *s.* Staid càile-nàduir.
Tempest, *s.* Doireann, doinionn, stoirm, ànradh, an-uair, gailionn.
Tempestuous, *adj.* Ànrach, stoirmeil, gailbheach, doinionnach.
Templar, *s.* Stuidear-san-lagh.
Temple, *s.* Teampull; leth-cheann.
Temporal, *adj.* Aimsireil; talmhaidh.
Temporality, *s.* Séilbh-thalmhaidh.
Temporals, *s.* Nithe saoghalta.
Temporalty, *s.* Am math-shluagh; séilbh neo-eaglaiseil.
Temporary, *adj.* Neo-mhaireann, neo-bhuan, siùbhlach; car ùine, ré seal.
Temporize, *v. n.* Cuir dàil, maillich; aontaich; géill do na h-amannaibh, imich a réir na h-aimsir.
Tempt, *v.* Buair, meall; brosnaich, feuch ri, thoir ionnsaidh; tàlaidh.
Temptation, *s.* Buaireadh, mealladh; cathachadh; brosnachadh.
Tempter, *s.* Buaireadair; mealltair; an t-aibhisdear, an diabhol.
Ten, *s.* Deich, deichnear.
Tenable, *adj.* So-ghleidheadh.
Tenacious, *adj.* Féin-bharaileach, dòchasach; cumailteach, leanailteach, righinn; spìocach, iongach, sporach, crìon, gann.
Tenacity, *s.* Leanailteachd, rìghneachd, cumailteachd.
Tenant, *s.* Tuathanach; fear-aonta.
Tenantable, *adj.* So-àitichte.
Tenantless, *adj.* Neo-àitichte.
Tenantry, *s.* Tuath-cheathairn.
Tench, *s.* Seòrs' éisg àibhne.
Tend, *v.* Gléidh, thoir an airc air, cum sùil air, fair, lean, treòraich; aom; siubhail a dh' ionnsaidh.
Tendence, Tendency, *s.* Aomadh; rùn, miann, seòladh, cùrsa.
Tender, *adj.* Maoth, anfhann, lag, fann, tais, bog; caomh, suairce, còir, caoimhneil, tlùsail, truacanta; caoin, mìn, òg, fiùranta.
Tender, *v. a.* Tairg, nochd.
Tender, *s.* Tairgse; long-fhreacadain.
Tenderhearted, *adj.* Teò-chridheach, tiom-chridheach, blàth-chridheach, tlùsail, truacanta.
Tenderling, *s.* Maoth-chabar.
Tenderness, *s.* Anfhainneachd; maothalachd; ùiread; caomhalachd, tlùs, caoimhneas, bàigh, truacantas; gràdh, gaol; cùram.
Tendinous, *adj.* Féitheach.
Tendon, *s.* Féith-lùghaidh.
Tendril, *s.* Maotharan, faillean.
Tenebrious, *adj.* Dorcha, ghuamach.
Tenement, *s.* Aitreabh, gabhail, &c.
Tenet, *s.* Barail-shuidhichte, beachd; punc-chreidimh.
Tennis, *s.* Cluich-cneutaig.
Tenon, *s.* Làmh.
Tenor, Tenour, *s.* Brìgh, bladh, ciall, seadh; rùn; staid, inbhe; modh; aomadh, claonadh, cùrsa; fuaim; fonn mheadhonach.
Tense, *adj.* Teann, rag, tarruinnte.
Tenseness, *s.* Tinnead, raigead.
Tension, *s.* Teannachadh, sìneadh, ragachadh, tarruinn.
Tent, *s.* Bùth, pubull, pàilliun.
Tentation, *s.* Deuchainn, buaireadh.
Tented, *adj.* Bùthach, pàilliunach.
Tenter, *s.* Cromag, dubhan.
Tenth, *adj.* Deicheamh.
Tenth, *s.* Deicheamh, deachamh.
Tenthly, *adv.* 'San deicheamh àite.
Tenuity, *s.* Tainead; caoile.
Tenuous, *adj.* Tana, caol, meanbh.
Tenure, *s.* Còir-fearainn, gabhaltas.
Tepefaction, *s.* Blàthachadh.
Tepid, *adj.* Meagh-bhlàth.
Tepidity, *s.* Meagh bhlàthas.
Tergeminous, *adj.* Trì-fillte.
Tergiversation, *s.* Dol air ais; cùl-

cheumnachadh, cur dheth ; car ; caochlaideachd, luaineachas.

TERM, *s.* Crìoch, iomall, ceann, ceann-crìche ; facal, briathar; ainm; cùmhnant ; ùine, tìm ; àm suidhe mòid.

TERM, *v. a.* Ainmich, gairm, goir.

TERMAGANT, *adj.* Buaireasach.

TERMAGANT, *s.* Ban-sglàmhrainn.

TERMINABLE, *adj.* So-chrìochnachadh.

TERMINATE, *v.* Crìochnaich.

TERMINATION, *s.* Crìochnachadh.

TERMLESS, *adj.* Neo-chrìochnach.

TERRACE, *s.* Barra-bhalla.

TERRAQUEOUS, *adj.* Talmhuisgidh.

TERRENE, TERRESTRIAL, *adj.* Saoghalta.

TERRESTRIAL, TERRESTRIOUS, *adj.* Talmhaidh, saoghalach.

TERRIBLE, *adj.* Eagalach, uabhasach, uabharra, fuathasach, oillteil.

TERRIER, *s.* Abhac, cù-tagraidh.

TERRIFIC, *adj.* Eagalach, uabhasach, uabharra, fuathasach, oillteil.

TERRIFY, *v. a.* Cuir eagal no oillt air, clisg, geiltich.

TERRITORY, *s.* Tìr, fearann, fonn, dùthaich, talamh.

TERROR, *s.* Eagal, oillt, uabhas ; culaidh-eagail, cùis-eagail.

TERSE, *adj.* Glan, cuimir, grinn.

TERTIAN, *s.* Fiabhras-critheannach.

TESSELATED, *adj.* Daoimeanach.

TEST, *s.* Deuchainn ; ceasnachadh.

TESTACEOUS, *adj.* Sligeach.

TESTAMENT, *s.* Tiomnadh.

TESTAMENTARY, *adj.* A réir tiomnaidh.

TESTATOR, *s.* Fear-tiomnaidh.

TESTATRIX, *s.* Ban-tiomnaidh.

TESTER, *s.* Sè-sgillinn ; brat-leapa.

TESTICLE, *s.* Magairle, clach.

TESTIFY, *v.* Thoir fianais, dearbh.

TESTIMONIAL, *s.* Teisteannas.

TESTIMONY, *s.* Fianais, dearbhadh.

TESTINESS, *s.* Frionasachd, frithearachd, crosdachd, càise.

TESTY, *adj.* Frionasach, crosda, snoigeasach, dranndanach, feargach, cas.

TETE-A-TETE, *s.* Ceann-ri-ceann ; còmhradh càirdeil, conaltradh.

TETHER, *s.* Teaghair, aghastar, taod.

TETTER, *s.* Frìd, miol-chrion.

TEWTAW, TOWTOW, *v. a.* Buail, bris.

TEXT, *s.* Ceann-teagaisg.

TEXTILE, *adj.* So-fhigheadh.

TEXTUARY, *adj.* A réir ceann-teagaisg.

TEXTURE, *s.* Figheadaireachd, fighe.

THAN, *adv.* Na (*erroneously spelt* "no").

THANE, *s.* Morair, iarla.

THANK, *v. a.* Thoir taing, thoir buidheachas.

THANKFUL, *adj.* Taingeil, buidheach.

THANKFULNESS, *s.* Taingealachd.

THANKLESS, *adj.* Mi-thaingeil.

THANKS, *s.* Buidheachas, taing.

THANKOFFERING, *s.* Iobairt-bhuidheachais, ìobairt-thaingealachd.

THANKSGIVING, *s.* Breith-buidheachas.

THAT, *dem. pron.* Sin, ud ; *rel. pro.* a ; *conj.* gu, gu'm, gun, gur, chum. *adv.* a chionn, do bhrìgh, a thaobh.

THATCH, *s.* Tubha, tubhadh.

THATCH, *v. a.* Tubh, dean tubhadh.

THATCHER, *s.* Tubhadair.

THAW, *s.* Aiteamh ; leaghadh.

THAW, *v.* Leagh ; dean aiteamh.

THE, *article, definite.* An, am, a, 'n.

THEATRE, *s.* Taigh-cluiche.

THEATRIC, THEATRICAL, *adj.* Cluicheil.

THEE, *pron. s.* Thu, thusa.

THEFT, *s.* Mèirle, goid, braide.

THEIR, *pron. poss.* An, am.

THEIST, *s.* Dia-chreideach.

THEM, *pron.* Iad, iadsan.

THEME, *s.* Stéidh, cùis, aobhar.

THEMSELVES, *pron.* Iad-féin.

THEN, *adv.* Air sin, air an àm sin, ar déigh sin ; uime sin, mata, mas eadh.

THENCE, *adv.* As a sin, ás an àite sin, o 'n àm sin ; o sin ; air son sin.

THENCEFORTH, *adv.* O 'n àm sin.

THENCEFORWARD, *adv.* O sin suas.

THEOCRACY, *s.* Dia-riaghladh, riaghladh freasdal Dé.

THEODOLITE, *s.* Inneal tomhais.

THEOGONY, *s.* Deé-ghinealachd.

THEOLOGIAN, *s.* Fear-aidmheil diadhachd, diadhaire.

THEOLOGICAL, *adj.* Diadhaireach.

THEOLOGIST, THEOLOGUE, *s.* Diadhair.

THEOLOGY, *s.* Diadhachd.

THEOREM, *s.* Barail ; ràdh fior, fìrinn; barail chum dearbhaidh.

THEORETIC, THEORETICAL, *adj.* Smuainteachail, beachdail, tionnsgalach.

THEORIST, *s.* Beachdair.

THEORY, *s.* Smuainteachadh, beachd; dealbh-inntinn, tionnsgnadh.

THERE, *adv.* An sin, an sud, san àite sin ; do 'n àite sin.

THEREABOUT, *adv.* Air feadh a sin, mu'n àite sin, mu sin ; mu'n tuairmeis sin, mu thimchioll.

THEREAFTER, *adv.* An déigh sin.

THEREAT, *adv.* An sin, aige sin ; air son sin ; 'san àite sin.

THEREBY, *adv.* Le sin, leis a' sin ; teann air a sin, dlù, am fagus.

THEREFORE, *adv.* Uime sin, air an aobhar sin, le sin, air son sin.

THEREFROM, *adv.* O sin, o sud, o' so, uaithe sin, uaithe so.

Therein, *adv.* An sin, ann, a staigh an sin, a steach an sin.
Thereinto, *adv.* A steach ann, ann.
Thereof, *adv.* Do sin, do so, dheth sin.
Thereon, *adv.* Air a sin, air so.
Thereout, *adv.* Á sin, a mach, ás.
Thereto, **Thereunto**, *adv.* Thuige sin, a chum sin, gu sin.
Therewith, *adv.* Leis a sin, air ball.
Therewithal, *adv.* A bharr, a thuileadh, a thuileadh air sin.
Thermometer, *s.* Teas-mheidh.
These, *pron. pl.* Iad, iad so.
Thesis, *s.* Argamaid, argainn. *Arg.*
They, *pron.* Iad, iadsan.
Thick, *adj.* Tiugh, garbh; reamhar.
Thick, *s.* Tiuighead, tiughalachd.
Thick, *adv.* Gu tric, gu minig; gu dlù.
Thicken, *v.* Tiughaich; dòmhlaich; neartaich; binndich, rìghnich; fàs tiugh, fàs dòmhail.
Thicket, *s.* Doire, dhlù-choille, badan.
Thickness, *s.* Tiughad, tiuighead, dòmhlachd, gairbhe; maoilead.
Thickset, *adj.* Dlù, air a' chéile.
Thief, *s.* Mèirleach, gadaiche.
Thiefcatcher, *s.* Maor-mheirleach.
Thieve, *v. n.* Goid, dean méirle.
Thievery, *s.* Méirle, braide, goid.
Thievish, *adj.* Bradach, tiolpach.
Thigh, *s.* Sliasaid, leis.
Thill, *s.* Càs-chùirn; càs-charbaid.
Thimble, *s.* Meuran.
Thin, *adj.* Tana, caol; finealta; seang; gann, tearc; bochd.
Thin, *v. a.* Caolaich, tanaich.
Thine, *pron.* Do, d', leat-sa.
Thing, *s.* Ni, rud, cùis; gnothach.
Think, *v.* Smaointich, saoil, baralàich, meòraich, measraich, meas, cuir an suim; cuimhnich, thoir fainear.
Thinking, *s.* Smaointeachadh; baralachadh; saoilsinn.
Thinness, *s.* Tainead; tearcad, teirce, teircead, ainmigead; caoilead.
Third, *adj.* An treas.
Third, *s.* An trian, treas cuid.
Thirdly, *adv.* Anns an treas àite.
Thirst, *s.* Pathadh, tart; ìotadh; tiormachd; ro-mhiann, ro-dhéidh, ro-gheall, dian-thogradh.
Thirst, *v.* Bi pàiteach, bi tartmhor.
Thirstiness, *s.* Pàiteachd, tartmhorachd, ìotmhorachd; tiormachd.
Thirsty, *adj.* Pàiteach; tartmhor, ìotmhor, tioram, déidheil.
Thirteenth, *adj.* An treas-deug.
Thirteen, *adj.* Trì-deug.
Thirty, *adj.* Deich thar fhichead.
This, *pron. dem.* So, an ni so.
Thistle, *s.* Cluaran, fòthannan.
Thistly, *adj.* Cluaranach.
Thither, *adv.* Thun a sin, an sin, gu ruig a sin, do 'n àite sin.
Thitherto, *adv.* Chum na crìche sin.
Thitherward, *adv.* Gu ruig a sin.
Thong, *s.* Iall, stiall, balt.
Thorax, *s.* Uchd, maothan.
Thoracic, *adj.* Maothanach.
Thorn, *s.* Dris, droigheann.
Thornback, **Thornbut**, *s.* Sgait.
Thorny, *adj.* Driseach, droighneach; stobach; deacair, draghail.
Thorough, *adj.* Iomlan, foirfe.
Thorough, *prep.* Trìd, tre, troimh.
Thoroughfare, *s.* Rathad, slighe.
Thoroughpaced, *adj.* Coimhlionta.
Those, *pron. plural* of *that.* Iad sud, iad sin; sud, sin, ud.
Thou, *the second pron. personal.* Tu, thu.
Though, *conj.* Ged; gidheadh.
Thought, *s.* Smaoin, smuain, aire, beachd, barail, saoilsinn, seadh, suim, cùram; dùil, dòchas, iomagain.
Thoughtful, *adj.* Smaointeachail, smuaireanach; iomaguineach, cùramach, cumhneach, dìomhair.
Thoughtless, *adj.* Neo-smaointeachail, neo-chùramach, neo-fhaicilleach; mi-shuimeil, faoin, baoth, gòrach.
Thoughtsick, *adj.* Iargaineach.
Thousand, *adj.* Mìle, deich ceud.
Thowl, *s.* Urracag, cnag; bac.
Thrall, *s.* Tràill; tràilleachd, daorsa.
Thraldom, *s.* Tràillealachd, daorsa.
Thrash, *v.* Buail; slacainn; gréidh; boicnich, dòrnaich, oibrich, saothraich; sùist, buail arbhar.
Thrasher, *s.* Buailtear.
Thrasonical, *adj.* Ràiteachail; bòsdal.
Thread, *s.* Snàthainn, toinntean.
Thread, *v. a.* Cuir snàthainn troimh.
Threadbare, *adj.* Lom, caithte.
Threat, *s.* Bagairt, maoidheadh.
Threaten, *v. a.* Bagair, maoidh.
Threatening, *s.* Bagradh, mùiseag.
Threatful, *adj.* Bagarrach.
Three, *adj.* Trì, triùir.
Threefold, *adj.* Trì fillte.
Threnody, *s.* Dan-corranaich.
Threshold, *s.* Stairseach.
Thrice, *adv.* Trì uairean.
Thrift, *s.* Deagh bhuil, sùrd.
Thriftiness, *s.* Fearas-taighe.
Thriftless, *adj.* Neo-shùrdail, neo-dhèanadach; stròghail.
Thrifty, *adj.* Sùrdail; gnìomhach, dèanadach, cùramach, gléidhteach.
Thrill, *v.* Toll; guin; cuir gaoir ann; dean fuaim geur; clisg, crith.

Thrive, *v. n.* Soirbhich; cinn, fàs.
Throat, *s.* Sgòrnan, sgòrnach. *Ir.*
Throb, *s.* Plosg, plosgart, ospag.
Throb, *v. n.* Dean plosgartaich, ploisg.
Throe, *s.* Ospag, uspag, éigin, greim; pian, saothair, frith-bhualadh.
Throne, *s.* Cathair, rìgh-chathair.
Throng, *s.* Dòmhladas, mòr-shluagh.
Throng, *v. n.* Dòmhlaich, teannaich; mùch; brùth, trus, cruinnich.
Throstle, *s.* Smeòrach.
Throttle, *s.* Sealbhan.
Throttle, *v. a.* Tachd, mùch.
Through, *prep.* Troi, tre, trìd.
Throughout, *adv.* Troimh; o cheann gu ceann; gu crìch, gu deiridh, anns gach àite, feagh gach àite.
Throughly, *adv.* Gu tŭr, gu h-uile.
Throw, *v.* Tìlg; thoir urchair, tilg sìos, leag; tilg air falbh.
Throwster, *s.* Fear-tacrais sìoda.
Thrum, *s.* Fuidheag.
Thrum, *v. a.* Dean dreangail chluiche.
Thrush, *s.* Smeòrach.
Thrust, *v.* Sàth; spàrr; put, pùc, purr, dinn, fuadaich, thoir ionnsaidh; torchuir, troi'-lot.
Thrust, *s.* Sàthadh, sparradh, pucadh, purradh, ionnsaidh ghuineach.
Thryfallow, *v. a.* Dean treas-threabhadh, dean treas-eilbheadh. *N. H.*
Thumb, *s.* Òrdag làimhe.
Thumb, *v. a.* Meuraich, làimhsich.
Thump, *s.* Buille, gleadhar, stràc.
Thump, *v.* Buail; slacainn, dòrnaich.
Thunder, *s.* Tàirneanach.
Thunder, *v.* Tàirneanaich; maoidh le briathraibh bòrb, dean tàirnthoirm, no stairirich.
Thunderbolt, *s.* Beithir.
Thunderclap, *s.* Bradh torrainn.
Thunderer, *s.* Tàirneanaiche.
Thunderstruck, *adj.* Buailte le dealanach; fo amhluadh; air grad chlisgeadh; fo oillt.
Thunderous, *adj.* Torrannach.
Thursday, *s.* Diar-daoin.
Thus, *adv.* Mar so, air an dòigh so.
Thwack, *v. a.* Buail, spuac, cnap.
Thwack, *s.* Buille, gleadhar, dòrn.
Thwart, *adj.* Crosgach, tarsainn; trasta, crosta, reasgach, draghail.
Thwart, *v.* Cuir an aghaidh; cuir tarsainn, thig tarsainn; bi 'n aghaidh, seas an aghaidh.
Thy, *pron.* of *thee.* Do, d', t'.
Thyme, *s.* Mionnt, meannt.
Thyself, *pron. recip.* Tu-féin, thu-féin, thu-fhéin, thusa-féin.
Tiar, **Tiara**, *s.* Crùn, coron, fleasg.
Tick, *s.* Creideas; earbsa; feursanan, ua-mial, mial-chon; aodach-adhairt; buille uaireadair.
Ticket, *s.* Cairt-chomharraidh.
Tickle, *v.* Diogail, ciogail; taitinn.
Ticklish, *adj.* Ciogailteach; deacair.
Tiddle, *v. a.* Dean mùirn, dean beadradh; mùirnich, breug, tàlaidh.
Tide, *s.* Seòl-mara, làn-mara, sruth, buinne-shruth, àm, ùin, tràth.
Tidewaiter, *s.* Maor-cuspainn.
Tidiness, *s.* Sgioltachd, sgiobaltachd.
Tidings, *s.* Naidheachd; sgeul.
Tidy, *adj.* Sgiolta, sgiobalta, cuimir.
Tie, *v. a.* Ceangail, snaim.
Tie, *s.* Ceangal, snaim, bann.
Tier, *s.* Sreath, breath, sreud.
Tierce, *s.* Togsaid-gu-'trian.
Tiff, *s.* Deoch; dod, snoigeas.
Tiger, *s.* Tìgeir, fiadh-bheathach mòr céin-thireach air chumadh cait.
Tight, *adj.* Teann; gramail, cuimir.
Tighten, *v. a.* Teannaich, daingnich, dìonaich, dlùthaich.
Tightness, *s.* Teinnead, daingneachd.
Tigress, *s.* Bann-tìgeir.
Tile, *s.* Criadh-leac.
Tiler, *s.* Tughadair, chriadh-leac.
Tiling, *s.* Tughadh chriadh-leac.
Till, *s.* Cobhan airgeid.
Till, *prep.* Gu, gus, gu ruig, thun.
Till, *v. a.* Àitich, treabh, ruamhair, oibrich, saothraich, saoithrich.
Tillable, *adj.* So-àiteach.
Tillage, *s.* Treabhadh, ar.
Tiller, *s.* Treabhaiche; ailm.
Tilt, *s.* Arm-chleas, bùth, sgàilean; còmhdach; aomadh.
Tilt, *v.* Rach an dàil, ruith an aghaidh; aom, còmhdaich, cathaich le cuinnsearaibh.
Timber, *s.* Fiodh; maide.
Timbered, *adj.* Fiodha.
Timbrel, *s.* Tìompan.
Time, *s.* Ùin, àm, aimsir, uair, tràth, tìm, ùine. *Arg.*
Time, *v. a.* Cùm tìm, tràthaich.
Timeful, *adj.* Tìmeil, tràthail.
Timekeeper, **Timepiece**, *s.* Tràthadair, uaireadair, uaradair. *N. H.*
Timeless, *adj.* Neo-thìmeil; roi'n àm, roi'n mhithich.
Timely, *adj.* An deagh àm; ann an deagh thràth, tràthail.
Timeserving, *adj.* Strìochdach, do'n tìm, do réir an àma.
Timid, *adj.* Gealtach, clisgeach.
Timidity, **Timorousness**, *s.* Gealtachd, sgàthachd, cladhaireachd, meath-chridheachd, athadh.

Timorous, *adj.* Eagalach, sgàthach.
Tin, *s.* Staoin, iarunn-geal.
Tincture, *s.* Dath, lìth; sùgh.
Tincture, *v. a.* Dath, cuir lìth air.
Tinder, *s.* Fadadh-spùinge.
Tine, *v. a.* Fadaich, lăs, cuir ri theine.
Tine, *s.* Fiacail cliath-chliathaidh.
Tinge, *v. a.* Dath, lìth; salaich.
Tingle, *v. n.* Gliong, dean gaoir, cluinn gaoir, cluinn fuaim, fairich crith-ghluasad.
Tinker, *s.* Cèard, dubh-cheard.
Tinkle, *v.* Gliong, dean gliongarsaich; thoir gliong air.
Tinman, *s.* Cèard-staoine.
Tinsel, *s.* Faoin-bhreaghas.
Tinsel, *adj.* Basdalach, soillseach.
Tint, *s.* Dath, lìth, neul, tuar.
Tiny, *adj.* Crìon, meanbh, beag.
Tip, *s.* Bàrr, binnein, biod.
Tip, *v. a.* Cuir mullach air; bean.
Tippet, *s.* Éididh-muineil.
Tipple, *v.* Bi déidheil air òl, dean pòit.
Tippler, *s.* Misgear, pòitear.
Tipsy, *adj.* Air mhisg, soganach, froganach, froidhleach.
Tiptoe, *s.* Corra-biod.
Tire, *s.* Sréad, sreath, breath; aodach-cinn, àirneis, acuinn.
Tire, *v.* Sgìthich, sàraich, dean sgìth; fàs sgìth; éid, sgeadaich.
Tired, *adj.* Sgìth, sgìthichte.
Tiresome, *adj.* Sgìtheachail.
Tirewoman, *s.* Ban-fhuaidhealaiche.
Tiringroom, *s.* Seòmar-sgeadachaidh.
Tissue, *s.* Òrneileìs.
Tit, *s.* Each beag; bean; eun.
Tithe, *s.* Deicheamh, deachamh; chàin; cléir-chàin, deachmhadh. *Ir.*
Titheable, *adj.* Buailteach do chàin.
Tither, *s.* Fear-trusaidh deachaimh.
Titillation, *s.* Giogal, ciogailt, diogladh, druideadh, drunnsail.
Title, *s.* Tiodal, ainm; còir, dlighe.
Title, *v. a.* Ainmich, goir, tiodalaich.
Title-page, *s.* Clàr-ainme.
Titmouse, **Tit**, *s.* Am mionnaran.
Titter, *v. n.* Dean fa-ghàire.
Tittle, *s.* Pong, pung; lideadh.
Tittle-tattle, *s.* Goileam; lonais.
Titubation, *s.* Tuisleachadh.
Titular, *adj.* Ainmichte.
To, *prep.* Do, a dh' ionnsaidh; ri, ris; gu; gus; chum, gu ruig; thun. *Sign of the infinitive.* A.
Toad, *s.* A mhial-mhâgach, màgach.
Toadstool, *s.* Balg-losgainn.
Toast, *s.* Deoch-slàinte; aran-caoin.
Toast, *v.* Òl deoch-slàinte; thoir deoch-slàinte; caoinich.
Tobacco, *s.* Tombaca.
Tobacconist, *s.* Fear reic tombaca.
Tod, *s.* Ochd puint fhichead olla.
Toes, *s.* Meòirean nan cas.
Together, *adv.* Le chéile, còmhlath, còmhluath, mar chòmhlath, li chéile, cuideachd; maraon; gu léir.
Toil, *v.* Saoithrich, oibrich; gabh saothair; sgìthich, sàraich.
Toil, *s.* Saothair, obair ghoirt.
Toilet, *s.* Bòrd-sgeadachaidh.
Toilsome, *adj.* Saoithreachail, goirt.
Toilsomeness, *s.* Sgìos.
Token, *s.* Cuimhneachan, tabhartas, comharradh; comhar. *Ps.*
Told, *part.* Dh' innis, thubhairt; dh' aithris; chùnnt.
Tolerable, *adj.* So-fhulang; meadhonach, an eatorras, cùibheasach; mar sin fhéin; mu 'n làimh.
Tolerance, *s.* Fulangas.
Tolerate, *v. a.* Fuilig, ceadaich.
Toleration, *s.* Fulang, comas.
Toll, *s.* Càin, cìs; buille cluig.
Toll, *v. a.* Beum no buail clag.
Tollbooth, *s.* Toll-bùth, toll-dubh.
Tomb, *s.* Tuam, tùnga, tùngais. *R. D.*
Tombless, *adj.* Gun uàigh; gun leac.
Tomboy, *s.* Caile-bhalach.
Tombstone, *s.* Tuam-leac, leac-laidhe, leac-lighidh, leac-uaghach.
Tome, *s.* Earrann-leabhair.
Ton, *s.* Tunna, cuthrom dà, mhìle punt; nòs, àird' an fhasain.
Tone, *s.* Fonn, fuaim; gleus.
Tong, *s.* Crambaid, teanga, bucail.
Tongs, *s.* Clobha, maide-briste. *Ir.*
Tongue, *s.* Teanga; cainnt, cànan.
Tongue, *v.* Troid; tachair ri.
Tonguetied, *adj.* Manntach, gagach.
Tonic, *adj.* Gleusach, guthach.
Tonnage, *s.* Tunna-chìs.
Tonsure, *s.* Bearradh, lomairt.
Too, *adv.* Cuideachd, fòs, mar an ceudna; tuilleadh 's a' chòir.
Took, *pret.* of *take.* Ghabh.
Tool, *s.* Ball-acainn, cùngaidh.
Tooth, *s.* Fiacail.
Toothach, *s.* Déideadh, cnuimh.
Toothless, *adj.* Gun fhiaclan.
Toothpick, *s.* Bior-fhiacal.
Toothsome, *adj.* Deagh-bhlasda.
Top, *s.* Mullach, bàrr, binnein, bidein, uachdar, druim, bràighe, roinn; gille-mirean.
Top, *v.* Barraich; thoir barrachd, bearraich, còmhdaich mullach; thoir barrachd, thoir bàrr, smàl.
Topaz, *s.* Clach-bhuidhe phrìseil.
Tope, *v. n.* Pòit, bi air mhisg.

Toper, *s.* Pòitear, misgear.
Topful, *adj.* Lom-làn, dearr-làn.
Topgallant, *s.* Baideal. *Md.*
Tophet, *s.* Ifrinn, an dù-shloc.
Topic, *s.* Ceann-còmhraidh, stéidh.
Topknot, *s.* Dos-cinn.
Topmost, *adj.* Uachdrach.
Topography, *s.* Tìr-chunntas, sgrìobhadh mu dhéibhinn àiteachan.
Topsail, *s.* Seòl-àrd, rò-sheòl.
Topstone, *s.* Clach-mhullaich.
Topsy-turvy, *s.* Bun-os-ceann.
Tor, *s.* Binnein cruach.
Torch, *s.* Leus, dòrn-leus.
Torment, *v. a.* Cràidh, pian, claoidh.
Torment, *s.* Cràdh, pian, pianadh, claoidh, àmhghar, dòrainn.
Tormentor, *s.* Claoidheadair, fear pianaidh, fear-léiridh.
Tormentil, *s.* Cara-mhil-a'-choin, leanartach, cairt-bhlàir. *Lew.*
Tornado, *s.* Ioma-ghaoth.
Torpedo, *s.* Orc-iasg.
Torpent, *adj.* Marbh, marbhanach.
Torpid, *adj.* Gun chlì, gun chàil.
Torpidness, *s.* Marbhantachd.
Torpor, *s.* Marbhanta, cion lùis.
Torrent, *s.* Beum-sléibhe, bras-shruth.
Torrid, *adj.* Teth, tioram, loisgeach.
Tort, *s.* Beud, dochan, cron.
Tortile, **Tortive**, *adj.* Sniamhanach, dualach, faineach, cuairteagach.
Tortoise, *s.* Sligeanach.
Tortuous, *adj.* Snìomhach, lùbach.
Torture, *s.* Cràdh, pian, claoidh.
Torture, *v. a.* Cràidh, pian, claoidh, sàraich, léir, cuir gu cràdh.
Tory, *s.* Fear taobh rìgh.
Toss, *v.* Luaisg, gluais, tilg, thoir urchair; tilg sios agus suas; tilg a null 's a nall; siùdain, seòganaich.
Tosspot, *s.* Pòitear, misgear.
Total, *adj.* Iomlan, uile; làn.
Totally, *adv.* Gu léir.
Totter, *v. n.* Crithich, crith, turamanaich, bi tuiteam.
Touch, *s.* Beantainn; buntuinn; mothachadh, feuchainn, deuchainn; cǎr; speal, greadan; suaip; buille; beagan, rud-eigin; làimhseachadh.
Touch, *v.* Bean do, buin do, buin ri, cuir meur air, cuir corrag air, laimhsich; drùigh air.
Touch-hole, *s.* Toll-cluaise.
Touching, *adj.* Drùighteach.
Touchstone, *s.* Clach-dearbhaidh.
Touchwood, *s.* Caisleach spuinge.
Touchy, *adj.* Crosda, frithearra, cas.
Tough, *adj.* Righinn; buan; teann.
Toughen, *v. n.* Rìghnich, dean righinn
Toughness, *s.* Rìghneachd, rìghnead
Tour, *s.* Turas, cuairt, astar.
Tourist, *s.* Fear-turais, fear-cuairt.
Tournament, *s.* Cath-chleasachd.
Tourniquet, *s.* Casg-fala.
Touse, *v.* Slàoid, tarruinn; reub, spìon.
Tow, *s.* Ǎsgart, pab; barrach. *Is.*
Tow, *v. a.* Slaoid, tre uisge.
Toward, *adj.* A ullamh, aontachail.
Toward, *adv.* Fagus, air aghaidh, deas.
Towards, *prep.* Chum; mu thimchioll.
Towel, *s.* Tubhailte, searadair.
Tower, *s.* Tùr, tòr, dùn, turaid; caisteal; daingneach; currac-àrd.
Tower, *v. n.* Itealaich gu h-àrd.
Towery, *adj.* Tùrach, turaideach.
Town, *s.* Baile-mòr; baile-margaidh.
Townclerk, *s.* Cléireach baile.
Townsman, *s.* Comh-bhailiche.
Toxical, *adj.* Nimheach, nimheil.
Toy, *s.* Ǎilleagan, déideag.
Toy, *v. n.* Cluich; dean mire, dean sùgradh, dean beadradh.
Trace, *v. a.* Lorgaich; rach air tòir; comharraich a mach.
Traces, *s.* Beairt-iall, beairt-dhreollaig, beairt-tharuinn, beairt-shlaoid.
Tracer, *s.* Lorgair, cù-luirg.
Track, *s.* Lorg, aile, frith-rathad.
Trackless, *adj.* Gun slighe, gun cheum.
Tract, *s.* Dùthaich; cùrsa; leabhran.
Tractable, *adj.* Soitheamh, soirbh; so-theagasg; aontachail, ciùin.
Tractableness, *s.* Soimeachas; socair.
Tractile, *adj.* A ghabhas bualadh a mach, so-bhualadh a mach.
Trade, *s.* Cèaird; ealain; co-cheannachd, malairt; cleachdadh, gnàths.
Trade, *v.* Dean ceannachd; malairtich.
Trader, *s.* Fear-malairt.
Tradesman, *s.* Fear-ceirde, fear-bùth.
Tradition, *s.* Beul-aithris, beul-oideas.
Traditional, **Traditionary**, *adj.* Beul-aithriseach, beul-iomraidheach.
Traduce, *v. a.* Cul-chàin, dean tarcuis.
Traducement, *s.* Cùl-chaineadh, tàir.
Traducer, *s.* Fear cùl-chàinidh.
Traduction, *s.* Tarruinn; aithrǐs.
Traffic, *s.* Ceannachd, bathar. *Arg.*
Trafficker, *s.* Fear-malairt.
Tragedian, *s.* Sgrìobhadair bròin-chluich, cleasaiche bròin-chluich.
Tragedy, *s.* Bròn-chluich.
Tragic, **Tragical**, *adj.* Brònach.
Tragicomedy, *s.* Cluich bròin-'s aoibhneis, cluich broin is aighir.
Trail, *v.* Slaoid, tarruinn; lorgaich.
Trail, *s.* Lorg; sguain, slaod.
Train, *v. a.* Tarruinn; meall; tog, àraich; teagaisg, ionnsaich; cleachd.

Train, *s* Mealladh ; cuideachd, buidheann ; slaod, earball, iomall ; òrdugh, cùrsa ; luchd-leanmhainn.
Trainbands, *s.* Dìon-fheachd.
Trainoil, *s.* Ola muice-mara.
Trait, *s.* Buille ; tuar, suaip.
Traitor, *s.* Fear-brathaidh.
Traitorly, Traitorous, *adj.* Brathach ; fealltach, slaoighteil.
Traitress, *s.* Bana-bhrathadair.
Trammel, *s.* Lìon ; ribe ; cuibhreach.
Trammel, *v. a.* Glac, rib ; grab, stad.
Trample, *v. a.* Saltair, breab.
Trance, Transe, *s.* Neul, plathadh.
Tranced, *adj.* Ann an neul.
Tranquil, *adj.* Sàmhach, sìochail, ciùin, fèitheil, sèimh, stòlta.
Tranquillity, *s.* Sàmhchair, ciùineas.
Tranquillize, *v.* Sithich, ciùinich.
Transact, *v. a.* Dean gnothach ; cuir air aghart, cuir gu dòigh.
Transaction, *s.* Gnothach, gnìomh.
Transcend, *v. a.* Rach thairis, thoir barrachd, thoir barr.
Transcendence, Transcendency, *s.* Barrachd, barrachas, barr-mhaise.
Transcendent, *adj.* Barrachdail.
Transcribe, *v. a.* Ath-sgrìobh.
Transcriber, *s.* Ath-sgrìobhair.
Transcript, *s.* Ath-sgrìobhadh.
Transcription, *s.* Ath-sgrìobhadh.
Transfer, *v. a.* Thoir thairis ; reic.
Transfer, *s.* Malairt ; toirt thairis.
Transferable, *adj.* So-thoirt thairis.
Transfiguration, *s.* Cruth-chaochladh, cruth-atharrachadh.
Transfigure, *v. a.* Cruth-atharraich.
Transfix, *v. a.* Troi'-lot, sàth.
Transform, *v. a.* Cruth-atharraich.
Transformation, *s.* Cruth-atharrachadh, cruth-chaochladh.
Transfuse, *v. a.* Coimeasg.
Transgress, *v.* Rach thairis ; ciontaich.
Transgression, *s.* Cionta, easantas.
Transgressive, *adj.* Ciontach.
Transgressor, *s.* Ciontach, peacach.
Transient, *adj.* Diombuan, siùbhlach, neo-mhaireann, caochlaideach.
Transientness, *s.* Diombuanas.
Transit, *s.* Eadar-dhol.
Transition, *s.* Imeachd, caochla.
Transitory, *adj.* Siùbhlach, diombuan, caochlaideach, neo-mhaireann.
Translate, *v. a.* Eadar-theangaich ; atharraich, tionndaidh.
Translation, *s.* Eadar-theangachadh.
Translator, *s.* Eadar-theangair.
Transluency, *s.* Trid-shoillseachd.
Translucid, Translucent, *s.* Trid-shoilleir, tre-shoillseach, glan.
Transmarine, *adj.* Thall thar chuan.
Transmigrate, *v. a.* Rach o thìr gu tìr.
Transmigration, *s.* Cian-imrich.
Transmission, *s.* Cur o àite gu àite.
Transmissive, *adj.* Air a chur sios o neach gu neach.
Transmit, *v. a.* Cuir o àite gu àite.
Transmutable, *adj.* Mùthach.
Transmutation, *s.* Tŭr-chaochla.
Transmute, *v. a.* Tur-chaochail.
Transom, *s.* Tarsannan, rùngas.
Transparency, *s.* Trìd-shoillse, glaine.
Transparent, *adj.* Trìd-shoilleir, glan.
Transpierce, *v. a.* Troi'-shàth.
Transpire, *v.* Rach an ceò ; bris a mach, thig am folais.
Transplace, *v. a.* Atharraich, cuir ás àite, cuir do dh' àit' eile.
Transplant, *v. a.* Ath-shuidhich.
Transport, *v. a.* Thoir o àite gu àite ; giùlain, iomchair, fògair, sgiùrs.
Transport, *s.* Long-ghiùlan ; iomchar, buaireadh ; éibhneas ; fògarach.
Transportation, *s.* Fògradh.
Transposal, *s.* Atharrachadh.
Transpose, *v. a.* Atharraich.
Transposition, *s.* Atharrachadh.
Transubstantiate, *v. a.* Brìgh-atharraich, brìgh-mhùth.
Transubstantiation, *s.* Brìgh-atharrachadh, brìdh-chaochla.
Transude, *v. n.* Rach seachad an ceò.
Transverse, *v. a.* Mùth ; caochail.
Transverse, *adj.* Crasgach, trasta.
Transversely, *adv.* Gu crasgach.
Trap, *s.* Ribe, painntear.
Trap, *v. a.* Rib, glac ; cuir an sàs.
Trap-door, *s.* Dorus-dìomhair.
Trappings, *s.* Rìmheadh ; briaghas.
Trash, *s.* Ni gun fhiù ; trusdaireachd.
Trashy, *adj.* Suarach, gun fhiù.
Travail, *v.* Bi ri saothair chloinne ; sàraich, claoidh, pian, sgìthich.
Travail, *s.* Saothair, éigin, obair, sgìtheachadh ; saothair chloinne.
Travel, *v.* Rach air-thuras, triall, siubhail thairis air ; falbh, gluais, imich ; saothraich, saoithrich.
Travel, *s.* Turas, taisdeal, siubhal.
Traveller, *s.* Fear turais, fear-astair, fear-sìubhail, coisiche, taisdea'aiche, fear gabhail an rathaid.
Travelling, *s.* Siubhal, imeac d.
Traverse, *adv.* Gu tarsainn,
Traverse, *adj.* Tarsainn, fiar.
Traverse, *v.* Seòl tarsainn, siu hail, triall ; coisich, imich ; grab, bac ; cuir crasgach, rannsaich.
Travesty, *adj.* Neònach ; baoth.
Tray, *s.* Sgàl, sgùil ; losaid.

Treacherous, *adj.* Mealltach.
Treachery, *s.* Ceilg, brath, foill.
Treacle, *s.* Dràbhag siùcair.
Tread, *v.* Saltair, ceumnaich; cliath.
Tread, *s.* Ceum; slighe, rathad.
Treadles, *s.* Casan-beaga breabadair.
Treason, *s.* Ar-a-mach, ceannairc.
Treasonable, *adj.* Foilleil.
Treasure, *s.* Ionmhas, maoin.
Treasure, *v. a.* Taisg, cuir seachad.
Treasurer, *s.* Fear-coimheid-ionmhais.
Treasury, *s.* Ionad an-ionmhais.
Treat, *v.* Socraich, cuir gu dòigh; labhair air; laimhsich; gnàthaich; gabh ri; cùmhnantaich; thoir cuirm.
Treat, *s.* Fleagh, cuirm, féisd. *Arg.*
Treatise, *s.* Seanachas, sgrìobhte.
Treatment, *s.* Gnàthachadh.
Treaty, *s.* Bann, cùmhnant; còrdadh; suidheachadh chùisean.
Treble, *adj.* Trì-fillte; binn, cruaidh.
Tree, *s.* Craobh, crann, dŏs.
Trefoil, *s.* An trì-bhileach.
Trellis, *s.* Obair-chliath.
Tremble, *v. n.* Crith, criothnaich.
Trembling, *adj.* Critheanach.
Trembling, *s.* Criothnachadh.
Tremendous, *adj.* Fuathasach, uabhasach, eagalach, uabharra, oillteil.
Tremor, *s.* Ball-chrith.
Tremulous, *adj.* Critheanach, eagalach.
Tren, *s.* Mòr-ghath éisg.
Trench, *v. a.* Cladhaich, claisich.
Trench, *s.* Clais-bhlàir, sloc, dìg.
Trencher, *s.* Trinnsear.
Trepan, *v. a.* Rib, glac, meall.
Trepan, *s.* Boireal; ribe, painntear.
Trepidation, *s.* Geilt-chrith.
Trespass, *v. n.* Ciontaich, peacaich.
Trespass, *s.* Cionta, peacadh, ainguidheachd, coire, easantas, briseadh-riaghailte, aindlighe.
Tress, *s.* Caisreag, ciabhag, bachlag, camag, dual, flann.
Tressy, *adj.* Bachlagach, camagach, caisreagach, ciabhagach, dualach.
Trestle, **Tressel**, *s.* Sorachan.
Tret, *s.* Luathsachadh tomhais.
Trevet, *s.* Trì-chasach.
Trey, *s.* An treas ball do chairtean no do dhìsnean.
Triad, *s.* Triùir; triear.
Trial, *s.* Deuchainn; dearbhadh; spàirn, strìth; buaireadh; cùis-lagha.
Triangle, **Trigon**, *s.* Trì-chearnag.
Triangular, *adj.* Trì-chearneach.
Tribe, *s.* Treubh, fine, cinneadh, clann, teaghlach, sliochd, sìol; seòrsa, pòr.
Tribulation, *s.* Trioblaid, àmhghar, teinn, teanntachd, an-shocair, éigin.
Tribunal, *s.* Cathair-breitheanais cùirt-lagha, mòd-ceartais.
Tribune, *s.* Ceann-feadhna Ròimheach.
Tributary, *adj.* Fo cheannsal.
Tribute, *s.* Cìs, càin; ùmhlachd.
Trice, *s.* Tiota; sealan; gradag.
Trick, *s.* Car, cleas, cuilbheart.
Trick, *v.* Meall, thoir an car á; sgeadaich, uidheamaich.
Tricking, *s.* Sgeadachadh, caradh.
Trickle, *v. n.* Sil, sruth, ruith.
Trident, *s.* Muirghe; coron-meurach.
Triduan, *adj.* Gach treas latha.
Triennial, *adj.* Gach treas bliadhna.
Trifle, *v. n.* Dean bàbhdaireachd, caith aimsir gu diomhain.
Trifle, *s.* Faoineas; rud beag, ni gun fhiù, ni suarach.
Trifler, *s.* Bàbhdaire.
Trifling, *adj.* Bàbhdach, gun fhiù; beag, crion, suarach.
Trifoliate, *adj.* Trì-dhuilleach.
Trigger, *s.* Iarunn-leigidh.
Trigon, *s.* Trì-shlisneag.
Trigonal, *adj.* Trì-oisneach.
Trigonometry, *s.* Tomhas nan-trian.
Trilateral, *adj.* Trì-shlisneach.
Trill, *s.* Caireall, crith, crith-cheòl.
Trillion, *s.* Muillean mhuillean de mhuilleanan.
Trim, *v.* Uidheamaich, gleus, deasaich, cuir gu dòigh; cuir an òrdugh; càirich, snas, ceartaich.
Trim, *s.* Uidheam, gleus, òrdugh.
Trim, *adj.* Glan, sgiobalta, speisealta, sgeinmeil; cuimir, cuanta.
Trimmer, *s.* Fear-leam-leat; geinn.
Trimming, *s.* Sgiamh, breaghas.
Trinity, *s.* An Trianaid.
Trinket, *s.* Àilleagan, seud.
Trio, *s.* Ceòl-triùir.
Trip, *v.* Cuir camacag; cuir bacag, tuislich, sleamhnaich; gabh ceum; rach am mearachd.
Trip, *s.* Bacag; tuisleadh, mearachd; turas beag, astaran.
Tripartite, *adj.* An trì earrannaibh.
Tripe, *s.* Maodal; grealach.
Triphthong, *s.* Trì-fhoghair.
Triple, *adj.* Trì-fillte.
Triplet, *s.* Trì do dh'aon seòrsa.
Triplicate, *adj.* Trìoblaichte.
Tripod, *s.* Stòl trì-chasach.
Tripoly, *s.* Gaineamh-gheur.
Tripping, *adj.* Iullagach, luath.
Trisyllable, *s.* Trì-shiola.
Trite, *adj.* As an fhasan; caithte.
Tritheism, *s.* Aoradh nan trì dia.
Triturable, *adj.* So-phronnadh.
Trituration, *s.* Pronnadh.

Triumph, *s.* Buaidh-chaithream; glòir; buaidh; gàirdeachas.
Triumph, *v.* Dean buaidh-chaithream, dean luathghair; faigh buaidh; giùlain buaidh gu tarcuiseach.
Triumphal, Triumphant, *adj.* Buadhach, buadhor; caithreamach.
Triumvirate, *s.* Riaghladh triùir.
Triune, *adj.* Tri-aon, mar an trionaid.
Trivet, *s.* Trì-chasach.
Trivial, *adj.* Faoin; suarrach; gun fhiù, gun seadh, gun suim, coitcheann.
Trod, Trodden, *part. pass.* of *to tread.* Saltairte fo chasaibh.
Troll, *v.* Ruidhil; ruith mu 'n cuairt; dean iasgach gheadas; cuir air falbh gu siùbhlach.
Trollop, *s.* Draip, sgliùrach, botrumaid, dubh-chaile, trusdar caile.
Troop, *v. n.* Ruith am buidheann; triall le cabhaig.
Troop, *s.* Buidheann, bannal, cuideachd; trùp, marc-shluagh.
Trooper, *s.* Trùpair, saighdear-eich.
Trope, *s.* Mùthadh seadh facail.
Trophied, *adj.* Cosgarra; sgeadaichte le buaidh-shuaicheantais.
Trophy, *s.* Craobh-chosgair.
Tropic, *s.* An grian-stad.
Tropical, *adj.* Samhlachail.
Trot, *v.* Trot; cuir na throtan.
Trot, *s.* Trot, trotail, trotan.
Troth, *s.* Creideas; fìrinn, briathar.
Trotter, *s.* Cas caorach.
Trouble, *s.* Buaireas, aimhreite; dragh, saothair; farran; éigin, aire, cruaidh chas, teanntachd, teinn; anshocair, àmhghar, truaighe, trioblaid.
Trouble, *v. a.* Buair; cuir dragh air, farranaich, cuir gu trioblaid, cuir thar a chéile, pian.
Troublesome, *adj.* Draghail; buaireasach, aimhreiteach, trioblaideach.
Troublesomeness, *s.* Draghalachd.
Trough, *s.* Amar, clàr.
Trounce, *v. a.* Cuir gu taic; peanasaich; lunndrainn, buail, dòrnaich.
Trowsers. *s.* Triubhas.
Trout, *s.* Breac, bricean.
Trow, *v. n.* Saoil, smuainich.
Trowel, *s.* Sgreădhal, trùghan.
Truant, *s.* Lùrdan; sgoilear leisg.
Truant, *adj.* Leasg, màirnealach.
Truce, *s.* Fosadh-còmhraig; anail.
Trucidation, *s.* Marbhadh, milleadh.
Truck, *v. n.* Dean malairt, iomlaidich.
Truckle, *v. n.* Strìochd, lùb, crùb.
Truculent, *adj.* Borb, garg, fiadhaich, gruamach; fuilteach.
Trudge, *v. n.* Triall air éigin.
True, *adj.* Fìreannach, fior, dìleas, tréidhireach; ceart, dligheach, cóir; deimhinn, cinnteach, seasmhach.
Truebred, *adj.* Do 'n t-seòrsa cheart.
Truehearted, *adj.* Ionraic, dìleas.
Trueness, *s.* Fìrinn, ionracas.
Truepenny, *s.* Fear-cinnteach, ceart.
Trull, *s.* Strìopach bhochd.
Truly, *adv.* Gu fìrinneach, gu dearbh, gu deimhinn; a theart rìreadh.
Trump, *s.* Trompaid; buadh-chairt.
Trump, *v. a.* Coisinn le buaidh-chairt.
Trumpery, *s.* Faoineas; faoin-chainnt.
Trumpet, *s.* Tròmbaid, triùmpaid, buabhall, stŏc, *Md.* and *Buch.*
Trumpet, *v. a.* Gairm, foillsich, dean aithnichte; séid le tròmbaid.
Trumpeter, *s.* Tròmbaidear.
Truncheon, *s.* Siolpan; bata.
Trundle, *s.* Ruithlean, roillean.
Trundle, *v. n.* Ruithil, roill; theirig car m'a char, car air char.
Trunk, *s.* Stoc, bun-craoibhe; cobhan, ciste, gnos, sròn; corp, còm.
Trunnions, *s.* Deilg-taoibh gunna-móir.
Truss, *s.* Crios trŭsaidh, braghairt, buinnseal; muillean.
Truss, *v. a.* Trus, ceangail.
Trust, *s.* Earbsa, dòchas, creideas.
Trust, *v.* Earb á, cuir dòchas ann, cuir muinghinn ann, creid, thoir creideas do, bi earbsach, bi cinnteach; bi 'n dòchas, bi 'n dùil.
Trustee, *s.* Ceileadair, fear-cùraim.
Trusty, *adj.* Dìleas, earbsach, ionraic, fìrinneach, fior, diongmhalta, daingeann, seasmhach, làidir.
Truth, *s.* Fìrinn; ionracas.
Try, *v.* Feuch, feuch ri; thoir ionnsaidh, cuir deuchainn air; dearbh, cuir gu deuchainn, ceasnaich, rannsaich, sgrùd, fidir.
Tub, *s.* Ballan, cùdainn, tŭba.
Tube, *s.* Pìob, feadan.
Tubercle, *s.* Plucan, guirean, buicean.
Tuberous, *adj.* Plucanach, buiceanach.
Tubular, Tubulated, Tubulous, *adj.* Pìobach, pìobanach, feadanach.
Tuck, *s.* Claidheamh-caol; eangach.
Tuck, *v. a.* Trus, criosraich.
Tucker, *s.* Eideadh-uchd mna.
Tuesday, *s.* Di-Màirt.
Tuft, *s.* Dos, dosan, babag, toipean, tolman, toman, bad, gasan, gasgan, badan, doire, garan.
Tufty, *adj.* Dosach, dosrach; topanach, badanach; gasganach; tolmanach, tomanach, doireach.
Tug, *v.* Spiol, spìon, tarruinn, dragh, slaoid; gleachd, dean strìth.

Tug, *s.* Spioladh, spionadh, spiodadh, draghadh, tarruinn, slaodadh.
Tugger, *s.* Long-shlaodaidh.
Tuition, *s.* Ionnsachadh, teagasg.
Tumble, *v.* Tuit, tuislich; tilg sios.
Tumble, *s.* Tuiteam, leagadh.
Tumbler, *s.* Cleasaiche-car; còrn.
Tumbrel, *s.* Cairt-innearach.
Tumefaction, *s.* Ăt, bòcadh.
Tumefy, *v. n.* Ăt, bòc, séid suas.
Tumid, *adj.* Ătmhor; làn, bòsdail, mòr-chuiseach, spagluinneach.
Tumorous, *adj.* Bòcach; spaideil, spagluinneach, mòr-chùiseach.
Tumour, *s.* Ăt; iongrachadh, màm, meall; spagluinn; mòr-chuis.
Tumult, *s.* Iorghuill, săbaid, aimhreite, buaireas, mi-riaghailt.
Tumultuary, *adj.* Iorghuilleach, aimhreiteach, săbaideach, mi-riaghailteach, troi'-cheile.
Tumultuous, *adj.* Iorghuilleach, săbaideach, aimhreiteach, buaireasach, mi-riaghailteach.
Tun, *s.* Tunna, da phìob.
Tune, *s.* Port, fonn, séis.
Tune, *v. a.* Gleus, cuir am fonn.
Tuneful, *adj.* Fonnmhor, binn.
Tuneless, *adj.* Neo-fhonnmhor, neo-bhinn, neo-ghleusta.
Tuner, *s.* Fear-gleusaidh.
Tunic, *s.* Casag leinibh.
Tunnage, *s.* Tunna-chìs; tomhas.
Tunnel, *s.* Luidheir; lìonadair.
Tup, *s.* Reithe; *v.* Put mar ni reithe.
Turban, *s.* Ceann-eideadh Turcach.
Turbary, *s.* Còir moinntich.
Turbid, *adj.* Tiugh, ruaimleach, neo-shoilleir, thar a chéile.
Turbidness, *s.* Ruaimleachd.
Turbinated, *adj.* Toinnte, sniomhte.
Turbot, *s.* Am bradan-leathann.
Turbulence, *s.* Buaireas; mi-riaghailt, aimhreite, troi'-chéile.
Turbulent, *adj.* Buaireasach.
Turd, *s.* Cac, inneir, aolach, salachar.
Turf, *s.* Sgroth, sgràth; tota, fàl, fòd [commonly written "fòid," the *gen. sing.* of fòd and fàd].
Turfy, *adv.* Fàileanach, gòrm.
Turcent, *adj.* Làn, ătmhor; gaothar.
Turgid, *adj.* Gaothar; ătmhor.
Turk, *s.* Turcach; *adj.* Turcach.
Turkey, *s.* Eun-Fràngach.
Turmeric, *s.* Dath-buidhe.
Turmoil, *v. a.* Bi cruaidh shaobhair; bi sgìth, bi sàraichte.
Turn, *s.* Tionndadh; lùb, car; cuairt; atharrachadh; pilleadh, pilltinn; grathunn, tacan; gnothach; cùis; tùrn, gniomh; faothachadh; aomadh, claonadh.
Turn, *v.* Pill, tionndaidh; iompaich; lùb; cuir mu 'n cuairt, cuir a cheann fodha, fàs, cinn; dealbh, cùm; mùth, atharraich, thig air t' ais.
Turncoat, *s.* Fear-leam-leat.
Turner, *s.* Tuairnear.
Turning, *s.* Tionndadh, càr, lùb.
Turnip, *s.* Sneup, neup, nèip. *Arg.*
Turnpike, *s.* Chachaileith-cìse.
Turnsol, *s.* An grain-ròs.
Turpentine, *s.* Bànbhìth giubhais.
Turpitude, *s.* Gràinealachd, olcas.
Turret, *s.* Turait; binnein; baideal.
Turtle, *s.* Calman, turtur.
Tush! *interj.* Bi d' thosd! uist! ĕist!
Tusk, *s.* Tosg, sgor-fhiacail.
Tut! *interj.* Tŭt! h-ŭd!
Tutelage, *s.* Oideas; togail suas.
Tutelar, **Tutelary**, *adj.* Dìonach.
Tutor, *s.* Oide-ionnsaich; tùitear.
Tutorage, *s.* Uachdranachd fir-foghluim, ionnsachadh; foghlum.
Tutoress, *s.* Ban-oid-ionnsaich.
Tuz, **Tuzz**, *s.* Ciabhag, badan fuilt.
Twain, *adj.* Dithis, càraid.
Twang, *s.* Srann; fuaim gheur.
Twang, *v. n.* Dean srann.
Twattle, *v. n.* Dean gobaireachd.
Tweak, *v. a.* Gòmagaich, teannaich.
Tweedle, *v. a.* Meuraich gu tlà.
Tweezers, *s.* Greimiche.
Twelfth, *adj.* An dara deug.
Twelve, *adj.* A dhà dheug.
Twentieth, *adj.* Am ficheadamh.
Twenty, *adj.* Fichead.
Twice, *adv.* Dà uair; dà chuairt.
Twig, *s.* Faillean, maothan, gineag.
Twilight, *s.* Eadar-sholus, camhanaich, camhanach, chamh-fhàir.
Twilight, *adj.* Dorcha, dubharach.
Twin, *s.* Leth-aon.
Twine, *v. a.* Toinn, dual, figh.
Twine, *s.* Sgéinnidh; toinntean; toinneamh, sniamh.
Twinge, *v. a.* Fàisg, toinn, cràidh.
Twinkle, *v. n.* Priob; boillsg.
Twinkling, *s.* Priobadh; crith-bhoillsge, dealradh, plathadh; gliosgardaich.
Twinling, *s.* Uan leth-aon.
Twirl, *v. a.* Ruidhil mu'n cuairt.
Twirl, *s.* Ruidhle, cuartalan.
Twist, *v. n.* Toinn, toinneamh, snìomh, figh, dualaich, cuir an amladh a chéile, bi sniomhte, bi toinnte.
Twist, *s.* Toinneamh, snìomh, car; toinntean, sreang, snàthain.
Twister, *s.* Fear-toinneimh, sniomhaire, sniomhadair; corra-shiamain.

Twisting, *s.* Toinneamh, sniomh.
Twit, *v. a.* Beum; maoidh, sgeig, mag, fochaidich, dean fanaid.
Twitch, *s.* Spioladh; spìonadh; guin.
Twitch, *v. a.* Spiol, spion, pioc; biorg.
Twitter, *v. n.* Dean diorrasan; sitrich, truitrich, crith; sgeig, măg, dean fàite, dean snodha.
Twitter, *s.* Diorrasan; sitrich.
Two, *adj.* A dhà, dà, dithis; càraid.
Twofold, *adj.* Dà-fhillte.
Twohanded, *adj.* Dà-làmhach.
Twopence, *s.* Dà-sgillinn.
Tympanum, *s.* Druma.
Type, *s.* Samhla, comhar; clò-litir.
Typical, *adj.* Samhlachail.
Typify, *v. a.* Samhlaich.
Typographer, *s.* Clò-bhuailtear.
Typographical, *adj.* Samhlachail.
Typography, *s.* Clò-bhualadh.
Tyrannic, **Tyrannical**, *adj.* Aintighearnail; smachdail, ceannasach; ainneartach, sàrachail; borb.
Tyrannise, *v. a.* Bi aintighearnail.
Tyranny, *s.* Ain-tighearnas.
Tyro, *s.* Foghlumaiche.

U

U, *s.* An t-aon litir thar fhichead do 'n Abidil.
Uberty, *s.* Pailteas, tairbhe.
Ubiquitary, *adj.* Uile-làthaireach.
Ubiquity, *s.* Uile-làthaireachd.
Udder, *s.* Ùgh, ùgh mairt.
Ugliness, *s.* Duaichneachd.
Ugly, *adj.* Grannda, duaichnidh.
Ulcer, *s.* Neasgaid, leannachadh; iongrachadh; bolg, leus, bucaid, spucaid, guirean, creuchd.
Ulcerate, *v.* Iongraich, leannaich.
Ulceration, *s.* Iongrachadh, creuchd.
Ulcerous, *adj.* Neasgaideach; leannachail, silteach, creuchdach.
Uliginous, *adj.* Féitheach, fliuch, bog, làthachail, làbanach, clàbarach.
Ultimate, *adj.* Deireannach.
Ultramarine, *adj.* Allmharrach.
Ultramarine, *s.* Dath-gòrm maiseach.
Umber, *s.* Dath-buidhe; seòrs éisg.
Umbles, *s.* Grealach féigh.
Umbo, *s.* Cop, cnap-sgéithe.
Umbrage, *s.* Sgàile, dubhar, dùbhradh, duibhre; leithsgeul; amharus, umhaill; corraich, fearg; mìothlachd.
Umbrageous, **Umbrose**, *adj.* Sgàileach, dubharach, dorcha.
Umbrella, *s.* Sgàilean-uisge.
Umpire, *s.* Breitheamh, breithe.
Un, *partc.* Neo; mi, eu, as, an, ana, do.
Unabashed, *adj.* Neo-nàraichte.
Unable, *adj.* Neo-chomasach.
Unacceptable, *adj.* Neo-thaitneach.
Unaccompanied, *adj.* Aonarach.
Unaccomplished, *adj.* Neo-chrìochnaichte, neo-oileanaichte, neo-ionnsaichte; bhuaidh, inntinn.
Unaccountable, *adj.* Do-innse, doaithris, do-chur an céill; iongantach, neònach, neo-fhreagarrach.
Unaccustomed, *adj.* Neo-chleachdte.
Unacquainted, *adj.* Aineolach.
Unactive, *adj.* Neo-theòma.
Unadmired, *adj.* Neo-urramaichte.
Unadorned, *adj.* Neo-sgeadaichte.
Unadvised, *adj.* Neo-chomhairlichte.
Unaffected, *adj.* Fìor, ionraic, neochealgach; còir; sìmplidh.
Unaffecting, *adj.* Neo-dhrùighteach.
Unaided, *adj.* Neo-chuidichte.
Unalienable, *adj.* Neo-bhuileachail.
Unallied, *adj.* Neo-chàirdeach.
Unalterable, *adj.* Neo-chaochlaideach; diongalta, maireann.
Unaltered, *adj.* Neo-atharraichte.
Unamendable, *adj.* Do-leasachadh.
Unamiable, *adj.* Neo-chiatach.
Unanimity, *s.* Aon-inntinn.
Unanimous, *adj.* Aon-inntinneach.
Unanswerable, *adj.* Do-fhreagairt.
Unappalled, *adj.* Neo-sgàthach.
Unappeasable, *adj.* Do-chasgadh.
Unapprehensive, *adj.* Gun amharus.
Unapproached, *adj.* Do-ruigheachd.
Unapt, *adj.* Neo-fhreagarrach.
Unaptness, *s.* Neo-fhreagarrachd.
Unargued, *adj.* Neo-chonnsaichte.
Unarmed, *adj.* Neo-armaichte.
Unartful, *adj.* Neo-ealanta, simplidh.
Unasked, *adj.* Gun iarruidh.
Unaspiring, *adj.* Neo-mhiannach.
Unassailable, *adj.* Do-bhualadh.
Unassisted, *adj.* Neo-chuidichte.
Unassuming, *adj.* Neo-stràiceil.
Unattainable, *adj.* Do-ruigsinn.
Unattempted, *adj.* Gun deuchainn.
Unattended, *adj.* Gun chuideachd.
Unauthorized, *adj.* Gun ùghdarras.
Unavailable, **Unavailing**, *adj.* Gun stà, gun mhath, faoin gun fheum.
Unavoidable, *adj.* Do-sheachanta.
Unaware, **Unawares**, *adv.* Gun fhios, gun fhaireachadh, gun aire, gun aithne; gu h-obann, gu grad.
Unawed, *adj.* Gun fhiamh, gun athad

UNBAR, *v. a.* Thoir an crann deth.
UNBEATEN, *adj.* Neo-bhuailte.
UNBECOMING, *adj.* Mi-chiatach.
UNBEFITTING, *adj.* Neo-fhreagarrach.
UNBELIEF, *s.* Ana-creideamh.
UNBELIEVER, *s.* Ana-creideach.
UNBENEVOLENT, *adj.* Neo-dhaonairceach, neo-mhathasach.
UNBENT, *adj.* Do-lùbadh.
UNBESEEMING, *adj.* Neo-chiatach.
UNBEWAILED, *adj.* Neo-chaoidhte.
UNBIDDEN, *adj.* Gun iarraidh, gun sireadh, gun chuireadh, neo-chuirte.
UNBIND, *v. a.* Fuasgail, tuasgail.
UNBLAMABLE, *adj.* Neo-choireach.
UNBLEST, *adj.* Neo-bheannaichte.
UNBODIED, *adj.* Neo-chorparra.
UNBOLT, *v. a.* Thoir an crann deth.
UNBOSOM, *v. a.* Leig ris; nochd
UNBOTTOMED, *adj.* Gun ghrunnd.
UNBOUGHT, *adj.* Neo-cheannaichte.
UNBOUNDED, *adj.* Neo-chrìochnach.
UNBREECHED, *adj.* Gun bhriogais.
UNBROKEN, *adj.* Neo-cheannsaichte.
UNBROTHERLY, *adj.* Neo-bhràthaireil.
UNBURDEN, *v. a.* Aotromaich.
UNBURIED, *adj.* Neo-adhlaicte.
UNBUTTON, *v. a.* Fuasgail putan.
UNCALCINED, *adj.* Neo-loisgte.
UNCALLED, *adj.* Gun chuireadh.
UNCAUGHT, *adj.* Neo-ghlacte.
UNCAUTIOUS, *adj.* Neo-aireachail.
UNCEASING, *adj.* Gun sgur.
UNCERTAIN, *adj.* Neo-chinnteach.
UNCERTAINTY, *s.* Neo-chinnteachd.
UNCHANGEABLE, *adj.* Neo-chaochlaideach, maireannach, buan.
UNCHARITABLE, *adj.* Neo-sheirceil.
UNCHARITABLENESS, *s.* Mi-sheircealachd, mi-charthannachd.
UNCHASTE, *adj.* Neo-gheimnidh.
UNCHRISTIAN, *adj.* Ana-crìosdail.
UNCIRCUMCISED, *adj.* Neo-thimchioll-ghearrta, gun timchioll-ghearradh.
UNCIVIL, *adj.* Mi-shuairce, borb.
UNCIVILIZED, *adj.* Borb, fiadhaich.
UNCLE, *s.* Brathair-athar no màthar.
UNCLEAN, *adj.* Neo-ghlan, peacach.
UNCLEANLINESS, *s.* Neo-ghloine.
UNCLERICAL, *adj.* Neo-chléireachail.
UNCLOUDED, *adj.* Neo-ghruamach.
UNCOCK, *v. a.* Cuir gunna bharr lagh.
UNCOLLECTED, *adj.* Neo-chruinnichte.
UNCOLOURED, *adj.* Neo-dhathte.
UNCOMBED, *adj.* Neo-chìrte.
UNCOMELINESS, *s.* Mi-chiatachd.
UNCOMELY, *adj.* Mi-chiatach.
UNCOMFORTABLE, *a.* An-shòcrach.
UNCOMMON, *adj.* Neo ghnàthach.
UNCOMMUNICATED, *adj.* Neo-bhuilichte.
UNCOMPLAISANT, *adj.* Mi-shuairce.
UNCOMPLETE, *adj.* Neo-chrìochnaichte
UNCOMPOUNDED, *adj.* Neo-mheasgte.
UNCOMPRESSED, *adj.* Neo-theannaichte.
UNCONCERN, *s.* Neo-chùram.
UNCONCERNED, *adj.* Neo-chùramach.
UNCONDITIONAL, *adj.* Neo-chùmhnantach, gun chùmhnanta.
UNCONFINABLE, *adj.* Neo-iomallach.
UNCONFIRMED, *adj.* Neo-dhaingnichte.
UNCONFORMITY, *s.* Neo-fhreagarrachd.
UNCONGEALED, *adj.* Neo-reòta.
UNCONJUGAL, *adj.* Neo-mharaisteach.
UNCONQUERABLE, *adj.* Do-cheannsachadh, do-chìosachadh.
UNCONSCIONABLE, *adj.* Neo-chogaiseach, mi-chogaiseach.
UNCONSCIOUS, *adj.* Neo-fhiosrach.
UNCOURTEOUS, *adj.* Mi-shuairce.
UNCOUTH, *adj.* Neònach, neo-mhìn.
UNCREATE, *v. a.* Cuir gu neo-bhith.
UNCREATED, *adj.* Neo-chruthaichte.
UNCROWN, *v. a.* Dì-chrùnaich.
UNCTION, *s.* Ungadh; taiseachadh.
UNCTUOUS, *adj.* Reamhar, sailleil.
UNCULLED, *adj.* Neo-thaghte.
UNCULTIVATED, *adj.* Fiadhaich, neo-àitichte; neo-foghluimte.
UNCUMBERED, *adj.* Neo-dhamhnaichte.
UNCURTAILED, *adj.* Neo-ghiorraichte.
UNCUT, *adj.* Neo-ghearrte.
UNDAN, *v. a.* Leig ruith le.
UNDAUNTED, *adj.* Neo-ghealtach.
UNDEBAUCHED, *adj.* Neo-thruaillichte.
UNDECEIVE, *v. a.* Cuir ceart.
UNDECEIVED, *adj.* Neo-mheallta.
UNDECIDED, *adj.* Neo-chinnteach.
UNDECISIVE, *adj.* Neo-chinnteach.
UNDECKED, *adj.* Neo-sgeadaichte.
UNDEFEASIBLE, *adj.* Seasmhach.
UNDEFILED, *adj.* Neo-thruaillidh.
UNDEFINED, *adj.* Neo-mhìnichte; gun chrìoch, neo-shònraichte.
UNDENIABLE, *adj.* Do-àicheadh.
UNDEPLORED, *adj.* Neo-chaoidhte.
UNDEPRAVED, *adj.* Neo-thruaillte.
UNDER, *adv.* and *prep.* Fo; an ìochdar.
UNDERBID, *v. a.* Tairg ni's lugha na luach, tairg fo luach.
UNDERGO, *v. a.* Fuilig, giùlain.
UNDERGROUND, *s.* Fo 'n talamh.
UNDERHAND, *adj.* Dìomhair; cealgach.
UNDERLINE, *s.* Iochdaran.
UNDERMINE, *v. a.* Cladhaich fodha; fo-chladhaich; cuir neach ás àite gun fhios, no le foill.
UNDERMOST, *adj.* Is ìsle, ìochdrach.
UNDERNEATH, *prep.* Fo, fodha.
UNDERPLOT, *s.* Fo-chluich.
UNDERPRIZE, *v. a.* Di-mheas

UNDERRATE, *v. a.* Di-mheas.
UNDERSELL, *v. a.* Reic fo luach.
UNDERSTAND, *v.* Tuig; thoir fainear.
UNDERSTANDING, *s.* Tuigse; ciall.
UNDERSTANDING, *adj.* Tuigseach, sgileil.
UNDERSTRAPPER, *s.* Ìochdaran.
UNDERTAKE, *v.* Gabh o's làimh
UNDERTAKER, *s.* Fear-gnothaich; fear a ghabhas adhlac os laimh.
UNDERTAKING, *s.* Gnothach, obair.
UNDERVALUE, *v. a.* Dì-mheas.
UNDERWOOD, *s.* Preasarnach, crìonach.
UNDERWORK, *s.* Ceartaichean.
UNDERWRITE, *v. a.* Fo-sgrìobh.
UNDERWRITER, *s.* Urrasaiche.
UNDERWRITTEN, *adj.* Fo-sgrìobhte.
UNDESCRIED, *adj.* Neo-fhaicinte.
UNDESERVED, *adj.* Neo-thoillteannach.
UNDESERVING, *adj.* Neo-airidh.
UNDESIGNING, *adj.* Neo-chealgach.
UNDESTROYED, *adj.* Neo-sgrioste.
UNDETERMINED, *adj.* Neo-shònraichte.
UNDIGESTED, *adj.* Neo-mhearbhte.
UNDIMINISHED, *adj.* Neo-lughdaichte.
UNDISCERNED, *adj.* No-fhaicsinn.
UNDISCERNIBLE, *adj.* Neo-fhaicsinneach.
UNDISCERNING, *adj.* Neo-thuigseach.
UNDISCIPLINED, *adj.* Neo-ionnsaichte.
UNDISCOVERED, *adj.* Neo-aithnichte.
UNDISCREET, *adj.* Gòrach, eu-crìonna, mi-chiallach, mi-shuairce.
UNDISGUISED, *adj.* Nochdte; fior.
UNDISPUTED, *adj.* Neo-chonnsachail.
UNDISTURBED, *adj.* Neo-bhuairte.
UNDIVIDED, *adj.* Neo-phàirtichte.
UNDO, *v. a.* Mill; sgrios; fuasgail.
UNDONE, *adj.* Caillte, neo-chrìochnaichte; neo-dheante, sgrioste.
UNDOUBTED, *adj.* Cinnteach; fior.
UNDOUBTEDLY, *adv.* Gu cinnteach, air chinnte, gun teagamh, gun amharus.
UNDRESS, *v. a.* Lom; rùisg.
UNDRESSED, *adj.* Neo-sgeadaichte.
UNDULATE, *v. a.* Udail mar thonn.
UNDULATION, *s.* Tonn-luasgadh.
UNDULATORY, *adj.* Tonn-luasgach.
UNDUTIFUL, *adj.* Mi-dhleasanach.
UNEASINESS, *s.* An-shocair; iomacheist; cùram; ro-chùram, aimheal.
UNEASY, *adj.* An-shocrach; neo-shocrach, aimhealach.
UNELIGIBLE, *adj.* Neo-roghnachail.
UNEMPLOYED, *adj.* Gun obair, 'na thàmh, dìomhanach.
UNENJOYED, *adj.* Neo-shealbhaichte.
UNENLIGHTENED, *adj.* Neo-shoillsichte.
UNENTERTAINING, *adj.* Neo aighearach.
UNEQUAL, *adj.* Neo-ionann.
UNEQUITABLE, *adj.* Neo-cheart.
UNEQUIVOCAL, *adj.* Soilleir.
UNERRING, *adj.* Neo-mhearachdach.
UNEVEN, *adj.* Neo-chòmhnard.
UNEVENNESS, *s.* Neo-chòmhnardachd.
UNEXAMPLED, *adj.* Neo-choimeiseil.
UNEXCEPTIONABLE, *adj.* Gun choire.
UNEXECUTED, *adj.* Neo-choimhlionta.
UNEXERCISED, *adj.* Neo-chleachdte.
UNEXHAUSTED, *adj.* Neo-thràighte.
UNEXPECTED, *adj.* Gun dùil.
UNEXPERIENCED, *adj* Neo-chleachdte.
UNEXPLORED, *adj.* Neo-rannsaichte.
UNEXPRESSIBLE, *adj.* Do-labhairt.
UNEXTINGUISHABLE, *adj.* Do-mhùchadh, nach gabh cuir ás.
UNFADING, *adj.* Neo-sheargte, buan.
UNFAILING, *adj.* Neo-fhàillinneach.
UNFAIR, *adj.* Mi-cheart, claon.
UNFAITHFUL, *adj.* Neo-dhìleas.
UNFASHIONABLE, *adj.* Neo-fhasanta.
UNFASHIONED, *adj.* Neo-chùmte.
UNFATHOMABLE, *adj.* Do-thomhas.
UNFATHOMED, *adj.* Neo-ghrùnndaichte.
UNFATIGUED, *adj.* Neo-sgìth.
UNFAVOURABLE, *adj.* Neo-fhàbharrach.
UNFED, *adj.* Neo-bhiadhta.
UNFEELING, *adj.* Neo thlusail.
UNFEIGNED, *adj.* Neo-chealgach, fìor.
UNFELT, *adj.* Neo-mhothaichte.
UNFERTILE, *adj.* Neo-thorrach.
UNFERMENTED, *adj.* Neo-oibrichte.
UNFETTERED, *adj.* Neo-chuibhrichte.
UNFINISHED, *adj.* Neo-chrìochnaichte.
UNFIRM, *adj.* Neo-sheasmhach, lag.
UNFIT, *adj.* Neo-iomchuidh.
UNFIT, *v. a.* Dean neo-iomchuidh.
UNFITNESS, *s.* Neo-iomchuidhead.
UNFIXED, *adj.* Neo-shuidhichte.
UNFLEDGED, *adj.* Gun itean.
UNFOLD, *v. a.* Fosgail; nochd, foillsich.
UNFORESEEN, *adj.* Neo-fhairichte.
UNFORGIVING, *adj.* Neo-mhathach.
UNFORMED, *adj.* Neo-chumadail.
UNFORSAKEN, *adj.* Neo-thréigte.
UNFORTIFIED, *adj.* Neo-dhaingnichte.
UNFORTUNATE, *adj.* Mi-shealbhach.
UNFREQUENT, *adj.* Ainmig, tearc.
UNFREQUENTED, *adj.* Neo-àitichte; fàs.
UNFRIENDED, *adj.* Gun charaid.
UNFRIENDLY, *adj.* Neo-chàirdeil.
UNFROZEN, *adj.* Neo-reòta.
UNFRUITFUL, *adj.* Neo-tharbhach.
UNFURL, *v. a.* Sgaoil, siùil, no brat.
UNFURNISHED, *adj.* Gun àirneis; neo-uidheamaichte, neo-dheasaichte.
UNGAIN, UNGAINLY, *adj.* Neo-chiatach; neo-eireachdail, mi-chuannta.
UNGENERATIVE, *adj.* Neo-thorrach.
UNGENEROUS, *adj.* Mi-shuairce, neo-fhialaidh, spìocach, crìon.
UNGENIAL, *adj.* Neo-bhaigheil.

UNGENTEEL, *adj.* Neo-eireachdail.
UNGENTLE, *adj.* Neo-shuairce.
UNGENTLEMANLIKE, *adj.* Neo-uasal; miodhoir, neo-mhodhail.
UNGIRT, *adj.* Neo-chrioslaichte.
UNGODLINESS, *s.* Mi-dhiadhachd.
UNGODLY, *adj.* Mi-dhiadhaidh.
UNGORGED, *adj.* Neo-lìonta.
UNGOVERNABLE, *adj.* Do-cheannsachadh, do-riaghladh, borb.
UNGOVERNED, *adj.* Neo-cheannsaichte.
UNGRACEFUL, *adj.* Neo-ghrinn.
UNGRACIOUS, *adj.* Neo-thaitneach.
UNGRATEFUL, *adj.* Mì-thaingeil; neo-thaingeil; neo-thaitneach.
UNGROUNDED, *adj.* Gun stéidh.
UNGUARDED, *adj.* Neo-dhìonta.
UNGUENT, *s.* Ungadh; ola.
UNHANDSOME, *adj.* Neo-thlachdmhor.
UNHANDY, *adj.* Neo-làmhchair.
UNHAPPY, *adj* Mi-shona, truagh.
UNHARMED, *adj.* Neo-dhochannaichte.
UNHARMONIOUS, *adj.* Neo-fhonnmhor.
UNHARNESS, *v. a.* Neo-bheairtich.
UNHEALTHFUL, UNHEALTHY, *adj.* Eus-lainteach, eucaileach, tinn.
UNHEARD, *adj.* Neo-iomraiteach.
UNHEEDED, *adj.* Gun mheas, gun suim.
UNHOLY, *adj.* Mì-naomha.
UNHONOURED, *adj.* Neo-onoraichte.
UNHOPEFUL, *adj.* Neo-dhòchasach.
UNHORSE, *v. a.* Tilg bhàrr eich.
UNHOSPITABLE, *adj.* Neo-aoidheil.
UNHURT, *adj.* Neo-chiùrrte, gun dochann, gun bheud.
UNHUSK, *v. a.* Plaoisg, faoisg.
UNICORN, *s.* Aon-adharcach, buabhall.
UNIFORM, *adj.* Aon-dealbhach.
UNIFORMITY, *s.* Riaghailteachd, co-ionannachd, aon-fhuirm. *Ir.*
UNIMAGINABLE, *adj.* Do-smuainteachadh, do-bharalachadh.
UNIMPAIRABLE, *adj.* Do-mhilleadh.
UNIMPAIRED, *adj.* Neo-mhillte.
UNIMPORTANT, *adj.* Fadharsach.
UNIMPROVABLE, *adj.* Do-leasachadh.
UNIMPROVED, *adj.* Neo-leasaichte.
UNINCLOSED, *adj.* Neo-dhìonte.
UNINDIFFERENT, *adj.* Neo-choidheis.
UNINFORMED, *adj.* Neo-ionnsaichte.
UNINGENUOUS, *adj.* Neo-ionraic.
UNINHABITABLE, *adj.* Do-àiteachadh.
UNINHABITED, *adj.* Neo-àitichte.
UNINJURED, *adj.* Gun chiorram.
UNINSPIRED, *adj.* Neo-dheachdte.
UNINSTRUCTED, *adj.* Neo-theagaisgte.
UNINSTRUCTIVE, *adj.* Neo-ionnsachail.
UNINTELLIGENT, *adj.* Aineolach.
UNINTELLIGIBLE, *akj.* Do-thuigsinn.
UNINTENTIONAL, *adj.* Neo-rùnaichte.
UNINTERESTED, *adj.* Gun seadh, coma.
UNINTERRUPTED, *adj.* Neo-bhacte.
UNINVESTIGABLE, *adj.* Do-sgrùdadh.
UNINVITED, *adj.* Neo-chuirte.
UNION, *s.* Aonachd; co-bhann.
UNIPAROUS, *adj.* Aon-bhretheach.
UNISON, *adj.* Aon-ghuthach.
UNISON, *s.* Aon-ghuth; gleus.
UNIT, *s.* Aon, a h-aon.
UNITARIAN, *s.* An-trìonaidiche.
UNITE, *v.* Ceangail; dlùthaich, aontaich, tàth, cuir ri chéile; gabh tàthadh, fàs mar aon.
UNITION, *s.* Aontachas; aontachadh.
UNITY, *s.* Aonachd, co-chòrdadh.
UNIVERSAL, *adj.* Coitcheann.
UNIVERSE, *s.* An domhan.
UNIVERSITY, *s.* Àrd-thaigh-foghlum.
UNIVOCAL, *adj.* Aon-ghuthach.
UNJUST, *adj.* Eucorach, mi-cheart.
UNJUSTIFIABLE, *adj.* Do-fhìreannachadh, do-dhìonadh.
UNKENNEL, *v. a.* Cuir á saobhaidh.
UNKEPT, *adj.* Neo-ghléidhte.
UNKIND, *adj.* Neo-chaoimhneil.
UNKINDNESS, *s.* Neo-chaoimhneas.
UNKNIGHTLY, *adj.* Neo-fhlathail.
UNKNIT, *v. a.* Sgar, sgaoil, fosgail.
UNKNOWING, *adj.* Aineolach.
UNKNOWN, *adj.* Neo-aithnichte.
UNLABOURED, *adj.* Neo-shaothairichte.
UNLACE, *v. a.* Fuasgail, sgaoil.
UNLADE, *v. a.* Aotromaich.
UNLADEN, *adj.* Neo-luchdaichte.
UNLAID, *adj.* Neo-leagte.
UNLAMENTED, *adj.* Neo-chaoidhte.
UNLAWFUL, *adj.* Mi-laghail.
UNLEARNED, *adj.* Neo-fhoghluimte.
UNLEAVENED, *adj.* Neo-ghoirtichte.
UNLESS, *conj.* Saor o; mur, mu's.
UNLETTERED, *adj.* Neo-ionnsaichte.
UNLEVELLED, *adj.* Neo-chòmhnard.
UNLIBIDINOUS, *adj.* Neo-chonnanach.
UNLICENSED, *adj.* Neo-cheadaichte.
UNLICKED, *adj.* Neo-imlichte; neo-chùmte, neo-sheamhsar.
UNLIKE, *adj.* Neo-choltach.
UNLIKELIHOOD, UNLIKELINESS, *s.* Eu-cosalachd; eucoltas.
UNLIKELY, *adj.* Eu-coltach.
UNLIMITED, *adj.* Neo-chrìochnach.
UNLOAD, *v. a.* Aotromaich.
UNLOCK, *v. a.* Fosgail glas.
UNLOOKED-FOR, *adj.* Gun dùil ris.
UNLOOSE, *v. a.* Fuasgail.
UNLOVELY, *adj* Neo-ionmhuinn.
UNLOVING, *adj.* Neo-ghaolach.
UNLUCKY, *adj.* Mi-shealbhar.
UNMADE, *adj.* Neo-dhèante.
UNMAIMED, *adj.* Neo-chiorramach.

UNMAN, *v.* Spŏth; dean tais, dean mi-fhearail, mì-mhisnich.
UNMANAGEABLE, *adj.* Do-cheannsachadh, do-riaghladh; trom.
UNMANLY, *adj.* Neo-fhearail, meata.
UNMANNERED, *adj.* Mi-mhodhail.
UNMANNERLY, *adj.* Neo-shìobhalta.
UNMARKED, *adj.* Neo-chomharraichte.
UNMARRIED, *adj.* Neo-phòsta.
UNMASK, *v. a.* Leig ris; rùisg.
UNMASKED, *adj.* Leigte ris; rùisgte.
UNMASTERED, *adj.* Neo-cheannsaichte.
UNMATCHABLE, *adj.* Gun choimeas.
UNMATCHED, *adj.* Gun leth-bhreac.
UNMEANING, *adj.* Gun seadh.
UNMEANT, *adj.* Neo-rùnaichte.
UNMEASURABLE, *adj.* Do-thomas.
UNMEASURED, *adj.* Neo-thomhaiste.
UNMEET, *adj.* Neo-airidh, neo-iomchuidh, neo-fheagarrach.
UNMELTED, *adj.* Neo-leaghte.
UNMERCIFUL, *adj.* An-tròcaireach.
UNMERITABLE, *adj.* Neo-airidh.
UNMINDED, *adj.* Neo-chuimhnichte.
UNMINDFUL, *adj.* Dì-chuimhneach,
UNMINGLED, *adj.* Neo-choimeasgta.
UNMIXED, *adj.* Neo-mheasgta, glan.
UNMOLESTED, *adj.* Gun dragh.
UNMOVEABLE, *adj.* Do-ghluasad.
UNMOVED, *adj.* Neo-ghluaiste.
UNMOURNED, *adj.* Neo-chaoidhte.
UNMUSICAL, *adj.* Neo-cheòl mhor.
UNNAMED, *adj.* Neo-ainmichte.
UNATURAL, *adj.* Mi nàdurra.
UNNAVIGABLE, *adj.* Do-sheòladh.
UNNECESSARY, *adj.* Neo-fheumail.
UNNEIGHBOURLY, *adj.* Neo-choimhearsnachail, neo-nàbachail; neo-chòir, neo-chaoimhneil, neo-choingheallach; neo-chòmpanta.
UNNERVATE, *adj.* Anfhannaichte.
UNNERVE, *v. a.* Anfhannaich.
UNNERVED, *adj.* Anfhann; tais.
UNNUMBERED, *adj.* Do-àireamh.
UNOBSERVABLE, *adj.* Do-fhaicinn.
UNOBSERVANT, *adj.* Neo-shuimeil.
UNOBSERVED, *adj.* Neo-bheachdaichte.
UNOBSTRUCTED, *adj.* Neo-bhacte.
UNOBTAINABLE, *adj.* Do-fhaotainn.
UNOCCUPIED, *adj.* Neo-shealbhaichte.
UNOFFENDING, *adj.* Neo-choireach.
UNOPERATIVE, *adj.* Neo-éifeachdach.
UNOPPOSED, *adj.* Neo-bhacte.
UNORDERLY, *adj.* Mi-riaghailteach.
UNORTHODOX, *adj.* Neo-fhallain.
UNPACK, *v. a.* Fuasgail, fosgail.
UNPAID, *adj.* Neo-phàighte.
UNPALATABLE, *adj.* Neo-bhlasda.
UNPARALLELED, *adj.* Gun choimeas.
UNPARDONABLE, *adj.* Gun leithsgeul, nach mathar; nach fhaodar a mhathadh, nach faigh mathanach.
UNPARDONED, *adj.* Neo-mhathte.
UNPARLIAMENTARY, *adj.* An aghaidh achd socraichte na pàrlamaid.
UNPARTED, *adj.* Neo-dhealaichte.
UNPARTIAL, *adj.* Dìreach, neo-chlaon, cothromach, neo-leth-bhreitheach.
UNPASSABLE, *adj.* Do-imeachd.
UNPAWNED, *adj.* Neo-ghealltainte.
UNPEACEABLE, *adj.* Buaireasach.
UNPENSIONED, *adj.* Neo-dhuaisichte.
UNPEOPLE, *v. a.* Dean fàs; sgrios.
UNPERCEIVABLE, *adj.* Do-mhothachadh, do-fhaireachdainn.
UNPERCEIVED, *adj.* Gun fhios.
UNPERFECT, *adj.* Neo-iomlan.
UNPERFORMED, *adj.* Neo-dhèanta.
UNPERISHABLE, *adj.* Maireannach.
UNPERPLEXED, *adj.* Gun amhluadh.
UNPETRIFIED, *adj.* Neo-cruadhaichte.
UNPHILISOPHICAL, *adj.* Neo-fheallsanta.
UNPILLOWED, *adj.* Gun chluasag.
UNPIN, *v. a.* Fuasgail dealg.
UNPITIED, *adj.* Gun truas ri.
UNPITYING, *adj.* Neo-thruacanta.
UNPLEASANT. *adj.* Mi-thaitneach.
UNPLEASED, *adj.* Mi-thoilichte.
UNPLEASING, *adj.* Mi-thaitneach.
UNPLIANT, *adj.* Do-lùbadh, rag.
UNPLOWED, *adj.* Neo-threabhta.
UNPOETICAL, *adj.* Neo-fhileanta.
UNPOLISHED, *adj.* Neo-liobhta; borb.
UNPOLITE, *adj.* Mi-mhodhail.
UNPOLLUTED, *adj.* Neo-thruaillte.
UNPOPULAR, *adj.* Neo-ionmhainn.
UNPRACTISED, *adj.* Neo-chleachdte.
UNPRAISED, *adj.* Gun iomradh.
UNPRECEDENTED, *adj.* Gun choimeas.
UNPREFERRED, *adj.* Neo-àrdaichte.
UNPREGNANT, *adj.* Neo-thorrach.
UNPREJUDICATE, *adj.* Neo-chlaon.
UNPREJUDICED, *adj.* Neo-leth-bhreitheach, neo-chlaon-bhretheach.
UNPREMEDITATED, *adj.* Neo-smuaintichte roi'-làimh, neo-shònraichte.
UNPREPARED, *adj.* Neo-ullamh.
UNPREPOSSESSED, *adj.* Gun taobh ri.
UNPRETENDING, *adj.* Neo-dhàna.
UNPREVENTED, *adj.* Neo-bhacte.
UNPRINCELY, *adj.* Mi-fhlathail.
UNFRINCIPLED, *adj.* Neo-chogaiseach.
UNPRINTED, *adj.* Neo-chlò-bhuailte.
UNPRIZED, *adj.* Neo-mheaste.
UNPROCLAIMED, *adj.* Neo-ghairmte.
UNPROFANED, *adj.* Neo-thruaillte.
UNPROFITABLE, *adj.* Neo-tharbhach.
UNPROLIFIC, *adj.* Seasg, aimrid.
UNPROPITIOUS, *adj.* Mi-shealbhach.
UNPROPORTIONED, *adj.* Neo-chumadail.

Unpropped, *adj.* Gun chùl-taic.
Unprosperous, *adj.* Mi-shealbhar.
Unprotected, *adj.* Gun dìon.
Unprovided, *adj.* Neo sholaraichte.
Unprovoked, *adj.* Neo-bhrosnaichte.
Unpruned, *adj.* Neo-ghearrta.
Unpublished, *adj.* Neo-fhoillichte.
Unqualified, *adj.* Neo-fhìr agarrach.
Unqualify, *v. a.* Dean neo-fhreagarra.
Unquenchable, *adj.* Do-mhùchadh.
Unquenched, *adj.* Neo-mhùchte.
Unquestionable, *adj.* Gun cheist.
Unquestionably, *adv.* Air chinnt.
Unquestioned, *adj.* Neo-cheasnaichte.
Unquiet, *adj.* Neo-fhoisneach.
Unracked, *adj.* Neo-shìolaidhte.
Unravel, *v. a.* Fuasgail, réitich.
Unread, *adj.* Neo-leughte.
Unready, *adj.* Neo-dheas.
Unreal, *adj.* Neo-fhìor, faoin.
Unreasonable, *adj.* Mi-reusonta.
Unreclaimed, *adj.* Neo-chìosnaichte.
Unreconciled, *adj.* Neo-réidh.
Unrecorded, *adj.* Neo-sgrìobhte.
Unrecounted, *adj.* Neo-aithriste.
Unreduced, *adj.* Neo-lughdaichte.
Unreformable, *adj.* Do-leasachadh.
Unreformed, *adj.* Neo-leasaichte.
Unrefreshed, *adj.* Neo-ùraichte.
Unregarded, *adj.* Gun sùim.
Unregererate, *adj.* Neo-ath-ghinte.
Unregistered, *adj.* Neo-sgrìobhte.
Unrelenting, *adj.* Neo-thruacanta.
Unrelievable, *adj.* Do-chòmhnadh.
Unremediable, *adj.* Do-leigheas.
Unrepented, *adj.* Neo-aithreachail.
Unrepining, *adj.* Neo-aithreach.
Unreplenished, *adj.* Neo-lìonta.
Unreproached, *adj.* Neo-chronaichte.
Unreproved, *adj.* Neo-achmhasanaichte.
Unrequested, *adj.* Gun iarraidh.
Unrequitable, *adj.* Neo-dhìolta.
Unresented, *adj.* Maite.
Unreserved, *adj.* Fosgarra.
Unresisted, *adj.* Gun bhacadh.
Unresolved, *adj.* Neo-shònraichte.
Unrestored, *adj.* Neo-aisigte.
Unrestrained, *adj.* Neo-smachdaichte.
Unrevealed, *adj.* Ceilte.
Unrevenged, *adj.* Neo-dhìolta.
Unrevoked, *adj.* Seasmhach.
Unrewarded, *adj.* Neo-dhuaisichte.
Unriddle, *v. a.* Tomhais; fuasgail.
Unrig, *v. a.* Rùisg dhet.
Unrighteous, *adj.* Eas-ionraic.
Unrightful, *adj.* Neo-dhligheach.
Unripe, *adj.* Anabaich, glas.
Unrivalled, *adj.* Gun choimeas.
Unrol, *v. a.* Fosgail, fuasgail.
Unroof, *v. a.* Thoir mullach dheth.
Unroot, *v. a.* Spìon á bhun.
Unrounded, *adj.* Neo-chruinn.
Unruffle, *v. n.* Bi ciùin.
Unruly, *adj.* Aimhreiteach.
Unsafe, *adj.* Neo-thèaruinte.
Unsaid, *adj.* Neo-ainmichte.
Unsalted, *adj.* Neo-shaillte.
Unsaluted, *adj.* Neo-fhàiltichte.
Unsanctified, *adj.* Neò-naomhaichte.
Unsatiable, *adj.* Do-shàsachadh.
Unsatisfactory, *adj.* Neo-thaitneach.
Unsatisfied, *adj.* Neo-thoilichte.
Unsavoury, *adj.* Mi-bhlasda; breun.
Unsay, *v. a.* Thoir air ais facal.
Unscholastic, *adj.* Neo-ionnsaichte.
Unschooled, *adj.* Gun sgoil.
Unscreened, *adj.* Neo-sgàilichte.
Unseal, *v. a.* Fosgail seula.
Unsealed, *adj.* Neo-sheulaichte.
Unseasonable, *adj.* Neo-thràthail.
Unseasonableness, *s.* Mi-thràth.
Unseasoned, *adj.* Neo-shaillt; neo-thràthail; neo-thiormaichte.
Unseconded, *adj.* Neo-chuidichte.
Unsecure, *adj.* Neo-thèaruinte.
Unseemly, *adj.* Mi-chiatach.
Unseen, *adj.* Neo-fhaicinte.
Unserviceable, *adj.* Gun stà.
Unsettle, *v. a.* Dean mi-chinnteach.
Unsettled, *adj.* Neo-shocrach, neo-shuidhichte, neo-shònraichte; luaineach, siùbhlach; caochlaideach; neo-àitichte; guanach, aotrom.
Unsevered, *adj.* Neo-sgarte.
Unshackle, *v. a.* Mi-chuibhrich.
Unshaken, *adj.* Neo-charaichte, neo-ghluasadach; daingeann.
Unshapen, *adj.* Neo-chumadail.
Unsheath, *v. a.* Rùisg, tarruinn.
Unsheltered, *adj.* Gun fhasgadh.
Unship, *v. a.* Thoir á luing.
Unshod, *adj.* Gun bhrògan.
Unshorn, *adj.* Neo-bhuainte.
Unsifted, *adj.* Neo-chriathairte.
Unsightliness, *s.* Duaichneachd.
Unsightly, *adj.* Duaichnidh.
Unskilful, *adj.* Mi-theòma.
Unskilfulness, *s.* Aineolas.
Unskilled, *adj.* Aineolach.
Unslaked, *adj.* Neo-mhùchta.
Unsociable, *adj.* Neo-chaidreach.
Unsoiled, *adj.* Neo-shalaichte.
Unsold, *adj.* Neo-reicte.
Unsolid, *adj.* Fàs; neo-ghramail.
Unsophisticated, *adj.* Ionraic; fìor.
Unsorted, *adj.* Neo-dhòigheil.
Unsought, *adj.* Gun iarraidh.
Unsound, *adj.* Mi-fhallain; grod.
Unspeakable, *adj.* Do-labhairt.

UNSPECIFIED, *adj.* Neo-ainmichte.
UNSPOILED, *adj.* Neo-chreachta, neo-mhillte ; neo-thruaillichte.
UNSPOTTED, *adj.* Gun bhall; gun smal.
UNSTABLE, *adj.* Neo-sheasmhach.
UNSTAINED, *adj.* Gun sal ; gun smal.
UNSTAUNCHED, *adj.* Neo-chaisgte.
UNSTEADFAST, *adj.* Mi-stéidheil.
UNSTEADY, *adj.* Neo-sheasmhach.
UNSTINTED, *adj.* Neo-ghann, fial, pailt.
UNSTRAINED, *adj.* Neo-éignichte.
UNSTRING, *v. a.* Lasaich, fuasgail.
UNSUBSTANTIAL, *adj.* Gun bhrìgh.
UNSUCCESSFUL, *adj.* Mi-shealbhar.
UNSUGARED, *adj.* Gun siùcar.
UNSUITING, *adj.* Neo-fhreagarrach.
UNSUITABLE, *adj.* Neo-iomchuidh.
UNSULLIED, *adj.* Gun truailleadh.
UNSUNG, *adj.* Neo-iomraiteach.
UNSUNNED, *adj.* Neo-ghrianaichte.
UNSUPPORTED, *adj.* Neo-chuidichte.
UNSUSPECTED, *adj.* Saor o amharus.
UNSUSPECTING, *adj.* Neo-amharusach.
UNSUSPICIOUS, *adj.* Gun umhaill.
UNSUSTAINED, *adj.* Neo-thaicichte.
UNSWAYED, *adj.* Neo-cheannsaichte.
UNSWEAR, *v. a.* Thoir mionnan air ais.
UNTAINTED, *adj.* Neo-thruaillichte.
UNTAMED, *adj.* Neo-challaichte.
UNTASTED, *adj.* Neo-bhlasta.
UNTAUGHT, *adj.* Neo-ionnsaichte.
UNTEMPERED, *adj.* Neo-chruadhaichte.
UNTENABLE, *adj.* Do-dhìon.
UNTENANTED, *adj.* Neo-àitichte.
UNTENTED. *adj.* Neo-fhritheilte.
UNTERRIFIED, *adj.* Gun sgàth.
UNTHANKED, *adj.* Gun taing.
UNTHANKFUL, *adj.* Mi-thaingeil.
UNTHAWED, *adj.* Gun aiteamh.
UNTHINKING, *adj.* Neo-smaointeachail.
UNTHOUGHT-OF, *adj.* Gun spéis.
UNTHREATENED, *adj.* Neo-bhagairte.
UNTHRIFT, *s.* Struidhear.
UNTHRIFTY, *adj.* Stròghail, sgapach.
UNTHRIVING, *adj.* Mi-shoirbheasach.
UNTIE, *v. a.* Fuasgail, lasaich.
UNTIED, *adj.* Fuasgailte, las.
UNTIL, *adv.* Gu ruig, gu, gus.
UNTILLED, *adj.* Neo-àitichte.
UNTIMELY, *adj.* Neo-thràthail.
UNTIMELY, *adv.* Roimh 'n àm.
UNTINGED, *adj.* Neo-dhàthte.
UNTIRED, *adj.* Neo-sgìth.
UNTITLED, *adj.* Neo-thiodalaichte.
UNTO, *prep.* Do, gu, chum, thun, a dh' ionnsaidh, gu ruig.
UNTOLD, *adj.* Neo-aithriste.
UNTOUCHED, *adj.* Neo-làmhaichte.
UNTOWARD, *adj.* Rag, reasgach, fiar.
UNTRACEABLE, *adj.* Do-lòrgachadh.
UNTRACED, *adj.* Neo-lòrgaichte.
UNTRAINED, *adj.* Neo-ionnsaichte.
UNTRANSPARENT, *adj.* Dorcha.
UNTRAVELLED, *adj.* Neo-choisichte.
UNTRIED, *adj.* Neo-dheuchainte.
UNTROD, *adj.* Neo-lòrgaichte.
UNTROUBLED, *adj.* Neo-bhuairte.
UNTRUE, *adj.* Neo-dhìleas.
UNTRULY, *adv.* Gu neo-dhìleas, gu fallsa, gu mealltach,
UNTRUTH, *s.* Breug ; sgleò.
UNTUNABLE, *adj.* Do-ghleusadh.
UNTURNED, *adj.* Neo-thionndaidhte.
UNTUTORED, *adj.* Neo-ionnsaichte.
UNTWINE, UNTWIST, *v. a.* Thoir as a chéile, thoir ás an fhighe.
UNUSUAL, *adj.* Neo-àbhaisteach.
UNVALUED, *adj.* Di-measte.
UNVANQUISHED, *adj.* Neo-cheannsaichte, neo-chlaoidhte.
UNVARIED, *adj.* Gun atharrachadh.
UNVARNISHED, *adj.* Neo-lìtheach.
UNVEIL, *v. a.* Leig ris, nochd.
UNVERITABLE, *adj.* Fallsa, breugach.
UNVERSED, *adj.* Neo-eòlach.
UNVIOLATED, *adj.* Neo-bhriste, slàn.
UNVISITED, *adj.* Neo-thaghaichte.
UNAWAKENED, *adj.* Neo-dhùisgte.
UNWARLIKE, *adj.* Neo-churanta.
UNWARNED, *adj.* Gun sanas.
UNWARRANTABLE, *adj.* Neo-cheadaichte, neo-laghal.
UNWARRANTED, *adj.* Neo-chinnteach.
UNWARY, *adj.* Neo-fhaiceallach; obann.
UNWASHED, *adj.* Neo-nighte; salach.
UNWASTED. *adj.* Neo-chaithte.
UNWEARIED, *adj.* Neo-sgìth.
UNWED, *adj.* Neo-phòsta.
UNWELCOME, *adj.* Neo-thaitneach.
UNWHOLESOME, *adj.* Neo-fhallain.
UNWIELDY, *adj.* Trom, liobasda.
UNWIND, *v. a.* Thoir as a chéile.
UNWISE, *adj.* Neo-ghlic, gòrach.
UNWONTED, *adj.* Aineamh, tearc.
UNWORTHY, *adj.* Neo-airidh.
UNWREATHE, *v. a.* Thoir ás an dual,
UNWRITTEN, *adj.* Neo-sgrìobhte.
UNWROUGHT, *adj.* Neo-oibrichte.
UNWRUNG, *adj.* Neo-fhàisgte.
UNYIELDED, *adj.* Neo-strìochdte.
UNYOKE, *v. a.* Neo-bheartaich.
UP, *adv.* Shuas ; gu h-àrd.
UP, *prep.* Suas ri bruthach.
UPBRAID, *v. a.* Maoidh ; troid.
UPHELD, *part.* Air a chumail suas.
UPHILL, *adj.* Ri bruthach, duilich.
UPHOLD, *v. a.* Cum suas, tog.
UPHOLDER, *s.* Fear taice.
UPHOLSTERER, *s.* Fear àirneisiche.
UPLAND, *s.* Airde ; aonach ; mullach.

Uplay, *v. a.* Càrn suas, cnuasaich.
Uplift, *v. a.* Tog suas, àrdaich.
Upmost, *adj.* Is àirde.
Upon, *prep.* Air, air muin.
Upper, *adj.* Uachdrach (*erroneously written* "uachdarach").
Uppermost, *adj.* Is uachdraiche.
Upraise, *v. a.* Tog suas, àrdaich.
Upright, *adj.* Tréidhireach ; ionraic ; dìreach 'na sheasamh, onarach, sìmplidh, ceart, cothromach, fior.
Uprightness, *s.* Tréidhireas, fireantachd ; seasamh dìreach.
Uprise, *v. n.* Éirich, suas.
Uproar, *s.* Gàire ; buaireas.
Uproot, *v. a.* Spìon á bhun.
Upshot, *s.* Co-dhùnadh, crìoch ; deireadh, ceann mu dheireadh.
Upside, *adv.* An t-uachdar.
Upstart, *s.* Ùranach.
Upstart, *v. a.* Leum suas.
Upward, *adj.* Suas, gu h-àrd.
Urbanity, *s.* Furmailt, suairceas.
Urchin, *s.* Cràineag ; isean, gàrlach.
Urethra, *s.* Fual-chuisle.
Urge, *v. a.* Earalaich ; spàrr ; aslaich ; brosnaich stuig ; cuir thuige ; teannaich ; fàisg, pùc, brùth.
Urgency, *s.* Cabhag ; earailteachd, feumalachd, fòghnadh.
Urgent, *adj.* Dian, earailteach, cabhagach, feumail.
Urger, *s.* Fear-earailteach ; earalaiche.
Urinal, *s.* Buideal-fuail.
Urinary, *adj.* Fualach, nùnach.
Urine, *s.* Maighistir, fual, mùn.
Urn, *s.* Poit tasgaidh luaithre nam marbh ; soigheach uisge.
Us, the *oblique case* of *we*. Sinn, sinne
Usage, *s.* Àbhaist, nòs, gnà ; càradh.
Usance, *s.* Riadh, ùin-réidh.
Use, *s.* Stà, math, feum ; dìol, gnàthachadh ; cleachdadh, nòs, àbhaist ; co-ghnàth ; riadh.
Use, *v.* Gnàthaich ; buin ri, dean feum ; cleachd ; bi cleachdte, giùlain, iomchair.
Used, *adj.* Gnàthaichte, cleachdte.
Useful, *adj.* Feumail, iomchuidh, freagarrach, stàmhor, tarbhach, math.
Usefulness, *s.* Feumalachd.
Useless, *adj.* Neo-fheumail, gun stà.
Usher, *s.* Fo'-mhaighstir ; gille-doruis.
Usher, *v. a.* Thoir a steach, thoir a stigh, feuch a steach, feuch a stigh.
Usquebaugh, *s.* Uisge-beatha.
Usual, *adj.* Coitcheann, tric, minig, gnàthach, gnàthaichte.
Usually, *adv.* Gu minig, a réir àbhaist, mar is trice.
Usurer, *s.* Fear-réidh, fear-ocair.
Usurious, *adj.* Riadhach ; ocarach.
Usurp, *v. a.* Gléidh gun chòir.
Usurpation, *s.* Glacadh gun chòir.
Usurper, *s.* Rìgh neo-dhligheach.
Usury, *s.* Airgead-réidh.
Utensil, *s.* Ball-acuinn, cungaidh beairt ; goireas, ball-àirneis.
Uterine, *adj.* Machlagach.
Uterus, *s.* Machlag, machlach.
Utility, *s.* Feum ; math, stà.
Utmost, *adj.* Iomallach, deireannach, is deireannaiche, is mò, is àirde.
Utmost, *s.* Meud, làn-oidhirp.
Utter, *v. a.* Labhair, abair, innis, nochd, cuir an céill ; reic ; sgaoil.
Utterable, *adj.* So-labhairt.
Utterance, *s.* Labhairt ; guth.
Utterly, *adv.* Gu tŭr, gu léir.
Uttermost, *s.* A chuid is mò.
Uttermost, *adj.* Is iomallaiche, is fhaide mach, is faid air fàlbh.
Uvula, *s.* Cioch-shlugain.
Uxorious, *adj.* Mùirneach mu mhnaoi.
Uxuriousness, *s.* Céile-mhùirn.

V

V, *s.* An dara litir thar fhichead do 'n Aibidil.
Vacancy, *s.* Fàslach ; failbhe ; àite falamh, àite fàs ; anail, clos, tàmh ; còs, bèarn ; neo-thoirt.
Vacant, *adj.* Fàs, falamh ; faoin.
Vacate, *v. a.* Falmhaich ; fàg ; dean faoin, cuir air chùl ; tréig.
Vacation, *s.* Uine shaor ; sgaoileadh ; tàmh, anail.
Vaccination, *s.* Cur breac a' chruidh.
Vacine, *adj.* Cruidh.
Vacuity, *s.* Failmhe, failbhe.
Vacuation, *s.* Falmhachadh.
Vacuous, *adj.* Falamh, fàs, faoin.
Vacuum, *s.* Falamhachd.
Vade-mecum, *s.* Leabhar-pòcaid.
Vagabond, *s.* Fear-fuadain.
Vagary, *s.* Faoin-dhòchas.
Vagrant, *s.* Fear-seacarain, diol-deirce, deirceach. *R. D.*
Vagrant, *adj.* Siùbhlach ; seachranach, iomrallach.
Vague, *adj.* Sgaoilte, faontrach.
Vail, *v.* Leig sìos ; ìslich ; géill.
Vails, *s.* Airgead doruis.
Vain, *adj.* Faoin ; diomhain ; neo-

éifeachdach, neo-tharbhach; falamh; fàs; uallach, stràiceil; suarrach; sgàileanta; bòsdail, spaglainneach.
Vain-glorious, *adj*. Ràiteachail.
Vain-glory, *s*. Ràiteachas.
Vale, *s*. Gleann, srath.
Valentine, *s*. Leannan; dealbh-gaoil.
Valerian, *s*. An trì-bhileach.
Valet, *s*. Gille-coise.
Valetudinarian, *s*. Neach tinn.
Valiant, *adj*. Treun, foghainteach, calma, làidir, neartmhor, misneachail.
Valiantness, *s*. Gaisge, tréine.
Valid, *adj*. Tàbhachdach; éifeachdach, comasach; cumhachdach, foghainteach, làidir; tarbhach.
Validity, *s*. Tàbhachd; éifeachd.
Valley, *s*. Gleann; glac, lag.
Valorous, *adj*. Gaisgeanta, curanta.
Valour, *s*. Gaisge, tréine, cruadal.
Valuable, *adj*. Luachmhor, prìseil.
Valuation, *s*. Meas, luach; fiach.
Value, *s*. Prìs, luach, fiach; toirt.
Value, *v. a*. Meas, prìsich, cuir meas.
Valve, *s*. Pìob-chòmhla; duilleag-doruis.
Vamp, *s*. Leathar-uachdair.
Vamp, *v. a*. Càirich, clùd, clùdaich.
Van, *s*. Toiseach-feachda; tùs.
Vane, *s*. Coileach-gaoithe.
Vanguard, *s*. Tùs-feachd.
Vanilla, *s*. Faoineag; seòrsa luibh.
Vanish, *v. n*. Rach ás an t-sealladh, falbh mar sgàile; sìolaidh air falbh.
Vanity, *s*. Diomhanas, faoineas; uaill.
Vanquish, *v. a*. Buadhaich, ceannsaich, cìosnaich, thoir buaidh; claoidh; faigh làmh-an-uachdar, cuir fo smachd; cuir fo cheannsal.
Vanquisher, *s*. Buadhaire.
Vantage, *s*. Tairbhe, làmh-an-uachdar, cosnadh, cothrom.
Vapid, *adj*. Neo-bhrìgheil, marbhanta, air dol eug; air bàsachadh mar leann.
Vaporous, *adj*. Smùideach, ceòthar.
Vapour, *s*. Deatach; ceo-gréine.
Vapours, *s*. Leanntras, liunntras.
Variable, *adj*. Caochlaideach.
Variableness, *s*. Caochlaideachd.
Variance, *s*. Aimhreite, cur a mach.
Variation, *s*. Caochla, dealachadh.
Variegate, *v. a*. Breac, breacaich, ballaich, balla-bhreacaich, stiallaich.
Variegated, *adj*. Breac, ballach.
Variety, *s*. Atharrachadh, caochla.
Various, *adj*. Eugsamhail, iomadach, iomadh, mòran; ioma-ghnèitheach.
Varlet, *s*. Crochaire; gàrlach.
Varnish, *s*. Slìob-ola, falaid.
Varnish, *v. a*. Slìobaich, falaidich.
Varnisher, *s*. Slìobaiche, falaidiche.
Vary, *v*. Caochail, eugsamhlaich, atharraich; breacaich, ballaich; rach a thaobh, claon.
Vase, *s*. Soire, soitheach.
Vassal, *s*. Ìochdaran; coitear.
Vassalage, *s*. Ìochdranachd.
Vast, *s*. Fàsach, ionad fàsail.
Vast, Vasty, *adj*. Mòr, ro-mhòr, ana-measarra, fuathasach; anabharrach, ana-cuimseach, aibhseach.
Vastness, *s*. Ana-cuimseachd, anmhorachd, anabharrachd.
Vat, *s*. Dabhach.
Vaticide, *s*. Mortair-bhàrd.
Vaticinate, *v. n*. Fàisnich.
Vault, *s*. Bogha; seileir; uamh, tuam.
Vault, *v*. Leum, gearr sùrdag; dean ruideis, tog bogha.
Vaulted, Vaulty, *adj*. Boghata.
Vaunt, *s*. Bòsd; spaglainn.
Vaunt, *v*. Dean bòsd, dean uaill.
Veal, *s*. Laoigh-fheoil.
Vecture, *s*. Giùlan, iomchar.
Veer, *v*. Tionndaidh, atharraich; rach mu 'n cuairt; cuir mu 'n cuairt; cuir timchioll; cuir tiomall.
Vegetable, *s*. Luibh, lùs.
Vegetate, *v. n*. Fàs mar lùs.
Vegetation, *s*. Fàs, luibhean.
Vegetative, *adj*. A' fàs mar luibh.
Vegete, *adj*. Làidir, lùghar, beò.
Vehemence, *s*. Déineas, déine, gairgead, deòthas, dealas, braisead.
Vehement, *adj*. Dian; déineachdach, borb, garg, deòthasach, loisgeanta, bras, dealasach, da-rireadh.
Vehicle, *s*. Càrn, carbad, cairt, inneal giùlain, inneal-iomchair.
Veil, *s*. Gnùis-bhrat, sgàile.
Veil, *v. a*. Còmhdaich, falaich, ceil.
Vein, *s*. Cuisle, féith; gnè; slighe; stiall; nàdur, inntinn, càil, sannt.
Veined, *adj*. Cuisleach, féitheach stiallach, snìomh-chuisleach, breac.
Vellicate, *v. a*. Spìon, spiol.
Vellication, *s*. Spìonadh, spioladh.
Vellum, *s*. Craicionn-sgrìobhaidh.
Velocity, *s*. Luathas, clise.
Velvet, *s*. Sìoda molach.
Venal, *adj*. So-cheannach, an geall air duais, sanntach; cuisleach, féitheach.
Venality, *s*. Brìobachd, sannt duaise.
Venatic, *adj*. Sealgach.
Venation, *s*. Sealg, faoghaid.
Vend, *v. a*. Reic, noch ri reic.
Vender, *s*. Reiceadair, fear-reic.
Vendible, *adj*. Reiceadach, so-reic.
Vendition, *s*. Reic.
Veneer, *v. a*. Còmhaich le fiodh tana.
Veneficial, *adj*. Nìmhneach, nimhe.

Venenate, *v. a.* Puinnseanaich.
Venerable, *adj.* Urramach, measail.
Venerate, *v. a.* Urramaich.
Veneration, *s.* Àrd-urram.
Venereal, *adj.* Drùiseil, macnusach.
Venery, *s.* Drùis; macnusachd.
Venesection, *s.* Leagail-fala.
Vengeance, *s.* Dìoghaltas; peanas.
Vengeful, *adj.* Dìoghaltach.
Veniable, **Venial**, *adj.* So-mhathadh, so-lughadh, ceadaichte.
Venison, *s.* Sithionn; fiaghach.
Venom, *s.* Nimhe, puinnsean.
Venomous, *adj.* Nimheil, mì-runach.
Venomousness, *s.* Nimhealachd.
Vent, *s.* Luidhear; fosgladh; toll-gaoithe, leigeil a mach.
Vent, *v. a.* Leig a mach; abair, labhair; dòirt a mach, thoir gaoth, foillsich; leig ruith le.
Ventilate, *v. a.* Fasgainn, fidrich.
Ventilation, *s.* Fasgnadh, fionnarachadh, cur ris a' ghaoith; fidreachadh, rannsachadh, sgrùdadh.
Ventilator, *s.* Fasgnadan.
Ventricle, *s.* Goile, bronnag; bolgan.
Ventriloquist, *s.* Brù-chainntear.
Venture, *s.* Tuaiream; cunnart.
Venture, *v.* Cuir an cunnart, cunnartaich; dùraig; gabh cuid cunnairt, rach an cunnart, thoir ionnsaidh.
Venturesome, **Venturous**, *adj.* Misneachail, dàna, neo-ghealtach.
Veracity, *s.* Fìreantachd, fìrinn.
Verb, *s.* Facal, briathar.
Verbal, *adj.* Faclach; beòil.
Verbatim, *adv.* Facal air son facail.
Verberate, *v. a.* Fri-bhuail; sgiùrs.
Verberation, *s.* Straoidhleireachd.
Verbose, *adj.* Briathrach, ràiteach.
Verbosity, *s.* Briathrachas.
Verdant, *adj.* Gorm; feurach, uaine.
Verdict, *s.* Breth-bharail.
Verdigris, *s.* Meirg umha.
Verdure, *s.* Feur-uaine; glasradh.
Verge, *s.* Slat-shuaicheantais; oir.
Verge, *v. n.* Aom, claon; teann ri.
Verification, *s.* Fìreannachadh.
Verifier, *s.* Dearbhair.
Verify, *v. a.* Dearbh; fìrinnich; daighnich, còmhdaich.
Verily, *adv.* Gu deimhinn, gu fior, gu firinneach, gu cinnteach, gu dearbha.
Verisimilar, *adj.* Cotlach, coslach.
Verisimiltude, **Verisimility**, *s.* Cosmhalachd, cosamhlachd.
Veritable, *adj.* Fìor, cinnteach.
Verity, *s.* Fìrinn dhearbhte.
Verjuice, *s.* Sùgh nan ubhall-each.
Vermiculation, *s.* Snìomhanachd.
Vermicule, *s.* Cnuimh, durrag.
Vermiculous, *adj.* Cnuimheagach.
Vermifuge, *s.* Fùdar-nam-biast.
Vermilion, *s.* Seòrsa deirg.
Vermin, *s.* Meanbh-bhéistean.
Verminous, *adj.* Béisteagach.
Vernacular, *adj.* Dùthchasach.
Vernal, *adj.* Earraich, céitein.
Vernility, *s.* Tràillealachd.
Versatile, *adj.* So-thionndadh; caochlaideach, luaineach; luasganach.
Versatility, *s.* Caochlaideachd.
Verse, *s.* Rann; dàn; duan; ceithreamh; earran; rannachd.
Versed, *adj.* Teòma, sgileil, eòlach, fiosrach, foghluimte, ionnsaichte.
Versification, *s.* Rannachd.
Versifier, *s.* Bàrd, duanaire.
Versify, *v.* Cuir an dàn, rannaich.
Version, *s.* Atharrachadh; eadartheangachadh; tionndadh, caochla.
Vert, *s.* Gorm-choille.
Vertebral, *adj.* Druim-altach.
Vertebre, *s.* Alt droma.
Vertex, *s.* Mullach; bior; binnein.
Vertical, *adj.* Dìreach os ceann.
Vertiginous, *adj.* Cuairteach, tuainealach cuairsgach, timchiollach.
Vertigo, *s.* Tuaineal; stùird.
Vervain, *s.* Crubh-an-leòghain.
Very, *adj.* Fìor, ceart; *adv.* Ro; glé.
Vesicle, *s.* Leus, builgein, guirein.
Vesicular, *adj.* Fàs, tolltach, còsach.
Vesper, *s.* Reannag-an-fheasgair.
Vespers, *s.* Fea garain. *Md.*
Vessel, *s.* Soitheach, long.
Vest, *s.* Siosta-còt, peiteag.
Vest, *v. a.* Sgeadaich, éid; gabh.
Vestal, *s.* Maighdeann-fhiorghlan.
Vestal, *adj.* Glan-maighdeannail.
Vestibule, *s.* For-dhorus.
Vestige, *s.* Lòrg; comharradh.
Vestment, *s.* Aodach, éideadh, earradh, trusgan; culaidh.
Vestry, *s.* Seòmar-eaglais; coinneamh fhoirfeach.
Vesture, *s.* Aodach, éideadh, earradh, trusgan, culaidh.
Vetch, *s.* Peasair-nan-each.
Veteran, *s.* Seann-saighdear.
Veterinarian, *s.* Spréidh-lighich.
Vex, *v. a.* Buair, cràidh, claoidh, sàraich, farranaich.
Vexation, *s.* Buaireadh, càmpar, aimheal, farran, àmhghar.
Vexatious, *adj.* Buaireasach, càmparach, farranach, aimhealach, draghalach, àmhgharach.
Vexatiousness, *s.* Aimhealachd.
Vial, *s.* Searrag ghlaine.

VIAND, *s.* Biadh, lòn.
VIATICUM, *s.* Biadh-siùbhail.
VIBRATE, *v.* Triobhuail; crath, crith.
VIBRATION, *s.* Triobhualadh, crith.
VIBRATORY, *adj.* Triobhualach.
VICAR, *s.* Biocair, co-arbha.
VICARAGE, *s.* Co-arbachd.
VICARIOUS, *adj.* Ionadach, an riochd.
VICE, *s.* Dubhailc; aingidheachd; droch-bheart; glamaire.
VICEGERENT, *s.* Fear-ionaid.
VICEROY, *s.* Fear ionaid rìgh.
VICINAGE, *s.* Nàbachd; dlùthas.
VICINAL, VICINE, *adj.* Fagus, dlù air.
VICINITY, *s.* Coimhearsnachd.
VICIOUS, *adj.* Dubhailceach, aingidh.
VICISSITUDE, *s.* Caochla, tionnda.
VICTIM, *s.* Iobairt; neach air a sgrios.
VICTOR, *s.* Buadhair, curaidh.
VICTORIOUS, *adj.* Buadhach, gaisgeil.
VICTORIOUSLY, *adv.* Buadhach.
VICTORY, *s.* Buaidh; làmh an uachdar.
VICTUAL, *s.* Lòn, biadh, beatha.
VICTUALLER, *s.* Biotailliche.
VICTUALS, *s.* Biotailt.
VIDELICET, *adv.* Is e sin ri ràdh.
VIDUITY, *s.* Bantrachas.
VIE, *v. n.* Dean strìth, dean spàirn.
VIEW, *v. a.* Beachdaich, amhairc air, dearc, feuch, gabh fradharc, gabh, beachd, gabh sealladh.
VIEW, *s.* Beachd, sealladh, fradharc; léirsinn, faicinn; dùil.
VIGIL, *s.* Faire; trasg, ùrnaigh-fheasgair; aoradh-oidhche.
VIGILANCE, *s.* Faiceallachd, furachras; beachdalachd, faire, caithris.
VIGILANT, *adj.* Faiceallach, furachail, aireachail, cùramach; caithriseach.
VIGOROUS, *adj.* Treun, làidir, calma, neartmhor, gramail, lùghor, beò.
VIGOUR, *s.* Tréine, spionnadh, treòir, neart, lùgh, comas, cumhachd.
VILE, *adj.* Salach, grannda, grâineil; truaillidh, dìblidh, suarrach, di-measda; aingidh, dubhailceach.
VILENESS, *s.* Truaillidheachd, suarr-achas, gràinealachd, trustaireachd, dìblidheachd, tàirealachd.
VILIFY, *v. a.* Maslaich; ìslich, dean tàir, salaich, truaill; màb, càin; di-mheas, dean suarrach.
VILL, VILLA, *s.* Taigh-dùthcha, taigh sàmhraidh, baile duin', uasail.
VILLAGE, *s.* Frith-bhaile, baile-beag.
VILLAGER, *s.* Fear frith-bhaile.
VILLAIN, *s.* Slaoightear, crochaire.
VILLANOUS, *adj.* Slaoighteil; dìblidh.
VILLANY, *s.* Slaightearachd, aingidh-eachd; cionta, coire; lochd, do-bheart.
VILLOUS, *adj.* Molach, ròmach, ròinn-each, giobach, cléiteagach.
VIMINEOUS, *adj.* Maothranach, slatag-ach, fiùranach, caolach, gadanach.
VINCIBLE, *s.* So-cheannsachadh.
VINDICATE, *v. a.* Fìreanaich, dìol; dearbh, dìon, cùm suas.
VINDICATION, *s.* Fìreanaichadh.
VINDICATIVE, *adj.* Dìoghaltach.
VINDICATOR, *s.* Fear-dìonaidh.
VINDICTIVE, *adj.* Dìoghaltach.
VINE, *s.* Fìonan, crann-fìona.
VINEGAR, *s.* Fìon-geur.
VINEYARD, *s.* Fìon-lios, gàradh-fìona.
VINE-PRESS, *s.* Fìon-amar.
VINOUS, *adj.* Fìonach.
VINTAGE, *s.* Fìon-fhoghar.
VINTAGER, *s.* Fìon-fhogharaiche.
VINTNER, *s.* Fìon-òsdair.
VINTRY, *s.* Fìon-mhargadh.
VIOL, *s.* Fidheall.
VIOLABLE, *adj.* So-chiùrradh.
VIOLATE, *v. a.* Ciùrr, mill, bris, dochainn; truaill, éignich.
VIOLATION, *s.* Milleadh, briseadh; éigneachadh; truailleadh.
VIOLENCE, *s.* Ainneart, fòirneart, éig-in, droch-ionnsaidh; déine; braise, deòthas, ciurram; cron, éigneach-adh, truailleadh.
VIOLENT, *adj.* Dian; ainneartach; ceann-laidir; garg, fòirneartach, borb, deòthasach.
VIOLET, *s.* Sail-chuaich, dail-chuach.
VIOLIN, *s.* Fidheall, fiodhall.
VIOLIST, *s.* Fìdhleir.
VIOLONCELLO, *s.* Fidheall-chruit.
VIPER, *s.* Nathair-nimhe, baobh.
VIRAGO, *s.* Aigeannach.
VIRENT, *adj.* Uaine, gorm, glas.
VIRGIN, *s.* Maighdeann, òigh, ainnir.
VIRGIN, *adj.* Maighdeannail, òigheil.
VIRGINAL, *s.* Òigh-cheòl.
VIRGINAL, *adj.* Òigheil, banail, màlda.
VIRGINITY, *s.* Maighdeannas.
VIRIDITY, *s.* Guirme, uainead.
VIRILE, *adj.* Fearail; duineil.
VIRILITY, *s.* Fearachas.
VIRTUAL, *adj.* Éifeachdach, feartach, buadach; nàdurail; brìgheil.
VIRTUALITY, *s.* Éifeachd.
VIRTUATE, *v. a.* Dean éifeachdach.
VIRTUE, *s.* Subhailc; deagh-bheus; buaidh; neart, comas; éifeachd.
VIRTUOSO, *s.* Fear-ionnsaichte.
VIRTUOUS, *adj.* Subhailceach; beus-ach, geimnidh; éifeachdach, cumh-achdach, comasach, slàinteil, math.
VIRULENCE, *s.* Nimhe; géire, gairge, falachd, gamhlas, mì-run, miosgainn.

VIRULENT, *adj.* Nimhneach; cnàmhtach, geur, garg, gamhlasach, mìrunach, miosgainneach.
VIRIS, *s.* Speach, nimh, ioghair.
VISAGE, *s.* Aghaidh, aodann, gnùis, sealladh, tuar, dreach.
VISCERATE, *v. a.* Thoir am mionach á.
VISCID, *adj.* Righinn, sticeach.
VISCIDITY, *s.* Leanailteachd.
VISCOSITY, *s.* Righneachd.
VISCOUNT, *s.* Biocas, morair.
VISCOUNTESS, *s.* Bana-bhiocas.
VISCOUS, *adj.* Glaodhanta, bìthanach.
VISIBILITY, VISIBLENESS, *s.* Faicsinneachd, leirsinneachd, soilleireachd.
VISIBLE, *adj.* Faicsinneach; soilleir.
VISION, *s.* Fradharc; sealladh, taisbean, foillseachadh; taibhs, tannasg; sgàile; bruadar, aisling.
VISIONARY, *adj.* Faoin, meallta, taisbeanach, baralach, dòchasach.
VISIONARY, *s.* Taibhsear, aisliche.
VISIT, *s.* Céilidh; coimhead.
VISIT, *v.* Fiosraich; taghail, thoir cēilidh, rach, a' choimhead.
VISITANT, *s.* Fear-céilidh.
VISITATION, *s.* Fiosrachadh, breitheanas; cuairt-rannsachaidh.
VISITER, VISITOR, *s.* Aoidh; dàimh. *Oss.*
VISOR, *s.* Cidhis, sgàile, cleith.
VISTA, *s.* Caol-shealladh, aisir.
VISUAL, *adj.* Fradharcach, léirsinneach.
VITAL, *adj.* Beathail, beò.
VITALITY, *s.* Beathalachd.
VITALS, *s.* Buill na beatha, neart.
VITIATE, *v. a.* Mill; truaill, salaich.
VITIATION, *s.* Truailleadh; milleadh.
VITIOUS, *adj.* Dubhailceach, truaillidh.
VITREOUS, *adj.* Glaineach, glaine.
VITRIFY, *v.* Fàs mar ghlaine.
VITRIOL, *s.* Uisge-loisgeach.
VITRIOLIC, *adj.* Mar uisge-loisgeach.
VITUPERATE, *v. a.* Coirich, cronaich.
VITUPERATION, *s.* Cronachadh, trod.
VIVACIOUS, *adj.* Maireann, buan, beò; mear, sgairteil, sùnntach.
VIVACITY, *s.* Beothalas, meanmnachd.
VIVID, *adj.* Beò; boillsgeanta, grad.
VIVIDNESS, *s.* Beothalachd, boillsge.
VIVIFIC, *adj.* Beothachaidh.
VIVIFY, *v. a.* Thoir beò; beothaich.
VIVIPAROUS, *adj.* Beò-bhreitheach.
VIXEN, *s.* Sionnach-boireann.
VIZ, *adj.* Is e sin ri ràdh.
VIZARD, *s.* Cidhis, sgàil.
VIZIER, *s.* Àrd-fhear-comhairl' an Turcaich, priomh-chomhairleach Turcach.
VOCABULARY, *s.* Facalair.
VOCAL, *adj.* G .thach, fonnar.
VOCALITY, *s.* Labhairt, cainnt.
VOCATION, *s.* Gairm, cèaird; rabhadh
VOCIFERATE, *v.* Glaodh, sgairt; beuc
VOCIFERATION, *s.* Glaodh, sgairt, beucail, sgairteachd; gàir, iolach.
VOCIFEROUS, *adj.* Beucach, sgairteach; stàirneach, glaodhach, guthach.
VOGUE, *s.* Fasan, gnàths, nòs.
VOICE, *s.* Guth, glaodh; guth-taghaidh; facal, sgairt, éigh, labhairt.
VOID, *adj.* Falamh, fàs, faoin.
VOID, *s.* Fàsalachd, falaimhe.
VOID, *v. a.* Falmhaich; tilg a mach.
VOIDABLE, *adj.* So chur air chùl.
VOLATILE, *adj.* Itealach, leumnach, grad-shiùbhlach; beò, beothail, spioradail, mear; caochlaideach; mùiteach; grad-thioram, lasanta.
VOLATILENESS, VOLATILITY, *s.* Gradthiormachd; luaineachd, caochlaideachd; beothalachd, iomaluaths.
VOLCANO, *s.* Beinn-theine.
VOLE, *s.* Buaidh-iomlan.
VOLERY, VOLARY, *s.* Sgaoth eun.
VOLILATION, *s.* Comas itealaich.
VOLITION, *s.* Toil, rùn, deònachadh.
VOLLEY, *s.* Làdach; *v.* Tilg a mach.
VOLUBILITY, *s.* Deas-labhairteachd, caochlaideachd; lonais beulais.
VOLUBLE, *adj.* Deas-chainnteach; luaineach, caochlaideach; siùbhlach.
VOLUME, *s.* Rola, leabhar, pasgan.
VOLUMINOUS, *adj.* Ioma-rolach.
VOLUNTARY, *adj.* Toileach, a dheòin.
VOLUNTEER, *s.* Saighdear-saor-thoile.
VOLUPTUARY, *s.* Ròicear, sòganiche.
VOLUPTUOUS, *adj.* Sòghmhor, sòghail.
VOLUPTUOUSNESS, *s.* Mi-stuamachd.
VOMIT, *v. a.* Tilg, sgeith, dìobhuir, tilg a mach, cuir a mach.
VOMIT, *s.* Tilgeadh, sgeith; dìobhuirt purgaid-thilgidh.
VORACIOUS, *adj.* Cìocrach, gionach; craosach, glutach, lonach.
VORACIOUSNESS, VORACITY, *s.* Cìocras, craosaireachd, glamaireachd, gionaichead lon, glutaireachd.
VORTEX, *s.* Cuairt-shlugan; coirecuairteig, faochag, cuairteag, cuinneag-thuaitheil, ioma-ghaoth.
VORTICAL, *adj.* Tuaitheallach.
VOTARESS, *s.* Ban-bhòidiche.
VOTARY, *s.* Fear-bòide.
VOTE, *s.* Guth-taghaidh.
VOTE, *v. a.* Thoir guth-taghaidh.
VOTER, *s.* Fear guth-taghaidh.
VOTIVE, *adj.* Bòideach.
VOUCH, *v. a.* Dearbh, còmhdaich, thoir fianais, tog fianais.
VOUCH, *s.* Fianais; dearbhadh; teisteannas, briathar.

VOUCHER, *s.* Fear dearbhaidh, fianais, teisteanas, dearbhadh.
VOW, *s.* Bòid, mòid, mionnan, guidhe, gealladh, mionnan-cùmhnainte.
VOW, *v.* Bòidich, mionnaich.
VOWEL, *s.* Foghair, guth.
VOYAGE, *s.* Taisdeal, turas-mara.
VOYAGER, *s.* Taisdealaich.
VULGAR, *adj.* Coitcheann ; gràisgeil ; ìosal, suarrach ; balachail ; neo-shuairce, mi-mhodhail.
VULGAR, *s.* Gràisg, pràbar.
VULGARISM, *s.* Trustaireachd.
VULGARITY, *s.* Gràisgealachd.
VULGATE, *s.* Bìoball laidinn Pàpanach.
VULNERABLE, *adj.* So-leònte.
VULNERATE, *v. a.* Leòn ; dochainn.
VULTURE, *s.* Fang, preachan.
VULTURINE, *adj.* Preachanach.

W

W. *s.* An treas litir thar fhichead do 'n Aibidil.
WAD, *s.* Cuifein ; muillean.
WABBLE, *v. n.* Gluais o thaobh gu taobh, dean luaghainn. *Lw.*
WADDING, *s.* Garbh-lìnig, cuifein.
WADDLE, *v. n.* Imich 's an turraman.
WADE, *v. n.* Rach troi' uisge.
WAFER, *s.* Abhlan, dèarnagan; breacag
WAFT, *v.* Giùlain ; iomchair troi' 'n adhar, snàmh.
WAFT, *s.* Crathadh bratlaich ri gaoith.
WAG, *v.* Crath, gluais ; crith, bog, seòg, siubhail.
WAG, *s.* Feer-an-cheairdeach.
WAGE, *v. a.* Feuch ri ; naisg geall ; thoir ionnsaidh, dèan.
WAGER, *s.* Geall ; tairgse bòide.
WAGER, *v. a.* Cuir geall, cuir an geall.
WAGES, *s.* Tuarasdal, duais.
WAGGERY, *s.* Fala-dhà, an-cheart.
WAGGISH, *adj.* Ain-cheartach, cleasanta ; sgeigeil, sgeigeach, magail, àbhcaideach.
WAGGLE, *v. n.* Dean turramanaich.
WAGGON, *s.* Cairt-mhòr.
WAGGONER, *s.* Cairtear.
WAGTAIL, *s.* Breachd-an-t-sìl, an glaiseun-seilich. *Arg.*
WAIF, *s.* Faotail ; ulaidh.
WAIL, WAILING, *s.* Caoidh, caoineadh, bròn, tuireadh, gul, gal.
WAIL, *v.* Dean-tuireadh, dean bròn, dean gal, caoidh, caoin, guil.
WAILFUL, *adj.* Tùrsach, brònach, muladach, dubhach, deurach.
WAIN, *s.* Feun, feanaidh, lòpan.
WAINSCOT, *s.* Cailbhe-fhiodh ; talninte ; darach-buidhe.
WAIST, *s.* Meadhon, cneas, crios.
WAISTCOAT, *s.* Siostacota, peiteag.
WAIT, *v.* Feith, fuirich, fritheil ; stad.
WAIT, *s.* Laidhe, plaid-laidhe.
WAITER, *s.* Gille-frithealaidh.
WAITS, *s.* Ceòl-òidhche.
WAIVE, *v. a.* Cuir gu taobh ; trèig.
WAKE, *v.* Dùisg, mosgail, fairich ; brosnach cuir chuige, bruidich ; dean caithris, dean faire.
WAKE, *s.* Fèill coisrigidh eaglais ; rotal luinge ; lòrg.
WAKEFUL, *adj.* Furachair, faicilleach ; aireachail, caithriseach.
WAKEN, *v.* Dùisg, mosgail, fairich.
WALK, *s.* Sràid ; rathad, slighe, imeach ; ceum sràide ; coiseachd, sràid-imeachd.
WALK, *v.* Coisich, imich, ceum, sràideasaich, sraid-imich ; spaidsearaich ; falbh, siubhail, triall.
WALKER, *s.* Coisiche ; oifigeach.
WALKINGSTICK, *s.* Lòrg, bata-làimhe.
WALKMILL, *s.* Mullean-luaidh.
WALL, *v. a.* Cuartaich le balla ; dìon, druid, callaidich, tog balla.
WALL, *s.* Balla ; callaid.
WALLET, *s.* Màileid, balg ; poca.
WALL-EYED, *adj.* Geal-shuileach.
WALLOP, *v. n.* Teas, goil, bruich.
WALLOW, *v. n.* Luidir, aornagaich, aoineagaich, aoineagraich, loirc.
WALNUT, *s.* Geinm-chnò.
WALTRON, *s.* An t-each-uisge.
WAN, *adj.* Glas-neulach ; glasdaidh.
WAND, *s.* Slat, slatag, maothan.
WANDER, *v.* Seachranaich, iomrallaich, rach air seachran, rach air iomrall ; rach am mearachd, rach air aimhreidh, rach air faontradh.
WANDERER, *s.* Seachranaiche, iomrallaiche, fògaraiche ; deòra, fearallabain, fear-fuadain.
WANDERING, *s.* Seachran, iomralladh, iomrall, faontradh ; allaban.
WANE, *v. n.* Beagaich, lughdaich ; searg, rach air ais, caith air falbh, crìon, fas sean.
WANE, *s.* [*of the moon,*] Earr-dhubh ; earradh, crìonadh, lughdachadh.
WANT, *s.* Uireasbhuidh, dìth, gainne, bochdainn, easbhuidh ; cion.
WANT, *v. n.* Bi dh' easbhuidh ; bi

an uireasbhuidh, bi am feum, bi as eugmhais; bi an dìth; sir, iarr; bi as aonais; fàilnich, thig gearr.

Wanton, *s.* Strìopach, siùrsach, gaorsach; druisear, trurstar.

Wanton, *adj.* Macnusach, feòlmhor, mear, meamnach; aotrom.

Wanton, *v. n.* Dean mire.

Wanty, *s.* Giort; crios-tarra.

War, *s.* Còmhrag cogadh; cath.

War, *v.* Còmhraig, cog; cathaich.

Warble, *v.* Canntairich; ceileirich.

Warbler, *s.* Ceileiriche; canntairiche.

Ward, *s.* Daingneach, àite-dìon, faire; freiceadan; leanabh fo thùitearachd; earrann, cearn glaise.

Ward, *v.* Dìon; cùm freiceadan; cùm air falbh.

Warden, *s.* Fear-gleidhidh.

Warder, *s.* Maor-coimhid.

Wardrobe, *s.* Seòmar-aodaich.

Wardship, *s.* Tùitearachd.

Wareful, *adj.* Furachair, fàicilleach.

Warehouse, *s.* Taigh-taisg.

Wares, *s.* Bathar, marsantachd. *Arg.*

Warfare, *s.* Cogadh, cath.

Warily, *adv.* Gu faicilleach.

Warlike, *adj.* Curanta, cogach; coganta, cathach, gaisgeil.

Warlock, *s.* Druidh, draoidh.

Warm, *adj.* Blàth; teth; teinnteach; feargach; dian, cas, lasanta; teòchridheach; caoimhneil.

Warm, *v. a.* Blàthaich, teò, teòthaich, teasaich, brosnaich, las.

Warming-pan, *s.* Aghann-blàthachaidh.

Warmth, *s.* Blàthas, blàs, déine, teasinntinn, deothas, dealas.

Warn, *v. a.* Thoir sanas, thoir rabhadh, thoir bàirlinn; thoir faireachadh.

Warning, *s.* Sanas, rabhadh, comhairle, faireachadh, bàirlinn; fios.

Warp, *v.* Tionndaidh a thaobh; rach gu taobh, atharraich, claon; crup; seac, lùb; dlùthaich; trus.

Warp, *s.* Dlùth; snàth-deilbhe.

Warrant, *s.* Barandas; comas.

Warrant, *v. a.* Urrasaich, barandaich, dean cinnteach, thoir barandas, rach an urras, deimhinnich.

Warrantable, *adj.* Barantach; làghail; dligheach, ceadaichte.

Warranty, *s.* Barandas, urras.

Warren, *s.* Broclach; faic.

Warrior, s. Mìlidh, curaidh, gaisgeach, laoch; cathach, fear-feachd, fear-cogaidh, saighdear.

Wart, *s.* Foinneamh.

Warty, *adj.* Foinneamhach.

Wary, *adj.* Faicilleach, curamach.

Was, *pret.* Bu, b', bha, bh'.

Wash, *v. a.* Nigh, glan, ionnlaid.

Wash, *s.* Bog, boglach, féith, uisge siabuinn; spùt; sŏs, bìadh-mhuc; sluisrich; nigheadaireachd.

Washer, *s.* Nìgheadair; sgùradair.

Washerwoman, *s.* Bean-nigheadaireachd, bean-nighe.

Washy, *adj.* Fliuch, àitidh, uisgidh; bog, tais, lag, spùtach, steallach.

Wasp, *s.* Connspeach, connsbeach.

Waspish, *adj.* Speachanta; speacharra, dreamach, dranndanach, crosda.

Wassail, *s.* Deoch, phòit.

Wassailer, *s.* Pòitear, misgear.

Waste, *v.* Caith, sgrios, struigh, cosg, mill; caith air falbh, lùghdaich, searg; rach an lughad.

Waste, *adj.* Fàs; uaigneach, dìthreabhach, sgriosta, mìllte; suarrach, gun stà; anabarrach, ro mhor.

Waste, *s.* Caitheamh, ana-caitheamh, struidheadh, strògh, diombuil; sgrios; fàsach, milleadh, lùghdachadh, fartas, asgart, dìthreabh.

Wasteful, *adj.* Caithteach; sgriosail millteach; cŏsgail, strùidheil, stròghail; uaigneach, fàs.

Waster, *s.* Strùidhear, milltear.

Watch, *s.* Faire, faireachadh; caithris; beachd, sùil; uaireadair; luchd-faire; freiceadan; forair. *Ps.*

Watch, *v.* Dean faire, cùm faire; suidh; cùm sùil, dean freiceadan, dìon, gléidh, coimhead, cùm; bi cùramach, bi faicilleach.

Watchet, *adj.* Gorm aotrom.

Watchful, *adj.* Cairiseach, furachair, faicilleach, faireil, aireach.

Watch-house, *s.* Tigh-aire, taighfaire; taigh-caithris, taigh-freiceadain, gainntir, toll-bùth.

Watching *s.* Caithris, faire.

Watchmaker, *s.* Uaireadairiche.

Watchman, *s.* Fear-faire, fear-caithris, gocmunn, gocuman.

Watchword, *s.* Ciall-chagar; diùbhras an airm, facal-faire.

Water, *s.* Uisge; bùrn; muir, mùn.

Water, *v.* Uisgich, fliuch; sil, fras.

Waterage, *s.* Airgead-aisig.

Watercresses, *s.* Biolaire an-fhuarain; an dobhar-lŭs.

Water-dog, *s.* Cù-uisge.

Waterfall, *s.* Eas, leum-uisge.

Waterfowl, *s.* Eun-uisge.

Watergruel, *s.* Brochan uisge, dubhbhrochan, stiùireag, easach. *Arg.*

Waterman, *s.* Portair, fear-asig

Water-lily, *s.* Billeag bhàite; bioras.

Watermark, *s.* Àird' an làin-mhara.
Watermill, *s.* Muileann-uisge.
Waterwork, *s.* Obair-uisge.
Watery, *adj.* Fliuch, uisgidh, bog.
Wattle, *s.* Slat-chaoil; sprogan coilich.
Wattle, *v. a.* Figh le caol.
Wave, *s.* Tonn, sùmainn, sùmaid, stuadh, lunn, bàrc.
Wave, *v.* Tog tonn; crath, luaisg; cuir dheth, fàg, tréig; cuir gu taobh, seachainn; giùlain; shéid, suas.
Waver, *v. n.* Bi 'n ioma-chomhairle, bi air udal, bi eadar da chomhairle, bi ann an teagamh, bi neo-shuidhichte.
Waverer, *s.* Fear-iomaluath.
Wavy, *adj.* Tonnach, stuadhach.
Wax, *s.* Céir, céir-sheillean.
Wax, *v.* Céirich; fas, mòr, cinn,
Waxed, Waxen, *adj.* Céireach,
Way, *s.* Rathad, slighe, ròd; car, bealach; aisridh, ceum; modh, seòl, dòigh, meadhon; astar.
Wayfarer, *s.* Fear-turais, fear-astair, fear-gabhail an rathaid.
Waylay, *v. a.* Dean plaid-laidhe, dean feall-fhalach, dean fàth-fheitheamh.
Waymark, *s.* Post-seòlaidh rathaid.
Wayward, *adj.* Bras, cabhagach, frithearra, dian, obann, reasgach, dreamluinneach, crosda, corrach.
We, *pron.* Sinn, sinne.
Weak, *adj.* Lag, fann; gun dìon.
Weaken, *v. a.* Lagaich, fannaich.
Weakling, *s.* Spreòchan.
Weakly, *adj.* Lag; fann, anfhann.
Weakness, *s.* Laigse, anfhannachd.
Weal, *s.* Math; sonas, soirbheachadh.
Wealth, *s.* Beairteas, saibhreas.
Wealthy, *adj.* Beairteach, saibhir.
Wean, *v. a.* Cuir bhàrr na cìche; caisg.
Weapon, *s.* Ball-airm, ball-deise.
Wear, *v.* Caith; lughadaich, claoidh, sàraich; cosg, cuir umad; cuir timchioll searg as.
Wear, *s.* Caitheamh; tuil-dhorus; àbh iasgach, cabhall, tàbhan.
Wearer, *s.* Fear-caitheamh.
Wearied, *adj.* Sgìth; air toirt thairis.
Weariness, *s.* Sgìtheas, sgìos, fannachadh; fadal, fadachd.
Wearing, *s.* Aodach, earradh.
Wearisome, *adj.* Sgìtheil; fadalach.
Weary, *adj.* Sgìth; claoidhte.
Weary, *v. a.* Sgìthich; fannaich; thoir thairis; sàraich; oibrich; caith; léir, claoidh.
Weasand, Weason, *s.* Stéic-bhràghaid; sgòrnan na-h-analach.
Weasel, *s.* Neas, nios.
Weather, *s.* Aimsir, àm, uair; sìde.
Weather, *v. a.* Seas ri; cùm ri, rach air fuaradh; cùm ri fuaradh, cuir fodha; cuir ri gaoith.
Weatherbeaten, *adj.* Sàraichte; cruadhaichte; cleachdte ri droch shìde.
Weatherboard, *s.* Taobh-an-fhuaraidh, taob na gaoithe.
Weathercock, *s.* Coileach-gaoithe.
Weathergage, *s.* Adhar-mheidh.
Weatherwise, *adj.* Sgileil mu'n aimsir.
Weave, *v.* Figh, dual, dlùthaich, amlaich, pleat; dean fighe.
Weaver, *s.* Breabadair; figheadair.
Web, *s.* Déilbhidh, éideadh.
Webbed, *adj.* Ceangailte le lìon.
Webfoot, *s.* Spòg-shnàmha.
Wed, *v. a.* Pòs, ceangail am pòsadh.
Wedded, *adj.* Pòsta.
Wedding, *s.* Pòsadh; banais.
Wedge, *s.* Geinn, deinn. *Ir.*
Wedge, *v.a.* Teannaich le geinn.
Wedlock, *s.* Pòsadh, ceangal-pòsaidh.
Wednesday, *s.* Dì-ciadain.
Weed, *s.* Luibh, éideadh-bròin.
Weed, *v. a.* Gart-ghlan.
Weeder, *s.* Gart-ghlanaiche.
Weedy, *adj.* Lùsanch; fiadhain.
Week, *s.* Seachduin.
Weekly, *adj.* Gach seachduin.
Weel, *s.* Poll-cuairteig; cabhall.
Ween, *v. n.* Saoil, smuainich.
Weep, *v.* Dean gul, dean caoidh, guil, caoin, dean tuireadh, dean bròn.
Weeper, *s.* Fear-bròin; geala-bhréidbròin, bàn-shròl-bròin.
Weeping, *s.* Gul, caoineadh, caoidh.
Weeping, *adj.* Deurach; snitheach.
Weevil, *s.* Leòmann, reudan.
Weft, *s.* Inneach, snàth-cuire.
Weftage, *s.* Fighe, pleatadh.
Weigh, *v.* Cothromaich; beachdsmuaintich, breathnaich.
Weighed, *adj.* Cothromaichte.
Weigher, *s.* Fear-cothromachaidh.
Weight, *s.* Cothrom; cudthrom; uallach, eallach, eire.
Weightiness, *s.* Truime, truimead, cudthromachd, chothromachd.
Weightless, *adj.* Aotrom; faoin, neo-throm; gun chothrom.
Weighty, *adj.* Tròm, cudthromach.
Welcome, *adj.* Taitneach; faoilteach, fàilteach, furanach, furmailteach.
Welcome, *s.* Fàilte, faoilte, fùran.
Welcome! *interj.* Fàilte! 's e do bheatha! 's e bhur beatha!
Welcome, *v. a.* Fàiltich; faoiltich, furanaich altaich beatha, cuir fàilt' air; cuir furain air.
Welcomer, *s.* Fear-fàilte.

WELD, *v. a.* Buail 'sa chéile.
WELD, WOULD, *s.* Am buidh-fhliodh.
WELDING, *s.* Tàth, tàthadh.
WELFARE, *s.* Sonas, àdh, slàinte.
WELKIN, *s.* Na speuran.
WELL, *s.* Tobar, fuaran, tiobairt. *Ob.*
WELL, *adj.* Math; ceart, gasta slàn, fallain, tarbhach, sona.
WELL, *adv.* Gu math, gu ceart; gu slàn, gu fallain; gu gleusda, gu gasda.
WELLADAY! *interj.* Mo chreach! mo thruaighe! mo ghunaidh! mo sgaradh! mo léireadh!
WELLBEING, *s.* Soirbheas; sonas, leas.
WELLBORN, *adj.* Uasal, inbheach, àrd.
WELLBRED, *adj.* Modhail; beusach.
WELLDONE! *interj.* Math thu féin! 'S math a fhuaradh tu, sin a lochain!
WELLFAVOURED, *adj.* Sgiamhach, ciatach, maiseach, eireachdail, bòidheach, tlachdmhor cuanda.
WELLNIGH, *adv.* Am fogus; ach beag, cha mhòr nach.
WELLSET, *adj.* Fuirbineach.
WELLSPRING, *s.* Tobar fhìr-uisg.
WELLWISHER, *s.* Fear deagh-rùin.
WELLWISH, *s.* Deagh-rùn.
WELT, *s.* Balt; oir, fàitheam.
WELT, *v. a.* Fàithem, faim.
WELTER, *v. n.* Aoirneagaich; luìdir.
WEN, *s.* Fŭth; fliodh.
WENCH, *s.* Siùrsach; caile.
WENCH, *v. n.* Bì ri siùrsachd.
WENCHER, *s.* Fear strìopachais.
WEND, *v. n.* Rach, imich, falbh.
WENNY, *adj.* Flŭthach; fliodhach.
WENT, *pret.* and *part.* of *go.* Chaidh.
WEPT, *part.* Ghuil, chaoin; caointe.
WERE, *pret.* of *To be.* Bhà, bu, b'.
WEST, *s.* An iar, an àirde 'n-iar, àirde laidhe na gréine, an taobh siar.
WEST, *adj.* Suas, shuas, siar.
WEST, *adv.* An iar, iar.
WESTERING, *adj.* Siar, gus an iar.
WESTERLY, WESTERN, *adj.* As an airde 'n iar, o 'n iar; chum na h-airde an iar.
WESTWARD, *adj.* Gu 's an airde 'n iar.
WET, *s.* Fliuiche, uisge, fliuchadh.
WET, *adj.* Fliuch, àitidh; bog, tais.
WET, *v. a.* Fliuch, uisgich.
WETHER, *s.* Mult, reithe spoite.
WETNESS, *s.* Fliuichead, fliuchalachd.
WETTISH, *adj.* A leth-char fliuch.
WEX, *v. a.* Cinn fàs mòr.
WHALE, *s.* Muc-mhara; orc. *Ob.*
WHARF, *s.* Laimhrig.
WHARFAGE, *s.* Cìs-laimhrig.
WHARFINGER, *s.* Fear-laimhrig.
WHAT, *pron.* Ciod; creud
WHATEVER, WHATSOEVER, *pron.* Ciod air bith, ciod sam bith, ge b'e air bith.
WHEAL, *s.* Guirean, spucaid, plucan.
WHEAT, *s.* Cruithneachd, cruineachd.
WHEATEN, *adj.* Do chruithneachd.
WHEEDLE, *v. a.* Meall le brìodal.
WHEEDLING, *adj.* Brìodalach.
WHEEL, *s.* Cuidhle, cuidheall, roth.
WHEEL, *v.* Cuidhil, ruidhil, roil, rol; cuir mu 'n cuairt, tionndaidh mu 'n cuairt, rach mu 'n cuairt.
WHEELBARROW, *s.* Bara-rotha.
WHEELWRIGHT, *s.* Saor-chuidhleachan.
WHEELY, *adj.* Cruinn; rothach, ruidhleanach, cearclach, cuairsgeach.
WHEEZE, *v. n.* Bi pìochanaich.
WHEEZING, *adj.* Pìochanach.
WHELK, *s.* Màighdealag; guirean, bocaid.
WHELM, *v. a.* Còmhdaich, cuibhrig.
WHELP, *s.* Cuilein.
WHEN, *adv.* C'uin? *i. e.* cia ùine? ciod an t-àm? 'nuair, air an àm.
WHENCE, *adv.* Cia ás? cò as? ciod ás? cò uaithe? c' arson? ciod uime?
WHENCESOEVER, *adv.* Ciod air bith an t-aite ás, ge b' e air bith cò ás.
WHENEVER, *adv.* Cho luath agus ceart cho luath 's, ge b' e uair.
WHERE, *adv.* C' àite? far.
WHEREABOUT, *adv.* Cia mu thimchioll?
WHEREAS, *adv.* A chionn gu, air a mheud 's gu, air a mheud 's gu'm, a chionn gu'm, do bhrìgh gun, a thaobh gur, do bhrìgh gur; a chionn gur; 'nuair; an àite sin.
WHEREAT, *adv.* Aige, aige sin; cò aige? ciod aige?
WHEREBY, *adv.* Leis; cò leis? leis an do.
WHEREVER, *adv.* Cia b' e air bith àite, c' àite sam bith, ge b' e àite.
WHEREFORE, *adv.* C' arson? ciod uime? air an aobhar sin, uime sin.
WHEREIN, *adv.* Far, anns an, anns am; c' àite? ciod ann? cò ann?
WHEREINTO, *adv.* A dh' ionnsaidh.
WHEREOF, *adv.* Do, cò dheth? cò leis? do dheth.
WHEREON, *adv.* Air, air an do; ciod air?
WHERESOEVER, *adv.* Ge b' e àite.
WHEREUNTO, *adv.* Ciad fàth? ciod do? ciod is crìoch do? c' arson? a dh' ionnsaidh.
WHEREUPON, *adv.* Air a sin.
WHEREWITHAL, *adv.* Cò leis? ciod leis? leis, le, leis an do.
WHERRET, *v. a.* Cuir dragh air.
WHERRY, *s.* Bàta dà chroinn.
WET, *v. a.* Geuraich; faobharaich.
WHET, *s.* Geurachadh; faobharachadh.
WHETHER, *pron.* Cò aca? cò dhiù.

WHETHER, *adv.* Co dhiù, ge b' e.
WHETSTONE, *s.* Clach-fhaobhair.
WHETTER, *s.* Fear-geurachaidh.
WHEY, *s.* Meòg, meug.
WHEYEY, WHEYISH, *adj.* Meògach, meògar, meugaidh.
WHICH, *pron. inter.* Cia ? ciod ?
WHICH, *pron. rel.* A ; nach, nith.
WHICHEVER, WHICHSOEVER, *pron.* Cia air bith, ciod air bith, ciod sam bith.
WHIFF, *s.* Tòth ; oiteag, séideag, osag.
WHIFFLE, *v. a.* Bi ann an iomchomhairle ; crath, crith ; sgap, sgaoil.
WHIFFLER, *s.* Gaoithean.
WHIG, *s.* Cuigse. *Mt.* and *R.D.*
WHIGGISH, *adj.* Cuigseach.
WHIGGISM, *s.* Cuigseachd.
WHILE, *v.* Cuir dheth aimsir; sìn ùine.
WHILE, *s.* Grathunn, tacan ; greis.
WHILE, WHILES, WHILST, *adv.* Am feadh, 'nuair, an àm, fhad 's ; am fad 's ré na h-ùine.
WHIM, WHIMSEY, *s.* Faoineachd ; faoin-dhòchas, amaideachd ; neònachas, faoineas, saobh-smuain.
WHIMPER, *v. n.* Dean sgiùganaich.
WHIMSICAL, *adj.* Faoin, neònach, iongantach, breisleachail.
WHIN, *s.* Conasg, conusg.
WHINE, *v. n.* Dean caoidhearan ; guil.
WHINE, *s.* Caoidhearan. *Md.*
WHINNY, *v. n.* Dean sitrich.
WHIP, *v.* Sgiùrsair, slat, cuip.
WHIP, *v.* Sgiùrs, tilip.
WHIPCORD, *s.* Còrd-sgiùrsaidh.
WHIPHAND, *s.* Làmh-an-uachdar.
WHIP-SAW, *s.* Tuireasg, sàbh-mòr.
WHIRL, *v.* Cuairtich, cuibhlich, ruidhil ; ruith mu'n cuairt.
WHIRL, *s.* Cuairt, cuibhle, ruidhil ; dol mu 'n cuairt, cuartag.
WHIRLIGIG, *s.* Gillemirean.
WHIRLPOOL, *s.* Cuairt-shlugan, faochag, cuairt-shruth, coire-tuaicheal.
WHIRLWIND, *s.* Ioma-ghaoth.
WHIRRING, *s.* Sgiath fharum.
WHISK, *s.* Sguab, sguabag.
WHISK, *v.* Sguab, sguab seachad.
WHISKER, *s.* Ciabhag.
WHISKY, *s.* Uisge-beatha.
WHISPER, *v. n.* Cogair, cagair.
WHISPER, *s.* Cogar, cagar, sanas.
WHISPERER, *s.* Fear-cagarsaich.
WHIST ! *interj.* Uist ! éisd ! bi do thosd ! tòst, bi sàmhach !
WHIST, *s.* Seòrsa cluiche air chairtein.
WHISTLE, *v.* Dean fead, feadairich.
WHISTLE, *s.* Feadag, feadan ; fead.
WHISTLER, *s.* Fear-feadaireachd.
WHIT, *s.* Mìr, dad ; smad, dadum.
WHITE, *adj.* Geal ; bàn, fionn.
WHITE, *s.* Gile, geal ; baine, gealagan.
WHITE, *v.a.* Gealaich, bànaich.
WHITEN, *v.* Gealaich, bànaich.
WHITENESS, *s.* Gile, gilead, bàinead.
WHITEWASH, *s.* Aol-uisg.
WHITHER, *adv.* C' àite ? ceana, cia 'n taobh ? ciod an car, ciod an rathad ? far, a dh' ionnsaidh.
WHITHERSOEVER, *adv.* Ge b'e air bith àite ; c' àlt' air bith.
WHITING, Cùiteag, phronn-chailc.
WHITISH, *adj.* A leth-char geal.
WHITLOW, *s.* Ana-bhiorach.
WHITSTER, *s.* Fear-gealachaidh.
WHITSUNTIDE, *s.* Caingis, Bealltuinn.
WHITTLE, *s.* Sgian, corc.
WHIZ, *v. n.* Srann.
WHIZZING, *s.* Srannail.
WHO, *pron. interrog.* Cò ?
WHO, *rel. pron.* A ; nach.
WHOEVER, *pron.* Cò air bith.
WHOLE, *adj.* Slàn, fallain ; iomlan ; uile, gu léir, uile gu léir.
WHOLE, *s.* An t-iomlan.
WHOLESALE, *s.* Reic-shlàn.
WHOLESOME, *adj.* Slàn, fallain.
WHOLLY, *adv.* Gu slàn ; gu tur ; gu h-iomlan, gu léir, gu buileach.
WHOM, *accus. sing.* and *plur.* of *Who.* A.
WHOMSOEVER, *pron.* Cò air bith ; aon air bith, neach sam bith.
WHOOP, *s.* Coileach-oidhche ; glaodh, gàir, iolach ; gàir-chatha.
WHORE, *s.* Siùrsach, strìopach.
WHOREDOM, *s.* Strìopachas.
WHOREMASTER, WHOREMONGER, *s.* Drùisear, fear-strìopachais.
WHORESON, *s.* Mac-dìolain.
WHORISH, *adj.* Strìopachail.
WHORTLEBERRY, WHURT, *s.* Braoileag.
WHOSE, *pron. interrog.* Cò ? cò leis ?
WHOSE, *pron. poss.* of *Who* and *Which.* Aig am beil.
WHOSOEVER, *pron.* Cò air bith.
WHY, *adv.* C'arson ? ciod uime ? cia fàth ? c' uige ? c' uime ?
WICK, *s.* Buaic, lasadan.
WICKED, *adj.* Olc, aingidh ; mallaichte, ciontach, peacach, dubhailceach.
WICKEDNESS, *s.* Aingidheachd ; olc, droch-bheart, peacadh, cionta.
WICKER, *adj.* Slatach, gadach.
WICKET, *s.* Caol-dhorus, dorus cumhann, fath-dhorus.
WIDE, *adj.* Farsuinn, leathann, mòr, leòbhar.
WIDEN, *v.* Leudaich, farsuinnich ; leathannaich ; fàs farsainn.
WIDGEON, *s.* An t-amadan-mòintich.

Widow, *s.* Banntrach.
Widower, *s.* Aonrachdan.
Widowhood, *s.* Banntrachas.
Width, *s.* Farsuinneachd; leud.
Wield, *v. a.* Làimhsich; stiùr.
Wieldy, *adj.* So-làimhseachadh.
Wife, *s.* Bean-phòsta, céile.
Wig, *s.* Pìorbhuic; fara-ghruag.
Wight, *s.* Neach; bith, urra.
Wight, *adj.* Uallach; iullagach.
Wightly, *adv.* Gu luath.
Wild, *adj.* Fiadhaich; borb; allaidh; allta; allmharra; fiadhain; fàs, garbh, neo-àitichte; mi-riaghailteach; mac-meanmnach, faoin.
Wild, *s.* Dìthreabh, fiadh-aite.
Wilder, *v. a.* Cuir air seachran.
Wilderness, *s.* Fàsach.
Wildfire, *s.* Teine-gradaig.
Wild-goose, *s.* Cadhan.
Wilding, *s.* Ubhal-fiadhain.
Wildness, *s.* Fiadhaichead, buirbe.
Wile, *s.* Car, cleas, cealg, cuilbheart.
Wilful, *adj.* Rag, reasgach, ceannlaidir, danarra; dùr, doirbh; ansrianta, dearrasach.
Wilfulness, *s.* An-toilealachd, reasgachd, rag-mhuinealachd.
Will, *s.* Toil, rùn, àill, gean, miann, togradh; deòin, roghainn; tiomnadh.
Will, *v. a.* Iarr; toilich; miannaich; rùnaich, sanntaich; togair, òrduich.
Willing, *adj.* Toileach, deònach, togarrach; miannach.
Willow, *s.* Seileach.
Will-with-a-wisp, *s.* Sionnachan.
Wily, *adj.* Eòlach, seòlta, culbheartach, sligheach, innleachdach.
Wimble, *s.* Tora, boireal.
Win, *v.* Coisinn; buidhinn, faigh.
Wince, Winch, *v. n.* Breab; tilg.
Winch, *s.* Maighdean-shniomhain.
Wind, *s.* Gaoth; soirbheas; anail.
Wind, *v.* Tionndaidh, toinn, lùb, trùs, tachrais; fàilich; rothainn; atharraich; rach mu'n cuairt.
Windegg, *s.* Ubh-maothaig.
Winder, *s.* Toinneadair, toinntear, fear-tachrais; cuidhle-thachrais.
Windflower, *s.* Lùs-na-gaoithe.
Windgun, *s.* Gunna-gaoithe.
Windiness, *s.* Gaotharachd.
Winding, *s.* Lùbadh; fiaradh, car.
Windingsheet, *s.* Marbh-phaisg.
Windlass, *s.* Ailig-ghuairneach, unndais; tachrasan.
Windle, *s.* Dealgan, fearsaid.
Windmill, *s.* Muileann-gaoithe.
Window, *v. a.* Uinneagaich.
Window, *s.* Uinneag.
Windpipe, *s.* Deteigheach, detioch; stéic-bràghad.
Windward, *adv.* Air fuaradh.
Windy, *adj.* Gaothar; stoirmeil, doinionnach; gaothach, aotrom.
Wine, *s.* Fìon.
Winepress, *s.* Fìon-amar.
Wing, *s.* Sgiath; cùl-taigh.
Wing, *v. a.* Cuir sgiathan air; falbh air iteig; leòn 's an sgéith.
Winged, *adj.* Sgiathach, luath.
Wink, *s.* Priobadh, caogadh, smèideadh.
Wink, *v. n.* Caog; priob, smèid; ceadaich, aontaich; leig seachad.
Winner, *s.* Fear-buanachadh.
Winning, *adj.* Tàirnneach, dlù-thairnneach, mealltach, ionmhuinn; maiseach; taitneach, ciatach; gaolach.
Winning, *s.* Cosnadh; buidhinn.
Winnow, *v.* Fasgain; glan, gréidh rannsaich; feuch; dealaich, sgar.
Winter, *s.* Geamhradh; dùbhlachd.
Winter, *v.* Geamhraich; cuir thairis no caith an geamhradh.
Winterly, Wintry, *adj.* Geamhradail, geamhrail, geamhrach.
Winy, *adj.* Fionach.
Wipe, *v. a.* Siab, sguab, glan.
Wipe, *s.* Siabadh, suathadh, glanadh; beum; buille, gleadhar.
Wire, *s.* Cruaidh-theud.
Wisdom, *s* Gliocas, tuigse, eòlas, ciall, tùr, eagnaidheachd; crìonnachd.
Wise, *adj.* Glic, eòlach, sicir, crìonna, ciallach, fiosrach, stòlda.
Wiseacre, *s.* Baothaire, burraidh.
Wish, *v.* Miannaich, guidh, togair; sanntaich, iarr, rùnaich, bi deònach.
Wish, *s.* Miann, àill, togradh; guidhe; toil, dùrachd, déigh; iarrtas.
Wisher, *s.* Fear-miannachaidh.
Wishful, *adj.* Togarrach, miannach, sanntach, déidheil, cionail.
Wisket, Whisket, *s.* Sgùile, sgùlan.
Wisp, *s.* Mùillean, boitein, sop.
Wistful, *adj.* Dùrachdach, smuainteach, aireach, cùramach.
Wit [to]. Is e sin ri ràdh.
Wit, *s.* Aigneadh, ciall, inntinn, tuigse, tùr, toinisg, meamna, mac-meamna, mac-meanmain; geur-labhairt; fear geur-chuiseach, fear geur-chainnteach, bearradair; fear tulchuiseach, fear mòr-thuigse; innleachd, tionnsgnadh.
Witch, *s.* Bana-bhuidseach, bandruidh, briosag. *Kk.*
Witchcraft, *s.* Buidseachd, rosachd, druidheachd; geasan, dolbh.
With, *prep* Le, leis, maille ri; ma

ri, cuide ris, am fochar. With me, thee, her, him, *leam, leat, leatha, leis;* with us, you, them, *leinn, leibh, leo.*

Withal, *adv.* Leis, mar ri.

Withdraw, *v.* Falbh, thoir air ais, thoir air falbh, rach a thaobh; cuir a thaobh; ais-chéimnich.

Withdrawing-room, *s.* Seòmar-taoibh.

Withe, *s.* Slat-chaoil; cual-chaoil.

Wither, *v.* Searg, seac, crìon, caith air falbh, sgreag, meath.

Withering, *s.* Seargadh, seacadh, crìonadh, sgreagadh.

Withers, *s.* Slinneanan eich.

Withhold, *v. a.* Cùm air ais, bac.

Within, *adv.* and *prep.* A steach.

Withinside, *adv.* An leth a steach.

Without, *prep.* Gun; as eugmhais; a mach, a muigh, an taobh a muigh.

Without, *conj.* Mur, saor; mur déan, mur bi, mur tachair.

Without, *adv.* Am muigh, a mach.

Withstand, *v. a.* Cùm ris, cùm an aghaidh, cùm roimh, seas ri.

Withy, *s.* Gad.

Witless, *s.* Gòrach; amaideach, eucéillidh, faoin, neo-thùrail.

Witling, *adj.* Fear leth-gheur.

Witness, *s.* Fianais.

Witness. *v.* Thoir fianais, dean fianais, dearbh le fianais, tog fianais.

Witted, *adj.* Geur, tùrail.

Witticism, *s.* Maol-abhachd.

Witty, *adj.* Geur, beumnach, aigneach, bearradach, tuigseach, tulchuiseach, geur-chuiseach, macmeamnach, geur-fhaclach; sgaiteach.

Wive, *v. a.* Pòs, gabh bean.

Wives, *s. pl.* of *wife.* Mnathan.

Wizard, *s.* Baobh; fiosaiche; drùidh.

Wo, *s.* An-aoibhneas; truaighe.

Woad, *s.* Seòrsa guirmein.

Woful, *adj.* Truagh, dubhach, brònach, muladach, tùrsach, cumhach, doilghiosach, an-aoibhneach.

Wolf, *s.* Madadhallaidh; mac-tìre; faol.

Wolfdog, *s.* Faol-chù.

Wolfsbane, *s.* Fuath-a-mhadaidh.

Woman, *s.* Bean; boireannach.

Womanish, *adj.* Banail, màlda.

Womanhater, *s.* Fear-fuathachaidh bhan, bean-fhuathaiche.

Womankind, *s.* An cinneadh banail.

Womanly, *adj.* Banail; mar mhnaoidh.

Womb, *s.* Machlag, bolg; brù.

Womb, *v. a.* Dùin; gin an uaigneas.

Women, *s. pl.* of *woman.* Mnài.

Wonder, *s.* Iongantas, neònachas.

Wonder, *v. n.* Gabh iongantas.

Wonderful, *adj.* Iongantach.

Wonderstruck, *adj.* Fo amhluadh.

Wondrous, *adj.* Neònach.

Wont, *v. n.* Gnàthaich, cleachd.

Wonted, *part. adj.* Gnàthaichte; coitcheann, cumanta, cleachdte.

Woo, *v.* Dean suiridhe, dean mire no beadradh; iarr; sir.

Wood, *s.* Coill, coille; fiodh, fiùdhaidh; iùdh, *and* iuch. *Ob.*

Woodbine, *s.* Eidheann-ma-cnrann; iadh-shat; deòthlag.

Woodcock, *s.* Coileach-coille, cromnan-duileag, creòthar.

Wooded, *adj.* Coillteach.

Wooden, *adj.* Fiodha, do dh fhiodh.

Woodhole, *s.* Toll-connaidh.

Woodland, *s.* Fearann-coilleach.

Woodland, *adj.* Coillteachail.

Woodlark, *s.* An riabhag-choille.

Woodlouse, *s.* Reudan, mial-fhiodha.

Woodman, Woodsman, *s.* Gìomanach; eunadair, sealgair; maor-coille.

Woodmonger, *s.* Fear-reic-fiodha, ceannaiche-fiodha.

Woodpecker, *s.* An lasair-choille, an snagan-daraich.

Woodsare, *s.* Smugiad-na-cuthaige.

Woodsorrel, *s.* Biadh-an-eòin, biadheunain, glaodhran, feada-coille.

Woodnymph, *s.* Annir-choille.

Woody, *adj.* Coillteach, doireach.

Wooer, *s.* Suiridheach, suiridhche.

Woof, *s.* Inneach, snath-cuir.

Wool, *s.* Clòimh, olunn.

Woolen, *adj.* Olla, do chlòimh.

Woolly, *adj.* Ollach, clòimheach.

Woolpack, *s.* Poca cloimhe.

Woolstapler, *s.* Ceannaiche-clòimhe.

Word, *s.* Facal, briathar; gealladh.

Word, *v.* Faclaich, deachd.

Wordy, *adj.* Briathrach; faclach.

Wore, *pret.* of *to wear.* Chaith.

Work, *s.* Obair, saothair, gnìomh, gothach cùis; dragh.

Work, *v.* Oibrich, saoithrich.

Worker, *s.* Oibriche.

Workhouse, *s.* Taigh-nam-bochd.

Workingday, *s.* Latha-oibre.

Workman, *s.* Fear-cèairde; fear-oibre.

Workmanlike, *adj.* Ealadhanta.

Workmanship, *s.* Obair, ealdhain.

Workshop, *s.* Bùth-oibre.

Workwoman, *s.* Ban-fhuaighealaich.

World, *s.* Saoghal, domhan, an cruinne; an cinne-daonna.

Worldling, *s.* Duine saoghalta.

Worldly, *adj.* Talmhaidh; saoghaltach, saoghalta, sanntach, spìocachteann-chruaidh.

Worm, *v.* Snìomh, toinn troimh.

Worm, *s.* Cnuimh, cnuimheag, durrag; cliath-thogalach.
Wormwood, *s.* Burmaid; burban.
Wormy, *adj.* Cnuimheach.
Worn, *part. pass.* of to *wear.* Caithte.
Worril, *s.* Feursanan.
Worry, *v.a.* Reub; stròic, beubanaich.
Worse, *adj.* Ni's miosa.
Worship, *s.* Urram, onoir, spéis.
Worship, *s.* Aoradh; urram.
Worship, *v.* Dean aoradh.
Worshipful, *adj.* Urramach.
Worst, *adj.* A's miosa.
Worsted, *s.* Abhras.
Wort, *s.* Brailis, seòrsa càil.
Worth, *s.* Fiach, luach, prìs; luachmhorachd, fiachalachd.
Worth, *adj.* Fiù, airidh, fiach.
Worthiness, *s.* Toillteannas; òirdheirceas; subhailc; mathas.
Worthless, *adj.* Suarrach, gun fhiù.
Worthlessness, *s.* Neo-fhiùghalachd.
Worthy, *adj.* Fiachail, fiùghail airidh, cubhaidh, toillteannach, cliùthoillteannach, òirdheirc.
Wot, *v. n.* Bi fiosrach.
Wove, *pret.* and *part.* of to *weave.* Dh' fhigh air fnige.
Woven, *part.* Fighte.
Would, *pret.* of to *will.* B' àill.
Wound, *s.* Lot, cneadh, creuchd, dochann, leòn, gearradh.
Wound, *v. a.* Leòn, creuchd, reub, lot, dochainn, cràidh, ciùrr.
Wound, *pret.* of to *wind.* Tachraiste.
Wrack, *s.* Bristeadh sgrios call.
Wrangle, *v. n.* Connsaich, deasbairich; cuir a mach, troid.
Wrangle, *s.* Connsachadh, trod.
Wrangler, *s.* Fear-connsachaidh.
Wrap, *v. a.* Paisg, trŭs; fill, cuairsg.
Wrapper, *s.* Filleag, còmhdach.
Wrath, *s.* Fraoch; corraich; fearg.
Wrathful, *adj.* Fraochanta, feargach, corrach căs, frithearra.
Wreak, *v. a.* Dean dìoghaltas.
Wreak, *s.* Dìoghaltas.
Wreakful, *adj.* Dìoghaltach.
Wreath, *s.* Blàth-fhleasg, coron, fleasg, figheachan; clàideag, lùbag, dual, camag; cuidhe.
Wreathe, *v. a.* Toinn, pleat, dual, cas, snìomh, cuairsg.
Wreathy, *adj.* Snìomhanach, cuairsgeach, leadanach, dualach.
Wreck, *s.* Long-bhriseadh; léirsgrios, bàthadh.
Wreck, *v.* Sgrios le ànradh cuain; bris, mill; bi air do bhriseadh.
Wren, *s.* Dreadhandonn.
Wrench, *v.a.* Toinn, snìomh; spìon.
Wrench, *s.* Toinneamh; snìomh, spìonadh, siachadh.
Wrest, *v. a.* Spìon; toinn, toinneamh, snìomh; éignich.
Wrest, *s.* Toinneamh; éigin.
Wrestle, *v. n.* Gleachd, dean strì.
Wrestler, *s.* Gleachadair, caraiche.
Wretch, *s.* Truaghan; crochaire.
Wretched, *adj.* Truagh, dòlum, bochd; dona, mi-shealbhar, dòruinneach, truaillidh, crìon, suarrach; dòlasach, doilghiosach, àmhgharach; leibideach, tàireil.
Wretchedness, *s.* Truaighe, donas.
Wriggle, *v.* Fri-oibrich; siùd, seòg.
Wriggling, *s.* Seòganaich, crathail.
Wright, *s.* Saor.
Wring, *v.* Fàisg; toinn, toinneamh; snìomh; sàraich, claoidh; gabh a dh' aindeoin, dean ainneart.
Wrinkle, *s.* Preas, preasadh, crupag, criopag, lorc, caisreag.
Wrinkle, *v. n.* Preas, Preasagaich, crup, cas, liurc, sream.
Wrinkled, *adj.* Preasagach; preasagaichte, casach, liurcach.
Wrist, *s.* Caol an dùirn.
Wristband, *s.* Bann-dùirn.
Writ, *s.* Sgriobhtur; reachd.
Write, *v.* Sgrìobh; gràbhail, geàrr.
Writer, *s.* Sgrìobhadair, ùghdar.
Written, *pass. part.* of to *write.* Sgrìobhte, air a sgrìobhadh.
Writhe, *v.* Toinn, toinneamh, snìomh; căs; cam, siach, fiar.
Writing. Sgrìobhadh.
Wrizzled, *adj.* Preasach, sreamach; seacte, seargte.
Wrong, *s.* Eucoir, eu-ceart, nearachd; dochair, coire.
Wrong, **Wrongly**, *adv.* Air aimhreith.
Wrong, *adj.* Eucorach, docharach, mearachdach, olc; coireach, cearr, air aimhreith, neo-chothromach, neo-chubhaidh.
Wrong, *v. a.* Dean eucoir air, dochannaich, bhalaich, ciùrr.
Wrongful, *adj.* Eu-corach, eu-ceartach, mearachdach, lochdach, ciontach, cronail, coireach.
Wrongheaded, *adj.* Caoch-cheannach, gòrach, amaideach, baoghalta, eucéillidh, mearachdach.
Wrongfully, *adv.* Gu neo-dhligheach, gu cronail, gu mi-cheart.
Wrote, *pret. part.* of to *write.* Sgrìobh.
Wroth, *adj.* Feargach, an corraich.
Wrought, *part.* Oibrichte; dèante.
Wrung, *part.* of *to wring.* Fàisgte.

Wry, *adj.* Cam, fiar, claon, crotach.

X

X, *s.* Ceathramh litir thar fhichead na h-aibidil.
Xerif, *s.* Flath Barbarianach.
Xebeck, *s.* Birlinn.
Xerocollyrium, *s.* Sàbh-shùl.
Xenodochy, *s.* Aoidheachd.
Xerophagy, *s* Biadh-tioram.
Xiphoides, *s.* Maothan.
Xylography, *s.* Gràbhaladh air fiodh.
Xystus, *s.* Rathad spaidsearachd.

Y

Y, *s.* Cùigeamh, litir thar fhichead, na h-Aibidil.
Yacht, *s.* Sgoth-luingeanach.
Yard, *s.* Gàradh; iadh-lann, lios, cùirt. Slat; slat-thomhais, slat-shiùil.
Yardward, *s.* Tomhas-slaite.
Yarn, *s.* Snàth; snàth-olla, abhras.
Yarrow, *s.* Eàrr-thalmhuinn.
Yawl, *s.* Geòla, bàta luinge.
Yawn, *s.* Meunan, mianan.
Yawn, *v. n.* Dean meunanaich.
Yawning, *s.* Meunanaich.
Yawning, *adj.* Meunanach, cadaltach.
Ycleped, *part.* Ainmichte.
Ye, *nominative plur.* of *thou.* Sibhse.
Yea, *adv.* 'S eadh; air chinnt.
Yean, *v. n.* Beir uan.
Yeanling, *s.* Uan, uanan, uainein.
Year, *s.* Bliadhna.
Yearling, *s.* Bliadhnach.
Yearly, *adv.* Gach bliadhna.
Yearn, *v. n.* Gabh truas, mothaich truas; fàisg, léir, cràidh.
Yearning, *s.* Truacantas, bàigh.
Yelk, Yolk, *s.* Buidheagan uibhe.
Yell, *s.* Sgrèach, sgriach, sgal, glaodh, sgairt, ulfhart, ràn, burral.
Yell, *v. n.* Sgrèach, sgriach, sgal, glaodh, sgairt, ulfhart, ràn, burral.
Yellow, *adj.* Buidhe.
Yellow, *s.* Dath-buidhe.
Yellowhammer, *s.* Buidheagbhuachair.
Yellowish, *adj.* A leth-char buidhe.
Yellowness, *s.* Bhuidhneachd.
Yelp, *s.* Tathunn, tathunnaich, comhartaich, deithleann.
Yelp, *v.n.* Dean tathunn, tathunnaich.
Yeoman, *s.* Tuathanach, fear gabhalach; leth dhuin'-uasal.
Yeomanry, *s.* Tuath-mheasail.
Yerk, *s.* Sgailleag, frith-bhuille, gleog, gleadhar; sitheadh.
Yerk, *v.* Buail gu grad, frith-bhuail; thoir sitheadh, sgiùrs, gabh air thoir grad leum.
Yes, *adv.* Seadh, 'se, tha, &c. &c.
Yest, Yeast, *s.* Beirm, cop.
Yesterday, *adv.* An dé.
Yesternight, *adv.* An raoir.
Yesty, Yeasty, *adj.* Beirmeach.
Yet, *conj.* Gidheadh, fòs, fathast.
Yet, *adv.* Fathast, fhathast; osbarr, tuilleadh fòs; *as yet;* gus a nise.
Yew, *s.* Iubhar, iuthar.
Yewen, *adj.* Iubhair.
Yield, *v.* Géill; strìoc; lub, feachd; thoir a mach; thoir suas, aontaich.
Yoke, *s.* Cuing, ceangal, slàbhraidh; càraid, dithis; daorsa, tràilleachd.
Yoke, *v. a.* Beartaich; cuingich, caraidich; sàraich, claoidh, ceannsuich, tràillich, cìosnaich.
Yoke-Fellow, *s.* Comh-oibriche.
Yon, Yonder, *adv.* Ud, an sud.
Yore, *adv,* O shean, o chian.
You, *pron. oblique case* of *ye.* Thu, thusa, tu; sibh, sibhse.
Young, *adj.* Òg; aineolach, lag.
Young, *s.* Òigridh; àl-òg.
Younger, *adj.* Ni's òige.
Youngest, *adj.* A's òige.
Youngish, *adj.* A leth-char òg.
Youngling, *s.* Ogan, maotharan.
Youngster, Younker, *s.* Òganach.
Your, *pron. sing.* Do, d' t'.
Your, *pron. pl.* Bhur, ur, 'r.
Yours, *pron. sing.* Leat, leatsa.
Yours, *pron. pl.* Leibh, leibhse.
Yourself, *pron.* Thu-féin.
Yourselves, *pron.* Sibh-féin.
Youth, *s.* Oigear; òige pàiste, òigeachd; òigridh, òganaich.
Youthful, *adj.* Òg, ògail, òigeil.
Youthly, Youthy, *adj.* Òg, ògail.
Yule, *s.* An Nollaig.
Yux, Yex, *s.* An ăileag

Z

Z. Sèathamh litir thar fhichead na h-Aibidil.

ZANY, *s.* Sgeigeir, cleasaiche.

ZEAL, *s.* Miann, eud; dian-dheòthas; dealas, deagh-dhùrachd.

ZEALOT, *s.* Eudair; Fear-tnuail; fear-leanmhainn, fear-dealaidh.

ZEALOUS, *adj.* Eudmhor, miannmhor, dealasach, deòthasach, dùrachdach, dian; teth, bras, togarrach.

ZEALOUSNESS, *s.* Dealasachd, dùrachd.

ZEBRA, *s.* An asal-stiallach.

ZECHIN, *s.* Òr naoi tastan.

ZENITH, *s.* Druim an adhair.

ZEPHYR, ZEPHYRUS, *s.* Tlàth-ghaoth; seamh-ghaoth; gaoth an iar.

ZEST, *s.* Blas; blas taitneach.

ZEST, *v. a.* Dean blasda.

ZIGZAG, *adj.* Carach; lùbach, cam

ZINC, *s.* Seòrsa miotailt.

ZODIAC, *s.* Grian-chrios.

ZODIACIAL, *adj.* Grian-chriosach.

ZONE, *s.* Crios; cearcall, cuairt; bann; cuairt do 'n talamh.

ZOOGRAPHER, *s.* Fear-sgrìobhaidh mu thimcholl ainmhidhean.

ZOOGRAPHY, *s.* Cunntas mu thimchioll cumadh agus nàduir ainmhidhean.

ZOOLOGY, *s.* Cunntas mu ainmhidhibh.

ZOOPHYTE, *s.* Beò-luibh.

ZOOTOMIST, *s.* Cairbh-sgathaich.

ZOOTOMY, *s.* Cairbh-sgathadh.

THE COMMON CHRISTIAN NAMES OF MEN AND WOMEN, IN ENGLISH AND GAELIC.

NAMES OF MEN.

THE NAMES IN ITALICS ARE THE ABBREVIATIONS, AS USED IN FAMILIAR DISCOURSE.

ADAM, ...Adhamh.
ADOMAN, ...Donnan.
ALBERT, ...Ailbeart.
ALEXANDER, *Ellic* .....Alasdair.
ALAN, ...Ailean.
ALPIN, ...Ailpein.
ANDREW, ...Aindrea.
ANGUS, ...Aonghas.
ARCHIBALD, ...Gilleasbuig.
ARTHUR, ...Art.
AULAY, ...Amhladh.
BANQUO, ...Bàncho.
BARTHOLOMEW, *Bat*...Parlan.
BEARNARD, ...Bearnard.
BENJAMIN, *Ben*. ....Beathan.
BRIAN, ...Brian.
CATHELD, ...Cathal.
CHARLES, ...Tearlach.
CHRISTOPHER, ...Gillecriosd.
COLIN, ...Cailean.
COLL, ...Colla.
CONALL,........ ....Connull.
CONSTANTINE, ...Conn.
DANIEL, *Donald* ....Dòmhnull.
DAVID, *Davie* ....Daibhidh.
DERMUD, ...Diarmad.
DUGALD, ...Dùghall.
DUNCAN, ...Donnachadh.
EDWARD, *Ned* ....Eideard.
EUGENE, ...Aodh.
EVANDER, ...Iomhar.
EWEN, ...Eòbhann.
FARQUHAR, ...Fearchar.
FERGUS, ...Fearghus.
FILLAN, ...Faolan.
FINGAL, ...Fionn.
FINLAY, ...Fionnladh.
FRANCIS, *Frank* ......Frang.
GEOFFRY, ...Goiridh.
GEORGE, ...Seòras.
GILLANDERS, ...Gilleanndrais.
GILBERT, ...Gillebard.
GILBRIDE, ...Gillebrìde.
GILLIES, ...Gilliosa.
GODFREY, ...Guaidhre.
GREGOR, ...Griogair.
HENRY, *Harry*..........Eanruig.
HECTOR, ...Eachunn.
HUGH, ...Ùisdean.
JAMES, *Jemmy*.........Seumas.
JOHN, *Jack* ....Iain.
JOSEPH, *Joe* ....Ioseph.
KENNEDY, ...Uarraig.
KENNETH, ...Coinneach.
LACHLAN, ...Lachunn.
LAWRENCE, ...Làbhruinn.
LEWIS, ...Luthais.
LUKE, ...Lucais.
LUDOVICK, ...Maoldònaich.
MAGNUS, ...Mànus.
MALCOLM,* ....Calum.
MARC, ...Marcus.
MARTIN, ...Màrtainn.
MATTHEW, *Mat*........Mata.
MAXWELL, ...Macsual.
MAURICE, ...Maolmuire.
MICHAEL, ...Mìcheil.
MUNGO, ...Mungan.

---

* "Malcolm" is a name of Celtic origin—from "*Maolcolum*," a votary of St Columba; as "*Maolmuire*" signifies a votary of the Virgin Mary. The English affix *bald*, is synonymous with the Gaëlic prefixes *maol* and *gille*,—"*Maol-ciaran*," a votary of St Kiaran, was in former times a Gaëlic proper name, but is now used only as descriptive of a person who is woe-begone and bending under sorrow. Examples of this use of the term will be found in the poetical compositions of Mary M'Leod, the celebrated poetess of Harris, and of Roderick Morrison, the famous blind harper of Lewis.

Murdoch, ...Murchadh.
Murphy, ...Muireach.
Nicolas, *Nic*..............Neacal.
Naughtan, ...Neachdann.
Niel, ...Niall.
Ninian, ...Ringean.
Niven, ...Gillenaomh.
Norman, ...Tòrmod.
Oliver, ...Olaghair.
Owen, ...Aoghann.
Paul, ...Pàl, Pòl.
Patrick, ...Pàdruig.
Peter, ...Peadar.
Philip, ...Philip.
Quintin, ...Caoidhean.
Richard, *Dick* ....Ruiseart.
Robert, *Bob* ....Rob.
Roderick, *Rory* ......Ruairidh.
Ronald, ...Raonull,
Samuel, *Sam* ....Samuel.
Somerled, ...Somhairle
Simon, ...Sìm.
Solomon, ...Solamh.
Stephen, ...Steaphan.
Taddeus, ...Taogh.
Thomas, *Tom* ....Tòmas.
Torquil, ...Torcull.
Walter, ...Bhaltair.
William, *Will* ....Uilleam.
Zachary, *Zach*.........Sachairi.

NAMES OF WOMEN.

Amelia, ...Aimili.
Anabella, ...Barabal.
Angelica, ...Aingealag.
Ann, *Nanny*............Anna.
Barbara, ...Barbara.
Beatrice, ...Beitiris.
Betsy, ...Beitidh.
Catharine, *Kate* ...Caitriana.
Christian, *Chris*......Cairistìne.
Cicely, *Cis*.............Silis.
Clare, ...Sorcha.
Clarisa, ...Caitir.
Diana, ...Diana.
Dorcas, ...Deòiridh.
Dorothy, *Dolly* ....Diorbhail.
Elgin, ...Eiliginn.
Elizabeth, *Bess*......Ealasaid.
Flora, ...Fionnaghal.
Frances, *Fanny* ....Fràngag.
Grace, ...Giorsail.
Helen, *Nelly* ....Eilidh.
Henrietta, *Harriet*.Eiric.
Isabella, *Bell* ....Iseabal.
Janet, ...Seònaid.
Jane, *Jean, Jenny*, ...Sìne.
Judith, ...Siubhan.
Louisa, ...Liùsaidh.
Lucretia, ...Lùereis.
Margaret, *Peggy* ....Mairearad.
Margery, ...Marsail.
Marion, ...Muireall.
Martha, *Patty* ....Moireach.
Mary, *Molly*...........Màiri.
Malvina, ...Malamhìn.
Mildred, ...Milread.
Eupham, ...Oighrig.
Rachel, ...Raònaild.
Sarah, *Sally* ....Mòr.
Sophia, ...Beathag.
Susanna, *Susan*.......Siùsan.
Uere, ...Eamhair.
Winifred, ...Ùna.